CANADA

FODOR'S TRAVEL PUBLICATIONS

are compiled, researched, and edited by an international team of travel writers, field correspondents, and editors. The series, which now almost covers the globe, was founded by Eugene Fodor in 1936.

OFFICES
New York & London

Fodor's Canada:

Editor: Gail Chasan
Area Editors: David Dunbar, Susan Learney, M.G. Mackay, Garry Marchant, Roger Newman, Barbara Peck, Valerie Ross, Margot Sammurtok, Ralph Surette, Colleen Thompson
Drawings: Brian Deines, Claude Detillieux
Cartography: Burmar Technical Corp., Mark Stein Studios, Pictograph

CONTENTS

CONTENTS

FOREWORD

Canada, a country larger than the United States, stretching from the Atlantic to the Pacific and up to the Arctic Ocean, offers a vast array of vacation possibilities—urban sophistication in Toronto, Montreal, and Vancouver; natural beauty in the Laurentians and the Georgian Bay area; wilderness adventure in the North; spectacular scenery from the Rockies to the Bay of Fundy. In the West, Victoria is very British; in the East, Quebec City is even more French.

Canadians are proud of their country and the editors of and contributors to *Fodor's Canada* reflect that pride. We have tried to provide a backdrop to the Canadian scene by describing the people of Canada, their government, land, and culture. Then, in an attempt to sort out some of the myriad choices Canada offers its visitors, we explore the country province by province. Each province has a fascinating story of its own, and we take you on a tour of some of each area's most interesting places. We have concentrated on giving you the broadest range of things to see and do in each province, and selections that we believe are safe, solid, and of good value to you. In addition, we have tried to offer a range of choices, so that you can decide what best suits your taste and pocketbook. We also have included a special insert on Calgary's 1988 Winter Olympics.

Chapters on Canada's Northwest Territories and the Yukon cover major points of interest but the accent here is on the wilderness, for the more adventurous.

The selections and comments in *Fodor's Canada* are based on the editors' and contributors' personal experiences and we have made every attempt to insure that the facts are up to date and accurate. Still, in a constantly changing world, mistakes will occur. We will value your comments and suggestions. Write to Fodor's Travel Publications, 201 East 50th Street, New York, NY 10022 or 9–10 Market Place, London W1N 7AG, England.

CANADA

BEAUFORT
SEA

QUEEN
ELIZABETH
IS.

ALASKA

YUKON
TERRITORY

Dawson •

• Inuvik
• Fort McPherson

Victoria
Is.

DISTRICT

O

N O R T H W E S T   T E R R

Yukon R.

⊙ Whitehorse

Mackenzie R.

Great
Bear Lake

DISTRICT OF
MACKENZIE

DISTRICT OF
KEEWATIN

ROCKY MTS.

Fort Nelson •

Great
Slave Lake

Slave R.

Peace R.

Uranium City
Lake
Athabaska

Wollaston
Lake

Churchill •

Prince Rupert •

Athabaska R.

ALBERTA

Reindeer
Lake

MANITOBA

Prince George •
BR.
COLUMBIA

• Jasper

⊙ Edmonton

Flin Flon

SASK.

R.

• Prince Albert

Lake
Winnipeg

Fraser R.

Lake Louise
Banff •

Saskatchewan R.

• Saskatoon

O

Vancouver I.

• Calgary

Lake
Winnipegosis

Lake
of the Woods

Victoria ⊙ • Vancouver

Columbia R.

Lethbridge •
• Medicine Hat

Trans Canada Hwy.

Regina •

Winnipeg •

PACIFIC
OCEAN

Red River

0   200   400

Scale of Miles

UNITED

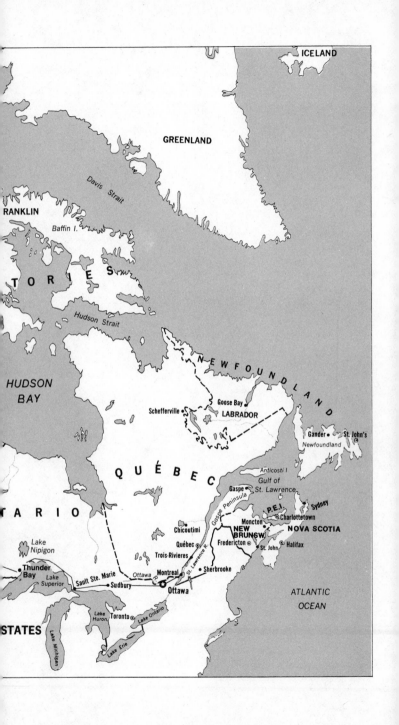

FACTS AT YOUR FINGERTIPS

PLANNING YOUR TRIP. Once you have decided to take a trip, it's time to get down to the details of making hotel and airline reservations and other arrangements. Consider using a travel agent to help you with trip planning and arrangements. (See travel agents section in this chapter.)

"Package tours" can be great money-savers, since they usually cover a variety of sightseeing stops, recommend selected restaurants, include tour guides, and offer the opportunity to meet other people in the group—for an all-inclusive rate. Tours of the fly/drive variety also are quite popular, since they offer a "do-it-yourself" opportunity.

If you plan to travel by car and you don't belong to an auto club, now is the time to join one. They can be very helpful about routings and providing emergency service on the road. If you plan the route yourself, make certain the map you purchase or get from your local service station is dated for the current year. The provincial tourist offices can be helpful here. Local chambers of commerce are also good sources of information.

WHAT WILL IT COST? Canada is one of the more expensive countries in the world for travelers, although the recent proliferation of budget accommodations such as hostels and campgrounds has made it possible to travel on an economy budget. Costs will vary from region to region. (The cities are generally more expensive than the countryside.) But the rise of the hotel, motel, and restaurant chains has leveled these differences somewhat.

Note: All prices quoted in this guide are in Canadian dollars unless otherwise noted.

The downtown areas of most cities have older hotels, formerly elegant, that have had to lower their prices to meet the competition on the outskirts. Often, however, they are quite adequate and may compare favorably with European, if not American, standards.

The prices in the table reflect average figures for the entire country. Adjustments may be necessary from province to province and from urban to rural locations.

Every province except Alberta, the Yukon Territory, and the Northwest Territories imposes a sales tax of anywhere between 4 and 12 percent on consumer goods, restaurant meals, and sometimes lodgings. A pleasant surprise, however, was the provincial government of Ontario's lifting of the 7 percent hotel room tax.

Typical Daily Budget for Two People

Room at a moderate hotel or motel	$70.00
Light breakfast for two at hotel or motel (incl. tip)	10.00
Lunch for two at an inexpensive restaurant (incl. tip)	15.00
Dinner for two at a moderate restaurant (incl. tip)	35.00
One sightseeing bus tour (two fares)	10.00
One cocktail apiece for two persons	8.00
Admission for two to one museum or historic site	10.00
	$158.00

In planning your budget don't forget to allow a realistic amount for recreation and entertainment expenses such as the rental of sports equipment, entrance fees to amusement parks, museums, galleries and historical sites; and tickets to movies, concerts, plays, and exhibitions. You'll also need to include souvenirs, extra camera film, and perhaps incidental medical fees that might not be covered by your insurance. Tipping will be another big extra; in some situations this can increase your costs by as much as 15–20 percent.

Picnicking is an excellent way to cut food costs. Most major scenic highways have well-maintained picnic and rest areas equipped with tables, benches, and trashcans, and often fireplaces, running water, and toilets.

SENIOR CITIZEN AND STUDENT DISCOUNTS.
Many attractions throughout Canada—and many hotels, motels, and restaurants—offer discounts to senior citizens and students. In most cases, showing a driver's license, passport, or some other proof of age will suffice—"senior" generally being defined as 65 or over. Museums, movie theaters, and even some stores will often post special senior-citizen rates. Some airlines give seniors a 10% discount on air travel. Those places offering student discounts are generally more stringent in their proof requirements—a high school or college ID, international student travel card, or evidence of age may be requested. Persons under 22 get a discount of up to 25% on air travel on a standby basis.

FACTS AND FIGURES. The country of Canada, the second largest in the world, covers 9,972,334 sq. km (3,850,318 sq. mi.). It is broken down into ten provinces plus the Yukon Territory and the Northwest Territories. The total population is approximately 24,341,181.

Note: References to Canadian areas are often defined as follows:

The Atlantic Provinces are Newfoundland, Nova Scotia, New Brunswick, and Prince Edward Island. Nova Scotia, New Brunswick and Prince Edward Island are often referred to as the *Maritime Provinces.*

The Central Provinces are Québec and Ontario.

The Prairie Provinces are Manitoba, Saskatchewan, and Alberta.

The Western Provinces include British Columbia with the Prairie Provinces.

The Northern Territories are the Yukon and Northwest Territories.

TOURIST INFORMATION. Each province and territory has its own tourism information office, as do the major cities. These offices also provide information on national parks and federal regulations, such as customs duties. With the exception of British Columbia, the Yukon, and Northwest Territories, all of the provincial tourism offices can be reached at the toll-free numbers listed below.

British Columbia: Tourism British Columbia, 1117 Wharf St., Victoria, B.C. V8W 2Z2; 604–387–1642.

Alberta: Travel Alberta, Box 2500, Edmonton, Alberta T5J 2Z4; 403–427–4321 or 800–661–8888.

Saskatchewan: Tourism Saskatchewan, Bank of Montreal Bldg., 2103 11th Ave., Regina, Sask. S4P 3V7; 306–787–2300, 800–667–7191 from U.S.

Manitoba: Travel Manitoba, 7th Floor, 155 Carlton St., Winnipeg, Manitoba R3C 3H8; 204–945–3777 or 800–665–0040.

Ontario: Ministry of Tourism and Recreation, Queenspark, Toronto, Ontario M7A 2E5; 965–4008 or 800–268–3735.

Québec: Tourism Quebec, P.O. Box 20000, Quebec City, Quebec G1K 7X2; toll-free 800–361–6490 (from Canada), 800–443–7000 (from U.S.).

Nova Scotia: Tourism Bureau, Box 130, Halifax, Nova Scotia B3J 2M7; 902–424–5000 or 800–565–7140.

New Brunswick: Tourism New Brunswick, Box 12345, Fredericton, New Brunswick E3B 5C3; toll-free 800–561–0123 (U.S. and Canada).

Prince Edward Island: Visitor Services Division, Box 940, Charlottetown, P.E.I., C1A 7M5; 902–892–2457 or 800–565–0243.

Newfoundland: Dept. of Development and Tourism, Box 2016, St. John's, Newfoundland A1C 5R8; 709–576–2830 or 800–523–6353.

Yukon: Tourism Yukon, P.O. Box 2703, Whitehorse, Yukon, Y1A 2C6; 403–667–5434.

Northwest Territories: Travel Arctic, Government of N.W.T., P.O. Box 1320, Yellowknife, N.W.T. X1A 2L9; 403–873–7400.

In addition, Parks Canada, Department of the Environment, Ottawa, Ontario K1A 1G2, 613–997–2800, handles information on national parks and national historic sites throughout Canada.

WHERE TO GO. Almost anywhere you point your finger on a map of Canada will provide the raw materials for an interesting tour. Here are some suggestions to help you narrow your choices and map out a tour.

Newfoundland. The route from Argentia to St. John's in Newfoundland offers bird sanctuaries at Cape St. Mary's and Witless Bay, the headquarters of pirate Peter Easton at Harbour Grace, and St. John's, the oldest city founded by Europeans on the North American Continent.

For the more rugged side of Newfoundland there is the route from Channel Port-aux-Basques at the end of the ferry from North Sydney, Nova Scotia, to St. John's. Along the way there are Deer Lake, Gros Morne National Park and Terra Nova National Park. The first park is an undeveloped wilderness and the second has interesting wildlife and rugged, forested highlands.

Prince Edward Island. Prince Edward Island is small enough to be taken in on one tour. The Blue Heron Drive will take you through Charlottetown, where Canada's independence was charted at a Confederation Conference in 1864, to Prince Edward Island National Park, with its water sports, nature trails and miles of beaches and bright sand dunes.

Nova Scotia. Nova Scotia offers a number of possibilities. West from Truro, a center of Scottish culture, there are the miner's museum of Springhill, the ruins of Fort Lawrence in Amherst, and (back to the east again) Pictou and the ferry to Prince Edward Island. To the northeast there are the antique steam engines of New Glasgow, the Gaelic-speaking community in Antigonish, the eighteenth-century Fortress Louisbourg, Sydney, and the historic Cabot Trail. To the southwest there is the boat building community in Lunenburg, the Citadel at Halifax, Captain Kidd's alleged buried treasure at Oak Island, the 40-foot tides of Windsor, and a recreation of the first Canadian settlement at Port Royal National Historic Park. In addition, there is the famous Lighthouse Route, 227 miles of rugged seacoast from Yarmouth to Halifax with pirate coves on one side of the road and scenic farms on the other.

New Brunswick. In northern New Brunswick you can take in the Acadian villages of Edmundston, St. Leonard, and Caraquet with its French-speaking population and its fine seafood. Grand Falls, with a 120-foot cataract, is also in the area. Clustered in the southern part of the province are the cities of St. John, Fredericton, and Moncton with the fascinating Bay of Fundy coastline.

Québec. Québec Province offers travelers everything from cities with an Old World flavor to raw wilderness. The Public Relations Department of the City of Montréal offers an excellent booklet that describes a 2.2-mile walk through the historic quarter of the city. It is worth the half day.

A tour of the Laurentian playground to the north of Montréal combines the unique food, culture, and language of La Belle Province with some of the most exciting canoe, camping, and skiing country in the world. A trip along the south shore of the St. Lawrence will take you through the old seignieuries, manor houses, and churches between Longueuil and Sorel. The Richelieu Valley is scenic farm country with markets and fairs in Valleyfield, Drummondville, and Sherbrooke. But for old French Canada you must explore the area between Montréal and Rivière du Loup, which takes in parts of both shores of the St. Lawrence. At Quebec City you can step back into the 18th century within the walls of North America's only remaining walled city, or you can visit the most famous shrine on the continent, at Sainte Anne de Beaupré, a short distance east. Finally, there is the Gaspé Peninsula at the mouth of the St. Lawrence River. Heading out onto the peninsula from Rivière du Loup you will pass fishing and farming villages, covered bridges, Forillon National Park (with its 22 species of whales), and shrines and missions.

Québec has been packaged in hundreds of forms, from a day tour to trips of a few weeks. The Québec Tourist Information Office can provide more information about these tours and the companies that run them, but it is safe to assume that you will pay at least $50 per person per day if you choose to travel that way.

Ontario. There are perhaps more ways to see Ontario than there are to see Québec. There are horseback tours, canoe tours, camping tours, fly/drive tours, tulip festival tours, and even houseboat tours. We'll stick here with tours by region, but there is no end to the ways you can see Ontario. There is a northern route through the Lake of the Woods country. There is the Lake Superior region including Sault Ste. Marie. There is northeastern Ontario with its fishing, camping, and canoeing. Stratford with its Shakespeare Festival is in the middle of the most English part of the world between Liverpool and Victoria. And the famous parks and gardens around Niagara Falls and the Niagara Peninsula are always a popular favorite.

Toronto and its environs offer a number of possibilities for well-planned tours. Another manageable trip would include Ottawa and the Ottawa Valley, which Champlain explored in the seventeenth century. Ottawa, Canada's capital, is a city that revels in pomp and pageantry, and has more museums and monuments than any other Canadian city. Upper Canada on the Heritage Highway includes the St. Lawrence Islands National Park and Upper Canada Village (a re-created Canadian village of about 1850). And these hardly cover the province's points of interest. Once again, write to the provincial tourist office for a list of tours and tour companies, if you want a package. If not, buy a map and plan your own.

Manitoba. Northern Manitoba is large. But if you are up to a 600-mile drive from Prince Albert to The Pas, Flin Flon, and Thompson and back again, you can catch the flavor of the frontier. If cities are more to your liking, try a walking tour of Winnipeg—along with short drives to the Icelandic village of Gimli and to Hecla Provincial Park.

Saskatchewan. There are a handful of ways to divide up Saskatchewan. In the north-central part of the province there is the area around Prince Albert and Prince Albert National Park that goes as far south as Saskatoon. Further south, in the triangle formed by Saskatoon, Swift Current, and Regina, you have Indian Country with impressive re-enactments of the Old West (i.e., Sitting Bull's escape after Little Big Horn) in Swift Current and Moose Jaw. Regina, the home of the Mounted Police, is the starting point for a trip through three provincial parks.

Alberta. In Alberta you can plan a trip to see dinosaur remains in the south-central badlands and at Dinosaur Provincial Park in the southeastern part of the province. Calgary and the area to the south have a western atmosphere celebrated each July during Stampede Week, the rich farmland of Lethbridge, and Waterton Lakes National Park. Edmonton was the starting point of the long road to the Klondike at the turn of the century, and its reminders of that period are worth a trip, especially if you include Elk Island National Park just outside the city. And finally there is the string of mountain parks: Willmore Wilderness Park, Jasper National Park, and Banff National Park—all full of sparkling lakes, streams, mountains, canyons, and forests.

British Columbia. British Columbia is more than Vancouver and Victoria. In the northern part of British Columbia there is wilderness, the fishing center of Prince Rupert, the model city of Kitimat, and the mining town of Prince George. Glacier National Park and its environs are a possibility for a compact trip. Vancouver and the Fraser Valley combine the sophistication of a large city with rural western life. Or you can combine Vancouver with Victoria (and the rest of Vancouver Island) to get two sophisticated cities and the Sunshine Coast.

Yukon Territory. If you don't mind driving and roughing it, you can take in almost all of the accessible parts of the Yukon Territory in one several-days swing. Start at Watson Lake on the British Columbia border and drive 270 miles up the Alaska Highway to Whitehorse, a gold rush center at the turn of the century and the capital of the Yukon today. Then it is a little less than 100 miles, a short drive (in these parts), to Haines Junction. From there it is 190 miles, almost half of it along the edge of Kluane National Park, to the Alaskan border and another 100 miles to Tetlin Junction, Alaska, where you can turn north toward the City of Gold, Dawson, on the Klondike River, about 180 miles away.

(In Dawson City you will find the only legal gambling casino in Canada, an establishment with the remarkable name of Diamond Tooth Gertie's.) About 222 miles more will bring you to Carmacks, a picturesque mining town, another 110 miles will take you back to Whitehorse.

Northwest Territories. The Northwest Territories are too large for a single trip. The one tour suggested for the newcomer to this vast and rugged world is confined to the southern region where summer temperatures are comfortable (and you *should* travel here in the summer). Going from Fort Smith, the old Hudson's Bay Company trading post, to Hay River, to Yellowknife will bring you past Wood Buffalo National Park—the world's largest national park—and Indian reservations, past waterfalls, onto the shores of Great Slave Lake, and into Eskimo artifact museums. It also just might whet the appetite for more of the North.

A number of organizations offer tours for your convenience. Among them are *Pacific Western Airlines,* Vancouver, B.C.; *Nortour,* Montreal, Quebec; *Horizon Holidays,* Toronto, Ont.; *Goligers Tours,* Toronto, Ont.; *Atlas Tours,* Whitehorse, Yukon; *Holidays by Majestic,* Edmonton, Alberta; *DeWest Tours, Ltd.* Vancouver, B.C.; *Society Expeditions,* Seattle, Wash.; *Special Odysseys,* Medina, Wash. See your travel agent for details.

WHEN TO GO. There is no *one* time to go to Canada. The country is too big and too diverse for anything as specific as that.

When you prefer to go will depend on what you like in the way of weather, sports, sightseeing, cultural events, and local color. Be sure to consult the section on *Seasonal Events,* because Canada's pageants, and fairs and festivals of every kind, from the cultural to the agricultural, should be an important part of your planning and enjoyment of this vast and varied country.

While it is impossible to generalize about the best seasons, the area along the border with the United States is most pleasant during May and June or September and October. While the summer heat can make travel in the temperate region uncomfortable, it is, however, an absolutely essential requirement for travel in the North—at least for those who prefer mosquitoes and other insects to the bitter cold. The summer months are also comfortable in the Rockies. And beautiful British Columbia is, of course, a delight year round.

Winter, though all but intolerable in the North, brings a tolerable dry cold to the Prairies. Autumn is most beautiful in the forests of the Atlantic Provinces and the West. And spring, even though it is the most beautiful time for the orchards, suffers in appeal because of the melting snow—especially during April.

SEASONAL EVENTS. In deciding when you will go and in determining your itinerary, you may want to take into account the various seasonal festivals and events that take place in Canada. The list below is by no means all-inclusive; it merely describes some of the more popular events. For exact dates and for more information write to the relevant provincial tourist office.

Newfoundland: *June:* Opening of rainbow trout and salmon fishing seasons. *July:* Summer arts festival in St. John's; Newfoundland Amateur Golf Championship at St. John's Bally Hally Golf Club; Canada's Day Pageant in St. John's. *August:* St. John's Annual Regatta. *September:* Newfoundland Golf Association Match Play Championship at the Bally Hally Golf Club in St. John's; Opening of hunting season. *September and October:* A variety of agricultural fairs and exhibitions throughout the province.

Prince Edward Island: *July:* The Potato Blossom Festival in O'Leary. *August:* Highland Games in Eldon; Old Home Week in Charlottetown; The Harvest Festival in Kensington; The Acadian Festival in Abrams Village.

Nova Scotia: *June:* Apple Blossom Festival in Annapolis Valley; Gala Kite Weekend at the Bell Museum at Baddeck; Festival of the Strait at Port Hawkesbury; Nova Scotia Tattoo at Halifax. *July:* Gathering of the Clans in Pugwash; Highland Games in Sydney; The Lobster Carnival in Pictou; The Annual Jamboree in Bras d'Or; Old Times Fiddling Contest in Dartmouth; Highland Games in Antigonish; Annual Piping Festival in Dartmouth; Acadian Day Festival in L'Ardoise; Nova Scotia Bluegrass and Oldtime Music Festival at Ardoise, Hants County. *August:* Nova Scotia Annual Gaelic Mod at St. Ann's, Cape Breton; Sam Slick Days at Windsor; International Air Show at Yarmouth; Blueberry Harvest Festival at Amherst. *September:* Joseph Howe Festival at Halifax; International Town Criers' Championship at Halifax; Fisheries Exhibition at Lunenburg.

New Brunswick: *May:* Festival of the Arts (Christ Church Cathedral) in Fredericton. *June:* Pioneer Days in Oromocto; Potato Festival in Grand Falls; Railroad Days in Moncton; Salmon Festival in Campbellton. *July:* Canada's Irish Cultural Festival in Chatham; Loyalist Days in Saint John; Lobster Festival in Shediac; Annual Antique Show & Sale in St. Andrews; Old Home Week at Woodstock. *August:* International Hydroplane Regatta at Cocagne; Miramichi Folk Song Festival at Newcastle; Acadian Festival at Carquet; Atlantic National Exhibition at Saint John. *September:* Lumberman's Days at Kings Landing.

Québec: *January:* International Bonspiel in Québec; National Skating Championship in Québec. *February:* Winter Carnival in Québec. *April:* Maple festivals throughout the province. *May:* Festival des Cantons in Sherbrooke. *June:* Man and His World Exhibition in Montréal (through September); St. Jean Baptiste Day Celebrations. *July:* Raftsman's Festival in Hull; Summer Festival in Québec; International Regatta in Valleyfield; Summer Festival in Rivière du Loup. *August:* National Folklore Festival in Chicoutimi; Kayak Canoe Races in Chicoutimi. *September:* Expo Québec in Québec City; Western Festival in St. Tite. *October:* Hunting Festival in St. Michel des Saints; Salon du Sport in Montréal; Snow Goose Festival in Montmagny. *December:* Salon des Métiers d'Art in Montréal; Salon des Artisans in Québec.

Ontario: *March:* Winter Fun Carnival in North Bay. *April:* the Guelph Festival in Guelph; Maple Syrup Festival in Elmira. *May:* Canadian Tulip Festival in Ottawa; Blossom Festival in Niagara Falls; Folk Arts Festival in St. Catherines. *June:* Shakespeare Festival in Stratford (through October); Metro Caravan ethnic fair in Toronto; Queen's Plate thoroughbred horse race in Toronto; Changing of the Guard at Ottawa's Parliament Buildings (through September). *July:* Fun in the Sun in Fort Frances; Highland Games in Cobourg; Highland Games in Brantford; Royal Canadian Henley Regatta in St. Catharines; Horse Show in St. Catherines. *August:* Miner's Festival in Cobalt; Bancroft Jamboree in Bancroft; Glengarry Highland Games in Maxville; Wikwemikong Indian Pow-Wow on Manitoulin Island; Six Nations Indian Pageant in Brantford; Highland Games in Fergus; Canadian National Exhibition in Toronto. *September:* Western Fair in London; Grape and Wine Festival in St. Catherines; Pioneer Festival in Toronto. *October:* Oktoberfest in Kitchener-Waterloo; Pioneer Day (Mennonite) Celebration in Jordan. *November:* Royal Winter Fair and Horse Show in Toronto.

Manitoba: *February:* Trappers' Festival in The Pas. *April:* Royal Manitoba Winter Fair in Brandon. *June:* Provincial Exhibition in Brandon; Nickel Days in Thompson; Red River Exhibition, Winnipeg. *July:* Trout Festival in Flin Flon; Winnipeg Folk Festival; Manitoba Stampede in Morris; Threshermen's Reunion in Austin; Northwest Roundup and Agricultural Fair in Swan River; National Ukrainian Festival in Dauphin. *August:* Pioneer Days in Steinbach; Opasquia Indian Days in The Pas; Icelandic Festival in Gimli; Corn and Apple Festival in Morden.

Saskatchewan: *March:* Winter Festival in Meadow Lake. *April:* Sportsman Show in Saskatoon. *May:* Ukrainian Folk Heritage in Saskatoon; Big Muddy Rodeo in Bengorigh; *June:* Antique Car and Gun Show in Weyburn; Ethnic Festival in Yorkton; Frontier Days in Swift Current; Pike Festival in Nipawin. *July:* Reunion Days in Indian Head; Rodeo in Wood Mountain; Saskatchewan

Stampede in Yorkton; Exhibition in North Battleford; Buffalo Days in Regina. *August:* Silver Spur Galaxy Horse Show in Lloydminster; Threshing Bee and Hobby Show in Maple Creek. *September:* Threshermen's Reunion in Frobisher. *October:* Western Canadian Amateurs Championship Fiddling Contest in Swift Current; Annual Goose Festival in Kindersley; Rodeo in Cutknife. *November:* Annual Carnival in Climax; Fall Carnival in Frontier; Annual Turkey Shoot in Kindersley; Western Canadian Agribition in Regina; Annual Winter Festival in Spalding; International Short Film and Video Festival, Yorkton.

Alberta: *May:* Festival of the Arts in Banff (through summer); International Horse Show in Calgary; Rodeo in Taber; Pioneer Days in Hanna. *June:* Big Horn Rodeo in Hinton; Agricultural Fair and Stampede in Rocky Mt. Horse; Rodeo Week in St. Albert; Stampede in Wainwright; Little Britches Rodeo in Didsbury. *July:* Stampede in Calgary; Midnight Days in Fort Macleod; Klondike Days in Edmonton. *August:* Lac Cardinal Stampede in Grimshaw; Indian Days in Banff. *September:* Rifleman's Rodeo in Panoka; Blueberry Festival in Fort McMurray.

British Columbia: *May:* Victorian Days in Victoria; Fraser River Canoe Marathon in New Westminster; Victoria Weekend Rodeo at Cloverdale; Oyster Festival in Denman Island. *June:* Stampede at Williams Lake; B.C. Salmon Derby in Howe Sound. *July:* Nelson's Curling Bonspiel in Nelson; Logger's Sports in Sooke; Sea Festival in Vancouver. *August:* Peach Festival in Penticton; Loggers' Sports Day in Squamish; Vancouver Island Exhibition in Nanaimo; Salmon Day in Vancouver; Pacific National Exhibition in Vancouver. *September:* Big Dam Canoe Race in Hudson's Hope; Gold Panning Taylor Day Festivities in Taylor; Rodeo in Lillooet. *October:* Oktoberfest in Vancouver.

Northwest Territories: *March:* International Curling Bonspiel at Inuvik; Caribou Carnival in Yellowknife. *April:* Toonik Tyme in Frobisher Bay. *June:* Pine Days in Pine Point.

Yukon Territory: *February:* Sourdough Rendezvous in Whitehorse; Ice Worm Squirm in Faro. *March:* Winter Carnival in Mayo; Spring Carnival in Dawson City. *August:* Discovery Days in Dawson City.

It is almost impossible to find any generalizations to cover such variety and ingenuity. Every region, every season, every occasion, every product, every activity is likely to have its own festival somewhere in this country. Almost the only thing you can do is decide when you can travel, where you want to go, and then begin to check into what will be going on there at that time. In addition to the events listed in this book, the various tourist offices and local chambers of commerce are gold mines of fascinating information.

 TRAVEL AGENTS. The critical issues in choosing a travel agent are how knowledgeable that person is about travel and how reliable his or her bookings are, regardless of whether you are looking for a package tour or planning to go it independently. The cost will be substantially the same whether you go to a major tour operator such as *Maupintour, American Express, Thos. Cook & Son* and *Olson's* or go to the small agency around the corner.

The importance of a travel agent is not merely for the making of reservations, however. A good travel agent booking a flight for a customer will know what general discounts are in effect based on how long your stay will be, how far in advance you are able to make your reservations, whether you are making a simple round trip or adding extra stops and other factors. He or she will also likely be able to suggest suitable accommodations or packages that offer the kind of services you want.

In the case of package tours, you want to be sure that the tour operator can deliver the package being offered. Here again, a travel agent can be helpful. Certainly the organizations named above have established their reputations based on reliability—the inevitable occasional foul-up notwithstanding.

Not all U.S. travel agents are licensed, as the laws vary from state to state, but membership in the American Society of Travel Agents (ASTA) is a safeguard. Similarly, U.K. agents belong to the Association of British Travel Agents (ABTA). Members prominently display ASTA or ABTA shields.

Make travel arrangements carefully. To avoid being victimized by fly-by-night operators who might claim better bargains, look for the ASTA member shield—the hallmark of dependable travel service. You'll find the shield on entrance doors, windows, and all office forms of the member agency you select.

ASTA membership indicates that the agent has been in business for a minimum of three consecutive years and is officially approved by the Society to sell tickets on behalf of airlines and cruise ships. ASTA agents also will arrange bookings for trains, buses, or car rentals. For further information write ASTA, 4400 MacArthur Blvd.; N.W., Washington, D.C. 20007, or call 202–965–7520.

HOW TO GET THERE. By commercial airline. Almost all of the international airlines have service into and out of Montréal and/or Toronto. You can fly to Canada from the major European capitals and from Central America, the Caribbean, and the Middle East on *Air France, Alitalia, Aeromexico, British Airways, El Al, KLM, Lufthansa, Sabena, Scandinavian Airlines, Air Maroc,* and *Swissair.* Also, *Air Canada* has service to several European capitals.

The major international airport on the West Coast is at Vancouver International, which has regular arrivals from many parts of the world.

Flying to Canada from the United States is a very simple matter. New York is connected with Toronto, Montréal, Québec, Ottawa, Halifax and other eastern cities. There are flights from Chicago to Winnepeg, Calgary, Toronto, Ottawa, and Montréal; and from Boston to Halifax, Yarmouth, St. John, Montréal, Toronto, and other cities. There are also direct links from Cleveland, Buffalo, Detroit, Pittsburgh, Miami, Tampa, Dallas, Houston, and Hartford to various points in eastern Canada.

On the West Coast you can fly from San Francisco and Los Angeles to Calgary, Edmonton, Vancouver, Toronto, and Montréal.

In between there are flights on regional airlines to Winnipeg from Minneapolis, Minnesota, and Fargo and Grand Forks, North Dakota; to Lethbridge, Alberta, from Great Falls, Montana.

Before booking a flight be sure to consult your travel agent to see if you are eligible for any of the economy, youth, or tour fares. (See the *Canada by Air* section.)

By private plane. Access to Canada by private airplane is relatively easy. All you need are a certificate of aircraft registration, an aeronautic certificate, a log book, and a valid pilot's license. Landing fees are moderate, but remember that the usual customs provisions are in effect whether you arrive by private plane or by some other, more mundane method. Visiting pilots should obtain a booklet, *Air Tourist Information—Air Canada,* from Transport Canada, AISP/A, Ottawa, Ont. K1A 0N8; 613–995–0197. Aeronautical charts are supplied by the Canada Map Office, 615 Booth St., Ottawa, Ont. K1A 0E9; 613–998–9900.

There are also a number of charter companies which will take you anywhere in Canada that has an airstrip or will make available a bush plane for travel in the North.

For details write to the appropriate provincial tourist office.

By car. Arriving in Canada by car offers you the most flexibility of any form of travel because it allows you to enter at your own convenience and to stop wherever, whenever, and however long you wish. (See *Canada by Car* section.)

You may bring your automobile into Canada free of duty for your own personal use for up to six months.

The U.S. Interstate Highway System leads directly into Canada at twelve points: US 95 from Maine to New Brunswick; US 91 and US 89 from Vermont to Québec; US 87 from New York to Québec; US 81 and a spur off US 90 from New York to Ontario; US 94, US 96, and US 75 from Michigan to Ontario; US 29 from North Dakota to Manitoba; US 15 from Montana to Alberta: and US 5 from Washington State to British Columbia.

Most of these connections and many of the less important ones, via national highways and state roads, hook up with the Trans-Canada Highway within a few miles.

The only routes from Alaska into Canada are the Alaska Highway (from Fairbanks), the Klondike Highway (from Skagway), and the Taylor Highway (to Dawson City).

By bus. The only bus company that makes long-distance runs from the United States to Canada is *Greyhound,* but its network of routes can get you from almost any point in the United States to any point in Canada. Inquire for information at your local Greyhound office. Sample fares run about $90 round-trip from New York to Montréal, and about $225 round-trip from San Francisco to Vancouver.

By rail. There are only three direct *Amtrak* connections with Canada: New York to Montréal, Buffalo to Toronto, and Chicago to Toronto. The one way coach fares from New York to Montréal run about $61; New York to Toronto with a change of trains at Buffalo runs about $72; Chicago to Toronto $68. A variety of excursion fares are available for round-trip fares so inquire first from Amtrak or your travel agent.

In addition to the three Amtrak direct routes, there are connecting services from many major cities along the U.S.-Canadian border. For information call or write to your nearest Amtrak office.

By yacht. Many Canadian cities allow entry by sea on private yachts and boats. Local marine authorities can advise you about the necessary documentation and procedure.

HINTS TO HANDICAPPED TRAVELERS. One of the newest and largest groups to enter the travel scene is the handicapped. There are millions of people who are physically able to travel and who do so enthusiastically when they know they will be able to move about with safety and comfort. A growing number of travel agents specialize in this market. Generally, their tours parallel those of the non-handicapped traveler but at a more leisurely pace, with everything checked out in advance to eliminate inconvenience. Important sources of information in this field are: The Travel Information Center, Moss Rehabilitation Hospital, 12th St. and Tabor Road, Philadelphia, PA 19141; *Easter Seal Society,* Director of Education and Information Service, 2023 Ogden Ave., Chicago, IL 60612. International Air Transport Association, 2000 Teel St., Montreal, Quebec H3A 2R4 publishes a free pamphlet, *Incapacitated Passengers Air Travel Guide.* Other publications giving valuable information about facilities for the handicapped are: *Access to the World,* by Louisa Weiss, published by Facts on File, 460 Park Avenue South, New York, NY 10016; and the annually revised guide *The Wheelchair Traveler,* by Douglass R. Annand, Ball Hill Road, Milford, NH 03055.

METRIC CONVERSION

Converting Metric to U.S. Measurements

Multiply:	by:	to find:
Length		
millimeters (mm)	.039	inches (in)
meters (m)	3.28	feet (ft)
meters	1.09	yards (yd)
kilometers (km)	.62	miles (mi)
Area		
hectare (ha)	2.47	acres
Capacity		
liters (L)	1.06	quarts (qt)
liters	.26	gallons (gal)
liters	2.11	pints (pt)
Weight		
gram (g)	.04	ounce (oz)
kilogram (kg)	2.20	pounds (lb)
metric ton (MT)	.98	tons (t)
Power		
kilowatt (kw)	1.34	horsepower (hp)

Temperature
  degrees Celsius   9/5 (then add 32)   degrees Fahrenheit

Converting U.S. to Metric Measurements

Multiply:	by:	to find:
Length		
inches (in)	25.40	millimeters (mm)
feet (ft)	.30	meters (m)
yards (yd)	.91	meters
miles (mi)	1.61	kilometers (km)
Area		
acres	.40	hectares (ha)
Capacity		
pints (pt)	.47	liters (L)
quarts (qt)	.95	liters
gallons (gal)	3.79	liters
Weight		
ounces (oz)	28.35	grams (g)
pounds (lb)	.45	kilograms (kg)
tons (t)	1.11	metric tons (MT)
Power		
horsepower (hp)	.75	kilowatts
Temperature		
degrees Fahrenheit	5/9 (after subtracting 32)	degrees Celsius

WHAT TO TAKE. First of all, don't try to pack at the last moment. Instead, begin in advance and make a list of things each member of the family will need; then check off the items as you pack them. You'll find it saves time and reduces confusion.

If you wear prescription glasses or contact lenses always take an extra pair or set; at the very least have a copy of your prescription. This is true of prescription sunglasses, too. A travel iron often comes in handy. Transparent plastic bags (large and small) are useful for wet bathing suits, socks, shoes, spillable cosmetics, and other easily damaged items. Plenty of photo film, suntan lotion, insect repellent, toothpaste, soap, and so forth, if purchased before you go, will help reduce those nuisance stops to pick up things you forgot. Binoculars, a compass, and a magnifying glass for reading those fine-print maps are all handy items which won't take up much space.

All members of the family should have a sturdy pair of shoes with nonslip soles. Keep them handy in the back of the car. You never know when you may want to stop and clamber along a rocky trail to fully enjoy the Canadian terrain.

Carry raingear in a separate bag in the back of the car (so no one will have to get out and hunt for it in the middle of a downpour).

If you're stopping en route, you'll find it's convenient to pack separately those few things you'll need for just an overnight stay. It saves unloading the entire car, only to reload it the next morning.

Apart from these general considerations, when you assemble your traveling wardrobe you need to take into account the temperature and weather of the region you're visiting. Light, loose-fitting clothing is best for hot areas. For the cold and snow, you'll want a very warm coat, gloves, hat, scarf or muffler, and even boots. In the North you can't have too much warm clothing, although you may not want to wear it all at once if you plan to engage in strenuous physical activity. A slicker or an umbrella is a must.

Finally, be wise about packing. Regardless of how or where you plan to travel, it is more convenient to travel light.

TRAVELING WITH CHILDREN. Minor medical problems can easily be handled with a good first-aid kit. Include the standard contents as recommended by the Red Cross, any special prescriptions required, spare glasses, a cough syrup, a stomachache remedy, a laxative, children's aspirin, an ophthalmic ointment, and antidiarrheal tablets (they travel more safely than liquid). One of the greatest triumphs of medical science, as far as traveling with children is concerned, is the individually packaged gauze pad pretreated with antiseptic and a mild local anesthetic. These are ideal for cleaning up scrapes and scratches. A tube of zinc oxide is a versatile aid for sun- and windburn, diaper rash, and minor abrasions. The dosage and directions for all medicines should be checked with your physician before departure. Pack the kit in a small shoulder bag so it can be kept handy.

Packing for children requires a little extra effort. Clothing should be simple, comfortable, and as versatile as possible. Wash-and-wear and stain-resistant fabrics will make life easier for mother. One of the handiest items is a box of small premoistened towelettes for impromptu clean-ups of hands and face. If a child is not yet a secure walker, it is a good idea to pack him too—in one of the back carriers that allow parents to carry the child while keeping their own hands free.

In your sightseeing, try to include something of interest to children. Public parks, zoos, aquariums, and amusement parks are perfect child-pleasers and often have special attractions for the kids. Canada is particularly rich in zoos. There are four in Québec (Charlesbourg, Granby, St. Felicien, and Montréal), three in Ontario (two in Toronto and one in Thunder Bay), two in Saskatchewan (Saskatoon and Moose Jaw), two in Alberta (Calgary and Edmonton), and one each in Manitoba (Winnipeg) and British Columbia (Vancouver). There are also wildlife parks in many areas. Beaches, circuses, and forts also make big hits with tiny tourists.

MONEY. The Canadian dollar, like the U.S. dollar, is divided into 100 cents, and coins and bills exist in the same denominations as in the U.S.—i.e., 1¢, 5¢, 10¢, etc.; $1, $2, $5, $10, etc.

Actual exchange rates fluctuate from day to day but the Canadian dollar is usually worth about 83 U.S. cents and about 49 British pence. In order to get the most for your money, convert it before you leave home. Waiting until you get to Canada can create problems. The banks, which are generally open only from 10 A.M. to 3 P.M. Monday through Friday, are sometimes not prepared to exchange foreign currency, and, even if you find one that will, it is not always convenient to go to a bank. Furthermore, hotels, stores, and restaurants may offer something less than the best rate. The best policy is to find the nearest Deak-Perera foreign exchange office. There are Deak bureaus in Vancouver (617 Granville); Toronto (10 King St. E. and 55 Bloor St. W.); and Montréal (1155 Sherbrooke St. W.).

There are no restrictions on the amount of money you may bring into or take out of Canada. Both Canadians and foreign visitors may convert money from Canadian tender to another currency or from a foreign currency to Canadian dollars as often as they want, in amounts as great as they want, either inside or outside Canada.

CREDIT CARDS. The main types of credit and bank cards widely accepted in Canada are *American Express, Carte Blanche, Diners Club, Visa* (formerly *BankAmericard* in the U.S. and *Chargex* in Canada) and *Master-Card.* If you don't already have a card, inquire locally to see where they are available in your area.

These cards have several advantages. Obviously they spare you the nuisance and risk of carrying large amounts of cash, or even traveler's checks, which are sometimes difficult to cash without full identification. They can be used to draw extra funds in case of emergencies, or to take advantage of sales and special opportunities. They can eliminate losses from unfavorable rates of exchange and commissions in hotels, restaurants and resorts, or from the need to change large sums to pay small bills. For people traveling on expense accounts, or seeking tax deductions for business and professional expenses, they provide the required records. They can make it easier to return unwanted merchandise to stores, because the store simply makes out a credit slip to your card's account.

Despite these conveniences, there are various special restrictions and charges that apply in particular cases and these can raise the final cost of an item to considerably more than what you expected or what the introductory brochure led you to expect.

TRAVELER'S CHECKS. These are the best way to safeguard travel funds. They are sold in various banks and financial companies in terms of American and Canadian dollars and, with proper identification, are as readily accepted as cash. *American Express* has offices throughout the U.S. and Canada; also widely accepted in Canada are *Thomas Cook* traveler's checks, represented by Canada Permanent Trust Company and Toronto Dominion Bank. *Deak-Perera Company* also issues traveler's checks in Canadian funds, although these may be harder to cash outside banks or major hotels.

 ENTERING CANADA. Customs regulations between the United States and Canada are among the most liberal in the world. Passing from one country to the other is usually a simple matter of presenting some valid and acceptable form of identification and answering a few simple questions about where you were born, where you live, why you are visiting Canada, and how long you will stay.

The identification need not be a passport, although this is certainly acceptable. You can also use a driver's license, birth certificate, draft card, Social Security card, certificate of naturalization, or resident alien ("green") card. Entry procedure for citizens of Great Britain, Australia, and New Zealand is similarly simple.

Canada allows British and American guests to bring their cars (for less than 6 months), boats or canoes, rifles and shotguns (but not handguns or automatic weapons) and 200 rounds of ammunition, cameras, radios, sports equipment, and typewriters into the country without paying any duty. Sometimes they will require a deposit for trailers and household equipment, but these are refundable when you cross back over the border. (This is to guarantee that you do not sell these items in Canada for a profit.) Needless to say, you may bring clothing, personal items, and any professional tools or equipment you need (if you work in Canada) without charge or restriction. It is also a good idea to carry your medical insurance and insurance for boats, vehicles, and personal luggage.

Some items are restricted, however. You need the contract for a rented car. And, if you are going to return home and leave behind a car you rented in the States, you have to fill out an E29B customs form. Tobacco is limited. Dogs, for hunting or pets, are duty-free, but you must bring a certificate from a veterinary inspector to prove that the dog has no communicable diseases. (Cats may enter without restriction.) All plants must be examined at the customs station to preclude the entry of destructive insects. Most important, Canadian officials are diligent in pursuing smugglers of narcotics and other illegal items.

 TIME ZONES. Canada spans six time zones, but only 4½ hours separate Newfoundland from the Yukon. This is because there is only ½ hour difference between Newfoundland Standard Time and Atlantic Standard Time. From East to West the six zones include the following regions of Canada:

Newfoundland Standard Time: Newfoundland.

Atlantic Standard Time: The Maritime Provinces, Labrador, most of Baffin Island, and Anicosti Island.

Eastern Standard Time: Québec Province (a few miles west of Thunder Bay) and all of Ontario east of 90° longitude.

Central Standard Time: Ontario west of 90° longitude, Manitoba, the Keewatin district of the Northwest Territories, and roughly the eastern half of Saskatchewan.

Mountain Standard Time: The rest of Saskatchewan, Alberta, those portions of the Northwest Territories directly to the north of Saskatchewan and Alberta, and the northeastern corner of British Columbia.

Pacific Standard Time: The rest of British Columbia and Yukon.

When the noon gun booms out in Vancouver's Stanley Park, it is: 1 P.M. in Calgary and Edmonton; 2 P.M. in Winnipeg; 3 P.M. in Toronto, Ottawa, and Montréal; 4 P.M. in Halifax, Charlottetown, and St. John, N.B.; and 4:30 P.M. in Newfoundland.

Daylight Savings Time (DST) is in effect in many parts of the country from the last Sunday in April to the last Sunday in October. The slogan "Spring forward, Fall back" is a good way to remember how to adjust your watch. If you're traveling a long distance within Canada, the optional use of DST from one area to another may increase the difference between time zones by an extra hour.

CANADA BY CAR. Canada's most important road, the Trans-Canada Hwy. (Hwy. 1), traverses just under 5,000 miles from Victoria, British Columbia, to St. John's, Newfoundland, using ferries to bridge coastal waters at each end.

Most of the Trans-Canada Hwy., as far east as Sydney, Nova Scotia, was constructed by 1962 after 12 years of widening old roads and building new stretches so that a single highway, now marked by signs with a white maple leaf on a green field, would cross the country from coast to coast. The finished product runs from Victoria through (or passing close by) Vancouver, Kamloops, Calgary, Regina, Winnipeg, Toronto, Montréal, Québec City, Fredericton, Halifax, and Sydney, ending at St. John's.

The second largest Canadian road, the Yellowhead Hwy. (Hwy. 16), follows the old Indian route from the Pacific Coast and over the Rockies to the Prairie. The main branch begins in Prince Rupert, British Columbia, and runs through Jasper National Park, Edmonton, and Saskatoon to its junction with the Trans-Canada Hwy. at Portage la Prairie, just over 50 miles east of Winnipeg. Traffic from Vancouver gains access to Hwy. 16 by its second branch, which begins at Kamloops.

Dawson Creek, British Columbia, just over the Alberta border, is the beginning of the 1,523-mile Alaska (Hwy. 2 in Alaska, Hwy. 1 in the Yukon, and Hwy. 97 in British Columbia). Two-thirds of this highway is in Canada and most of it is unpaved. The Alaska Hwy. goes through Fort St. John and Fort Nelson before crossing the northernmost Rockies, where it rises to over 4,000 feet above sea level. Then it enters the Yukon at Watson Lake, proceeding to the Alaska border via Whitehorse and Haines Junction. The last stretch, in Alaska, terminates at Fairbanks.

These primary arteries, along with the complex of roads in southeastern Ontario, around Toronto, bear most of the traffic in Canada. Along with connecting routes—such as the one between Calgary and Edmonton—they will take you anywhere you want to go in the populated areas.

North of the population centers roads become fewer and less developed. The unpaved Mackenzie Highway runs north from central Alberta to Yellowknife, Northwest Territories, and the Dempster Highway connects Dawson City and Inuvik.

Speed limits vary from province to province, but they are usually within the 50–60 mph (90–100 kilometers per hour) range outside the cities. The price of gasoline varies more than the speed limit. And Canada is much farther along in adopting the metric system than the United States. Distances are shown in kilometers, and liquids, including gasoline, are usually sold in liters. (There are 3.78 liters in a U.S. gallon.) (Comprehending the cost of gas in liters may be confusing but no less so than understanding your purchases in terms of the old Imperial gallon—the equivalent of 1.2 U.S. gallons or 4.5 liters—which, to confuse the traveler even further, is still in use in many places.)

The price of gasoline ranges from 40¢ to 52¢ per liter. Ontario prices are the norm, dropping slightly in Québec, Manitoba, Saskatchewan, and British Columbia but rising slightly in the Atlantic provinces, the Yukon and the Northwest Territories. The only "bargain" is in Alberta, where the absence of a provincial tax drops the cost. Regular gas is a few cents less in all provinces, unleaded premium a few cents more. And, needless to say, prices could jump higher at any time.

If you drive your own car into Canada from the United States, you should get a Canadian Non-Resident Inter-Province Motor Vehicle Insurance Liability Card, which is available from insurance companies in the States. The best source of information and advice about automobile insurance is *The Insurance Bureau of Canada*, 181 University Ave., Toronto, Ont. M5H 3M7; (416) 362–2031. Your U.S. driver's license is valid throughout Canada. Drivers from other countries are urged to obtain an International Driver's License before they come to Canada. These are available through various motor clubs in your native country.

Québec is the only province with toll roads (25 cents to 50 cents per gate on the Laurentian and Eastern Townships auto routes). In a number of places you will have to take a ferry to get where you are going by car.

Obviously you can't take your car from the mainland to Newfoundland or Prince Edward Island without a ferry. But ferry travel has become a popular form of recreational travel on both coasts and even on the Great Lakes.

If you are a member of AAA, you can dial 1–800–336–HELP for emergency road service in Canada.

CAR RENTALS. If you come to Canada by air or rail and want to rent a car, you can deal through *Hertz, Avis,* and *Budget Rent-A-Car,* whose rates are comparable to those in the States. They all have stations at major airports and you can reserve your car before you leave home.

However, if you are looking for a bargain or a recreational vehicle, try: *Tilden Rent-A-Car,* 1485 Stanley St., Montréal, Québec H3A 1P6, (514) 842–9445 in Canada.

 CANADA BY AIR. *Air Canada,* the state-owned airline, operates in every province. Aside from *Air Canada,* the major domestic carriers are *CP Air, Eastern Provincial Airways, Norcanair, Nordair, Pacific Western Airlines, and Québecair.* There are regularly scheduled flights to every major city and to most smaller cities, including many in the Yukon and the Northwest Territories.

In addition to the regular flights in the North, there are also a number of charter airlines and fly-in airports. Check with the territorial tourist agencies for charter companies and with the District Controller of Air Services in the territorial (and provincial) capitals for the locations of air bases that allow private flights and for regulations.

Major international credit cards are generally accepted by airlines. Best to check ahead, though.

Be sure to identify all bags by firmly affixing your name to the outside and inside. The airlines will not accept them for checking otherwise. Name tags ensure a faster tracing of misdirected luggage. They also avoid the possibility of picking up someone else's bag.

Canada is a huge country. The airplane has shrunk it considerably and the flying time between coasts is tolerable. However, service to smaller cities is often only once or twice a day. Therefore, you may encounter long stopovers when trying to reach your destination.

Fly/Drive. As an alternative to waits in airports, you may want to consider a fly/drive package, which offers a different way to satisfy a deeper curiosity. Most airlines, in conjunction with car-rental companies, offer these combination opportunities to most parts of the country all year round.

All you have to do is decide where you want to go, and what you would like to see and do. Then visit your travel agent, who will have a large selection of fly/drive packages from which you can make a choice.

Fly/drive package rates and flexibilities vary considerably. Generally, they cover one or more cities plus the use of a rented car for a specified number of days.

Car usage also varies. For example, with some packages you can drive an unlimited number of miles free. With others you get a specified number of miles free, then must pay an additional charge per mile for the overage. Gas is generally not included, but insurance is.

Some packages offer plans for small groups and a choice of hotel accommodations. Some even offer motor homes, if you're interested in roughing it. Check into special children's rates as well.

Before booking, though, check with your agent about where to pick up the car (at airport or other station), and about the time it will take you to arrive at your hotel to meet your reservation. If you are not going to pick up the car

at the airport, check ahead on airport limousines and bus and taxi service to
your hotel.

For More Information. In Ontario: *Aeronautical Information Services,
P/T,* Transport Canada, Place de Ville, Ottawa, Ont. K1A 0N8. **In British
Columbia:** *CP Air,* One Grant McConachie Way, Vancouver International
Airport, B.C. V7B 1V1. **In Atlantic Canada:** *Eastern Provincial Airways,* Box
178, Elmsdale, Nova Scotia B0N 1M0. **In Saskatchewan:** *Norcanair,* Hanger
2, Mobile 3, Saskatoon, Sask. S7M 5X4. **In Québec:** *Québecair,* Montréal
International Airport, P.O. Box 490, Dorval, Que., H4Y 1B5; *Air Canada,*
Place Air Canada, Montréal, Québec H2Z 1X5; *Nordair,* 1320 Graham Blvd.,
Town of Mount Royal, Québec, H3P 3C8; *CP Air,* 1500 Atwater, Montreal,
Quebec. **In Alberta:** *Pacific Western Airlines,* 615 18 St. SE, Calgary, Alberta
T2E 6J5. **In Manitoba:** *Pacific Western Airlines,* 570 Fenny Rd., Winnipeg,
Manitoba, R3H 0T7 204–632–2811.

CANADA BY RAILROAD. Transcontinental rail service is provided by *Via Rail Canada.* It takes about four
days and four nights to cross Canada by train. The line
also runs shorter routes between major eastern cities. In
addition there are smaller lines which operate within individual provinces.
Information is available from the lines listed below. Or you can check with your
travel agent or with the provincial tourist agencies for these local lines.

There are no trains at all in the Northwest Territories or the Yukon.

Both sleeping-car and coach accommodations exist on most trains. Both
classes allow access to dining cars. Sleeping-car passengers, however, can enjoy
comfortable parlor cars, drawing rooms, bedrooms, and roomettes. Fares are
reasonable. (Vancouver to Montréal fares range from under $250 for coach to
a little over $400 for a roomette. And a variety of round trip, advance purchase,
youth, senior citizen, family and group rates reduce fares anywhere up to 50
percent.

Canrailpass offers flat-rate passes for 8, 15, 22, and 30 days that can result
in substantial savings.

For More Information. In Nova Scotia: *Via Rail Canada,* 24-hour service:
800–561–3952 or 800–361–7773. **In Québec:** *Via Rail Canada,* Rail Travel
Bureau, Central Station, Montréal, P.Q. H3C 3N3; *Cartier Railway,* Gaganon,
Quebec, G0G 1K0; *Québec Central Railway,* 780 CP Rail Terrace, Sherbrooke,
Quebec, J1H 1T8; *Québec North Shore and Labrador Railroad,* 100 Retty St.,
Sett-iles, Quebec; G4R 3E1. **In Ontario:** *Algoma Central Railway,* P.O. Box
7000, Sault Ste. Marie, Ont. P6A 5P6; *Ontario Northland Railway,* 195 Regina
St., North Bay, Ont. P1B 8L3. **In British Columbia:** *British Columbia Railway,*
P.O. Box 8770, Vancouver, B.C., V6B 4X6. **In Alberta:** *Rail* 10004 104 Ave.,
Edmonton, Alberta, T5J 0K1. **In Manitoba:** *Via Rail Travel Center,* room 101,
123 Main St., Winnipeg, Manitoba R3C 2P8.

Also contact *Amtrak,* National Railroad Passenger Corp., 400 North Capitol
Street, N.W., Washington, D.C. 20001.

CANADA BY BUS. The long-distance bus system in
Canada is important because it services towns without
airports and rail lines. It reaches into almost every populated area of the country.

The **Atlantic Provinces** have the *St. John's Transportation Commission* and
a number of smaller companies in Newfoundland, the *SMT System* in New
Brunswick and Prince Edward Island, and *Acadian Lines* and the *Mackenzie
Line* in Nova Scotia.

Québec has long-distance bus routes along both banks of the St. Lawrence,
on the Gaspé, in the eastern townships, up into the Laurentians, and out to the
northwestern part of the province.

Ontario is equally well served by *Colonial Coach Lines, Gray Coach Lines,
Greyhound, Ontario Northland, Grey Goose Bus Lines,* and *Chatham Bus Lines.*

Greyhound, Grey Goose, Eagle, Beaver, Manitoba Motor Transit and *North
Star Bus Line* leave **Manitoba.** *Greyhound, Saskatchewan Bus Company, Cross-
land Coachways, Beacon Bus Line, Leader-Climax Bus Line, Moose Mountain
Bus Line,* and *Safe-T Motor Coach Line* all have routes in parts of **Saskatche-**

wan. *Greyhound, Coachways, Red Arrow,* and *Cardinal Coach Lines* cover **Alberta.** And *Greyhound, Coachways, Vancouver Island Coach Lines, Pacific Coach Lines, Squamish Coach Lines, Misty Islands Transportation Co., Barkerville Stage Lines, Lillooet Coach Lines,* and *Cranbrook Golden Bus Lines* will take you where you want to go in **British Columbia.**

Greyhound ventures into selected areas in the **Northwest Territories,** and *Coachways* goes into the **Yukon.** *Alaska Coachways* offers regular service to Fairbanks and Anchorage, Alaska, from the Canadian border.

Canada's two major carriers, *Voyageur* and *Greyhound,* offer several cost-cutting options. Greyhound's *Ameripass,* modeled after European rail passes, permits unlimited travel on any Greyhound line in North America, except Mexico, Alaska, and Vancouver Island. A 7-day pass costs over $250 (Canadian); 15 days, about $350; 30 days, about $500. For long-distance bus travel in Canada, another alternative is Voyageur's excursion discount plan. To qualify, you must leave any day except Friday and return within five days. The regular return rate between Toronto and Montréal, for example, drops about 25% if these conditions are met.

Addresses for bus lines: *Acadian Lines,* 6040 Almon St., Halifax, Nova Scotia B3K 5M1. *Gray Coach Lines,* Toronto Bus Terminal, 610 Bay St., Toronto, Ontario M5G 1M5. *Greyhound Lines of Canada Ltd.,* 222 First Ave., S.W., Calgary, Alberta T2P 0A6. *Pacific Coach Lines,* 150 Dunsmuir Street, Vancouver, British Columbia V6B 1W9. *Saskatchewan Transportation Company,* Transportation Building, 2041 Hamilton St., Regina, Saskatchewan S4P 2E2. *Voyageur Colonial Ltd.,* 265 Catherine St., Ottawa, Ontario K1R 7S5.

ACCOMMODATIONS. Although there are many establishments available for the traveler across Canada, they vary substantially in accommodations. If you do not have reservations, it is wise to begin looking for a suitable place to stay early in the afternoon and not run the risk of having to settle for pot luck later in the day when most motorists have decided to settle in for the night. If you have reservations, you should advise the establishment in advance if you expect to arrive late, since, otherwise, some places will not hold reservations after a certain hour.

Reserve well in advance for hotels and motels in popular resort areas at peak seasons. Also, many cities, in any season, may be hosting conventions or special events at the time you arrive. Planning your trip early will either provide you with the accommodations you want to give you plenty of time to make alternative arrangements.

A number of hotels and motels have one-day laundry and dry-cleaning services, and many motels have coin laundries. If your hotel does not have these services or a barbershop or beauty salon, there will almost certainly be local establishments nearby. Just ask your hotel clerk.

Most motels, but not all, have telephones in the rooms. However, if you want to be sure of room service, you will be better off in a hotel.

Many motels, even some in central cities, have swimming pools.

You can assume free parking at motels, motor hotels, and country and resort hotels. But you will pay for parking at most city hotels, although certain establishments do have free parking.

Cribs for the children are almost always on hand—sometimes at no cost, but more frequently at a minimal charge. Cots to supplement the beds in your rooms will also involve a minimal charge. The better hotels and motels generally add a moderate charge for moving an extra single bed into your room.

Chains. In addition to the hundreds of excellent independent hotels and motels throughout the country, there are also many fine establishments in both categories that belong to chains. A major advantage of the chains is the ease with which you can make reservations—either one at a time en route, or all at once in advance. If you are staying at a member hotel or motel, the management will be delighted to secure you a booking at one of its affiliated hotels or motels for the coming evening—at no extra cost to you.

Categories: Hotels and motels in this guidebook are listed according to area and price. The price categories (*Super Deluxe, Deluxe, Expensive, Moderate,* and *Inexpensive*) are based on the cost in Canadian dollars of a room for two people. The actual prices reflected in the categories vary with the region and are listed at the beginning of each accommodation section.

HOSTELS. As students have known for years, hostels are comfortable, clean, inexpensive places to stay when traveling on a tight budget. But hostels are not just for young people. Adults—even families—are welcome at many of Canada's 60 hostels.

The Canadian Hostelling Association was established in 1933. It is a non-profit organization whose aims are to help all, but especially young people, to a greater knowledge and appreciation of the countryside, particularly by providing accommodations for them while traveling.

A hostel offers simple overnight accommodation. It is open to everyone, and is a common meeting place for people from every nationality and background, particularly those interested in traveling off the beaten track. A hosteler may stay up to a maximum of three consecutive nights, though in some hostels this may be longer. In Canada, the cost of overnight accommodation ranges from $3 to $12 person. Meals, where available, are extra. Many hostels have a kitchen and most provide blankets, pillows, cooking utensils, and cleaning equipment. Guests are often expected to help with hostel chores during their stay. Only those holding current membership cards are admitted to youth hostels. Canada generally has a fee differential for non-members. In addition, a CHA card represents membership in the international organization—valid in some 50 countries.

For information write the *Canadian Hostelling Association,* Place Vanier, Tower A, 333 River Rd., Ottawa, Ont. K1L 8H9.

FARM VACATIONS AND BED-AND-BREAKFAST ACCOMMODATIONS. Two interesting low-cost options are farm vacations and the increasingly popular bed-and-breakfast lodging available throughout Canada. For as little as $15 a day, Canadians will put you up and feed you in their own homes. In addition to saving money, you'll get a closer look at the land and its people. The big-city version of this type of accommodation is the guest house, common in Toronto, Montréal, and Québec. These are usually well-maintained private homes with rooms available on a daily or weekly basis. Most are listed in local phone books or newspapers. Standards of quality vary widely, so compare homes early in the day before making your choice. Private bathrooms are rare, and some proprietors lock up early, a practice that could put a damper on your plans for a night on the town.

Two excellent sources are *Fodor's Bed & Breakfast Guide,* which has listings for seven Canadian provinces, and John Thompson's *Country Bed and Breakfast Places in Canada,* which lists more than 160 places from Gertie Legge's "Hospitality Home" in Heart's Delight, Newfoundland, to Olga Maye's single room in Oliver, British Columbia.

Eight provinces have farm vacation associations, which distribute lists of guest farms, inspect facilities, and handle consumer complaints: **National:** Canadian Country Vacations Association, Hopewell Hill, N.B. E0A 1Z0; **Alberta:** Travel Alberta, Box 2500, Edmonton, Alberta T5J 2Z4 (specify Alberta Country Vacations brochure); **Saskatchewan:** Saskatchewan Farm Vacations Assoc, Box 24, Bateman, Saskatchewan S0H E0E; **Manitoba:** Manitoba Farm Vacations Assoc, Box 2580, Winnipeg, Manitoba R3C 4R3; **Ontario:** Ontario Farm Vacations Assoc, RR #2, Vankleek Hill, Ontario K0B 1R0; **Québec:** Agricotours, 525 ave. Viger, Montréal, Québec H2L 2P1; **New Brunswick:** New Brunswick Farm Vacations Assoc, R.R. 1, Harcourt, Kent County, New Brunswick E0A 1T0; **Nova Scotia:** Nova Scotia Farm and Country Vacations Assoc, Halls Harbour, Kings County, Nova Scotia B0P 1J0; **Prince Edward Island:** P.E.I. Visitor Services Division, Box 940, Charlottetown, P.E.I. C1A 7M5.

DINING OUT. The general rule for metropolitan areas is to make reservations in advance whenever possible for midday and evening meals. In other areas the lack of reservations may not pose any problem for lunch, but remember that at dinnertime most travelers have settled in a particular place for the evening and will quickly fill up the nearby restaurants. If you prefer a motel, life is simpler if the motel has a restaurant, since their hours are more accommodating to early and late traffic. If it doesn't, try to stay at one located near a restaurant.

Although universal dress standards have become more casual, some restaurants, particularly the better ones and those in heavily populated areas, are relatively fussy about customers' dress, especially in the evening. If you have any doubt about acceptable dress at a particular restaurant, call ahead. But as a general rule, a neatly dressed customer—and in major metropolitan cities, a more conservatively dressed customer—usually will not experience any problems.

Restaurant chains serving fast foods have begun to spring up in Canada and will be instantly recognizable to the motoring public by their specific type of food if not by their outer signs. The popularity of these chains makes low prices and high-speed service possible. While the menu may be limited, the average lunch or dinner ranges from under $3 to about $5, and you can carry out the food or eat it on the premises.

Categories: Restaurants in this volume are divided into five price categories: super deluxe, deluxe, expensive, moderate, and inexpensive. As a general rule, restaurants in metropolitan areas tend to be higher-priced, although many restaurants that feature foreign cuisine are often surprisingly expensive. In Ontario particularly (and in Toronto especially), one finds almost every kind of ethnic restaurant: Chinese, French, Japanese, Spanish, Italian, Greek, Jewish, etc.

We should also point out that space limitations make it impossible to include every establishment worth sampling. We have, therefore, included those we consider among the best within each price range.

As with hotels and motels, while the names of the various categories are standard in this volume, the prices listed under each category may vary from area to area. Again, this variance reflects local price standards.

NIGHTLIFE. In the large cities of Montréal and Toronto the problem is never what to do in the evening but how to choose from among the hundreds of attractions available. Whatever form of entertainment you fancy, these cities inevitably offer something to suit your taste.

Theater thrives all over Canada, but especially in Toronto, Montréal, and more recently, Vancouver. Dance is one of the most popular art forms and there are performances in every large city.

Nightclub and jazz entertainment are also popular in the cities. To find out what is going on in a city consult the local papers or entertainment brochures.

Outside the big cities, there is still a good deal of nighttime entertainment, especially in areas that cater to tourists. Most often, however, evening entertainment in smaller cities will be confined to weekends and the local hotels and larger motels. (Your desk clerk is probably the best source of information about what's going on.)

TIPPING. There is no law in Canada that says you must leave a tip for service. However the unwritten laws of custom make tipping necessary more often than not. Tipping is a personal thing, your way of expressing appreciation of someone who has given you attentive, efficient, and personal service. Because standards of service in Canada are uneven, you should, when you get genuinely good service, reward it. And when you feel that the service you got was indifferent or surly, don't hesitate to recognize this by the size, or withholding, of your tip. Remember that in many places those who serve you are paid very little and depend on tips for part of their income. This is supposed to give them an incentive to serve you well. These days, the going rate on restaurant service is 15 percent on the amount *before* taxes. Tipping at counters is not universal, but many people leave at least 50¢, and 10 percent when it comes to anything over that. For bellboys, 50¢ per bag is usual. For one-night stays in most hotels and motels you leave nothing. If you stay longer, at the end of the stay leave the maid $1.00–$1.50 per day, or $5.00 per person per week for multiple occupancy. If you are staying in an American Plan hostelry (meals included), $2.00–$3.00 per person for the waitress or waiter is considered sufficient, and is left at the end of your stay. However, if you have been surrounded by an army of waiters, sommeliers, and stewards, add a few extra dollars and give the lump sum to the captain or *maître d'hôtel* when you leave, asking him to allocate it. Outside of Canada and the United States, it is customary for restaurants and nightclubs to add a percentage for service to your bill. In Canada this practice is permitted only with the consent of the customer. If a tip is added without your knowledge and consent, you can refuse to pay it.

For the many other services you may encounter in a hotel or resort, figure roughly as follows: doorman, 50¢ for taxi handling, $1.00 for help with baggage; bellhop, 50¢ per bag, more if you load him down with extras; parking attendant, $1.00; bartender, 15 percent; room service, $1.00; laundry or valet service, 15 percent; barbers, $1.00; Shoeshine attendants, 50¢; hairdressers, $2.00.

Transportation: Taxi and limousine drivers in Canadian cities expect 15 percent. Car-rental agencies, nothing. Bus porters are tipped 50¢ per bag, drivers nothing. On charter and package tours, conductors and drivers usually get $10.00 per day from the group, but be sure to ask if this has been already figured into the package cost. On short local sightseeing runs, the driver-guide may get 50¢–$1.00 per person, more if he has been especially helpful or informative. Redcaps, 50¢ per suitcase. Tipping at curbside check-in is unofficial, but same as above.

Railroads suggest you leave 10–15 percent per meal for dining-car waiters, but the steward who seats you is not tipped. Sleeping-car porters get about $2.00 per person per night. Baggage porters are tipped 50¢ per bag, depending on how heavy your luggage is.

 NATIONAL PARKS. There are 28 Canadian National Parks, divided among five regions. For complete information on facilities and accommodations write to the central office in Ottawa, the relevant regional office, or the headquarters of the park you with to visit: *Parks Canada,* Department of the Environment, Ottawa, Ont. K1A 1G2.

Atlantic Region

Parks Canada—Atlantic Division, Upper Water St., Halifax, N.S. B3J 1S9; (902) 426–3457.

Cape Breton Highlands National Park (367 square miles) has skiing, swimming, salmon fishing, hiking trails, rocky coastline, forests, and a Scottish atmosphere. (Ingonish Beach, Cape Breton, N. S. B0C 1L0; 902–285–2270.)

Fundy National Park (almost 80 square miles) includes oddly formed sandstone cliffs punctuating lovely beaches. (P.O. Box 40, Alma, N. B. E0A 1B0; 506–887–2000.)

Gros Morne National Park (750 square miles) contains the Long Range Mountains, lakes that look like fiords, a rugged coast, and heavy forests. (P.O. Box 130, Rocky Harbour, Bonne Bay, Nfld. A0K 4N0; 709–458–2417.)

Kejimkujik National Park (147 square miles) features rolling woodland and fishing lakes. (P.O. Box 36, Maitland Bridge, Annapolis County, N. S. B0T 1N0; 902–242–2770.)

Kouchibouguac National Park (87½ square miles) includes swimming, campgrounds and offshore sandbars in the bay. (Kent County, N.B. E0A 2A0; 506–876–2443.)

Prince Edward Island National Park (7 square miles) is a strip of Gulf of St. Lawrence coast 25 miles long, with the warmest beaches north of the Carolinas. (P.O. Box 487, Charlottetown, P.E.I. C1A 7L1; 902–566–7050.)

Terra Nova National Park (153 square miles) surrounds Bonavista Bay with its inlets, its boreal forest on the land side, and its enormous icebergs floating into the Bay to melt. (Glovertown, Nfld. A0G 2L0; 709–533–2801.)

Québec Region

Parks Canada—Québec Region, 3 Buade, P.O. Box 6060, Québec City, Québec G1R 4V7 (418) 694–4042.

Forillon National Park (92.8 square miles) on the tip of the Gaspé region is an incomplete park situated in a region of seascapes and preserved French Canadian villages. (P.O. Box 1220, Gaspé, P.Q. G0C 1R0; 418–368–5505.)

La Mauricie National Park (210 square miles) in the Laurentians is largely undeveloped and heavily wooded. (P.O. Box 758, Shawinigan, P.Q. G9N 6V9; 819–536–2638.)

Ontario Region

Parks Canada—Ontario Region, P.O. Box 1359, Cornwall, Ont. K6H 5V4; (613) 933–7951.

Georgian Bay Islands National Park (5.4 square miles on 40 islands) is characterized by rock formations created by glaciers and old forests. (Box 28, Honey Harbour, Ont. P0E 1E0; 705–756–2415.)

Point Pelee National Park (6 square miles) sticking into Lake Erie contains a 14-mile-long beach and a sanctuary for 100 species of birds. RR #1. (Leamington,Ont. N8H 3Z4; 519–326–3204.)

Pukaskwa National Park (725 square miles) attempts to preserve the wilderness of northern Ontario and its wildlife. (Box 550, Marathon, Ont., P0T 2E0; 806–229–0801.)

St. Lawrence Islands National Park (1.6 square miles) includes a tip of the mainland, 18 wooded islands, and 80 rocky inlets in excellent boating water. (P.O. Box 469, R.R. #3, Mallorytown Landing, Ont. K0E 1R0; 613–923–5261.)

Prairie Region

Parks Canada—Prairie Region, 391 York Ave., Winnipeg, Man. R3C 4B7; 204–949–2290.

Auyittuq National Park on Baffin Island (8,290 square miles) is in the planning stages and includes fiords along Cumberland Peninsula mountains, ice floes and glaciers, and polar bears, seals, and whales. (Pangnirtung, N.W.T., X0A 0R0 819–473–8962.)

Kluane National Park (8500 square miles) in southwestern Yukon is full of high mountains, glaciers, ice fields and lakes. Travel without a guide is discouraged. (Mile 1019, Alaska Highway, Haines Junction, Y. T. Y0B 1L0; 403–634–2251.)

Nahanni National Park (1840 square miles) lies around the South Nahanni River, which few travelers have ever navigated, with its canyons, Virginia Falls, and nearby hot springs. (Postal Bag 300, Fort Simpson, N.W.T. X0E 0N0; 403–695–3151.)

Prince Albert National Park (1496 square miles) surrounds Lake Waskesiu and its fauna and flora are representative of the Prairie Region. (P.O. Box 100, Waskesiu Lake, Sask. S0J 2Y0; 306–663–5322.)

Riding Mountain National Park (1150 square miles) sits on a plateau 1,500 feet above the countryside and has over 50 lakes. (Wasagaming, Man. R0J 2H0; 204–848–2811.)

Wood Buffalo National Park (17,300 square miles), the largest national park in the world, is larger than a number of countries and provides a haven for about 8,000 bisons and about 50 of the nearly extinct whooping cranes. (Fort Smith, N.W.T. X0E 0P0; 403–872–2649.)

Western Region

Parks Canada—Western Region, 220 4th Ave., SE, Calgary, Alberta T2P 3H8; 403–231–4440.

Banff National Park (2564 square miles) is the oldest and best-known Canadian National Park. It runs through the Continental Divide and has snow-capped mountains, ski slopes, hot springs, deep valleys, glaciers and lakes. (Box 900, Banff, Alta. T0L 0C0; 403–762–3324.)

Elk Island National Park (75 square miles) is the home of a 600-head bison herd, aspen and spruce forests, and is surrounded by level farmland and numerous lakes. (Site 4, R.R. #1, Fort Saskatchewan, Alta. T8L 2N7; 403–998–3781.)

Glacier National Park (521 square miles) is in the Selkirk Mountains and contains over 100 glaciers as well as hemlock and cedar forests and excellent fishing streams. (P.O. Box 350, Revelstoke, B. C. V0E 2S0; 604–837–5155.)

Jasper National Park (4200 square miles) takes in high peaks in the Rockies, large rivers, rapid streams, hot springs, ice fields, and ski slopes. (Box 10, Jasper, Alta. T0E 1E0; 403–852–6161.)

Kootenay National Park (543 square miles) is a narrow valley on the western slopes of the Rockies and includes colossal Sinclair Canyon and Radium Hot Springs. (P.O. Box 220, Radium Hot Springs, B. C. V0A 1M0; 604–347–9615.)

Mount Revelstoke National Park (100 square miles) on the rugged western slopes of the Selkirks is a mountaintop park with ski slopes and alpine meadows. (P.O. Box 350 Revelstoke, B. C. V0E 2S0; 604–837–5155.)

Pacific Rim National Park (250 square miles) on the western slope of Vancouver Island is most famous for sandy Long Beach and the sea lions living on rocky offshore islets. (P.O. Box 280, Ucluelet, B. C. V0R 3A0; 604–726–7721.)

Waterton Lakes National Park (203 square miles) adjoins Glacier National Park in Montana. It includes flat meadows and towering mountains in a striking contrast of prairie and alpine terrain. (Waterton Park, Alta. T0K 2M0; 403–859 –2262.)

Yoho National Park (507 square miles)—"How Wonderful," in the local Indian language—has spectacular Yoho Glacier, Lake O'Hara, Takkakaw Falls, and a famous pass through the Rockies following Kicking Horse River. (P.O. Box 99, Field, B. C. V0A 1G0; 604–343–6324.)

These by no means cover all the parks in Canada. The provinces have their own systems of parks. Information about them can be obtained from the pertinent provincial tourist office.

CAMPING. If you own a tent, trailer or recreational vehicle, camping may be the cheapest way to travel. There are more than 2,000 campgrounds in Canada, from simple roadside turn-offs with sweeping mountain vistas to fully equipped facilities with groomed sites, trailer hookups, recreational facilities, and vacation-village atmosphere. Many of the finest are in Canada's 28 national and more than 300 provincial parks. Here it is first-come, first-served, with nominal overnight fees. Commercial campgrounds offer more amenities, such as electrical and water hookups, showers, even game rooms and grocery stores, but usually charge more per night. Nevertheless, camp fees are a bargain compared to the cost of hotel or motel accommodation.

It pays to arrive early and to make your camping stops in areas that have a number of parks or privately owned campgrounds. If one is full, there is likely to be space in another. It pays also to check how long you can stay, and plan your travels accordingly. Provincial tourist offices publish lists of their area's private and public camping facilities. In addition, the AAA and its Canadian affiliate, the CAA (1775 Courtwood Crescent, Ottawa, Ont. K2C 3J2), publish a series of guidebooks to campgrounds in North America.

If all you need is a clear patch of ground to pitch a tent, then you can simply pull off the road on millions of square miles of Crown lands and simply set up camp.

For listings of private and public campgrounds, contact the tourist office of the province you plan to visit. Brochures and other information on national and provincial parks are also available from the National and Provincial Parks Association of Canada, 69 Sherbourne St., Box 313, Toronto, Ontario M5A 3X7.

PARTICIPANT SPORTS. Canadians are enthusiastic about all kinds of sports. We will discuss hunting, fishing, and canoeing elsewhere, but the range of sporting activities for both spectators and participants goes well beyond these three staples.

Swimming is excellent all over the country, whether off the Atlantic coast of the Maritime Provinces, in the thousands of lakes all over the country, or on the Pacific coast of Vancouver Island.

Tennis too is popular throughout the country. There are dozens of golf courses in every province that welcome tourists. And there are about two dozen golf tournaments in Canada, the most important of which is the Canadian Open.

There is skiing wherever there are mountains, and there are helicopter skiing trips in Alberta and British Columbia.

Sailing is common on both coasts and rentals are available in many places. Nova Scotia offers a unique attraction for divers. There are about 3,000 wrecked ships off the coast of Nova Scotia, some of them containing treasure. The provincial Department of Tourism will provide details on the locations of wrecks and where to buy or rent equipment. If you're lucky, you could pay for your trip.

Canada also offers the full range of winter sports: ice skating, tobogganing, snowmobiling, dogsledding, etc. But skiing is probably the most popular winter sport. There are slopes in every province, but those in Québec, Alberta, and British Columbia are the best. The Rockies are also particularly good for climbing and hiking.

Horseback riding is popular all over Alberta.

For something completely unique you might even try curling, either as a spectator or a participant. Best described as lawn bowling on ice, curling has two teams, of four players each, who compete by sliding large stones toward a mark in the center of a circle or "house."

 SPECTATOR SPORTS. Professional organized team sports are widespread. The addition of Toronto and Vancouver franchises in the North American Soccer League has brought new attention to that sport. But baseball, football, and hockey deserve special mention.

Baseball, long a favorite, increased dramatically in popularity when the major leagues expanded into Montréal in 1969. In 1977 the opening of the Montréal Expos' new home at Olympic Stadium and the initial season of the New American League franchise, the Toronto Blue Jays, further stimulated Canadian interest in the game. There are also minor league teams in Vancouver, Edmonton, Calgary, Lethbridge, and Medicine Hat.

Canadian football differs from the game as it is played in the United States. It allows only three downs, employs a 110-yard field, and permits 12 players per team. British Columbia, Calgary, Edmonton, Hamilton, Montréal, Ottawa, Saskatchewan, Toronto, and Winnipeg all field teams in the professional Canadian Football League.

Hockey, however, is still the most popular sport in Canada. Montréal, Toronto, Vancouver, Edmonton, Calgary, Québec and Winnipeg are represented in the National Hockey League. Hockey goes far beyond the major leagues in Canada, however. Moncton, N.B., and Nova Scotia have teams in the American League. And there are junior leagues (for the 16- to 20-year-olds) in Québec, Ontario, and Western Canada. Schools and clubs sponsor teams everywhere, and pick-up games are ubiquitous.

There are rodeos all over the Prairie Provinces, especially in Alberta.

There is thoroughbred racing in Ontario, Manitoba, Saskatchewan, Alberta, and British Columbia during the spring, summer, and fall. In Québec, Newfoundland, and the other Atlantic Provinces there are a number of harness racing tracks, especially on Prince Edward Island where it is the most popular spectator sport. There is also stock car racing in Manitoba, Saskatchewan, and on Prince Edward Island.

Colleges compete in basketball, football, soccer, swimming and diving, volleyball, wrestling, and hockey, among others. Baseball is extremely popular all over the country; lacrosse is played in Ontario, and rugby and cricket in British Columbia.

 CANOEING. Canada has thousands of miles of rivers and streams. While some of them are mild and gentle, many include rapids and falls. Some of them are great rivers in developed areas, but many more are fast streams running through wilderness. Your degree of expertise and experience will dictate where you will canoe. Beginners will look for waterways in more settled areas. The real pro will head north to the streams and rivers that flow into the Arctic Ocean. The Canadian Government Travel Office offers maps, information, and advice for those in either category. Provincial tourist offices and the federal Department of Northern Development and Indian Affairs can also be of assistance, especially in locating an outfitter to suit your needs.

The Humber and Lloyds-Exploits Rivers in **Newfoundland** are rugged and for experts only. The Kanairiktok River in Labrador is for novices, but Goose River in the same area is only for those familiar with line hauling and portage.

Canoeists on **Prince Edward Island** will have to bring their own gear and will find no river longer than 18 miles.

There are many fine waters for canoeing in Nova Scotia, especially in Kejimkujik National Park.

In **New Brunswick** there are four main canoeing rivers: the St. John, the St. Croix, the Miramichi, and the Restigouche. Each has a number of tributaries feeding into it. Other waterways in the province are used primarily for fishing and do not offer canoeists much of a challenge.

The provincial government of **Québec** has largely restricted canoeing to the confines of provincial and national parks, but this action has hardly limited the sport, since there are 8 major drainage basins flowing through the parks. Other river systems in Québec are off limits at certain times of the year because of pulp driving. It's best to inquire first from the provincial tourist office. A third group of waterways, near James Bay, is restricted by Hydro Québec, the power company.

Canoeing in **Ontario** is an industry. There are nine major drainage basins in northern Ontario and four in southern Ontario. There are dozens of outfitters and hundreds of miles of rivers and lakes, ranging in difficulty from the simplest to the most difficult.

The nine basic drainage basins in **Manitoba** all flow into or out of Lake Winnipeg, and all of them are well charted. The Hayes River and Seal River basins offer the longest trips (about 600 miles each), while others in the province are as short as 10 miles.

The **Saskatchewan** routes are concentrated into three major systems: the Saskatchewan River System, the Churchill River system, and the Lake Athabaska system. Each offers its own special pleasures, but the last of them includes 6 old fur trade canoe routes, which add an extra, romantic, dimension to canoeing there.

Alberta offers canoeists the most varied terrain in Canada. There are rugged mountains, flat plains, and Pre-Cambrian Shield terrain. The Bow River in Banff National Park is perhaps the most popular canoe route in the province.

British Columbia is almost as varied as Alberta. The range of routes is from the easiest novice streams to the treacherous whitewater Thompson River, where updendings are almost inevitable and where at least three canoes should travel together to assure rescues.

Three rivers in the **Yukon** —the Yukon, the Teslin, and the Stewart—can be tackled by those of intermediate skill. But the Big Salmon, the Klondike and others should not be attempted without considerable experience. All nonresidents must register with the Mounted Police in Whitehorse, for their own protection.

Only the most experienced canoeists should try the rivers of the **Northwest Territories** —and even for them rivers like the Coppermine, the South Redstone, the South Nahanni, the Kazan, and the Dubawnt can be dangerous.

 FISHING. Each Canadian province offers something for the fisherman. Bag limits, seasons, and licensing regulations vary from province to province. Prospective anglers should inquire at provincial tourist offices in advance.

Newfoundland offers cod, mackerel, salmon, and sea trout in the Atlantic and speckled trout and rainbow trout in the 30 percent of Newfoundland that is water. The booklet *Hunting and Fishing Guide* is available from the Dept. of Development and Tourism, Box 2016, St. John's, Newfoundland A1C 5R8; (800) 523–NFLD.

The same species are available on **Prince Edward Island.** The deep-sea fishing—especially for tuna—is best in the eastern part of the province. The *Fish and Wildlife Branch,* P.O. Box 2000, Charlottetown, P.E.I. C1A 7N8, 902–892–0311, is the primary source of information.

Nova Scotia has the most stringent freshwater restrictions in Canada, but the availability of Atlantic salmon, speckled trout, and striped bass make the trouble worthwhile. Nonresidents, for instance, are required to hire a guide for each three fishermen. Going for saltwater fish such as mackerel, cod, swordfish, and bluefin tuna is also popular—and almost as restricted. Inquire at Fisheries and Oceans, Box 550, Halifax, Nova Scotia B3J 2S7; (902) 426–5952.

The salmon, trout, and black bass in **New Brunswick** are abundant and fine. However, many of the streams and rivers are leased to private freeholders, either individuals or clubs. A daily license is available for some waters. Inquire at the *Fish and Wildlife Branch,* 349 King St., P.O. Box 6000, Fredericton, N.B. E3B 5H1; (506) 453–2440.

The lakes of **Québec** hold trout, bass, pike, and landlocked salmon (called "ouananiche"). The tributaries of the St. Lawrence River teem with brook trout and landlocked salmon. Licenses can be exclusive, as in New Brunswick, or to individuals. And, although the season varies with the species and the location, you may fish for most species in most places from June 15 through Labor Day—provided you have a license. Further information is available from *The Department of Recreation, Fish, and Game,* Place de la Capitale, 150 St. Cyrille Blvd. E., 15th Fl., Québec, P.Q. G1R 4Y1; (418) 643–2266.

Just about every kind of North American freshwater game fish is available in some part of **Ontario.** Bass, perch, trout, walleye, salmon, muskies, pike, and whitefish in all their forms can be had either within a short drive of Ontario or deep in the wilderness. Unfortunately, the variety of regulations is almost as great as the variety of fish. Get full details from *The Wildlife Branch, Ministry of Natural Resources,* 99 Wellesley St. W., Room 3304, Whitney Block, Queen's Park, Toronto, Ont. M7A 1W3; (416) 965–4251.

Manitoba offers lake trout, brook trout, pike, grayling, walleye, Hudson Bay salmon, and smallmouth bass. It also offers a winter fishing season, but some areas require a guide. (You can even hunt whales, with a camera, out of Churchill.) *The Game and Fisheries Branch* of the Department of Mines and Natural Resources, P.O. Box 24, 1495 James St., Winnipeg, Man. R3H 0W9, (204) 945–6784, issues licenses and offers assistance.

The lakes and rivers of *Saskatchewan* hold lake trout, pike, grayling, perch, and walleye. The small streams contain trout, whitefish, and splake. The *Fisheries Branch,* 3211 Albert St., Regina, Sask. S4S 5W6, (306) 565–2700, will provide details.

Alberta is a paradise for sportsfishermen with its trout in streams; pike, walleye, and perch in lakes, grayling, goldeye, and whitefish in rivers. Fishing is permitted in the mountain national parks, but regulations are different from those for waters outside the parks. The *Fish and Wildlife Branch,* 9945 108th St., Edmonton, Alta. T5K 2C9, 403–427–0326, is the primary source of information.

The salmon fishing in **British Columbia** is unparalleled, even though only two of the five available species may be taken in nontidal waters. There are also plentiful char, grayling, whitefish, bass, perch, and nine varieties of trout in the streams and rivers. The *Fish and Wildlife Branch,* 780 Blanchard St., Victoria, B.C. V8V 1X5, 604–387–1628, will tell you everything you need to know about fees and regulations.

The **Yukon Territory** has a wide variety of trout, salmon, grayling, and pike even in waters right off the main roads, so fishermen don't have to go into the remote wilderness. For up-to-date information write: *Tourism Yukon.* Box 2703, Whitehorse, Y.T. Y1A 2C6; (403) 667–5434.

Commercial fishing dominates the **Northwest Territories,** especially at Great Slave Lake. But there are still sufficient amounts of game fish, most spectacularly the giant lake trout in Great Bear Lake. Information is available from *Travel Arctic,* Yellowknife, N.W.T. X1A 2L9; (403) 873–7400.

 HUNTING. Bag limits and firearms regulations vary widely from province to province. Handguns are not allowed anywhere, but nonresidents may take any other equipment they need into any province. Guides are required in many places and available almost everywhere. Provincial offices listed in the section on fishing can also be helpful.

The following list gives some idea of the variety of game available.

Newfoundland: moose, caribou, bear, rabbit, snipe, wild goose, and duck.

Prince Edward Island: small game only.

Nova Scotia: moose, caribou, bear, wildcat, fox, raccoon, rabbit and hare, marten, beaver, mink, otter, weasel, muskrat, ruffed grouse, partridge, pheasants, duck, snipe, and woodcock.

New Brunswick: deer, rabbit, ruffed grouse, spruce, partridge, migratory game birds, bear, bobcat, fox, raccoon, skunk, porcupine, groundhog, and crow.

Québec: moose, deer, bear, caribou, wolf, small game, partridge, goose, ptarmigan, pheasant, grouse, and waterfowl. (A warning here. Much of Québec's best hunting areas are under lease, although many leaseholders permit individuals to come onto their preserves for a fee.)

Ontario: deer, moose, black bear, small game, grouse, and waterfowl.

Manitoba: deer, moose, bear, and caribou.

Saskatchewan: deer, elk, moose, caribou, deer, bear, and a variety of birds.

Alberta: moose, deer, caribou, bear, coyote, antelope, wapiti, mountain sheep and goat, elk, waterfowl, and pheasant and other birds.

British Columbia: mountain goat and sheep, black and grizzly bear, moose, wapiti, caribou, deer, wolf, cougar, and waterfowl. (The difficulty of reaching the north central part of British Columbia is amply rewarded by the abundance of game.)

Yukon Territory: moose, caribou, black and brown bear, mountain goat and sheep, grouse, ptarmigan, goose, and duck.

Northwest Territories: The large game here includes black, grizzly, and polar bears; barren-ground, Peary, and woodland caribou; mountain goat; moose; muskox; Dall's sheep; wolf; and wolverine.

Other Useful Addresses. In British Columbia: *B.C. Fish and Game Assoc.,* 780 Blanchard St., Victoria, B.C. V8V 1X5. **In Alberta:** *Alberta Fish and Game Assoc.,* 6024–103rd St., Edmonton, Alta. T6H 2H6. **In Manitoba:** *Winnipeg Game and Fish Assoc.,* 301–289½ Garry, Winnipeg, Man. **In Ontario:** *Ontario Federation of Anglers and Hunters,* Box 28, 169 Charlotte St., Peterborough, Ontario K9J 6Y5. **In Québec:** *Montréal Anglers and Hunters,* 319 St. Zoteque Est., Montréal, Qué. H2S 1L5.

HOLIDAYS. National public holidays in Canada are: New Year's Day (January 1); Good Friday (the Friday before Easter); Easter Monday (the Monday following Easter); Victoria Day (the Monday preceding May 25); Canada Day (July 1); Labour Day (the first Monday in September); Thanksgiving Day (the second Monday in October); Remembrance Day (November 11); Christmas Day (December 25).

In recent years there has been a tendency to observe some holidays on the nearest Monday to the actual date. Remember, though, that many stores and resort attractions remain open on holidays even though banks, schools, and government offices may close. Remembrance Day, for instance, is a school and government holiday in some provinces; stores shut in others.

In addition to the national holidays there are also a number of provincial holidays.

Newfoundland: St. Patrick's Day, (March 17); St. George's Day (around April 23); Discovery Day (second to last Monday in June); Memorial Day (July 3); Orangemen's Day (July 12); and Boxing Day (December 26).

Nova Scotia: Sir John A. MacDonald's Birthday (January 11); Boxing Day (December 26).

New Brunswick: Boxing Day (December 26).

Prince Edward Island: Boxing Day (December 26).

Québec: Epiphany (January 6); Ash Wednesday (first day of Lent), Ascension Day (40 days after Easter), St. Jean Baptiste Day (June 24); All Saints' Day (November 1); and Immaculate Conception (December 8).

Ontario: Civic Holiday (first Monday in August); Boxing Day (December 26).

Manitoba: Civic Holiday (first Monday in August); Boxing Day (December 26).

Saskatchewan: Boxing Day (December 26).

Alberta: Alberta Heritage Day (first week in August); Boxing Day (December 26).

British Columbia: British Columbia Day (first week in August); Boxing Day (December 26).

Yukon Territory: Discovery Day (third Monday in August).

Northwest Territories: Civic Holiday (first Monday in August); Boxing Day (December 26).

BUSINESS HOURS. Opening times for stores, shops, and supermarkets are similar to those in the United States: 9 A.M. to 6 P.M., Monday through Saturday, although in major cities, supermarkets are often open as early as 7:30 A.M. and stay open until 9 P.M.. Blue laws (enforced Sunday closings) are in effect in much of Canada, so don't expect to get much souvenir shopping done on Sunday. Retail stores are generally open on Thursday and Friday evenings; most shopping malls till 9 P.M. The trend with Canadian banks is away from the traditional business hours of 10 A.M. to 3 P.M., Monday through Friday, and toward extended hours and Saturday-morning openings. Many banks offer automated tellers at any hour. Drugstores in major cities are often open until 11 P.M. and convenience stores are often open 24 hrs. a day, 7 days a week.

LIQUOR LAWS. Rules and regulations governing what kinds of alcoholic beverages may be sold, at what hours and to whom, vary from province to province.

In *Newfoundland* the legal drinking age is 19 and women are permitted in taverns and cocktail lounges.

On *Prince Edward Island* liquor stores are open six days a week for upwards of 12 hours a day. The legal drinking age is 18.

New Brunswick allows women in taverns, and you must be 19 to buy alcohol.

Nova Scotia allows women in all drinking establishments. The legal age to buy alcohol is 19.

In *Ontario* the drinking age is 19, but some communities are completely dry and others impose severe restrictions.

Québec does not allow women in taverns, and the few liquor stores close early. But cocktail lounges and cabarets stay open until 2 A.M. and 3 A.M., respectively, in Montréal. The legal drinking age is 18.

Mixed-company drinking is legal everywhere in *Manitoba* except in beer parlors. The legal drinking age is 18.

Mixed drinking is legal for anyone in *Saskatchewan* over the age of 19.

Alberta imposes no drinking restrictions on women, and the liquor prices are the lowest in Canada. The legal age is 18.

British Columbia allows mixed drinking for those over 19.

The Yukon permits drinking for anyone 19 and over.

In the *Northwest Territories* the legal drinking age is 19. Communities in N.W.T. vote on whether they want to be dry or wet, and they may vacillate. If you are concerned, check before you go to places in far-flung areas.

MAIL. Stamps can be purchased at any post office in Canada, often from your hotel desk, or from coin-operated vending machines located in transportation terminals, banks, and some shops (stationers and drugstores, for example). They cost the same from a machine as from the post office, but the machines only sell in 50¢ lots. Postal rates are listed in the table below. Post offices are usually open during business hours and sometimes on Saturday mornings.

Stamped mail can be posted in the letter drops at the post office, in the letter chutes of some hotels and office buildings, in the red mailboxes on many street corners. Or you may leave it with the hotel desk clerk, who will post it for you.

If you expect to receive mail while traveling, you can have it addressed to you in care of your hotel(s).

There is no separate air mail rate for the letters or postcards posted in Canada for delivery within the country or to the United States. Mail for distant points is automatically airlifted. The following postal rates, in Canadian money, were in effect as of March 1987, but they are subject to change—usually up, not down—so check when you buy stamps to be sure.

Letters & Postcards

Within Canada	36¢ for the first ounce
To the United States	41¢ for the first ounce
Air Mail to all other countries	70¢ for the first ounce and for Mailgrams

TELEPHONE. Coin-operated telephones are available almost everywhere. To use the coin telephone, just follow the instructions on the phone box. Local calls usually cost 25¢ and can be dialed directly. If you don't reach your party, your money is refunded to you automatically when you hang up.

For long-distance calls, have plenty of coins available unless you are calling "collect." The operator may ask for enough change to cover the initial time period before she connects you. To place a call outside Canada, dial "0" and ask for the overseas operator. You can, however, dial any point in the United States from most places in Canada directly.

In hotels, your switchboard operator will either place your outside call for you, or tell you how to dial directly from your room. The telephone charges will be added to your hotel bill (although many times local calls are free), and you will pay for them when you check out.

TELEGRAPH. To send a telegram to a destination anywhere within Canada, ask for assistance at your hotel, or go to the nearest CNCP telegraph office. Overseas cablegrams can also be dispatched by CNCP.

LEAVING CANADA. U.S. Customs. American citizens and other residents of the U.S. who visit Canada for more than 48 hours and who have claimed no exemption during the previous 30 days are entitled to bring in duty free up to $400 (retail value) worth of foreign purchases. The items may be intended for personal use or as gifts for those back home. They all count, even if some are personal effects you have already worn.

All your purchases are to accompany you, and it is wise (and simpler when inspection time comes) to try to put everything, or as much as possible, into one suitcase or carryall.

Also try to keep your purchase receipts together and handy, in case you have to produce them.

Members of a family can pool their exemptions because each separate member, including all minors, is entitled to the $400 exemption.

Small gifts under $50 in value may be mailed home to friends duty-free, but not more than one package to any one address. Such packages cannot contain perfumes, tobacco, or liquor. The outside of such a package must be marked: "Unsolicited Gift, value under $50," followed by the contents of the package.

Packages mailed to yourself are subject to duty. Your best bet, again, is to carry everything with you. Further information will be provided by the nearest U.S. Customs office or by U.S. Customs Service, Washington, D.C. 20229.

Great Britain. You may bring into the U.K. the following goods duty-free: 200 cigarettes, or 100 cigarillos, or 50 cigars, or 250 grams tobacco; plus one liter of alcohol of more than 38.8% proof, or 2 liters of alcohol not more than 38.8% proof, or 2 liters of fortified or sparkling wine and 2 liters of still table wine; plus 50 grams of perfume and ¼ liter of toilet water; plus other goods to the value of £28.

AN INTRODUCTION TO CANADA

by
SUSAN LEARNEY

Exciting, clean, and safe cities; unique blends of cultural and regional traditions; richly varied natural splendor—Canada is much more than simply the "other half" of North America. Canada's relatively peaceful evolution has given it a different national outlook than that of the United States. The flavor of Canada is richly spiced by the French and British influence, a diversity of ethnic groups, and native peoples. Natural resources provide everything from daily bread to industry, and some of the world's most spectacular scenery is easily accessible. Canada is huge, larger than the United States, and second only to the Soviet Union. (In the United States, a population ten times that of Canada's lives in a land area smaller than Canada's 9,972,334 square kilometers [3,850,318 square miles] and still praises its wide open spaces!) Canada's perimeters are defined by 6,400 kilometers (4,000 miles) of undefended border shared with the United States, and 60,000 kilometers of coastline (excluding islands) along three oceans.

The Canadian Identity

Peace, order, and good government are the principles that color Canadian attitudes. A modest lot, Canadians typically wonder if there *is* such a thing as a Canadian identity. There is, and it's wonderfully complex.

Friendly relations with its huge neighbor are fundamental to Canada's sense of identity. The sheer length of the border makes it indefensible for a population the size of Canada's, and it is crossed continually by a flow of cultural influences. But Canada is neither simply American, nor simply French and British. The province of Quebec is a political and social entity unique in North America. The French culture of Quebec, along with strong French cultures staunchly maintained in other provinces (notably, Ontario, Manitoba, Saskatchewan, and New Brunswick), is of major importance to the sense of being Canadian. Unlike the great "melting pot" to the south, Canada tends to retain visible cultural and ethnic identities through the generations. Within the larger cities, distinct ethnic communities maintain a life of their own, such as the Chinatowns of Vancouver and Toronto and Toronto's Little Italy, Portuguese, and Greek communities.

The Canadian population is about 25 million. Of these, English-speaking people are in the majority (about 60 percent). French-speaking (Francophone) people form the largest minority (about 25 percent). Native peoples represent about 2 percent and new Canadians about 13 percent of the population.

Canadian Definitions

To born-and-bred Canadians, perhaps the dominating influence is a strong sense of regional identity. Vast distances between major centers and industrial development based on specific resources have both fostered differing regional outlooks. The word "Canadian" has a different meaning to an Ontarian living in the manufacturing, political power, and population base of the country than it does to a British Columbian seemingly cut off from the rest of the country by vast mountain ranges. When easterners use the term "western Canada," they often mean everything as far as the west coast. But British Columbians, to themselves, are just that—British Columbians. (It's often said with a slight swagger.) Living their daily lives in full view of the oceans and the mountains, Vancouver residents seem almost more Californian than Canadian, though in Victoria, British tradition prevails. Really, western Canada is the prairies. Albertans do consider themselves part of western Canada, but not "just" part of the prairies. After all, they have the mountains. Western Canadians, involved in primary resource-based industry, have long felt frustrated by their great distance from the money power of eastern Canada. They often feel a greater north–south affinity to the western United States than to the rest of Canada.

"Eastern Canada" comprises the central provinces of Ontario and Quebec. Ontarians consider their province to be the heart of the country, and Quebec knows it's unique! From Canada's earliest history, Quebecers have felt themselves to be a separate part of the Canadian identity, but after mighty struggles, especially in the last twenty years, they are now finding the idea of political separation less tenable. Canada is officially bilingual, but *the* language of Quebec really is French. (Don't be deterred, though, from an exploration of Quebec's uniqueness. Any honest effort with the language is rewarded, especially in the larger cities.) The Atlantic provinces are "the Maritimes." A way of life largely based on the sea has historically given Maritimers concerns that are different from those of the inland power bases of Ontario and Quebec. Maritimers still refer to Ontario as Upper Canada, reflecting the trauma of the historic shift of political and economic power to central Canada.

In the North, an entirely different set of values from those of southern Canada is largely based on daily survival and of native ways. To northerners of any province or territory anything south of the true north is simply "Southern Canada"—far less rugged and, therefore, less "Canadian."

The country and its people are probably best understood in terms of the forces of nature and man that shaped Canada physically and historically.

SEVEN NATURAL WONDERS

Over the millenia, nature has worked many miracles in Canada. The combined forces of Ice Age glaciers, volcanoes, and earthquakes thrust up the jagged mountain peaks of the west. Glacial retreat and erosion smoothed the prairies, created inland valleys, and rounded the contours of the eastern mountains. At the end of the last Ice Age, about 12,000 years ago, Canada was left with millions of lakes and rivers (about 15 percent of the world's fresh water) and seven distinct natural regions.

Cordillera

The Cordillera area of Canada includes all of British Columbia as well as parts of the Yukon, Northwest Territories, and Alberta. Its landscape varies from coastal rain forests to Canada's most rugged scenery. There are more climatic variations in this region than any part of Canada. Here are the gentle English gardens of Victoria, the wilderness of Kluane National Park, and the market gardens of the Okanagan. Here, too, are the mammoth Douglas firs of the British Columbia logging industry, coal mining, and the grazing lands of the British Columbia and Alberta beef industries.

The oldest parts of the region are the gently rolling interior plateaus, formed by erosion many millions of years ago. The youngest parts are the twenty mountain systems, which include the famous Rockies. The Rockies are composed of sedimentary rock, thrust up less than 58 million years ago, then eroded by glaciers. The highest peak in the Rockies is Mount Robson (3954 meters/12,972 feet). The Yukon's St. Elias mountain range in Kluane National Park is still being formed by the same thrusting action. In this range are Canada's two highest peaks, Mt. Logan (5951 meters/19,524 feet) and St. Elias Mountain (5489 meters/18,008 feet). The world's greatest concentration of icefields and glaciers still surround Mt. Logan.

Interior Plains

The plains cut a curving swath southeast from the Northwest Territories, through the northeast corner of British Columbia and most of Alberta, crossing southern Saskatchewan and Manitoba. The area varies from treeless tundra to the semi-arid grasslands of the Canadian prairies, with coniferous forests and parkbelt regions in between. Some of the world's best grain-growing land is here, and a thriving potash industry is located in Saskatchewan. Here, too, are the unique Cypress Hills, and some of the most significant dinosaur remains ever found in the world. South of the Peace River, the terrain is similar to the southern plains, permitting the northern-most agriculture in the world. Three separate areas define the southern plains, or prairie.

Dominating the Alberta plain, sloping down from the Rocky Mountain foothills, is rolling terrain, formed of hummocky moraine (accumulations of sediment deposited by glaciers). The Badlands of Alberta were formed by the dissection of soft, underlying rock.

The large flat areas of the Saskatchewan plain were formed from glacial lakes, filled in by glacial deposits. The Cypress Hills, in the southeast corner, were one of the few areas in Canada not completely covered by glaciers.

The Manitoba plain, the lowest and flattest of the areas, is perhaps up to 600 million years old, and is covered by glacial lake silts and clay.

Canadian Shield

The Shield, covering 46 percent of the country's land area, cradles James Bay and the lower portion of Hudson Bay, curving in a rough U-shape through much of Ontario and northwest through northern Manitoba and Saskatchewan, the northeast corner of Alberta, and part of the Northwest Territories. To the northeast, it curves through much of Quebec and all of Labrador. The Shield contains some of the oldest rock in the world, dating from the Pre-Cambrian era (more than 600 million years ago). Time and the scouring effects of the last glaciation (100,000 to 6,000 years ago) have weathered the Shield into an out-doorsman's paradise, with a landscape of rolling forested hills, magnificent rocky outcrops, and a plethora of lakes and rivers. Here is much of the scenery painted by Ontario artists known as "the Group of Seven," a hunting and fishing paradise, and the varied recreations of Quebec's Laurentian Hills.

Hudson Bay Lowlands

The small area sandwiched between the Shield and Hudson Bay, about 60 percent of which lies beneath Hudson and James Bays, is composed of bedrock covered by marine and glacial sediments dating from about 7,500 years ago. Hilly near the Shield, the land flattens out near the coast into marshes strewn with glacial boulders and level plains with many ponds.

The St. Lawrence Lowlands

The Lowlands include the extreme southwestern and southeastern portions of Ontario (divided by the southerly tip of the Shield) and a narrow strip of southern Quebec along both shores of the St. Lawrence River. Here, in some of the finest agricultural land in Canada, are the Niagara Peninsula, the market gardens of eastern Ontario, and the farms of the early seigneurs of Quebec. This area has had the greatest population density in Canada from prehistoric times. Today it's home to Canada's two largest cities, Toronto and Montreal.

The landscape of the Lowlands varies from the limestone and dolomite plateaus of the western portion, bisected by the Niagara escarpment, to the rolling hills of the central portion, which are covered by glacial and marine deposits, to the relative flatness of the eastern portion, which has a base of sedimentary rock.

The Maritimes

Through Quebec's Gaspé region, New Brunswick, Nova Scotia, Prince Edward Island, and Newfoundland, continues the Appalachian topography of Vermont and New Hampshire. In this region are Cape Breton's picturesque Cabot Trail, coastal sand dunes accompanied by some of the best beaches in the country, and the famous red soil of Prince Edward Island. The forests supplied the early shipbuilding industry and timber trade. Some of the world's finest potatoes are grown in New Brunswick and Prince Edward Island, in finely grained, mineral-rich soils formed by the breakdown of weaker rocks. The mountains and highland areas are formed of stronger rock, dating from 480–280 million years ago. They follow a Z-shaped path from the Quebec/ United States border to the Gaspé, running across New Brunswick and appearing in the highlands of Cape Breton and along the western fringe of Newfoundland.

The Arctic

Contrary to popular belief, the Arctic region makes up only about one-quarter of Canada's land area! The true Arctic includes coastal plains, lowlands, portions of the Canadian Shield, and treeless tundra. The zone between the Shield and the Cordillera, gracefully sloping to the Arctic Ocean, is 570–225 million years old. Islands in this part of the Arctic were formed from sedimentary rocks, which were folded and then eroded. The mainland east of Great Bear and Great Slave Lakes is part of the Canadian Shield, with its center flooded by Hudson Bay. The eastern rim of the Arctic includes northern Labrador, Baffin, and Ellesmere Islands. It is mountainous with coastal fjords, and it is about 5 percent covered with glaciers.

Even in the treeless tundra, over 900 plant species thrive. Just below the closely matted, seemingly delicate vegetation, the permafrost glistens. Perennially frozen ground, permafrost ranges from a few meters (several yards) thick in the southern Arctic to 500 meters (1,640 feet) thick in the north. Two distinctive features of the Arctic landscape are tundra polygons—tortoise shell patterns of cracks, sometimes up to 30 meters wide, with ice wedges below— and pingos (ice-covered, conical hills). Over 1,500 pingos have been counted in the Tuktoyaktuk area of the Mackenzie River. In the Arctic, freshwater lakes and rivers are ice-free in the south from July to October and in the far north from July to August.

HISTORICAL OVERVIEW

The Original Canadians

From its earliest beginnings, man's contact with Canada has concentrated on the land's wealth of natural resources. At some time during the last Ice Age (ending about 12,000 years ago), migrators crossed a land bridge between Siberia and Alaska, and moved south to the western United States. Known as Paleo-Indians, these people moved north and westward, following retreating continental glaciers. Within a thousand years, they had occupied at least the southern portion of all provinces except Newfoundland. The Bluefish Caves in the Yukon hold the earliest known traces of these peoples. As the glaciers disappeared, several different environments evolved. The Paleo Indians developed differing lifestyles, based on the environmental conditions of each region.

On the west coast, an abundance of salmon and other sea life for food permitted the Indians to develop a sophisticated culture, and to evolve the art forms evident in Northwest Coast Indian art today. In the valleys between the mountain ranges, early bison hunters adapted to the hunting of wapiti and caribou, while other groups relied on salmon from the rivers.

The bison hunters of the Plains area were able to maintain their lifestyle for thousands of years, virtually unaltered until the appearance of Europeans, and in some cases, well into the late nineteenth century. Among their descendants are the mighty Blackfoot. Weaponry evolved from spears to bows and arrows, and hunting techniques improved to include buffalo pounds and jumps (cliffs over which herds of buffalo were driven, before being slaughtered). Guns introduced by early fur traders and the arrival of horses from Mexico around 1730 caused a revolution in hunting, traveling, and warfare.

The area of greatest prehistoric population density was Central Canada, where the Paleo Indians developed the only prehistoric lifestyle in Canada based on agriculture. Among their descendants were the Iroquois and Algonquin peoples encountered by early fur traders and missionaries.

On the east coast, a way of life based on seal and walrus hunting evolved into essentially a fishing and hunting economy in both coastal and interior regions. Descendants of these peoples included the Micmac and Maliseet.

In the Arctic, two distinct cultures emerged, the Paleo Indians and the Paleo Eskimos, who derived about 4,000 years ago from eastern Asia. From the Mackenzie River to Hudson Bay, the ancestors of the modern Athapaskan peoples were Plains Indians who had led a caribou-hunting way of life for about 7,000 years.

The coasts and islands of the Arctic were occupied by Paleo Eskimos, who very likely crossed the Bering Strait in open boats, and then spread rapidly across Alaska and Canada, down the coast of Labrador, and into Newfoundland. They lived largely on caribou, muskoxen, and seals. Among their descendants were the people of the Dorset culture, efficient whale hunters who produced some striking carvings in ivory and wood. They were displaced about 800 years ago by the Thule culture, which introduced skin boats for open-water hunting and dog sleds. Much of the Inuit culture we know today develops from this period.

Contact with Europeans began in the early 1500s and, ultimately, brought profound changes to the Indians. Many changed their lifestyles from food hunting to fur trapping to satisfy the demands of the fur traders. As a result, they became dependent on the fur traders for food and livelihood. Through Indian intermarriage with French fur traders, the Métis people evolved, and for years found a home in neither camp. Others, like the Cree, became middlemen between fur traders and the Athapaskans of the northwest. Some Indians migrated westward, into strange territories and lifestyles, fleeing the onrush of settlement.

The greatest culture shock, however, was felt by the Plains peoples, whose lifestyle had been virtually frozen in time before the Europeans arrived. Deaths from European illnesses ravaged their numbers. The introduction of guns and horses led to overhunting and near extinction of the buffalo, the mainstay of their lives. More and more settlers encroached on their lands. In a short period of time, the Indians had through treaties surrendered their ancestral lands in return for a life of dependence on government.

At first contact with Europeans, the Indian population (excluding Inuit) was about one million. By 1867, it was 112,000, including Métis and Inuit, and it declined yearly until 1920.

The Modern Native Population

The native population has been growing rapidly since the 1920s. Today there are close to 400,000 Indians, 100,000 Métis, and 25,000 Inuit. About 70 percent of Indians still live on reserves, where the federal government provides housing, education, and social programs. Many still follow traditional lifestyles, based on hunting, fishing, and trapping. Increasingly over the past twenty years, Indians and many of the Métis have moved to the cities, taking their chances in twentieth-century urban society.

The Inuit peoples have remained largely in the north, where their lifestyle has altered dramatically in the twentieth-century. Snowmobiles, air travel, and modern communications have reduced the isolation of small communities. Discovery of oil and mineral deposits has led to calls for land claim compensation. The Inuit's introduction to a money economy began in the 1940s through government-run cooperatives. Today, one of the most visible and successful of these acts as the central marketing agency for Inuit art.

More and more, Canadian native peoples are seeking to control their own destinies. Organizations such as the Dene Nation, the Métis National Council, and Inuit Tapirisat, each speak with a collective voice on matters affecting both the future of native peoples, such as settlement of land claims, and the preservation of their traditional cultures.

The Coming of Europeans

Europeans were exploring Canada, and exploiting its resources in the early 1500s. Basques and French fishermen hunted whales in the Gulf of St. Lawrence and hauled in cod off the Grand Banks of Newfoundland. On the west coast, Spanish explorers were leaving their legacy in place names such as Alberni, Mount Bodega, and Quadra. Early explorers were searching for a Northwest Passage through the New World to the fabled riches of the Orient.

In 1534, Jacques Cartier penetrated the Gulf of St. Lawrence up the river as far as modern Quebec city. He claimed all the territory he discovered for France. The colony of New France began to grow, as did the area that became known as Acadia (the Gaspé of Quebec, and portions of New Brunswick, Nova Scotia, and Prince Edward Island). Catholic missionaries followed the settlers. One of the most renown was the Jesuit, Jean de Brebeuf, martyred in 1649 by warring Iroquois at his mission, Ste. Marie among the Hurons, near modern Midland, Ontario.

The search for the Northwest Passage continued. Along the way, a lucrative fur trade between the French and the Indians developed, and by the late eighteenth century, satisfying the European market for furs had become a goal in itself. Voyageurs paddled their canoes farther and farther along Canada's inland waterways in the search for furs.

Ironically, it was a proposal by two French fur traders that launched the British influence in Canadian history and altered the complexion of the country. In the early 1600s, Pierre Radisson and Medard de Groseillers wanted to start a fur trading company to penetrate the vast interior via Hudson Bay. The idea found no backers in France, but financial support finally came from Britain. The Hudson's Bay Company (HBC) was founded in 1670 with a charter that gave it administrative and trading rights in all the territory whose waters drained into Hudson Bay—about half of the country! The area was named Rupert's Land, after a cousin of Charles II who helped promote the idea.

The HBC set up trading posts on the shores of the bay to receive furs from the Indians. But it fought with the French for control of its southern lands, as France and Britain were fighting for control of New France. Britain finally succeeded in 1763. New France became British North America, and was divided into the provinces of Upper and Lower Canada (present-day Ontario and Quebec). Over a period of time, the Acadians were deported by the British government, about half trekking to Louisiana, where they are now known as Cajuns. The saga of their grueling journey is remembered in Longfellow's *Evangeline*. (Over succeeding generations, many Acadians returned and today form a distinct presence in the Maritimes.)

French settlers in Lower Canada, however, were permitted to retain their language, religion, and government, but under careful control. The effects of that decision color Canadian politics to this day.

Following the American Revolution, British Loyalists flooded into the British colony, notably to the Maritimes and present-day Ontario. In the Maritimes, they more than doubled the existing population, and two new provinces, New Brunswick and Cape Breton, were added to British North America. Loyalists formed the first substantial population base in Upper Canada, and Ontario's traditions of conservative thinking date back to this era.

Meanwhile, in the fur trade fierce competition was growing between the HBC and a rival faction of Scottish fur traders, who had formed the North West Company (NWC) based in Montreal. Instead of waiting for the Indians to come to their posts, as did the HBC, the NWC followed over land and water routes to the fur-rich interior. They forced the HBC to set up interior trading posts for the first time. The competition resulted in ever increasing exploration of Canada, as fur traders pushed farther and farther west, establishing trading posts and seeking the best water routes to transport their treasure.

Two memorable expeditions by Alexander Mackenzie, a NWC trader based at Lake Athabasca, finally completed the overland exploration of Canada from coast to coast. In 1789, he followed the Mackenzie River all the way to the Arctic ocean. In 1793, he reached the Pacific, traveling via the Peace River and through the mountains, to reach in a few short months the west coast at Bella Coola, in British Columbia. The HBC was not far behind, and within a few years, it was conducting a fur trade with coastal Indians, albeit by the sea rather than overland.

Over the next few years, David Thompson, first for the HBC then for the NWC, explored the rivers and mountain passes of western Canada, intent on opening up trade with the Indians in the interior west of the Rockies. His maps, based on his own explorations, became the first truly comprehensive view of the vast western territory of Canada.

Eastern Canada, from 1812–1815, was the battleground for the war between the United States and Britain. With a few decisive victories on either side and considerable involvement by Canadian militia and Indians, the war helped cement the boundary, politically and emotionally, between Canada and the United States as far west as Lake Superior.

David Thompson's early survey work formed the basis for the western boundary, drawn as far as the summit of the Rockies. The colony of New Caledonia was started by the HBC on Vancouver Island in anticipation of the remaining boundary settlement, which came through the Treaty of Oregon in 1846 and through subsequent negotiations between Britain and the United States.

In the nineteenth century, the provinces of British North America matured, developing differing economies and diverging political interests. In the Maritimes, shipbuilding and the timber trade were thriving, but the large, vocal population bases were in Upper and Lower Canada. Support grew within these two provinces for the concept of self-government, just at a time when Britain was losing interest in the business of managing its colonies. After a series of trial-and-error governments, the four provinces of Ontario, Quebec, New Brunswick, and Nova Scotia were joined, in 1867, by an Act of British Parliament, into the Confederation of Canada.

Rupert's Land was sold by the HBC to the government in 1869, and was divided into the province of Manitoba and the Northwest Territories in 1870. New Caledonia, which had seen an influx of settlement following the discovery of gold along the lower Fraser River in the 1850s, joined the Confederation as British Columbia in 1871. Prince Edward Island followed in 1873.

Construction of a national railway (the Canadian Pacific Railway, or CPR) began, and enthusiastic government immigration policies followed to help spread settlement throughout the west. Metis concerns over encroaching settlements led ultimately to the Riel Rebellion of 1885, which was put down by the recently created North West Mounted Police. In 1880, Britain had handed over the Arctic islands to Canada. In 1898, the Yukon was split off from the Northwest Territories. Alberta and Saskatchewan were created from the remaining southern portion in 1905. The last of the provinces, Newfoundland, remained a British colony until 1949, when it joined the Confederation.

The history of Canada has been called the triumph of transportation over geography. Canada's vast natural waterways were fundamental to the success of the fur trade, and it was through their exploration that Canada's interior was first opened up. Natural waterways were the preferred transportation routes until the advent of the railways in the 1880s, and they were the only viable transportation routes to Canada's north well into the twentieth century. Although man-made waterways, such as the Rideau Canal and the Trent–Severn system, were built as alternate supply routes after the War of 1812, they were never used for their intended military purpose. It wasn't until 1954 that human improvements on nature reaped real benefits, culminating in the massive St. Lawrence Seaway project, built cooperatively by the United States and Canada.

Ad Mare usque ad Mare

But it was the building of railroads that truly made Canada a nation "from sea to sea." Prince Edward Island joined the Confederation because Canada promised to assume its huge debt, amassed during railway construction. And it was on the promise of a national railway that British Columbia joined the Confederation. The Canadian Pacific Railway made settlement of the west viable, especially after the Indians surrendered their lands. As the railway proceeded west, modern Canadian cities sprang up, forming links in the chain across the southern part of the country. Rushed to completion in 1885, the CPR permitted the mass movement of troops that put down the Riel Rebellion. The problems of accurate timekeeping over the railroad's vast distance led the world's adoption of international time zones. And it was the discovery, during construction of the CPR, of the sulphur springs at Banff that led to the formation of Canada's National Parks System, and the start of major tourism in Canada.

Following the CPR, branch railways and new lines opened up new areas for settlement and resource development. Railways were directly responsible for the development of northern Ontario's mining industry, and the expansion of CPR lines opened up coal mining areas in the Rockies.

Road systems complemented the network of railway lines, often following Indian footpaths and wagon trails, sometimes paralleling the railroads, especially through mountain passes. The Trans-Canada Highway, dreamed of since 1910, was finally opened in 1962, crossing the country with the aid of coastal ferries. The first road traffic to the far north began during World War II, with construction of the Alaska Highway. The Mackenzie Highway now links Edmonton with Yellowknife, and Canada's most northerly highway, the Dempster, links Dawson City, in the Yukon, and Inuvik, in the Northwest Territories.

But air transportation is the biggest single factor in the opening of the Canadian north in the twentieth century. The sagas of Canadian bush pilots, often former flying aces of the world wars, have added their own colorful page to Canadian history.

The Twentieth Century

In the twentieth century, Canada solidified its nationhood, and evolved into a modern industrial nation. In 1914, Britain's declaration of war automatically included all of her colonies, but by 1918, Canada signed the Armistice on her own behalf. In 1931, Canada was given nominal independence by Britain, but it wasn't until 1982 that Canada formally proclaimed her own Constitution, completing the road to independence.

Modern Canadian industry continues to rely heavily on natural resources, particularly in Western Canada. Agriculture is still fundamental to the economy of the prairies, as is the petroleum industry to Alberta and fisheries and forestry to British Columbia. Eighty percent of the manufacturing industry, and therefore the power base of the country, is located in Ontario and Quebec. The tourism industry is burgeoning in all parts of the country.

Approaching the Twenty-first Century

Canada continues to evolve, both politically and industrially. The political structure of the country as it now stands has been in place for only forty years. Debate goes on over provincial status for the Yukon Territory, the separation of the Northwest Territories into east and west, and the division of northern and southern Ontario into separate provinces. Major land claims and questions of aboriginal rights have yet to be settled, and the special status of native peoples has not yet been fully addressed by the new constitution or the Charter of Rights.

Like other developed countries, Canada's biggest industrial growth is currently not in the resource or manufacturing sectors but in the management of information. As it approaches the twenty-first century, Canadian industry is expanding towards a new era.

THE CANADIAN SCENE

The Canadian Constitution

Government and law in Canada operate by a combination of unwritten traditions and written law. Canadians governed themselves successfully for over a hundred years without, for example, a written description of the rights and freedoms of individuals. Until 1982, the only written constitution was an Act of British Parliament, the British North America (BNA) Act of 1867, setting out the terms of Canadian Confederation. The Constitution Act, proclaimed in 1982, defines rights and freedoms, but comprises the complete constitution of Canada only when read together with the BNA Act, and taking into account the multitude of precedents and unwritten principles of British Parliamentary tradition.

Political Parties

There are three federal political parties, two of which date from the Confederation era, the Liberals and the Progressive Conservatives (PCs). The socialist New Democratic Party (NDP), a relative newcomer as a national party, had its origins in the western dustbowl of the Great Depression. The Liberals and the PCs have more or less traded power since Confederation. From time to time, while never having formed a government, the NDP has strongly influenced government policy, especially during periods of minority government.

Each party employs its own mechanism for choosing a party leader. If his party wins a national election, the leader becomes the prime minister. (There have been no female party leaders to date.) The leader continues to head the party, even in election defeat, so long as that leadership satisfies the party membership.

Provincial parties mirror the federal parties, with some important regional differences. The principle of leadership with resulting governmental office in the case of victory is the same.

Government Structure

Canada is a strong federal state, combining the checks and balances of the American system with the traditions of British Parliament. Specific responsibilities are assigned to the provinces; for example, education, family law, roads, and ownership of natural resources. All unspecified power rests with the federal government. For example, in the twentieth century this has included control of new technologies such as television and telecommunications.

The head of the executive branch is the governor general. As the Queen's representative in Canada, the role is of great symbolic importance, but the functions have become largely ceremonial, such as the swearing-in of cabinet ministers, administering the system of Canadian Honors, and opening sessions of Parliament. Since 1952, Canadians have held this position. The first woman governor general, Jeanne Sauve, was named in 1984.

Canada has a pluralist government. Real executive power rests with the elected prime minister and his cabinet. The prime minister leads the majority party in the legislature and also leads the cabinet in the formulation of government policy. Prime ministers can call an election at any time, largely at their own discretion. They choose cabinet ministers from among members of their own party, usually with individual expertise and regional interests in mind. Cabinet ministers must be members of either house of the legislative branch. Ministers are responsible for specific "portfolios," such as housing, finance, and external affairs. They establish government policy, introduce most legislation, make judicial and diplomatic appointments, and are responsible for the finances of government.

The bicameral legislature consists of the House of Commons and the Senate. The House has 310 "seats" allocated on a population basis. Members (MPs) are directly elected by Canadian citizens for a possible five-year term. They propose and enact legislation. Independent members are sometimes elected, but the vast majority are party-affiliated. Cabinet ministers are most often chosen from the House of Commons.

The Senate has 104 members, appointed by the prime minister, on a regional basis. Among other qualifications, they must be at least thirty years old, and must retire at age seventy-five. Senators provide "sober second thought" on legislation passed by the Commons, and also protect the regional interests of the country. They rarely reject legislation, but they do propose amendments to it. Provincial governments echo the structure of the federal system, with a lieutenant-governor, as the Queen's provincial representative, and an elected premier and cabinet holding the real executive power. Legislative assemblies are the elected provincial equivalent of the Commons. There are no provincial senates.

The two territories are under direct federal control. In both territories, the responsibilities of the territorial governments roughly parallel those initially given to the provinces. Both governments are headed by a federally appointed commissioner, and have an elected body. In the Northwest Territories, the Territorial Council has twenty-four elected members, with no party affiliations. The commissioner traditionally follows the political lead of the Council but is not required by law to do so.

The Yukon Territory is more politically advanced. In 1979, the federal government transferred power from the commissioner to an Executive Council, consisting of members of the Legislative Assembly. The Commissioner must follow the direction of the Council on almost all matters. The twelve members of the Legislative Assembly are affiliated with various political parties.

Municipal governments are under the jurisdiction of the provinces. Municipal powers are determined by each provincial government, which directly regulates some responsibilities, such as municipal planning and finance.

The judicial system in Canada is separate from the executive and legislative branches of government. All Canadian judges are appointed. Judges of the provincial Superior Courts and the Supreme Court of Canada are appointed and paid by the federal government. Provincial and municipal governments appoint the judges of the lower courts, as well as magistrates, justices of the peace, sheriffs, coroners, and other officers of the courts.

Federal courts are courts of appeal on matters concerning the whole country. The Supreme Court is the ultimate appeal court. Its nine judges (three of whom are from Quebec) hear cases, at their discretion, that deal with matters important to the country as a whole or that involve some important aspect of law, such as interpreting the new Charter of Rights or determining a province's right to enact particular legislation. Other federal courts hear appeals on matters of taxes, patent and copyright law, and maritime law. Superior courts are the provincial courts of appeal.

All courts in Canada, except those of Quebec, enforce Common Law, based on British legal tradition. Quebec enforces Civil Law, also known as the Napoleonic Code, which derives from Roman law in the time of Emperor Justinian.

The Musical Ride and Other Police Forces

Contrary to their Hollywood image, red-coated "Mounties" do not stride across Canada rending the wilderness with song! They do enforce the law in many parts of the country, though, and are of great symbolic importance to the country. Their scarlet tunics hark back to the historic good relations between the British army and the Indians, a tradition which the Royal Canadian Mounted Police (RCMP) quickly made its own. As the North West Mounted Police, their presence in western Canada from 1874, before major settlement took place, prevented the kind of frontier violence that pervaded the American West. The North West Mounted Police established a tradition of law and order, maintained largely without force of arms, that helps give Canada its "clean and safe" image today.

The provinces are responsible for public policing and delegate local policing to the municipalities. The largest municipal force is the Metropolitan Toronto Police. Through contractual arrangements with the provinces, the RCMP provides provincial policing, such as highway patrols, and local policing of small communities, to all provinces, except two. Ontario and Quebec have their own provincial forces. The RCMP also polices the two territories and federal and diplomatic buildings. It handles criminal investigation related to organized crime, narcotics, and commercial fraud; maintains national criminal records; and provides advanced training to other forces. In 1984 the intelligence operations of the RCMP were taken over by a civilian agency, the Canadian Security Intelligence Service.

The world-famous Musical Ride of the RCMP has its origins in the mandatory riding training once given to all recruits. This stirring spectacle enlivens many a Canadian festival each year.

Canadian Armed Forces

Unique in the world is the unified Canadian Armed Forces. The separate army, navy, and air force were integrated in 1968 with a common uniform and badge system, administrative support, and training. Three distinct service identities have begun to reemerge, though, and in 1984, separate uniforms were reintroduced. The Canadian Armed Forces currently comprise about 85,000 men and women. Conscription has been used only during the two world wars. The governor-general is the commander-in-chief of the Canadian Armed Forces.

Education

Because education is a provincial responsibility, there are twelve autonomous education systems in Canada. Ninety-five percent of all Canadian pupils are enrolled in "public" schools, totally supported by provincial and municipal tax dollars. "Separate schools" (usually Roman Catholic) are maintained by the tax dollars of citizens who specify their preference, and by varying degrees of provincial subsidy. Newfoundland has three distinct denominational public systems. In Quebec, the public system is Roman Catholic, the separate system is Protestant. A small number of pupils are enrolled in private or alternative schools in the country. Until 1960s most higher education was offered by private universities, and only a few colleges, such as the prestigious Ryerson Polytechnical Institute. Provincially supported universities in seven provinces, and a host of technical and community colleges across the country, were established in 1960, largely as a result of federal funding made available for the construction of new schools, institutes, and adult training centers.

The federal government has its greatest effect on education through funding to the provinces. But the Official Languages Act (1970), which declared Canada officially bilingual, directly affected the growth of second-language instruction across Canada. Particularly in the last five years, the growth in English-speaking Canada of total-immersion-style French-language education has been striking.

ENTERTAINMENT AND THE ARTS

Canadian cities offer the cosmopolitan nightlife of cabarets, nightclubs, and the performing arts. In the smallest communities, there are weekend dances and social gatherings. Spectator sports are popular all over the country. Regular season football and hockey, to name but two, draw regular large crowds, and their championship games (the Grey Cup and the Stanley Cup Playoffs) attract crowds that swell the seams of the host cities. There is pari-mutuel betting in all provinces. There is, at the least, a bingo hall in almost every community, and casinos are found at fairs and festivals in many provinces.

The arts in Canada have exploded onto the international scene in the past twenty-five years, directly paralleling the history of the Canada Council, a federal agency, and the increased sophistication of Canadian audiences. The Canada Council provides direct financial aid to all aspects of the arts from children's theater to the publishing industry, including grants to individuals and professional institutions. The commemoration of Canada's Centennial in 1967, and the centennial birthdays of several provinces have seen a proliferation of museums and galleries across the country. Today, a multitude of museums, galleries, and centers for the performing arts showcase the talents of Canadians.

Festivals

There are almost 200 major festivals each year in Canada, and a host of minor ones. Most take place in the summer, but they can be found throughout the country at any time of year, celebrating everything from the time of year itself to indigenous foods, history, ethnic origins, and the arts.

The Quebec Winter Carnival is renowned for its Mardi Gras–style celebration of the Canadian winter. The Yellowknife Annual Midnight Golf Tournament celebrates the 24-hour sunshine on the longest day of the year. Kitchener–Waterloo's Oktoberfest celebrates both the harvest and the Mennonite food traditions of the area. Good examples of ethnic festivals are Prince Edward Island's Fête Acadienne; the National Ukrainian Festival in Dauphin, Manitoba; and the Gathering of the Clans in Pugwash, Nova Scotia. The unique Northern Games roam through the Northwest Territories, from town to town, with Inuit and Dene games, dances, competitions and displays. Multi-cultural festivals like Toronto's Caravan, Edmonton's Heritage Days, and Regina's Mosaic are increasingly popular. Some festivals have historical themes, like Edmonton's Klondike Days and Saint John's Loyalist Days. Others have their roots in Canadian history. Canada's oldest permanent festival, the Canadian National Exhibition, began as southern Ontario's agricultural fair. The Calgary Stampede keeps alive the cowboy skills of the western cattle business.

The drama productions of the Stratford and Shaw Festivals along with the music of Toronto's Mariposa Folk Festival and Edmonton's Jazz City all boast their own audiences of aficionados. The Banff Festival of the Arts is renowned for its summerlong celebration of theater, music, and visual arts.

Theater

Live theater flourishes across Canada, from small repertory companies to the internationally acclaimed productions of the Shaw Festival and the Stratford Festival. Musical theater thrives at the Theatre in the Dell and the Bayview Playhouse, both of Toronto, and at the renowned Charlottetown Festival in Prince Edward Island, among others. Readily accessible to visitors are the lunch and dinner theaters, such as Solar Stage in Toronto, the hugely successful Stage West in Edmonton, and City Stage in Vancouver. A growing trend in the 1980s is summertime outdoor theater, with performances held in park settings in the open air or in tents.

More uniquely Canadian works are being performed, for increasingly receptive audiences, than ever before. And Canadian performers such as Kate Reid, Christopher Plummer, Hume Cronyn, and Kate Nelligan are increasingly well-known internationally. French-language theater tends toward distinctly regional themes, not only in Quebec, but also in provinces with strong French cultures. In the Maritimes, it tends to deal with the Acadian experience in a modern context, while in Manitoba, French-language theater is one of the most visible aspects of the French culture.

Music

Canadian taste in popular music covers everything from the stylings of Paul Anka to the Heavy Metal sounds of Chilliwack. Many Canadian singers, such as Anne Murray, Joni Mitchell, Neil Young, and Bruce Cockburn, have "made it big" beyond the Canadian border. Folksingers Ian and Sylvia Tyson's "Four Strong Winds" was perhaps one of the first songs to explore the Canadian temperament. Gordon Lightfoot, the composer of such songs as "Early Morning Rain," has moved easily from folk to pop.

Canadian country-and-western singers tend to sing more traditional ballads and story songs than American singers. Tommy Hunter, almost a legend in his own time, has maintained his popularity for over twenty-five years.

The biggest name in Canadian jazz is pianist Oscar Peterson, but the best-known in the United States might be trumpeter and bandleader Maynard Ferguson. Jazz is played in the nightclubs of most major cities, such as the Cellar (Vancouver), Yardbird Suite (Edmonton), George's Spaghetti House (Toronto), and La Jazzteck (Montreal).

Chamber music is played in the traditional manner by the York Winds and the Montreal Brass Quintet. There are avant-garde chamber groups such as the Vancouver New Music Society and New Music Concerts of Toronto. A breath of fresh air is blown through Canada by the Canadian Brass—superb musicians with a highly successful international career. Noted for their on-stage hilarity, they have performed with leading symphony orchestras and have made many recordings. One of the finest symphony orchestras in Canada is the Montreal Symphony (its Carnegie Hall debut was in 1976); its recordings, made in the church at St. Eustache, Quebec, have won the orchestra many awards. There are several other fine orchestras in the country, such as the Toronto Symphony, the Vancouver Symphony, the Winnipeg Symphony (which plays for the Royal Winnipeg Ballet), and the Edmonton Symphony. The reputation of the National Art Centre Orchestra in Ottawa has continued to grow for twenty years.

Although almost every major city has an opera association, the Canadian Opera Company of Toronto is one of the most successful. Maureen Forrester, one of North America's most sought-after contraltos, was appointed Chairperson of the Canada Council in 1983, a fine tribute to her interest in the arts. Tenor Jon Vickers is in such international demand that he rarely has the chance to perform in his own country.

One of Canada's greatest contributions to classical music has been the work of the late Glenn Gould. He drew immediate attention with his recording of Bach's *Goldberg Variations*. In 1981 he recorded his new interpretation of "the Goldbergs"—it was his farewell to piano solo recording. His next interest, conducting small ensembles in experimental taping sessions, was cut off by his untimely death in 1982.

Dance

Modern dance is reaching wider Canadian audiences than ever before. One of the most successful companies is the Toronto Dance Theatre, founded by three one-time students of Martha Graham. The Anna Wyman Dance Theatre is highly successful in Vancouver. There are three main ballet companies, and several regional ones, in the country. The oldest is the renowned Royal Winnipeg Ballet. (Royal is a designation that may be used only on the approval of the Queen). The

Royal Winnipeg Ballet has maintained a repertoire designed to have broad appeal and has won medals in Paris and ovations in the USSR.

The National Ballet of Canada, founded in 1951 with Toronto backing, by Celia Franca, offers a broad repertoire, but bases its reputation on lavish productions of nineteenth-century favorites such as *Swan Lake* and *Sleeping Beauty*. Regular guest appearances by Rudolph Nureyev helped the National achieve international acclaim and further the careers of Karen Kain and her partner, Frank Augustyn.

Les Grand Ballets Canadiens had its roots in the launching of French-language television, evolving later into live performances. Founded in 1958 by Ludmilla Chiriaeff, it now offers a varied repertoire representing the best of classical tradition and modern dance.

Film

There has been a great increase in Canadian film production over the last twenty years, largely due to the creation by the federal government of the Canadian Film Development Corporation, which offers substantial tax incentives to investors in the Canadian film industry. A change in management in 1978 has seen the focus shift from "film as art" to film as commercial industry. Foreign stars and directors have been used more often to insure box office successes such as *The Changeling, Who Has Seen the Wind?,* and *The Apprenticeship of Duddy Kravitz. Scanners* established David Cronenberg's reputation in the genre of horror films.

Canada's reputation in film animation has evolved over the past forty years. The National Film Board of Canada has won major awards, including three Oscars, for its animated shorts. The box office hit *Heavy Metal* was the work of former National Film Board animator Gerald Potterton. Crawley Films of Ottawa has produced some animated series for American television, such as *Return to Oz.*

Art

Canadian painting has responded in diverse ways to outside influences, regional historic differences, and distances between major centers. A Canadian identity burst forth in the 1920s in the work of the "Group of Seven," who held jobs in Toronto and made painting exhibitions to northern Ontario. At the same time, a regional style was developing in Quebec, based on a 300-year attachment to the land. On the west coast, the work of Emily Carr reflected a profound sense of the British Columbian landscape and the influence of west coast Indian art. During the 1940s, young abstract painters in Montreal such as Albert Pellan felt more affinity for the European influence of Paris. In the 1950s the early works of Harold Town and the late Jack Bush, both of Toronto, reflected the abstractionism of New York City. Western centers such as the Banff Centre School of Fine Arts and the Emma Lake workshops in Saskatchewan tried to fight the problem of isolation from major centers.

Today, Canadian painting strives to maintain its identity in the face of strong influences, both from Europe and the United States, but several painters have maintained their roots. On the west coast, the surrealism of Jack Shadbolt is affected by the same factors that inspired Emily Carr. In the Maritimes, Alex Colville has raised realist art to a new standard, evoking stark images of his locale and influencing the works of Christopher and Mary Pratt. One of Canada's most imaginative artists is Michael Snow, who has moved from painting into multimedia art forms.

Native Art

A current resurgence of native art has resulted from an increased interest by artists in Canadian traditions, combined with a ready market for their highly distinctive work. Native art falls into two separate categories, Indian and Inuit.

There are two preeminent schools of Indian art. The Woodlands artists of eastern Canada are "legend painters," whose works are narrative or descriptive of mythological characters. The works of Norval Morriseau, an Ojibwa from northern Ontario, and Jackson Beardy, an Ojibwa from Manitoba, are credited with the upswing of interest in Woodlands art.

Northwest coast Indian art is highly formalized, based on traditions that have evolved over a period of 3,000 years. The distinctive feature is the form line, a continuous flowing line used in a prescribed manner for figure outlines as well as in interior design elements. A strong revival of the traditional art forms began in 1958 when Bill Reid, a Haida Indian, began to recreate Haida totem poles for the Upper British Columbia Museum of Anthropology. About 200 hundred artists are now producing works, including carvings, jewelry, and weavings that are highly prized by collectors.

In addition to the two main groups, there is a scattered group of people who are artists first who "happen to be Indian" also. Their work, like that of the late Arthur Shilling or Alex Janvier, still shows an unmistakable link with Indian traditions.

As we know it, Inuit art dates from the late 1940s, although its traditions can be traced to the Middle Dorset period, A.D. 400–500. Soapstone and ivory carvings have become world-famous, as have wall hangings, but prints provide the greatest return for investment-minded collectors. Inuit art is illustrative or narrative, depicting survival techniques and the lifestyles of the north. Styles vary according to the location of production, that is, Cape Dorset, Baker Lake. The works of Jessie Oonark of Baker Lake are renowned, combining traditional Inuit images with the symbolism of her Christian beliefs. Five of her children are recognized as artists in their own right.

As the popularity of Inuit art has increased, prices have soared. It is widely imitated, usually at lower prices through mass production. The real thing is marketed by Arctic Cooperatives Ltd., one of the more successful Inuit co-ops.

A TASTE OF CANADA

Canadian cuisine ranks among the best in the world for its quality and variety. The wealth of foodstuffs produced in their own country means that Canadians pay less for their food than any other country in the world except the United States. They also eat out at least one-third of the time, which may account for the wide range of dining-out experiences available, ranging from *haute cuisine* in the finest traditions to casual, corner coffee shop and take-out places. It may also account for the growing international acclaim of Canadian chefs. During the 1980s, the Canadian Chefs de Cuisine have consistently won top awards in international competitions. In 1984, the Chefs took the Frankfurt World Culinary Olympics by storm, winning first place with twenty-four gold medals.

The Canadian food industry has the highest standards in the world for hygiene and sanitation. From afternoon tea to caribou steaks under the midnight sun, Canadian restaurants await your pleasure.

A Well-Balanced Diet

Canadians can stay healthy eating only foods produced in their own country. Some of the world's finest beef is produced in Canada, as is pork, lamb, and veal. Venison, caribou, and other game are plentiful. There is an abundance of freshwater fish—trout, walleye, pike, pickerel, to name a few—and a wealth of seafood, from Malpeque oysters and Atlantic lobster to British Columbian salmon. Excellent fruits and vegetables from British Columbian's Okanagan Valley and Ontario's Niagara Peninsula are complemented by a wide variety of indigenous berries from across the country, world-famous Prince Edward Island potatoes, and grains from the prairies.

Some Mouthwatering Reading

A multitude of Canadian cookbooks has been published in recent years, enhancing domestic eating pleasure. Jehane Benoit's *Encyclopedia of Canadian Cuisine* spans the whole spectrum of Canadian ingredients, while Helen Gougeon's *Good Food* has a French-Canadian flavor. *Food that Really Schmeck's* is Edna Staebler's famous contribution from the Mennonite heritage of southwestern Ontario. Worth a good look are the *Northern Cookbook* by Eleanor A. Elkis, Bernard Assiniwi's *Indian Recipes,* and the works of Elizabeth Baird, which focus on the food heritage of Canada's pioneers.

A Sampling of Canadian Ingredients

The multi-cultural makeup of Canada's population has added many new dishes to Canadian tables, and imported goods to the food stores. But the food traditions of Canada trace their beginnings to pioneer adaptations of favorite recipes to suit local ingredients. A typically Canadian cuisine is difficult to define as a Canadian is, but regional specialties are not. Try to sample at least some of the following:

British Columbia: Fish and shellfish of many kinds. Salmon, crab, shrimp, black cod, and halibut are among the best. Lamb, from the marshes of Saltspring Island, is served with mint sauce, not mint jelly. Try cheddar cheese from Armstrong or, from the Okanagan Valley, a wealth of produce—cherries, peaches, pears, apples, and vegetables.

The Prairies: World-famous grain-fed beef from the Alberta foothills—juicy thick steaks and chuckwagon stew. Alberta lamb and pork. Honey from the Peace country. Grab the chance when you can to try succulent buffalo steaks. In Saskatchewan, a variety of grains, especially wheat. Whitefish, trout, pickerel. Gamebirds such as partridge and prairie chicken. Saskatoon pie with thick cream, made from a berry that gave its name to the city. From Manitoba, smoked Winnipeg goldeye. Wild rice, caviar, and whitefish. Local honey from the Dauphin area.

Ontario: Freshwater fish from three-quarters of a million lakes. Try whitefish, lake trout, pike, and smelt. Fruits and vegetables from the Niagara Peninsula. Macintosh applies from their place of origin in eastern Ontario. Ontario cheddar cheese. Succulent ears of corn, roasted or steamed, dripping with melted butter.

Quebec: Maple sugar: Try it as maple syrup on hotcakes, hard blocks of maple sugar candy, or in sugar pie. Try it as taffy, cooled on the snow in spring forests. Brome Lake Duckling. Oka and Ermite cheeses. Pork is essential to the rural French-Canadian meal. Try it as a spiced pork spread called *cretons,* or in *tourtiere,* a minced pork pie, or try French Canadian pea soup flavored with a ham hock or salt pork. For some of the finest classic French cuisine in North America, sample even the most modest of restaurants in Quebec City.

Maritimes: In New Brunswick, steamed fiddleheads with melted butter. Salmon, oysters, lobster, clam. Dulse (a dried seaweed snack). Blueberries, strawberries, and rhubarb. In Prince Edward Island, don't miss a chance to visit a church lobster supper. Try soused mackerel, or Malpeque oysters, and some of the finest potatoes in the world. In Nova Scotia, there are famous Digby scallops, tuna, and swordfish. Apples from the Annapolis Valley. Mahone Bay steamed brown bread. Lunenburg sausage or blueberry grunt. In Newfoundland, if you ask for fish you'll be served cod. Try baked cod cheeks, cod tongues, or seal-flipper pie. Try a bakeapple berry pie, rich in vitamin C.

The Arctic: For a hearty appetite there are juicy char-broiled caribou steaks. Arctic char is a special treat, with a flavor like salmon but more delicate. Sample the many types of wild berries, including wild blueberries and soapberries.

Thirst Quenchers

Canadians are among the great beer drinkers in the world. Regular strength Canadian beer contains five percent alcohol by volume, although light beers are becoming increasingly popular. Canadian beer is produced in all provinces except Prince Edward Island, by four major breweries—Molson, Carling, Labatt, and O'Keefe—and several regional breweries, such as Old Fort (British Columbia), Rocky Mountain (Alberta), Amstel (Ontario), and Moosehead (Nova Scotia and New Brunswick).

In a few provinces, a growing trend is the establishment by restaurants of small brewhouses, producing small quantities of natural beers for sale on their own premises.

Wine making in Canada dates back to the 1600s when early Jesuit missionaries made their own sacramental wines. Today, wine is produced in seven provinces, but the two main centers are the Niagara Peninsula and the Okanagan Valley.

The first vines were planted in Canada in 1857 at St. Davids, in the Niagara area. Eighty percent of Canada's wine grapes are now grown in the peninsula. The British Columbia wine industry began on Vancouver Island where there was a surplus of loganberries, then expanded to lakeside irrigated grape plots in the Okanagan Valley. Over half of the wine made in Canada is now produced from hybrids of *vinefera* vines, which are used in European wine making. Of about forty-five varieties of grapes grown, the main ones are Concord, de Chaunac, Niagara, Elvira, and Foch.

In 1983 Canadian wines won thirty-five medals in international competitions. Small wineries now specialize in higher quality wines, such as Pinot Noir, Cabernet Sauvignon, and Gewurztraminer. The largest wineries make sparkling wines, sherries, ports, and reds. In major Canadian cities of the 1980s, dry white wines have become extremely popular.

Canada also has a wide range of imported wines. Alberta, with no domestic wine industry and therefore no tarriff protection, has the lowest prices in the country on imported wines. Quebec shows a definite preference for imported French wines. Many wines unavailable elsewhere in North America can be found in Quebec restaurants and liquor stores.

Canada's first recorded distillery produced rum from molasses at Quebec City in 1769. Canadian spirits were in great demand in the United States as early as 1861, and the distilling industry grew tremendously during American prohibition. Today one of the two largest distilling companies in the world, Canadian Seagrams, remains Canadian, while ownership of the other, Hiram Walker, has recently passed into British hands. Canadian blended rye whiskies and other products are internationally known for their quality and consistency. For those of sterner stuff, there is the acquired taste of spruce beer and Newfoundland Screech.

ONTARIO

The Heartland of Canada

by
VALERIE ROSS

Valerie Ross has written for most major Canadian publications and is currently entertainment editor at Maclean's, *Canada's national magazine.*

Ontario is an old Iroquois word meaning "shining waters." The province contains 156,670 square kilometers (68,490 square miles) of fresh water—one quarter of all there is in the world.

The waters of the St. Lawrence Seaway and the Great Lakes bound Ontario for a thousand miles on its populous and affluent southern rim. Here its waterways are plied by hulking ocean tankers, lake cruisers, and pleasure craft. But the majority of Ontario's lakes are empty of traffic, except for blue expanses crossed by the occasional lone canoe. West of Kenora and Rainy River, the Ontario-Manitoba border runs north through forest, tundra and Arctic plain. Ontario's eastern boundary is the Ottawa River and then a line of ever-diminishing trees straggling up to the barren saltwater shores of James and Hudson Bays.

The sheer immensity of Ontario (an area of almost a half-million square miles) makes it hard to discern a character. Inside one political boundary you will find frontier mining towns like South Porcupine, the gentle pastoral scenery of Kitchener's Mennonite farm communities, flashing neon sophistication of midtown Toronto, and gray stone conservatism of townships around Kingston.

The scenery varies tremendously and so do the people. Ontario, with nine million people, is the most populous province in English Canada. It's home to wealthy industrialists, Indian and Métis trappers, celebrated artists, solitary bush pilots, WASP gentry and immigrants of all colors and creeds. It has more Germans than Nürnberg, more Italians than Florence, more Blacks than Bermuda. The province is as big as two Texases, three Japans or France, Germany, and Italy combined. As a traveler in a province this big and this diverse, the best you can do is scratch the edges and marvel at the rest—like the first explorers who glimpsed its vastness more than three and a half centuries ago. Ontario's "shining waters" were their routes.

Greed and God and the First Explorers

In 1610 Henry Hudson sailed through Arctic waters into Hudson Bay and claimed the land for the British Crown. Meanwhile, the French were beginning to explore the Great Lakes shoreline and backwoods river systems in the south. Between those first French and English explorers stretched thousands of square miles of forest, marsh and rock, sparsely populated by tribes of farmers—Iroquois and Huron —and hunters—Algonquin, Cree, and Eskimo.

The Europeans intruded on their lands for a mixture of reasons: greed for land for their respective crowns; greed for the natural wealth (furs, fish, lumber, and minerals) the region promised; religious zeal; and the simple challenge of curiosity.

Two very different, but very typical, men were French-born Étienne Brûlé and Father Jean de Brébeuf.

Brûlé, a lieutenant of the explorer Samuel de Champlain, was not yet 17 years old when he made his first sortie from the French settlement at Québec into the western wilderness. He is credited with being the first white visitor to Lake Ontario, Lake Erie, Georgian Bay, Sault Ste. Marie, and the north shore of Lake Superior. Rascally and audacious, he traveled extensively with his Indian guides, speaking their language, making love to the women, quarreling with the men, until in 1632 he was murdered and reportedly eaten by some exasperated Hurons.

By contrast, Father de Brébeuf was a calm, dedicated Jesuit who lived for 12 years among the Hurons. He built a mission school and hospital, advised their farmers and ministered to their sick, all the while hoping patiently for converts. The site of the early Jesuit mission has been reconstructed at Ste. Marie Among the Hurons, near Midland.

In 1649 de Brébeuf was captured by the Hurons' enemy, the Iroquois, and horribly tortured and martyred by them. Father de Brébeuf has since been canonized by the Catholic Church.

After the death of de Brébeuf and his fellow missionaries, French settlement in Ontario was limited to the occasional fortified trading post. But exploration continued, and from Ontario trading posts and friendly Indian villages, the expeditions of La Salle, Joliet and Father Marquette set out for the American Midwest and down the Mississippi. The French naturally claimed the land they found for their king, and by the end of the century their claims had almost surrounded the fledgling British colonies of New England. Strategically, this was bad; economically, worse, for it gave the French a huge advantage in the profitable fur trade. The British waited for their chance. When the Seven Years' War broke out in Europe, British troops based in what was to become the United States conquered French forts in Ontario and Quebec, and in 1756 the western regions of New France passed to the British Crown and became Upper Canada.

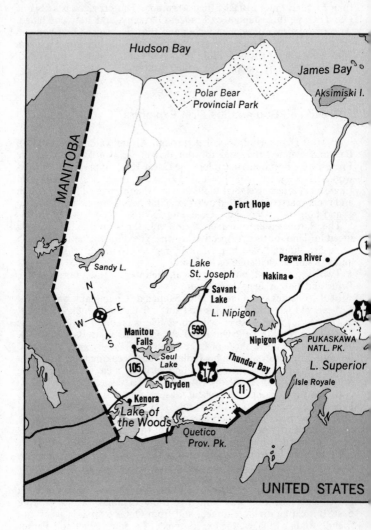

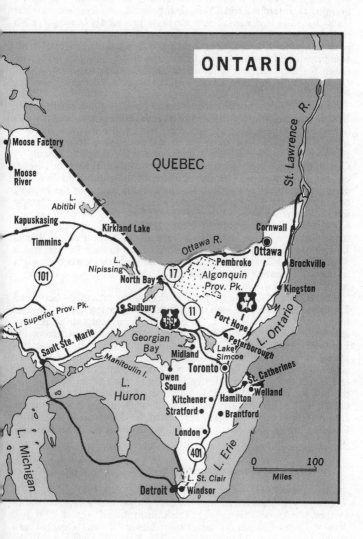

ONTARIO

QUEBEC

Moose Factory

Moose River

L. Abitibi

Kapuskasing

Kirkland Lake

Timmins

L. Nipissing

North Bay

101

L. Superior Prov. Pk.

Sudbury

Sault Ste. Marie

Georgian Bay

Manitoulin I.

Midland

L. Huron

Owen Sound

Kitchener

Stratford

London

L. Michigan

Detroit

L. St. Clair

Windsor

St. Lawrence R.

Cornwall

Ottawa R.

Ottawa

Brockville

Pembroke

Algonquin Prov. Pk.

Kingston

17

11

Port Hope

Peterborough

Lake Simcoe

L. Ontario

Toronto

St. Catherines

Hamilton

Welland

Brantford

401

L. Erie

0   100
Miles

Loyalists: the Backbone of Ontario

The American War of Independence had a profound effect in shaping Ontario. Waves of pro-British refugees flooded into the region, bringing their families and slaves, their political conservatism and their staunch loyalty to Britain. The motto of the province is *Ut incepit fidelis sic permanet* ("Loyal she began, loyal she remains"). The colonial government tried to help the Loyalist refugees with grants of land, equipment, and livestock, but there is no doubt that the going was tough for the Germans who settled around Adolphustown (Bay of Quinte) and Berlin (now Kitchener), the Scots at Glengarry, and the British who settled all across the province.

Just as 1776 marks the coalescence of the American spirit, so the British-American war of 1812–14 marks the real beginning of Canada's determination to survive as a country. In fact, the war was simply a series of skirmishes that hardly changed the borders of its participants. But those skirmishes played a major role in shaping the identity of Canadians. Their heroes are not revolutionaries but rather the defenders of the Crown, who fought at Queenston Heights and Fort Michilimackinac, and the British Troops who retaliated for the burning of York (Toronto) by putting Washington to the torch. Many Ontario forts which saw action in the War of 1812 have now been reconstructed. You may also notice the Laura Secord chain of candy stores throughout the province; they're named after a heroine of the War of 1812, a Massachusetts-born female counterpart to Paul Revere. Laura Secord trekked 20 miles through enemy lines and thick woods at night to warn the nearest British troops that the Yankees were coming—indeed, at her farm at Queenston.

The War of 1812 brought more settlers to the province—Scots and English soldiers and German mercenaries who, having fought, decided to stay, and soon after them, the Irish. Driven to emigrate by poverty and famine at home, the Irish poured into Canada both from the Protestant north and the Catholic south. But once here the Protestants joined the powerful Orange Lodge, greatly strengthening the pro-British conservatism of the province while Irish Catholics remained poorer and far less influential politically. On July 12, the Orange holiday, you can still see parades of Protestants in some Ontario communities. The old fights live on through the symbolic white horse, orange sashes, Union Jack banners and drum corps, and the descendants of the Irish Catholic immigrants offer pithy partisan observations from the sidelines.

The Fight for Good Government

Surprisingly, it wasn't one of the fighting Irish, but a Scotsman, William Lyon Mackenzie, who led the fight for democratic reform of Ontario's colonial government. The Constitutional Act of 1791 had divided Upper Canada (Ontario) from Lower Canada (Québec), and established an elected legislative assembly. But real power lay with the body over it—a legislative council run by a self-perpetuating clique of rich Anglicans so closely related in philosophy and marriage that they were called the Family Compact. The system was rife with patronage for members of the Compact which Mackenzie, through his outspoken newspaper, the *Colonial Advocate,* attacked vigorously. In retaliation, several young men from Toronto's finest families dumped his printing presses into Toronto harbor.

Mackenzie was elected five times to the Legislature and five times he was expelled—sometimes bodily. Finally, in 1837, coordinating with rebellious democrats in Québec, Mackenzie staged open rebellion. A ragtag group of men marched on Toronto from Montgomery's Tavern at the north end of Yonge Street, only to be dispersed by the muskets of the British army. Mackenzie fled to the States; two other rebel leaders were caught, tried and hanged. It appeared the Family Compact had triumphed.

In a very real sense, however, Mackenzie's revolt succeeded. As a result the colonial government was reformed, elected representatives given real political power and democracy established in Ontario.

Ethnic Diversification

Throughout the 19th century, waves of immigrants kept arriving, settling and adding to the blend of Ontario's character. Many sailed from the British Isles, bringing traditions of beef-and-potatoes cooking, a hardy ambition to make a lot of money, and a taste for whiskey and beer.

A lot of drinking went on in pioneer Ontario. In winter a town's main streets would be lined with barrels of alcohol; as the water content froze the ice was lifted out, leaving a strong brew behind. The temperance efforts of Methodist ministers eventually brought in Ontario's famously repressive liquor laws. For a long time, no Sunday drinking was allowed. Many local townships in Ontario are still "dry" and technically, you still cannot picnic with wine in a public place. (Interestingly, Ontario never had full prohibition. From here in the Roarin' Twenties, bootleg whiskey was smuggled over the border to Detroit, turning several Canadian families into dynasties of multimillionaries. But later immigrant groups greatly altered Ontario's attitudes to liquor—and, thank goodness, improved the quality of its local wines.

Jews and Eastern Europeans came to Ontario towards the middle of the 19th century (settling in Toronto, Hamilton, and around southwestern Ontario). Chinese and Italians were brought in as laborers. Of special pride to Ontarians is one group of immigrants who arrived in the 1840's, 50's and 60's—runaway Blacks from the Southern states. They traveled by the Underground Railroad to freedom in Canada where the slave trade had been outlawed since 1793. In Southeastern Ontario at Windsor and Niagara-on-the-Lake there are plaques commemorating the Underground Railroad's "terminals," while near Dresden is the home and grave of Rev. Josiah Henson (an inspiration for Harriet Beecher Stowe's *Uncle Tom's Cabin*).

Confederation and Commerce

Among the Fathers of Canadian Confederation—the men who joined separate British colonies into the independent Dominion of Canada—none were more influential than Ontarians. George Brown (crusading first editor of Toronto's powerful paper *The Globe and Mail*), Oliver Mowat, premier of Ontario and the hard-drinking Kingston lawyer, Sir John A. Macdonald, were architects of Confederation; incidentally they ensured that Ontario would play a dominant role in its politics. John A. Macdonald went on to become Canada's first prime minister and the driving force behind the construction of the transcontinental railway which brought the west into the new Dominion.

The railways changed the lives of Ontario settlers. Previously towns had depended on the waterways for transport and power for their struggling flour and saw mills. Sir John's creation, the Canadian Pacific Railway (which spanned the province by 1888), opened up Ontario's manufacturing, resource, and trade potential. The coming of electricity accelerated Ontario's development. The province has always lacked major fuel resources. Then, in 1906, businessmen prevailed on the provincial government to step in as the federal government had done with the construction of the transcontinental railway. As a result, Sir Adam Beck established the Hydro Electric Power Commission (now Ontario Hydro) which was soon providing a surplus of cheap energy. One effect of such fruitful cooperation between state and business is that policies that smack of socialism south of the border, such as government-run oil companies, medicare, or public television, often make sense to both ends of the political spectrum in Canada. Now Ontario Hydro has become one of the world's greatest hydroelectric enterprises. Hydro operates nuclear stations—the two largest are at Pickering (east of Toronto) and near Port Elgin—and coal-based stations which bring the province-run corporation into frequent conflict with environmentalists concerned about acid rain.

Hydro spurred the growth of pulp and paper manufacture (now a major industry), mining, refining and manufacturing. As a result Ontario has continued to grow rich and powerful. It produces almost half the manufactured goods in Canada, including most of the automobiles (at Oakville, Oshawa, and Windsor). The "Golden Horseshoe"—the heavily populated and wealthy semicircle from Oshawa through Toronto to steel-producing Hamilton—is the center of this wealth and industry.

The Land of Precious Metals

For generations, Northern Ontario was known as God's country because few others seemed to care about it. But in the past few decades it has proved to be rich in mineral wealth. At the beginning of this century, there were gold and silver rushes at Cobalt, Kirkland Lake and Porcupine Lake. They are still major mining centers. Sudbury now produces most of the world's platinum and more than a fifth of the world's nickel output. Rich uranium discoveries around Algoma, Blind River, and Bancroft within the last 25 years have fueled the research and development of nuclear power.

Waterways have always played a major role in Ontario's history, but of unparalleled importance is the 2,000-mile-long St. Lawrence Seaway, handling grain (from the giant terminals at Thunder Bay), ore (from Sault Ste. Marie), and manufactured goods (from the Golden Horseshoe). The seaway, opened in 1961, accounts for a 500 per cent increase in the port of Toronto's overseas consignments alone.

With the decline of world oil prices, Ontario has regained its traditional economic, political, and cultural domination over such English-speaking provincial rivals as Alberta. In Ontario are the headquarters of English-language C.B.C. television, private television and film production; here is the home of the National Ballet, the Canadian Opera Company, the National Gallery. Out of 282 seats in the federal House of Commons, 95 are occupied by members from Ontario. The Toronto Stock Exchange, largest in Canada, is among the top five on the continent.

But its people are the basis of Ontario's wealth. Post-war immigrants have poured into Ontario from Asia and Europe (including refugees from Hungary, Vietnam, and Latin America), swelling the province's population to nine million. Once Loyal Orange and True Blue, Ontario has become a colorful spectrum—still loyal to its founders' principles of order and respect, but combining with them tolerance, friendliness, and an appetite for life.

EXPLORING TORONTO

"Toronto is not a city generally attractive to the traveller" wrote the great English novelist Anthony Trollope in 1862, while poet Rupert Brooke lamented "the depressing thing is that it will always be what it is, only larger."

Fortunately for the provincial capital, these learned men reckoned without the dramatic changes wrought by time, wealth, and thousands of immigrants. Once known as Muddy York, later—disparagingly—as Toronto The Good, it is now a city of over 2 million souls, of old tree-lined streets, safe pleasant parks, galleries and cafés, low crime rates, renovation and innovation.

The city has several symbols including a squirrel mascot and an official coat of arms. But the image of the city used most to stamp Toronto's identity on T-shirts, park benches, and souvenir ashtrays is of its bivalved city hall. It is a view that you will see if you stand in Nathan Phillips Square, just south of the building. The square, named after a Toronto mayor, is the center of activity even in winter, when the reflecting pool becomes a skating rink, and is as jammed on New Year's Eve as Times Square in New York City. In summer, Nathan Phillips Square is the site of ethnic festivals, outdoor art shows, free concerts, and people-watching. It's an excellent place to begin a Toronto walking tour.

To your east looms the old City Hall, a pile of Victorian Gothic stones, complete with clocktower, gargoyles (said to be portraits of early city fathers) and the architect's name (E. J. Lennox) carved into stone tracery under the eaves. Built in 1899, it now houses courts.

In front of you is the new City Hall, a clam-shaped design of Finnish architect Viljo Revell which was completed in 1965. Every day of the week City Hall offers conducted tours. There is an information booth and art displays in its front lobby. In front of the main entrance stands "The Archer," a Henry Moore bronze sculpture purchased by some of Toronto's rich to complement Revell's architectural design.

On the west side of the square is the beautifully restored Osgoode Hall, the headquarters since 1832 of the Law Society of Upper Canada. It once housed Ontario's Supreme Court. Particularly beautiful are Osgoode Hall's main lobby with its Corinthian columns, stained glass, and elaborately tiled floor, and the 40-foot vaulted ceiling of the second floor library. The wrought-iron fences in front still feature the original cow-gates, complexly shaped to keep out wandering cattle.

At the northwest corner of City Hall Square, behind Osgoode Hall, a passageway leads past the New Courthouse and fountains to University Avenue. Here is the American consulate. A plaque (at 555 University Avenue) marks the birthplace of silent screen star Mary Pickford. At 426 University Avenue stands the Royal Canadian Military Institute, a private officers' club with an excellent collection of pistols, sabers, swords, and the cockpit of the Red Baron von Richthofen's Fokker D-VIII (he was shot down by a Canadian flying ace in 1918).

Gentlemen, Scholars and Immigrants

Turn west three blocks on Dundas Street until you reach the Art Gallery of Ontario. Its back entrance—overlooking a small leafy park where old men play chess in summer—is known as The Grange. Built in 1817, The Grange is a Georgian manor home, once belonging to

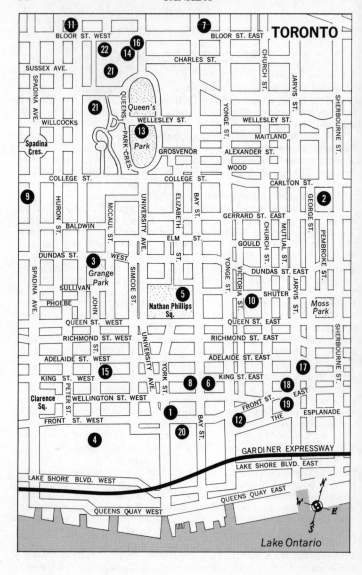

Toronto—Points of Interest

1) Airport Bus Departure (Royal York)
2) Allan Gardens
3) Art Gallery
4) C. N. Tower
5) City Hall
6) Commerce Court
7) Cumberland Terrace
8) Toronto Dominion Centre
9) Kensington Market
10) Mackenzie House
11) Medical Arts Building
12) O'Keefe Centre
13) Parliament Buildings
14) Planetarium
15) Royal Alexandra Theatre
16) Royal Ontario Museum
17) Saint James Cathedral
18) St. Lawrence Centre for the Arts
19) St. Lawrence Market
20) Union Station
21) University of Toronto
22) Varsity Stadium

members of Upper Canada's ruling Family Compact. Later it housed Toronto's first public art gallery. The Art Gallery of Ontario has since moved next door, but shares a courtyard restaurant and its hours of opening with The Grange.

East and west along Dundas Street stretches Toronto's Chinatown: first-class restaurants and shops offering candied roses, pickled seaweed, porcelain and jade. Keep heading west and you'll come to Spadina Avenue, the ladder to success of Toronto's immigrants. As the original Anglo-Saxon gentry moved farther up the street, Jewish immigrants moved in at the southern end. One notable site is Switzer's Delicatessen (322 Spadina Avenue). Upstairs is the room where "Red Emma" Goldman, the anarchist feminist, died in May, 1940. One block west (between Dundas and College) Kensington, the old Jewish market, teems with live rabbits, smoked salmon, hundreds of local and imported cheeses, old men selling homemade halvah. As groups of immigrants have prospered and moved north, new ones have taken their place. Today Kensington shoppers can also choose from among Portuguese, West Indian, and Chinese goods.

At Spadina and College are clubs and bars offering jazz and blues. They're overshadowed to the north of the intersection by a batlike Gothic building. Constructed in 1875 as Knox college, this sinister-looking building later became Connaught Laboratories; here the first penicillin and polio vaccine were manufactured.

Turn east from Spadina along College Street. You're entering the University of Toronto campus. On the north corner is the former Central Library, now the university bookstore and student center; the corner of College and St. George Street (#33 St. George) boasts the Macdonald-Mowat House. Now the International Student Centre attached to the University of Toronto, 33 St. George Street's airy, high-ceilinged rooms were once home to Canada's first prime minister, Sir John A. Macdonald, and to Sir Oliver Mowat, premier of Ontario at the end of the 19th century. The main campus of the century-and-a-half-old University of Toronto lies east of St. George, north of College Street. University College (which dominates the north side of King's College Circle) was built in 1859. Its leafy quadrangle, gargoyles, vaulted halls, carved bannisters and patterned tile floors give it special charm. The round tower at the west end is reported to be haunted.

To the east of University College is the small domed tower of the old Observatory building. Now that Toronto's David Dunlap Observatory has moved north to Richmond Hill, the old building has become the headquarters of the University's Students' Administrative Council.

To the northeast is Hart House, a Gothic-style student center, with a paneled, Oxford-style Great Dining Hall, built between 1911 and 1919 by the Massey family of whom it used to be said, "Toronto has no social classes/only the Masseys and the masses." The family also gave Toronto its fine old concert hall on Shuter Street, and a beautiful piece of modern architecture, Massey College at Devonshire Place just north of Hart House.

The University of Toronto, one of the largest and best in the country, is known for research (penicillin, pablum, and the electron microscope were developed here), scholarship, and power. Canadian prime ministers, e.g. the long-ruling Mackenzie King and Nobel Peace Prize winner Lester B. Pearson, are among its graduates.

Yorkville

Avenue Road and Bloor marks the edge of Toronto's shopping and coffeehouse district, Yorkville. An independent village until 1883, Yorkville was Toronto's bohemia in the 1950's and 60's. Its clubs hosted then-unknown folk singers like Gordon Lightfoot and Joni Mitchell. Some of Yorkville's architecture is new (for example the Hazelton Lanes, Cumberland Court, and York Square café-boutique-and-garden complexes). Some of it is sandblasted Victoriana, like the houses and galleries on Scollard Street and Hazelton Avenue. Of special interest is a renovated church-turned-boutique-arcade at the corner of Hazelton and Scollard.

A side trip: 15 to 20 minutes' walk northwest of Yorkville is Casa Loma, a millionaire's folly built between 1911 and 1914 by Sir Henry Pellatt. Known in financial circles as "Pellatt the Plunger," Sir Henry spent three million dollars to equip his 98-room castle. He installed one of the first private elevators anywhere plus gold-plated bathroom fixtures, an 800-foot-long underground passageway to huge stables, and porcelain troughs for horses. The cost of castle-living broke Pellatt in the 1920's. And except for a brief stint as a hotel, the castle stood empty and deserted until 1937 when the Kiwanis Club took over. During World War II it served as an army intelligence headquarters.

The castle features an organ with 60-foot high pipes in the Great Hall; Sir Henry and Lady Pellatt's bedrooms (totally refurnished); views from the east-end Scottish tower and west-end Norman tower, and a small museum which includes a lock of Métis rebel leader Louis Riel's hair.

A fifteen-minute walk southwest of Casa Loma takes you to Markham Village, another boutiques-and-art-galleries shopping area one block west of Bathurst and Bloor. Or head southeast to Yorkville, Bay Street (Canada's Wall Street of high finance), and Yonge Street, which is probably the most colorful way to get back downtown.

Yonge Street

Yonge Street is billed as "the longest street in the world." Under various names it stretches from the north shore of Lake Ontario 1,000 miles further north. Yonge Street was first laid out by Lt. Governor John Graves Simcoe almost 200 years ago. The ill-fated rebels of 1837 marched down this street. Now it is a shopping strip which runs the gamut from pricey to tawdry, as you will see if you head south from Bloor. Maple Leaf Gardens, at Yonge and College Streets, is the home of the Toronto Maple Leafs hockey team. It has also hosted practically every other sort of entertainment, from Sunday-night wrestling to the Bolshoi Ballet and Bob Dylan. Below College, Yonge Street turns into a strip of bargain book and record stores and raunchy movie houses. Two of Toronto's major department stores are at the intersections of Yonge and Dundas and Yonge and Queen. On the north side, the Eaton Center, a huge glassed-in mall, stretches right up to Dundas Street. The Metropolitan Toronto Convention and Tourist Bureau is headquartered here. Behind the Eaton Center hides the tiny, pretty Church of the Holy Trinity, built in 1847 when an anonymous English benefactress willed the land to the Anglican Church in perpetuity. East across Yonge Street along Dundas a block or two (at 82 Bond Street) is the old Mackenzie House, where the rebel leader died in 1861. The house has been restored to its 1850's finery and includes the flatbed printing press which Mackenzie's ghost is said to haunt.

Still east of Yonge but farther south, a plaque at 60 Richmond Street East marks the site where in 1879 Sir Sandford Fleming read a paper to the Canadian Institute outlining his plan for a worldwide standard time system.

The big building on the southwest corner of Yonge and Front Streets is the old central post office. Beyond it, soaring 1,815 feet, is the world's tallest free-standing structure, the CN Tower (CN is Canadian National, the publicly owned rail and communications corporation). From the CN Tower's 1,100-foot-high revolving restaurant and observation pod visitors can see about 75 miles on a clear day.

East of Yonge on Front Street are two of Toronto's main theater complexes. The first is the O'Keefe Centre, home of the National Ballet. The second, to the east of it, is the St Lawrence Centre, which houses two theaters. Farther on lies the 170-year-old St. Lawrence farmers' market (open Saturdays for the sale of fish, fresh produce, and home preserves). Attached to the market is another of Toronto's early city halls, the St. Lawrence Hall, built in 1844 and recently restored to its former splendor. It was here that Jenny Lind, the Swedish songbird sang, Sir John A. Macdonald boomed out speeches at stormy political rallies and P. T. Barnum once displayed midget Tom Thumb.

Museums, Parks, Art Galleries

One of the quickest ways to escape the downtown smog is to catch a ferry to Toronto Islands. Ferry docks are at the foot of Yonge Street. The ferries sail to three destinations. Ward's Island is where a remnant residential community retains private homes. Centre Island has bicycle and boat rentals, outdoor pubs, beaches, a zoo, a children's amusement area and farm, and sailing clubs. Hanlan's Point's beaches are less crowded, and you can watch the planes take off from Island Airport. In summer the islands host ethnic festivals. The islands may also be seen from cruise boats that depart from the bottom of Yonge Street. For licensed pilots, Island Rent-a-Plane is located at 545 Lakeshore Boulevard.

From the willow-lined parks of the islands, you can see how the tallest of Toronto's buildings cluster around Bay Street. Bay is Canada's Wall Street, the financial district and headquarters to many of the country's most powerful corporations. Bay Street is dull to walk up, however; you will do better to head west from Bay on King. Past University Avenue, one eccentric Toronto millionaire has opened a row of good, inexpensive beef and seafood restaurants and financed the resurrection of the grand old Royal Alexandra Theatre. Across from the "Royal Alex" rises Toronto's new concert hall named after the newspaper baron, Roy Thomson. Farther west along King Street are a couple of good restaurants and wholesale clothiers. To the south lie the CN Tower and Old Fort York. At Fort York you can see drills and cannons demonstrated by its scarlet-clad guard. Fort York was the scene of Toronto's fiercest battle in 1813. Seventeen hundred Americans defeated Toronto's 700-man defense force. Retreating, the Canadians set fire to the gunpowder barrels lest the fort fall into American hands. The explosion was tremendous. When the smoke cleared, 38 American soldiers lay dead. The American occupation of York lasted less than a week. Though Torontonians remember it for the burning of their legislative buildings, many of the soldiers were gentlemen conquerors, even returning books they had borrowed from local libraries!

Farther west are the grounds of the Canadian National Exhibition (the world's largest annual exhibition, it's open from mid-August to Labor Day in September). The "Ex," as it has been known for almost a century, features craft shows, ferris wheels, butter sculptures, the latest model cars and appliances. Off-season some of the Ex Grounds' attractions are open, like the Hockey Hall of Fame (where the Stanley Cup is displayed), Canada's Sports Hall of Fame, Scadding Cabin, a restored log house (built 1794), and the Marine Museum of Upper Canada. Housed in century-old army barracks, the Museum displays

Eskimo kayaks, a fully restored tug, and working models of Ontario's canal systems.

To the south of Exhibition Park is Ontario Place, a waterfront amusement park. Ontario Place has man-made beaches and picnic spots plus the world's largest indoor movie screen (offering spectacular experimental films), a children's playground with climbing ropes, punching bags and dunking pools. And it has the Forum. The Forum is an outdoor amphitheatre where symphony orchestras or rock groups play for 8,000 fans stretched out on the grass under the stars.

West of Ontario Place and the CNE are some small public beaches and landing places for small craft. To reach one of Toronto's most pleasant city parks, turn north at Parkside Drive (subway stops: Keele, High Park). High Park contains a small zoo, floral gardens and abstract sculpture dotted throughout 400 acres of treed, rolling hills. In the heart of the park, you'll find Grenadier Pond. It's named for a Redcoat Grenadier who drowned in it a century and a half ago. Now it's a cheerful, pretty spot, with boat rentals and gardens along its shores. At the Regency-style Colborne Lodge (built in 1836) in the middle of the park you can see sketches and paintings of architect John Howard (the original owner).

Back in downtown Toronto, you'll find other pleasant parks. Queen's Park is one of the main downtown parks, and the well-fed black and brown squirrels who live here think it's just fine. The park has the same name as the pink Romanesque Provincial Parliament Buildings to the south. It is flanked by the Sigmund Samuel Canadiana Gallery, the McLaughlin Planetarium, Victoria University in the University of Toronto, and St. Michael's College. The equestrian statute in the middle of the park is a recent addition; King Edward VII was first unveiled over 60 years ago in Imperial India. He was brought to Canada just decades ago when the independent Indians no longer wanted him.

The Sigmund Samuel Canadiana Gallery (14 Queen's Park Crescent West) contains an early Canadian paneled room, plus a fine collection of drawings, prints, crafts, and antique furniture. Nearby, the McLaughlin Planetarium houses permanent exhibits of the development of astronomy, model solar systems, solar wind, meteorite matter. It also features a domed theater where a 150-lens film projector creates astronomical films-in-the-round.

The newly expanded and renovated Royal Ontario Museum is next door: about 5,000,000 human artifacts and natural wonders, including one of the world's best Chinese collections (20 galleries' worth and, at street level, behind a glass wall, the renowned Ming Tomb Complex); a six-story West Coast Indian totem pole; intriguingly instructive models in the geology and palaeontology galleries (including skeletons of 70-million-year-old dinosaurs); and toy-and-snack shops for children.

Toronto, a major center of the Canadian and international art scene, has many excellent private galleries. They are clustered around Yorkville, north of Queen's Park, Markham Village, Yonge Street and the Art Gallery of Ontario. It also boasts two excellent public galleries, the already mentioned Art Gallery of Ontario and the McMichael Canadian Collection in Kleinburg (a 20-mile drive northwest of Toronto).

The McMichael Collection, a beautiful 30-room log-and-stone gallery, houses major works by the Group of Seven, a movement of early 20th-century landscape painters. In addition to their colorful, dramatic canvases, and those of their associates, you can see carvings and crafts by Indian and Eskimo artists. The setting is perfect: lofty art-lined rooms smelling of warm wood look out on the rolling woods of the Humber River Valley. A recent $9 million renovation has made the gallery fireproof, and climate controlled. All levels are now accessible to the handicapped.

Scientists at Play

One of the city's most popular playgrounds is the Ontario Science Centre, a hands-on museum with chess-playing computers, musical instruments for visitors to bang, and glass booths of chicks breaking out of their shells. You can watch the workings of television studios, electrical storms, and simulated moon-landings. The center also contains an excellent film library and theater. It's all housed in a spectacular modern building clinging to the slopes of the Don Valley at Don Mills Road and Eglinton Avenue.

Many of Toronto's parks are linked through the city's ravine systems and the Don Valley north of the Science Centre joins some particularly beautiful ones. You can walk from the Wilket Creek-Sunnybrook Park chain (where there are public riding stables) north to Edwards Gardens. Once a private estate, Edwards Gardens is now 35 acres of rustic paths, bridges and flowerbeds; here, too, is the Civic Garden Centre of Toronto with a fine gardener's library.

A bus from Eglinton subway (or a drive west to Jane Street then north to Keele) will take you to Black Creek Pioneer Village, where small-town Ontario of the 1840's has been re-created. Guides in period costume show you around an operating mill, schoolhouse and general store.

The inventiveness manifested by the new Metro Zoo has astonished Toronto. It's really a park for animals; the people are kept apart. Five thousand creatures roam around in 710 acres of forest, plain and river valley where botanists have simulated African savannah, Malayan rain forest and polar tundra. The people, on the other hand, must keep to footpaths or board silent, slow-moving trains so as not to disturb the zoo's full-time inhabitants.

PRACTICAL INFORMATION FOR TORONTO

HOW TO GET THERE. By air: Many major international carriers (*KLM, Air France, Alitalia, El Al, American Airlines, Eastern Airlines*) land at Lester B. Pearson International Airport. *Air Canada* and *Canadian Pacific* link Toronto to international and intraprovincial centers.

By Train: *Via Rail* links with *Amtrak* at Montréal, Windsor and Buffalo.

By bus: The bus terminal is at 610 Bay St. Service to all points in Ontario and beyond is provided by *Eastern Canadian Greyhound Lines Ltd., Gray Coach Lines, Voyageur Colonial,* and others.

By car: the Macdonald Cartier Freeway (Hwy. 401) passes through Toronto on an east-west axis. Hwys. 11 and 400 are major routes north. The Queen Elizabeth Way curves southwest from Toronto, linking it to Hamilton, Niagara Falls, Fort Erie, and New York State.

ACCOMMODATIONS. In Toronto, they range from clean budget establishments to royal suites. Recently there has been a trend toward construction of middle-priced hotels with smaller rooms and fewer frills, providing clean, modern accommodation and basic services. Tariffs for double occupancy are categorized as follows: *Deluxe,* more than $140; *Expensive,* more than $100, less than $140; *Moderate,* between $80 and $100; *Inexpensive,* less than $80.

Most places accept the following major credit cards: American Express, MasterCard and Visa; others may also be honored. Not all establishments accept credit cards, therefore we suggest you call for information.

Deluxe

Four Seasons. 21 Avenue Rd. M5R2G1 (416–964–0411). You may see rock star Elton John under the foyer's chandelier or it may be the Prime Minister. Rooms are bright and airy with good midtown views. In summer the outdoor pool is a popular meeting spot. There's an indoor pool, too. All in the fashionable, overpriced Yorkville district. Wheelchair accessible.

Toronto Hilton Harbour Castle. 1 Harbour Sq. M5J 1A6 (416–869–1600). A spectacular view of Toronto Harbour, an indoor pool, first-class restaurants on the premises, and a jet-setting clientele account for this new complex's prices. Wheelchair accessible.

King Edward Hotel. 37 King St. E. M5C 1E9. (416–863–9700). It's been splendidly restored since The Beatles and Liz and Dick stayed there in the late 1960's, and is now a palace of marble and mushroom velvet, saunas, first-class restaurants, handy to the best theaters.

The Sheraton Centre. 123 Queen St. W., M5H2M9 (416–361–1000). Across from City Hall, has almost 1,500 rooms, some of which look out on the rooftop pool; an indoor waterfall; a shopping arcade; and the longest bar in North America.

Westin Hotel. 145 Richmond St. W. M5H 3M6 (416–869–3456). A Trader Vic's. Indoor/outdoor pool, expensive modern décor.

Expensive

L'Hotel. 225 Front St. W.; M5V 2X3 (416–597–1400). Connects Metropolitan Toronto Convention Centre to the CN Tower. Indoor pool.

Park Plaza Hotel. 4 Avenue Rd. M5R 2E8 (416–924–5471). Since the 1930's the quiet quality of this hotel has attracted Prince Phillip, Rudolf Nureyev—quite a range. Great rooftop bar. Scheduled for a massive renovation.

Royal York. 100 Front St. M5J 1E3 (416–368–2511). For years it was Toronto's top-of-the-line. Old but gracious, with a shopping arcade, a huge nightclub and a smaller, but excellent jazz club on the ground floors. Some deluxe rooms. Wheelchair accessible.

Windsor Arms. 22 St. Thomas. M5S 2B9 (416–979–2341). This small hotel in the expensive Bloor St. shopping district is a real find. The absence of indoor-pool-type frills is more than made up for by individually decorated rooms, some of the best restaurants in the city.

The Bradgate Arms. Corner Avenue Rd. and St. Clair; M4V 2G6 (416–968–1331). The oldest apartment building in town, it has a European, small hotel feel to it and antiques in many of the rooms.

Moderate

The Carlton Inn Hotel. 30 Carlton St. M5B 2E9 (416–977–6655). This central, serviceable hotel, right next door to Maple Leaf Gardens, has 535 rooms, indoor pool and sauna.

The Delta Chelsea Inn. 33 Gerrard St. W. M5G 1Z4 (416–595–1975). The pleasant rooms are fully equipped with color TV and private bath—some have kitchenettes. The reason they're less expensive is their slightly smaller size. Indoor pool. Right downtown. Some expensive rooms.

Roehampton Place Hotel. 808 Mount Pleasant Rd. M4P 2L2 (416–487–5101). An outdoor pool, some rooms with individual saunas, lounge and dining room. Slightly too far north to be central, but handy to public transport, shopping, restaurants.

The Brownstone. 15 Charles St. E.; M4Y 1S1 (416–924–7381). On a quiet side street near the city's best shopping and restaurant area.

Inexpensive

Karabanow Guest House. 9 Spadina Rd. M5R 2S9 (416–923–4004). Discounts in the winter; clean, cheerful old house beside subway and within walking distance of Yorkville.

Toronto International Hostel. 223 Church St. at Dundas. M5B 1Z1 (416–368–0207). Open to all ages. Shared rooms; midnight curfew. Lowest rates in town.

Neill-Wycik College. 96 Gerrard St. E. at Church St. M5B 1G7 (416–977–2320). Open only in summer. Single, double and family accommodations available in this 22-story co-operative residence. Popular roof deck for sunning. Downtown location.

TELEPHONES. Toronto and the Golden Horseshoe cities of Hamilton, St. Catharines, and Niagara Falls are in area code 416. Pay phone booths cost 25¢.

HOW TO GET AROUND. By public transport: Tokens are available at subway stations, cigar stores and sundries stores on bus and streetcar routes. Buses and streetcars will only take exact fares. The subway is fast, clean and relatively pleasant. It crosses midtown on Bloor St.'s east-west axis and runs north and south on Yonge St., and the Spadina-University line. Transfers are free. Call 393–INFO (that's 4636) for transit information. If you're staying for a month, do buy a "Metropass"—a photo-identity card that entitles you to unlimited rides—after you've paid the initial $43.50.

By taxi: The rates start at $1.55, increasing by 20¢ each 260 meters. For complaints call: 488–2221. The biggest city-wide companies are *Metro, Diamond* and *Co-op.* Smaller companies are equally efficient.

From the airport: Limousines will take you down in style. They're generally waiting outside the arrival level. Airport buses will take you downtown to the Royal York Hotel for about $7.50. Other hotels run buses from the airport; their fares vary. There are also Airport Express buses run by Gray Coach, which for $4.00 will take you from the airport to the Islington Stop on the east-west subway line, for about $4.50 to the Yorkdale Stop on the Spadina line, and for about $5.00, to the York Mills Stop on the Yonge line.

TOURIST INFORMATION. The *Metropolitan Toronto Convention and Visitors Association* has a good general city map and a quarterly publication on what's happening. Toronto Eaton Centre Galleria, Suite 110, Box 510, Toronto M5B 2H1 (Telephone: 979–3143).

SEASONAL EVENTS. January-February. New Year's Eve is celebrated by crowds skating in front of City Hall. There are weekend sleigh rides at Black Creek Pioneer Village.

The International Boat Show and The Farm Show come to the Coliseum in Exhibition Park. Exact dates may vary yearly.

In **March,** the Coliseum hosts the Quarter-Horse extravaganza, Quarterama, with many riding classes, an auction and a stallion parade, as well as the Canadian National Sportsmen's Show.

April brings crafts lovers to the Winter's End Craft Show, and do-it-yourself repairmen and interior decorators to the National Home Show in Exhibition Park.

On the **May** 24th weekend, fireworks at Ontario Place celebrate the birthday of Queen Victoria.

In **June,** it's time for the running of the Queen's Plate, the oldest stakes in North America. Metro International Caravan begins; it's a 9-day salute to the food, drink, and dance of the city's ethnic communities. Centre Island is the site of the International Picnic, known for the Miss Bikini Pageant, a pizza-eating contest, soccer games, and music.

Toronto's West Indians get a weekend to themselves in mid-**July:** it's Caribana, with parades, music, and mardi-gras atmosphere.

August marks the opening of the Canadian National Exhibition, and also the Players Tennis Championships.

In **November,** the Royal Agricultural Winter Fair opens. Out at Black Creek Pioneer Village, kids help adults spin, bake, and sing in preparation for Christmas.

TOURS. The *Toronto Stock Exchange* is at Stock Exchange Tower, 2 First Canadian Place, shadowed by the high office towers of high finance. This exchange handles over two-thirds of the volume of trading in Canada, and offers free presentations year-round at 2:00 P.M.

Free guided tours leave the front desk of the new *City Hall* daily, at frequent intervals. The *Provincial Parliament,* built of pink sandstone Romanesque style

TORONTO SUBWAY NETWORK

MC COWAN
SCARBOROUGH CENTRE
MIDLAND
ELLESMERE
LAWRENCE EAST
KENNEDY
WARDEN
VICTORIA PK.
MAIN ST.
WOODBINE
COXWELL
GREENWOOD
DONLANDS
PAPE
CHESTER
BROADVIEW
CASTLE FRANK
SHERBOURNE
BLOOR-YONGE

DANFORTH AVE.

Airport Bus Departure Point

YONGE ST.

FINCH
SHEPPARD
YORK MILLS
LAWRENCE
EGLINTON
DAVISVILLE
ST. CLAIR
SUMMER-HILL
ROSEDALE

WELLESLEY
COLLEGE
DUNDAS
QUEEN
KING

BAY UNIVERSITY AVE.

MUSEUM
QUEEN'S PK.
ST. PATRICK
OSGOODE
ST. ANDREW

ST. GEORGE
SPADINA

UNION

BATHURST
DUPONT
ST. CLAIR WEST
CHRISTIE
EGLINTON WEST
OSSINGTON
GLENCAIRN
DUFFERIN
LAWRENCE WEST
LANSDOWNE
YORKDALE — Airport Bus Departure Point
WILSON
DUNDAS WEST

BLOOR ST.

KEELE
HIGH PARK
RUNNYMEDE
JANE
OLD MILL
ROYAL YORK
ISLINGTON — Airport Express Bus departs from here
KIPLING

are close by Queen's Park subway. There's also a visitors' gallery high above the Debates chamber.

See Toronto from the air: *Toronto Airways Ltd.* (416–493–6221) takes off with sightseers aboard from the Buttonville airport, Hwy. 7 and Woodbine Ave. Or you can see Toronto by trolley seven days a week except in Dec., Jan., and Feb., when the trolley runs on weekends only, or by the *Shipsands,* a 51-passenger vessel that tours Toronto Harbour from mid-April to the end of October.

Or see Toronto from a three-masted sailing ship: call *Empire Sandy Cruise,* 416–364–3244. Glass-topped sightseeing boats also provide 1-hour cruises of the waterfront, and of duck hideaways in the lagoons of Toronto Islands. Board at the foot of Yonge St. Toronto Harbor and Islands Boat Tours reserves for its one-hour tour of the harbor islands. Telephone: 416–364–2412.

For a free 3½-mile tour of Toronto's east harbor and headlands call the *Toronto Harbour Commission* (416–863–2000). On summer Sundays tours leave from the foot of Leslie St.

Tour through Casa Loma, the lavish and quirky home of Toronto's eccentric millionaire, Sir Henry Pellatt. No guided tours are offered. Instead, knowledge-able people are stationed throughout the castle to answer your questions. Call 416–923–1171.

The *Pickering Nuclear Generating Station* offers free tours with well-informed guides and a Star Trek display of computer games, all designed to make you feel more comfortable about nuclear power. Children must be accompanied by an adult. Group tours must be arranged in advance. Call 416–839–0465. Should you care to tour a water filtration or sewage treatment plant, Metro Toronto Works will be happy to make the arrangements. Just call 416–392–8209.

Three guided walking tours of the University of Toronto's midtown campus start from Hart House at Queen's Park and Wellesley St., June through August, at 10:30 A.M., 12:30, and 2:30 P.M. U. of T.'s Community Relations office number is 416–978–6564.

 CHILDREN'S ACTIVITIES. *The Ontario Science Centre,* 770 Don Mills Rd., has the ultimate in toys—millions of dollars' worth of educational, experimental, participatory machines and exhibits, like a computer with which you can play tic-tac-toe, a static electricity machine that is quite literally hair-raising, or a model of the rain cycle.

The exhibits at the *Royal Ontario Museum* and next door to it the *McLaughlin Planetarium* are both imaginatively designed, and bright older children can occupy themselves here quite happily for hours. Children under six are not admitted to the *Planetarium Theatre.* The ROM has a special children's cafeteria downstairs. The McLaughlin Planetarium, the ROM and the Science Center are more fully described under "Museums and Galleries."

Canada's Wonderland has 370 acres of rather un-Canadian cartoon animals come to life, 5 roller coasters, a saltwater circus with dolphins, and an artificial mountain.

The *CN Tower,* the world's largest freestanding structure, has impressive views from the top and offers a simulated shuttle flight to Jupiter, called Tour of the Universe. The "flight" lasts an hour but starts every fifteen minutes. Children must be at least three feet tall to enjoy it.

Harbourfront is great, day or night: craft shows, antique sales, dance (watching or doing), sailing, jazz. There are always exciting activities specially designed for children—everything from computer camps to free workshops in such crafts as papermaking or glass blowing. Children will also enjoy Harbourfront's seasonal events. Call (416–364–5665) for information.

Centre Island has a special children's park where kids can ride swan-shaped boats or an old-fashioned merry-go-round, or play with the animals in the *Centreville Farm.* Take the Centre Island ferry from the foot of Bay St.

The *Toronto Islands* are a great place for children to run off excess energy; so is the *Children's Village Playground* at Ontario Pl., with its ropes to swing on and foam rubber to land in. Closed winters.

Ontario Place is open from mid-May to Labor Day. In its winter season, the *Toronto Symphony* performs special children's concerts: *Peter and the Wolf, Carnival of the Animals,* etc. Call Roy Thomson Hall for details. (416–593–4828).

Toronto is also the home of *Young People's Theatre,* which coordinates several companies of professional actors who tour schools; their 468-seat YPT Centre opened in the fall of 1977 at the corner of Front and Frederick Sts., the first center for the performing arts for children and teens in Canada. They have also showcased music, puppetry, mime, and dance.

Children can see the 19th century come alive in the general store, blacksmith's shop and 28 other reconstructed buildings at *Black Creek Pioneer Village,* open from March to December. It's at Jane St. and Steeles Ave. W. Admission, at $4 for adults and $2 for children, is well worth the price. Weekend events vary with the season.

Historic *Fort York* (East of the Canadian National Exhibition grounds) is a good bet. Better: the 700-acre *Metro Zoo* where animals roam free in faithfully re-created natural environments, which humans tour by silent electric trains, on foot or on cross-country skies in winter.

There are some excellent toy shops in the *Ontario Science Centre* and the *McLaughlin Planetarium.* Among the other good toy stores are *The Toy Shop,* 62 Cumberland; *Little Dollhouse,* 617 Mt. Pleasant, specializing in miniatures; and *The Creative Child,* 47A Colborne St.

SPORTS. Professional sports: The *Toronto Blue Jays* bring American Baseball League games to Toronto; the stars of Canadian professional sports, the *Toronto Argonauts,* play Canadian Football League games in the CNE Stadium. *The Toronto Maple Leafs'* games are held at Maple Leaf Gardens, 60 Carlton St. E., where you can also catch the Ontario Hockey Association's Toronto *Marlboroughs.* **Horse-racing:** *Greenwood Racetrack* at Queen and Coxwell is relatively central, but Toronto's other horse-racing center, *Woodbine Racetrack,* is a brisk drive away at Highway 27 in Malton. **Golf:** Toronto has many public 18-hole golf courses, including *Don Valley Golf Course,* 4200 Yonge Street, and *Dentonia Park Par 3,* at Victoria Park subway station. **Tennis:** Thirty-nine public parks have tennis courts, but at some you must bring your own net. **Swimming:** There are large—and popular—public swimming pools in or near *Christie Pits* (subway: Christie), *Broadview, Don Valley, High Park, Monarch Park,* and *Eglinton* at Avenue Rd. Swimming in Lake Ontario is supervised on Toronto Island, the beaches in the east end, and Sunnyside west of Ontario Pl., but not all beaches are open for swimming, due to unacceptable levels of pollution. Call Public Health (416–392–7466) for information. **Boating:** The water is cold; you may be happier sailing. For information about public launching spots call Metro Parks (416–392–7259). **Winter sports:** In winter, they'll also give you information about the city's 75 outdoor rinks and cross-country skiing on the islands or in the city's ravine systems. **Bicycling:** There are some excellent *cycling routes* in Toronto, notably the path in Central Don Park and the Martin Goodman Trail along the lakeshore. **Fishing:** In the conservation areas that surround the city, *fishermen* can even get in some decent angling.

HISTORIC SITES. Toronto was settled by a few French traders as early as 1730; a granite monument in the grounds of the Canadian National Exhibition marks the site of the original *Fort Rouillé.* The *Scadding Cabin,* also on the CNE grounds, is the oldest remaining building in Toronto. Preserved as a late 18th-century residence, open afternoons Wednesday-Sunday, summer. East of the CNE grounds, on Garrison Rd., lies the restored military fort of the War of 1812, *Fort York.* The Guard exercises daily. After the 1793 Toronto Purchase, development from wooded ravines to settlers residences began. The old town was bounded by Ontario, Parliament, Duke and King St. Close to these original city limits is the *Old City (St. Lawrence) Hall,* a graceful classic with ornamental plaster and glittering chandeliers built in 1850, many years after the town had grown. At King St. E. is historic *Little Trinity Church,* which was built in 1844 for Irish immigrants.

The magnificent pink sandstone and granite *Provincial Parliament Building* in Queen's Park was built in the late 1800s for Ontario's legislators and is still the seat of provincial government today. House is in session roughly from Oct.–Dec. and Feb.–June, but visitors can tour daily, year-round.

None of the original buildings survive, but the southeast downtown area has many old architectural and historic curiosities: among them *The Enoch Turner*

Schoolhouse (1848), 106 Trinity St., behind Little Trinity Church. The school provided Toronto's first free education. A small admission price treats you to a typical 19th-century Toronto schoolday. Open weekdays.

Toronto's *First Post Office* (1834) is part of a historic block of buildings at 260 Adelaide St. E. (Adelaide and George St.). Still a working postal substation, it offers replicas of 1833 and 1834 cancellations for mail sent from this office. Costumed guides help visitors write letters with quills and sealing wax. Writing materials of the early 19th century are for sale. Open daily, 10 A.M. to 4 P.M. Wheelchair access from parking lot. For information, call (416–865–1833).

Many early Toronto residences, such as the *Parshall Terry House* at Todmorden Mills and *Colborne Lodge* (1836), have been restored and opened to the public. The Parshall Terry House dates back to 1798, although it has been refurnished in the 1830s style. Colborne Lodge was the home of surveyor, architect, and art teacher John Howard. His watercolors are on the walls of this Regency-style house in the middle of High Park. *The Grange*, behind the Art Gallery at 317 Dundas St. W., is a gentleman's manor in the style of the 1830's—polished wood and delicate wallpaper—where English man of letters Matthew Arnold was once entertained. For many years it was Toronto's art gallery.

Spadina, at 285 Spadina Rd., is the 1866 mansion of financier James Austin, overlooking a lovely English-style garden. Next to it is *Casa Loma*, the extravagant castle built in 1911 by Sir Henry Pellatt. Wheelchair access.

Osgoode Hall (Queen St. at University Ave.) has been the home of the Law Society of Upper Canada since 1832. But its serious occupants haven't dimmed the airy, chandeliered, Corinthian-pillared charm of this impressive public building. *Montgomery's Inn* (Dundas and Islington) once served travelers journeying from the west into Toronto. Now open daily, its Loyalist-era comforts have been restored. Call (416–236–1046) for information on events and activities.

Cornell House (Brimley Rd. and Lawrence Ave.) was built in 1850. The clothes and kitchen utensils of its 19th-century occupants, on display, make Cornell House a disarmingly personal museum. Open late May to mid-October, Wednesdays, Saturdays, and Sundays. *Gibson House*, at 5172 Yonge St., features daily demonstrations of crafts and cooking from the 1830's. Its original owner was one of the rebels who supported William Lyon Mackenzie, and was forced to spend a decade in exile in the United States. The ghost of the man responsible for the rebellion of 1837 is said to haunt *Mackenzie House*, 82 Bond St. Furnishings of the 1850's, plus Mackenzie's former printing press in the basement, would make the journalist-turned-rebel feel right at home.

Many of the fathers of Canadian Confederation lived in Toronto. Their homes are commemorated by Provincial Plaques. Editor and politician *George Brown's house* on Beverly St. is now the home of the Metropolitan Toronto Association for the Mentally Retarded; the mansion in which *Sir John A. Macdonald* and *Sir Oliver Mowat* lived at 63 St. George St. is now the International Student Centre. You're welcome to look in.

 LIBRARIES. Every book in the University of Toronto's enormous system of colleges, schools and institutes is catalogued in the main *John Robarts Library*. The students call this lofty modern $48 million pile dominating the corner of St. George and Harbord Sts. "Fort Book." Here too is the *Thomas Fisher Rare Books Library*, with over 200 books inked before the year 1500. You need a special permit to get in. The Metropolitan Toronto Public Libraries system boasts among other things an excellent multilingual collection and one of the most complete collections of Sherlock Holmes tomes and the works of his creator, Sir Arthur Conan Doyle. You'll find them at the *Metropolitan Toronto Library*, one block above Yonge and Bloor.

The country's largest military library is hidden away in the *Canadian Military Institute*, 426 University Avenue. Gardeners may find the books they need at the *Civic Garden Centre* in Edwards Gardens. The *Law Society of Upper Canada's Library*, on Osgoode Hall's second floor, is a neoclassical paneled room with fireplace, squeaking floors and books.

MUSEUMS AND GALLERIES. Recently imaginative administrations, charged with the new spirit of civic enthusiasm, have made Toronto's museums and galleries come alive as well-loved and well-used focal points of community cultures.

Museums. The *Royal Ontario Museum,* at Avenue Rd. and Bloor (subway: Museum) has one of the finest Chinese collections in the world; its Ming Tomb Complex, relocated behind a glass wall, is dramatically illuminated and visible from Bloor St. There's also a good Egyptian collection which includes 2,000-year-old jewelry, mummies, and models; rooms of European furnishings and musical instruments and a well-organized ethnology section. A children's store, a gift shop with reproductions, and two cafeterias on the premises offer a pleasant tour break. Don't overlook the well-presented geology, minerology, or ethnology displays, or the West Coast totem poles which soar on either side of the central staircase. Closed Christmas and New Year's.

The *Sigmund Samuel Canadiana Gallery* specializes in early Canadian furniture and antiques. Silver, glass, coins and wooden sculpture complement the paneled rooms of rich wooden furnishings. It's at 14 Queen's Park Crescent and is open seven days a week, admission free.

The *McLaughlin Planetarium* is next door to the Royal Ontario Museum, north of the Sigmund Samuel Museum. Open daily, it familiarizes visitors with the development of astronomy through a tunnel that leads past exhibits and diagrams into a huge domed theater. Here hour-long films broadcast the heavens onto a curved screen. You lie back in your tilted chair and marvel. The planetarium admission price includes theater entrance. Closed Mon., Christmas Day, and New Year's Day.

Opposite the ROM is the *George M. Gardiner Museum of Ceramic Art,* featuring pre-Columbian, Italian Maiolica, English Delftware, and 18th-century porcelain from Europe and England. Open daily all year except Mon. and national holidays. The *Marine Museum of Upper Canada* is housed in officers' quarters that date from 1841. The atmosphere is nautical, the exhibits entertaining—everything from an old Eskimo kayak to a tug in dry berth. Open daily. Because the museum is on the grounds of the Canadian National Exhibition, it's best to drive there. Go along Lakeshore Blvd. and turn into the CNE Grounds. While you're there, the *Sports and Hockey Halls of Fame* are close by. The latter is the permanent home of the Stanley Cup and fans can also view hockey memorabilia like Bobby Hull's stick.

The HMCS *Haida,* a destroyer that served Canada in World War II and the Korean War is yet another museum near the CNE. It's afloat off the east end of Ontario Place.

The *Museum of the Queen's Own Rifles of Canada* is not a large museum, but if the fanciful architecture of Casa Loma has attracted you, it's worth a visit to the castle's third floor to look at the museum's weapons, medals, and memorabilia of the 1885 Northwest Rebellion, including rebel Louis Riel's moccasins and the hood he wore at his hanging. Open daily. Casa Loma also houses an antique car collection.

Todmorden Mills Museum, 67 Pottery Rd., is a four-building complex on the site of an early mill. The old brewery has changing exhibits; there's a collection that will delight the hearts of old railway buffs in the Don Station building; and the Parshall Terry House has been refurnished the way it looked in 1837 when Toronto rebels marched against the local government. The fourth building is a restored house circa 1867. Open May through December, Tuesdays to Sundays and holiday Mons.

Historic *Fort York* northeast of the CNE grounds is a living museum. The scarlet-clad guards drill, parade and fire their cannon daily, all year. In the original buildings, maps, films, models, uniforms and equipment recall the fort's heyday when it guarded Toronto during the War of 1812.

Galleries. Toronto is becoming ever more interested in art. In addition to the AGO's (Art Gallery of Ontario) schedule of special shows, there are little galleries practically all over downtown. A Henry Moore bronze dominates the southwest corner of Dundas and McCaul streets. That's your introduction to the *AGO,* which was expanded in the 1970s to include the world's largest public collection of Henry Moore's work (plasters, sketches, and bronzes). Expansion also permitted exhibition of the important Zacks Collection of 20th-century painting and sculpture and the evocative works of Tom Thomson and the Group of Seven school of Canadian landscape painters; Tintoretto's "Christ Washing

His Disciples' Feet," Rubens' "The Elevation of the Cross," some rosy Renoir women, an Augustus John portrait of a vivid woman with amazing red hair, a Rodin nude, Claes Oldenburg's giant soft "Hamburger." 317 Dundas St. W. Closed Mondays, Christmas Day, and New Year's Day. Opposite the AGO is the Ontario Crafts Council, whose first floor is a gallery where you can see objects and art handmade from a variety of materials.

The Art Gallery at Harbourfront is the city's public alternative gallery. Its imaginative young staff cram in everything from the best of Swedish furniture design to installations by West Coast street graffiti artists. It moved to larger quarters in May 1987; its alternate name is the *Power Plant.*

As for some of the smaller private galleries, here is a sampling of the best: *Mercer Union,* 333 Adelaide St. W., 5th floor, is a non-profit space run by artists; it is committed to providing exhibition space to leading-edge drawings, paintings, and installations by many of the city's less commercial artists. There is a concentration of good galleries in one former office building at 80 Spadina Ave. Here are located the *Leo Kamen Gallery,* the *Olga Korper Gallery, Toronto Image Works,* the *Toronto Photography Workshop,* and the *Albert White Gallery,* which stocks internationally famous artists such as Picasso, David Hockney, and Joan Miro, as well as primitive art.

Try *Mira Godard Gallery* at 22 Hazelton, for internationally acclaimed moderns (Ben Nicolson, Jean McEwen); *Moos Gallery* at 136 Yorkville (Canadian modern); *Albert White Gallery* (25 Prince Arthur), all of which are in the Yorkville area.

Nancy Poole's Studio, 16 Hazelton, features exclusively Canadian work—like the nostalgic works of magic realist John Boyle, Tony Urquhart's fanciful sculptures or Kim Ondaatje's cool prints. Closed Mondays.

Jane Corkin Gallery, 144 Front St. W., is a gallery of photographic art. The *Innuit Gallery,* 9 Prince Arthur, specializes in Eskimo art. *Limited Editions,* 136 Yorkville, sometimes carries Dali, Delacroix, and Miro prints.

More avant-garde works are to be found at *YYZ Artists' Outlet* 116 Spadina Ave., and *The Funnel,* 507 King St. E.

The Isaacs Gallery, 832 Yonge St., is one of the guardians of contemporary Canadian art. Here you'll see anything from William Kurelek's almost primitive realism to Denis Burton's word and image fantasies. Closed Mondays.

Bau Xi, 340 Dundas W., with modern Canadian works, is right across from the Art Gallery of Ontario. Closed Mondays.

Toronto Fine Arts Gallery, 145 King St. W., carries fine French lithographs, Aubusson tapestries, limited-edition prints. Monday to Friday.

Not quite a museum and not exactly a gallery, *The Ontario Science Centre* houses over 500 fascinating exhibits in a striking modern complex that descends the slope of the Don Valley. How musical instruments make sound; how a TV studio works; what causes genetic mutation; computers, and colonies, geiger counters, miniature rain storms—they're all here. Open daily. Don Mills Rd. and Eglinton Ave.

 MUSIC AND DANCE. If you've checked the local papers or magazines, it hasn't escaped you that Toronto is a musical city. It's home base of the *National Ballet, The Canadian Opera Company,* the *Toronto Symphony,* and many smaller but excellent companies and groups.

For over a decade the active *Guitar Society* has been bringing the world's best concert guitarists, lutenists, and groups to Toronto audiences.

The *Royal Conservatory of Music,* 273 Bloor St. W., is an old neo-Gothic pile of stone where solo concerts and workshops are regularly held. The *Royal Conservatory Orchestra* holds annual concert series in the Church of the Redeemer. For details call (416–978–5470).

The *Edward Johnson Building,* partially hidden by the McLaughlin Planetarium south of Avenue Rd. and Bloor is the home of the University of Toronto's *Faculty of Music.* Its two theaters, *Walter Hall* and the *MacMillan Theatre* have esoteric concerts—renaissance songfests or electronic sounds, for example, for its learned audiences. The Edward Johnson Building also runs an excellent chamber music program. You may hear Toronto's well-known *Orford Quartet.* The *Tallis Choir,* a chamber choir of 30 voices directed by founder Peter Walker, is well known for performances of Renaissance and Baroque music. The *Choirs of St. Mary Magdalene* (416–531–7955) have an international reputation for the quality of their live and recorded performances. In addition to regular Sunday services, they give occasional recitals. They are under the direction of Robert Hunter Bell.

Other excellent choirs include the *Toronto Children's Chorus* (416–929–5580), the *Toronto Mendelssohn Choir* conducted by Elmer Iseler (416–598–0422), and the smaller *Elmer Iseler Singers.*

Massey Hall may not be beautiful, but acoustically it's one of the best concert halls in North America. It has been replaced by the huge new *Roy Thomson Hall* as the winter home of the *Toronto Symphony.*

In summer, the Toronto Symphony moves to the *Ontario Place Forum,* where the *Hamilton Philharmonic* is also a regular guest. The acoustics are not great at the Forum unless you can get one of the 2,000 amphitheater seats; but you can still hear the music while you gaze at the night stars if you sprawl out on the grassy hills that surround the Forum.

During the academic year, York University runs concerts at the *Burton Auditorium* and in its college theaters.

The *National Ballet of Canada* is headquartered in Toronto, and performs at the O'Keefe Centre. The city's other dance venues include *Premiere Dance Theatre,* 235 Queen's Quay W. (third floor) and *Ryerson Theatre,* 43 Gerrard St. E. The O'Keefe also hosts musicals and opera—indeed, it is home to the Canadian Opera Company until the COC moves into its new building some time in 1989. And it caters to more pop tastes too, with the likes of Tom Jones and the Muppet Show.

Next door to O'Keefe Centre, are the two stages of the *St. Lawrence Centre for the Performing Arts.* Lavishly renovated, the new main theater is home to *CentreStage Company,* which produces dramatic and comedic works. The smaller *Jane Mallett Theatre* hosts solo musicians, chamber groups and dance companies. Here you can hear *The Chamber Players of Toronto.*

Consult newspaper listings for the performances of the active modern troupe, *The Toronto Dance Theatre.* For experimental dance/art, check out *The Funnel,* on King St. E. at Parliament.

In summer, try Toronto island ferries' *Jazz-on-the-Lake* cruises for a lively evening of drinking and listening to good Dixieland. For information on the free jazz, folk, pops and classical summer concerts in the parks, Harbourfront Park, and City Hall Square, consult newspaper listings.

 THEATER AND REVUES. The twelve-million-dollar *O'Keefe Centre,* at 1 Front St. E., is a 3,155-seat cavern, a regular off-Broadway tour stop. The O'Keefe Centre, owned by Metropolitan Toronto, is next door to the *St. Lawrence Centre,* 27 Front St. E., a publicly supported showcase for Canadian theater, community forums, small concerts. It is home to the resident CentreStage company, under whose name current productions are listed. CentreStage produces classics and Canadian drama. In summer, Theatre Plus, the city's only subscription summer theatre, takes over the St. Lawrence Centre.

Another major theater, the *Royal Alexandra,* is privately owned and has been lovingly restored to its turn-of-the-century splendor. Its booking policy is aggressive and often its Broadway-destined plays star international talents like Liv Ullmann and Laurence Olivier. It's at 260 King Street West, across from Toronto's new concert hall, *Roy Thomson Hall.*

Some of the best of Canadian and contemporary international theater is featured at *Theatre Passe Muraille,* 16 Ryerson Ave., the *Toronto Workshop Productions,* 12 Alexander St., the *Tarragon Theatre,* 30 Bridgman St., *Toronto Free Theatre,* 26 Berkeley, and *Bathurst Street Theatre,* 736 Bathurst St. *Young People's Theatre,* 165 Front St. E., specializes in puppet shows, concerts, musicals, and plays for children. Major ticket agent: Bass, Telephone: 698–2277.

Second City Fire Hall, 110 Lombard, is the home of Toronto's satirical Second City Revue. Other revues entertain after-dinner audiences at restaurants like *Old Angelo's,* 45 Elm St., *The Teller's Cage,* in the Commerce Court complex at King and Bay Sts., and *Theatre-in-the-Dell,* 300 Simcoe St.

 SHOPPING. You can get pretty well everything in Toronto, from antique radio parts to bathrobes lined in ranch mink, if you've got the money and the time to hunt. The biggest retail stores are *Eaton's, Simpson's* (both are on Yonge between Queen and Dundas Sts. and in suburban shopping plazas), and *The Bay,* better known as The Hudson's Bay Company.Its biggest store is at Yonge and Bloor Sts. *Yorkdale, Sherway Gardens, Square One,* and *Scarborough Town Centre* are among the biggest suburban shopping centers, but you can shop in underground plazas in the heart of the city, too. The *Toronto Dominion Centre* at King and Bay Sts. has 54 stores, a cinema and restaurants; it links up to the *Commerce Court Mall, First Canada Place,* and others. Over at the corner of Dundas and McCaul streets is another mall, *Village by the Grange.* Its boutiques stock more eccentric wares—perhaps because it is adjacent to the Ontario College of Art. Currently, the city's most expensive shopping complexes include *Hazleton Lanes* at Yorkville and Avenue Rd. and *Queen's Quay,* at Harbourfront.

Toronto's villages come alive in summer. *Yorkville* and *Markham Villages* (the former at Bloor St. and Avenue Rd., the latter at Bloor and Bathurst) are colorful streets of renovated Victoriana with art galleries, gourmet shops, antique stores, and outdoor cafés. Markham Village has a shop devoted to art books at bargain prices; Yorkville, galleries, several bath boutiques, expensive toy shops, and women's clothing stores with used and new high fashion. A new and increasingly upscale shopping strip has taken over the once run-down Queen St. West shopping strip, with trendy restaurants, designer clothing stores, and new wave music clubs pushing out the greasy-spoon eateries and junk shops.

In the ManuLife Centre (south corner of Bay and Bloor Sts.) *Birk's* and *Creed's* cater to Toronto's wealthy. Birk's sells mainly jewelry; Creed's carries designer clothes (Sonia Rykiel, Missoni), furs, and a small line of Maud Frizon's extraordinary shoes. Diagonally across from the ManuLife Centre is *David's,* Toronto's best and probably most expensive shoe store. For bargains in clothes or anything else, you'll do better strolling through the city's three Chinatowns— the first is a strip along Dundas west of Bay, which extends all the way to Spadina; north and south on Spadina lies the second; the third is in the east end, around Broadview and Gerrard. *Hercules* army surplus, 577 Yonge St., *La Mode de Vija,* 601 Markham St., or the incredible *Honest Ed's* at Bathurst and Bloor. The Queen-Jarvis-King area abounds in antique and junk stores. The *Jazz & Blues Record Centre* at 66 Dundas E. is a mecca for serious buffs. *Bakka,* 282 Queen Street West, carries only science fiction, albeit broadly defined.

RESTAURANTS. Toronto used to close its sensible meat and potatoes eating establishments early—perhaps because people were so bored. But in the last decade, with the influx of immigrants, money and education about such matters, fine food has become a passion for Torontonians. Good restaurants in all price ranges and all types of cuisines still meet with the approval of an increasingly educated, critical palate. Critics including France's *Gault et Millaud* rate Toronto as one of the best dining cities on the continent.

Restaurants have been categorized on the basis of a typical dinner with appetizer, entrée, and dessert. Drinks, tax and tips are excluded. *Deluxe* costs more than $50 per person; *Expensive* is $30 to $50; *Moderate* is $18 to $30, and *Inexpensive* is less than $18. And a restaurant that is "licensed" is, of course, licensed to serve liquor.

Most places accept the following major credit cards: American Express, MasterCard and Visa; others may also be honored. Not all establishments accept credit cards, therefore we suggest you call for information.

Canadian

Expensive

Babsi's. 1371 Lakeshore Dr. W. (416–823–3794). Owned by Herbert Sonzogni, one of Canada's best chefs, it concentrates on local ingredients such as pheasant in barberry and maple syrup.

Moderate

Montréal Bistro. 65 Sherbourne St. (416–363–0179). French-Canadian favorites like pea soup in a charming country atmosphere. Great bar adjacent.

Inexpensive

Newfoundlander. 185 Danforth Ave. (416–469–1916). "Newfie" dishes like "brewis" (cod and fried potatoes) and "screech" (dark, overproof rum).

Chinese

Moderate

The Pink Pearl. 142 Dundas Street W. (416–977–3388). Authentic Hong Kong cuisine, comfortable elegance. Try the fried stuffed crab claw; Rainbow in Crystal Fold, shark's fin soup. Licensed. Can become expensive.
Kowloon Dim Sum, 187 Dundas W. (416–977–3773).

Inexpensive

Ho Yuen. 105 Elizabeth St. (416–977–3449). If you're serious about Chinese food, this gritty, unlicensed restaurant is for you. The setting is not elegant, the line-ups a bother, the lobster in ginger and garlic is breathtaking. A find, an adventure, a gem. Can be more expensive.

French

Deluxe

Auberge Gavroche. 90 Avenue Rd. (416–920–0956). The atmosphere is elegant-rustic, the entrées famous for their smooth herbed sauces, the waiters very French.

Expensive

Gaston's. 35 Baldwin St. (416–596–0278). The rooms are narrow and pretty; the mussels, rabbit and seafood can be delicious. There is a charming backyard patio for open-air dining on hot summer nights.
Les Copains. 48 Wellington Ave. E. (416–869–0898). A good bistro with pommes frites, steaks, duck, turn-of-the-century graphics on the walls, and jazz downstairs.
Maison Basque. 15 Temperance St. (416–368–6146). Service can be frustrating, but salmon, grouper, lamb, inexpensive wines, and rich Basque cake make up for it.

Moderate

La Chaumiere. 77 Charles E. (416–922–0500). For two generations it has served ample portions, well-prepared, prix fixe.
Le Select. 328 Queen St. W. (416–596–6405). Casual atmosphere, jazz, *coq au vin*, good salads, and a clientele of local Francophones.
Le Pigalle. 315 King St. W. (416–593–0698). Upstairs, Marcel's Bistro (416–596–8600). Both offer splendid French cooking, with sweetbreads, steaks, good wine and liqueur lists, grilled lamb, bourgignons, moderate prices. Expect line-ups.

Greek

Expensive

Anesty's. 16 Church St. (416–368–1881). A white-walled garden and bar, Greek lamb, pastries, tzadziki.

Moderate

Ellas. 702 Pape Ave. (416–463–0334). Visit the kitchen and choose moussaka, roast lamb, spicy vegetables and a feta salad. Licensed.
Byzantium. 401 Danforth Ave. (416–466–2845). For less than $9 you get a heaping plate of eggplant, okra, and lamb.

Indian

Moderate

Moghal Restaurant. 563 Bloor W. (416–597–0522). North Indian cuisine, specializing in tandoori dishes. Licensed.

Inexpensive

Sher-E-Punjab. 341 Danforth Ave. (416–465–2125). A good curry house. Licensed.

International Cuisine

Deluxe

The Restaurant, Three Small Rooms. 22 St. Thomas St. (416–979–2341). Its low-key comfort, extensive wine list and classic cooking have earned it an international reputation.

The Palmerston. 488 College St. (416–922–9277). A narrow, severe-looking place which is very serious about food: it was founded by one of the city's most adventuresome young chefs, Jamie Kennedy. The menu mixes tart, bitter, and exotic flavors with a deft touch on sole, lamb, beef. Licensed.

The Beaujolais. 165 John St. (416–598–4656). Two west coast chefs skilled in Canadian versions of California nouvelle cuisine offer a wonderful pizza with Mexican peppers and goat cheese, or a plate of hors d'oeuvres featuring vegetables some Canadians have never heard of. Licensed.

Fenton's. 2 Gloucester St. (416–961–8485). There is a fine food shop adjacent to three rooms of restaurants. One of the rooms is a cozy cellar; another has an open fireplace, another is a courtyard full of trees hung with lamps. The food is inventive if a bit pretentious: cold Stilton soup, chicken stuffed with ginger, syllabub. Good wine, liquor list.

Italian

Expensive

Noodles. The address is 60 Bloor St. W. but the entrance is around the corner on Bay St. (416–921–3171). As with a Fellini Film, you will either love Noodles or hate it. A pink neon and chrome décor works a warm magic in this futuristic Italian restaurant. Soups like cream of watercress or iced cucumber, followed by rich linguini, basil and garlic-tinged ravioli, imaginative spinach, endive or celery root salads, good veal, plump fowl and seductive desserts.

Orso. 106 John St. (416–596–1989). With its turquoise-and-pink interior, it looks like an Architectural Digest eatery. Luckily, the food is tasty and includes vitello tonato, grilled fish, carpaccio. Licensed.

Pronto. 692 Mt. Pleasant. (416–486–1111). A grand piano, wallful of Italian art posters, an uptown clientele. The delight of the nouvelle cuisine is as much in the presentation as in the taste. Their bread is poor and service can be slow—otherwise a delight.

Trattoria Giancarlo. 41 Clinton St. (416–533–9619). In summer there are tables outdoors. Inside, a black-and-white tile interior and fresh flowers. Specialties include fresh pasta with three kinds of mushrooms, quail braised with rosemary and giant shrimp, split and grilled.

Moderate

La Bruschetta. 1325 St. Clair W. (416–656–8622). A family-run establishment with Tuscan specialties and seafood.

Sabatini's. 1248 St. Clair W. (416–653–7169). The room at the back offers entertainment and is packed on weekends. Recommended dishes include the fried calamari, mussels, linguini. Licensed.

Inexpensive

Porretta's Pizza. 97 Harbord. (416–920–2186). Best pizza in town.

Jewish-Middle Eastern

Moderate

Aida's. 597 Yonge St. (416–925–6444). This tiny restaurant offers the city's fattest felafels, and is also noted for its fried eggplant and chicken livers in garlic. Not licensed.

Jerusalem. 955 Eglinton W. (416–783–6494). Middle Eastern delights like hummus and shish kebab. Licensed.

Scandinavian

Moderate-Expensive

Copenhagen Room. 101 Bloor W. (416–920–3287). Lunch here is a joy: tartar with caviar and fried Camembert open-faced sandwiches. In the evening, prices shoot up. Can become expensive.

Seafood

Moderate

Ed's Seafood. 276 King St. W. (416–977–3938). King crab legs, lobster tails, lots of atmosphere. No blue jeans. Gentlemen must wear jacket and tie.

The Old Fish Market. 12 Market St. (416–363–0334). Big brick rooms accommodate all the people who are attracted by conch, crab, mussels and salads at reasonable prices.

Whistling Oyster. 11 Duncan St. (416–598–7707). Shellfish are a bargain here at Happy Hour. Fish, affordable, is also very good. Licensed.

Spanish-Latin American

Moderate

Don Quijote. 300 College St. (416–922–7636). The chicken is rich, the squid delicate, the mussels, shrimps, and paella delicious. Afterwards go upstairs for Spanish coffee and flamenco dancing. Licensed.

Sombreros. 438 Parliament St. (416–968–1731). Toronto is new to Mexican food and this is one of the few places which makes its own tacos rather than importing them. Fillings include pork with orange juice, combined with three cheeses and hot peppers. Licensed—and the margaritas are recommended.

The Willow. 193 Danforth Ave. (416–469–5315). The tacos here taste authentically of corn. Fillings include beef spiced with cumin and cauliflower with raisin. Licensed.

The Boulevard Cafe. 161 Harbord St. (416–961–7676). This popular spot serves South American grilled food: meat, fish, and some spicy soups. Also good is its creamy rice pudding. Licensed, and there's a patio.

Steak Houses

Expensive

Barberian's. 7 Elm St. (416–597–0335). It's cozy, attractive and practically an institution. It's open late, too.

Hy's. 73 Richmond W. (416–364–3326). A library atmosphere and delicious appetizers (*e.g.,* chopped liver, ribs). The steaks are good too. Businessmen love it. There's another Hy's at 133 Yorkville where the crowd is jet-set, sort of.

Moderate

The Keg Mansion. (416–964–6609). Jarvis at Wellesley. The setting—the former mansion of the Massey family—outshines the food. The steaks and ribs are good value and the service young and excessively cheerful.

Other

Moderate

The Hop and Grape. 14 College St. (416–923–2715). A wine bar upstairs, pub downstairs, with savory fare. Smoked goldeye, salmon mousse, steak'n'kidney pie.

The Parrot. 325 Queen St W. (416–593–0899). One of the city's real finds, this restaurant changes its menu and its decor frequently but it is always hip, affordable, imaginative, and tasty. It emphasizes dishes cooked with a light touch—chicken grilled with mango, goat cheese salads, indulgent desserts.

Inexpensive

Switzer's Delicatessen. 322 Spadina Ave. (416–596–6900). Diner-style booths and a wide selection of good, affordable deli food. The corned and baby beef sandwiches are probably the best in the city. Service is fast and friendly.

West End Vegetarian. 2849 Dundas W. (416–762–1204). This unlicensed restaurant has a gourmet veggie menu that changes daily. Kids welcomed.

 NIGHTCLUBS AND BARS. Toronto is a good jazz and blues town, but has its share of dark, comfortable, quiet places to talk. Best known—and darkest—of these is *The Twenty Two,* 22 St. Thomas St., which features piano entertainment in the evenings.

Noodles Wine Bar, 60 Bloor W. (416–920–2186), is crowded despite the fact that not all would find its high-tech decor comfortable. *Chick'n'Deli,* 744 Mount Pleasant (416–489–4161), offering wings and traditional jazz, and *Meyer's Deli,* on Yorkville Ave. (416–960–4780), which also features jazz, live and late into the night.

There are other hot music spots scattered across the city. One of the livelier is *Albert's Hall,* upstairs at the Brunswick House, 481 Bloor W. (416–964–2242), which specializes in blues and R & B, Dixieland and old-fashioned rock 'n' roll. Acts at the *Bam Boo,* 312 Queen St. W. (416–593–5771), range from reggae to performance art, with country funk too. The *Beverly,* 240 Queen W. (416–598–2434), and the *Cameron,* 408 Queen W. (416–364–0811), are artists' hangouts and the music may range from raunchy to fringe. Uptown, *Club Blue Note* at 128 Pears Ave. (416–921–6034) showcases the best in North American rhythm'n'blues. *The Copa,* at Yorkville and Bellair (416–922–6500), is such a hot spot that its late night celebrations have sparked a lively battle with local ratepayers. *The Diamond* is at 410 Sherbourne St. (416–927–9010), and offers a restaurant, dance floor, video club, and forum for everything from live rock to fashion shows. And then there is the good old *El Mocambo,* 464 Spadina Ave. (416–961–8991), a mecca for blues fans. Since The Rolling Stones played here some years ago, the "Elmo" has attracted big-name groups. Get tickets early.

Joe Allen, one of the successful New York-based chain is popular; it's hidden away at 86 John St. (416–593–9404). *Grossman's,* 379 Spadina Ave. (416–977–7000), looks grotty with its terrazzo floors, gloomy paint job, and rows of pickled eggs in jars. But the jazz is funky and the crowd faithful. *The Horseshoe,* 368 Queen W. is one of the centerpieces of the Queen St. strip, and its acts range from punk to country to performance art. *The Rivoli,* 334 Queen St. W. (416–596–1908), is more likely to feature new-wave poets, but also offers music as well. The City offers a true font of Canuck culture: *The Newfoundlander,* a restaurant, bar, and, on weekends, Maritime country music spot. On Danforth east of Broadview (416–469–1916).

There are big, expensive nightclubs in town and frequently they feature big, expensive entertainers. One of the most popular is the Royal York Hotel's huge, elegant old *Imperial Room,* which features the likes of Ella Fitzgerald and Tina Turner. Call (416–368–2511) for information. *Water's Edge Cafe,* York Quay Centre, 235 Queen's Quay W. Big band or country, there is likely to be a dancing crowd here.

EXPLORING OTTAWA

In 1858, Queen Victoria astounded Canada by choosing Bytown, a backwoods lumbering town, to be the capital of the new Dominion. Typically, her compromise site pleased neither French-Canadians (who were arguing for Québec City) nor English (who supported Kingston and Toronto). At any rate, Bytown was renamed Ottawa, an Indian word meaning "a place of buying and selling." The name is perhaps a caution to the city's thousands of federal politicians and civil servants.

From a remote village with a population of 7,500 at the time of Confederation, "Westminster in the wilderness" has blossomed into a lively cosmopolitan capital of over 650,000 people. The verb "blossom" is in Ottawa's case quite literal: the city is full of gardens and parks. Every May, to commemorate Canada's hospitality towards the exiled Dutch royal family during World War II, the government of Holland sends three million gorgeous tulips, 600,000 daffodils, and half a million crocuses to paint Confederation Square, the banks of the Rideau Canal and Parliament Hill.

When Bytown became Canada's capital, land values were modest, to say the least. The government paid $3,750 for the original 29-acre site which became Parliament Hill. A quick decision was made to award an $800,000 contract to architects Thomas Fuller and Chilion Jones, and the neo-Gothic Parliament Buildings were erected on a 150-foot promontory overlooking the Ottawa River by 1700 laborers whose pay ranged from 80¢ to $2.45 a day.

The Peace Tower, in the center block of the complex, is the natural place to begin a walking tour of Ottawa. The tower is a 291-foot-high neo-Gothic structure which replaced the original Centre Block after it was gutted by fire in 1916. Ten-foot gargoyles project from each corner of the tower under the four-faced clock. Inside, there's a monument to Canada's war dead, a lookout and a 52-bell carillon. The 22,400-pound Bourdon Bell strikes the hour.

Changing of the Guard

Around the Peace Tower stretch Parliament Hill's acres of brilliant lawn. The Eternal Flame in the center symbolizes Canadian unity. It is rumored to have gone out six times since it was first lit in Canada's centennial year, 1967. All coins tossed in the surrounding fountain are given to charity. Every summer day in front of the Peace Tower—weather permitting—the 30-minute-long changing of the guard ceremony is performed at 10 A.M., complete with pipes, drums, bearskin hats, and the flashing red coats of the Governor General's Foot Guards and the Canadian Grenadier Guards of Montreal. If you are too late for that ceremony, then at noon, Monday to Saturday, you can hear the blast of the noon gun at Major's Hill—within earshot, or a short walk from Parliament Hill, along Wellington past the Chateau Laurier, then left on Sussex or MacKenzie.

To the sides of the Peace Tower and Centre Block are the East and West Blocks, their copper roofs oxidized to blue-green above gray sandstone. Both are part of the original complex which first housed Parliament in 1866 (a year before Nova Scotia and New Brunswick joined Québec and Ontario in Confederation). They partially escaped the fires half a century ago which devastated the Centre Block. Above the doorway of the East Block's main (150-foot-high) tower are carved the Coats-of-Arms of the two provinces of United Canada. On the western façade a carriage porch of cut freestone stands out from the building. At the northern end of the East Block is the entrance to the prime minister's office. The East Block is open to the public on Sundays only.

The Senate, the House of Commons, and the office of the leader of the opposition are all located in the Centre Block. Austere, dignified, the limestone-and-oak hall of the House of Commons is the scene of the debates of Canada's 282 elected members of Parliament. The public is welcome to observe House debates and Question Period (usually the liveliest part of the proceedings) which take place daily when the House is in session. In the Centre Block's blazing gold-and-crimson Senate Chamber the Governor-General (the Queen's representative in Canada) reads the speech from the Throne at the opening of each session of Parliament. The Centre Block also houses the Library (completed

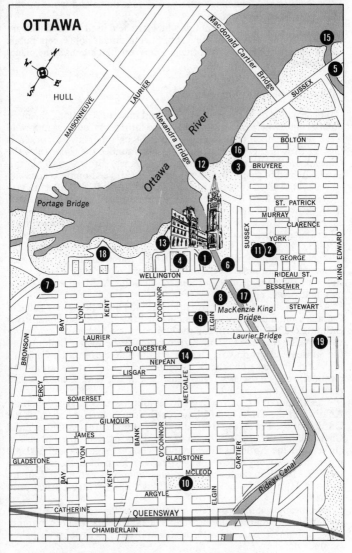

Ottawa—Points of Interest

1) Bytown Museum
2) Byward Market
3) Canadian War Museum
4) Centennial Flame
5) City Hall
6) Chateau Laurier
7) Garden of the Provinces
8) National Arts Centre
9) National Gallery
10) National Museum of Man
11) Canadian Ski Museum
12) Nepean Point
13) Parliament Buildings
14) Place Bell Shopping Mall
15) Rideau Falls
16) Royal Canadian Mint
17) Sightseeing Boat Cruises
18) Supreme Court of Canada
19) University of Ottawa

1876) with its rich paneling, echoing 132-foot dome and white marble statue of Queen Victoria.

Commons Committee meetings which are held in the West Block are also open to the public, but the rest of the building is not (except public washrooms in the northeast corner). The West Block houses the offices of members of Parliament.

Statues of Founding Fathers

The grounds of Parliament Hill abound in statues. Among the more notable figures here immortalized are two fathers of Confederation who were assassinated: behind the Centre Block's northwest corner is George Brown, the Toronto journalist who founded the *Globe* (now the *Globe & Mail* and Canada's national newspaper). Brown was a reformer who helped to shape the Liberal Party. He also championed runaway slaves who wished to settle in Canada. He died in 1880 after an employee he had fired from the newspaper shot him. Diagonally across from Brown is the Irish-born Thomas D'Arcy McGee, another political reformer who drew the wrath of the Irish immigrant Fenian group for criticizing their tactics. One Fenian, acting on his own, shot McGee in 1868. The statue of Sir Wilfred Laurier, Canada's first Francophone (French-speaking) prime minister, can be found in the extreme east corner of the grounds. At the southeast corner of Centre Block, is the statue of the hard-drinking visionary, Sir John A. Macdonald, Canada's first prime minister.

Across Wellington Street from the Parliament Buildings are some of Canada's unofficial policy-influencing institutions, the National Press Building (150 Wellington), and the United States Embassy. Continuing along Wellington across Bank Street, you pass the Justice Building and the Supreme Court on your right. Here the public can watch Canada's highest court make final and far-reaching decisions on constitutional, criminal, and civil cases. The Bank of Canada (and Canada's gold reserves) are on your left.

The Memorial Arch over Lyon Street joins the neoclassical Veterans' Affairs and the Trade and Commerce Buildings. Straight ahead is the Garden of the Provinces, flanked by St. Peter's Lutheran Church and Christ Church Cathedral. Across from the garden are the Public Archives and the National Library (with 400,000 volumes and 100,000 more in microcopy). The rounded bronze form of a Henry Moore sculpture stands in the foyer; etched glass windows on the first floor are by John Hutton who created the windows of Coventry Cathedral in England.

Now head back towards Parliament Hill via Sparks Street pedestrian mall, where fountains, sculpture and café tables have replaced automobiles, bringing thousands of browsers and tourists to shop on balmy summer days.

Emerging from the Sparks Street Mall you'll face Confederation Square, and the dense, heroic bronze figures of Canada's War Memorial. Unveiled by King George VI in 1939, the Memorial commemorated the 66,655 Canadian dead of World War I. Ironically, the Memorial was completed on the eve of World War II. The 70-foot-high Memorial is the work of Vernon March. To your left is Parliament Hill; to your right one of Canada's grand old hotels, the Château Laurier, which looks like an oversized, gray-turreted baronial castle; straight ahead of you is a deep gorge where manual locks can lift boats 79 feet up from the Ottawa River to the Rideau Canal. Follow the steps down the gorge to Bytown Museum in Ottawa's oldest stone building, erected 1826–27. A pedestrian and bicycle path has been built around the base of Parliament Hill on your left. It's a recent addition: the original pathway,

Lovers' Walk, was closed in the 1930's because the earth moved—landslides.

Civil Servants on Skates

The old railway station (now the Government Conference Centre) and the National Capital Commission, the federal agency responsible for enhancing Canada's capital (and incidentally a good place to get information on the city) face you from the far side of the Rideau Canal. Closer are the 2,300-seat opera house, 800-seat theater and experimental stage of the National Arts Centre, a complex modern building hung with vines and gardens. The Arts Centre also features a pleasant waterside café where on winter days you can watch the unusual but typically Ottawan sight of briefcase-carrying civil servants skating to work along the Rideau Canal.

Walk past the Chateau Laurier, turn left to William Street and the Byward Market, where, since 1846, local farmers have hawked cheeses, pickles, fresh produce, and cut flowers. Head up Sussex Drive. Here the National Capital Commission has restored many of the original Georgian and Victorian shopfronts. Now they are boutiques, art galleries, and cafés.

If you turn left off Sussex Drive towards Alexandra Bridge, you'll find yourself at Nepean Point, a small public park with a big beautiful view. The view encompasses the odd duality of the capital's character. Behind you, on an imposing bluff rising out of the Ottawa River are the gray spires and distinguished blocks of Parliament Hill; across the river, a tangle of industrial buildings and neon: Hull, Québec, which for a long time was, frankly, the most interesting part of Ottawa, Ontario. Ottawa's relationship with Hull is symbiotic. It has relied on the Québec lumbering town to alleviate its burdens of state—and in fact Hull still has many of the capital's finest French restaurants and liveliest nightclubs.

But, spurred by the city's raunchy reputation and relatively high crime rate, Hull is cleaning up its taverns. Back in Ottawa, Notre Dame Basilica (1841–46) stands on the corner of Sussex Drive and St. Patrick. The beautiful wooden decorations inside were executed by Philippe Parizeau, who also worked on the National Library. The Canadian War Museum at 330–350 Sussex Drive is next door to the Mint (which produces all of Canada's coin currency). The Mint also has a good display of historic coinage. Tours are available by appointment.

Ballroom, Rink and Cricket Pitch

Sussex Drive skirts the Ottawa River above limestone bluffs. Monumental institutional architecture gives way to the elegant leafy streets of Rockcliffe Park, the home of many governmental officials, embassies, and official residences. The prime minister's residence (24 Sussex Drive) is a gray stone mansion built in 1868. It was acquired by the government in 1943 and Prime Minister Louis St. Laurent became its first prime ministerial occupant in 1950.

Government House (or Rideau Hall), the official residence of the Governor-General, is across a park from the prime minister's residence, on MacKay Street. Built in 1838, it has its own ballroom, skating rink and cricket pitch.

Final stop: the Central Experimental Farm, where the government conducts cross-breeding and fertilization projects, and where you can wander among 1,200 acres of flowerbeds, gardens, brand-new plants and an arboretum of approximately 1,700 different trees and shrubs. They even grow marijuana here—for controlled laboratory use only. It is also a favored spot for newlyweds to have their portraits taken. The farm is open every day from 8:30 A.M. until dusk.

Parliament recesses for the summer, but politics remains the city's driving force. Indeed, the real Ottawa is inaccessible to tourists. It includes a humming gossip network, strategic tables in certain restaurants such as the Chateau Grill and Les Saisons in the Westin Hotel, and parties in the private homes of Rockcliff. Still, Ottawa has charms for the apolitical tourist, too. In May, the city astounds with its millions of flowers. In late August, the Central Canada Exhibition brings a horse show, a grandstand show and a midway to town. In winter, skaters swarm on the Rideau Canal, Parliament Hill is floodlit on frosty nights, theatergoers glitter in the foyer of the National Arts Centre and skiers escape to the snowy slopes of the Gatineau Hills.

PRACTICAL INFORMATION FOR OTTAWA

HOW TO GET THERE. By air: Ottawa Uplands Airport is an international airport. There are direct flights from New York via *Eastern Airlines,* from Montréal via *Nordair, Canadian Pacific* and *Air Canada,* and from Toronto via *Canadian Pacific* and *Air Canada.*

By train: *Via Rail* runs day, express and overnight trains from Toronto; it also operates an Ottawa-Montréal route. The train station is at the Alta Vista interchange off the Queensway.

By bus: *Voyageur Colonial* is the major inter-city service. Its terminal and the Ottawa bus station are at 265 Catherine St.

By car: The *Trans-Canada Highway* links Ottawa with Montréal from the east and goes west through Sault Ste. Marie, Thunder Bay, and into Manitoba. *Highway 7* is the scenic central route between Ottawa and Toronto.

ACCOMMODATIONS. Most of Ottawa's hotels serve a governmental clientele. They therefore tend to be a little more expensive, with an emphasis on quiet comfort, than hotels in other Ontario centers. But there are hotels and motels to suit all pocketbooks in the area, most of them within walking distance of major sights and museums. Rates for double rooms are categorized as follows: *Deluxe,* more than $110; *Expensive,* $90–$110; *Moderate,* $55–$90; *Inexpensive,* less than $55.

Most places accept the following major credit cards: American Express, MasterCard and Visa; others may also be honored. Not all establishments accept credit cards, therefore we suggest you call for information.

Deluxe

Château Laurier. 1 Rideau St. K1N 8S7 (613-232-6411). It's old, gracious and very much a Canadian institution. The large, airy rooms have recently been refurnished but the dark paneled lobby has been allowed to retain its nostalgic elegance. Right beside Parliament Hill and the Rideau Canal, the Château has an indoor pool, boutiques, and lounges with entertainment. Wheelchair accessible.

Delta Ottawa. 361 Queen St. K1R 7S9 (613-238-6000). Noted for its comprehensive health club facilities including an indoor pool and sauna and its proximity to Parliament Hill. Wheelchair accessible.

Skyline Ottawa. 101 Lyon St. K1R 5T9 (613-237-3600). With a younger, livelier clientele and a good rooftop bar. The hotel also has an indoor pool and wheelchair access.

Moderate

Hotel Roxborough. 123 Metcalfe St. L1P 5L9 (613-237-5171). A 150-room hotel catering to business clients. It gives its guests a complimentary continental breakfast and newspapers.

Moderate

Best Western Macies Ottawan Motel. 1274 Carling Ave. K1Z 7K8 (613–728
–1951). With its outdoor pool, spa, whirlpool, babysitting services, and waterbeds, this west-end hotel caters to young families and couples. Family operated, 116 rooms, with sauna, whirlpool and exercise area.

Lord Elgin. 100 Elgin St. K1P 5K8 (613–235–3333). Because of its reasonable prices, its pleasant, older atmosphere and its downtown location, this hotel
remains extremely popular. The rooms are smaller but comfortable and fully
serviced.

Inexpensive

Journey's End. 1252 Michael St. K1J 7T1 (613–744–2900). Near Hwy 417,
this is a smaller, well-run hotel in a reliable chain.

L'Auberge du Voyageur Inn. 2200 Montréal Rd. K1J 6M5 (613–746–4653).
Small, suburban, with 40 rooms and TV. There are exotic dancers in the lounge,
so not all families will feel comfortable here.

TELEPHONES. Ottawa, Kingston, and the cottage
country between—including the Rideeau Lakes district
—all lie within area code 613. Some government telephones, on local call rates with Ottawa, actually lie in
area code 819—because their offices are on the Hull, Québec, side of the Ottawa
River.

HOW TO GET AROUND. By bus: There are two bus
systems in Ottawa, the *Rideau-Carleton Regional Transit Commission,* and *La Commission de Transport de la
Communaute Regionale de l'Outaouais;* a bus loop joins
Ottawa, Hull, and the two systems. Tickets must be purchased in specially
designated neighborhood stores, or a cash fare is required (no change given). For
further information and a public transportation map contact the Ottawa-Carleton Transportation Commission at 294 Albert St. (613–741–4390).

By taxi: Major cab lines, like *Blue Line* and *Diamond,* run a good citywide
service.

From the airport: An airport limousine bus service run by *Blue Line* takes
visitors to and from the airport and major downtown hotels. Taxi fares from
the airport are a good deal more expensive, but should stay under $20.

TOURIST INFORMATION. Canada's Capital Visitors and Convention Bureau is in 222 Queen St., 7th floor, a block south of the Sparks St. Mall.
Telephone: (613) 237–5158.

SEASONAL EVENTS. Winterlude, each **February,**
culminates a week of speed skating, snow sculpting,
horse races on ice and bed races (?!) with fireworks. The
Festival of Spring in **May** brings musical events,
parades, beer gardens, and more fireworks. **July** 1 is the celebration of Canada
Day, culminating a variety show televised from Parliament Hill, with fireworks,
of course. Festival Ottawa is a midsummer performing arts festival. In late
August, the Central Canada Exhibition opens its midway, horseshow, and
agricultural exhibits.

TOURS. The Rideau Canal winds through the heart of
the city and falls to the Ottawa River below Parliament
Hill. Two of the most pleasant sightseeing expeditions
are run by *Paul's Boat Lines,* which take visitors on
1¼-hour cruises of the Rideau Canal or ½-hour cruises of the Ottawa River.
Riverboats can be boarded below the Bytown Museum; canal boats dock across
from the National Arts Centre at 3244 Riverside Dr., Ottawa. Call (613–733–
5186). Tours are available in English or French, and are operated from mid-May
to mid-October. Or take a 3-hour cruise of the Rideau Lakes (Saturday-night
Dinner Dance Cruises available in mid-summer). Contact *Ottawa Riverboat*

Company, 316 Dalhousie (613–232–2888 and 617–235–8409), for 1¾-hour cruises on the Ottawa River.

Double-decker buses cover a 27-mile sightseeing circuit leaving from Confederation Square, mid-May to the end of October. In the fall, special trips are offered into the Gatineau Hills in Québec to see the brilliant autumn colors. For further information contact *Gray Line Sightseeing Tours,* (613–741–6440). From April to October, their 2-hour National Capital Tour shows visitors Parliament Hill, the Central Experimental Farm, Hog's Back Falls, various embassies, etc. From July to early September, the tour is expanded to include an optional viewing of the Changing of the Guards on Parliament Hill. The *Ottawa-Carleton Transportation Commission* runs seven daily bus tours around the capital from May to October. You can take a horse-drawn wagon ride through the Central Experimental Farm, weather permitting.

GARDENS AND PARKWAYS. The 3½-mile-long parkway which runs beside the Rideau Canal—it's called *Queen Elizabeth Driveway*—has cycle paths, shady spots to stop and watch the water, and in May, Ottawa's famous tulips. The largest flowerbeds are at Dow's Lake.

There is a two-mile parkway through the *Central Experimental Farm,* which connects with scenic, residential Island Park Drive. The farm has ornamental gardens and an arboretum with over a thousand different trees and shrubs among its 1,200 acres. Open May to September.

Rockcliffe Driveway runs along river cliffs to garden rockeries. Here you can picnic in Rockcliffe Park.

The 8.2 acres of *Nepean Point* offer a splendid view of Parliament Hill and the Ottawa River.

Hog's Back Park, 54 acres, contains the pretty Hog's Back Falls. There is a path at the base of Parliament Hill, and across the canal, behind Chateau Laurier, you can find Major's Hill Park with its noon gun salute.

CHILDREN'S ACTIVITIES. Ottawa's *Museum of Science and Technology* is for children of all ages who want to twist knobs, pull levers, turn dials and watch the laws of physics, astronomy and meteorology come to life. There are locomotives, vintage autos, and model ships too. The Museum is on 35 acres of parkland, 1867 St. Laurent Blvd., and is closed Mondays from mid-September to mid-May.

The Ottawa Parks Recreation Branch organizes children's activities—*puppet shows, theater groups* and *celebrations* in its parks. Other regional administrations run similar programs: *Nepean Parks and Recreation* and *Gloucester Recreation and Parks.*

The public *libraries* offer story hours, puppet shows, and films. Also check with Gloucester Public Libraries and Nepean Public Libraries.

The *Museum of Canadian Scouting,* 1345 Baseline Rd., is full of artifacts of interest to those members and ex-members of packs. Open all year, Monday to Friday except holidays.

Children also enjoy the daily 10 A.M. changing of the guards on Parliament Hill. One of Canada's outstanding summer attractions.

Slide-A-Ride is a 350-foot-long flume, just 8 miles south of town on Hwy. 31 at Poplar Grove. Mini-golf, too.

Your children might be interested in seeing metals being stamped into coins at the *Royal Canadian Mint,* 320 Sussex Dr. Tours are held Monday to Friday except holidays.

SPORTS. Ottawa has been a sports-minded town since its lumberjack days. Games of the *Ottawa Roughriders,* Canadian Football League pros, are popular. There are lots of opportunities to be active, as this list shows:

Boats can be rented at Dow's Lake on the Rideau Canal, rowboats at the corner of Fifth Ave. and Queen Elizabeth Driveway. There is good **swimming** at Gatineau Park in Quebec, but swimming in the Ottawa River is not advised. **Cycling** is extremely popular. On Sundays, Queen Elizabeth Driveway and Colonel By Drive are both closed to traffic until noon for cyclists. It seems that everyone from cabinet ministers to kids takes advantage of the city's 65 miles of bicycle paths. Path maps are available from the National Capital Commission, 48 Rideau, near Parliament Hill. In winter, the paths become urban **cross-country ski** trails. The hills around Ottawa offer good **downhill skiing.** One of the major Ontario resorts is at Mount Pakenham. Highway 15 south of 17. On sunny winter weekends, it's possible to see 50,000 **skaters** on the Rideau Canal. Public **golf** courses in the National Capital region include National Capital Commission Golf Centre and Pine View Municipal Golf Course. There are public **tennis** courts at City View and West Ottawa, but don't be surprised to find them heavily subscribed. Ottawa has two **racetracks.** When the Connaught Park is closed, chances are you can still find some action at the Rideau-Carleton Raceway on Albion Rd.

 HISTORIC SITES. Ottawa is a relatively young city. Settlement began here in 1809, but until 1867, when Queen Victoria chose it as Canada's capital, it remained a tiny lumbering town. Consequently, its historic sites are only a couple of generations old.

Laurier House, 335 Laurier Ave. E., residence of two Canadian prime ministers, was built in 1878. It has been refurnished in period style. Closed Mondays all year.

Here too is the study where Prime Minister William Lyon Mackenzie King ran the country throughout the dark days of the Second World War by communing through seances with his dead mother.

At *Kitchissippi Lookout* on Island Park Dr., a plaque commemorates the Canadian rivermen who were recruited in 1884 to negotiate the dangerous cataracts of the Nile River and relieve British General Charles Gordon in the siege of Khartoum.

A statue of Samuel de Champlain, the French explorer, geographer, and governor of New France, gazes across the city from *Nepean Point.*

You can tour Ottawa's 8 locks where the Rideau Canal pours into the Ottawa River, simply by scrambling down the north side of the Château Laurier Hotel grounds. Or head along Sussex Drive past the Pont MacDonald Cartier bridge to Rideau Falls. "Rideau" is French for "curtain" and the double falls here form a striking curtain of water. In the 19th century, this was a major industrial site of water-powered textile and lumber mills, foundries, and breweries. Two historic sites here have become restaurants: *The Mill,* a former grist mill on the south bank of the river at 555 Ottawa River Parkway, and *Le Castor* at 449 Sussex Drive. Le Castor is the site of a former hotel where the legendary Joe Mufferaw, the Ottawa Valley Giant, allegedly left his boot prints on the ceiling.

There are many old, charming villages within the National Capital Region. At Almonte, west of the city, an old gristmill has been restored and now contains a fine collection of pioneer artifacts. The *Mill of Kintail* is closed from October to May and Tuesdays.

Moorside, the summer home of Canada's longest-serving prime minister, the occultist MacKenzie King, is open to the public. It's in the middle of Gatineau Wilderness Park.

At Manotick, *Watson's Mill* dating from 1859 has been restored and opened to visitors.

Nearby, at Richmond, there's an old church, *St. John's Anglican,* which was built in 1823 and old stone houses, one built in 1828.

 MUSEUMS AND GALLERIES. Museums. As we go to press, several museums are closed for renovation. The *National Gallery of Canada* will reopen near Nepean Point in a new home—a glass cathedral complex designed by Israeli-Canadian architect Moshe Safdie—by the summer of 1988. The *National Film Board* Gallery is also looking for a new home. The *National Museum of Man* will reopen on completion of a sweeping new complex designed by Canadian Métis architect Douglas Cardinal.

The Bytown Museum is a stone commissariat store constructed in 1827. It's between Château Laurier and Parliament Hill and is open from May to September. Most of its 3,500 artifacts relate to the building of the Rideau Canal, the development of Ottawa, and the personal history of Colonel By, an engineer in charge of the building of the canal. Open May to September except Sundays and holidays.

At the *Museum of Canadian Scouting,* 1345 Baseline Rd., the lives of Lord Baden-Powell and his movement in Canada are remembered through old photos, insignia and so forth, which should be of interest to scouts and former scouts. Open all year, Monday–Friday except holidays.

At the *National Museum of Science and Technology,* 1867 St. Laurent Blvd., you can participate in many of the displays of meteorology, physics, and astronomy. From mid-September to mid-May, the museum is closed on Mondays.

The *National Aviation Museum* has over 100 aircraft inside three World War II hangars at Rockcliffe Airport, including the early Canadian "Silver Dart." Closed Mondays from mid-September to mid-May.

Some of the specimens date back three hundred years to the French-Indian bush wars at the *Canadian War Museum,* 330 Sussex Dr. Photos, maps, flags, models, a Sopwith Camel, Indian clubs, and one of the finest medal collections in the world can be seen daily all year except Mondays, Labour Day to April. Open holiday Mondays.

Philatelists will enjoy the *National Postal Museum* at 180 Wellington Street. Old photographs, old mailbags and pouches, ornate brass letter balances, hand canceling hammers, and a priceless collection of stamps make this an intriguing place to browse even for non-philatelists. There's even an old general store and post office, circa 1885, reconstructed right down to the weathered floorboards, tin boxes of medicinal herbs, glass jars, crocks and earthenware. At the counter of the store you can buy the latest mint stamps, first-day covers, and postcards. If you mail one from the store's Victorian mailbox, it will receive the special Postal Museum cancellation. Open all year daily except Christmas Day and Mondays.

There are old photographs and ancient skis at the *Canadian Ski Museum,* 457A Sussex Dr. Open all year Tuesday to Saturday, afternoons. Closed holidays.

The *National Library* and *Public Archives* displays its books, films, paintings, watercolors, engravings, photographs, and maps at 395 Wellington St., every day all year.

Galleries. Among the private art galleries are *Wells Gallery,* 459 Sussex Dr., for contemporary painting, graphics, and sculpture, the *S A W Gallery,* 55 Byward Market, where exhibitions range from representational watercolors to the more challenging forms of video art. *Giraffe* at 67 Sparks St. carries artifacts and crafts from Africa and Asia, including masks, tapestries, and funerary figures, as does the *Ufundo Gallery* at 541 Sussex Dr. The *Wallack Gallery* at 203 Bank St. caters to corporate collectors.

MUSIC AND THEATER. The three-theater complex of the *National Arts Centre* is the focus of the city's cultural life. Here you can enjoy dinner before a ballet or symphony in the 2,300-seat opera theater, drama in an 800-seat, thrust-stage theater, or something more avant-garde in the 300-seat experimental studio. Music, dance, and two resident (French and English) drama companies play here. The *National Arts Centre Orchestra* is a 45-member symphony conducted by Franco Mannino. The Centre stands among gardens and walkways by the side of the Rideau Canal just south of Confederation Square.

The University of Ottawa's music department sponsors concerts throughout the academic year.

SHOPPING. *Sparks Street Mall* is a traffic-free shopping street in the heart of the city, and in summer its crowds are attracted as much by the rock gardens, fountains, outdoor tables and art exhibitions as they are by the shops. Eskimo sculpture and Eskimo and Indian prints and crafts can be purchased at *Snow Goose Handicrafts,* 40 Elgin St. *Canada's Four Corners,* 93 Sparks St., carries native and Canadian crafts. *Pierre l'Artisan* (at the St. Laurent shopping mall) offers jewelry, crafts, Canadiana. Look at the jewelry, furniture, pottery, leatherwork, and prints; they are the work of excellent local craftsmen. The *Wells Gallery,* 459 Sussex Dr., sells quality ceramics, glass, and fine art. *Byward Market,* just around the corner on York St., is one of the most colorful places to shop for fresh fruit, vegetables, and cheeses. The *Bayshore Shopping Centre* is a two-level mall with over 100 shops.

Embassy wives buy their finery at expensive import shops like *Peacock Imports,* 219 Bank St., *Capune Ltd.* (for imported knitwear), and *Puchi Mode*

Internationale, both at Place de Ville. Richard Robinson, whose boutique, *Maison de Haute Couture,* is at 423 Sussex Dr., has designed for former Prime Minister Pierre Trudeau's ex-wife. Also try *Sarah Clothes,* 46 Elgin, for more off-beat, Asian imports. *Kanal* at Elgin and Frank offers handmade clothing for women and men. *Justine,* 537 Sussex Dr., carries designer gowns and suits, imported and Canadian.

Downtown Ottawa has been restructured by the *Rideau Centre,* a new development of 200 stores and shops. Rideau and Sussex Sts. don't look the same, now that the two-level complex is linked by an overhead walkway to *The Bay. Ogilvy's, Eaton's, Simpson's,* and *Holt Renfrew* are other popular stores. *Howarth's,* 89 O'Connor St. has men's and women's Aquascutum coats. Scottish kilts, mugs, and heraldry knick-knacks are available at the *Family Coat of Arms* shop, 55½ William St. *All Things Small* at 380 Elgin St. stocks handcrafted miniatures, doll houses, and furnishings.

 RESTAURANTS. For many years Ottawa's restaurants shared the fate of local cultural and night life—they struggled along in the shadow of Hull. While Hull still boasts many of the finest French and international cuisine restaurants—like La Ferme Colombia or L'Echelle de Jacob—now Ottawa has many restaurants to be proud of too. And if you are planning a summer picnic, you couldn't do better than to drop by the *Kardish Delicatessen,* 979 Wellington St., for smoked meat and strong dill pickles, or the *Byward Market* and surrounding bakeries.

Cost categories per person are for dinner including hors d'oeuvre, entrée, and dessert. Drinks and tips are not included. *Expensive,* more than $25 per person; *Moderate,* between $15 and $25; *Inexpensive,* less than $15.

Most places accept the following major credit cards: American Express, MasterCard and Visa; others may also be honored. Not all establishments accept credit cards, therefore we suggest you call for information.

CENTRAL EUROPEAN

Moderate

A Touch of Europe. 1792 Bank St. (613–521–6650). Noted for Stroganoff, thick goulash soup, and bratwurst and sauerkraut. Can be expensive.

Chinese

Moderate

Yangtze. 700 Somerset (613–236–0555). No decor to speak of—just a reputation for good Cantonese cooking and dim sum lunches. Licensed.

Pine Tree Village. 354 Elgin (613–232–6126). Northern Chinese cuisine features delicious Peking duck, hot and sour soup, curry-style dishes.

Shanghai. 651 Somerset St. W. (613–233–4001). Specialties include pickerel fried with almonds and shallots, soft noodle (chow mein), and chicken fried with ham. Licensed for wine and beer.

French-International

Expensive

Cafe Henry Burger. 69 Laurier, Hull (819–777–5646). Small, old, and charming, it offers the French classics.

Chez Jean Pierre. 210 Somerset W. (613–235–9711). Jean Pierre Muller, the cook for 17 years at the home of the U.S. Ambassador, has finally established his own, first-rate French restaurant. Licensed.

Le Jardin. 127 York St. (613–238–1828), in an old house in the market area. A classically conservative interior, baroque music, and a classic chef, whose touch with scallops, scampi, sole, vegetables and cheesecake is legendary—and award-winning.

Les Saisons. 11 Colonel By Dr. (613–560–7000). Thronged with bureaucrats having power lunches. The elegant, floral decor complements classic French cuisine.

The Mill. 555 Ottawa River Pkway. (613–237–1311). An historic grist mill has been renovated and now serves French and Canadian classics.

Moderate

Café Casa Blanca. 87 George St., Market Mall (613–233–3190). French-Moroccan food: couscous, cornish hen with prunes, hot pepper salads with cumin. Great waiters and French chansonnier tapes, but a rather dull setting.

Inexpensive

Le Café. In the National Arts Centre off Elgin at Wellington (613–594–5127). Known for its homemade ice cream, this informal but charming place to eat, especially near the windows overlooking the Rideau Canal. Light meals, leafy salads and delicate quiches. Licensed. Open only in summer.

Italian

Moderate to Expensive

Il Vagabondo. 186 Barrette St. (613–749–4877). The Cappellozzi family make their own pasta, grate their own cheese, and keep the menu short in order to do it justice.

Mamma Teresa. 300 Somerset (613–236–3023). It's extremely popular because its veal dishes (with wine sauce, or vermouth or lemon or cheese or . . .) are invariably good. Mamma's zabaglione is also recommended.

Japanese

Expensive

Japanese Village Steak House. 170 Laurier Ave., W. (613–236–9519). There's something about the lightly fried shrimps, teriyaki chicken, steak and lobster that make them particularly good here. Maybe it is because they are cooked in front of you by showman chefs.

Moderate

Suisha Gardens. 208 Slater (613–236–9602). One of Ottawa's many popular Japanese restaurants.

Mexican

Moderate

Guadala Harry's. 18 York St. (613–234–8229). Mexican furniture and a re-created Spanish-style streetfront. Tacos and tequila.

Seafood

Moderate to Expensive

The Seven Seas. 87 George St. (613–237–7819). Scallops, sole, clams, shrimp, and a conscientious cook.

Moderate

Friday's. 150 Elgin (613–237–5353). So popular with the civil servants at lunch it should be listed in the government telephone directory. Roast beef, steak, seafood. Can be expensive.

Hayloft Steak House. 200 Rideau (613–232–7161). It's part of a chain which handles big flavorful steaks in a cheerful barnboard atmosphere.

Hayloft Portside. 202 Rideau St. (613–236–6863). Affordable seafood. Licensed. Part of the chain next door.

Mother Tucker's Food Experience. 61 York St. (613–238–6525). Recommended by readers for its good value in steak and seafood. Licensed.

The Place Next Door. 320 Rideau St. (613–232–1741). Owned by Dave Smith—his brother, Jack, owns the locally famous deli which this place is next door to—the restaurant draws celebrities such as Frank Sinatra for its steaks. Licensed.

Other

Nate's. 316 Rideau St. (613–236–9696). *The* deli in town.

BARS AND NIGHTLIFE. *Zoe's Bar,* in the Chateau Laurier, 1 Rideau St. (613–232–6411), moire walls, overstuffed chintz chairs, flowers, and elegance. The house specialty is a drink called the Cocktail Zoe: champagne and blackberry liqueur. *Brandy's,* 126 York St. (613–234–5088), on the Byward Market, is a popular disco. *Molly McGuire's* is an Irish pub on Rideau St. at number 257 (613–235–1972).

Stoney Monday's is a popular rock and dance spot in the Byward Market, at 62 York St. (613–236–5548). A college crowd.

The best clubs for partying into the small hours are in Hull. Among the liveliest: *the Vogue,* 86 Promenade du Portage (819–777–7522); *Le Zinc,* 191 Promenade du Portage (819–778–0462); and the once-infamous, now renovated, *Le Nouveau Chez Henri,* 179 Promenade du Portage (819–777–2741).

EXPLORING SOUTHERN ONTARIO

Most of Ontario's first French, English, and Loyalist settlers entered the province from the southeast. You can retrace some of their routes on Southern Ontario's Heritage Highways. Highway 2, parallel to Highway 401, is smaller than the cross-Ontario freeway but more picturesque. It's the original nineteenth-century route that linked Québec and Kingston to "Muddy York" (Toronto) in the west. And with appropriate detours it can afford you a good glimpse into many of Southern Ontario's diverse attractions.

Cornwall, headquarters of the St. Lawrence Seaway, is a bilingual city of 45,900, which connects via the international bridge to Rooseveltown, New York State. For pedestrians only: Pitt St. Mall, whose pools and fountains are built of local limestone. West on Highway 2 before Morrisburg is Upper Canada Village, a faithful re-creation of an Ontario community in the early 1800's. When the construction of the St. Lawrence Seaway flooded some old riverside communities, the historic buildings were moved to the site of the Battle of Crysler's Farm, a dramatic military engagement. It was a British victory or an impasse, depending on who tells the tale. Twenty-five hundred Americans arrived on the Canadian shore in the autumn of 1813 and were met by 800 Redcoats sent down from Kingston. After what historians have called a "smart but indecisive action," 181 British lay dead, while 300 Americans were killed or wounded. There is no echo of musketry in the peaceful, mid-19th-century Upper Canadian town that has been re-created at Crysler's Farm. You can tour the site by horsedrawn boats, oxcarts, or on foot and visit a general store, church, tavern, or schoolmaster's house. In most of the buildings there are contumed guides waiting to answer your questions. (Upper Canada Village is open from mid-May to mid-October.) Morrisburg also has an antique car museum (one mile west of Upper Canada Village on Highway 2) and the Upper Canada Migratory Bird Sanctuary, a 3,500-acre refuge, nine miles east of the town. It is open daily from April to November.

Highway 2 runs beside the St. Lawrence River section of the 2,300-mile-long Seaway. Sixty-five hundred homes had to be moved, along with 18 cemeteries and 35 miles of highway, to accommodate the flood of water along this particular stretch of Seaway. Iroquois, a tiny village now boasts a major set of locks, through which massive lakers carry tens of thousands of tons of grain and ore.

Farther on, at Prescott, Fort Wellington and the Old Lighthouse (both of which saw action in the War of 1812) are now restored and open to the public. Canadian, American, and French regiments perform period drills dressed in period costume in mid-July. You can also visit Prescott's old wooden chapel (the Blue Church, built 1845). In its cemetery are the graves of many early settlers, including Barbara Heck, founder of Methodism in North America.

Brockville (named after Sir Isaac Brock, hero of the War of 1812) is an entry point to the St. Lawrence Parks Commission's Islands Park. The park offers both mainland campgrounds and island camps accessible by boat. You can rent boats at Brockville, or take a boat tour from Rockport, Kingston, Gananoque or Ivy Lea through the Thousand Islands. Hill Island, near Ivy Lea, features Never Never Land, a children's playground. Adults have their playgrounds too. Boldt Castle, once the summer residence of a nostalgic and wealthy German, rises like a Rhine Valley château on an island near Gananoque.

The Spirit of Colonialism

The city of Kingston, solid and enduring like the gray limestone of which it is built, is over 300 years old. It was founded in 1673 by Count Frontenac, the governor of New France, and was guarded by Old Fort Henry, once the principal military stronghold of Upper Canada. Here from mid-May to mid-October you can see a splendid display of infantry, cavalry, artillery, and naval equipment. Muzzle-loading cannon cast in 1874 blast salutes, and red-coated army cadets execute the traditional changing of the guard.

There is a real spirit of Upper Canadian colonialism about the city. This is immediately apparent in the title of the town's newspaper, the *Kingston Whig-Standard.* As well, Martello towers guard the harbor. Gray and solid, they are structures similar to those the British erected to guard the coasts of their other colonies. The "Limestone City" is the home of Canada's Royal Military College, the Military College Museum (housed in a Martello tower in the city's other military defenses at Fort Frederick), the old and venerable Queen's University, and Bellevue House, a Tuscan-style villa, once the home of Canada's first prime minister, Sir John A. Macdonald. The old town has another side, however. It offers a Hockey Hall of Fame, a Canadian Forces Communications and Electronic Museum (with kit shop) at Vimy Barracks, Highway 2 East, plus bookshops, cafés, art/craft galleries and lively local theater, all patronized by Kingston's university community.

Situated at the point where the Rideau Canal system and Lake Ontario join the St. Lawrence River, Kingston is very much a harbor town. In 1976, it was the site of the XXI Olympiad's yachting events. In late August, the former Olympic site becomes the site of North American training regattas. Its 19th-century naval glory is recalled at the old shipbuilding yards (now on Royal Military College grounds), the century-and-a-half old Rideau Canal locks at Kingston Mills and the bright sails and riggings of the pleasure craft clustered in the city's harbor. From Kingston, boat lovers can also enjoy paddlewheel tours on the licensed, three-tiered *Island Queen* (trips daily, mid-May to September) and motor launch tours through the Thousand Islands.

Don't leave Kingston without dropping by the Pump House Steam Museum. The museum, housed in an imposing pile of Victorian limestone on the waterfront, has the biggest working-order steam exhibit in the world (open June 15 to Labour Day, daily, except Fridays).

North of Kingston is resort country—the Rideau Lakes. Mallards and blue-winged teal skim the warm water; boats cruise through the Rideau Canal. In the heart of the Lake district, Perth is the site of Ontario's last fatal duel, fought in 1833 over the honour of one Miss Hughes. Her fiancé, Robert Lyon, died in the exchange of shots.

The White House

Take Highway 33 west and stop by the White House at Collin's Bay. Built in 1793, it is one of the best remaining examples of a Loyalist home. There's another, near Bath, built in the 1780's by Loyalist Jeptha Hawley. Then drive on into the out-of-the-way pastoral countryside of the Prince Edward County Peninsula. Much of the peninsula was settled by German refugees from the American War of Independence; their early tribulations in the half-surveyed wilderness are recalled at the Loyalist Museum at Adolphustown. Two-and-a-half miles north, at Hay Bay, is a Quaker Burying Grounds which dates from 1784.

Picton (population 4,300) is the county center. Its original Greek revival courthouse, built in 1832, where Sir John A. Macdonald once practiced law, is still in use. The Prince Edward County Peninsula is rich in historic sites; it also offers some beautiful lakeside campsites, like the breezy dunes of Sandbanks and North Beach Provincial Parks (11 miles west of Picton).

Belleville has a fine yacht harbor on the Bay of Quinte, plus golf, swimming, even a local flying club.

In Belleville you can visit the handsome Hastings County Museum at Glanmore, a French rococo-style Victorian mansion. The museum displays European and Oriental furniture and a rather unusual assembly of lighting devices that date back to the Stone Age (257 Bridge St. E.). Belleville also produces some first-rate Canadian cheddar cheeses.

Highway 62 north from Belleville takes you into mining and lumbering country. Seventy miles on is Bancroft, a geologists' paradise, with its annual early-August "Gemboree" and its abundance of local amethyst, beryl, garnet, magnetite, rose quartz, tourmaline, and zircon mineral deposits. River raft trips on white water (i.e., rough water) are available. And for simple picnic outings, there is a splendid spot at Eagles' Nest Lookout, 600 feet above the town of Bancroft.

Head west again on Highway 2. There is a licensed restaurant in the century-old home of silent movie star Marie Dressler at Cobourg. And on summer afternoons, a band plays concerts in the town park near Cobourg's restored Palladian-style Victoria Hall.

Cobourg and its neighboring city, Port Hope, are both rich in architecture, particularly the 19th-century mansions of wealthy Americans who summered here. If you turn North from Highway 2 up Highway 28, traveling through the Great Pine Ridge and Kawartha Lakes vacation regions, you'll come to Peterborough, a university town of 61,000 people. Besides the intricate modern architecture of Trent University, Peterborough offers the Kawartha Downs standardbred racetrack, the second highest hydraulic lift locks in the world on the Trent-Severn Waterway and the annual Peterborough Summer Festival (aquatic events, music and theatre, early July). On Saturday morning, pick up some fresh fruit and baked goods at the local Farmers' Market in Morrow Park, then drop by Century Village (a restored pioneer village) to picnic and swim in the Indian River.

Six-Foot Mound Snakes

Picnickers mingle with archeologists at the Serpent Mounds Provincial Park (south of Peterborough at Keene). Here a mysterious six-foot-high man-made mound snakes across the landscape. Northeast of Peterborough at Nephton are unusual black symbols painted on the white rock. Both sites are believed to have been left by prehistoric Indian peoples 2,000 years ago. The parks are open mid-May to mid-September.

Farther north are the Kawartha and Haliburton Highlands, unsurpassed camping and cottage country culminating in the wilderness of Algonquin Provincial Park. In between are pretty little towns like Lakefield, where Prince Andrew of the British Royal family attended the prestigious local boys' school. In summer, theatergoers flock to Lindsay's Academy Theatre, which specializes in comedy. Haliburton has four 9-hole golf courses.

Sixty-five miles east of Toronto, Heritage Highway 2 merges with the fast-moving Macdonald-Cartier Freeway (Highway 401). The traffic thickens as you approach Oshawa. Oshawa's General Motors plant is the biggest automobile manufacturing center in the country. Adults and accompanied children can tour the plant, then drop by the Canadian Automotive Museum (99 Simcoe Street, South) to view a collection of 50 motor vehicles, some dating back to 1900. Around that time Colonel Sam McLaughlin was designing his own version of the horseless carriage; later he became president of General Motors of Canada. His 55-room estate, Parkwood, is open June–August except Mondays, September–November and April–May except Saturdays and Mondays. Although the mansion has opulent touches (an indoor pool, a tiled private barbershop, a gilded Steinway grand piano, and an organ hidden by silk-paneled walls), the real attractions are the greenhouse and gardens.

The Grand Prix of Canada

If Oshawa is the commercial car capital of Canada, Mosport to the north has become synonymous with auto racing. The Canadian Grand Prix has been held on its ten-corner 2½-mile wooded circuit. On race weekends, expect crowds of up to 50,000.

Highway 401 west brings you past the mammoth nuclear power station at Pickering into Toronto. Many towns of the surrounding area (like Newtonville, Uxbridge, Sutton, Aurora, Cheltenham, Caledon) are known to antique collectors as great places to browse. Others, like Bradford in Holland Marsh, are farming and produce centres. Farther out from Toronto are small cities: Orillia, Barrie, Midland, Guelph and Kitchener.

Barrie, a thriving city of 44,000, is situated on the shores of Lake Simcoe, less than an hour's drive from Toronto. Barrie is another lake-oriented town. In winter, it attracts ice fishermen and, at its Winter Carnival, ice motorcyclists, dog sledders, and other winter-sport sensation seekers. The town offers straw hat theater at the Gryphon Theatre, floodlit harness racing at Barrie Raceway, and lakeside regattas.

Highway 27 leads you to other local attractions: scenic caves and a summer slide at Collingwood, Ontario's largest ski center. Indian crafts and pioneer artifacts on exhibition at the Simcoe County Museum and an old log house next door. At Shanty Bay you can see an unusual rammed-earth construction church built in 1838.

Leacock and Orillia

At the turn of the century Orillia, Barrie's sister city at the junction of Lakes Simcoe and Couchiching, was a flourishing resort drawing regular vacationers from as far away as Memphis, Tennessee. Humorist Stephen Leacock immortalized Orillia's golden years in *Sunshine Sketches of a Little Town,* still recommended reading for ramblers through small-town Ontario. Leacock is buried at Sutton, in St. George's Church, along with novelist Mazo de la Roche. You can visit Leacock's summer home, a lovely white colonial-style house off Highway 12B, from June to September in Orillia. Children might prefer the falcon and hawk shows at Golden Creek Game and Bird Farm, Hwy. 11, South Sparrow Lake Rd., daily in summer.

North of Orillia, the gentle landscape changes to the granite-and-pine scenery of the Canadian Shield. You are in Muskoka, a resort region whose population triples in summer. Among Muskoka's sights are Santa's Village (at Bracebridge, open all summer); the 40-foot totem pole on Canoe Lake (a memorial to artist Tom Thomson, who disappeared here half a century ago), and Muskoka Pioneer Village at Huntsville.

Gravenhurst, a holiday town on Lake Muskoka, is the birthplace of Norman Bethune, a Canadian doctor who treated Mao Tse-tung's army of peasant revolutionaries and became a hero in the Peoples' Republic of China. Visitors from China make a pilgrimage to Bethune's birthplace. North American visitors to Gravenhurst are attracted by summer theater at its restored Opera House, by lakeside Sunday evening concerts and by cruises aboard the *S.S. Segwun.*

Midland, on the south shore of Georgian Bay, is another pretty port town. It's also the site of the original French mission, Ste. Marie Among the Hurons. Jean de Brébeuf and five other Jesuit priests were murdered near here by Iroquois; they were canonized by the Catholic Church. Thousands of Roman Catholics attend the daily masses at Martyrs' Shrine, the twin-spired church which overlooks a reconstruction of the Jesuit mission. At Midland's Little Lake Park, a full-scale replica of a Huron village adjoins the Historic Huronia museum (late May to mid-October). The Wye Marsh Wildlife Centre on the outskirts of Midland is a 2,500-acre wildlife haven. Naturalists will guide you through (late May to Labour Day).

Home of the British Navy

At Penetanguishene, 3 miles northeast of Midland, British forces established a naval headquarters in 1817. Guides costumed as sailors and soldiers show you through officers' quarters, garrison reserve and work areas (late May to Labour Day). Boat cruises through (some of) the 30,000 islands of Georgian Bay are available from the foot of the Penetanguishene Town Dock. West of Penetanguishene, 9-mile-long Wasaga Beach stretches in the curve of Nottawasaga Bay. Despite record high water levels that have eaten away much of the beach, the town has many pleasures, including hot dog stands and pinball arcades. At Wasaga's Nancy Island Historic Site, you can watch the recreation of an 1814 naval battle in an electronic theater. The schooner *Nancy,* once called the most beautiful ship on the Great Lakes, was a vital supply ship in the War of 1812. In 1814, an American naval squadron discovered the *Nancy* hidden up the Nottawasaga River and set her on fire. Her charred hull and the complete wheelhouse of a Great Lakes steamer are among the artifacts displayed.

Collingwood, past the far end of the beach, is a major ski resort in winter. The Blue Mountain chairlift affords you a superb view of Georgian Bay, and there is a 3,000-foot sled-run descent. The Collingwood area is also noted for its Blue Mountain pottery (you can tour the pottery works) and for good antique hunting.

The next big port town along Georgian Bay is Owen Sound. Worth a visit are the County of Grey and Owen Sound Museum, with its Algonkian Indian and pioneer artifacts, and the Tom Thomson Memorial Art Gallery, featuring oils, drawings, and mementos of the influential Canadian landscape painter. Inglis Falls, 80 feet high, and a local beauty spot, can be reached by taking Highway 6 south from Owen Sound.

Georgian Bay is enclosed by the limestone spit of the Bruce Peninsula. Hikers on the 430-mile Bruce Trail which runs along the Niagara
escarpment from Niagara Falls to the Bruce Peninsula discover Tobermory, a tiny fishing village at the peninsula's tip. Here scuba divers can
explore old shipwrecks in the Fathom Five Provincial Park, or scram-
ble among weird, wind-shaped rock formations on Flower Pot Island.
From late April to Labour Day, a ferry connects Tobermory to
Manitoulin Island (discussed in "Exploring Northern Ontario"). The
trip aboard the 600-passenger *Chi-Cheemaun* ("Big Canoe") usually
takes less than 2 hours.

From Tobermory to Sarnia, Lake Huron washes against quiet beaches and resort towns like Port Elgin, Grand Bend (with excellent summer theatre at the Huron County Playhouse) and Goderich.
Kincardine has pipe band concerts in summer. At Douglas Point visitors can tour the Bruce Nuclear Power Development. At Sauble Beach
they can swim off a 7-mile strip of fine sand. Sarnia, which connects
via international bridge to Port Huron, Michigan, is an oil refining and
petrochemical center.

The Golden Horseshoe

The Ontario that lies between Lake Huron, Lake Erie, and Lake
Ontario is rich—economically, culturally and historically. The Golden
Horseshoe, stretching from Oshawa east of Toronto to Oakville,
Hamilton, St. Catharines and Welland around the western end of the
Lake, is where much of the cultural and economic wealth is concentrated. Oakville, just west of Toronto on the Queen Elizabeth Way (the
Golden Horseshoe's main artery), is one of the wealthiest communities
in Canada. The reason for Oakville's yachts and stately homes is the
presence of the Ford Motor Company. You can tour the Ford plant
(by reservation 416–845–2511). Bronte Creek Provincial Park, with its
bicycle paths, playgrounds, hiking trails and tractor tours and a restored turn-of-the-century farmhouse, is also worth a visit.

Hamilton is Canada's steel capital. The city's spectacular entrances
—over the Burlington Skyway from the north, or via the Royal Botanical Gardens on the south—make Hamilton proper look gritty and
industrial by contrast. But Hamilton is a tough, vital city with strong
traditions. Chief among them is steel manufacturing; the flaming stacks
of the Stelco and Dofasco plants dominate the bay area. But football—
the Canadian variety—is also a prominent feature of Hamilton life and
you can visit the Canadian Football Hall of fame in City Hall Plaza.
Surprisingly, Hamilton is also known for sweeping expanses of parks.
The Royal Botanical Gardens, in the city's north end, are comprised
of 2,000 acres of garden and parkland. Strollers stop for refreshment
at the Tea House overlooking the rock garden. Nearby, the marshes
and gullies of Cootes Paradise provide a sanctuary for wildlife. Dundurn Castle, built between 1832 and 1835 by a pre-Confederation
Canadian prime minister, Sir Allan Napier McNab, has gardens where
in summer you can enjoy concerts and children's theater. Hamilton's
McMaster University recently acquired the papers of 20th-century
philosopher Bertrand Russell. Tuesdays to Saturdays the Central
(farmers') Market bustles with local produce. Hamilton, which has
lived with the reputation of being a tough industrial city, is also proud
of its glittering performing arts center, Hamilton Place, home of the
Hamilton Philharmonic Orchestra, and its boutique and restaurant
shopping area, Hess Village.

St. Catharines, in the heart of Canada's fruit belt and major wine-
producing region, celebrates the harvest with the ten-day Niagara
Grape and Wine Festival at the end of September. An old city, it was

originally settled by the Loyalist troops of Butler's Rangers, who disbanded here in 1784. Loyalist nostalgia for Britain is also recalled in the Royal Canadian Henley Regatta, North America's largest rowing regatta which St. Catharines hosts in early August. The city has its attractions throughout the year, among them the locks of the Welland Canal and Rodman Hall's Art Gallery of graphics, sculpture, and tapestries at 109 St. Paul Crescent.

Tecumseh and General Brock

From St. Catharines, it's just a short drive to Queenston. Queenston, a typically pretty Southern Ontario town won its place in history during the War of 1812. The invading American forces landed here, securing Queenston Heights. British General Sir Isaac Brock scanned the Heights, and believing them to be held by only a handful of Yankee gunners, cried "Follow me, boys!" and led his cheering militiamen in a charge uphill. The attempt failed, and Brock, the hero who had captured American Forts Detroit and Michilimackinac, was shot and killed; the 210-foot Brock monument commemorates the place on which he fell. At one point in the 1812 War, the Stars and Stripes flew over the Heights. They were later recaptured by the British with the help of Indian allies. Brock, in spite of his uphill charge, was regarded as the most competent general on the British side, which may not speak well of their competence. Near Queenston stands the Laura Secord home, restored to the condition in which Secord left it on the night she warned British troops of a surprise attack by the Americans. North of Queenston, at Niagara-on-the-Lake, the critically acclaimed Shaw Festival continues to delight audiences each summer. Some visitors observe a pleasant tradition: to follow a matinee at the Festival Theatre with a stroll through town for ice cream or a drink in a sidewalk cafe. Niagara-on-the-Lake also features the Niagara Apothecary shop, a pharmacology museum where apothecary glass is lined up above oldfashioned walnut and butternut fixtures, outdoor cafés, curio shops, and the Niagara Fire Museum, where some of the fire-fighting equipment displayed dates back to 1816. Fort George (1797) and the McFarland House, a Georgian brick home built in 1800, both restored, are nearby on the Niagara Parkway.

Don't confuse the pretty 19th-century charms of Niagara-on-theLake with the commercial glories of Niagara Falls, once a honky-tonk paradise for publicity seekers (who tight-roped across the Falls or went over in barrels) and honeymooners, who watched hand-in-hand from the side. The honeymooners still come, but now it's to visit the Wax Museums, rock tunnels, boat rides, public gardens, 520-foot-high Skylon Tower with its revolving restaurant, and, of course, the magnificent white curve of the 186-foot-high falls themselves. At night the Falls are illuminated. Horseshoe Falls on the Canadian side is separated from the American Falls by Goat Island. Take the *Maid of the Mist* boat tour under the falls from 5920 River Road or descend by elevator and tunnel to the water's edge at 4330 River Road—it's called the Niagara Daredevil Gallery and is open May to October.

Just west of town sprawls Marineland and Game Farm at 7657 Portage Road. A mammoth roller coaster and an even bigger parking lot may be your first view of the place, but inside the gates lies an amusement park of considerable variety. Flower beds and picnic spots surround a petting zoo, kiddie rides, and a small stadium where several times a day a cast of dolphins and killer whales puts on a delightful show—frequently splashing members of the audience sitting near the front.

Old Fort Erie, with its drawbridge, moat and cannon, guards the town of the same name 20 miles south of Niagara Falls. Fort Erie also offers some of the best thoroughbred racing in Ontario. Crystal Beach on Lake Erie is a beachside carnival town locally famous for its Comet Coaster. Port Colborne handles the area's serious business. One of the world's largest single locks marks the southern end of the Welland Canal. In the country north of the Erie shore, tobacco is grown.

Home of Alexander Bell

Brantford, northeast of Port Dover on Highway 24, is named after Joseph Brant, the loyalist Mohawk chief who brought the Six Nations Confederacy into Canada after the American War of Independence. Brantford's other famous son is Alexander Graham Bell, whose homestead is open to the public all year, daily, except Mondays from Labour Day to mid-June. Canadians claim he invented the telephone and made his first long distance calls here in Southern Ontario.

Brantford is rich in Indian traditions. The oldest Protestant church in Ontario, Her Majesty's Chapel of the Mohawks, was built here in 1785. The Brant County Museum has an excellent collection of Six Nations artifacts. Another attraction is Chiefswood, the classical-style 1850's home of Mohawk chief George Johnson; now it's also a literary shrine to Indian poet Pauline Johnson. In June, at Alberton, near Brantford, there's a major archery competition. In August, the nearby reservation hosts a Six Nations Indian Pageant.

West of Brantford is London, a city of about 266,000. Chosen by Colonel (later Lieutenant Governor) John Graves Simcoe as Upper Canada's future capital, it has turned instead into an academic, industrial and commercial center. Despite its white-collar, conservative reputation, London contains a surprising range of attractions—including a pioneer-era brewery, a turn-of-the-century opera house that now houses a first-rate theater, a respected regional art gallery, and a river—named the Thames, of course—cruised by paddle-wheel boats. London's Fanshawe Park with its dam, reservoir, Pioneer Village, swimming, hiking, golfing and sailing is also on the banks of the Thames. Eldon House, built in 1834, has been restored and is open from March to November; if you have children, you should also drop by Ska-Nah-Doht, a reconstructed long house Indian Village (Longwoods Road Conservation area) and Storybook Gardens in Springbank Park, complete with miniature trains and Old MacDonald's Farm.

St. Thomas, south of London, is known as "the Garden City"—visitors to the floral displays and fountains of Pinafore Park and Waterworks Park can see why. Nearby, at the Southwold Earthworks, is the only double-walled Indian village and fort in Canada.

Each summer, the town of Stratford is transformed into one of North America's major theater capitals. Its company enjoys an international reputation for quality as British and American guest stars and directors join many of Canada's finest actors to present works from Shakespeare to Gilbert and Sullivan. Like London's Thames River, the name of Stratford's river, the Avon, echoes its English counterpart. Around noon in theater season, its swans are forced to compete for space on the riverbanks with picnickers. When the theaters open, the crowds disappear to enjoy some of the finest productions of Shakespearian drama in the world. Stratford is a pleasant old town with leafy streets, cafes, gift shops and an art gallery (on Romeo Street). Fryfogel's Inn (1844), 8½ miles east of Stratford on Highway 8, was a stop over for stagecoaches on the old Huron Road.

East of Stratford are the twin towns of Kitchener and Waterloo. Original German settlers have left their stamp on the city. Kitchener's ten-day Oktoberfest is an annual beer-drinker's bonanza. As well, the Seagram Museum—a showcase of the wine and spirits industries—is an architectural gem. More sober influences also appear in this region of Ontario. Here live many of Canada's Amish and Mennonites. Strict Mennonites still drive horse-drawn buggies; conveniences of all kinds are antithetical to their defiantly self-sufficient way of life. The baked goods, delicious preserves, and handicrafts of the Mennonite women are plied at the Kitchener Farmers' Market on Saturdays.

Travel west of Kitchener on Highway 401. And don't overlook the town of Aberfoyle as you turn off on Highway 6. Every summer Sunday, bargain hunters flock to Aberfoyle's flea market, where acres of stalls crammed with junk produce some surprising bargains.

Guelph, a lovely old gray stone university and manufacturing town, is dominated by the spires of its Church of Our Lady Cathedral (modeled after the Cathedral of Cologne). Guelph has a waterfowl park, an electric railway museum, a museum for poet John McCrae—most famous for his poem *In Flanders Fields*. McCrae also wrote the poem paraphrased by U.S. President Ronald Reagan in the wake of the Challenger shuttle tragedy: "They have slipped the surly bonds of earth to touch the face of God." Just north of Guelph is Elora. It's a picturesque village clinging to the sides of a limestone gorge. Many of its 19th-century shops have become antiques and crafts stores.

Highway 401 slices through southwestern Ontario. It takes just over three hours to drive the 185 miles from Guelph to Windsor on the border. It's worth a detour to visit Dresden (16 miles north of Chatham), where you can visit the home of Reverend Josiah Henson, a runaway slave. Henson, who founded Canada's first vocational school as a rehabilitation service for other runaway slaves, is supposedly the model of Harriet Beecher Stowe's *Uncle Tom's Cabin*. At any rate, that's what the Dresden slave museum is called.

The Route of Rum-Runners

Windsor is Canada's southernmost city. In the roaring twenties it was a main rum-running route to Prohibition America. Now it's a heavily industrialized center with close ties to Detroit's automobile industry but the verve of its earlier days lives on in its restaurants and nightclubs. The city has a good art gallery (with an excellent collection of Inuit art), an all-seasons harness raceway, and an abundance of industrial tours (Bell Canada, Ford Motor Company and the Hiram Walker Distillery, which produces Canadian Club rye). Don't miss the Sunken Gardens and fountains at Jackson Park. They are especially beautiful by night when the ornamental lighting goes on. François Bâby House, now the Hiram Walker Historical Museum, was the headquarters of the invading American army in 1812. It has been handsomely restored. South of Windsor, at Leamington, you can enter Point Pelee National Park. Canada's southernmost point, it is on the same latitude line as the French Riviera. It's a 4000-acre marsh and forest sanctuary for over 300 species of birds. You can explore the park by taking a boardwalk stroll for over half a mile past thick marsh grass to an observation tower. From here you can birdwatch in silence or enjoy the sunsets for which Point Pelee is famous. However, its most astoundingly beautiful sight probably occurs in late September when tens of thousands of orange Monarch butterflies rest at Point Pelee before migrating south.

EXPLORING NORTHERN ONTARIO

Northern Ontario, its inhabitants will proudly tell you, is a province unto itself. The line from Ottawa to Kenora that roughly separates north from south is over 1,000 miles long. Most of the land in between is the rugged, 2½-billion-year-old igneous and metamorphic rock-face of the Canadian Shield, dotted by innumerable freshwater lakes. People here are tough frontiersmen, descendants of native hunting peoples, French and English traders, Italian laborers, Scandinavian trappers. Northern Ontario's winters are long and harsh, its summers balmy, and its autumns brilliant. The area is a paradise for hunters, fishermen, and those who simply seek isolation and austere grandeur.

The best way to see northern Ontario is probably by canoe or bush plane. But to get there, you'll be taking the Trans-Canada Highway. Although the roadside scenery can be dazzlingly beautiful in fall, winter and spring, please bear in mind that many museums and other attractions are open only between May and September.

From the nation's capital, Highway 17 follows the route of the early *coureurs de bois* north beside the Ottawa River. The Ottawa is now a major logging river, down which log booms are transported from lumber camps to the pulp mills at Hull. At Almonte (a short detour south of Highway 17 on Highway 44), you'll find the Mill of Kintail, a picturesque stone mill dating from 1830. A century after it was built it became the home of sculptor and fitness educator Dr. R. Tait McKenzie, who designed the medallions that are awarded in Olympic Games. Many of his sculptures of athletes in action are displayed here alongside the older pioneer artifacts.

In summer, cottagers flock to Renfrew, 61 miles west of Ottawa on Highway 17. Children can play among life-sized fairytale figures at Storyland (open May to October), while their parents browse in the Cross Canada Craft Shop. Native crafts for sale include basketry, prints and carvings from the Golden Lake Reserve (July–August). Near Renfrew, from the Champlain Lookout, miles of surrounding woods and water are visible—but it isn't until you get to Cobden, 20 miles farther on, that your path crosses that of the 17th-century French explorer. Here a plowboy stumbled across what historians agree was Champlain's astrolabe, a navigation instrument his party lost almost four centuries ago.

Heading west, you'll pass Pembroke (its small zoo is open in summer), a Canadian Forces base at Petawawa, and Chalk River, site of one of the first atomic fission stations in the world. You can tour Chalk River's Nuclear Laboratories (open from June to Labour Day) and see an atomic reactor at work.

A hundred and ninety miles northwest of Ottawa lies Mattawa, a bilingual town of about 3,000 people. Mattawa was once a major portage on the Ottawa River route of the fur traders. The next big community is the city of North Bay. Each February, North Bay holds a dog-sledding, log-chopping, sleigh-riding extravaganza, the francophone community's Bon Homme Winter carnival. The rest of the year, its population of 50,000 is swelled by vacationers attracted to its golf courses, its mile-long sand beach, and its reputation for great hunting and fishing.

The Trans-Canada Highway splits at North Bay. If you follow the Superior Route, you'll find the landscape more beautiful, the food and lodging better. The rather barren Northern Route is slightly faster.

The Northern Route

Ninety miles north of North Bay, in 1903, Fred Larose threw his hammer at a passing fox and struck silver ore instead. He precipitated a Silver Rush now celebrated by the town of Cobalt in its 10-day-long Miners' Festival (held each July). Cobalt also has an excellent Mining Museum, open from May to October.

A tiny town just after Kirkland Lake illustrates the cocky independence of Northern Ontarians' character: during World War II, when patriots suggested Swastika change its name from Adolf Hitler's hated symbol to something more Canadian, inhabitants demanded, "Why? It's been ours longer. Let *him* get a new symbol."

Timmins, to the southwest, is Canada's biggest city—at least in area (1,260 square miles). Timmins is centered in one of the most productive zinc and silver regions in the world. You can tour the mines in summer months. Nearby, the town of Porcupine has an outdoor mining museum. Cochrane is a major outfitting center for sportsmen and the southern terminal of the famous Polar Bear Express.

The train from Cochrane is the only land access to Moosonee, 186 miles north on the shores of James Bay. The Polar Bear Express follows the route of a French soldier, the Chevalier de Troyes. In 1668, he led a tiny expedition up chilly northern rivers and captured the unsuspecting English trading post at Moosonee's twin city, Moose Factory, for the French Crown. The train from Cochrane takes you through Northern Ontario's fertile Clay Belt, past the massive Hydro Dam at Otter Rapids, through muskeg and forest. As you approach the Tree Line, the scraggly pine get smaller and smaller, then disappear.

Moosonee and Moose Factory, founded more than 300 years ago by the Hudson's Bay Company, are both genuine frontier towns, and some of their buildings date back to the early 18th century. St. Thomas Church has a beaded moosehide altar cloth and hymn books in the Cree language. Moosonee is also the gateway to Ontario's largest and most rugged park, Polar Bear Provincial. To visit it, you'll require a special permit and a chartered plane. Polar and black bear, moose, caribou, and Arctic fowl abound in the park.

West of Cochrane on Highway 11, are the pulp and paper town of Smooth Rock Falls, Kapuskasing (the Kleenex capital), and Hearst, a sawmill town with a lively French-speaking population. Hearst is also noted for moose hunting and for the pickerel (walleye) that teem in its local waters.

Hundreds of miles of forest, deserted beaches, and rock (where rockhounds can find agate, quartz, fool's gold, flint and fossils) dominate the scenery to Nipigon, where the Northern and Southern routes merge again. The last few miles of the Northern route skirt Lake Nipigon by tall cliffs. From the Nipigon River, west of the highway, 14-pound brook trout and 30-pound lake trout have been taken.

The Southern (Superior) Route

Take Highway 17 west from North Bay. As you approach Sudbury, the landscape becomes positively lunar—in fact, American astronauts trained for their moon walk here. (Outsiders joked that the astronauts were in town to see what the moon looked like; in fact, they came to see "shatter cones"—geological formations that resulted from a giant meteorite's crashing into the earth's surface here. The mineral wealth of the Sudbury Basin—nickel, cobalt, copper, gold, and platinum—is believed to be the result of that meteorite crash.) Sudbury is noted for its polluted air, the orange glow of molten metal on its slag heaps, and its nickel production (commemorated by a 30-foot-high Canadian 5¢ piece, made, oddly enough, of stainless steel). The walls of the magnificent new museum, Science North, with hands-on physics, biology, and geology exhibits, are hewn from solid rock.

West of Sudbury, the "World's Nickel Capital," is Elliot Lake, which styles itself the "World's Uranium Capital." Early in 1953, prospectors, geologists, and bush pilots flew a secret mission into the area. When news of their uranium discovery broke, Elliot Lake's mines were contracted to produce over a billion dollars' worth of the metal. A well-planned model community sprang out of the wilderness, but by 1960, when the uranium boom was over, it nearly became a well-planned model ghost town. Recent contracts with the Ontario government may revitalize operations.

You might also want to take a detour from Espanola (30 miles before Elliot Lake). From Espanola, you can head south to Manitoulin Island. "Manitou-lin" ("God's home") is the world's largest freshwater island and contains more than 100 lakes of its own. Tourists have been visiting it for more than a century, drawn by the island's miles of pastel birch forests, cliffs, and beaches. Manitoulin has pretty little port towns, waterfalls and beaches, restored jailhouses, lighthouses, churches and other museums, and two culturally active Indian Reserves. Both Ojibwa communities hold summer festivals. The area is rich in Indian history and artifacts. Archeologists working at Sheguiandah have suggested that Manitoulin was the site of one of North America's earliest native cultures.

Next is Sault Ste. Marie, a city of about 82,000 people. The "Soo" derives its name from *sault*, the French word for rapids—and from which the English expression "shoot the rapids" comes. Across the St. Mary River rapids lies Sault Ste. Marie's twin city, Sault Ste. Marie, Michigan; they're joined by the International Bridge.

Even before explorer Étienne Brulé arrived here in 1622, the rough water between Lake Superior and Lake Huron was a meeting and trading center for the Ojibwa Indians. For the early trader-explorers, the Soo was the gateway to the west. In fact one Frenchman, figuring he would shortly reach China, arrived here wearing "damask silk robes." On seeing the hilly wilderness around him, he discarded his finery for buckskin. The French explorer, Father Marquette, established a mission here in 1689. Later it became a major post of the Nor'West and Hudson's Bay Companies. During the War of 1812, the men of Sault Ste. Marie, with the crucial support of their Indian allies, aided in the capture of the American Fort Michilimackinac. In retaliation, the Canadian settlement was destroyed by American naval forces in 1814. The oldest stone house in Northern Ontario, the Soo's Ermatinger House, was built that year after the departure of the Americans by fur trader Charles Oakes Ermatinger for his Ojibwa wife, Charlotte Kallawabide, and has been beautifully restored.

The Soo locks on the Canadian side of the St. Mary River were built in 1870 to facilitate the movement of troops west to crush Louis Riel's second rebellion. The building of the locks increased the city's wealth in trade; following the discovery of iron ore in the Algoma district, the first steel plant in Ontario opened here in 1902. Italian laborers (paid at the rate of 17¢ an hour) were brought in to man the mills. Their descendants include talented local restaurateurs, delicatessen operators, and 1970s hockey great, Phil Esposito.

The Soo is the place to begin Northern Ontario's other great rail adventure, the Agawa Canyon Tour. You catch the Algoma Central Railway train before breakfast (in peak summer months, its served aboard the train), then settle back and watch as the train twists around great hulking hills and slopes of river gorges, rattles over 130-foot-high trestle bridges and then, four hours later, plunges into the Agawa Canyon. In winter, the frozen lakes are crisscrossed by the tracks of otters' slides across the ice. Waterfalls, frozen into white sheets, are streaked with yellow and blue mineral deposits. Trappers and skiers flag down the train and jump aboard. In autumn, the hillsides blaze with scarlet and gold. Any time of year, it's a colorful trip, and if you make arrangements with the railway personnel in advance, you can be dropped by the side of the track to head off into the bush and camp. The train makes the trip six days a week and will pick you up again at an appointed time.

North of the Soo is some of Ontario's most spectacular scenery as the highway winds along the hilly north shore of Lake Superior. You can find Indian pictographs painted on the rock north of Agawa Bay Scenic Lookout, in Lake Superior Park.

A huge statue of a Canada goose welcomes you to Wawa ("Wild Goose"), the center of Algoma's iron mining industry. Here you can tour the pit heads of abandoned mines, watch the Magpie River drop 75 feet at Magpie High Falls, or poke around the area's Indian sites. There's an outsized thermometer by the highway at White River (population 847) proclaiming it the most frigid spot in Canada where the mercury once fell to —72°F (or —58°C). Why White River should covet this uncomfortable distinction is unclear, but it's hotly (or coldly) contested by Hawk Junction, just north of the Agawa Canyon near Wawa. Incidentally, White River, Hawk Junction, and Chapleau (a bush pilot center) are all jumping-off points for sportsmen bound for the bush.

From scenic Aquasabon Gorge near Terrace Bay, it's another 130 miles to Thunder Bay. Before you arrive, take another detour to Silver Islet (41 miles east of Thunder Bay) and visit a tiny abandoned mining community. Once the site of one of the world's richest silver mines, it is now inhabited by cottagers. The old general store is open for business in summer.

Now the sight of Thunder Bay's huge grain elevators greets you. Thunder Bay is in the geographical center of Canada. A billion bushels of prairie wheat are stored here, then shipped east through the St. Lawrence Seaway. Across from the grain and freight bustle of Thunder Bay's waterfront looms Nanibijou, the Sleeping Giant. Nanabijou was the Ojibwayan Prometheus: he stole fire from heaven and gave it to man. The son of the West Wind and an ally of the Thunderbird, he was a handsome Indian brave. In fact, because of errors in the work of the 19th-century scholars who first began compiling the Nanabijou tales, the poet Longfellow confused his story with that of Hiawatha, incorporating elements of both into his epic poem.

Thunder Bay offers first-class skiing. At Big Thunder Jump there are 70- and 90-meter jumps—among the highest in the world. One of five local ski areas, Mount McKay, is operated by the Fort William Indian band. If you visit in summer, you can gather gemstones at an amethyst mine (open May to October), or visit Fort William, a fur-trading community which has been restored to its early 19th-century state. Costumed artisans work in the blacksmith's shop, candle factory, bakery, and canoe repair sheds. Thunder Bay's other attractions include Centennial Park's replica of a logging camp, a good local museum with Indian and early military artifacts, and Magnus Theatre, a vigorous regional company with a reputation for mounting successful original Canadian plays and musicals. The International Friendship Garden is really a series of gardens reflecting the characters of the city's different ethnic groups. Eighteen miles beyond Thunder Bay is Kakabeka Falls. According to legend, an Ojibwa princess once led a band of Sioux warriors over the 128-foot drop and saved her people. The site is a pleasant place to picnic.

At Shabaqua Corners the Trans-Canada Highway splits again. The Southern Route (Highway 11) goes through Atikokan, the access point to Quetico Provincial Park. Nearby, a whole lake has been drained and turned into open pit iron mines. The highway travels through forest, followed by a three-mile causeway which leapfrogs across Rainy Lake's islands to bring you into Fort Frances. Fort Frances has an official museum, a reconstructed trading fort at Pither's Point Park, and paper-making tours of the Boise Cascade Canada Ltd. plant.

After Nestor Falls, the water to your west is Lake of the Woods, whose shoreline twists through so many peninsulas and indentations that it is longer than the Lake Superior shore. This makes Lake of the Woods a natural site for the International Sailing Association Regatta (held every summer in Kenora).

At Kenora, the southern Highway 11 links up with the northern Highway 17 route. If you have followed 17, the way has been flatter, less scenic. But Highway 17, too, has its points of interest; for example, the bald eagles that abound near such bush pilot headquarter towns as Ear Falls, Sioux Lookout and Red Lake. At Kenora, ½-hour's drive to the Manitoba border, you're 1,280 miles west of Cornwall in eastern Ontario. Set your watch back an hour—you've traveled into a new time zone.

PRACTICAL INFORMATION FOR ONTARIO

HOW TO GET THERE. By air: Pearson International and Ottawa Uplands are major international airports, served by most international carriers as well as *Canadian Pacific* and *Air Canada*.

By car: Ontario is easily accessible by car. From Michigan in the southwest, the MacDonald-Cartier (Hwy. 401) connects Windsor, London, Toronto and Kingston. From New York State, the Queen Elizabeth Way connects Fort Erie and Niagara Falls with Hamilton and Toronto. Ontario is connected to Québec via Hwys. 401 and 417 (Québec Hwy. 40, which splits at Dorion). Hwys. 17 and 11 cross northern Ontario. Hwy. 17 exits via Manitoba, Hwy. 11 via Minnesota.

By train: Ontario is served by cross-Canada *Via Rail* service. There are rail connections with the United States at Windsor/Detroit and Fort Erie/Buffalo.

By bus: *Greyhound Lines* link Ontario to other provinces and to the United States.

ACCOMMODATIONS. Hotel rates vary greatly in Ontario. Bear in mind that rates will go up as you get closer to (or in) large cities and may depend on season, as well. Because it is such a large province, we are breaking it down by Southern Ontario and Northern Ontario. Most places accept the following major credit cards: American Express, MasterCard and Visa; others may also be honored. Not all establishments accept credit cards, therefore we suggest you call for information.

SOUTHERN ONTARIO

Southern Ontario has everything from lush resorts to serviceable motels to antique-filled inns. Information at time of writing has been checked, but vacationers are warned to inquire in advance about rates and services. Where hotels are unlicensed it is sometimes permissible to provide your own liquor. These categories indicate price only and are daily rates for two people in double occupancy. *Deluxe,* more than $110; *Expensive,* $80–$109; *Moderate,* $55–$79; *Inexpensive,* less than $55.

ALGONQUIN PARK. *Deluxe.* **Arowhon Pines.** Hunstville, POA 1KO (705–633–5661). On Little Joe Lake. Artist Tom Thomson was entranced by the scenery. So are the guests, but they also return for the beach, boat rentals and comfortable rooms and cottage units furnished in pine. Guides are available for longer canoe trips. Not licensed. Meals included in the price. The kitchen is first-rate—the owner's daughter is one of Canada's leading food and restaurant critics.

ALTON. *Deluxe.* **The Millcroft Inn.** John St., Alton, Box 89, ION 1AO (416–791–4422). A beautiful job of restoring an old mill overlooking the water. This 42-room inn has fireplaces in its rooms, an outdoor pool, golf, tennis, and first-rate food. Licensed. Very popular; reserve ahead.

APSLEY. *Inexpensive-Moderate.* **Harbour Hill Cottages.** Hwy 504, RR1. KOL 1AO (705–656–4652). High on a hill overlooking Chandos Lake, these simple, older housekeeping cottages offer good summer and winter accommodation for families. There's a sandy swimming place for kids; nearby golf, cross-country ski or hiking trails.

BALA. *Moderate-Expensive.* **Roselawn Lodge.** River St., Box 347, POC 1AO (705–762–3353). A pretty clapboard complex of lodge and cottages with a beach on the Moon River, boat rentals and an unlicensed dining room.
Trafalgar Bay Cottages. River Rd. (705–762–5266). A cluster of well-appointed cottages, some of them 2-story with log construction and balconies, overlooking two good swimming beaches on a quiet bay of the Moon River.

BANCROFT. *Moderate.* **Sword Motor Inn.** Hwy 62, KOL 1CO (613–332–2474). It's one of the larger complexes in the area with TV, licensed dining room, and golf nearby. On the property, facing the water, there's a beach, and an outdoor pool for folks who prefer less natural water.

BARRIE. *Inexpensive.* **Journey's End.** L4N 5M3 (705–722–3600). A 60-room motel, clean and good value.
Lake Simcoe Motel. 114 Blake St. L4M 1K3 (705–728–3704). 20 rooms on a beach with waterskiing.

BAYFIELD. *Moderate.* **The Little Inn.** Main St., Box 100, NOM 1GO (519–565–2611). Built around 1830, this Victorian hotel has guest rooms and a marvellous licensed dining room. It's handy to tennis, swimming, and walking by the Lake Huron shore.

BENMILLER. See **GODERICH.**

BRACEBRIDGE. *Deluxe.* **Tamwood Lodge.** R.R.1, POB 1CO (705–645–5172). Six miles west on Lake Muskoka, it's a rustic complex of lodge and cottages built of logs. An indoor pool substitutes for the beach on rainy days.
Moderate. **Holiday House.** 17 Dominion St. Box 1139. POB 1CO (705–645–2245). 17 rooms and outdoor pool, overlooking Muskoka River. Recommended for families.

BROCKVILLE. *Moderate.* **Best Western White House Motel.** R.R.1, K6V 5T1 (613–345–1622). Two miles east of Brockville on Hwy. 2, it's a quiet family-operated, riverside motel with outdoor pool, TV and good licensed dining room.

BURLEIGH FALLS. *Inexpensive—Moderate.* **Stricker's Cottages.** Hwy. 28, KOL 1KO (705–654–3547). Among the birches, you'll find eleven housekeeping cottages on a beautiful stretch of water.

CHATHAM. **Best Western Wheels Inn.** Hwy. 2, Box 637, N7M 5K8 (519–351–1100). The building is designed around indoor gardens. The licensed dining room has a Victorian flavor to it. The 354 rooms are air-conditioned and have

TV. There are indoor and outdoor pools, golf, and tennis. Families come here for exercise facilities as much as for relaxation.

COLLINGWOOD. *Moderate–Expensive.* **Blue Mountain Inn.** Blue Mountain Pk. Rd. L9Y 3Z2 (705–445–0231). The inn has been a popular spot for almost a generation of skiers. Its rooms are older, but have a rustic flavor.
Moderate. **Beaconglow Motel.** Hwy. 26 and RR3, Hwy. 26, L9Y 3Z2 (705–445–1674). Family units, whirlpool, outdoor pool, playground.
Heidelberg Inn. 461 Hume St. L9Y 1W8 (705–445–4280). Outdoor pool, buffet, 32 rooms.

CORNWALL. *Inexpensive—Moderate.* **Colonial Manor Hotel.** 1618 Vincent Massey Rd. K6H 5R6 (613–933–5100). A small motel set on treed lawns.

DORSET. *Moderate.* **Nordic Inn.** Hwy. 35, POA 1E0 (705–766–2343). The inn is owned by a Finnish family and specializes in cross-country skiing. It also has licensed dining facilities and rooms with TV.

ELORA. *Moderate—Deluxe.* **The Elora Mill Inn.** 77 Mill St., Box 218, NOB 1SO (519–846–5356). The roar of a waterfall is muffled in 22 tastefully renovated rooms, licensed dining.

FERGUS. *Moderate.* **The Breadalbane Inn.** 487 St. Andrew's St. N1M 1P2 (519–843–4770). The six rooms are small, but comfy places to read the Inn's tattered old copies of *Country Life.* Sauna, excellent dining room, splendid garden in which to sip your before-dinner apéritif.
Hotel La Placia. 280 Bridge St. N1M 1P6 (519–843–3115). A newly renovated country inn.

GANANOQUE. *Moderate—Expensive.* **Gananoque Inn.** 550 Stone St., Box 626, K7G 2A8 (613–382–2165). On the St. Lawrence River. A 90-year-old renovated mansion overlooking the water. There are 37 fully serviced rooms and 3 cottages.
Caiger's Resort. On the 1000 Islands Pkwy. KOE 1RO (613–659–2266). It is not elegant, but it is comfortable and the home-cooked food in the dining room is very good. This quiet resort caters to serious fishermen and their families.

GODERICH. *Deluxe.* **Benmiller Inn.** R.R.4, N7A 3Y1 (519–524–2191). Two mills on the banks of Sharpe's Creek have been expensively restored. The beamed sitting rooms look out on gardens or, in winter, cross-country ski trails. Reservations a must.
Inexpensive–Moderate. **Hotel Bedford.** 92 Courthouse Sq. N7A 1M7 (519–524–7337). An historic hotel which has been modernized, some of its 29 rooms have fireplaces.

HALIBURTON. *Expensive—Deluxe.* **Sir Sam's Inn.** Hwy. 18, Eagle Lake, KOM 1MO (705–754–2188). The only thing wrong with this lovely old mansion —once the private retreat of a corrupt federal minister of defense—is that it does not welcome children. Its dance floor, bar, beach, pool, and excellent retaurant are for adults only.
Inexpensive. **Haliburton Forest Reserve.** On Kennisis Lake. R.R. 1, KOM 1SO (705–754–2198). A lodge in the middle of the wilderness with spartan bunkhouse-type accommodation on the edge of Algonquin Park. Swimming, boat rentals and simple dining.

HALLS LAKE. *Moderate.* **Cherokee Resort.** R.R.2, Minden. KOM 2KO (705–489–2879). Well-equipped housekeeping cottages amid the pines overlooking a waterfront full of swimming kids and boaters. Good hiking, cross-country skiing nearby.

HAMILTON. *Moderate—Expensive.* **Royal Connaught Hotel.** 112 King St. L8N 1A8 (416–527–5071). Hamilton's grand old hotel has catered to conventions, football fans and honeymooners for several generations. Two hundred and eight rooms have TV and all facilities. Licensed lounges, dining room.

HUNTSVILLE. *Expensive.* **Billie Bear Lodge.** R.R.4, POA 1KO (705–635–2441). On Bella Lake. There are 6 rooms in the main log-built lodge, but Billie Bear's real charm is its 21 cottages with fieldstone fireplaces. Aircraft charter service and fly-in fishing are provided. Beach, boat rentals.

JONES FALLS. See **RIDEAU LAKES.**

KINGSTON. **The Prince George.** 200 Ontario St. K7L 2Y9 (613–549–5440). A real find, this renovated 100-year-old hotel overlooking the waterfront has antique pine in the rooms, balconies, and saunas, and a good restaurant.

KITCHENER. *Moderate.* **Valhalla Inn.** King St., Box 4, N2G 3W9 (519–744–4141). Indoor pool, 130 rooms, and a superb brunch make this a favorite stopping place for families enroute to the Stratford Festival.
Walper. 1 King St. N2G 1A1 (519–745–4321). The grand old Walper is open again, its 111 rooms newly renovated.

LONDON. *Moderate.* **Golden Pheasant Motel.** Hwy 22, R.R.5, N6A 4B9 (519–473–4551). 40-plus rooms, near Storybook Gardens and Indian reserve.
Inexpensive. **Rainbow Motel.** Southdale Rd. R.R. 1, N6A 4B5 (519–685–3772). An outdoor pool, golf nearby, and 23 quiet rooms. It's rated very highly among travelers to the area.

MAGNETAWAN. *Moderate.* **Woodland Echoes Resort.** Nipissing Rd. POA 1PO (705–387–3866). Magnificent scenery, a beach, and fireplaces in most rooms.

MEAFORD. *Moderate.* **Fisherman's Wharf.** 12 Bayfield St. NOH 1YO (519–538–1390). Overlooking the docks. Good restaurant, close to public beach. Small.

NEWBORO. *Expensive.* **Stirling Lodge.** General Delivery, KOG 1PO (613–272–2435). On Hwy. 42 in town. A hotel since the 1830s, it has a huge verandah with gliders; the stone hotel overlooks the Rideau Canal Trails.

NIAGARA FALLS. *Moderate—Expensive.* **The Brock Sheraton Hotel.** 5685 Falls Ave. L2G 3K6 (416–357–3090). A popular place to stay, with an outdoor pool, golf, babysitting services, licensed dining room and TV in its 248 air-conditioned rooms.
Inexpensive—Expensive. **Michael's Inn.** 5599 River Rd. L2E 3H3 (416–354–2727). Overlooks Niagara Gorge and Rainbow Bridge. Pubs on the premises are popular. Its 130 rooms have air conditioning and TV, and there's an indoor pool.

NIAGARA-ON-THE-LAKE. *Moderate—Expensive.* **Prince of Wales,** 6 Picton St. LOS 1JO (416–468–3246). An old hotel, renovated with real charm—tasteful graphics, ornate wallpapers, a comfortable elegant lounge and dining room, and TV in its 94 rooms.
Moderate. **Oban Inn.** 160 Front St. LOS 1JO (416–468–2165). From the Oban's spacious front porch you can gaze out over the Niagara River and Lake Ontario. It's a gracious old small-town inn with good dining facilities and modern conveniences (TV, air conditioning, convention facilities).
Moderate. **Moffat Inn.** 60 Picton St. LOS 1JO (416–468–4116). An 1835 inn has been renovated with flower gardens and fireplaces; 22 rooms.

NORMANDALE. *Inexpensive.* **Union Hotel.** R.R. 1, Vittoria. NOE 1WO (519–426–5568). Just 3 guest rooms with quilted rugs and antiques; a big verandah in front and home-cooked meals in the dining room. Reservations are important.

PETERBOROUGH. *Moderate.* **Red Oak Inn.** 100 Charlotte St. (705–743–7272). Grouped around a solarium with swimming pool are 183 rooms. Also whirlpool and sauna facilities. Good for families.

PICTON. *Expensive–Moderate.* **Isaiah Tubbs Inn.** R.R. 1, West Lake Rd. (613–393–5694 or 800–267–0525). A country inn turned resort, located on acres of woods, with a heated pool and gym.

PORT CARLING. *Expensive.* **Clevelands House.** On Lake Rosseau, Muskoka Rd. POB 1GO (705–765–3171). Golf, outdoor pool, rooms with TV, a licensed dining room known in the area for its good food and service. Tennis and boating are specialties. It's an older resort on spacious grounds.

PORT DOVER. *Inexpensive.* **Erie Beach Hotel.** Walker St. NOA 1NO (519–583–1391). You're in a time warp here, lost in the early 1950s decor, with the honkytonk midway and beach just out the front door. 18 rooms, real charm.

RIDEAU FERRY. *Expensive—Deluxe.* **Hotel Kenney,** in town. KOG 1HO (613–359–5500). In Jones Falls on Whitefish Lake. There's a view of the locks from the licensed dining room, an outdoor pool, boat rentals, babysitting, 37 rooms with TV, and one cottage. The setting is especially pleasant.
Inexpensive. **Rideau Ferry Inn,** in town. KOG 1WO (613–267–2152). Near Perth on Big Rideau Lake. The view through the colonial-style licensed dining room adds to the middle-aged clientele's enjoyment of this comfortable resort's features: outdoor pool, natural shoreline, boat rentals, guides available for fishing expeditions, and 16 rooms, 3 cottages with TV. Readers report that the dining room's grasp sometimes exceeds its reach.

STRATFORD. *Expensive.* **The Jester Arms.** 107 Ontario St. N5A 3HI (519–271–1121). 107 Ontario St. A small hotel wiht lots of charm. Pub attached.
Expensive. **The Raj.** 123 Church St. (519–271–7129). An elegant bed-and-breakfast owned by a graduate of the Art Institute of Chicago, who has filled it with Victorian and East Indian antiques. Reservations a must.
Moderate—Expensive. **Victorian Inn.** 10 Romeo St. N. N5A 5M7 (519–271–4650). Only one block from the Festival Theatre, it overlooks a parking lot. But beyond lie a golf course and the Avon River. The lounge has a small fireplace and there's also an indoor pool and sauna. Reservations essential in Festival season.

TOBERMORY. *Moderate.* **Tobermory Lodge.** Harbour Rd. NOH 2RO (519–596–2224). Lodge rooms or semi-detached chalets. Modern, well-appointed, with outdoor pool, by scenic Tobermory Harbour.

WASAGA BEACH. *Moderate.* **Hotel Waldhorn.** Mosley and 32nd Sts. LOL 2PO (705–429–4111). Welcome to Bavaria West. The fact that the rooms are adjacent to a popular beer garden and a highway mean it's not peaceful; but its 21 rooms are well-equipped and just a short stroll from the world's largest freshwater beach.

WINDSOR. *Moderate.* **Ivy Rose Motel.** 2885 Howard Ave. N8X 3Y4 (519–966–1700). A large comfortable motel with 69 rooms and an outdoor pool.

YOUNG'S POINT. *Inexpensive–Moderate.* **Old Bridge Inn.** Hwy. 28 at the locks (705–652–8507). Four of the 10 guest rooms overlook the water. Attractively renovated rooms do not have private baths. Good restaurant attached.

NORTHERN ONTARIO

Although there are modern and even deluxe accommodations available in northern Ontario's larger centers, many communities can only promise you comfortable clean quarters—no frills such as air conditioning and television. Remember, many tourists bring their own accommodation, *i.e.,* camping gear, with them. The categories used in this survey are price categories only. They are for double occupancy: *Deluxe,* more than $90; *Expensive,* $65–$89; *Moderate,* $55–$64; *Inexpensive,* less than $55.

ALBAN. *Moderate—Expensive.* **Hotel Beausejour.** Hwy. 64. POM 1AO (705–857–2193). Licensed dining room gets lively on weekends. 8 rooms, 6 cottages on French River.

ATIKOKAN. *Expensive—Deluxe.* **Camp Quietico.** Hwy. 11 POT 1 CO (807–929–2266). 7 rooms, 8 cottages; beach on Eva Lake. Excellent fishing, spring and fall bear hunts.
Moderate. **Perch Lake Resort.** 2 km (1 mi.) west of Hwy. 11 on Perch Lake Rd. POT 1CO (807–597–2828). Six housekeeping cottages with fireplaces overlook a beach on Perch Lake.
Inexpensive. **Hillcrest Resort.** 35 km (22 mi.) east on Hwy. 11. POT 1CO (807 929 3441). On Duncan Lake, it has a beach, boat rentals and guides. Five housekeeping cottages open May to October.

BLIND RIVER. *Moderate—Expensive* **North Shore Motel.** 6 km (4 mi.) north on Hwy. 555, Lake Duborne Rd. POR 1B0 (705–356–2249). Bavarian atmosphere, licensed dining lounge plus an indoor pool, sauna, 25 air-conditioned rooms with TV and 2 cottages.
Inexpensive. **Old Mill Motel.** Hwy. 17, POR 1B0 (705–356–2274). With a downtown location right on the waterfront.

BURKS FALLS. *Moderate.* **Pickerel Lake Lodge.** Pickerel Lake Rd. POA 1CO (705–382–2025). Eleven rooms, 11 cottages with fireplaces. It's a pretty setting and handy to a beach. Hunting and fishing packages available.

CALLENDAR. *Moderate–Expensive.* **Sunset Cove Lodge.** Hwy. 654, turn onto Sunset Cove Dr. POH 1HO (705–752–2820). German cooking, fireplaces, big sandy beach.

COCHRANE. *Moderate–Expensive.* **Northern Lites Motel.** Hwy. 11, POL 1CO (705–272–4281). One of the most popular places to stay overnight if you are bound north on the Polar Bear Express. 41 rooms, TV. Forty-one rooms have private bath, air conditioning, TV. There's golf nearby.

DEEP RIVER. *Inexpensive.* **Moore's Lodge and Motel.** Hwy. 17, KOJ 1PO (613–584–2861). Hwy. 17. 14 waterfront cottages on the Ottawa River.

EAGLE RIVER. *Deluxe.* **Lindmeier's North Shore Lodge.** Hwy. 594, POV 1SO (807–755–2441). Fly-in to Eagle Lake. Rustic décor in the main lodge and 20 cabins. Dining facilities plus a complete outdoor program: boat rental, beach and guides available for hunting and fishing expeditions. European Plan available.

ENGLISH RIVER. *Moderate.* **Meade's of English River.** Hwy. 17, POT 2YO (807–0120). Fourteen rooms and 7 cottages overlooking the river. Dining room, boat rentals, guided fishing trips.

ESPANOLA. *Moderate.* **Clear Lake Inn.** Hwy. 6, POP 1CO (705–869–1748). 13 rooms and a beach on the lake.

FORT FRANCES. *Moderate.* **The Fisheries.** Hwy. 11 to Armstrong Rd. P9A 3M6 (807–481–2534). Six cottages, with fireplaces, by Rainy Lake. Hunters and fishermen are the main customers.

FRENCH RIVER. *Moderate.* **Hartley Bay House.** POM 1AO (705–857–2038). Home-cooked meals and 10 cabins with fireplaces.

IGNACE. *Inexpensive.* **Cobblestone Resort.** Hwy. 17, POT 1TO (807–934–2345). On Raleigh Lake. Seven cottages are built of round stones—the construction is quite unusual. There are also 24 rooms, a coffee shop, a beach and boat rentals.

KAPUSKASING. *Inexpensive.* **Rufus Lake Rainbow Lodge.** Fergus Rd. P5N 2Y5 (705–337–1299). 7 cottages on a beach.
Two Bridges Motel. Hwy. 11, P5N 2Y5 (705–335–2281). 23 rooms. A popular stopover for people taking the Polar Bear Express. Wheelchair access.

KENORA. *Moderate–Expensive.* **Travel-Inn Resort Motel.** Hwy. 17 east, P9N 1K2 (807–468–3155). Its 34 air-conditioned rooms have TV's and there's a licensed dining room, outdoor pool and indoor pool and sauna.

MATTAWA. *Moderate–Expensive.* **Breton's Motel.** Hwy. 17, POH 1VO (705–744–5536). 14 rooms and a dining room open 24 hours—a clean comfortable stop for all-night travelers on the Trans-Canada Highway.

MORSON. *Moderate.* **Buena Vista Resort.** Hwy. 621, POW 1MO (807–488–5652). On Lake of the Woods. Five rooms, 7 cabins with air-conditioning, dining, beach, boat rentals.

NESTOR FALLS. *Inexpensive–Moderate.* **Nestor Falls Motel.** Hwy. 17, POX 1KO (807–484–2223). Overlooking Kakabikitchiwan Lake (also known as Little Pine Lake), beach nearby.

NEW LISKEARD. *Moderate.* **Breault's Motor Hotel.** Hwy. 11, POJ 1PO (705–647–7357). French-Canadian wood furniture in lobby. Indoor pool, sauna, whirlpool. Dining room and cocktail bar. Rooms have color TV.

NORTH BAY. *Moderate.* **Sunset Park Motel.** 641 Lakeshore Dr. P1A 2E9 (705–472–8370). On a secluded beach on Lake Nipissing, the hotel is still within walking distance of shopping.

SAULT STE. MARIE. *Moderate–Expensive.* **Best Western Water Tower Inn.** 360 Great Northern Rd. P6A 5N3 (705–949–8111). 153 rooms, sauna, indoor pool, babysitting, fireplaces in rooms.
Moderate–Expensive. **Empire Inn.** 320 Bay St. (705–759–8200). A pool, sauna, and whirlpool in this modern motor hotel make it popular with business travelers. Close to the Agaw Canyon Train.

SIOUX NARROWS. *Moderate–Expensive.* **Rod and Reel.** Hwy. 71, POX 1NO (807–226–5240). Six rooms, 10 cottages overlooking a beach by Whitefish Bay. Fireplaces

SMOOTH ROCK FALLS. *Moderate.* **Moose Motel.** Hwy. 11, POL 2BO (705–338–2777). Its 30 rooms with private bath and TV don't seem remarkable, but the proprietors are scrupulous and thoughtful.

SUDBURY. *Moderate–Expensive.* **Peter Piper Inn.** 151 Larch St. P3E 1C8 (705–673–7801). Some of its 45 rooms have private sauna. Good licensed dining room, central location; "the Prime Minister's Suite," too.
Moderate. **Cassio's Hotel.** 1145 Lorne St. P3E 4S8 (705–674–4203). Thirty-six rooms, hearty restaurant, facilities for wheelchairs.

TEMAGAMI. *Moderate.* **Scandia Inn.** Hwy. 11, POH 2HO (705–569–3644).

THESSALON. *Expensive.* **Melwel Lodge.** Melwel Rd. P0R 1LO (705–842–2141). Fourteen miles northeast on Big Basswood Lake, the big, rustic lodge with its good dining facilities plus 11 comfortable cabins with TV and fireplace look out on a beach and boating facilities. Guided trips available. American Plan.

THUNDER BAY. *Expensive.* **Red Oak Inn.** 555 Arthur St. P7E 5R5 (807–577–8481). One hundred eighty-two rooms with indoor sauna, near airport, routes to skiing. Regarded locally as the best restaurant, businessman's and family hotel.

Ramada Inn Prince Arthur. 17 N. Cumberland St. P7A 4K8 (807–345–5411). Nicely renovated old railway hotel. View of Thunder Bay's harbor. Inuit prints in comfortable rooms. Central, too. Great restaurant attached.

TIMMINS. *Moderate.* **Ramada Inn.** 1800 Riverside Dr. P4N 7J5 (705–267–6241). One hundred twenty rooms with TV, air conditioning, indoor pool, licensed dining room, babysitting.

WAWA. *Moderate.* **The Wawa Motor Hotel.** 100 Mission Rd. POS 1 KO (705–856–2278). Eighty rooms with TV, coffee shop, licensed dining room, fireplace. Ten log cottages accommodating 12 guests. Indoor pool and sauna.

HOW TO GET AROUND. By car: An excellent road map with index on top is available at Tourist Information Offices. Twenty-four-hour road condition information is available at (416) 235–1110 and could be vital in winter driving conditions. U.S. drivers' licenses are valid in Ontario, but you should bring your owner's registration or copy of rental contract. The U.S. AAA is affiliated with the Ontario Motor League, which has offices in 28 centers across the province. Speed limits: 60 mph or 100 km./hr. on freeways; 50 mph or 80 km./hr. on two-lane highways; 30 mph or 50 km./hr. in urban areas. Also bear in mind that many gas stations close at 7 P.M. and on Sundays. And that wearing seatbelts in automobiles is compulsory for all passengers for whom belts are available. Infants must be strapped into car seats.

The Trans-Canada Highway crosses Northern Ontario. Major links are Highways 11 (from Toronto) and 417 (from Montréal).

By train: *Via Rail* operates all across the province. In addition, the *Ontario Northland Railway* connects Cochrane to James Bay and the *Algoma Central Railway* serves the Algoma District north of Sault Ste. Marie. The *Polar Bear Express* connects Cochrane with Moosonee.

By bus: *Voyageur Colonial, Trailways* and *Gray Coach* are among the major carriers in Southern Ontario. *Gray Goose* and *Ontario Northland Transportation Commission* cross the north.

By air: *Air Canada* and *CP* fly intraprovincially. Northern Ontario is serviced by *Air Canada* which serves North Bay, Sudbury, Sault Ste. Marie, Timmins. *NorOntair, Austin Airways, Transair* and *Bradley Air Service* fly into smaller communities and fishing and hunting resorts. *Bush pilots* may be hired in northern centers like Ear Falls, Chapleau, Fort Frances, Hearst, North Bay and Temagami.

FACTS AND FIGURES. The name *Ontario,* adopted in 1867 when the province joined the Confederation, is an Iroquois word which means "the shining waters" or "beautiful lake." The provincial flower is the white trillium. The Provincial Coat-of-Arms is a green shield with three maple leaves surmounted by the Red Cross of St. George. Above the crest stands a black bear; the sides are supported by a moose and a deer. Beneath the shield is a scroll bearing the provincial motto; *Ut Incepit Fidelis Sic Permanet* ("Loyal she began, loyal she remains"). The Provincial capital is Toronto. The population of Ontario is over 8,900,000. The province covers 412,582 square miles.

Ontario's winters can be extremely cold in the north to cool in the extreme south. Its summers are warm, but in the north temperatures drop after sunset.

TOURIST INFORMATION. The central clearing house of tourist information is the *Ministry of Tourism and Recreation.* In Ontario you may contact its Ontario Travel division, Queen's Park, Toronto, Ontario M7A 2R9 (telephone: 416–965–4008). Call during business hours, Monday to Friday.

Travel Information. In *Southern Ontario,* Ontario Travel Information beside Hwy. 400 Northbound at Barrie is open year-round. So are travel information offices on Brookdale Ave. in Cornwall, at 5355 Stanley Ave. in Niagara Falls, at 110 Park St. E. in Windsor, at the Garden City Skyway and QEW in St. Catharines and at Bluewater Bridge in Sarnia.

In *Northern Ontario,* there are travel information offices open all year in Fort Frances, 400 Central Ave. and Sault Ste. Marie at 120 Huron St.

Year-round travel information centers are open from 8:30 A.M. to 4:30 P.M. (4 P.M. Saturdays), later in summer.

Ski information is available from the *Ontario Ski Resort Association,* 124 Milner St., Willowdale, Ontario M2P 1B3, and from *Ontario Travel,* Queen's Park, Toronto M7A 2E5. Up-to-the-minute snow condition reports are available from Central Ontario (705–726–0932) or Central and Southern Ontario (416–963–2992). The *Canadian Ski Instructors Alliance* supervises most ski instruction in Ontario; most areas are patrolled.

Fishing and **hunting** enthusiasts flock to Ontario for its muskie, trout, goose, pheasant, moose, deer, and bear. Fishing and hunting are seasonal however. For fishing information contact the *Sport Fisheries Branch, Ministry of Natural Resources,* Queen's Park, Toronto. Information about fishing in lakes which may be polluted is available at *Ministry of the Environment,* Information Services Branch, 135 St. Clair Ave. W., Toronto M4B 1P5. Fishing and hunting maps available from *Ministry of Natural Resources,* Public Service Centre, Toronto M7A 1W3. Hunting licenses are available at over 40 Natural Resources District offices or can be purchased at some sporting goods stores or outfitters. Hunting dogs from the U.S. need certification from a licensed vet of rabies vaccinations at least 30 days before entering.

Campers can obtain camping permits at the entrance to Ontario's 128 provincial parks. To plan a trailer trip contact the *Ministry of Tourism and Recreation,* Queen's Park, Toronto M7A 2R9. There are size limits for trailers traveling on Ontario highways (maximum length, car and trailer, 65 feet). The Province of Ontario has a Human Rights Code, providing for fair and equal treatment of all visitors by public resorts, restaurants, hotels, motels, beaches pools, parks, and campsites. Contact *Ontario Human Rights Commission,* 400 University Ave., Toronto (telephone: 416–965–6841) for inquiries.

TIME ZONES. Ontario spans two time zones. West of Thunder Bay, the province runs on Central Standard Time. East of and including Thunder Bay, it is on Eastern Standard Time (the same zone as New York City, Miami, and Montréal).

BUSINESS HOURS AND HOLIDAY CLOSINGS. Bank hours are 10 A.M. to 3 P.M., Monday–Thursday, 10 A.M. to 5 P.M. on Friday. Many banks offer self-serve, automated tellers for simpler transactions; customers with clearance use special cards to gain access to accounts. Many post offices are open 9–5 and on Saturday mornings (smaller ones run by one person may close for lunch). Small shops close Sundays and Mondays. Larger shops are open 6 days a week, and Thursday nights until 9. Some government ministries are on staggered hours (8:30 A.M. to 4:30 P.M. or 9:30 A.M. to 5:30 P.M.). Almost *nothing,* except convenience stores, restaurants, theaters, and specially designated tourist areas, opens in Ontario on Sundays.

SEASONAL EVENTS. January–February: Cross-country skiers compete in the *Muskoka Loppet* (snow conditions permitting). In mid-January *Niagara Falls* holds its Winter Festival (broomball, arts and crafts, Old Timers Hockey Tournament). In late January or early February, the Canadian Ski Jumping Championships are held at Thunder Bay. From *Sault Ste. Marie,* the Agawa Canyon snow train takes you into a wilderness of frozen waterfalls and forests hung with icicles. The *Bon Soo Winter Carnival* (Sault Ste. Marie)

opens with a torchlight parade, followed by polar bear swimming, sled dog races at the end of January and early February.

North Bay holds its Winter Fur Carnival in late February. Near the end of the month *Georgian Peaks* hosts the Pontiac Cup ski races.

March: *Kenora* holds winter festivities.

April: Join in a "sugaring-off" at the Algoma Maple Festival, *St. Joseph's Island*. Or take a hayride into the maple bush at the *Elmira* Maple Syrup Festival (mid-April) then sample syrup and pancakes or Mennonite cooking.

May: Early in May the *Niagara region* bursts into bloom, and you can celebrate spring at the Niagara Falls Blossom Festival (parades, ethnic dances, sporting events). *Ottawa's* flowers follow later—three million tulips set off the Ottawa/Outaouais Festival of Spring (fireworks, flea market, regattas). Early in May, the *Guelph* Spring Festival schedules first-class opera, concerts, films, and art exhibitions. *St. Catharines* throws an ethnic extravaganza—its Folk Arts Festival in late May. The Shaw Drama Festival season begins at *Niagara-on-the-Lake*. The last Saturday of the month, the Mennonite communities near *Kitchener-Waterloo* and *New Hamburg* sell food and crafts for overseas relief. The 24th of May, Queen Victoria's birthday, is celebrated with fireworks.

June: *Welland* celebrates its Rose Festival with parades, boat races and fiddle contests. The internationally acclaimed *Stratford* Shakespearean Festival begins its season. *Fort Frances* hosts a "Fun-in-the-Sun" festival, bathtub derby, water skiing contest, parade and horse show.

July: Across Ontario, fireworks mark the national Canada Day (July 1). It's also the beginning of the *Windsor/Detroit* International Freedom Festival and *Ottawa's* cultural Festival Ottawa. At *Mosport,* the Canadian Grand Prix brings world championship motorcycle racers to Southern Ontario.

August: Participants have the most fun at the *Lake of the Woods* International Sailing Regatta (beginning of the month). *Cobalt's* Miners Festival (first week in August) features French-Canadian step-dancing and a canoe marathon. Also check the Bancroft Gemboree, in *Bancroft,* and the Wikwemikong Pow Wow on *Manitoulin Island.* There's sweet music at *Shelburne's* Canadian Open Old Time Fiddlers' Contest—antiques, crafts and a parade, too. A forest amphitheater in the *Brantford Reserve* turns into the Six Nations Pageant mid-August weekends. The Glengarry Highland Games in *Maxville* are the largest such celebration in North America. The Royal Canadian Henley Regatta, the largest rowing course in North America, is seen in *St. Catharines* in early August. A second Highland Festival is held in *Fergus* later in the month.

September: Clowns and musicians stroll among the crowds and industrial exhibits at *London's* century old Western Fair. Wine-tasting parties headline *St. Catharines'* Grape and Wine Festival (mid-September) along with steel bands, ethnic dancing, art displays and parades. The *Algoma* Arts Festival brings music, theater and displays to Sault Ste. Marie (mid-September to the end of the month). The Canadian Grand Prix for formula cars is run at *Mosport.*

October: Gemutlichkeit Uber Alles: oompah bands, beerhalls and dancing at Oktoberfests in *Kitchener-Waterloo* and *London.* The Canadian Thanksgiving weekend is the best time to enjoy the *Muskoka* and *Haliburton* Cavalcades of Colour (parades and fairs throughout the regions).

November: Early in November, 240 varieties of flowers bloom at Parkwood's Fall Flower Show (*Oshawa*).

December: Celebrate an Old Tyme Christmas at *Port Hope* (antique show, carolling, sleigh rides). Victoria Park blazes with lights for skaters and strollers in *London's* Winter Wonderland. And colored lights illuminate *Niagara Falls* and its usual winter formation, the Ice Bridge.

 TOURS. There's a wide choice of tours to show you Ontario—everything from cultural sorties into the theaters of Festival country to whitewater kayak trips down wild northern rivers. All tour operators must be registered with the Ministry of Consumer and Commercial Relations. For a complete list of tours available throughout the province, write to the Ministry of Tourism and Recreation, Queen's Park, Toronto, ON M7A 2R9. We mention a few examples of what's available.

Packages available include weekend specials from Windsor to Toronto or Niagara Falls which include rail transportation, accommodation, and Continental breakfast. Contact *Can-Am Travel Ltd.,* 3000 Town Centre, Suite 2340, Southfield, MI 48075 (313–353–9740 or 800–482–0629).

Gray Line Sightseeing Tours, 610 Bay St., Toronto, ON M5G 1M5 (416–979–3511), runs tours around Toronto plus excursions to the Kitchener Mennonite Farmers' Market or Georgian Bay's 30,000 islands.

All Star Tours Ltd., Box 24, 1400 Bishop St., Cambridge, ON N1R 6V5 (519–623–3030), runs 3-day package trips to enjoy Ottawa's tulips and cruise the Ottawa River.

P.M.C.L. Tours, 475A Bay St., Midland, ON L4R 1L1 (705–526–5438), takes you through Huronia to Midland and includes a visit to the Martyr's Shrine, recently visited by the Pope, and Sainte Marie among the Hurons, a fascinating recreation of an early French settlement.

You can cruise Trent Severn Waterway by private cruiser houseboats. *Go Vacations,* 129 Carlingview Dr., Rexdale, ON M9W 5E7 (416–674–1880), rents houseboats and motor homes.

Ontario has two well-known, well-loved rail adventures. The *Algoma Central Railway,* 212 Queen St. E., Box 814, Sault Ste. Marie, ON P6A 5X8 (705–254–4331), operates year-round. There is a day-long trip through spectacular Agawa Canyon in the summer, a snow tour in the winter, and a 2-day trip to Hurst year-round on varying schedules. Among operators organizing tours on the railway are: *Denure Tours Ltd.,* 71 Hount Hope St., Lindsay, ON 9V 5N5 (705–324–9169), offering fall color tours through the Agawa Canyon, and *Algoma Holiday Tours,* 212 Queen St. E., #101, Sault Ste. Marie, ON P6A 5X8 (705–942–2113), with package tours including accommodation. You can also deal directly with the railway.

Ontario Northland Railway, 195 Regina St., North Bay, ON P1B 8L3 (705–472–4500 or 800–268–9281) runs the Polar Bear Express, an unforgettable experience, from Cochrane to Moosonee. Aside from the barren grandeur of the tundra and muskeg scenery and the curiosities of Moose Factory and Moosonee, the excitement of the trip is often provided by local hunters, trappers, and Métis who spin stories to pass the time aboard the train. *Overland Tours,* Box 100, Agincourt, ON M1S 3C6 (416–291–7334), is one of several operators organizing tours on the express.

For the adventurous: *Wildwaters,* 119 N. Cumberland St., Thunder Bay, ON P7A 4M3 (807–345–0111), leads one-two–week canoe trips into Northern Ontario as far as Hudson Bay and sea kayaking trips on Lake Superior. *Goway Travel Ltd.,* 40 Wellington St. E., Toronto, ON M5E 1C7 (416–863–0799), offers wilderness, overland, and canoe trips for young adults.

NATIONAL PARKS. Boat services from Honey Harbour take you to the 50 islands of *Georgian Bay Islands National Park* in the heart of historic Huronia. There is also boat access from Tobermory, only 3 miles from the weirdly-shaped rock pillars of Flowerpot Island. Scuba divers can explore the wrecks of sunken lake vessels, while naturalists will enjoy the abundance of wildfowl (wood ducks, black ducks, coots, mergansers and scaup), and wildlife. The fishing is good and many of the beaches deserted. Admission is free. Camping is by permit only and is limited to 14 days. Contact the Superintendent, Georgian Bay Islands National Park, Box 28, Honey Harbour. Open May through September.

Point Pelee National Park is the southernmost mainland point in Canada—on the same latitude as Northern California or the French Riviera. Four thousand acres of rolling dunes, virgin forest, and marshland attract thousands of visitors each year—from naturalists to over 350 species of migratory birds. In late September Point Pelee is a stopover for thousands of brilliant Monarch butterflies. The sight is dazzling. A boardwalk winds 3,100 feet into the marsh to a 20-foot observation tower—or you can rent rowboats and canoes to discover the park's wildlife. In summer a park naturalist is on duty to answer your questions about the woodland nature trail. Maps, sketches, and displays offer further explanations at the Park Nature Centre. Point Pelee Park is six miles south of Leamington. No family camping; group camping for organizations. Contact Superintendent, Point Pelee National Park, R.R.1, Leamington. Open from April to Labor Day.

Pukaskwa National Park, 725 square miles, is the largest national park in Ontario. Near Marathon, on the north shore of Lake Superior, the park encompasses Tip Top Mountain, whose 2,120-foot elevation makes it one of the highest points in the province. The landscape is typical of the Canadian shield: rugged islands, wild rivers and lakes where caribou, moose, deer, mink, otter, marten, lynx, bobcats and wolves roam. Archeologists are also investigating the sites of prehistoric pit culture Indian inhabitants. The park is still being developed. For information apply to the Park Superintendent, Pukaskwa National Park, P.O. Box 550, Marathon, Ontario P0T 2E0. Season: from June through September.

St. Lawrence Islands National Park consists of 17 islands, 80 rocky islets, and a mainland base. At the Mallorytown Landing (between Kingston and Brockville) you can explore the Nature Exhibit or the Brown's Bay wreck exhibit before boarding a boat for the islands. The park offers a naturalist program during summer months to help you discover the wildlife of the area—ring-billed gulls, blue herons, a variety of ducks. Boats can be rented, water taxis hired, or docking facilities are available. Serviced camping at Mallorytown Landing and Central Grenadier. Campgrounds open mid-May to mid-October, park open all year. Contact: Superintendent, St. Lawrence Islands National Park, Box 469, R.R. #3, Mallorytown, Ontario K0E 1R0.

PROVINCIAL PARKS. The province operates 128 parks; 98 have campsites available on a first-come, first-served basis. Permits are available at park entrances for a fee. Some parks have facilities for mobile homes; all have some form of sanitation provisions. Frequently there are sheltered cooking and dining areas. Electric power costs a small additional sum at those parks which offer it. Riders of motorcycles and trail bikes must wear helmets and keep to the main park roads. Some provincial parks ban liquor in spring.

Algonquin Park was first designated a protected area in 1893. It is still a virtually untouched wilderness. Although Hwy. 60 crosses the southwest corner of the park, most of its 2,955 square miles of forest and lake are accessible only by canoe or on foot. On Hwy. 60 near the East Gate Entrance, the Logging Museum illustrates lumber activities in the area. Canoe outfitting, stores, restaurants and some excellent lodgings are available within the park. Camping, fishing. Admission charges. Season mid-May through mid-October. For information, apply Superintendent, Algonquin Provincial Park, Algonquin P.O., Ontario.

Arrowhead: 2,162 acres near Huntsville on Hwy. 11. Year-round camping, swimming, hiking, snowshoeing, and cross-country skiing. Spectacular lookouts at Big Bend, Stubb's Falls.

Batchewana: 418 acres north of Sault Ste. Marie on Hwy. 17. Day-use only (no camping). One mile of sandy beach along Lake Superior.

Blue Lake: 873 acres on Hwy. 17 west of Dryden. Fishing, swimming, 70-mile canoe loop. In spring the park blooms with moccasin flowers.

Bon Echo: 16,417 acres on Hwy. 41 north of Napanee. Camping facilities range from drive-in spots with showers to remote campsites accessible only by canoe or overnight hike. Swimming, fishing. Granite cliffs 375 feet high at Mazinaw Lake, which can throw back a loud echo, give the park its name. Indian rock paintings.

Chutes: 270 acres on Hwy. 17 west of Espanola. By the Aux Sables River waterfalls. Swimming, hiking, trout fishing nearby.

Craigleith: Small (126 acres) shoreline park on Hwy. 26 in Blue Mountain area near Collingwood. Swimming is dangerous because of rocks, where fossils and formations delight geologists.

Darlington: 360 acres. Hwy 401 east of Oshawa. Camping and picknicking. Duck hunting and waterfowl weekends in fall.

Devil's Glen: 150 acres. Take Hwy. 24 south from Collingwood. The ¾-mile Mad River Trail connects with the Bruce Trail.

Esker Lakes: 7,680 acres on Hwys. 11 and 66 north of Kirkland Lake. Many lakes afford good canoe routes. Beach, hiking trails, rock-collecting.

Ferris: 503 acres on Hwy. 30 and on Trent Severn Waterway near Campbellford. Campgrounds in open and wooded areas which form part of the large Peterborough Drumlin Field.

Fitzroy: 435 acres on Hwy. 17 west of Ottawa. Swimming at sandy beach, boating, angling for smallmouth bass and yellow pickerel. Small pioneer cemetery.

Holiday Beach: 521 acres on Lake Erie. Take Hwy. 18A south from Windsor. Good beach, picnic grounds, some camping. Stocked fish pond. Waterfowl hunting in season. Canada goose sanctuary nearby.

Inverhuron: 545 acres. Take Hwy. 21 south from Port Elgin. Day-use only (no camping). Trails, beach, swimming, boating. Site of prehistoric Indian camps and pioneer town.

Ipperwash: 201 acres. Take Hwy. 21 north from Sarnia. Children's programs, family campgrounds, sandy beach.

Ivanhoe Lake: 3,000 acres. Take Hwy. 101 west from Timmins. One of the best sandy beaches in northeastern Ontario. Swimming, boating.

Lake-on-the-Mountain: 256 acres. Take Hwys. 401/14/33 to Prince Edward County. Day-use only, no swimming. A spring-fed lake with a mysterious source and a spectacular view.

Lake Superior: Large (512 square miles) and accessible via Hwy. 17 north from Sault Ste. Marie. Camping and picnic grounds and Indian rock paintings near Hwy. 17. Interior camping accessible by canoe or on foot.

Long Point: 849 acres. Take Hwy. 3 south from Tillsonburg then 59. Sandy beach, picnic area, bass fishing, viewing of waterfowl migration.

MacLeod: 200 acres. Take Hwy. 11 east from Geraldton. This former gold-mining area is ideal for viewing moose and collecting rocks. Swimming, fishing for pike and pickerel (walleye).

Marten River: 1,034 acres. Take Hwy. 11 north from North Bay. Boating, game fishing, children's wading pool. Sawmills and exhibit of early logging industry nearby.

Missinabi Lake: 157,334 acres. Take Hwy. 11 from Chapleau, then north. Rough access road, bad for trailers. Indian rock paintings, large lake with good beaches.

Neys: 8,150 acres. Take Hwy. 17 west from Marathon. In spite of the fine beach, Lake Superior is cold for swimming. Fishing is excellent. Good hiking, great lookouts. Caribou herd in the park.

Pancake Bay: 1,151 acres on Hwy. 17 north of Sault Ste. Marie. The swimming is cold at good Lake Superior beach, but rainbow trout attract fishermen.

Petroglyphs: 2,500 acres on Hwy. 28 north of Peterborough. Day-use only (no camping). Hiking trails to waterfall, large concentration of prehistoric Indian rock paintings.

Point Farms: 582 acres. Take Hwy. 21 north from Goderich. Enjoy barn dances, sing-alongs, horseshoe tossing in the restored barn or try out the fitness trail, baseball diamond, and beach.

Polar Bear: 9,300 square miles, accessible only by charter aircraft from Moosonee (250 miles to the south). All provisions and equipment must be carried in. There are no means of outside communication. Access points and travel areas within the park have been chosen to minimize disturbance of abundant wildlife—polar bear, black bear, red fox, Arctic fox, wolf, bearded seal, moose, caribou, Arctic loon, Canada goose, snow goose, northern phalarope. The weather varies from the surprisingly balmy odd day in summer to severe winters. Chilling sea fog frequently engulfs the land and has discouraged tree growth near coast of Hudson Bay. Polar Bear Provincial Park is open in summer only; to get a special permit of admission, contact the District Manager, Ministry of Natural Resources, P.O. Box 190, Moosonee, Ontario P0L 1Y0.

Presqu'ile: 2,170 acres. Take Hwy. 401 west from Cobourg, then Hwy. 30. Migratory birds displayed in small museum, and good birdwatching in spring and fall. Picknicking, boating and swimming on long sandy beach.

Quetico: 1,750 square miles of wilderness accessible via Dawson Trail Campgrounds, Hwy. 11, 30 miles east of Atikokan. Quetico is a favorite for canoeing. Local outfitters offer comprehensive service. Game fishermen are attracted by lake trout, northern pike and pickerel (walleye), bass and some sturgeon. Resident mammals include black bear, moose, wolves and white-tailed deer. A natural history museum outlines the park's flora and fauna. Season: June through September. Contact: District Manager, Ministry of Natural Resources, Atikokan, Ontario.

Rondeau: 11,456 acres. Take Hwy. 3 west from Leamington, then Hwy. 51. At the interpretive center, the Carolinean forest (walnut, sassafras, and tulip trees) and the park's animal inhabitants are explained in exhibits. Swimming, boating, cycling, hiking, waterfowl hunting in season.

Sandbanks: 1,802 acres. Take Hwy. 401 to Trenton, then Hwy. 33. A 5-mile sandbar between Lake Ontario and West Lake. Spectacular dunes, beach, swimming, and boating.

Serpent Mounds: 70 acres. Take Hwy. 7 to Peterborough then south to Keene. Campsite overlooks Rice Lake. Archeological exhibits, prehistoric Indian burial mounds, fishing, access to Trent-Severn Waterway.

Wasaga Beach: 344 acres. Take Hwy. 27 then 92. Day-use only (no camping). Museum of the Upper Lakes on Nancy Island outlines naval history, local battles of War of 1812. Swimming, cross-country skiing, boating.

Windy Lake: 293 acres. Take Hwy. 144 north from Sudbury. Long beach, swimming, boating, fishing, golf course adjacent to park.

This is only a partial list of Ontario's parks. There are also recreational areas operated by 38 conservation authorities, and 3 parks commissions, plus roadside picknicking, camping, and public recreation centers.

For more information: a complete list of parks, campsites, and picnic grounds is available from: Provincial Parks Information, Whitney Block, Queen's Park, Toronto, Ontario M7A 1W3 or contact a District Tourism Office.

FARM VACATIONS AND GUEST RANCHES. Ontario has many working farms that take in guests. Some specialize in holidays for children, others attract adults with their home-cooking, crafts facilities or proximity to cultural events and country auctions. For up-to-date information listing host farms, write to the *Ontario Vacation Farm Association,* R.R. 2, Vankleek Hill, Ontario K0B 1R0.

Specific questions, reservations and vacation arrangements can only be made directly with your host. Usually a nonrefundable deposit of 10 per cent is payable when you make your reservation. Meals are usually included with rates and at most farms children over 12 are charged the adult rate. Your host may prefer to limit the consumption of alcohol on his premises. That's his perogative —check with him.

CHILDREN'S ACTIVITIES. Children seem to be happiest when they're participating with their bodies as well as their minds. In Ontario you can provide them with a wide range of activities, happily exhausting and pleasantly instructive. Some provincial parks run special youth programs or offer children's playground facilities.

At **Bronte Creek,** 25 miles west of Toronto, there's a farm where children can see and touch the donkeys, sheep and cows or play in a hay-filled barn, fully equipped with ropes to swing on. There is also a huge swimming pool and nature trails through a forest. Here you can take them on a tractor or wagon ride through the park, or introduce them to turn-of-the-century life at the park's *Spruce Lane Farm.* You're welcomed into the farmhouse by the smell of baking bread or the strains of the parlor organ.

There's a children's playground and snack shop at *Blue Mountain Scenic Caves,* 5 miles west of **Collingwood** on Hwy. 26. The caves, once the home of an early Huron tribe, can also be reached by chairlift.

More caves outside **Eganville** (21 miles south of Pembroke); the *Bonnechere Caves* are full of fascinating fossils and stalactites. While you're in the area, Ontario's only *"magnetic hill"* is at **Dacre,** at the junction of Hwy. 132 and 41. Be ready for questions about the behavior of your car. If you point your car downhill and release the brakes, it will roll back up.

There are special facilities for children at some provincial parks, including *Ipperwash* on **Lake Huron.** Take Hwy. 21. Farther north on Hwy. 21, at *Point Farms,* a restored barn, a baseball diamond, and a horseshoe pitch keep children happy and busy.

Rushing River east of **Kenora** in the heart of Canadian Shield country has a playground; so does *Sioux Narrows* to the south, where you can also show children Indian pictographs or take them boating on *Lake of the Woods.* **Wasaga Beach** is a superb stretch of sand for running, jumping or flopping down in the sun. Drivers get there via Hwy. 27 and 92. Nearby is a sound and graphics recreation of the War of 1812 at the *Museum of the Upper Lakes.*

Provincial parks with "themes"—bird-watching, Indian culture, skills programs in camping or canoeing—have visitor service centers which provide interpretive information about the parks. For example, *Sibbald Lake* and *Balsam Lake* have star-watches; there's a 38-foot replica of a Canoe d'Maître and a small fur trade museum at *Samuel de Champlain Park,* while at *Quetico* and

Point Pelee, naturalists are on duty to answer your child's questions about the wildlife.

At **Rockton,** 11 miles northwest of Hamilton, there's a different sort of park—the *African Lion Safari,* which also features an elephant compound, an ostrich pen, and a pet's corner where children can pet the pets. *Marineland and Game Farm* in **Niagara Falls** (open all year) is famous for its trained dolphins. Its summertime aquarium show also stars a killer whale.

Niagara Falls appeals to grown-up children; small ones will also get a kick out of climbing into raincoats for the *Maid of the Mist* boat trip. The boat passes directly in front of the Falls. Helicopter rides over the Falls cost $10 per person for a 12-minute trip. Children under 3 are free. If they are accompanied by adults, children can get into Niagara Falls' Panasonic Centre and Marine Museum free. High-speed elevators whisk visitors to a tower 665 feet above the Falls, where a wax museum and dining rooms compete with the spectacular view. Niagara Falls' other joys for kids include waxworks, fantasy museums, and a *Daredevil Hall of Fame* in the City Museum.

Niagara Falls doesn't have a monopoly on fantasy; another version of it is available at **Niagara-on-the-Lake.** Children's events are included in the *Shaw Festival.* The town has a fire equipment museum, including 19th-century engines, which will fascinate kids.

There are many children's gardens throughout Ontario. In **London's** *Storybook Gardens,* children can take rides in a miniature train or meet fairytale characters and live animals of Old MacDonald's Farm. **Stratford's** *Shakespeareland* features 60 large-scale replicas of famous buildings from England's Stratford-upon-Avon (open mid-May through September). **Ivy Lea,** near Gananoque has its *Never Never Land* (Victoria weekend in late May–Labor Day in September); more fairytales come to life at **Renfrew's** *Storyland.* Here a telescope on top of the lookout provides a great view of the surrounding woodlands. In **Dorset,** there's a 100-foot *observation tower* from which children can scan the Haliburton Highlands. Not far away, in **Bracebridge,** they can take miniature trains, paddle wheel boats or covered wagons through *Santa's Village.* These parks' seasons run from mid-June to September.

Windsor's *Bob-Lo* is a large amusement park with 40 rides and attractions. On an island in the Detroit River, it is accessible by ferry. Canada's largest amusement park is outside **Fort Erie** at *Crystal Beach.* The gigantic Comet Coaster is among 40 rides featured. *Old Fort Erie,* nearby, has the original ditches, drawbridge and guns. Guards in 19th-century uniforms drill daily.

Meanwhile, at the other end of the province, the soldiers are also drilling at **Kingston's** *Old Fort Henry.* While you're in the area, your child can experience the life style of a century ago at *Upper Canada Village* in **Morrisburg.** Oxcarts, miniature trains or horse-drawn boats take them past the church, bakery, smithy, and even an old hotel where meals are served.

Older children will never forget a trip through the glowing red and black interior of a *steel plant.* In **Hamilton,** *Stelco* guides visitors through the stages of steelmaking. (Visitors must be 15 or older.) Telephone in advance to confirm your visit. If they enjoyed that, they may also take themselves on a tour of the *Hershey Chocolate plant* in **Smiths Falls,** or a 7½-hour tour, with lumberjack lunch, through the *Abitibi pulp and paper* operations in **Iroquois Falls.** (Children under 8 not allowed, but babysitting services are available.)

There are *Indian pow-wows* in **Sumer, Brantford** and **Manitoulin Island.** Another great way to introduce native culture is to visit **Ska-Na-Doht,** a reconstructed Indian Village with 70-foot long bark-covered long houses, or the timber palisaded *Huron Village* in **Midland.**

Sportsminded kids will get a kick out of visiting **Hamilton's** *Canadian Football Hall of Fame,* the *Hockey Hall of Fame* in **Toronto** and the *Canadian Ski Museum* in **Ottawa.** If they have ever asked you what a *gelandesprung* is, you can find out here.

 SUMMER SPORTS. In summer, Ontario lives out-of-doors. Campers, hikers, and naturalists find wildlife and the wide-open spaces that keep bringing them back. **Canoeing:** If you don't own a canoe, you can rent or buy one, along with all the other supplies needed for a trip. Complete outfitting services provide canoes, life jackets, camping and cooking equipment, food supplies, maps, fishing licenses and tackle, and guides. The canoeing season runs from the May thaw or breakup to the November freeze-up. Lists of outfitters should be available at regional tourism and Ministry of Natural Resources offices. Packaged canoe trips are also offered. Contact: *Algonquin Canoes Routes Ltd.,* Box 187, Whitney, K0J 2M0 (613–637–2699); *Algonquin Outfitters,* R.R.1 Oxtongue Lake, Dwight P0A 1H0 (705–635–2243); Bud Dickson's *Canoe Canada Outfitters,* Box 1810, Atikokan, P0T 1C0 (807–597–6418); or the *Outfittings Co-ordinator, National and Provincial Parks Association of Canada,* 69 Sherbourne St., Toronto (416–366–3494). Some provincial parks specialize in wild river routes.

Package holidays: Experienced bush pilots, usually flying prop planes capable of lake landings, provide a province-wide air service to take you to the best fishing and hunting spots. For further information, contact *NorOntair,* 195 Regina St., North Bay, Ontario, P0B 8L3, *Austin Airways,* Timmins Airport, Box 1160, or *On Air Ltd.,* Thunder Bay Airport, P7E 3N9.

Package fly-in holidays are also available and there are many excellent fly-in lodges from which to base your swimming, fishing, sailing, canoeing vacations. Hunting and fishing licenses are available at Natural Resources district offices.

Cycling: Some bicycle shops will rent cycles for cross-Ontario exploration, and as cycling becomes more popular, more metropolitan regions are providing cycling trails.

Horseback riding: There are over a hundred horseback riding establishments in Ontario, not counting the private pony and hunt clubs whose red-coated, blue-blooded members may flash across your trail in pursuit of fox. Among those establishments that provide horse rentals and trails: (in Central Ontario) *Skyline Tourist Park,* 920 Skyline Rd., Ennismore, near Peterborough; *Lakeview Farm* R.R. #3, Port Carling; *Rouge Hill Stables,* Port Union Rd. and Hwy. 2 on the beautiful Rouge Valley near Toronto; *Palomino Ranch,* Carlisle. In Eastern Ontario, similar facilities are available at *St. Alban's Stable,* Box 577, Brockville K6V 5V7 (613–342–6006). *Circle "N" Ranch,* R.R. #3, Pembroke. In Northern Ontario, *Wagonwheel Ranch,* R.R. #1, St. Charles, near Sudbury; *Rolling Valley Equestrian Centre* on Gordon Lake Rd. in Chelmsford; *Ferme d'Equitation,* in Hearst, and The Royal Ranch, R.R. #2, Timmins, all offer rentals and other services.

Golfing: There are over 300 golf courses in Ontario. Some larger public ones are *Ava,* in Brantford; *Tyandaga Municipal Golf and Country Club,* Burlington; *Lee* in Cochrane; *Kitchen Creek Golf and Country Club* in Fort Frances; *Chedoke Civic* in Hamilton; *Doon Valley* near Kitchener; *Thames Valley* in London; *Upper Canada* in Morrisburg; *Countryside* in Sudbury; *Chapples* in Thunder Bay.

Racing: Southern Ontario's two major drag strips are at Cayuga and St. Thomas, but Mosport, north of Bowmanville, is Canada's capital of car racing. The *Canadian Grand Prix* brings Formula I World Champions to the hilly, well-serviced woodlands of Mosport Park. Here fans can also enjoy *Can-Am* and motorcycle races on most weekends in summer and early fall. Stock car enthusiasts watch the rubber burn at Delaware International Speedway in London.

Horse-racing: The *Queen's Plate* is to Canada what the Kentucky derby is to the United States—venerable tradition and heady excitement. It kicks off the racing season at Toronto's Woodbine Racetrack in June. Other racetracks throughout the province are Ottawa's *Rideau Carleton,* the picturesque track at *Fort Erie* which opened in 1897; the modern, glass-enclosed *Flamboro Downs* near Hamilton; *Sudbury Downs;* Peterborough's *Kawartha Downs,* which holds standardbred racing virtually all year long.

Boating: St. Catharines' *Royal Canadian Henley Regatta* is one of North America's largest rowing regattas. Many yacht clubs run sailing schools in summer and often marinas will rent sailboats, powerboats, and water ski equipment.

Scuba diving: Local outfitters in Tobermory will equip you for scuba diving among Georgian Bay wrecks. For information on scuba diving call the *National Association of Underwater Instructors, Canada,* at 416–493–6284.

Professional sports: The recently established *Toronto Blue Jays* are members of the American Baseball League, and they are building up Ontario's appetite for pro **baseball,** especially after their terrific, near-pennant-winning season in 1985. **Football** has a longer tradition in this country. The *Hamilton Tiger Cats* and the *Ottawa Roughriders* were the stars of the Canadian Football League, recently eclipsed by the hard-working *Toronto Argonauts.* Strong semi-pro **soc-**

cer teams have sprung up in other centers, among them Hamilton, Kitchener, and Windsor.

Other sports: You can enjoy tennis, squash, table tennis, badminton, kayaking, scuba-diving or sky diving in Ontario if you've got the energy and the inclination. For more information, contact the *Sports Centre Inc.*, 1220 Sheppard Ave., E, Toronto telephone: 416 495–5000.

PRIVATE CAMPGROUNDS AND TRAILER SITES. There are over a thousand privately owned campgrounds and trailer sites. All are inspected and licensed by the provincial government or municipal authorities. For a comprehensive booklet listing private campgrounds, write to *Travel Information, Ministry of Tourism and Recreation,* Third Floor, Hearst Block, Queen's Park, Toronto M7A 2E5.

At private campgrounds daily rates vary depending on the facilities available. Although trailers' size is limited on Ontario highways (65 feet long including car), oversize permits are available from *Oversize-Overweight Permit Section,* Ontario Ministry of Transport and Communications, Queen's Park, Toronto, Ontario. Many provincial parks and private campgrounds have sewage and pump-out facilities.

HIKING TRAILS. Day and weekend hiking trips are becoming increasingly popular with Ontarians and visitors. On Saturdays and Sundays the trails can be relatively crowded with hikers, campers, picnickers, and naturalists. At all times, people are asked to remember that since many trails cross private property, you are only crossing it on the goodwill of the farmers.

Algonquin Park Highland Hiking Trail: A 22-mile loop with a shorter 11-mile loop, suitable for snow shoeing and cross-country skiing in winter, guides you through the woods of Algonquin Park. The park also features the Western Uplands hiking trail. Contact the Ministry of Natural Resources, Box 219, Whitney, Ontario K0J 2M0.

Arrowhead Park north of Huntsville has miles of cross-country ski trails, good for summer hikes.

The Bruce Trail: White blazes on trees, fenceposts, and rocks mark the trail. Blue blazes indicate campsites and lookouts. The Trail's 430 miles (680 km.) stretch along the limestone Niagara Escarpment from the orchards of Niagara Falls to the cliffs and bluffs at the end of the Bruce Peninsula. Write to: Bruce Trail Association, 33 Hardale Crescent, Hamilton, Ontario L8T 1X7.

Ganaraska Trail: A geologist's wonderland, the trail extends northwest from Port Hope to connect with the northeast section of the Bruce Trail. Through historic Huron, French, and English pioneer country, the trail's access points are marked by a brown arrowhead symbol on a white square. It's also ideal for cross-country skiing and snow shoeing. For information write to Ganaraska Trail Association, Box 1136, Barrie, Ontario L4M 5E2.

Grand Valley Trail: This trail, suitable for day hikes only, stretches 80 miles (128 km.) from the Scottish-flavored village of Elora through Mennonite country to Brantford, and the famous Mohawk's Reserve. There is overnight camping at Conservation Parks only. Contact Grand Valley Trail Association, Box 1233, Kitchener, Ontario N2G 4G8.

High Falls Hiking Trail: on Manitoulin Island, off Highway 6 north of the village of Manitouwaning. There are restrooms and picnic tables at the top and the landscape is spectacular. Also on the island is *Cup and Saucer Hiking Trail,* overlooking the North Channel, accessible off Highway 540. The trail is adjacent to the West Bay Indian Reserve, and features gorgeous views over the channel and eastward over Georgian Bay. There is also an adventure trail for the daring: it features narrow passes, ledges, and a chimney opening for slim hikers to squeeze through.

Rideau Trail: The trail stretches 241 miles (406 km.) from the marshes of Little Cataraqui near Kingston to the Chaudière Falls, Ottawa along the route of the historic Rideau Canal. Access points from the highway are marked with orange triangles. Blue triangles indicate loops and side trails. Contact the Rideau Trail Association, P.O. Box 15, Kingston, Ontario K7L 4V6.

Voyageur Trail: In the process of being constructed, this trail will stretch from Manitoulin to Gros Cap, west of Sault Ste. Marie. Three sections of the trail have been completed. For further information contact Voyageur Trail Association, Box 66, Sault Ste. Marie, Ontario P6A 5L2.

Other trails in Ontario include *Thames Valley Trail,* c/o Thames Valley Trail Association, 403 Lansing Ave., London, Ontario N6K 2J2; *Guelph Trail,* c/o Guelph Trail Club, Box 1, Guelph, Ontario N1H 6J6; *Quinte-Hastings Recreational Trail,* stretches 250 miles from Outlet Provincial Park to Lake St. Peter. Contact Quinte-Hastings Recreational Trail Association, R.R. #7, Belleville, Ontario K8N 4Z7.

 WINTER SPORTS. You can always pass a pleasant Ontario winter sipping hot cider by a roaring fire—but remember, there's also a world of Alpine skiing, cross-country skiing, snowmobiling, hockey, sleigh riding, ice-fishing, curling, even winter camping awaiting you outside. Don't forget these telephone numbers for up-to-the-minute snow condition reports: 416–963–2992 for alpine conditions and 416–963–2911 for cross-country.

Skiing: The Canadian Ski Instructors' Alliance standardizes the high quality instruction available at many resorts and slopes. Commercial slopes are patroled by the Canadian Ski Association. A complete list of Ontario's more than 400 slopes is available from *Ontario Travel,* Queen's Park, Toronto M7A 2R9. Major sites in the southern part of the province are near Ottawa, Collingwood, Huntsville, Barrie; major northern sites are at Kirkland Lake, Sault Ste. Marie, and Thunder Bay, which also features two of the world's largest (70- and 90-meter) ski jumps. Remember, 90 meters is about 300 feet—just watching the professional jumpers can be an exhilarating sport.

Cross-country skiing is becoming increasingly popular, and at many ski centers is complemented by snow shoeing and tobogganing facilities. Rented equipment and snacks are available at most centers. The *Muskoka Loppet* in early January is one of Canada's largest cross-country ski events.

Snowmobiling as a sport was invented here, and many international snowmobile races are held at Owen Sound and Lindsay (mid- to late January), and Eganville, Orangeville, and Jordan (February). For your protection the law requires that you wear a safety helmet whenever you board a snowmobile.

Winter camping, skiing, snow shoeing: Half of Ontario's parks remain open in winter for winter camping, skiing, and snow shoeing. Most are clustered in the southern part of the province. Write to the *Ministry of Natural Resources,* Parks Branch, Queen's Park, for a complete list.

Ice-fishing, people are discovering, can mean sitting comfortably in a stove-heated hut waiting for the trout, whitefish, perch, and pike to nibble. Major fishing centers are Lakes Simcoe and Couchiching (near Barrie), Lake Nipissing (near North Bay), Boshkung and Kennesis Lakes (near Haliburton), and Manitoulin Island.

Hockey: Winter is hockey time in Canada—*Toronto's Maple Leaf Gardens* is the place to catch the National Hockey League stars in action. When you watch the games of Ontario's Junior A Leagues you are probably watching the Wayne Gretskys and Phil Espositos of tomorrow—that's where they got started.

Ice skating: Most municipalities have skating rinks or natural facilities; among the most picturesque places to skate are Ottawa's Rideau Canal (stroking side by side with the civil servants), Toronto's City Hall Square, or Harbourfront by the lake, and London's Victoria Park.

Curling bonspiels are held throughout the province from December to February.

Racetracks are open in winter at *Windsor Raceway* (harness racing), London's *Western Fair Raceway* (harness), and Campbellville's huge *Mohawk Raceway.* For a list of winter carnivals, races, and events—don't forget the *Canadian National Sportsmen's Show* in March in Toronto—write to *Ontario Travel,* Queen's Park, Toronto M7A 2R9, or call (416) 965–4008 for information.

 MUSEUMS AND PUBLIC GALLERIES. Almonte: R. Tait McKenzie sculpted the athletes you see on Olympic medallions. He was also a great Canadian surgeon and the father of physical education in Canada. His words are displayed in the 1830's mill he restored and made his home, *Mill of Kintail Museum and Conservation Area* off Highway 29, north of Almonte. Open mid-May to mid-October daily.

Amherstburg: After the British evacuated Detroit in 1796, they constructed earthwork defenses and fortifications at Amherstburg's *Fort Malden.* The fort saw action in the War of 1812, and for years after continued to be Canada's main military base in the southwest. Open all year except December 25–January 1.

In King's Navy Yard visit the *Park House Museum,* the oldest (1799) house in the area. It was moved from Detroit to its present site and refurnished. The *North American Black Historical Museum,* adjacent to the Nazery AME Church (one of the first Black parishes in the area), is at 281 King St., west off Hwy. 3 (Sandwich St.). The museum contains old slave shackles, early farm implements, and songbooks.

Belleville: In the grandeur of a restored Victorian mansion you can browse through the *Couldrey Collection* of furniture and art, or pore over an unusual collection of lighting devices from prehistoric times to gas lamp days. *Hastings County Museum,* 257 Bridge Street, Belleville. Open all year daily, except Mondays.

Bowmanville: *Bowmanville Museum* (37 Silver Street) has a collection of century-old toys that will delight children of all ages. At the 1861 residence-turned-museum there are also displays of musical instruments, arts and crafts, and room after Victorian room of period furnishings. Open mid-April–mid-December, Tuesday–Saturday.

Brantford: At the *Brant County Museum,* the history of the Six Nations loyalist Indians Joseph Brant led to Canada after the American War of Independence comes alive. The museum also illustrates the lives of Alexander Graham Bell, the Mohawk poetess E. Pauline Johnson, and novelist Thomas B. Costain. Drop by 57 Charlotte St. It's open all year Tuesday–Saturday except holidays; May–Labour Day closed Mondays.

Base Borden/Barrie: The *Canadian Forces Base* at Base Borden is open to visitors all year, daily except Monday. Huge Allied Sherman Tanks and German panzers from World War II line the roads and there are more guns and vehicles at the museum. (Hwy. 90, west from Barrie.)

Cochrane District: The *Cochrane Railway and Pioneer Museum* displays model trains, photos and Indian and Eskimo handicrafts in old Ontario Northland and Canadian National Railway cars. Open mid-June to Labour Day, daily.

Cornwall District: Thomas Edison installed the electrical equipment you can see at the *United Counties Museum.* Settlers produced the maps, toys, and early local pottery. There are also Indian artifacts from the flooded Sheik Island site on display. Open May to October.

Other museums: The *Invarden Regency Cottage* is the finest Regency (1816) cottage architecture in the province. You'll find its 14 rooms on Hwy. 2 at Boundary Rd. (April–November). The *Living Museum and Indian Village* was built by the North American Indian Traveling College on Cornwall Island. Mid-May–September.

Elliot Lake: Models of uranium mines can be seen at the *Elliot Lake Mining and Nuclear Museum,* 45 Hillside Drive North, Elliot Lake. Open June to September, daily; October–May, Monday–Friday.

Elmira: Handmade doll costumes and antique dolls are on display at *The House of Dolls,* 28 South St. W. Open all year.

Guelph: The *University of Guelph Art Gallery,* open daily September to mid-July. In the permanent collection are over 400 items—paintings, graphics, and prints from 1800 to the present. *Halton County Streetcar and Electric Railway Museum,* 9 km. north of Hwy. 401 on Guelph Line. You can ride some of the old streetcars.

Hamilton: A gorget presented to a loyalist Mohawk chief (Joseph Brant) by an English king (George III) is among the Indian artifacts from 10,000 B.C. to the present day exhibited at the *Joseph Brant Museum,* Burlington. Open all year daily. Open Sundays in July and August only. A special children's collection of toys and dolls can be seen at the *Dundas Historical Society Museum,* 139 Park St. W. in Dundas. Open Monday to Friday. In Hamilton, check out the adults' toys at the *Canadian Football Hall of Fame,* City Hall Plaza. Open daily. Hamilton also has two art galleries. At 123 King St. W., the *Art Gallery of Hamilton's* permanent collection of Canadian, American, and European painters is worth a visit. Open all year daily except Mondays and statutory holidays. The *McMaster University Art Gallery* is noted for its excellent collection of German Expressionist prints. Monday to Thursday, closed Fridays and weekends. *Dundurn Castle,* a 19th-century mansion with adjacent gardens and aviary, is open all year, afternoons. On summer nights there is a Son-et-Lumière display. *Whitehern,* built in the 1840's, has been carefully restored to its upper-middle-class stuffy splendor. Ask the guide to tell you the story of the McQuesten family who lived here.

Haileybury: The *Temiskaming Art Gallery* concentrates on works by Northern artists. Open year-round, admission free. Call 705–672–3707.

Kapuskasing: *Ron Morel Memorial Museum:* More railway coaches, this time including steam engines and 19th- and early 20th-century railway memorabilia. Open mid-June–Labour Day, daily, afternoons.

Kenora District: *Lake of the Woods Museum* by Memorial Park houses Indian and pioneer artifacts. But the museum in **Ear Falls** has an intriguing collection of artifacts from pioneer bush pilot days, housed in an old log building. Open mid-May to September, daily.

Kingston: There are many museums in Kingston, among them Sir John A. Macdonald's home, *Bellevue House* on Centre St. Open all year daily, except holidays from October to April. The *Pump House Steam Museum* holds a collection of intricate machines, model engines, and two monster pumps, circa 1892. The museum is at 23 Ontario St, open June 15 to Labour Day, daily. *The Canadian Forces Communications and Electronic Museum* has equipment displays and a kit shop. At Vimy Barracks, Hwy. 2 E. At the *Royal Military College Museum,* the Douglas Small Arms and Weapons Collection is displayed. The Museum is located in the Martello Tower, Fort Frederick, and is open June to Labour Day. *Old Fort Henry* is a living museum, where infantry cadets perform daily drills and, Mondays, Wednesdays and Saturdays in July and August (weather-permitting), execute the colorful "Sunset Ceremonial." May 15 to October 15. The *Agnes Etherington Art Centre* on the old gray stone campus of Queen's University has circulating exhibitions on view. Open all year, daily except Mondays and holidays. It has also inherited part of the excellent Zacks collection of contemporary Canadian sculpture and nonfigurative art.

Kirkland Lake: Built in 1919, the Sir Harry Oakes Chateau now houses the *Museum of Northern History,* focusing on natural history, mining and local history. Open year-round. Call 705–568–8800.

Kitchener–Waterloo District: The little town of **Doon** on a wooded hilltop near Kitchener has its own school of fine arts. It also has the *Doon Pioneer Village,* open May to October. *Enook Galleries,* 16 Young St., features Indian and Eskimo prints. At the University of Waterloo, there's a *Museum of Games* —over 1,000, including Indian bone games and Japanese drinking games.

Lindsay: *Victoria County Historical Museum* features an apothecary shop, a toy store, a doctor's office, and early Canadian glass and oil lamps. May 24–Labour Day, daily except Mondays. Afternoons only.

London: *Eldon House* at 481 Ridout St. dates from 1834. In summer, its old garden is open, too. The *Labatt Pioneer Brewery,* 150 Simcoe St., shows early methods of beer-making. The *London Regional Art Gallery,* 421 Ridout St., is a beautiful modern structure overlooking the Thames River. It houses changing national and international exhibitions.

Markham: *Markham Museum* is located among 22 acres of restored buildings including the oldest church in the township of Markham. The museum occupies the old Mount Joy School and displays a collection of Indian and pioneer artifacts. On Hwy. 48 north of Hwy. 7. Open afternoons, Tues.–Sun., longer in the summer months after June 15. Call 416–294–4576.

Milton: *Ontario Agricultural Museum:* Over 25 buildings and displays show Ontario's rural and agricultural history. Open daily mid-May to Thanksgiving. At Hwy. 401, Interchange 320B.

Moosonee: *Moose Factory Museum Park:* This museum has been built on the site of an early trading post. A forge, a gun powder magazine, and Hudson's Bay Company exhibits chronicle the development of the 300-year-old trading center. Open June–October daily.

Morrisburg: *Upper Canada Village*'s more than 40 buildings make it a living museum. You can travel by oxcart to candlemaking or bread baking demonstrations, sample the atmosphere of early 19th-century churches and taverns, visit lovingly refurnished residences of the period 1785–1865. Open May 15 to October 15.

Niagara Falls: A 6 × 28 foot mural, "The Canadian Pioneer," and a 160-panel series, "The Passion of Christ," bring the sharp lines and vivid colors of Canadian master William Kurelek to the *Niagara Falls Art Gallery and Mu-*

seum. The five-level gallery also has changing exhibitions and art films. Queen Elizabeth Way. Open all year, closed Tuesdays. Admission charge.

Oshawa: Over 50 vintage cars, some Canadian-designed, are on display at the *Canadian Automotive Museum* (99 Simcoe St., S.). Open all year, daily.

The works of one of the most influential movements in nonfigurative painting in Canada, "Painters Eleven," form just part of the *Robert McLaughlin Gallery's* collection. Modern Canadian works are complemented by changing exhibitions of internationally known artists. Civic Centre. Admission free. Open daily all year.

Parkwood, mansion of the Canadian auto manufacturer R.S. McLaughlin, who sold out to General Motors, is magnificent. Gardens open, too, June–Labour Day daily except Mondays.

Owen Sound: A 26-foot birchbark Express canoe is part of the Indian and pioneer collections displayed at 975 Sixth Street East—the *County of Grey and Owen Sound Museum.* Open mid-January to mid-December, Tuesday through Sunday. The brilliant, thick-stroked canvases of the influential Canadian landscape painter Tom Thomson, and his sketches, letters, and drawings are hung in *Tom Thomson Art Gallery,* 840 First Ave. W., Owen Sound, and can be seen afternoons except Mondays in July and August.

Peterborough: Rare pioneer homespun, toys, photos, fossils, and an animated model of the Trent-Severn Waterway are just part of the collection of the *Peterborough Centennial Museum* on Hunter St. E. Open all year, daily. Fourteen restored pioneer buildings comprise Peterborough's other museum, *Century Village.* Open mid-May to Thanksgiving; special demonstrations on Sundays. July and August, daily. Other times, Wednesdays, Saturdays, and Mondays. Peterborough's *Art Gallery* is at 2 Crescent St. by Little Lake.

St. Catharines: *Rodman Hall,* 109 St. Paul Crescent, features tapestries, glassware, paintings, and graphics as well as exhibitions of Canadian and international artists. Open Tuesday, Thursday to Sunday. More china and weaving are displayed at the *St. Catharines Historical Museum,* 343 Merritt St., along with prints and relics from the War of 1812, and old photos and scale models relating to the construction of the Welland Canal.

St. Thomas: Colonel Thomas Talbot, an English backwoods despot, ruled the settlers on his grant of land with an iron fist in an iron glove. His life is recorded in exhibits on display at 32 Talbot St., in the renovated residence of a pioneer physician. Open all year daily.

Sarnia: You can clamber around a former Great Lakes oil tanker's center castle and explore the officers' quarters, masters' quarters, wheelhouse, signal flag locker, etc. in the *Pilot House Museum* in Corunna on Hwy. 40 south of Sarnia. Open mid-May to October, daily.

Sault Ste. Marie: A century-old church, a pioneer log cabin, a barn and a school make up the *St. Joseph Island Museum* complex just east of Sault Ste. Marie. Open June through September, Wednesdays, Saturdays, and Sundays, 2 to 5 P.M. July and August. Also visit the 1814 *Ermatinger House,* built by a fur trader for his Indian princess wife.

Remnants of the fur trade canoes, battleships, and freighters that plied the Great Lakes are on display at Sault Ste. Marie's *Marine Museum,* 41 Lake St., Bellevue Park, open July 1 to Labor Day. The *Art Gallery of Algoma* is at 10 East St.

Smiths Falls: The *Heritage House Museum* depicts upper-middle-class life in Ontario circa 1867–1875. Here you can investigate a two-story privy, a brick bake oven, and Smiths Falls artifacts. For information, call 613–283–8560.

Stratford: Every month a new and impressive exhibition is mounted by *The Gallery,* 54 Romeo St. North. Open May to September, daily; closed Mondays from Labour Day to May. Also features films, lectures, and concerts.

There's a 1/10-scale reproduction of Stratford-upon-Avon—including the Garrick Inn and Anne Hathaway's cottage—at *Shakespeareland. Fryfogel's Inn,* 8½ miles east of Stratford on Hwy. 7, has been made into a museum. Costumed hostesses guide you through the stagecoach inn past 5 rooms of exhibits. Open July to Labour Day, daily, noon to 6 P.M., except Monday.

Sudbury. *The Laurentian University Museum and Art Centre,* John St. at Nelson, consists of 3 galleries and a restored 1906 home.

Science North encourages you to explore the world of science as a participant. Discover minerals from the Sudbury Basin or count the number of lightning strikes during a storm in the Weather Station. For information, call 705–522–3700.

Thunder Bay: A wide assortment of old stoves, player pianos, outboard engines, Edison record players—if it sounds like a general store, that's part of the *Thunder Bay Founders' Museum*, too. Hwy. 61. Open June 15 to September 15, daily. *Lakehead University* has an art gallery, open daily. *The National Exhibition Centre*, Keewatin at Red Lake Rd., features Indian art.

Timmins: The *Ukrainian Historical and Cultural Museum* documents the lives of Ukrainian immigrants who were drawn to Northern Ontario by the discovery of gold and silver. Open year-round. Call 705–264–3393.

Wasaga Beach: A sound and graphics show dramatizes the American's burning of the *Nancy*, a supply schooner which served the British in the War of 1812 at the *Nancy Island Historic Site*. There are models and artifacts inside the museum, and the charred hull of the *Nancy* outside. Open late May to Labour Day.

Whitby: The former *Grand Trunk Railway Station* (early 1900's) has become Whitby's Art Gallery. "The Station" features traveling exhibits from the Art Gallery of Ontario plus a good display of local crafts. Open daily except Monday.

MUSIC. There are over 30 symphony orchestras plus 18 youth orchestras in Ontario. The largest and most polished are the excellent *Toronto Symphony*, the *Hamilton Philharmonic*, the *London Symphony Orchestra*, and the *National Arts Centre Orchestra of Ottawa*. The *Guelph Spring Festival* is an annual event held in late April and early May in **Guelph**. In the past the festival has featured chamber and solo concerts by ranking musicians from violinist Yehudi Menuhin to jazzman Moe Koffman. Ticket prices vary. International and local jazz, opera and pops artists are showcased in the concert series of the **Stratford** and **Shaw** Festival programs. Check **Ottawa** and **Peterborough** Festivals (spring-summer) for quality concerts. The *Shaw's Festival Theatre* at **Niagara-on-the-Lake** also runs a winter weekends concert series. Early August is the time to catch fiddlers at the *Open Old Time Fiddlers' Contest* in **Shelburne** and the pipe bands at **Kincardine**. Out-of-door summer concerts at **Hamilton's** *Dundurn Castle* and *Toronto's Ontario Place* range from pops to classical. There are bluegrass festivals at **Carlyle** and Burk's Falls. Fall brings symphony season to **Toronto, Hamilton** and **Ottawa;** late fall, the performances of the *National Ballet* and the *Canadian Opera Company*.

SHOPPING. Canada's richest province naturally has some of the best shopping—everything from native crafts to antique junk to tens of thousands of dollars' worth of fur coats. Major retail stores are *The Bay* (The Hudson's Bay Company), *Eaton's, Simpson's, Ogilvy's,* and *Holt Renfrew*. They are clustered in major urban centers and their suburban branches carry the same lines of manufactured clothes and goods.

Native arts and crafts. Eskimo soapstone carvings and prints are available at Toronto's *Innuit Gallery of Eskimo Art*, 9 Prince Arthur Ave., which sells soapstone sculpture (from $50), prints, wall hangings, scrimshaw—or etched ivory—and other Eskimo antiquities. *Inukshuk Gallery*, in Waterloo, also specializes in Eskimo art. At *The Three Bears*, Niagara Falls, *The Canadian Craft Shop*, Kingston, and *The Snow Goose*, Ottawa, you can find both Eskimo and Indian work.

Indian crafts (moccasins, beadwork, traditional basketry often fashioned from fragrant sweet grass, silverwork, wood carvings, and Native prints) are available at centers like *Courtney's* on St. Joseph Island, east of Sault Ste. Marie. The *Cross Canada Craft Shop*, 11 miles west of Renfrew, carries Eskimo and Golden Lake Reserve Indian carvings and crafts. In Sault Ste. Marie's *The Loon's Nest*, quilts, dolls, puppets, homemade jams, weaving, pottery, Indian mittens and moccasins, and fine batiks are improbably jumbled in a modern shopping mall.

Canadian crafts. Many excellent Canadiana crafts centers are dotted across the province. Check Gananoque, Pakenham Perth, and Westport in eastern Ontario. In Kingston, the *Canadian Shop of Kingston and Gallery* carries glass, ceramics, tapestries, jewelry, toys, and Native crafts. There's a café behind the store where you can relax after browsing. *Chez Piggy* is a restaurant off King St. with boutiques all around the courtyard. *Cooke's Olde World Shop* on Lower Brock St. is a century-old general store with wood floors carrying gourmet teas, coffees, etc. *The Peanut Gallery* in Burk's Falls is the place where Northern Ontario craftsmen display their ceramics, metal, and woodwork.

In central Ontario, quilts, rugs, needlework, and crafts are sold in Cookstown, Dwight, Bond Head. Maple sap flows from sugar maples throughout central and southern Ontario in the spring, but in Orillia, Shaw's Pure Maple Products sells syrup, candy, butter, and sugar, all of maple, year-round. How sweet it is!

Elmira is in real Mennonite country. At *The Sap Bucket,* double-bed, down-filled quilts go for about $200, for a tiny fraction of that price you can take some Mennonite tradition home in the shape of an odd, charming little apple doll. The Sap Bucket also carries stained glass, wooden toys, and works by the Waterloo Potters' Guild. In London *The Canadian Craftsman* carries some jewelry and ceramics. Also check crafts shops in Bronte, Campbellville, Beamsville, and Dundas when in southwestern Ontario. For hand-processed candy with a tradition going back to the 1890s, look into *The Candy Shop,* 26 Brunswick St., Stratford. Stratford also offers china, hand-crafted works, old clothing, and Shakespeare memorabilia to the hordes of Festival visitors. At the *Pillar and Post Shoppe* in Niagara-on-the-Lake you can find work by over 150 local craftspeople. There's even a carpentry workshop and smithy on the premises, where pine replicas of traditional furniture, hardware and lighting fixtures are produced.

Gems and minerals. Bancroft is a center for geologists and in its two local rock shops you can pick up rose quartz, garnet, zircon, and beryl. You'll also find the books, tools, and advice you need to go out hunting for your own. In Thunder Bay's *Amethyst Mines,* you either chip your own gems and pay for what you take with you, or browse for already polished gems and jewelry in the mine's rock shop. Hwy. 17 at East Loon Rd.

Antiques. Antique hunters are more common in Ontario than game hunters. They flock to *flea markets* in Burlington (weekends at 1400 Plains Rd. E.), Aberfoyle (Sundays in spring, summer, and fall) and Hamilton (on Sundays). The little towns of southeastern Ontario are a treasure trove for people in search of pressback chairs, dry sinks, oak tables; sharp-eyed collectors can even find relatively rare pieces of Ontario pine. Some of the best antiques are to be found in roadside, family-owned stalls around Cobourg, Peterborough, Marmora, Hastings, and Belleville. Another good bet—and a lot of fun—is to get a list of country auctions from local papers and general stores. *Clappison's Corner's* offers antiques and junk at the Circle flea market, every Sunday on Highway 5. In Toronto, antique sellers congregate every day, except Monday. On weekends as many as 200 stalls may be open. Free. *Trans Canada Antiques* in Sault Ste. Marie claims to have Northern Ontario's largest selection of antique oak, walnut, and mahogany furniture. Corner 5th Line and Hwy. 17 N.

 LIQUOR LAWS. Anyone over 19 may buy liquor. Liquor is sold in Provincial Liquor Control Board Outlets. Domestic beer is available at Brewers' Retail. Domestic wines are sold through company stores. On Sundays, alcohol is served from noon to 11 P.M. On other days drinking hours are 11 A.M. to 1 A.M.

 RESTAURANTS. Dining out in Ontario means big helpings of plain food of the meat and potatoes variety, and, if you're lucky, fish or home-baked goods. You can also find tasty ethnic cooking in an area not otherwise noted for its cuisine. In both Southern and Northern Ontario, price categories for a dinner for one of appetizer, entrée and dessert, are: *Deluxe,* more than $35; *Expensive,* $22–$34; *Moderate,* $15–$22, *Inexpensive,* less than $15.

Most places accept the following major credit cards: American Express, MasterCard and Visa; others may also be honored. Not all establishments accept credit cards, therefore we suggest you call for information.

ALGONQUIN PARK. *Expensive.* **Arowhon Pines.** off Hwy. 60 (705–633–5661). You can take second helpings in this pine-paneled rustic dining room, and you may very well want to: the chef, imported from Toronto for the summer, concentrates on a choice of three entrées each night and gives them his full attention. Roasts especially good. Not licensed. Season: May to October.

ALTON. *Expensive.* **The Millcroft Inn.** John St. (416–791–4422). Imaginative soups and entrées, fresh fish, herbs from the garden, good wine list. Overlooks a waterfall.

BARRIE. *Moderate–Expensive.* **Maude Koury's Steak House.** 126 Collier St. (705–726–6030). Four small, darkly wall-papered rooms and a conservative menu oriented toward beef. Licensed.

BRAMPTON. *Expensive.* **Trattoria Via Veneto.** 21 Queen St. (416–453–4333). E. Northern Italian cooking with gnocchi al vodka and veal in pernod.

BRACEBRIDGE. *Moderate.* **Holiday House.** 17 Dominion St. (705–645–2245). Steak and kidney pie ribs and a salad bar in a big old clapboard dining room overlooking Bracebridge Falls. Licensed.

CALABOGIE. *Moderate–Expensive.* **The Whippletree Shanty.** In town (613–752–2428). Steaks, kebabs, burgers and two big fireplaces overlooking Lake Calabogie. Licensed.

CALEDON. *Expensive.* **Caledon Inn.** (416–584–2891). The dining room has cedar beams and an old stone fireplace. Menu limited. Roast beef, homemade pies, high tea. No license. Reservations necessary.

COBOURG. *Moderate–Expensive.* **Dressler House.** 212 King St. (416–372–5243). Continental menu. Dinners, served in the house of former silent movie star Marie Dressler, include fresh trout and homemade desserts. A terrace open for dining in summer.

COLLINGWOOD. *Expensive.* **The Spike and Spoon.** 637 Hurontario St. (705–445–2046). Fresh flowers, a prix fixe menu, gazpacho, Stroganoff, Dutch apple pie. Licensed.
Inexpensive–Moderate. **Aquafarms.** Near Feversham, call for directions (519–922–2817). This is a working trout farm with a small bright dining room attached. The kids can fish. The restaurant serves smoked trout, fish chowder, grilled trout, homemade pies for dessert. Licensed. Worth the trip.

DORSET. *Moderate.* **Cedar Narrows.** (705–766–2344.) The main dining room which serves German dishes overlooks Lake of Bays. You can retire to a log lounge with a big fireplace for your coffee and liqueurs after your meals. Licensed.

ELORA. *Moderate.* **Cafe Flore.** Mill St. (519–846–5631). Basque cooking, served cafeteria style, includes chicken with peppers and tomatoes, beef stews with wine and onions, basque cakes filled with custard. Some of the tables in this small restaurant overlook the river. Licensed.

FERGUS. *Expensive.* **The Breadalbane Inn.** 487 St. Andrew St. (519–843–4770). A 125-year-old mansion whose owners serve good English meaty dishes and play jazz tapes. An outdoor patio garden is open for drinks.

GANANOQUE. *Moderate.* **Golden Apple.** In town. (613–382–3300). Highly recommended, but very popular, so reserve. In summer, a garden is your first introduction to this old and much-loved restaurant. Fresh vegetables complement good homestyle entrées (beef, lamb, fish). Relishes and desserts especially good. Licensed.

GODERICH. *Deluxe.* **Benmiller Inn.** Benmiller Village (519–524–2191). Overlooking Sharpe's Creek. There's a view of water and gardens outside; inside, a stone-floored dining room in a restored, 100-year-old mill serves rainbow trout, sirloin, fresh vegetables. Licensed.

HALIBURTON. *Expensive.* **Sir Sam's Inn.** Eagle Lake (705–754–2188). Children are not allowed. There is a long elegant dining room overlooking the water and some ambitious cooking, such as cornish hen with green grapes. Licensed.

HAMILTON. *Expensive.* **Lo Presti's.** Jackson St. (519–528–0205). It looks old-fashioned with its flock wallpaper. But the cook's touch is deft with veal and pasta. Licensed.

Moderate. **The Old Country Restaurant.** 1360 King St. E. (416-547-2572). Open-spit cooking of lamb, pork, chicken; Hungarian stews and Greek/Yugoslavian appetizers and desserts. The staff is very friendly. Licensed.

KINGSTON. *Moderate–Expensive.* **The River Mill.** 2 Cataraqui St. (613–549–5759). On the banks of the Catarqui River, the dining room affords a lovely view. Some dishes are better than others. The hits include homemade pâté and rabbit stew.

Chez Piggy. 68 Princess St. (613–549–7673). Fresh vegetables, sophisticated but light menu, homemade desserts. A courtyard setting and a license. Operated by rock musician Zal Yanofsky, formerly of The Lovin' Spoonful.

KITCHENER. *Moderate–Expensive.* **Walper Terrace Hotel.** 1 King St. W. (519–745–4321). A grand hotel since the beginning of the 19th century, the Walper has just reopened with four dining rooms. Bavarian food and rich desserts remain its forte. Licensed.

Expensive–Deluxe. **The Brittany.** 24 Eby St. (519–745–7001). Specialties include sweetbreads sauteed in brandy and seafood. The house is very plainly decorated; the emphasis is on the cooking. Licensed.

Expensive. **Café Mozart.** Queen St. (519–578–4590). Wonderful tortes and pastries with coffee.

KLEINBURG. *Deluxe.* **The Doctor's House and Livery.** Off Hwy. 27 (416–893–1615). Roast duckling, old-fashioned service. Licensed.

LONDON. *Expensive.* **Auberge du Petit Prince.** King St. (519–433–9394). A reputation for good French cuisine, but it has recently changed owners.

Moderate. **The Mug House.** 1544 Dundas St. (519–453–9355). Helpings are huge, families welcome, the atmosphere noisy and cheerful. Soups, hamburger, and steak. Licensed.

MEAFORD. *Moderate.* **The Fisherman's Wharf.** 12 Bayfield St. (519–538–1390). You can eat freshly prepared lake fish overlooking the docks full of fishing boats. Licensed.

Moderate–Expensive. **The BackStreet Cafe.** 27 Nelson St. Off Hwy. 26 (519–538–4455). Fish, chicken, veggie dishes, home cooked, in a nice, funky licensed restaurant frequented by theater-goers.

NIAGARA FALLS. *Moderate.* **Betty's 2.** Victoria St. (416–357–2655). This is no-nonsense, no-frills, dependably good home cooking. Steak or turkey dinners, real whipped cream in the desserts. Licensed.

The Old Stone Inn. 5425 Robinson St. (416–357–1234). A 1904 flour mill renovated, now serving beef and seafood on oak tables. Sometimes a harpist entertains.

NIAGARA-ON-THE-LAKE. *Deluxe.* **Prince of Wales.** 6 Picton St. (416–468–3246). In summer the airy, elegant restaurant expands into a greenhouse. The menu is imaginative (*e.g.,* watercress soup) and tasty (*e.g.,* fresh trout). A good wine list complements your dinner and there is a comfortable lounge next door.

Expensive. **The Oban Inn.** 160 Front St. (416–468–2165). A former officer's mess, the renovated inn overlooks a lawn and the lake. Pine furniture in a warm old-fashioned dining room. Classic beef and poultry entrées. Licensed.

NORMANDALE. *Moderate.* **The Union Hotel.** Vittoria. (519–426–5568). Specialties are stuffed pork tenderloin and local perch. Homemade desserts change daily. There's a grand verandah on which to sit afterward and digest. Unlicensed. Reservations important.

ORANGEVILLE. *Expensive.* **Greystones.** 63 Broadway (519–941–1301). A conservative Anglo menu: beef, trout, beans wrapped in bacon.
   Inexpensive–Moderate. **The Paradise.** Off Main St. (519–941–4910). centre of town. Home made fries, real hot turkey sandwiches, fresh-baked desserts, a license too.

ROCKWOOD. *Moderate–Expensive.* **La Vielle Auberge.** 262 Main St. (519–856–4170). Local salads in summer, good daily specials and local baked goods all year round.

ROSEMONT. *Moderate.* **Globe Restaurant.** South side of Hwy. 89 in town (705–435–6981). Canadian standards (roast beef, steak-and-kidney pie) served before one of the inn's two fireplaces. Licensed.

ST JACOB'S. **The Stone Crock.** 41 King St. (519–664–2286). Mennonite country cooking: buffet or platters of schnitzel and sausage from which diners are welcome to sample repeatedly.

STRATFORD. *Expensive.* **The Church.** 70 Brunswick (519–273–3424). One-hundred-year-old church has been beautifully converted into a restaurant offering pâté of fresh lamb, lake trout, veal, sweet soufflés. Licensed. The Church is heavily subscribed; book ahead.
   Moderate–Expensive. **The Jester Arms.** 107 Ontario St. (519–271–1121). Start with an afternoon tea of English scones jam and thick cream. The dinner menu is equally Anglo-Saxon, with lamb and mint pie, plus the usual prime ribs. Licensed.

TERRA COTTA. *Expensive.* **Terra Cotta Inn.** King St. (416–453–8261). Terrace, 4 dining rooms, pub, country setting. Open for lunch, afternoon tea, dinner. English and Victorian décor.

WILLIAMSFORD. *Moderate.* **Gerard's Feed Mill.** Hwy. 6 (519–794–3102). A 19th-century grist mill overlooking the Saugeen River, offering Indonesian rice and peanut dishes as well as Dutch and Canadian cooking. Licensed.

WINDSOR. *Expensive.* **The Mason-Girardot Manor.** 3203 Peter St. (519–253–9212). A restored 1877 manor house with a curving black walnut staircase. The cooking is Mediterranean—Cypriot to be precise—with moussaka, kebabs, and lamb. Licensed.

NORTHERN ONTARIO

DRYDEN. *Moderate–Expensive.* **Riverview Inn.** 148 Earl Ave. (807–223–4320). A log hotel overlooking the Wabigoon River. Beef and fish, licensed.

ESPANOLA. *Moderate.* **Goodman's Motel.** Hwys. 17 and 6 (705–869–1020). Homemade soup and home-fries to go with the German cooking. Licensed.

FORT FRANCES. *Moderate.* **Rainy Lake Hotel.** 235 Scott St. (807–274–5355). Local pickerel (walleye) is a speciality in this older hotel dining room, but there is also seafood, beef. Licensed.

KENORA. *Expensive.* **Kenwood Hotel.** 15 Chipman St. (807–468–8913). Giant servings of local walleye or monumental steaks. Licensed.
   English Inn. In Kenricia Hotel, 155 Main St. (807–468–6461). There's a painting over the fireplace which adds to the atmosphere of this older hotel dining room. Prime rib, Lake of the Woods walleye pickerel, steak plus a salad bar. Licensed.

MANITOULIN ISLAND. *Moderate.* **Huron Sands Motel.** 20 Sunova Beach Rd. (705–476–4600). In Providence Bay. Home cooking with fresh local ingredients in a bright, comfortable room. Not licensed.

MATHESON. *Expensive.* **Kiss Motel.** Hwy. 11 west of town. (705–273–2812). Central European dishes like paprikash, spicy pork. Not licensed, but very popular.

NORTH BAY. *Moderate–Expensive.* **Champlain Trails.** 300 Lakeshore Dr. (705–476–3636). A surf and turf restaurant with an open fireplace and good Greek daily specials. Licensed.

ROSSPORT. *Moderate–Expensive.* **Rossport Inn.** Rossport Loop (807–824–3213). A 100-year-old inn overlooking the town harbor. The inn serves local fish and imported seafood such as lobster and scallop. Licensed.

SAULT STE. MARIE. *Expensive.* **Cesira's.** 133–137 Spring St. (705–949–0600). Two older, oak-trimmed houses joined together, serving pasta, veal steak. Licensed.
   Moderate–Expensive. **Thymely Manner.** 531 Albert St. (705–942–5076). The Sicoli family serves generous portions of homemade antipasto, fresh lake trout, fresh-made pasta, entrées with local wild mushrooms. Highly recommended.

SUDBURY. *Moderate.* **The Peter Piper.** 151 Larch St. (705–673–7801). Fresh fish, Italian and Greek items on the menu. It is a local favorite. Licensed.

THESSALON. *Moderate–Expensive.* **The Horseshoe Inn.** 179 Main St. (705–842–2138). A 100-year-old hotel where the cooking leans to old standards: beef and local fish in season. Licensed.
   Moderate. **The Round Barn.** Brownlee Rd. east of town on Hwy. 17 (705–842–3341). It is natural for a farm to present a menu based on seasonal fruits and vegetables—including chunky vegetable soups, salads, and homemade jams for tea. Unlicensed.

THUNDER BAY. *Expensive.* **Airlane Motor Hotel.** 698 west Arthur St. (807–577–1181). Fresh Lake Superior trout, fresh vegetables, steaks. Licensed.
   Uncle Frank's Supper Club. RR4 Hwy. 61, out of town (807–577–9141). The restaurant looks like a 1950s supper club—which it is. Ask for Uncle Frank. He cuts his own steaks and serves them up with some fine home cooking in this comfortable, popular restaurant. Licensed.
   Inexpensive. **Hoito.** 314 Bay St. (807–345–6323). Finnish cooking (mojjaka, a fish soup, and smorgasbord sandwiches) in an unpretentious and unlicensed setting.
   Kanga's. 379 Oliver Rd. (807–344–6761). First and foremost, a sauna, with restaurant attached, for after-sauna soups and chocolate cheesecakes.

QUEBEC

La Belle Province

by
DAVID DUNBAR

David Dunbar, a former Montrealer who now lives in New York, writes about travel for such publications as Travel & Leisure, Reader's Digest, *the Toronto* Globe and Mail, *and the Boston* Globe, *as well as for CBC Radio. He is a member of the Society of American Travel Writers. This chapter also includes material contributed by Bernadette Cahill, Pauline Guetta, Janet Kask, Betty Palik, and Barbara Peck.*

What makes Quebec so different from all other provinces of Canada is its strong French heritage. Not only is French spoken everywhere (English is spoken too), but many of the local customs and traditions have their roots in Roman Catholic France rather than in Anglo-Protestant Great Britain.

Visitors love Quebec—for its French character, for its peacefulness, for its great beauty, for its storied past. For those who love history, Quebec City is unlike any other in North America, with its old-world feeling, its ramparts, and its winding, cobblestone streets. For those who want fun and excitement, Montreal is as cosmopolitan as New York, as chic and as French as Paris. For those who yearn for the serenity of nature, that too is in Quebec, in its uncountable lakes, streams, and rivers, in its great mountains and deep forests, in its rugged coastline, and in its farmlands and villages.

QUEBEC HISTORY

In 1534 a young French sea captain named Jacques Cartier set out to find the Northwest Passage to China around the American continent, but he discovered eastern Canada instead. On his second trip, the following year, he came back looking for gold. But this time he found a wide river, sailed down it, and arrived at Stadacona, an Indian village, on the site of today's Quebec City. The village perched on the cliffs overlooking a *kebec*, the Indian word for "narrowing of the waters." Then he sailed upstream and disembarked at Hochelaga (which became Montreal), where he was greeted by more than a thousand surprised Indian natives.

First Inhabitants

When Cartier took his wrong turn, the fierce and mighty Iroquois lived south of the St. Lawrence River and east to the Richelieu River. The Naskapi hunted in what is now eastern Quebec. The members of this tribe who lived toward the south, between the St. Maurice River and present-day Sept-Îles, were called Montagnais (mountain men) by the French. Other tribes of southern Quebec were the Algonquin, Huron, Malecite, and the Micmac.

French Cities

Seventy-three years passed after Cartier's visit before the French returned. Samuel de Champlain arrived in 1608 determined to build a French settlement close to Stadacona, with a commanding view of the river. His people built a two-story, wooden *"Habitation"* on the riverbank beneath the cliffs of Cape Diamond, then constructed a fortress atop the Cape. Known as the "Father of New France," Champlain did more than any other explorer to map the northern United States and the Canadian interior. He also did much to encourage settlement in the vast region.

In 1642 Paul de Chomedey, Sieur de Maisonneuve, came to the island where Hochelaga once had existed, and to the mountain that Cartier had named Mont Réal, in order to establish a Jesuit mission for the Indians. He and his followers built a small palisaded settlement and named it Ville-Marie de Montreal. In gratitude for their success, they later erected a huge cross on the mountaintop. Today a brightly lit cross, visible for miles, stands on the site.

The Seigneuries

In 1663 King Louis XIV of France proclaimed Canada a crown colony. To bolster defenses he sent out the famous Carignan-Salières regiment. He also appointed a succession of military governors and civil intendants.

Jean Talon, the first intendant, offered large grants of land, or *seigneuries*, to officers of the Carignan-Salières regiment if they settled discharged veterans on the land. He also offered land to aristocrats in the colony if they promised to settle tenants, or *habitants*.

The land was allotted in a unique fashion. Rectangular strips, each about 1 mile deep and about 60 miles wide, fronted a lake, road, or riverbank. The houses and farm buildings were built along a road through the seigneury, giving the impression of a continuous village street. As the front *"rang"* filled up, further allotments were made in a second rang behind it. This pattern of long and narrow farms is still evident in the Quebec countryside. The habitants were not only close-knit, they were also deeply religious. The Roman Catholic Church took on an importance that went beyond religious functions. Priests and nuns also acted as doctors, educators, and overseers of business arrangements between the habitants and between French-speaking traders and English-speaking merchants. An important doctrine of the church in Quebec was *survivance,* the survival of the French people and their culture. Couples were told to have large families, and they did. Ten and 12 children in a family were the norm, not the exception.

War with England

The Algonquins and the Hurons carried beaver pelts out from the interior and sold them to the French at boisterous trade fairs in Montreal. But the Iroquois, who coveted the fur routes, fought bitter wars against those tribes and terrorized the French settlers. Eventually, toward the end of the seventeenth century, the French made peace with the Iroquois, and Ville Marie prospered. Its location was ideal, at the meeting of the mighty St. Lawrence and Ottawa rivers. By the early 1700s, about 9,000 French colonists and native people lived in the town.

The first half of the 18th century saw a series of wars in Europe and in the New World between England and France. The Seven Years' War began in 1756. France sent the commander, Louis Joseph, Marquis de Montcalm, to secure the southern frontier of New France and consolidate the new territory of Louisiana. In 1759 the British dispatched to Quebec City a large invasion fleet carrying an army commanded by James Wolfe.

The British bombarded the city for weeks, reducing it nearly to rubble and attempted several times to land on shore. With summer drawing to a close, Wolfe decided on one more attack. With about 4,000 men, he rowed upriver to a cove behind the city and climbed the cliff face in the darkness, bringing his army right against the walls of Quebec. The French emerged from their stronghold to battle on the Plains of Abraham.

The fate of Canada was decided in a vicious battle that lasted 30 minutes. The British won, but both leaders were mortally wounded. Today, a unique memorial honors these two leaders—the only statue in the world commemorating both victor and vanquished of the same battle. Three years later the Treaty of Paris ceded Canada to Britain. France gave up the new country and kept her Caribbean sugar islands, which were believed to be of more value.

In 1774, the British Parliament passed the Quebec Act, giving full authority to the Roman Catholic Church, maintaining the seigneurial landlord system, and providing for civil justice under the existing French law. In general, it ensured the survival of the traditional Quebecois way of life.

The Conscription Crisis

The entente between the French and English existed until World War I. At the outbreak of the war, the two groups felt equally supportive of the two European motherlands. Even a French regiment was created, the Royal 22nd ("Van Doos"). But two things ended the uneasy arrangement between French and English.

In 1915, Ontario passed Regulation 17, severely restricting the use of French in its schools. The anti-French stand created open hostility. The flow of French Canadians into the army became a trickle. Then Prime Minister Robert Borden ordered conscription of childless males

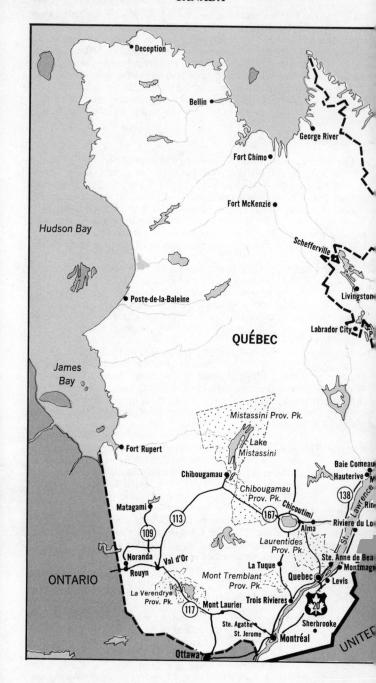

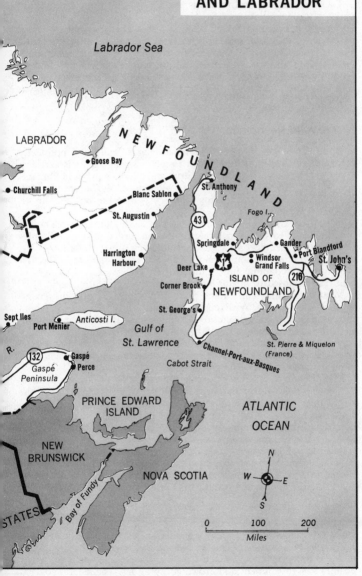

QUÉBEC, NEWFOUNDLAND AND LABRADOR

Labrador Sea

LABRADOR

NEWFOUNDLAND

• Goose Bay

• Churchill Falls

St. Anthony●

Blanc Sablon●

St. Augustin●

Fogo I.

43

Springdale● ●Gander

Harrington Harbour●

Windsor
Grand Falls●

Port Blandford●
●St. John's

Deer Lake●

ISLAND OF
NEWFOUNDLAND

216

Corner Brook●

Sept Iles●

Port Menier● *Anticosti I.*

St. George's●

Gulf of
St. Lawrence

St. Pierre & Miquelon
(France)

R.

132

●Gaspé

Gaspé
Peninsula

●Perce

Channel-Port-aux-Basques

Cabot Strait

PRINCE EDWARD
ISLAND

ATLANTIC
OCEAN

NEW
BRUNSWICK

N

W   E

S

NOVA SCOTIA

STATES

Bay of Fundy

0   100   200
Miles

to reinforce the ailing Canadian corps, which formed the shock troops of the British Empire and died horribly, by the thousands. A wider conscription law loomed in Ottawa. The outcry in Quebec was led by nationalist journalist and politician Henri Bourassa. The nationalists claimed that conscription was a device to diminish the French-speaking population. When, in 1917, conscription did become law, Quebec was ideologically isolated from the rest of Canada.

The crisis led to the formation of the Union Nationale provincial party in 1936, initially a reformist party. Under its leader Maurice Duplessis, it held control till 1960 and was characterized by lavish patronage, strong-arm methods, fights with Ottawa, and nationalistic sloganeering. Duplessis believed that to survive, Quebecers should remain true to their traditions—a culture founded in religion and an economy founded in agriculture. Duplessis deterred industrial expansion in Quebec, which went to Ontario, and slowed down the growth of reformist ideas until his death.

The Quiet Revolution

Under Duplessis, Quebec had fallen economically and politically behind Canada's English majority. French-language schools and universities were supervised by the church and offered courses in humanities rather than in science and economics. As a result, few Francophones (French-speaking Quebecers) held top positions in industry or finance.

In 1960 the Liberal Party under Jean Lesage swept to power. Though initially occupied with social reform, it soon turned to economic matters. In 1962 Lesage's minister of natural resources, René Lévèsque, called for nationalization of most of the electricity industry—the first step toward economic independence for Quebec. The financiers of Montreal opposed it, but ordinary Quebecers were enthusiastic.

Meanwhile American capital poured into Quebec, as it did everywhere else in Canada. With it came American cultural influence, which increased Quebecers' expectations of a high standard of living. English-speaking citizens remained in firm control of the large national corporations headquartered in Montreal. Few Francophones were promoted to executive status. Successive provincial governments became increasingly irritated by the lack of progress.

The discontent led to a dramatic radicalization of Quebec politics. A new separatist movement arose that hoped to sever Quebec from the rest of the country. The most extreme faction of the movement was the Front de Libération du Québec (FLQ). It backed its demands with bombs and arson, culminating in the kidnap-murder of Quebec Cabinet Minister Pierre Laporte in October 1970.

The federal government in Ottawa, under Prime Minister Pierre Elliot Trudeau, himself a French-speaking Quebecer, imposed the War Measures Act. This permitted the police to break up civil disorders, arrest hundreds of suspects, and led to the arrest of the murderers of Laporte.

The political crisis ended but it left vibrations that jangled all of the country. The federal government redoubled its efforts to correct the worst grievances of the French Canadians. Federal funds flowed into French schools outside of Quebec to support French Canadian culture in the other provinces. French Canadians were appointed to senior positions in government and crown corporations. The federal government increased its bilingual services to the population dramatically.

In Quebec from the mid-1970s, the Liberal government and then the Parti Quebecois, elected in 1976, headed by René Lévesque, replaced the English language with the French language in Quebec's economic life. In 1974 French was adopted as the official language of Quebec. This promoted French language instruction in the schools and made French the language of business and government. The Parti Quebecois followed up in 1977 with the Charter of the French Language, which established deadlines and fines to help enforce the program to make French the chief language in all areas of Quebec life. The charter did bring French into the workplace; it also accelerated a trend for English companies to relocate their headquarters outside Quebec, particularly in and near Toronto.

The Parti Quebecois proposed to go further by taking Quebec out of confederation, but maintaining economic ties with the rest of Canada. A referendum was held in 1980 for the authority to negotiate a sovereignty association with the rest of Canada. But Quebec voters rejected the proposal by a wide margin. In the last provincial elections, held in the fall of 1985, the Parti Quebecois government was itself defeated at the polls by the Liberals.

QUEBEC'S CULTURAL LIFE

The French Canadians of Quebec, often called "Latins of the North," have a wonderful ever-sparkling joie de vivre, especially at the more than 400 festivals and carnivals they celebrate each year. The largest festival splash is on June 24, which was originally the Feast of Saint John the Baptist. Now it is called "La Fête Nationale," or National Day. Everyone celebrates the long weekend by building roaring bonfires and dancing in the streets.

Words and Music

In the early 1900s, Quebecers sang songs from France and the United States. Then came Félix Leclerc, who, in the 1950s, traveled the province with simple songs celebrating the uniqueness of Quebec. He sang of everyday life: of farmers, log drivers, and lumberjacks. The effect was to make Quebecers proud of their heritage and culture. Gilles Vigneault also rose to popularity with his traditional melodies and provocative lyrics.

Raymond Lévesque established Quebec monologue as an art form. Other monologuists appeared, most notably Yvon Deschamps. Monologues and *chansons* took hold of French Quebecers' imaginations and were credited with helping to elect the separatist Parti Quebecois in 1976 by proclaiming to a wide audience that Quebec was for the Quebecers.

Their efforts were paralleled in literature. In 1960 a new kind of writing appeared, fierce and satirical. *The Impertinences of Brother Anonymous,* written by a teaching brother, Jean-Paul Desbiens, satirized the French educational system and thus sparked a fiery debate on the social, religious, and academic realities of the day.

Novelists like Gabrielle Roy *(The Tin Flute),* Anne Hébert *(Kamouraska),* Marie-Claire Blais *(Une Saison dans la vie d'Emmanuel),* and Yves Thériault *(Agaguk)* came to attention with books about the frustrations of Quebec society. Other novelists, like Hubert Aquin, Jacques Godbout and Réjean Ducharme, as well as dramatist Michel Tremblay, produced important reflections of Quebec society.

Certainly not all Quebec writing is French. Many of Mordecai Richler's short stories and novels *(The Apprenticeship of Duddy Kravitz)* and Leonard Cohen's novels *(Beautiful Losers)* and poems *(The Spice-Box of Earth)* sprang from their experiences in Montreal. Hugh MacLennan of Montreal's Concordia University, is one of the best-known novelists and essayists in Canada. His novels *Two Solitudes* (1945) and

Return of the Sphinx (1967) are about interactions between French and English in contemporary Quebec. More recently, playwright David Fennario has written about French and English working-class Montreal *(On the Job, Balconville)* to great acclaim.

Visual Arts

Tourists in Old Montreal and Old Quebec are quickly attracted by artists working in the open, in the Paris tradition. These open-air artists are the most obvious evidence of Quebec's modern painters, of whom a number are well-known.

In the early 1900s, Quebec's impressionists, such as James Wilson Morrice, Maurice Cullen, and Marc-Aurèle Suzor-Côté, produced highly prized canvases. Then came Alfred Pellan, "Quebec's Picasso," who started the "Automatistes" school, largely impressionistic but with strong social and political overtones. In the 1950s Jean-Paul Riopelle, an abstract painter, gained international stature. Separate from this school was Jean-Paul Lemieux, whose nostalgic and impressionistic style has special appeal to Quebecers.

A second school emerged in the late 1950s, "Les Plasticiens," whose hard-edged style gained strength through the work of Guido Molinari. Recent years have seen a realist school emerging, characterized by painstaking devotion to detail. Graphic art is also flourishing.

In the field of sculpture, Quebec has produced wood carvings for its churches since the 17th century. Today this skill is kept alive by a sculptors' school run by Médard Bourgault in Saint-Jean-Port-Joli.

In addition, very moving and beautiful sculpture made from stone, bone, and ivory is produced by the Inuit in northern Quebec. These works are distributed through cooperatives run by the Inuit themselves and are sold in specialized galleries. Inuit carvings all bear an igloo tag and a number, issued by the federal government. Lower priced imitations carved by whites in the south do not carry this tag of authenticity.

MONTREAL: CANADA'S SECOND CITY

Nearly half of Quebec's 6 million people live in or near Montreal, with 2.5 million in the Greater Montreal area. Canada's second-largest city (after Toronto) is an island city 51 kilometers (32 miles) long and over 16 kilometers (10 miles) across at its widest.

Indians and Europeans alike settled here because three converging rivers made Montreal a natural communications and transportation center. From here voyageurs could portage past the roiling, unnavigable Lachine rapids to rejoin the St. Lawrence further west, and press on to the heart of the continent.

North and northwest, intrepid travelers found the Ottawa River. The Richelieu River led south to Lake Champlain and the headwaters of the Hudson River. All around lay a fertile plain, its soil deposited by the last ice age.

In 1639 a group of zealous lay Catholics—convinced that native North Americans formed the lost tribe of Israel whose conversion would hasten Christ's second coming—formed the Société de Notre-Dame de Montreal, to convert the natives to Christianity. In May 1642 Paul de Chomedey, sieur de Maisonneuve, landed with 40 settlers. The group included Jeanne Mance, who set up the colony's first hospital. De Maisonneuve named the settlement "Ville-Marie de Montreal," later shortened to Montreal.

The little colony suffered from constant danger, as the Iroquois fought bitterly until the treaty of 1701. In spite of hardship from weather, war, and pestilence, settlers survived, and penetrated into the continent. Some sought furs and other valuable commodities, some explored for a direct route to China, and still others wanted converts, but all discovered more and more of the new land.

Throughout the French regime Montrealers extensively explored and mapped the continent. Men like LaSalle, d'Iberville, Jolliet, Marquette, Duluth, Lamothe-Cadillac and La Vérendrye extended New France from Hudson Bay to the Gulf of Mexico and the Rocky Mountains. They discovered, explored, or settled at least 35 of the American states, leaving 4,000 French geographical names throughout the United States as reminders of their exploits.

During the 18th century, European powers battled to control the Americas. French and English colonies waged constant war, culminating in the English victory at Quebec City in 1759, when Montreal became the capital of New France for the few months until, in 1760, the French surrendered the city without a fight. The French regime officially ended in 1763. At that time Montreal's population had reached 5,000, almost entirely French.

Fifteen years later, because almost all Quebecers had French roots, members of the American Continental Congress in New England believed the inhabitants would welcome an American army to liberate them from the British. In November 1775 General Richard Montgomery led his Continental Army troops into Montreal. They headquartered at Château Ramezay (now a museum). Colonel Benedict Arnold and General Richard Montgomery, as well as Benjamin Franklin, stayed there. The French population, however, declined the invitation to become the fourteenth state. After suffering conclusive defeat at Quebec City, the Americans retreated from Canada in June 1776.

American forces also tried to take Montreal, and Canada, during the war of 1812–14, but in 1813 Colonel de Salaberry's forces beat them back at Châteaugay, just south of Montreal. Again, during the American Civil War, the North threatened to invade Canada after a party of twenty-odd Montreal-based Confederate soldiers raided St. Alban's in Vermont. Fortunately, no war ensued.

After the British conquest, a small group of Scots and English reorganized the fur trade, which dominated the city's economic life throughout the 18th century. Traders sent *coureurs de bois* and *voyageurs* out to trap and trade in the wilderness. In time, the smaller companies formed the North West Company, competing with the older Hudson's Bay Company. The rivals eventually merged in 1821, but by then other forms of commerce and transportation had evolved.

Development of Communications

Montreal progressed rapidly after it incorporated as a city in 1832. It became the capital of the United Canadas (Upper and Lower) with the 1841 Act of Union, but lost that title to Kingston, Ontario, in 1849. (Ottawa is now Canada's capital city.) Montreal, however, retained economic supremacy. As commerce in furs dwindled, lumber and then wheat became major exports. The city emerged as a shipping and railway giant. By 1900 Montreal, with a population of 370,000, was by far the country's major metropolis.

Over the years tensions rose and fell between the city's two main groups. The Francophones saw that they needed to learn English to get ahead, which made them feel like second-class citizens in their own province. Since then, French has become Quebec's official language. In Montreal, street signs, traffic directions, and outdoor publicity are

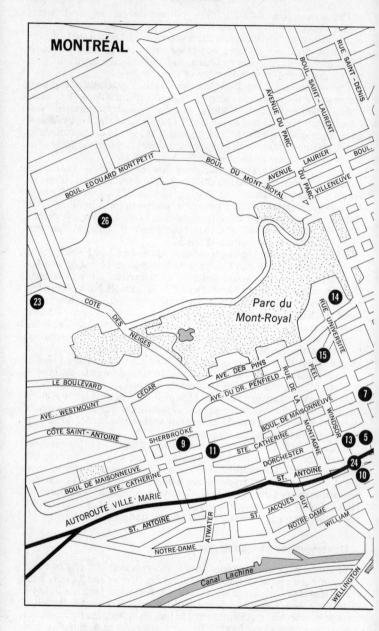

MONTRÉAL

Montreal — Points of Interest

1) Aquarium
2) Bonsecours Market
3) Botanical Garden
4) Canadian Broadcasting Company
5) Central Station
6) Chateau Ramezay
7) Christ Church Cathedral
8) City Hall
9) Congregation Notre-Dame Mother House
10) Dow Planetarium
11) Forum
12) Garden of Wonders

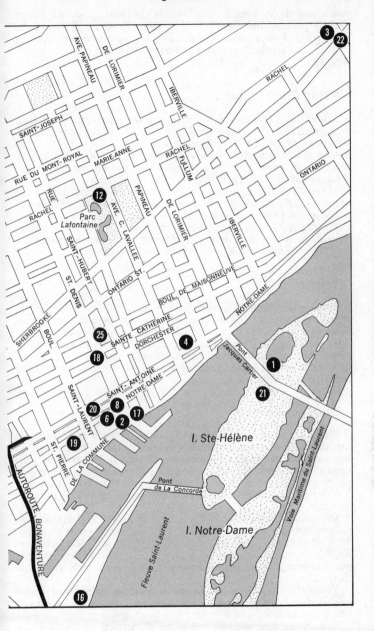

13) Marie-Reine-du-Monde Cathedral
14) McGill Stadium
15) McGill University
16) Museum of Contemporary Art
17) Notre-Dame-de-Bonsecours Church
18) Notre-Dame-de-Lourdes Church
19) Notre-Dame Church
20) Old Court House
21) Old Fort
22) Olympic Stadium
23) Oratoire St.-Joseph
24) Post Office
25) Quebec University
26) University of Montreal

predominantly in French. Montreal is the world's second largest French-speaking city, after Paris. Now, about 70 percent of the population speaks French, with the majority of the remaining speaking English, and nearly all speaking at least a few words of one another's language.

Métro, Expo, Olympics

Recent decades brought Montreal vibrant international development, placing it in a global spotlight. In 1967 the city hosted North America's first officially recognized world's fair, Expo 67. Over 50 million people from 70 nations participated during the six-month run, recalled each summer with the ongoing Man and His World fair and the amusement park, La Ronde.

Also in 1967, the city constructed a colorful and efficient subway, the Métro. A building boom dramatically changed the city's skyline and added a new underground dimension.

The city hosted the 21st Olympic games in 1976, building a unique "flying saucer" stadium seating 72,358, and a complex that includes a six-pool swimming arena, and Vélodrome for cycling.

Tourism

Each year, Montreal welcomes more than 5,000,000 visitors. In recent years the city has drawn millions of visitors to cultural attractions, such as the 1985 Picasso exhibit at the Montreal Museum of Fine Arts, the Egyptian treasures and artifacts of Ramses II, and festivals of art, movies, and music, as well as popular events like the annual fireworks show, La Ronde amusement park, and free dancing and band concerts in the city's many parks.

Exploring Montreal

People often compare Montreal with Paris. You will instantly recognize the Gallic heritage, particularly in people's love of fun, dedication to good food and wine, and, of course, the fact that almost everyone speaks French. But, in reality, comparing Montrealers to French people because they speak the same language is like saying that New Yorkers or Kansans resemble Londoners because they speak the same language.

Montreal is . . . different. But it is clean and organized, so that most visitors feel safe and comfortable as they discover the city's charms. Most downtown hotel and restaurant employees speak excellent English. In other areas they try if they can, for Montrealers jealously guard their reputation as good hosts and are happy to welcome you as their guest.

You will soon discover that Montreal is comprised of many vibrant neighborhoods, or *quartiers,* each with its own charm. Of the island's two dozen or more quartiers here is a small selection:

Downtown, you will find boutiques, department stores, and museums. Montreal's Fifth Avenue is Sherbrooke, roughly between University and St. Mathieu, and all streets between leading down to Dorchester. (Montrealers often leave off the rues, streets, and avenues, making street names serve equally well in French and English.) On Sherbrooke between University and McTavish, you will find the handsome colonnade called the Roddick Gates, marking the entrance to McGill University's campus, which opened in 1821 and is one of the city's two English-language universities (with Concordia University on nearby de Maisonneuve).

Further west on Sherbrooke, at the corner of Drummond, you find the Ritz-Carlton Hôtel and, at Mountain Street, Holt Renfrew, an exclusive department store. The Montreal Museum of Fine Arts stands on the north side of Sherbrooke. Boutiques, galleries, and restaurants line the south side of Sherbrooke, and all the side streets. Indeed, Crescent, Mackay, and Bishop streets house some of the trendiest bars, restaurants, and clubs, while the Hôtel de la Montagne, a baroque luxury hotel enjoyed by many beautiful people, stands on Mountain.

Continuing west, past Guy and Atwater streets, you arrive in the City of Westmount, one of the 28 municipalities belonging to the Montreal Urban Community.

Westmount is proud of its Victorian municipal library (built to celebrate Queen Victoria's 1899 jubilee), pretty municipal greenhouses (free entry), and bowling green. You will find many fine boutiques and restaurants, such as Les Près and Encore une Fois (health food—bring-your-wine) in the Victoria Avenue-Sherbrooke area. Similar delights abound on Greene Avenue, and in Westmount Square, where many European couturiers have boutiques.

Many handsome homes line the steep and winding roads leading up the slopes of Westmount, which is topped by a bird sanctuary and Westmount Lookout, from which you can see the St. Lawrence River and the Adirondack Mountains of New York. On the other side rises the main tower of the huge Université de Montreal (begun in 1928), designed by art déco architect Ernest Cormier.

Just over the border from Westmount, on the northeast corner of Atwater and Ste-Catherine, stands the Montreal Forum, home of the Montreal Canadiens ice hockey team. From here take a cab a few streets down Atwater to browse among the antique stores on Notre-Dame Ouest between Atwater and McGill College avenues. They specialize in items like old duck decoys, Napoleonic mementos, and especially Quebec pine antique furniture.

Back in the downtown area east of Crescent, Mackay, and Bishop streets, Ste-Catherine boasts several major department stores including Ogilvy's (where a Scottish highlander pipes you out at closing time), Simpson's, Eaton's, The Bay, and Birk's. Within this area you will also find some of the world's finest (and most reasonable) furriers, many of whom produce furs for the world's great couture houses.

Further east on Ste-Catherine stands the city's main performing arts center, Place des Arts (PdA) with three theaters seating a total of 5,000. Opposite PdA you will find Complexe Desjardins, with offices and the luxury Hôtel Meridien on the upper levels, and boutiques and restaurants circling a handsome atrium of plants and fountains at the center.

PdA and Complexe Desjardins link up to the "underground city," connected to the Métro, which reaches to the four corners of the city and under the St. Lawrence River to the south shore. Downtown pedestrian passageways lead to hotels and parking garages. Packed with shops, boutiques, cafes, street musicians (who must obtain permits to play), and bustling, well-dressed people, the underground city proves popular as well as practical—in bad weather no one need set foot outside.

Buildings linked this way include Place Ville-Marie, the Château Champlain and Queen Elizabeth hotels, and convention centers like the Palais des Congrès and Place Bonaventure. The latter also serves as a year-round merchandise mart and showcase for manufacturers and industries. Atop you will find the Bonaventure Hilton International Hôtel, with its unusual year-round outdoor pool and Japanese garden.

From here you can reach the city's Latin Quarter by Métro, surfacing at Berri-de Montigny station on St-Denis. Main center for students is the modern University of Quebec at Montreal, which retains as its façade the historical old cathedral (St-Jacques) that originally stood there. St-Denis has a typical student-quarter atmosphere, with book stores, art galleries, and bistros frequented by poets and artists. In summer musicians in town for the Jazz Festival gather for jam sessions, part of an outdoor frolic enjoyed by thousands. Off St-Denis, 19th-century homes on St-Louis Square surround a fountain and flower market. The square's west side leads to Prince Arthur, a pedestrian mall lined with restaurants, many of them inexpensive, and outdoor cafes, where you watch *le monde* go by to the strains of street musicians.

From there you can take a cab to Place Jacques-Cartier in Old Montreal, many of whose historic sites are described elsewhere (See "Historic Sites").

Or, you might return via Métro to Place d'Armes station, and visit the Palais des Congrès and exhibition hall. Just outside, a stroll along Lagauchetière through Chinatown leads to Blvd. St-Laurent (St. Lawrence Boulevard) and to Complexe Guy Favreau, which contains a small cinema where documentaries by the award-winning National Film Board of Canada are screened.

Within the city, you should also visit the Parc LaFontaine area, including the small zoo in the park, and Château Dufresne on the corner of Sherbrooke and Pie IX ("Pie Neuf," for Pope Pius Ninth), which houses fine collections of decorative arts. In this same area you will find the Botanical Gardens and Olympic Park site of the 1976 Olympic Games, and still a much-used sports center.

Other interesting areas include Plâteau Mont-Royal, on the east side of Mont-Royal, once mainly a Greek and Jewish area, but now increasingly popular with all groups. Avenue Parc, in particular, is the newest "in" spot for nightlife, restaurants, and bistros. Neighboring Outremont, an area with many fine old houses, caters to the carriage trade, offering lively little restaurants, boutiques, the Cinéma Outremont (French repertory), and the ubiquitous bistros. East of the Plâteau, you will find Blvd. St-Laurent, through which every immigrant group passes. It, too, is gradually becoming more upscale—even the old fish market (Waldman's) has been bought by a grocery chain. But on the streets east of St-Laurent, you can still see rows of houses whose outside staircases twist up to second-story apartments, and marvel how generations of people can manage them in icy weather.

Outside the city you will find much to do, from the amusement park thrills of La Ronde on Île Ste-Hélène (accessible by the Métro of the same name), to the West Island towns usually referred to as "the Lakeshore." From Lachine (whose rapids roil in the St. Lawrence, ideal for jet-boat rides), the old road hugs the shoreline west to the tip of the island at Ste-Anne de Bellevue and Senneville. Charming developments and old properties line the road, which winds through the picturesque villages of Dorval, Pointe Claire, Beaurepaire, Baie d'Urfé, and Ste-Anne de Bellevue.

As you will see, Montreal's geography, food, wine, atmosphere, and, above all, the people, make it a city like no other. When you visit you are sure to agree with the local sentiment: "Vive la différence!"

PRACTICAL INFORMATION FOR MONTREAL

HOW TO GET THERE. By Plane. Some 60 airlines use Montreal's two commercial airports. *Dorval* receives mainly domestic flights. *Mirabel International Airport* handles overseas planes. Canada's main airlines include *Air Canada, CP Air, Wardair,* and *Quebecair,* which goes to Quebec City, New York, Boston, and many points within the province served by no other commercial line. Major American airlines flying into Dorval include: *American Airlines, Delta, Eastern, Republic, United,* and *U.S. Air.*

By Boat. The Montreal Yacht Club, Port Ste.-Hélène, CP 20, Station M, Montreal, PQ H1V 3L6. Open from mid-May to mid-October; facilities for boats up to 19.5 m (65 ft) long (871–1595).

By Bus. Bus companies including Greyhound, Voyageur, and Voyageur—Colonial from throughout the U.S. and Canada use Montreal's downtown Voyageur Bus terminal, 505 Blvd. de Maisonneuve Est, Montreal, PQ H2L 4R6 (514–842–2281).

By Train. From Gare Centrale (Central Station) downtown on Dorchester at Mansfield (514–871–1331), VIA Rail trains leave for all Canadian destinations, and AMTRAK (800–426–8725 or 4AMTRAK) serves U.S. cities. Commuter trains use both Central and Windsor Station, located on Peel at Lagauchetière streets.

By Car. Montreal is accessible from the east and west via highways 20 and 40, and from the south via highways 10 and 15. Three major expressways lead to the U.S.: Route 91 to Boston, Route 87 to New York, and Route 89 to Vermont.

TOURIST INFORMATION. The *Greater Montreal Convention and Tourism Bureau,* 174 Notre-Dame Est, Montreal, PQ H2Y 1C2 (514–871–1595) or *Tourisme-Quebec,* Maison de Tourisme, 2 Place Ville-Marie, Room 70, Montreal, PQ H3B 2C9 (514–873–2015).

In summer stop by the downtown information kiosk on the north side of Dominion Square, open June 1 to Labor Day, 9 A.M.–6 P.M. Year-round you can walk into the Greater Montreal Convention and Tourism Bureau, close to Montreal's City Hall, and the Maison de Tourisme (addresses above). At big hotels, the Montreal Convention Centre, and tourist kiosks, a video screen displays data on shows, sports, exhibitions, upcoming events, and history. Simply push a button on an Info-Montreal terminal for free access. Good sources for latest data on coming events include the Friday and Saturday editions of Montreal's daily papers, *La Presse* and *Le Devoir* in French, and the *Gazette* in English. You can also buy *Montreal* magazine (English). Many hotels and some restaurants give away *En Ville* (bilingual) and *Montreal Scope.* Wanderlust Publishing, Ltd., puts out *Montreal Cuisine,* with menus, prices, and recipes from great local restaurants; $12.95 at newsstands. Write Box 1471, Montreal, PQ H5A 1H5 (871–9122).

TELEPHONES. Montreal and surrounding areas' code is 514. You pay 25 cents for a local call on a public telephone, with no time limit. Reach directory assistance by dialing 411.

EMERGENCY TELEPHONE NUMBERS. For police, fire department, and ambulance (called "Urgence Santé"), dial 911; 24-hour drugstore service, 527–8827; dental clinic (523–2151), open seven days 8 A.M.–11 P.M.; *Montreal General Hospital* (937–6011); the *Quebec Poison Control Centre* can be reached at 800–463–5060; other local *poison-control* centers are at the Montreal Children's Hospital (934–4456) and at l'Hôpital Ste-Justine pour enfants (345–4600); *Touring Club de Montreal—AAA, CAA, RAC* (288–7111).

HOW TO GET AROUND. From the Airports. Dorval is 22.5 km (14 mi.) from downtown, and Mirabel 54.5 km (34 mi.). You'll easily find taxis at both airports. **From Dorval,** fares run about $20 to the city. *Aerocar* (397–9999) buses leave Mon.-Fri. every 20 minutes, Sat., Sun., every half hour, for the Voyageur bus terminal at Berri de Montigny Métro station, with stops at the Sheraton Centre, Chateau Champlain, Le Grand Hotel, and the Queen Elizabeth Hotel. Return trip makes same stops. Fare $6. If you travel light and do not mind stairs, take the bus and the Métro: Board autobus 204 for nearby Dorval Gardens Shopping Centre, then take express bus 211 to Lionel-Groulx Métro station for the ride downtown, total fare $1 or one bus/Métro ticket. Limousine service is provided by *Contact Limousine Service* (631–5466) and *Murray Hill Limousine Service buses* (937–5311). **From Mirabel,** taxis to downtown cost about $50. *Aerocar* (397–9999) provides buses, at $9 per person, between the airport and Place Bonaventure Métro station (behind Central Station) with no stops; and between airports, also at $9.

By Subway and Bus. You'll easily spot entrances to Le Métro, Montreal's safe, clean, and quiet underground transportation system, by the foot-square signs with a large white arrow on a blue ground. There are five lines and 54 stations. Call 288–6287 (AUTOBUS) for bilingual help to reach points served by the MUCTC (Montreal Urban Community Transit Commission). Le Métro runs 5:30 A.M.–12:30 A.M. daily. Fare $1, or six tickets for $5 at Métro stations. Bus drivers take only exact fare or tickets.

By Taxi. Fares start at $2, with 70 cents for each additional kilometre and 25 cents a minute for waiting. Montreal's major taxi companies include: *Diamond* (273–6331); *La Salle* (277–2552); *Champlain* (273–2435); *Co-op* (725–9885); *Regal* (484–1171); *Veterans* (273–6351).

By Rental Car. You will find rental firms at the two main airports, railway stations, and major hotels. Main local car rental services include: *Avis Rent-a-Car* (514–866–7906); *Hertz* (514–842–8537); and *Budget-Rent-a-Car* (514–937–9121). For a local bargain, check out *Tilden Rent-a-Car* (514–878–2771). The phone directory's Yellow Pages list smaller companies renting cars or trucks.

 HINTS TO HANDICAPPED TRAVELERS. Write to The Greater Montreal Tourist Convention and Bureau, 155 Notre-Dame Est, Montreal, PQ H2Y 1B5 (871–1595), for the folder, "Useful Information for the Handicapped." Most restaurant guides and tourist pamphlets list facilities for the handicapped. Many streets have wheelchair ramps. Shopping centers and main tourist and entertainment centers allot primary parking areas to handicapped people's vehicles bearing special stickers. You can get wheelchair help from *Kéroul,* 4545 ave. Pierre de Coubertin, Montreal, PQ H1V 3R2 (252–3104), Mon.—Thurs., 9 A.M.–5 P.M.; Friday., 9 A.M.—noon. Reach the *Canadian National Institute for the Blind* (CNIB) at 1010 Ste-Catherine Est, Montreal, PQ H2L 2G3 (284–2040), Mon.—Fri., 8:30 A.M.—noon; 1–4:30 P.M. Reserve at least 24 hours ahead for transportation for people in wheelchairs from Voyageur Bus Service, 505 blvd. de Maisonneuve Est, Montreal, PQ H2L 1Y4 (514–842–2281).

 SEASONAL EVENTS. March. Sample maple sugar products at *sugaring-off parties* on farms near Montreal (call Tourisme Quebec at 873–2015). **May.** The *Benson & Hedges International Fireworks Competition* lights up the skies for several weeks with classic and pyromusical fireworks. At La Ronde amusement park on Île Ste. Hélène. Tickets ($8–$15) through Ticketron or AMARC, Administration Pavilion, Île Notre Dame, Montreal, PQ H3C 1A9 (872–6212). In late May attend the *Montreal International Mime Festival,* when masters from a dozen countries lead 23 stage productions, 30 street shows, and five 40-hour workshops. Box 267, de Lorimier Station, Montreal, PQ H2H 2N6 (526–0452).

June. *Montreal International Music Competition* (285–4380). Younger visitors enjoy the *Quebec International Puppet Festival* early in June, at the provincial children's theater, La Maison-Théâtre, 255 Ontario Est, Montreal, PQ H2X 1X6 (288–7211). Top Formula 1 drivers compete for the world championship at *Grand Prix Labatt of Canada.* Write to Grand Prix Labatt, Bassin Olympique, Île Notre-Dame, Montreal, PQ H3C 1A9 (871–1421). Late June features

Montreal's International Jazz Festival, with 1,000 musicians from 15 countries participating in a ten-day series of indoor and outdoor shows. Besides big names, you will find many brilliant lesser-knowns, as well as acrobats, jugglers, and street performers. Tickets from Ticketron and from Montreal International Jazz Festival, 355 Ste-Catherine Ouest, Suite 301, Montreal, PQ H3B 1A5 (871–1881). Antique buffs note the annual three-day *antique show,* held each June in Place Bonaventure, Box 1,000, Montreal, PQ H5A 1G1 (933–6375). June 24 is *la Fête nationale des Quebecois,* Quebec's national Festival, formerly Saint Jean Baptiste Day, an official provincial holiday when neighbors get together for parades, street dancing, and bonfires.

July. The jazz beat (see June) continues, followed by giggles with the *"Just-for-Laughs Festival."* Some 60 comics from a dozen countries give four nights of English performances and five in French. Tickets from Ticketron and Festival du Rire, 63 Prince Arthur Est, Montreal, PQ H2X 1B4 (845–3155). **August.** *Player's Challenge Tennis Championships.* The world's best players. Odd years (1989 and 1991) the men play; even years (1988 and 1990) the women take over. At Jarry Tennis Stadium. Tickets from $4 to $2,000 for a box for four. Player's Challenge Tennis Canada, 5253 ave. Parc, Suite 610, Montreal, PQ H2V 4P2 (273–1515). In late August Montreal's *International Film Festival* shows movies representing cinematography's every trend, in North America's only competitive film festival recognized by the International Federation of Film Producers' Assoc. Write to Festival des Films, 1455 blvd. de Maisonneuve Ouest, Suite 109, Montreal, PQ H3G 1M8 (848–3883).

September. *Montreal International Marathon,* a 42.195-km (26.2-mi) course. Some 12,000 take part. Registration, $10. Write to Montreal Marathon, Box 1570, Station "B", Montreal, PQ H3B 2L2 (879–1027). **October.** In Chinatown, *Festival of the Harvest Moon.*

TOURS. City tours by bus leave all year from Dominion Square on Peel below Dorchester. For sightseeing tours call *Murray Hill* (937–5311) or *Gray Line of Montreal* (280–5327). A company called *Les Montrealistes,* Box 457, Station A, Montreal, PQ H3C 2T1 (744–3009), organizes bus and walking tours of cultural and tourist attractions in Montreal districts daily during summer. *Guidatour,* Box 575, Station N, Montreal, PQ (844–4021) provides licensed guides, and escort services for arrivals and departures, and also organizes traditional and specialized tours for individuals and groups, in several languages.

Boat Cruises. *Montreal Harbor Cruises,* Box 1085, Place D'Armes, Montreal, PQ H2Z 2C7 (842–3871), run three vessels offering a variety of tours of the mighty St. Lawrence River from early May to late September. Prices range from about $5 for one-hour sunset cruises to over $20 for ten-hour cruises to Sorel. (children half-price). Choices include three-hour "Love Boat" cruises with live orchestra and Sunday breakfasts, and 90-minute moonlight cruises.

Calèche Rides. All year you can rent a horse-drawn carriage from starting points at Dominion Square, Place d'Armes or on Mont-Royal. You can hail a *calèche* in Old Montreal around Bonsecours and Gosford, and de la Commune streets. Hourly cost $30 (844–1313 or 845–7995).

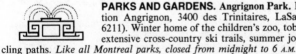

PARKS AND GARDENS. Angrignon Park. Métro station Angrignon, 3400 des Trinitaires, LaSalle, (872–6211). Winter home of the children's zoo, tobogganing, extensive cross-country ski trails, summer jogging, cycling paths. *Like all Montreal parks, closed from midnight to 6 A.M.*

Ile-Ste-Hélène. An island park reached by Métro (Île-Ste-Hélène station) or by car from Jacques-Cartier Bridge. In winter you can cross-country ski and snowshoe. In summer jog, walk, picnic, and swim in outdoor pools.

Jardin botanique (Botanical Garden). (872–1400). On blvd. Pie IX, above Sherbrooke, is the world's third-largest garden, after London's and Berlin's. Some 26,000 different species of plant life are displayed in 30 outdoor gardens and ten greenhouses. Unique collections include more than 400 varieties of bonsai (miniature trees) and 1,700 orchid varieties. Open daily 9 A.M.–6 P.M. Free admission to grounds. Admission to greenhouses: adults, $3; seniors, ages 5–7, and handicapped, $1.50; under 5 admitted free.

LaFontaine Park. rue Sherbrooke Est at Papineau (Métro Papineau) (872–6211), includes a lagoon where you can rent boats by the hour. Or visit the children's zoo and playground area.

La Ronde Amusement Park. Île-Ste-Hélène (Métro stop Île-Ste-Hélène) provides fun for all. You will find many attractions—games of chance, an old Quebec village with craft workshops, restaurants, and boutiques. View the city and river from on high in the overhead minirail. Recent spruce-ups include Western Fort, giant water slides, an antique, hand-carved merry-go-round, live entertainment, and the world's highest double-tack roller coaster, aptly named "The Monster"—*"c'est terrifiant!"* From May to early June, weekends, holidays only. Mid-June-Labor Day, Mon.–Sat., noon–2:30 A.M., Sun., holidays, 10 A.M.–midnight. Various admission packages range in price from about $8–$35 (for a family pass). For data on day passes, call 872–6222.

Les Floralies. On Île-Notre-Dame, via Métro to Île-Ste-Hélène (872–6093). Huge outdoor international flower show makes sweet-scented background for strolling musicians, free open-air concerts. Mid-June–September. Free.

Mont-Royal. Known fondly as "the mountain" to Montrealers, topped by a 30.5-meter (100 ft) illuminated cross, Mont-Royal rises 233 meters (764 ft) above sea level in the heart of the city. The 19th-century landscape architect Frederick Law Olmsted, who also designed New York's Central Park, insisted that Mont-Royal remain natural. Montrealers use their mountain park widely for recreation. They jog and hike all year round. In summer they cycle around Beaver Lake or feed the ducks and sail miniature boats. In winter they use the little ski run, toboggan, and skate on the small lake. Other attractions include horse-drawn carriage and sleigh rides, the Universal Museum of Hunting and Fishing, and a chalet lookout giving a panoramic view extending south to Vermont. Picnic and snackbar facilities. Get there by car, or number 11 bus from Mont-Royal Métro station. No public transport service to adjoining Westmount lookout or bird sanctuary topping Westmount. But by cab or car, turn up Belvedere Road from Côte-des-Neiges. From here, on a clear day you can see the Adirondack Mountains in New York State.

 PARTICIPANT SPORTS. Montrealers' many sports vary with the season. In summer you will find **cycling**, on paths in more than 20 areas, many in parks. Guided cycle tours of historic Lachine Canal, 10:30 A.M., Sat.–Sun., during the summer (872–6211). Rent good bikes from Cycle Peel, 6665 St-Jacques, Montreal, PQ H4B 1V3 (486–1148). You can **jog** on Mont-Royal and in most other city parks.

Most **golf** clubs are private. Call 873–2015 for a list of courses. Public courses include: *Fresh Meadows,* 505 Golf Beaconsfield, Pointe-Claire, PQ H9W 2E5 (697–4036) and *Golf Le Village,* 4601 rue Sherbrooke Est, Montreal, PQ H1X 2B1 (872–2781). A nine-hole municipal course.

There are two **rafting** outfitters: *Lachine Rapids Tours Ltd.,* 105 rue de la Commune, Montreal, PQ H2Y 2C7 (284–9607 or 843–4745). Daily from Victoria Pier at rue Berri. Jet boat every two hours, May–mid–Sept., 10 A.M.–6 P.M. Daily rubber rafting, mid-June–mid-Sept. Adults, $25. Youths 10–18, $20. Six to 10 years, $10. *Voyageur-Lachine,* from Quay 34, St.-Joseph Blvd. at 32nd Ave., Lachine (634–7877 or 637–3566). Mid-May–Sept., 9 A.M.–7 P.M. Mon.–Fri., $15. Sat., Sun., $18.

You can play **tennis** all year in Montreal—in winter in indoor health clubs. Summer outdoor courts include: Parc Jeanne-Mance, north of avenue des Pins at avenue Parc; Parc Lafontaine, rue Sherbrooke Est at Calixa-Lavallée (872–6211).

You can **skate** all winter at 29 illuminated outdoor rinks, 23 indoor arenas, and every neighborhood park maintains a skating and/or hockey rink. Try pretty *Angrignon Park,* 7050 de la Vérendrye Blvd., and *Beaver Lake* on Mont-Royal (872–6211).

Parc Mont-Royal provides a small **downhill ski** run. You will find **cross-country** trails and good snowshoeing throughout the city's parks and golf courses, notably: *Île Notre-Dame* and *Île Ste-Hélène,* (both at Man and His World) and *Parc Mont-Royal.* These, plus Angrignon, Ahuntsic, and Parc LaFontaine, also hold great **toboggan slides.**

SPECTATOR SPORTS. Hockey. The Canadian Ice Hockey Club, Les Canadiens, has won 23 Stanley Cups. Regular season, Oct.–Apr.; playoffs, Apr., May at The Montreal Forum, 2313 Ste. Catherine Ouest, Montreal, PQ H3H 1N1 (932–6181).

Football. Les Alouettes, Canadian football, Olympic Stadium, June–late Nov. Montreal Football Club, Box 100, Station M, Montreal, H1V 3L6 (253–8088). Tickets from $5 (bleachers)–$18.50.

Baseball. The Montreal Expos play at Olympic Stadium. Mid-Apr.–Oct. Montreal Baseball Club, Ltd., Box 500, Station M, Montreal, PQ H1V 3L6 (253–3434 or 800–351–0658).

Harness Racing. Blue Bonnets race track, Jean Talon and Decarie Blvd. (Métro Namur). 7440 Decarie Blvd., Montreal, PQ H4P 2H1 (739–2741). Open year-round; closed Tues. and Thurs.

HISTORIC SITES AND HOUSES. You will find much of Montreal's rich cultural legacy permanently preserved within the heritage area of Old Montreal, near the port, and around Place d'Armes. To explore the area thoroughly takes several days, but the city provides a free 28-page walking-tour guide detailing all the interesting points. Special landmarks are listed here.

Bank of Montreal. 129 St-Jacques Ouest (877–6892). Montreal's oldest bank faces Place d'Armes. Worth a visit for its ornate, black marble-columned main hall. Numismatists find the tiny museum particularly interesting. Displays include a detailed reconstruction of the bank's first branch (featuring period office equipment), an extensive currency collection, and 19th-century mechanical savings banks. Mon.–Fri., 10 A.M.–4 P.M. Admission free.

Bonsecours Market (Marché Bonsecours). rue St-Paul, one of the city's oldest streets. The market, with its handsome dome and colonnades, is the street's most impressive building, but all the neighboring buildings have been well restored and house boutiques, offices, and restaurants. The restored market (1845) is now used as municipal offices.

Centaur Theatre. 453 St-François-Xavier (288–3161). English theater housed in Montreal's first Stock Exchange Building, with its stately colonnaded facade.

Château Dufresne. 2929 Jeanne-d'Arc, corner of blvd. Pie IX and Sherbrooke Est (259–2575). A classic mansion, built in 1918 for the Dufresne family. Permanent and visiting exhibits of decorative arts, plus Victorian and Edwardian furnishings. Wed.–Sun., 11 A.M.–5 P.M. Adults, $2; students, 75 cents; seniors, $1; children under 12, handicapped, free.

Château Ramezay. 280 Notre-Dame Est (861–3708). Built in 1705 for Claude de Ramezay, France's eleventh governor of Montreal, it was the base of the American occupying forces in 1775–76. Benjamin Franklin slept here. Interior shows 18th-century nobleman's residence, complete with original furniture, household articles, prints, paintings, weapons, tools, and miscellany. Exhibits of fur trade, English influence, 19th-century Canadiana and Quebec's Indians. Tues.–Sun., 10 A.M.–4:30 P.M. Adults, $2; under 16 and seniors, 50 cents.

City Hall (Hôtel de Ville). 275 rue Notre-Dame Est, and opposite Château Ramezay, is a massive example of Renaissance architecture, adapted to 19th-century needs. Finished in 1877, it overlooks Place Vauquelin's pretty fountain and Champ-de-Mars, the old military training ground, now a city parking lot. The fine, domed old courthouse (1849) on the other side of Place Vauquelin, houses CIDEM, Montreal's economic development department, and home of CIDEM-Tourisme (155 Notre-Dame Est) where you write, call, or visit for tourist information (871–1595).

Maison du Calvet. 400 St-Paul Est, corner of Bonsecours. One of the finest examples of domestic architecture of the French regime, with all window and door frames of cut stone. Pierre Calvet was a Huguenot merchant and justice of the peace, imprisoned for years for giving information to American general Montgomery. Built around 1725, the house was restored by Ogilvy's department store to commemorate its 100th birthday in 1966. Now an epicurean food shop.

Nelson's Column. Place Jacques-Cartier. British Admiral Lord Horatio Nelson won the battle of Trafalgar in 1805. The column is the oldest existing monument celebrating the victory, and predates London's Nelson. He looks down over a lively scene, including a flower market, strolling musicians, jugglers, artists, and people sipping and dining in outdoor cafes. A charming cobblestoned square, where calèches line up to take you exploring. Before boarding, tour the square, noting plaques on the heritage houses at nos. 433, 404–410, and 407.

Place d'Armes. Between Notre-Dame and St-Jacques, Montreal's old financial district. A detailed tribute to Maisonneuve stands dramatically in the center, marking, some say, the exact spot where the city's founder grappled in mortal combat with the Iroquois chieftain, and won. To the south stands Notre-Dame Basilica, opened in 1829. West of the church is Seminaire de St-Sulpice, established in Montreal in 1685. You will notice the remarkable fine woodwork clock (1710).

Place Royale. The city's oldest landmark, bearing an obelisk declaring that Champlain named the square. Maisonneuve's settlers laid the city's foundations here, erecting the first homes, a fort, a chapel, and a cemetery.

Sir George Étienne-Cartier House. 458 Notre-Dame Est (283–2282). Run by Parks Canada, this is a restored property constructed in 1862. Actually two houses, which the Cartier family lived in successively. Now, you can see one elegantly furnished for the affluent folk like the Etienne-Cartiers. The other contains contemporary exhibitions. May–Sept., daily, 9 A.M.–5 P.M. Sept.–May, Wed.–Sun., 10 A.M.–5 P.M. Free.

HISTORIC RELIGIOUS SITES. In 1881 Mark Twain noted that in Montreal "you couldn't throw a brick without hitting a church." Indeed, Montreal holds more churches than Rome, with more than 450 on the island.. Following are some of the more historically interesting religious sites.

Cathedral-Basilica of Mary, Queen of the World and St. James the Greater. Dorchester at Mansfield, opposite the Queen Elizabeth Hotel (866–1661). A replica of St. Peter's Basilica of Rome, built from 1870–1894 by Bishop Ignace Bourget, the city's second bishop. Statues atop the cathedral recall the patron saints of the archdiocese in 1894. Open daily from, 7:00 A.M.–about 7:15 P.M.

Christ Church Cathedral. 635 St-Catherine Ouest (879–1996). The Anglican cathedral (1851) is pure Gothic. Note the stained glass, gargoyles and angels, and Coventry Cross, made from nails salvaged from the ruins of Britain's Coventry Cathedral, bombed in 1940.

Church of St. Andrew and St. Paul. Sherbrooke at Redpath (3415 Redpath Ave.) (842–3431). Presbyterian, regimental church of the Black Watch (Royal Highland regiment of Canada). Fine stained glass, including two Tiffany windows. Fine Sunday choir. Open for Sunday morning services; to view the church at other times, call the church office, open daily 9 A.M.–5 P.M., to make an appointment.

Grand Séminaire de Montreal. Sherbrooke at du Fort, built on the site where Messieurs de St-Sulpice constructed a fort protecting early settlements from the Iroquois. The twin towers form two of the city's oldest structures.

Grey Nuns' Museum. 1185 rue St-Mathieu (937–9501), at the community's Mother House. Collection includes textiles, embroidery, lace, paintings, and sculptures, mostly from 18th century. Wed.–Sun., 1:30–4:30 P.M. Free. Groups by appointment.

Notre-Dame Basilica. Place d'Armes (849–1070). Noted neo-Gothic architecture, double-tiered galleries, three rose stained-glass windows. Huge Cassavant organ. Notre-Dame's museum, entrance at 430 rue St-Sulpice (842–2925) holds religious articles including a small silver statue donated by King Louis XV of France. Church open 8 A.M.–6 P.M. for visitors. Museum, Sat., Sun., 10 A.M.–5 P.M.

Notre-Dame de Bon-Secours Chapel. 400 rue St-Paul est (845–9991). Called "the sailors' church," because it holds the carved ships that sailors left as votive offerings. A small, charming church, with observation tower over the St. Lawrence. Memorable statue of Virgin Mary, arms outstretched to the port. Basement museum shows 58 scenes of life in old Quebec and of Blessed Marguerite de Bourgeoys, who founded the Congregations de Notre-Dame order and the first girls' school (1653). Open Tues.–Fri., 9–11:30 A.M., 1–4:30 P.M.; Sat., Sun., 9 A.M.–11:30 P.M.; closed Mon. Admission: adults, $1, children, 25 cents. Via Champ-de-Mars Métro.

St. Joseph's Oratory. 3800 Chemin de la Reine-Marie (Queen Mary Road) (733–8211). Two million pilgrims visit the world's biggest shrine dedicated to St. Joseph, started in 1904 as a tiny chapel for Brother André, a humble, uneducated doorman, credited with many miraculous cures. Finished in 1967 entirely from public subscription, its massive green copper dome is visible for miles. Highlights include stations of the cross, the original chapel, Brother André's tomb, and two museums, one containing hundreds of crutches from people claiming cures. Oratory open 6:30 A.M.–10 P.M. Summer organ concerts, Wed., 8 P.M. $3.50. Boys' choir, Sun., 11 A.M. (summer only). Museum open daily, 10 A.M.–5 P.M. Admission free. Also, art museum containing religious paintings and artifacts. Donations accepted.

Séminaire St-Sulpice. On Place d'Armes, next to Notre-Dame Basilica. Built by the Sulpicians in 1685, and is the city's oldest building still standing. Bears the oldest (1710) public clock in North America. The seminary is closed to the public.

La Visitation du Sault-au-Recollet. 1847 Blvd. Gouin Est (388–4050). Montreal's oldest church, 250th anniversary in 1986. Sanctuary and vestry date to 1680; the Louis XV nave, to 1749. Wood sculpture and gilding at their elaborate best. Daily, 8 A.M.–4:30 P.M.

 MUSEUMS. Cinémathèque Quebecoise. 335 de Maisonneuve est (842–9763) Canada's main technical film museum. Equipment from mid-19th century. Photographs and drawings from animated films. Free. Movies, $1.50. Open daily except Mon., 6–9 P.M.; Sun., 2:30–4:30 P.M.

David Macdonald-Stewart Museum. Old Fort, Île Ste-Hélène (861–6701). Military and household items of 19th century; military maneuvers. May–Sept., daily, 10 A.M.–5 P.M. Sept.–May, Tues.–Sun., same times. Adults, $2; children, $1.50. Phone first.

Lachine Historical Museum. 1255 Saint-Joseph Blvd., corner of 12th Ave. Lachine (637–7433). Take 191 bus from Lionel-Groulx Métro. Artifacts of Canada's fur trade. Sept.–April, Wed.–Sun., 10 A.M.–noon, 1–5 P.M. Mid-May–Sept., daily (except Monday A.M.), 9 A.M.–noon, 1–5:30 P.M. Closed Jan., Feb. Free. Always call first.

McCord Museum. 690 Sherbrooke Ouest (392–4778 weekdays or 392–4774 weekends). Fine collections of artifacts of all principal North American native peoples. Huge totem pole dominates entry. See 19th-century art, costumes, and objects including William Notman photographic archives showing Montreal's past. Wed.–Sun., 11 A.M.–5 P.M. Adults, $1; students, seniors, 75 cents. Families, $2.

Montreal History Centre. 335 Place d'Youville (845–4236). The old fire station depicts Montreal from 17th century to the present. Tues.–Sun., 10 A.M.–3:30 P.M. Adults, $2; seniors, children, $1.

The Montreal Museum of Fine Arts. (MMFA) 1379 rue Sherbrooke Ouest (285–1600). Canada's oldest museum, founded 1860. Quebec's main fine arts museum. Big international collections, world-class exhibitions. Tues.–Sun., 11 A.M.–5 P.M. Thurs., 11 A.M.–9 P.M. Adults, $2; students (16–25 with ID cards), 75 cents, youths, 12–15, 50 cents; children under 12, handicapped, seniors, free; families, $4.

Musée d'Art Contemporain. Cité du Havre (873–2878). Today's art in myriad forms. Library. Tues.–Sun., 10 A.M.–6 P.M. Free.

Musée d'Art de Saint Laurent. 615 Ste. Croix Blvd., Saint Laurent (747–7367). Quebec's early arts and crafts. Periodic thematic exhibitions, guided tours and concerts. Sun., Tues.–Fri., noon–5 P.M. Admission free.

Musée Marc-Aurèle Fortin. 118 St-Pierre (845–6108). One of the few museums dedicated to one person's work, an original, outstanding, impressionist. Tues.–Sun., 11 A.M.–5 P.M. Adults, $2; students, seniors, 75 cents.

Saidye Bronfman Centre. 5170 Côte-Ste-Catherine (739–2301). Montreal's liveliest, most controversial and interesting contemporary art often shown here. Vibrant art school, workshops, lecture/discussion programs, theater (see "Stage"). Mon.–Thurs., 9 A.M.–9 P.M. Fri., 9 A.M.–3 P.M. Free.

GALLERIES. You will find art galleries and boutiques in many parts of the city, including Old Montreal, Westmount around Victoria Avenue, the St-Denis area, and downtown near the Montreal Museum of Fine Arts. Hours vary with exhibits. Many close Sun., Mon. Long-established galleries include: *Canadian Guild of Crafts,* 2025 rue Peel (849–6091). Nonprofit, handicrafts, art, especially Eskimo art. *Continental Gallery Inc.,* 1450 rue Drummond (842–1072). *Dominion Gallery,* 1438 rue Sherbrooke Ouest (845–7833). *Eskimo Art,* 1434 rue Sherbrooke ouest (844–4080) devoted exclusively to Eskimo art. *Walter Klinkhoff Gallery,* 1200 rue Sherbrooke Ouest (288–7306, 288–5972). *Elca London,* rue 1616 Sherbrooke ouest (931–3646). *Verre d'Art,* 1518 rue Sherbrooke Ouest (932–3896). Art glass. *Theo Waddington,* 1504 rue Sherbrooke Ouest (933–3653).

 ARTS AND ENTERTAINMENT. Montrealers support arts and culture with enthusiasm and sophistication. Montreal's English daily, the *Gazette,* lists art, entertainment, lectures, and auditions on Saturday. For tickets call your local Ticketron outlet or Ticketron in Montreal, 300 Léo Parizeau, 5th Floor, Montreal, PQ H2W 2N1 (288–3651). Ticket arrangements vary with show.

The main performing arts complex, *Place des Arts (PdA),* 1501 rue Jeanne Mance, Montreal, PQ H2X 1Z9 (842–2112), holds three concert halls. Salle Wilfrid Pelletier seats 3,000. Théâtre Maisonneuve is a traditional 1,300-seat theater, and Théâtre Port-Royal seats 800. Salle Wilfrid Pelletier presents major visiting performing groups and the Orchestre Symphonique de Montreal (OSM). Two halls present plays, recitals, ballet, and other performances; Théâtre Port-Royal presents plays only. Prices average $20. Box office, Mon.–Sat., noon–9 P.M. Place des Arts' Sunday programs start at 11 A.M. (box office opens 10:30 A.M.) Nov.–May, at $5 for lectures with slides; $1.50 for *Sons et brioches* ("brunch concerts"), plus $1.50 for light breakfast *(brioches et café)*. Miniconcerts suitable for children are held on Saturdays at 11 A.M., Jan.–May. In summer Basilica Notre-Dame in Old Montreal holds Mozart concerts.

MUSIC. *Orchestre Symphonique de Montreal* (842–3402) stars at PdA twice most weeks in the October–May subscription concert season. Tickets at $11–$29 available one month ahead through the box office only. Occasionally tickets available same night. PdA also hosts the McGill Chamber Orchestra (935–4955). *Pollock Concert Hall,* 555 Sherbrooke Ouest, Montreal, PQ H3A 3E3 (392–8224), attached to McGill University, offers classical, light classical, and chamber music, often free. Arrive early. *Opéra de Montreal* (521–5577). Produces four operas each winter at PdA. Seats cost $15–$45.

DANCE. Several dance groups perform in the city, including *Les Grands Ballets Canadiens,* (849–8681) and *Les Ballets Jazz,* at PdA.

Traditional folk dancing. During the summer, folk-dance societies give free performances in city parks. Join them with or without a partner. Call tourist information centers for details. Ethnic folk dancing continues all winter. For instance, Quebec folk dancers meet the third Saturday each month, 8:30 P.M., 4805 ave. Christophe-Colombe (598–8295). Year-round, about 1,500 people dance western-style with the Montreal Area Square Dance Association, Box 906, Pointe Claire-Dorval (744–5036). You can do-si-do at clubs for singles, golden-agers, and couples.

STAGE. Montreal hosts two permanent English theaters, some 10 French theaters, and, occasionally, Yiddish, German, and Hungarian, plus visiting groups, all listed in the *Gazette,* as well as *En Ville,* and *Montreal Scope,* distributed free by many hotels and tourist information centers.

English theaters: *Centaur.* 453 St-François-Xavier (288–3161). Often new plays and experimental theater, Sept.–June, two stages, in original Montreal Stock Exchange Building, Old Montreal. *Saidye Bronfman Centre,* 5170 Chemin de la Côte-Ste-Catherine (739–2301). Reopened fall 1986, revamped and rebuilt, offers exciting program of international theater Sept.–June. The Saidye's Yiddish Theatre group performs plays by leading Jewish writers. (Other English-language theater listed under "Dinner theaters.")

French theaters: *Théâtre Denise Pelletier,* 4353 Ste-Catherine Est (253–8974). *Théâtre de Quat-Sous,* 100 ave. des Pins Est (845–7277). *Théâtre du Nouveau Monde,* 84 Ste-Catherine Ouest (861–0563). *Théâtre du Rideau Vert,* 4664 St-Denis (844–1793).

Dinner theaters: Elegant dinner productions renewed interest in Montreal's English theater. Combinations of theater and/or dinner at various prices, ranging from about $12 for the show-only to over $40 for show, dinner (without wine, tips, or tax), parking. Enthusiasts find this a great excuse to dress up and enjoy a night on the town. Note that drinks usually cost about $4.50.

Arthur's Café Baroque. Queen Elizabeth Hotel, 900 Blvd. Dorchester Ouest (861–3511). Elegant setting for light suppers and drinks. Musical comedies in French and English, operettas, and leading jazz musicians in jam sessions. Closed Mon., Tues. Cover, Wed.–Sun., $12; Sat., $15.

Le Festin du Gouverneur. In the old fort at Île Ste-Hélène (879–1141). Great for groups. Enjoy light operatic airs beautifully rendered. A merry 17th-century frolic in the military barracks mess hall, where copious food comes second to the entertainment. Around $30, including half-liter of wine. Free parking. Reservations necessary.

La Diligence. 7385 Blvd. Décarie (731–7771). Thurs.–Sun. Two dinner theaters plus a restaurant. Light musical comedies and plays in English, local comedians and performers, plus name entertainment—Eartha Kitt, Al Martino. Prices: $30–$45, depending on show.

Le Caf'Conc. Hôtel Château Champlain, 1050 de la Gauchetière ouest (878–9000). Las Vegas-style Parisienne cabaret, with lots of oo-la-la.

Puzzles Scene. Hôtel du Parc, 333 Prince Arthur ouest (288–3733). Light comedy in English.

ACCOMMODATIONS. Unless otherwise noted, establishments accept American Express, MasterCard, and Visa. You can call free to most hotels. Before calling long-distance (514 area code), check 800–514–555–1212 for toll-free numbers. All hotel people speak English, French, and often other languages.

Ask about packages, particularly for weekend visits Nov.–May. Some deluxe hotels offer two nights and three days, including two full breakfasts, for $75–$125 per person, based on double occupancy, subject to availability.

Price categories, based on double occupancy without meals, run as follows: *Super Deluxe,* over $175; *Deluxe,* $130–$175; *Expensive,* $90–$130; *Moderate;* $70–$90; *Inexpensive,* $70 and less. All deluxe hotels offer super-deluxe floors and many expensive hotels hold deluxe accommodations.

Super Deluxe

L'Hôtel Ritz-Carlton. 1228 Sherbrooke Ouest, Montreal, PQ H3G 1H6 (514–842–4212). 241 rooms. On fashionable rue Sherbrooke. Five-star hotel. with fine restaurant. In summer, dine by a garden complete with duck pond.

Le Quatre Saisons (The Four Seasons). 1050 Sherbrooke Ouest, Montreal, PQ H3A 2R6 (514–284–1110). 302 rooms. Elegant, spacious, well-appointed. Fine cuisine, with one of the city's best wine lists; piano bar; well-equipped fitness center; 24-hour room service. Fashionable area.

Deluxe–Super deluxe

Bonaventure-Hilton International. 1 Place Bonaventure, Montreal, PQ H5A 1E4 (514–878–2332). 400 rooms. Unusual luxury hotel atop convention facilities, with rooftop garden and outdoor heated pool used even in subzero weather (swimmers wear bathing caps in winter), parking. Resort atmosphere with gardens. Fine restaurants, entertainment.

Centre Sheraton Montreal. 1201 Blvd. Dorchester Ouest, Montreal, PQ H3B 2L7 (514–878–2000). 827 rooms. Elegant new hotel, 40 suites, indoor pool, entertainment.

Château Champlain. (CP Hotels), 1 Place du Canada, Montreal, PQ H3B 4C9 (514–878–9000). 616 rooms. Gorgeous hotel overlooking park. Free health club with pool, saunas, whirlpool, exercise area, for guests only. Attractions/services include boutiques, movie theater, fine dining, entertainment.

Hôtel du Parc. 3625 ave. du Parc, Montreal, PQ H2X 3P8 (514–288–6666). 455 rooms. Live music in Puzzles (except Sun.), three cinemas. Adjoining Nautilus health club, includes squash, tennis, gyms, pool, saunas, whirlpools, steam baths.

Hôtel de la Montagne. 1430 de la Montagne, Montreal, PQ H3G 1Z5 (514–288–5656). 132 rooms. Baroque, trendy, action-packed, entertainment, disco, fine cuisine, summer pool.

L'Hôtel Méridien. 4 Place Desjardins, Montreal, PQ H5B 1E5 (514–285–1450). 601 rooms. Business center, pool, sauna, babysitting, opposite PdA. Over shopping plaza. Direct underground walkway to Le Palais des congrès (Montreal Convention Center).

La Reine Elizabeth (The Queen Elizabeth). 900 Blvd. Dorchester Ouest Montreal, PQ H3B 4A5 (514–861–3511). CN hotel, 1,070 rooms. Directly linked to underground city. Valet parking, boutiques, fine restaurants, including *The Beaver Club,* entertainment.

Expensive

Château de l'Aéroport. Box 60, Aéroport Internationale de Montreal, Mirabel, PQ J7N 1A2 (514–476–1611). CP hotel. Next to Mirabel International Airport. 365 rooms. Pool, sauna, whirlpool, two squash courts, luxury hotel/resort atmosphere. Dining rooms.

Holiday Inns. (800–465–4329). The following expensive Holiday Inns offer air-conditioning, parking, indoor pools, saunas, boutiques, meeting rooms, dining rooms, and cafes. *Downtown Holiday Inn Centre-Ville.* 420 Sherbrooke Ouest, Montreal, PQ H3A 1B4 (514–842–6111). 486 rooms. *L'Hôtel Place Dupuis.* 1415 St-Hubert, Montreal, PQ H2L 3Y9 (514–842–4881). 359 rooms. Pool, sauna. *Le Richelieu, Est.* 505 Sherbrooke est, Montreal, PQ H2L 1K2 (514–842–8581).

Le Grand Hôtel. 777 University, Montreal, PQ H3C 3Z7 (514–879–1370 or 800–361–8155). 737 rooms. Former Hyatt-Regency; near Old Montreal, connected to the Stock Exchange. Spa, steam bath, indoor pool, aerobic dance classes. Revolving rooftop restaurant with live entertainment, quartet, dinner-dancing.

Montreal Airport Hilton International. 12,505 Côte-de-Liesse, Dorval, PQ H9P 1B7 (514–631–2411). 483 rooms. Free shuttle to and from Dorval Airport, two minutes away. Executive floor, health club, indoor/outdoor pool, summer garden bar. Dining, entertainment.

Moderate

Hôtel Château Versailles. 1659 Sherbrooke Ouest, Montreal, PQ H3H 1E3 (933–3611). 70 rooms. Fine, European-style hotel run by same family for over past 28 years. Handsome Edwardian décor on quiet section of elegant Sherbrooke. Special weekend rates October–May. Do reserve.

Ramada Inns. *Ramada Inn Airport.* 6600 Côte-de-Liesse, St-Laurent, PQ 2 H4T 1E3 (514–737–7811 or 342–2262). 220 rooms, indoor pool, patio. *Ramada Inn Centre-Ville.* 1005 rue Guy, Montreal, PQ H3H 2K4 (514–866–4611). 205 rooms downtown. Outdoor pool, sauna, exercise rooms, piano bar, restaurants. *Ramada Inn Parc Olympique.* 5500 Sherbrooke Est, Montreal, PQ H1N 1A1 (514–256–9011). 236 rooms. Near Olympic Games site, stadium. Pool, nightclub.

Inexpensive

Le Baccarat. 475 Sherbrooke Ouest, Montreal, PQ H3A 2L9 (514–842–3961 or 800–361–4973). 200 rooms. Near McGill University.

Le Royal Roussillon. 1610 rue St-Hubert, Montreal, PQ H2L 3Z3 (514–849–3214). 104 rooms.

Château de l'Argoat. 524 Sherbrooke Est, Montreal, PQ H2L 1K1 (514–842–2046). Family-run, 27 rooms, near Latin Quarter, Métro, Voyageur bus terminal. Popular with Europeans. Rooms with bath, under $40.

BED AND BREAKFAST. B&Bs cost about $30–$45 for singles, and $40–$65 for doubles. Deposit, required with reservation, usually refundable if cancellation received seven days before arrival. Reservation bureaus include: *Montreal Bed & Breakfast,* 4912 Victoria, Montreal, PQ H3W 2N1 (514–738–9410), which also covers the Laurentians and Eastern Townships; *Downtown Bed & Breakfast–Montrealers at Home,* 3458 ave. Laval, Montreal, PQ H2X 3C8 (514–289–9749); *Bed & Breakfast de Chez-nous,* 5386 ave. Brodeur, Montreal, PQ H4A 1J3 (514–485–1252); and *Ginette Houle,* 5151 Côte St-Antoine, Montreal, PQ H4A 1P1 (514–484–7802).

YS AND YOUTH HOSTELS. Montreal's youth hostel downtown: **l'Auberge de jeunesse de Montreal.** 3541 Aylmer, Montreal, PQ H2X 2B9 (514–843–3317). Members, $9 nightly, nonmembers, $12. L'Auberge sleeps 108 people in rooms—most reserved for men only or for women only—with four to 12 beds. Some rooms available for couples and families.

YWCA. 1355 Blvd. Dorchester Ouest. Montreal, PQ H3G 1T3 (514–866–9941). Women residents only. Men may use cafeteria. Overnight singles, $23–$38; doubles, $38–$50. Choose room only, room with sink, or room with private bath. Reserve for best choice. Oct.–May, stay seven nights, pay for six. Cafeteria open 7:30 A.M.–P.M. Pool, sauna, whirlpool, fitness classes, no extra charge for guests.

YMCA. 1450 rue Stanley, Montreal, PQ H3A 2W6 (514–849–8393). Accepts women as well as men. Book at least two days in advance. Women must book seven days ahead—there are fewer rooms with shower (at $42.50) for women. Anyone staying summer weekends must book a week ahead. Men's room rates: $26 (no shower), $42.50 for single, and $50 double. Add $8 per person up to five people, with full bathrooms.

 RESTAURANTS. Montrealers study restaurants with the same enthusiasm with which some people follow sports. Following is a brief selection of Montreal's 2,000 restaurants arranged according to type of food and price. The price categories, based on the cost of a full meal for one person, without tip, tax, or wine, are: *Super Deluxe,* over $40; *Deluxe,* $30–$40; *Expensive,* $20–$30; *Moderate,* $12–$20; *Inexpensive,* less than $12. Unless otherwise noted, some or all major credit cards are accepted.

Chinese

Expensive–Deluxe

Abacus II. 2144 Mackay (933–8444). Spicy Szechuan and Hunan fare served in swish decor that draws beautiful, well-heeled folk. Tues.–Sat., noon–3 P.M., 6 P.M.–midnight. Closed Mon. New York Bar open 5 P.M.–1 A.M.; live entertainment.

Inexpensive–Moderate

La Maison Kam Fung. 1008 Clark (866–4016). Over 700 seats. Gold, red, and black Chinese-dragon décor. At lunchtime dim-sum waitresses sing out names of dishes served from wagons they wheel between the tables. Pick miniportions from over 100 delicacies, at $1.50–$2 each. No dim sum evenings. Full dinner, $10–$20. Dim sum, Mon.–Sat., 11 A.M.–3 P.M., Sun., 10 A.M.–3:30 P.M. Dinner, Mon.–Sat., 3 P.M.–midnight; Sun., 3:30–midnight.

Inexpensive

You will find many other low-priced Chinese restaurants—such as *Le Jardin Lung Fung,* 1071 rue St-Urbain, (879–0622), and *Fung Shing Restaurant,* 1102 blvd. St-Laurent (866–0469), where full meals cost under $12—in Chinatown, which extends roughly from east and west of Bleury to blvd. St-Laurent, south from blvd. Dorchester to Lagauchetière. No credit cards.

French and Belgian

Deluxe–Super Deluxe

Les Chenêts. 2075 Bishop (844–1842). Possibly the city's most expensive restaurant, with the biggest wine cellar. French classics. *Diner gastronomique* for two at $155 includes half-bottle white wine with fish course, a whole bottle of red with the meat. Table d'hôte lunches, $6.50. Mon.–Fri., noon–11 P.M. Sat., Sun., 5:30–11 P.M.

Les Halles. 1450 Crescent (844–2328). Montreal's Establishment loves the glossy décor, perfect textures of fish and lamb. Business lunches. Liquor license. Mon.–Fri., 11 A.M.–11 P.M., Sat., 5–11 P.M. Closed Sun.

Expensive–Deluxe

See also below, under "Hotel Dining Rooms."

Chez la Mère Michel. 1209 Guy (934–0473). Business clientele appreciates the rustic French provincial décor, well-appointed cellar, traditional (and some new) French dishes. Liquor license. Tues.–Fri., 11:30 A.M.–2:30 P.M., 5:30–10:30 P.M. Mon. and Sat., 5:30–10:30 P.M. Closed Sun.

La Chamade. 1453 Bélanger Est (727–7040). Least expensive of the fine owner-chef restaurants. Liquor license. Tues.–Fri., noon–2 P.M. Tues.–Sat., 6–10 P.M. Closed Sun., Mon.

Le St-Amable. 188 rue St-Amable (866–3471). In old fieldstone house, Old Montreal. Classic French. Big on flambéing. Business lunches. Liquor license. Mon.–Fri., noon–3 P.M.; daily, 6–11 P.M.

La Marée. 404 Place Jacques-Cartier (861–8126). Next to St-Amable, also in a heritage fieldstone house. Classic French, like cherries jubilee. Liquor license. Mon.–Fri., noon–3 P.M.; daily 6–11:30 P.M.

Le Fadeau. 423 St-Claude (878–3959). Comfortable old Norman-style house, often brilliant nouvelle cuisine. Often rated tops. Gourmet samplings of many specialties, at $45 per person. Liquor license. Mon.–Fri., noon–3 P.M., 5:30–11:30 P.M. Sat., 6–12 P.M.; Sun., 6–11 P.M.

La Picholette. 1020 St-Denis (843–8502). Divine Victorian house. Food to die for. Honest. Business lunches, Mon.–Fri. Liquor license. Mon.–Fri., 11:30 A.M.–2:30 P.M.; 5:30–11 P.M. Sat., 5:30–11 P.M. Closed Sun.

Moderate–Expensive

Le Caveau. 2063 rue Victoria (844–1624). Note this Victoria stands downtown, near McGill. Reliable, comfortable, amiable, and affordable. Liquor license. Open Mon.–Fri, 7:30 A.M.–11 P.M. Sat., noon–midnight; Sun., 4:30–11 P.M.

L'Exprèss. 3927 St-Denis (845–5333). Quintessential modern bistro. Noisy, bright, lots of mirrors; everyone in overdrive. Wonderful cakes, cheese, nouvelle cuisine. Low wine markup. Dinners under $20. 8 A.M.–2 A.M. Sam. Sun., 2 P.M.–midnight.

L'Odéon. 4806 ave. Parc (273–4088). Bistro imported from Brussels. Perhaps the city's best bistro cuisine. Liquor license. Tues.–Sun., 6:30–11:30 P.M. Bar open till 1 A.M.

Inexpensive-Moderate

La Duchesse Anne. 6390 rue St-Hubert (273–4352). Métro Beaubien, northeast shopping area. Genuine wafer-thin crêpes from Brittany. French country-inn décor. Liquor license. Tues.-Fri., 11:30 A.M.–3 P.M.; Tues., Wed., Sun., 5–9 P.M.; Thurs.–Sat., 5–10:30 P.M. Closed Mon.

Le Paris. 1812 Ste-Catherine Ouest (937–4898). Good little French restaurant. Fresh market produce only. Liquor license. Open Mon.–Sat., noon–3 P.M.; 5–10 P.M.

Le P'tit Port. 1813 Ste-Catherine Ouest (932–6556). Fish and seafood. Bring wine. Tues.–Fri., noon–10:30 P.M. Sat. 6–10:30 P.M.

Restaurant Julien. 1191 Union Ave. (871–1581). Near downtown hotels, shops. Pretty décor. Nouvelle cuisine. Wine bar. 11:30 A.M.–3 P.M.; 6–10:30 P.M.

Hotel Dining Rooms

You will find some of the most elegant dining (mostly French) in Montreal's fine hotels. They vie jealously to keep their clientele on the premises by offering soft background music (sometimes harp or piano), fine and often innovative cuisine, and service at competitive prices. Dinners are in the *Expensive–Super Deluxe* range. Popular Sunday brunches (reservations necessary) cost around $20; children usually half price. All hold liquor licenses and accept credit cards. The selection includes:

The Beaver Club. The Queen Elizabeth, 900 blvd. Dorchester Ouest (861–3511). Local lions dine among fur-trade artifacts, as they did at the original 18th-century club. Sunday brunch, $19, two sittings, 11:30, 1:30. Open daily from 12 A.M.–3 P.M.; 6–11 P.M.

Café de Paris. L'Hôtel Ritz-Carlton, 1228 Sherbrooke Ouest (842–4212). Classical French food and service. Pianist.

Le Castillon. Bonaventure-Hilton International, Place Bonaventure (878–2332). Unusual 17th-century French castle décor, overlooking rooftop garden. Business lunch, Mon.–Fri., $10.50–$25. Dinner $25 and up. Sunday brunch. 11 A.M.–2:30 P.M.; Mon.–Fri., noon–2:30 P.M.; nightly 6–11:30 P.M.

Lutétia. Hotel de la Montagne, 1430 de la Montagne (288–5656). Baroque mezzanine restaurant overlooks cabaret, piano bar, and lots of action. Sunday brunch. Mon.–Sat., 7–11:30 A.M.; noon–3 P.M.; 6–11:30 P.M. Sun. 11:30 A.M.–3 P.M.

Le Neufchâtel. Château Champlain, Place du Canada (878–9000). Elegant country *château* décor. Harpist. A la carte dinner, $45. House wine. Mon.–Sat., 6–10 P.M. Closed Sun. Sun. brunch at rooftop L'Escapade, 10:30 A.M.–2:30 P.M.

Le Point de Vue. Centre Sheraton, 1201 Dorchester Ouest, (878–2000). Harpist, Mon.–Sat., 6–10:30 P.M. Closed Sun.

Le Restaurant. Le Quatre Saisons, 1050 Sherbrooke Ouest (284–1110). A la carte dinner $20–$30. "Alternative cuisine" available for people monitoring calorie, cholesterol, and sodium intake. Daily, 7 A.M.–11 P.M.

Greek

You will find many Greek restaurants dotted throughout the city, most in the pedestrian mall around Prince Arthur. Many favorites in traditionally Greek avenue du Parc area.

Moderate-Expensive

Molivos. 4859 ave. du Parc (271–5354). Seafood by the pound, extras à la carte. Dinner about $10–$30. Liquor license. Daily, 11 A.M.–midnight.

Milos. 5357 ave. du Parc (272–3522). Shrimp, fried squid, and charcoal-broiled fish flown in from New York, four-pound lobsters. A la carte. Dinner about $20. Liquor license. Daily, 11 A.M.–3 P.M.; 5 P.M.–1 A.M.

Indian

Moderate

Le Taj. 2077 Stanley (845–9015). Elegant. Attracts well-dressed people. Tandoori dishes and north Indian fare. Main dishes, $8.95–$15. Buffet lunch, Mon.–Fri. $8. Liquor license. Daily, 11:30 A.M.–2:30 P.M., Sun.–Thurs., 5–11 P.M. Closes midnight Fri., Sat.

Inexpensive–Moderate

New Delhi. 5014 Ave. du Parc (279–0339). Authentic northern Indian. Liquor license. Mon.–Fri., 11:30 A.M.–2 P.M., Mon.–Thurs., 5–11 P.M.; Fri., Sat., Sun., 5 P.M.–midnight.

New Punjab. 4026A Ste-Catherine Ouest (932–9440). New family-run restaurant holds much promise. Liquor license. Daily, 11 A.M.–11 P.M.

New Woodlands. 1241 rue Guy (933–1553). Real south Indian vegetarian fare, plus meat and fish curries. Try masala dosa, big, crisp, and lacy crêpes. Liquor license. Summer, daily, 11:30 A.M.–11 P.M. Winter, 11:30 A.M.–3 P.M., 5–11 P.M.

Italian

Moderate–Expensive

La Sila. 2040 St-Denis (844–5083). Draws rave reviews for ambiance, service, and innovative fare. Liquor license. Dinner only, Mon.–Sat. 5:30–11 P.M. Closed Sun.

Lo Stivale d'Oro. 2150 Mountain St. (844–8714). Critics heap praise on this warm and romantic echo of Italy. Regional Italian and continental cuisine. Liquor license. Mon.–Fri., 11:30 A.M.–3 P.M., 5P.M.–midnight; Sat., noon–midnight; Sun., 5–11 P.M.

Restaurant Baci. 2095 McGill College Avenue (288–7901). Opened in 1985, and worth watching. Pianist plays evenings from Wed.–Sat. Mon.–Sat., 11 A.M.–midnight; Sat., 5:30 P.M.–midnight. Closed Sun.

Inexpensive–Moderate

Le Piémontais. 1145A de Bullion (861–8122). Lively and sympatico little downstairs ristorante. Liquor license. Mon.–Fri., 11 A.M.–midnight; Sat. 5 P.M.–midnight. Closed Sun.

Deli and Jewish-Style

Vaad Hair, 5491 Victoria Ave., Westmount (739–6363), supplies lists of true kosher restaurants.

Inexpensive

Balkans & Lennox. 359 ave. du President Kennedy (845–9494). Unpretentious décor, motherly service. Small, kosher-style. Mon.–Fri., 6 A.M.–8 P.M.; Sat., 6 A.M.–2 P.M. Closed Sun.

Beauty's. 93 ave. Mont-Royal Ouest (849–8883). New York diner atmosphere. Wholesome breakfast food all day. Big for Sunday brunch. No liquor license. Mon.–Fri., 7 A.M.–6 P.M., depending on demand. Sat., 7 A.M.–5 P.M. Sun., 8 A.M.–5 P.M. No credit cards.

Ben's. 990 blvd. de Maisonneuve Ouest (844–1001). Serves smoked meat. Open Sun.–Wed., 7 A.M.–4 A.M.; Thurs., Fri., Sat., 7 A.M.–5 A.M.

Brisket's. 2055 Bishop (843–3650). Ice-cream-parlor décor in cozy downtown house. One of Montreal's claims to culinary fame rests on smoked meat. Here they cure their own. Classic smoked-meat sandwiches. Draft beer. Cherry coke. Friendly service. Liquor license. Sun.–Wed., 11 A.M.–10 P.M. Thurs.–Sat., 11 A.M.–midnight in winter, and until 1 A.M. in summer.

Main St. Lawrence Steak House Delicatessen. 3864 blvd. St-Laurent (843–8126). Home-cured smoked meat. No liquor license. Never closes.

Schwartz's Montreal Hebrew Delicatessen. 3895 blvd. St-Laurent (842–4813). Lunch-counter style. Montreal smoked meat cured here. No liquor license. Sun.–Thurs., 9 A.M.–12:45 A.M.; Fri., 9 A.M.–1:45 A.M.; Sat., 9 A.M.–2:45 A.M. No credit cards.

Québec

Expensive

Les Filles du Roy. 415 Bonsecours (849–3535). Features Quebec cooking in traditional Quebec décor. 11:30 A.M.–midnight.

Pâtisseries

In case you have a *pâtisserie* attack, here are three treatment centers, offering divine pastry and coffee. None hold liquor licenses or accept credit cards. Opening hours vary. *Au Duc de Lorraine,* 5002 Côte-des-Neiges (731–4128). Closed Mon., Rockland Shopping Centre, Town of Mont-Royal (731–8229). Closed Sun. *LeNôtre,* 1050 Laurier Ouest (270–2702). Closed Mon. Also at 2072 Drummond (842–4000). Closed Sun. *Pâtisserie de Nancy,* 5655 Monkland (482–3030). Closed Mon.

Vegetarian

Inexpensive

Le Commensal. 2115 St-Denis (845–2627) and 680 Ste-Catherine Ouest (871–1480). Inventive veggie fare, sold by weight, so salads cost less than curried rice. You can bring wine to the St-Denis cafe, which opens daily 6 A.M.–2 A.M. The Ste-Catherine outlet, which holds a liquor license, opens daily from 11 A.M.–midnight.

 NIGHTLIFE AND BARS. The big hotels all offer entertainment, from full-fledged cabarets and dinner theater to dancing to live music between shows. The *Ritz-Carlton,* 1228 Sherbrooke Ouest (842–4212), has a ground-floor bar *(très élégant),* with pianist in evening dress, where you nibble on smoked salmon. The most soigné gentlefolk trip the light fantastic on the Ritz' tiny dance floor. You will find a boggling assortment of bars and nightlife in five main areas: first, the trendy, traditionally Anglophone (but really cosmopolitan) Bishop/Crescent streets—no jeans here; second, the Latin Quarter of rue St-Denis above Ste-Catherine as far north as rue Rachel; third, the Laurier Boulevard/St-Laurent area; fourth, the newly awakening (and "in") avenue Parc/St-Joseph quarter; fifth, rue Prince Arthur at Boulevard St-Laurent.

L'Air du Temps, 191 St-Paul Ouest (842–2003). Victorian, with lace and petit point, winding staircase, wood paneling, at this well-established jazz bar offering fine groups and soloists. Imported Paris Métro car provides intimate corners for private conversations. $5 cover.

Biddle's. 2060 Aylmer (842–8656). Montreal's annual Jazz Festival attracts the world's greats, but many live and work here, namely, bassist Charlie Biddle's trio, with pianist Oliver Jones, and guest. Great ribs-and-chicken. Biddle and Jones play Wed.–Sat. from 10:30 P.M. Other live music earlier. No cover.

Business Bar. 3510 St-Laurent at Milton (849–3988). Alternative disco, like basement parking garage, all cement, glass, and steel *au naturel*. Holds 300 people. Sun–Thurs., 10 P.M.–3:30 A.M.; Fri., Sat., 9 P.M.–3:30 A.M. $4 cover.

The Cock'n Bull. 1944 Ste-Catherine Ouest (933–4556). British-style pub, with good fare. Double Diamond and Guinness beer on draft. ll A.M.–3A.M. Live music Thurs.–Sat.

Club de Danse Ira Murra, Enrg. 3981 St-Laurent Suite G1 (842–4761). The Laflèches learned to dance from Arthur Murray's brother, Ira. For $2.50 you get coffee and foxtrot, rhumba, waltz, and chacha, Sat., from 9 P.M. Closed July/Aug. Rusty? Then come at 7:30 P.M. for lessons, $40 for 10 hours ("never a contract"). No liquor served.

Du Côté de Chez Swann. 57 Prince Arthur (844–1019). Fri., Sat. meet the young crowd—ages 18–35. Weekdays, average age rises. Three-floor bar, discos, one with dance floor for 250 people, stage. Quiet area, too. Daily, 5 P.M.–3 A.M. Cover $3. Thurs.–Sat.

Les Foufounes Electriques. 97 Ste-Catherine est (845–4584). At "The Electric Bums," new wave "alternative" disco/stand-up bar. Wear whatever here. Stage, room for 300. Black walls glow in black light. Mix of go-go, tango, poetry readings, theater, mime, magic, action painting, and latest sound. Most avant-garde bar in town. Not for faint-hearted. 10 A.M.–3 A.M. Cover charge varies with events.

Le Grand Café. 1720 St-Denis (849–6955). Downstairs, restaurant. Upstairs, live talent, including pianists, jazz, comedians. Tues.–Sat., from 9 P.M. Last set at 2:15 A.M. Cover charge. $3–$5.

Grumpy's. 1242 Bishop (downtown) (866–9010). Sedate pub with warm atmosphere, mainly well-dressed, over-35 crowd. Mon.–Sat., 3 P.M.–3 A.M.; Sun., noon–3 A.M.

Lux. 5229 St-Laurent (271–9272). Extraordinary bar-restaurant-tobacconist (exotic Turkish and Egyptian brands), and newsstand. Every kind of magazine you could possibly want. Wine by glass; dazzling tubular décor with grillwork. Like a Parisian "drogstore," never closes.

The Old Dublin Pub. 1219A University (861–4448). Irish, British beer on tap—Guinness, Tartan Bitter, Bass Ale, Harp Lager. Live entertainment, darts, sing-songs. Mon.–Sat., 11:30 A.M.–3 A.M.

Old Munich. 1170 St-Denis (288–8011). Montreal's biggest (and loudest) German beer hall. Bavarian food and entertainment. Liveliest on weekends and holidays.

Puzzles' Bar. Hotel du Parc, 333 Prince Arthur Ouest (288–3733). Big, comfortable arm chairs, many plants, live jazz on Thurs.–Sat., 9:30 P.M.–1:30 A.M. Open daily 11:30 A.M.–3 A.M.; closes 1 A.M. Sun. No cover.

La Ricane. 177 Bernard Ouest (279–3977). Neighborhood bar serves bargain food *la bouffe*. Montreal Storytellers hold forth in English alternate Tuesdays. Fri. and Sat. night jazz. Daily, 4 P.M.–3 A.M.

Spectrum de Montreal. 318 Ste-Catherine Ouest (861–5851). A former movie theater with seats replaced by tables, chairs, and bar, holds 1,000 people who pay about $16 for latest rock, jazz, pop *spéctacles*. Opens 8 P.M. for 9 P.M. show; sometimes second show around 10:30 P.M. Closes about midnight. Giant screen for latest music videos.

Thursday's. 1449 Crescent (849–5634). Lots of action at this giant stand-up bar. Vast disco downstairs always lively. Cover charge.

Woody's Pub. 1234 Bishop (395–8118). Dance floor. Well-heeled crowd, aged 24–40. Young crowd. Upstairs, The Comedy Nest showcases stand-up comics. Shows Thurs., 9 P.M.; Fri., Sat., 9 P.M., 11 P.M.; Sun., 8:30 P.M.

QUEBEC CITY: GIBRALTAR OF

NORTH AMERICA

Birthplace of French-colonial North America, this jewel of a city perched high on a cliff overlooking the St. Lawrence River is so rich with charm, history, and natural beauty that it is an experience not to be missed when touring the province. The old, walled city is so full of architectural treasures—many dating back to the 17th century—that UNESCO recently declared it a site of "outstanding universal value," ranking with Egypt's pyramids and India's Taj Mahal.

Quebec's history is inextricably tied to its strategic position high above the narrowing of the St. Lawrence River. Its value as a military fortress was first realized by the founder of New France, Samuel de Champlain, who began the settlement in 1608. Champlain built Fort St-Louis in 1620, at the highest point of the cliff known as Cap Diamant. The Comte de Frontenac took over the colony's administration in 1672 and started building the walls after the British navy demanded his surrender in 1690. (Frontenac reportedly told an emissary from British Admiral William Phipps, "My answer will come from the mouths of my cannons.")

These early defense systems would be rebuilt and improved several times during the next two centuries, resulting in the walled city that earned Quebec the name, "Gibraltar of North America."

The fortress was used to defend the colony against the British (until Quebec fell to General James Wolfe in 1759) and later against the Americans, who made several attempts to capture the stronghold, first in 1775 and again during the War of 1812. To ward off further American invasions, the British built the Citadel, a giant star-shaped bunker on Cap Diamant.

Religion was central to the colonists' lives and played a vital role in the settlement of Quebec. In the early 17th century religious orders established hospitals, churches, and centers of learning. Sister Marie de l'Incarnation and Madame de la Peltrie founded the first school for girls in North America. François-Xavier de Montmorency Laval was named bishop of the diocese extending to the Pacific and the Gulf of Mexico. He founded the Séminaire de Quebec which eventually became Laval University. The colonists completed what is now the oldest standing cathedral in North America—Notre Dame de la Victoire—in 1678.

In the meantime, the town became a thriving center of trade and commerce, with fur trading the major activity. Eventually, fishing, logging, and shipbuilding flourished. The suburb of Lauzon across the St. Lawrence has one of the world's largest shipyards. A major port today, Quebec exports Canadian grain and imports general cargo from around the world.

Today the biggest employer in Quebec, the provincial capital, is the government. The 30,000 civil servants who live and work here make up the bulk of its labor force. Many also work in the city's hospitals and educational institutions.

A seat of government since its beginnings, the city has political traditions that run strong and deep. Politics are as important to Quebecers as hockey and good food, and the fine art of rhetoric can be heard when the National Assembly sits from March to June and from September to December.

With a population of 500,000, Quebec has all the advantages of a middle-sized city, including manageable traffic and easy access to the countryside. Beautiful Laurentian lakes and mountains and some of the finest ski slopes and trails anywhere are only a 20-minute drive from downtown.

The term *joie de vivre* has been used to death to describe Quebecers' legendary love for a good time, but the ambiance of lively talk, laughter, and general enjoyment is indeed a fact of life here—and it is infectious. Walk down the Grande Allée any summer evening—or winter evening, for that matter—and you will hear it drifting out of the dozens of bars, bistros, and discotheques.

While Quebec is indisputably and proudly French-speaking, most natives—especially those in the tourism business—also speak English. Many British, Scottish, and Irish soldiers married into French-speaking families. Their influence is unmistakable in the jigs, reels, and ballads of Quebec's folk culture. In fact, Quebecers will tell you they speak three languages—French, English, and hospitality.

Exploring Quebec City

There is so much to do and see in Quebec and vicinity, it is best to line up your sightseeing priorities before you set out. Canada's destiny was shaped on the famous battlefield, the Plains of Abraham, now a national historic park. The image of General James Wolfe and his army of 4,000 men crossing the St. Lawrence and scaling the cliffs under the Plains on the moonless night of 13 September 1759 lives in the memory of every Canadian schoolchild. Both generals Wolfe and the Marquis de Montcalm died heroes' deaths in the battle along with 2,000 soldiers. The Citadel, Martello Towers, and other fortifications built to protect the city from American invasions are part of the remarkable fortifications system in the park.

Just outside the walled city is modern Quebec, with high-rise hotels and government buildings blending with architecture of the past. The Grande Allée, the main thoroughfare leading to the old city and flanked by mansions, is now the center of cafe society and nightlife with its lively strip of sidewalk restaurants and bars. On the left (as you enter the city) the Grande Allée borders a complex of government buildings, including the stately, 19th-century Hôtel du Parlement, seat of the provincial government, and Le Pigeonnier ("Pigeonhole") Square, where the city's pigeon population earns a Good Housekeeping award for sticking to its specially built "pigeon condos."

Le Grande Théâtre on St. Cyrille Street, home of major theatrical events here, was designed by architect Victor Prus as a project honoring Canada's 1967 Centennial. A huge (and controversial) three-part mural called "Death, Space, and Liberty" by Spanish-born artist Jordi Bonet—Quebec's answer to Mexican muralist Diego Rivera—stands in the main foyer.

Entering the old, walled city—the only one in America north of Mexico—is like entering a time warp. The walls and great, arched gates lead you to a world so different (at least by North American standards) you may wonder if you have not strayed into a movie set by mistake. Extremely proud of their heritage, Quebecers have preserved dozens of buildings, battle sites, and monuments, some dating back to the 17th century. The result is a charming blend of winding, cobblestone streets and old houses reminiscent of Europe.

Old Quebec's location on a steep hill gives it a "split-level" character, dividing it into *Haute Ville* (Upper Town), the colonial era's residential area, and *Bas Ville* (Lower Town), center of commerce and shipping. Central meeting place for the community was Place d'Armes, the

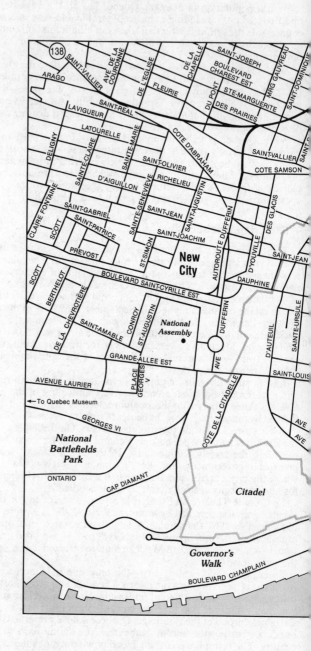

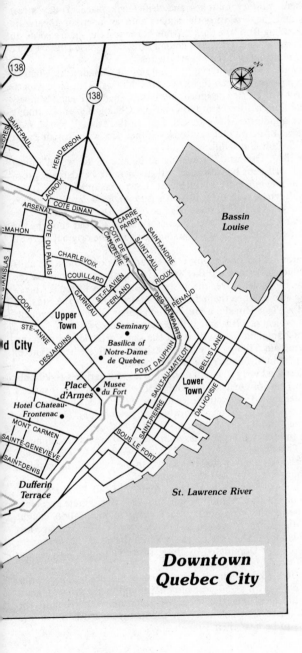

Downtown
Quebec City

square where military marches and drills took place. Today street musicians and jugglers turn the square into an open-air theater in summer. Leading from rue Sainte-Anne bordering the square is rue du Trésor, a narrow lane where the colonial treasury house *(trésor)* once stood. Today artists sell their work there.

Probably the most photographed building in Canada, the Château Frontenac, a massive, green-turreted castle, dominates the city. American architect Bruce Price designed the classy Canadian Pacific Railway hotel where Queen Elizabeth and Madame Chiang Kai-shek, among many other dignitaries, have stayed. During the Second World War, U.S. president Franklin Delano Roosevelt met here with British Prime Minister Winston Churchill.

Built in 1838, Dufferin Terrace has to be one of the world's most elegant and well-kept boardwalks, with its pergola bandstand, green railings, and magnificent view of the St. Lawrence and Lower Town. Linking the Terrace with Place d'Armes is *Promenade des Gouverneurs* (Governors' Walk). The Terrace sits above *Cap Diamant* (Cape Diamond, so named, the story goes, because Jacques Cartier thought the quartz he discovered there was diamonds), site of the original Fort St. Louis.

An elevator (called *funiculaire*) travels up and down the steep cliffs between Dufferin Terrace and Bas Ville. The stouthearted can make the same trip on the fabled "Breakneck Steps"—named by intrepid American tourists who climbed them and survived—which scale the cliffs. At the bottom is Place Royale, a multimillion dollar Quebec government restoration project of 17th- and 18th-century buildings standing on the site where Champlain first settled. In the same area, local artists restored Champlain Village, now an artists' cooperative where some of the province's finest handicrafts can be found.

Île d'Orléans, a lovely island of farmlands and six parishes 16 kilometers (9 miles) east of Quebec via Route 138, was one of New France's earliest settlements. Here you can visit more old houses, churches, and museums and pick your own strawberries (watch for "Cueillez vos fraises" signs) and apples in season.

The Montmorency Falls *(Chutes Montmorency)* are further along on route 138. This gorgeous 83-meter (272 feet) waterfall (one and a half times as high as Niagara Falls) is well worth the journey. In winter it forms a giant ice cone called the "sugar loaf."

Sainte-Anne-de-Beaupré is also on route 138, 40 kilometers (24 miles) east of Quebec. A million pilgrims visit this tribute to Sainte Anne, mother of the Virgin Mary, each year. Colonial sailors caught in a devastating storm prayed to Sainte Anne and were saved, according to popular lore. They set up the original shrine at the site where they reached land. Dominated by the giant romanesque basilica, the shrine is North America's largest.

On route 369, 7 kilometers (4 miles) north of Quebec in Loretteville, is Huron Village with a 250-year-old chapel, old manuscripts, a giant tepee, and liturgical museum. The Arouanne museum recounts the evolution of the tribe, which moved to the spot from southern Ontario in the 1600s to be near their French allies.

PRACTICAL INFORMATION FOR QUEBEC CITY

HOW TO GET THERE. By Plane. Quebec's International Airport, in suburban Ste-Foy, 19 km (12 mi.) from downtown Quebec City, was enlarged and remodeled in 1984. It handles regular service to Canadian and U.S. cities via *Air Canada, Quebecair, Quebec Aviation,* and *CP Air.* Air Canada flies regularly from Quebec to Montreal, New Orleans, Baton Rouge, Houston, Dallas, Austin, Halifax, London, (Ontario), Edmonton, Calgary, Brussels, and Paris.

By Bus. *Voyageur, Inc.* provides hourly service daily between Montreal and Quebec from 6 A.M.–1 A.M. and regular service between Quebec and several other centers from two terminals: Downtown terminal, 225 Charest Blvd. Est (418–524–4692), and Ste-Foy terminal, 2700 Laurier Blvd., Ste-Foy.

By Train. *VIA Rail* travels daily to and from Montreal to Quebec's recently renovated 19th-century CPR (Canadian Pacific Railway) station, Gare du Palais, 450 rue St-Paul (418–524–6452) and suburban Ste-Foy, 3255 Chemin de la Gare, (418–692–3940).

By Car. From Montreal, highways 40 and 138 will take you on a leisurely route through Trois-Rivières and several picturesque villages. Superhighway 401 from Toronto continues into Hwy. 20 to Quebec—about 3½ hours from Montreal. U.S. highways 87 in New York, 89 in Vermont, and 91 in New Hampshire connect with Hwy. 10—Quebec's Eastern Townships Autoroute—which also joins with Hwy. 20. From Maine motorists may take highways 201, 173, and 73 to Quebec, or a longer riverside route via Hwy. 95 to highways 1, 2, and 185, joining with Hwy. 20 at Rivière du Loup, northeast of Quebec.

By Boat. Founded as a trading center, the city continues to flourish as a major Canadian port and plays host to cruise and cargo ships alike. Quebec offers docking facilities and complete services for boaters. Call Sociéte du Port de Quebec (418–648–3645) or write to Ports Canada, 150 Dalhousie, Box 2268, Quebec, PQ G1K 7P7.

TOURIST INFORMATION. You will find an excellent selection of information at one of two major tourism centers in downtown Quebec. *Tourisme Quebec* at 12 rue Ste-Anne (418–643–2280 or 800–443–7000) is open daily June-Aug., 8:30 A.M.–8:30 P.M. Sept.-May daily, 9 A.M.–5 P.M. Or write to CP 20,000, Quebec, PQ G1K 7X2. The *Quebec City Region Tourism and Convention Bureau,* 60 rue d'Auteuil, Quebec, PQ G1R 4C4 (418–692–2503), is open daily, early June-Labor Day, 8:30 A.M.–8 P.M. April and May, Sept. and Oct., Mon.-Fri., 8:30 A.M.–5:30 P.M. Nov.-April, 8:30 A.M.–5 P.M. A second office at 3005 Blvd. Laurier, Ste-Foy, PQ G1V 2M2 (651–2882) is open daily 8:30 A.M.–6 P.M., 8 P.M. in summer.

To find out what is going on daily while you are there, check out the city's two daily, French-language newspapers, *Le Journal de Quebec* (A.M.) and *Le Soleil* (P.M.). The English-language *Chronicle Telegraph* appears on Wednesdays. Other sources of information in English are CKMI-TV, Channel 5, and radio station McCBVE, 104.7 FM (6 A.M.–1 A.M.).

TELEPHONES. The area code for Quebec is 418. Cost of a local call is 25 cents, with no time limit. **Emergency Numbers:** *City police* (691–6123); *provincial police* (623–6262); *24-hour emergency medical service* (687–9915); *Health-info* (648–2626); *Hôtel-Dieu Hospital* (694–5042); *Jeffrey Hale Hospital* (683–4471); *emergency dental service,* Mon.-Fri., 8 A.M.–5 P.M. (653–5412); *24-hour poison center* (656–8090); *pharmacy,* daily until 2 A.M., 4266 Charlesbourg Ave. (623–1571); *24-hour maritime search and rescue* (872–2859); *air search and rescue* (800–267–7270); *road conditions* (643–6830); *24-hour weather* (872–2859).

HOW TO GET AROUND. From the airport. The Quebec Airport is 19 km (12 mi) from downtown. Taxis, available just outside the airport exit near the baggage claim, cost around $20 and an airport bus leaving every two hours and stopping at major hotels is $6.75 for the 20-minute trip to downtown Quebec.

By Bus. *Quebec Urban Community Transit* buses run regularly every 15–20 minutes in town and cost $1.20 (exact change) for adults, 65 cents for children. For information, call 627–2511.

By Taxi. Drop rate is $1.50 and 70 cents per kilometer thereafter. Taxi companies are listed in the yellow pages. Among them are: *Taxi Quebec*, 975 8th Ave. (522–2001), and *Taxi Coop de Quebec*, 302 3rd Ave. (525–5191).

By Rental Car. Car rentals are reasonable, with special weekend rates averaging $30–$35. Insurance costs about $10 daily. Quebec is served by the major firms including *Avis* (airport, 872–2861; downtown, 523–0041); *Budget* (airport, 872–9885; downtown, 692–3660; toll-free, 800–268–8970); *Hertz* (airport, 871–1571; downtown, 694–1224; toll-free, 800–268–1311); *Holiday* (downtown, 667–0129; Ste-Foy, 656–1411); *Rent-A-Wreck* (683–2333); *Tilden* (airport, 871–1224; downtown, 694–1727); *Sears* (Ste-Foy, 694–1685).

HINTS TO HANDICAPPED TRAVELERS. The Quebec Urban Community's publication *Access to Métro Quebec* has a comprehensive list of stores, tourist attractions, restaurants, and lodging with special facilities for handicapped travelers. Write in advance or pick up a copy at the Quebec city Region Tourism and Convention Bureau, 60 rue d'Auteuil, Quebec, PQ G1R 4C4 (418–692–2503). Most street corners have wheelchair ramps and strictly enforced parking for the disabled marked with blue and white wheelchair signs. Kéroul, 4545 Pierre Coubertin or CP 1,000, Succursale M, Montreal, PQ H1V 3R2 (514–252–3104) lists special tours, as well as orthopedic centers, for the disabled.

WINTER CARNIVAL. Renowned as the world's biggest winter carnival, Quebec's version of the pre-Lenten Mardi Gras festival is an anti-February-blues bash without rival. The ten-day event usually beginning the first week in February has become famous for its celebration of snow and ice, phenomena the natives here take pride in transforming into everything from giant sculptures to a spine-chilling luge run. The festival turns this city of 17th-century châteaus and fortresses into a magical snow-covered Disneyworld complete with an ice castle, a queen and six duchesses, parades, and gala balls. Founded 33 years ago by a group of local businessmen to "beat the winter blues," the event now draws as many as 1½ million tourists and features more than 100 indoor and outdoor events including concerts, special exhibitions, and nightly dances.

Among the major highlights is the ice-sculpture competition on Place du Palais. Created by local artists and others from as far afield as Mexico and Switzerland, the massive works of art are judged by the Carnival's host, "Bonhomme Carnaval," a huge snowman dressed in the traditional red tuque and woven belt of Quebec's early "habitants." (Another dazzling sculpture competition on rue Ste-Therese in Lower Town features work by local residents.)

The carnival's conventional athletic events range from hockey tournaments and speed-skating marathons to provincial swimming, racquetball, and volleyball competitions. More unusual competitions include torch and acrobatic skiing, dogsled racing, and the famous international canoe race across the St. Lawrence in which participants do battle with large chunks of floating ice.

Accommodations in major hotels, the YWCA, and youth hostels are generally booked solid at least a month in advance, though last-minute vacancies are often available in suburban inns, motels, and bed-and-breakfast arrangements in private homes. (Major hotels often raise their rates as high as 30 percent during the Carnival.) If you are willing to rough it with your own towel and sleeping bag, you can stay in a downtown church basement for $7.50. A lodging committee on duty around the clock during the event matches visitors with accommodations, usually within four hours. Call (418) 524–8441 for information. For further details, write to the Carnival's head office at 290 rue Joly, Quebec, PQ G1L 4T8 (418–626–3716).

OTHER SEASONAL EVENTS. Late January. *Quebec International Bonspiel.* Quebec curling clubs. Six-day international curling tournament (688–1225). **February.** *International Pee-Wee Hockey Tournament.* Quebec Coliseum, Exposition Park. For 10–12-year-olds from Canada, the U.S., and Europe. Lasts ten days (656–3372). **Mid-April.** *International Book Fair.* Centre municipal des congrès de Quebec, Place Quebec (658–1774). **First two weeks in July.** Quebec's annual Summer Festival features a dazzling variety of concerts, stage shows, and other special events, including many special children's activities. **July 26.** *Feast of Ste-Anne.* Ste-Anne-de-Beaupré Basilica. Torchlight parade (827–3781). **End of July-early August.** *Quebec handicraft exhibition and sale.* Jardins de l'hôtel de ville (City Hall) (694–0260). **End of August-early September.** *Agricultural Fair.* Parc de l'Exposition. The province's biggest. Also trade and industrial show. Lasts two weeks (694–0260). **Early December.** Salon des artisans de Quebec *(Quebec Crafts Show)* Centre municipale des congrès de Quebec, Place Quebec. Lasts 15 days (694–0260).

TOURS AND SPECIAL-INTEREST SIGHTSEEING. Bus. *Gray Line* (627–2351) offers guided tours of Quebec City, Montmorency Falls, Ste-Anne-de-Beaupré, Île d'Orléans, and combination city tours and harbor cruises. Prices range from about $11–$16 for adults, half that for children. City tours run year-round, others from May-Oct., or June-Labor Day, depending on tour. Other bus lines with competitive prices and similar tours are: *Maple Leaf Sightseeing Tours* (688–9742); *Contact-Quebec,* which also offers fall foliage tours (692–2801); *Old Quebec Tours* (872–9226); *Orbitour* (692–1223); *Visite touristique de Quebec* (653–9722). *Visites Touristiques Fleur-de-Lys* (658–9635).

Boat. St. Lawrence cruises—including moonlight cruises of Quebec harbor—are offered by *Quebec Maritimes Excursions* (692–1678) and *M/V Louis Jolliet* (692–1159). The *Quebec-Levis ferry* (692–0550) takes 15 minutes and runs every half hour. For whale-watching excursions (July-Oct.) contact the *Société Linnéene du Quebec* (653–8186) or *Lower St. Lawrence Tourist Assoc.* (867–1272).

By Antique Car. *Les Tours d'Antan Inc.,* 396 Principale, St-Étienne, Lévis, PQ G0S 2L0 (831–1678).

By Calèche. These horse and carriage rides cost about $30–$35 (667–9029).

By Foot. *L.L.M. Tours,* 2216 Chemin du Foulon, Sillery, PQ G1T 1X4 (658–4799).

PARKS AND GARDENS. Bois-de-Coulonge. Grande Allée Ouest and Holland St. A summer theater now stands on the grounds of this former seigneurial domain and mansion of lieutenant governors since Confederation. Lieutenant Governor Paul Comptois died in the fire that destroyed the mansion in 1966. Open 24 hours. Free.

Cartier-Brébeuf Park. 175 rue de l'Espinay (648–4038). Operated by Parks Canada, this extensive green space was named after Canada's discoverer Jacques Cartier, who spent the winter of 1535–6 at the site, and Father Jean de Brébeuf, a founder of the Jesuit Order in New France. Special features are a replica of Cartier's flagship *La Grande Hermine,* guided tours, and an information center explaining Cartier's voyages. The park offers picnic sites, canoeing, skating, cross-country skiing, cycling paths, and calèche rides. May 14-Labor Day, Tues.-Sun., 9:30 A.M.–5 P.M. Sept.-May, visitors center only, Mon.-Fri., 10 A.M.–4 P.M. Closed Christmas-New Year's Day. Free.

Joan of Arc Park. Laurier Ave. and Place Montcalm. A statue of the 15th-century heroine on horseback dominates this park belonging to the Battlefields Park Commission. French formal gardens surround the statue and square. Open 24 hours. Free.

Le Jardin des Gouverneurs. Behind the Château Frontenac. Outdoor theater and dance take place in the park in summer. A statue of generals James Wolfe and the Marquis de Montcalm honors both heroes.

Montmorency Park. East of Quebec via the Montmorency-Dufferin Autoroute (440), Autoroute de la Capitale (40), and Hwy 138, this recreation spot faces the spectacular Montmorency Falls. Several picnic areas provide beautiful scenic views. The Natural Stairway Park nearby has nature paths and trails along the Montmorency River. June-Labor Day, 8:30 A.M.–8:00 P.M.

Van den Hende Gardens. Between blvd. Hochelaga and Autoroute du Vallon, Ste-Foy (656–3333). Developed by prominent horticulturist Roger Van den Hende. this 15-acre botanical garden belongs to the Laval University Faculty of Agriculture and features some 2,500 species of plants. Open June-Sept. Free.

ZOOS. The Quebec Zoological Gardens. 8191 ave. du Zoo, Charlesbourg (622–0312). On the bank of the Du-Berger River seven miles north of Quebec on Route 73, the zoo specializes in native Canadian fauna but features exotic species too. More than 900 species of birds and several hundred mammals live in the 30 developed acres of the 90-acre woodland site. (There is a "petting zoo" for youngsters.) Mid May-mid June, 9 A.M.–6 P.M. daily; mid June-early Sept., 9 A.M.–7 P.M. daily; rest of year, 9 A.M.–5 P.M. daily. Adults, $1.50; children, 25¢; family rate, $3.

The Quebec Aquarium. 1675 du Parc, Ste-Foy (659–5264). This modern circular building stands on a cliff overlooking the St. Lawrence in Aquarium Park, a terraced woodland offering spectacular views of the river and country-side. The aquarium features native and foreign saltwater species, marine mammals, and reptiles, as well as nature films. Cafeteria is open year-round, picnic tables from mid-May to Sept. Seals' feeding time is 10:15 A.M. and 3:15 P.M. Daily from 9:00 A.M.–5 P.M. May 15–Labor day until 7 P.M. Adults, $2, children, 50 cents. Half price, Nov.–Apr. 30.

PARTICIPANT SPORTS. Sports enthusiasts can enjoy anything from snowshoeing to windsurfing in the Quebec region, though alpine and cross-country skiing are the main attractions here. *Village des Sports,* 1869 blvd. Valcartier, Valcartier, route 371 north of Quebec (844–2212), offers a complete range of sports activities including roller-skating, cycling, horseshoe throwing, volleyball, badminton, trampoline, waterfall and water slides (summer), toboggan slides and lifts, cross-country skiing and snowshoeing, rubber tube sliding, and skating paths (winter).

Curling. *Club de curling Jacques-Cartier* (643–4431); *Club de curling Etchemin* (839–9067); *Club de curling Victoria* (656–0403).

Cycling, jogging. *Battlefields Park* and *Parc du Mont-Ste-Anne,* among others, have extensive cycling and jogging paths.

Golf. Quebec and suburban centers offer 18 golf courses, several open to the public. Reservations (including clubs and motorized carts) during summer months are essential and members generally book weekends well in advance. Closest to downtown Quebec is *Club de Golf Métropolitain,* 1575 ave. Chauveau (872–9292).

Fitness centers. *Pavillon d'Éducation physique et des Sports,* campus universitaire, Université Laval (694–7224); *YWCA,* 855 ave. Holland (656–2155); *En Forme,* 330 rue Ste-Hélène (529–1329); *Fitness 2,000,* 3 Place du Quebec (525–9909).

Horseback Riding. *Ranch El Paso,* 24 blvd. du Lac, Ste-Brigitte-de-Laval (825–2630); *Ranch JJ,* 506 rue Jobin, Lac-St-Charles (849–8986); *Centre d'équitation Le Paddock,* 8622 ave. Royale, Château-Richer (824–3351).

Racquet sports. Tennis attire required at all clubs. Reserve and bring your own equipment, as racquets are not always available. *Club de Tennis & Squash Montcalm Inc.,* 901 blvd. Champlain (687–1250); *Club Tennisport Inc.,* 4200 blvd. Hamel, Ancienne Lorette, (872–0111); *Raquetball Laurentien Inc.,* 5050 blvd. Hamel Ouest, Ste-Foy, (871–5051).

Downhill skiing. Five major ski centers within 40 km (25 mi) of Quebec, including Mont-Ste-Anne, site of several World Cup international ski competitions, offer lifts, jumps, and extensive trails for downhill and cross-country skiing. Downhill: *Mont-Ste-Anne,* Beaupré (827–4561); *Le Relais,* 1084 blvd. du Lac, Lac Beauport (849–3073); *Mont-St-Castin,* 82 Tour du Lac, Lac Beauport (849–6776); *Ski Stoneham,* 1420 ave. Hibou, Stoneham (848–2411); *Mont-Hibou,* 825 ave. Hibou, Stoneham, (848–3283).

Cross-country skiing. *Centre l'Éperon,* 506 Tour du Lac, Lac Beauport (849–2778), *Le Saisonnier,* 78 Chemin du Brûlé, Lac Beauport (849–2821); *Club Mont Tourbillon,* 55 Montée du Golf, Lac Beauport (849–4418); *Manoir du Lac Delage,* 40 ave. du Lac, Lac Delage (848–2551); *Camp Mercier,* Stoneham (848–2422); *Centre Le Refuge,* 1186 rue Emond, St-Adolphe, (848–3329); *Cap*

Rouge, Centre de ski de fond, 4473 rue St-Félix, Cap Rouge (653–9381); *Parc du Mont-Ste-Anne* (826–2323).

Skibus: A special municipal bus service (627–2511) leaves from downtown Quebec and Ste-Foy daily (except Christmas and New Year's Day), Dec. 21–Jan. 5, and weekends through the end of March, for Lac Beauport, Stoneham, and Mont-Ste-Anne. $2.50.

Sailing. *Vieux Port de Quebec,* rue Abraham Martin (692–0043); *Parc nautique Levy,* 205 rue St-Laurent (833–9421). *Yacht Club de Quebec,* 1061 blvd. Champlain (681–4617); *Marina de la Chaudière,* Chemin du Bac (839–7939).

Ice-skating. *Château Frontenac,* St. Charles River.

SPECTATOR SPORTS. Hockey is the abiding passion here, and Quebec is proud of its own *Nordiques.* The National Hockey League team's fancy skating can be seen at home games during the season at Le Colisée de Quebec, parc de l'Exposition, 2205 ave. du Colisée (694–7110), Sept.-May. During the summer you can watch harness racing at the Hippodrome de Quebec, also at the parc de l'Exposition (524–5283).

HISTORIC SITES AND HOUSES. It would be hard to find another area on the continent that boasts more historic sites and houses than Quebec City and its neighboring suburbs. (The towns of Charlesbourg, Neuville, and Beauport have restored entire districts' 17th- and 18th-century homes.) Following are some of the major attractions.

Artillery Park. 2 rue d'Auteuil (648–4205). Part of the city's fortification system, the defense complex in the park includes 20 buildings ordered after the fall of Louisbourg in 1745. First acting as headquarters for the French garrison, the buildings were taken over by the British in 1759. The garrison played an important role in the city's defense system during the American seige of Quebec in 1775–76. A cartridge factory on the site produced munitions for the Canadian army from 1880–1972 when restoration began. Visitors reception and interpretation center provides slide shows, guided tours. July, Aug. Daily except Monday, 10 A.M.–5 P.M. Free.

Battlefields Park. Between Grande Allée and Champlain Blvd. Also known as the Plains of Abraham, this 250-acre expanse of green on a cliff overlooking the St. Lawrence is a national historic preserve. A free 20-minute guided bus tour (June-Sept.) with 13 stops includes an exhibition center with slide show explaining historic battles and the city's Martello towers. Picnic areas, jogging, and bicycle paths. Free parking on Montcalm Ave. Open 24 hours. For group reservations and other information call 648–3506.

Château Frontenac. Inaugurated in 1893 and completed in 1925 when a central tower was added, the grand hotel was designed by American architect Bruce Price.

The Citadel. Battlefields Park. (648–3563). The bunker on Cap Diamant, called the "largest set of fortifications in North America still occupied by troops" (Canada's Royal 22nd Regiment), includes 25 buildings. The Musée militaire (regimental museum) in the complex has military exhibits from the 17th to 20th centuries. Museum tours are part of Citadel guided tours. Changing of the Guard, mid-June-Labor Day, daily at 10 A.M., weather permitting. Beating the Retreat, June 23-Labor Day, Tues., Thurs., Sat., Sun., 7 P.M., weather permitting. Cannon firings from Prince of Wales bastion daily at noon and 9:30 P.M. Adults $2.25, children $1.

Fortifications. 2 rue d'Auteuil (648–3564 or 648–7016). The history of Old Quebec's fortifications is recounted on guided tours leaving from the Poudrière de l'Esplanade (Esplanade Powder House). The 4.6 km (3 mi) walls are a National Historic Park. May 15–Oct. 31, 10 A.M.–5 P.M. Closed Mon. and Tues. Free.

Gare du Palais. 450 rue St. Paul. This splendid 19th-century train station was renovated and reopened through popular demand, after a decade of disuse. Future plans include an "Intermodal" station for buses and trains.

Hôtel du Parlement. (643–7239). The seat of Quebec's government, the National Assembly was designed in French Renaissance style by Eugene Étienne-Taché and built between 1877–86. Life-sized solid bronze statues of Quebec heroes stand at various points on the building's front wall, and Taché wrote "Je me souviens" ("I remember")—later to become a nationalist motto—

above the front door. (The motto was a response to disparaging remarks by Britain's Lord Durham, who claimed that French-Canadians had no history.) Bilingual guided tours last 30 minutes. July and Aug., daily 10 A.M.–5:30 P.M. Other months, weekdays only, 9 A.M.–4:30 P.M. Free. Parking in lots near government buildings G and H.

Krieghoff House. 115 Grande-Allée Ouest. Cornelius Krieghoff, one of Canada's best-known landscape artists, settled in Quebec in 1852. The Amsterdam-born painter married a Quebecer and lived in this house for several years. Not open to visitors.

Martello Towers. Battlefields Park (648–3506). The British erected four Martello towers after the American War of Independence. Three of the four towers still stand. Exhibit at Martello Tower No. 2, corner of rue Taché and rue Laurier; daily, 10 A.M.–8 P.M., Wednesday, noon–8 P.M. Exhibition center on towers, Martello Tower No. 4, rue Lavigueur; daily, 11:30 A.M.–6 P.M. Wednesday, noon–6 P.M. Free.

Notre Dame Basilica. 16 rue Buade (692–2533). The original basilica was built in 1647, on the site of Champlain's original Notre Dame-de-la-Recouvrance church built in 1633 and destroyed by fire in 1640. Partially destroyed during seige of Quebec in 1750, it was rebuilt from 1768–71.

Montcalm Monument. Built jointly by France and Canada to commemorate Louis-Joseph Montcalm, commander of the troops in New France.

Place-Royale. A multimillion-dollar renovation project by the Quebec government, the original site of Champlain's settlement is now a group of restored 17th- and 18th-century buildings, called the largest concentration of houses from this period in North America. Several houses are open to the public. Others are shops and restaurants. Among notable buildings are Notre-Dame-des-Victoires church, built in 1688, Maison Chevalier and Îlot la Cetière—archaeological remains of Champlain's settlement. Visitors information center is at La Maison Soumandre, 29 rue Notre Dame (643–6631). Free.

St. Louis Gate. Corner of rue d'Auteuil and rue St. Louis. Originally built in 1693, the gate was demolished and rebuilt several times. Architecture is the same as the original.

Le Vieux-Port. 36½ rue St-Pierre (692–0043). Currently being restored by a $100-million federal government restoration project. Plans for the 72 acres of parkland on the site of Quebec's original port include a Museum of Civilization now under construction, a theater and several parks. Open to visitors. Group tours by reservation.

The Wolfe Monument. Wolfe Ave., just off Grande Allée Ouest. Erected on the spot where General James Wolfe died. His 4,500 British troops won the battle of the Plains of Abraham after having lost the Battle of Montmorency in the summer of 1759.

 MUSEUMS AND GALLERIES. Quebec and its suburbs are a museum buff's paradise, with literally dozens of exhibits, with everything from historical to contemporary art galleries. What follows is only a sampling.

Centre d'Artisinat Amerindien et Inuit. 17 rue Desjardins (392–3056). Amerindian and Inuit art.

L'Empire de Madame Belley. (Moving at press time. Call 628–8916 for new address.) Madame Belley, a designer, clairvoyant, and eccentric, lived from 1905 to 1980 and made a name for herself by creating and wearing extravagant clothes. Her remarkable collection drew record-breaking crowds when shown at the Musée du Quebec in 1971. The exhibit is billed as the biggest private costume museum in Canada. Daily tours for groups with reservations in summer, 10 A.M.–10 P.M.; 1–5 P.M. in winter. Closed Mon. Adults $3, students and over 65, $2.50, children under 12 with adult, free.

Galerie du Musée. 24 blvd. Champlain (643–7975). Contemporary art featuring Quebec and foreign artists, in historic Amiot and Langlois houses. Closed Mon., Tues. Open Wed., Sat., Sun., noon–6 P.M. Thurs., Fri., noon–8:30P.M. Free.

Maison Chevalier. 60 Marche Champlain, Place Royale. Early Canadian furniture and art. Open year-round. Closed Mon. Free.

Musée du Fort. 10 rue Ste-Anne (692–2175). A sound and light show re-enacting the Battle of the Plains of Abraham on a 450-square-foot model of 18th-century Quebec. Bilingual narration. Three shows morning and afternoon;

call for hours. Closed Dec. 1–20. Adults, $3; students, $1.50; children under 6 free.

Musée de Cire. 22 rue Ste-Anne (692–2289). North American historical figures in wax. Daily, 10 A.M.–5:30 P.M.

Musée du Quebec. Battlefields Park (643–4103, 643–2150). Built in 1933. Commemorates 300th anniversary of founding of Quebec. Permanent collections of sculpture, paintings, antique furniture and Quebec folk art, visiting collections of Canadian and foreign art. Daily, 10 A.M.–6 P.M., Wed. until 10 P.M. Closed Mon. Guided tours arranged by reservation.

Musée du Séminaire de Quebec. 9 rue de l'Universite (692–2843). Permanent collections of Quebec, European, and Oriental art, scientific instruments, stamps, and currency. May 1–Oct. 31, daily 10 A.M.–4 P.M. Sunday, 10 A.M.–5 P.M. Nov. 1–April 30, daily 11:00 A.M.–4 P.M. Sundays, 11 A.M.–5 P.M. Closed Mon. Adults, $2; students and over 65, $1; family, $5. Children 12 and under free.

Musée des Ursulines. 12 rue Donnaconna (694–0694). Furniture and silverware from the 17th and 18th centuries. Centre Marie-de-L'Incarnation, near the museum, exhibits objects belonging to the founder of the convent and girls' school. Open year-round except Dec., Tues.-Sat., 9:30 A.M.–noon, 1:30–5 P.M. Sun., noon–5:30 P.M. Closed Mon. Adults, $1; students and seniors, 50 cents; family rate, $2.50.

Voûtes du Palais. 1033 rue des Prairies (691–6092 or 691–6285). Underground vaults. Information center. Tues.-Sun., 12:30–5 P.M. Guided tours, groups only. Free.

ARTS AND ENTERTAINMENT. Music, dance, and opera. *Le Grande Théâtre de Québec,* 269 blvd. St-Cyrille (643–8131) is Quebec's theatrical pièce de résistance. It is the home of the Quebec Symphony Orchestra, Canada's oldest. Leading artists perform in the Salle Louis-Fréchette. Other concert halls are *Bibliothèque Gabrielle-Roy,* 350 rue St-Joseph (some free concerts); *Colisée* (Coliseum), Parc de l'Exposition, 2205 ave du Colisée (694–7110); *l'Institut canadien* 37 rue Ste-Angèle (692–2135) (some free concerts); *le Palais Montcalm,* 995 place D'Youville (670–9011); *La Salle Albert Rousseau,* CÉGEP Ste-Foy, 2410 Chemin Ste-Foy (659–6710); *Théâtre de la Bordée,* 1091½ rue St-Jean (694–9631); and *Théâtre Le Petit Champlain,* 68 rue Petit Champlain (692–4398).

Theater: *Grande Théâtre,* Salle Octave-Crémazie; *Salle Albert-Rousseau* and *Théâtre de la Bordée* (see above); *Théâtre de la Cité Universitaire,* Université Laval, Cité Universitaire, Ste-Foy (656–3333). **Summer theaters.** *Théâtre du Bois-de-Coulonge,* rue St-Louis, Sillery, (681–4679, 681–0088 in summer, 692–3041 off-season); *L'Anglicane,* 33 rue Wolfe, Levis (833–8831); *Théâtre La Fenière,* 1500 de la Fenière, Ancienne-Lorette (872–1424, summer, 651–3218 off-season); *Théâtre de l'Île,* 342 rue Galendor, St-Pierre, Île d'Orléans (878–3581); *Théâtre Paul-Hébert,* 1451 ave. Royale, Île d'Orléans (829–2202, summer, 523–2163, off-season); *Implanthéâtre,* 2 rue Crémazie, (529–2183). Remember, most but not all productions are in French.

Film. Repertory: *La Boîte à films,* 1044 3 ave. (524–3144), $3.50, $2 over 65 and under 14; *Cartier,* 1019 rue Cartier (525–9340), shows films in English; $3.50, $2 over 65 and under 14; *Clap,* 2360 Chemin Ste-Foy, (653–3750), $3.75, $2 over 50 and under 14. Films usually in French, sometimes with English subtitles.

ACCOMMODATIONS. Because tourism is a major industry here, Quebec City's large variety of hotels, motels, tourist homes, and inns offer a total of 8,000 rooms and at a broad range of prices. During high tourist seasons—May-Sept. and the Winter Carnival in February—reservations are advised. Prices listed here are for May-Oct. While rates in larger hotels and motels generally stay the same all year, smaller establishments often lower their rates $10–$20 from Nov.-April. During Winter Carnival, however, rates often go up as much as 30 percent above those listed here. Categories, based on double occupancy rates, are as follows: *Deluxe,* $140–$200; *Expensive* $100–$140; *Moderate,* $75–$100; *Inexpensive,* under $75. For a complete listing of accommodations in the Quebec City region, write to the Quebec City Region Tourism and Convention Bureau, 60 rue d'Auteuil, Quebec, PQ G1R 4C4 (692–2471).

Deluxe

Château Frontenac. 1 rue des Carrières, Quebec, PQ G1R 4P5 (418–692–3861). 500 rooms (some only expensive). One of oldest luxury hotels in Canada, parking, air-conditioning, antique furniture in public rooms, excellent restaurants.

Loews le Concorde. 1225 Place Montcalm, Quebec, PQ G1R 4W6 (418–647–2222 or 800–463–5256). 424 rooms, overlooking Battlefields Park, panoramic views of city and countryside, indoor and outdoor pools (indoor pool is in another building), sauna, restaurants including rotating l'Astral on 28th floor, room service. Interesting modern architecture.

Expensive

Auberge des Gouverneurs. 690 blvd. St-Cyrille, Quebec, PQ G1R 5A8 (418–647–1717 or 800–463–2820). 379 rooms, parking, sauna, dining room, outdoor pool.

Hilton International Quebec. 3 Place Quebec, Quebec, PQ G1K 7M9 (418–647–2411 or 800–268–9275). Just outside the walls of the old city. 563 rooms, some *deluxe,* parking, indoor and outdoor pools, good restaurants.

Moderate

Auberge du Trésor. 20 rue Ste-Anne, Quebec, PQ G1R 3X2 (418–694–1876). 21 rooms, some *inexpensive,* parking, air-conditioning, downtown location.

Auberge Ramada Inn. 1200 rue de LaVigerie, Ste-Foy, Quebec, PQ G1W 3W5 (418–651–2440). 100 rooms, some *inexpensive,* free parking, air-conditioning, dining room, coffee shop, outdoor pool.

Auberge Universel Wandlyn. 2955 blvd. Laurier, Ste-Foy, PQ G1V 2M2 (418–653–8721). 140 rooms, air-conditioning, dining room, indoor pool.

Château Bonne-Entente. 3400 Chemin Ste-Foy, Ste-Foy, Quebec, PQ G1X 1S6 (418–653–5221). 102 rooms, free parking, air-conditioning, outdoor pool.

Holiday Inn. 395 rue de la Couronne, Quebec, PQ G1K 7X4 (418–647–2611). 233 rooms, free parking, dining room, coffee shop, indoor pool.

Hôtel Clarendon. 57 rue Ste-Anne, Quebec, PQ G1R 3X4 (418–692–2480). 93 rooms, *inexpensive to moderate,* downtown location, parking, excellent restaurant.

Maison Au Jardin du Gouverneur. 16 rue Mont-Carmel, Quebec, PQ G1R 4A3 (418–692–1704). 17 rooms, parking, air-conditioning.

Manoir des Remparts. 3½ rue des Remparts, Quebec, PQ G1R 3R4 (418–692–2056). 35 rooms, parking.

Inexpensive

Château de la Terrasse. 6 Place Terrasse Dufferin, Quebec, PQ G1R 4N5 (418–694–9472). 18 rooms, parking, kitchenettes, excellent view.

Hôtel Château Laurier. 695 Grande Allée est, Quebec, PQ G1R 2K4 (418–522–8108). 55 rooms, *inexpensive to moderate,* air-conditioning, central location.

Hôtel le Manoir d'Auteuil. 49 rue d'Auteuil, Quebec, PQ G1R 4C2 (418–694–1173). 17 rooms, some *moderate,* parking.

Hôtel Le St-Laurent. 3135 chemin St-Louis, Ste-Foy, PQ G1W 1R9 (418–653–4941 or 800–463–4752). 82 rooms, *inexpensive to moderate.* Free parking, air-conditioning, outdoor pool.

 BED AND BREAKFAST. For homes away from home at reasonable prices, contact one of the following: *Bed and Breakfast–Bonjour Quebec,* 395 blvd. Monaco, Quebec, PQ G1P 3J3 (418–527–1465); *Bed and Breakfast in Old Quebec,* contact François Begin, 300 rue Champlain, Quebec, PQ G1K 4J2 (418–525–9826, ext. 8711); *Gite Quebec,* 3729 ave. Le Corbusier, Ste-Foy, PQ G1W 4R8 (418–651–1860); *Hebergement Bed & Breakfast Quebec,* 72 rue Ste-Ursule, Suite 103, Quebec, PQ F1R 4E8 (418–692–2801). Rates average between $40–$50 per night for two people. For farmhouse bed and breakfast and family farm vacations, contact *Vacances-Familles/Agricotours,* 1661 ave. du Parc, Ste-Foy, PQ G1W 3Z3 (418–658–0576).

YS AND HOSTELS. Quebec has one Y and several youth hostels. The *YWCA* at 855 ave. Holland, Quebec, PQ G1S 3S5 (418–683–2155) has rooms for men and women, Sept.-May.; women only, May-Sept. Prices are $30 for two people, $20 for one. Reasonable cafeteria meals: breakfast, 7–9 A.M., $2; dinner, 5–6:30 P.M., $3.25; weekend brunch, 9 A.M.–1 P.M., $3.25.

The city's largest hostel, *Centre international de séjour,* 19 rue Ste-Ursule, Quebec, PQ G1R 4E1 (418–694–0755) has 200 beds and charges International Youth Hostel members $8 per night, nonmembers $10. Open all year. Membership costs $18 per year.

Others in similar price range are *Auberge de la Paix,* 31 rue Couillard, Quebec, PQ G1R 3T4, near Château Frontenac, May-Oct., 56 beds (418–694–0735); *Auberge de la Haute-Ville,* 1190 Claire-Fontaine, Quebec, PQ G1R 3B3 (418–525–9233); and *La Belle Étoile,* 1100 de la Chevrotière, Quebec, PQ G1R 3J5 (418–525–5874).

RESTAURANTS. True to the French culture, Quebecers consider fine cuisine a matter of honor. The city's 300 restaurants give it the distinction of having more eateries per capita than any other city in the country. The specialties here are French and continental cuisine. Seafood is also favored and deliciously prepared. Inexpensive home-style fare can be found at one of the city's many *brasseries*—Quebec's version of the British pub.

Restaurants are listed according to the price of a complete dinner not including drinks, tax, and tip. *Super Deluxe,* $30 and up; *Deluxe,* $25–$30; *Expensive,* $20–$25; *Moderate,* $12–$20; *Inexpensive,* under $12. Unless otherwise noted, restaurants take some or all major credit cards.

Super Deluxe

Le Champlain. Château Frontenac, 1 rue des Carrières (692–3861). Waiters dressed in 16th-century attire, elegant décor, and occasionally, a harpist combined with good food and a first-rate wine cellar guarantee a memorable eating experience. French cuisine. Dinner and Sunday brunch.

Clarendon Hotel. 57 rue Ste-Anne (692–2480). Provincial government hotel inspectors give the main dining room in this elegant vintage hotel top rating. French nouvelle cuisine. Breakfast, lunch, and dinner daily.

Le Croquembroche. Quebec Hilton. 3 Place Quebec (647–2411). Reputedly the city's best hotel cuisine. French. Lunch and dinner daily.

A la table de Serge Bruyère. 1200 rue St-Jean (694–0618). Food critics say this restaurant specializing in nouvelle cuisine is second to none in the city. Reservations essential. Dinner. Closed Sunday and Monday. AE.

Deluxe

L'Astral. Hôtel Loews le Concorde, 1225 Place Montcalm (747–2222). Definitely worth the trip for a stunning view of the city—especially under night lights—from the hotel's 28th floor. The revolving restaurant slowly turns as you dine so you do not miss anything. Piano bar. Continental, French cuisine. Excellent table d'hôte (full course) meal for $24. A la carte is *deluxe.* Brunch and dinner.

La Chaumière. 22 rue Couillard (692–2051). Fine French cuisine in an 18th-century house. Dinner, Tues.-Sat. only.

Le Marie Clarisse. 12 rue Petit-Champlain (692–0857). Seafood, nouvelle cuisine, warm atmosphere, excellent fare. Lunch *(moderate–expensive)* and dinner. Closed Sunday. AE.

Expensive

Café de la Paix. 44 rue Desjardins (692–1430). Elaborate French cuisine, seafood in an intimate Parisian atmosphere. Lunch and dinner.

Chalet Suisse. 32 rue Ste-Anne (694–1320). Specializes in such Swiss standards as fondue and raclette, which the owners introduced to Quebec some 30 years ago. This 4-room complex in three beautifully renovated houses is best known as the favored hangout of politicians and journalists. Lunch *(moderate)* and dinner daily.

Le Deauville. 300 blvd. Laurier, Ste-Foy (658–3644). Friendly atmosphere, good steaks and seafood. Lunch and dinner.

Le Paris-Brest. 590 Grande Allée Est (529–2243). Top-rated continental cuisine. Lunch and dinner.

Chez Umberto. 770 rue de l'Alverne (527–4442). Good Italian food for connoisseurs. Intimate setting. Lunch *(moderate)* and dinner.

Moderate

Aux Anciens Canadiens. 34 rue St-Louis (692–1627 or 694–0253). Authentic Quebec dishes in La Maison Jacquet, one of the city's oldest houses, built in 1675 and later the home of prominent 19th-century novelist Philippe-Aubert de Gaspé—best known for his novel *Aux Anciens Canadiens.* Good full-course lunch available for $6; dinner is *moderate–expensive.* Reservations recommended; private rooms available for groups.

Anse-aux-barques. 28 blvd. Champlain (692–4674). Excellent fresh seafood, grills, shipboard décor. Lunch and dinner.

Restaurant d'Europe. 27 rue St-Angèle (692–3835). Excellent French and Italian cuisine. Lunch and dinner daily.

Restaurant Gambrinus. 15 rue du Fort (692–5144). Italian food and seafood specialties in a lovely dining room with carved wood and plants.

Chez Guido. 73 rue Ste-Anne (692–3856 or 692–3857). French and Italian cuisine. Lunch and dinner.

Wong's. 19 rue Buade (692–2409). Good quality Chinese food and attractive decor. Lunch and dinner.

Inexpensive

Pacini. 22 côte de la Fabrique (692–4199). A wide range of spaghettis and several other pastas to choose from. Higher priced dishes are especially tasty. Lunch and dinner.

Au Petit Coin Breton. 655 Grande Allée Est (525–6904). Breton-style pancakes. Open 10 A.M.–11 P.M.

 NIGHTLIFE AND BARS. Quebec has plenty to offer in this department, whether it be throbbing discos or intimate *boites à chansons*—small nightclubs with singing or musical acts. The Grande Allée just outside the city gates is the action center, with its two-block strip of bars, outdoor cafes, and discotheques. The Old City tends to specialize more in piano bars and jazz clubs. Natives say much of the local population moves to the bars and discos of suburban Ste-Foy in winter. Cover charges are not the rule in night spots here. (The price of your drinks generally covers entertainment.) For specific shows, consult the two daily newspapers, *Le Soleil* or *Le Journal de Quebec.*

Discos. *Disco le Cabaret,* Hôtel Loews le Concorde, 1225 Place Montcalm (647–2222) is the "in" dance scene. You cannot get near it on a Saturday night unless you arrive sometime before 9. Wear a jacket and tie (natty dressers come here to see and be seen). Also in the chic and trendy category is *Disco l'Eden,* Quebec Hilton, 3 Place Quebec (647–2411). Others are: *Le Beaugarte,* 2590 blvd. Laurier, Ste-Foy (651–5000); *Chez Dagobert* (disco-rock), 600 Grande Allée Est (522–0393); *Chez Rasputine* (waiters dressed as monks), 2960 blvd. Laurier, Ste-Foy (659–4318); and *Disco-bar Vendredi 13* (Friday the 13th), 1018 rue St-Jean (694–0611).

Ballroom and folk dancing. *Soirée de Danse Moderne et Canadienne,* 155 blvd. Charest Est (647–5858). Sat., 8 P.M., orchestra. Admission $3.

Jazz. Tops in this category is the *Hôtel Clarendon's* elegant *bar l'Emprise* 57 rue Ste-Anne (692–2480), where the art deco is genuine. Quality performers make early arrival a must on weekends. Others are *Bar le Jazzé,* 19 rue St-Pierre, Place Royale (694–1244); *Bar Élite,* 54 rue Couillard (692–1204), no cover charge, no minimum.

Bars. *Bar La Bourgeoise L.M. Inc.* 5930 ave. Charlesbourg (623–4996). Orchestra on weekends; *Bar LaGrande* 1114 Cartier (529–9767). Piano bar daily; *Bar-Spectacles Ainsi-Soit-Il,* 1135 Cartier (522–5370); *Saint-Charles Bar Spectacles.* 545 1 ave. (647–1777). Progressive rock shows Thurs.-Sun.

EXPLORING QUEBEC PROVINCE

Quebec has recently been divided into eighteen tourist regions. Each has a Regional Tourist Association which provides an information bureau and organizes budget-minded, all-inclusive tours. The system is coordinated through a central government agency, Tourisme Quebec. Although each of Quebec's 18 regions is blessed with scenic splendors and myriad opportunities for vacation adventure, the following areas—L'Estrie, the Laurentians, Charlevoix, and the Gaspé Peninsula —have remained especially popular over the years, providing generations with holiday pleasure.

L'Estrie-Garden of Quebec

This region has many of the attractive qualities of New England— covered bridges, village greens, white church steeples, welcoming country inns, and quiet backroads winding past fields and farms. L'Estrie comes by these characteristics honestly: the area was settled by Loyalists fleeing north after the American War of Independence.

The gateway to the region is the eclectic town of Granby, an industrial city with a dozen European fountains, including a 3,200-year-old Greek fountain on Leclerc Boulevard and a Roman fountain in Pelletier Park. Granby also has a car museum with Canada's finest collection of antique autos and an outstanding zoo. An international song festival in October and a gastronomic festival in September highlight the town's social season.

Nearby Mont Bromont is equipped for night skiing, which makes an impressive spectacle for motorists driving along Highway 10 on a winter's evening. The 18-hole golf course, one of the finest in the region, remains popular even in winter—for its cross-country ski trails.

Farther east, Mont Orford dominates the western part of Mont Orford Provincial Park. Almost 20 ski slopes wind through the woods on its southern face; a chairlift whisks skiers in winter and sightseers in summer to the summit of the 738-meter (2,400-foot) peak. For the past 30 summers some 300 students have come to the Orford Arts Center to study and perform classical music. The center also welcomes artisans—potters, painters, sculptors, lacemakers—who organize art exhibitions throughout the summer.

Another appealing aspect of L'Estrie is its cluster of sparkling lakes, with their strange mixture of euphonious Indian names (Massawippi, Memphrémagog, Mégantic) and harsher English designations (Brome, Brompton, Stukely).

You can enjoy Memphrémagog's "beautiful waters" (the meaning of its Indian name) on the cruise boat *L'Aventure*. One of the highlights of the trip is the abbey of St-Benoit-du-Lac, which sends a slender bell tower up above the trees like a Disneyland castle. Built on a wooded peninsula in 1912 by the Benedictines, the abbey is home to some 60 monks who produce all their own food. They sell apples from their orchards as well as distinctive cheeses: Ermite, St-Benoit, and ricotta.

After the Civil War, nearby Lac-Massawippi became a favorite summer haunt of wealthy Southerners, who rusticated in the cool North without the annoyance of Yankees. Several of the homes they built here have been converted into gracious inns, including the Manoir Hovey and the Hatley Inn. North Hatley, at the northern end of the lake, still attracts visitors with its antique shops and the region's only English-language theater productions, at a converted barn called The Piggery.

The August milk festival in Coaticook, to the southeast, is a reminder that L'Estrie is one of Quebec's most productive dairy regions. The festival fun includes a fashion show in which bovine beauties model the latest in agricultural haute couture.

Cookshire to the north is best known for its annual bread festival, when the June air around town is scented with the rich aroma of fresh-baked loaves. Visitors come to watch the townswomen prepare traditional family recipes and bake the bread in outdoor ovens, and admire Cookshire's fine 19th-century buildings.

Sherbrooke, the unofficial capital of L'Estrie, was founded by Loyalists in the 1790s. Local greenhouses turn out 50,000 annuals each year; some 15,000 grace a park near the Renaissance-style courthouse and another 25,000 form an abstract design along rue King Ouest, the main drag. The University of Sherbrooke's arts center offers a full range of cultural activities.

The Laurentians: A Vacationland as Old as the Hills

Some parts of the world give new life to expressions that have lost their meaning through time and overuse. Such is the case with the area of Quebec northwest of Montreal. The phrase "pretty as a picture" might have been made for the Laurentians. Year round, its spectacular scenery awaits, ready to be framed by the camera's lens or captured on canvas with the artist's brush. Well developed for tourists, with numerous world-class resorts that cater to the most expensive tastes, nestling at lakesides among woods and mountains, it is the embodiment of the phrase "playground of the rich."

This area is one place where you can really capture the meaning of the expression "old as the hills," for the Laurentians are among the most ancient mountains in the world, formed during the Pre-Cambrian Age more than 600 million years ago. Long ages of glacial erosion have left in their wake sweeping valleys; gentle, rounded mountains; and a complicated lacework of lakes and rivers.

The Laurentians, the best-developed resort area in the whole of Canada, owes its growth to the vision and encouragement of a nineteenth-century priest, Curé Labelle, who saw the potential of the mountains and lakes—where farming had limited possibilities—as a recreation area. Most of the Laurentian resorts lie between St-Jérome and Ste-Agathe. There is also a busy resort at Mont Tremblant.

Water and weather combine to provide a multitude of sporting opportunities. In summer, the countless lakes are dotted with a rainbow of sails of a flotilla of craft, while the hills echo with the hum of powerboats, their passengers thrilling to the wind in their faces, or their waterskiers being put through their paces. At a "lower tech" pace, swimmers can relax on the innumerable beaches, and pedal- or tour-boat enthusiasts can take a leisurely outing around the resort lakes.

Off the water, amateurs of horseback riding, tennis, and golf have plenty to gratify their appetites. Many resorts offer competitive packages concentrating on specific sports, while the whole region is a cycling challenge.

In winter, when the landscape turns white, downhill skiing (*ski alpin*), cross-country skiing (*ski du fond* or *ski randonnée*), snowshoeing, and skating opportunities abound. Sleigh rides and snowmobile touring afford the less agile the chance to take an equal part in the winter activities. Again, a wide variety of competitively priced packages are available.

Charlevoix: Quebec's Switzerland

Charlevoix stretches along the St. Lawrence River's north shore east of Quebec City from Ste-Anne-de-Beaupré to the Saguenay River. Often called the "Switzerland of Quebec," Charlevoix embraces long rolling mountains rising from the sea and a succession of valleys, plateaus, and cliffs cut by waterfalls, brooks, and streams. The roads wind into villages of picturesque old houses and huge tin-roofed churches.

The name Charlevoix (pronounced, approximately, "Shar-le-vwah") comes from New France's first historian, a Jesuit father. Explorer Jacques Cartier landed in 1535. The first colonists arrived from France during the 17th century. They developed a thriving shipbuilding industry which lasted until fairly recently, specializing in the schooners *(goélettes)*, which hauled everything from logs to lobsters up and down the coast in the days before trailer trucks. You will see abandoned goélettes on many beaches.

The region starts 33 kilometers (20 miles) east of Quebec City, at Ste-Anne-de-Beaupré. Each year more than a million pilgrims come to the region's most famous religious site, Ste-Anne-de-Beaupré Basilica, dedicated to the Virgin Mary's mother.

Only eight kilometers (five miles) further on, in October and May 100,000 greater snow geese gather at the Cap Tourmente wildlife preserve and nature interpretation center. Other parts of the region offer whale-watching cruises. You can sometimes spot seals, whales, and dolphins from ferries and on land. Bring those binoculars!

Active hikers, cyclists, joggers, campers, skiers of all types, and snowshoers, as well as walkers and painters, all enjoy the region's three main ski areas: Parc du Mont-Ste-Anne, on the World Cup downhill ski circuit; Mont Grand Fonds, with a vertical drop of 335 meters (1,000 feet), 13 slopes, and 135 kilometers (84 miles) of cross-country trails; and three-peaked Le Massif, including the province's highest vertical drop (800 meters, 500 feet). Here, you bus 30 minutes to the top, and a guide leads you down through powder snow.

Baie-St-Paul, Charlevoix's earliest settlement (1628) after Beaupré, proves popular with hang gliders and artists. You will find artists and artisans working in old *habitant* houses. Here, the high hills circle a wide plain holding the village beside the sea. Many of Quebec's greatest landscape artists portray the area, as you will see at the art center, June to September. At town-center Maison Otis, a stone house built in 1858, has been converted into what many describe as the area's finest inn/restaurant.

At Baie-St-Paul, choose between the open, scenic coastal drive (Route 362) or the faster (and also lovely) Route 138 to Pointe-au-Pic, La Malbaie, and Cap-à-l'Aigle. This section of Route 362 provides memorable views of rolling hills—green, white, or ablaze with fiery tones, depending on the season—meeting the broad expanse of the "sea," as people call the St. Lawrence estuary.

A secondary road leads sharply down into St-Joseph-de-la-Rive, with its line of old houses hugging the mountain base on the narrow shore road. Here, you discover peaceful inns and restaurants, like l'Auberge Sous les Pins ("under the pines"). Nearby Papeterie St-Gilles produces unusual handcrafted stationery, using a 17th-century process. A small museum commemorates the days of the St-Lawrence goélettes.

You take the ferry from St. Joseph to Île aux Coudres, the island where Jacques Cartier's men gathered hazel nuts *(les coudres)* in 1535. Since then, the island produced many a goélette, and former captains now run several small inns. Larger inns feature folk-dancing evenings.

Many visitors like to cycle the 16-kilometer (10-mile) circuit around the island, visiting inns, a windmill, an old schooner, and boutiques selling paintings and local handicrafts like household linens.

Continuing on Route 362, you will come to one of the most elegant and historically interesting resorts in all Quebec. La Malbaie was known as Murray Bay in an earlier era when wealthy Anglophones summered there and in the neighboring villages of Pointe-au-Pic and Cap-à-l'Aigle.

The regional museum—Musée Laure-Conan—traces its history as a vacation spot in a series of exhibits and is developing an excellent collection of local paintings and folk art.

Once called "the summer White House," this area became popular with both American and Canadian politicians in the late 1800s. Ottawa Liberals and Washington Republicans often partied decorously through the summer with members of the Quebec judiciary.

American civil governor of the Philippines William Howard Taft built the first of three summer residences in Pointe-au-Pic in 1894. He became the 27th United States president in 1908, then Chief Justice in 1921. Local residents still fondly remember the Tafts, and the parties they threw in their elegant summer homes. Interestingly, local people refer to Americans, like all English-speaking people, as "Les Anglais."

Now many Taft-era homes serve handsomely as inns and hotels, guaranteeing you an old-fashioned coddling with extras like breakfast in bed, whirlpool baths, gourmet meals, and free rides to the ski centers in winter. Many serve lunch and dinner to nonresidents, so you can tour the area going from one gourmet's delight to the next. The cuisine, as elsewhere in Quebec, is genuine French, rather than a hybrid invented for North Americans.

The road, the views, and the villages continue all the way up to Baie-Ste-Catherine, at the mouth of the Saguenay fjord. Pretty Port-au-Persil harbors a small, inexpensive inn of the same name, founded by the Taft's former head cook.

Gaspé Peninsula: Wild Beauty "Where the Land Ends"

Jutting into the stormy Gulf of St. Lawrence like the battered prow of a ship, the Gaspé Peninsula remains an isolated region of unsurpassed scenic beauty. Sheer cliffs tower above broad beaches, and tiny coastal fishing communities cling to the shoreline. Inland rise the Chic-Choc Mountains, Eastern Canada's highest, the realm of woodland caribou, black bear, and moose.

Jacques Cartier landed here in 1534, but it wasn't until the early 1800s that the first settlers arrived. Today, the area still seems unspoiled and timeless, a delight for travelers dipping and soaring along the spectacular coastal highways, or venturing on river-valley roads to the forested interior.

The largest colony of gannets in the world summers on the Gaspé's Bonaventure Island, off Percé. Windsurfers and sailors enjoy the breezes around the Gaspé; there are windsurfing marathons in Baie des Chaleurs (at Carleton) each summer. "Gaspé" is the name of the town at the peninsula's tip as well as the name most Anglophones give to the region. The most famous sight hereabouts is the huge fossil-embedded rock off the town of Percé that the sea pierced ("a percé") thousands of years ago. Geologically, the peninsula is one of the oldest lands on earth. A vast, mainly uninhabited forest covers the hilly hinterland. Local tourist officials help you find outfitters and guides to fish and hunt large and small game. The Gaspé features four major parks, Port Daniel, Forillon, Causapscal, and Gaspé Park, covering a total of 2,292 square kilometers (885 square miles).

Small fishing and farming villages ring the 270-kilometer (150-mile) Route 132 that hugs the dramatic coastline. The region boasts Quebec's longest ski season and highest peaks. For instance, Ste-Anne-des-Monts offers the only heli-skiing east of the Rockies, with deep powder, open bowl and glade skiing clear into June on peaks that rise to 823 meters (2,700 feet). Other centers operate from mid-November to May.

The Gaspé was on Jacques Cartier's itinerary—he first stepped ashore in North America in the town of Gaspé—but Vikings, Basques, and Portuguese fisherfolk came long before. You'll find the area's history told in countless towns along the way. Acadians, displaced by the British from New Brunswick in 1755, settled in Bonaventure. Paspébiac still has a gunpowder shed built in the 1770s to help defend the Gaspé from American ships. United Empire Loyalists settled New Carlisle in 1784. Fishing magnates from the Channel Islands Jersey and Guernsey dominated the peninsula's business until fairly recently, as you'll see at the museum in Gaspé town.

Townspeople in some Gaspé areas speak mainly English, but most *Gaspésiens* speak slightly Acadian-accented French.

PRACTICAL INFORMATION FOR

QUEBEC PROVINCE

TOURIST INFORMATION. Tourisme Quebec publishes a variety of brochures, maps, and directories to help visitors plan vacations. To obtain this helpful information, contact *Tourisme Quebec,* Box 20,000, Quebec City, PQ G1K 7X2 (514–873–2015, 800–443–7000 from eastern and midwest U.S., 800–361–6490 from Ontario and the Maritimes, and 800–361–5405 from within the province).

For your convenience the Quebec government maintains the following information offices in American cities: Délégation du Quebec, Peachtree Center Tower, 230 Peachtree St. N.W., Suite 1501, Atlanta, GA 30303 (404–581–0488); Délégation du Quebec, 53 State St., 19th Floor, Boston, MA 02109 (617–723–3366); Délégation du Quebec, 35 East Wacker Dr., Suite 2052, Chicago, IL 60601 (312–726–0683); Délégation du Quebec, 700 South Flower St., Suite 1520, Los Angeles, CA 90017 (213–689–4861); Délégation du Quebec, 17 West 50th St., Rockefeller Center, New York, NY 10020 (212–397–0200); Bureau de tourisme du Quebec/Quebec Government Office of Tourism, 1300 19th St. N.W., Suite 220, Washington, DC 20036 (202–659–8990 or 8991).

In Canada a Gouvernement du Quebec tourism office is located at Toronto's Eaton Center, 20 Queen St. W., Suite 1004, Toronto, Ont. M5H 3S3 (416–977–6060).

Tourisme Quebec operates permanent information offices at 2 Place Ville-Marie, Bureau 70 (i.e. Office 70, corner of Cathcart and University), Montreal, PQ H2B 2C9 (514–873–2015) and at 12 rue Sainte-Anne (near Place d'Armes), Quebec City, PQ G1R 3X2 (418–643–2280).

The ministère du Loisir, de la Chasse, et de la Pêche (ministry of recreation, hunting, and fishing) can provide much useful information on outdoor recreation in Quebec. Contact the office at 150 blvd. St. Cyrille Est, Quebec City, PQ G1R 4Y1 (418–643–3127).

TELEPHONES AND EMERGENCY NUMBERS. Three area codes crisscross the province: Montreal and its environs, 514; Quebec City, Gaspé, and eastern Quebec, 418; Eastern Townships and northern Quebec, including Hull, 819. For directory information, call 411 locally or (area code)–555–1212.

Bell Canada, Quebec's telephone company, charges 25 cents for local pay telephone calls. Have lots of change handy if you plan to make long distance calls; to do so, dial 0–(area code)–telephone number direct within Canada and the United States, or dial 0 for operator-assisted calls.

 LIQUOR LAWS. The minimum drinking age in Quebec is 18. The province's public drinking hours are the most liberal in Canada. Taverns and brasseries serve liquor from 8:00 A.M. to midnight, Monday to Saturday. All other licensed establishments are permitted to remain open from 11:00 A.M. to 3:00 A.M. daily.

Beer and selected wines are sold at corner grocery stores (*dépanneurs*) throughout the province. The sale of liquor and wine is regulated by the provincial government and largely distributed through "Société des Alcools" stores, which are open from 10:00 A.M. to 6:00 P.M., Monday to Wednesday, 10:00 A.M. to 9:00 P.M. on Thursday and Friday, and 10:00 A.M. to 5:00 P.M. on Saturday. Provincial liquor stores close on Sundays and holidays.

If you plan a night on the town, walk, ride public transit, or take a taxi to your hotel. Quebec has tough antidrunk-driving laws. If motorists exceed the legal blood alcohol limit of 0.08 percent, they face stiff fines, a few hours behind bars of a different kind, and risk losing their driver's licenses.

 HINTS TO HANDICAPPED TRAVELERS. Since the International Year of the Handicapped, Quebec is more aware of the special needs of physically handicapped travelers. Most public buildings, churches, restaurants, and hotels now have wheelchair access ramps, washrooms, and telephones. Bus, train, and airport terminals have automatic doors for easier entry. Sidewalks dip at corners to facilitate street crossing by wheelchair. Many of the province's tourism brochures include information for handicapped travelers.

In major centers, public transportation is available for wheelchair-bound travelers. Voyageur, the provincial bus company, offers interprovincial wheelchair transportation. Contact the nearest office listed in the local telephone directory's white pages, or write: Voyageur Inc., 505 blvd. de Maisonneuve Est, Montreal, PQ H2L 1Y4. Reserve access 24 hours ahead.

If you plan a vacation, these handy reference guides may help: *Access to the World: A Travel Guide for the Handicapped* by Louise Weiss, from Facts on File, 460 Park Ave. S., New York, NY 10016, which covers travel by air, bus, train, car, and recreational vehicle as well as accommodations, tours, travel organizations, and more; *The Incapacitated Passengers Air Travel Guide* from The International Air Transport Association, 2000 Peel St., Montreal, PQ H3A 2R4, deals with international airline travel; *A Guide for the Disadvantaged* published by Transport Canada, Tower C, 21st Floor, Place de Ville, Ottawa, Ont. K1A 0N5.

 CAMPING. In Quebec most campgrounds and trailer parks are run by private owners but the Ministère du Loisir, de la Chasse, et de la Pêche operates at least 60 campgrounds on provincial lands. All sites, general information, and regional camping and caravaning associations are listed in a free publication, "Quebec Camping," available from Tourisme Quebec, Box 20,000, Quebec City, PQ G1K 7X2.

Provincial park campgrounds have a variety of sites available from full-service, developed spaces to rustic, wilderness locales. Maximum stays are usually limited to 14 days. Group sites for nonprofit organizations are also available. At some provincial campgrounds you can purchase monthly or seasonal passes to campsites where you intend to set down roots for an extended stay. The maximum number of campers per site is six.

Senior citizens (over 65) camp for half-price in provincial parks and reserves. Special discounts are offered for stays longer than seven days, as well as monthly or seasonal campsite rentals. Canoe camping spots cost about $6 per night per site.

For information about camping in Quebec's three national parks, contact Parks Canada, Information Services, 3 Buade St., Box 6060, Haute Ville, Quebec City, PQ G1R 4V7 (418–648–4177).

FISHING. The sparkling waters of over one million virgin, wilderness lakes and rivers tempt anglers to cast for myriad sport fish. In the St. Lawrence River you can troll for fierce, fighting muskie. Spin for quick-jumping ouananiche, landlocked salmon, in the presteen Lac-Saint-Jean or Lac Tremblant, or fly fish the magnificent, wild Gaspé rivers for Atlantic salmon. In Quebec's arctic regions, you can cast for the exotic char, whose whitish-pink flesh is a gourmet delight. Rainbow, brook, brown, speckled, sea, lake, and the unique Quebec red trout are some of the sport fish that attract avid fly fishermen.

Nonresidents must hire an outfitter and use a guide north of the 52nd parallel; south of this point, the decision is up to you. You must have a fishing license (available at most sporting goods stores) before unpacking your rod and reel. You can fish most species in most places from June 15 to Labor Day. During the winter, ice fishing is popular.

Write Tourisme Quebec, Box 20,000, Quebec City, PQ G1K 7X2 for copies of the following valuable guidebooks: "Quebec Fishing Guide," which highlights Quebec sport fish species as well as tackle, popular fishing methods, and general information; and "Quebec Fishing, Hunting, and Trapping," a listing of regulations, limits, zones, and license costs.

 WINTER SPORTS. The proliferation of winter sports in Quebec may surprise you. In the Laurentians alone, there are more than 2000 km of well-groomed cross-country ski trails. Each February more than 100 Nordic ski enthusiasts participate in the 140-km Lachute to Hull cross-country ski marathon. There are more than 95 alpine ski centers where you can enjoy a day's outing; most are located within two hours of Quebec's major urban centers.

Ice skating, tobogganing, snowmobiling, snowshoeing, and even dog sledding are popular ways to keep fit and warm during Quebec's long winter months. And, of course, there are those great Canadian pastimes: curling, broomball, and ball, or street hockey.

SNOWMOBILES. To snowmobile in Quebec, you must hold a membership card or daily pass issued by an authorized representative of a snowmobile club. Such passes are readily available from one of more than 260 local organizations. You must carry your snowmobile permit and registration certificate with you. Every snowmobile owner must maintain a minimum insurance coverage of $35,000, wear a protective helmet and only ride on marked snowmobile trails. Drivers under 18 may not cross public roads unless they have an automobile driver's licence. When your snowmobile is in operation, headlights and other running lights must be on.

For information about snowmobile tours offered by private companies, contact Tourisme Quebec (see "Tourist Information.") Request a copy of Quebec's Snowmobiling Guide and Transport Quebec's map of the Trans-Quebec Trail Network, including its nine circuit routes. The Canadian Council of Snowmobile Organizations may also help you to locate valuable regional resources. Write: 2596 de Vigny, Mascouche, Quebec, J7K 1W4 (or call 514–474–1177).

 ACCOMMODATIONS. Quebec offers weary travelers a variety of accommodations, from large resort hotels in the Laurentians to shared dormitory space in rustic youth hostels near the heart of Gaspé. We list a selection for L'Estrie, the Laurentians, Charlevoix, and Gaspé. Establishments are listed alphabetically according to their town and each is given a price category based on double occupancy. The categories vary by region.

Lilies and Forks. The provincial government rates all inns and the hotels, awarding up to six lilies for comfort, and four forks for cuisine, ambiance and service in hotel restaurants. The lilies mean: one for basic comfort; two for average comfort; three for good comfort; four for above-average comfort, and five for very good comfort. Hotel restaurants are classified with awards of forks, as follows: One fork for satisfactory cuisine, service and ambiance; two forks for good; three for very good, 4R for excellent (on a regional basis); and four for excellent. The government inspectors do not throw their forks around lightly, so even one or two forks can mean that the cuisine is quite good. Perhaps the waiters or waitresses did not wear fancy uniforms, or the décor may lack excitement. In general, restaurants with more forks charge more for meals.

L'ESTRIE

The categories, for double rooms, are: *Deluxe,* $75–$125; *Expensive,* $50–$75; *Moderate,* $35–$50; and *Inexpensive,* under $35. A number of the inns offer MAP.

AYER'S CLIFF. Hotel Ripplecove Inn. *Deluxe* (MAP). Box 246, Ayer's Cliff, PQ J0B 1C0 (819–838–4296). 11 rooms in main inn, plus cottages. On the shore of Lake Massawippi, surrounded by century-old white pines. Four lilies; three forks.

COMPTON. Hotel Domaine St-Laurent. *Expensive.* Box 180, Chemin Cochran, Compton, PQ J0B 1L0 (800–567–2737 or 819–835–5464). This rambling Tudor inn, formerly a girls' school, has 80 rooms and suites. Villas on the grounds add another 100 rooms. Indoor pool, sauna, spa, tennis, cross-country ski trails. Three lilies; three forks.

GRANBY. Motel Le Granbyen. *Expensive.* 700 rue Principale, Granby, PQ J2G 2Y4 (514–378–8406). A modern 65-unit motel just a few blocks from downtown and near the Granby Tourist and Convention Bureau. Four lilies.

LAC-MÉGANTIC. Motel Panorama. *Moderate.* 3284 rue Laval, Lac-Mégantic, PQ G6B 1A4 (819–583–2110). Excellent food, TV, 37 rooms. Three lilies; two forks.

NORTH HATLEY. Auberge Hatley Inn. *Deluxe* (MAP). Box 330, North Hatley, PQ J0B 2C0 (819–842–2451). Originally built in 1903 as a summer retreat for a southern gentleman, this outstanding inn has the finest dining in the region. Chef Guy Bohec is a member of Quebec's prize-winning gastronomic team. Four lilies; four forks.
Le Manoir Hovey. *Deluxe* (MAP). Box 60, North Hatley, PQ J0B 2C0 (819–842–2421). This replica of George Washington's Mount Vernon was built at the turn of the century by an Atlanta businessman. The elegant appointments and first-rate cuisine make this one of the region's finest inns. Cross-country skiing, downhill nearby. Windsurfing, pedalboats, canoes, tennis, and hiking in summer. Extensive frontage on Lake Massawippi. 36 rooms. Three lilies; four forks.

SHERBROOKE. Hotel Le Président. *Expensive.* 3535 rue King Ouest, Sherbrooke, PQ J1L 1P8 (800–361–6162 or 819–563–2941). Indoor pool, free parking, TV. Five lilies; three forks.
Motel L'Ermitage. *Moderate.* 1888 rue King Ouest, Sherbrooke, PQ J1J 2E2 (819–569–5551). Outdoor pool. Three lilies.

STRATFORD. Hotel Stratford. *Inexpensive.* 175 ave. Centrale Nord, Stratford, PQ G0Y 1P0 (418–443–2636). Near Parc de Frontenac. One lily.

SUTTON. Hotel-Motel Horizon. *Inexpensive.* Chemin Mont-Sutton, Sutton, PQ J0E 2K0 (514–538–3212). Near Sutton ski area. Indoor pool, TV, 48 rooms. Three lilies.

THE LAURENTIANS

Price categories, based on the cost of a double room, are: *Super Deluxe,* $180 and up; *Deluxe,* $130–$180; *Expensive,* $90–$130; *Moderate,* $50–$90; and *Inexpensive,* $50 and below. Many inns offer AP or MAP. For an explanation of the province's lily and fork rating system, see *Facts at Your Fingertips.*

LAC-DES-PLAGES. Hôtel Mon Chez-Nous. *Moderate.* rue Principale, Lac-des-Plages, PQ J0T 1K0 (819–426–2186). Cross-country skiing, lake fishing, skidoo, snowmobile trails, skating nearby, water sports, good beach, organized activities. 35 rooms, and four cabins on the lake.

MONT-ROLLAND. Auberge Mont-Gabriel. *Deluxe* (MAP). Autoroute 15, Sortie (Exit) 64, Mont-Rolland, PQ J0R 1G0 (514–229–3547). 1200-acre estate, 159 rooms. Tennis, ski week and weekend packages.

MONT-TREMBLANT. Auberge Cuttle's Tremblant Club. *Deluxe–Super Deluxe.* Lac-Tremblant, PQ J0T 1Z0 (819–425–2731). Lakeside. Skiing, tennis, swimming, fishing, golf.
    Station du Mont-Tremblant Lodge. *Expensive–Deluxe.* Mont-Tremblant, PQ J0T 1Z0 (819–425–8711, 514–861–6165 from Montreal, 800–567–6761 else-where). "The only hotel at the foot of the big mountain." Chalets, apartments. All winter sports facilities. Ski schools.
    Hôtel-Motel Chalet des Chutes. *Deluxe* (MAP). CP # 1, Lac-Tremblant, PQ J0T 1Z0 (819–425–2738). Near lake, waterfalls. Tennis, golf, all skiing locally.
    Hôtel-Motel Villa Bellevue. *Moderate–Expensive* (MAP). Mont-Tremblant, PQ J0T 1Z0 (819–425–2734 or 800–567–6763 from Ontario, Quebec, and the Maritimes). Lakeside, with all water sports; tennis; skiing.

MORIN HEIGHTS. Auberge Hollandaise. *Moderate.* 796 Route St-Adolphe, Morin Heights, PQ J0R 1H0 (514–226–2009). Two lakes nearby for wind-surfing, swimming. Cross-country skiing.
    Hôtel The Carriage House. *Inexpensive.* Route 329 Nord, 486 route St-Adolphe, Morin Heights, PQ J0R 1H0 (514–226–3031). Lake, windsurfers, canoes for guests, winter sports, cross-country trails.

ST-JOVITE. Gray Rocks Inn. *Deluxe–Super Deluxe* (MAP). Box 1000, St-Jovite, PQ J0T 2H0 (819–425–2771, 514–861–0187 from Montreal, or 800–567–6767 from Ontario, Quebec, and the Maritimes). About the oldest of the Laurentian resorts. Extensive landscaped grounds on lakefront. Water sports, children's program, golf, all winter sports. Private airstrip and seaplane anchor-age.

ST-SAUVEUR-DES-MONTS. Auberge St-Denis. *Moderate–Expensive.* Box 1229, 61 rue St Denis, St-Sauveur-des-Monts, PQ J0R 1R0 (514–227–4766). All sports available locally.
    Motel Mont-Habitant. *Inexpensive–Moderate.* 12 blvd. des Skieurs, St-Sau-veur-des-Monts, PQ J0R 1R0 (514–227–2637, 800–363–3612). On private lake. Some of the 25 rooms have fireplaces. Tennis, water and winter sports.

STE-ADELE. Hotel Le Chantecler. *Deluxe–Super Deluxe* (MAP). CP 1048, Chemin du Chantecler, Ste-Adele, PQ J0R 1L0 (514–229–3555, 800–363–2420 (Quebec). Cross-country and downhill skiing, pool, tennis, squash, horseback riding, and golf. Lakeside beach.
    Motel Altitude. *Moderate–Expensive.* CP 1234, Route 117, Ste-Adele, PQ J0R 1L0 (514–229–6616 or 800–363–3683 from Ontario and Quebec). 45 min from Montreal. Near all winter sports. 52 rooms, 22 with fireplaces. Swimming pools, squash, sauna.

STE-AGATHE-DES-MONTS. Le Manoir d'Ivry. *Inexpensive.* 3800 chemin Renaud, Ste-Agathe-Nord, PQ J8C 2Z8 (819–326–3564). Lakeside, all-season accommodation in a *fin-de-siècle* manor house near Parc Mont-Tremblant. Winter and summer sports and water sports.

VAL-DAVID. Parker's Lodge. *Inexpensive–Moderate (AP).* 1340 Chemin Lac-Paquin, Val-David, PQ J0T 2N0 (819–322–2026). Near lake. Cross-coun-try and downhill skiing. Instructors. Swimming, boating, golf nearby.
    Hôtel La Sapinière. *Deluxe–Super Deluxe (AP).* CP 190, 1244 chemin de la Sapinière, Val-David, PQ, J0T 2N0 819–322–2020, 514–866–8262 from Mont-real, or 800–567–6635 from Quebec and Ontario. 70 rooms with private bath. Canoeing, golf, biking, nature trails, tennis, all winter sports, equipment rentals. One of the very best hotels in the whole area.

VAL-MORIN. Far Hills Inn. *Deluxe* (MAP). Rue Far Hills, Val-Morin, PQ J0T 2R0 (819–322–2014, 514–866–2219, or 800–567–6636 from Canada and eastern U.S.). Principally cross-country. Lakeside, water sports, equipment available for guests, local club for tennis and squash.

CHARLEVOIX

BAIE-ST-PAUL. Maison Otis. *Expensive-Deluxe.* 23 rue St-Jean-Baptiste, Baie-St-Paul, PQ G0A 1B0 (418–435–2255). Many rate this one of the region's best. The old stone house in a picturesque village proves a romantic setting for fine nouvelle cuisine dishes, all market-fresh. Lunch on the terrace in summer only. Gourmet dinners. The 28 well-appointed rooms (some with whirlpool baths, fireplaces, antique furniture), garnered four lilies. Four forks for cuisine.
    Le Dery Hotel and Motel. *Moderate.* 896 blvd. Monseigneur de Laval, Baie-St-Paul, PQ G0A 1B0 (418–435–3910). European French cuisine, lunch and dinner. 18 rooms, three lilies, three forks.

CAP-A-L'AIGLE. Auberge des Peupliers. *Deluxe–Super Deluxe* (MAP). 381 rue St-Raphael, Cap-a-l'Aigle, La Malbaie, PQ G0T 1B0 (418–665–4423). Charming old farmhouse with original antiques, beautiful dining room, genuine Quebec fare from owner's family recipes. New section features very comfortable rooms. 21 rooms, four lilies, three forks.
    Auberge la Pinsonnière. *Deluxe–Super Deluxe.* 124 rue St-Raphael, Cap-a-l'Aigle, La Malbaie, PQ G0T 1B0 (418–665–4431). Swimming pool, private beach, view over the St. Lawrence and back across the bay to Pointe-au-Pic. Classical music in rooms. Highest government rating both for the comfort of its 24 rooms (five lilies) and cuisine (four forks).

LES EBOULEMENTS. Auberge de Nos Aieux. *Inexpensive–Moderate.* 183, Route 362, Les Eboulements, PQ G0A 2M0 (418–635–2483). *Nos Aieux* means "our forefathers." This is an exceptionally lovely village. Partial access for handicapped people. 42 rooms. Three lilies for comfort, one fork.

ÎLE AUX COUDRES. Auberge la Coudrière. *Moderate–Expensive.* 244 rue Principale, Île aux Coudres, PQ G0A 2A0 (418–438–2838). Typical Quebec fare, folk dancing. Seasonal. Three lilies for its 49 rooms. Two forks.
    Hôtel Cap aux Pierres et Motels. *Moderate–Expensive.* 220 rue Principale, Île aux Coudres, PQ G0A 2A0 (418–438–2711 or 800–361–6162). Pool, tennis, traditional Quebec fare, folk dancing. Seasonal. Four lilies, 98 rooms. Two forks.
    Hôtel St-Bernard. *Inexpensive–Moderate.* 35 rue Royale Ouest, Île aux Coudres, PQ G0A 1X0 (418–438–2261). Seasonal. One lily for its 14 rooms. Reasonably priced Quebec fare. No credit cards.

LA MALBAIE. (See also Cap-à-l'Aigle and Pointe-au-Pic.) **Manoir Charlevoix.** *Moderate–Expensive.* 1030 rue St-Etienne, La Malbaie, PQ G0T 1J0 (418–665–4413). Fine old pine-paneled hotel perched on rocks. European French cuisine (two forks). 42 rooms (three lilies);

POINTE-AU-PIC. Auberge des Falaises. *Expensive–Deluxe.* 18 blvd. des Falaises, Pointe-au-Pic, PQ G0T 1M0 (418–665–3731). A most romantic dining room and terrace overlooking the bay. Nine-course gourmet dinners. Nouvelle cuisine with local produce, lamb, smelts, rabbit (four forks). 12 rooms (four lilies).
    Manoir Richelieu. *Expensive–Deluxe.* 181 ave. Richelieu, Pointe-au-Pic, PQ G0T 1M0 (418–665–3703, 800–463–2613). Biggest hotel in the region, a remnant of the days when rich visitors arrived by the "white boats." Several dining rooms, entertainment, golf, tennis, swimming pools. 325 rooms, four lilies, two forks.
    Auberge les Sources. *Expensive–Deluxe.* 8 ave. des Pins, Pointe-au-Pic, PQ G0T 1M0 (418–665–6952). Fine old Taft-era house overlooking water. European French cuisine. 20 rooms, four lilies, two forks.
    Auberge au Petit Berger. *Deluxe–Super Deluxe* (MAP). 1 Côte Bellevue, Pointe-au-Pic, PQ G0T 1M0 (418–665–4428). The "little sheepfold," is actually several old houses turned into very comfortable rooms, some with whirlpool

baths. Special packages for tennis players, golfers. 20 rooms, four lilies, three forks.

Auberge la Petite Marmite. *Expensive.* 63 rue Principale, Pointe-au-Pic, PQ G0T 1M0 (418–665–3583). Small seven-room inn, two lilies, two forks.

GASPÉ PENINSULA

Price categories, based on the price of a double room in high season, are: *Deluxe,* over $70; *Expensive,* $50–$70; *Moderate,* $30–$59; and *Inexpensive,* under $30.

CARLETON. Baie Bleue. *Expensive–Deluxe.* Route 132, Carleton, P.Q. G0C 1J0 (418–364–3355, 800–361–6162). Part of Hôte, the Quebec chain of 36 quality motels and hotels run by individual innkeepers. 85 motel units, heated outdoor pool, sandy beach, near golf, tennis, fishing, hiking, windsurfing. Rates 5 lilies, 4 forks for dining room.

PASPÉBIAC. Auberge du Parc. *Moderate–Expensive.* C.P. 40, Paspébiac, P.Q. G0C 2K0 (418–752–3355). Seasonal. Near tennis, historic building, artists' colony. On beach. Motel units, and inn with magnificent old staircase, fine views. 3 lilies, 2 forks.

PERCÉ. La Normandie. *Moderate.* CP 129, Perce, PQ G0C 2L0 (418–782–2112). 30 modern and comfortable units, all overlooking the great pierced rock. Beach. Fine dining, with 3 forks for gourmet cuisine, 4 lilies for well-appointed rooms.

 BED-AND-BREAKFAST. Scattered in a variety of settings and sites, these guest houses are usually family homes with a pleasant atmosphere and clean, comfortable rooms. The style, standards, and price of these accommodations vary widely. Private bathrooms are a luxury; in most places the facilities are down the hall. Breakfast arrangements vary; the hostess may serve a homemade French-Canadian meal with pancakes, preserves, Canadian back bacon, and other delights, or ask you to prepare a do-it-yourself meal with supplied ingredients.

Two terrific guidebooks will help you to find bed-and-breakfast accommodation in Quebec. John Thompson and Pat Wilson's handy *Traveller's Guide to Bed-and-Breakfast Places in Canada* has over 40 provincial listings, from Auguste and Anne Simard's 800-acre dairy farm in Lac-St-Jean to a 110-year-old Victorian antique-furnished town house overlooking the heart of Montreal (available from Grosvenor House, 1456 Sherbrooke St. W., 3rd Floor, Montreal, PQ H3G 1K4, for about $12). A guide to farm vacations, country inns, and B&Bs, *Les Sejours et Les Promenades à la ferme, les gîtes du passant et les tables champêtres* is published and distributed free by the ministère du Loisir, de la Chasse, et de la Pêche (see "Tourist Information").

 RESTAURANTS. Whether you enjoy a croissant and espresso at a sidewalk cafe, sample North America's finest nouvelle cuisine, or order *poutine,* a streetwise mix of homemade french fries *(frites)* from a fast-food emporium, dining in Quebec is an unforgettable experience. You do not simply "eat out"; restaurants are an integral slice of Quebec life.

We suggest a few restaurants for each of the sections covered here. As for the accommodations, establishments are listed alphabetically by town, and each description includes a price category based on the cost of a complete three course meal for one, not including beverage, tax, or tip. The actual prices represented by the categories vary by region and are given at the beginning of each section.

"Forks"—These are part of the provincial rating system and are explained above at the beginning of the accommodations section.

L'ESTRIE

Expensive, $20–$25; *Moderate,* $12–$20; *Inexpensive,* under $12.

BELOEIL. Restaurant Rive Gauche. *Expensive.* 1810 blvd. Richelieu, Beloeil, PQ J3G 4S4 (514–467–4477). Outstanding French cuisine along the banks of the Richelieu. Daily 7:30 A.M.–10:30 P.M.

CARIGNAN. Au Tournant de la Rivière. *Expensive.* Autoroute 10, Exit 22, Carignan (514–658–7372). Housed in an old farmhouse, this exquisite restaurant features fanciful nouvelle cuisine by chef Jacques Robert. Open 6:30–9:00 P.M. for dinner; closed Mon. and Tues.

GLEN SUTTON. Auberge Glen Sutton. *Inexpensive.* RR 4, Glen Sutton J0E 1X0 (514–538–2000). The only restaurant hereabouts serving Mexican food. Wed.–Sun., 4:00–9:30 P.M.

MAGOG. Auberge de l'Etoile. *Moderate.* 1133 rue Principale Ouest, Magog, PQ J1X 2B8 (819–843–6521). One of the region's best. Specialty of the house is Brome Lake duckling, prepared by chef Bernard Leroy. Daily, 7:00 A.M.–11:00 P.M.

MANSONVILLE. Petite Europe. *Inexpensive.* Route 243, Mansonville, PQ J0E 1X0 (514–292–3523). Central European cuisine served in a stylish chalet. Open daily, 5–9 P.M.

SHERBROOKE. Au p'tit sabot. *Expensive.* 1410 rue King Ouest, Sherbrooke, PQ J1J 2C2 (819–563–0262). Specialty: Quebec wild boar prepared by award-winning chef, Sylvio Clement. 11:30 A.M.–2:00 P.M., 5:00–10:00 P.M. Closed Sun.

THE LAURENTIANS

Three and even four fork restaurants are common in many of the hotels. Many restaurants offer table d'hote menus that considerably reduce expenses. The categories here are: *Super Deluxe,* $80–$100; *Deluxe,* $60–$80; *Expensive,* $40–$60; *Moderate,* $20–$40; and *Inexpensive,* under $20.

MONT TREMBLANT. Auberge du Coq de Montagne. *Inexpensive–Moderate.* Lac Moore, Mont-Tremblant (819–425–3380). Wholesome Italian food from the kitchens of this auberge. Dinner, 5:30–9:30 P.M., to 10 P.M. weekends. No AE.

ST-JOVITE. La Table Enchantée. *Inexpensive to Moderate.* Route 117 nord, Lac Duhamel, St-Jovite (5 km north of St-Jovite). (819–425–7113). Quebec cuisine. Dinner, 5–11 P.M. Tues.–Sun.

STE-ADELE. Le St-Trop. *Moderate–Expensive.* 251 rue Morin, Ste-Adele (514–229–3298). French cuisine in a lakeside setting. Dinner, Wed.–Mon. 7 P.M.–midnight; lunch, 12:30–2:30 P.M. Sun. Closed Mon. in winter.

STE-AGATHE. Chez Girard. *Moderate.* 18 rue Principale Ouest, Ste-Agathe (819–326–0922). French cuisine in a small traditional auberge. Lunch, 11:30 A.M.–2:00 P.M.; dinner, 5–9 P.M., Tues.–Sun.
　　Eberhard's Chatel Vienna. *Moderate.* 6 rue Ste-Lucie, Ste-Agathe (819–326–1485). Viennese and continental cuisine in a lakeside setting. Dinner, 5–10 P.M. Tues.–Fri. Lunch and dinner, noon–11 P.M., Sat., noon–9 P.M., Sun. Closed Apr. and Nov.

STE-MARGUERITE. La Clef des Champs. *Moderate.* 875 Chemin Ste-Marguerite, Ste-Marguerite (514–229–2857). Gourmet French cuisine in a family-owned hillside restaurant. Dinner, 5:30–10:30 P.M., Tues.–Sun. and holiday Mon. Closed for vacations after Easter.

VAL-DAVID. Hôtel La Sapinière. *Super Deluxe.* 1244 chemin de la Sapinière, Val-David (819–322–2020). Classic continental cuisine. Lunch, 12–2 P.M.; dinner, 6:30–8:30 P.M. daily.

Auberge Le Rucher. *Moderate–Expensive.* 2368 rue de l'Église, Val-David (819–322–2507). Excellent French cuisine. Dinner, 6–9 P.M. Closed Apr.

Auberge du Vieux Foyer. *Moderate–Expensive.* 3167 Montée Doncaster, Val-David (819–322–2686). International cuisine. Lunch, 12–3 P.M.; dinner, 6–8:30 P.M. Daily, June–Oct. and mid Dec.–Easter. Weekends only the rest of the year. Closed Nov. and Apr.

CHARLEVOIX

In Charlevoix, you dine best in the inns, manors, and hotels, although you can find many good, inexpensive snack bars and cafes for light repasts. Regional fare includes a unique bean soup, made with a local legume called *gourgane*, fresh seafood of all kinds, locally raised fresh lamb, rabbit, Quebec meat pies *(tourtières)*, and deserts like sugar pie, which tastes somewhat like an English treacle tart or an American pecan pie without the pecans. Most dining rooms open from about noon to 2:30 or 3 P.M., and from 5:30 or 6 P.M.–8:30 or 9 P.M. Reservations are essential, so check times when you call to reserve. Price categories for a complete dinner for one (not including beverage, tax, or tip) at the inns listed in the accommodations section are: *Super Deluxe,* over $35; *Deluxe,* $24–$35; *Expensive,* $18–$23; *Moderate,* $8–$18; and *Inexpensive,* under $8. Because most restaurants offer *table d'hôte*—complete meals, usually with hors d'oeuvre or soup, a main dish, and dessert—the prices often range through two categories. All the hotels hold liquor licenses, so do not bring your own wine.

A good restaurant not associated with an inn, and so not listed above, is:

Le Mouton Noir. *Moderate–Inexpensive.* rue du Quai, Baie-St-Paul (418–435 –3075). Open 11 A.M.–9 P.M. daily, but closed from 2–5 P.M. in winter. Charlevoix specialties, wild-rabbit pie, veal scallop, lamb, and homemade Merguez sausages.

GASPÉ PENINSULA

CARLETON. Le Vivier. *Inexpensive–Moderate.* Route du Quai off route 132 (418–364–6122). Fresh lobster and salad bar.

PARC NATIONALE DE LA GASPÉSIE. Auberge Gîte du Mont Albert. *Expensive.* Route 299 (418–763–2288). Three forks.

PERCÉ. Auberge du Gargantua. *Expensive.* 222 route des Falls (418–782–2852). Four forks.

Hotel Bonaventure-sur-mer. *Expensive.* (418–782–2166.) Excellent cuisine, but hotel is closed in winter.

NEW BRUNSWICK

Natural Habitat for Sports Lovers

by
COLLEEN THOMPSON

Author of New Brunswick Inside Out, *a native's view of the province, travel writer Colleen Thompson has journeyed extensively throughout the Atlantic provinces. She is a regular contributor to various U.S. and Canadian magazines and newspapers, a travel columnist for the Saint John* Telegraph-Journal, *and a sometimes radio commentator.*

For years this scenic and varied province has been ignored by tourists who whiz through to better known Atlantic provinces. In some ways it's been a blessing in disguise because today's motorists who leave the major highways to explore the 2,240 kilometers (1,400 miles) of unspoiled sea coast, pure inland streams, pretty towns and historical cities, are finding an innocent area almost free of tourist hype. Residents who bask in an unhurried way of life still think of tourists as welcome visitors. It makes for a charming vacation.

The dual heritage of New Brunswick (35 percent of its population is Acadian French) provides an added bonus. Within a 400-kilometer (250-mile) drive from north to south, you can vacation in both the Acadian and the Loyalist regions, making New Brunswick a bargain . . . two vacations for the price of one.

New Brunswick is where the great Canadian forest, sliced by sweeping river valleys and modern highways, meets the sea. It is an old place in New World terms, and the remains of a turbulent past exist in delightfully quiet nooks.

More than half the province is surrounded by coastline. The rest of it is nestled into Quebec and Maine. The dramatic Bay of Fundy, which has the highest tides in the world, sweeps up the coast of Maine, around the enchanting Fundy Isles at the southern tip of New Brunswick, and on up the province's rough and intriguing south coast. To the north and east, home of the French Acadian heritage, it's the gentle and warm Gulf of St. Lawrence that washes the quiet beaches.

For all that, New Brunswick is also a province of inland attractions. Its land mass and its human side are dominated by the Saint John River Valley—a strip of gentle farmland with sweeping views, and genteel communities with a captivating heritage. The capital, Fredericton, is built on the river's banks and it enters the sea at Saint John, the province's main industrial city.

Spring is a glorious time—the greening of the land begins in April and by June the meadows are vivid with the purple and gold of violets (the province's official flower) and dandelions. Throughout June, the roads are almost empty of tourist vehicles, yet it is one of the loveliest of months in New Brunswick.

Summer is hot, more so in the inland cities such as Fredericton where the average temperature of 21°C (70°F) can sometimes soar to 35°C (95°F). But this is the time of festivals; and almost every community has some sort of celebration, often featuring foods and activities associated with its region.

The warm weather makes the lakes, the pure rivers, and the seaside even more delightful with plenty of water activities such as swimming, wind surfing, sailing, tubing, canoeing, even rafting, and sand-castle-building competitions.

In the fall, especially October, the country is ablaze with some of the most magnificent color in North America. In September, which is still warm, the roads are again uncrowded and touring is delightful. It's also theater season when Fredericton's Playhouse presents professional productions.

Winter begins in November and by January is usually severe with lots of snow. Winter sports are plentiful with both downhill and cross-country skiing popular. The province has extensive skiing facilities with many annual competitions and championships. Ice fishing is another winter pastime, and you'll see clusters of tiny shacks on lakes and rivers. Some operators offer sleigh rides, snowmobile tours, ice fishing, and skiing all in one package. Clear air, unbroken snow, and ice-crystal-hung trees make this season exceptionally beautiful in New Brunswick.

Certain foods and seasons are often well paired in this maritime province. In April, when the sap begins to flow, maple sugar camps offer pancake breakfast in the bush.

In the spring, the tourist must sample New Brunswick's delicacy, the fiddlehead fern, picked fresh alongside the rivers and streams. Eaten as a vegetable (boiled, then drenched with lemon butter, salt, and pepper), fiddleheads are delicious, with something of an artichoke taste, and they go well with spring's bony fish, shad and gaspereaus.

Salmon, which used to be a spring staple, is still available but quite costly. Lobster is the Maritimer's favorite dish, eaten on shore preferably, not at the table. Indeed, all shellfish coming from the Bay of Fundy and Gulf of St. Lawrence waters are especially tasty. Look for oysters, scallops, clams, crab, and mussels. And don't overlook dulse, a salty seaweed eaten like potato chips. Wash down these hearty native dishes with rich Moosehead beer, brewed in Saint John (a strictly local beer for decades, it is now a well-known export), and you'll have feasted well, New Brunswick style.

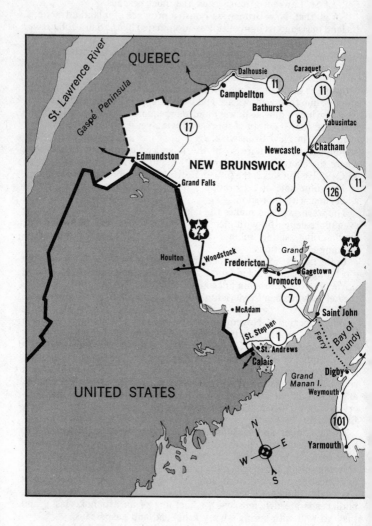

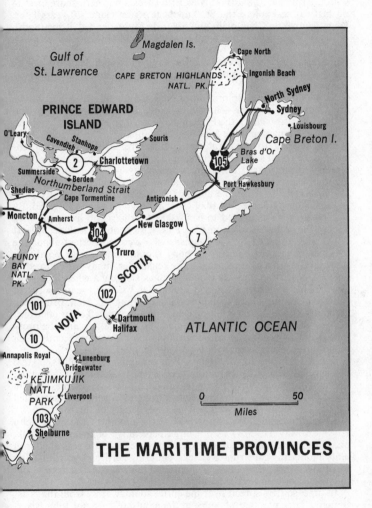

Magdalen Is.

Gulf of
St. Lawrence

Cape North

CAPE BRETON HIGHLANDS
NATL. PK.

Ingonish Beach

North Sydney

PRINCE EDWARD
ISLAND

Sydney

Louisbourg

O'Leary

Cavendish
Stanhope
Souris

Cape Breton I.

2

Charlottetown

Summerside
Berden

Bras d'Or
Lake

105

Shediac
Northumberland Strait
Cape Tormentine

Port Hawkesbury

Moncton
Amherst

Antigonish

New Glasgow

104

7

2

Truro

SCOTIA

FUNDY
BAY
NATL.
PK.

102

101

NOVA

Dartmouth
Halifax

ATLANTIC OCEAN

10

Annapolis Royal
Lunenburg
Bridgewater

KEJIMKUJIK
NATL.
PARK

Liverpool

0   50
Miles

103

Shelburne

THE MARITIME PROVINCES

A Quiet History

While the red-bearded Vikings may have been familiar with the shores of New Brunswick's Fundy Isles in the Passamaquoddy Bay, history records the first white explorer as Jacques Cartier who traded with the Micmac Indians on New Brunswick's northern shore in 1534 on his way to explore the St. Lawrence River. Some 70 years later, when Samuel de Champlain and Sieur de Monts landed at the mouth of the St. John River they were casually greeted by an elderly Indian chieftain, the same Chief Membertou who had met Cartier on his first North American adventure. The Indian population in New Brunswick today is about 6,000, spread throughout the province in various reserves.

Throughout their exploration of New Brunswick (then part of the area known as Acadia—embracing Nova Scotia, Cape Breton, and Prince Edward Island), the French maintained good relationships with both the Micmacs and the Maliceets who inhabited the St. John River Valley. Hoping to pre-empt the land before the English, they encouraged French settlers, opening up the rich fur trade to them. Their strategy deteriorated, however, when many of the French fought among themselves, a situation that allowed the English to launch successful attacks from Maine and establish their own settlements.

Finally, in 1713, the Treaty of Utrecht ceded Acadia to England. By 1755 there were estimated to be 10,000 Acadians still living in Nova Scotia (the area of New Brunswick and Nova Scotia). Of these, at least 7,000 were expelled by the English, who were concerned about the loyalties of this ever-increasing body should another war break out between France and England. Of the remainder, many were forced to flee to Québec and faraway places, such as Louisiana where the name Acadian has been corrupted to "Cajun." Yet, within 20 years many had returned, settling along the shores, especially in the New Brunswick communities of Cocagne, Shippagan, and Caraquet. Today one third of New Brunswick's population is made up of Acadians and the province is officially bilingual although attempts have only recently been made to familiarize residents with both languages.

The close of the Revolutionary War brought the Loyalists, 50,000 of them, loyal to Great Britain in deed or spirit. Because of the influx, the area known as Nova Scotia was divided into two colonies, and in 1784, the province of New Brunswick came into being. It was named for the Houste of Brunswick, of the royal family of the time.

Three thousand Loyalists arrived at the mouth of the Saint John River on May 11, 1783 . . . a large percentage of them gentlefolk, unaccustomed to deprivation. Here they were forced to seek shelter in tents and hastily constructed shacks, enduring hardships with amazing fortitude. Aged and infirm, women and children suffered deeply and many died of cold and exposure.

In time, settlers spread over the entire country away from the coast though a large number remained at the mouth of the Saint John River, founding the city which now bears that name. The hardy Loyalist spirit and the French persistence have made the New Brunswicker what he is today . . . stubborn, resourceful, fun-loving, sometimes rowdy, usually gracious—and fiercely independent.

The Great Outdoors

A province of great geographical variety, New Brunswick claims 1,400 miles of seacoast, including the hauntingly beautiful Fundy Isles, acres of rolling agricultural land along its rivers, and a rugged highland interior—forests, secluded lakes and mountains.

Crisscrossed with rivers, the province is a fisherman's heaven, offering Atlantic silver salmon, speckled trout, and black and striped bass. Said to offer the best bass fishing in North America, the season starts in mid-May with the Big Bass Tournament at Mactaquac, upriver from Fredericton. The Miramichi, the Restigouche, and the Nashwaak Rivers are prized by sport fishermen the world over.

Deep-sea fishing is also available for the avid sportsman. Canoeing, hiking, bird-watching—and more recently, whale-watching and windsurfing—are popular summer pastimes.

New Brunswick is still largely unsettled—88 percent of the province is forested lands. Inhabitants have chosen the easily accessible area around rivers, ocean, and lakes, leaving most of the interior to the pulp companies. In fact, the view from a plane will make you think that New Brunswick is still an unspoiled wilderness with little sign of civilization. But its towns and cities, some of the first to be founded on the continent, have emerged through centuries as cultured centers of learning and government, their respect for the past as acute as their awareness of the future.

How New Brunswick Makes a Living

Lumbering, a major source of income since the days of pit props and ships' masts, has taken a back seat to the mineral industry in recent times. Zinc, lead, and potash are the major minerals. Fishing remains the major occupation along the shores while the rich agricultural lands of the upper Saint John Valley turn out profitable potato crops each year. Saint John is a major port and industrial city. The largest oil refinery in Canada is located there. Tourism also generates considerable economic activity. Manufacturing is mostly done on the small scale, and it is diverse.

FREDERICTON

The seat of government for New Brunswick's 710,900 residents has been the inland city of Fredericton on the St. John River since 1785. Loyalist to the core and named for Frederick, second son of George III, the city is the pride of the province. Tree-lined, resting sedately on the bank of the river, it was never a true frontier town. From the first town plan, the wealthy and scholarly Loyalists set out to create a gracious and beautiful place.

Its predecessor was the early French settlement of Ste.-Anne's Point established in 1642 during the reign of the French governor, Villebon, who made his headquarters at the junction of the Nashwaak and the Saint John. From Fort Nashwaak—now only a memorial cairn—he launched many successful raids into Maine, which caused great resentment among the English. Villebon left Fort Nashwaak in 1698, but the memory of the English was long and some forty years later a raiding party known as Hazen's Massachusetts Rangers burned the small village to the ground, killed most of the men, and carried the women and children off to Boston. The city of Fredericton rose from the ruins of this small French village.

Exploring Fredericton

Called the City of Stately Elms, Fredericton became an elegant British garrison town starting in 1825 when the military quarters were established there. A look at the military compound (including officer's quarters, enlisted men's barracks, guardhouse, and parade ground) is a must for any visitor interested in the city's past. Now designated a federal historic site, the military compound has been restored. Although the inside houses government offices, some parts, such as the guardhouse, are open to the public.

At present, the officer's quarters houses the York-Sunbury Historical Museum (largest community museum in the province, displaying many mementos of the past including replicas of 19th-century Fredericton homes), reconstructed with authentic furnishings of the period. You'll also find there the remains of one of Fredericton's legends. Staring at you from its glass case at the top of a staircase is the famous Coleman Frog, allegedly discovered in nearby Killarney Lake by hotelier Fred Coleman. Weighing 42 pounds, it was dispatched to an untimely death by a dynamite charge set by some disgruntled fishermen. Coleman had the frog stuffed; for forty years it sat in the lobby of his hotel on Queen Street where visitors were held spellbound by the stories of how it used to thrive on a diet of buttermilk, June bugs, fireflies, and whiskey fed to it by Fred and his friends. Resurrected from someone's garage after the old Barker House closed, it now holds a place of honor in the museum; and, of course, with a slight smile on its froggy face it never reveals its secret . . . which only Fred Coleman knew. Hoax or miracle? You'll have to decide for yourself. Call (506) 455–6041. Open 10:00 A.M.–6 P.M. Small admission.

Because of the gifts showered upon it by former New Brunswicker Lord Beaverbrook, multimillionaire, British peer, and newspaper baron, Fredericton has many fine buildings. On lower Queen Street, just two blocks from the Military Compound, you'll see the Playhouse, a gift of the Beaverbrook and the Dunn Foundation (former New Brunswicker Sir James Dunn, steel magnate and also Beaverbrook's close friend). The Playhouse (home of Theatre New Brunswick), built in 1964, provides year-round professional theater to city and province. Call (506) 458–8344.

The Beaverbrook Art Gallery across the street will delight you with the wealth of its collection, including works by many of New Brunswick's noted artists as well as Salvador Dali's giant canvas *Santiago el Grande* (a huge painting bought especially for the Gallery's opening in 1959 by Sir James Dunn), canvasses by Reynolds, Turner, Hogarth, Gainsborough, the Canadian Group of Seven, and even works by Sir Winston Churchill. The Gallery houses a large collection of Graham Sutherland (47), and the largest collection in any institution of the works of Cornelius Krieghoff, famed Canadian landscape painter, known for his portrayals of Canadian life in the early 1800s. Call (506) 458–8545. Open 10 A.M.–5 P.M., Tues.–Sat., noon–5 P.M., Sat. and Mon. Admission: adults, $2; students 50 cents.

The Provincial Legislature, built in 1880, is across the street from the Gallery. Open to the public, it offers guided tours at no cost, except when the Legislature is in session. When the House is in session, the public may view the proceedings from the public gallery, where you must also examine Sir Joshua Reynolds' portraits of George III and Queen Charlotte which flank the Throne.

In the back room of the Legislature, near the handsome spiral staircase, is the Legislative Library which contains two interesting and rare items. The first is a copy of the *Domesday Book*, the first census ever written, commissioned by William of Normandy in 1087. (This edition was printed in 1783.) Then turn to the four-volume set of the rare king-size Audubon bird books, more than three feet high, containing 435 hand-colored pictures (1834). Call (506) 453–2338. Open 8:30 A.M.–4:30 P.M., Mon.–Fri. Free.

At the triangle of Queen, Church, and Brunswick Streets, about a block from the Legislative Building, you'll find the Christ Church Cathedral, Fredericton's pride. Completed in 1853, it is a beautiful building, one of the best examples of decorated Gothic architecture in North America and the first new cathedral foundation built on British soil since the Norman Conquest. Inside you'll find a clock known as "Big Ben's little brother" designed by Lord Grimthorpe, probably as the test-run for London's famous timepiece. While there, watch out for the ghost of Mrs. Medley, wife of the first bishop, John Medley. She's often seen crossing the lawn to enter the Cathedral by the west door. Open to public, free.

The University of New Brunswick (located at the end of University Avenue on a hill overlooking the city), is ancient by Canadian standards. Established in 1783, when it was called the College of New Brunswick, it later became known as Kings College until 1859, when it became the University of New Brunswick. Today the campus also includes St. Thomas University, a small but steadily growing institution. Site of many firsts, the University of New Brunswick campus had the first astronomical observatory (the Brydon Jack Observatory) in Canada. The building is now an observatory museum called The Brydon Jack Museum. The university initiated the first engineering school in Canada and the second forestry school. With an active enrollment in the sciences and arts as well, the university has come a long way since the first two B.A. degrees were awarded in 1828. Enrollment today is approximately 8,000.

On Woodstock Road, surrounded by spacious lawns, you'll find Old Government House, built in 1828 as a residence for the province's lieutenant governors. The classic old Georgian building has housed many famous guests, for example, the Prince of Wales (later Edward VII) who stayed here in 1860 when he visited New Brunswick as a young man of 19. Dancing all night at one of the city's gaiest balls, he won the hearts of all the women. Unfortunately, now that Government House is headquarters for the RCMP, it is not generally open to the public. It is, however, being restored and future plans are to open one wing for public inspection.

John James Audubon stayed here two years later as the guest of the Governor and painted his famous Pine Finch on the grounds. (You can view it at the Legislative Library.)

A walking tour of Fredericton's historic homes is available at bookstores.

But for a true understanding of New Brunswick's background and history, visit Kings Landing, located about 23 miles west of Fredericton on the Trans-Canada Highway. Challenging the imagination of visitors, this reconstructed village—55 buildings including homes, inn, forge, store, church, school, and working farm—is designed to illustrate life in the central Saint John River Valley between 1790 and 1870. The winding country lanes, creaking wagons, old houses, and the smell of freshly baked bread will pull you back a century or more to when the sound of the motor car was unknown. The costumed staff will answer your questions, and the Kings Head Inn is a friendly spot to rest your feet and quench your thirst with a draft of cold beer or a sip of wine. The restaurant upstairs serves old-fashioned traveler's fare such as cold cuts and hot meat pie. Just around the corner in a barn, the King's Theatre offers some of the funniest "mellerdrama" you've ever witnessed.

PRACTICAL INFORMATION FOR FREDERICTON

HOW TO GET THERE. By air: Both *Air Canada* and *CP Air* service Fredericton airport at Lincoln (5 miles from Fredericton), with connecting flights from most major airlines.

By car: Follow the Trans-Canada Hwy. from Québec; U.S. 95 and Trans-Canada Hwy. from Houlton, Maine; Hwy. 3 and Trans-Canada Hwy. from Calais, Maine; Trans-Canada from Nova Scotia.

By train: *Via Rail* has daily rail liner service to and from Halifax through Saint John and Moncton. At Moncton it makes connections with the *Ocean Limited* train which travels Halifax-Montréal.

By bus: *SMT* bus service within the province provides regional transportation. Most major bus companies in USA and Canada connect with SMT.

ACCOMMODATIONS. Hotels and motels in and around Fredericton are not luxurious but are adequate with friendly service. A 10% sales tax will be added to your bill. Rates are based on double occupancy as follows: *Expensive,* over $43 and *Moderate,* $30–43.

Most places accept the following major credit cards: American Express, MasterCard, and Visa; others may also be honored. Not all establishments accept credit cards, therefore we suggest you call for information.

Auberge Wandlyn Inn. *Expensive.* 58 Prospect St. W., Box 214, Fredericton, NB E3B 4Y9 (506–452–8937). 116 pleasant rooms, good dining room, cozy bar, heated pool. Close to three shopping malls, many restaurants, three theaters. Major credit cards.

The Diplomat Hotel. *Expensive.* 225 Woodstock Rd., Box 634, Fredericton, NB E3B 5A6 (506–454–5584). 100 pleasant rooms, many with balconies overlooking pool, good dining room, intimate indoor bar, and popular pool bar, often patronized by Fredericton residents. Outdoor jazz cafe in summer. Major credit cards.

Howard Johnson Motor Lodge. *Expensive.* Box 1414, Fredericton, NB E3B 5E3 (506–472–0480). On Rte. 2 (Trans Canada Hwy.). Pleasant rooms, good dining area, indoor court with pool and bar. Major credit cards. On the north side.

Keddy's Motor Inn. *Expensive.* Forest Hill Rd., Box 1510, Fredericton, NB E3B 5G2 (506–454–4461). Pleasant rooms (120 units), lively lounge-bar, dining-room, pool. Close to university. Major credit cards.

The Lord Beaverbrook Hotel. *Expensive.* 659 Queen St., Fredericton, NB E3B 5G2 (506–455–3371). Popular pool bar, good main dining room and steakhouse. River Room bar draws civil servants, politicians, visiting VIPs at lunch and happy hour. Major credit cards.

The Condor Motel. *Moderate–Expensive.* Woodstock Rd. W., Box 801, Fredericton, NB E3B 5B4 (506–455–5537). Adequate rooms, small dining room, heated pool. Major credit cards.

City Motel. *Moderate.* 1216 Regent St., Fredericton, NB E3B 3Z4 (506–455–9900). Better than average rooms, good small dining room. Close to shopping center, theaters, restaurants. Major credit cards.

The Fredericton Motor Inn. *Moderate.* 1315 Regent St., Fredericton, NB E3B 3Z4 (506–455–1430). Excellent value—nice rooms, good dining room, pleasant decor.

Happy Apple Acres Bed and Breakfast. *Moderate.* R.R. #4, Fredericton, NB E3B 1A1 (506–472–1819). Five charming rooms in a country setting.

HOW TO GET AROUND. By bus: Fare in city, 75¢. *Fredericton Transit* buses travel across the river to Nashwaaksis, Marysville, Barker's Point and New Maryland. Catch a Fredericton Transit bus by the Military Compound on Queen St. for Silverwood. (An Edmundston bus from the SMT terminal on Regent will take you there too as well as to Oromocto and Lincoln.)

By taxi: As many taxis do not have meters, you could end up sharing a cab with other people. Some meter cabs are available, however.

From the airport: A limousine service is provided to the Lord Beaverbrook Hotel.

TOURIST INFORMATION. Tourist Office, City of Fredericton, telephone 452–9426. Provincial Tourist Information Centre, on Trans-Canada Hwy., open June to September, tel. 458–8331.

Province: Department of Tourism, Recreation, and Heritage, 7th floor, Carleton Place, corner Carleton and Kings Sts., Box 12345, Fredericton, NB E3B 5C3. U.S. and Canadian residents call toll-free, 1–800–561–0123.

RECOMMENDED READING. Fredericton was the home of the late Alden Nowlan, the award-winning poet and novelist. *Bread, Wine and Salt, Between Tears and Laughter,* and *I'm A Stranger Here Myself* are collections of his poems; his book of stories, *Miracle at Indian River,* and his novel *Various Persons Named Kevin O'Brien* offer the most penetrating view available of rural life in the Maritimes. Fredericton has always been a center for writers, from the early Loyalist poet Jonathan Odell to contemporary novelist Kent Thompson (*The Tenants Were Corrie & Tennie*) and a group of poets centered around UNB and *Fiddlehead* magazine. New Brunswick has been more given to poetry and less to fiction than Nova Scotia, but younger writers like David Adam Richards (*Blood Ties, The Coming of Winter*) and Raymond Fraser (*The Black Horse Tavern*) may be changing that fact. A well-beloved writer of nonfiction is Stuart Trueman (*An Intimate History of New Brunswick, The Fascinating World of New Brunswick*). W.S. MacNutt has written histories of New Brunswick and of the Atlantic provinces generally. *History of Fredericton —the Last 200 Years* by W. Austin Squires gives a readable "human" history of the capital city. Another historian of note is A.F. Bailey (*Culture and Nationality*) who is also a poet (*Thanks for a Drowned Island*). *New Brunswick Inside Out* by Colleen Thompson is an invaluable handbook for visitors to the province and to Fredericton.

CITY PARKS. Three hundred acres of wooded land at *Odell Park* off Waggoner's La. Nature trails, picnic tables with barbecue pits and wood, play equipment, duck pond, and deer enclosure. *Wilmot Park* on Woodstock Rd.—picnic tables, wading pool, playground, free tennis courts. Swimming at Queen Square and Henry Park.

SPORTS. The river is widely used for sculling, wind surfing, sailing, etc. Tennis is popular, as are golf, cycling, curling, and hockey (Fredericton is home for the NHL Quebec Nordiques farm team Express). There is a Sports Hall of Fame at Queen and Carleton streets.

TOURS. *Heritage Tour Guide Service,* Box 23, Garden View Acres, R.R. # 6, Fredericton, NB E3B 4X7 (506–459–5950), helps with city tours. A walking guide is available at tourist information centers and City Hall, on Queen St.

THE ARTS. Fredericton is a small city (population about 46,000) and its cultural facilities are not extensive, although they are of nationally recognized quality.

The Beaverbrook Art Gallery, Queen St. (458–8545), in fact, is internationally known, with a collection of works by Turner, Krieghoff, Gainsborough, Dali, and the Group of Seven, plus rotating exhibits.

The Playhouse, also on Queen St., is the home of *Theater New Brunswick* (458–8344), which brings professional live theater to the city. TNB also tours the province.

The York Sunbury Historical Museum and Officers Square, again on Queen St. (455–6041), is the city's main museum. It is part of a downtown historical restoration and features local and military history.

SHOPPING. New Brunswick is famous for crafts, and Fredericton has many studios and artisans' sales rooms. *Aitkens Pewter,* 81 Regent St., and *Pewtercraft,* 582 Brunswick St., offer beautiful pewter holloware, goblets, belt buckles, jewelry and authentic reproductions of ancient folk dishes. After browsing you can sample ice cream or a snack on the back porch at Aitkens. *Shades of Light Studio and Gift Shop* on Regent St. features stained glass and other local crafts.

The Regent Craft Gallery, 71 Regent St.; wide variety of quality local crafts and works of local artists.

The *Boyce Country Market* on George St. operates every Saturday morning offering everything from crafts to home baked doughnuts and breakfast at Goofy Roofy's. An outdoor café, operating out of the market in the summer (in winter it goes indoors), it is an incredible experience as politicians, scholars, actors, musicians and writers come in to partake of Roofy's special omelets.

An elaborate booklet describing crafts in New Brunswick and listing all craftspeople is available from various tourist bureaus and offices.

RESTAURANTS. Restaurants in Fredericton have improved a lot in recent years; a few are very good. Price categories, based on the cost of three-course meal for one, not including tax (10%), tip, or beverage, are: *Expensive,* over $16; *Moderate,* $11–$16; and *Inexpensive,* under $11.

The Coffeemill. *Expensive.* In Fredericton Shopping Mall on Prospect St. (459–3463). The seafood is good, and the other food is generally good, too. Major credit cards.

Eighty-Eight Ferry. *Expensive.* 88 Ferry St. (472–1988). Charming old-home decor, excellent food, friendly owners. Drinks served in the garden. Highly recommended.

The Maverick Room. *Expensive.* Queen St. (455–3371). Located in the basement of the Lord Beaverbrook Hotel and open only at night (from 6 P.M.). Steaks are a specialty, the spareribs are excellent, the atmosphere dim, and the wines marked up. Major credit cards.

Victoria and Albert. *Expensive.* 636 Queen St. (458–8310). Seafood and steaks in Victorian England decor. Major credit cards.

La Vie En Rose. *Moderate.* 594 Queen St. (455–1319). Small cafe specializing in tempting desserts and exotic coffees.

Martha's. *Moderate.* 625 King St. (455–4773). Hungarian dishes in cosy atmosphere. Excellent salad bar, fresh bread. Major credit cards.

Mei's Chinese Restaurant. *Moderate.* 74 Regent St. (454–2177). Excellent Szechuan food, understated, comfortable decor, in small restaurant.

Pat's Gourmet. *Moderate.* Lower St. Mary's (472–0992). Excellent Asian food of all varieties. Major credit cards.

Bar B Q Barn. *Inexpensive.* 540 Queen St. (455–2742). Ribs, fish and chips, and fried scallops. A family spot.

The Luna Steakhouse. *Inexpensive.* 168 Dundonald St. (455–4020). Leans toward Greek-style cuisine. Brochettes of chicken especially good, great garlic bread.

Ming Restaurant. *Inexpensive.* 1185 Smythe St. (452–2828). Good variety of Chinese and Canadian food, pleasant restaurant, excellent for family eating.

NIGHTLIFE. In Fredericton, the most popular spots are the *River Room* at the Lord Beaverbrook Hotel where they feature folksingers; private clubs and discos such as *The Cosmopolitan Club,* where you have to be signed in at the door. *The Chestnut Inn* has dining and live bands. The *Poacher's Lounge* at the Diplomat Motel on Woodstock Rd. is popular. So is *Hilltop* on Prospect St. The *Riverview Arms,* Lincoln Rd., and the *Rolling Keg* on King St. are taverns serving steaks and featuring loud music.

SAINT JOHN AND ITS VALLEY

Saint John, on the Bay of Fundy at the mouth of the Saint John River, is the largest city in New Brunswick. The Saint John River forms 75 miles of the border with Maine. The Saint John River Valley itself is a scenic delight. Rolling hills of rich agricultural land and the blue sweep of the winding Saint John make the drive excellent viewing. From St. Leonard to Woodstock lies New Brunswick's famed potato belt. Note the endless fields of potatoes and the squat, half-underground potato storage houses. Though Grand Falls is itself largely French speaking, from there on down the river, the French tongue is replaced by English everywhere.

At Grand Falls, site of a large and beautiful cataract, you may want to inspect the wells in the rocks, deep holes worn by the action of the water, some with a diameter of 16 feet and a depth of 30 feet. One of the town's interesting features is its wide main street, formerly a military parade ground. As the residents built their homes around it to view the proceedings, it gradually became the center of town.

The legend of Malabeam, part of the town's history, is the story of a young Indian maiden who led her Iroquois captors to their deaths over the falls rather than take them to her village. In memory of her courage, old boats filled with flowers are occasionally sent over the falls during the town's annual celebration of the Potato Festival. Local history is depicted at the Grand Falls Historical Museum.

Exploring the Saint John River Valley

At Woodstock, the alternate route to Fredericton (Route 105 on the other side of the Saint John River) takes you through typical small communities over an uncrowded road. It's easy to cross back to the Trans-Canada Highway at Mactaquac where the road leads over the dam. Since the building of the hydroelectric dam over the river, the valley has changed even as far away as Woodstock. While many of the Saint John River islands have disappeared, the area of the headpond has become quite lovely. A provincial park has been established at Mactaquac, probably the most comprehensive in all of New Brunswick. Visitors can enjoy everything from golfing on the 18-hole professional course to swimming, hiking and sailing. The campground is so popular that cars line up, sometimes all night, to claim the first empty camp lot in the morning. Your best bet is to get there early. There are 300 campsites, supervised recreation, two beaches, two marinas, as well as a licensed lodge with dining room. There's an Antique Arms Museum featuring antique firearms, trout fishing pond, and horseback riding nearby. If Mactaquac campsites are full, there are several other good campgrounds in the area.

Load your camera for Hartland. Here you'll find the longest covered bridge in the world—1,282 feet in length. Many of New Brunswick's covered bridges have been destroyed in recent years but the Department of Highways is now seeking to protect the 78 or so that still exist. The Courtyard mall is located at the end of the covered bridge at Hartland. It's a real courtyard with places for lunch.

Woodstock, population 5,068, named for a novel by Sir Walter Scott, is also called the "hospitality town." It was an axiom in the old days that "no traveller, known or unknown, shall pass through the community without sharing its hospitality." That tradition remains strong today. You'll experience it especially at the annual Old Home Week celebrations in July when most of the Saint John River Valley residents participate.

There is a 9-hole golf course and during the summer months a farmers' market is held on Fridays at the Stewart parking lot where homemade foods may be purchased. Harness racing takes place at Connell Park.

The Old Courthouse (c. 1833) has been carefully restored by an interested community . . . it's been a coaching stop, a social hall, a political meeting place, and the seat of justice for the area. The guides have many tales to tell of famous trials held here. An excellent duty-free shop is located at the Houlton-Woodstock border.

Between Woodstock and Meductic, you'll find excellent German food at the John Gyles Motel on the Trans Canada Highway (Route 2 here).

Just below Woodstock at Meductic, young John Gyles, 9-year-old son of a New England judge, was held captive by the Maliceets for 6 years. His diary, reconstructed by New Brunswick writer Stuart Trueman, makes interesting historical reading.

There are two roads from Fredericton to Saint John. Route 7 is straight and dull for its 68 miles. The other, Route 102, leads along the Saint John River through some of the province's loveliest country. At Oromocto, the site of Canadian Armed Forces Base Camp Gagetown, largest military base in Canada, there's a reconstruction of Fort Hughes, an 1871 blockhouse which stands on the bank of the Oromocto River, and a fine military museum. You'll also find there a shopping mall and a beautifully laid out town, often called Canada's model town.

Along the river you'll notice fine craft shops, tearooms, and small car ferries—from Jemseg to Upper Gagetown, Crystal Beach to Westfield, Clifton to Gondola Point, Gagetown to Lower Jemseg, Evandale to Hatfield Point, and Hampstead to Wickham. These cable-ferries are free, will take trailers and pickup campers, and provide you with a little respite from driving or a chance to look at the country on the other side. Grand Lake, for instance, offers camping in a provincial park, with freshwater swimming off sandy beaches.

Closer to Saint John, the Evandale ferry takes you to Belleisle Bay and the Kingston Peninsula—a lovely landscape. At Gagetown, the Steamers Stop Inn provides pleasant dining over the river and rents six rooms.

At Gagetown, stop and have a look at the Queens County Museum, the former home of Sir Leonard Tilley, one of the Fathers of Confederation. While there, stop in at the Loomcrofters, one of Canada's better suppliers of handwoven goods. It's located in a 200-year-old blockhouse. The area is known for its many craftsmen. Colpitt's Marina at Gagetown provides yachting necessities. Steamer Stop Inn has pleasant dining and six charming rooms. Many artisans shops can also be found here.

Canada's Oldest City

Saint John is old . . . the oldest incorporated city in Canada, with the special weatherbeaten quality of any port city. When Champlain and de Monts landed here in 1604 on St. John the Baptist Day, it must have appeared a primitive spot. But not so primitive as it seemed to the three thousand Loyalists who poured off a ship one May morning in 1785 to find nothing but rocks and forests for shelter. Babies were born in windswept tents that first chill winter as their parents fought to stay alive. But they were a tenacious lot and, by the following year, most had built snug little homes, oddly furnished perhaps, with silver and crystal, damask cloths and lean-to beds. From those beginnings Saint John has emerged as a thriving industrial and port city, a tribute to its hardy Loyalist forebears. A recent face-lift and a new harborfront development have improved its appearance, and its history is fascinating.

Fiercely loyal to the British Crown, the early residents even laid out King Square in the design of the old Union Jack. Each year in July, a reenactment of the Landing of the Loyalists is held during the Loyalist Day celebrations. A costumed city joins in a colorful event that is the envy of many other communities.

Saint John (the spelling is never abbreviated) has the advantage of a year-round harbor. Ships from all over the world dock here, continually stimulating the economy. Among the outstanding enterprises are those run by the Irving family, descendants of a New Brunswick industrialist, K.C. Irving, who established the Irving pulp mill, the Irving Oil refinery, and a steel and drydock industry.

Exploring Saint John

From across the harbor, Saint John looks like a colorful version of a tiny Boston, although its hilly streets might have you thinking more of a micro-San Francisco, complete with historic island in the bay. In this case it's Partridge Island, not Alcatraz, but its history is just as solemn. Hundreds of Irish immigrants died there in the 1840s when it was used as a quarantine station for over 30,000 people escaping the Potato Famine at home. The Irish heritage here is obvious, and the Irish Festival held in March each year is one of the more boisterous in the province. (March 16–22)

Up until a few years ago, the buildings around the waterfront huddled together, as though humbled by crumbling facades and a century of grime. Even though the city has always had the mystique of any seaport, it was not pretty. Now, like Cinderella ready for the ball, Saint John has astonished its neighbors, and even its own residents, with its emergence as one of the more charming of the cities of New Brunswick.

A major renovation and preservation project has done it, as well as a tremendous surge of civic pride.

Old warehouses have been reclaimed and made part of an enchanting waterfront development. Whole business blocks are being restored. A harborfront walk leads past a tug boat (twice reclaimed from the sea) now used as a bar. The Market Square complex of boutiques and restaurants uses the original warehouses as its exterior. A gem of a Hilton, the company's smallest, furnished and decorated with New Brunswick–made furniture and antiques, perches over the harbor.

In 1986, Canada Games left the city with a major aquatic center, and the old main street (King Street) has been set with red brick and lit with old-fashioned lamps. A 1913 theater, where Ethel Barrymore, Harry Houdini, Gracie Fields, and John Phillip Sousa entertained, has been bought and restored by public campaign. Skywalks and underground passages join most of this to City Hall, the new Delta Hotel, and Brunswick Square, an adjoining shopping mall.

There are a number of side trips from Saint John. One of them along the coastal Route 111 takes you to St. Martins, a delightful seaside village.

Following Route 1 NE from Saint John, you pass the engaging dairy town of Sussex, through rolling countryside to Penobsquis, where you may turn off to Fundy National Park, 80 square miles of sea-conditioned playground skirting the Bay of Fundy.

The coast road up to Moncton takes you over covered bridges and along rocky coasts. At Hopewell Cape, you'll find the famous giant flowerpot, one of many rock formations carved by the action of the Fundy tides.

New River Beach Provincial Park is located right on the southern Fundy shore where rolling breakers come roaring in. New Brunswickers swim in it but—a word to the wise—the Fundy water is usually chilly.

The peaceful hideaway fishing villages of Maces Bay, Dipper Harbour, and Chance Harbour are still much the same as they have been for centuries but residents fear a change since the advent of the nuclear reactor plant at nearby Point Lepreau. If you drive into the area, you'll find a great little tea room. The Fundy Haven, right on the cliffs overlooking the bay. Marvelous, inexpensive seafood!

PRACTICAL INFORMATION FOR SAINT JOHN

HOW TO GET THERE. By air: Both *Air Canada* and *CP Air* make connections with most major airlines. Airport 10 miles east of city.

By car: From Nova Scotia by ferry from Digby; by road from Nova Scotia through Moncton via Rte. 1, from Fredericton via Rte. 7, from Calais, Me. via Rte. 1.

By train: *Via Rail* has service daily to Fredericton, Moncton, Halifax, and Montreal. Connections for Montréal can be made at Moncton.

By bus: SMT bus service within the province provides regional transportation. Most major bus companies in USA and Canada connect with SMT.

ACCOMMODATIONS. In the summer, tourist accommodations tend to be at a premium in Saint John so it is best to reserve ahead to ensure a place to stay. Price categories are the same as for Fredericton. Rates are based on double-occupancy as follows: *Expensive,* over $43; *Moderate,* $30–43; *Inexpensive,* under $30.

The Delta Brunswick Inn. *Expensive.* 39 King St., Saint John, NB E2L 4W3 (506–648–1981). New downtown hotel atop Brunswick Square. Good dining room. Bar, banquet and convention facilities. Major credit cards.

Hilton International Saint John. *Expensive.* One Market Square, Saint John, NB E2L 4Z6 (506–693–8484 or 800–361–6140). Part of Market Square, overlooking harbor. Mammoth convention facilities, including a Medieval Great Hall. Adjoining shops, restaurants, bars, library. Major credit cards. This, the smallest Hilton, is charmingly furnished in Loyalist style.

Holiday Inn. *Expensive.* 350 Haymarket Square, Saint John, NB E2L 3P1 (506–657–3610). 128 rooms. Dining room, heated pool. Major credit cards.

Howard Johnson Motor Lodge. *Expensive.* Box 790, Saint John, NB E2L 4C1 (506–642–2622). At Chelsey Place. Caters to families, with special facilities for children. Major credit cards.

Keddy's Motor Inn. *Expensive.* Portland and Main streets, Saint John, NB E2K 4H8 (506–657–7320). 137 rooms, heated pool, bar, dining room, and steakhouse. Major credit cards.

Park Plaza Motel. *Moderate.* 607 Rothesay Ave., Saint John, NB E2H 2G9 (506–633–4100). Dining room and bar.

The Trellis Bed and Breakfast. *Inexpensive.* 4247 Manawagonish Rd., Saint John, NB E2M 3X8 (506–696–5397). Two air-conditioned rooms in pleasant home.

HOW TO GET AROUND. Airport limousine: Between airport and Delta or Hilton Holiday Inn. $5.
Taxi: individual fares.
Bus: Good community service.
City Guide: Available at Tourist Info. Center, Reversing Falls and at Sydney St. Tourist Bureau.

TOURIST INFORMATION. *Tourist Information Center,* 20 Hazen Ave. (506–658–2855). *City Hall tourist information:* 506–658–2814. *Reversing Falls:* 506–672–1198.

SEASONAL EVENTS. *Loyalist Days,* held each summer during the third week of July, commemorates the arrival of the Loyalists in 1783 and the landing is re-enacted in full pageantry and costume. *Festival By The Sea,* in Aug., is a mammoth bringing together of cultures from one end of the country to the other. You'll see Indian dancing to square dancing in colorful ceremonies.

SPECIAL INTEREST TOURS. Three major walking tours have been developed to familiarize visitors with the town and its history. The Loyalist Trail retraces the footsteps of Loyalist city founders. The Victorian Stroll takes you past elegant old homes. Prince William's Walk explores the merchant heritage (Benedict Arnold once ran a store here). The Tourist Information Center provides information. See also "Historic Sites," below.

CITY PARKS. *Rockwood Park,* within the city limits, is an excellent place for kids and adults alike. It surrounds several lakes, has a "children's farm" as well as Atlantic Canada's only exotic zoo, which includes many animals on the endangered species list. Also golf, swimming, and other facilities.

ZOO. Cherrybrook Zoo. Rookwood Park (506–693–1440) Open every day 10 A.M. to dusk, admission: adults, $2.50; students, $1.75; under 12, $1.25. Has a petting farm for small children who can familiarize themselves with gentle animals such as fawns and a wide range of exotic animals from around the world.

SPORTS. Saint John has year round harness racing, some excellent golf courses, tennis courts and several good beaches in the area. *The Aquatic Center,* adjoining City Hall, is a major world class facility for all kinds of water sports with slides, swinging ropes, warm-up pool, Olympic size pool, whirlpools, and a cafe. (642–7946; hours, 6:30 A.M.–10 P.M., admission: adults, $3.50; child, $2.50).

MUSEUMS. *New Brunswick Museum.* 277 Douglas Ave. Phone 693–1196. Admission: adults, $2; students, 50 cents. Open 10 A.M.–5 P.M. The first museum to be built in Canada, it is still recognized as one of the best of its size. You'll see the figurehead from the bad luck ship built in Saint John's famous shipyards—a ship that is said to have killed a man on every voyage. Along with impressive artifacts, there are native animals displayed in natural surroundings, costumes, even a collection of dolls, some Egyptian relics, and an impressive art gallery.

HISTORIC SITES AND POINTS OF INTEREST.
Items of interest that you'll visit on the walking tours
(See "Tours") are: *the spiral staircase* in the Old Courthouse, Sydney St., (admission free, open during business
hours). Built of tons of unsupported stone, it ascends for three stories and is of
special interest to architects and engineers. *Trinity Church,* 115 Charlotte St.,
phone 693–8558. Open to public and dates back to 1877 when it was rebuilt after
the Great Saint John Fire. Inside, over the west door, note the coat of arms, a
symbol of the Monarchy rescued from the council chamber of the Colony at
Massachusetts Bay. The coat of arms was deemed a worthy "refugee" and set
in its place of honor in the church. *Old Loyalist House,* 120 Union St., phone
652–3590, is open through the week 10 A.M.–5 P.M.; Sun., 2–5 P.M., or any time
by appointment. Admission: adults, $2; children, 25 cents. Built in 1810 by
Daniel David Merritt, a wealthy Loyalist merchant, the house retains all its past
beauty with authentic period furniture and eight fireplaces. *The Old City Market,* Charlotte St. or Germain St., built in 1876, runs a full block and offers a
wide variety of products including red fresh-cooked lobster, great cheeses, dulse,
inexpensive snacking, and the friendly chatter of the marketplace. (Open Mon.
to Fri. 8:30 A.M.–5:30 P.M.; Sat. 8:30 A.M.–9 P.M.) *Market Slip,* where the Loyalists
landed in 1783, is the site of *Barbour's General Store,* phone 658–2939. Free and
open 9:30 A.M.–5 P.M., this is a fully stocked 19th-century shop redolent of smells
of the past; tobacco, pickles, smoked fish, peppermint sticks, and the unforgettable tang of dulse, the edible seaweed New Brunswickers love to chew. Beside
the store is an *1800s Red School House* (same hours) and over toward Market
Square is the *Ocean Hawk II,* the tugboat turned bar where you can savor fresh
oysters and watch the sun set on St. John harbor.

Other sights to visit are the *Old Loyalist Burial Grounds,* at the top of King
Street. At one corner in adjacent King Square, you'll find a strange mass of
metal on the ground. It is actually a great lump of melted stock from a hardware
store across the street which was demolished in Saint John's Great Fire of 1877
when 115 buildings were destroyed.

The Carleton Martello Tower, Charlotte Ext. West, phone 672–5792, is open
9 A.M.–5 P.M. after July 1 and up to Sept 1, 9 A.M.–8 P.M. Admission free. It was
built in 1810 as a precaution against American attack. Costumed guides point
out 8-foot thick walls and pose for photographs. The view from its walls is
almost as fine as that from *Fort Howe* (Magazine St.), a reconstructed fortress
on a cliff overlooking the harbor. Reached via a winding road, it is believed to
be near the site of Fort LaTour, a French stronghold resolutely defended by
Madame La Tour from her absent husband's fur-trading rival. Finally, surren-
dering on the condition that the lives of her men would be spared, the unfortunate woman was betrayed and forced to watch them all put to death. She died
shortly after of a broken heart, it is said . . . a romantic fate befitting her former
profession as star of the Paris stage. Always open; free.

Tourist brochures tout the charms of *Reversing Falls Rapids* and everyone
who visits Saint John should see it, more for its interest than its beauty. Now
somewhat tarnished by the effluent of a pulp mill on the bank, and occasionally
blanketed by a less than sweet stench from the same mill, this phenomenon is
nevertheless worth a look. It's actually a series of rapids and whirlpools at
which, twice a day, the Fundy Tides attempt to push the river water back
upstream. When the tide flow weakens and ebbs, the river once again pours out
over the rock ledges and the rapids appear to reverse themselves. A tourist
information center is located here with an excellent free film on the falls.

SHOPPING. As in the rest of the province, it's the little
antique stores and craftshops that provide the best shopping. You'll find them sprinkled around the downtown
area. Prince William Street offers interesting browsing in
excellent antique shops and craft boutiques. Brunswick Square and Market
Square in new harbourfront development offer airy shopping with many top
quality boutiques. And there's the Old City Market between Charlotte and
Germain Streets. It bustles with activity six days a week, and always stocks
delicious local specialties such as maple syrup and fresh lobsters.

RESTAURANTS. Several good, new restaurants of gourmet caliber have popped up in recent years. Try the ones specializing in seafood. Price categories per person are as follows: *Expensive,* over $16; *Moderate,* $11–16; *Inexpensive,* under $11. Drinks, tax, and tip are not included.

Most places accept the following major credit cards: American Express, MasterCard, and Visa; others may also be honored. Not all establishments accept credit cards, therefore we suggest you call for information.

The Continental. *Expensive.* Level III, Historical Properties, Market Square. European cuisine with pizzazz, served on china and silver. Major credit cards. Phone 642–1157.

Mallard House. *Expensive.* In Delta Brunswick Hotel (648–1981). Gracious dining with excellent food and service.

Turn of the Tide. *Expensive.* In The Hilton Hotel beside Market Square. Elegant dining overlooking the Saint John Harbour. Phone 693–8484. Major credit cards.

The House of Chan. *Moderate-Expensive.* Hilyard Place (near Keddy's and Howard Johnson's). Great luncheon buffet. Good Chinese and Canadian dishes. Lobster and steak specialties. Major credit cards. Phone 693–7777.

Grannan's. *Inexpensive.* Market Square. Spills out over sidewalk in summer. Terrific desserts. Nice bar. Raw oyster bar. Phone 642–2225. Major credit cards.

Incredible Edibles. *Inexpensive.* 177 Prince William St. (693–0209 or 642–2382). Excellent lunch spot with great salads, pizzas, linguine, etc. Outdoor dining in summer.

NIGHTLIFE. Although Saint John occasionally offers dinner shows in places like Market or Brunswick Square (check with tourist office for dates), the nightlife, with the exception of theater or special summer attractions, is centered around discos, taverns, and lounges.

The Squire's Tap, Holiday Inn, quiet friendly bar sometimes featuring singers.

Grannan's, Market Square. Good gathering place in nautical atmosphere.

Tugboat Ocean Hawk II, for oysters, drinks, and socializing. Market Square.

1880 Club, 134 Sydney St., in a restored 19th-century building. Features dancing, dining, and a games room.

Brigantine Lounge, Hilton, overlooks the harbor, has a pianist and is preferred by the more sophisticated set. *Barlow's Lounge.* small, intimate, is off the lobby in the Delta Hotel.

For more boisterous surroundings, try *Baldy's,* Market Square, popular and central. *Lighthouse Bar,* also in Market Square, in an actual lighthouse, is cozy.

EXPLORING NEW BRUNSWICK

As you cross the Québec border into New Brunswick (a large, new tourist information center has been built here, with displays, audiovisual presentations, etc.), you'll find yourself in the mythical Republic of Madawaska. As we delve into its history, we learn that in the early 1800's the narrow wedge of land which makes up most of Madawaska County is coveted by Québec on one side and New Brunswick on the other. On top of that, the U.S. claimed it as well. Seeking to retain it for New Brunswick, Governor Sir Thomas Carleton found it easy to settle with Québec. He rolled dice all night with the Governor of North America at Québec, who happened to be his brother. Sir Thomas won at dawn . . . by one point. Settling with the Americans was more difficult. The border had always been disputed; even the lumbermen engaged in combat, brandishing peavies as weapons and otherwise harassing each other from both sides of the border. Finally, with the Treaty of Webster-Ashburton, in 1842, the British flag was hoisted over Madawaska county. It is said that one old-timer, tired of being asked which country he belonged to, replied: "I am a citizen of the Republic of Madawaska." So Madawaska exists to this day with its own flag (an independent eagle on a field of white) and coat-of-arms. On rare occasions someone is honored with membership in the Republic, a unique mark of respect.

Edmundston, Capital of Madawaska

Edmundston has always depended on the wealth of the deep forest land surrounding it; even today the Fraser Company's paper mill provides the major source of employment. It was in these woods that the legend of Paul Bunyan was born, and the feats of a strong young Madawaskan embroidered. Tales were spread to Maine and even to the west coast. Other lands, other people have tried to claim him for their own . . . but Paul Bunyan was born and raised in the forests and lumber camps of Madawaska County.

Formerly called Petit Sault because of the small rapids which existed here, the town was renamed Edmundston after a visit by Sir Edmund Head, one-time Lieutenant Governor of the province.

Since Edmundston is not really an Acadian town, most of its French population has come from neighboring Québec. The first French settlers arrived here in the 19th century, followed closely by the British, especially the Scots. That combination gives this happy, thriving city a unique background. The main language is French, but most people are bilingual, not to mention exuberant. The French from Madawaska are often called "Brayons." The annual midsummer Foire Brayonne festival (lumberjack competitions, folk dancing, handcraft exhibits, and other events) is one of the most popular festivals in New Brunswick. It is held annually during the last week of July.

Examine the two churches which dominate the skyline. The Roman Catholic Cathedral of the Immaculate Conception is regarded as one of the better examples of its particular style of architecture in eastern Canada, and the Church of Our Lady of Sorrows contains some beautiful woodcarvings, notably those of the Fourteen Stations of the Cross created by noted New Brunswick artist Claude Roussel.

At the College of Saint Louis-Maillet, the religious paintings of another native son, Claude Picard, decorate the walls. On the campus too, the Galerie Colline displays touring art exhibitions.

About 20 miles out of Edmundston on Route 120 is a very popular recreation area, the Lac Baker Provincial Park with swimming, watersports, and camping.

For other diversions, skiing is popular on the slopes of nearby Mount Farlagne, the 18-hole golf course is well recommended by residents, and you'll enjoy the old car museum on the grounds of Les Jardins Provincial Park. The new Madawaska Regional Museum has displays on regional history and sports an art gallery.

THE FUNDY COAST

Route 1, leading along the Bay of Fundy from St. Stephen to Saint John, is one of New Brunswick's most interesting drives. St. Stephen (a small border town named for a surveyor, not a saint) has always enjoyed such good relations with its neighboring American town of Calais that during the war of 1812, while the rest of Canada and the United States were in conflict, St. Stephen obligingly lent gunpowder to Calais for its Fourth of July celebration. Each summer there is an international festival held jointly in the two towns. The Charlotte County Historical Society Museum, describing the area's Loyalist ancestry, is located here.

The first week of August in St. Stephen is Chocolate Festival, fitting for the town that invented the chocolate bar. The Chocolatiere on Water St. provides famed Ganong's hand-dipped chocolates.

At Oak Bay, outside St. Stephen, you'll find a little provincial park complete with beach, shaded camping grounds, and barbecue pits stocked with plenty of wood.

Take the jog off Route 1 to St. Andrews, a town every visitor to New Brunswick should see. Long the summer resort of the affluent (mansions ring the town), it's also a fisherman's town. Little has changed in the last two centuries. Of the town's 550 buildings, 280 were erected before 1880. Of these, 14 have survived from the 1700s. Indeed, some ingenious Loyalists who settled here brought their homes with them, piece by piece, from Castine, Maine, across the Passamaquoddy Bay. The Old English character of the town is preserved and enhanced by many of the town's businesses.

A walking-tour map is available from the tourist information center on Water St. . . . follow it to some of the town's most interesting buildings. One of these, Greenock Church, is an architect's delight. Stuart Trueman called it "the church that was born of an insult" in his book *The Fascinating World of New Brunswick*. The church was the result of a remark passed at an 1822 dinner party regarding the inability of the "poor" Presbyterians to have a church of their own. Presbyterian Captain Christopher Scott took exception to the slur. Sparing no expense, he erected an admirable building with a green oak tree carved on its tower in honor of his birthplace, Greenock, Scotland. The new Ross Memorial Museum on Montague Street features one of the finest antique collections in eastern Canada.

A drive up Joe's Point Road takes you to the Huntsman Marine Aquarium, an offshoot of the Federal Fisheries Research and Biological Station nearby. You'll see the shells of the two giant lobsters, Bonnie and Clyde, and be intrigued by the tank holding many varieties of marine life under a sign which says "Please Touch." Playful seals love to entertain the small fry and the film on current off-shore research is thoroughly engrossing.

The blockhouse on the shore is a restoration of one of five built in the area during the War of 1812. It's only 68 miles from St. Andrews to Saint John so take advantage of the route by taking some side trips to the numerous little coastal villages along the way. St. George, for instance, has one of the oldest Protestant graveyards in Canada as well as a fish ladder running up the side of the dam across the Magaguadavic River which flows through the town. And in nearby Lake Utopia (a scenic recreation area) lives the fabled Lake Utopian monster. He's been seen for generations . . . a rival for Scotland's Loch Ness monster.

Black's Harbour boasts the largest sardine cannery in the British Commonwealth. Nearby Pennfield the landing site of the British aviator Mollison, when he made the first nonstop, east-west crossing of the Atlantic.

The Fundy Isles

New Brunswick's Fundy Isles are true escapist retreats. It's hard to beat their windswept hospitable charm. Grand Manan, largest of the three, is the farthest away. It's a two-hour ferry ride from Black's Harbour, but you might see spouting whales, sunning porpoises, or a rare puffin on the trip out. It will be immediately apparent that the island's main preoccupation is fishing. The circular herring weirs dot the coastal waters and fish sheds and smokehouses appear along the shores. Names like Swallowtail, Southern Head, Seven Days Work, and Dark Harbour are as romantic as the island air, and the friendly folk speak with an accent all their own.

Grand Manan

About 20 miles of road lead from Southern Head to Northern Head, each Head with its own lighthouse perched high on jagged cliffs above the rocky surf. The famous American author Willa Cather spent her summers here and some of her novels were written on Grand Manan.

You'll want to visit Dark Harbour where no sun shines until late morning when it finally rises over the high hill that shades the harbor. The home of New Brunswick's dulse industry, it is here that dulse harvesters gather the purple seaweed from rocks left dry at low tide. They dry it in the sun on a natural rocky breakwater, and send it to mainland stores where it is purchased by New Brunswickers who enjoy the salty goodness of dried seaweed. The natives eat it like candy, but the visitor needs a little time to acquire the taste.

At Red Point, you'll find two different geological phenomena. Because of a long ago underwater upheaval, you will stand in one spot and note, on one side, 16-million-year-old volcanic material and on the other, the 6-billion-year-old sedimentary rock of the continental mass.

Welcome bird watchers! The island is known as an ornithologist's wonderland. Even John James Audubon came here in 1831 to study the various species; in fact, the rare puffin is the symbol of Grand Manan. If you'd like a close look at puffins, take a boat trip to Machias Seal Island, about 2 hours away by boat. Bird-watching tour packages are available to Grand Manan throughout the summer months. Contact Tourism New Brunswick for information. Whale-watching expeditions are also available through the Marathon Inn and the charming bed and breakfast The Compass Rose.

The Manan Island Inn and Spa, also located here, offers kelp herbal wraps and other spa amenities.

Anchorage Provincial Park on Grand Manan offers picnic, camping and hiking facilities. Hiking on Grand Manan generally is a very popular activity for tourists.

At the Grand Manan Museum, formerly the dwelling of Moses Gerrish, one of the first three settlers on the island, you'll be able to see many stuffed specimens of the island's birds as well as a large collection of artifacts from the ocean's bottom—the only residue of vessels wrecked in the waters of the Fundy Isles.

Campobello and Deer Islands

Neatly manicured, preening itself in the Bay, Campobello Island has always had a special appeal to the wealthy and the famous. It was here that the Roosevelt family spent its summers. The home of Franklin Delano Roosevelt, former president of the United States, is now maintained as a lovely museum in his honor. Located in the center of Roosevelt International Park, a joint project of the Canadian and American governments, President Roosevelt's home was the setting for the movie *Sunrise at Campobello*. A few miles away, a gracious mansion known as the Owens home is open to the public, and for overnight guests. Built by Captain William Owens in 1767, it has 21 rooms and nine fireplaces.

Herring Cove Provincial Park has camping facilities and a 9-hole golf course. And Campobello Island Estates is developing the island, creating tennis courts, boat ramps, and selling lots. You can book rooms at Campobello Club Lodge throughout the week but weekends are reserved for serious buyers.

Connected to Lubec, Maine, by an international bridge, Campobello may still be approached from the other side by toll ferry from Deer Island.

An easy 20-minute free ferry ride from Letete near St. George brings you to Deer Island for a relaxing visit. You'll enjoy exploring the fishing wharves like those at Chocolate Cove. You'll find the world's largest lobster pound at Northern Harbour (owned by Conley's), and you'll want to walk through an interesting park at Deer Point, where you catch a toll ferry to nearby Campobello. If you listen carefully you may be able to hear the sighing and snorting of "the Old Sow," the second largest whirlpool in the world. If you can't hear it, you'll be able to see it, just a few feet off shore.

Exploring the island takes only a few hours. . . . it's 7½ miles long, varying in width from 3 miles to a few hundred feet at some points. If you decide to spend the night you might be interested to know that Deer Island is located exactly on the 45th parallel and one of the motels at Fairhaven is named just that and has a good seafood restaurant.

THE ACADIAN COAST

From the Nova Scotian border at Aulac, along New Brunswick's northern shore, across the top of the province to Charlo, the Acadians settled on what is now known as the Acadian region.

Moncton

The city of Moncton has become the unofficial capital of Acadia and much of its history is interwoven with that of the Acadian people. Moncton, settled by Dutch and German families from Pennsylvania, was originally called Petitcodiac by the Indians, meaning the "river that bends like a bow." When the deeply religious Acadians came along they built a chapel and for a while the area was known as La Chapelle. Later it became Le Coude or The Elbow because the river bends so sharply here. Even to this day, one sometimes hears it called "The Bend."

In 1755, Lt. Colonel Robert Monckton finally captured nearby Fort Beausejour, bringing to an end the French occupation of the area. Moncton took his name, dropping the "K" over the years. After the Expulsion, a number of Acadians returned to areas around Moncton, settling most noticeably in Cocagne, Shediac and Grand Digue. Today in Moncton names like Belliveau, Blanchard, and Gaudet are mixed with Steeves (formerly Stief), Trites (Trietz), and Lutes (Lutz).

Once famous for shipbuilding, Moncton gradually became the province's main railway center and is now known as the "hub of the Maritimes" because all railroads seem to lead there. It is a natural center for sales and distribution throughout the Maritimes. A commercial town, its skyline has changed in recent years as economic activity increased.

The population is almost evenly divided between Catholics and Protestants, and churches dot the landscape. It is unfortunate that few historic buildings remain to tell the tale of Moncton's early days. The New Brunswick Telephone tower and the 11-story Assumption Building, containing City Hall and the adjoining the Beausejour Hotel, dominate the downtown area which has lately been beautified. Red brick courtyards, lovely Victorian lampposts, and hanging baskets of flowers have created a charming Main Street. Laid out on the flat marshy land on the banks of the muddy Petitcodiac River, Moncton has many homes that were built by railroad men, sturdy, solid, and enduring homes but with little architectural interest. Still there are a few interesting structures to be seen.

Walk out King Street and around to Mountain Road and you'll find, on Stedman Street, the oldest building in Moncton, a delightful little hall called the Free Meeting House, founded in 1821 by a group who believed in a common place of worship for the residents. Even the little graveyard beside it has been preserved. It has been the home of every denomination in the city, including Protestant, Roman Catholic, and Jewish.

Don't be startled by what you see next! The square modern building across the street has a strange old-fashioned entrance, completely out of keeping with the local architecture. But it happens to be the façade of the original town hall and it has been incorporated into the design of the new Moncton Civic Museum. Once inside the museum, railway enthusiasts and history buffs will delight in the steam engine mementos. And the curator will let you ring the huge cast iron bell. The museum has taken a forward step toward preserving some of the area's past.

One of Moncton's special attractions is the famous Tidal Bore. Viewed best from Boreview Park on Main Street, this low wall of water, which comes in right on time as befits any railroad town, is caused by the tide surging through the narrow entrance of the Petitcodiac River. As it rolls up the river it fills the wide muddy trench from bank to bank.

Moncton's Magnetic Hill—a rare optical illusion—must be seen to be believed. Drive down the hill to the white post. Turn off your motor, but put the car in neutral. As you gaze in astonishment at the steep hill behind you, your car will back up in such a hurry that you may be tempted to use your brake.

At Centennial Park, once more the steam engine reigns supreme. Crawl right up into the cab of the locomotive which is permanently on display there, and pretend your name is Casey Jones.

A drive through the spacious and modern campus of the University of Moncton will take you to the door of the Acadian Museum where you'll find artifacts and historical displays which present a clear picture of what life was all about in the days of the early Acadian settler. The ancient tools and primitive utensils are there along with the interiors of barns, schools and houses, all lovingly and beautifully reproduced.

Following the shore roads from Aulac to Moncton, you'll also follow the Trans-Canada Highway. On the way you'll pass the site of Fort Beausejour, a national historic site. Built by the French in 1751, and captured by the English in 1755, it was originally known as Fort Cumberland—the scene of the final battle for English supremacy in this region.

Sackville, a small university town, with the only harness shop in North America still producing handmade horse collars (and visitors welcome), is worth a short detour to the southeast from Moncton. Home of Mount Allison University, an arts oriented institution, Sackville is reminiscent of many old English villages. The Owens Art Gallery, on campus, is open to the public. A walk around town will also divulge other small galleries and fine crafts shops.

Shediac

From Moncton it's only 20 miles to the town of Shediac, home of King Lobster, where each July the Shediac Lobster Festival takes place. The beaches, especially at the provincial park, are long, fine-sanded, and shallow, with water warmer than anywhere else on the coast.

Fishing is the major industry and you can find fresh lobster, cooked or uncooked, at Paturel's Fish Processing Plant; the nearby *Shore*

House, run by Paturel's, offers fresh seafood. At Shediac, you can also find excellent and reasonably priced seafood at the *Fishermen's Paradise* and fine dining at *Chez Francoise* in the old Tait Mansion. There's also an "All You Can Eat Lobster Feast" near the giant waterslide park where electric wagons take you on to the beach, free.

Traveling up the shore towards Bathurst you'll pass through the fishing villages of Cocagne, scene of international hydroplane races in the summer and the Acadian Bazaar, usually in August; Buctouche, noted for the quality of its oysters; Richibucto and Rexton (the latter the birthplace of Andrew Bonar Law, first and only prime minister of Britain to be born outside the British Isles). At Richibucto there's a new museum of local history covering the storied Richibucto River and Kent County.

Kouchibouquac National Park, recently developed, has camping facilities and a marvelous beach, with long miles of sandbar washed by the warm waters of the Northumberland Strait. It also has excellent recreational facilities: canoeing, hiking, and others. Lobster suppers are offered at the park's restaurant, Bon Acceuil.

In 1959, 35 fishermen were drowned in a sudden squall off Point Escuminac in one of New Brunswick's worst fishing disasters. A monument created by Claude Roussel, one of the province's foremost artists, has been erected on the shore. It depicts three fishermen starkly outlined against the sea behind them. This route is highly recommended for Acadian color.

Chatham and Newcastle

Chatham and Newcastle, both early lumbering towns, are the exceptions on this Acadian coast, largely retaining the characteristics of the Irish, Scottish, and English immigrants who settled there. Anyone who lives along the Miramichi River is known as a "Miramichier" and proud of it. It's a region of folklore and superstition, of ballads and boisterousness, nourished by pride of ancestry. The hospitality is renowned and the friendly people still wave as you drive by.

Chatham, once a great shipbuilding area, was the home of Joseph and Henry Cunard, who came from Nova Scotia to build wooden ships. At one time the Cunards employed almost everybody, if not in the shipyards, then in the forests, cutting masts for the great ships. Joseph Cunard, flamboyant and wealthy, drove a coach-and-four, ordered peacocks for his lawns, and sent riders ahead to spread the word of his coming whenever he returned from his frequent visits to England. When the coming of the steam engine ruined his business, the area took a long time to regain its former prosperity. The building of a jet training school and air base in the region infused new life into the economy and today Chatham is thriving once again. The history of the area is related through exhibits at the Miramichi Natural History Museum. Loggie House is a late Victorian, Second Empire-style home furnished in antiques from the period. It functions as a cultural center in winter and is open to visitors in summer.

Max Aitken, the son of a poor Presbyterian minister, and later Lord Beaverbrook (a name he took from a brook running near his home), lived his boyhood years in Newcastle. Eventually a multimillionaire, owner of the London *Daily Express,* confidante of kings and politicians, and at one time minister of aircraft production in Churchill's wartime cabinet, Beaverbrook traveled a long way from his early beginnings in New Brunswick. One of his many bequests to Newcastle was his childhood home, the Old Manse, now a functioning library. He encouraged its custodian, the late Dr. Louise Manny, to record the hundreds of folksongs and "come all ye's" of the area and helped her set up an annual folksinging festival which takes place in July every year. His ashes are held in the bottom of his statue in the middle of the town square. One of the province's more exuberant events is the Great Miramichi Raft Race, held each summer on a Saturday in mid-Aug.

Outside Chatham on Route 11 is the MacDonald Farm, a major restoration of an 1830's working farm.

Three miles west of Newcastle is the Enclosure, the site of the graves of the first settlers, part of a lovely provincial park, largely donated to the province by Lord Beaverbrook.

The shortest route from Newcastle to Bathurst is the inland Route 8 but this route has little of interest.

The road along the shore is more rewarding. You'll pass through small communities with intriguing names such as Burnt Church, named for an ancient English raid; and Tracadie, once a leper colony. The Tracadie Museum, located in the Town Hall, commemorates this part of Tracadie's past. There is a new museum of local history at Tabusintac and a new marine museum at Shippagan, which is a major provincial facility. It depicts the history of the fishing industry and portrays the lives of the area's fishermen. Shippagan, typical of the north shore fishing villages, offers superb opportunities for photographers. This entire shore has fine beaches. You might want to take the free ferry to Miscou Island, where you can beachcomb along deserted beaches. Accommodations there consist of campgrounds and cabins.

Caraquet

Caraquet, a lively Acadian town, is prosperous and busy. You'll find a wooden shipbuilding factory, fish and crab packing plants, and a market on the wharf peddling fish and shellfish fresh from the boats at very good prices.

Down by the Fisheries School, the Acadian Museum perched over the water offers an interesting and informative encounter with area history. You'll even find a small handicraft shop tucked in one corner where you can pick up a hooked rug or a woven napkin for a reasonable price.

West of Caraquet is the Acadian Village, a restoration of 30 buildings, which depicts the Acadian lifestyle in New Brunswick between 1780 and 1880. Also, if you're in Caraquet around mid-August, it's worth staying for the Acadian Festival, a cultural event featuring the Blessing of the Fleet, Acadian folksinging, L'Acadie en fête, and various other unique celebrations. Caraquet is also the province's most popular port for deepsea sport fishing, especially for the bluefin tuna. At Grand Anse, a new museum, the Pope's Museum, has displays of the history of the Popes, a replica of the Vatican, and a collection of religious attire. Admission: $2. Open 10 A.M.–6 P.M.

From Caraquet to Bathurst the seacoast reminds one of France's Brittany coast, and the design of the occasional house or barn along the way heightens that impression. As you drive along Route 11, the rocky shores of the Gaspé across the Chaleur Bay are clearly visible; at Pokeshaw, notice the curious flat-topped rock. Its dead trees are usually covered with birds, giving it the name "Bird Island."

Bathurst to Dalhousie

Bathurst (population 17,000) has recently found its wealth in mining. Nearby discoveries of iron, lead, and zinc have stimulated industries of all kinds. Always a happy town, it pleased both Jacques Cartier when he visited here in 1534 and also Champlain when he bartered for clothes right off the Indians' backs during his business trip. A century later another tourist from France, Nicholas Denys, liked it so well he settled at the mouth of the Nipisiquit River on Bathurst Bay where he ran a fish and fur-trading business as well as a mill. Bathurst has been a busy town ever since.

In colonial days, the area was known as St. Peters, but religion evidently yielded to politics when, in 1826, the town became Bathurst, after the Earl of Bathurst who was then Colonial Secretary.

As friendly and hospitable a town as it is busy, Bathurst has a special charm. Perhaps it comes from a happy blending of French and English, although the population breakdown always depends on the background of the person asked—English-speaking people say it's 60/40 English and the French say it's 60/40 French. Bathurst also has a war museum operated by the Royal Canadian Legion.

The beach at Youghall, where you'll find a provincial park and camp grounds, winds all the way around Bathurst Bay and the water in summer is warm. That's why Cartier named it *Baie de Chaleur* (Bay of Warmth).

One of the most popular pasttimes in the area is eating lobster on the beach. On a clear night, as you stare out to sea, you might see the phantom ship. All along the Bay of Chaleur from Bathurst to Campbellton, the ship has been sighted. No satisfactory explanation for this phenomenon has been given but descriptions have been pretty much the same: a burning sailing ship, sometimes with sailors scurrying about the flaming rigging; finally the ship disappears, still aglow, beneath the waves. Some say it's the ghost of a French ship lost in the Battle of the Restigouche; others claim it's a reflection of heat waves. Whatever it is, many have sighted it during the years—even a Sunday school teacher and his whole class. So keep your eyes on the Bay of Chaleur. You, too, might see the phantom ship! There's also an excellent marina and yacht center.

Just west of Bathurst on Route 11, there's an Acadian crafts center attached to La Fine Grobe restaurant offering classes in the fine arts and crafts, with full board. (Box 219, Nigadoo, NB E0B 2A0, phone 738–3138). At Belledune there's a huge smelter which processes the ores from the mineral fields and looks startlingly futuristic. You'll travel along Jacquet River, where a charming provincial park is situated right on the shore. At Eel River Crossing, you can join right in with your shovel to dig some of the finest clams in the world. Just across the long stretch of sand bar, the local Indians run a small handcraft shop.

In Dalhousie and Campbellton, Scottish and Irish settlers mingled with the Acadians to settle the area. Just as in the Newcastle/Chatham district, it's sometimes hard to pick out the accent. Is it French or Irish?

Dalhousie, a year-round port, is also the home of one of the province's largest industries, the newsprint mill of the New Brunswick International Paper Company. Large ocean-going ships stop here on their way to Europe. The Chaleur History Museum on Adelaide Street features local history of the area.

Campbellton

Campbellton (population about 10,422) retains the charm of a pioneer town. Nestling at the foot of Sugarloaf, a perfectly rounded mountain, it is reminiscent of lumbermen, river drives, and seagoing vessels. Still the headquarters for fishing outfitters for the famous salmon rivers of the region, the town is fast forging ahead into modernity. The new Restigouche Gallery is a major provincial exhibition center. The theater in the modern high school/trade school complex presents plays of professional quality. Theatre New Brunswick also brings its touring productions here where they are always well received.

The all-season Sugarloaf Provincial Park has an excellent ski hill and lodge. Newest winter sport wrinkle is an Alpine slide. Just across the river in Québec, Federal archeologists have been using a diving bell to bring up artifacts from the Battle of the Restigouche, the last naval engagement of the Seven Years' War fought off Campbellton in 1760. A summer salmon festival is held here from late June to early July.

Route 17, known locally as the Stuart Highway, cuts through the central forest where communities are sparse. The road, though narrow, is good, cutting across hills and valleys for 100 miles to the small town of St. Leonard.

PRACTICAL INFORMATION FOR
NEW BRUNSWICK

HOW TO GET THERE. By air: Airports serviced by *CP Air* and *Air Canada* at Moncton, Fredericton, and Saint John; *CP Air* also flies to Charlo, near Dalhousie, from Moncton, Chatham and Montréal.

By car: By car ferry from Prince Edward Island, Trans-Canada Hwy. from Nova Scotia, Trans-Canada Hwy. from Québec, Interstate 95 to Houlton, Me., U.S. 1 to Calais, Me.

By train: Regular *Via Rail* passenger service from Moncton to Montréal and Halifax, with links via ferry to Prince Edward Island and Newfoundland.

By bus: *SMT* within the province connecting with most major bus lines.

ACCOMMODATIONS. New Brunswick has a number of officially designated "Heritage Inns"—places built mostly in the last century and having some local historic significance. They have either antique china or furniture or some other quaint touch and they provide accommodations that vary from homey to elegant, sometimes in the inexpensive category. They are noted as Heritage Inns in the following listing.

Price categories are based on double-occupancy. *Expensive,* over $40; *Moderate,* $30–40; *Inexpensive,* under $30.

Most places accept the following major credit cards. American Express, MasterCard and Visa; others may also be honored. Not all establishments accept credit cards, therefore we suggest you call for information.

BATHURST. Keddy's Motor Inn. *Expensive.* 80 Main St., Bathurst, NB E2A 1A3 (506–546–6691; 800–561–0040 in NB). 89 units, dining room, bar, coffee shop.

Atlantic Host Hotel. *Expensive.* Box 910, Bathurst, NB E2A 4H7 (506–548–3335). 106 units, swimming pool, dining room.

Danny's Motor Inn. *Moderate.* Box 180, Bathurst, NB E2A 3Z2 (506–548–6621). 40 units (4 housekeeping), good dining room, tennis courts, beach nearby.

Fundy Line Motel. *Moderate.* 855 Ste. Anne St., Bathurst, NB 2EA 2Y6 (506–548–8803). 52 units, excellent dining room, long corridors, and unique rooms in former seminary.

BUCTOUCHE. Buctouche Bay Inn. *Inexpensive.* Box 445, Buctouche, NB E0A 1G0 (506–743–2726). A Heritage Inn. 11 units, nice location, dining room, and bar.

CAMPBELLTON. Caspian Motel. *Expensive.* Box 489, 26 Duke St., Campbellton, NB E3N 3G9 (506–753–7606). 60 units, pool, sauna, spa, dining room, and bar.

Howard Johnson Motor Lodge. *Expensive.* 157 Water St., Campbellton, NB E3N 3H2 (506–753–5063). On Rte. 11. Comfortable and friendly. Dining room.

Fundy Line Motel. *Moderate.* Roseberry St., Campbellton, NB E0A 1A0 (506–753–3395). 77 adequate rooms, excellent dining room.

CAMPOBELLO. Friars Bay Motor Lodge. *Moderate.* Welshpool, Campobello, NB E0G 3H0 (506–752–2056). Near the sea. 10 units, licensed dining room.

The Owen House. *Inexpensive.* Welshpool, Campobello, NB E0G 3H0 (506–752–2977). A Heritage Inn. Nine rooms in historic old home. Bed and breakfast.

Quoddy View Cabins. *Inexpensive.* Wilson's Beach, Campobello, NB E0G 3H0 (506–752–2981). Seven units (five housekeeping), near beach.

CARAQUET. The Motel Savoie. *Expensive.* 139 Blvd. Ste. Pierre, Caraquet, NB E0B 1K0 (506–727–3845). Comfortable and modern. Restaurant on premises.

Motel du Village. *Moderate.* Box 1116, Caraquet, NB E0B 1K0 (506–732–2982). 20 attractive units, dining room, and bar.

Hotel Paulin. *Inexpensive.* 143 Blvd. Ste. Pierre, Caraquet, NB E0B 1K0 (506–727–9981). A Heritage Inn. Old hotel (established 1887), with no pretensions, but charming in an off-beat other-century way. Dining room has a reputation for good, low-cost seafood.

DALHOUSIE. Cedar Lodge Motel. *Moderate.* Box 1089, Dalhousie, NB E0K 1B0 (506–684–3363). About 12 miles from Campbellton. 32 units, some overlooking the Baie des Chaleurs where a ghostly ship is said to sail. Excellent dining room, small bar, and dance floor with band.

DEER ISLAND. Fairhaven Bed and Breakfast. *Moderate.* Fairhaven, Deer Island, NB E0G 1R0 (506–747–2962). Two units.

The 45th Parallel Motel and Tourist Home. *Inexpensive.* Fairhaven, Deer Island, NB E0G 1R0 (506–747–2231). Ten units (3 housekeeping). Good seafood restaurant.

West Isles World. *Inexpensive.* Lambert's Cove, Deer Island, NB E0G 1R0 (506–747–2961). Two rooms, pool, boat tours.

EDMUNDSTON. Auberge Wandlyn Inn. *Expensive.* 919 Canada Rd., Box 68, Edmundston, NB E3V 3K5 (506–735–5525). Pool, good dining room, bar.

Howard Johnson Motor Lodge. *Expensive.* 100 Rice St., Edmundston, NB E3V 1T4 (506–739–7321). Good restaurant, bar, and adjoining major shopping center.

Motel le Brayon. *Moderate.* Rue de Rocher, Ste. Basile, NB E0L 1H0 (506–263–5514). On the TCH. Charming motel with some chalets and friendly operators who serve breakfast and lunch or dinner, if requested.

FUNDY NATIONAL PARK. Caledonia Highlands Inn and Chalets. *Expensive.* Fundy National Park, Box 99, Alma, AlbertCo., NB E0A 1B0 (506–887–2930). 44 units.

Fundy Park Chalets. *Inexpensive.* Alma, NB E0A 1B0 (506–887–2808). 29 housekeeping units, dining room, pool.

GAGETOWN. Steamer's Stop Inn. *Moderate.* Front St., Box 155, Gagetown, NB E0G 1V0 (506–488–2903). A Heritage Inn. Seven rooms, decorated in old country style with lovely view over river. Good dining room.

GRAND FALLS. Motel Pres du Lac. *Expensive.* Box 1170, Grand Falls, NB E0J 1M0 (506–473–1300). 96 units, (three housekeeping), dining room. Small bar. Pool. Pleasant.

GRAND MANAN. Grand Manan is a small and very personal place. Expect accommodations to be likewise. A Government liquor store operates on the island and some dining rooms serve beer or wine.

The Marathon Inn. *Expensive.* North Head, E0G 2M0 (506–662–8144). A Heritage Inn. Hundred-year-old hotel overlooking the ferry landing. Built by a sea captain. Rooms furnished with antique furniture. Heated pool, tennis. Headquarters for whale-watching expeditions, bird watching, and photography packages. Rates include breakfast and dinner.

The Compass Rose. *Moderate.* North Head, Grand Manan, NB E0G 2M0 (506–662–8570). A Heritage Inn. Charming old house with annex overlooking the sea, near ferry landing. Rates include breakfast. Workshops, such as print-making, sometimes offered in packages.

Grand Harbour Inn. *Inexpensive.* Grand Harbour, Grand Manan, NB E0G 1X0 (506–662–8681). Six rooms in pleasant old house. Rates include breakfast.

MONCTON. Auberge Wandlyn Motor Inn. *Expensive.* Magnetic Hill, R.R.8, Moncton, NB E1C 8K2 (506–384–3554 or 800–561–0000). Rooms plain but comfortable. Pool, good dining room, small bar.

Hotel Beausejour. *Expensive.* 750 Main St., Box 906, Moncton, NB E1C 8N8 (506–854–4344 or 800–561–0040). 317 rooms, decorated in old Acadian theme with thick carpeting and plenty of comfortable and attractive furniture. Pleasant bar, coffee shop, dining room, and pool.

Howard Johnson Motor Lodge. *Expensive.* Magnetic Hill, Box 5005, Moncton, NB E1C 8R7 (506–384–1050 or 800–654–2000). On TCH. Dining room, bar, lounge, pool.

Keddy's Brunswick Hotel. *Expensive.* 1005 Main St., Box 282, Moncton, NB E1C 8N6 (506–854–6340 or 800–561–0040). 197 rooms, newly renovated. Dining room, lounge/bar. Centrally located.

Rodd's Park House Inn. *Expensive.* 434 Main St., Moncton, NB E1C 1B9 (506–382–1664 or 800–565–0201). 97 units. We recommend the new part. Great view of Bore. Good, moderately priced breakfasts. Pool.

Hotel Canadiana. *Inexpensive.* 46 Archibald St., Moncton, NB E1C 5H9 (506–382–1054). A Heritage Inn in downtown Moncton with 73 rooms, a fine antique collection, and a homey atmosphere.

NEWCASTLE. Auberge Wandlyn Motor Inn. *Expensive.* 365 Water St., Box 411, Newcastle, NB E1V 3M5 (506–622–3870). 73 units, pleasant dining room.

The Wharf Inn. *Expensive.* Jane St., Box 474, Newcastle, NB E1V 3M6 (506–622–0302). Excellent motels with 53 units, pool, and licensed lounge.

Castle Lodge Tourist Home. *Inexpensive.* 152 Castle St., Newcastle, NB E1V 2L7 (506–622–2442). Five units in old Victorian home right on Town Square.

OROMOCTO. The Oromocto Hotel. *Moderate-Expensive.* 100 Hershey St., Oromocto, NB E2V 1J3 (506–357–8424). 46 units (20 housekeeping), small bar, good dining room.

SACKVILLE. The Marshlands Inn. *Moderate.* 73 Bridge St., Box 1440, Sackville, NB E0A 3C0 (506–536–0170). A Heritage Inn with 16 units and an impressive collection of 19th-century furniture. You'll enjoy the special Marsh-lands breakfast. Make reservations well in advance.

A Different Drummer. *Inexpensive.* 146 W. Main St., Box 188, Sackville, NB E0A 3C0 (506–532–4405). Six units in lovely old home, with friendly hosts.

SHEDIAC. Chez Françoise. *Moderate.* 96 Main St., Shediac, NB E0A 3G0 (506–532–4233). Nine rooms, some with balconies, in a beautiful old mansion. Excellent restaurant.

Neptune Hotel. *Moderate.* Main St., Box 1000, Shediac, NB E0A 3G0 (506–532–4299). 33 comfortable units near fine sand beach.

Hotel Shediac. *Inexpensive.* Main St., Box 279, Shediac, NB E0A 3G0 (506–532–4405). 30 rooms in a Heritage Inn, a grand old hotel of yesteryear. Near the finest beaches in New Brunswick. Good seafood restaurant.

SHIPAGPAN. Motel Shippagan. *Moderate.* Box 260, Shippagan, NB E0B 2P0 (506–336–2276). Licensed dining room. Modern surroundings.

ST. ANDREWS. The Algonquin Hotel. *Expensive.* St. Andrews, NB E0G 2X0 (506–529–8823 or 800–268–9411). A venerable CP hotel and a local landmark, 193 rooms, pool, dining room, pub, dance hall, tennis courts. Modified American plan.

The Rosemount Inn. *Expensive.* R.R. 2, St. Andrews, NB E0G 2X0 (506–529 –3351). A Heritage Inn. Huge old home, pool, and lots of crystal and antiques. Especially lovely interior, pretty dining room.

Tara Manor. *Expensive–Moderate.* 559 Mowett Dr., St. Andrews, NB E0G 2X0 (506–529–3304). A Heritage Inn. Early American and French Provincial decor. Former home of Canadian politician C. D. Howe. Putting green, lavish bedrooms (19 units), coffee shop. Specify inn or motel. Excellent dining room.

Best Western Shiretown Inn. *Moderate.* Box 145, 218 Water St., St. Andrews, NB E0G 2X0 (506–529–8877 or 800–387–3400). A Heritage Inn. One of the oldest operating inns in Canada. Large, old, high-ceilinged rooms, dining room, bar, coffeeshop. Old English pub. Homemade bread.

The Pansy Patch. *Moderate.* 59 Carleton St., St. Andrews, NB E0G 2X0 (506–529–3834). Exceptional bed and breakfast in charming early-Canadian home.

ST. STEPHEN. Auberge Wandlyn Inn. *Expensive.* 99 King St., St. Stephen, NB E3L 2C6 (506–466–1814 or 800–561–0000). Comfortable, good dining room.

Liz's Place Bed and Breakfast. *Inexpensive.* 14 Watson St., St. Stephen, NB E3L 1Y5 (506–466–3401). Three units.

WOODSTOCK. Auberge Wandly Inn. *Expensive.* Box 1191, Woodstock, NB E0J 2B0 (328–8876 or 800–561–0000). Pool, good dining room.

John Gyles Motor Inn. *Moderate.* R.R.1, Woodstock, NB E0J 2B0 (506–328 –2698). On the TCH, to the east. Great view of valley. Excellent German restaurant. New units.

Atlantic Inns Ltd. *Inexpensive.* R.R. 6, Woodstock, NB E0J 2B0 (506–328– 6688). 27 units, restaurant.

Cosy Cabins. *Inexpensive.* R.R.1, Woodstock, NB E0J 2B0 (506–328–3344). In town. Dining room, pool, beach, studio of Woodstock weavers.

HOSTELS. Hostels are located in Saint John, Fredericton, Moncton, Shediac, Tracadie, Caraquet, Bathurst, Campbellton, and Edmundston. All operate from 6 P.M. to 9 or 10 A.M., doors closing for the night around midnight—except in Moncton (11 P.M.), Shediac (11:30 P.M.), and Saint John (1 A.M.). Costs less than $5 a night except in Moncton, Fredericton and Saint John, where it is slightly higher. Meals are extra—breakfast, about $1, and some serve dinner early in the evening for under $2. Hostel provides bunk and foam mattress, usually dorm-style. Most have travel information. For details, write New Brunswick Hostel Association, R.R. 4, Douglas, New Brunswick. Telephone: (506) 453–4869 (9–5 P.M.), 472–1597 (evenings and weekends).

TELEPHONES. The telephone area code for all of New Brunswick is 506.

TOURIST INFORMATION. *Municipal Information Centres:* Belledune on Rte. 11, 552–5220; Bertrand on Rte. 11, 727–2126; Buctouche, 743–5719; Caraquet, 727 –6234; Clair, Main St., 992–2181; Dalhousie, Inch Arran Park, 684–5352; Edmundston, 739–8191; Eel River Crossing, 826–3086; Fredericton, 452–9426; Grand Anse, on Rte. 11, 732–5481; Grand Falls, Madawaska Rd., 473–4538; Hampton, Old King's County Jail, 832–3335; McAdam, 784–3574; Moncton, Magnetic Hill, 384–6833; Neguac, on Rte. 11, 776–8907; Oromocto, Miramichi Rd., 357–5730; Plaster Rock, Main St., 356–2196; Richibucto, Legion St., 523–6642; Riverview, Court House, 386–8874; Rogersville, Monument Assumption, 775–2502; Shediac, Corner of Rte. 11 and Rte. 15, 532–1136; Sussex, Four Corners, 433–4553; St. Andrews, Water St., 529–3000; St. George, Brunswick St., 755–3721; Saint John, Hazen Ave., 658–2855; Tracadie, City Hall, 395–9244.

Provincial Tourist Bureaus: At Aulac on the Trans-Canada Hwy., 536–0923; Bathurst, 548–9344; Campbellton at Sugarloaf Park, 753–5413; Campobello, 752–2997; Chatham, 773–5628; Edmundston on the Trans-Canada Hwy., 735–6103; Fredericton on the Trans-Canada Hwy., 455–3092 or 455–3099; Moncton on the Trans-Canada Hwy., 384–8608; Newcastle, 622–0303; Penobsquis on the Trans-Canada Hwy., 433–4326; St. Andrews at Waweig on Rte. 1, 466–4858; Saint John at the Reversing Falls, 672–1198; St. Leonard on the Trans-Canada Hwy., 423–6324; St. Stephen, 466–1139; Woodstock on Rte. 95, 328–3419.

Or write for information to: *Dept. of Tourism,* Box 12345, Fredericton, New Brunswick, Canada E3B 5C3; (506) 453–2377, 800–561–0123 from Canada and U.S. or 800–442–4442 from within New Brunswick.

TIME ZONE. The province is on Atlantic Time—one hour in advance of Eastern Time.

 SEASONAL EVENTS. Food festivals abound all summer, celebrating the harvests of scallops, salmon, lobsters, oysters, clams, and important vegetables like potatoes and Brussels sprouts. Other festivals celebrate heritage, music, crafts, athletics, and old home weeks. For dates and locations, contact *Dept. of Tourism.* Likewise for schedules of Atlantic Symphony Orchestra performances and art gallery exhibitions.

 SPECIAL INTEREST TOURS. At Brunswick Mining and Smelting you can visit "the underground city," almost 3,000 feet down in a mine which produces zinc, lead, silver, and copper.

Boat Tours: Fundy Isles Marine Enterprises, 529–3688. Shediac—Romeo's Marine, 532–6444. Point-du-Chene—Moyak Marine, 532–4098. Dalhousie—Chaleur Phantom, 684–4219. In the Caraquet area there are numerous boat tour operators. Ask for information locally, or from Tourism New Brunswick. Paddlewheeler tours on St. John River at Fredericton. Harbor Tours sometimes available in Saint John. Check at Tourist Information Center, Reversing Falls, 635–1238.

Bird-watching is a special attraction on Grand Manan Island. There are over 240 species of sea birds that nest there. It's also a paradise for rockhounds, painters, nature photographers, and hikers—not to mention whale watchers! Bicyclists contact Carl White, 408 Princess Drive, Bathurst, New Brunswick, for information regarding special bicycle tours. Tours for all of these activities can be arranged by telephoning 800–561–0123.

 PARKS AND CAMPING. New Brunswick has two national parks. *Fundy National Park* fronts the Bay of Fundy—about 13 km. (8 mi.) of shore with an inland area of tall timber, lakes, and streams. There is a motel and chalets inside the park. It opens when the fishing season does—the third weekend in May.

Kouchibougouac National Park stretches 25 km. (15 mi.) along the Gulf of St. Lawrence shore. It's a panorama of forest, marshes, tidal lagoons, meandering rivers, sand dunes, and—especially—a vast and sweeping beach along much of its length. Canoes, bicycles, and boats may be rented on site.

Mactaquac, north of Fredericton, is the major provincial park. It has extensive camping facilities, golf, and other summer and winter sports facilities. *Sugarloaf* in the north is a year-round facility with the accent on skiing and other winter activities while *Mount Carleton* offers much wilderness and primitive camping facilities. There are smaller provincial parks throughout New Brunswick.

Miscou Island has camping facilities and cabins. Contact Miscou Island Campground and Cabins, Miscou Centre. Phone 344–8352.

Camping fees in provincial and national parks are generally between $6 and $10, depending on services. Private campgrounds may charge a bit more. The province's accommodations guide lists them all. The Avis Rent-a-Car company also rents tents and camping kits along with cars throughout the Maritime provinces.

FARM VACATIONS. About two dozen farms in the province take on people who wish to experience a farm vacation. Most cater to families, but some will take children alone. Contact *Dept. of Tourism,* Heritage and Recreation.

SPORTS. Golf: New Brunswick has 31 golf courses, most with pro shops and rentals, as well as restaurants and shower facilities. Most are uncrowded.

Fishing and hunting: Charters for deepsea fishing are mostly concentrated in the Caraquet area, where angling for the bluefin tuna is a glamour activity. New Brunswick is also known internationally for its salmon and bass fishing, although its multitude of lakes abound in other freshwater species as well.

Hunting for deer, bear, and small game can be arranged. You will need a licensed guide and a nonresident hunting license for yourself. (Trius Tours Ltd., 455–8400) organizes bear-hunting expeditions. So does Fundy Outfitters, Box 16, Hillsborough, NB E0A 1X0 (734–2424).

Tourism New Brunswick has a fishing and hunting guidebook listing outfitters and other relevant information.

Winter sports: New Brunswick is a growing destination for winter vacationers. It has dependable deep snow and is abuzz all winter with skiing, snowmobiling, ice-fishing, and other activities over great open spaces. Canada East Tours (548–3447) in Bathurst organizes snowmobiling holidays.

Sailing: For the yachting enthusiast, there are the extensive and gorgeous waters of the lower Saint John River and Grand Lake. Yachts can be rented at *Maritime Yachts,* Box 27, R.R. 3, Site 4, Fredericton, N.B. (453–4388) or at *Fundy Yachts,* Dipper Harbour, Box 490, R.R. 2, Lepreau, N.B. (659–2769). Houseboat rentals are available from Houseboat Vacations, P.O. Box 2088, Sussex, N.B. E0E 1P0, or phone 433–4801 or 433–1609. Fredericton Rowing Club, Aquatic Centre, holds clinics and regattas for rowers.

For details on any of the above, contact Tourism, Recreation, and Heritage, New Brunswick, P.O. Box 12345, Fredericton, New Brunswick E3B 5C3; 453–2377, 800–561–0123 from Canada and U.S., or 800–442–4442 from within New Brunswick.

MUSEUMS. The province has a couple of dozen museums apart from the major ones found in Saint John and Fredericton. In particular there's the *Acadian Historical Village* and the *Acadian Museum* in **Caraquet,** the *Pope's Museum* in Grand Anse, plus the *Acadian Museum* at the University of Moncton campus in **Moncton**—all depicting the history of the Acadian people. *Eglise St.-Henri* at **Barachois** is an old wooden church converted to a museum also on the Acadian theme. Most small museums are on local history, but some have specific themes. For example, *Miramichi Salmon Museum,* **Doaktown** the *Central New Brunswick Woodsmen's Museum* at **Boiestown,** the *Automobile Museum* at **Edmundston,** and the *Fundy Antique Car Museum* at **Hopewell Cape,** Hillsborough-Salem Railway operates 1-hour steam locomotive trips in summer, the *Marine Museum* at **Shippagan,** and the *Sportsman's Museum* at **Shediac.** The *Grand Manan Museum* has an interesting collection of birds and geological exhibits. The *Tracadie Historical Museum* pays tribute to those who dedicated their lives to a leper colony that once existed there. The *Moncton Museum* is another fairly large museum of provincial scale.

New Brunswick also has some 9,000 homes designated as "historic." Some can only be viewed from the outside, but some have exhibits and are open to the public. Check the Tourism New Brunswick publication *Historic Faces.*

SHOPPING. Bathurst's one unique store, *Frank's Furs,* specializes in designing and making fur coats in larger sizes.

In **Edmundston,** *Chiasson's Furs* offers stunning furs designed with the French flair.

Moncton's shopping is some of the best in New Brunswick—five spacious malls and numerous pockets of shops in downtown Moncton. Among the crafts to look for are the yarn portraits of La Sagouine, "the old sage" of Buctouche.

The sayings of an old Acadian woman as she goes about her daily chores were made famous in Antonine Maillet's novel *La Sagouine.*

St. Andrews has great English and New Brunswick woolens, lots of English bone china, and marvelous wool yarn at *The Sea Captain's Loft, Cottage Craft,* and *Saint Andrews Woollens.* Rare and out-of-print books, antiques, etc. at the *Pansy Patch,* a stunning old home across from the Algonquin Hotel. Quality crafts are at *La Baleine* on Water St., and antiques can be found at the *Trading Post,* also on Water St.

Fredericton's artist's studios and craftpeople are noted for their work.

At **St. Leonard,** be sure to visit the studio/store of the *Madawaska Weavers,* whose handwoven items are known the world over. Handsome skirts, stoles, and enchanting ties are some of the items for sale.

At **St. Stephen,** *Quartermain's Ltd.,* a long-standing business where you can browse for hours among quality Canadian and British goods. *Le Chocolatier* is Ganong's outlet for hand-dipped chocolates.

In the studio of *Peter Hummel-Newell,* you'll find exquisite pieces of jewelry made from real New Brunswick wildflowers.

The *Directory of New Brunswick Craftsmen & Craft Shops,* available from the Department of Youth, Culture, and Recreation, Handcrafts Branch, Box 6000, Fredericton, N.B. or from tourist bureaus, will direct you to potters, weavers, glass-blowers, jewelers and carvers all over the province.

In summer, handcraft courses are offered at various locations throughout the province.

Shopping hours. Downtown shopping runs from 9 A.M. to 5 or 6 P.M. Monday–Saturday, and up to 9 P.M. on Fridays. The shopping malls are open 10 A.M. to 10 P.M. six days a week, except in Moncton where they close at 6 P.M. Saturday nights.

Holiday closings during the summer season occur on Victoria Day (3rd Monday in May), Canada Day (July 1), New Brunswick Day (1st Monday in August), and Labor Day. Thanksgiving (2nd Monday in October) and Remembrance Day (November 11) are also local holidays.

LIQUOR LAWS. The minimum legal drinking age in New Brunswick is 19.

RESTAURANTS. Expect surprisingly good dining in some places in rural New Brunswick, in others just average. Price categories: *Expensive,* over $15; *Moderate,* $10–15; *Inexpensive,* under $10. A 10% provincial tax will be added to your bill.

Most places accept the following major credit cards: American Express, MasterCard, and Visa; others may also be honored. Not all establishments accept credit cards, therefore we suggest you call for information.

BATHURST. La Fine Grobe. *Expensive.* Located at Nigadoo, near Bathurst (783–3138). French and traditional Acadian cuisine at its best. Fine buffet; special drink of the house—old Acadian recipe from Prohibition times called Le Caribou. Art and craft gallery with folksingers.

Danny's Restaurant. *Moderate.* On Rte. 134 (548–6621). Good food, plainly served. Generous lobster cocktails, friendly service in serene dining room.

Ship's Galley. *Moderate.* Fundy Line Motel, 855 Ste. Anne St. (548–8803). Some of the area's best seafood in attractive dining room.

CAMPBELLTON. Fundy Line Motel Dining Room. *Moderate.* Roseberry St. (739–3395). Good, plain food. Excellent steak and salmon.

Caspian Hotel Dining Room. *Moderate.* 26 Duke St. (753–7606). Good food, pleasant room.

CARAQUET. Hotel Paulin. *Moderate.* 143 Blvd. St. Pierre (727–9981). Excellent seafood and home-cooked Acadian dishes.

Le Poirier. *Moderate.* Blvd. St. Pierre (727–4713). A new restaurant with a good initial reputation. Seafoods a specialty.

CHATHAM. La Portage. *Moderate.* Richibucto Rd. (773–6447). Good steak.

DALHOUSIE. The Cedar Lodge Dining Room. *Moderate.* Rte. 11 (684–3363). Excellent food. The apple pie is highly recommended.

EDMUNDSTON. Le Baron. *Expensive.* 174 Victoria St. (739–7822). Excellent food; pâté à la maison, crêpe Suzettes flamed at your table.

The Wandlyn. *Expensive.* 919 Canada Rd. (735–5525). Good food, comparable to Le Baron. Piano bar, dancing.

FORT BEAUSEJOUR. Drury Lane Steakhouse. *Moderate.* In Aulac, near Fort Beausejour (536–1252). Steak, clam chowder with home-baked rolls, steamed clams—all excellent.

GRAND MANAN. The Compass Rose. *Moderate.* North Head (662–8570). Seafood in home-cooked style. Afternoon tea.

The Marathon. *Moderate.* North Head (662–8144). Dinner at six. Set menu. Bread baked fresh daily. Good food. Homey and friendly.

MONCTON. Chez Jean Pierre. *Expensive.* 21 Toombes St. (382–0332). Features Provençal cuisine (stuffed baby pig, quail in raisin sauce, and others). Major credit cards.

The Windjammer. *Expensive.* 750 Main St. (506–854–4334). The most elegant dining room in the Beausejour Hotel. Private booths and portholes with real fish swimming around in them. Although expensive, service is slick and food is good. Châteaubriand recommended. Major credit cards.

Cy's. *Moderate-Expensive.* Main St. (382–0032). Noted seafood restaurant which richly deserves its reputation. The seafood platter, one of the specialties, will amaze you with its quality and quantity. Lobster a specialty, of course, and a great view of the tidal bore from a window table. Major credit cards.

Papa Joe's. *Moderate–Expensive.* 111 St. George St. (854–9947). Fair food. Fiddleheads available, steaks are good; try some of the flaming coffees. Major credit cards.

Two Brothers. *Moderate–Expensive.* Petitcodiac, 30 miles outside Moncton (east) (756–8111). Good food in 1860 home. French and local seafood. Licensed. Major cards.

Ming Garden Restaurant. *Moderate.* 797 Mountain Rd. (855–5433). Interesting Cantonese-Canadian food, the best in the Maritimes. One dish, chunks of fresh lobster, wrapped in thin slices of chicken, deep fried and served with oyster sauce should be tried. Open till 2 A.M. weeknights, 3 A.M. weekends. Major credit cards.

Le Cave à Pape. *Inexpensive-Moderate.* 236 St. George St. (855–0581). Excellent French and Acadian cuisine. Major credit cards.

NEWCASTLE. The Wandlyn Dining Room. *Moderate.* 365 Water St. (622–2847). Small, cozy, good.

PERTH-ANDOVER. York's Dining Room. *Moderate.* (273–2847). Deserves special mention. A uniquely New Brunswick establishment, York's serves gargantuan helpings of excellent home-cooked foods in an unassuming dining room.

SACKVILLE. Marshlands Inn. *Expensive–Moderate.* 73 Bridge St. (536–0170). Fine old inn serving traditional English and New Brunswick foods such as steak and kidney pie, seafood, fiddleheads, in mahogany panelled dining room with antique lined walls.

SHEDIAC. Chez Francoise. *Expensive–Moderate.* 93 Main St. (532–4233). Glowing old-fashioned dining rooms in old mansion. Cuisine *a la francais* with accent on fresh seafood of the region.

Paturel's Shore House. *Moderate.* At Cape Bimet a few miles east of Shediac. (532–4774). Lobster and seafood.

Shediac's Fisherman's Paradise. *Moderate.* Main St. (532–6811). Good seafood in the heart of lobster country.

ST. ANDREWS. The Algonquin Hotel. *Expensive.* (529–8823). Excellent lobster dinners on weekends. Open dances in the casino on some Saturday nights.

Conley's Lighthouse. *Expensive.* (529–3082). Good fresh lobster in all forms, boiled, stewed, or on rolls.

L'Europe Dining Room. *Expensive.* King St. (529–3818). Superb dining— excellent food, good service.

The Rossmount. *Expensive.* R.R.2 (529–3351). Elegant decor. The specialties are lobster and Bay of Fundy fish. Reservations suggested.

Tara Manor. *Moderate–Expensive.* 559 Mowatt Dr. (529–3304). Good dining room with friendly service.

The Shiretown. *Moderate.* 218 Water St. (529–8877). Fairly good food, interesting lunchtime buffet.

Whale of a Café. *Inexpensive.* Water St. (no phone). Excellent chowder, lobster chunks in fresh croissants.

ST. STEPHEN. Auberge Wandlyn Inn. *Moderate.* 99 King St. (466–1814). Small, cheerful dining room with good standard fare.

WOODSTOCK. Auberge Wandlyn Inn. *Expensive.* Junction routes 2 and 95 (328–8876). Large, pleasant dining room, good food.

John Gyles Motor Inn. *Moderate.* R.R.1 (328–6688). Excellent German cuisine in attractive surrounding.

NIGHTLIFE. In **Edmundston,** some of the hotels that offer live entertainment are *Charlies Bar* at the Wandlyn Motel, *The Riverside* and the *New Royal* (the last two have been known to offer strip shows), or the bars at the *Praga* tavern atmosphere with canned music.

In **Moncton** for dressed-up stepping out, the hottest spot is the *Cosmopolitan Club* in the old courthouse on Main St. *The Beaus and Belles* lounge in the Beausejour Hotel is an attractive spot decorated in Gay Nineties style where you can have a snack with your drink. *The Coach Room Lounge,* Keddy's Motel, dark, quaint and quiet. Perfect spot for a quiet tête-à-tête. *Lamplighter Room* in the Howard Johnson's Motor Inn is pleasant and congenial.

In **St. Andrews,** two swinging bars in the Algonquin Hotel offer nightly entertainment. Quiet drinking in the *Shiretown Inn,* Water St., like a small English pub.

NOVA SCOTIA

Old Legends—New Attractions

by
COLLEEN THOMPSON, RALPH SURETTE,
and ALAN FREEMAN

Colleen Thompson is a travel writer based in New Brunswick. Ralph Surette is a writer based in Halifax and Alan Freeman is based in Toronto.

Early settlers called their new homeland Nova Scotia, Latin for "New Scotland," and it bears more than a passing resemblance to its bonnie namesake across the sea. Not only does it woo visitors with the skirl of bagpipes and the saucy flirt of a kilt, but you'll see the similarities in dramatic highlands, winding blue rivers, flower-filled valleys, and timeless sea-swept villages. Names like Inverary, New Glasgow, and Clyde appear on the map. Heather grows naturally on a slope in Halifax, and the purple Scotch thistle found by the roadside is a nostalgic link with the old country. Colorful clouds of lupins fill ditches, climb hills, cover meadows, and turn whole sections of highway into Scottish country gardens.

And Scottish-like, indeed, is the famous Fundy fog which sometimes creeps in from the bay to cover the land with an anonymous blanket of mist. Just the kind of weather in which you might expect to glimpse the lanterns of the *Marie Celeste,* a ghostly ship whose crew disappeared mysteriously in the middle of the sea. Occasionally she's reported off these shores although she has long lain on the bottom near some faraway shore.

219

Although it is said there are more clans represented in Nova Scotia than in Scotland itself, it is not all Scottish. In Cheticamp and Margaree, in Cape Breton, and from Yarmouth to Digby on the Evangeline trail, the language of the friendly Acadians is French. In Lunenburg and New Germany, on the south shore, the food and warm hospitality shows more than a bit of German and Dutch background. And 5,400 of the original people, the Micmac Indians, still live on a number of reserves around the province.

There's something about the way this lobster-shaped peninsula juts out into the Atlantic that gives it an air of dreamy isolation. Because it almost touches the Gulf Stream on the Northumberland Strait shore, the seawater there is warmer than most of the New England coast.

Made up of the beautiful mountainous island of Cape Breton and the agricultural, seafaring peninsula which is attached to New Brunswick, Nova Scotia reaches out toward Maine. Between green clad capes and bold headlands are countless beaches. The whole province, second smallest in Canada, is only 560 kilometers (350 miles) long with no part more than 56 kilometers (35 miles) from the sea. Motoring is therefore ideal on wide paved roads with informative road signs to make it easy to find your way to even the most secluded spots.

From tiny towns nestled between apple orchards or dominated by a lighthouse, to lovely Halifax, the capital, and one of Canada's more sophisticated maritime cities, you'll find Nova Scotia historic, scenic, and refreshing.

The Vikings may have seen its shores around A.D. 1,000. One of the oldest European settlements in North America was established at Port Royal, on the Bay of Fundy, in 1605. And the area was of pivotal importance during the French and English wars of the seventeenth and eighteenth centuries that determined the future of Canada. The French fortress at Louisbourg, Cape Breton, one of the most ambitious historical reconstructions ever undertaken in Canada, and the Citadel, which dominates downtown Halifax, are but two of the many fortified remains of that period.

The Tides of History

As early as 1518 and again in 1523, French expeditions tried—with no success—to establish permanent settlements in the area. The first Europeans to colonize the region were French explorers de Monts and Champlain who secured their "Habitation" in 1605 near present day Port Royal and called it Acadia. Eight years earlier, British navigators John and Sebastian Cabot had stopped briefly on the northern tip of Cape Breton, claimed the entire continent for England, and then moved on. It was not until 1621, when King James I of England and VI of Scotland granted the province to Sir William Alexander, that the British made their first attempt to settle in Nova Scotia, the first British colony to possess its own flag. Derived from the original arms presented by King James, it is made up of the blue cross of St. Andrew with a shield depicting the red lion of Scotland. A new order of knighthood—the Baronets of Nova Scotia—was created and each knight was awarded a grant in the new territory. Although the scheme to colonize the area failed after a few years, the Order still exists.

The French were more successful at colonization but less so at retaining their territory. The entire region was the scene of continuing French/British conflict for supremacy over all of Canada in the 17th and early 18th centuries until the Treaty of Utrecht transferred Nova Scotia to British rule in 1713. Cape Breton Island (a separate province until 1820) remained French for a short time thereafter.

Although the French struggled to preserve their beachheads in the British part of the province, disaster struck in 1755 when they were driven from the province by British troops who questioned their loyalty. Some journeyed to Quebec, Prince Edward Island, or Cape Breton Island; others set out for Louisiana where their descendants are known today as "Cajuns," a corruption of "Acadians." Henry Wadsworth Longfellow, 19th-century American poet, immortalized the tragedy of the forced evacuation in *Evangeline:* "Waste all those pleasant farms and the farmers forever departed!" In return Acadians immortalized both Longfellow and *Evangeline.* There are stone monuments to the poet and his creation in the Grand Pré National Historic Park, although according to historians Longfellow never set foot in Nova Scotia.

The Acadians' lands were quickly settled with thousands of New England "planters," who were British Empire Loyalists escaping the American Revolution. The Acadians who managed to return to their former holdings found them occupied. Moving further down the Nova Scotia coast, they settled the area between Yarmouth and Digby—where the Acadian language and traditions are maintained to this day.

The Treaty of 1763 gave Britain permanent possession of Nova Scotia and most of what is now eastern Canada; France relinquished all claims, including Cape Breton Island, except for the tiny islands of St. Pierre and Miquelon which remain French Departments to this day.

Until 1784, Nova Scotia included what is now the province of New Brunswick. Following the influx of tens of thousands of United Empire Loyalists to the enlarged Nova Scotia, the separation of the New Brunswick portion was accomplished.

Early in 1800, the Highland Scots began to arrive; within 30 years more than 50,000 had settled in Cape Breton, and Pictou and Antigonish counties. Present-day Scots have maintained their Highland tradition, taking a fierce pride in the Gaelic language, the kilt, bagpipes, and traditional dances. Today, no parade in Nova Scotia is complete without a pipe band, (bagpipe, that is), and throughout the summer there are numerous Highland Games, gatherings, and concerts.

After the American Revolution, about 25,000 American colonists, with strong ties of allegiance to England, migrated to Nova Scotia where they founded Shelburne. In the war of 1812, Nova Scotia was the leading British base in North America.

The colony became the first one in British North America to achieve representative government—government elected by the people. That happened in 1758. In 1848 it became the first part of Canada to achieve "responsible" government—in which the cabinet was chosen from the elected members rather than appointed by the crown.

Industry in Nova Scotia

Nova Scotia has a highly diversified economy. Manufacturing takes many forms—from electronics to textiles to steel—in both large and small plants. Fishing is obviously a major activity, but so are forestry, agriculture, and even tourism. One interesting note with regard to forestry is that the county of Lunenburg is considered the Christmas tree capital of North America. Hundreds of thousands of cultivated firs are shipped from there every autumn. Manufacturing is dominated by the French multinational company, Michelin Tires Ltd., which has three tire-making plants in the province. Another dominating installation is the steel mill at Sydney, which employs several thousand people. Sydney is the only other city in the province apart from Halifax and Dartmouth, which form one metropolitan area. Shipbuilding and ship repair are also important throughout the province, while Halifax, of course, is a major Canadian port and naval base.

Mining has been an up and down affair over the decades. There was a short-lived gold rush in the late 1800's, then a decline, and now there's a revival in mining generally. Around the turn of the century, Nova Scotia was a major gold producer. Today there is evidence of this prosperity in heaps of mine tailings and abandoned pits on remote back roads in areas such as Moose River Gold Mines off Highway 7, or at The Ovens, near Lunenburg, where there's a local museum on gold mining.

Coal mining has had a checkered history in Nova Scotia, bringing vast fortunes to a few industrialists and little more than bitter memories to the miners early in the 20th century. As oil became more common, the collieries declined, and in 1969, the Canadian government set up the Cape Breton Development Corporation to wind down the mines and transfer the miners to other work. After the rapid rise in oil prices since 1973, coal has again become a valued resource. Several new mines have been opened in the Cape Breton coalfield, employing thousands of miners.

Tourists may take mine tours in Springhill, a town built above the deepest coal mines in Canada, and in Cape Breton at Glace Bay and Sydney Mines. The Miners' Museum at Glace Bay has an excellent layout and display area, including reproductions of typical early buildings from the mining towns.

History Preserved and Polished

The province abounds in historic homes, building sites, and other attractions that have been maintained or restored by the provincial and federal governments. There are eight specially designated tourist routes that cover most of the areas of interest. These follow mostly the old trunk highways that wind their way through the villages and towns. Traffic is usually light on these roads, since the province also has a network of modern superhighways for through traffic.

The South Shore (Lighthouse Route) between Halifax and Yarmouth is often called the quintessential Nova Scotia. It features intriguing fishing villages and small towns nestled in a sometimes rugged, sometimes gentle coastline loaded with seafaring tradition. Near Mahone Bay, for instance, there's the famous Oak Island money pit—an ingeniously designed pit believed to have held pirate treasure but which defies sure explanation to this day. Peggy's Cove—the province's showpiece fishing village—is on this route. So is Lunenburg, site of the Fishermen's Museum, a small town which is pretty well the Canadian capital of the fishing tradition.

The Annapolis Valley route (Evangeline Trail) takes you past Annapolis Royal, the site of Samuel de Champlain's 1605 settlement; the entire downtown has recently received an historic facelift with numerous old buildings being restored. Nearby is North America's first tidal power plant on the Annapolis River. The valley is also a very scenic drive.

The Fundy Shore (Glooscap Trail) runs along the site of the world's highest tides, where ships rest on the bottom and fishermen collect their catch on foot at low tide. The cliffs contain a wealth of fossils, especially near Joggins. And Cape Blomidon Provincial Park located here is as lovely a spot as you'll find anywhere.

The Eastern Shore (Marine Drive) follows the ever-captivating Atlantic coast from Halifax to Cape Breton, with a high point at Sherbrooke Village, the province's main 19th-century reconstructed historic village.

The Northumberland Shore (Sunrise Trail) has plenty of beach and warm water for swimming—the only part of the province that has it.

Cape Breton has three trails. There's the Cabot Trail with its breathtaking views—one of the most gripping marine drives on the continent. The Fleur-de-Lis Trail goes to the reconstructed fortress at Louisbourg and some Acadian parts of Cape Breton, while the Ceilidh (pronounced *kay-lee*) Trail takes you to places like St. Ann's, Baddeck, and other centers of the province's rich Scottish-Gaelic heritage.

The Climate

Weather in Nova Scotia depends on the area. Inland, the temperatures tend to be more extreme, roughly −10 to −1°C. in January and 11 to 29°C. in summer (13–30°F. in January and 52–75°F. in summer), than temperatures along the coast. Along the coast, weather tends to be more variable, particularly in winter, changing as much as 23°C. (45°F.) over an eight-hour period. Precipitation may be snow inland and rain along the coast. While the ocean causes variable weather, it also warms the land, keeping the province relatively warm in winter and cooler in the summer.

Each season brings its own pleasures. In the spring (mid-April to the end of May), days are mild, nights are cool. A season of crocuses, tulips, and budding trees. Average temperatures: 7 to 14°C. (45–58°F.).

Summer (June, July, August) is time for fun in the sun. Even the hottest summer day is cooled in the evenings by soft ocean breezes. Be prepared for the occasional summer shower and, for comfort, take a light sweater for evening. Temperatures range from 18 to 32°C. (65–90°F.).

No part of Nova Scotia—54,390 sq. kms. (21,000 square miles)—is more than 56 kms. (35 miles) from the sea. During July, August, and even into early September the many sandy beaches are well used. For comfort, saltwater swimming should be restricted to the Northumberland Strait coast where water temperature will reach up to 21°C. (70°F.). On the other coasts the water temperature is distinctly cool, and so cold in the Bay of Fundy as to be dangerous to swimmers. A number of beach areas on all coasts have been developed by the provincial government and several have supervised swimming areas. These vary from year to year. Check with the Department of Tourism for an up-to-date list.

Indian Summer (September) is one of the favorite times of year for travelers to Nova Scotia. Days are warm, but not hot; evenings crisp, but not cold. Expect temperatures from 18 to 23°C. (65–75°F.), cooling to 15°C. (60°F.) at night.

Autumn (October) brings on Nova Scotia's most colorful season. Leaves turn first in the inland areas; then, in a predictable 2-week period, the vibrant colors spread to the coast. Temperatures hover between 13 and 18°C. (55–65°F.), cooling at night.

Autumn travel has become more popular in recent years. During July and August, accommodations and the better service facilities are usually taxed to the limit, and charge high season rates. After September 1, the traffic flow dwindles considerably and travel operations become less crowded.

Particularly in the Cabot Trail region of Cape Breton and certain sections of the Annapolis Valley, the brilliant autumn leaves combined with clear, crisp weather bring out native Nova Scotians as well as visitors. The best fall colors can usually be seen during the first two weeks of October, depending on the preceding weather.

In winter, November days are blustery and snowfalls begin in time for a white Christmas. Snows are intermittent and rarely predictable from December through March.

Cape Breton/Cabot Trail

With dramatic seascapes, rugged highlands, and lovely, old fishing villages, Cape Breton, the island part of Nova Scotia, is the province's most popular tourist area. The Cabot Trail, some 278 kms. (172 miles) of mountain and sea on a circular loop, is one of the most spectacular day drives in North America in any season. The controversy that rages as to whether one should drive the trail in a clockwise or counterclockwise direction is usually settled in favor of the clockwise direction. This puts the sun to the side of the car or behind it, and allows driving on the "inside"—next to the mountain rather than the cliff, so that the steepest grades are descended rather than climbed. Part of the Cabot Trail lies within the Cape Breton Highlands National Park, but no entrance fee is required unless specific Park facilities are to be used.

The Bras d'Or Lakes form a large inland salt lake which has become popular with yachting enthusiasts. Most of them headquarter at the Baddeck Yacht Club and spend days cruising the sheltered inland sea.

Cape Breton has a history of chronic unemployment due to the unsteady fortunes of the coal and steel industries. As a result, much of the Sydney—Glace Bay industrial area and environs have acquired a permanently depressed appearance. Yet the people are friendly and the place has its own rough charm. The traditions of steelworking and coalmining are cherished despite the hard times they evoke.

The Scottish tradition is still very strong in Cape Breton, particularly around the Baddeck-Iona region. Many people still speak Gaelic and the Gaelic College in St. Ann's is unique on this continent with its summer courses in piping, highland dancing, and Gaelic language.

HALIFAX

Founded in 1749 by Lord Cornwallis, Halifax—capital of Nova Scotia, largest city in the Atlantic Provinces, and one of the oldest cities in Canada—today combines the best of the colonial heritage with contemporary life.

Originally a military and naval base designed to defend the British colonies and also to counteract the defenses raised by the French at Cape Breton Island at Louisbourg, Halifax—built on a small peninsula —protected its harbor by a series of fortifications including the Citadel, which became the mightiest fortress in British North America and is now an historic site.

A Spectacular Harbor

Enjoying the benefits of one of the finest harbors in the world, Halifax is joined to the city of Dartmouth to the northeast by two suspension bridges. The "old bridge," the Angus L. Macdonald Bridge, was opened in 1955 and is some 1597 meters (5,239 feet) long. The "new bridge," the A. Murray McKay Bridge, was opened in 1970. The toll on both bridges starts at 25¢ for cars in either direction. The tollbooths are on the Dartmouth side of the bridges.

At the foot of both cities is the harbor where the shipping of the world ties up. The busy container port often operates around-the-clock.

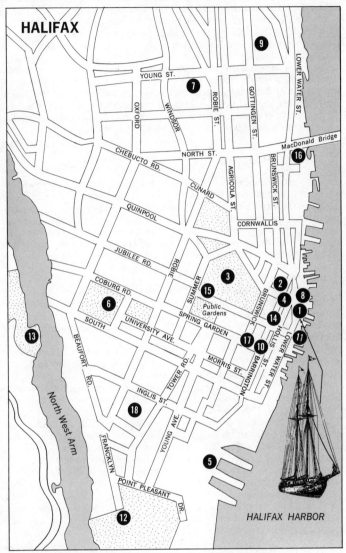

Halifax—Points of Interest

1) Bluenose II Wharf
2) Chateau Halifax
3) Citadel
4) City Hall
5) Container Port
6) Dalhousie University
7) Exhibition Grounds
8) Fisherman's Market
9) Fort Needham
10) Government House
11) Maritime Museum
12) Martello Tower
13) Memorial Tower
14) Neptune Theater
15) Nova Scotia Museum
16) Old Dutch Church
17) St. Mary's Basilica
18) St. Mary's University

While one ship may be loading grain for eastern Europe, another is off-loading automobiles from the Orient at the Autoport.

Halifax/Dartmouth is the home of the Canadian Forces Maritime Command (Atlantic), and the sleek gray warships are a common sight under the two massive suspension bridges spanning the harbor.

Together, Halifax and Dartmouth form the largest metropolitan area east of Montréal. With a population of some 280,000 people, they are the major urban center for almost half of Nova Scotia as well as the business, financial, educational (also medical; most of the major hospitals are located here), and shopping center for Atlantic Canada. The area is also the seat of provincial government and headquarters for most government offices, both federal and provincial.

"Historic Properties"

The combination of old and new in Halifax is nowhere more apparent than in and around the area known as *Historic Properties*. Only one block away is the ultramodern Scotia Square, a shopping-office-apartment-hotel complex. High-rise office and apartment buildings spear the skyline in downtown Halifax, yet Historic Properties is only a few steps away. A joint development of the City of Halifax, Historic Properties Ltd., a Halifax company, and the federal department of Indian and Northern Affairs, the area has 12 buildings, of which several date back to the early 1800's.

When the area was originally built in the 1800's, it was the center of business for the young city. The Privateer's Warehouse was a stone building which housed the cargoes captured by Nova Scotia schooners serving as privateers until the captured ships and cargoes could be auctioned off by the Admiralty.

Collins Bank was the headquarters of Nova Scotia entrepreneur Enos Collins. When Collins died in 1871, he was reported to be the richest man in British North America.

The block of North American Renaissance buildings on Granville Street, between Duke and Buckingham, was constructed after the great Halifax fire of 1859, which razed the area. Designed by William Thomas, architect, of Toronto, the buildings were not all built at the same time but all exhibit a common theme and exterior format. Some of the storefronts which still remain were fabricated of cast iron and were probably designed by Bogardus. The only way to tell if they are metal is to test with a magnet. While many of the details of the architectural extravagances of the 1870's have been obliterated by time, the original elegance may still be seen in the tall windows and storefront designs. That part of Granville Street is now a strictly pedestrian area.

Between June and October in Historic Properties you can hear the town crier, take helicopter, sternwheeler, walking, and bus tours, *Bluenose II* tours, and enjoy numerous special events, such as historical feasts of the 1840s.

Saved by the People

Early in the 1960's, the Historic Properties area was slated for demolition to make way for a superhighway along the waterfront. A successful campaign by civic groups saved the area from the wrecker's ball and the City of Halifax, which owns most of the property, called for redevelopment plans to restore the buildings to their original appearance on the exterior, while retaining commercially usable interiors.

The buildings have nooks and crannies in interesting locations, arches and odd-shaped windows, stucco and wooden beams—all of those beautiful "useless" architectural appendages which modern designers seem to eliminate in their functional steel and glass buildings.

The buildings of Historic Properties once again hear the footsteps of Haligonians (inhabitants of Halifax) and visitors alike walking the old cobblestone streets and shopping for wares in shops featuring handmade articles—leather, wood, glass, and ceramic. There are law offices, federal and provincial government offices, the campus of the Nova Scotia College of Art and Design, and restaurants and pubs. Nova Scotia's floating ambassador, the schooner *Bluenose II,* docks at Privateer's Wharf, just as vessels tied up there 200 years ago. Instead of loading the exotic plunder of faraway countries, *Bluenose II* lowers the gangplank for visitors to enjoy a cruise out in Halifax Harbour during summer afternoons and evenings.

One block up from Historic Properties is the new Barrington Hotel, which continues the tradition of revitalizing old buildings. Its exterior was rebuilt with the original granite from the façade of an entire city block, but the interior contains a modern hotel and two levels of boutiques, craftshops, restaurants, and some of the city's finest stores. It is also linked to Scotia Square, the main downtown shopping, hotel and office complex.

A couple of blocks to the south along Upper Water Street is a new waterfront development that includes the Maritime Museum of the Atlantic. Displays that describe Nova Scotia's golden age of sail, when the province's flag was seen in ports around the world, dominate. The main display is docked outside, however. It's a 900-ton hydrographic ship, the *Acadia,* which charted the Labrador and Arctic coasts early in this century. Admission to all these attractions, free.

Between the museum and Historic Properties, the Halifax-Dartmouth ferries chug in and out of a new terminal. It's a cheap (35¢) sightseeing tour in itself.

Plenty of Open Space

With such development in the middle of the downtown core, one might assume that the Halifax/Dartmouth metro area is not an entirely relaxing place in which to live and work. Although there is the hustle and bustle associated with any city, both cities are blessed with hundreds of acres of open green park and recreation space as well as salt- and freshwater recreation areas which can be used by the area's residents.

The North West Arm, Halifax Harbour, and Bedford Basin are dotted with pleasure boats of all shapes and sizes during the season which runs from spring to "frostbite" time in November. Dartmouth has no less than 22 lakes within the city limits.

No Longer Drab

Halifax was once appropriately known as the "gray city." Its dour and somber appearance has been replaced since the mid-60's with the establishment of new business and shopping centers, a night life which is interesting, and the vibrant atmosphere associated with a growing city.

Part of the drab reputation that once tagged the city comes from its long history as a military port. Here, roaming press gangs kidnapped unsuspecting young men from the streets and forced them into service aboard British naval ships.

Fort Needham, a long hill in the north end of Halifax, has been developed as a memorial park and offers a panoramic view of the area devastated in the Great Halifax Explosion on December 6, 1917. The explosion, the largest single man-made blast prior to the atomic bomb, was caused when a munitions ship collided with another vessel in the harbor. Two thousand fatalities were recorded, 10,000 more suffered serious injuries, 25,000 were left homeless, and the shockwave was felt in the town of Truro, more than 60 miles away.

One of the most pleasant spots in summertime Halifax is the Public Gardens on Spring Garden Road. Preserving much of the original landscape design (1753), the 18 acres have formal gardens, a large pond for ducks, geese and swans, lawns, a wide variety of exotic plants and trees, fountains, and plenty of park benches for quiet enjoyment. At noon, take in the front lawn of the Halifax Regional Library on Spring Garden Road. Live entertainment, either structured or impromptu, makes a snack from the street vendors or at one of the nearby restaurants that much more relaxing and enjoyable.

Most visitors to Halifax take one of the excellent water tours. The famous *Bluenose II* sailing schooner takes passengers on harbor cruises from Privateer's Wharf, as does a company called Halifax Water Tours. Harbour Island Tours leaves from the new Marine Museum of the Atlantic and takes passengers to historic and mysterious McNab's Island at the harbor mouth for a two-hour walking tour.

The best view of the city is from the ring-road around the top of the Citadel, the old fort which dominates the Halifax skyline near the waterfront.

Fairview, a suburb of Halifax, has its own recollections. It was here that recovered victims of the *Titanic* disaster (1912) were buried.

Halifax in Sun and Rain

Summer evenings bring out locals and visitors along the pathways of the Commons in the center of Halifax to enjoy amateur sports or just to walk about.

Halifax is a quiet, clean, and pleasant city but a couple of cautions are in order. Food and accommodations can be expensive and parking is a problem in the downtown area of Halifax. The best bet is to head for either the Scotia Square Parking Garages which usually have some space, or the Historic Properties parking area on the waterfront.

In the rain, take refuge in the provincial pioneer and military museums inside the Citadel and the Nova Scotia Museum on Summer Street; the latter features natural history and has supervised programs, mainly for children. The new Marine Museum of the Atlantic on Lower Water Street displays the seagoing tradition of the east coast. The Dartmouth Heritage Museum exhibits early history, while the suburban Cole Harbour Heritage Farm features agricultural history. Art galleries at St. Mary's, Dalhousie, and Mount St. Vincent universities, as well as the New Art Gallery of Nova Scotia, have regular exhibitions.

One can even don rainwear on damp days and walk to Point Pleasant Park's Black Rock to watch ships come and go only a few hundred yards away. Ship watching is equally pleasant in fine weather. Be sure to look for some of the Scottish heather here—apparently the only location in North America where the plant grows wild. The seeds came from mattresses shaken out by British sailors many decades ago.

Halifax is a city to explore. The old and new stand side by side in a fine blend. The only shots to be fired from the Citadel are the cannon announcing the arrival of noon each day—a custom which is still preserved, much to the shock of unwary passersby.

PRACTICAL INFORMATION FOR

HALIFAX/DARTMOUTH

HOW TO GET THERE. By Plane. *Air Canada* provides regular, daily flights to Nova Scotia from New York, Boston, Toronto, Montreal, and St. John's, NF, with world-wide connections through all these gateways except St. John's. *CP Air's* Canadian and worldwide routes connect in Toronto and Montreal and some fly nonstop to Halifax. They also fly throughout the Atlantic provinces and provide a direct link with Amsterdam.

By car: Most highways in Nova Scotia lead to Halifax/Dartmouth. Hwys. 3/103, 7, 2/102 and 1/101 terminate in the twin cities. Hwy. 104, the Trans-Canada Hwy. from Amherst at the New Brunswick border joins Rtes. 2/102 at Truro.

By bus: Within Nova Scotia, Halifax is served by *Acadian Lines Limited;* along the South Shore only, service is operated by *MacKenzie Bus Lines. Greyhound,* from New York, and *Voyageur Inc.,* from Montreal, connect with *SMT* in New Brunswick which, in turn, connects with *Acadian Lines* in Nova Scotia at Amherst; intraprovincial bus lines link most major communities.

By train: *Via Rail* passenger services serve Halifax from most major Canadian centers. From the United States, *Amtrak* connections may be made in Montréal.

ACCOMMODATIONS. Accommodation in Halifax/Dartmouth is generally comfortable and reservations are a necessity any time of year. Reservations can be made by calling the toll-free numbers listed in the *Tourist Information* section. Hotel/motel rates in Halifax/Dartmouth, based on double occupancy, are categorized as follows: *Expensive,* $44 or more; *Moderate,* $33 to $44; *Inexpensive,* less than $33.

The 10% provincial sales tax is added to all hotel/motel rates.

Most places accept the following major credit cards: American Express, MasterCard and Visa; others may also be honored. Not all establishments accept credit cards, therefore we suggest you call for information.

Halifax

Expensive

Auberge Wandlyn Inn. 50 Bedford Hwy., NS B3M 2J2 (902–443–0416). About 15 min. from downtown. 74 rooms, some with a good view over Bedford Basin. Coffee bar, licensed dining room. Pets permitted. Off-season rates, Oct.–June. All major credit cards.

Best Western Dresden Arms. 5330 Artillery Pl., NS B3J 3G6 (902–422–1625). 94 rooms in pleasant surroundings off the main street but still downtown. Dining room usually good. Pool, sauna, whirlpool, and exercise area. Major credit cards.

Chateau Halifax. 1990 Barrington St., NS B3J 1P2 (902–425–6700 or 800–268–9411). A CP hotel, with 305 rooms. The rooms are better than average, but the corridors are dark and narrow. Heated indoor–outdoor pool, sauna, dining room, pub, and lounges. The best part of this hotel is that it is part of the big Scotia Square shopping–office complex. All major credit cards.

Citadel Inn. 1960 Brunswick St., NS B3J 2G7 (902–422–1391 or 800–565–7162). 189 excellent rooms, quiet lounge, and dining room. Patronized by businesspeople and sales personnel. All major credit cards.

The Delta Barrington. 1875 Barrington, NS B3J 3L6 (902–429–7410 or 800–268–1133). Part of a shopping and convention complex incorporating the reconstructed facade of an entire historic city block. No charge for children under 18 sharing their parents' room. All major credit cards.

Halifax Sheraton. 1919 Upper Water St., NS B3J 3J5 (902–421–1700). About 350 rooms. Elegant hotel on the harborfront with the Cafe Maritime, a fine restaurant, live piano entertainment in the lobby, and docking space for yachts.

Holiday Inn. 1980 Robie St. (at the Willow Tree), NS B3H 3G5 (902–423–1161). Better-than-average Holiday Inn, with 237 rooms, indoor pool, sauna, rooms for the handicapped, dining room, lounge, and pub. All major credit cards.

Keddy's Halifax Hotel. 20 Margaret's Bay Rd., NS B3N 1J4 (902–477–5611). About 15 min. from downtown, in Armdale. Part of a chain. About 125 units (7 efficiencies), of adequate quality; pool, sauna. Off-season rates, Nov.–May. All major credit cards.

The Lord Nelson Hotel. 1515 St. Park St., NS B3J 2T3 (902–423–6331). A local landmark, opposite the Public Gardens. 320 rooms, popular lounge. Major credit cards.

The Prince George Hotel. 1725 Market St., NS B3J 2X1 (902–425–1986 or 800–565–1567). New and luxurious, over 200 rooms, restaurants, lounges, pub, pool, sauna, exercise rooms. Connected by tunnel to World Trade and Convention Center and Metro center.

Inexpensive

Waken'n Eggs Bed and Breakfast. 2114 Windsor St., NS B3K 5B4 (902–422–4737). Three rooms in Victorian home. Private or shared bath. Full breakfast included.

YMCA. 1656 S. Park St. NS (902–422–6437). 68 pleasant rooms for men with full use of Y facilities: sauna, pool, gym, and squash. Downtown location. Visa only.

YWCA. 1239 Barrington St. NS (902–423–6162). 12 pleasant rooms for women, with use of Y facilities. No credit cards.

Dartmouth

Expensive

The Atlantic Inn. 739 Windmill Rd. B3B 1C1 (902–469–0810). 92 units near Dartmouth Industrial Park. Coffee shop, licensed dining and lounge. Off season rates October to April. All major credit cards.

Holiday Inn. 99 Wyse Rd. at MacDonald Bridge, B3A 1L9 (902–463–1100). 120 rooms with no surprises; dining room with less than adequate food and lounge. Outdoor pool. Off-season rates October to May. All major credit cards.

HOW TO GET AROUND. Walking or bicycling is a good way to get around many areas of downtown Halifax and Dartmouth. In downtown Halifax, in particular, parking may be a problem during the business day.

By taxi: Taxi rates start at $1.20 and meter up based on mileage and time combined. A crosstown trip should cost about $4.00 to $5.00, depending on traffic. Hailing taxis on the street is often difficult. Call a stand and have the taxi pick you up.

By bus: The *Metropolitan Transit Commission* operates a bus system covering the entire metropolitan area. Basic fare is 60¢, and exact change is needed. Call 426–6600 for information.

By ferry: The *Dartmouth Ferry Commission* operates two passenger ferries from the George Street terminal in Halifax to the Portland Street terminal in Dartmouth. Ferries operate from 6 A.M. to midnight on half-hour and hourly schedules. Fare for a single crossing is 35¢. Call 466–2215 for schedules and information.

TOURIST INFORMATION. *For Nova Scotia.* Write Nova Scotia Department of Tourism, P.O. Box 130, Halifax, Nova Scotia, Canada, B3J 2M7. Phone: (902) 424–4247.

Call-toll free: in continental U.S.A. (except Alaska and Maine), 1–800–341–6096; in Maine, 1–800–492–0643; Canada-wide, 1–800–565–7166; in the Maritime Provinces, 1–800–565–7105; in Newfoundland and Québec, 1–800–565–7180; in Ontario, 1–800–565–7140; in British Columbia, 112–800–565–7166. You can also make hotel and motel reservations through these numbers.

Tourist information desks are located on the ferries to Nova Scotia from Port-aux-Basques and Argentia, Nfld. At Bar Harbour and Portland, Me., tourist-information desks are inside the ferry terminals. These ferries go to Yarmouth on a daily basis. And the N.S. Department of Tourism operates a tourist information center at Port Hastings on the Cape Breton side of the Canso Causeway (625–9991), and at Pictou, a few miles from the landing of the Wood Island Ferry from P.E.I. (485–6213).

You will find provincially operated tourist bureaus at Yarmouth and Digby near the ferry wharves; at Antigonish on the Trans-Canada Hwy.; near the Halifax International Airport; at Amherst near the New Brunswick border; and at the Pictou Rotary a few miles from the ferry landing from Prince Edward Island. Most are open from 8 A.M. to 8 P.M. from mid-May to the end of October, and at the Red Store, Historic Properties, Halifax, year-round. You're generally no more than 15 miles from a tourist bureau anywhere in the province.

For Cape Breton: Write The Cape Breton Tourist Association, 20 Keltic Dr., Sydney River, N.S., Canada B1S 1P5. Telephone (902) 539–9876.

From June to September the Tourist Association distributes a free monthly guide to events and places called *What's Happening,* which you'll find in restaurants, motels, and tourist bureaus.

Park information centers are located at both the Ingonish and Cheticamp entrances to Cape Breton Highlands National Park.

The Red Store, Historic Properties, Halifax—The City *of Halifax,* the *National Parks Department* and the *Nova Scotia Department of Tourism* all operate information centers in the Red Store. For city information, call 421–8736; for provincial information call 424–4247; for national parks information call 426–3436. Offices open year-round. Also, there's a year-round information center at Halifax International Airport (861–3184).

The City of Dartmouth operates a tourist bureau on Thistle St. from mid-May to mid-October. Call 421–2319 during the open season, and 421–2220 off-season.

Throughout the province there are some 40 tourist information bureaus run by local municipalities and boards of trade.

RECOMMENDED READING. The novels of Thomas Raddall (and, to some extent, Will R. Bird) give a vital and colorful account of the province's rich history. Raddall's *Halifax: Warden of the North* has been called a model of local history. The speeches, essays and poems of Joseph Howe are compiled in several anthologies; Howe was the greatest political and intellectual leader in 19th century Nova Scotia. Thomas Chandler Haliburton's *The Clockmaker* set out to scourge the Bluenoses for their want of thrift and industry; it became the first Canadian book to achieve international fame. Haliburton learned his satiric trade in part from Thomas McCulloch, a pioneer clergyman, satirist and educator (among other things, he was the first president of Dalhousie University), whose sharp satiric portrait of Pictou, *The Stepsure Letters,* is still in print and still funny.

The fiction of Ernest Buckler (particularly *The Mountain and the Valley* and *Oxbells and Fireflies*) and of Charles Bruce (*The Channel Shore*) are meditative, beautifully written portrayals of the traditional Nova Scotian lifestyle. Helen Crieghton's *Bluenose Magic* and *Bluenose Ghosts* reveal the depth of folklore in the province.

Recent Nova Scotia fiction includes Chipman Hall's *Lightly,* Alistair MacLeod's *The Lost Salt Gift of Blood,* and Susan Kerslake's *Middlewatch.* Recent nonfiction may be represented by Harry Bruce's *Lifeline,* the story of the Maritime ferry system, and by Silver Donald Cameron's account of the great fishing strike of 1970/71, *The Education of Everett Richardson.* Jim and Pat Lotz have written a comprehensive volume, *Cape Breton Island. Nova Scotia in Your Pocket* by John Prince is a good general guide.

BUSINESS HOURS. Most stores are open between 9 or 10 A.M. until 9 P.M., Wednesdays, Thursdays, and Fridays. On Monday, Tuesday, and Saturday, they close at 6 P.M.

Banks are open 10 A.M. to 3 P.M. generally; most stay open until 4 P.M. Thursdays and Fridays, while some stay open until 5. A few banks in the shopping centers keep shopping center hours.

SEASONAL EVENTS. Every year the N.S. Department of Tourism publishes a *Calendar of Events,* free on request, which describes provincial festivals and events. Some highlights:

May: Antique Show & Sale, Halifax; Late May: Apple Blossom festival, Kentville area (one of the major Nova Scotia festivals: it includes dances, parade, sports, entertainment).

June: Mid-June: Annual Summer Antique Sale, Halifax; the Nova Scotia Tattoo, Metro Centre, Halifax.

July: In Dartmouth, the Festival of Piping; later in the month, Halifax Natal Day (road races, rock concerts, band concerts, parade in the morning, children's program, barbecue, sports events, rock dance, fireworks).

August: Halifax and Dartmouth Natal Day Celebrations; Mid-August: Halifax Citadel Festival of History.

September: The Joseph Howe Festival (oratorical contest, pony express ride, pancake breakfasts, open-air and craft markets, dances, concerts, beer fests, parade, whaler races, bazaar, multicultural concert, town crier championships, and international dory races).

October: Antique Show and Sale, with paintings by maritime artists, Halifax; International Town Crier Championship at Halifax.

FREE EVENTS. The programs listed in the *Children's Activities* section are free. So is entry to all the city's museums and other public cultural facilities. Participation in the various cultural festivals is without charge. And the Sunday-afternoon band concerts at the Public Gardens are free as well.

TOURS. Both the *Metropolitan Transit Commission* and *Gray Line* (operated by Acadian Bus Lines) have coach tours of Halifax, each lasting about two hours. The Gray Line tour may be boarded at the Acadian Lines terminal on Almon Street, and at most major hotels. For times and information call 454–9321. *Halifax Transit* tours may be boarded at Historic Properties. Call 421–6600 for full information. Cost of both tours is about $4.00 ($1.50 for children).

Halifax Water Tours operates an excellent 2-hour boat tour of Halifax Harbour and the Northwest Arm leaving from Privateers Wharf four times daily, June 16–September 9, with fewer tours daily starting June 1 and lasting to Oct. 13. The tour boat is comfortable and licensed; commentary by the hostesses is very good. For information and times call 423–7783 or 425–1271. The cost is about $6.00 per person ($2.00 for children).

During most of July, August, and September, visitors may enjoy a sail on a Halifax Harbour cruise aboard *Bluenose II,* the 143-foot replica of the famous Nova Scotia sailing schooner. A 2-hour sail costs about $9.00 per person ($4.00 for children, $4.50 for senior citizens) and the vessel leaves from her wharf at Historic Properties. For information on sailing times, call 422–2678, or 424–4247.

One unique package involves a sail to McNab's Island, at the mouth of Halifax Harbour, for a 2-hour walking tour. The name of the company is *Harbour Island Tours,* and it leaves twice daily through most of the summer from near the Maritime Museum of the Atlantic. Phone 422–9523.

Further information on day charters, boat rentals and cruises can be obtained from the Nova Scotia Department of Tourism's publication, *Sports and Activities,* P.O. Box 456, Halifax, N.S. B3J 2R5.

The Halifax, Dartmouth, or Provincial tourist bureaus have details of a number of well-organized self-drive tours of the area. Walking tours of historic sites in downtown Halifax and Dartmouth are available.

A non-guided tour of Halifax Harbour is as simple as taking a trip on the Dartmouth Ferry on a bright, sunny day. The round trip costs 50¢ and takes 45 minutes to an hour. Passengers can sit outside on the top of the ferry.

A Cyclist's Guide to Nova Scotia is available from N.S. Tourism and local sports stores. Halifax is an easy city to explore by bike.

PARKS. *Point Pleasant Park* covers the entire tip of the peninsula of the City of Halifax. As it is a natural woodland park, automobile traffic is banned. Surrounded on three sides by saltwater, there are trails, picnic areas, a swimming beach, and a number of partially ruined fortifications.

Fort Needham, a hill in the north end of Halifax, has been developed as a small park.

Fleming Park on the North West Arm is known locally as "The Dingle." The area was donated to the city by Sir Sandford Fleming, a railroad builder who also invented Standard Time. The tall tower was built to commemorate the first elective assembly held in the British colonies. The view from the top of the tower overlooking the Arm and the City makes the many steps well worth your while.

The Citadel, where candlelit tours and "Cavalier" dinners are sometimes offered (check with Dept. of Tourism), as well as *Horseshoe Island Park* in Halifax are also pleasant.

Many of the 22 lakes in Dartmouth have small parks, beaches, and picnic areas along the shores.

The Halifax Commons is a large area in the center of the city with children's playground, wading pool, ball fields, tennis courts lighted for night play, and lots of grassy area.

GARDENS. The *Halifax Public Gardens,* 18 acres of color in the heart of the City, is a favorite spot for relaxation for visitors and Haligonians. Landscaped originally in 1753, these gardens are among the oldest on the continent. In addition to trees and shrubs from every corner of the globe, there are fountains, a bandstand, and a large pond with various waterbirds. One corner has been set aside as a children's area.

The gardens are open mid-May to mid-November, 8 A.M. to sundown daily. No admission charge.

CHILDREN'S ACTIVITIES. During July and August, the Halifax and Dartmouth Recreation Departments operate summer programs at *school playgrounds,* the *Halifax Commons,* and at the *Dartmouth Lakes.* The playground facilities, including swings and other equipment, wading pool and playground fields at the Halifax Commons may be used without charge.

Dartmouth and Halifax have supervised swimming at many of the lakes and Halifax has supervised salt water swimming at *Point Pleasant* and *Flemming Parks.*

The Nova Scotia Museum, 1747 Summer St., in Halifax has special children's programs throughout the year. Call 429–4610 for information. Free.

For children of all ages, fishing from a waterfront wharf or breakwater on the incoming tide usually yields some small but interesting specimens of salt water fish.

For complete information, call Halifax Recreation at 426–6426; or Dartmouth Recreation at 469–9211.

SPORTS. Halifax is the home of the American Hockey League *Nova Scotia Voyageurs,* a farm team of the Montréal Canadiens. The team plays more than 20 home games from November to April against international competition. For information on game dates and tickets, call 453–4015.

College-level sports events take place throughout the school year. For full information, contact the Halifax Tourist Bureau.

Hard surface *tennis* courts, lighted for night play, are available at the Halifax Commons. For *sailing* enthusiasts there are five yacht clubs in Halifax/Dartmouth. *Canoeing* is a popular sport in Dartmouth and is centered on Lake Banook and Micmac Lake.

Bicycle tours available from Bicycle Nova Scotia, 5516 Spring Garden Road, P.O. Box 3010 Halifax, N.S. B3J3G6 Phone: 425–5450.

For full information on all sports in the Halifax/Dartmouth area, contact the tourist bureau in either city.

HISTORIC SITES. Halifax has three surviving military installations, all of British origin, which once served as essential elements of the defense against the French threat at Louisbourg. The *Citadel,* a star-shaped fort, was begun in 1749. A third version, completed in 1828, now has an excellent military museum and a commanding view of the Nova Scotia capital. Open year-round. Other installations, built in the late 1700's, include the *Prince of Wales Martello Tower* and the *York Redoubt,* which was modified and used throughout the 19th century as part of the harbor defense. Open June 1 to September 30. Telephone: 426–5080. There are also ruins of other fortifications in Point Pleasant Park.

The *Naval Dockyard* on North Barrington St. was begun in 1757 and is still in operation.

Charles Dickens called *Province House* on Hollis St. "a gem of Georgian architecture." The building is still used as the province's legislature and has an excellent library. It is the oldest existing legislative building in Canada.

A number of Halifax churches are historically significant. *St. Matthew's Church* on Barrington St. is very old and has a fine interior. One of the earliest ministers was the great-grandfather of U.S. president Grover Cleveland. *St. George's Round Church* on Brunswick St. was built in 1800 and is a rare example of circular ecclesiastical architecture. *St. Mary's Basilica* on Spring Garden Rd. is a fine granite structure, reputed to have the highest granite spire in the world. *St. Paul's Church* on Barrington St., built in 1749, is the oldest Protestant church in Canada. The *Old Dutch Church* on Brunswick St., built in 1756, was the first Lutheran Church in Canada.

Admission is free to all historic sites.

  MUSEUMS AND GALLERIES. Museums: The *Halifax Citadel National Historic Park* is a hilltop fortress built in 1828 on the site of earlier fortifications dating back to the city's founding in 1749. Dominating the city and offering excellent views, The Citadel houses the Army Museum, depicting the history of colonial warfare. Kilted soldiers drill and there is a unique gift shop. On the fortress grounds is the Old Town Clock, originally built in 1803, and now the unofficial symbol of the city. Parking outside the fortress is limited. There's a tea shop and occasionally a candlelit evening tour and special dinners. Admission free. Open 9 A.M. to 8 P.M., June to October; 10 A.M. to 5 P.M., the rest of the year.

The *Marine Museum of the Atlantic,* 1675 Lower Water St. The seagoing tradition, housed in a restored chandlery and dockside warehouse. It includes, docked outside, the hydrographic ship *Acadia,* which was used to chart the coasts of Labrador and the Arctic earlier in this century. Summer: 9:30 A.M.–5:30 P.M.; Tues. until 8 P.M.; Sun. 1–5:30 P.M. Call 429–8210 for additional information.

The *Maritime Command Museum,* Admiralty House, CFB Stadacona, on Gottigen at Almon St., has military artifacts; open year-round. Free. Phone 472–7740 for hours.

The *Nova Scotia Museum* 1747 Summer Street in Halifax features both permanent exhibits on *Man and His Environment* and general and natural history exhibits of Nova Scotia. Many parts of the museum feature "touch and feel" sections and there are special areas for children's activities. Open daily; call 429–4610 for opening and closing times.

The *Dartmouth Heritage Museum and Art Gallery* 100 Wyse Rd. (463–3183), features displays on early life in Dartmouth and the surrounding area. The art gallery features permanent and traveling exhibits. Open Mon.–Fri., 9 A.M.–9 P.M.; Sat., 9 A.M.–6 P.M.; Sun., 2–5 P.M. Free.

Other museums include *Province House,* the seat of the Nova Scotia government and the oldest legislative building in any Canadian province; *Prince of Wales Martello Tower; York Redoubt National Historic Park;* and the *Public Archives of Nova Scotia* at the corner of Robie St. and University Ave.

Galleries: The *Art Gallery of Nova Scotia,* 6152 Coburg Rd., is the main non-commercial gallery. Open 10 A.M.–5:30 P.M., Mon., Wed., Fri. & Sat.; Tues. & Thurs., 10 A.M.–9 P.M.; Sun., noon–5:30 P.M. Call 424–7542. Free. Others are located at the *Dartmouth Heritage Museum, Mount Saint Vincent University, Dalhousie University* and *St. Mary's University.*

Of the several commercial galleries in Halifax, the best are *Manuge Galleries* on Hollis St. near Sackville; *Zwicker's Gallery* on Doyle St. near Brunswick; *Gallery 1667* in the Promenade Block from the Potomac Bldg., Historic Properties; and *Atlantic Art Gallery* at Hollis and Duke Sts. *Three Oaks Corporation,* 3 Albert St. in Dartmouth is owned and operated by Tom Forrestall, a popular Canadian realist, and his works are featured in this pleasant gallery.

Admission to any of the private or public museums or galleries is free.

MUSIC AND THEATER. The *Rebecca Cohn Auditorium* (sometimes referred to as the *Dalhousie Arts Centre*) is one of Halifax's centers for live concerts and musical presentations featuring international artists, year round. Call 424–2298 for box-office information and bookings.

Major musical presentations in Halifax take place at the *Metro Centre,* a new sports and cultural complex located downtown. For up to date information on what's playing where, check with the Halifax Tourist Bureau.

Neptune Theatre is Nova Scotia's only professional live theater group. Most of their presentations are given at *Neptune Theatre* on Sackville St. Most of the plays are in repertory and offer comedy and drama, both modern and traditional. For box office and information call 429–7300.

A better-than-average amateur group known as the *Kipawo Showboat Company* performs at the new amateur playhouse at Historic Properties. Members perform mostly musicals. What they lack in professional polish they make up in enthusiasm, offering an evening of theater that is fun.

SHOPPING. There are several specialty shopping areas in Halifax. The Spring Garden Rd. area is the older one with more traditional goods, particularly British imports. The newer and more exquisite area is actually in the oldest part of Halifax— *Historic Properties* and the *Barrington Inn* complex —where you can find fine crafts in such stores as the Pewter House, Nova Pine, and The Eskimo Gallery, as well as top line manufactured goods. A block away, in the *Scotia Square* complex, is the city's main downtown mall for day-to-day shopping. The principal suburban shopping centers are *Micmac Mall* in Dartmouth and the *Halifax Shopping Center,* the *Maritime Mall,* and *Bayer's Road Shopping Center* in Halifax.

RESTAURANTS. Dining out in Halifax/Dartmouth is usually good to excellent in the better restaurants. Many restaurants are set in refurbished historic homes or other restored quarters.

Service is generally good in the better restaurants, although it can be slow, especially if the place is busy. Your waiter or waitress can usually suggest the best items on the daily menu or the specials of the day.

Restaurants are categorized on the basis of full course dinner, with drinks, tax and tips excluded: *Expensive,* over $17; *Moderate,* $12–$17; *Inexpensive,* under $12. A 10% provincial tax will be added to all meals over $3.00.

Most places accept the following major credit cards: American Express, MasterCard and Visa; others may also be honored. Not all establishments accept credit cards, therefore we suggest you call for information.

Halifax

Expensive

Clipper Cay. Phone: 423–6818. Historic Properties. Restaurant with the best location, over-looking Privateer's Wharf and Halifax Harbour. Ask for window table with a harbor view. The *Cay Side* (429–5639), downstairs, has lunch outdoors on the wharf during summer months. All major credit cards (both restaurants).

Fat Frank's. 5411 Spring Garden Rd. (423–6618). Edwardian atmosphere, gourmet dining (Fat Frank's boasts it can prepare any known dish on demand). Lunch and dinner. Seats only 55, so reservations, especially in summer, are recommended. Major credit cards.

The Henry House. 1222 Barrington St. (423–1309). Dining room in historic granite building. Food is excellent and the atmosphere classic Georgian. Call

for reservations. Dress casual, but no dungarees. All major credit cards. Specialty: Champlain's Feast (dinner Theatre).

Moderate-Expensive

Old Man Morias. 1150 Barrington St. (422–7960). Open year-round. Hellen-
ic cuisine (spitted lamb, moussaka, etc.) served in renovated townhouse. Licensed. Major credit cards.

Moderate

DA's. Dresden Arms Motor Hotel, 5530 Artillery Pl. (422–1625). Good food
in pleasant dining room. Try the Maid's Brunch at lunchtime. Call for reserva-
tions. All major credit cards.
The Gondola Restaurant. 5175 South St. (423–8719). Features authentic
Italian cuisine in trattoria-style surroundings; terrace dining during summer.
Start with appetizer of spaghetti and continue from there. Call for reservations.
Major credit cards.
The Hermitage. South Park St. at Inglis St. (421–1731). Swiss and French
décor and cuisine. Major credit cards.
O'Carrolls. 1860 Upper Water St. (423–4405). Oysters a specialty and sea-
food is excellent.
Pepe's. 5680 Spring Garden Rd. (429–7321). Superb surroundings and food
to match. A bright and cheerful restaurant. Major credit cards.
Pino's. 1225 Bedford Rd. (835–8453). Same owners as the Gondola restau-
rant. Good Italian food.
Rosa's Cantina. Argyle and Sackville (422-7535). Authentic Italian cuisine.
Ryan Duffy's Steakhouse. 40 Spring Garden Rd. (421–1116). Getting good
reports for steaks and atmosphere.
Sanford's. In *The Brewery,* Lower Water St. (423–4560). Sanford's offers
natural foods, crêpes and quiche. American Express and Visa only.
    Other fine moderate restaurants are **Five Fishermen,** Argyle St.; **Thackery's,**
Spring Garden Rd.; **Lawrence of Oregano's,** Argyle St.; **My Apartment,** Argyle
St.; and an excellent little café called **Quelque Chose,** serving quiche, salads,
light dinners and mouthwatering desserts, Hollis St.

Inexpensive

Georgio's. Prince George Hotel, Market St. (425–1986). Newest hot spot;
meals, lounge.
Privateer's Warehouse. Phone: 422–1289. Historic Properties, Lower Deck
and Middle Deck for lunch. 11:30 to 2:30. Sandwiches, chowder, sauerkraut,
and sausage with beer are the specials. Informal atmosphere popular with young
professionals, secretaries, and students. The Upper Deck dining room is in the
Inexpensive category for lunch and the *Moderate* category for dinner, but the
average quality of the food does not make up for the lack of atmosphere. Major
credit cards.
The Silver Spoon. 1865 Hollis St. (429–6617). Historic Properties. A fine
touch with seafood and desserts.

 NIGHTCLUBS AND BARS. Nightlife in the area tends
to be centered in downtown Halifax with a variety of
clubs and bars offering entertainment, food, and congenial surroundings.
    Most popular nightspots at the moment are: *Harbourside,* Sheraton Hotel,
Water St.; *Georgio's,* Market St.; *Rosa's Cantina,* Argyle and Sackville; *My
Apartment,* Argyle St.; and *Privateers Warehouse,* in Historic Properties. The
Lower Deck on the ground floor is a tavern with beer only and accordion music.
The Middle Deck on the second floor is a bar with light jazz music. Both Decks
are usually packed on weekends so get there early. Cover charge on weekends.
    The *Misty Moon,* Barrington St., is for dancers. Most lounges have some kind
of dance floor and music. At *Ginger's,* a pub at Hollis and Morris, you find
Atlantic talent including, occasionally, Rita MacNeil.
    For a quiet drinking place, try the *Victory Lounge* in the Lord Nelson Hotel
on South Park and Spring Garden Rd.
    The Split Crow, corner Duke and Granville, a decorous pub popular with
young professionals.

PRACTICAL INFORMATION FOR CAPE BRETON

 HOW TO GET THERE. By air: *Air Canada* has direct flights to Sydney from Halifax, Toronto, Montréal, and Québec City with connections to international flights. *CP Air* has flights to Sydney from Montréal, Newfoundland, New Brunswick, and Prince Edward Island. Sydney is also the connecting airport for flights to the French islands of St. Pierre and Miquelon which lie off the south coast of Newfoundland. *Air St. Pierre* (with *CP Air*) operates a year-round schedule of flights to France's last North American possessions.

By boat: Regular ferry service connects North Sydney with Port-aux-Basques, Newfoundland. A summer service is operated to Argentia, Newfoundland. For information and reservations, contact any *CN Marine* ticket office in Canada (800–565–9470) or (800–432–7344) Maine, or (800–341–7981) continental U.S. or your travel agent.

By bus: Daily bus service to Cape Breton from Halifax is operated by *Acadian Lines Limited* which connects with other bus lines throughout the country.

By car: The automobile (camper, motorcycle, or other recreational vehicle) must cross the Canso Causeway if approaching Cape Breton from mainland Nova Scotia. The toll is $1.50 per vehicle, payable only when entering Cape Breton.

By train: *Canadian National* operates train service to Sydney and intermediate points from Halifax and Truro. For information and reservations, contact any *Via Rail* ticket office. (800–561–3952 in Canada; Amtrak in U.S.)

 ACCOMMODATIONS. Accommodations in Cape Breton are generally comfortable with at least one excellent seasonal hotel. Hotel/motel rates in Cape Breton, based on double-occupancy, are categorized as follows: *Expensive,* $39 or more; *Moderate,* $30 to $39; *Inexpensive,* under $30. Reservations for accommodations throughout Cape Breton and Nova Scotia can be made by dialing the toll-free numbers listed under "Tourist Information" in the "Exploring Halifax-Dartmouth" section.

The 10% provincial sales tax is added to all hotel/motel rates.

Most places accept the following major credit cards: American Express, MasterCard and Visa; others may also be honored. Not all establishments accept credit cards, therefore we suggest you call for information.

BADDECK. *Expensive:* **Inverary Inn.** Box 190, Baddeck, NS B0E 1B0 (902–295–2674). One of the best places to stay in Cape Breton. About 80 motel units, efficiency units, and cottages. Dining room is licensed. Private beach and children's playground. Open May 1–November 1. Off-season rates October 15–May 15. Major credit cards.

Silver Dart Motel. Box 399, Baddeck, NS B0E 1B0 (902–295–2340). Good view over Bras d'Or. Licensed dining room. Open mid-May–mid-October. Off-season rates before June 15. About 80 efficiency units available; pets permitted. Major credit cards.

Moderate: **Telegraph House.** Chebucto St., Box 8, Baddeck, NS B0E 1B0 (902–295–9988). 47 rooms, some with family arrangements. Traditional place to stay; open year-round. Dining room.

CHETICAMP. *Moderate:* **Acadian Motel.** Main St., Box 11, Cheticamp, NS B0E 1H0 (902–224–2640). 16 units; licensed lounge and dining room. Open year-round; off-season rates October 30–May 15. Major credit cards.

Laurie's Motel. Main St., Box 1, Cheticamp, NS B0E 1H0 (902–224–2400). 31 units; pets permitted. Breakfast and dinner available to registered guests. Open year-round, except weekends, mid-October–mid-May; off-season rates mid-October–mid-June. Major credit cards.

IONA. *Expensive:* **Highland Heights Inn.** Rte. 223, Box 19, Iona, NS B0A 1L0 (902–622–2360). Comfortable atmosphere and friendly hosts. 26 units;

licensed dining room with good food. Open May 1–October 31; off-season rates September 15–July 1. Croquet, hiking, birdwatching. Major credit cards.

LOUISBOURG. *Inexpensive:* **Greta Cross Bed and Breakfast.** 81 Pepperell St., Box 68, Louisbourg, NS B0A 1M0 (902–733–2833). 3 rooms; breakfast included. Evening meal by request.

MARGAREE HARBOUR. *Moderate:* **Duck Cove Inn.** Margaree Harbour, NS B0E 2B0 (902–235–2658). 24 units; licensed dining room. Canoe rentals; horseshoe; giant checkers; deep-sea fishing; river salmon and trout fishing, guides available. Open June 1–October 31; off-season rates are in effect October 15–June 15. Major credit cards.

Whale Cove Summer Village. RR 1, Margaree Harbour, NS B0E 2B0 (902–235–2202). 30 modern deluxe housekeeping and overnight cottages. Laundry facilities, store, playground; deep-sea and freshwater fishing nearby. Open mid-June–mid-October. Major credit cards.

ST. PETER'S. *Inexpensive:* **Macdonald's Hotel.** Box 70, St. Peter's, NS B0E 3B0 (902–535–2997). 15 rooms in renovated house just off Rte. 4. Pets permitted; open year-round; licensed dining room. Major credit cards.

SYDNEY. *Expensive:* **Auberge Wandlyn Inn.** 100 Kings Rd., Sydney, NS B1S 1A1 (902–539–3700, 800–561–0000). About 70 units; coffee shop; licensed dining room; games room. Part of chain offering clean but usually plain accommodations. In converted nursing institution which is adequate for the purpose, but its architecture is odd. Pets permitted with permission from manager. Major credit cards.

Best Western Cape Bretoner Hotel. 560 Kings Rd., Sydney, NS B1S 1B8 (902–539–8101). About 50 units; licensed dining room. Major credit cards.

Holiday Inn of Sydney. 480 Kings Rd., Sydney, NS B1S 1A8 (902–539–6750). Typical Holiday Inn located a bit away from downtown area. About 120 rooms; coffee bar and dining room are both of minimum quality and service; cocktail lounge and bar, one with live entertainment; pool. Open year-round; off-season rates October 1–May 31. Major credit cards.

Keddy's Motor Inn. 600 Kings Rd., Sydney, NS B1S 1B9 (902–539–1140). Part of a chain noted for inconsistent quality, particularly in food service. Licensed dining room. Off-season rates November 1–April 30. Major credit cards.

Moderate: **Vista Motel.** 140 Kings Rd., Box 1232, Sydney, NS B1P 6J9 (902–539–6550). About 60 comfortable, plain units. Off-season rates October 15–June 1. Major credit cards.

 HOSTELS. Canadian Hostelling Assoc. (Nova Scotia office, P.O. Box 3010, 5516 Spring Garden Rd., Halifax, N.S., B3J 3G6, 425–5450) has information on hostels in Halifax, Chester, Liverpool, Shelburne, Yarmouth, Annapolis-Royal, Wentworth, New Glasgow, Antigonish, Wolfville, Seal Island, and Cape Breton.

BED AND BREAKFAST. More than 50 Cape Breton families participate in the bed-and-breakfast program. Rates for private bedroom in the family home are about $16 a night for one, $18 per night for two, including full breakfast the following morning. For visitors on a budget or wanting to meet some very hospitable people, this is an excellent program.

Participating families display a distinctive bed-and-breakfast sign. For reservations or listings of bed-and-breakfast locations, contact the Cape Breton Tourist Information Bureau, 20 Keltic Dr., Sydney River, Nova Scotia; the Cape Breton Development Corporation, Box 1750, Sydney, NS B1P 6T7 or the Nova Scotia Department of Tourism.

HOW TO GET AROUND. From the airport: Transportation from Sydney airport is operated by *Briands Cabs.* A one-way trip is about $3.00 to downtown hotels. Briand's Cabs and *Bill's Yellow Cabs* operate scheduled tours of the Cabot Trail and to the Fortress of Louisbourg.

Car rental: Rent-a-car agencies are located at the airport and most also have downtown offices. Cars should be reserved in advance, particularly during the summer season.

By bus: Several small bus companies operate local service to communities in Cape Breton from Sydney. For up-to-date schedules, contact the Cape Breton Tourist Board (902–539–9876).

By car: Using your own transportation is still the best way to get around Cape Breton. Most highways are paved and in good condition, although secondary roads may be winding and hilly. The local people know the roads and will drive faster than most visitors. Pull over and let them pass if they seem to be tailgating—it makes everyone happier and a lot safer.

By ferry: Two car ferries operate on route 223—one at Little Narrows and another at Grand Narrows. Both operate 24 hours a day on a 10- to 15-minute schedule. Fare for each passage is about 50¢ per vehicle.

TOURIST INFORMATION. The Department of Tourism operates a tourist information center at Port Hastings (625–9991) at the entry point to Cape Breton by highway. The Cape Breton Tourist Board has bureaus at Baddeck, Louisbourg, Margaree Forks, Martinique, St. Peter's, and Sydney Mines. Otherwise, all Nova Scotia tourist bureaus have information on Cape Breton. Or write: Nova Scotia Department of Tourism, P.O. Box 130, Halifax, Nova Scotia B3J 2M7.

For information on seasonal events, camping parks and national parks, regional theater, and other bits of practical information for Cape Breton see the *Practical Information for Nova Scotia* section.

TOURS. Tours by passenger car to Louisbourg, Miner's Museum, Bell Museum, and the Cabot Trail are operated by *Cape Breton Tours,* 263 Esplanade, Sydney; call 564–6200 or 564–6151. Operates from mid-May to September 20. *Yellow Cabs Ltd.* operates tours to the same Cape Breton destinations from May 15 to October 15. Address is 10 Pitt St., Sydney; call 564–4481 or 564–8161. Contact operators for rates, duration, and departure times.

Cape Breton is part of many coach tours operating from points in the United States and Canada. For information, contact a travel agent or the Nova Scotia Department of Tourism.

RESORTS. The Keltic Lodge P.O. Box 70, Ingonish Beach, NS B0C 1L0 (902–285–2880). One of the province's most elaborate resorts. It has 32 rooms in the main lodge, 40 motel rooms, and 24 cottages. It has convention space, sitting rooms with fireplaces, and there's evening entertainment in a licensed lounge. It operates year-round and features a wide array of indoor and outdoor activities—golf, skiing, fishing, tennis, swimming and so on. European Plan and Modified American Plan (dinner and breakfast included). Two-, three-, five- and seven-day packages available. Major credit cards.

The **Dundee Resort,** R.R. 2, West Bay, NS B0E 3K0 (902–345–2649). Located in Dundee, overlooking the Bras D'Or lakes, is more modest. It has 39 fully equipped housekeeping cottages, swimming pool, marina, tennis, 9-hole golf course, pro-shop, licensed dining room and lounge. Major credit cards.

SPORTS. Several Cape Breton waters, ranging from quiet rivers to expert white water runs, are highly regarded by **canoeing** enthusiasts. The Cape Breton Tourist Association has several good publications and maps. For canoe route information, contact Canoe Nova Scotia, P.O. Box 3010 South, Halifax, N.S. (425–5450), or the Nova Scotia Bookstore, 1597 Hollis St., Halifax, N.S.

Golf courses come in various sizes and ratings from several good nine hole courses like the professionally designed lakeside course at Dundee (off Rte. 4) to the championship 18 hole Cape Breton Highlands in the National Park. **Tennis** is also a popular sport; a number of communities have outdoor courts open to the public.

Scuba divers find Louisbourg Harbour and waters off southern Cape Breton excellent for wreck hunting. Contact Jim Wilson at Dive Cape Breton Ltd., P.O. Box 130, Louisbourg, or call 733–2877 for information on underwater tours of 1–5 days.

Hikers will find a variety of trails in the national park. There's a booklet on hiking called *Walk Cape Breton* available at tourist bureaus. **Anglers** may seek Atlantic salmon and trout in streams and rivers. Angling regulations are available from the Nova Scotia Department of Tourism.

Yacht rentals for **sailing** the 450 square mile Bras d'Or Lakes are available from: Baddeck Marine & Sports (sloop daysailers & charters), 295–2434; Bras d'Or Charter (all types of sailboats), 295–2756; Anchors Aweigh (paddleboats, canoes, tours) in Baddeck, 295–2713 and on *The Balaema*, a 32-ft. diesel schooner out of Margaree Harbour, 235–2943. Cruises to Bird Islands ($6 a person) by Boularderie Cruises in Big Bras d'Or, 674–2384.

For those who bring their own boat, launching ramps are located at a number of sites along the Bras d'Or. Check with the tourist information bureau for the closest one.

The Nova Scotia Department of Recreation operates supervised **swimming** at Port Hood Beach, Inverness Beach, Dominion Beach, and East Bay Beach.

For **skiing** during the winter months, the Cape Smokey Ski Centre at Ingonish on the Cabot Trail operates three major runs of about one mile each. The biggest drop is about 1,000 feet. Snow from December to mid-April. Double chairlift and pony. Call 285–2880 for snow conditions.

For specific information, contact the Cape Breton Tourist Board or the Nova Scotia Department of Tourism.

 MUSEUMS AND HISTORIC SITES. Cape Breton has a number of local history museums and several very unique museum complexes which will appeal to visitors.

Mining coal has long been a way of life in Cape Breton. The first recorded mining operation was by the French who, in 1720, dug into an exposed coal seam at Port Morien. The site of this mine and other 19th-century operations is the first stop on the *Three Mine Tour* in the Glace Bay area. Two hundred million year old fossils can be seen in the coal face at the walk-in mine. Open from noon to 8 P.M. during July and Aug.

The second stop is at the *Miners Museum* in Glace Bay which displays a 200-year history of mining in the area. Visitors can walk into the Ocean Deeps Colliery with a veteran miner accompanying each group. The Men of the Deeps, an internationally known miners' choral group, sing weekly in summer evening concerts. Check with museum for times. The mining area has a very low roof in places and, although quite safe, is definitely not for claustrophobics. Helmets and protective shawls are provided. The adjoining *Miner's Village* has a replica of the company store and company housing. The Miner's Village Restaurant is licensd and serves seafood prepared by local women—nice surroundings with coal oil lamps. The museum, located at Quarry Point in Glace Bay, is open daily, mid-June to mid-September, from 9 A.M. to 8:30 P.M., and the rest of the year on Wednesday from 9 A.M. to 9 P.M., and Thursdays to Sundays from 9 A.M. to 5 P.M. The restaurant is open 9 A.M. to 9 P.M. daily, year-round (Reservations: 849–9344). Tour costs about $1.75 for adults and 75¢ for children, $1.00 for students. Museum free.

The third mine is the *Princess Colliery* in *Sydney Mines* where visitors descend 682 feet to the pit bottom before being hoisted back to the surface in coal boxes on the mine railway. Protective clothing is provided. Quite safe but not for the claustrophobic or the faint of heart. Open during July and August from 11 A.M. to 7 P.M. Admission is about $2.00 for adults.

The *S&L Railway Museum* in Louisbourg is in a restored 1895 railway station. Open June 15 to Sept. 30, daily. Free. Special tours, by appointment.

The *Old Sydney Museum* in the St. Patrick's Church Building is open daily, June to mid-Oct. Free.

The *Garrison Church*, circa 1784, in Sydney, Charlotte at Nepean St., allegedly the oldest parish in Cape Breton, was built with stones from the wrecked buildings of Louisbourg.

In Sydney, *Cossitt House,* is the restored residence of Rev. Ranna Cossitt, the oldest house in Sydney, built around 1787. Open May 15 to October 15.

In Baddeck, the *Alexander Graham Bell Museum* has excellent displays of the works of the inventor of the telephone and the first airplane to fly in the British Empire. A replica of Bell's schooner-sized Hydrofoil, along with the dismembered original are on display. Free admission. Open May 20 to October 15 from 9 A.M. to 9 P.M. and October 15 to May 15 from 9 A.M. to 5 P.M., except holidays. Tel. 295–2069.

Victoria County Archives & Museum in Baddeck offers well-organized archives of local history. Free. Open summer months to the public.

Fortress Louisbourg, at Louisbourg, is the most ambitious restoration project ever undertaken in Canada. The original fortress, constructed by the French 1720–45, was the major French fortification in Acadia and a focal point of struggle between the French and English until its total destruction by the English in 1760. Restored homes are "inhabited," and the lifestyle is that of 1750, complete with town "characters." A new interpretive center was opened in 1976 and provides a long range view of the fortress, looking much as it did in 1750. If you are a history, architecture, or restoration buff, plan to spend at least a half day there. A park bus takes visitors from the interpretive center to the Fortress proper. 733–2280. Bus fare is included in the fee which is about $2.00 for adults and about 50¢ for children. A maximum family rate of about $4.00 gets everybody in.

The *Nova Scotia Highland Village* on Rte. 223 at Iona is a collection of refurbished and reconstructed buildings—a carding mill, forge, country store, school and cabin—recalling the early Scottish settlers to the area. Open June 15 to Sept. 15, 10 A.M. to 5 P.M. daily. Admission is about 50¢ for adults and 25¢ for children. The *Acadian Museum* in Cheticamp is more of a handcraft shop and village center. Local women demonstrate Acadian-style rug hooking, weaving, and spinning. Snack bar.

The *Margaree Salmon Museum* at North East Margaree has a collection of fishing paraphenalia used on the famous Margaree River in search of the fighting Atlantic salmon. Open 9 A.M. to 5 P.M. daily, mid-June to mid-October. Admission for adults is about 50¢, children 25¢.

In Margaree, the *Museum of Cape Breton Heritage* has a collection of Scottish, Acadian and Indian household items, and arts and crafts. Free. Closed Sundays.

The *Gaelic College of Celtic Folk Arts and Highland Crafts* at St. Ann's on the Cabot Trail welcomes visitors to the daily concerts and the grounds. Bagpipes and drums only. Small charge for the evening concerts; afternoon practice sessions are free. For information, call 295–2877.

St. Ann's has the *Giant MacAskill Highland Pioneers Museum.* Free. Open June 1–October 15 from 9 A.M. to 5 P.M.

South Cape Breton. In Arichat, the *Le Noir Forge* (off Rte. 4 on 320), a restored 18th-century stone blacksmith shop with working forge. Open June 15 to Sept. 15; Mon. to Sat., 9–12 A.M., 1–5 P.M.; Sun., 1–4 P.M. Free.

The *Nicholas Denys Museum* in St. Peter's (Rte. 4) has implements and artifacts from as far back as 1638. Adults 50¢, children 25¢. Open June 1 to September 30 from 9 A.M. to 5 P.M.

The *Marble Mountain Museum & Library* in Marble Mountain (off Rte. 105 or Rte. 4 at Cleveland) shows the history of limestone quarries and the business of Marble Mountain. Free. Open in summer months only.

 MUSIC. Much of the music of Cape Breton takes a traditional form—bagpipes, fiddle, guitar, and piano with voices singing folk style songs in English, French, or Gaelic. Throughout the summer visitors will find Scottish concerts at places such as *Broad Cove* and traditional Scottish Ceilidh's (kay'lees) in various Cape Breton communities.

The *Gaelic College* at St. Ann's has daily concerts by students. Afternoon session, from about 2 to 3 P.M.; evening session, from about 7 to 8 P.M. most days during July and August. For exact times, contact the Cape Breton Tourist Association at 20 Keltic Dr., Sydney River, or the nearest local tourist bureau.

The *Gaelic Mod* at St. Ann's in early August and *Iona Highland Village Day,* usually the first weekend in August, are excellent showcases for Scottish and other Cape Breton talent in dance, piping, and traditional music.

Every second year in early July, the village of Glendale (in Inverness County just off Rte. 105) hosts a weekend festival of Cape Breton fiddling and stepdancing, with fiddlers returning to Cape Breton from all over the continent. *The* music event of the year in Cape Breton when it's held. Look for Scottish concerts in Frenchvale, Cheticamp, Mabou, St. Ann's and summer festivals in Marion Bridge, St. Joseph du Moine, Wycocomagh, Margaree, Petit de Grat, and Louisbourg—and for Cape North's *Blueberry Festival: Action Week & Highland Games* in Sydney; the *Community Bazaar* in Arichat; *Highland Dancing* festival in St. Peter's (Rte. 4); the *Richmond Exhibition* in Louisdale (off Rte. 4); and the *Festival of the Strait,* a week-long celebration in Port Hawkesbury. N.S. Department of Tourism's *Calendar of Events,* or local newspaper supplements, will give you exact dates and times.

The *Men of the Deeps* is a male choir made up of coalminers from the Cape Breton area. They have toured many North American centers and have also toured China. Tourist information bureaus have schedule.

RESTAURANTS. Dining out in Cape Breton can be something of an adventure in the specialty restaurants and a taste delight (French cuisine) in the island's best dining room.

Ask your waiter or waitress to suggest the best items on the daily menu or the specials of the day.

Most places accept the following major credit cards: American Express, MasterCard and Visa; others may also be honored. Not all establishments accept credit cards, therefore we suggest you call for information.

Restaurants are categorized on the basis of a full-course dinner, with drinks, tax, and tips excluded: *Expensive,* over $15; *Moderate,* $10–15; *Inexpensive,* under $10.

CHETICAMP. *Moderate.* **Acadian Museum,** Main St., Cheticamp (224–2170). Serves delicious old Acadian food in tiny restaurant.

Harbour Restaurant. Box 400, Main St. (224–2042). Specialties: steak, seafood.

INGONISH BEACH. *Expensive.* **Keltic Lodge Dining Room.** Phone: 285–2880. International cuisine and an excellent choice of menu—all for the one table d'hôte price. Good wine selection. Strict atmosphere of resort luxury: Jackets for men; women requested not to wear casual attire at dinner (e.g., no daytime pant suits, jeans, etc.). Open mid-June to mid-October. Reservations necessary. The Lodge's Coffee Shop, open 8 A.M. to 10 P.M., is moderately priced. Major credit cards.

IONA. *Moderate:* **Highland Heights Inn.** Phone: 622–2360. Scottish home-style cooking, with fresh fish in season. Atmosphere of a Scottish inn with huge stone fireplace in dining room, overlooking the Bras d'Or at Grand Narrows. Licensed. Major credit cards.

LOUISBOURG. *Expensive:* **L'épée Royalle.** Phone: 733–2441. In Fortress; 18th-century French dining with 18th-century animation. Open June to September from 11 A.M. to 8 P.M. daily. Licensed. Major credit cards.

L'Hotel de la Marine. Phone: 733–2441. Part of the Fortress Louisbourg restoration, the dining room has been recreated to portray the lifestyle of Louisbourg of the 1740's. Food is prepared from authentic 18th-century French recipes and served in that informal style. Atmosphere is excellent; food is wholesome and interesting. Open from about 11 A.M. to 8 P.M. from June to Sept. Phone 733–2280. Major credit cards.

Moderate: **Anchors Aweigh Restaurant.** 1095 Main St. (733–3131). Next to Railway Museum and tourist bureau. Licensed. Specializes in fresh Atlantic seafood.

Grubstake Restaurant. 1274–1276 Main St. (733–2844). Pleasant surroundings, good food. Credit cards.

Inexpensive: **Lobster Kettle,** Seafood by the wharf. Phone 733–2877. Visa only.

MARGAREE HARBOR. *Moderate:* **Schooner Restaurant "Marian Elizabeth."** Phone: 235–2317. Aboard a former fishing schooner built in Nova Scotia in 1918; now permanently beached in Margaree Harbour. Licensed with seafood specialties. The chowder is usually excellent; the atmosphere is an experience. Open June 15 to mid-October. Call for reservations.

SYDNEY. *Expensive.* **Petit Jean.** 233 Esplanade Rd., Sydney (539–4671). Tries to be French; succeeds moderately well. Lunch on Monday to Friday only from noon–2 P.M.; dinner daily 6 P.M. to 10 P.M. Call for reservations.
   Moderate: **Joe's Warehouse.** 424 Charlotte St. (539–6686). Good food. Cabaret on lower floor called *Smooth Herman's.* A fun place.
   Peaches and Cream. 403 Charlotte St. (539–2599). Terrific desserts.
   Inexpensive: **Venice Pizzeria.** On Welton St. (539–4973). Try their Mexican food.

SYDNEY MINES. *Moderate:* **The Cauldron.** Phone: 736–6823. Located at the Princess Tourist Mine. Open daily May to September. Home-cooked-style food with daily specials.

WHYCOCOMAGH. *Moderate:* **Village Inn.** Phone: 756–2002. Home-cooked meals in tiny country inn. Old-style friendly service and delicious food. Licensed. Make reservations. Major credit cards.

PRACTICAL INFORMATION FOR NOVA SCOTIA

HOW TO GET THERE. By car: The Trans-Canada Hwy. eastbound will deliver you to Nova Scotia by the overland route through New Brunswick, entering the province at Amherst.
   By ferry: Visitors may also reach Nova Scotia by one of the six-car ferry connections from Maine, New Brunswick, Prince Edward Island, and Newfoundland.
   Passenger and vehicle ferry service is operated between Yarmouth, Nova Scotia, and Portland, Maine, by *CN Marine* and by *Prince of Fundy Cruises.* A one-way trip takes between 10 and 12 hours. Cabins, dining facilities, entertainment, and recreation are available on both ferries. Advance reservations must be made for both vessels, especially during the summer season. Contact Prince of Fundy Cruises at the International Terminal in Portland. Call (207) 775–5611. CN Marine may be booked through any CN ticket office in Canada or by calling toll-free in Maine (800) 432–7344 or toll-free (800) 341–7981 in mid-Northeastern United States. Or contact a travel agent for bookings. There is also a CN Marine passenger and vehicle ferry service between Yarmouth and Bar Harbour, Me. Crossing time: six hours. Same telephone information as for Portland ferry.
   CN Marine also operates frequent vehicle and passenger service between Saint John, New Brunswick, and Digby, Nova Scotia. The 40-mile crossing takes about 2½ hours. Make reservations in advance, especially for summer months. Book through any CN ticket office in Canada or by calling toll-free in Maine (800) 432–7344 or toll free in mid-Northeastern United States or book through a travel agent.
   The ferry service between North Sydney, Nova Scotia, and the Newfoundland ports of Argentia (summer service) and Port-aux-Basques (year-round service) is also operated by CN Marine. The crossing to Port-aux-Basques takes about 6 hours; to Argentia about 18 hours. Cabins, dining, entertainment, and recreation facilities are available on the vessels. Bookings may be made at the above CN Marine numbers or through a travel agent. Make reservations for Argentia, especially during the summer season, and on the Port-aux-Basques night service. Reservations are not accepted on the Port-aux-Basques day service.
   Passenger and vehicle service between Wood Islands, Prince Edward Island, and Caribou [near Pictou], Nova Scotia, is operated from May to late December by *Northumberland Ferries Limited.* The 14-mile crossing takes about an hour.

Lunch-counter facilities are available but there are no cabins. Reservations are not accepted and the line-ups may take several hours during the summer season. It is best to cross early [first ferry leaves at 6 A.M. in summer] or late in the evening. For information, contact Northumberland Ferries, P.O. Box 634, Charlottetown, P.E.I., or call (902) 894–3473. In Caribou, Nova Scotia (902) 485–9015.

By train: *Via Rail* provides train service to Nova Scotia from major centers across Canada. *Amtrak* from New York makes connections with CN in Montréal.

By bus: Service to most Nova Scotia areas is provided by *Acadian Lines* and other bus companies. Connections are made at Amherst, Nova Scotia, and with the ferries at Yarmouth, Digby, Caribou and North Sydney, Nova Scotia.

By air: *CP Air* flies to Halifax and Sydney, Nova Scotia, from centers within Atlantic Canada and from Toronto and Montreal. *Air Canada* also flies into Halifax, Yarmouth, and Sydney from Atlantic centers—Montréal, Québec, and Toronto. *CP Air* and *Air Canada* have extensive national and international connections.

ACCOMMODATIONS. Accommodations are generally good and friendly throughout the province. Reservations can be made by calling the toll-free numbers listed under "Tourist Information" in the "Practical Information for Halifax/Dartmouth" section. Rates based on double-occupancy. *Expensive,* over $39; *Moderate,* $30–39; *Inexpensive,* under $30.

A 10% provincial tax will be added to your bill.

Most places accept the following major credit cards: American Express, MasterCard and Visa; others may also be honored. Not all establishments accept credit cards, therefore we suggest you call for information.

AMHERST. *Expensive:* **Auberge Wandlyn Inn.** Trans Canada Highway at Victoria St. exit, Amherst, NS B4H 3Z2 (902–667–3331, 800–561–0000). 60 units outside of the town beside the highway. Clean, comfortable accommodations with large fields for children. Two miles from New Brunswick–Nova Scotia border. Coffee shop, licensed dining room and lounge, heated outdoor pool. Off-season rates October–June. Pets with permission. Major credit cards.

ANNAPOLIS ROYAL. *Moderate:* **Bread and Roses Country Inn.** 82 Victoria St., Annapolis Royal, NS B0S 1A0 (902–532–5727). 9 rooms each with private bath. Library; fireplace in drawing room. Breakfast available. No smoking.

Royal Anne Motel. Box 400, Annapolis Royal, NS B0S 1A0 (902–532–2323). 20 units (3 housekeeping), licensed restaurant, gardens and open lawns. Pleasant surroundings near most historical sites in the area. Off-season rates mid-September–mid-June. Pets allowed with permission. Credit card: Visa only.

AULD COVE. *Moderate:* **The Cove Motel.** Auld Cove, NS (902–747–2700). Secluded, on peninsula; licensed dining room overlooking the Strait of Canso, near the Canso Causeway; 31 units including 12 chalets; pets permitted. Major credit cards.

BRIDGETOWN. *Expensive:* **Bridgetown Motor Hotel.** 83 Granville St. E., Box 478, Bridgetown, NS B0S 1C0 (902–665–4491). 33 units, comfortable accommodation; licensed dining, and lounge with bar shaped like distillery barrel. Sauna, pool, table tennis. Off-season rates mid-September–June. Attended pets permitted. Major credit cards.

BRIDGEWATER. *Expensive:* **Auberge Wandlyn Inn.** 50 North St., Bridgewater, NS B4V 2W6 (902–543–7131). 75 units off Highway 103 (exit 12). Clean, comfortable accommodations. Coffee shop, licensed dining room and lounge; indoor pool and sauna; gift shop. Off-season rates October–June. Pets with permission. Major credit cards.

DIGBY. *Expensive:* **The Pines Resort Hotel.** Box 70, Shore Rd., Digby, NS B0V 1A0 (902–245–2511). 90 rooms in main lodge; 60 in cottages. Elegant resort; fireplaces and sitting rooms. Tennis, pool, excellent golf. Fine service and gracious dining.

Moderate–Expensive: **Admiral Digby Inn.** Box 608, Shore Rd., Digby, NS B0V 1A0 (902–245–2531). 40 units; licensed dining room and lounge; indoor pool. Major credit cards.

Moderate: **Mountain Gap Inn.** Digby, NS (902–245–2277). Large motel. Some cottages with one to two bedrooms. Pool, tennis, beach; bar, dining room.

KENTVILLE. *Expensive:* **Auberge Wandlyn Inn.** RR 1, Coldbrook, NS B4N 3V7 (902–678–8311, 800–561–0000). 75 rooms, clean, comfortable accommodations. Coffee shop, licensed dining room and lounge, pool, playground, golf green, horseshoe pit, games room, pool table; pets with permission. Off-season rates October–June. Major credit cards.

LUNENBURG. *Inexpensive:* **Bluenose Lodge.** Box 339, 10 Falkland St., Lunenburg, NS B0J 2C0 (902–634–8851). 9 rooms with bath; licensed dining room; deep-sea fishing excursions arranged; displays local crafts. Major credit cards.

NEW GLASGOW. *Expensive:* **Heather Motor Inn.** Foord St., Stellarton, NS B0K 1S0 (902–752–8401). 76 clean and comfortable units off Hwy. 104 (exit 24); licensed dining room with good seafood and lounge. Open year-round; pets permitted. Major credit cards.

Moderate: **Peter Pan Motel.** 390 Marsh St., New Glasgow, NS B2H 4S6 (902–752–8327). 54 units; good buy. Bar, dining room, pool.

PORT DUFFERIN. *Moderate:* **Marquis of Dufferin Lodge and Motel.** RR 1, Port Dufferin, NS B0J 2R0 (902–654–2696). 14 units overlooking the Atlantic, 8 miles east of Sheet Harbour on Hwy. 7. Adjacent restaurant; pets permitted. Off-season rates. October–May. Major credit cards.

TRURO. *Moderate:* **Tidal Bore Inn.** RR 1, Truro, NS B2N 5A9 (902–895–9241). 24 clean and comfortable rooms; in the viewing area for the tidal bore rapids; licensed restaurant. Open mid-May–mid-October; off-season rates before mid-June. Major credit cards.

WESTERN SHORE-OAK ISLAND CHANNEL. *Expensive:* **Best Western Oak Island Inn.** West Shore, Lunenburg Co., NS B0J 3M0 (902–627–2600, 800–528–1234). 71 rooms, comfortable and well appointed. Ocean view overlooks the marina and Oak Island treasure island. Licensed dining room and lounge. Pool, marina, sailboat rentals, deep-sea fishing charters. Open year-round. Major credit cards.

WINDSOR. *Moderate to Expensive.* **Old Stone House,** Newport Landing (902–757–2604). 3 rooms in a Bed and Breakfast. Delightfully furnished house dates from 1690.

WOLFVILLE. *Expensive:* **Old Orchard Inn.** Phone: 902–542–5751. 74 rooms and 30 chalets with 10 efficiency units; comfortable with a spectacular view over the Annapolis Valley from the main building. Licensed dining and lounge, with nightly entertainment; coffee shop. Pool, sauna, tennis, nature trails, playground. Motel open year-round; chalets open May–October. Major credit cards.

Moderate–Expensive: **Blomidon Inn.** 127 Main St., Wolfville, NS B0P 1X0 (902–542–9326). 21 rooms in lovely old mansion. Breakfast included. Excellent dining room.

YARMOUTH. *Expensive:* **Manor Inn.** Box 56, Hebron, Yarmouth Co., NS B0W 1X0 (902–742–2487). Colonial mansion on Hwy. 1 with rose garden, estate, and lakefront. 29 rooms; licensed dining room and lounge with entertainment; pets permitted. Open mid-June–October. Major credit cards.

Rodd's Grand Hotel. Box 220, 417 Main St., Yarmouth, NS B5A 4B2 (902–742–2446 or toll free 800–565–0207 Maritimes; 800–565–1430 U.S. eastern seaboard). 138 clean and comfortable rooms near the ferries from Portland

and Bar Harbor, Maine. Licensed dining room and two lounges; pets permitted. Major credit cards.

 BED AND BREAKFAST. Nova Scotia also has a well-developed bed-and-breakfast program. Private homes take overnight guests for as little as $15 to $22 a night. In the towns they go by the name of "guest homes." The provincial accommodations guide, available at tourist bureaus, lists them all.

TELEPHONE. The long-distance area code for the entire province (plus neighboring Prince Edward Island) is 902.

 HOW TO GET AROUND. By car: Major highways in Nova Scotia are good to excellent. The routes tend to follow the coastline and the three-digit routings [e.g. 104] are the faster, but less scenic, roads. Most of the 10 routes are paralleled by the older and more scenic highways. During the summer months, Nova Scotia's unpaved highways are usually in very good condition and, aside from raising some dust, make for quiet and scenic drives.

As in the rest of Canada, summer is "highway repair time" and motorists are cautioned to be alert for the flag-people with warnings of road works ahead.

Car-rental agencies are located at both the Halifax International and Sydney airports, all Nova Scotia entry points, and in the cities of Halifax and Sydney. Reservations are necessary during the summer months and may be made through local agency offices or a travel agency.

By train: *Via Rail* serves many major centers in Nova Scotia and Via Rail operates a daily service from Halifax to Digby. For the traveler, train service in Nova Scotia is inconvenient at best. The tracks usually run through the least interesting scenery and service is not frequent. Bookings may be made at any CN ticket office in Canada or through a travel agency.

By bus: *Acadian Lines Ltd., MacKenzie Bus Line Ltd.,* and *Zinck's Bus Company Ltd.* operate daily service to all parts of Nova Scotia. Information and bookings may be made through a travel agent or by contacting Acadian Lines Limited, 6040 Almon Street, Halifax, Nova Scotia, (902) 454–9321, or an Acadian Lines office.

By air: Both *Air Canada* and *CP Air* have flights between Sydney and Halifax several times daily. In Halifax, contact Air Canada at 429–7111 and *CP Air* at 465–2111. In Sydney, call Air Canada at 539–6600 and *CP Air* at 564–4545. Bookings may be made through any travel agency. The flight between the two cities takes about 40 minutes.

TIME ZONE. Nova Scotia is on Atlantic Time (1 hour in advance of Eastern Time).

 SEASONAL EVENTS. The **winter** season in Nova Scotia is a time of performances by Neptune Theatre and the Atlantic Symphony in *Halifax* and on tour. **Winter** carnivals are held at the major universities in *Halifax, Wolfville,* and at *Antigonish* as well as at larger centers with service club sponsorship.

During **March** and **April** (maple sugar weather) the *Glooscap* Maple Sugar Festival invites visitors to the sugar bush for pancake suppers and maple candy.

As **May** turns into **June,** the Apple Blossom Festival is celebrated in the Annapolis Valley towns of *Kentville, Wolfville,* and *New Minas.* In May and June the Blessing of the Fleet is held in many French villages— *Meteghan, Main-á-Dieu, Petit de Grat*—before the boats begin the inshore and offshore fishing season. Scottish Concert and Dance, with performers from around the Maritimes, is held annually in *Pictou.* Rhododendron Sunday in *Kentville* in mid-June brings out the flower lovers. The landing of explorer John Cabot in 1497 is remembered in late June at *Cape North* in an annual pageant.

Festivals and events ranging from week-long galas to community suppers are held throughout the summer months in all parts of Nova Scotia. The Department of Tourism can provide complete lists with dates. Many of the festivals have an ethnic background—Scottish or Acadian—or feature local fishery or agricultural fairs and exhibitions. Some events have special foods—such as lobster carnivals and steer barbecues—which provide excellent informal dining at minimal costs.

July 1, as well as being Dominion Day, is also the Gathering of the Clans in *Pugwash* and the beginning of the multi-cultural festival known as the Festival of the Strait in *Port Hawkesbury.* The first week sees the Annual Lobster Supper Weekend in *St. Peter's.* The *Sydney* Highland Games take place in early July, as do the Maritime Old Time Fiddling Contest in *Dartmouth,* the *Pictou* Lobster Carnival, the *Antigonish* Highland Games, and the Acadian Festival of *Clare* held at Meteghan River. In *Kingston,* two steers are barbecued in mid-July.

The *Margaree* Summer Festival is held in late July. The fictional clock salesman, Sam Slick, is remembered in the home town of his creator during Sam Slick Days and Regatta in *Windsor* at that time, and the Acadian Day Festival in *L'Ardoise* and the East Pictou Annual Fair in Thorburn are held in late July.

Once again in a Scottish vein, the Gaelic Mod is the attraction at the Gaelic College in *St. Ann's* early in **August** when the South Shore Exhibition in *Bridgewater* begins the series of agricultural fairs and exhibitions throughout the province. In *New Glasgow* early in August kilts swirl at the Festival of the Tartans and at Highland Village Day in *Iona.* The Piper's Picnic in *Earltown* is the scene for pipe bands, highland dancing and a gathering of the clans. In mid-August rockhounds from many parts of North America congregate in the *Parrsboro* area for the annual Rockhound Round-up. The *Canso* Regatta, the traditional *Johnstown* Milling Frolic, the Highland Summer Festival in *Inverness,* and Scallop Day in *Digby* are other local events in mid-August.

Throughout July and August there are Scottish concerts and many communities have a Ceilidh (kay-lee) with piping and fiddling and Gaelic folk singing.

During early **September** the blueberry is king in the *Amherst* area during the Blueberry Festival, while in *Lunenburg* the Nova Scotia Fisheries Exhibition celebrates the harvest from the sea. The international dory races also take place now.

TOURS AND SPECIAL INTEREST SIGHTSEEING. *Nova Tours Ltd.* operates several bus tours per season through Nova Scotia. For departure dates and rates, telephone 902–429–3702. Other operators offering bus tours through Nova Scotia and other Maritime Provinces are *Evangeline Tours,* Wolfville (902–542–9109); and *Atlantic Tours,* Saint John, New Brunswick (902–657–6386). Also *Bridges Tours,* Halifax (902–422–8462), and *Village Bus Tours,* P.O. Box 35, Cornwallis, Nova Scotia B05 1H0.

The Nova Scotia Department of Tourism can provide complete information on guided and self-guiding tours of the province.

The Canada Department of Agriculture Research Station in Kentville conducts poultry and horticultural research on its 650-acre site. Open Monday to Friday from 8:30 A.M. to 5 P.M.

Wildlife parks with native animals and birds in natural open settings are operated by the province at Shubenacadie, about 48 kms. (30 miles) from Halifax on Rte. 102, at Upper Clements on Rte. 1 between Annapolis Royal and Digby, and near Marion Bridge, about 20 miles from Sydney. Open May 1 to end of October from 8:30 A.M. to 7:30 P.M. daily. Wear walking shoes and take a camera. A good way to entertain children.

NATIONAL PARKS. The two national parks in Nova Scotia offer you great contrasts. Cape Breton Highlands National Park is high and forested with sheer cliffs dropping off into the sea. Kejimkujik National Park is inland —a hilly forested area with many lakes.

Cape Breton Highlands is partially ringed by the spectacular Cabot Trail. The interior of the Park is wilderness and inaccessible by normal means. The 950 sq. kms. (367 square miles) area has numerous rivers which provide good fishing and the forest is home to many animals. Facilities in the park are available for fishing (provincial regulations apply), excellent hiking with nature trails starting at the highway, canoeing, and camping including a trailer park. There are also an interpretive center and a very good 18-hole championship golf course. Rates for golf are about $5 per day and about $25 weekly. A number of saltwater beaches on the eastern coast offer excellent swimming.

Cape Breton Highlands is both a summer and winter park, with extensive skiing facilities and other winter activities. For more information, contact the Superintendent, Cape Breton Highlands National Park, Ingonish Beach, Cape Breton, Nova Scotia B0C 1L0.

Kejimkujik (ke-jim-kú-gik) National Park is in the western part of the province and is reached by Hwy. 8 between Liverpool and Annapolis Royal. A former Micmac Indian reservation, the park was named for the largest lake.

The 381-sq.-km. (238-square mile) park has a relatively mild winter climate combined with many lakes inhabited by a wide range of reptiles and amphibians. Essentially a wilderness, Kejimkujik has well-marked canoe routes into the interior with primitive campsites.

There are park facilities for camping, boating and boat rentals, hiking (nature trails), fishing (under provincial regulations), and freshwater swimming. There is also an interpretive center. Many animals live in the park and in the adjoining Tobeatic Game Sanctuary. Deer are often seen.

Kejimkujik has one minor problem—dog ticks, introduced into the area by the hunting dogs used by United States hunters earlier in the century. Although the ticks do not carry disease and are easily removed from the skin, tight-fitting clothing and a thorough examination after being in the woods are necessary. During midsummer, the pest declines in numbers and is virtually gone by autumn. Visitors with dogs and other domestic animals must be careful to avoid a tick infestation on the pet. Visitors who avoid the heavy woods are not likely to have any problem.

For additional information on Kejimkujik National Park, contact the Superintendent, P.O. Box 36, Maitland Bridge, Annapolis County, Nova Scotia B0T 1N0.

Both national parks have a user fee of about $1.00 per vehicle per day, $2.00 for a 4-day pass, and $10.00 for an annual pass valid for all Canadian national parks. There is no charge for vehicles passing through Cape Breton National Park on the Cabot Trail.

Camping fees in both parks range from about $4.50 to about $8.00 per day depending on the facilities.

 PROVINCIAL CAMPING PARKS. Provincial campgrounds are located throughout the province. All have well-managed facilities and all except Beaver Mountain have picnic sites.

Battery. 114 acres, almost 2 kms. (one mile) north of St. Peter's on Rte. 4. Features hiking trails.

Beaver Mountain. 329 acres off Rte. 104 at Beaver Mountain Road between New Glasgow and Antigonish.

Blomidon. 1667 acres, 16 kms. (10 miles) north of Canning on Rte. 1. Has a spectacular lookout over the Bay of Fundy with the world's highest tides.

Boylston. 225 acres, 6½ kms. (4 miles) north of Guysborough on Rte. 16.

Caribou. 78 acres, 8 kms. (5 miles) north of Pictou on Rte. 106 near the ferry from Prince Edward Island. Has hiking and swimming area.

Ellenwood Lake. 281 acres, 19 kms. (12 miles) northeast of Yarmouth on Rte. 340. Has hiking trails and a boat-launch ramp. Lake swimming.

Five Islands. 1020 acres, 24 kms. (15 miles) east of Parrsboro on Rte. 2 along the Bay of Fundy coast. Has hiking trails and unique scenery.

Graves Island. 123 acres, 3 kms. (2 miles) east of Chester on Rte. 3.

Laurie. 71 acres, 40 kms. (25 miles) north of Halifax on Rte. 2. Has hiking trails and boat launch ramp.

Mira River. 216 acres, 24 kms. (15 miles) south east of Sydney on Rte. 22. Has boat launch ramp and hiking trails along the river.

Porter's Lake. 216 acres, 19 kms. (12 miles) east of Dartmouth on Rte. 7. Has hiking trails and boat launch ramp on the lake.

Risser's Beach. 18 acres, 27 kms. (16 miles) south of Bridgewater on Rte. 331. Has an interpretive center and one of the best beaches in Nova Scotia, but the water is cool at the best of times.

Salsman, 26 acres, 13 kms. (8 miles) south of Goshen off Rte. 316; *Saltsprings,* 76 acres, 24 kms. (15 miles) west of New Glasgow; and *Valleyview,* 134 acres, 5 kms. (3 miles) north of Bridgetown off Rte. 1, have no facilities except for camping and picnics, although *Valleyview* does have an excellent view over the lower Annapolis Valley farming country.

Smiley's. 100 acres, 13 kms. (8 miles) east of Windsor on Rte. 14; and *Wentworth,* 243 acres at Wentworth Centre on Rte. 104, have hiking trails.

The Islands. 62 acres, 5 kms. (3 miles) west of Shelburne, on Rte. 3; and *Whycocomagh,* 503 acres, east of the community of Whycocomagh on Rte. 105, having hiking trails and boat launch ramps.

These provincial recreation areas are open from mid-May to mid-October. Most have water, toilet facilities, fireplaces, and firewood or some of these; many have sewage disposal stations. Camping fees at most recreation areas begin at about $5 per day depending on the facilities.

A number of provincial camping parks and day-use parks (without camping areas) are spotted around the province overlooking scenic views or by the water.

 BEACHES. The Nova Scotia Department of Recreation operates supervised beaches in the following areas: on the Northcumberland Strait coast at Heather Beach, Caribou Beach, Melmerby Beach; on the Nova Scotia Atlantic coast at Summerville Beach, Rissers Beach, Queensland Beach, Crystal Crescent Beach, Lawrencetown Beach, Martinique Beach, Clam Harbour Beach and Taylor Head Beach. There is a supervised swimming area in Kejimkujik National Park with freshwater swimming. There is also supervised freshwater swimming at Ellenwood Lake Beach and both fresh and saltwater beaches in the Cape Breton National Highland Park.

In addition, there are dozens of unsupervised beaches ranging from small strips to huge sandy beaches such as Mavililette Beach at Cape St. Mary about 24 kms. (15 miles) north of Yarmouth. On the Northcumberland Strait coast, the summer water temperature is in the 18–21°C. (65–70°F.) range, quite pleasant for swimming. The Atlantic coast water temperatures range from distinctly cool to dangerously cold.

 FARM AND COUNTRY VACATIONS. More than 40 Nova Scotia families are members of the farm and country vacation program. This includes farmers, fishermen, and rural people who have opened their homes to guests on a year-round or seasonal basis.

Country vacation guests live, eat, and become part of the host family for a few days or weeks. Guests may take part in the farm activities or go fishing with the host. Many country vacation homes have swimming, fishing, and hiking facilities on or near their property.

Guests are advised to take along old clothes and extra shoes and boots. Paying for the vacation is more easily done on arrival. Ask before bringing along the family pet.

Costs range from about $85 to $125 per person per week; children under twelve from about $50 to $60 per week. Includes three home-cooked, home-grown meals plus snacks each day. Reservations should be made early and directly with the country family chosen. Information and listings of families in the program may be obtained from the Nova Scotia Department of Tourism or at individual tourist bureaus.

 RESORTS. *Expensive:* **Liscombe Lodge.** At Liscombe Mills, on Hwy. 7/Marine Dr. (902–779–2307, in winter, 902–424–3258). 35 units, including cottages and chalets. Tennis, boat, and canoe rentals, lawn games, deep-sea and freshwater fishing, marina. Major credit cards.

The Pines Resort Hotel. At Digby (902–245–2511). 90 bedrooms in main lodge, 60 more in deluxe cottages. Licensed dining room with dress regulations in effect. Live entertainment, outdoor swimming pool, floodlit tennis courts, 18-hole golf course, other activities. Modified American Plan optional (breakfast and dinner). Major credit cards.

Moderate: **The Mountain Gap Inn.** At Smith's Cove near Digby. (902–245–2277). 100 motel units and 12 cottages. Licensed lounge and dining room. 25 acres of landscaped ground with tidal-beach frontage. Swimming pool, tennis courts, conference and convention facilities. Major credit cards.

White Point Beach Lodge. At Hunt's Point, near Liverpool. (902–354–3177). 300-acre beach resort with ocean beach, freshwater lake, heated pool, golf course, tennis courts, boating facilities. 24 rooms in lodges and 40 cottages with one to three bedrooms. Major credit cards.

 CHILDREN'S ACTIVITIES. With many picnic and recreation areas, the main highways tend to follow the coast where children can safely explore beaches and rocks.

The wildlife parks at Shubenacadie, near Halifax/Dartmouth, in Upper Clements near Digby and at Marion Bridge, near Sydney, are good for a half day each. No admission fee.

Many of the provincial parks have special areas for kids, and many of the commercial camping parks have playgrounds. At Cabotland, Cape Breton, at the junction of Rte. 105 and the Cabot Trail, there is a children's farm with pettable animals, pony rides and other attractions.

Fishing can provide hours of enjoyment. Saltwater fishing requires no license and in most places youngsters can fish from the local wharf with some hope of a catch.

Bryce and Sylvia Milne, Grand Pré, Nova Scotia, have a large farm with riding horses and lots of pets. The Milnes are members of the farm and country vacation program, but they take only children—up to three at a time. Cost is about $125 per week per child, which includes everything. Address: P.O. Box 31, Grand Pré, N.S. 3OP 1M0; 542–3054.

 SUMMER SPORTS. Boating: During the summer Nova Scotians take to the water. Nova Scotia's most famous ship, the *Bluenose II*—a reproduction of the original race champion fishing schooner, *Bluenose I*—sails daily except Mondays from the Privateer's Wharf in Halifax for 2-hour harbor cruises. Call 424–4247 for information. Halifax Water Tours offers tours of Halifax Harbour and environs, starting from Historic Properties. Phone 423–7783. Guided walking tours of the islands of Halifax Harbour take place May 15 to September 25. Boat leaves from near the Maritime Museum of the Atlantic. Call 422–9523. Along the *South Shore,* the Oak Island Inn Marina at Western Shore, Lunenburg County (627–2600) gives tours of the Mahone Bay area and charters large and small sailboats. In Dayspring, R.R.3, Bridgewater, in Lunenburg County, Brian Stokes has a 34-foot ketch, two lasers, and 18-foot keel sloops available, with or without crew; he also gives sailing lessons. 543–3658. In Chester, Lunenburg County, you can take 2½-hour cruises on the *Buccaneer Lady,* a 50-foot cabin cruiser, sailing from the Buccaneer Lodge in Chester (275–5255). In Mahone Bay, Whitehouse Marine Ltd. (627–2641 in-season, 861–3418 off-season) charters a crewed boat, sailing out of Oak Island Marina. Marriotts Cove Charter (275–4886) has bare boat or skippered charters in the Mahone Bay—St. Margaret's Bay area aboard the 25-foot diesel auxiliary ketch *Ailsa III.* In Lunenburg, *Timberwind,* an authentic 35-foot gaff-rigged sailing schooner, sails daily, June to late September, from the Lunenburg Fisheries Museum four times a day. $8.50 per person. Charters also available. Phone 634–8966. Along the *Northumberland Shore,* contact the Tatamagouche Tourist Bureau in Tatamagouche, Nova Scotia, for information.

The Nova Scotia Dept. of Tourism's brochure *Nova Scotia Sports and Activities* has additional information on marinas, charters and rentals.

Canoe route information is available from the Nova Scotia Government Bookstore, 1597 Hollis St., Halifax. The publication, *Canoe Routes of Nova Scotia,* is available from Canoe Nova Scotia, P.O. Box 3010 South, Halifax, N.S. Phone 425–5450. Cost: $9.25.

Golf: Nova Scotia and Cape Breton have 38 golf courses as well as driving ranges and miniature golf courses, all described in *Nova Scotia Sports and Activities,* available, free, from the N.S. Dept. of Tourism.

Tennis is popular and many private clubs have excellent courts. For a list of public courts, contact the Nova Scotia Department of Tourism.

Bicycling: *Bicycle Tours in Nova Scotia* is available for $3.50 postpaid. Write to: Bicycle Nova Scotia, P.O. Box 3010 South, Halifax, N.S.

Other Sports: The Tourism Department will also supply complete information on other popular activities such as *hiking, flying, skiing, snowmobiling, scuba diving, fishing* in both fresh- and salt-water, and *hunting.*

CAMPING OUT. Nova Scotia has a large number of private and provincial (government) campgrounds througout the province. The provincial recreation areas listed in the previous section all have camping facilities, as have the two national parks.

Private campgrounds are inspected by the provincial department of tourism and licensed if they pass inspection. The better campgrounds display the "Approved Campground" sign issued by the Department of Tourism. The awarding of the approval sign is based on an operation displaying a high degree of cleanliness, comfort, and hospitality over and above the necessary minimum for licensing.

Minimum charge at most private campgrounds is about $5.00; the maximum is dependent on the services provided. Provincial recreation area campground charges begin at about $4.00; and, in the national parks, at about $3.50. The national parks also have a user permit of about $1 per vehicle per day, $2 for a four day pass, and $10 for an annual pass valid at all Canadian national parks.

Camping in Nova Scotia is allowed only at designated camping areas. No camping is allowed in picnic areas, day use parks, or along public highways.

 WINTER SPORTS. Skiing, particularly cross-country, is becoming more popular in Nova Scotia but the province does not have the heavy and consistent snowfall necessary to make it a great ski area. January, February, and March usually provide the best snow, but it is not unusual for snow to be wiped out by a warm rain early in the season.

Other sports: *Ice skating, ice boating,* and *snowshoeing* are also popular winter sports.

Contact the Nova Scotia Department of Tourism for information.

 HISTORIC SITES. The first permanent European settlement north of the Gulf of Mexico was at Port Royal in what is now Nova Scotia. Here, in 1605, the French explorers Champlain and de Monts established their *Habitation,* or trading post, which stood until Virginian raiders scattered the French and leveled the buildings in 1613.

To reach the Habitation compound, now rebuilt, follow Rte. 1 toward Annapolis Royal and turn off to the right (if approaching Annapolis Royal from the east) just before crossing the Annapolis Causeway.

Fort Anne National Historic Park in Annapolis Royal documents part of the two-century French-English struggle for North America. Check open hours; call 532–5197.

Longfellow's poetic story of Evangeline and Gabriel, two Acadians driven apart by the French-English struggles, has its memorial at *Grand Pré National Historic Site* near Wolfville. The interpretive center has displays and artifacts. Call 542–3631.

Fort Edward, in the town of Windsor, has the oldest surviving blockhouse in Canada. Call 426–5080.

With the exception of Fortress Louisbourg (see *Practical Information for Cape Breton*) there is no admission charge to any National Historic Sites which are usually open from mid-May to mid-October, 9 A.M. to 8 P.M., though times may vary with the site. For material on any of the sites, contact Parks Canada— Atlantic Region, 5161 George Street, Halifax, NS B3J 1M7, (902–426–3405).

The Nova Scotia Museum operates the following sites in the province:

Perkins House in **Liverpool** is a fine restored New England-style example of the Nova Scotia lifestyle prior to the American Revolution. In **Shelburne,** the *Ross-Thompson House* has been restored with trade items of the day.

Uniacke House, at **Mount Uniacke** near Halifax, presents one of the finest examples of the architecture and furnishings of the early 1800's to be found in North America. Thomas Chandler Haliburton, creator of the famous Sam Slick stories, completed his home in **Windsor** in 1836. *Haliburton House. "Clifton,"* is now open to the public. *Lawrence House* in **Maitland** was the home of the builder of Nova Scotia's largest wooden ship. The gracious Georgian brick house of Charles *Prescott* was completed about 1814 at **Starr's Point** near Wolfville. The early 19th-century home of *Thomas McCulloch* in **Pictou** has fine examples of carved interior woodwork.

The Museum also operates three historic mills in Nova Scotia. The *Wile Carding Mill* in **Bridgewater,** water-wheel driven, is unchanged since the days of the mid-1800's. The *Woolen Mill* in **Barrington** shows how the wool was woven into bolts of twills and flannels, blankets and suitings. The *Balmoral Grist Mill* at **Balmoral Mills** is one of the oldest operating mills in the province, dating from 1860. Visitors may purchase sample bags of stone ground flours and meals. A pleasant picnic ground overlooks the mill pond and falls.

The historic homes and mills are open from mid-May to mid-October, 9:30 A.M. to 5:30 P.M. daily. No admission charge.

Sherbrooke Village on Rte. 7 is a living village museum—a restoration of a 19th-century lumbering and gold-mining community. The inhabitants of the village still live in their homes within the "museum" and all of the buildings are staffed by costumed residents "working" at their trades. Wear walking shoes and try the excellent home-made soup or other fare at Bright House or What-Cheer-House. Open May 15 to October 15, 9:30 A.M. to 5:30 P.M. daily. Adult admission is $1.50; children enter free.

Ross Farm Museum, on Rte. 12 about 19 kms. (12 miles) north of Chester Basin, is a living museum which illustrates advances in farming from 1600 to 1925. Wear comfortable shoes or boots and old clothes. Adult admission is $1.50, children under 14 about 25¢. Family admissions are about $3.50. Open mid-May to mid-October, 9:30 to 5:30 daily. Open by appointment only the remainder of the year; 389-2210.

Museums on the Tourist Trails

Evangeline Trail (reached by Hwys. 1 and 101). In Yarmouth, the *County Historical Society Museum & Research Library* displays ship models and paintings, and the *Firefighters Museum* which illustrates the history of firefighting in the province; in Clementsport, the *Old St. Edwards Church Museum* (1797) is built like a ship of hand-hewn timbers; *North Hills Museum* at Granville Ferry has English furniture and bric-à-brac from the Georgian (1714–1830) period; in Annapolis Royal, the already-mentioned historical sites and the *O'Dell Inn & Tavern* and *The McNamara House* are restored buildings from the 19th and 18th centuries; in Middleton, the *Phinney Clock Collection* at the *Annapolis Valley MacDonald Museum,* an exhibit of 115 clocks and 52 watches, most of them brought to Nova Scotia by original settlers; in Wolfville, the *Historical Museum* features historical material from the New England Planters and Loyalists; in Hantsport, the *Churchill House and Maritime Museum* (1860) has a collection of shipbuilding tools, nautical instruments, old ships' logs and pictures.

Lighthouse Route (reached by Hwys. 3 and 103). The *Acadian Museum,* West Pubnico, tells of local history; *The Old Meeting House,* which is the oldest nonconformist church building in Canada (1766), and the *Cape Sable Historical Society Archives,* both in Barrington; in Lockeport, the *Little School Museum* is a restoration project housing a local history collection; in Bridgewater, the *Des Brisay Museum and Park,* which is the oldest municipally owned museum collection in Nova Scotia; the *Fort Point Museum* in La Have, a former lighthouse keeper's house; in Parkdale, the *Parkdale-Maplewood Museum* which emphasizes the German heritage of the area; in Blockhouse, the *Roaring 20's Museum* houses Nathern Joudrey's private collection of antique cars; in Lunenburg the *Lunenburg Fisheries Museum* and the *Aquarium* which is aboard two former fishing vessels and a one-time rumrunner; and via Rte. 332 from Lunenburg is the site of an old-time goldrush with monuments, caverns and a museum at the *Riverport-Ovens Natural Park.*

Glooscap Trail (reached by Hwys. 2 and 215). In Minudie, the *Amos Seaman School Museum,* which is housed in a restored one-room schoolhouse; the *Geological Museum* in Parrsboro has minerals and semiprecious stones from the region; in Springhill, visitors can go down into an actual mine and dig coal from the face at the *Miners' Museum;* in Truro, the *Colchester Historical Society Museum;* in Walton, the *Walton Museum* of local history; and on Rte. 14 the *South Rawdon Museum* has a small collection reflecting the former local temperance movement in a one-time Sons of Temperance Hall.

Sunrise Trail (reached by Hwy. 6). The *Sunrise Trail Museum* in Tatamagouche features memorabilia of the local-born giantess Anna Swann; in Pictou, the *Micmac Museum* is located next to a 17th-century Micmac burial ground and is the largest archeological discovery of its kind in Eastern Canada; in New

Glasgow, the *Pictou County Historical Museum* which features "Samson", the first steam locomotive used in Canada; and in nearby Stellarton, the *Mining Museum & Library;* in MacPherson Mills, *MacPherson's Mill & Farmstead* has a water-powered grist mill and restored farm buildings.

Marine Drive Trail (reached by Hwys. 7, 316, 16 and 344). In Musquodoboit Harbour, the *Railway Museum* is housed in a 1917 CNR station and features two restored railway cars; in Jeddore Oyster Pond, the *Fisherman's House & Museum* illustrates the life of the inshore fisherman from 1890–1920; in Sheet Harbour the *Marine Gallery Museum* has local history collected; and in Sherbrooke, the whole center of the village has been restored as a living museum; in Guysborough town, the *Old Court House* (1843) and in Canso town, the *Canso Museum* features a special marine exhibit and a widow's-walk.

MUSIC. With the vast Scottish heritage, bagpipe music and Gaelic songs are an important part of Nova Scotia culture. Although Gaelic is spoken only by a small minority, the skirl of the pipes has been adopted by Nova Scotians of every background. Scottish concerts are held throughout the summer months in a number of communities. If you find an announcement for a ceilidh (pronounced kay-lee), that means a Scottish concert. Check *"Seasonal Events"* section earlier in this chapter, the newspaper events supplements, and Nova Scotia Tourism's *Calendar of Events.*

REGIONAL THEATER. Live amateur theater is alive and well in Nova Scotia. The *Kipawo Show Boat Company* in Wolfville (542–3500 or 3542) is the best-known, but the *Mulgrave Road Co-op Company* in Mulgrave, *Mermaid Theatre* in Wolfville, *Theatre Antigonish* in Antigonish, the *Deaf-Gypsy Mime Company* in Centreville, *Savoy Theatre* in Glace Bay, and *Mermaid Theatre* in Dartmouth also are making themselves known. Some of these companies tour the province, putting on two or three productions a year. Also the puppet theater, *Canadian Puppet Festivals* in Chester (275–3171 or 3430), has drawn critical acclaim. The department of tourism or the department of culture can tell you more.

SHOPPING. Nova Scotia's shopping centers tend to be uninspiring, not much different from anything you might find anywhere else in North America. The exciting shopping and fascinating browsing is found in the shops of craftspeople all over the province—where you'll find everything from blacksmiths in East Dover, silversmiths in Waverley, to leaded glass hanging ornaments in Purcells Cove, to wooden toys in Middleton, pewter in Wolfville, pottery in Arichat, apple dolls in Halifax. The N.S. Dept. of Culture, Recreation and Fitness (P.O. Box 864, Halifax, N.S. B3J 2V2; phone 902–424–4061) or the Dept. of Tourism will send you the Handcraft Directory, an excellent guide to the craftspeople of Nova Scotia.

Antique stores proliferate all over Nova Scotia and Cape Breton. One of the better—and more genuine—ones is *Dana Sweeny Antiques* in Mahone Bay.

Another source of unique shopping and browsing experiences (and, likely, good stories from the shopkeepers) are the hundreds of tiny, rural general stores in villages all over the province. In these you might find anything from yardgoods to harnesses, sou'westers to weird ointments—well worth poking around in these stores.

The largest shopping center in the province is MicMac Mall in Dartmouth off the A. Murray Mackay Bridge. It is also the largest east of Montréal. Next is Scotia Square in Halifax, which has dozens of chain stores as well as dozens of specialty shops; the next largest is the Woolco shopping center in Sydney, on the highway as you go in on Rte. 4. Here, you'll be able to get recordings of local but well-known musicians like Lee Cremo or the Men of the Deeps, The Steel City Players, "Rise & Follies of Cape Breton" or the Glendale Concert albums.

LIQUOR LAWS. The legal drinking age in Nova Scotia is 19 years. Bottled alcoholic beverages are sold only in Nova Scotia Liquor Commission (NSLC) retail stores, located in most major communities. NSLC hours vary from place to place, but they are usually open from 10 A.M. to 5 P.M. weekdays and Saturdays, and to 9 P.M. on Friday evenings, and all are closed on Sundays.

Beer and alcoholic beverages by the glass are sold in licensed restaurants (food must also be ordered) and in licensed lounges (cocktail lounge, a bar with entertainment, only the name is changed). Beer by the bottle and draught beer by the glass are sold in taverns and beverage rooms, which often offer surprisingly good snacks and light meals. Open hours average from 10 A.M. to midnight. Licensed lounges average from 11 A.M. to 2 A.M.

There are no restrictions on women entering taverns in Nova Scotia, although the atmosphere in some taverns tends to be a bit rough.

A few "dry" areas still remain in Nova Scotia, but barriers are falling rapidly and the "wets" are prevailing. For a list of dry districts, contact the Nova Scotia Department of Tourism.

RESTAURANTS. The food in most Nova Scotia restaurants in well prepared—especially the seafood. In the past few years the standard of cuisine and its presentation have improved greatly.

Service is generally good in the better restaurants although it can be slow, especially if the place is busy.

Restaurants are categorized on the basis of a full-course dinner, with drinks, tips and tax excluded. *Expensive,* over $15; *Moderate,* $10 to $15; *Inexpensive,* under $10.

A 10% provincial tax will be added to all meals over $3.

Most places accept the following major credit cards: American Express, MasterCard and Visa; others may also be honored. Not all establishments accept credit cards, therefore we suggest you call for information.

ANTIGONISH. *Moderate–Expensive:* **Lobster Treat Restaurant.** 241 Post Rd. (863–5465). On the Trans Canada Hwy. Undistinguished looking on the outside, a pleasant surprise inside. Seafood specialties; licensed.

BRIDGETOWN. *Moderate:* **Continental Kitchen.** Granville Ferry, RR 1 (665–2287). Spotlessly clean, excellent food prepared in a country style, huge portions. Licensed. Be sure to make reservations early in the day.

CHESTER. *Expensive:* **The Captain's House.** 129 Central St. (275–3501). Restored to its early 1800s elegance. Specializes in the fine Maritime recipes. An experience. Major credit cards.
Rope Loft. Phone: 275–3430. One of the best views in the province. Food usually excellent; licensed. Bring a camera. Open noon–10 P.M. summer season only. Reservations recommended; seafood specialty. Major credit cards.

DIGBY. *Expensive:* **The Pines Resort Hotel Dining Room.** Shore Rd. (245–2511). Usually good food served in large dining room of older resort hotel. Pleasant grounds overlooking Digby harbor; dancing. Specialty is Digby scallops. Major credit cards.

LISCOMBE MILLS. *Expensive:* **Liscombe Lodge Dining Room.** Phone: 779–2307. A good dining room in this resort overlooking the Liscombe River. Stone fireplace often lit for dinner; specialty is fresh salmon caught in nearby river; licensed. Call for meal hours and reservations. Open May–mid-October. Major credit cards.

LUNENBURG. *Moderate.* **Boscowen Inn.** 150 Cumberland St. (634–3325). Restored Victorian mansion. Emphasis on seafood.
Mug Up Chowderhouse. 128 Montague St. (634–3118). Noted for its food.

MAHONE BAY. *Expensive.* **Zwicker Inn.** 662 Main St. (624–8045). Renovated old post house of 1805. Charming atmosphere with wide range of excellent food, especially seafood.

NEW GLASGOW. *Expensive:* **Heather Motel Dining Room.** Foord St. Stellarton (752–8401). Clean, comfortable place with friendly service and usually good food. Licensed. Call for reservations. Major credit cards.

SHERBROOKE VILLAGE. *Moderate:* **The Bright House.** Main St. (522–2691). A licensed dining room serving lunch and dinner; specializes in roast beef. Open May–October. Visa and MasterCard accepted.
Inexpensive: **What Cheer House.** In historic Sherbrooke Village living museum. Turn of the century village inn with hearty seafood chowder, beef stew, home-baked beans and bread. Not licensed. Lunch and tea only.

TRURO. *Expensive:* **Glengarry Motel Dining Room.** 138 Willow St. (895–5388). Features home cooking in large dining room. Major credit cards.
The Village Estate, 164 Farnham Rd., Bible Hill (895–3809). Licensed dining room on historic estate. Good wine cellar.

WOLFVILLE. *Expensive.* **Blomidon Inn.** 127 Main St. (542–9326). Lovely old mansion. Dining room provides fresh country seasonal produce. Excellent.

YARMOUTH. *Expensive:* **Harris' Seafood Restaurant.** (Restaurant on the right side of the highway is run by the same people but is a short order place.) Phone: 742–5420. Possibly the best seafood in Nova Scotia. Lobster is a specialty. Call for reservations.
Manor Inn. Rte. 1 (742–2487). Good food in pleasant surroundings. Beer garden, dining room in manor with folk singers. Licensed. Steak and lobster especially good. Call for reservations.
Moderate: **Rodd's Grand Hotel.** 417 Main St. (742–2446). Ordinary hotel dining room except for hot lobster sandwich—big chunks of creamed lobster served on toast. Live entertainment and dancing except on Sundays. Major credit cards.

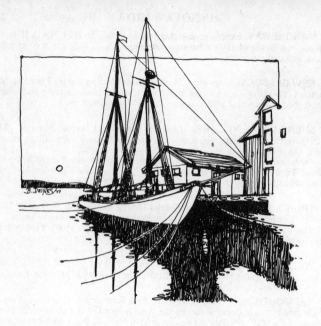

PRINCE EDWARD ISLAND

Vacation Province

by
RALPH SURETTE and MARGOT SAMMURTOK

*Ralph Surette is a freelance journalist living in Nova Scotia. He writes
for a number of Canadian magazines and is a regular commentator on
Canadian Broadcasting Corporation Radio. Margot Sammurtok is a
public relations consultant and free-lance editor who lives in Halifax and
is very involved with tourism in the Atlantic provinces.*

Prince Edward Island (P.E.I.) is cradled on the waves of the Gulf of
St. Lawrence, off the coasts of New Brunswick and Nova Scotia. This
precious island province has enchanted people for nearly 2,000 years.
From about A.D. 100, the Micmac Indians canoed from the mainland
across Northumberland Strait for summers of fishing. Eventually they
settled here (and are still represented here on four reservations), calling
the island Abegweit, which means "cradled on the waves." French
explorer Jacques Cartier, on sighting the island in 1534, called it "the
fairest land 'tis possible to see!" When the British took possession more
than two hundred years later, Edward, Duke of Kent, was impressed
enough to give it his name. But those who live there, and those who
visit, know it simply (and fondly) as "the Island."

The Island is naturally beautiful. The red sandstone cliffs of the
southern coastline, topped by rich green fields and trees, give summer
visitors arriving by ferry across Northumberland Strait their first im-
pressions of the lasting beauty of the province. The north shore, with
its white, silky sand that makes up much of the Island's 800 kilometers

(500 miles) of beaches along with the immaculate communities that form part of the gently rolling inland landscape offer a contrasting beauty.

That the Island has retained its popular appeal over the centuries is a tribute not only to its enduring beauty, but also to the friendly, hardy residents (many of them descendants of the early settlers), who live and work harmoniously while maintaining their individual heritages. Just 244 kilometers (140 miles) tip-to-tip, and from 6.4 kilometers (4 miles) to 64 kilometers (40 miles) across, Prince Edward Island is permanent home to 123,000 Islanders.

The Island appeals to its inhabitants in much the same way that it attracts visitors, offering its lovely land, relaxing lifestyle, clean environment, and wide range of diversions. The Island residents have industriously developed their agricultural, coastal, and educational resources while maintaining a highly desirable lifestyle and retaining a stubborn pride in their heritage—British, French, Scottish, and Micmac Indian—evidenced in the many local museums that dot the province and in the number of cultural festivals held throughout the tourist season.

Agriculture

Prince Edward Island has been described as two huge beaches separated by potato fields. An apt, if oversimplified, description. Farmland makes up about 49 percent of the land area. Potatoes are the major crop, occupying about 70,000 hectares (170,000 acres). The Island is self-sufficient in its production of grain and waving fields of barley, oats, wheat, and other grains are a feast for the eye with their summer hues of brown and yellow and green. Many vegetables and strawberries, blueberries, and raspberries are grown. There is a good-sized livestock population, too. The Islanders take great pride in their reputation for producing high-quality, disease-free crops and livestock.

Tourism

Tourism adds $65 million annually to the Island's economy. More than 600,000 visitors come to this vacation island annually and more than 70 percent come again. Small wonder. A reasonable drive from Montreal, New York, or Toronto; an easy drive from Halifax, Bangor, or Boston, Prince Edward Island is readily accessible via ferries. There is modern car and passenger service from points on mainland New Brunswick and Nova Scotia, and from the Magdalen Islands. There are flights from major cities on the Canadian mainland and from Bangor, Maine. The tourist season is May to October with the greatest concentration of visits taking place in the summer months; but conventions have helped to increase year-round "tourist" visitations.

Prince Edward Island offers visitors a very broad range of activities and attractions. Not surprisingly, many of them relate to water. There is sportfishing, boardsailing (wind surfing), boating, and other watersports on inland and coastal waters. The Island's 1,760 kilometers (1,100 miles) of coastline offer 800 kilometers (500 miles) of Class A beaches, huge sand dunes, and some of the warmest salt water north of Florida. Ten golf courses (seven of them 18-hole) offer ocean or riverside settings. Harness racing, horseback riding, camping, festivals, lobster suppers, and repertory theater add to the available pleasures, not to mention the sightseeing possibilities: museums, art galleries, historic homes, and—for the children—a surprising number of amusement and theme parks within minutes of most major crossroads.

What the visitor will find most distinctive are the historic and personal elements: the enduring French Acadian influence; the vestiges of Micmac, English, and Scottish settlements; vacation farms that offer visitors the unique experience of sharing accommodations—and chores —of their farm family hosts; homes/studios of the many local craftsmen (some of whom provide free demonstrations of their craft), where travelers can stop awhile and talk with the artisans and, of course, buy their works; the serenity of the low inland hills; and, above all, an essentially rural island personality that sets this island apart from similar but more commercial holiday destinations.

The sense of remoteness is one of the Island's most appealing features. Many of the facilities are oriented to the natural environment, and tourists are invited to "discover an Island." There are numerous federal, provincial, and private camping and trailer sites. There are more than 5,440 kilometers (3,880 miles) of paved roads in the province to make exploration easy, including the three scenic drives called Lady Slipper Drive, Blue Heron Drive, and Kings Byway. The routes loop around western, central, and eastern Prince Edward Island, each following the coastline of the Island's three major land divisions formed naturally by the bays and rivers. These divisions are also the approximate boundaries of the province's three counties, Prince, Queens, and Kings.

Islanders encourage visitors to allot at least one day for each drive. Relaxation is the watchword and side trips are the rule since distances between attractions are short and almost every road eventually leads to a major highway. Each drive features access to beaches, parks, camping grounds, scenic lookouts, towns, villages with notable historic or special attractions, and places where you can buy fresh seafood and vegetables.

Although Prince Edward Island is very much part of the modern world, it has retained the relaxed pace and human qualities of an earlier age. Islanders are not only friendly but thoroughly hospitable, preferring unpretentious comfort, homey accommodations, and traditional food from land and sea. Food should be a treat, as a mainstay of the dinner table is lobster, brought in daily from the deep waters off the coast when the season permits. The lobster supper, an Island tradition, is a unique dining experience and should be sought out when touring along the North Shore. Other seasonal treats are the famous Malpeque oysters (once farmed exclusively in Malpeque Bay but now cultivated throughout coastal Prince Edward Island); strawberries and blueberries, which thrive on the Island's sandy soil; and the plenteous homegrown vegetables that invariably surprise the visitor because of the Island's small size and short growing season.

Fisheries

Fishing is Prince Edward Island's third industry, with lobsters the most profitable of the more than 30 varieties of fish (including cod, sole, herring, scallops, and tuna) yielded up by the waters surrounding and crisscrossing the Island. The inshore fishery adds about $50 million to the Island's annual economy.

History is Sparsely Recorded

Except for scattered monuments, restorations, recreated villages (some frankly commercial), gravestones and the like, there are few visible reminders on Prince Edward Island of the earliest European settlements. But the Island did experience a history of quarrelsome confrontations between those early rivals France and England in the race to exploit and colonize North America. The heritage of both remains.

The French came first but took their time in settling here. Jacques Cartier discovered Prince Edward Island in 1534, but his countrymen did not establish an outpost on Ile St. Jean, as they named it, until 1663. A more complete settlement was established in 1720 by Compte St. Pierre and a band of 300 at Port La Joie, across the harbor from what is now Charlottetown, the capital of Prince Edward Island. (Today, the site of Port La Joie is part of Fort Amherst National Historic Park.) France hoped that the new settlement would draw from the Acadian (French) settlements in what is now Nova Scotia, but there was little migration until the French were forced to leave, following the fall of Louisbourg on Cape Breton Island, Nova Scotia, to the English. The English Lord Rollo arrived with ships and men to take possession of the Island, and in 1763 Prince Edward Island changed hands from French to English. Its name was Anglicized to the Island of Saint John, and Charlotte Town (it was two words then) was named its capital. In 1769 the Island gained independence from Nova Scotia. In 1799 it was renamed Prince Edward Island in honor of Prince Edward (later Duke of Kent). Soon after, settlers began arriving from the Scottish Highlands, Ireland, and England.

A Peaceful Beginning

There is little indication of any major strife here between the early French settlers and the Island's Micmac Indians. The tribe—made up of small groups, each with its own chief—did not live in permanent villages, preferring instead to move from place to place as hunters and fishermen. Today, about 400 Micmac Indians remain on the Island's four reservations where they have found it difficult to maintain their native culture. By comparison, descendants of some of the early Acadians also remain on the Island but retain their identity in a number of ways, notably in their food, their music, and their language. The Acadians are often considered to speak a debased form of French. They do not. Though many English words have crept into their speech over the years, their language is still basically good eighteenth-century provincial French, just as the distinctive accents of Newfoundland often prove to be pure eighteenth-century Devon or Dorset.

The population of the Island grew during the American Revolution, particularly at its end when British Loyalists were forced to leave the newly established United States and flee to Canada. It was during this period that the Island officially became a Crown Colony and was renamed Prince Edward Island. One of the more durable settlements was established by Scotland's Lord Selkirk, who arrived in 1803 with three ships of pioneers from the Scots Highlands. Restored log cabins and other shelters, as well as the group's church built in 1824, may be seen in the Belfast district of the Island, where there are also a number of descendants of the original settlers.

For most visitors, the Island's development in the first half of the nineteenth century has a more visible significance since a number of the homes, churches, government structures, monuments, and sites of historic or colorful interest can actually be seen and visited. Province House, in Charlottetown, is probably the most revered of these, having been the site of the 1864 conference of Confederation planners. Their deliberations led, three years later, to the union of all the British North American colonies into a united Canada, although Prince Edward Island did not join the Confederation until 1873. The imposing structure still serves as the province's legislature and still dominates the architecture of downtown Charlottetown.

A more contemporary symbol is Green Gables House, which served as the setting for Lucy Maud Montgomery's well-known novel, *Anne of Green Gables*. Situated at Cavendish, in the center of the Island's North Shore, the house should be visited by devotees of the book and other works by the author, although in other respects it is an unremarkable Island farmhouse. Nearby, Green Gables Post Office is the Island's most popular center for stamps and postmarks during the summer.

EXPLORING CHARLOTTETOWN

The provincial capital and Prince Edward Island's only city, Charlottetown, reflects its Loyalist heritage even in its name (after Charlotte, stylish consort of England's George III). It is often referred to as "the Cradle of Confederation," a reference to the conference held here in 1864 that led to Canada's unification.

Essentially a small city with a population of 15,300 (30,000 if you include surrounding areas), Charlottetown has no smokestack industry, in the traditional sense. Its main activities center around government, tourism, and private commerce, and in these capacities it functions as a service center for the surrounding districts. While these new suburbs were springing up, the core of Charlottetown remained unchanged and the waterfront was restored to recapture the tempo and appearance of earlier eras. The waterfront area now includes the Prince Edward Convention Centre and hotel, several off-Broadway-type restaurants, and handcraft and retail shops. The yacht club and marina are also focal points of the waterfront.

The facades of the old red brick buildings and the gingerbread architecture of the wood houses lining Charlottetown's side streets are other pleasant reminders of the past. The Prince Edward Island Museum and Heritage Foundation has strengthened this image of earlier days by restoring an entire block of row housing on Great George Street across from St. Dunstan's Basilica.

The exceptionally handsome—and modern—Confederation Centre of the Arts, opened in 1964 as Canada's national memorial to the Fathers of Confederation, houses an art gallery and museum, provincial library, memorial hall, two theaters (one of which is the 1,100-seat main stage theater), and a restaurant. From June to October, the Confederation Centre's Charlottetown Festival offers excellent professional entertainment, including the annual world-famous musical, *Anne of Green Gables*.

Two nearby churches are particularly noteworthy. St. Paul's Anglican Church, east of Province House, is the oldest (1747) Protestant church on the Island. Its baptismal register includes the name of Margaret Gordon, sweetheart of author Thomas Carlyle and heroine of his masterpiece, *Sartor Resartus*.

St. James Presbyterian Church, better known as "the kirk," has impressive stained-glass windows and ancient relics from the island of Iona, one of the earliest Christian sites in Scotland. A block of granite resting on a marble slab embedded in the north wall of the kirk came from St. Mary's Cathedral on Iona. It also has an intriguing legend. On the day in 1853 when the ship *Fairy Queen* went down in Northumberland Strait, the kirk was empty, but the kirk's bell, so the story goes, was heard to toll many times. A townsman who heard it claimed to have seen three women, bareheaded and barefooted, disappear through the locked doors of the kirk. Later it was learned that three female members of the congregation were lost in the wreck.

South of Province House, on Great George Street, stands St. Dunstan's Basilica, seat of the Roman Catholic diocese in the province. It is not only one of the largest edifices of its kind in eastern Canada, but contains an impressive altar along with many beautifully executed Italian carvings.

St. Peter's Cathedral, in the northwest corner of Rochford Square, was erected in 1879 and consecrated by the Lord Bishop of Nova Scotia. The church chapel (1888) was designed by W.C. Harris, with murals by his famous brother, Islander Robert Harris.

Victoria Park, overlooking the expanse of water in Charlottetown Harbour at the southernmost tip of the city, is the setting for several notable buildings. Located on a hill between white birches is the old Government House, a mansion built in 1835 as the official residence for the province's lieutenant governors. Across the street from the mansion stands Beaconsfield, a house designed by W.C. Harris; it's an excellent example of Victorian architecture. Built in 1877, it houses the Prince Edward Island Museum and Heritage Foundation offices, the Centre for Genealogical Research, and a bookstore specializing in publications about the Island. Periodically, Island artifacts are on display, and the interior design of this gracious old home is worth a visit.

Also in Victoria Park and overlooking the harbor is Fort Edward, built in 1805. It is one of a series of fortifications constructed along the Charlottetown harbor entrance, and has a six-gun battery. From here one can look across the harbor mouth to Fort Amherst, now a National Historic Site.

The University of Prince Edward Island is located in the provincial capital and is a popular spot for people of all ages. The university offers Elderhostel programs along with its regular summer educational programs.

Exploring Routes near Charlottetown

For a rewarding coastal drive, take Route 1 out of Charlottetown and Route 19 around Fort Amherst National Park, site of the old French fort. On the way, you'll drive through Cornwall, a spot where it is said a mermaid came ashore one day. Described "as big as a small girl," she talked to no one and allowed no one to get close. After about an hour in the July sun, she slipped back into the ocean.

At New Haven on Route 1, Fairyland is one of the many attractions that cater especially to children.

At Hampton, watch for Route 116, which takes you to the shore and to Victoria Provincial Park. No matter where you travel in this section, the scenery is delightful. Nearby Victoria-by-the-Sea is a quaint old English community. When you are here, take a drive around Augustine's Cove.

SCENIC DRIVES THROUGH
PRINCE EDWARD ISLAND

There are three scenic drives in Prince Edward Island, roughly corresponding to the province's three counties of Prince, Queens, and Kings. The drives are outlined on highway maps in red, blue, and purple, respectively, and highway markers are color-keyed accordingly. The scenic drives are comprehensively described in the brochure *Explorer's Guide to P.E.I.*, which can be obtained at any of the ten provincial Visitor Information Centres (VICs), at most privately owned tourist operations and at some car rental agencies. As you loop through the province with the help of this colorful guide, you will discover the highways, byways, and waterways that lend such distinction to this vacation province. Each drive is more or less a continuous circle, so the driver may start or stop at any point or travel in either direction. All together, the scenic drives take in the entire coast of Prince Edward Island and also provide easy access to inland areas and communities. Most highways are paved, with some short stretches of smooth red clay. With few exceptions, roads are evenly surfaced and well maintained for comfortable drives.

Lady Slipper Drive

The scenic Lady Slipper Drive is 288 kilometers (135 miles) long and follows the coast of western P.E.I., swooping past bright red sandstone cliffs and silver sand dunes and rolling through the lush green meadow lands. It takes its name from the delicate Lady Slipper Orchid, the official floral emblem of the province. The highway marker is a white square with a red border and a red orchid in the center.

The region encircled by the drive is made up of small and very old villages (with the exception of Summerside, the largest P.E.I. community designated as a town, and second in size to Charlottetown), still adhering to a more traditional way of life. This western region is the home of the Island's Acadians, descendants of the original French settlers. In addition to the strong Acadian presence, Micmac Indians, farms, Irish moss, and oysters are pronounced influences in the region.

At Summerside

You can preview your tour of this region at the Lady Slipper Visitor Information Centre at Wilmot on Route 1A, 2 kilometers (1.2 miles) east of Summerside, where staff are available to answer questions and help with reservations. Proceed west to Summerside. An annual event here is the eight-day Summerside Lobster Carnival in mid-July. The Carnival is actually a combination fair and festival, with exhibits of livestock, agriculture, and handicrafts as well as parades, beauty contests, harness racing, a midway, and, of course, lobster suppers (chicken too). Specific dates of the Carnival are available from the Island's Visitor Information Centres or from the Summerside Area Tourist Association.

From Summerside follow the Lady Slipper Drive signs on Route 1A to St. Eleanors; then turn west on Route 2 to Miscouche. Here, the Acadian Museum of P.E.I. has a collection of artifacts dating from before the 1800s which relate to Acadian lifestyles over the years. There are household and farm implements as well as other domestic items. The red stone monument behind the museum stands over a collective Acadian grave transferred from River Platte in 1839.

Following the northern route of the Drive, proceed up Route 12 to Rosehill, then turn right onto Route 123, and continue along the road that curves around the cape—jutting into Malpeque Bay, center of the Island's oyster-farming industry. The road rejoins Route 12, which then winds along the western shore of the Bay, across rivers and harbor inlets, and through small and large ports serving as harvest centers for other catches of the Island's important fishing industry.

The Green Park Shipbuilding Museum & Historic House, a provincial historic park at Port Hill, merits a visit. There is a mansion here that was the onetime home of a shipbuilding family named Yeo, and the park area is now a permanent museum. The mansion, built in 1865, has been restored and refurnished. An interpretive center houses displays and artifacts from those early wooden ships, and there is a shipyard with a display of a wooden vessel under construction. Informal tours of the house are conducted and demonstrations are given of domestic life during the 1860s.

On Route 163 off Route 12 is the Lennox Island Micmac Indian Nation scenic reservation. St. Ann's Catholic Church was built in 1869; the altar railing, plant stand, and chair, made by local Micmacs, is on display at the Arts & Craft Shop which specializes in local and Canadian crafts, collector, and one-of-a-kind items.

Farther north is Alberton, one of several major deep-sea charter fishing ports along Lady Slipper Drive (others included are Skinner's Pond and Conway Harbour Inlet). Deep-sea fishing outings can be a family affair and all you need are warm clothing and a lunch. Most trips last four hours, with cod, mackerel, halibut, herring, and hake the usual catches. Cost is $10 per person or more. The cost for tuna chartering is usually $300 per eight-hour day for upwards of six persons, and there are often special rates for children. The boat captain will supply all the tackle and bait and you don't need a license.

Leavitt's Maple Tree Craft Shop in Alberton specializes in turned Bird's-eye maplewood products. The craftspeople here are always ready to talk with visitors, and bird's-eye maple blanks can be purchased for home lathes. There is also a variety of finished wood products. Also in Alberton, the Alberton Museum features local and provincial artifacts and relics, housed in what was Alberton's first courthouse, built in 1878. It focuses on the silver fox industry, which thrived here in the early part of this century, but also has Indian relics, farm and trade implements, glass, china, books, and other artifacts.

At nearby Northport is Sea Rescue Park overlooking Northport harbor. The park is the site of the restored lifeboat station from which Northport seamen performed a daring rescue of survivors from a foundering sailing vessel during a storm in the fall of 1906. There are picnic tables, washrooms, water tap, and a children's playground.

North Cape

Lady Slipper Drive continues past Cape Kildare, where French explorer Cartier reportedly first got a close look at the Island, then proceeds to the northwestern-most tip of the Island named, appropriately, North Cape. This is the home of the Atlantic Wind Test Site, a national laboratory for testing and evaluating wind-driven generators. An audiovisual presentation is shown regularly in the site's visitor center.

Motoring down the western coastline, you will drive through Skinner's Pond and, a bit farther south, Miminegash at the head of the river of the same name, considered one of the better inland fishing areas in the western part of Prince Edward Island.

The next 48 kilometers (30 miles) or so of the Lady Slipper Drive follow the quietly attractive western and southern coastline. For a more sightworthy route, leave the Drive at Campbellton and take Route 145 to Route 2, turning right at Bloomfield to St. Anthony, and right again on Route 143 to Howlan. From here, Route 148 takes you to the farming community of O'Leary and the Prince Edward Island Potato Museum. There is a log barn with old farm implements, a building displaying local history with pictures of original residents, documents, and household artifacts, and a third building which is a little red schoolhouse transferred from Alaska, P.E.I.

At Coleman, you are again on Lady Slipper Drive and should take the southern route back to Summerside in order to visit the Acadian Pioneer Village at Mont-Carmel. The restoration includes a church, priest's house, blacksmith shop, homes, barn, and store. The buildings are furnished with artifacts and restored items relating to the life of the French settlers of the early nineteenth century. To enjoy Acadian food, visit the restaurant on the site and try *Fricot* (Acadian stew) or Râpure (a meat and potato dish). Prices are reasonable. A French-language dinner theater, *La Cuisine Â Mémée,* portrays the uniqueness of the Acadian culture through its traditional humor and entertainment.

Blue Heron Drive

Circling the Island's center segment and roughly outlining Queens County, Blue Heron Drive is 190 kilometers (114 miles) long. It takes its name from the Great Blue Heron, a stately waterbird that migrates to Prince Edward Island each spring to nest in the shallow bays and marshes; you are likely to see several herons along the route. The highway marker is a white square with a blue border and a blue heron in the center.

From Charlottetown, Blue Heron Drive winds through farmland to the North Shore fishing villages, spectacular beaches of Prince Edward Island National Park and the Cabot Provincial Park, through Anne of Green Gables country, and along the south shore with its red sandstone seascapes and historic sites.

You might follow this suggested route: Drive north from Charlotte-town in a counterclockwise direction, follow Route 15 to Brackley Beach, a pivotal intersection for access to the roughly 40 kilometers (25 miles) of North Shore beaches that comprise the National Park. Symbols on the road map will advise you of available facilities (campsites, beaches, day-use parks, fishing).

Lobster Suppers

This is the region where you must sample the Island's distinctive lobster supper. Popular places for lobster suppers are New London, New Glasgow, St. Ann's Church in Hope River, Fisherman's Wharf in North Rustico, Stanhope Beach Lodge, and Rosebank Hall in Rose-bank.

At Brackley Beach, Blue Heron Drive turns left and follows Route 6 across Oyster Bed Bridge to South Rustico with its historic Farmer's Bank, chartered in 1864. Farmers and fishermen were its directors, and it prospered for thirty years by providing cheap credit to help the people of this predominantly Acadian community gain economic independence. Rustico, in fact, took its name from one of its early French settlers, René Rassicot, who came from Normandy. Townspeople claim that the world's first automobile was driven in this community in 1866, when Father Belcourt drove around in a "strange, noisy contraption."

South Rustico is also the home of Jumpin' Jack's Old Country Store Museum, an authentic old country store that dates back to the 1800s and features cracker barrels, fish barrels, egg crates, a checkerboard, potbellied stove, and countless other items purchased and used by the residents' forefathers. It is also the home of the world-famous racing pigs. Free admission, but donations are welcome and entitle you to membership in Jumpin' Jack's pig-racing club.

Anne of Green Gables Country

Farther along Route 6 is Cavendish and the farm famous as the setting for Lucy Maud Montgomery's best-loved novel, *Anne of Green Gables*. Green Gables House is situated on the edge of the challenging 18-hole Green Gables Golf Course in the national park. The house is open to the public (admission is free) and offers bilingual guide service.

Blue Heron Drive continues along Route 6 for about 11 kilometers (7 miles) to New London (you may want to see the white cottage where Lucy Maud Montgomery was born) and then turns north onto Route 20. Drive north along Route 20 to the French River district near New London harbor, where there are two pioneer-era cemeteries, Yankee Hill and Sims, located within 300 yards of each other. They contain tombstones of a number of residents who died between 1816 and 1843. Farther along the highway is Park Corner, where those who have read the stories of Pat of Silverbush (more of Lucy Maud Montgomery) might enjoy a visit to the Anne of Green Gables Museum at Silverbush. Lucy Maud was married here, and many personal effects are on display.

Historic Malpeque

Crossing over from Queens to Prince County, you come to Malpeque, one of the truly historic corners of Prince Edward Island. The French settled in this area in the early 1700s; before them, the wandering Micmac Indians camped here. Traces of their weapons and implements can still be found in Malpeque. In 1765, when the English sent Captain Samuel Holland to survey the new colony, he recommended that "Princetown," as he called the settlement, be made capital of Prince County (although it subsequently reverted to the Indian name). Five years later came the first sizable migration of Scots; many of their descendants live here today.

The Malpeque Gardens, proclaimed by many to be the loveliest in Atlantic Canada, feature 400 colors and varieties of dahlia, rose gardens, sunken gardens, an old-fashioned windmill, and a glass behive, among other things. The famous Malpeque oysters, originally farmed in adjacent Malpeque Bay, are shipped to seafood distribution centers throughout North America.

From Malpeque, follow the route to the southern coast and watch carefully for the Blue Heron Drive signs, since the highway route numbers change several times. At Cape Traverse, east of Borden, you'll find a monument to the ice boat—the only way to travel to the mainland in the winter before 1917. Still farther east is Augustine Cove, an exceptionally attractive inlet, and beyond that Victoria-by-the-Sea, a quaint Old English community where you might enjoy a two-hour sail out of Victoria harbor on a traditional schooner—one of the last coastal working vessels—for about $12.50 a person. Across the harbor is Victoria Provincial Park, a scenic setting for camping and picnicking.

Just beyond is DeSable and from here there are two major routes back to Charlottetown. The Blue Heron Drive continues along the red sandstone coastline to the end of the peninsula that faces Charlottetown south of its harbor. Just before this point is Fort Amherst National Historic Park, site of Port La Joie, the first French settlement and, later, of Fort Amherst (English), built in 1758. Today only the earthworks of the fort remain. The bilingual interpretive staff of the V.I.C. provide an audiovisual presentation detailing the social, political, and military history of the area.

At the tip of the peninsula is Rocky Point and the Micmac Indian Village. Displays at the village include birchbark wigwams and canoes, handmade hunting and fishing implements, and life-size sculptures of Indians and animals. Of special interest is the museum, which holds actual tools and weapons used by the first inhabitants of the Island.

The final leg of Blue Heron Drive backtracks a short way down the north side of the peninsula, then crosses the West River, and continues to Cornwall, where it connects with the Trans-Canada Highway (TCH) back to Charlottetown.

The alternate return from DeSable is more or less an inland drive along National Route 1 (TCH) and is generally more entertaining as well as scenic. At Bonshaw, just beyond DeSable, is the Car Life Museum which houses one of Eastern Canada's finest displays of antique and special-interest cars from 1898–1959, farm machinery from the early 1800s to the early 1900s, and farm tractors from 1914–1939. All exhibits are restored to their original performance and appearance. Farther along the highway is Strathgartney Provincial Park, a scenic area for tenting with a stunning view of the surrounding countryside. Route 1 continues through New Haven and Fairyland, an attraction for children; then it rejoins the Blue Heron Drive at Cornwall for the last several miles into Charlottetown.

Kings Byway Drive

The Kings Byway Scenic Drive is named after Kings County which includes the entire eastern end of the province. The drive is 375 kilometers (225 miles) long and takes visitors through some of the oldest and most interesting areas of Prince Edward Island. Many of the attractions recall early days of the Island settlers and the pioneering spirit they brought with them. There are red-banked and white sand beaches, the "singing sands" at Basin Head, highly photogenic lighthouse points, fisheries, and the "Tuna Capital of the World" at North Lake.

The Kings Byway is considerably longer than the other two drives. If you want to see it all, you should plan on staying overnight once or twice along the route. The Kings Byway highway marker is a white square bordered in royal purple with a crown in the center.

There are many major sights and attractions along the way, beginning at Charlottetown and heading south. The agricultural heritage of the Island's rural communities is highlighted at Orwell Corner Historic Village, an officially designated historic site near Orwell. A living farm museum, the site contains a combined store, post office, school, church, farmhouse, and barns. Farming methods are those of former years, and there are old-fashioned musical evenings and hayrides. Farm life of the early inhabitants is also highlighted at MacPhail Provincial Park at nearby Orwell. The home of Sir Andrew MacPhail, a noted Prince Edward Island physician and author, is surrounded by picnic grounds open to the public.

Farther along the route is Flat River, where the Flat River Crafts Studio specializes in good pottery. Visitors may chat with the craftspeople as they watch them at work. The *Mirana,* a 40-foot Newfoundland schooner, offers daily cruises on Northumberland Strait, leaving from Wood Islands.

Continuing along the coast, Kings Byway circles Murray Head peninsula, the southeastern-most tip of the Island, and passes through a number of special communities lining the large Murray Harbour inlet. At the community of Murray Harbour is the Log Cabin Museum depicting the lifestyle of the Island during the last century, with many well-preserved implements and household necessities of both local and European manufacture. The building itself is made of logs and finished with hand-split island shingles. In Murray River, the Handcraft Co-Op Association shop on Main Street is one of the largest and most complete handcraft retail outlets on the Island. A different type of souvenir of the Island is provided by Captain Garry Herring aboard whose boat you can tour the Murray River and Harbour. Some of the sea life on hand are seals, seagulls, blue herons, cormorants, and arctic terns. Within walking distance of Murray River is the Northumberland Mill and Museum, on Route 4. This restored grist mill, water-powered, is set in a scenic park and picnic area with waterfalls, fishing, and swimming nearby. The museum is a replica of the country store which stood on the site until the turn of the century and served the busy shipbuilding area around Murray River. And at Murray Harbour North, at the upper corner of the bay, wildlife fanciers may want to seek out Seal Cove Campground from which to view a natural seal colony just off-shore.

Just beyond the crossing at Sturgeon River, which happens to be a popular waterway for rainbow trout, Route 317 will take you to Milltown Cross and two of the Island's more unique wildlife attractions. At Buffaloland Provincial Park herds of North American buffalo and white-tailed deer graze in a 100-acre enclosure. Nearby is Moore's Migratory Bird Sanctuary, a haven for migrating waterfowl, including the Canada goose, blue goose, and black duck. Bird watchers may explore the nature trails, and there is trout fishing in the back pond after July 1. Although privately operated, the sanctuary is free. $2 fishing fee.

Rejoin Kings Byway by taking Route 4 from Milltown Cross north to Montague, where the Garden of the Gulf Museum features an interesting collection of old firearms, along with displays of farm tools and household items. Waterways cut deep into this eastern coast of Prince Edward Island north of Montague, forming a number of unusual seascape peninsulas. One of the more popular views is bordered by the Brudenell and Cardigan Rivers, the site of the 1,400-acre Rodd's Brudenell River Resort.

Continue north on Route 4 and turn right on Route 3 to Georgetown and the P.E.I. Brass Rubbing Centre located in the crypt of the Holy Trinity Church, one of the oldest and prettiest churches on P.E.I. You can make your own rubbings from facsimiles of medieval brasses in English country churches.

As the Byway follows the heavily indented coastline north, duplicating scenery and sights, you may want to bypass part of this by taking Route 4 north to Dingwells Mills, then turning right on Route 2, which rejoins the Byway at Rollo Bay West. You will pass the town of Souris, home of the Island's only midshore dragger fleet, also the docking port for a daily passenger service between P.E.I. and the Magdalen Islands. Moving more directly up the coast, you should not overlook the Basin Head Fisheries Museum, established in 1973 to preserve the heritage of the Island's fisheries, notably that of the inshore fishermen. Displays of equipment, artifacts, and exhibits illustrate how the small boats were used and the types of fish they caught. The boat shed houses a small-craft display, and a canning factory features a new marine aquarium.

The smoke house, fish-box factory, and fishermen's sheds are all situated next to one of the Island's finest sand-dune systems. While at Basin Head, experience the "singing sands" of the beaches (said to sing because the sand squeaks loudly when walked upon).

Tuna Capital of the World

The Byway now proceeds to the tip of the Island, East Point, then around to North Lake, major port for the Island's big-game fishermen who battle the giant bluefin tuna. Some of the giants run to almost 1,200 pounds and can fight for hours before being brought to gaff. The North Lake Tuna Charter Association has a number of properly equipped tuna boats which charter for about $300 per day for a maximum party of eight. Most charters leave at 10 A.M. If you want to try standby, show up early at the wharf and you may be able to join a party for a share of the cost. Take a lunch and warm clothing; if a tuna is on the line, you may be out long past the normal 6 P.M. returning time. The tuna is the property of the boat captain. The angler is photographed beside the fish after the weigh-in; that's his or her trophy.

It has been said that the railroad on Prince Edward Island was built and paid for by the mile, wandering along for many miles without getting very far. Although the passenger service no longer operates, there is a railway museum that preserves the memories. A gift of Canadian National Railways, the Elmira Railway Station dating from 1911 has been refurbished and features photographic displays and railroading artifacts. Elmira is a short side trip south of North Lake, on Route 16A.

The Kings Byway routing back to Charlottetown follows the north shore of Kings County, crossing the Morell River (good salmon fishing), and crossing back into Queens County at St. Andrews. If you are in a hurry, you can skip a portion of the Byway by remaining on Route 2, rejoining the Byway at Dunstaffnage. For antique car buffs, the Spoke Wheel Museum here has a 1916 Buick believed to be the only one still in existence. This private collection includes many other models and vintages.

On the final leg of the Byway, flower fanciers may want to turn off at Route 25 for a very short detour to Jewell's Country Gardens and Pioneer Village. An original Island pioneer village, an antique glass museum and five acres of beautiful flowers are featured here. Specialties of the formal gardens are begonias and fuchsias.

PRACTICAL INFORMATION FOR

PRINCE EDWARD ISLAND

HOW TO GET THERE. By Plane. *CP Air* has direct flights to Charlottetown Airport from Toronto, Montreal, and Halifax daily. *Air Canada* has one-stop (Ottawa) service from Toronto and also from Boston and New York, stopping at Halifax where you change to CP Air for the short flight to the Island. *Bar Harbor Aviation* flies from Bangor to Halifax, where you change to the CP Air flight to the Island. Schedules and other information are available from all three airways. Many of the larger hotels and resorts in Prince Edward Island will meet guests at the airport if prior arrangements are made. A limo service will take passengers from the airport to major motels in Summerside.

By Car Ferry. Two ferry services operate regularly between Prince Edward Island and the mainland. One sails from Cape Tormentine, New Brunswick, and docks at Borden, Prince Edward Island; the other sails from Caribou, Nova Scotia, and docks at Wood Islands, P.E.I. Current sailing schedules can be found on the back of the Visitors Map. Ferries have snack bars and newsstands. Ferry service is also available to the Magdalen Islands via Souris.

By Train. Transports passengers by bus to the train in Moncton, New Brunswick, from Charlottetown and Summerside.

ACCOMMODATIONS. Double-occupancy rates in Prince Edward Island are categorized as follows: *Expensive*, $50 or more; *Moderate*, $35–$50; *Inexpensive*, under $35. The 10% provincial sales tax is applied to all accommodation rates. Reservations should be made in advance through any P.E.I. Visitor Information Centre (VIC). A listing of all accommodations, including the many comfortable farms, guest homes, and cottages on the Island, can be obtained from P.E.I. Visitor Services Division, Box 940, Charlottetown, P.E.I. C1A 7M5. You can make reservations by calling toll-free (800–565–7421) from Nova Scotia or New Brunswick from mid-May to October 31 (subject to change).

Most places accept the following major credit cards: American Express (AE), MasterCard (MC), and Visa (V); others may also be honored. Not all establishments accept credit cards, therefore we suggest you call for information.

ALBERTON. *Moderate.* **Westerner Motel.** Box 138, Alberton, P.E.I. C0B 1B0 (902–853–2215). Comfortable housekeeping cottages and motel units. Free use of pedal boats, canoes, row boats. Near golf course and beach. Open year-round. Off-season rates Sept. 30–June 1. MC, V, AE accepted.

BRACKLEY BEACH. *Expensive.* **Shaw's Hotel and Cottages.** Brackley Beach, P.E.I. C0A 2H0. (902–672–2022). Adjacent to National Park. Overnight units and non-housekeeping cottages. Rates include two meals a day. Pets allowed only in cottages. Sailboats, windsurfing, beach nearby. Open June 10–Sept. 20.

Moderate. **Centennial Cottages.** Winsloe, RR 1, P.E.I. C0A 2H0 (902–672–2729). Nine two-bedroom cottages; housekeeping; nearly 6 km (3½ mi.) from beach; located on active farm with animals; 8 km (5 mi.) to 18-hole golf course. Lobster suppers nearby. MC, V accepted. Open June 1–Oct. 15.

Millstream Cottages. Brackley Beach, Winsloe, RR 1, P.E.I. C0A 2H0 (902–672–2186); *winter* (902–672–2718). 14 one- and two-bedroom housekeeping cottages. Free boating and trout fishing. Barbecues, picnic tables, fireplace, wood supplied. Beach 2 km (1.2 mi.). No pets. No credit cards accepted. Open June 1–Sept. 30.

Inexpensive–Moderate. **Bayview Farm Apartments and Cottages.** Brackley Beach, Winsloe, RR 1, P.E.I. C0A 2H0 (902–672–2328) Seven housekeeping cottages. Clam digging, picnic tables, swings, and barbecues on premises. No pets. MC, V accepted.

BRUDENELL. *Inexpensive–Moderate.* **Fraser's Deluxe Housekeeping Cottages.** Montague, RR 5, P.E.I. C0A 1R0 (902–838–2453). Ten two- and three-bedroom housekeeping cottages. River beach on property. Open June 1–Oct. 31. No credit cards accepted.

CAVENDISH. *Moderate–Expensive.* **Anne Shirley Motel and Cabins.** Cavendish, P.E.I. C0A 1N0 (902–963–2224); *winter,* 31 Bolger Dr., Charlottetown, P.E.I. C1A 7T2 (902–892–9612). One- and two-bedroom overnight and housekeeping units. Play area, heated pool, barbecues, picnic tables. Beach, golf, fishing, other attractions nearby. Open June 1–Sept. 25. V, MC, AE accepted.

Bay Vista Motor Inn. Breadalbane, RR 1, P.E.I. C0A 1E0 (902–963–2225); *winter,* North Wilshire, RR 1, P.E.I. C0A 1Y0 (902–675–3238). Social gathering spot, overnight and housekeeping units, lounge, pool, 4.8 km (3 mi.) to beach and golf course, other attractions nearby. Open mid-June–mid-Sept. AE, V, MC accepted.

Cavendish Maples Cottages. Green Gables P.O., Cavendish, P.E.I. C0A 1N0 (902–963–2818); *winter,* Site 9, Box 21, Charlottetown, RR 7, P.E.I. C1A 7J9 (902–892–6991). Nine two-bedroom cottages and two one-bedroom cottages with sundecks. Within walking distance of horseback riding, children's attractions, lounge. Heated pool; beach 2 km (1.2 mi.). Pets on leash permitted. Open late May to late Sept. V, MC accepted.

Ingleside Lodge. Hunter River, RR 2, P.E.I. C0A 1N0 (902–963–2431); *winter*, 7 Noble Ct., Georgetown, ON L7G 1M5 (416–877–5640). 16 one- two- and three-bedroom housekeeping cottages, some with fireplaces. On Rte 13 at entrance of National Park. Near Green Gables golf course, tennis, beach. Pets on leash permitted. Open June 1–Sept. 15. No credit cards accepted.

Inexpensive–Moderate. **Shining Waters Lodge and Cottages.** Cavendish, P.E.I. C0A 1N0 (902–963–2251). Rustic lodge with 10 rooms; one-, two-, and three-bedroom housekeeping cottages. Heated swimming pool; ocean beach at hand. Barbecues, weekend campfires, adventure playground. Open May 1–Oct. 15. V accepted.

Inexpensive. **Marco Polo Inn.** Box 9, Hunter River, P.E.I. C0A 1N0 (902–963–2352); *winter,* (902–964–2223). Six overnight units. 2 km (1.2 mi.) to Cavendish beach. Marco Polo Land facilities available to guests. Licensed dining room and two heated swimming pools on premises. Pets on leash allowed. Open June 27–Sept. 7. MC, V accepted.

CHARLOTTETOWN. *Expensive.* **The Charlottetown Hotel.** Rodd Inns, Resorts, and Hotels, Box 159, Charlottetown, P.E.I. C1A 7K4 (902–894–7371) or (800–565–0207) from within the Maritimes, or (800–565–1430) from the U.S. eastern seaboard. Dining room, lounge, indoor tropical pool; features Charlottetown Festival packages. No pets. Open year-round. Off-season rates Nov. 1–May 31. V, AE, MC, EnRoute accepted.

Dundee Arms Motel and Inn. 200 Pownal Street, Charlottetown, P.E.I. C1A 3W8 (902–892–2496). Inn furnished in antiques; motel is modern. Excellent dining in its licensed dining room. No pets. Open year-round. Off-season rates Oct. 1–May 31. AE, V, MC, EnRoute accepted.

The Inn on the Hill. Box 1720, Charlottetown, P.E.I. C1A 7N4 (902–894–8572). Downtown area; 5 km (3 mi.) from airport. Babysitting arranged; trained pets permitted. Open year-round, Off-season rates before July 7 and after Sept. 13.

The Kirkwood Motor Hotel. 455 University Ave., Charlottetown, P.E.I. C1A 4N8 (902–892–4206). Two restaurants, lounge, heated indoor pool. Bilingual. Open year-round. Off-season rates Oct. 15–May 31. Pets permitted on leash. All major credit cards accepted.

MacLauchlan's Motel (Best Western). 238 Grafton St., Charlottetown, P.E.I. C1A 1L5 (902–892–2461). Overnight and housekeeping units. Licensed dining room, lounge, indoor pool, sauna. Pets on leash permitted. Open year-round. AE, MC, AC, V accepted.

Prince Edward Hotel and Convention Centre. 18 Queen St., Charlottetown, P.E.I. C1A 4A1 (902–566–2222). In Harbourside, Olde Charlottetown. Central; restaurant, lounge, indoor pool, saunas. Open year-round. Off-season rates before June 1 and after Oct. 15. All major credit cards accepted.

Rodd's Confederation Inn. Box 651, Charlottetown, P.E.I. C1A 7L5 (902–892–2481). Junction of Routes 1 and 2 in West Royalty. Heated outdoor pool, sundeck. Licensed dining room and lounge. Pets permitted. Golf packages available. Open year-round. Off-season rates Nov. 1–May 31. V, AE, MC, EnRoute accepted.

Rodd's Royalty Inn and Conference Centre. Rodd Inns, Resorts and Hotels, Box 2499, Charlottetown, P.E.I. C1A 7K7 (902–894–8566) or (800–565–0207) within the Maritimes, or (800–565–1430) from the U.S. Eastern Seaboard. Excellent accommodations, heated indoor pool, games room, saunas, licensed dining room and lounge. Festival theater packages available. Open-year round. Off-season rates Nov. 1–May 31. V, MC, AE, and EnRoute accepted.

Wandlyn Inn. Box 9500, Charlottetown, P.E.I. C1A 8L4. (902–892–1201). Licensed dining room, lounge; coffee shop; heated outdoor pool. Pets permitted on leash. Open year-round. Off-season rates Oct. 31–May 31. AC, AE, MC, DC, V accepted.

Moderate. **Holiday Island Motor Lodge.** 307–309 University Ave., Charlottetown, P.E.I. C1A 4M5. (902–892–4141). Overnight and housekeeping units. Licensed dining room and lounge. 20 minutes from North Shore beaches. Pets on leash permitted. Open year-round. Off-season rates Nov. 1–Apr. 30. Bilingual. AE, V, MC, and EnRoute accepted.

Inexpensive. **Sherwood Motel.** Located in Sherwood on Rte. 15, Brackley Point Road, R.R. 1, Winsloe, P.E.I. C0A 2H0 (902–892–1622). Opposite airport. Trained pets permitted. Licensed dining room, harness racing, 18-hole golf course all within 3 km (1.8 mi.). Open year-round. Off-season rates Sept. 1–June 30. V, MC accepted.

Court Bed & Breakfast. 68 Hutchinson Court, Charlottetown, P.E.I. C1A 8H7 (902–894–5871). Two overnight units, full breakfast included in rates. Licensed dining room 4 blocks, all amenities nearby, ocean beach 24 km (14.4 mi). No pets. Open June 1–Sept. 15. No credit cards accepted.

Hostel. *Canadian Hostelling Association's* main hostel is at 151 Mt. Edward Rd. (902–894–9696). Showers, kitchen facilities. Under $10 a night.

DARNLEY. *Inexpensive–Moderate.* **Penderosa Beach Cottages.** Penderosa Beach, Darnley, P.E.I. C0B 1M0 (902–836–3301). Two three-bedroom A-frame chalets; 20 one- and two-bedroom cottages. Ocean beach on premises; boat launching on lake shore; windsurfing rentals; hay rides. Pets on leash permitted. No credit cards accepted. Open May 15–Sept. 30.

KENSINGTON. *Inexpensive.* **Blakeney's Bed & Breakfast.** 15 MacLean Ave., Box 17, Kensington, P.E.I. C0B 1M0 (902–836–3254). Two overnight units. Overlooks Malpeque Bay; North Shore beaches, Malpeque Gardens, deep-sea fishing, all nearby. Open year-round. No credit cards accepted.

KINGSBORO. *Moderate–Expensive.* **Sea Breeze Motel.** Rte. 16, 11 km (6.6 mi.) east of Souris overlooking Basin Head harbor, Souris, RR 2, P.E.I. C0A 2B0 (902–357–2371). Overnight and housekeeping units. Home-style cooking in licensed dining room on premises. White sand beach 2 km (1.2 mi.), Basin Head Fisheries Museum at hand; "Tuna Capital of the World" at North Lake 13 km (10 mi.) away. Playground. Pets on leash permitted. V, MC accepted. Open year-round.

MALPEQUE. *Moderate.* **Malpeque Harbour Cottages.** 112 Pownal St., Charlottetown, P.E.I. C1A 3W5 (902–836–5203); *winter* (902–892–3810). Seven two-bedroom housekeeping cottages with sundecks. Overlook the sea, sand dunes, and fishing harbor of Cabot Provincial Park. Pets on leash permitted. Open June 15 to Labor Day (early Sept.). No credit cards accepted. $100 deposit required.

MILL RIVER EAST. *Moderate–Expensive.* **Lady Slipper Cottages.** Box 8, Alberton, P.E.I. C0B 1B0 (902–859–2261); *winter* (902–853–2229). On Rte. 172, off Lady Slipper Drive. Two-bedroom deluxe cottages, three-bedroom summer home. 3 km (1.2 mi.) from golf course and resort. Bay beach. Pets on leash permitted. No credit cards accepted. Open June 1–Sept. 30.

MONTAGUE. *Moderate.* **Lobster Shanty North.** Box 158, Montague, P.E.I. C0A 1R0 (902–838–2463). One of the better places to eat and stay on the King's Byway. Features good dining with seafood specialties in a rustic licensed dining room that extends into the lounge bar overlooking the Montague River. 27 km (17 mi.) to ocean beach, 11 km (7 mi.) to Brudenell golf course. Open year-round. Wheelchair facilities. AE, MC, V accepted. Quiet pets permitted.

Inexpensive. **Lane's Tourist Court.** Box 548, Montague, P.E.I. C0A 1R0 (902–838–2433). Nine housekeeping units. Near center of Montague. Quiet, scenic atmosphere. Children's playground. Supervised beach nearby. No pets. Open May 15–Oct. 15. V, MC accepted.

NORTH LAKE. *Inexpensive.* **Bluefin Motel.** North Lake Harbour, P.E.I. (C0A 1K0 (902–357–2599); *winter* (902–583–2214). 11 overnight units. Clean, comfortable accommodation near the North Lake tuna fishing area. Ocean beach, lake clamming within 150 meters (500 feet) of the motel. Small leashed pets permitted. Open June 15–Oct. 15. No credit cards accepted.

NORTH RUSTICO. *Inexpensive–Moderate.* **St. Lawrence Motel.** North Rustico, Hunter River RR 2, P.E. C0A 1N0 (902–963–2053); *winter,* Howard

& Edna Zimmer, 125 Donahue Road, North Granby, CT, U.S. 06060 (203–653 –2706). 15 one-, two-, and three-bedroom housekeeping units. Located on Gulf Shore Road in the National Park (toll-free to the motel guests). Golf range, putting, bicycle rentals, deep-sea fishing, licensed dining room 2 km (1.2 mi.), beach nearby. Bilingual. Open May 20–Oct. 15. V, MC accepted.

POOLES CORNER. *Moderate.* **Kingsway Motel.** Box 307, Montague, P.E.I. C0A 1R0 (902–838–2112). Small, modern motel. Licensed dining room, good food, home-cooked variety; cozy lounge bar. The river beach and golf course at Brudenell Resort are 5 km (3 mi.) away. Open year-round. Pets on leash permitted. V, MC, AE accepted.

RUSTICOVILLE. *Expensive.* **The Pines Motel.** Rusticoville, P.E.I. C0A 1N0 (902–963–2029). Overnight and housekeeping units. Beach 4 km (2.4 mi.). Deep-sea fishing. Licensed dining room. Open May 15–Oct. 15. No credit cards accepted.
 Moderate–Expensive **Chalets Grand-Pre.** Rusticoville, Hunter River RR 2, P.E.I. C0A 1N0 (902–963–2616). Housekeeping cottages and motel units. Heated pool. Playground on premises. Deep-sea and tuna fishing arranged. Beach 3 km (1.8 mi.). Supervised pets permitted. Open June 1–Oct. 1. No credit cards accepted.

SOURIS. *Inexpensive.* **Souris West Motel & Cottages.** RR 4 Souris West, P.E.I. C0A 2B0 (902–687–2676). Small, comfortable motel and cottages overlooking Colville Bay. *On parle francais ici.* Open year-round. Pets permitted. Tuna, deep-sea fishing; licensed dining room, beach 2 km (1.2 mi) No credit cards accepted.

SOUTH RUSTICO. *Moderate–Expensive.* **Rustico Resort Ltd.** Hunter River, RR 3, P.E.I. C0A 1N0 (902–963–2357); *winter;* 108 Renfrew Ave., Ottawa, ON K1S 1Z8 (613–232–1965). 10 housekeeping cottages, 12 housekeeping motel units, 18 overnight units. 180 acres with free golf, tennis, heated pools, swimming in the bay, trail rides, lounge. Babysitting arranged. Open May–Sept. No pets. No credit cards accepted.
 Moderate. **Barachois Inn.** Box 1022, Charlottetown, P.E.I. C1A 7M4 (902–963–2194). 6 overnight units in a beautifully restored 15-room 19th-century home with a view of Rustico Bay and Winter River. No pets, no smoking. Breakfast extra. Open May–Oct. Reservations, deposit required. No credit cards accepted.

STANHOPE. *Moderate–Expensive.* **By-the-Bay Cottages.** Stanhope, P.E.I. C0A 1P0 (902–672–2307). 8 housekeeping units on Bay Shore Road, Rte. 25, overlooking water. Clam digging, lobster suppers, deep-sea fishing, windsurfing, and golf nearby. Picnic tables, large play area. Leashed, small dogs permitted. Babysitting arranged. Open June 1–Sept. 15. No credit cards accepted.
 Inexpensive–Moderate. **Del-Mar Cottages.** Little York R.R. 1, P.E.I. C0A 1P0. (902–672–2582). 6 housekeeping units on Gulf Shore Road in National Park, facing ocean beach. Babysitting arranged. Golf course, windsurfing, deep-sea fishing nearby. No pets. Licensed dining room 2 km (1.2 mi.). Open June 1–Sept. 30. No credit cards accepted.

SUMMERSIDE. *Expensive.* **Garden of the Gulf Motel/Quality Inn.** 618 Water St. E., Summerside, P.E.I. C1N 2V5 (902–436–2295). Heated outdoor pool, 9-hole golf course and bay beach on property. Babysitting arranged. Adjacent restaurant. Pets on leash permitted. Open year-round. Off-season rates Sept. 30–June 1. AE, MC, V accepted.
 Moderate–Expensive. **The Linkletter Motel.** 311 Market St., Summerside, P.E.I. C1N 1K8 (902–436–2157). Downtown area. Tuna and deep-sea fishing charters, car rental agency, travel agency, coffee shop, licensed lounge. Beach 6 km (3.6 mi.). Pets permitted. Open year-round. Off-season rates Jan. 1–May 31. All major credit cards accepted.
 Moderate. **The Glade Motor Inn & Cottages.** Rte. 1A, 6 km (3.6 mi.) from Summerside, Box 1387, Summerside, P.E.I. C1N 4K2 (902–436–5564). Horseback riding, nature trails, heated outdoor pool. Coffee shop, restaurant

and lounge on premises. Cottages open June 1–Oct. 1. Motel and inn open year-round. Off-season rates Aug. 24–July 1. Pets permitted. MC, V, AE accepted.

Silver Fox Inn. 61 Granville St., Summerside, P.E.I. C1N 2Z3 (902–436–4033). Central to downtown. Six rooms with private baths. Bay beach 3 km (1.8 mi.), licensed dining room within walking distance. No pets. Open year-round. Off-season Sept. 30–June 1. V, MC, AE accepted.

Inexpensive. **Cairns' Motel.** 721 Water St. E., Summerside, P.E.I. C1N 4J2 (902–436–5841). Golf, riding academy, drive-in theater nearby. Open year-round. Off-season rates Sept. 15–June 24. No credit cards accepted.

Faye & Eric's Bed & Breakfast. 380 MacEwen Rd., Summerside, P.E.I. C1N 4X8 (902–436–6847). Exceptional accommodations. Three "regular" rooms, self-contained housekeeping unit, and self-contained "Royalty Suite" with Jacuzzi whirlpool bath, other extras. Private kitchen for guests, licensed dining room and shopping within walking distance. Beach 5 km (3 mi.). Open year-round. No pets. No credit cards.

MacQuarrie's Lighthouse Motel. 802 Water St., Summerside, P.E.I. C1N 4J6 (902–436–2992). Housekeeping and overnight units. Near shopping, golf, beaches. Licensed dining room, nearby. Open year-round. V, MC, EnRoute accepted.

TIGNISH. *Inexpensive.* **Murphy's Tourist Home & Cottages.** 325 Church St., Tignish, P.E.I. C0B 2B0 (902–882–2667). Housekeeping and overnight units. Breakfast served on request. Large playground. Dining room, beach nearby. Pets permitted on leash. Open June 1–Sept. 30. V accepted.

UIGG. *Inexpensive–Moderate.* **Dunvegan Farm Motel and Bed & Breakfast.** On Rte. 24, 30 km (18 mi.) east of Charlottetown, Vernon Bridge RR 2, P.E.I. C0A 2E0 (902–651–2833). Noted for friendly hospitality. On a working farm with cows, horses, poultry, and pets. Motel equipped for housekeeping. Rooms available in farm home. Breakfast served on request. Controlled pets permitted. Open year-round. Off-season rates from Labour Day to June 25. No credit cards accepted.

MacLeod's Farm Bed & Breakfast. Uigg, Vernon P.O., P.E.I. C0A 2E0 (902–651–2303). Noted for homemade bread and biscuits, jam. On 100-acre mixed farm, Rte. 24, 30 km (18 mi.) northwest of Wood Islands ferry. Three overnight units, one housekeeping unit with wheelchair ramp. Breakfast served on request. No pets. Open June 15–Sept. 30. No credit cards accepted.

VICTORIA. *Inexpensive–Moderate.* **Victoria Village Inn.** Victoria-by-the-Sea, P.E.I. C0A 2G0. (902–658–2288). Licensed dining room. Sailing cruises, ocean beach, clam digging, crafts and theater nearby. Open year-round. Off-season rates Oct. 15–May 15. All major credit cards accepted.

Inexpensive. **Dunrovin Cottages, Lodge and Farm.** Victoria P.O., P.E.I. C0A 2G0 (902–658–2375). Eight housekeeping cottages, two overnight units in lodge. Home-cooked meals in lodge by arrangement. Animals, children's activities. Seafood restaurant, playhouse nearby. Pets on leash permitted. Baby-sitting and deep-sea fishing arranged. Open June 21–Sept. 8. No credit cards accepted.

WOOD ISLANDS. *Inexpensive–Moderate.* **Meadow Lodge Motel.** Wood Islands, Belle River P.O., P.E.I. C0A 1B0 (902–962–2022). Clean, comfortable accommodation. Near picnic area and ocean beach at Wood Islands Provincial Park. 2 km (1.2 mi) from Wood Islands ferry. Small leashed pets permitted. Open May 15–Oct. 13. Off-season rates Sept. 1–June 30. MC, V accepted.

WOOD ISLANDS EAST. *Inexpensive–Moderate.* **Netherstone Inn.** Box 1053, Montague, P.E.I. C0A 1R0 (902–962–3200). Overnight and housekeeping units. Picnic tables, playground, trout pond with canoes. Licensed country dining room. Open June–Sept. V, MC, AE accepted.

YORK. *Inexpensive.* **Vessey's Housekeeping Units.** York, P.E.I. C0A 1P0 (902–892–2168). Quiet place only 8 km (5 mi.) from Charlottetown. Three overnight units, one housekeeping apartment. No dogs permitted. No credit cards accepted. Open June 15–Sept. 15.

TELEPHONES. The Island has one long-distance telephone area code throughout (902).

TIME ZONE. Prince Edward Island is on Atlantic Time (one hour ahead of Eastern Time).

HOW TO GET AROUND. By bus. Double-decker, London-style buses tour Charlottetown and visit the North Shore daily, with departures from Confederation Centre. *Island Transit Co-operative Ltd.* operates a bus service from Charlottetown to Tignish, Charlottetown to Souris, and Charlottetown to New Glasgow, Nova Scotia.

By limousine. Service is available by reservation to South Shore points of interest, with departure from Charlottetown Hotel.

By horse and buggy. Horse-and-carriage tours of Olde Charlottetown, Victoria Park. From corner of Great George and Richmond Streets. $18 and up.

On foot: In Charlottetown, most attractions are within walking distance of one another. A booklet entitled *Walks in Charlotte Town* is a useful guide. It's available in many bookstores or at the P.E.I. Heritage Foundation.

By car. As tour operations in Prince Edward Island are generally not extensive, visitors arriving by air in Charlottetown might want to tour the province by rented car. Rental agencies such as *Avis, Budget, Hertz,* and *Tilden* are located at the Charlottetown Airport. Some car-rental agencies maintain small branches in Summerside. During the summer months, it is advisable to book your car rental in advance through a travel agency or the local branch of the rental agency.

HOW TO REACH LADY SLIPPER DRIVE. By car. From Charlottetown, take Rte. 2 to Summerside. Rte. 2 intersects Lady Slipper Drive at the tiny village of Traveller's Rest. Follow the red signs showing the silhouette of a lady slipper orchid.

HOW TO REACH THE BLUE HERON DRIVE. By car. From Charlottetown (following the blue heron sign), continue in a counterclockwise direction on Rte. 19, or take 15 north to Rte. 6 at Cavendish.

By ferry. The ferry service from Cape Tormentine, New Brunswick, docks at Borden, P.E.I., about 27 km (17 mi.) from Lady Slipper Drive. From the ferry, turn west onto Rte. 10 to join the drive at Reads Corner. For ferry information, contact CN Marine, Borden, P.E.I. The service from Cape Tormentine takes about 45 minutes. From June–Sept. there are numerous daily crossings from 6:30 A.M. to 1:00 A.M. Less frequent daily crossings during remainder of the year.

HOW TO REACH KINGS BYWAY DRIVE. By car: From Charlottetown, take Rte. 1 (TCH) east across Hillsborough Bridge and follow the purple crown Kings Byway signs. From Cavendish and the National Park area, take Rte. 6 east and go around Kings Byway Drive in a clockwise direction. The ferry from Caribou, Nova Scotia, to Wood Islands, Prince Edward Island, lands visitors about 1.5 km (1 mi.) from Kings Byway. Turn east or west at Wood Islands. For ferry information, contact Northumberland Ferries Ltd., 54 Queen St., Charlottetown, P.E.I. C1A 7L3. From June–Sept. there are numerous daily sailings. Reduced sailings from Sept. 3 to Dec.

TOURIST INFORMATION SERVICES. The government maintains ten visitor information centers in Prince Edward Island. There are two VICs on the mainland— one at Aulac, New Brunswick, and one at Caribou, Nova Scotia. The main VIC is located in the Royalty Mall on University Avenue in Charlottetown (902–368–4444). Open-year round. The others are located at Alberton on Rte. 12 (902–853–2555); Borden (at the ferry terminal), Rte. 1 (902–855–2090); Brackley Beach, Rte. 15 (902–672–2259); Cavendish, Rte. 13

(902–963–2639); Pooles Corner (near Montague), Rtes. 3 & 4 (902–838–2972); Souris, Rte.2 East (902–682–3238); Stanhope, Rte. 25; Wilmot (near Summerside), Rte. 1A, (902–436–2551); and Wood Islands, Rte. 1 (902–962–2015). There are municipal information centers operated in Kensington, New London, Portage, and Abram-Village. The provincial VICs operate from May through Oct.

Dial-the-Island reservations and information system. This arrangement makes it easy for you to call ahead to plan your trip, secure any information you may need, and make reservations. Just call the central reservations office while en route to the Island. From New Brunswick or Nova Scotia, dial toll-free (800–565–7421). It is in effect from mid-May to Oct. 31. Once on the Island, a network of two-way radios at VICs gives you valuable assistance with travel needs.

RECOMMENDED READING. Prince Edward Island is the home of Atlantic Canada's most famous and successful author, the late Lucy Maud Montgomery, whose *Anne of Green Gables* and its successors are worldwide favorite books for girls. Montgomery's life and work are the basis of a small sub-branch of the tourist industry in P.E.I.

Reshard Gool is a poet, novelist *(Price)* and essayist *(Portrait and Gastroscopes,* with Frank Ledwell), and publisher. His Square Deal Press publishes many Island poets and playwrights; it has also published Christopher Gledhill's *Folklore of P.E.I.* and the reminiscences of a folksy former premier, Walter Shaw's *Tell Me the Tales.* A comic novel is Jeffrey Holmes's *The Highjacking of the P.E.I. Ferry.* A worthwhile memento of an Island visit is *Memories of the Old Home Place* by W.P. Bolger, Wayne Barrett, and Anne MacKay.

SEASONAL EVENTS. Alberton. The *Prince County Exhibition* takes place in late Aug.

Charlottetown. The *Charlottetown Festival,* one of Canada's summer highlights, takes place yearly from June to Oct., presenting a series of plays in the Confederation Centre of the Arts. Two full-scale musicals playing in repertory six nights a week, Mon.–Sat., along with that perennial musical favorite, *Anne of Green Gables,* are among the performances. Special exhibitions of art are presented in the Art Gallery. For information on the summer season, write to: Confederation Centre for the Arts, Box 848, Charlottetown, P.E.I. C1A 7L9. *Harness racing* is a year round sporting pastime at the Charlottetown Driving Park; pari-mutuel betting is available. A regatta takes place on *Natal Day,* in mid-June. *Country Days* and *Old Home Week* is held in early Aug.

Eldon. *Highland Games and Gathering of the Clans* takes place in early Aug.

Montague. *Welcome to Summer Celebrations* is held in late June.

O'Leary. The *Prince Edward Island Potato Blossom Festival* takes place in late July.

Oyster Bed Bridge. Stock car races in mid-July. Drag races in early Aug.

Summerside. The *Cape Egmont Yacht Race* is held in June. *Harness racing* takes place from May to late fall at the Summerside Raceway. Pari-mutuel betting available. The *Lobster Carnival and Livestock Exhibition* takes place in late July.

Tyne Valley. The *Oyster Festival* occurs in early Aug.

Exact dates of festivals and events change yearly. Check dates and details in the 1987 schedule of events, available from P.E.I. Visitor Information Centres.

TOURS. *Abegweit Sightseeing Tours* offer a *Charlottetown Tour* of the old and new capital city on a double-decker, London-style bus; six one-hour tours daily, including Sun.; adults, $3.75; children under 12, $1.00. They also offer a *South Shore Tour* by limousine (reservations required) and a daily *North Shore Tour* by bus leaving the Confederation Centre in mid-morning, returning late afternoon. Adults, $17; children under 12, $8.50. Prices include all admissions and are subject to change. Contact: 157 Nassau St., Charlottetown, P.E.I. C1A 2X3 (902–892–9966).

Guide Service of Prince Edward Island (Division of Abegweit Tours) offers a guide service only, bilingual on request, your motorcoach or private automobile. Three tours or a combination: four-hour *Gateway Tour,* out of Borden, $63; six-hour *North Shore Tour,* $53; and one-hour *Charlottetown Tour,* $25. Contact: 157 Nassau St., Charlottetown, P.E.I. C1A 2X3 (902–894–9966).

Gulf Tours offer step-on tour guides and special tour packages. Bilingual service on request. Four tours available: six-and-one-half-hour *North Shore Tour,* $55; six-hour *Lady Slipper Drive Tour,* $65; *Lucy Maud Montgomery Tour,* $65; and one-hour *Charlottetown Tour,* $25. Rates quoted are for guide service only. Will build special packages, rates on request. Contact: Kensington RR 1, P.E.I. C0B 1M0 (902–836–5418).

Murphy's Tour Service is a professional ground operator service offering complete packages to tour operators. General rates, bilingual guides and private automobile tour rates available on request. Contact: 455 University Ave., Charlottetown, P.E.I. C1A 4N8 (902–892–0606).

 PROVINCIAL PARKS. Along the Kings Byway, a small herd of North American bison is the feature attraction at the 100 acre *Buffaloland Provincial Park* on Rte 4, 6 kms. (4 miles) south of Montague. There is also a small picnic area.

Fantasyland Provincial Park on Rte. 348, near Murray River, has a nice picnic area, swimming, clam-digging, and boating facilities. For the children, there are giant replicas of fairytale characters and a playground.

The *Lord Selkirk Provincial Park,* on Rte. 1, east of Eldon, has a campground, picnic area, swimming, posted hiking trails, and clam-digging flats.

An excellent beach with supervised swimming is available, at the *Panmure Island Provincial Park* on Rte. 347, off Rte. 17 on the south side of Cardigan Bay. This recreation park also has campsites, picnic area, clam-digging flats, and a laundromat. Good for small-boating.

Sir Andrew MacPhail Provincial Park at Orwell is a day-use park on Rte. 1, 32 kms. (20 miles) from Charlottetown. The 143 acres of natural woodland has nature trails, fishing in the pond, a picnic area.

Near the Wood Islands Ferry Terminal is the *Wood Islands Provincial Park.* A day-use park, it overlooks the ocean and has a picnic area and a children's playground.

The *Marie Provincial Park* is another day-use park on the bank of the Marie River 3 kms. (2 miles) east of Morell on Rte. 2. Picnic and small recreational areas along the green riverbank.

Red Point Provincial Park and *Campbell's Cove Provincial Park,* both on Rte. 16, offer tenting sites and swimming for visitors to King County. Supervised beach.

The *Northumberland Provincial Park* is a complete camping and day-use park with supervised swimming and bathing houses with showers on the sheltered salt water beach. There are picnic areas, a children's playground, a laundromat, recreation hall, and clam-digging flats. On Rte. 4, 3 kms. (2 miles) east of Wood Islands Ferry Terminal.

Another day-use park with a playground is *Bloomfield Provincial Park* on Rte. 2 near St. Anthony. Picnic area, washroom, and shower facilities.

A great picnic site with a view is *Campbellton Provincial Park* on the high cliffs overlooking Northumberland Strait, 2½ kms. (1½ miles) south of the junction of Rtes. 14 and 145 at the village of Campbellton.

Cedar Dunes Provincial Park, 18 kms. (11 miles) south of O'Leary on Rte. 14 at West Point, has a long sandy beach, playground, evergreen groves, tenting and trailer sites.

Jacques Cartier Provincial Park honors the French explorer who landed here in 1534. On Rte. 12, 8 kms. (5 miles) north of Alberton. Facilities include campground and beach, with a clam-digging and trout fishing area nearby.

Green Park Provincial Park in Port Hill near Tyne Valley has a interpretive center and a shipbuilding museum. Also a campground with shower and washroom facilities.

Cabot Provincial Park on Rte. 20 has a sandy beach, campground, 24-hour supervision and laundromat on the premises.

Along Blue Heron Drive, *Victoria Provincial Park* on Victoria Harbour, Rte. 10, has a good picnic area. There is swimming here and also at *Argyle Shore Provincial Park.*

Bonshaw Provincial Park on Rte. 1 offers a 32-km. (20-mile) hiking trail. Beginning at West River Bridge near St. Catherine, it goes on to Victoria, winding through large woodlots, fields, and country roads. Never far from roadways, the trail may be hiked in sections. *Strathgartney Provincial Park,* nearby, offers picnic and tenting facilities, as well as a 9-hole golf course.

The *Devil's Punch Bowl Provincial Park* near Granville, on Rte. 254, is a day-use park with a short hiking trail which leads to the spring from which the park got its name.

Scales Pond Provincial Park, Rte. 109, is the site of the Island's largest hydroelectric operation which began in 1798 and closed in 1963.

The Prince Edward Island Visitor Information Centres supply information, locations, opening and closing dates for other smaller day-use and camping provincial parks with picnic, beach, swimming, and other attractions.

 GARDENS. Good red earth has made the entire province a garden spot during summer months. *Jewell's Gardens and Pioneer Village* at **York,** off Kings Byway on Rte. 25, specialize in begonias and fuchsias. An antique glass museum, an old country store, and a children's playground are nearby. Open daily, mid-June to mid-Oct. Admission: adults $3.50, children under 13 free.

Malpeque Gardens on Rte. 20 features brilliant varieties of dahlias and dozens of floral arrangements. An old-fashioned windmill irrigates the gardens. Open June 21 to August 31, daily 9 A.M. to 8 P.M.; 9 A.M.–5 P.M. during Sept. and Oct. Admission: adults $2.25; children under 14, $1; preschoolers free.

 FARM VACATIONS AND FARM TOURIST HOMES. For visitors seeking less commercial accommodations, farm vacation and tourist homes offer both an economical way to spend a holiday and an opportunity to meet the people of an area and live among them for a time. Farm tourist and vacation homes take guests on a daily or weekly basis. Some of the homes are on working farms; others are in rural areas. Guests stay in spare rooms, share meals, activities, and even chores with the host family.

Daily rates, ranging from about $20 to $25 per day for two people, may include home-cooked country meals and a snack before bed. Most farm homes have special rates for children.

In general, farm pets do not welcome visiting pets. Check before you come. Bring old clothes and shoes or boots for everyone, especially the children. Farm families usually go to bed early and rise early. Pay for your farm holiday in advance—it's easier to do business before you've become friends.

The P.E.I. Visitors Information Centres have complete listings of farm vacation and tourist homes with rates. Make reservations well in advance directly with the farm family hosts, especially for an extended stay.

 RESORTS. *Very Expensive.* **Dalvay-by-the-Sea** at Grand Tracadie north of Charlottetown by the P.E.I. National Park. 25 rooms in manor surrounded by rolling green lawns, two cottages. American plan with American and French cuisine in dining room. Babysitting arranged. Two tennis courts, bowling greens, ping pong, driving range, canoeing and trout fishing on premises. Ocean beach 200 yards. Open mid-June–mid-Sept. Contact: Box 8, York, P.E.I. C0A 1P0 (902–672–2048); *winter* (902–672–2546).

Expensive. **Rodd's Mill River Resort** at Woodstock in western P.E.I. on Rte. 2, 57 km (34 mi.) from Summerside. 80-room hotel resort. 18-hole championship golf course, six tennis courts, canoeing, wind surfing, bicycling, fitness center, heated indoor pool, lounges, licensed dining room. Open May–late Oct. V, AE, MC, EnRoute accepted. Contact: Rodd Inns, Resorts & Hotels, Box 395, O'Leary, P.E.I. C0B 1V0 (902–859–3555). Nov.–Apr.: Box 432, Charlottetown, P.E.I. C1A 7K7 (902–892–7448). Dial toll-free within the Maritimes (800–565–0207) year-round; from the U.S. eastern seaboard (800–565–9077).

Rodd's Brudenell River Resort at Roseneath on the east end of the Island, offers an excellent family holiday location. 50 riverside chalets, 18-hole championship golf course, tennis courts, canoeing, trail riding, lawn bowling, heated outdoor pool, kiddies' pool, licensed lounge and dining room. Playground. Some pets permitted. Open June through mid-Oct. AE, V, MC, EnRoute accepted. Contact: Box 22, Cardigan, P.E.I. C0A 1G0 (902–652–2332); Nov.–Apr.: Box

432, Charlottetown, P.E.I. C1A 7K7 (902–892–7448). Dial toll-free within the Maritimes (800–565–0207) year-round; from the U.S. eastern seaboard (800–565–9077).

CHILDREN'S ACTIVITIES. Beaches, playgrounds, and parks throughout the province offer excellent activities and facilities for children. Other points of interest include:

Burlington near Kensington: *Woodleigh Replicas,* displays scale models of famous castles and cathedrals, including the Tower of London. Some are large enough to enter and walk around in.

Bonshaw: *Bonshaw 500* has karting for all members of the family. Children drive their own karts. Picnic tables; playground.

Cavendish: *The Royal Atlantic Wax Museum* has life size wax figures of famous people from Josephine Tussaud.

Green Gables House is the famous farm home in Lucy Maude Montgomery's *Anne of Green Gables.*

Rainbow Valley as described in L.M. Montgomery's *Rainbow Valley,* has a Children's Farm, a playground, Fantasy Area, Flying Saucer, boating lakes, and a giant water slide.

Sandpit has Can Am racing for skilled and young drivers, bumper boats, miniature golf, and "soft play" world for little folks.

DeSable: *House of Dolls* exhibits miniature dolls of famous people from many nations. Also, children's corner.

Harrington: *Pinehills Playground* has large play area with long slide, maze, haunted cave, swings, Indian area, and prehistoric animals.

Murray River: *The Toy Factory* offers tours of a small factory that specializes in toy making.

North Rustico: *The Wildlife Park,* complete with picnic area, has fine collection of native animals and wild birds.

Rocky Point: *Micmac Indian Village* has Indian Trail and authentic Indian Village.

Stanley Bridge: *Cap'n Bart's Adventure Park* contains a full-size reproduction of space shuttle *Columbia* complete with mini science lab in cargo bay. Mountain climbing and Adventure Forest.

Marineland Aquarium and Manor of Birds has fine collection of mounted birds; fish tanks; seal pool; butterflies.

Woodstock: *Mill River Fun Park* offers family fun. Water slides, giant pirate ship, adventure trail, animal barn, children's theater, clowns.

Also check under *Festivals and Events, Provincial Parks,* and *Camping* in this section.

SPORTS. P.E.I. is sports-oriented. On an island of golf courses, one of the best known in Atlantic Canada is the championship Brudenell Golf Course, located in the resort complex at *Roseneath.* The Belvedere course in *Charlottetown,* the Mill River championship course on Lady Slipper Drive, and the Summerside Golf Club Course (all are 18-hole courses) are also among the best.

The Green Gables Course, part of the National Park, surrounds the home of the storybook character Anne of Green Gables, in the *Cavendish* area.

The *Rustico* Golf Course is flanked by trees and waterholes overlooking Rustico Bay. An 18 holer, it is near recreational activities of all kinds.

The *Stanhope* Golf and Country Club is situated near Prince Edward Island National Park.

A 9-hole course, the Glen Afton, is located on the south coast near the historic *Fort Amherst* site. Another 9-hole course, Forest Hills Golf Course, is located on Rte. 6 in *Cavendish.*

The *Strathgartney* links offer a par three, nine-hole course.

Bicycling. Its small size and veinwork of quiet country roads make P.E.I. a natural attraction for the cyclist. Bicycles can be rented at MacQueen's Bike Shop, 430 Queen St., *Charlottetown* (892–9843) or at Summerside Advance Rental, 133 Water St., *Summerside* (436–3867); cost: about $12 daily, $30 weekly at both places. Bicycles can also be rented at *Rent-a-Bike* in Cavendish and *Stanhope Beach Lodge* in Stanhope. Provincial VICs supply information on bicycle parts, repairs, rentals, and cycling packages. More information from *P.E.I. Cycling Association* (902–566–1154) and *Sport P.E.I.* at (902–894–8879).

Canoeing is also growing in popularity in the province's many meandering tidal estuaries—a delight of rolling sandbars and quiet havens. Visitor information bureaus can tell you where to rent canoes.

Hiking and cross-country skiing are a pleasure on the low rolling terrain of Prince Edward Island. There are hiking trails and numerous nature walks.

Devil's Punch Bowl Trail —one mile long, located between the Rattenbury Rd., Rte. 254, and South Granville—down an old horse and carriage road through hardwood forests. Easy enough for children.

Bonshaw Hills Trail —20 miles long, from West River Bridge (near St. Catherines) to Victoria, not far from Borden.

P.E.I.'s national park has several trails. And in winter there are four loop-style cross-country ski trails.

Information on hiking and cross-country ski trails is available from the P.E.I. Department of Tourism.

Fishing. The Island has some of the best salt- and freshwater fishing in eastern Canada. *Freshwater fishing* for brook trout and white perch is usually no more than a few minutes' walk across a field. The trout season runs from mid-April to September 30, with a limit of 20 trout a day. Non-resident fishing licenses cost $12, obtainable from the Fish and Wildlife Division in Charlottetown or any other license vendor; guides are not required. All the inland fisheries are fine places to catch brook trout. For rainbow trout, fish the Dunk, Cardigan, and Sturgeon Rivers and two inland lakes—Glenfinnan and O'Keefe. In recent years salmon fishing has been rejuvenated on the Morell River.

Saltwater or *deep-sea fishing* can be a family outing. Most trips last 4 hours and most fishing ports have boats available for charter. The cost is about $10 per person. The boat captain supplies all tackle and bait. Boats listed by the Visitor Information Centres have passed rigorous safety standards set by the federal government. Reservations can be made in advance by phhone. A boat list is available at the nearest Visitors Information Centre or at a wharf displaying the deep-sea fishing sign.

Tuna fishing is serious sport in P.E.I. The North Lake area on the Kings Byway is still the giant bluefin capital of the island. On the Blue Heron Drive, North Rustico, and Malpeque Harbour are tuna fishing ports. On King's Byway there are two other tuna ports: Morell Harbour and Savage Harbour. Tuna charters are roughly $300. Further information on tuna charters and other deep-sea fishing arrangements is available from any P.E.I. Visitors Information Centre. Or write Tourism Services Division, P.O. Box 940, Charlottetown, P.E.I., C1A 7M5. The Fish and Wildlife Division, P.O. Box 2000, Charlottetown, P.E.I., Canada C1A 7N8 will also have any additional information you need.

Along with golf and fishing, another top sport is **harness racing.** Two major tracks—at Charlottetown and Summerside—feature competitions from all over Canada and the U.S. A fast growing sport is windsurfing. P.E.I. is considered by North American experts to have the best summer windsurfing waters in North America.

Other popular sports are tennis, swimming, boating, and horseback riding, available at a good number of resorts, campgrounds, and at the national park.

 CAMPING. For a small island, P.E.I. has a good number of private and provincially operated campgrounds for tenting, tailering, and camping. Check open dates for each campground. Unless stated otherwise, reservations may be made directly with the camping area.

Along the Kings Byway, at Roseneath, near Brudenell Resort, is the *Brudenell River Provincial Park*, on Rte. 3 between Pooles Corner and Georgetown. The 90-acre park has 94 unserviced sites and 12 two-way hookups. Campers can use the 18-hole Brudenell golf course and the fresh water beach on the Brudenell River. Open mid-May to mid-October. Reservations not accepted.

For campers who prefer saltwater beaches, *Seal Cove Campground* at Murray Harbour North has a saltwater beach on the premises and another ocean beach just a short distance away. Located 16 kms. (10 miles) from Murray River via Rtes. 4 and 17, the 25-acre campground has 17 unserviced sites, 25 two-way hookups, and 60 three-way hookups. Open June 1 to Oct. 15.

For the camper with an interest in history, the *Lord Selkirk Provincial Park* commemorates the Scottish settlers who broke the land here in 1803. Located 1½ kms. (1 mile) east of Eldon, just off the Trans-Canada Hwy., the 50-acre camping portion of the park has 52 unserviced sites and 20 two-way hookups. Among other amenities is the nearby reconstructed Lord Selkirk Settlement, saltwater beach, picnic sites, marked hiking trails, and clam-digging flats within the park. Open from the beginning of June to September 6. Reservations not accepted.

Jacques Cartier Provincial Park has 24 unserviced sites and 12 two-way hookups on 22 acres. Located 6 kms. (4 miles) from Alberton off Rte. 2 at Kildare Capes. Ocean beach on premises. Reservations not accepted. Open June to Labor Day.

One of the best ocean beaches is at *Cedar Dunes Provincial Park,* 24 kms. (15 miles) from O'Leary. The 100-acre park has 36 unserviced sites and 10 two-way hookups. Reservations not accepted.

Green Park Provincial Park, which includes a wooden shipbuilding museum and restoration, is 32 kms. (20 miles) west of Summerside, on Rte. 12. There are 66 unserviced sites and 24 three-way hookups with an ocean beach on the premises. Reservations not accepted. June to Labor Day.

About 6½ kms. (4 miles) west of Summerside on Rte. 11, *Linkletter Provincial Park* has 52 unserviced sites and 32 two-way hookups. Saltwater beach on the premises. Reservations not accepted. Open mid-May to mid-September.

Along Blue Heron Drive, beach camping is excellent in the campsites of Cavendish, Brackley, and Stanhope, all part of the National Park. The privately owned Cavendish Sunset Campground has a swimming pool, tennis courts, ocean beach, and a miniature golf course. Reservations accepted.

At *Blythwood Trailer Park,* Cavendish, pets permitted on leash, mini-bikes not permitted; ocean beach, and 18-hole golf course.

At *Rustico Island Campground,* a section of the national park, 5 kms. (3 miles) west of Rte. 15 on Gulf Shore Rd., you'll find 113 developed acres and 148 unserviced sites. There's an interpretative program, outdoor theater, ocean beach, and 18-hole golf course. Reservations not accepted.

The *Prince Edward Island National Park* runs 25 miles along the coastline and beaches of the North Shore. Excellent beaches, campgrounds, and sporting facilities.

Another section of the national park at Stanhope on Gulf Shore Rd. has 5 developed acres with 103 unserviced sites and 14 three-way hookups. An interpretive program, ocean beach, and 18-hole golf course are available. Washing machines on site. Reservations not accepted.

Camping fees range from $5.50 to $12 daily, depending on the type of site. Private trailer park daily rates average $8 a day.

Note: Camping on Prince Edward Island is restricted to organized camping grounds. It is against the law to camp on a beach or on property not designated as a camping area.

The P.E.I. Visitors Information Centres have listings of campgrounds with rates at their bureaus.

 MUSEUMS AND HISTORIC SITES. P.E.I. Tourism's brochure *Visitor's Guide* describes and illustrates museums and historic sites by County, and is available by request, at no charge from the provincial tourism department. Some highlights—In **Charlottetown**, historically important *Province House* now houses the province's legislature; *Beaconsfield* is headquarters for the Prince Edward Island Museum and Heritage Foundation; and *Old Charlottetown* houses a wide variety of old shops, museums, stores, craft centers, restaurants, churches, and homes.

The Kings Byway Dr. will take you through many attractions that recall the early days of the Island and the early settlers' pioneering spirit. (See *Kings Byway Drive* section earlier in this chapter for additional Museums and Historic Sites).

The agricultural heritage of rural P.E.I. is re-captured at the *Rural Life Museum* near **Orwell.** Open for the summer season, 10 A.M. to 6 P.M. Admission: adults $1.50; children 50¢.

The *Log Cabin Museum* at **Murray Harbour** depicts the Island's 19th-century lifestyle. Open July 1 to Labor Day, 9 A.M. to 7 P.M. daily. Admission: adults, $1; children, 50¢; under 6, free.

An interesting collection of old firearms is one of the features at the *Garden of the Gulf Museum* in **Montague.** Open June 27 to September 16, 9:30 A.M. to 5 P.M., Monday–Saturday, 1 to 5 P.M., Sundays. Admission: adults, about $1.00; children under 12, 50¢. Displays and photographs in the *Fisheries Museum* at *Basin Head* show how small boats were used by early fishermen. Open mid-June –Sept. 1 from 9 A.M. to 5 P.M. daily, Sept. 1–Sept. 30 open 5 days a week. Admission: adults, $2.00; children under 12, free.

Antique car buffs might visit the *Spoke Wheel Car Museum* at **Dunstaffnage.** Open June 1 to September 15, 9 A.M. to 8 P.M., during July and August; 10 A.M. to 6 P.M., the remainder of the season. Admission: adults $3.00; children 1 to 6, $1.00; pre-schoolers, free.

Along Lady Slipper Drive, *Green Park Provincial Park* at **Port Hill** commemorates a 19th-century shipping complex. Admission: adults $1.50, children under 12 free. Open daily 10 A.M. to 6 P.M. June 21–Sept. 1. Check for hours after September 6. A campground is also part of the park.

At **Northport,** *Sea Rescue Park* has picnic tables, washrooms, water tap, and a children's playground. Sea Rescue Park is open from June 1 to October 31, from 9 A.M. to 10 P.M. daily. Free.

The *Acadian Museum* at **Miscouche** has an impressive collection of 17th-and 18th-century household, farm, and other domestic implements portraying the Acadian lifestyle over the years. Open from June 23 to Sept. 19, Sundays 1:00–5:00 P.M. and rest of week, 9:30 A.M.–5 P.M. Adults, $2.00; children, $1.00; under 12, free.

(See *Lady Slipper Drive* section earlier in this chapter for additional information.)

Blue Heron Drive passes the historic *"Farmers' Bank"* (chartered in 1864) at **South Rustico.**

The **French River District** has two pioneer era cemeteries, *Yankee Hill* and *Sims.*

At **Bonshaw** just beyond DeSable is an interesting *Car Life Museum.* Open May 24 to mid-Sept.; July and August, 9 A.M. to 9 P.M. daily, May, June and Sept. 10 A.M. to 5 P.M. Admission: adults, $3.00; children 6–14, $1.25; pre-schoolers, free.

At **Rocky Point** across the harbor from Charlottetown, the earthworks of the historic *Fort Amherst* (formerly Port La Joie, 1720) are a reminder of 18th-century occupation. Interpretative center, audiovisual display, picnic area. Open June 1–Oct. 15, 9 A.M.–5 P.M. daily. Free admission.

One mile east on Rte. 19, a *Micmac Village* has been re-created . . . birchbark canoes, wigwams, and an Indian craftshop. Open June 1–Sept. 15. Hours from 9:30 A.M.–7 P.M., July and Aug. From 10 A.M.–5 P.M., June and Sept. Admission: Adults, $2.50; children, $1; under 6 years free.

 ART GALLERIES. *The Confederation Centre Art Gallery and Museum* at the Confederation Centre in Charlottetown, is one of Canada's premier art museums. It is dedicated to the work of Canadian artists and hosts major exhibits from Canada, the U.S. and overseas. Its permanent collection includes the country's largest collection of paintings by Robert Harris (1849–1919), Canada's foremost portrait artist. Admission $1; family, $2; group, $5. Open year-round. July and Aug. from 10 A.M.–8 P.M.; Sept. to June from 10 A.M.–5 P.M., Tues. to Sat.

The Great George Street Gallery at 88 Great George St., Charlottetown, is a nonprofit gallery run by artists and supported by the national and provincial governments. It provides a program of exhibitions by local and regional artists, plus some special events. Admission free. Open year-round.

Holland College School of Visual Arts Gallery at 50 Burns Ave., West Royalty, features exhibitions by local artists and craftspeople. Open year-round. Admission free.

Pavilloner Art Gallery in the CP Prince Edward Hotel and Convention Centre, Queen and Water St., Charlottetown, exhibits national, Maritime, and local artists; also English marine art and other 18th- and 19th-century works, Open year-round. Mon.–Sat., 10 A.M.–8 P.M.

THEATER. During July and August, the **Charlottetown** Festival at the Confederation Centre for the Arts includes the P.E.I. perennial, *Anne of Green Gables,* plus a number of other, usually musical, productions. Feature plays are staged six nights a week in the 1,100-seat *Main Stage Theatre.* International concert artists are featured Sunday evenings on Main Stage. The adjacent *Cameo Theatre* cabaret productions of Canadian musicals six nights a week.

The King's Playhouse at **Georgetown** on Rte. 3, 30 miles (50 km.) east of Charlottetown, provides professional summer theater. Three plays in repertory plus variety concerts. Open daily, July and Aug.

The Governor's Feast at *The Wandlyn Inn* restaurant on Rte. 1 near **Charlottetown** is light dinner theater featuring the governor of 1842 and retinue. Similarly, there's *The Flyer's Feast,* bouncing 1940's stuff, at *The Brothers Two* restaurant on Rte. 1A near **Summerside.**

Victoria Playhouse in Victoria-by-the-Sea also offers repertory theater nightly during July and Aug.

La Cuisine à Mémé at the Acadian Pioneer Village, Mont-Carmel, offers charming French-language Acadian dinner theatre.

SHOPPING. Since colonial times, handcrafted items have been valued by P.E.I. inhabitants and craftspeople excel at jewelry making, wood carving, pottery, enameling, leather work, quilting, and weaving—just a few of the crafts executed with great skill. The P.E.I. Craftsmen's Council, Inc., P.O. Box 1573, **Charlottetown,** P.E.I. C1A 7N3 (tel. 892–5152), or the P.E.I. Visitors Information Centre can supply full information on outlets and types of crafts available.

Along Lady Slipper Drive, look for turned Bird's-eye maple wood products at the Leavitts' Maple Tree Craft Shop in **Alberton.** Open year-round, 8 A.M. to 5 P.M., Monday–Saturday.

Lennox Island Indian Arts and Crafts on **Lennox Island,** Rte. 163, has MicMac beadwork, moccasins, masks, turtle rattles and other crafts.

One major stop is the Acadian Pioneer Village at **Mont Carmel,** a restored early 19th-century community. Also visit the restaurant on the site and try an Acadian soup or potato dish. The restaurant is open from 10 A.M. to 11 P.M. daily. Prices are reasonable. The museum village is open from mid-June to mid-Sept., 10 A.M. to 7 P.M. daily.

For good pottery, visit the Flat River Crafts Studio on Kings Byway Drive. Open year-round, daily, 9 A.M. to 9 P.M.

One of the largest and most complete handcraft shops in P.E.I. is the Wood Islands Handcraft Co-Op on Main St. in **Murray River.** All the Island crafts are represented in this retail outlet on Kings Byway, which is open from June to Sept.

In **Charlottetown,** there's the Island Craft Shop located at 146 Richmond St. This shop contains a wide selection of island crafts. Open year-round from Monday to Saturday, 9 A.M. to 5 P.M. In July and August it's Monday to Saturday, 9 A.M. to 8 P.M.

Shopping malls are open 10 A.M. to 10 P.M., Monday to Saturday. Other stores throughout the province generally open at 9 A.M. and close at 5 or 5:30 P.M. On Friday evenings, most stores stay open until 9 P.M. Country stores generally open earlier and close later.

Holiday closings: Good Friday, Easter Monday, Victoria Day (in mid-May), July 1 (Canada Day), Labor Day (September 3), Thanksgiving (October 8), and Remembrance Day (November 11).

RESTAURANTS. The Island offers plenty of plain, wholesome, home-cooked food with friendly (often slow) service in an informal setting. In Charlottetown, however, good formal dining can be had in at least half a dozen restaurants.

The legal drinking age is 18. Liquor stores are open six days a week for about 12 hours a day.

Restaurants are categorized on the basis of full course dinners; drinks, tax, and tip are excluded. *Expensive,* over $25; *Moderate,* $20–$24; *Inexpensive,* under $20. A 10% provincial tax will be added to all meals over $2.00.

Most places accept the following major credit cards: American Express, MasterCard and Visa; others may also be honored. Not all establishments accept credit cards, therefore we suggest you call for information.

Every effort is made to ensure that the list of restaurants is up to date, but they come and go so quickly that it is always a good idea to call before going far out of your way.

BRACKLEY BEACH. *Inexpensive:* **Shaw's Hotel.** Sumptuous menu, from appetizers to desserts. Menu changes each day; call for menu and reservations. Phone 672–2022.

CAVENDISH. *Moderate:* **Chez Yvonne.** Good food, all home cooking; has its own garden, fresh vegetables. Phone 963–2070.

Fiddles & Vittles. Fresh shellfish, chowder, and steak. Open 4–9 P.M.; licensed. Phone 963–2225.

Marco Polo Inn. Well-known; good food. Phone 963–2351. Major credit cards.

Inexpensive: **Cavendish Arms.** Steak and seafood, licensed; Irish and modern music; dancing. Phone 963–2732.

CHARLOTTETOWN. *Expensive:* **The Confederation Dining Room,** Charlottetown Hotel. Elegant surroundings, pleasant food. Phone 894–7371. Major credit cards.

Lord Selkirk Dining Room. Feast on gourmet delicacies in the formal dining room of the Prince Edward Convention Centre. Phone 566–2222. Major credit cards.

Griffin Dining Room in the Dundee Arms Inn. Situated in a Victorian home. Checked tablecloths, fireplace, good food. Licensed. Chef has a special knack with locally caught fish. Phone 892–2496. Major credit cards.

Lock Stock and Barrel at the Confederation Inn. Good but not ritzy. Phone 892–2481. Major credit cards.

Moderate: **Caesar's Italy.** Italian foods plus local steaks and seafoods. A casual place with a salad and soup bar. Phone 892–9201. Major credit cards.

Casa Mia. Situated in old home. Quiet. Italian and Canadian food. Phone 892–8888. Major credit cards.

Claddagh Room. A must for the best seafood in town. Phone 892–9661. Major credit cards.

Garden of the Gulf Restaurant. Good food served in the elegant surroundings of the Prince Edward Convention Centre. Phone 566–2222. Major credit cards.

Off Broadway Cafe. Tucked away in old Charlottetown. Homemade specials. Phone 892–0632.

MacLauchlan's Motel. Scottish atmosphere. Home-style cooking. It has gained popularity in recent years for its accent on traditional island dishes. Phone 892–2461. Major credit cards.

The Rodd Royalty Inn. An uncomplicated but fairly attractive menu of steaks and seafoods. Phone 894–8566. Major credit cards.

Inexpensive–Moderate: **Pat's Rose and Grey Room.** Canadian and Italian menu. Phone 892–2222.

Inexpensive: **Cedar's Eatery.** Delicious Canadian and Lebanese cuisine. Phone 892–7377.

Maxwells. Specializes in hot or cold lobster plate dinner and Porter House steak dinner. Children's menu available. Phone 894–3137.

Town & Country. Good family restaurant, take-out available. Phone 892–2282.

CORNWALL. *Inexpensive–Moderate:* **Hans & Peter's Lobster Smorgasbord.** More than just lobster, and all you can possibly eat at one price. Open 4–9 P.M., 7 days a week Phone 566–2241.

Inexpensive: **Bonnie Brae.** Good family restaurant, Canadian and international fare. Phone 566–2241.

GRAND TRACADIE. *Expensive:* **Dalvay-By-The-Sea Hotel.** Located 3½ miles off Rte. 25 (near Stanhope). One of the Island's most elite eating places. Built as a summer home for a wealthy American who later sold it to his coachman (in lieu of 7 years' wages, according to locals), it has a large staircase and elegant interior. Excellent seafood. Reservations preferred but not always necessary. Phone 672–2048. Major credit cards.

KENSINGTON. *Moderate:* **Recreation Center.** Homemade food; not elegant but good.

KINGSBORO. *Moderate:* **Seabreeze Motel.** Good dining room, licensed; features home cooking with seafood specialties. Open year-round. Phone 357–2371.

MONTAGUE. *Moderate–Expensive:* **Lobster Shanty North.** One of the best places to eat on the Kings Byway. Dining room has rustic décor that extends into the lounge bar overlooking the Montague River. Licensed, and features seafood, particularly lobster. Open year-round. Phone 838–2463.

MONT CARMEL. *Moderate:* **Étoile de Mer** in the Acadian Pioneer Village. Specializes in Acadian dishes—Râture and meat pies. Try Acadian stew or a potato dish. Open mid-June to mid-September, 10 A.M. to 11 P.M. daily.

MORELL. *Moderate:* **Village Diner.** Features home-cooked meals and specials every day. Overlook the rough atmosphere and enjoy the food. Licensed with adjacent lounge bar. Open year-round.

POOLES CORNER. *Moderate:* **Kingsway Motel.** Licensed dining room, good food and a cozy lounge. Open year-round. During off-season—dancing. Phone 838–2112. Major credit cards.

ROSENEATH. *Expensive:* **Brudenell Resort Restaurant.** Usually good service and good food in the resort complex. Licensed. Two lounge bars adjacent. Open June 1 to September 3. Phone 652–2332. Major credit cards.

RUSTICO. *Moderate–Expensive:* **Fisherman's Wharf Restaurant.** Open mid-May to October. 7 A.M.–10 P.M. daily. Seafood and special mussel chowder. Phone 963–2669.

SOURIS. *Inexpensive:* **Bluefin Restaurant.** Plain food in unpretentious surroundings. Licensed with adjacent lounge bar featuring entertainment. Open year-round. Phone 687–3271.
Platter House. Enjoy the best fresh-cooked seafood in eastern P.E.I. while looking out over the lovely Colville Bay. Phone 687–3340.

SUMMERSIDE. *Moderate–Expensive:* **Brothers Two.** Steaks and seafood, scallops a specialty. Open and airy atmosphere, pleasant service. Licensed. Dancing. Also "Flyer's Feast," specializing in Island seafood served by a cast of talented performers who dine, dance and perform during feast. 6 P.M. to 9 P.M., Monday to Saturday. Phone 436–9654.
Moderate: **Linkletter Motel.** Licensed; specialty is good buffet at noon weekdays & on Friday evenings. Phone 436–2157. Major credit cards.
Papa David's. Seafood, mostly in a cozy waterfront setting. Phone 436–4606. Major credit cards.

LOBSTER SUPPERS. You *must* sample the lobster suppers. Usually served in church halls or community centers, they are an Island tradition.
Silver Fox Curling and Yacht Club Lobster Suppers (licensed), open July 1–Aug. 15, 4 P.M.–8 P.M. daily. Phone 902–436–3209; manager Jim Grant.
New Glasgow Lobster Suppers (licensed) open June 1–Oct. 20, 4 P.M.–8:30 P.M. daily. Phone 902–964–2870.
New London Lions Lobster Suppers (licensed), open June 2–mid-Oct., 4 P.M.–8:30 P.M. daily. Phone 902–886–2599 or 886–2526.
Fisherman's Wharf (licensed), North Rustico, Rte. 6. Open June 1–mid-Oct., 4 P.M.–10 P.M. daily. Phone 902–963–2669. Reservations accepted.

Rosebank Hall, Rosebank. Open June 1–Sept. 29. By reservation for large groups only. Phone 902–894–8589 or 902–569–2434; manager, Abe Zakem.

St. Ann's Church Lobster Supper (licensed), Rte. 224 between Stanley Bridge & New Glasgow. Open June 18–Sept. 15, 4 P.M.–8:30 P.M. daily except Sun. Phone 902–964–2385 or 902–964–2053.

Stanhope Beach Lodge Lobster Smorgasbord (licensed), Stanhope, on Rte. 25. Open June 6–Sept. 2, 4:30 P.M.–8:30 P.M. daily. Reservations advised. Phone 902–672–2047 or 902–672–2975.

Cardigan Lobster Suppers, on Rte. 321. Open June–Oct., 4 P.M.–9 P.M.

Northumberland Lobster Suppers, Fishermen's Loft, Northumberland Arena, Murray River. Open July and Aug., 3 P.M.–8 P.M. on Fri., Sat., and Sun.

Cape Cannery Lobster Suppers, Little Pond, Rte. 310, Kings Byway. Open summer months, 4 P.M.–9 P.M. from Thurs. through Sun.

 NIGHTCLUBS, BARS, LOUNGES. A lounge in P.E.I. is a fully licensed bar which usually has some live entertainment part or all of the week. Some lounges also have a limited food menu during certain hours of the day. All are closed on Sundays.

Charlottetown: *The Tudor Lounge,* Charlottetown Hotel, is quiet, popular on Friday evenings. *The Smuggler's Jug,* Confederation Inn. Rustic beams, quiet background music. *Page One,* Rodd Inn. Cozy, dim and attractive, small lounge. *Olde Dublin Pub,* rollicking Irish music and great pub food. *The Gallows Lounge,* small, built on Gallows Hill with rather macabre gallows décor; daily happy hours. *The Tackroom.* Small bar, great drinks. *Sea Shell Lounge* (large and plush) and *Crossed Key Bar* (small and intimate), both in Prince Edward Hilton hotel.

Summerside: *Regent Lounge.* Disco to 2 A.M. weekends, 1 A.M. weeknights. *Scrooge's Lounge* above Clovie's Restaurant, closes at 1 A.M. *Papa David's Lobster Trap Lounge,* disco to 2 A.M. weekends, 1 A.M. weekdays. *Friday's Lounge* and *Capt. Grady's Pub* are both in Brothers Two restaurant.

NEWFOUNDLAND AND LABRADOR

An Early European Beachhead

by
RALPH SURETTE and MARGOT SAMMURTOK

Perhaps the legendary Leif Ericson was among the Viking crew and passengers of the Norse longship that came ashore and formed a settlement, sometime about A.D. 1000, on a point of land on the northern tip of Newfoundland. Perhaps not. At least we know that the half-barbarian, half-literate adventurers were the first discoverers of Newfoundland—and possibly the first Europeans who landed on North American shores. While the Norsemen made several voyages to this area during the next 100 years, it was not until 1497 that John Cabot, sailing from Bristol on the west coast of England, found the almost invisible niche in the rock leading into a protected harbor. Legend has it that he arrived on St. John's Day, and thus named the port St. John's.

Nearly a hundred years passed and the "new found land" remained unknown in Europe except to a handful of Bristol merchants and the fishermen employed by them. For a century, these westcountry men carried back the rich harvest from the Newfoundland fishing banks, even establishing seasonal colonies from which to support the fishery. Yet little is known of this early period of exploration. For years, the West of England fishermen sought to conceal their profitable voyages from the scrutiny of a tyrannical Crown in order to avoid payment of oppressive taxes. But the trade became too large and too prosperous to be hidden for long; in 1583 Sir Humphrey Gilbert claimed the land for Elizabeth I. To reinforce his claim, he set up a trading stall on what is now the St. John's waterfront, and opened it up for business. Sir Humphrey also distinguished himself by bringing from England the first professional dancers and musicians to play in the New World; these were the "hobby horses and Morris dancers and many like conceits" who performed on shore at St. John's on August 5, 1583.

Hard Times for Settlers

Gilbert's claim for Britain ended the laissez-faire days of international fishing off the coast of Newfoundland by 30,000 fishermen from half a dozen nations who operated in relative peace and security. It began the infamous era of the Fishing Admiral which was to last for another century. The Fishing Admiral was the first captain to sail into any Newfoundland harbor each year. This distinction allowed the fortunate skipper to set himself up as a total despot for the season, thereby creating unceasing turmoil between permanent settlers and English adventurers.

It was also the time of bitter dispute between the merchant overlords in Devon and the English west country and the would-be colonists. Settlement in Newfoundland was against the law and anyone who tried colonization was laying his life on the line. The colonists could see the rich future in settlement and pursuit of the rich inshore fishery. The merchants could see the colonists rapidly wresting control of the rich trade in salt fish away from the motherland.

In 1711, the colony was placed under the rule of Naval Governors and the Fishing Admirals' empire was dissolved. Although harsh legislation had been enacted, settlement had continued during the reign of the admirals. Around the bays and inlets were tiny settlements and individual families. Most could be reached only by boat and signs of habitation were usually well hidden from outsiders. Sometimes known as "the lost men," these tiny communities were enlarged by further groups of settlers, some successful, some doomed.

Though harsh anti-colonization laws were passed and repealed from time to time at the whim of the British monarchy, Newfoundland settlements became a fact. Some credit for their survival may go to the New England colonies who aided and abetted a settlement policy for many years.

Dominion to Colony to Province

In 1811 the British government legalized permanently the granting of land and the building of houses in the colony. By 1855, Newfoundland had become a self-governing Dominion within the British Commonwealth.

By 1934, having weathered the growing pains of a new country, a world war, and the first years of the Great Depression, Newfoundland was bankrupt. There was no alternative but to become a British colony once again with a commission government to administer its affairs. With the advent of World War II, however, Newfoundland found itself in the middle of supply lines from North America to Europe, and the Allies poured money and men into Newfoundland to spur on the effort of building bases where only wilderness had existed before. The problem was no longer to find money, but to find men to do the work.

Prosperous throughout the war and the post war period, Newfoundland again considered its future. To join the nation of Canada, with Newfoundland on its front doorstep, seemed the logical choice to many Newfoundlanders. Finally, after a bitter and stormy campaign and

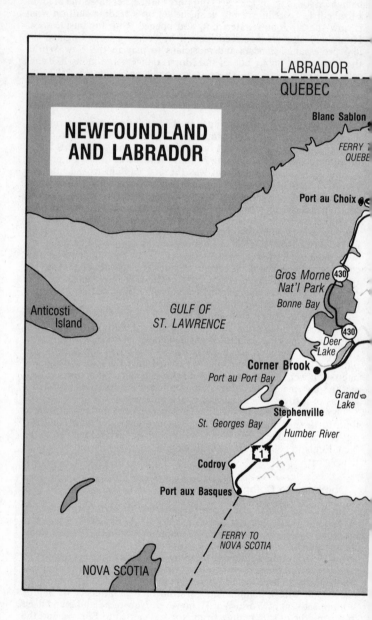

NEWFOUNDLAND AND LABRADOR

LABRADOR
QUEBEC

Blanc Sablon

FERRY QUEBE

Port au Choix

Gros Morne Nat'l Park
Bonne Bay

GULF OF ST. LAWRENCE

Anticosti Island

Deer Lake

Corner Brook
Port au Port Bay

Grand Lake

Stephenville

St. Georges Bay

Humber River

Codroy

Port aux Basques

FERRY TO NOVA SCOTIA

NOVA SCOTIA

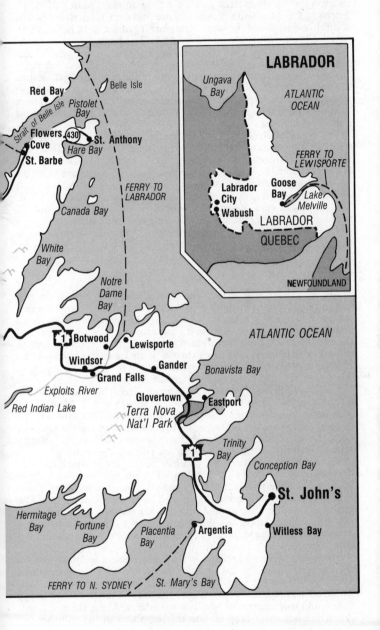

referendum, Newfoundland joined Confederation on March 31, 1949, becoming Canada's tenth province. Since that time, it has developed its natural resources and, in some part, rearranged the once isolated out-port society which made up most of Newfoundland.

Settlement in the larger communities, university and trades educa-tion, and modernization of the fishing, forestry, and mining industries characterize the contemporary directions of the province. Yet, despite the encroachments of 20th-century living, Newfoundland and New-foundlanders have managed to retain their special personality and their culture, a combination that makes Canada's newest province a most unique acquisition.

The Newfoundland flag—a new one proclaimed in 1980—has two triangles (representing Labrador and the Island of Newfoundland) and stylized ornamentations representing the Christian, and Beothuk and Naskapi Indian backgrounds of the province. The colors are blue (the sea) and red (human endeavor) on a background of white (snow). It replaces the Union Jack which had served as the provincial flag before. The provincial coat of arms—developed in 1637, lost, rediscovered, then finally adopted officially in 1928—is a red shield quartered by the white cross of Saint George. The quarters contain the white unicorns of England and gold lions of Scotland.

A Craggy Isle

Newfoundland, an island off the coast of northeast North America and situated between the Gulf of St. Lawrence and the Atlantic Ocean, is separated from the mainland by the Strait of Belle Isle on the North and Cabot Strait on the southwest. Labrador, the northeast corner of the continent, is the province's mainland section. To neglect to mention the massive land area of this province is to leave the unsuspecting traveler unprepared for his journey. In terms of the United States, only Alaska, Texas, and California are greater in size.

Largest of the four Canadian Atlantic provinces, Newfoundland has a total area of 405,720 sq. kms. (156,648 square miles). Most of the province's population of 620,000 is concentrated on the island—in the cities of St. John's, the capital, and Corner Brook, and in the towns of Gander and Grand Falls. The Labrador towns of Goose Bay/Happy Valley, Wabush, and Labrador City are also on the upswing.

Visitors flying overhead have commented that the province seems to be made up of bodies of water surrounded by bits of land. Indeed, about 10 percent of the province is lakes and streams—thousands of them!

Labrador is mountainous, dotted with lakes, and cut by rivers. The mountains are ancient, ground blunt by the passage of glaciers eons ago. Most of the slopes are forest covered up to the tree line with a hardy, slow-growing spruce, suited to endure severely cold winters and short summers.

The island of Newfoundland is also mountainous and lake-strewn. On the west coast, the flat, forested mountains form an escarpment some 2,000 feet high which plunges sharply into the sea at the coast. In the central region, the mountains give way to low land and boggy forests and more ranges of hills and mountains. Along the east coast, the mountains again drop off into the sea, although the cliffs are not as steep as on the opposite coast.

It was this forbidding landscape which made the fishery the chief economic mainstay of Newfoundland for 450 years. With the riches of the Grand Banks there for the taking and an inshore fishery which yielded vast quantities of cod and other fish, there was no need to look inland. Even today, agriculture tends to be concentrated in smaller operations and in areas such as the Codroy Valley in the west coast.

The inland riches of Newfoundland now lie in the forests and under the barren rock and in the tumbling water. Forestry, mining and the production of hydroelectricity are major industries. Newfoundland has generally the highest unemployment rate of Canada and is considered its poorest province. But the discovery of huge oilfields on the Continental Shelf may change all that.

Newfoundland is in a unique time zone, one-half hour earlier than Atlantic Canada. The weather varies widely as the province extends more than 1200 kms. (750 miles) north to south. In St. John's, average summer temperatures range from 21°C (70°F) to roughly 13°C (55°F) at night. In the north, the summer temperatures follow about the same range, although the season is shorter. Winter temperatures in St. John's are about 0°C (32°F) by day, dipping to about −7°C (20°F) at night. On the west coast of the island and in Labrador, winter temperatures can fall to −45°C (−50°F).

Another unique geographical fact is that the island part of the province has no skunks, snakes, or ragweed pollen.

Words ...

The visitor to Newfoundland is charmed by the unique speech of the outport people, the originality of their idiom, and the dialects that one hears only in this province. The St. John's accent has an Irish quality (the name of the city is pronounced "sin jahns," with the accent at the end); accents in places like Harbour Main, Ferryland and Placentia are similar. In the north, one listens to a Dorset or Devon dialect of three centuries ago complete with words and idioms long forgotten in England. Then there are the traditional figures of speech that have been retained through four centuries of settlement. Words like "ballycater" —ice formed on the shore by spray or little cakes of sea ice; "cuddy"—a covered space in the bow of a boat, and "kinkhorn"—a person's Adam's apple. "Sparbles" are headless nails, and a "yaffle" is an armful of dried fish—the word used as a unit of measure—a yaffle of fish.

In 1811, immigration to Newfoundland became legal. The isolated settlers kept the words of their own times, and passed them on to succeeding generations. Absence of books and formal literacy helped preserve the old words. Terms relating to the sea and the fishery were kept to the forefront and if a suitable word did not exist, one was made up "right off the bat."

... and Music

Newfoundland seems to have more folk songs than any other part of Canada, most of them with an Irish flavor. Many old folk songs were brought from Britain with the settlers through 300 years of illegal and legal settlement. Another group of songs originated in Newfoundland —songs of the sea, of love affairs, the eternal triangle, and the loss of a lovelorn man or maiden.

One of the most prolific of later-day Newfoundland folk song writers was Johnny Burke whose home was a gathering place for many of the finest singers in Newfoundland. Born in 1851, he lived here with his sister until his death in 1930. Burke's most popular piece was *The Kelligrew's Soiree,* the story of an all-out party in the community of Kelligrews, just outside St. John's.

Dancing is part of Newfoundland musical heritage. Local square dances are full of movement, rhythm, and grace. When no one is available to play on a fiddle or jew's-harp, somebody has to furnish "chin-music."

A Modern City

But Newfoundland is not all mountains and folk music. St. John's, its capital, is a flourishing, contemporary city, symbolizing new directions of the province (and the country). It is a pleasure to visit.

EXPLORING ST. JOHN'S

St. John's is situated on the eastern coast of the Avalon Peninsula, an "H"-shaped promontory jutting out by a spindly isthmus from the southeast corner of the Island of Newfoundland. Because of its strategic location almost halfway between Montreal and Europe, St. John's has long been connected with shipping across the North Atlantic. Lying almost on top of one of the world's richest fishing banks, the old city has been a second home to European fishermen for more than four centuries. A walk along St. John's waterfront, even today, reveals a polyglot culture that adds great vitality to the life of the city.

John Cabot, as noted earlier, arrived in 1497, naming the harbor St. John's and the whole island New Founde Isle before sailing off to the Canadian mainland.

Six years later, the British Bristol Company tried, without success, to plant a colony on Cabot's new found harbor in the New World. But more hardy people were to follow. In 1583, Sir Humphry Gilbert proclaimed the land for Elizabeth I, announcing that anyone daring to disobey the rule of Her Majesty would have his ears cut off. By this time St. John's was a prosperous town—the rocky walls of the harbor sheltering the fishing fleets of many nations. Well-established merchants did a thriving business and the town was ruled by the law of the Fishing Admiral.

Despite the harsh winters and a forbidding landscape, St. John's was coveted by several European nations over the centuries including the Dutch, Portuguese, Spanish, French and British. Thus, the city was periodically besieged by contending nations as well as attacked several times by freelancing pirates. The final shots of the Seven Years' War between the French and English were fired in St. John's in 1762.

Under strong British rule, St. John's settled into a comparatively quiet and stable way of life. The merchants traded and prospered. The fishermen struggled and barely made a living. The cosmopolitan character of the city broadened and international history continued to be played out around the old port. The "townie" of St. John's (as distinguished from the "bayman" who lived outside the town) cast a curious eye at these events, but refused to become overly excited. So he took it in stride when Guglielmo Marconi received the first wireless signal from across the ocean at his receiver atop Signal Hill in St. John's in 1901; and few well-wishers cheered Alcock and Brown when they took off from Lester's Field to complete the first trans-Atlantic flight in 1919. And it seemed only natural to the "townie" that Roosevelt and Churchill should choose to meet on the quiet waters of nearby Placentia Bay to draft the terms of the Atlantic Charter.

Two world wars brought successive waves of uniformed "mainlanders" from Canada as well as seafaring men of a dozen nations to walk the steep cobblestone streets along the waterfront, waiting to board convoy ships for Europe. Many young men and women joined the much-decorated Newfoundland fighting units and merchant marine, and died in defense of the countries which had given life to their city centuries before.

St. John's was probably closer to the wars than most North American cities. During World War II, German U-boats constantly cruised the waters off Newfoundland in search of allied shipping and convoys, torpedoing ships only a few miles outside St. John's harbor.

After the signing of the Lend-Lease agreements, St. John's became familiar with the uniform and accents of United States military personnel as Britain exchanged leases on territory in return for American shipping and hardware with which to continue the war. The complex by the shores of Quidi Vidi (pronounced *Kiddy-Viddy*) Lake was built by the United States and known as Pepperell Air Force Base. It has since been returned to the city, and renamed Pleasantville, and is now office space for various government agencies, apartment buildings, a hospital, and other institutions.

Following the last war, a new era began for Newfoundland and for St. John's, which was named capital of North America's oldest territory and Canada's youngest province. This change (which some Newfoundlanders still regard, with good humor, as the time when Canada joined Newfoundland) was to have a dramatic effect on the new province and especially on St. John's.

Old City, New Life

The old city—one of the oldest in the New World—rapidly became the showplace of the province. As it took its place as Newfoundland's leading retail, wholesale, and service center, a major ocean port, and a focus of transportation, its citizens benefited economically. With expansion of its shipbuilding, fish processing, and manufacturing industries, a new and more contemporary lifestyle began to emerge.

The townie took the changes, both good and bad, with a philosophical attitude. Mainlanders arrived by the boatload and "tried to teach us their way." But the city simply sighed, and made room for them, and proceeded to turn them into Newfoundlanders.

The sprawling campus of Memorial University is a far cry from the tiny college-school of only a few years ago. New housing and high-rise buildings have changed the skyline. The discovery of oil offshore has changed the economic base; but attitudes have remained traditional in many ways and the citizenry retains its unique character. Though friendly and hospitable to all visitors, the people are hardy to the point of stubbornness. How else to account for their unbounded resilience in the face of extreme hardship and a succession of tragedies over the years? The original settlers were mostly fishermen from the villages of Devon, Cork, Dorset, Somerset, and Waterford. Their descendants survived England's harsh policy toward permanent settlement only to watch their city captured and plundered four times and finally leveled by fire in 1817. Indeed, St. John's was the first North American city to have been totally destroyed by fire. Fire struck again in 1846 and, for the third time, in 1892 when 13,000 people were left homeless. Yet today, St. John's is alive and well, as cosmopolitan as London or Montréal and as English as Victoria.

Tea is still the favorite nonalcoholic drink, with rum in first place for those who like something a bit stronger. English biscuits are still preferred over mainland cookies and many offices still close for lunch between 12:30 and 1:30. Living is still leisurely and everyone celebrates all the provincial and federal holidays with a few extra of their own, such as St. Patrick's Day and Orangemen's Day. One special non-holiday event is Bonfire Night—Guy Fawkes Night—on November 5th. Gambling is a Newfoundland passion—bingo, wheels of fortune,

and raffles for live turkeys and pigs at Christmas are well attended.
Every townie is expected to go trouting, or angling, and he enjoys his
leisure, extending hospitality to any who will enjoy it with him.

Water Street, running quite naturally along the waterfront, is probably the oldest street in North America. In the shops and stores one
can purchase everything from an anchor to a needle. Secretaries in the
latest fashions mingle with fishermen in rubber boots and school children in English-style uniforms. Even if you do not buy, it is interesting
to walk the length of the street. Stop at the Living Room Café in
newly-restored, historic Murray Premises and enjoy your tea with the
locals.

A number of walking and self-drive tours have been developed for
St. John's and the surrounding area. The best way to see St. John's is
on foot even though the hilly streets, as the natives say, go in only two
directions—up and down. A heritage foundation has restored many of
the quaint clapboard houses in the downtown core.

A publication entitled *Everyman's Complete St. John's Guide* costs
about $3.00 and offers several detailed walking and self-drive tours.
And remember—when you journey outside the city, take your camera
or your sketch book! (For further information, see *"Special Interest
Tours"* under Practical Information for St. John's.)

No matter what time of year you visit St. John's and whatever
historic sites you choose to see, your most enduring memory will be of
the people. St. John's has an accent all its own—mainly Irish and a bit
English, with unusual idioms spicing the conversation. The accent is
soft and expressive, tumbling off the tongue; most visitors will come to
adopt it during their stay, even in spite of themselves.

Find any excuse to start a conversation with a total stranger. Your
new friend will accompany you, just to keep you on track, pointing out
all the sights along the way. And if you ask a few questions about the
old city, you may have found a friend for your entire visit to St. John's.

PRACTICAL INFORMATION FOR ST. JOHN'S

HOW TO GET THERE. By Plane. *CP Air* and *Air
Canada* operate regularly scheduled flights to St. John's
from points throughout Canada, the U.S. and within
Newfoundland. New regional carriers *Air Atlantic* and
Air Nova connect from many points throughout the Maritime and Atlantic
regions.

By car. St. John's is the eastern terminus of the Trans-Canada Hwy. (TCH—
Hwy. 1) from Port-aux-Basques and also of the car ferry from North Sydney,
Nova Scotia. Visitors taking the other ferry from North Sydney to Argentia,
Newfoundland, follow highway 100 to the intersection with TCH. Turn east
toward St. John's. This latter ferry service operates only during the summer
months. Reservations required on both services and must be picked up 1½
hours before sailing. For reservations and information write to Marine Atlantic,
Reservations Bureau, Box 250, North Sydney, NS B2A 3M3 (902–794–7203).
Toll free in Canada, Ontario, and Quebec (800–565–9411), Nova Scotia, New
Brunswick, and Prince Edward Island (800–565–9470); in Newfoundland, (800
–563–7701); in continental U.S. (800–341–7981); in Maine, (800–432–7344) and
for the hearing impaired in continental North America (800–794–8109).

By bus. Motorcoaches operated by *TerraTransport* (709–737–5912) carry
passengers from the ferry terminals to St. John's. For tickets and information,
contact any VIA Rail ticket office (agents for TerraTransport) in Canada; see
also the "How to Get There" section in Practical Information for Newfoundland and Labrador.

ACCOMMODATIONS. St. John's has changed considerably since the discovery of oil off the shores of Newfoundland. Accommodations are sometimes hard to come by, and reservations are recommended. Most St. John's hotels are on the expensive side. There are some "Hospitality Homes," however, that provide inexpensive accommodation. Double-occupancy rates are as follows: *Expensive,* \$46 or more; *Moderate,* \$35–45; *Inexpensive,* under \$35. A 12% provincial tax will be added to your bill.

Most places accept the following major credit cards: American Express (AE), MasterCard (MC), and Visa (V); others may also be honored. Not all establishments accept credit cards, however, and we suggest that you call for information.

Expensive

Airport Inn. Airport Road, Box 9432, St. John's, NF (709–753–3500). Plain, comfortable accommodations near airport, 9 km (5 mi.) from downtown. Dining room, lounge. Pets allowed. Major credit cards accepted.

The Battery Hotel. ("The Inn with the View"). 100 Signal Hill, St. John's, NF A1A 1B3 (709–726–0040). Dining room, lounge, indoor pool, and sauna. Pets allowed. Major credit cards accepted.

Best Western Travellers Inn. Kenmount Road, St. John's, NF A1B 3P9 (709–722–5540); toll free in Canada (800–528–1234). Comfortable accommodations. Dining room, lounge, night club. Major credit cards accepted.

Chateau Park. 7 Park Avenue, Mount Pearl, St. John's, NF A1N 1J1 (709–363–7725; toll free 800–563–9300). Excellent dining and lounge facilities. Major credit cards accepted.

Holiday Inn Government Centre. 180 Portugal Cove Road, St. John's, NF A1B 2N2 (709–722–0506). Dining room, coffee shop, heated pool. Licensed patio (in season). Major credit cards accepted.

Hotel Newfoundland. Cavendish Square, Box 5637, St. John's, NF A1C 5W8 (709–726–4980). Dining room, lounges, pool, sauna, squash courts. Babysitting can be arranged. Major credit cards accepted.

Hotel St. John's. 389 Elizabeth Avenue, St. John's, NF A1B 1V1 (709–726–0092). Dining room, lounge. Pets allowed. Major credit cards accepted.

Kenmount Motel. 479 Kenmount Road, St. John's, NF A1B 3P9 (709–722–5400). Comfortable. Dining room, lounge. Pets permitted. Major credit cards accepted.

Lester Hotel. 12 Blackmarsh Road, St. John's, NF A1E 1S3 (709–579–2141). Dining room, lounge, sauna. Pets permitted. Major credit cards accepted.

Moderate

Greenwood Lodge & Motel. 53 Greenwood Crescent, Mount Pearl, St. John's, NF A1N 3J1 (709–364–5300). Breakfast room, lounge, picnic tables, BBQ, country surroundings. Ramps and some rooms equipped for paraplegic visitors. Pets allowed. V, MC accepted.

Parkview Inn. 118 Military Road, Box 1212, St. John's, NF A1C 5N9 (709–753–2671). 18 rooms with private baths. Dining room, snack bar. Open year-round. Downtown location. No credit cards.

Skyline Motel. 479 Kenmount Road, St. John's, NF A1B 3P9 (709–722–5400). Plain, comfortable accommodations. Dining room, lounge, wheelchair accessible. Pets allowed. Major credit cards accepted.

Inexpensive

Bonaventure House. 34 Bonaventure Avenue, St. John's, NF A1C 3Z5 (709–753–3359). Two units. Nice dining room.

The Olde Inn. 157 LeMarchant Road, St. John's, NF A1C 2H4 (709–722–1171). Bed & breakfast, 14 rooms.

Prescott House. 19 Military Road, St. John's, NF A1C 2C3 (709–753–6036). Three units.

HOW TO GET AROUND. From the Airport. *Gulliver's Taxi* operates a taxi/limo service from the St. John's Airport to downtown hotels. Cost is about \$4.00 per person. **Car Rental.** Major car rental agencies have desks at the St. John's airport and in some hotel lobbies. Advance booking recommended through a travel agent or the local office of the rental agency. Most agencies will deliver cars to St. John's hotels.

By Bus. The *Metrobus* system operates throughout St. John's and into the outlying areas. Routes start operating between 6:45 A.M. and 8:00 A.M. and stop running between 6:00 P.M. and 12:30 A.M. depending on the route. Passengers must have exact fare as drivers do not carry change. Fares subject to change. ($10.80 at press time). For information, call (709–722–9400). Metrobus also offers special tours and out-of-town charters. A number of small operators run services to other regions of the Avalon Peninsula. Contact the nearest tourist information office for routes and timetables or call the St. John's tourism office.

By taxi. Taxis do not generally "cruise" in St. John's. It is usually necessary to call one of the stands and have the cab meet you.

TOURIST INFORMATION. *St. John's Tourist Chalet,* TCH (709–568–5900). *St. John's Tourist Commission,* City Hall, New Gower St. (709–722–7080). *Tourist Information Desk,* Colonial Building, Military Road at Bannerman Road (709–753–9380). *Tourist Information Desk,* Confederation Building, Confederation Parkway (709–576–3630). *Tourist Information Desk,* Newfoundland Museum, Duckworth St. (709–576–2461). *Provincial Department of Development,* Tourism Branch, Confederation Building (709–576–2830 or 800–563–6353). *Hospitality Newfoundland* (709–722–2000).

TELEPHONES. The area code for St. John's and all Newfoundland, including Labrador, is the same: 709.

TIME ZONE. St. John's is on Newfoundland Time, as is the rest of the island—that is, one half-hour in advance of Atlantic Time and 1½ hours ahead of Eastern Time.

RECOMMENDED READING. The indispensable book for tourists in Newfoundland is Harold Horwood's *Newfoundland,* a superb account of the people, traditions, resources, and places of the province. Horwood is the greatest Newfoundland writer, a novelist (*Tomorrow Will Be Sunday, White Eskimo*) and biographer (*Bartlett: The Great Canadian Explorer*) and nature historian (*The Foxes of Beachy Cove,* a minor masterpiece). Ray Guy is a brilliant humorist whose mordant wit is collected in *You May Know Them As Sea Urchins, Ma'am* and the award-winning *That Far Greater Bay.* Guy has been known to shake Newfoundland governments. Other contemporary novels are Percy Janes's *House of Hate* and Gordon Pinsent's *The Rowdyman.* Kevin Major, national and international award-winning author of adolescent and young adult books, is required reading for anyone wanting to gain insight into growing up in Newfoundland. His works, *Hold Fast, Far From Shore,* and *36 Exposures* are available at bookstores featuring Canadian authors and at any Canadian bookstore.

Poet Al Pittman's *Down by Jim Long's Stage* and the plays of Michael Cook are published by Newfoundland's own Breakwater Books, a venture that has achieved remarkable national stature despite its youth and distance from major markets. Former premier Joey Smallwood compiled *The Book of Newfoundland,* and his memoirs *I Chose Canada* include a lively account of the campaign that brought Newfoundland into Confederation in 1949. Cassie Brown specializes in marine disasters; her *Death on the Ice,* about a catastrophe at the famous (or infamous) seal hunt in 1914, was an international success. Paul O'Neill's *The Oldest City* is a detailed history of St. John's.

Those who combine a love of language with a love of history will appreciate the *Dictionary of Newfoundland English,* the result of the collaborative efforts of G.M. Story, W.J. Kirwin, and John D.A. Widdowson.

SEASONAL EVENTS. In **February** and **March** there are *winter carnivals* in many Newfoundland towns and villages. In **February,** the *Kiwanis Music Festival;* in **April,** the *Provincial Drama Festival.* In **May,** the *Newfoundland Kennel Club All-Breed Championships,* and the *Lion's Trade Fair.*

May to **October,** *sailing races* around St. John's, including the annual Regatta, said to be the oldest continuous sporting event in North America. **June,** the *St. John's Day* civic celebrations. **July** features the *Fish, Fun & Folk Festival* in Twillingate, *ForestFest* in Springdale, and *Hangashore Folk Festival* in Corner Brook. In **August,** there is the *Newfoundland and Labrador Folk Arts Festival,* of international repute. From **mid-July** to the end of **August,** the Newfoundland Militia perform a colorful *military tattoo* on Signal Hill on Tues., Thurs., Sat., and Sun. at 3 and 7 P.M. weather permitting. Musket and cannon fire, military drill, and the red uniforms of the militiamen make this an exciting performance. In **September,** the *Newfoundland Amateur Golf Championship.*

TOURS. *Overland Tours* (709–576–4412), the *St. John's Transportation* (709–722–9400), *Newfoundland Historic Trust* (709–754–1742), *Newfoundland Nature Tours* (709–754–2052), *Fleetline Tours* (709–722–2608), and *McCarthy's Party* (709–854–5705) has bus tours of the island and the city and environs. *Harbour Charters* (709–754–1672) and *Lucky Strike Boat Charters* (709–3940) take passengers sightseeing and fishing in the harbor and beyond.

SPECIAL INTEREST TOURS. A number of **walking/ driving tours** of St. John's are available at the tourist information desks or by mail from the *St. John's Tourist Commission,* City Hall, New Gower St., St. John's. Self-guided driving tours to outlying areas of the city and environs include tours to Marine Drive/Pouch Cove, Portugal Cove/St. Phillips, and Petty Harbour/ Maddox Cove. All these drives offer dramatic seacoast scenery and take you to fishing villages and inland forested regions.

A well-marked **nature trail** starts at King George V Park and leads walkers for some distance along the river and ponds to an area outside the city. Inquire at the travel information desk for the best place to begin the trail.

For **bicyclers,** a cycle path begins at Kent's Pond, just west of the junction of Portugal Cove Rd. and Confederation Pkwy., leading through the woods and coming out on Higgin's Line.

Eight-day nature excursions to make "human contact" with the **whales,** porpoises, and dolphins that abound off eastern Newfoundland are offered by *Ocean Contact Ltd.* Reservations needed well in advance. Contact Box 10, Trinity, Trinity Bay, NF A0C 2S0 (709–464–3269). Shorter excursions and daily expeditions also available.

Newfoundland has three important **seabird sanctuaries**—one on Gull Island in Witless Bay, 30 km (18 mi.) south of St. John's on Rte 10; one at Cape St. Mary's, approximately 193 km (120 mi.) southeast of St. John's; and one on the Funk Island, 80 km (50 mi.) off the northeast coast of Newfoundland.

The best time to go to *Gull Island* is June 15 – July 15 and the best way to reach the island 5 km (3 mi.) offshore is by making arrangements with *Bird Island Charters* (see *Tours,* above). Special permission is needed to land. The best time for *Cape St. Mary's* is June 15 – Aug. 15. A rough 16 km (10 mi.) road branches off Rte. 100 about 3.2 km (2 mi.) past St. Bride's and leads to Cape St. Mary's. The bird colonies at Cape St. Mary's are viewed from a spectacular clifftop lookout. A trip to *Funk Island* is a major expedition and is only available to *bona fide* scientists with a permit. Further information from the Department of Development and Tourism.

PARKS. C.A. Pippy Park—4,000 acres on the city's northern boundary—is St. John's favorite open-air recreation spot, and a marvelous place to take children. There are extensive woodlands with nature trails, picnic areas, campgrounds, golf course, a small botanical and wildlife reserve, playground, and children's farm. The Memorial University campus, the Confederation Building and several other noteworthy buildings are within the park's confines.

Another favorite relaxation spot for residents and visitors is **Bowring Park,** in the west end. It has a year-round playground with wooded areas, open fields, swimming pools in summer, and skating rink in winter. Bannerman Park, on Bannerman Rd. behind the Colonial Building, has an outdoor pool and playground. **Quidi Vidi Picnic Ground** on the north shore of Quidi Vidi Lake has tables and fireplaces for picnics. **Cochrane Pond** and **Butterpot Provincial Parks** are within easy driving distance of St. John's on the TCH. With the exception of the provincial parks, there is no entrance fee to any St. John's park.

PARTICIPANT SPORTS. For **golf,** the *Bally Hally Golf and Country Club* is a private club but visitors can play. Green fees $18 (709–753–6090). Also in St. John's is the municipal *Pippy Park Golf Club,* a public 9-hole golf course. Green fees $6 (709–753–7110).

Ice skating during the winter and **roller skating** during the summer at the half-dozen arenas and rinks in town. **Bicycling** is becoming popular. The St. John's Club has tours Wednesdays and Sundays. All invited.

For **swimmers,** there are outdoor summer pools at Bowring Park, Waterford Bridge Rd. (709–364–3880); Bannerman Park, Bannerman Rd. (709–753–4655); Victoria Park, Water St. (709–726–8181). Indoor year-round pools are located at the Torbay Recreation Centre at St. John's Airport (709–737–2792); Downtown Boys and Girls Club, Water St. (709–753–7080); Mount Pearl Swimming Pool, Park Avenue (709–368–0128); and Wedgewood Park Pool, 45 Gleneyre (709–753–0570); and the Aquarena (709–754–1977).

SPECTATOR SPORTS. Regatta Day on Quidi Vidi Lake is St. John's big holiday of the year. Called for the first Wednesday in Aug., or the first fine day following, it is the oldest (1826) sporting event in North America still being held. It is probably the only civic holiday that is decided at 7 A.M. on the morning of the holiday. Townies listen to their radios for the magic phrase "The races are on!" that signals the holiday. Thousands crowd the lakeshore to watch the events as teams of oarsmen and oarswomen in racing shells compete up and down the lake, and to gamble on the games of chance at the booths set up throughout the area. If the weather is inclement, the townies go to work and listen each morning at the same time until they hear the magic phrase—uttered on the first fine morning after the first Wednesday in Aug.

The **Avalon Raceway** at Gould's, 16 km (10 mi.) from St. John's, has harness racing Wed., Sun., and holidays, spring to fall, on a variable schedule. Usually at 7:45 P.M., but better check for times.

HISTORIC SITES AND SIGHTS. Signal Hill National Historic Park is probably the focal point in St. John's. At the top, the Cabot Tower, near where (the precise spot is marked by a plaque) Marconi received the first overseas wireless message, has become a symbol of the city. The bleak and rocky headland was the site of early forts as well as the last battle of the Seven Years' War in North America. Here you will have a breathtaking view of St. John's and the harbor as well as the last landfall before Europe. In spring, large white and turquoise Arctic icebergs, known as "growlers," can sometimes be sighted. Gibbet Hill near Deadman's Pond was the site of the old gallows. The Interpretive Centre halfway up Signal Hill offers another great view of the city and the harbor; it also has a number of interesting displays and artifacts that document the city's history. There are interpretive walks and lookouts in the park. Obtain information from the Interpretive Centre—open 9 A.M. to late evening in summer.

The **Sir Humphrey Gilbert Memorial** is a plaque set below the National War Memorial on Water St., and it marks the spot where Sir Humphrey planted the Royal Standard of Elizabeth I in 1583 and claimed Newfoundland for England; the **National War Memorial,** whose figures represent freedom, was unveiled on July 2, 1924. The **Queen's Battery,** overlooking the harbor entrance just below the crest of Signal Hill, dates back to the 18th century when France and England were still struggling for possession of Newfoundland, to the time of the last battle on Signal Hill in 1762 when the English took St. John's. **Chain Rock Battery** was located at the narrowest part of the harbor entrance. In the late 1700s, a large chain was put between Chain and Pancake Rocks so that two capstans could be used to raise it to obstruct enemy vessels. During World War I, a chain boom was used to protect ships in the harbor, and then in World War II, the place was used for an anti-submarine net.

The Anglican **Cathedral of St. John the Baptist,** a fine example of North American church Gothic architecture, was started in 1816, destroyed by fire in 1842 and again in 1892, then restored with the present building in 1905. The clergy is pleased to provide information. The **Basilica of St. John the Baptist,** started in 1841 and finished in 1850, is made of limestone and Irish granite. It is built in the shape of a cross, with 138-foot towers, and holds 2,000 people.

MUSEUMS. Newfoundland Museum on Duckworth St. opposite Cathedral St. has a number of artifacts from shipwrecked vessels, displays of early settlements in Newfoundland, and the only known relics of the Beothuk Indians, a vanished race that once roamed the island. Open six days a week, 9 A.M.–5 P.M., Mon.–Fri.; 9 A.M.–9 P.M. on Thurs.; 10 A.M.–6 P.M., Sun. and holidays. Admission free.

The **Newfoundland Museum at the Murray Premises** on Water St., a downtown branch of the main museum, has displays of the province's sea-going history, a natural history exhibit, plus a collection of military firearms, equipment, uniforms, and other exhibits. Open seven days a week, 9 A.M.–5 P.M., Mon.–Fri.; 10 A.M.–6 P.M. Sat.–Sun.

The **Anglican Cathedral** (with a small museum) on the corner of Gower St. and Church Hill, is rated one of the finest examples of ecclesiastical architecture in North America. Its museum is located behind the small organ screen to right of the altar. Usually open when cathedral is open.

Commissariat House, a provincial historic site, is a former military residence and rectory restored to the style of the 1830s.

ART GALLERIES. The *Memorial University Art Gallery* at the Arts and Culture Centre has lectures, films, and other presentations, in addition to art exhibits. *The Gallery,* 284 Duckworth St., deals in Canadian paintings, prints, and sculpture. Other galleries featuring local artists are: *Rostotski,* 296 LeMarchant St.; *Spurrell Gallery,* 87 Longs Hill; *Finishing Touch,* 127 Queens Road.

THEATER AND MUSIC. Live theater in St. John's is not necessarily abundant, but it is lively. *CODCO* is one group that has caught national attention. *The Resource Centre for the Arts* is a venue for original theater and dance. More formal plays, including Shakespearean presentations, are staged at the auditorium of the *Arts and Culture Centre* at Memorial University, and also at the Little Theatre at the university. The Arts and Culture Centre is the city's main stage and also hosts symphony orchestras, jazz concerts, and the like. Call (709–737–3900) for information.

SHOPPING. Newfoundland handcrafts have an international reputation. It is the home of such exotica as Grenfell parkas, Labrador jewelry, and so on. St. John's abounds in craftshops—most of them being concentrated in the commercial area along Duckworth St. Restored Murray Premises has excellent quality shops. The *Newfoundland and Labrador Crafts Development Association,* 265 Duckworth St., has a complete list of craft shops, products, and information on prices. The *Department of Development and Tourism,* Confederation Building, also has booklets listing crafts and outlets. The Avalon Mall and the Village Shopping Centre are the main shopping malls. Malls are mostly open Mon.–Sat., 10 A.M.–10 P.M. Other shopping areas open Mon.–Sat., 9 A.M.–6 P.M. except Fri. night when they stay open to 9 P.M. Most stores are closed Victoria Day (late May), Memorial Day (late June), Labor Day, Thanksgiving, St. George's Day (late Apr.), Discovery Day in mid-June, Orangemen's Day in early July, and Remembrance Day (Nov. 11). (All holidays come under the Shop Closing Act. Only convenience stores remain open.)

RESTAURANTS. Dining out in St. John's can be a pleasant experience if one samples the various Newfoundland dishes and chooses wisely from the menu. Seafoods tend to be the best choice. Expect them to be prepared in a fairly traditional manner—wholesome but not too exciting. Most of the better restaurants can provide small side orders of traditional food such as cod tongues, scrunchions (bits of fat pork, crisply fried), fish and brewis, or seal flipper.

Service is generally good in the better restaurants although it can be slow, especially if the place is busy. Strike up a conversation with your waiter, who can often provide you with an enjoyable meal and friendly humor.

Restaurants are categorized on the basis of the price of a full-course dinner, drinks, tax, and tips excluded: *Expensive,* over $16; *Moderate,* $10–$16; *Inexpensive,* less than $10. A 12% provincial sales tax will be added to your bill.

Most places accept the following major credit cards: American Express (AE), MasterCard (MC), and Visa (V); others may also be honored. Not all establishments accept credit cards, therefore we suggest you call for information.

Expensive

Cabot Club. (709–726–4980). Elegant dining in the new Hotel Newfoundland. Overlooking St. John's Harbour with a view of the Narrows. Major credit cards.

Stone House Restaurant. 8 Kenna's Hill (709–753–2380). Traditional and innovative dishes. Reservations. Major credit cards.

Moderate–Expensive

The ACT III Restaurant. (709–754–0790.) At the Arts and Culture Centre. Quality dining in a relaxed atmosphere. Major credit cards.

The Battery. On Signal Hill. (709–762–0040.) One of the best; ask for a window table overlooking St. John's at night. North American menu with Newfoundland specialties. Organ music most nights during dining. Major credit cards.

The Colony. 64 Portugal Cove Rd. (709–753–9510). Continental menu specializes in seafood and local dishes. Major credit cards.

Explorers' Restaurant at the Fishing Admiral. 203 Water St. (709–753–6203). Good food, featuring live lobster from the tank, cod, caplin, prime rib of beef.

290 Restaurant. 290 Duckworth St. (709–722–1290). Seafood specialties and French cuisine. Favorable reviews in many North American publications. Major credit cards.

Moderate

Colonial Inn. In community of Topsail on Hwy. 3 just outside St. John's (709–722–6933). Good but limited menu. Fireplace, nice, little bar, cozy. Major credit cards. Reservations.

Casa Grande. 108 Duckworth Street (709–753–6108). A fine Mexican food restaurant. Major credit cards.

Inexpensive–Moderate

McGregor's. 28 Cochrane St. (709–754–2413). Open 12 noon to 12 midnight, 7 days a week. Major credit cards.

Inexpensive

Captain's Cabin. (709–726–3280.) Cafeteria in Bowring's Department Store on Water St. has nice view of harbor and waterfront. Specialties, Newfoundland dishes and Irish coffee.

The Blue Door Cafe. 252 Duckworth St. (709–726–7822). Relaxing atmosphere, friendly service, varied menu.

NIGHTLIFE. A St. John's pub crawl is a cultural experience in itself. It's a city that expresses itself, rather in an Irish way, in its multitudes of ebullient lounges, taverns, and bars. The minimum legal drinking age in Newfoundland is 19.

Albert's. Baird's Cove. Features latest in top 40's and videos.

Capricorn's Bar. George St. Live music, Friday and Saturday.

Captain's Quarters. Holiday Inn, is heavy on the distinguished nautical atmosphere.

Christian's. 23 George Street. Relaxing bar, specializing in coffees and wines.

Club Max. 130 Water St. The St. John's interpretation of New York's Studio 54. Lively, loud disco.

Corner Stone. Corner of Queen and George Streets. In a historic building, this night spot offers quality entertainment weeknights, dancing and featured entertainment on weekends. Box office information (709–754–1410). Quiet bar downstairs.

Damien's Pub. 892 Water St. Friendly pub on one level; more intimate surroundings on another level in "Damien's Den."

The Duke of Duckworth. 325 Duckworth St. Old English-style pub.

Mingles. 53 Harvey Road. A lively singles bar.

The Narrows. Hotel Newfoundland. A quiet bar overlooking the hotel's garden. Piano music daily.

Pepper's. 193 Water St. Another lively spot. Dancing.

Raffles Pub. 379 Duckworth St. A neighborhood pub.

Schroeder's Piano Bar. 8 Bates Hill. Reminiscent of the era of the "cafe society," patrons gather around the grand piano.

Silver Knight Lounge. Airport Inn. Live entertainment nightly.

Stone House Wine Bar. 8 Kenna's Hill. Espresso, cappuccino, and a large range of specially imported French wines. No reservations accepted.

Sundance Saloon. corner of George St. and Adelaide St. Western theme.

Trapper John's Museum 'n' Pub. 2 George St. Unique pub with museum atmosphere. Patrons who consume 3 oz. of dark rum receive an Honorary Lifetime Membership Certificate.

EXPLORING NEWFOUNDLAND AND LABRADOR

Newfoundland's West Coast

The west coast begins at the ferry terminal and fishing town of Port-aux-Basques, a name that reveals the Basque past of Newfoundland.

On Table Mountain, just a few miles north of Port-aux-Basques on the Trans-Canada Highway (Highway 1), is a big yellow and black wind-warning sign: "Notice. Dangerous winds up to 120 miles per hour known to occur next 10 miles." The sign explains that if drivers have difficulty handling their cars they should wait or turn back "as high winds [are] known to blow trains from rails, and overturn motor vehicles." In characteristic Newfoundland style, no punches are pulled in wording the sign. The wind, funneled by the Long Range Mountains on one side and the open sea on the other, can blow a terrific gale across the plateau. The ground-hugging bushes and stunted, twisted trees quietly attest to the might of the wind.

Safely across Table Mountain, the mountains rise, forested and quiet, one after another toward the horizon. Cottages nestle beside the lakes here and there. Privacy is the rule—there are enough lakes to go around.

The town of Stephenville was one of those created by World War II. Under the lend-lease agreement between Britain and the United States, land for an air base was turned over to the U.S. military. The complex was named Harmon Field and thousands of American military people at one time or another set foot in Newfoundland. The field and buildings were eventually turned back to the Newfoundland government and are used today as a commercial airport. A liner board mill was opened here during the 1960s, went bankrupt in the 1970s, but now has opened again as a paper mill. Forestry is the town's main industry.

Corner Brook, the "western capital," is the center of Newfoundland's west coast. At the mouth of the Humber River, the city is a major pulp and paper producer and retail distribution center for half of Newfoundland. Corner Brook is on the Humber River, which teems with salmon during the season. Journeying north past Deer Lake, you should stop to enjoy the grandeur of Bonne Bay and Gros Morne National Park. To reach the park, turn off the Trans-Canada Highway to Highway 430. Highways in the park region are maintained by the Parks Department.

North from Gros Morne Park, Highway 430 follows the coast for nearly 640 kilometers (400 miles) to St. Anthony. Although the highway is well maintained, this is not a journey for the faint-hearted in the winter. During the summer it is a trip to be long remembered. The road passes through tiny villages at the foot of forested mountains beside the sea. The country is wild and if the interior looks uninhabited, that is because it is the domain of moose, bear, and other animals. If the drive gets tiring, a night at Cow Head or Hawke's Bay is a good idea.

At Port au Choix, the National Historic Park is dedicated to the ancestors of Indians and Inuit who lived here 4,000 years ago. The Viking ruins at L'Anse-aux-Meadows National Park, recently placed on the World Heritage list by UNESCO, have been preserved and housed for viewing. Standing on the barren headland, one can imagine the high-prowed longship bringing the Norsemen across the sea from Greenland as they sought the legendary Vinland.

At St. Barbe, a small ferry takes cars across the Strait of Belle Isle to the coast of Labrador at Blanc Sablon, Quebec. A 48-kilometer (30-mile) drive brings one to the Pinware River Provincial Park for fishing and a view of one of the world's last frontiers. Check with a Newfoundland tourist center for ferry times and fishing regulations.

In general, the west coast has rather different weather from the central and east. Temperatures on the west coast tend to drop lower in winter and rise higher in summer, and areas such as the Marble Mountain Ski area may have more than 150 inches of snow on the ground at the end of the season.

Central and Eastern Newfoundland

Looking at a map of Newfoundland, one sees that the interior of the province is marked by an absence of roads and that communities along several hundred miles of the south coast have no roads, in or out. With Newfoundland entering confederation as late as 1949, it might be said that highway development had some catching up to do. The highway across the island, now known as Highway 1 (TCH—the Trans-Canada Highway), was for many years gravel surfaced and paved only in sections. To cross the province was something of an adventure. By the mid-1960s, the paving was completed and work has been directed at improving the remainder of the trunk roads. Most communities are now serviced by paved roads.

The paving of the TCH linked the east and west coasts and has assisted in opening up the central portion of the island. West from Deer Lake, the highway runs through what seems to be deserted country—forests of spruce, occasional bogs, and mountains in the background. Most of the exits turn to the seacoast. Pick an exit, find yourself a tiny community with a name like Sop's Arm or Harry's Harbour, and stop a while.

The twin towns of Windsor and Grand Falls straddle the TCH halfway across the province. Both are paper towns and retail centers for the surrounding area. The Mary March Museum in Grand Falls has displays of logging and natural history of the region. Mary March was the Christian name given to Demasduit, a young Beothuk Indian woman captured by John Peyton, Jr., near Grand Falls. Demasduit, who died in 1820, may have been the last survivor of a tribe that probably numbered around 5,000.

The town of Botwood at the mouth of the Exploits River might have become a world aviation capital. Prior to World War II, the aviation industry was undecided as to the merits of flying boats versus land-based aircraft. With the outbreak of war, the superiority of the wheeled airplane became evident, and Botwood, which had been scheduled to become a major flying boat base, became the victim of technology. The town of Gander, only 91 kilometers (57 miles) away and at the time just a small air station, was expanded as the airbase for the trans-Atlantic air ferry service and the first North American landfall when passenger crossings were being made by propeller-driven aircraft. A small museum in the Gander airport portrays the long history of trans-Atlantic aviation in Newfoundland and displays models of many of the early aircraft.

One of the best drives on Newfoundland's east coast is along the Eastport Peninsula. Take Highway 310 at Glovertown, follow the partly graveled road to the community of Salvage, and stop at the tiny local history museum. The museum was created by purchasing a house and all of the furnishings, fixtures, and fittings from a retired fisherman and his wife. The couple was given a new completely furnished home nearby. Beaches, a shipyard, and even a community called Happy Adventure are there for the tourist's pleasure.

Labrador

Labrador, one of the last North American frontiers, has been called "the land that God gave Cain." Icy and desolate in winter, it has an austere charm in summer. It has few people but is rich in minerals, water, wildlife, and forests. Still relatively unexplored, Labrador is a land of mystery and power. Its land mass constitutes the larger part of the province of Newfoundland.

Goose Bay and the adjacent community of Happy Valley were once bustling and busy. Goose Bay was built as a ferry station for aircraft during World War II. The United States obtained the base under the lend-lease arrangement, and British and Canadian forces also owned portions of the base. Recently, the U.S. has cut back on the use of the base, but several NATO countries now use the area for training purposes. The commercial airport uses part of the base facility, and the community is a service center for the various outposts up and down the Labrador coast. "Goose" is also the jumping off point for anglers and hunters taking bush planes into private lakes and rivers. Visitors can reach Goose Bay only by plane or by Marine Atlantic coastal boat.

Wabush and Labrador City are twin mining towns on the Labrador–Quebec border which produce about fifty percent of Canada's iron ore. They are pleasant company towns with relatively few facilities for tourists except the Smokey Mountain Ski Club which attracts the hardier cross-country skiers. The area boasts one of the world's best cross-country ski ranges, at which international competitions are held occasionally.

Labrador's main appeal for tourists is fishing and a limited amount of hunting. Salmon, Arctic char, trout, and northern pike are fished. See *Practical Information* section on "Fishing" and other related sections at end of this chapter for further details.

PRACTICAL INFORMATION FOR
NEWFOUNDLAND AND LABRADOR

 HOW TO GET THERE. By Plane. *CP Air* operates scheduled jet services to a number of Newfoundland centers including St. John's, Gander, Corner Brook, Goose Bay, Churchill Falls, and Wabush, from Toronto, Montreal and other eastern Canadian points. *Air Canada* operates scheduled jet flights from Toronto, Montreal and eastern Canadian points to St. John's and Stephenville. *Air Atlantic* and *Air Nova* operate connector flights within the Maritimes. *Quebecair* operates scheduled jet flights from Montreal to Wabush.

By Car. With the exception of some 80 km (50 mi.) of highway from Blanc Sablon, Quebec, to Red Bay, a partially paved road link from Baie Comeau, Quebec, to Labrador City, and local roads in Goose Bay and Wabush/Labrador City, Labrador has no roads. The island of Newfoundland has about 9,654 km (6,000 mi.) of highway, including the 906 km (565 mi.) TCH from Port-aux-Basques to St. John's. Most main roads, including the Trans-Canada, are paved; most secondary highways are paved but some are still gravel surfaced.

By Ferry. From North Sydney, Nova Scotia, to Port-aux-Basques, Newfoundland, there is a daily year-round car/ferry service (with up to five crossings per day in summer). A crossing takes about six hours. During the summer season, it is best to travel early in the day and early in the week. Cabins, restaurants, bars, cinema, and a tourist bureau are available during the summer. Reservations are required on all crossings and must be picked up at the ferry terminal 1½ hours before sailing.

Marine Atlantic also operates a summer service from North Sydney, Nova Scotia, to Argentia, Newfoundland—an 18-hour mini-cruise for visitors with some room for cars. The service runs from mid-June to mid-Sept., three days per week. Cabins, a restaurant and bar, cinema, and tourist bureau are available. Reservations are required and must be picked up 1½ hours before sailing at the ferry terminal. For information and reservations, contact Marine Atlantic, Reservations Bureau, Box 250, North Sydney, NS B2A 3M3 (902–794–7203); toll free in Canada, Ontario, and Quebec (800–565–9411); Nova Scotia, New Brunswick, and Prince Edward Island (800–565–9470); in Newfoundland (800–563–7701); in continental U.S. (800–341–7981); and in Maine (800–432–7344). In continental North America the hearing impaired can call 800–794–8109.

By Train. Train service to Newfoundland is operated by *VIA Rail* through the ferry crossings from North Sydney, Nova Scotia, to Port-aux-Basques, Newfoundland. Connections can be made to VIA Rail by Amtrak from New York. Since Newfoundland had operated under the British rail system, all trains in the province ran on narrow-gauge tracks. The alternative to replacement of all track and antiquated rolling stock was to discontinue passenger service by rail during the 1960s and institute an efficient service by motor coaches (known in Newfoundland as "road cruisers"). Road cruisers reach most major communities in Newfoundland adjacent to the TCH.

Marine Atlantic provides a toll-free telephone service (see "By car" section). VIA Rail offices in eastern Canada also have information. Or see your travel agent.

By Bus. Most major bus lines throughout North America connect with *Acadian Lines* in Nova Scotia to take visitors to the ferry in North Sydney, Nova Scotia. For information, see your local bus line agent or your travel agent.

 ACCOMMODATIONS. Visitors to Newfoundland will find traditional, comfortable accommodation throughout the province. In the larger centers, the motels may appear more modern, but they cannot exceed the hospitality of the smaller properties. Most lodgings are small and have a dining room and/or bar as part of the business. Some of the older properties may not have private bathrooms in all units; you must specify if you wish a private bath. Usually, the owners live on the property and welcome guests personally.

Double occupancy rates in Newfoundland are categorized as follows: *Expensive,* $40 or more; *Moderate,* $30–$40; *Inexpensive,* under $30. The 12 percent provincial sales tax will be applied to all accommodation rates.

Most places accept the following major credit cards: American Express (AE), MasterCard (MC), and Visa (V); others may also be honored. Not all establishments accept credit cards, therefore we suggest you call for information.

BURGEO. *Moderate–Expensive.* **Sou'Wester Inn.** Route 480. Box 339, Burgeo, NF A0M 1A0 (709–886–3309). Accommodations by the sea. Lots of atmosphere. Adequate dining room.

CHURCHILL FALLS. *Expensive.* **Lobstick Lodge and Motel.** Box 86, Churchill Falls, LB A0R 1A0 (709–925–3235). Dining room, lounge, picnic tables, playground. Sports fishing and guide service nearby. Open June 1–Sept. 30.

CLARENVILLE. *Expensive.* **Holiday Inn.** Box 967, Clarenville, NF A0E 1J0 (709–466–7911). Coffee shop, dining room, lounge. Outdoor pool. Wheelchair accessible.
Moderate–Expensive. **Restland Motel.** Cabot Highway off Route 1, Clarenville, NF A0E 1J0 (709–466–7636/2287). Private pool, restaurant, lounge, playground, fishing/hunting nearby.

CORNER BROOK. *Expensive.* **Bridge Way Motel.** Riverside Drive, Corner Brook, NF A2H 6J2 (709–634–4378). Route 440. Sun deck, BBQ, picnic tables, outdoor pool.
   Glynmill Inn. Cobb Lane, Box 550, Corner Brook, NF A2H 6E6 (709–634–5181). Steak house, dining room, lounge. Pets allowed.
   Holiday Inn. 48 West Street, Corner Brook, NF A2H 2Z2 (709–634–5381). Outdoor pool. Wheelchair accessible. Restaurant, lounge.
   Hotel Corner Brook. Main Street, Box 398, Corner Brook, NF A2H 6E3 (709–634–8211). Dining room, lounge. Pets allowed.
   Mamateek Motor Inn. TCH, Corner Brook, NF A2H 6G7 (709–639–8901). Dining room, lounge, coffee shop. Hunting/fishing/skiing/golf nearby.
Inexpensive. **Jones Hospitality Home.** 11 Noseworthy's Road, Corner Brook, NF A2H 3T6. Just 1½ km (1 mi.) off Arterial Road (709–785–7461). Two rooms. Dining room; marina and park nearby. No credit cards.

DEER LAKE. *Expensive.* **Deer Lake Motel.** Box 820, Deer Lake, NF A0K 2E0 (709–635–2108) or toll-free (800–563–2144) from within the province. Basic accommodations. Dining room, lounge, coffee shop. Car rental office.
   Driftwood Inn. Box 58, Deer Lake, NF A0K 2E0 (709–635–5115). Home style cooking a specialty of the house. Pioneer Pub, with display of old style items. Coffee shop, dining room. Major credit cards.

DUNVILLE. *Expensive.* **Northeast Arm Motel.** Box 219, Dunville, NF A0B 1S0 (709–227–3560). About 8 km (5 mi.) from Argentia/North Sydney Ferry Terminal. Lounge, dining room, games room, playground. Hunting, fishing nearby. V, only.

EASTPORT. *Moderate–Expensive.* **Eastport Efficiency Units.** Site 18, Box 8, Eastport, Bonavista Bay, NF A0G 1Z0 (709–677–2458); Sept.–June (709–677–3417). 32 units. 20 serviced trailer lots available. Swimming pool, tennis court, sport equipment rentals. Lounge, restaurant. Playground, picnic tables. Beach swimming, boating, fishing, hunting nearby.
   Squire's Housekeeping Units. Eastport, Bonavista Bay. Contact: Traytown, NF A0G 4K0 (709–677–3224). Beach swimming nearby. Fishing. Playground. Pets allowed. Credit cards accepted.
   White Sails Cabins. 20 km (12 mi.) from Rte. 1; Eastport, NF A0G 1Z0 (709–677–3400). Housekeeping units. Beach, playground, boating, fishing. Pets allowed on leash.

FORTUNE. *Moderate.* **Seaview Motel.** Box 620, Fortune, NF A AOE1LO (709–832–1411). Basic accommodation with restaurant and lounge. 1 km (½ mi.) from St. Pierre Ferry.

GANDER. *Expensive.* **Albatross Motel.** Box 450, Gander, NF A1V 1W8 (709–256–3956) or toll-free (800–563–4894). Over 100 rooms. Wheelchair accessible. Excellent seafood dining room; lounge. Pets allowed. Golf course nearby.

Holiday Inn. 1 Caldwell St., Gander, NF A1V 1T6 (709–256–3981). Typical Holiday Inn. Nice, cozy cocktail lounge. Coffee shop and dining room. Outdoor pool. Paraplegic facilities.

Hotel Gander. 100 TCH, Gander, NF A1V 1P5 (709–256–3931). Over 100 rooms. Wheelchair accessible. Dining room, coffee shop, lounge. Boating, fishing, golf, playgrounds nearby.

Sinbad's Motel. Bennett Drive, Box 450, Gander, NF A1V 1W6 (709–651–2678) or toll-free (800–563–4894). Efficiency and motel units. Fully wheelchair accessible. Dining room, lounge. Recreational services, golf course nearby. Pets allowed. Major credit cards.

Moderate. **Airport Inn.** TCH, Gander, NF A1V 1P6 (709–256–3535). 64 rooms, 8 housekeeping units. Food service nearby. Beach swimming, boating, golf, playgrounds, fishing, etc., nearby. Pets allowed. Major credit cards.

GLOVERTOWN. *Expensive.* **Janbu Motel.** Box 252, Glovertown, Bonavista Bay, NF A0G 2L0 (709–533–6726). Basic accommodation. Dining room, lounge, games room.

Moderate–Expensive. **Rest A While Hotel.** Main Street, Glovertown, NF A0G 2L0 (709–533–2500). Dining room, lounge. Fishing nearby.

Inexpensive. **Ackerman's Hospitality Home.** Glovertown, NF A0G 2L0 (709–533–2811). Friendly hosts.

GOOSE BAY. *Expensive.* **Labrador Inn.** Box 58, Station "C", Goose Bay, LB NF (709–896–3351). 62 units. Children under 12 free. Dining room. Cocktail lounge. Major credit cards.

Royal Inn. 5 Royal Avenue, Happy Valley, Labrador, NF A0P 1E0 (709–896–2456). 15 efficiency and housekeeping units. Continental breakfast included. Children under 12 free. V, only.

GRAND BANK. *Moderate.* **Granny's Motor Inn.** 5 km (3 mi.) from St. Pierre Ferry Terminal; Box 809, Hwy. By-Pass, Grand Bank, NF A0E 1W0 (709–832–2180). 10 rooms, lounge, licensed dining room. V, only.

The Thorndyke. 33 Water Street, Grand Bank, NF A0E 1W0 (709–832–0820). 5 rooms. Children under 12 free. No private baths. Captain's home (turn of the century). No credit cards.

GRAND FALLS. *Expensive.* **Car-Sans Hotel.** 78 Lincoln Road, Grand Falls, NF A2A 2J3 (709–489–5324). 8 rooms, lounge and dining room.

Highliner Inn. Route 1, Box 748, Grand Falls, NF A2A 2M4 (709–489–5639). 20 housekeeping units. Lounge. Golf course nearby. Major credit cards.

Mount Peyton Hotel/Motel. Route 1, 214 Lincoln Rd., Grand Falls, NF A2A 1P8 (709–489–2251) or toll free (reservations only, 800–563–4894). Over 150 units. Dining room, steak house, lounge. Pets allowed. Hunting/fishing nearby. Major credit cards.

Inexpensive. **Town and Country Inn.** Box 477, Grand Falls, NF A2A 1Z1 (709–489–9602). 9 rooms, Continental breakfast included. Lounge. Games room. 6 Church Road.

HARBOUR GRACE. *Expensive.* **Hunt's Hotel "By the Sea."** Box 675, Water Street, Harbour Grace, NF (709–596–5156). Dining room, lounge. Ocean view.

Inexpensive–Moderate. **Pike's Hotel.** Box 100, Harbour Grace, NF A1A 2M0 (709–596–5072). 14 motel and 7 hotel rooms; adequate restaurant, separate dining room plus lounge.

HAWKE'S BAY. *Expensive.* **Maynard's Motor Inn.** Hawke's Bay, NF A0K 3B0 (709–248–5225). 20 motel, 12 housekeeping units. Wheelchair accessible. Restaurant and cocktail lounge. Viking Trail tours. Salmon outfitters. Major credit cards.

LABRADOR CITY. *Expensive.* **Carol Lodge.** 215 Drake Avenue, Labrador City, NF A2V 2B6 (709–944–3661). 22 housekeeping units, 2 rooms. Downhill skiing, golf, playground, fishing, hunting nearby. Major credit cards.

LEWISPORTE. *Expensive.* **Brittany Inns.** Box 689, Lewisporte, Notre Dame Bay, NF A0G 3A0 (709–535–2533). Hotel, motel, and housekeeping units. Hospitable staff; good service. Dining room and cocktail lounge.

MARYSTOWN. *Expensive.* **Motel Mortier.** P.O. Box 487, Marystown, NF A0E 2M0 (709–279–1600). Wheelchair accessible. Coffee shop. Pets allowed. Major credit cards.
   Moderate. **Seaway Lodge.** Box 1201, Villa Marie Drive, Marystown, NF A0B 2M0 (709–279–1139). Dining room, lounge/bar. Breakfast included in rate.

NAIN. *Expensive.* **Atsanik Lodge.** Box 10, Nain, Labrador, NF A0P 1L0 (709–922–2910). Dining room, lounge bar. Trout fishing; hunting nearby.

PLACENTIA. *Moderate–Expensive.* **Harold Hotel.** Main Street, Placentia, NF A0B 2Y0 (709–227–2107). Basic accommodations in older hotel. Dining room, lounge, playground. V, only.

PORT-AUX-BASQUES. *Expensive.* **Grand Bay Motel.** Box 538, Port-aux-Basques, NF A0M 1C0 (709–695–2105). Basic accommodation 2 km (1 mi.) from CN Ferry Terminal. Dining room and lounge. Pets allowed. Major credit cards.
   Hotel Port-aux-Basques. 2 km (1 mi.) from CN Ferry Terminal; Box 400, Port-aux-Basques, NF A0M 1C0 (709–695–2171). Restaurant, coffee shop, cocktail lounge. Pets allowed. Major credit cards.

PORT UNION. *Expensive.* **Seaport Inn.** Port Union, Trinity Bay, NF A0C 2J0 (709–469–2257). Hotel and motel. Good food in dining room; licensed. V, MC accepted.

ROCKY HARBOUR. *Expensive.* **Gros Morne Cabins.** Box 151, Rocky Harbour, NF A0K 4N0 (709–458–2020). Housekeeping units. Picnic tables, recreation area and playground. Swimming, cross country skiing nearby. Open year-round.
   Ocean View Motel. Box 129, Rocky Harbour, NF A0K 4N0 (709–458–2730). 22 rooms. Dining room, lounge. Movie rentals. Pets allowed. Western Brook Pond & Bonne Bay boat tours available. Major credit cards. Open year-round.

ST. ANTHONY. *Expensive.* **St. Anthony Motel.** Box 237, St. Anthony, NF A0K 4S0 (709–454–3200). Basic accommodation; dining room and cocktail lounge. Major credit cards.
   Vinland Motel. Box 400, St. Anthony, NF A0K 4S0 (709–454–8843). Motel and housekeeping units. Basic accommodation; dining room, cocktail lounge. No pets. Major credit cards.
   Moderate. **Decker's Tourist Home.** St. Anthony, NF A0K 4S0 (709–454–3664). Modest accommodation, but all meals included in daily rate.

STEPHENVILLE. *Expensive.* **Hotel Stephenville.** Box 301, 213 Oregon Dr., Stephenville, NF A2N 2Z4 (709–643–5176). 50 units. Licensed dining room; cocktail lounge. Pets allowed. Major credit cards.
   Island Inn. Box 194, 75 West Street, Stephenville, NF A2N 2Y9 (709–643–5616). Breakfast only. Bar service; no dining room. Major credit cards.

White's Hotel/Motel. 14 Main Street, Box 386, Stephenville, NF A2N 2Z5 (709–643–2101). Children under 18 years free if sharing room with parents. Dining room; lounge. Major credit cards.

TERRA NOVA NATIONAL PARK. *Moderate.* **Weston's Terra Nova National Park Chalets.** Terra Nova National Park (Newman Sound), Glovertown, Bonavista Bay, NF A0G 2L0 (709–533–2296); off-season address: Box 309, Gander, NF, A1V 1W7 (709–651–3434). 24 housekeeping cabins. Licensed dining room. Maid, babysitting service. Camping, sporting equipment rental. Golf course, supervised swimming. Pets allowed on leash (at all times).

TRAYTOWN. *Moderate.* **Ledrew's Housekeeping Cabins.** Traytown, Bonavista Bay, NF A0G 4K0 (709–533–2553). Lovely spot, open-year round. Playgrounds, kiddies pool, sea trout fishing, boat charters.
Traytown Tourist Cabins. Traytown, Bonavista Bay, NF A0G 4K0 (709–533–2246) during season; off-season call (709–464–3634). Housekeeping units. Pets allowed on leash. Terrific spot for children—beach swimming nearby; canoeing, paddle boats, BBQ sites. Licensed lounge. Open May 1–Sept. 30.

TRINITY. *Moderate.* **Trinity Cabins.** Box 54, Trinity, Trinity Bay, NF A0C 2S0 (709–464–3657); off-season call (709–464–3720). Housekeeping units. $2 each child under 12. Groceries, playground, outdoor pool. Pets allowed on leash. Beverage room. Drive-in and travel-trailer park. Open mid-May to Sept. 30.
The Village Inn. Trinity, Trinity Bay, NF A0C 2S0 (709–464–3269). Licensed dining room. Kayak rentals, boat charters and whale-guide services arranged. Film shows, presentations, lectures on marine life.

TWILLINGATE. *Expensive.* **Anchor Inn Motel.** Box 550, Twillingate, Notre Dame Bay, NF A0G 4M0 (709–884–2776). Basic accommodation in motel with dining room and cocktail lounge. V, only.

WOODY POINT. *Expensive.* **Stornoway Lodge.** Woody Point, Bonne Bay, NF A0K 1P0 (709–453–2282). 10 motel units; dining room and cocktail lounge.
Moderate. **Victorian Manor Hospitality Home.** Box 165, Woody Point, Bonne Bay, NF A0K 1P0 (709–453–2485). 4 rooms in private home. Dining room with good, home-cooked meals. Open year-round. View of Gros Morne and Bonne Bay.

 HOW TO GET AROUND. By Car. With the exception of a few miles of highway from Blanc Sablon to Red Bay and local roads in Goose Bay and Wabush/Labrador City, the Labrador area of Newfoundland has no roads suitable for normal vehicles. The island has about 9,654 km (6,000 mi.) of highway, including the 906-km (565-mi.) Trans-Canada Hwy. (signposted throughout Newfoundland as "TCH") from Port-aux-Basques to St. John's. Secondary roads are generally paved; some gravel-surfaced roads remain, but they are usually in good condition in summer.

By Bus. Because Newfoundland operated under the British rail system, the trains in the province ran on narrow-gauge track. Passenger service by rail was discontinued during the 1960s and a bus service is operated by *TerraTransport.* Known as "roadcruisers," the buses reach most major communities in Newfoundland adjacent to the TCH. For information, contact VIA Rail (see information for trains in "How to Get There" section), call TerraTransport (709–737–5916) in St. John's or a travel agent.

By Plane. *CP Air* operates jet passenger flights connecting St. John's, Gander, Corner Brook (via Deer Lake and Stephenville airports), Goose Bay, Churchill Falls, and Wabush/Labrador City. **Charters:** *Labrador Airways,* Box 13485, Station A, St. John's, NF, A1B 4B8 (709–896–8113). *Gander Aviation,* Box 250, Gander, NF (709–256–3421). *Newfoundland Labrador Air Transport Limited,* Box 3, Corner Brook, NF (709–686–2521) or (709–635–3574). *Gracefield Aviation Limited,* Box 55, Stephenville, NF, A2N 2Y7 (709–643–2014).

By Boat. One of the most interesting ways to see Newfoundland and Labrador is by one of the Marine Atlantic coastal boats. The south coast service has sailings from Argentia to Port-aux-Basques, calling in at a number of tiny ports along the way. Many of these ports are not connected to the highway system and the boat brings in the mail, freight, and passengers. Operates year-round.

The North Coast and Labrador Marine Atlantic boats service many tiny isolated communities on the Labrador coast from Lewisporte as a starting point. Sailings from spring thaw (mid-May to mid-June) until mid-Nov.

A round trip on one of the Labrador boats can take up to a week, covering some 1,600 nautical miles and calling at up to 40 communities.

The coastal steamer service operated by Marine Atlantic provides passenger and freight connections to the many settlements in Newfoundland and Labrador not reached by road or railway. Trips on these boats offer extremely interesting vacation travel, passing through numerous picturesque coastal villages. Reservations on this service can only be made from within the Province of Newfoundland by contacting *Marine Atlantic Reservations Bureau*, Box 520, Port-aux-Basques, NF A0M 1C0 (800–563–7381).

TOURIST INFORMATION. Travel information on Newfoundland and Labrador can be obtained from *Department of Development and Tourism*, Box 2016, St. John's, NF A1C 5R8 (toll free 800–563–6353). Or, while in St. John's, call (576–2830).

Tourist Information Chalets are conveniently located along the TCH. (Hwy. 1). They are: Port-aux-Basques (709–695–2262); Corner Brook (709–639–9792); Deer Lake (709–639–2202); Springdale (709–673–3110); Grand Falls (709–489–6332); Clarenville (709–466–3100); Marystown (709–279–3830); Dunville (709–227–5602); Notre Dame Junction (709–535–8547); Twillingate (709–629–7207); Whitbourne Junction (709–759–2170); and Stephenville (709–647–9208). Tourist desks are also located on the ferries sailing from North Sydney, NS, to Port-aux-Basques and Argentia and at the ferry terminal at North Sydney.

SEASONAL EVENTS. January to March, is winter carnival time in many Newfoundland towns and villages. The biggest carnivals are held in Corner Brook, Mount Pearl, and Labrador City. Parades, snow sculpture, skiing, and other outdoor events and lots of parties are featured. **Mid-April,** Newfoundland and Labrador Drama Festival.

From spring to fall there are weekly harness horse racing cards at Goulds near St. John's. Also at Meadows Raceway near Corner Brook.

In the 1920's the late Johnny Burke wrote a song about the Kelligrews Soiree, a party to end all parties. In **July,** the village of Kelligrews on Conception Bay relives the soiree and the town of Placentia holds an annual regatta for the surrounding area. Twillingate is the site for the Fish, Fun, & Folk Festival, while Springdale holds a ForestFest.

On **July** 1 there are Canada Day celebrations in Corner Brook, Grand Falls, Paquet, and other communities. In mid-**July** Stephenville holds the Stephenville Theatre Festival.

August features a number of civic festival days in various Newfoundland towns including a festival of traditional French culture, music and dance at Cape St. George.

During **September** and **October,** regional agricultural exhibitions and fairs are held throughout Newfoundland.

All-Breed Dog Championship Shows are held at St. John's in **May,** at Corner Brook in **July,** and in Harbour Grace on the Labor Day weekend.

TOURS. Newfoundland's tourist industry is greatly geared to the traveler—especially the adventurous one. *Wildland Tours* offers a variety of one-day and three-day packages. A three-day family adventure by boat, bus, and foot takes you to Witless Bay, Trepassey, and Cape St. Mary's. Whales, caribou, moose, puffins, and gannets are some of the wildlife to be seen. One-day tours to any one of the above destinations include a hearty mid-day meal. There are specialty tours for bird watchers, salmon anglers and others, and city tours with guides are also available. Contact: Wildland Tours, Box 383, Station "C," St. John's, NF A1C 5J9 (709–722–3335).

Viking Trail Tours offers a 7-day, 6-night excursion to the Great Northern Peninsula of Newfoundland, a breathtakingly beautiful region and site of the only known Viking colony in North America. Minimum land cost $700 per person. Contact: Maynard's Tours, A Division of Maynard's Motor Inn, Hawke's Bay, NF A0K 3B0 (709–248–5225).

Labrador Straits Tours offers a "Labrador Weekend Tour (three-nights, two-days), including an Indian burial site and the archeological site at Red Bay where Basque whalers headquartered over four centuries ago. Minimum individual land cost, $142. And the "Labrador-Northern Peninsula Tour" (five-nights, four-days), including the town of St. Anthony, home of the world-famous Grenfell Mission; L'Anse-aux-Meadows National Historic Park, site of Viking settlement dating back to A.D. 1000; Port au Choix National Historic Park, site of ancient burial ground of Maritime Archaic Indians about 4,000 years ago; and the rugged beauty of the fjords and mountains of Gros Morne National Park. Minimum individual land cost, $400. Tour can be done in reverse, giving visitors a weekend in Labrador. Contact: Labrador Straits Tours, L'Anse au Clair, LB A0K 3K0 (709–931–2332).

There are boat tours and charters available in a half-dozen places; there are organized canoe tours and "safaris" to the province's gripping interior; there's a "Trap Line Tour" by dogsled in Labrador; and there is wilderness sightseeing by air available. There are 22 self-guided auto tours, fully described in the Department of Development and Tourism's booklet "Newfoundland and Labrador Auto Guide." And, of course, there are a half-dozen companies offering bus tours to various parts of the province. The Department of Development and Tourism will supply brochures on request, or you can pick them up at tourist bureaus.

 NATIONAL PARKS. Newfoundland is a wild, rugged, and beautiful land of mountains, lakes, forests, and wildlife. That description is also appropriate for the province's two national parks: Gros Morne National Park and Terra Nova National Park.

Gros Morne National Park covers 1,942 sq. km (750 sq. mi.) of seacoast and mountain about 120 km (75 mi.) north of Corner Brook. The mountains of the area drop sharply into the sea; the escarpment is sometimes 610 m (2,000 ft.) high. A tiny ferry carries cars across Bonne Bay from Woody Point to Norris Point at the foot of flat, gray, bald Gros Morne which rises 806 m (2,644 ft.) above the village. The park is a veritable paradise for camping, wilderness hiking, and sightseeing.

Gros Morne National Park was the home region for a number of peoples including Archaic Indians (4,500 years ago), Inuit about 1,000 years ago, and, more recently, the Beothuk Indians until the time of their extinction in the early 1820s.

The park features more than 159 unserviced camping sites, heated washrooms and showers, kitchen facilities, picnic areas, swimming, hiking, boat facilities, fishing and wilderness backpacking as well as a sewage disposal station. The maximum stay permitted in a campground is two weeks.

The Park Information Centre near Rocky Harbour has a large facilities and activities map for easy reference, with staff to answer questions. During the summer, a free interpretive program is offered by the park naturalist staff which includes conducted hikes and illustrated talks.

Activities in the park include hiking in the summer and snowshoeing and cross-country skiing in the winter. The well-marked hiking trail to the top of Gros Morne offers a commanding view of Bonne Bay and the Long Range Mountains. Fishing for salmon and brook trout are popular in the lakes and streams while mackerel and cod can be taken in the salt water. Fishing regulations are available from park officials and local merchants in the villages.

For swimmers, a large sandy beach at Shallow Bay offers saltwater bathing in water which can reach 21°C (70°F) during July and Aug. The mouth of Western Brook is also suitable for swimming and has a small sand beach.

Camping fees are $8 for semi-serviced sites and $5 for unserviced sites but are subject to small increases. For additional information, write The Superintendent, Gros Morne National Park, Rocky Harbour, Newfoundland.

Terra Nova National Park is Canada's eastern-most national park, covering 396 sq. km. (153 sq. mi.) of forested hills and lakes on Bonavista Bay. The park is about 232 km (145 mi.) northwest of St. John's and 79 km (48 mi.) southwest of Gander, on the TCH.

The surface of Terra Nova Park was scoured and gouged by the glaciers of the Ice Age; from convenient lookouts visitors can see six or more lakes, all at different altitudes, on the sides of the surrounding hills. In the park's bogs are a variety of wildflowers including the province's official flower, the pitcher plant. This unique plant is a carnivore that traps, drowns, and digests insects. Arctic char can be caught by patient anglers, and brook trout are common in the streams. Whales and seals frequent the ocean shore. The park is home to numerous sea and land birds as well as animals of all sizes from moose to mink.

Park naturalists have developed an extensive interpretive program that includes guided hikes, boat tours, and illustrated talks. During the summer, swimming, canoeing, boating, hiking, and fishing are popular. Winter activities include cross-country skiing, winter camping, and showshoeing.

Serviced campsites are available at Newman Sound and Malady Head on a "first come" basis. Open year-round. Motel and restaurant facilities are available at Charlottetown and Newman Sound, at villages within the Park, or at various villages just outside the Park boundaries during the summer months.

Except for through highway traffic, an entrance fee to Terra Nova Park will be charged. Daily entry fee is $3. Newman Sound fee is $8 per night ($40 per week). Malady Head is $7 per night ($35 per week). The overnight boat-docking fee is from $4 to $20 depending on the length of boat.

Staff at the Park Information Centre, located at the headquarters area just off the TCH, can direct visitors to facilities and special events. For additional information, write: Superintendent, Terra Nova National Park, Glovertown, NF A0G 2L0.

 PROVINCIAL PARKS. One good way to enjoy the great outdoors in Newfoundland is to use the network of provincial parks—43 camping parks, 15 day-use parks and 19 "Natural Scenic Attractions" parks. All 77 parks have picnic areas; most have swimming facilities and well marked trails for hiking or strolling.

From mid-July to mid-August, the fresh water lakes and salt water ponds on the shore are at their best for swimming, usually between 16–20°C (60–70°F). Open salt water can be uncomfortably cold.

Three types of parks have been designated in Newfoundland: (1) Camping parks, which have both camping and day use facilities. The maximum stay is 24 consecutive days and requires a camping permit costing $5 per day; plus you will have to buy a $10 vehicle-entry permit, which is valid for all provincial parks throughout the season. The vehicle permit fee for one day is $2. No reservations for camping are accepted. (2) Day-use parks have no camping facilities. (3) Natural Scenic Attractions are parks with special scenic qualities or natural significance. They have ample parking and walking trails, and some have interpretation centers. Anyone 65 years or over is admitted free to all provincial parks upon proof of age. Angling is permitted in all parks and is subject to the provincial regulations. For licensing information, see park staff. No hunting is allowed in the parks.

Although the parks offer outdoor living at its best, there are some drawbacks such as black flies, mosquitos, and various other pests. The underbrush has been cleared as much as possible, however, to allow freer circulation of air. When picking a picnic site, try for one with a good breeze. A commercial insect repellent is often helpful.

The following provincial parks offer a good sample of Newfoundland outdoors:

Aspen Brook. Day-use only with small pool for swimming. Highway 1 at Aspen Brook, 11 kms. (7 miles) west of Windsor.

Backside Pond. Near Whiteway on Hwy. 80; 51 campsites, picnic area, swimming, hiking trail, trout and saltwater fishing. The Atlantic Cable Museum at nearby Heart's Content tells the story of trans-Atlantic communication.

Barachois Pond. On Hwy. 1 about 64 kms. (40 miles) south of Corner Brook, is one of the largest parks in the system. Swimming, boating, angling for salmon and trout, and water skiing on lake. Guided walks and evening programs by park naturalist; 158 campsites with dumping station. Hiking on Erin Mountain Hiking Trail for spectacular views.

Bellevue Beach. Hwy. 201 at Bellevue on Isthmus of Avalon. Picnic area, swimming, and boating in a protected barachois pond. Angling for trout and saltwater fish; 77 campsites.

Beothuk. Rte. 1 at Rushy Pond, just west of Windsor; 64 campsites, picnic and swimming, boating and trout fishing on Rushy Pond. Reconstructed logging camp open June 1 to September 6, 10 A.M. to 8 P.M. Admission included in permit fee.

Blow Me Down. At Lark Harbour on Hwy. 450, about 48 kms. (30 miles) west of Corner Brook; 27 campsites, picnic areas. Hiking trail to lookout over Bay of Islands. Saltwater angling.

Blue Ponds. Hwy. 1 about 32 kms. (19 miles) west of Corner Brook. Twin limestone lakes for swimming, hiking, picnic area; 37 campsites and trout streams.

Butter Pot. Probably Newfoundland's most popular park, on Hwy 1, about 32 kms. (20 miles) from St. John's. Freshwater beach, hiking trails to two spectacular lookouts, guided nature walks, interpretive center, picnic areas, 122 campsites, dumping station, and trout fishing.

Catamaran. Hwy. 1, about 48 kms. (30 miles) west of Windsor, on Joe's Lake; 55 campsites, picnic area, swimming, and boat launch. Trout fishing.

Chance Cove. On Hwy. 10 near Cape Race. Camping park with picnic area, 25 campsites, swimming, trout and saltwater fishing. Bay seals live along the shallows during certain seasons.

Cheeseman. Hwy. 1 just north of Port-aux-Basques and the CN ferry to Nova Scotia; 103 campsites, picnic area, swimming, trout and saltwater angling. Try beachcombing on the Cape Ray Sands.

Cochrane Pond. Hwy. 1 about 16 kms. (10 miles) south of St. John's. Day-use park with picnic areas, swimming, and trout angling in pond.

Crabbes River. Hwy. 1 near intersection of Hwy. 405; 32 campsites, picnic area. Good salmon and trout fishing.

Dildo Run. Highway 340 on New World Island. Take highway from Trans-Canada toward Lewisporte and continue toward Twillingate; 31 campsites, picnic sites, swimming, and saltwater fishing.

Duley Lake. Labrador City, Labrador; 100 campsites, sandy beach on lake with swimming, boating, and trout fishing.

Father Duffy's Well. Hwy. 90 about 24 kms. (15 miles) south of Holyrood. Day use only. Shrine dedicated to 19th century Irish priest.

Fitzgerald's Pond. Hwy. 100, about 32 kms. (20 miles) east of Argentia. Near CN ferry to Nova Scotia and Castle Hill National Historic Park; 24 campsites, picnic, swimming, and hiking. Angling for salmon and trout.

Flatwater Pond. Hwy. 410 to Baie Verte, about 40 kms. (25 miles) north from the Trans-Canada Hwy.; 25 campsites, picnic area, freshwater swimming, boat launching, trout angling.

Frenchman's Cove. Near Garnish on Hwy. 213. Burin Peninsula. Salt- and freshwater swimming, picnic sites, 81 campsites, trout and saltwater fishing, bird-watching.

Freshwater Pond. Hwy. 220 near Burin. Sandy beaches and freshwater swimming, 30 campsites, picnic areas, boat launch, salmon and trout fishing.

Glenwood. A day-use park on Hwy. 1, just west of Gander. Picnics, trout fishing, and fresh water swimming.

Grand Codroy. Hwy. 406, off Hwy. 1, about 40 kms. (25 miles) north of Port-aux-Basques; 25 campsites, picnic area, and freshwater swimming. Canoeing, salmon and trout angling.

Gushues Pond. Hwy. 1 about 48 kms. (30 miles) from St. John's. Two ponds for swimming; trout fishing and boating; 117 campsites.

Holyrood Pond. Hwy. 90 on St. Mary's Bay, more than 96 kms. (60 miles) south of the village of Holyrood. Long, narrow saltwater pond for warm salt water bathing, boating, trout and saltwater fishing; 15 campsites and picnic area.

Indian River. Hwy. 1 near Springdale. Canoeing on river, swimming, hiking, salmon and trout fishing, picnic area; 49 campsites.

Jack's Pond. Hwy. 1 near Arnold's Cove on Avalon Isthmus. Freshwater boating, swimming, trout fishing, picnic area; 74 campsites.

Jonathan's Pond. Hwy. 330 about 16 kms. (10 miles) north of Gander. Birch forest, boating, swimming, 96 campsites and picnic area.

LaManche Valley. Hwy. 10, about 48 kms. (30 miles) south of St. John's; 51 campsites, picnic area, hiking, swimming, trout and saltwater fishing. Waterfall and bird-watching.

Lockston Path. Hwy. 236 on the Bonavista Peninsula; 20 sheltered campsites, fresh water beach, picnic area, swimming, boat launch.

Mary March. On Hwy. 370 to Buchans. Named after Mary March, the last known Beothuk Indian, who was captured nearby. Red Indian Lake provides good swimming, trout fishing and swimming. Picnic sites and boating; 26 campsites.

Mummichog. Hwy. 1, about 24 kms. (15 miles) north of Port-aux-Basques. Named after a small fish found in the brackish waters of the lagoon; 38 campsites, picnic area, swimming, boat launch, and hiking trails. Salmon and trout fishing in stream.

Northern Bay Sands. Hwy. 70, about 24 kms. (15 miles) north of Carbonear. Fresh and saltwater swimming; 42 campsites, picnic area, and saltwater fishing.

Notre Dame. Hwy. 1, about 32 kms. (20 miles) east of Bishops Falls. Swimming, picnic area, and 100 campsites with dumping station.

Otter Bay. Hwy. 1, about 24 kms. (15 miles) east of Port-aux-Basques; 5 campsites, picnic area, swimming, trout and saltwater fishing.

Piccadilly Head. Hwy. 463 on the Port au Port Peninsula; 50 campsites, picnic area, hiking, swimming on a long sandy beach, and saltwater fishing.

Pinware River. Take the ferry from Flowers Cove on Hwy. 430 to the Labrador coast and follow Hwy. 510 toward Red Bay for about 48 kms. (30 miles). Camping park at the mouth of a good salmon river. 15 campsites. Trout and saltwater fishing, too.

Pipers Hole River. Camping park on Hwy. 210 near Swift Current. 30 campsites. Picnic area, scheduled salmon river, hiking trail. No swimming.

Pistolet Bay. Hwy. 437 near St. Anthony. Canoeing country with 27 campsites, picnic area, swimming, salmon and trout fishing; near L'Anse au Meadows Viking settlement and historic park.

River of Ponds. Hwy. 430 near the village River of Ponds; 40 campsites, picnic area, swimming, boat launch, salmon and trout angling; exhibit of whale bones.

Sandbanks. At the community of Burgeo. Accessible by boat or by hiking a half mile. 8 campsites, picnic area, and swimming at sandy beaches; trout and saltwater fishing.

Smallwood. Hwy. 320 north of Gambo; 27 campsites, picnic area, fine salmon angling; working model of a watermill.

Sop's Arm. Hwy. 420 near the village of Sop's Arm on White Bay; 25 campsites, picnic area, salmon, trout and saltwater fishing.

Squires Memorial. Hwy. 422 near Deer Lake. One of the larger provincial parks; 159 campsites, picnic area, good salmon fishing, boat rental facility. Reserve the night before. Cost about $6 per day.

Square Pond. Hwy. 1 near Gambo; 93 campsites, picnic area, swimming, boat launch, hiking, salmon, trout and Arctic char angling.

Windmill Bight. Hwy. 330 near Cape Freels on Bonavista Bay; 29 campsites, picnic area, fresh- and saltwater swimming, salmon, trout and saltwater fishing. Good place to watch for icebergs.

Natural Scenic Attraction parks, a Newfoundland specialty, are especially worthwhile. There are 19. Here are a few:

The Arches. North of Gros Morne National Park on Rte. 430. Natural rock archway created by tidal action.

Cataracts. Hwy. 91, 100 kms. (60 mi.) southwest of St. John's. A deep river gorge with two waterfalls. Stairs and walkways.

Deadman's Bay. Hwy. 330. Grand coastline; spot to watch for in early summer.

Dungeon. Rte. 238 near Bonavista. Features a sea cave with a natural archway carved by tidal action. A restored 19th-century lighthouse nearby.

Eastport North Beach. Hwy. 310. Excellent beach and scenery on Eastport Bay. Terra Nova National Park and craft shops nearby.

French Islands. Hwy. 220 south from Grand Bank. Excellent view of St. Pierre and Miquelon islands, owned by France.

Maberly. Rte. 238 near Bonavista. A sea bird colony nesting on an off-shore island is visible from the jagged shore.

Northeast Arm. Hwy. 310 off Glovertown. Spectacular ocean view overlooking Terra Nova National Park from across the water.

Point La Haye. Hwy. 90 about 150 kms. (90 mi.) southwest of St. John's. Historic beach utilized by Basque fishermen in centuries past for drying their catch.

CHILDREN'S ACTIVITIES. Keeping children occupied in Newfoundland should present little problem, but do not look for amusement parks or fully equipped playgrounds except in the larger centers. Concentrate on the network of provincial and national parks.

Obtain a fishing license for the family and pack a couple of rods and reels for hours of entertainment. Sturdy footwear and clothing make hiking and walking easier in the parks.

A trip to a fishing village in mid- to late afternoon should put visitors at the wharf in time to see local fishermen cleaning their catch and carting away the fish. Nature walks and lectures at the parks will hold the attention of older children and a camera may keep a child involved for the entire trip.

SUMMER SPORTS. Sports in Newfoundland tend to be the outdoors variety. **Water sports** such as water skiing, canoeing, power boating, and sailing are popular activities. There are **harness horse racing** cards at the Avalon Raceway in Goulds, near St. John's, from spring to fall every Sunday and Wednesday evening and at other unscheduled times. There is also great interest in **golf, tennis, bowling, roller skating,** and **rowing** in centers where facilities are available.

Golf courses include the Grand Falls Golf and Country Club and the Blomidon Golf and Country Club in Corner Brook. Nine hole courses are located at Stephenville and Labrador City. Check with local tourist information centers for rules on visitors at each course.

Newfoundland is a **canoeists'** paradise. The tourism department offers a list of about twenty routes, ranging in length from 12 to 336 kms., and they should be consulted about current restrictions on forest travel in the fire season. Canoe tours to the deep interior are arranged by some outfitters. Canoes can be rented at numerous places. Check with the tourist bureaus.

See sections on "Fishing" and "Hunting" for information on these sports.

FISHING. Newfoundland is one of the best fishing areas in North America. Brook trout can be found in most streams and salmon populate many of the larger rivers. In saltwater, codfish can be jigged and sea trout, flounder, tuna, mackerel and caplin can be caught. Deep-sea tuna fishing is also available.

Nonresidents must have a valid fishing license. For salmon fishing they must be accompanied by a licensed guide. Inland fishing licenses are available from most service stations, sporting goods stores, hardware stores, and department stores. Nonresident salmon fishing licenses cost about $40 for the season. Family salmon licenses are about $60 for the season. Salmon may be taken by artificial fly only during the season from June 20 to August 31 on the Island of Newfoundland and from June 20 to Sept. 15 in Labrador.

Nonresident trout licenses cost $10 for individuals for the season and $15 for a family. The license covers all rivers except those indicated as scheduled rivers. These are usually well marked. Salmon licenses are required for these waters. Special licenses from park officials are required for fishing in Terra Nova National Park. The open season for rainbow trout is June 1 to September 15. The season for all other trout is January 15 to September 15.

Licensed guides are required for all fishing in Labrador where the fishing waters are usually located far from habitation and are reached by bush plane. The season for Arctic char, northern pike, and trout other than rainbow trout is January 15 to September 15 in unscheduled rivers in Labrador.

The bag limit for trout in Newfoundland and Labrador is 24 per day per license, or the number of trout totaling 10 pounds in weight plus one trout, whichever is the lesser. The limit for lake trout is four per day; northern pike, 24 per day; Arctic char, 4 per day.

Several dozen outfitters in both Newfoundland and Labrador operate special fishing cabins for the more serious sportsmen. They are listed in the *Hunting and Fishing Guide,* obtainable from any tourist bureau or by writing Department of Development and Tourism, Province of Newfoundland, P.O. Box 2016, St. John's, Newfoundland. This kind of fishing is expensive; expect to pay $1,000 a week or more.

HUNTING. The *Hunting and Fishing Guide* describes hunting opportunities (see "Fishing" section). Basically, Newfoundland is famous for its moose and bear hunting. This, however, is for the serious hunter. You will need a licensed guide who also functions as an outfitter.

CAMPING OUT. Complete information on camping in Newfoundland Provincial Parks may be found in the "Provincial Parks" section.

Sixteen private campgrounds-trailer parks are in operation in Newfoundland.

Complete information on camping in Newfoundland's two national parks is in the *National Parks* section.

WINTER SPORTS. The west coast of Newfoundland averages 152 inches of snow per year with average temperatures in the -12 to $-4°C$. range (10 to 25°F). Ski runs over a mile long with drops of at least 213 meters (700 feet) make Marble Mountain Ski Resort one of the best ski areas in eastern Canada. The resort is about 24 kms. (15 miles) from Corner Brook on Hwy. 1.

The Smokey Mountain Ski Club in Labrador City can be reached only by air to Wabush/Labrador City. The hill has 5 trails and one open slope. The longest run is 299 meters (4,500 ft.) with a 1,372-meter (980 foot) vertical drop. Three of the trails are lit for night skiing.

Although many Newfoundland communities have indoor arenas or outdoor rinks for **ice skating,** ponds and lakes are excellent for outdoor skating in most areas.

Curling is a growing sport in Newfoundland and local and regional bonspiels are held throughout the winter months. Major curling clubs are located in St. John's, Gander, Grand Falls, Corner Brook, Labrador City, and Stephenville. Snowmobiling is also a popular sport in winter. In Labrador, snowmobiles have been used as a prime source of winter transportation for some years now, replacing the traditional dog teams in the remote sections of the province.

HISTORIC SITES. *Cape Spear* is the closest North American point to Europe and the site of one of Canada's oldest surviving lighthouses, built in 1836. During World War II, a coastal battery was constructed here. Crashing waves and the sight of so much open sea make this 16-km. (10-mile) drive south from St. John's worthwhile. Open year round, with a guide service from June to Sept.

The remains of both French and British fortifications may still be seen at the *Castle Hill National Historic Park* at Placentia. Originally built by the French to protect their colony, the fortifications were taken over by the British in 1713. An interpretive center contains displays and artifacts. Guided tours are available from June to September.

Prior to the 1960's, scholars had long sought tangible evidence of *Viking settlements* in North America. Helge and Anne Stine Ingstad, over a seven-year period, excavated the area near L'Anse aux Meadows on the tip of Newfoundland's Great Northern Peninsula where they thought the Vikings had landed. Their patience was rewarded with positive evidence of Viking settlement at least 1,000 years ago. The dig site can be viewed by visitors. A reception center and museum are at the site.

The *Port au Choix National Historic Park* is located on an important Maritime Archaic Indian (and later Dorset Eskimo) burial ground. The interpretive center portrays the lifestyle of the people who lived here 4,000 years ago. Port au Choix is on Hwy. 430, about 8 kms. (5 miles) north of the community of Port Saunders.

MUSEUMS. There are many—for history buffs and fishermen: *Ferryland Museum.* General history museum in one of the oldest settlements in province. Open during summer months in courthouse. *Hibb's Cove Fishermen's Museum.* Fishing artifacts in typical Newfoundland fishing village combined with arts and music center. Open summer months. *Heart's Content.* History of the trans-Atlantic communications cable which first came ashore here. Open summer months. *Trinity Museum and Archives.* Local artifacts and papers. Open summer months. *Bonavista Museum.* Local history. Open summer; winters by appointment. *Salvage Museum.* Local history in fisherman's house. *Greenspond Museum.* Local history displayed in courthouse. Open summer months. *Durrell Museum.* Local history; open summer months. *Twillingate Museum.* Local history in old Anglican Rectory. Open summer months. *Cow Head Museum.* Local history; open year round. *Grand Falls, Mary March Regional Museum.* Local history of the logging industry and natural history. Named after Demasduit (named Mary March by her captors), the last known Beothuk Indian who was captured in the region. Open year-round. Grand Bank. *Southern Newfoundland Seamen's Museum.* Displays relating to the fishery on the south coast. Open year-round. *Gander Airport Aviation Exhibit.* Displays and history of pioneer aviation, trans-Atlantic and domestic, located in airport terminal building. Open year-round. The *Conception Bay Museum National Exhibition Centre* at Harbour Grace which is located in the old Court House displays traveling exhibits along with its own permanent collection, and it is open year-round. In Wesleyville, you can explore local history in the *Wesleyville Museum,* and the *Durrell Museum* in Durrell has local history and also artifacts from World War I. The *Fishermen's Museum* in Musgrave Harbour is also a local history museum, as is the *Placentia Area Museum* in Placentia.

MUSIC. Newfoundland has its own indigenous rhythms, mostly of Scottish and Irish derivation, and you'll find them everywhere—in local festivals, in nightclubs, bars and taverns, and at local concerts.

SHOPPING. For the most part, goods and services tend to be slightly more expensive in Newfoundland than elsewhere in Canada. The same general range of merchandise is available as on the mainland.

Newfoundland handcrafts, such as knitted goods, woven items, and clothing are usually good purchases because of the quality of the product.

Other unique Newfoundland items include: Labradorite jewelry (Labradorite is a quartz-like rock which takes a high polish), earrings of codfish ear bones (quite attractive), seal skin products, and Eskimo and Indian carvings.

Store hours are roughly the same as for St. John's, except that some stores outside St. John's may be closed on Mondays. Holidays closings are roughly the same, except for local civic holidays. See the "Shopping" section in *Practical Information for St. John's.*

LIQUOR LAWS. The legal drinking age is 19.

RESTAURANTS. In general, the best places to dine in Newfoundland (outside of St. John's) are the hotels and motels which usually combine accommodation, a cocktail lounge, and dining room or restaurant.

At best, dining out in Newfoundland is something of an adventure. Visitors should sample home-cooked food and specialties of the area and the season. Fish and salt meat dishes are the best bets everywhere—expect it to be wholesome and hearty, rather than delicate and gourmet-style. Restaurants are categorized on the basis of full-course dinners, drinks, tips and tax excluded: *Expensive,* over $13; *Moderate,* $8–$13; *Inexpensive,* less than $8.

The 12% provincial sales tax will be added to your bill.

Most places accept the following major credit cards: American Express, MasterCard and Visa; others may also be honored. Not all establishments accept credit cards, therefore we suggest you call for information.

CORNER BROOK. *Expensive:* **The Carriage Room.** In the Glynmill Inn. Newfoundland dishes and all types of fish. Licensed.

The Wine Cellar. On Cobb Lane. Steaks and Italian food. Licensed.

GANDER. *Moderate:* **Albatross Motel.** Seafood platters. Licensed.
Sinbad's. Canadian food. Licensed.

GRAND FALLS. *Expensive:* **Mount Peyton Hotel.** Canadian food. Licensed.

MANITOBA

Home of Hudson's Bay Company

by
ROGER NEWMAN

Roger Newman, proprietor of Western News Service, Winnipeg, has written extensively for Canadian and U.S. periodicals.

Manitoba is known as the multi-cultural province because of the number and variety of ethnic groups that are represented in its population of about 1,070,000. Traditionally, these groups have been encouraged to preserve their cultures, with the result that Manitoba is the home of some of North America's largest ethnic festivals, a few of which have become national and international tourist attractions.

The biggest of these is Folklorama, which dominates life each August in Winnipeg, the province's capital. It is an Expo-like festival of nations with more than forty pavilions spread throughout the city. The week-long festival starts with a parade and concludes with a variety show capped by the crowning of Miss Folklorama in the Winnipeg Convention Centre. In between the opening and closing, Winnipeggers and their visitors make the rounds of the pavilions, sampling the food, drink, entertainment, and handicrafts of the world's different cultures. More than a million visitors have been welcomed at the pavilions since Folklorama's debut in 1970 as one facet of Manitoba's centennial celebrations.

Other major ethnic festivals include: the Festival du Voyageur in the French-speaking Winnipeg suburb of St. Boniface in mid-February; Canada's National Ukrainian Festival at Dauphin in Western Manito-

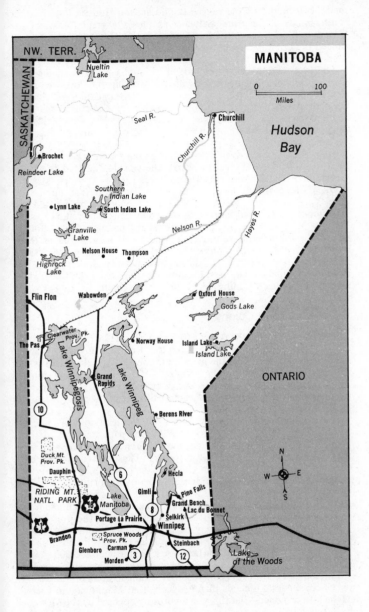

MANITOBA

| 0 | 100 |
Miles

NW. TERR.

SASKATCHEWAN

Nueltin Lake

Seal R.

Churchill

Churchill R.

Hudson Bay

Brochet

Reindeer Lake

Southern Indian Lake

Lynn Lake

South Indian Lake

Granville Lake

Nelson House

Thompson

Highrock Lake

Nelson R.

Hayes R.

Flin Flon

Wabowden

Oxford House

Gods Lake

The Pas

Clearwater Prov. Pk.

Lake Winnipegosis

Grand Rapids

Norway House

Island Lake

Island Lake

Lake Winnipeg

ONTARIO

10

Duck Mt. Prov. Pk.

Dauphin

6

Berens River

Hecla

RIDING MT. NATL. PARK

Lake Manitoba

Gimli

8

Pine Falls

Grand Beach

Lac du Bonnet

Portage la Prairie

Selkirk

Winnipeg

N

W   E

S

Brandon

Spruce Woods Prov. Pk.

Carman

Steinbach

Glenboro

3

12

Lake of the Woods

Morden

ba at the end of July; and the annual Icelandic Festival in Gimli, on Lake Winnipeg, in early August. These festivals—plus year-round performances by many other cultural groups—give Manitoba a rich cosmopolitan flavor that is lacking in some other regions of Canada.

It all started more than 12,000 years ago when the ancestors of Manitoba's native Indian people migrated to the region from Asia. By 1600, four distinct Indian tribes lived in the 251,000-square-mile territory that was to become Manitoba. In the north, the Chipeweyans made their homes on the rugged tundra around Hudson Bay. Farther south, bands of Cree and Salteaux roamed the great forests of the Canadian Shield; while the famous buffalo hunters, the Assiniboines, ranged the broad plains to the southwest along the present Canadian-United States border.

The first white man to set foot in Manitoba was the Englishman Captain Thomas Button, who wintered two ships at Port Nelson on Hudson Bay in 1612. He, and then other European explorers, chanced upon the Hudson Bay area while searching for a northern sea trade route to the Orient. Instead of a sea route to the riches of the East, they discovered a land abundant with animals and game—and the lucrative fur trade began.

Soon, the lakes and rivers of Northern Manitoba were being explored by a host of adventurers from across the world—the Radissons, the Grosselliers, the Kelseys, and the LaVerendryes.

One of the most adventurous was Pierre Gaultier de Varennes, Sieur de la Verendrye, who arrived in 1738 at the junction of the Red and Assiniboine rivers, the future site of Winnipeg. La Verendrye established a fur-trading post, Fort Rouge, at the junction in an effort to extend the French empire in North America. It became the center of a thriving fur trade which pitted the North West Company against the Hudson's Bay Company. The ultimate winner was the Hudson's Bay Company, which has survived for more than 300 years and ranks today as one of Canada's leading department store chains.

The Red River Colony

Fur trading started to give way to farming in 1812 when Lord Selkirk arrived from Scotland to establish the Red River Colony, a permanent agricultural settlement at the junction of the Red and the Assiniboine. The settlement was built at the instigation of the Hudson's Bay Company, which wanted to combat the ever-increasing cost of importing food from overseas and thereby gain a competitive edge over its fur-trading rivals.

But trouble flared, pitting Hudson's Bay Company officials and the Selkirk Settlers against the North West Company and the Métis, a people of white and Indian blood, mostly French-speaking, who were the descendants of the early fur traders. The quarreling reached a climax in 1816 with the Seven Oaks incident, which left twenty-two people dead, including Robert Semple, the governor of the Red River Colony. The colony survived, however, and the agriculture industry started to flourish in western Canada. Soon, it was the richness of the region's farmland that was attracting immigrants to the prairies.

The Hudson's Bay Company was the principal influence and authority on the prairies until 1870, when it agreed to relinquish its vast holdings of western Canadian land for a payment of 300,000 pounds sterling from the Canadian government. Three years earlier—in 1867 —Canada had come into being through a confederation of four eastern provinces. Federal officials then proposed that Manitoba join Canada as the fifth province—but this was vigorously opposed by the Métis, led by Louis Riel.

There followed the famous Riel Rebellion, pitting the adherents of the Métis leader against Canadian authorities. The uprising, one of the few major battles in western Canada's otherwise peaceful history, was put down, and Louis Riel was hanged.

As a result, Manitoba became a Canadian province on July 15, 1870. Over the years, the status of Louis Riel has changed from villain to hero. A statue of the Métis leader is now one of the principal attractions on the grounds of the Manitoba Legislative Building in Winnipeg.

Tourists also visit Riel's grave in the churchyard of St. Boniface Cathedral in suburban Winnipeg, as well as the Riel family house on the Seine River, which has been designated a national historic site.

Four years after the province's founding, Winnipeg was incorporated in 1874. With a population of about 12,000, the city flourished as the first prairie agricultural service center in Canada; development really accelerated in 1882 when the transcontinental railroad started operating across Canada. The arrival of the railroad, coupled with a program of land grants to homesteaders, set off a flood of immigration into the province. By the turn of the century, Manitoba's population had increased to 255,000, while wheat production had reached 50,000 bushels annually.

But the politics of the 1890–1900 period left an open wound on the province that is still not healed today. In 1890, the Manitoba Legislature passed the Public Schools Act, which ended government financing of private Catholic Schools and also abolished teaching in the French language. In the same year, legislators also passed Manitoba's Official Language Act, which prohibited the use of French in the province's courts and also in the legislature's debates and proceedings.

These two bills were perceived as an injustice by Manitoba's French-speaking minority, as well as by Catholic parents anxious to send their children to religious schools. Both groups have fought for almost a hundred years to reverse the legislation of 1890. The first changes were made in the 1960s when Conservative Premier Duff Roblin started to share public school services with private parochial schools, mainly Catholic and Jewish. Then, in 1970, French was reinstated as a language of instruction in Manitoba public schools.

Nine years later, the Supreme Court of Canada ruled invalid Manitoba's Official Language Act of 1890, saying that a provincial legislature had no right to overturn a federal statute which set up Manitoba as a bilingual English-French province in 1870. The Supreme Court has given Manitoba until 1989 to translate its statutes into French.

French-speaking organizations are still pressing for extended government services in their own language, and supporters of private schools continue to seek full government funding of their schools.

Slow but Steady Growth

Since 1900, Manitoba has maintained a slow but steady rate of economic growth. Today, the province has about 1,070,000 citizens, more than 50 percent of them living in Winnipeg. Agriculture remains an important contributor to the province's prosperity, but low grain prices in the 1980s have meant that many of Manitoba's 20,000 farmers are struggling for survival.

This would be extremely serious except that the province has diversified its economy over the years, adding a wide range of secondary industries. Just about all types of manufacturing and processing are represented in Manitoba, with the sole exception of an automobile manufacturing industry.

The province's principal industries are garment-making, furniture-making, construction, food-processing, electronics, aerospace, tourism, and machinery manufacturing. Most Manitobans, however, work in the service industry—more than 300,000 of the 490,000 people who make up the province's labor force. Major employers in this sector include banks, insurance companies, retail stores, hotels and restaurants, schools, universities, and government. Since the recession of 1982, the province's economy has gradually recovered and ranked near the top in Canada from 1985 to 1987.

Rich in Resources

While not as rich in natural resources as neighboring Alberta and Saskatchewan, Manitoba, the eastern-most of the three prairie provinces, does have significant mineral deposits in its north. Major nickel, copper, and zinc mines are operated by INCO Ltd. at Thompson, by the Hudson's Bay Mining and Smelting Company Ltd. at Flin Flon, and by Sherrit-Gordon Mines Ltd. at Ruttan Lake. These mines are now operating on a regular basis after shutdowns during the recession of 1982–83. But the continuing weakness of international mineral prices is limiting activity and prompting some mines to close for longer than usual summer holidays.

Potential new gold deposits are luring prospectors to the north because of recent gains in price. SherrGold Inc. opened a new mine at Lynn Lake in 1986; other companies opened two more gold mines in the same vicinity in 1987.

Northern Manitoba is also the site of the multi-billion-dollar Nelson River power development being built by Manitoba Hydro, the province's publicly-owned power utility. In 1985, Hydro started building the $1.8-billion Limestone generating station, the fourth in a chain of seven power plants on the Nelson, the province's last harnessable waterway.

Limestone is the first Nelson project to be undertaken since 1977 when work was halted because of excess generating capacity in the province. However, recent export power sales to the United States have led to the resumption of construction. Because of these sales, Hydro hopes to start work soon on the $3-billion Conawapa Station, downstream from Limestone, guaranteeing the province a decade of hydro construction and creating substantial business for Manitoba contractors and manufacturers of machinery.

Fishing and forestry are other industries that are dominant in the province's north. And in southwestern Manitoba—centred around the town of Virden—a small oil industry has flourished for more than thirty years. About 200 wells have been drilled in each of the last three years, but the slumping international price of oil has reduced activity.

The People of Manitoba

As Western Canada gained renown as one of the world's best grain-growing areas, immigrants began to flock to Manitoba. The province's first great influx of settlers was largely English-speaking, from eastern Canada and the United States. Then, in 1874, the first Mennonites arrived from Russia. They were followed in 1875 by numerous Icelanders and French-speaking families from Quebec and France. By 1891, there had also been substantial migration from Britain, and the ethnic flavor was further enhanced that year by the arrival of the vanguard of substantial numbers of Ukrainians.

By 1911, Manitoba's population had swelled to 461,394 versus the 152,506 of twenty years earlier. But after that, growth moderated and it has taken seventy-five years for the population to double to 1,070,000 today. At last count, almost 400,000 Manitobans were of British origin. Other principal ethnic groups in the province are: German, Ukrainian, French, North American Indian and Inuit, Polish, Dutch, Scandinavian, Hungarian, Jewish, and Italian. In recent years, large numbers of Asian, Philippine, Vietnamese, and South American immigrants have added to the cosmopolitan flavor of the province.

For almost twenty-five years following World War II, Manitobans elected traditional free enterprise-supporting Liberal and Conservative provincial governments. But there was a big change in 1969 when the New Democratic (Socialist) Party squeezed into power, ousting an eleven-year-old Conservative administration.

The New Democrats, led by Premier Ed Schreyer—now Canada's Ambassador to Australia—were re-elected in 1973 before losing in 1977 to a resurgent Conservative Party headed by Sterling Lyon. Because of a slumping economy, the Conservatives, in turn, were ousted in November 1981 with the New Democratic Party regaining power this time under the leadership of Howard Pawley.

Mr. Pawley, a lawyer from the rural town of Selkirk, narrowly won a second five-year term in March 1986 with a three-seat majority over the Conservatives. When the New Democrats were first elected in 1969, they were something of a novelty in that they were Manitoba's first socialist administration and only the second government of this kind to be elected anywhere in North America. But they have now been in power in the province for fourteen of the last eighteen years and by 1990, they will have extended their streak to sixteen out of twenty years.

Manitoba is as culturally and industrially advanced as any North American province or state, although the relatively small population means that things are on a smaller scale. The Universities of Manitoba and Winnipeg (both in the capital city)—plus the University of Brandon, 125 miles west of Winnipeg—provide for the province's higher education needs. In other centers throughout Manitoba, community colleges and technical schools all have full enrollments.

EXPLORING WINNIPEG

In just over 112 years, Winnipeg has developed from a tiny fur-trading outpost into one of Canada's most sophisticated urban communities. Its population totals almost 700,000.

Because water transportation was the most convenient method of getting goods to market from that region in the 1870s, the fur companies set up their trading posts at the junction of the Red and Assiniboine Rivers. From this spot Winnipeg has spread out in all directions to become a great city.

Red River Ox Carts

Winnipeg, however, was only a tiny village in 1870 when the Canadian Government created the province of Manitoba. At that time, there were only 215 inhabitants and 18 business establishments. By 1874 Winnipeg had 1,879 citizens, 100 businesses, and 27 manufacturing enterprises. This rapid growth prompted civic leaders that year to incorporate Winnipeg, an event that was commemorated with extensive centennial celebrations in 1974.

Since its inception, Winnipeg has been the primary manufacturing, warehousing, and distribution center for western Canada. In the early days, goods stored in the city were hauled by Red River ox carts to surrounding farms, villages, and hamlets. These carts were also used as early as 1850 on the first regular trade route linking Winnipeg with St. Paul, Minnesota. The carts were subsequently outmoded by Red River paddlewheel steamers; these, in turn, were replaced by a Winnipeg–Minneapolis railroad in 1878.

In 1882, Winnipeg became a mainline point on the first east–west Canadian railroad. Rapid development was taking place at this time,

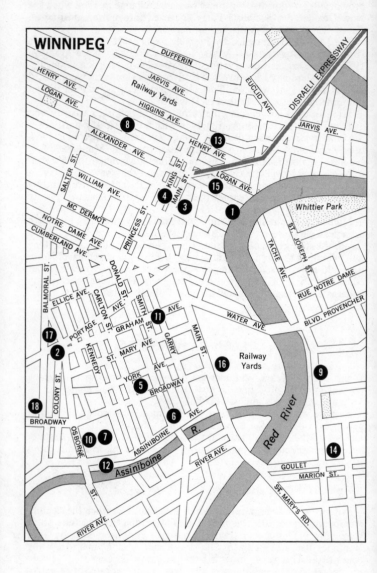

Winnipeg—Points of Interest

1) Alexander Dock
2) Art Gallery
3) Centennial Center (Museum of Man and Nature-Concert Hall-Planetarium)
4) City Hall
5) Convention Center
6) Dalnavert-MacDonald House
7) Federal Building
8) Ivan Franko Museum
9) La Verendrye Monument
10) Legislative Building
11) Post Office
12) Riel Monument
13) Ross House-first Post Office
14) St. Boniface Cathedral and Museum
15) Ukrainian Cultural Center
16) Union Station
17) University of Winnipeg
18) Winnipeg Stadium

and the city blossomed as the leading financial, industrial, and retail center for the territory stretching from Lake Superior to the Rocky Mountains.

A Place of Ethnic Diversity

At about the same time, agriculture started to make a major impact on Winnipeg's economy. Following the first shipment of wheat from Manitoba in 1876, numerous grain-trading businesses began springing up in the city as traders realized that the prairies were destined to become one of the world's major grain-producing areas. The Winnipeg Grain Exchange—now the Winnipeg Commodity Exchange—was established in 1887 and its busy trading floor is still one of the main tourist attractions in the city.

Winnipeg's greatest burst of expansion took place between 1901 and 1914. Population increased by 100,000 as European and American immigrants flocked to the prairies, attracted by the success stories that were flowing back from the western Canadian frontier. This wave of immigration brought substantial numbers of Ukrainians, French-Canadians, Germans, Poles, and Scandinavians, creating an ethnic diversity that remains one of the city's principal characteristics.

Instead of falling into the "melting pot," the various ethnic groups maintained their traditions and languages. Consequently, Winnipeg, each year, is the scene of a large number of ethnic festivals, including the Festival du Voyageur in February and Folklorama, a city-wide Expo-type of celebration staged in August by all of the city's ethnic groups.

A New Building Boom

The 1900–14 period was also the era when Winnipeg's downtown took shape. The arrival of so many immigrants at the turn of the century created an enormous demand in the city for residential accommodation, office buildings, and manufacturing space. Winnipeg became the home of numerous construction firms, as well as for companies supplying lumber, steel, brick, stone, and building supplies of all kinds. Winnipeg experienced another building boom in the early 1970s. This was precipitated by the need to replace original downtown buildings that had decayed with age.

The burst of construction started when James Richardson and Sons Ltd., the prominent Winnipeg investment and grain dealers, erected the thirty-four-story Richardson Building at Portage and Main, the key downtown intersection. The thirty-two-story Winnipeg Commodity Exchange Tower and a twenty-five-story Bank of Montreal regional headquarters have also been completed at Portage and Main in recent years and are two of more than two-dozen new highrises that have given Winnipeg a radically altered skyline.

Unfortunately, economic recession halted the construction boom in the early 1980s. But with the recovery starting in 1983, building picked up and more than $500 million-worth of projects were in progress in the downtown district in 1986. These include the Portage Place shopping mall, which will have more than 200 stores; a $9-million building for the Royal Winnipeg Ballet; a $35-million head office for the Investors Group, Canada's most successful mutual fund company; and a three-tower, $65-million apartment development that will be known as Fort Garry Place.

While Winnipeg is putting on a modern face, it still has the finest collection of turn-of-the-century office buildings and warehouses in Canada. Most of these structures are in the city's Exchange District, which annually welcomes thousands of tourists drawn by its open-air market, numerous fine restaurants, and boutiques.

The Canal and Winnipeg

Winnipeg suffered a severe economic blow in 1914 when the Panama Canal was opened. Prior to that, the city was the main warehousing and distribution center for goods moving to all parts of western Canada. To the detriment of Winnipeg, the canal proved to be a cheaper route for shipping to British Columbia and Alberta.

Offsetting this blow to some extent, Winnipeg has slowly but surely developed into the major manufacturing center for the prairie region. The city has large secondary industries that make clothing, furniture, food products, farm machinery, machine tools, electronic parts, and a host of other goods. This diversity and balance give Winnipeg a measure of economic stability often not present in communities dependent on one or two key industries.

A Major Performing Arts Center

On a cultural and recreational level, Winnipeg is proud of facilities that rank with most large cities in North America. The beaches of Lake Winnipeg—one of the world's largest freshwater lakes—are within fifty miles of the city. The city itself has more than a hundred parks and close to thirty golf courses, while the Birds Hill provincial park and beach is just outside Winnipeg's boundaries.

Downtown, there is abundant night life, with the Rorie Street Marble Club being the "in" spot for the younger set.

Desotos caters to the second-time-around 50s nostalgia crowd; the new Sheraton and Relax hotels have added an extra dimension to Winnipeg dining. Altogether, the city has more than a hundred hotels, plus a convention center with several restaurants that can host gatherings of 8,000 delegates.

As far as the performing arts are concerned, Winnipeg is unique for a community of its size. The city is the home of six professional performing arts companies that regularly present everything from drama and ballet to symphony and opera. Some of these companies, such as the Royal Winnipeg Ballet and the Manitoba Theatre Centre, have won international reputations for the quality of their presentations.

The professional companies, together with the city's numerous amateur theatrical groups, have made Winnipeg the major performing arts center on the prairies.

The city's other cultural attractions include a multi-million dollar civic library, the Winnipeg Art Gallery and the Manitoba Museum of Man and Nature with its adjacent planetarium.

PRACTICAL INFORMATION FOR WINNIPEG

HOW TO GET THERE. By air: Airlines serving the Winnipeg International Airport include *Air Canada, CP Air, Northwest Airlines* and *Pacific Western.* Charter and regional companies provide connections to the province's other major centers and *Perimeter Airlines* has scheduled flights to Dauphin, the Lake Winnipeg communities, and Red Lake, Ont.

By car: Trans-Canada Hwy. 1 passes through Winnipeg on its east-west route. Hwy. 75 runs south to connect with main highways in North and South Dakota and Minnesota, and intersects Hwy. 1 in the south end of the city.

MANITOBA

By train: *Via Rail,* Canada's government-subsidized rail passenger service, serves Winnipeg providing daily east-west runs from its station at Broadway and Main. Two trains leave Winnipeg westbound each day. One travels to Vancouver via Regina and Calgary. The other goes to Prince Rupert via Saskatoon and Edmonton.

By bus: There is *Greyhound* bus service from as far away as New York City. Other lines running to Winnipeg include *Beaver* and *Grey Goose.* The Greyhound/Grey Goose terminal is at 487 Portage Ave.

 ACCOMMODATIONS in Winnipeg still include some well-preserved establishments that couple modern conveniences with traditional service. Many new hotels and motels have been built in recent years, especially in the downtown area, and there are plans for more.

Accommodations are listed according to the following price categories, based on double-occupancy: *Deluxe,* \$70 to \$130; *Expensive,* \$50 to \$69; *Moderate,* \$35 to \$49; *Inexpensive,* under \$35.

Most places accept the following major credit cards: American Express, MasterCard, and Visa; others may also be honored. Not all establishments accept credit cards, therefore we suggest you call for information.

Deluxe

Birchwood Inn. 2520 Portage Ave., Winnipeg, MB R3J 3T6 (204–885–4478 or 800–665–0352). Licensed dining room, cocktail lounge and coffeeshop. Indoor swimming pool, sauna. Easy access to airport. Major credit cards.

Delta Winnipeg. Portage at Smith St., Winnipeg, MB R3C 0B8 (204–956–0410 or 800–268–1133). Centrally located. Licensed dining room, cocktail lounge, beverage room, indoor swimming pool. Indoor walk-through to the T. Eaton Co., two theaters, babysitting. Major credit cards.

International Inn. 1808 Wellington Ave., Winnipeg, MB R3H 0G3 (204–786–4801). Convenient for airport. Cabaret, indoor swimming pool, restaurant, color TV. Major credit cards.

Marlborough Inn. 331 Smith St., Winnipeg, MB R3B 2G9 (204–942–6411). Three licensed dining rooms, a cocktail lounge with entertainment. Convention and banquet facilities, free parking for registered guests. Major credit cards.

Sheraton Winnipeg. 161 Donald St., Winnipeg, MB R3C 1M3 (204–942–5300 or 800–325–3535). Winnipeg's newest hotel. Licensed dining room, cocktail lounge, indoor swimming pool. Major credit cards.

Holiday Inn Downtown. St. Mary's and Carlton, Winnipeg, MB R3C 3J2 (204–942–0551 or 800–465–4329). Popular with conventioneers. Connected by a walkway to the Convention Centre. Cabaret, cocktail lounge, licensed dining room, convention and banquet facilities, indoor pool, sauna and recreational area. Major credit cards.

The Holiday Inn, Winnipeg South. 1330 Pembina Hwy., Winnipeg, MBR3T2B4 (204–452–4747 or 800–465–4329). Restaurant, cocktail lounge, indoor swimming pool, satellite TV.

The Westin Hotel. Two Lombard Pl., Winnipeg, MB R3B 0Y3 (204–957–1350 or 800–268–3000). Modern highrise in the heart of the business district. Connected underground to the Lombard Concourse. Several restaurants and bar. Enclosed guest parking, year-round swimming pool. Major credit cards.

Expensive

The Brittany Inn. Carlton and Ellice., Winnipeg, MB R3B 1Y1 (956–0100 or 204–943–1375 collect). Convenient location. Banquet facilities, meeting rooms. Licensed dining room, cocktail lounge, entertainment, guest parking. Major credit cards.

Charterhouse. 330 York Ave., Winnipeg, MB R3C 0N9 (204–942–0101). Centrally located with dining room, lounge, coffeeshop and outdoor pool. Major credit cards.

Niakwa TraveLodge. Trans-Canada Hwy. E. at St. Anne's Rd., Winnipeg, MB R2M 0Y5 (204–255–6000 or 800–255–3050). Dining room, cocktail lounge, beverage room, beer vendor, coffeeshop, entertainment. Bowling alley, golf course across the street. Guest parking. Major credit cards.

Polo Park Inn. 1405 St. Matthews., Winnipeg, MB R3G 0K5 (204–775–8791). Modern motel, convenient for shopping, airport and sports. Dining and drinking facilities. Recreation center for bowling, billiards, swimming and sauna. Major credit cards.

Viscount Gort Flag Inn. 1670 Portage Ave., Winnipeg, MB R3J 0C9 (204–775–0451 or 800–661–1460). Sauna, lounge, licensed dining room and color TV. Major credit cards.

Windsor Park Inn. 1034 Elizabeth Rd., Winnipeg R2J 1B3 (204–253–2641). Recently upgraded suburban hotel; a fun place with indoor pool and waterslide, color cable TV, a restaurant, and three bars that offer entertainment.

Moderate

Assiniboine Gordon Inn on the Park. 1975 Portage Ave., Winnipeg, MB R3J 0J9 (204–888–4806). Licensed dining room, cocktail lounge, beverage room, Visa.

Curtis Gordon Motor Hotel. 1011 Henderson Hwy., Winnipeg, MB R2K 2M2 (204–334–4355). Licensed restaurant, beverage room, beer vendor, entertainment, dancing, guest parking. Visa.

Downs Motor Inn. 3740 Portage Ave., Winnipeg, MB R3K 0Z9 (204–837–5831). Modern facilities convenient to shopping and racetrack. Dining room, lounge, and beverage room. Country/Western entertainment. Major credit cards.

Grant Motor Inn. 635 Pembina Hwy., Winnipeg, MB R3M 2L4 (204–453–8247 or 800–665–0087). Beverage room, cocktail lounge, entertainment, licensed dining room, guest parking. Major credit cards.

St. Regis Flag Inn. 285 Smith St., Winnipeg, MB R3C 1K9 (204–942–0171). Dining room, coffeeshop, beverage room. Major credit cards.

Inexpensive

Aberdeen Hotel. 230 Carlton St., Winnipeg, MB R3C 1P5 (204–942–7481). Good downtown location, comfortable rooms, poor service.

Chalet Hotel. 611 Archibald St., Winnipeg, MB R2J 0X8 (204–237–8901). An out-of-the-way hotel frequented by colorful cattlebuyers and cowboys.

Norwood Hotel. 112 Marion St., Winnipeg, MB R2H 0T1 (204–233–4475). Fine place to eat, drink, and listen to good music. Visa.

Osborne Village Motor Inn. 160 Osborne, Winnipeg, MB R3L 1Y6 (204–452–9824). Located in a quaint remodeled shopping and restaurant area and within walking distance of downtown.

HOW TO GET AROUND. By bus: Maps of the bus system are available at the Lombard Place concourse under Portage and Main, and at 421 Osborne St. *D.A.S.H. bus service:* from 11:00 A.M. to 3:00 P.M., Monday to Friday. Buses travel a continuous route through the downtown and into the warehouse area and charge no fare. Regular city transit runs from 6:00 A.M. to 1:30 A.M. Monday to Saturday and from 7:00 A.M. to midnight on Sunday. Fares are 40¢ for seniors and children, and 90¢ for adults; exact change required.

By taxi: There is metered taxi service, and also a limousine service from the airport to all major downtown hotels.

TOURIST INFORMATION. Travel Manitoba Visitor Reception Centre at the Legislative Building, downtown (204–945–3777).

TOURS. Visitors may tour the *Legislative Building* at Broadway and Osborne. Made of native Tyndall stone, the building contains the legislative chambers, offices of the premier and cabinet ministers and some departments of government. Atop the 240-foot-high dome of the Legislative Buildings is the Golden Boy, one of the best known symbols of Manitoba.

The Centennial Centre on Main St. N., comprising the Concert Hall and the Planetarium, schedules tours of the concert hall (phone 956–1360) and arranges tours for the planetarium as well. The Concert Hall and Planetarium portions of the centre were completed during 1967, Canada's Centennial Year.

City Hall tours can be arranged by phoning the mayor's office at 986–2196. *Winnipeg Commodity Exchange,* Portage Ave. and Main St.—one of the largest in the world—is open to visitors Monday through Friday. Guides are available.

Winnipeg Art Gallery, 300 Memorial Blvd., offers tours some evenings and weekends. Phone 786–6641. Exhibits are changed regularly and feature collections of traditional and contemporary Canadian, American, and European art. The *Winnipeg Mint,* said to be the most modern in the world, has been designed so that the public can see how money is made. Tours weekdays.

Paddlewheel Riverboat Cruises along the Red River operate each summer, taking excursions to Lower Fort Garry. In conjunction, double-decker London buses conduct daily tours of the city, departing from major downtown hotels.

The *River Rouge Pleasure Ship* offers afternoon and evening cruises along the Red and Assiniboine rivers, while the 1,500-ton *Lord Selkirk* plies the Red north of Redwood Bridge.

SPECIAL INTEREST TOURS. *The Living Prairie Museum,* 2795 Ness Ave., Winnipeg, MB R3J 3S4 (204–832–0167), is a unique chance to explore some of the little remaining tall-grass prairie on the plains. You'll be amazed by the amount and variety of wildflowers. The museum *is* the prairie; the "reception center" has displays to give you background information. Well worth even a short visit. Self-guided and naturalist-led tours. Open weekdays: noon–5 P.M., May, June, and Sept.; 10 A.M.–6 P.M. July and Aug. The rest of the year the museum is open weekdays, 9 A.M.–1 P.M., basically only business hours because there is little interest in the prairie in the winter.

CITY PARKS. The 362 acres of *Assiniboine Park* include an English Garden, a conservatory, miniature railroad, a zoo, and a refreshment pavilion. Adjacent to *Assiniboine Park* is the *Assiniboine Forest,* where deer and waterfowl roam free. *Kildonan Park,* popular for tobogganing and ice skating, also features the *Rainbow Stage,* Canada's only active semi-outdoor theater.

CHILDREN'S ACTIVITIES. Children always enjoy a trip to the zoo, and Winnipeg has one of the finest in Canada—the *Assiniboine Park Zoo. The Planetarium* in the Centennial Centre offers exciting programs that are both educational and fun. *The Manitoba Museum of Man and Nature,* also in the Centennial Centre, features displays explaining the history and prehistory of man. June through September, the *Prairie Dog Central* makes a two-hour steam train excursion from Winnipeg to Grosse Isle. The train departs from C.N.R. St. James Station, 1661 Portage Ave., Sunday. Or maybe your children would like to board one of Winnipeg's cruise ships and enjoy the sights along the Red and Assiniboine Rivers. *Fun Mountain Water Slide Park* has four twister slides that will plummet you into a large heated swimming pool. *The City of Winnipeg Library Department* holds story hours, films, and puppet shows in library branches. A telephone call to the Centennial Library (986–6432) will steer you to the nearest and most convenient.

SPORTS. Spectator. You'll see all your favorite sports in Winnipeg, starting in summer when the Winnipeg Blue Bombers take on the opposition football teams at the Winnipeg Stadium. The Winnipeg Jets play in the National Hockey League and draw big crowds. Professional wrestling and boxing and college basketball, hockey and volleyball are also popular in the city. Thoroughbred horse racing and exciting harness races thrill crowds year-round at Assiniboia Downs. **Participant.** Those who like to get into the action find an excellent selection of golf courses and tennis courts in all areas of the city. The city operates three indoor and numerous outdoor swimming pools for the aquatic crowd. The Pan Am Pool on Grant Ave. houses an aquatic museum. The Winnipeg Roller Rink at Portage Ave. and Langside St. also offers an evening of active entertainment, as do the Hamelin St. roller rink in Fort Garry, the McPhillips St. rink in the north end and the Transcona roller rink. Curling clubs provide interesting winter spectator sport. The Tourism Industry Association of Manitoba can give you further information on these. Write 232–375 York Ave., Winnipeg, R3C 3J3 or phone 204–943–1551.

HISTORIC SITES. Milestones of Winnipeg's past are traced through historic sites in all parts of the city. Nothing speaks for the city's early years as eloquently as its many beautiful old churches.

Grant's Old Mill, overlooking Portage Ave. near the Grace Hospital, is a watermill built on the site of the Red River Settlement's first mill. Stone-ground flour made at the mill is available for purchase. Open daily June 1 to September 1, and weekends in May, September, and October.

Knox United Church on Edmonton at Qu'Apelle St. in downtown Winnipeg is one of the city's oldest churches, yet retains a modern look. Construction of the church was begun in 1914, but because of World War I, the building was not completed until 1917. Knox welcomes visitors to its Sunday services. Open to the public daily at 8 A.M.

Kildonan Presbyterian Church, John Black Ave., the first church of that denomination in western Canada, was completed in 1854 under the direction of the Rev. John Black, the first resident Presbyterian minister in that region.

St. Boniface Basilica, Tache Ave., is the oldest cathedral in western Canada. Its exterior has survived several fires and the interior has been rebuilt as a modern chapel. On the grounds are the graves of Father Provencher and Louis Riel.

A monument to the memory of *Thomas Simpson* who, with *Peter Warren Dease,* between 1837–39, carried out important explorations in the Arctic regions, stands at Main St. and St. John's Ave.

In *Kildonan Park* a plaque commemorates the first steam-powered vessel to reach Fort Garry via the Red River from the south. The *S.S. Anson Northup* arrived at the settlement June 10, 1859.

In a park adjacent to 100 Main St., a tablet commemorates four fur-trade forts once built on this site at the forks of the Red and Assiniboine Rivers. They were Fort Rouge, Fort Gilbraltar, and the first and second Fort Garry. The north gate of the latter still stands.

Opposite the CPR Station on Higgins Ave., a cairn marks the site of the Hudson's Bay Company's *Fort Douglas,* built to protect the Red River Settlement.

Ross House, 140 Meade St., is the first post office in the Red River Settlement.

A small stone shaft on north Main St., in West Kildonan commemorates the *Battle of Seven Oaks* in which Governor Robert Semple of the Hudson's Bay Company and 20 Selkirk settlers were killed by rival traders of the North West Company.

On Tache Ave., opposite St. Boniface Hospital, the *La Verendrye Monument* honors Pierre Gautier de La Verendrye, the first white man to travel west by the Great Lakes chain to reach the forks of the Red and Assiniboine Rivers.

Dalnavert-MacDonald House, the restored Victorian home of Sir Hugh John MacDonald, former premier of Manitoba, is located at 61 Carlton St. Open throughout the year. Guided tours.

LIBRARIES. The *University of Manitoba* and the *University of Winnipeg* both have their own libraries. *Dafoe Library,* the main library at the U. of Man., contains 4,000 volumes of rare books and manuscripts, including the manuscripts of Fredrick Philip Grove, the well known Canadian novelist. It also houses the papers of John Dafoe, the prominent Winnipeg editor for whom the library is named. *The Ukrainian Arts and Crafts Museum,* 1175 Main St., also has a rare book section, the majority of which deal with 17th-century literature and folklore written in the Ukrainian language. An excellent collection of volumes concerning art history and fine arts is at the *Winnipeg Art Gallery,* 300 Memorial Blvd., along with a large number of periodicals and reports. The *Winnipeg Public Library,* on Graham Ave., has an extensive Canadian section, including early writings on Manitoba's history. The *Ukrainian Cultural and Educational Centre,* 184 Alexander Ave. E., contains one of the largest Ukrainian-related libraries in North America.

MUSEUMS AND GALLERIES. The varied ethnic backgrounds of Winnipeg's population, and the history of Manitoba, are reflected in the city's museums and galleries.

Museums. Largest and most well known of these is the *Manitoba Museum of Man and Nature,* 190 Rupert Ave. It is a unique and interpretive center that uses graphics, specimens, reconstructions, and audiovisual presentations of the human and natural history of the province. There are also galleries depicting the beginnings of earth and the universe, the history and prehistory of man's existence, and Winnipeg's environment, past, present, and future. The newest gallery, *Touch the Universe* is filled with hands-on activities for all ages. Open daily.

The Historical Museum of St. James-Assiniboia, 3180 Portage Ave., contains pioneer material relating to the history of the area. Daily April 1 to September, Sunday October 1 to March 31.

Naval Museum H.M.C.S. Chippawa, 51 Smith St. (943–7027), contains a collection of British and Canadian naval artifacts dating from World War I to the present. Open by appointment only. Admission is free.

Riel House, 330 River Road (257–1783 or 233–4888). A look at the cultural, social and economic lives of the Lagimodiere and Riel families of the 1880s.

Royal Winnipeg Rifles Museum, Room 208 Minto Armoury, 969 St. Matthews (783–0880). Uniforms, weapons and artifacts portraying the history of the oldest military unit in Western Canada.

The *St. Boniface Museum,* 494 Tache, is housed in Winnipeg's oldest building, with displays and artifacts depicting the history of Manitoba's French minority. Year-round.

Seven Oaks House, ½ block east of Main St. on Rupertsland Ave., Open seasonally. The oldest habitable house in Manitoba. Built in 1851 and containing furnishings and artifacts from that era.

Ukrainian Cultural and Educational Centre, 184 Alexander Ave. E., is an historical and ethnographic museum, art gallery, and library.

Western Canada Aviation Museum, 958 Ferry Rd. (775–8447), displays vintage aircraft and related memorabilia.

Galleries. Canada's third-largest art gallery, the *Winnipeg Art Gallery,* 300 Memorial Blvd., is housed in one of the most up-to-date structures in North America. It contains a permanent collection, gallery shop, art rental and sales gallery, library, restaurant, education and exhibitions program. Open six days a week.

The Medea, in Winnipeg's popular Osborne Street Village, is the city's first cooperative gallery. Browsing encouraged.

FILM. The National Film Board of Canada screens top-notch Canadian films at its cinema at 245 Main Street. Admittance is free. Information about the time, date, and subject of each screening can be obtained from the NFB at 949–4129.

In addition there are numerous privately owned cinemas in Winnipeg. They include: Capital 1 and 2 (942–6020), Cinema 3 (783–1097), Cinema Gallery (786–7811), Cine-Plex 1, 2, 3, 4, 5, 6 and 7 (943–6149), Convention Centre (947–0783), Epic (943–8261), Garden City 1 and 2 (338–8747), Garrick 1, 2, 3 and 4 (942–2034), Grant (453–4084), Kings (888–1344), Northstar 1 and 2 (943–0089), Metropolitan (942–7710), Odeon (943–4743), Park (452–3118), Polo Park (786–3100), St. Vital Cinema 6 (256–3901), and Towne Cinema 1, 2, 3, 4, 5, 6, 7 and 8 (947–2848).

Movies are rated by a censorship board. "General" movies are recommended for family viewing. "Mature" movies are designed for adult entertainment but anyone may see them. Movies rated "Adult Parental Guidance" may be viewed by minors only if a parent is in accompaniment. "Restricted Adult" movies are just that—restricted to adult viewing only.

Monthly, from September to April, travelogs are screened at the *Centennial Concert Hall* by the CBO (475–9055) and the Rotary Club (942–6654).

PERFORMING ARTS. Winnipeg has earned its reputation as a cultural center, encouraging the development of ballet, theater and other cultural activities.

Dance. *The Royal Winnipeg Ballet,* Canada's first ballet company was established in 1938, and has since become a professional company, winning two gold medals at the International Dance Festival in Paris. In addition to performances from October to May, the company stages a series of free, outdoor summer concerts in Assiniboine Park, called Ballet in the Park. *Winnipeg's Contemporary Dancers* was founded in 1964 by Rachel Browne. It became a fully professional company in 1970. Its performances, dedicated to bringing the best in modern dance entertainment to North America, are scheduled from October to April.

Music. *Winnipeg Symphony Orchestra* holds a season of concerts, from Sept. to April in the Manitoba Centennial Concert Hall. It gives an occasional concert in Kildonan Park, Labor Day weekend. *The Manitoba Opera Association* gives a season of three operas at the Centennial Concert Hall. Other ethnic and cultural groups perform regularly during the summer in Assiniboine and Kildonan parks. *University of Manitoba's School of Music* gives free concerts throughout the year. The *Manitoba Chamber Orchestra* holds a series of concerts during the winter at Westminster Church.

Stage. *The Manitoba Theatre Centre* is one of the leading regional theaters in North America. From October through April, it presents a series of outstanding plays featuring a full professional staff, including Canada's leading actors. *Prairie Theatre Exchange* stages performances at its own theater, 166 Princess St. The new *Gas Station Theatre* in Osborne Village is always busy with professional and amateur companies. They are listed in the local telephone directory. *Rainbow Stage,* western Canada's only semi-outdoor theater, presents musicals during July and August. A special event at the end of March is the *Theatre for Children* at the Winnipeg Art Gallery.

SHOPPING. In addition to nationally known department stores such as *Eaton's, Sears,* and *The Bay,* there are a variety of interesting shops and boutiques. Osborne Village is a neighborhood crammed with stores and workshops selling treasures that would be difficult to find anywhere else. Everything from weaving yarn to necklaces of New Mexican silver to Western Canadian contemporary art is sold here. Just south of downtown, it's the perfect place for afternoon browsing. *Polo Park,* on Portage Ave. in the west end, has recently doubled in size to 200 stores and ranks as the most modern enclosed shopping mall in Winnipeg. Other major enclosed centers are *Unicity* on Portage Ave. in St. James; the *St. Vital Centre* on St. Mary's Rd. at Bishop Grandin Blvd. in St. Vital; *Kildonan Place* on Regent Ave. in East Kildonan; and *Garden City* on McPhillips St. in the North End. They will be joined in Sept. 1987 by *Portage Place,* an enclosed mall with 200 stores in the heart of the downtown district. The Exchange District, near city hall, has many boutiques and offers an open-air market on Saturdays from May to September. The *Winnipeg Convention Centre* also has a host of boutiques and specialty shops on its second level, as does *Winnipeg Square* beneath the Portage and Main concourse.

DINING OUT. In Winnipeg is an opportunity to experience the cuisine of the many and diverse cultures that typify this city. The atmosphere in most Winnipeg restaurants is one of casual informality. Restaurants are categorized on the basis of their own medium-priced full-course dinners per person; drinks and tips excluded. *Deluxe,* $40 and higher; *Expensive,* $30–40; *Moderate,* $20–30; *Inexpensive,* under $20.

Most places accept the following major credit cards: American Express, MasterCard, and Visa; others may also be honored. Not all establishments accept credit cards, therefore we suggest you call for information.

American and Canadian

Moderate

Haynes' Chicken Shack. 257 Lulu. (774–2764). Authentic Southern fried chicken, mouthwatering BBQ spareribs, and deep-fried shrimp. No credit cards.

Inexpensive

Kelekis. 1100 Main St. (582–1786). Homemade French fries, hamburgers, and hot dogs cooked by the same family for the past 55 years.

Chinese

Moderate

Mandarin. 613 Sargent Ave. (775–7819). Pleasant atmosphere. Northern Chinese cuisine.

Shanghai. 240 King St. (943–7700). Fine Chinese food, seven days a week. Equipped for banquets and take-out orders. Licensed. Major credit cards.

Inexpensive

Kum Koon Garden. 426 Main. (943–4655). Extensive selection of dim sum dishes. Recommended by the Chinese residents of Winnipeg. Visa.

River Mandarin. 252 River Ave. (284–8963). Northern Chinese dishes. Outdoor patio dining in summer.

Continental

Deluxe

Dubrovnik. 390 Assiniboine Ave. (944–0594). Continental-Yugoslavian. An elegant dining spot located in a renovated, stately old Winnipeg residence. The food is consistently excellent and the service prompt and cheerful. An extensive menu, with stuffed veal or pork the chef's specialty. Major credit cards.

The Royal Rib Room (942–0101). Charterhouse Hotel, Hargrave St. and York Ave. Specialties include onion soup and prime ribs of roast beef. The roast beef is always tender and good-tasting. Extensive wine list. Major credit cards.

Victor's. Elegant dining in the Osborne Village boutique district (284–2339). Executive Chef Heinz Kaltenfeld offers a menu that features bouillabaisse, veal dishes, and rack of lamb. Joanna's Happy Cake is a favorite dessert. 454 River Ave. Sister restaurants, **Pantages** on Portage Ave. and **Amici's** on Broadway, are also tops. Major credit cards.

Westin Hotel. 2 Lombard Pl. (957–1350). A complete dinner section of the menu offers Cornish game hen, prime roast beef, and river trout with shrimp. Includes soup, salad, and dessert. Two-star entrées are fresh lobster from the restaurant's tanks and an excellent rack of lamb. Major credit cards.

Expensive

Churchill's. Marlborough Inn, 331 Smith St. (942–6411). Posh dining room for the romantically inclined. Food adequate. Major credit cards.

Hy's. 216 Kennedy St. (942–1000). A veteran eating establishment but still one of the best in town. This is the place for steak, beef, lamb and ribs. Cheese bread and toast is a specialty. Can be expensive. Major credit cards.

Moderate

Old Swiss Inn. 207 Edmonton St. (942–7725). One of Winnipeg's best and most reliable restaurants. It is small and inviting, with a menu that offers several fish dishes, and the chef's special, shrimp sautéed in butter at the table. The steak is excellent. Major credit cards.

Oliver's Old Bailey Restaurant. 185 Lombard Ave. (943–4448). A luxurious restaurant decorated with antique furnishings and fixtures. Specialties are scampi, Australian lobster tail, and grilled steak. Desserts include good cheesecake and very good sabayon Marsala. Major credit cards.

Picasso's Cafe & Bar. 615 Sargent Ave. (775–2468). Attracts the Yuppie and artistic crowds who appreciate the coziness and excellent cuisine. Fresh seafood is a speciality, but traditional dishes are also available. Major credit cards.

Danish

Moderate

Bistro Dansk. 63 Sherbrook St. (775–5662). Charming, small and casual. Homemade soups, bread and pastries. All authentic Danish meals, including frikadeller (Danish meat patties). Visa.

Inexpensive

Kronborg. 1875 Pembina. (261–1448). Small family restaurant with delicious home-cooking and 64 varieties of open-faced sandwiches. Visa.

East Indian

Inexpensive

Ardjuna. 457 Notre Dame Ave., (942–5440). Specializes in Indonesian pork sate, lumpia egg rolls, marinated chicken, and Dutch croquettes. Wine and beer licence.

French

Expensive

La Grenouillère. 150 Provencher Blvd. (233–0422). St. Boniface. Cozy restaurant. Best of the specialties include frog's legs, milk-fed veal, and sole. Major credit cards.

Moderate

La Veille Gare. Provencher Ave. and Des Meurons St., St. Boniface (237–7072). Continental French food is the speciality here. This restaurant, fashioned from an old railway station, features attractive, luxurious decor. Flamed pepper steak and veal sweetbreads are two popular entrées. This restaurant also has a wide selection of wines. Major credit cards.

Greek

Moderate

Homer's. 520 Ellice Ave. (774–9123). A Greek restaurant with a pleasant atmosphere and good food that caters to Winnipeg's television crowd. Major credit cards.

Hungarian

Moderate

Hungarian Restaurant. 174 Isabel St. (775–4790). Comfortable atmosphere. Try the veal meatball dish served with noodles, the goulash or the breaded rabbit and half-pheasant. Cosmopolitan wine list.

Italian

Inexpensive

Da Mamma Mia Pizzeria. 631 Corydon Ave. (453–9210). Best Italian pizza in town. Major credit cards.

Mona Lisa. 1697 Corydon Ave. (452–4916). Great pizza and pasta. Restaurant walls are an art gallery for local artists. Decor changes as artists change. Licensed. Major credit cards.

Moderate

Cibo's. 283 Bannatyne (943–4922). In the heart of Old Market Square. Seafood specials and pasta include excellent fettuccine with shrimp and broccoli. Dancing upstairs until 1 A.M.

Japanese

Moderate

Tokyo Joe's. 132 Pioneer (943–5796). Korean/Japanese. Specialties include steak tartar and pickled cabbage. Pleasant atmosphere. Wine license. Major credit cards.

Yamato. 667B Stafford (452–1166). Excellent Japanese food. Liquor license.

Mexican

Inexpensive

Chi-Chi's. 1460 Maroons Rd. (775–0351) and 1590 Regent (661–6776). House specialties include chimichangas, chajitas, and fried ice cream. Licensed. Major credit cards.

Lunch and Light Specialty Dinners

Moderate

Garden Crêperie. 349 York Ave. (957–0221). Casual, easy and light dining with rolled crêpes the specialty. Fully licensed. Major credit cards.

Tony Roma's, 203 Kennedy. (949–9426). Good barbecued ribs at acceptable prices. Licensed. Major credit cards.

Inexpensive

Basil's. 117 Osborne St. in the Osborne Village (453–8440). Open-faced European sandwiches, cheese plates and variety of specialty coffees. Excellent pastries. Wine license. Visa only.

The Fork, 218 Sherbrook St. (774–2289). A fondue bistro with a cozy atmosphere. The perfect place to spend a relaxing evening with friends.

 NIGHTLIFE. Winnipeg's entertainment scene is as vibrant as the city itself, catering to a variety of moods and predilections. For a night of dancing, *Elboes* in the Downtown Holiday Inn (942–0551) is a popular spot. Dress is casual. Those who like taped and live dance music and are members of the trendy young in-crowd gravitate to the *Rorie Street Marble Club,* 65 Rorie St. (943–4222) or *BlueJeans Cabaret,* 1133 Portage Ave. (772–0454). The older 1950s and 1960s nostalgia crowd gathers at *Desotos,* 171 McDermot Ave. (943–4444). In the suburbs, the hot spots are *Night Moves Cabaret* in the Windsor Park Inn, 1034 Elizabeth Rd. (253–2641), and *Scandal's Fun Club* in the Norlander Hotel, 1792 Pembina Highway near the University of Manitoba (269–6955).

Comedy clubs are also in vogue in the city; try *Rumors Comedy Club* in Gallagher's Bar and Grill, 2025 Corydon Ave. (453–8216), or *Yuk Yuk's,* 2nd floor, 108 Osborne St. (475–9857).

Situated in the midst of Winnipeg's business district, *The Old Bailey,* 185 Lombard Ave. (943–4448), attracts the office crowd for drinks after five. *The Hollow Mug* in the International Inn (786–4801) presents musical revues followed by dance music. Other popular night clubs include the *Club Morocco,* 575 Portage Ave. (772–2578), the *Rose and Crown* in the Marlborough Inn (942–6411), and the *Norwood Nightclub,* 112 Marion St. (233–4475).

EXPLORING MANITOBA

The history of Manitoba is interwoven with the era of exploration in North America and the development of the fur trade. As a fur-trading center, the region was involved in the imperial struggle between France and England. Since those days, the province has attracted immigrants from all over the world, and today it is noted for its diverse cultural strains. The influence of still strong ethnic roots has uniquely shaped its towns and influenced its countryside.

A Water Highway

The Red River was the main transportation route and the focal point for settlers in the 18th and 19th centuries. Today, the river offers a beautiful scenic drive and a journey into Manitoba's pioneering past.

From Winnipeg's Perimeter Highway 101, take Metro Route 52 (Highway 9) and drive northeast. There is an interesting side trip on Highway 410 (St. Andrews Road), three quarters of a mile east to River Road. There you will see the lovely St. Andrews Church, built in the early 1880's. Some original furnishings remain, including kneeling benches covered in buffalo hide. Nearby, the Red River House Museum contains artifacts of a former Hudson's Bay Company fur trader and explorer.

To see a re-enactment of pioneer life as it was more than 100 years ago in the environs of Lower Fort Garry, continue northeast on River Road back to Hwy. 9, then go north. The approach to the fort is impressive—huge stone walls and cannons pointing menacingly across the Red River.

One of the oldest stone-built, fur-trading forts in North America, its history is preserved within the original buildings which are stocked with period furniture and mementos of the early days. Members of the fort's staff, dressed in the fashions of the old days, play their roles of early residents of the fort. There's even a blacksmith who has forging tools and horsehoes in his smithy.

Continuing north on Highway 9, you will reach Selkirk, a haven for pleasure craft, fishing fleets, and freighters. There is a popular marine museum in the town. A reminder of the early settlers is the huge replica in the municipal park of a Red River cart. The town is famous for its Highland Gathering in July.

The Western Shore

Lake Winnipeg is a large and shallow lake with a variety of beaches. Winnipeg Beach is a popular vacation area; it has a wide beach and a wayside park that provides picnic and boating facilities.

North again on Highway 9 brings you to Gimli. The town was founded in 1875 and is the second largest Icelandic community outside of Iceland. This fishing town has even more to offer than its harbors and beaches. Its annual Islendingadagurinn festival is held the first week in August. To further explore the town's origins, don't miss the Gimli Historical Museum and the giant Viking Statue in town.

Hecla Provincial Natural Park is the site of another Icelandic settlement. Its large Gull Harbour Resort reflects the early Icelandic architectural styles. From Gimli the route to the island is via Highways 8, 234 and 233. The rugged shoreline scenery resembles that of the Maritimes and the marshy areas have a profusion of wildlife and flora. On the island there is plenty for the visitor to do: a rich history to be studied, camping and sports facilities to be enjoyed and teeming wildlife to be observed.

The Far Shore

Across the lake, on the east side, there are more fine beaches and tour spots. Grand Beach, on Highway 59, attracts thousands of Manitobans on weekends and is reputed to have the finest sand this side of Hawaii. Other popular beaches on this highway are Victoria, Albert, Belair, and Patricia. The biggest town on the east side is Pine Falls on Highway 11 where the 82,000-kilowatt generating station is open to visitors. You can also see over the Abitibi-Price paper plant; tours are provided by appointment.

You have a choice of continuing north on Highway 11 for a taste of more expansive beaches, or you can go south on that highway to view more of Manitoba Hydro's power plants. The stations at Winnipeg River and Seven Sisters offer tours. The mining town of Lac du Bonnet is a good center for sportsfishermen; angling equipment is also available. A side trip along Highway 211, west, will give the opportunity to take in the atomic energy plant at Pinawa.

The main leg of this tour continues south on Highway 11. Turn west on Highway 307 to reach Seven Sisters, the largest of the six power stations on the Winnipeg River; it is open to visitors. This road will take you into Whiteshell Provincial Park where recreational and camping facilities blend into a scenic, pre-Cambrian setting of sparkling lakes and jackpine forests. At the junction of Highway 1 and Highway 44, turn west for West Hawk Lake. Some 365 feet deep, this deepest lake in Manitoba is believed to have been formed by a meteor about 150 million years ago. Follow Highway 301 out of the park, but do take time to explore Falcon Lake.

Heritage Odyssey

Southern Manitoba is full of ethnic variety and historic interest. To explore this area, take Highway 1 from Winnipeg until you reach Highway 12, then go south to Steinbach. This town's Mennonite Village Museum is located about 1½ miles north of the town on Highway 12; here you can see the sights and hear the sounds of a Mennonite village of 1874. You can even taste the sort of foods the villagers ate in those days by visiting the Big Red Restaurant. In early August, the village holds its Pioneer Days Festival to honor its Mennonite forefathers who emigrated from Russia in the 1870's.

To visit St. Pierre, home of the Frog Follies in early August, drive west on Highway 52, then north on Highway 59. The typical French-Canadian town of St. Mâlo can be reached farther south on Highway 59. Displays illustrating the history of this predominantly French-Canadian district can be seen at the Pioneer Museum. The St. Mâlo recreation area includes beach, picnic, and camping facilities.

To visit Morris, home of the Manitoba Stampede, go north on Highway 59, then head west on Highway 23. Traveling from Winnipeg, Morris is 30 miles south on Highway 75. Direct from Calgary's Stampede, this well-known event features rodeos, chuckwagon races, and an exhibition in mid-July.

Western Manitoba

See the longest swinging footbridge in Canada at Souris, 20 miles south of Brandon. It is 582 suspense-filled feet of faltering footsteps. There is first-class swimming and boating at Killarney.

PRACTICAL INFORMATION FOR MANITOBA

HOW TO GET THERE. By Air: Manitoba's largest airport is in Winnipeg. It is served by *Air Canada, CP Air,* and *Pacific Western Airlines.* Additionally, *Northwest Airlines* flies in from Minneapolis and offers connections with other major U.S. cities.

By Car: A circle highway route, originating in the United States, is linked to the Manitoba highway system. In the southeast, Hwy. 75 runs to Winnipeg from the U.S. border and connects with Trans-Canada Hwy. 1. To the southeast, Hwy. 10 runs from the border, passing through Brandon and continuing north to Dauphin, The Pas, and Flin Flon.

By Train: The main lines of the *Canadian Pacific* and *Canadian National* railroad systems serve Winnipeg, Portage La Prairie, and Brandon. Canadian

National also provides services from Winnipeg to the northern regions of the province through Dauphin, The Pas to Thompson and Churchill on Hudson Bay. But passenger service has been transferred to *Via Rail,* a government agency.

By Bus: Service is provided by two mainline bus companies, *Grey Goose* and *Greyhound,* and several local companies.

 ACCOMMODATIONS in Manitoba range from the deluxe to inexpensive, but in the smaller towns it is sometimes difficult to find anything but the most basic accommodation. The price categories in this section are based on double occupancy. *Deluxe,* over $60; *Expensive,* $40 to $59; *Moderate,* $25 to $39; *Inexpensive,* under $25. All have dining facilities.

Most places accept the following major credit cards: American Express, MasterCard, and Visa; others may also be honored. Not all establishments accept credit cards, therefore we suggest you call for information.

BRANDON. *Deluxe.* **Royal Oak Inn.** 3130 Victoria Ave., Brandon, MB R7A 4Z7 (204–728–5775). Indoor solarium, pool, and sauna. Excellent dining room. Lounge, tavern and entertainment. Major credit cards.
Rodeway Inn. 300 - 18th St. N., Brandon, MB R7A 2V6 (204–728–7230). Saunas and game room are two special features of this motel. Major credit cards.
Victoria Inn. 3550 Victoria Ave., P.O. Box 458, Brandon MB R7A 5Z4 (204–725–1532). Pool, sauna, cocktail lounge, and licensed dining room. Major credit cards.
Expensive: **Canadian Inn.** 150 - 5th St., Brandon, MB R7A 3K4 (204–727–6404). Indoor pool, licensed dining room, coffee shop, cocktail lounge. Major credit cards.

CARMAN. *Moderate.* **Carman Motor Hotel.** Box 1439, 44 Centre W, Carman MB R0G 0J0 (204–745–3733). Well known for its open steak pit, where you cook your own steak.

DAUPHIN. *Expensive:* **Rodeway Inn Motel.** Hwy. 10 S, Box 602, Dauphin MB R7N 2V4 (204–638–5102). Indoor pool, sauna whirlpool. Color TV. Self-serve breakfast nook. Major credit cards.

FLIN FLON. *Deluxe:* **Kelsey Trail Motor Inn.** Hwy. 10, Box 220, Flin Flon MB R8A 1M9 (204–687–7555). Full range of comforts and conveniences. Indoor pool, licensed dining room, and beverage room. Major credit cards.

GIMLI. *Moderate:* **Viking Motor Hotel.** NW 7th and Centre, Box 131, Gimli, MB R0C 1B0 (204–642–5181). Licensed dining room, sauna, cocktail lounge and beverage room. Color TV, air conditioning. Major credit cards.

HECLA PROVINCIAL NATURAL PARK. *Deluxe:* **Gull Harbour Resort Hotel.** General Delivery, Riverton, MB R0C 2R0 (204–475–2354 or 800–442–0497). Lounge, adult games room, indoor pool, sauna, deck and play area, gymnasium, 18-hole golf course, lake swimming facilities, snowshoe and cross-country ski trails. Amphitheater, marina. Major credit cards.

LAC DU BONNET. *Moderate:* **Lakeview Motor Hotel.** 57 Park, Box 189, Lac Du Bonnet, MB R0E 1A0 (204–345–8661). Licensed restaurant and beverage room. Major credit cards.

LA RIVIÈRE. *Moderate:* **Chalet Motel.** SW 25 - 3 - 10 W, La Riviere, MB R0G 1A0 (204–242–2172). Convenient to ski hills. Air-conditioned, color TV, cocktail lounge and licensed dining room. Fishing licenses can be bought here. Major credit cards.

MINNEDOSA. *Moderate:* **Valley Motor Hotel.** 28 Main St., Box 238, Minnedosa MB R0J 1E0 (204–867–2741). Licensed dining room, beverage room, cocktail lounge, and coffeeshop. Indoor pool, color TV. Major credit cards.

MORDEN. *Expensive:* **Morden Motor Inn.** 780 Thornhill, Box 1177, Morden, MB R0G 1J0 (204–822–6272). Licensed restaurant and dining room, cocktail lounge, sauna, and color TV. Major credit cards.

PINAWA. *Expensive:* **Pinawa Motor Inn.** Lot 147, Box 340, Pinawa, MB R0E 1L0 (204–753–2279). Licensed dining room, coffeeshop, and beverage room. Major credit cards.

PORTAGE LA PRAIRIE. *Expensive:* **Best Western Manitoba Inn.** Hwy. 1 and Yellowquill Tr., P.O. Box 867, Portage la Prairie, MB R1N 3C3 (204–857–9791). All facilities, including swimming pool. Major credit cards.
   Westgate Inn Motel. 1010 Saskatchewan Ave. E., Portage la Prairie, MB R1N 0K1 (204–239–5200). Color cable TV. Choice of waterbeds, queen-sized beds. Kitchenettes in some units. Major credit cards.
   Westward Village Inn. 2401 Saskatchewan Ave. W., Box 385, Portage la Prairie, MB R1N 3L5 (204–857–9745). Across from major shopping center. Dining and lounge facilities; newly opened.
   Moderate: **Midtown Motor Hotel.** 177 Saskatchewan Ave. W., Portage la Prairie, MB R1N 0P5 (204–857–6881). Licensed restaurant, dining room, and beverage room. All major credit cards accepted.

RIDING MOUNTAIN NATIONAL PARK. *Deluxe:* **Elkhorn Ranch.** Mooswa Dr. W., Box 40, Wasagaming, MB R0J 2H0 (204–848–2802). Indoor pool, licensed dining room, and cocktail lounge. Major credit cards.

STEINBACH. *Moderate:* **Frantz Motor Inn.** Hwy. 52 E., Box 2558, Steinbach, MB R0A 2A0 (204–326–9831). Licensed dining room, cocktail lounge, and beverage room. Visa only.

THE PAS. *Expensive:* **La Verendrye.** 1326 Gordon, Box 510, The Pas, MB R9A 1K6 (204–623–3431). Dining room, lounge. Color TV. Major credit cards.
   Wescana Inn. 439 Fischer Ave., Box 2519, The Pas, MB R9A 1M3 (204–623–5446). Dining room, cocktail lounge and beverage room. Major credit cards.

THOMPSON. *Expensive:* **Burntwood Motor Hotel.** Selkirk Dr., Thompson, MB R8N 0N1 (204–677–4551). Choice of dining and drinking facilities. Major credit cards.
   Mystery Lake Motor Hotel. Cree Rd., Thompson, MB R8N 0N2 (204–778–8331 or 800–442–0429). Large hotel with choices in dining and drinking facilities. Limousine service to airport. Major credit cards.

WHITESHELL PROVINCIAL NATURAL PARK. *Deluxe:* **Keystone Resorts Ltd.** Lot 3, West Hawk Lake, MB R0E 2H0 (204–349–2250). Coffee shop, outdoor pool, color T.V., fishing licenses, tackle and bait available. Major credit cards.

HOW TO GET AROUND. By air: *Pacific Western,* a major interprovincial airline, serves centers throughout Manitoba, Saskatchewan, and Alberta. *CP Air* provides regional service to Thunder Bay, Sault Ste. Marie, and Toronto, all in Ontario. Other regional and charter companies offer flights to areas in the province.
   Car rental: Car rental companies such as *Avis, Budget, Hertz,* and *Tilden* have facilities in all major centers, as well as a number of the smaller centers.

MANITOBA FACTS AND FIGURES. Manitoba's name originated with the Indian words Manitou bau—Strait of the God—describing the Lake Manitoba Narrows. It is often called Friendly Manitoba. Its floral emblem is the crocus; the Coat-of-Arms, "Vert on a rock a buffalo stantant proper, on a Chief Argent the Cross of St. George"; the provincial flag, a red ensign bearing Manitoba's coat-of-arms. The Great Grey Owl—in abundance here—has recently been adopted as the provincial bird.

Winnipeg, population of over 600,000, is the provincial capital. The population of Manitoba is more than 1,000,000.

TOURIST INFORMATION. Tourist Information, Travel Manitoba is ready to answer any questions you might have. You will find them at the Legislative Building, Broadway and Osborne, Winnipeg, Manitoba R3C 0V8.

Seasonal Reception Centres are in operation from mid-May to September at six border and highway locations.

Camping, fishing, canoeing, hunting, winter recreation, and complete tourism information can be obtained by writing to: Travel Manitoba, Dept. 6001, 7th Floor, 155 Carlton St., Winnipeg, R3C 3H8.

The *Manitoba Vacation Guide* is available free of charge at all government information centers. It includes information on hotel and motel facilities, campgrounds, points of interest, historic sites, museums, recreational and sport facilities, and so on.

SEASONAL EVENTS. January: *Snowmobile races* start off the year in a number of Manitoba communities. Curling fans enjoy the *Manitoba Curling Association Bonspiel*—the world's largest bonspiel—usually held the last week of January. *Ukranian Christmas* in early January is the occasion for a series of special dinners and entertainment events in Winnipeg and other Manitoba communities.

February: The *Canadian Power Toboggan Championship Races,* featuring top racers from Canada and the U.S., are hosted in Beausejour. Held in conjunction with the races, the *Beausejour Winter Farewell* is highlighted by the crowning of Miss Power Toboggan. The *Festival du Voyageur* in St. Boniface features a costume ball, ice sculpture, and many other winter activities. In The Pas, tourists and residents alike enjoy the *Northern Manitoba Trappers' Festival.*

Both the University of Manitoba and Winnipeg present winter festivals around a theme chosen as current and of particular interest to the students and the community.

March: The *Manitoba Music Competition Festival,* Canada's largest music festival, is held in Winnipeg.

April: The *Royal Manitoba Winter Fair,* including livestock judging and horse shows, is staged in Brandon at the beginning of the month. Also in Brandon, the *Brandon Music Festival* is held at the West Man Auditorium. Annually on Easter Sunday, the *Aurora Snow Festival* in Churchill heads into a week of dog team and snowmobile races.

May: The *Shrine Circus* comes to the Winnipeg Arena at the beginning of May. Racing enthusiasts enjoy stockcar racing at *Winnipeg Speedway,* starting in mid-May and continuing to September.

June: The rural French-speaking community celebrates St. Jean Baptiste Day during Fête Franco-Manitobaine, in La Broquerie. In Winnipeg, the *Red River Exhibition* features carnival attractions and stage shows at the end of June. The International Peace Gardens on the Manitoba/North Dakota border, hosts the *International Music Camp* featuring jazz concerts, drama and workshops.

July: The *Winnipeg Folk Festival* presents three days of music in Birds Hill Park. In July and Aug., *Rainbow Stage,* the only outdoor theater in western Canada, presents musicals in Winnipeg's Kildonan Park. Dancing, drumming and piping are presented at the *Manitoba Highland Gathering.* At Assiniboia Downs in Winnipeg, horse lovers gather for the *Manitoba Derby.*

This is the month for Manitoba's famous rodeos and festivals. There's the *Manitoba Stampede* in Morris, the *Threshermen's Reunion* in Austin, the *Annual Manitoba Sunflower Festival* in Altona, *Thompson Nickel Days* in the northern mining community of Thompson, and *Steinbach Pioneer Days,* an ethnic Mennonite celebration, in Steinbach. Workshops in painting and music are scheduled for the *Holiday Festival of the Arts* in Neepawa. Three days of rodeo and exhibits are featured at the *Northwest Round-up and Agricultural Fair* in Swan River at the end of July. The football season, starring the *Winnipeg Blue Bombers,* starts in July and continues to November.

August: Gimli presents the *Icelandic Festival of Manitoba* early in the month. *Harness racing* gets under way at Winnipeg's Assiniboia Downs. Winnipeg's cultural mosaic is well represented at *Folklorama,* a week of music, dancing and foods from many lands at pavilions located throughout the city. Morden's *Corn and Apple Festival* continues Manitoba's festival tradition during the last days of the month. In Dauphin, it's the *Canada's National Ukrainian Festival,* and in Boissevain, the *Canadian Turtle Derby.*

October: *Hockey,* featuring the *Winnipeg Jets,* starts at the Winnipeg Arena and continues through March. The Royal Winnipeg Ballet and the Manitoba Theatre Centre begin performances.

November: Brandon stages the *Brandon Agricultural Exhibition* at Keystone Centre. And, for the pleasure of both children and adults, there is the Santa Claus Parade, held near the end of the month in Winnipeg.

December: The Winnipeg Symphony celebrates the Christmas season with its annual *Christmas Fantasy* presentation and the Royal Winnipeg Ballet delights the entire family with its annual presentation of The Nutcracker.

TOURS. Tours are available in Winnipeg and surrounding areas and also to Manitoba's northland. *Via Rail's Hudson Bay Explorer Tours*—a five-day, combined train and plane tour to sub-Arctic Churchill, and the Arctic Islands. Contact your travel agent or the Via Rail Passenger Sales Office for information and reservations.

Grayline Bus/Paddlewheel Boat Tours, 1048 Main St. (204–339–1696), has package tours around the city, including paddlewheel riverboat cruises on the Assiniboine and Red Rivers.

River Rouge Ltd., Nairn Ave., arranges tours on its *River Rouge* and *Lady Winnipeg* river cruise ships, as well as on its three double-decker buses. And, if you want to sail around on your own yacht, call M.S. *Black Hawk Charter Cruise* in Selkirk. *FunShip Cruise Lines* offers cruises on the 1,500-ton *Lord Selkirk* north on the Red River from Redwood Dock (284–3031).

INDUSTRIAL TOURS. *Whiteshell Nuclear Research Establishment* has general tours of the plant during summer, including a portion of the reactor building and laboratories, 10 A.M. and 2 P.M. daily, except Sundays. Expectant mothers and children under 12 are not allowed to make the tour, but they may see films and displays in the information center.

Abitibi-Price Paper Co., Pine Falls, on the Winnipeg River is open for tours Monday to Friday, providing advance notice is given. Camp and picnic grounds are located across the river from the town. Visitor tours are available at several of Manitoba Hydro's power plants—Pine Falls, Seven Sisters, and Pointe du Boise. All stations are accessible by road.

NATIONAL PARKS. *Riding Mountain National Park,* a 1,150-square-mile parkland area in western Manitoba, includes both evergreen and hardwood forests, prairies, rolling hills, valleys, lakes and streams. Plateaus rise to heights of 2,480 feet above sea level and tower 1,100 feet above the surrounding countryside. Black bear, white-tailed deer, moose and elk, and numerous other smaller animals roam the park. Beaver are to be found in streams in many places in the area. A carefully controlled herd of buffalo grazes in a 1,314-acre enclosure and provides an ever-popular attraction for visitors. A special observation area affords a good view of these animals in their natural habitat.

Lakes and streams offer good fishing. Northern pike (a prime species in the region), walleye, whitefish, and lake trout flourish in cold waters such as Clear Lake, while rainbow and brook trout are among those found in Lake Katherine and Deep Lake. Clear Lake, the largest in the park, also offers opportunities for sailing and waterskiing.

The resort town of Wasagaming is the focal point of vacation activity in the park. In the town, visitors have a choice of theater, bowling, tennis, a natural history museum, and formal gardens. There is also an 18-hole golf course in the locality. A variety of good accommodation is available. Wasagaming and several of the lake areas in the park have campgrounds for both tents and trailers.

The park is bisected by Hwy. 10 and it can also be reached using Hwy. 5.

PROVINCIAL PARKS. Plenty of opportunity here for relaxation or adventure among the forests, lakes, streams, and rolling hills. Hiking, picnicking, canoeing, camping—whether you like to stray from the beaten path and rough it, or make use of the excellent facilities in Manitoba's provincial parks, you'll find what you are looking for regardless of season.

Recreation areas are provided with facilities for winter sports, including ski slopes and tows, motels and other types of accommodation. Groups of more than 40 persons are advised to make reservations at least a week in advance.

Provincial parks include:

Agassiz Provincial Forest, 50 miles east of Winnipeg, is reached by Hwys. 44 and 15. There are several picnic sites along the highways crossing the area.

Asessippi Provincial Park covers 5,000 acres beside the lake formed behind the Shellmouth Dam at the junction of the Shell and Assiniboine Rivers near the Saskatchewan border. It is reached by Hwy. 83 and is designed for water vacation activities.

Belair Provincial Forest has 164,920 acres of timberland. North Star Trail, the main route, begins just north of Stead off Provincial Rd. 219 and exist on Hwy. 59 near Grand Beach Provincial Park. The forest may also be entered a little farther north on Hwy. 59. This trail exits on Hwy. 11. Trails are being improved for public use and are accessible by most vehicles.

Birds Hill Provincial Park, 14 miles north of downtown Winnipeg on Hwy. 59, comprises 8,300 acres. The park includes an 80-acre man-made lake dotted with small islands and is suitable for swimming. A large tenting and trailer campground with modern facilities is provided. A commercial riding stable is also located in the park. Throughout the winter, group hay rides may be booked and for cross-country skiing enthusiasts, equipment may also be hired through the stable.

Clearwater Provincial Park, north of The Pas on Hwy. 10, is a 147,000-acre area surrounding Clearwater Lake—said to be one of the three true bluewater lakes in the world. (There are two modern campgrounds.)

Cormorant Provincial Forest, located 30 miles northeast of The Pas along the Hudson Bay railroad, adjoins Clearwater Provincial Park. It includes a fishing and hunting lodge.

Duck Mountain Provincial Park, comprises a 492-square-mile area in the Duck Mountain Provincial Forest northwest of Dauphin. Its 73 lakes have good fishing and it has excellent camping facilities.

Grand Beach Provincial Park covers over 59,000 acres, and is located 57 miles north of Winnipeg via Hwys. 59 and 12. Private cottages, a motor hotel, and camping facilities are available.

Grass River Provincial Park is the ultimate for wilderness camping. It consists of 565,000 acres of roadless terrain. The park is entered from Hwy. 10 at Cranberry Portage or from Provincial Rd. 231 along its southern boundary.

Hecla Provincial Park is only a few hours' drive north of Winnipeg via Hwy. 8 and Provincial Rds. 234 and 233. The park includes the Lake Winnipeg islands of Hecla, Black, Deer, and several smaller islands as well as the lake area in the vicinity. Hecla Island is joined to the mainland by a causeway. Golfing, resort accommodation complete with indoor pool, tennis courts, and convention facilities.

Porcupine Provincial Forest, north of Swan River adjoining the Saskatchewan boundary, is reached by Hwy. 10 and forestry roads. The lakes and rivers provide good sport for fishermen; facilities for picnicking and tenting are available.

Sandilands Provincial Forest is located between the southern boundary of Agassiz Forest and the United States border. Main access is by Hwy. 12 and the Trans-Canada Hwy. E. Picnic sites are situated within the area.

Spruce Woods Provincial Park, thirty miles east of Brandon and between the Trans-Canada Hwy. W. and Hwy. 2, covers 90 square miles. One of the newest provincial parks, it provides modern campground and picnic facilities. This is the eastern segment of the Spruce Woods Provincial Forest, and its 57,000 acres are well wooded with aspen and spruce trees. Spruce Woods Provincial Forest itself is 25 miles east of Brandon between Hwys. 1 and 2. The park and forest may be reached from the communities of Glenboro on Hwy. 2 or through Carberry on the Trans-Canada Hwy. from the north.

Turtle Mountain Provincial Park, one of the smaller provincial parks, covers 47,000 acres of rolling, forested hills and fertile valleys along the International border in the southwest corner of the province. One of its main attractions is the world's largest garden dedicated to peace: the International Peace Garden. The park has a total of 29 lakes.

Whiteshell Provincial Park, a 1,065-square-mile park, comprises the major vacation area of the eastern region. Lakes, rivers, and streams in the area provide ample opportunity for fishing, hunting, camping, and other outdoor activities. The park includes one of Canada's most modern recreational townsite developments at Falcon Lake, with tennis, an 18-hole golf course and a ski resort. Falcon Lake resort is 90 miles east of Winnipeg on the Trans-Canada Hwy. Two other resort areas are on Falcon Lake, a popular spot for waterskiing, sailing, and fishing. The Whiteshell has numerous campgrounds and picnic sites, plus modern accommodation in lodges and motels.

 GARDENS. *The International Peace Gardens,* at the junction of Hwy. 10 and North Dakota 3, cover an area of 2,300 acres in the Turtle Mountains Provincial Park. Dedicated to international peace and goodwill, the formal gardens surround ornamental spillways originating from a series of lakes. The Centennial Pavilion in the garden commemorates Canada's 100th birthday. Named for Errick F. Willis, it was built as a memorial to the former Lieutenant-Governor of Manitoba. A permanent feature of the garden is the nondenominational Chapel of Peace financed by the General Order of the Eastern Star. The Chapel stands astride the international border, overlooking the panels of the formal gardens. No charge for admission to the gardens.

Morden's *Experimental Station* opens its gates each summer during its open house. Tours of the exotic, beautiful and/or agricultural facilities yield botanical oddities and hardy farm plantings.

 FARM VACATIONS AND GUEST RANCHES. Manitoba offers hospitality on more than 50 host farms, most of which accommodate visitors both in winter and summer. Activities range from helping with the chores to just plain relaxing. Many farms offer all the traditional holiday activities of fishing, golfing, swimming and boating, with the additional bonuses of old-fashioned hayrides and country-style barbecues. A vacationer can either "live in" with meals supplied or camp on the property with meals on request. Some host farms prefer children only, senior citizens, convalescents, or adults only, while others accommodate one-day touring groups, trailers, or a family holiday lasting a week or more.

For further information, contact Travel Manitoba, Dept. 6001, 7th Floor, 155 Carlton St., Winnipeg, MB R3C 3H8, or the Manitoba Farm Vacations Association, 525 Kylemore Ave., Winnipeg, MB R3L 1B5 (204–475–6624).

The Hostelling Association of Manitoba offers accommodation in Winnipeg, and Glenboro. To make arrangements, telephone: (204–788–5364). The Bed-and-Breakfast Association also offers hospitality to visitors in members' homes. For information, write the association at 7 Sandale Dr., Winnipeg R2N 1A1 (204–256–6151).

 CHILDREN'S ACTIVITIES. Ride on the *Prairie Dog Central,* hitched on to an old-time steam locomotive. It runs from Winnipeg to Grosse Isle. Kids love the four wooden coaches and the caboose. Adults will enjoy this glimpse of the past. Refreshments and souvenirs aboard.

Take a closer look at Manitoba's wildlife. *Alf Hole Goose Sanctuary,* near **Rennie,** Hwy. 4, for a close range look at Canada geese. *The Delta Marsh* near **Portage La Prairie** is one of the largest and best-known waterfowl staging marshes in North America, and it is closely rivaled by the *Netley Marshes* near **Petersfield. Flin Flon,** where the 25-acre park is home to many species of wildlife. The zoo at **Winnipeg,** one of the world's finest, with more than 100 animal species. Many monkeys. See *Aunt Sally's Farm* there for the young animals. Zoo is open year round; Aunt Sally's Farm open during summer months.

For three to five weeks each summer, beginning in late June, the *strawberries* are ripe for the plucking. U-Pick signs mark the location of farms which allow families to pick their own sweet berries for nominal charge. For further information call: Citizen's Inquiry, 800–282–8060 or 945–3744.

 SUMMER SPORTS. Sports enthusiasts will find every type of summer sport in Manitoba, for both spectators and participants.

Fishing: The 90,000 lakes in the province offer ample opportunity for good sport. There are more than a dozen varieties of gamefish native to Manitoba's waters, including northern pike, walleye, and smallmouth bass.

Hunting: There is an abundance of wildlife ranging from white-tailed deer and elk to black bear and all types of game.

Hiking: The province has many exciting trails to explore. The *Amisk* trail in Whiteshell Provincial Park, one of the more challenging trails, runs through pre-Cambrian country and is bridged over a moss swamp. Those more interested in geology and plantlife should explore the interpretive trails. A printed pamphlet explaining the vegetation and wildlife along the way is available at the start of the trail.

Watersports: Manitoba's rivers and lakes are excellent for canoeing, swimming, sailing, and other watersports. For the sea lovers, the 3-mile stretch at *Grand Beach* is one of the finest sandy beaches in North America.

Golf: Golfers will find numerous, challenging courses in all parts of the province, including *Falcon Beach Golf Course,* and the *Sandy Hook Golf Course, Riding Mountain* and the *Hecla Provincial Course.*

Riding and racing: Horse lovers can either go riding at one of the many fine stables in the province, or head for *Assiniboine Downs,* Winnipeg, for the thoroughbred and harness racing. The *Manitoba Derby* is run mid-July.

 CAMPING OUT. Private and government-operated campgrounds abound throughout the province with facilities for both tents and trailers. There are more than 5,000 private and 5,000 public campsites ranging from simple to fully serviced facilities; some are complete with restaurants, laundromats, stores and other features. For further information about camping facilities, contact Travel Manitoba, Dept. 6001, 7th Floor, 155 Carlton St., Winnipeg, MB R3C 3H8.

 WINTER SPORTS. Every region in the province provides excellent facilities for active participation in winter sports. The number of ski resorts in Manitoba has grown considerably since it was begun by a handful of Winnipeggers 40 years ago. Some of them, with facilities including modern chalets and high powered snow-making equipment, are among the best in Canada. *The Falcon Lake Ski Resort* has always been popular with beginners and intermediate skiers. Located 96 miles east of Winnipeg, the resort offers equipment rentals, a ski shop, and certified ski instruction. In Manitoba's central region, *Birch Ski Resort, Holiday Mountain Ski Resort, Snow Valley Resort,* and *Stony Mountain Ski Park* are favored ski areas. In the west, the major ski centers are *Mount Agassiz, Mount Glenorchy,* and *Mark Valley Ski Resort,* and in Manitoba's north, *Mystery Mountain* and the *Ptarmigan Ski Club* offer a wide range of facilities. (Some of the resorts also have tobogganing, skating, and snowmobile rentals.)

Many of Manitoba's parks are catering to the growing enthusiasm for cross-country skiing, and numerous trails have been developed. In Winnipeg and other centers, ice hockey and wrestling are among the main sports attractions.

HISTORIC SITES. Arnes: *Stefansson Memorial Park* honors the Arctic explorer—one of the first to report to the Canadians on climatic conditions in the Northwest Territories.

Betula Lake: Near Betula Lake in *Whiteshell Provincial Park* are large stone figures arranged on the base rock in the shapes of turtles, snakes, fish, and birds. These ancient mosaics were used by the Ojibwa Indians in ceremonies associated with their Medicine Society.

Emerson: *Fort Dufferin,* 2 mi. N of Emerson. From this fort, in 1874, the newly-organized North West Mounted Police began their historic trek to bring law and order to the western plains. The site is marked by a cairn.

Gardenton: The first Ukrainian Greek Orthodox church to be erected in North America is located 5 mi. E of Hwy. 59. The first Ukrainians on the continent settled here.

Gimli: The first permanent Icelandic settlement was established at *Gimli,* October 1875. The townsite was named for the home of the gods in Norse mythology.

Lockport: *St. Andrew's Church,* Provincial Rd. 410 and River Rd., was built in the early 1800s and is the oldest stone church in western Canada still used for worship.

Morris: The *Morris River,* known as the Scratching River in 1801, was the site of North West and XY companies, fur-trading posts. Settlement began here in 1874, where the trail from Pembina crossed the river.

Pilot Mound: On Hwy. 3, *Old Mound,* is the site of prehistoric burial grounds. Later, it was used as a signal hill by the Assiniboine Indians. It was also a prominent landmark for explorers and settlers traveling through southern Manitoba.

Poplar Point: *Ste. Anne's Church* (1864) on Hwy. 26, is one of the oldest log churches in continuous use in western Canada.

Portage La Prairie: Marked by a cairn, *Fort La Reine* was built by La Verendrye as a base from which he left the rivers and ventured onto the plains, seeking the "white" Indians near what are now Bismark and Mandan, North Dakota.

Selkirk: *Lower Fort Garry* is one of the oldest stone-built fur trading posts in North America. Built in the 1830's by the Hudson's Bay Company, it was once a center for the western fur trade and for exploration to the Northwest Territories. It later became a training base for the Royal Canadian Mounted Police.

Souris: *Souris River Fur Trade Post*—seven of these were built between 1785 and 1832 by the North West, Hudson's Bay and XY companies. A cairn marks the site.

Steinbach: In 1873, eight townships were set aside in the Steinbach vicinity for the exclusive use of *Mennonite* settlers from Russia. More than 50 villages were founded by 1923.

Swan River: From 1787, when the first trading post was built near Swan River, until 1821, the *Swan River Valley* was the scene of intense rivalry and competition between the North West and the Hudson's Bay companies.

Winnipeg Area: *La Barriere,* a half mile south of St. Norbert, Hwy. 75, where the Metis followers of Louis Riel turned back emissaries of William McDougall, first Lieutenant-Governor of Manitoba. On the Trans-Canada Hwy., 13 mi. W of Winnipeg, near Headingly, marks the *Principal Meridian.* The land survey system for all of western Canada started from this point. Both sites are marked by cairns.

 MUSEUMS AND GALLERIES. Austin: *Manitoba Agricultural Museum* depicts pioneer life in the form of a pioneer village complete with machines, tools and household effects.

Brandon: *Brandon Allied Arts Center,* 638 Princess Ave., has yearly programs of changing exhibits, paintings, prints and handicrafts. Lovers of wildlife and conservation will find plenty to enthuse over at the *B. J. Hale Museum of Natural History* in the Arts and Library Building at Brandon University. A special feature is the collection of 400 mounted birds representing 250 species, and the mammal collection that includes northern animals in a setting of ice and snow. Open daily except Sun. and holidays.

Commonwealth Air Training Plan Museum, No. 1 Hangar, McGill Field is dedicated to the retrieval, restoration and display of aircraft and artifacts used in training. The British Commonwealth Air Training Plan has been called "Canada's greatest single contribution to the Allied victory in W.W. II."

Boissevain: *Moncur Gallery of Prehistory* (534–2433) is an exciting new gallery featuring ancient artifacts, text and maps depicting life of the people of Turtle Mountain before agricultural settlement.

Carmen: *Dufferin Historical Museum* in Kings Park contains a wide array of pioneer photos, artifacts and antiques. Located near swimming, golf, picnic and camping facilities.

Churchill: At the *Eskimo Museum* you will see Eskimo artifacts and survival tools in stone, bone, ivory and metal, as well as wildlife exhibits. Open year-round, no charge.

Dauphin: *Fort Dauphin Museum* is a recreation of a fur trade fort including log building, pioneer house and school house dating from 1892.

Dugald: Just 25 min. from downtown Winnipeg, the town has built a permanent home for its famous *Dugald Fashion Collection,* one of the country's most extensive and beautiful costume collections, with clothing dating back to Western Canada's earliest history.

Elkhorn: *Manitoba Automobile Museum* has 80 antique cars, plus pioneer objects.

Gimli: *Gimli Historical Museum* also displays Ukrainian and Icelandic pioneer materials.

Killarney: *J.A. Victor David Museum* features articles of Indian and pioneer life and natural history.

Morden: *Morden and District Museum* offers a varied display of prehistoric fossils and specimens going back as far as 70 million years, Piggot papers, and antique furniture.

Neepawa: *Beautiful Plains* features pioneer and Indian exhibits. Open July to September.

Portage La Prairie: Hundreds of items illustrating Manitoba's history are in the *Fort la Reine Museum and Pioneer Village.* The complex embraces a fort, log home, school, church, and two major display buildings.

St. Georges: *Le Musee St. Georges Museum* is 75 miles NE of Winnipeg off Hwy. 1. It is a bilingual museum filled with antiques and furnishings of early French Canadian settlement in Manitoba.

St. Joseph: *Musee St. Joseph Museum* is 4 miles off Hwy. 75 on No. 201. Bilingual museum of domestic and agricultural material relating to the pioneers of the region. Includes a display building, two historical houses, a school, a blacksmith shop, machine sheds and a general store.

Selkirk: Plenty of history at the *Lower Fort Garry National Historic Park Museum,* once a central provisions and supply depot for the fur trade in Northwest Canada. Built in the 1830's. Restored buildings and contemporary facilities open mid-May to mid-October.

Shilo: *The Royal Regiment of Canadian Artillery Museum,* Canadian Forces Base, portrays the regiment's history with a display of guns, ammunition, uniforms, medals and historical documents. Tours arranged by written request.

Souris: *Hillcrest Museum* is an historic home of unique architecture with furnished period rooms and pioneer material.

Steinbach: A replica of a Mennonite village with historic, completely furnished buildings is located in Steinbach. The *Mennonite Village Museum* includes an original log house, windmill, blacksmith's shop, general store, antiques and manuscripts.

Stonewall: *Stonewall Quarry Park* is set in an abandoned quarry. Limestone formations, towering kilns and varied wildlife are highlighted through displays, trails and guided events.

Swan River: *Swan Valley Museum* houses collections of native and local pioneer materials in five separate buildings.

Virden: *The Pioneer Home Museum of Virden and Districts* is a large brick house depicting life in the Victorian era. Year-round tours by appointment.

Wasagaming: *Riding Mountain National Park Interpretive Centre* interprets the rich and natural history of the park through displays and audio-visual programs. Located in a beautiful log building dating back to the 1930's.

Winkler: *Pembina Threshermen's Museum* shows how it was, with steam threshing equipment in working order and pioneer antiques and artifacts.

 MUSIC. *The Winnipeg Symphony* gives over a dozen concerts in the Centennial Concert Hall between October and May, in addition to an occasional open-air concert in Winnipeg's Assiniboine Park.

The annual *Winnipeg Folk Festival* attracts top folk artists from across the continent who gather at Birds Hill Provincial Natural Park for three days of workshops and entertainment each July.

A sister event, *The Children's Festival,* is held every year in May or June in Kildonan Park. International children's entertainers perform in huge tents for the younger set.

At the *International Peace Gardens,* an annual music camp and workshop is held featuring a round of summer activities including jazz concerts and drama.

 SHOPPING. Major stores in Winnipeg, such as the *Hudson's Bay Co.,* and *Eatons,* offer the vacation shopper everything from the smallest necessities to fine china, British woolens, silverware, and jewelry. Branches of these stores will be found in the *Polo Park Shopping Centre, Kildonan Place, St. Vital, Garden City,* and similar centers throughout Manitoba.

The city and provincial centers have a variety of unusual shops and boutiques. Just north of *The Pas* is an Indian handicraft shop where the visitor can watch Indian women making moccasins, mukluks, jackets, other clothing and jewelry. For that special souvenir, you may find what you are looking for at the *Rock Shop.* Here you can choose from a fine line of costume jewelry made from the rock from a local quarry. Also, you can buy an inexpensive permit to collect your own rock.

Sales tax is six percent in Manitoba.

 LIQUOR LAWS. The legal drinking age in Manitoba is 18. Liquor may be purchased by the bottle or the case from Government Liquor Commission stores and beer from government-approved vendors. Wine and liquor prices have been rising steadily in Manitoba.

 RESTAURANTS. Rural Manitoba offers a wide choice of restaurants ranging from ultra-expensive to moderately-priced with good home-cooked food.

Most of the best restaurants outside Winnipeg are located in hotels and motels. Brandon, the province's second largest city, has an excellent selection of restaurants, as does Portage La Prairie, halfway between Winnipeg and Brandon. There are also a number of first-class eating places catering to tourists in the Whiteshell, Lake Winnipeg and Clear Lake resort areas. Generally, price ranges per person for a meal are: *Expensive,* $25 and up; *Moderate,* $15–$24; *Inexpensive,* under $15.

Most places accept the following major credit cards: American Express, MasterCard and Visa; others may also be honored. Not all establishments accept credit cards, therefore we suggest you call for information.

Southern Manitoba

BRANDON. *Expensive:* **North Hill Inn.** 10th and Braecrest Dr. Phone 727–4455. Dining room sits atop a hill and overlooks the lights of the city. Dancing and entertainment are featured. There is also a lounge and a nine-hole golf course.

Royal Oak Inn. 3130 Victoria Ave. Phone 728–5775. First-class selection of dining, lounge, and café facilities.

Suburban Restaurant, 2604 Victoria Ave. Phone 728–3031. Long established top-grade restaurant offering a varied menu.

Victoria Inn. 3650 Victoria Ave. Phone 725–1532. Features dining room, lounge, and tropical café overlooking the swimming pool.

Moderate: **Kokonas Restaurant.** 1011 Rosser Ave. (727–4395). Very good international cuisine with Greek specialties.

The Keg. 1836 Brandon Ave. (725–4223). Rustic dining room features steak and seafood.

Inexpensive: **Smitty's Restaurant.** Brandon Shopper's Mall, 18th St. Phone 728–0690. Second location in Brandon Gallery (727–4972). Caters to families. Major credit cards accepted.

CLEAR LAKE. *Expensive:* **Elk Horn Ranch Resort Hotel.** Mooswa Dr. Phone 848–2802. Open year-round, featuring fully-licensed dining room and cocktail lounge with wheelchair service.

DAUPHIN. *Inexpensive:* **Dauphin Community Inn.** 104 Main N. Phone 638–4311. Licensed restaurant and beverage room.

King's Hotel. 204 Main N. Phone 638–3620. Light snacks to full course meals in the dining room and adjoining cocktail lounge.

La Verendre Steak House. 26 1st Ave. N.W. Phone 638–5220. Steak and seafood. Elegant dining on a budget.

LAKE WINNIPEG AREA. *Moderate:* **The Golden Falcon Restaurant.** 72 First Ave., Gimli. Phone 642–8868. Features varied menu. Entertainment on weekends in this pretty Lake Winnipeg town.

The Moonlighter. Winnipeg Beach Provincial Park. Phone 389–4605. Fine dining overlooking the lake. Fully Licensed. Reservations accepted.

Inexpensive: **Viking Motor Hotel.** N.W. 7th and Centre, Gimli. Phone 642–5181. Cocktail lounge and dining room facilities.

MINNEDOSA. *Moderate:* **Valley Motor Lodge.** 28 Main N., Phone 867–2741. Fully licensed restaurant adjoining indoor pool and sauna.

PORTAGE LA PRAIRIE. *Expensive:* **Best Western Manitobah Inn.** Highway No. 1 and Yellowquill Trail. Phone 857–9791. A Best Western Hotel with dining room, lounge, enclosed pool and recreation area.

Moderate: **Midtown Motor Inn.** 177 Saskatchewan Ave. W. Phone 857–6881. Good dining facilities in the heart of the downtown district.

Northern Manitoba

FLIN FLON. *Expensive:* **Bakers Narrows Lodge.** Bakers Narrows near Flin Flon. Phone 637–6087. Good accommodation and lodging catering to hunters and fishermen.

Kelsey Trail Motor Inn. No. 10 Highway. Phone 687–7555. Dining and beverage rooms, indoor pool, sauna.

SWAN RIVER. *Moderate:* **Valley Hotel.** 703 Main E. Phone 734–3497. Beverage room and licensed restaurant.

Westwood Inn. Highway 10 N. Phone 734–4548. Restaurant, cocktail lounge, convention facilities, indoor pool.

THE PAS. *Moderate:* **Wescana Inn.** 439 Fischer. Phone 1–800–442–0400. Full dining and beverage facilities in a modern hotel.

THOMPSON. *Expensive:* **Mystery Lake Motor Hotel.** Cree and Selkirk. Phone 778–8331. Licensed dining room, lounge, and beverage room.

Moderate: **Burntwood Motor Hotel.** Selkirk Ave. Phone 677–4551. Licensed dining room and lounge, beer vendor.

Eastern Manitoba

FALCON LAKE. *Expensive:* **Falcon Lake Resort and Club.** Lake Blvd. Phone 349–8400. Open year-round, offers first-class dining and imbibing facilities to summer campers and winter cross-country skiers.

GRAND BEACH. *Moderate:* **Grand Beach Inn.** Grand Beach Rd. Phone 754–2554. Dining and beverage room at popular Lake Winnipeg resort.

LAC DU BONNET. *Inexpensive:* **Lakeview Motor Hotel.** 57 Park N. Phone 345–8661. Beverage room and licensed restaurant on the shore of the Winnipeg River.

PINAWA. *Moderate:* **Pinawa Motor Inn.** Lot 147. Phone 753–2279. Beverage and dining room, licensed and air-conditioned.

PINE FALLS. *Inexpensive:* **Paper Motor Hotel.** Highway 304, St. George. Phone 367–2261. Licensed dining room and cocktail lounge.

SASKATCHEWAN

by
ROGER NEWMAN

Saskatchewan—which joined Canada a scant eighty-two years ago—is a province of contrasts. Vast stretches of prairie farmland, a rugged northern wilderness, and increasingly sophisticated urban communities are all to be found within its 251,700 square miles of territory. Above all, Saskatchewan is Canada's largest producer of grain and is nicknamed "the Wheat Province." This is because 60 percent of the country's wheat, as well as most other major crops, are grown each summer on millions of acres of Saskatchewan farmland.

Centuries ago, long before mankind set foot in the region, Saskatchewan was covered by giant bodies of water. Their sediments form the rich and fertile grain belt that today extends right across the southern half of the province. Geographically, Saskatchewan is in the center of the three prairie provinces bordered by Manitoba on the east, Alberta on the west, the Northwest Territories on the north, and Montana and North Dakota on the south. Roughly the shape of a rectangle, the province extends for 761 miles from north to south and has an average width of 335 miles.

While Saskatchewan is mainly associated with the prairies and grain growing, the terrain is far from flat and barren. The scenic hilly Qu' Appelle Valley runs through part of the southern prairie district. The Cypress Hills, some with an elevation of 3,000 feet above sea level, are in the southwest; while the badlands are in the southeast due south of Regina, the province's capital.

The badlands—a region of sandstone buttes, sharp cliffs, and rough-hewn caves—were part of Butch Cassidy's outlaw trail from Canada

350

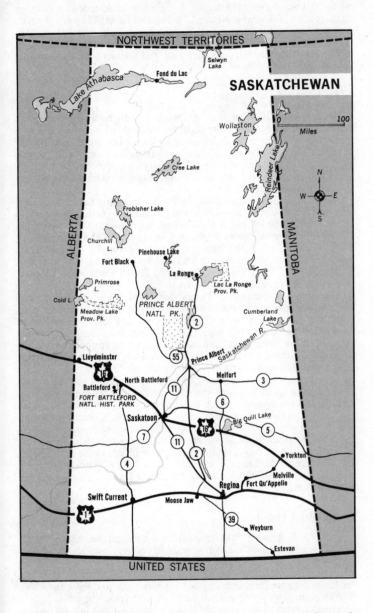

to Mexico. At the turn of the century, the area was a haven for cattle rustlers, horse thieves, and stagecoach robbers because of its forbidding terrain and proximity to the United States border.

Northern Saskatchewan offers another contrast—it is a land of lakes and forests interrupted only by remote fishing camps and tiny settlements. There are more than eighty million acres of wilderness and enough lakes for an angler to fish a different one every day for a century. Fishing, canoeing, camping, and hunting are excellent in the north and good everywhere else. A visitor to Saskatchewan can stop at more than 300 campgrounds, 17 provincial parks, 91 regional parks, and the Prince Albert National Park, a jewel in the northern wilderness. In winter, Saskatchewan also caters to the outdoor enthusiast, with many cross-country ski locations and sixteen sites for downhill schussing.

An Urban Environment

With a population now exceeding one million, Saskatchewan in recent years has become increasingly urbanized, with many rural residents and other newcomers flocking to the eleven cities that dot the province. The two largest, Regina and Saskatoon—each with populations of about 170,000—have a great rivalry and offer the urban attractions and amenities that are to be found in major metropolitan centers in North America.

Regina, the province's capital, is the main training center for Canada's national police force—The Royal Canadian Mounted Police—and is also the home of the Saskatchewan Roughriders, the province's professional football team. Saskatoon is the site of the University of Saskatchewan and is the principal supply center for the province's potash and uranium mining industries. Other cities are Moose Jaw, Prince Albert, Swift Current, Yorkton, North Battleford, Estevan, Weyburn, Lloydminster, and Melville.

The people of Saskatchewan are descended from immigrants who came from the United Kingdom, Germany, the Ukraine, Scandinavian countries, France, the Netherlands, and Poland. There is also a vibrant Native Indian community whose art work and handicrafts are in keen demand at the twenty-five craft fairs that are held annually across the province. Interestingly, Saskatchewan residents have the highest life expectancy of any Canadians—78.64 years for females and 71.13 for males. Perhaps this is because of Saskatchewan's dry climate which lowers humidity and softens the effect of extreme temperatures. July and August are typically beach weather, with temperatures peaking in the high 80s (Fahrenheit). Blue skies and memorable sunsets in summer and sunshine with less than fifty inches of snow in winter characterize the weather. Rain is rare during the hot months, usually coming in the form of brief but dramatic thunderstorms late in the day. There's plenty of sunshine, however, especially in the city of Estevan in southeast Saskatchewan. This is Canada's Sunshine Capital, averaging 2,560 hours a year.

Industrial Might

From the beginning, Saskatchewan's economy has been based on the natural wealth of the land. Agriculture has always been the province's largest industry—accounting as it does for about half of Canada's total grain production. Currently, Saskatchewan farmers are hoping for better times because their industry has been in a slump during the 1980s due to poor growing conditions and low grain prices.

Saskatchewan also has other rich resources—Canada's largest reserves of heavy oil and over half the world's known recoverable reserves of potash. The province's north is the site of uranium mining, pulp and paper production, and commercial fishing and trapping. But like agriculture, these resource industries tend to have their ups and downs, and both oil and potash prices have nosedived in the 1980s because of oversupply on world markets.

To counterbalance cyclical commodity prices, Saskatchewan has developed significant manufacturing, construction, tourist, and service industries. Regina is a city of civil servants who work for the provincial government and almost forty provincially owned corporations that market everything from auto insurance to hydroelectric power. In 1987, it also became the site of Canada's first heavy oil upgrading plant; while Saskatoon is nurturing an expanding high-tech and computer industry that has been spawned by its university.

Tepee Rings and Rock Carvings

The first inhabitants of Saskatchewan, some 20,000 to 30,000 years ago, were Paleo-Indians who crossed from Asia to North America to hunt and forage. When the first white man, Henry Kelsey, arrived almost 300 years ago, he found Saskatchewan occupied by various tribes of Indians—Chippewa in the north, Blackfoot in the central parklands, and Assiniboines in the south. Although actual historical evidence of these tribes is limited to a few tepee rings and rock carvings, their presence is remembered by the lyrical names they gave Saskatchewan rivers, lakes, hills, and settlements. Pick up a map of Saskatchewan and you'll find them—Pasquia Hills, Katepwa, Nipew Lake, Wataman River. In fact, the name Saskatchewan comes from the Cree word "Kisiskatchewan," which means "the river that flows swiftly."

The Fur Adventure

On the heels of the explorers came fur traders in search of both fur and adventure. Competition was fierce, and to protect their assets, the fur trading companies were forced to establish trading posts inland. The first post built in Saskatchewan was Cumberland House in 1774 by Samuel Hearne for the Hudson's Bay Company. The North West Company was not far behind, however, and as the fur trade flourished, more forts were established by the two rival companies, usually a short distance from each other and in direct competition. Finally, in 1821, the rivals merged under the name of the Hudson's Bay Company and held a monopoly on the fur trade until the 1870s when it was abandoned for the more lucrative agriculture.

The original fur-trading posts are the sites of many of Saskatchewan's present-day cities—and their overland routes to new homesteads have become the province's highways.

Provincial Status

The first permanent settlers were Métis, of mixed Indian and European blood, from Manitoba's Red River Valley. However, in 1872, when the Canadian Government offered free land to all who wanted it, a flood of settlers from all over the world began to move into the empty plains. The construction of the Canadian Pacific Railway and the establishment of the North West Mounted Police, forerunner of the Royal Canadian Mounted Police, brought even more newcomers. Settlements were formed, local governments set up, and, in 1905, Saskatchewan and its 250,000 people became a Canadian province. The first Saskatchewan legislature was opened in Regina on March 29, 1906.

By 1910, waves of colonists were arriving, attracted by free or cheap homesteads and the province's rich agricultural land. There was an era of relative prosperity until the 1930s when the Great Depression and a series of crop failures hit Saskatchewan, forcing thousands of farm families off the land and leaving them destitute. This is still remembered as the "Dirty Thirties" or the "Dust Bowl" era in the province.

The hardships of those times prompted Saskatchewan voters to elect North America's first Socialist government in the 1940s, and to maintain it in office—with a single break—until 1982.

Since 1982, the province has had a Conservative government led by Premier Grant Devine, a University of Saskatchewan agricultural economics professor. Devine won a second four-year term in 1986 but the Socialists, known as the New Democratic Party, increased their representation in the Legislature and now constitute an effective opposition.

The Last Canadian Conflict

Any historical sketch of Saskatchewan would be incomplete without mention of the famous Riel Rebellion. The seeds of this rebellion were sown in Manitoba's Red River Valley in 1812 when the Métis living there learned that the land did not necessarily belong to the men born and living on it. More and more settlers arrived and, in 1869, when surveyors ran lines across Métis strip farms, the Metis rebelled and formed a provisional government under Louis Riel.

The Canadian government moved quickly, making Manitoba a province and setting aside 1,400,000 acres for Métis settlement. Riel was exiled, and when the government offered scrip—entitling each holder to 240 acres of land—the leaderless Métis, not understanding its value, failed to collect or sold the land for a fraction of its worth. Further demoralized by the loss of freighting jobs due to the cessation of steamboat operations, the Métis headed for the South Saskatchewan River Valley in Saskatchewan. They survived there for almost fifteen years on mediocre farmland. They petitioned the government for land rights but were ignored, and finally, in 1884, they sent for Louis Riel. Riel's moderate reform program garnered no sympathy from Ottawa, and so, knowing of an impending solar eclipse, he told the Métis and Indians that if God were on their side, He would blot out the sun on March 16. Of course, the divine sign occurred, and three days later Riel formed a provisional government with Gabriel Dumont as his commander-in-chief. The first clash occurred at Duck Lake on March 26, 1885, between a Métis Indian band and a 100-member force of police and volunteers. Militia units were organized in Ontario and Québec, and 850 men led by Major General Frederick Middleton went west by Canadian Pacific Railway. With several impressive victories to his credit, Dumont wanted to harass Middleton's forces, but Riel convinced him to stand and defend Batoche.

Middleton and his main force arrived at Batoche on May 8, and for three days the Métis Indians held the edge in the battle. On the fourth day, Middleton's troops attacked, using the new multibarreled Gatling gun, and in two hours Batoche was taken. The Métis' attacks against the Gatling gun with muzzle-loaders using nails and gravel as ammunition were hopeless. Riel escaped but surrendered a few days later. He was tried for treason and hanged at Regina. Dumont fled to the United States, where he joined Buffalo Bill's Wild West Show. He returned to Batoche after being granted amnesty and died there in 1906.

The Riel Rebellion was the last armed revolt in Canada. Batoche is a national historic site and underwent a facelift for the rebellion's 100th anniversary.

EXPLORING REGINA

Although situated on the treeless prairie, Regina is full of trees. The

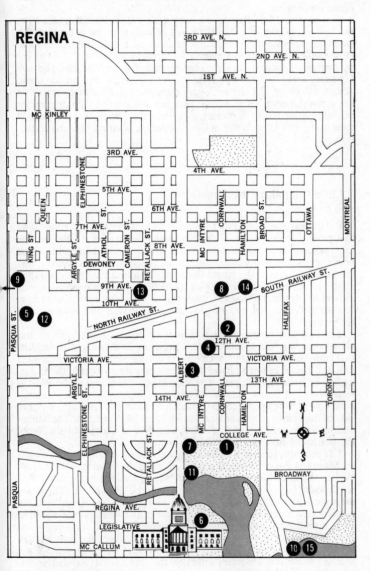

Regina—Points of Interest
1) Art Gallery
2) City Hall
3) Court House
4) Dunlop Art Gallery
5) Exhibition Auditorium
6) Legislative Buildings
7) Museum of Natural History
8) Post Office
9) RCMP College
10) Saskatchewan Center of the Arts
11) Speakers Corner
12) Agridome (Regina Pats)
13) Taylor Field (Sask. Roughriders)
14) Union Station
15) Wild Bird Sanctuary

city's heart is a 2,500-acre park called Wascana Centre, the Indian name for Regina.

Founded in 1882, Regina was originally called Pile of Bones from the Indian practice of piling the bones of buffalo in the belief that this would ensure that they would always come back to be hunted for food. It was officially renamed Regina (the formal Latin title of the Queen) by Princess Louise in honor of her mother, Queen Victoria. The surrounding area is world-famous for the production of high-quality bread wheat. However, the city no longer depends to such a large extent on the grain industry; its economic base has widened to include a major oil refinery and manufacturing establishments, including the largest steel mill (IPSCO) in Western Canada, and agriculture-related production plants.

Little Chapel on the Square

Regina has always been in the midst of Canadian history. From 1882 to 1905 it was the capital of the Northwest Territories. In 1903 it was incorporated as a city, and two years later became the capital of the newly formed Province of Saskatchewan. Also during this period it was the headquarters for the Royal Canadian Mounted Police, known then as the Northwest Mounted Police. In 1920 the force's head office was moved to Ottawa, but Regina continued as a training center, and today 1,000 recruits a year are taught law enforcement and investigation techniques.

The R.C.M.P. depot division contains barracks, sport facilities and classrooms, a scientific laboratory, a museum, and a chapel. This "Little Chapel on the Square" is well worth a visit. Built in 1883 as a mess hall and converted to a chapel fourteen years later, it gives the visitor a glimpse back into the past. The stained glass windows depict Northwest Mounted Police members—one sounding reveille; one standing, head bowed, rifle upside down in mourning position. The flags on either side of the chapel flew over Fort Walsh from 1875 to 1880. The baptismal font is in memory of a Mountie who died at Cutknife Hill, one of the battles of the Riel Rebellion.

The museum furnishes a chronological history of the Royal Canadian Mounted Police. There is a uniform worn by Superintendent J. M. Walsh, the man who negotiated with Sitting Bull when the Sioux fled to Canada following the Battle of the Little Big Horn. There are displays depicting the hunt for "the mad trapper of Rat River" and the crucifix that Louis Riel, the Métis leader of the Northwest Rebellion, carried to the hanging scaffold on November 6, 1885.

In Barracks Square a monument commemorates the first voyage through the Northwest Passage by the R.C.M.P. patrol boat *St. Roch,* a tablet honoring Mounties killed in the line of duty, and 2 sevenpounder muzzle-loading cannons dating back to 1808. Beyond the square is a cemetery almost as old as the force.

History buffs visiting Regina in July and August can often see a reenactment of Louis Riel's trial for treason, in Saskatchewan House, once the residence of lieutenant governors. A life-size statue of Riel by John Nugent may be seen near the Legislative Buildings in Wascana Centre.

You might also be drawn to IPSCO Zoo, a short distance north of Regina, and if you are a football enthusiast, Regina's Taylor Field is the home of the Saskatchewan Roughriders of the Canadian Football League.

A Unique Agribition

If you enjoy getting close to the land, don't miss the Canadian Western Agribition. It is held in Regina in late fall every year and, besides the traditional livestock shows and sales, features a "Mexabition" of equipment, inventions, gadgets, house and garden amenities and products, and do-it-yourself ideas, to mention a few. A championship rodeo is also held, and if you miss this rodeo, visit Saskatchewan in August when Buffalo Days are held in Regina, a pioneer celebration with ten days of horse races, band concerts, midway and grandstand entertainment.

Parks and Museums

A visit to Regina would not be complete without exploring the parks within the city: Wascana Park, in the southern portion of the city situated on the banks of Wascana Lake (formed by damming Wascana Creek); Victoria Park in the center of the city, where a monument commemorates the inauguration ceremony for the Province of Saskatchewan on September 4, 1905; and King's Park, which has a golf course and is located a short distance out of the city proper.

Wascana Park, containing over 2,500 acres, has an impressive list of things to see and do. Here rests Diefenbaker Homestead, the boyhood home of John G. Diefenbaker, Canada's thirteenth prime minister; the Legislative Buildings, built between 1908 and 1912 of Tyndall stone and some 34 kinds of marble, the Saskatchewan Archives with memorabilia of the early history of the province and the Northwest Territories; the Saskatchewan Center of Arts for live-theatergoers. Also picnic and barbecue areas, band shells, swimming and boating facilities, and a bird sanctuary on Willow Island in Lake Wascana which can be reached by ferry from Wascana Park. The Museum of Natural History is dedicated to the pioneers of the Province. Graphic displays and habitat groups show Saskatchewan's varied landscape, plant and wildlife.

A Trip to History

An interesting side trip out of the confines of Regina itself can be taken to Last Mountain House Historical Park simply by driving on Highways 11 and 20 five miles past Craven, a distance of 26 miles. Here you can see the house built by Issac Cowie in 1869, as well as the men's house, ice cellar, and other buildings.

PRACTICAL INFORMATION FOR REGINA

HOW TO GET THERE. By air: *Air Canada, Pacific Western,* and *Norcanair* service Regina.

By car: Access to Regina from eastern and western Canada is on the Yellowhead and Trans-Canada Hwys. From the United States Hwys. 6, 47, and 39 provide access.

By bus: *STC* and *Greyhound* serve Regina.

By train: *Via Rail* through Regina on an east/west axis and through the more scenic route via Saskatoon on an east/west axis.

ACCOMMODATIONS. Based on double-occupancy, without meals, price categories are as follows: *Expensive,* $60 to $130; *Moderate,* $40–60; *Inexpensive,* under $40.

Most places accept the following major credit cards: American Express, MasterCard and Visa; others may also be honored. Not all establishments accept credit cards, therefore we suggest you call for information.

Expensive

Chelton Inn. 11th Ave. and Rose St., Regina, SK S4P 0J2 (306–569–4600). Extra-large rooms, fully licensed restaurant, refrigerators and bar sinks in each room.

Hotel Saskatchewan. Victoria Ave. and Scarth St., Regina, SK S4P 0S3 (306–522–7691). Old atmosphere, restaurant and dining room, lounge, entertainment.

Regina Inn. Victoria Ave. and Broad St., Regina, SK S4P 1Y2 (306–525–6767). Restaurant and dining room, lounge, entertainment, confectionery.

Sheraton Centre. Broad and Victoria., Regina, SK S4P 0R1 (306–569–1666). Lounge, dining room, indoor resort complex and meeting rooms.

Moderate

Imperial 400 Motel. 4255 Albert St., Regina, SK S4S 3R6 (306–584–8800). Indoor pool, whirlpool, sauna, dining room and lounge.

Landmark Inn. 4150 Albert St., Regina, SK S4S 3R6 (306–586–5363 or 800–667–8191). Two restaurants; extra-large rooms.

Vagabond Motor Inn. 4177 Albert St., Regina, SK S4S 3R6 (306–586–3443). Beverage and cocktail rooms, dining room, entertainment, pets permitted.

Westwater Inn. Victoria Ave. and Broad St., Regina, SK S4P 0P9 (306–757–0663). Dining room, coffee shop, cocktail lounge with entertainment.

Inexpensive

Plains Motor Hotel. 1965 Albert St., Regina, SK S4P 2T5 (306–757–8661). Beverage and dining rooms.

Prairie Inn Motel. 1020 Albert St., Regina, SK S4R 2PH (306–525–3535). Modern rooms, restaurant.

Relax Inn. 1110 Victoria Ave. E., Regina, SK S4P 0N7 (306–565–0455 or 800–661–9563). 190 modern rooms, limited food service.

HOW TO GET AROUND. Maps of bus routes are available from the *Transit Department,* and tours by *Prairie City Tour Guides Ltd.* (949–5727) are also regularly scheduled. Regina also offers commercial taxi services. *Saskatchewan Transportation* offers regular service to nearly every place in the province.

TOURIST INFORMATION. *Tourism Saskatchewan,* a branch of the Department of Tourism and Small Business, is located at 2103 11th Ave., Regina, S4P 3V7. The *Regina Chamber of Commerce* at 2145 Albert St. will also provide information.

TOURS. Sightseeing and industrial tours are available in Regina. Ask *Tourism Saskatchewan* (306–787–2300 or 800–667–7191) for further information. Among the 28 auto tours listed by *Tourism Saskatchewan,* several include Regina. Bus tours are scheduled daily during June-September. Custom group tours and special-interest tours may also be arranged. *Saskatchewan Transportation* (306–787–3340), the province's largest bus company, offers a number of tours.

CITY PARKS. *Wascana Centre,* some 2,500 acres of parkland in southern Regina, has an impressive list of things to do and see—picnic and barbecue areas, band shells, swimming and boating facilities in Wascana Lake, a bird sanctuary on Willow Island. Within the Centre's boundaries are many features significant in the past, present and future of Saskatchewan. The seat of the provincial government, in the stately Legislative Building, is set in 167 acres of government grounds, the largest in the world. The University of Regina is located on a 330-acre site in the center. There are also a number of historical sites located in this park area—bus tours are available. Information on the Centre may be obtained on site at the Information Guide office.

Victoria Park: a small daytime park for relaxing and taking walks into the heart of downtown.

SPORTS. Regina is home of the *Saskatchewan Roughriders* of the Canadian Football League. Their games are held at Taylor Field. In the winter the *Regina Pats Junior A* team plays a full schedule of games at the Agridome.

HISTORIC SITES. *Little Chapel on the Square*—located at R.C.M.P. depot, originally a mess hall converted to a chapel—has been preserved to give the visitor a glimpse of history. Also on the depot grounds can be found *Barracks Square* with a monument commemorating the maiden voyage through the Northwest Passage (by R.C.M.P. vessel *St. Roch*). Tours are conducted.

In Wascana Centre the *Diefenbaker Homestead,* boyhood home of Canada's thirteenth Prime Minister. This three-room frame house, built in 1906, was moved from Borden, Saskatchewan, in 1967. Open from May to September.

LIBRARIES. The Regina Public Library has branches conveniently located throughout the city. Films, discussion groups and lectures are regularly scheduled at the Central Library, 2311 12th Ave.

MUSEUMS AND GALLERIES. Regina is an interesting place for museums and art galleries. **Museums.** *The Museum of Natural History,* located on Albert St. and College Ave., built in 1955, is dedicated to the pioneers of Saskatchewan. Open all year. *The R.C.M.P. Museum,* located at depot, provides history of R.C.M.P. Open from June to Sept. *Government House,* 4607 Dewdney Ave., a former residence of the province's Lieutenant-Governors, has rooms restored to turn-of-the-century elegance. Open year-round. Also of interest are the *Plains Historical Museum,* 1801 Scarth St., and the *Saskatchewan Sports Hall of Fame,* 2205 Victoria Ave.

Galleries. *Dunlop Art Gallery,* located in the Regina Public Library, 12th Ave. and Lorne St., has displays of paintings, sculptures, and handicrafts by local artists. *The Norman Mackenzie Art Gallery,* located on the University campus, College Ave. at Scarth St., has collections of English, American, and Canadian painters, as well as early Egyptian, Chinese, and Greek sculpture. *Gallery on the Roof,* 13th Floor, Sask. Power Bldg., 2025 Victoria Ave., features the work of Saskatchewan artists and provides a panoramic view of Regina.

PERFORMING ARTS. The *Regina Symphony Orchestra* regularly performs at the Saskatchewan Centre of the Arts, Regina's cultural and convention center. Ballet, opera, and visiting variety artists also appear regularly at the Centre. The *Globe Theatre's Adult Company* is the province's first professional drama group, performing in the 200-seat Globe Theatre as well as in other centers. *Regina Modern Dance Works* performs contemporary works in their theater on Osler St.

SHOPPING. Several centers, including the *Golden Mile* Plaza on Albert St. S., comprised of 36 stores, and the *Sherwood Plaza* in the northwest district, offer visitors a wide selection of goods from which to choose, both imported and locally handcrafted. New *Cornwall Centre* in downtown area features *Eatons, Sears,* and two-floor enclosed mall with close to 100 stores.

 DINING OUT. Restaurant price categories are for hors d'oeuvres or soup, entrée and dessert. Not included are drinks, tax, and tips. Restaurants are classed as: *Deluxe,* $40 and up; *Expensive,* $30–40; *Moderate,* $20–$30; *Inexpensive,* under $20.

Most places accept the following major credit cards: American Express, MasterCard and Visa; others may also be honored. Not all establishments accept credit cards, therefore we suggest you call for information.

Expensive

C.C. Lloyd's. 1907 11th Ave. (569–4650). Casually elegant dining in a 1930s New York atmosphere.

Celebrations Restaurant. 669 Albert St. (358–7092). Brand new restaurant featuring music-hall entertainment.

The Diplomat Steak House. 2032 Broad St. (359–3366). The "newest" place to go for luxury dining. Steak and seafood.

Hotel Saskatchewan. Victoria and Scarth (522–7691). Good evening atmosphere, where a variety of hors d'oeuvres, soups, salads, and desserts complement the main entrée. Entertainment is featured on the weekends.

Regina Inn Restaurants. Broad and Victoria (757–0663). Be prepared to choose from a large selection of foods, décor, and price ranges.

Moderate

The Brother's Theatre Restaurant. 1867 Hamilton St. (569–4600). Features live dinner music and European and Chinese cuisine.

Cellar Dining Room. Sheraton Centre, 1818 Victoria Ave. (569–1666). Fully licensed, modern. Also try *Coffee Plaza,* a coffee shop in the same hotel.

The Copper Kettle. 1953 Scarth St. (525–3544). Open for lunch and evening dining. Lunchtime features pizza and smoked meats. Evening dining, in the steakhouse, features steak and lobster and specialty salads. It is renovated and friendly service is notable.

Keg Restaurants. Two locations at Albert St. (585–1717) and Hamilton St. (352–9691). A broad selection of seafood and beef cuts in a friendly "party" atmosphere.

Landmark Inn. 4150 Albert St. (586–5363). *Coco's* dining room has a relaxed atmosphere with an excellent assortment of cuisine.

Pirate's Cove. 11th St. near Albert (359–0880). Caters to lovers of seafood.

Tumbler's Bar and Restaurant. Whitmore Park Mall (586–1920). Good food and drink in the suburbs.

Inexpensive

B-Bop Café. 1834 Scarth St. (352–3991). Trendies and Yuppies gather at this club and restaurant.

Bartleby's Dining Emporium. 1920 Broad St. (565–0040). Antique décor and tops in atmosphere. No reservations necessary.

Bonzinni's. Albert St. at Gordon Rd. (586–3553). Great Italian food, especially the pasta.

Elephant and Castle Restaurant. 2102 11th Ave., Cornwall Centre (757–4405). Place to rest your feet in a major shopping center.

Geno's. 1515 Albert St. (949–5455) and in the Gordon Road Shopping Centre (585–0366). Two locations with fine Italian food.

Plains Flag Inn. 1965 Albert St. (757–8661). Dining room features noon smorgasbord, evening buffet, and full menu.

NIGHTCLUBS AND BARS. For an evening on the town Regina offers enough variety to accommodate everyone's taste, with a dozen night spots within walking distance of Broad and Victoria, the city's busiest section. *W.H. Shooters* on Broad St. (525–3525) draws western music lovers; *The Brother's Theatre Restaurant,* 1867 Hamilton St. (522–1659), features the Regina Jazz Society every second Friday night; *The French Quarter* in the Sheraton Centre, Broad St. and Victoria Ave. (569–1666) presents live brassy bands, and *The Manhattan,* 2300 Dewdney Ave. (359–7771), is a flashy, dressy nightclub featuring top-40 hits.

EXPLORING SASKATOON

Saskatoon, the "City of Bridges," with six bridges spanning the South Saskatchewan River, with a population of approximately 170,000 ranks in size with Regina and is a university center. It began in 1883 as a temperance colony . . . twenty years later its population was only 113 people. It would appear the early pioneers were not for abstinence!

Since Saskatoon's development has been mainly in the twentieth century, town planning has ensured wide, tree-lined streets and industrial development on the fringe. Saskatoon marks the ending of the prairie and the beginning of northern Saskatchewan's parklands.

Here, as in the Regina area, wheat production is an important activity; a 5.5-million-bushel grain elevator located in Saskatoon attests to this. It is a major distribution point, has a good industrial sector including foundries, machine shops, woodworking plants, sheet metal works, tanneries, creameries, potash-uranium, and petroleum-related industries, and one of the West's major meat-packing plants.

Parks, Museums, and Art Galleries

If you are interested in Saskatchewan history and Canadian artists, Saskatoon is a must on your stopping list. Memorial Art Gallery, just off 11th Street, has over 50 paintings on display by Canadian artists, including Homer Watson, John William Beatty, and James Henderson. This gallery is a war memorial.

Farther northeast, along the west bank of the South Saskatchewan River, is the Mendel Art Gallery and Conservatory. Sculptures, flowers, and a collection of works by Canadian artists, including Group of Seven artists, are displayed here.

Directly across the river from the Mendel Gallery is the University of Saskatchewan, founded in 1907, which now has an annual enrollment of about 20,000 students. A number of interesting displays are open to the public here: Marquis Hall Art Gallery; W. P. Herbarium, containing plants, mosses, liverworts, and lichens; Victoria School—Saskatoon's first school, built in 1887, containing replicas of original furniture and equipment. The university is also the site of the John G. Diefenbaker Centre, which displays mementos of the career of the Saskatchewan-based former Canadian Prime Minister.

Museums depicting Ukrainian history, crafts, and costumes as well as one of Canada's largest collections of antique automobiles and agricultural machinery, furniture, and artifacts are located in Saskatoon. The Western Development Museum has recreated a street with buildings, implements, and cars indicative of communities found in Saskatchewan in 1910. It is known as Main Street, Boom Town, Saskatchewan.

Saskatoon has its own symphony orchestra which performs regularly. Moreover, the city's Centennial Auditorium frequently offers Broadway plays, opera and Grand Ole Opry.

There are some 17 parks for the summer visitor, including Diefenbaker Park, Victoria Park, Gordon Howe Park Complex, and Lief Ericksen Park. All offer recreational facilities in close proximity to the South Saskatchewan River. There are also a number of golf clubs within the city.

Pioneer Days—And All the Fun!

Every July, for seven days, the city of Saskatoon celebrates Pioneer Days in conjunction with the Saskatoon Exhibition, known as the biggest pioneer show in North America. There are history pageants, antique farm equipment demonstrations, antique car displays, threshing competitions, harness racing, and livestock and agriculture shows. This is all in addition to the midway and grandstand of the exposition.

A Man-Made Mountain?

Yes! truly, made by man—300 feet high and 700 feet at the base. This is Blackstrap Mountain, a ski resort 25 miles south of Saskatoon and well worth a visit. It was built in 1971 for the Canadian Winter Games, and its main ski run is 1,400 feet long.

PRACTICAL INFORMATION FOR SASKATOON

HOW TO GET THERE. By Plane. *Air Canada, Norcanair,* and *Pacific Western* service Saskatoon.

By Car. Access via the Yellowhead Hwy. and Trans-Canada Hwy. from the east and west and Hwy. 6 and 11 from the south.

By Train. *Via Rail* has service from Regina into Saskatoon, and has recently reestablished Trans-Canada east-west service through Saskatoon.

By Bus. *STC* and *Greyhound* serve Saskatoon.

ACCOMMODATIONS. Based on double occupancy, price categories are as follows: *Expensive,* $50 and up; *Moderate,* $40–50; *Inexpensive,* under $40.

Most places accept major credit cards; however, not all establishments accept credit cards, therefore we suggest you call for information.

Expensive

Bessborough Hotel. 601 Spadina Crescent, Saskatoon, SK S7K 3G8 (306–244–5521). Dining room, coffeeshop and lounge. Banquet facilities and swimming pool.

Holiday Inn. 90 22nd St. E., Saskatton, SK S7K 3X6 (306–244–2311). Restaurant and dining room, lounge, entertainment, indoor pool, and sauna.

Imperial "400" Motel. 610 Idylwyld Dr. N., Saskatoon, SK S7L 9Z9 (306–244–2901). Restaurant and dining room, lounge, indoor pool, sauna, and whirlpool. Limousine service from the airport.

Ramada Renaissance. 405 20th St. E., Saskatoon, SK S7K 6X6 (306–665–3322). Saskatoon's newest hotel brings a touch of international elegance. It features dining, entertainment, and a gigantic water slide.

Saskatoon Inn. 2002 Airport Dr., Saskatoon, SK S74 6M4 (306–242–1440). All facilities for luxury living, including queen-size beds. Handy to airport.

Sheraton-Cavalier Motor Inn. 612 Spadina Crescent, Saskatoon, SK S7K 3G9 (306–652–6770). Restaurant and dining room, lounge, entertainment. Swimming pool, sauna.

Moderate

Park Town Motor Hotel. 924 Spadina Crescent, Saskatoon, SK S7K 3P7 (306–244–5564). Dining room, lounge, entertainment.

TraveLodge. 106 Circle Drive W., Saskatoon, SK S71 4L6 (306–242–8881 or 800–255–3050). Restaurant and dining room, lounge; also motel units available.

Inexpensive

King George Motor Hotel. 157 2nd Ave. N., Saskatoon, SK S7K 2A9 (306–244–6133). Restaurant and dining room, lounge, and entertainment.

Skybird Motel. 16 33rd St. E., Saskatoon, SK S7K OR6 (306–244–4055). 19 units and 11 light housekeeping; pets allowed.

Yellowhead Motor Inn. 1715 Idylwyld Dr., N., Saskatoon, SK S7L 1B4 (306–244–5552). Saskatoon's newest budget motor inn; free local phone calls.

HOW TO GET AROUND. By Bus: The *Saskatoon Transportation Co.* (STC) and *Sightseeing Tours* provide adequate access to the city proper.

TOURIST INFORMATION. *Tourism Saskatchewan* in Regina at 2103 11th Ave. has up-to-date information. The *Saskatoon Board of Trade* will also provide information.

TOURS. Auto tours of Saskatoon and the surrounding area have been mapped by *Tourism Saskatchewan.* Organized bus tours, group, and special-interest tours are also available. *Northcote River Cruises* offers cruises on the Saskatchewan River, boarding from behind the bandstand south of the Bessborough Hotel. Adults, $5.00; children, $2.00.

SPECIAL INTEREST TOUR. On the university campus a collection of Saskatchewan and Arctic plants can be found at the W. P. Herbarium.

PARKS. Saskatoon has a number of parks along the South Saskatchewan River system. Most have picnic facilities, benches to relax on, golf courses, and pools. *Forestry Farm Park,* located northeast of the city, has over 300 animals.

SPECTATOR SPORTS. For sports fans, the *Saskatoon Junior Blades* of the Western Hockey League and the University of Saskatchewan football and hockey teams play regularly during their respective seasons.

HISTORIC SITES. *Barr Colony Campsite:* a plaque marks the campsite of 1,500 colonists en route to Lloydminster led by Rev. Isaac M. Barr. *The Stone Victoria School,* built in 1887 as Saskatoon's first school, is located on the University campus.

MUSEUMS AND GALLERIES. Galleries. *Mendel Art Gallery and Conservatory* features a permanent display of Canadian and European artwork set amidst flower arrangements. Open year-round. *The Art Gallery* across from city hall and the *St. Thomas More Gallery* on the University of Saskatchewan campus offer paintings by regional artists. The *Photographers' Gallery,* also with monthly exhibit changes, features Canadian and local work. Open September to April.

Museums. *Museum of Anthropology and Archeology,* located in Arts Building on University campus, has displays showing man's evolution, prehistoric man in Saskatchewan, and settlement of the West. *Ukrainian Arts and Crafts Museum,* located in the Mohyla Institute, exhibits costumes, tapestries, and handicrafts of Ukrainian people. *Western Development Museum,* located close to Exhibition Grounds at 2610 Lorne Ave. S., displays the kind of community that grew up throughout Saskatchewan in pioneer days. One of largest collections of agricultural machinery and antique autos.

THEATER. The 25th Street House and *Persephone,* Saskatoon's professional theater companies, each present a season of main stage productions each winter. Drama productions are also presented regularly at the University of Saskatchewan.

SHOPPING. A variety of shopping opportunities are open to visitors to Saskatoon. *The Confederation Park Plaza* has 34 stores and the *Midtown Plaza* has a similar number. Saskatoon also has a good selection of handicraft and specialty shops.

DINING OUT. Restaurant price categories are for hors d'oeuvres or soup, entrée, and dessert. Not included are drinks, tax, and tips. *Deluxe,* $40 and up; *Expensive,* $30 and up; *Moderate,* $20–30; *Inexpensive,* under $30.

Most places accept the following major credit cards: American Express, MasterCard and Visa; others may also be honored. Not all establishments accept credit cards, therefore we suggest you call for information.

Expensive

The Bessborough. 601 Spadina Crescent (244–5521). Diversified dining in the *Samurai* Japanese restaurant, the *Treetops* tearoom, and the *Aerial's Cove* for evening dinner. Fresh seafood flown in from the Maritimes is a feature of the menu.

Lucci's. 3rd Ave. (653–0188). French and European dishes; entertainment.

Smugglers. 416 21st St. E. (665–0012). Menu features prime rib and salad bar in a nautical atmosphere.

Villy's. Sasktoon Square Penthouse (244–0955). Extensive menu in comfortable surroundings and a magnificent view of the city and river.

Moderate

Artful Dodger. 119 4th Ave. S. (653–2577). Old English pub décor with a menu to match.

Blue Diamonds. 1428 22nd St. W. (652–8044). Family restaurant featuring steak, seafood, pasta, Greek dishes, and pizza.

Cave. 8th St. (374–5090). Popular restaurant with good pizza.

Cousin Nik's. 1100 Grosvenor (374–2020). Greek cuisine in a Mediterranean decor.

Earl's. 2nd Ave. (664–4060). Gourmet burgers.

Saskatoon TraveLodge. 106 Circle Dr. (242–8881). West. Located just off the main highway a few minutes from the airport and downtown Saskatoon. The fully licensed *Captain's Table* dining room features specialties and a children's menu.

Shaheen's Curry. 135 20th St. W. (244–8807). Award-winning Indian Restaurant.

Inexpensive

Imperial 400 Motel. 610 Idylwyld Dr. N. (244–7722). Rich Mediterranean décor of the motel dining room creates the setting for family dining.

NIGHTCLUBS AND BARS. *Das Clubbers,* 303 Pacific Ave. (652–5512), and *Sliders,* 301 1st Ave. N. (664–1900), are two of Saskatoon's hot spots. Live entertainment is featured at *Lorenzo's* in the Sheraton-Cavalier, *Club Soda* in the Capri Hotel, and at *Cousin Nik's* (8th St.; 374–2020) and *The Artful Dodger* (119 Fourth Ave. S.; 653–2577). *Texas T.,* 8th Ave. E. (373–8080), is popular with the country music set.

EXPLORING SASKATCHEWAN

Are you looking for an interesting and different vacation, especially for a family? You'll find it in Saskatchewan, on one of the many vacation farms. All you need are your old clothes, a camera, and an "I'm willing to try anything" attitude.

The Saskatchewan Farm Vacations Association has a list of 30 farm families willing to share and show you their farm. You will need reservations. Don't be afraid of getting lost on country roads—once in the province there are information centers to help you.

The whole family—including the children—will be able to help with the chores—gather eggs, feed the chickens, care for the small farm animals—and take in some of the surrounding scenery and fresh air. Have you ever smelled fresh mowed hay or watched a prairie sunset? You can on a Saskatchewan farm.

Another unique Saskatchewan vacation idea is a northern canoe or fishing trip. Water accounts for one-eighth of the province's area and the greater part of this water lies in the sparsely-populated northern half. If you're planning a canoe trip, be prepared to meet a varied wilderness environment. The country is forested, the water bodies vary from rock-bound lakes to tea-colored sloughs, shallow marshlands, and boiling rapids. Numerous islands dot the lakes, and an abundance of wildlife—deer, bear, moose, loons, grebes, ducks, muskrat, beaver, mink, and otter—inhabit the area. Even the rare bald eagle can be observed.

While canoeing, it is quite likely you will meet or see native Indians, as many Crees who live in frontier settlements and on reserves fish during the summer. Most speak some English, and they will certainly provide information.

Some 56 canoe trips have been mapped out giving starting and finishing points, number of portages, length of trip in days and miles, and features to note along the way. Detailed information is available from Saskatchewan Tourism or individual outfitters. Seven of these adventures are for canoeists not ready to tackle more difficult routes. All but two have starting points which can be reached by road; these two require fly-in by chartered aircraft.

Canoe trips are of two basic types: the loop, which returns the traveler to his starting point, and the circuit, which does not finish at its origin.

Angling is a major attraction to many canoeists. Northern waters abound with pike, pickerel, and perch, and farther north, with grayling and lake trout. However, if you are not a canoeist, there are some 200 drive-in and fly-in fishing camps. Arrangements for accommodations and transportation can be made by your travel agent or airline. Of course, you will need a license and a regulation guide, and these can be obtained from the fishing camp, sporting goods stores, or Saskatchewan Tourism.

Touring

There are a number of fascinating trips to take in Saskatchewan by vehicle, planned or otherwise. By planned, we mean that the Saskatchewan government has come up with 28 planned auto tours through the southern prairies, the central parklands, the wilderness north, as well as city tours of Regina and Saskatoon. The tours include vacation farms, industrial tours, museums, geological and historical attractions, and parks. A complete list of these tours can be found under the section *Practical Information for Saskatchewan,* but let's take one out of Regina, the province's capital: on Highway 10, White City at Mile 8 is the location of Dad's Cookies—stop and take a look. At Mile 16 Balgonie, a collection of old-time tractors is on display. Travel northeast on Highway 10 to Mile 45—view the fabulous Qu'Appelle Valley made famous by the poetess E. Pauline Johnson. The twin lakes of Pasqua and Echo are the setting for Echo Valley Provincial Park, where you can enjoy swimming, boating, and a host of other activities.

Traveling on the south side of Echo Lake, to your right, directly at the bottom of the hill, make a stop at the Fish Culture Station, open daily, to learn what's involved in caring for millions of fish from the time they hatch until they stock provincial waters. Continue driving on the south side of Echo Lake to the town of Fort Qu'Appelle, where the museum is open. A museum is joined to an original 1864 Hudson's Bay Company post and displays Indian artifacts and Hudson's Bay Company articles.

From Fort Qu'Appelle turn south on Highway 10 and then right just before the top of the hill and take a side trip to the vacation farm of Harman's Western Playground. It is easily spotted for its rodeo-style structure. Echo Valley Centre, also on the north side of the lake, is now the home of Saskatchewan Summer School of the Arts, and each weekend during the summer session, public concerts and displays of students' work are held. Travel north on Highway 35 to Mile 55—Huber's Manufacturing—where tours are offered of their operation in the manufacture of Christmas decorations, gardening tools, and other items.

With the lush valley of the Qu'Appelle behind, take Highway 22 west through typical farming country to Earl Grey at Mile 96. Here, the Centennial Museum displays old machinery, pioneer items, and turn-of-the-century books and catalogues. This museum is open evenings or by request. West on Highway 22 and west again on Highway 220 brings you to Mile 121—Rowan's Ravine Provincial Park, where the big thing is swimming at the long sandy shores of Last Mountain Lake. Four miles south is the Lakeside Museum with a collection of Indian and pioneer artifacts. Traveling east on Highway 220 and southeast on Highway 332, you will arrive at Mile 142, Last Mountain House Historic Park. Established in 1869 by the Hudson's Bay Company, the post was a major trading center for two years. The master's house has been rebuilt, and other buildings marked. Picnic facilities are on the site.

Traveling southeast take note of the market gardens in the Qu'Appelle Valley between Craven on Highway 20 and Lumsden on Highway 11; stop for some fresh produce. Return to Regina at Mile 164 via Highway 11.

If you do not like to follow a planned route, a good map and a willingness to camp are all you need. Saskatchewan has eighteen provincial parks with campsites and picnic areas as well as two national parks, regional parks, and campgrounds scattered throughout the province. They are open from May to September; a few remain open year-round, but services are limited. The provincial parks have well-marked nature trails, slide presentations, talks on wilderness survival, swimming, canoeing, sailing, and fishing. If you do not wish to camp, there are some cabins for rent. Side trips from these provincial parks may be taken—"little England on the Prairies," better known as Cannington Manor, the site where Sitting Bull and 5,000 American Sioux Indians set up camp following their victory at the Battle of the Little Big Horn, or that geological oddity, the Cypress Hills. Museums, wheat fields, badlands, game farms, dams, Indian carvings, *roches moutonnées,* antique cars and machinery, early architecture, virgin wilderness, wildlife, freaks of nature are all within reach.

It becomes abundantly clear that Saskatchewan is a paradise for outdoor people, but there is something here for everyone. Cities and towns offer many activities—museums, live theater, sports activities, nightspots, art galleries, fine cuisine, exhibitions, fairs, rodeos, carnivals, natural history exhibits, and libraries.

PRACTICAL INFORMATION FOR
SASKATCHEWAN

HOW TO GET THERE. By air: Saskatoon and Regina have the major airports. *Air Canada* and *Pacific Western* serve the major cities, and *Norcanair,* a regional carrier, the smaller centers.

By car: East/west access to southern Saskatchewan on the Trans-Canada Hwy. through Moosomin to Regina from the east and Swift Current, Moose Jaw, and Regina from the west; to northern Saskatchewan on Hwy. 16 from the west through Lloydminster, North Battleford, Saskatoon, and Hwy. 16, from the east through Langenburg and Yorkton. Access from the United States into the eastern part of the province can be obtained through Port of Estevan/Noonan, North Dakota, on Hwys. 47 and 39, and North Portal/Portal, North Dakota, on Highway 39, both going through Estevan, Weyburn, Moose Jaw to bisect the Trans Canada; through Port of Regway/Raymond, Montana, on Hwy. 6 to Regina. Access into the western part of the province from the United States through Port of Climax/Turner, Montana, on Hwy. 37 and the Trans-Canada to Swift Current, Port of Monchy/Morgan, Montana, on Hwy. 4 to Swift Current. Altogether there are 13 ports of entry between the United States and Saskatchewan.

By train: Transcontinental passenger service of *Via Rail* crosses Saskatchewan daily, making connections with Regina, Moose Jaw, and Swift Current on its Southern east/west run, and between Saskatoon, Melville and Biggar on its Northern east/west run.

By bus: Saskatchewan is well served with bus routes. Several companies, including *Greyhound Lines of Canada* and *Saskatchewan Transportation Company* (STC), maintain passenger service as well as express and charter service to all their points of call.

ACCOMMODATIONS. Double-occupancy rates are categorized as follows: *Deluxe,* $50 and up; *Expensive,* $35 to $49; *Moderate,* $30 to $34; *Inexpensive,* under $30. These rates are subject to a 5% provincial sales tax. (There are accommodations in the smaller towns around Saskatchewan and although they have not been listed in this guide, they are basically adequate, with inexpensive rates.)

Most places accept the following credit cards: American Express, MasterCard and Visa; others may also be honored. Not all establishments accept credit cards, therefore we suggest you call for information.

ESTEVAN. *Expensive:* **Derrick Motor Hotel.** 125 4th St., Estevan, SK S4A 0T3 (306–634–3685). Dining room, beverage room, and 70 rooms.

Fai's Motel. Hwy. 39 E. on South Service Rd., Estevan, SK S4A 2A6 (306–634–2693). Newly renovated, adjoins service station.

Swank Motel. Hwy. 39 W., Estevan, SK S4A 2A7 (306–634–2691). 21 modern housekeeping rooms.

FORT QU'APPELLE. *Moderate:* **Country Squire Motor Hotel.** Jct. Hwy. 10 and Bay St., Box 699, Fort Qu'appelle, SK S0G 1S0 (306–332–5603). Modern rooms, restaurant, and beverage room.

Valley Trails Motel Ltd. Old Hwy. 35, Fort Qu'appelle, SK S0G 1S0 (306–332–5757). 11 rooms.

LLOYDMINSTER. *Moderate:* **Capri Motor Inn.** 5615 50th Ave., Lloydminster, SK S9V 0P4 (403–825–5591). Beverage room, dining room, entertainment. 60 rooms.

Prince Charles Motor Inn. 50th Ave. and 49th St., Lloydminster, SK T9V 0W5 (403–875–2216). Beverage room, restaurant, cocktails, dining room, entertainment, pets allowed.

MOOSE JAW. *Expensive:* **Harwood's Moose Jaw Inn.** 24 Fairford E., Moose Jaw, SK S6H 0C7 (306–692–2366). Beverage room, restaurant and dining room, cocktails, entertainment, pets allowed, indoor swimming pool, and sauna. 100 rooms.

Heritage Inn. 1590 Main St., Moose Jaw, SK S6H 7N7 (306–693–7550). Extensive facilities, include pool and miniature golf.

Moderate: **Parke Lodge Motor Hotel.** Jct. Hwy. 1 and 2, Moose Jaw, SK S6H 4P8 (306–692–0647). Licensed dining room. Indoor pool and courtyard, whirlpool and sauna. Tastefully decorated in the Old English style of the Tudor reign. Also coffeeshop. 82 rooms, 10 light housekeeping.

NORTH BATTLEFORD. *Moderate:* **Beaver Brook Lodge.** Hwy. 16, North Battleford, SK S9A 3E6 (306–445–7747). Licensed steakhouse, electric heat, coffee shop.

Beaver Motor Hotel. 11th Ave. at 100th St., North Battlefield, SK S9A 2Y3 (306–445–8115). Downtown location near theaters, shopping, and waterslide. Nightly entertainment.

Capri Motor Hotel. 992 101st St., North Battleford, SK S9A 2Z6 (306–445–9425). Restaurant, beverage and cocktail rooms. 91 rooms.

PRINCE ALBERT. *Expensive:* **Pines Motor Inn.** 3245 2nd Ave. W., Prince Albert, SK S6V 5G1 (306–922–1333). 78 extra-large rooms. Sauna, whirlpool, indoor swimming pool, dining room, coffee shop, cocktail lounge.

Moderate: **Coronet Motor Hotel.** 3551 2nd Ave. W., Prince Albert, SK S6V 5G1 (306–764–6441). Beverage and cocktail rooms, restaurant and dining room, indoor pool, sauna and whirlpool, pets allowed. 101 rooms.

Prince Albert-Imperial 400 Motel. Hwy. 2 S., Prince Albert, SK S6V 5G2 (306–764–6881). Enclosed pool, lounge and dining room. 139 rooms.

Inexpensive: **Porter's Motel.** 2½ mi. S. on Hwy. 2., Prince Albert, SK S6V 5E9 (306–764–2374). Pets allowed. 12 units.

SWIFT CURRENT. *Expensive:* **Best Western Swift Motel.** 160 Begg St., Swift Current, SK S9H 0K4 (306–773–4668). Outdoor barbecues, picnic tables, heated pool, pets allowed. 55 units, 13 light housekeeping.

TraveLodge Motel. Hwy. 1, E., Swift Current, SK S9H 2A3 (306–773–3101). Outdoor barbecues, heated pool and sauna. 49 rooms.

Moderate: **Rodeway Inn Motel.** 1200 Begg St. E., Swift Current, SK S9H 4C9 (306–773–4664). Restaurant, sauna, whirlpool. 28 rooms, all wheelchair-accessible.

WEYBURN. *Moderate:* **Weyburn Inn.** 5 Government Rd., Weyburn, SK S4H 0N8 (306–842–6543). 2 dining rooms, 2 lounges and pool. 50 rooms.

Inexpensive: **Andy's Motel.** 3 2nd Ave. S.W., Weyburn, SK S4H 2J3 (306–842–4647). 24 rooms, dining nearby.

King George Hotel. 3rd St. and Railway Ave., Weyburn, SK S4H 0V9 (306–842–2662). Redecorated.

YORKTON. *Moderate:* **Corona Motor Hotel.** 345 Broadway W., Yorkton, SK S3N 2X1 (306–783–6571). Restaurant and dining room, beverage and cocktail rooms, entertainment, swimming pool. 85 rooms.

Holiday Inn. 110 Broadway E., Yorkton, SK S3N 2V6 (306–783–9781). Restaurant and dining room, entertainment, cocktail room, pool, 92 rooms.

Imperial "400" Motel. Broadway and Dracup, Yorkton, SK S3N 2V6 (306–783–6581). Restaurant, indoor swimming pool. 99 rooms.

Inexpensive: **Yorkton Hotel.** 14 2nd Ave. N., Yorkton, SK S3N 1G2 (306–782–2421). Beverage room, restaurant, and pets allowed. 23 modern and 20 not-so-modern rooms.

HOW TO GET AROUND. By plane. *Air Canada* and *Pacific Western* provide national service into the larger cities. *Norcanair* provides service into the smaller centers and also operates a charter service. It has offices in Cluff Lake, Fond du Lac, La Ronge, Prince Albert, Regina, Saskatoon, Stoney Rapids, Uranium City, and Wallaston.

By car. Saskatchewan has more miles of road than any other Canadian province. The southern part of the province is a gridiron of hard surface roads, and there are miles and miles of graveled and graded roads to the smaller towns and villages.

By train. Service is available to some major centers in Saskatchewan on an east/west axis.

By bus. Bus service is good in Saskatchewan. The largest carrier in the province is *Saskatchewan Transportation Company* (STC). Its buses average 10,000 miles a day on 30 regular routes covering about one third of the provincial highway system. This company also offers a wide variety of tours.

FACTS AND FIGURES. Saskatchewan was derived from the Cree word *Kisiskatchewan,* meaning "the river that flows swiftly." Nicknamed "the wheat province" because of the great volume of cereal grains grown. The provincial flower is the western red lily *(lilium philadelphicum andium)* and the provincial bird is the prairie sharp-tailed grouse *(pedioecetes phasianellos campesetris).* Saskatchewan has one provincial motto: *Honi soit qui mal y pense,* "Evil be to him who evil thinks." Regina is the provincial capital, and the provincial population is one million. Saskatchewan has sunny cold winters with an average snowfall of 50 inches, and short warm summers.

TOURIST INFORMATION. *Tourism Saskatchewan,* 2103 11th Ave. in Regina, can supply up-to-date travel information on campsites, towns and cities, activities and attractions, tours, accommodations, fishing, and canoeing from June to September. The phone number is 787–2300 during regular office hours. There are toll-free lines for in-province calls—1–800–667–7538 is the number. If you are outside the province, call 800–667–7191.

Information can also be obtained by writing *Department of Tourism and Small Business,* 2103 11th Ave., Regina, Saskatchewan S4P 3V7.

Also during the summer months (May to September) information centers are open throughout the province with travel counselors available to provide free information and travel planning services. These centers are located on the main access routes into Saskatchewan:—Trans-Canada Hwy: in various campgrounds: east approach—near Manitoba border at Fleming; west approach—Maple Creek Junction of Hwys. 1 and No. 21 and in the Maple Creek Campground; Yellowhead Hwy. (Hwy. 16): east approach—Langenburg; west approach—Lloydminster. From the United States, Hwy. 39: North Portal just beyond the Canadian Customs Office.

For tourists not traveling by car, air facilities maps can be purchased from the Central Survey & Mapping Division, Department of Highways, 1855 Victoria Ave., Regina, Saskatchewan.

Remember *Tourism Saskatchewan* of the Department of Tourism and Small Business, Regina, is the place to contact for any information you require on Saskatchewan, or you can go through your travel agent, carrier, auto club, or local chambers of commerce.

SEASONAL EVENTS. For up-to-the-minute information on annual events and special events, contact *Sask-Travel.*

January: The winter months are the time for curling bonspiels, winter carnivals, snowmobile racing, and winter sports such as downhill and cross-country skiing and snowshoeing. A three-day mid-January winter carnival with snow mobile races takes place at Humboldt.

February: Estevan, Fort Qu'Appelle, Lloydminster, Melfort, and Prince Albert all celebrate their winter carnivals during this month. Prince Albert's hoopla is highlighted by a championship dog derby, an event where 8-dogteams compete with each other in a 3-day, 48-mile race. "King Trapper" is also chosen, the winner of a marathon of log sawing, wood chopping, flour carrying, and bannock baking. Estevan holds International 250 Snowmobile Race from Regina to Minot.

March: Again this is a month for winter carnivals and curling bonspiels—Craik, Kelvinton, Kyle, Meadow Lake all celebrate this month.

April: An Easter-week Pee Wee Hockey Tournament at Weyburn, a music festival at the end of the month in North Battleford, and *carnivals* at Lloydminster and North Battleford round out this month.

May: Moose Jaw is the setting for an international band festival put on by the local Kinsmen. It is one of the continent's biggest band events and attracts over 70 bands and 5,000 musicians. Saskatoon's Vesna Festival is an annual spring multicultural festival patterned after Regina's Mosiac celebration, held the same month.

June: The summer months are swamped with shows and expositions. In North Battleford, a Those Were The Days Festival is an annual event. Pioneer machinery and tools are operated; the outdoor pioneer village and 40,000 square feet of indoor displays are there for browsing. It is held in late June and an exhibition, parade, and harness racing also take place. In Regina, a unique event takes place from mid-June to August—The Trial of Louis Riel, the leader of the Northwest Rebellion of 1885, is reenacted three times weekly at Saskatchewan House. Moose Jaw holds a biannual air show on the Canadian Forces base there.

July: In Saskatoon the week-long Pioneer Days, called the biggest pioneer show in North America, takes place with historical pageants, pioneer equipment and machinery demonstrations, antique displays, harness racing, and livestock and agricultural shows. Saskatchewan's biggest rodeo is also held this month in Swift Current with parades, street dancing, and a fair. The Saskatchewan Craft Festival in Battleford brings the best crafts people together.

August: The town of Craven's big rodeo and Regina's Buffalo Days Exhibition, ten days of pioneer celebration, horse racing, barbecues, picnics, band concerts, midway and grandstand entertainment make this a good month to visit Saskatchewan.

September: Visit the Harvest Festival in Swift Current put on by the Chamber of Commerce. Stop by the Moose Jaw Wild Animal Regional Park—300 acres with buffalo, elk, yak, deer, and antelope as well as a children's zoo. September-October Swift Current holds Western Canadian Olde Tyme Fiddling Contest. Thresherman's Show in Yorkton draws contestants from across the prairies.

October: The Tomahawk Rodeo at Cutknife is presided over by the world's largest tomahawk—54-foot, 6-ton fir handle and 2,500-pound fiberglass blade. A film festival at Yorkton, a turkey shoot at Unity, and the Pineland Mexpo at Prince Albert finish off this month.

November: The Mexabition in Saskatoon in November and in Regina in late November and early December is an annual event. In Regina it is held in conjunction with the Agribition, an international livestock show. Agricultural equipment, inventions, gadgets, house amenities and products, lawn and garden accessories, and equipment, as well as the livestock shows and sales, are featured.

December: This month is the time to visit the cities of Saskatchewan where Christmas events are happening. Bands, symphonies, choirs all present special concerts.

TOURS. There are 28 auto tours mapped out by *Tourism Saskatchewan*. They have been listed below, and if more detailed information is required, you can contact the above department. Rental accommodations, campgrounds, points of interest, and industrial tours are plotted on each tour.

Tour 1. Maple Creek, Cypress Hills Provincial Park, Fort Walsh Historic Park, Swift Current.

Tour 2. Maple Creek, Gull Lake, The Great Sand Hills.

Tour 3. Moose Jaw, Assiniboia, Wood Mountain Historic Park.

Tour 4. Buffalo Pound Provincial Park, Lake Diefenbaker recreation area.

Tour 5. Moose Jaw, Big Muddy Badlands, Wilcox.

Tour 6. Regina, Fort Qu'Appelle, Rowan's Ravine and Echo Valley Provincial Parks, Last Mountain House Historic Park.

Tour 7. Swift Current, Saskatchewan Landing Provincial Park, Kindersley.

Tour 8. Saskatoon, Lake Diefenbaker recreation area, Mount Blackstrap, Manitou Beach.

Tour 9. North Battleford, Saskatoon, Rosetown.

Tour 10. Indian Head, Fort Qu'Appelle, Katepwa Provincial Park, Melville.

Tour 11. Lloydminster, Cut Knife, North Battleford.

Tour 12. Foam Lake, Touchwood Hills Historic Park, Rowan's Ravine Provincial Park, Lanigan.

Tour 13. Wynyard, Quill Lakes, Kinistino, Humboldt.

Tour 14. Lloydminster, Fort Pitt and Steele Narrows Historic Parks, St. Walburg, North Battleford.

Tour 15. Moose Mountain Provincial Park, Weyburn, Estevan, Cannington Manor Historic Park.

Tour 16. Moose Mountain Provincial Park, Broadview, Esterhazy, Moosomin.

Tour 17. Duck Mountain and Good Spirit Provincial Parks, Yorkton, Esterhazy.

Tour 18. Duck Mountain Provincial Park, Porcupine Hills, Hudson Bay.

Tour 19. Greenwater Lake Provincial Park, Tisdale, Kelvington.

Tour 20. Greenwater Lake Provincial Park, Carrot River, Hudson Bay, Wildcat Hills Wilderness Area.

Tour 21. Saskatoon, Batoche, Duck Lake.

Tour 22. Prince Albert, Prince Albert National Park, MacDowall, Waskesiu Lake.

Tour 23. Prince Albert, Nipawin Provincial Park, Creighton, Denare Beach.

Tour 24. Prince Albert, La Ronge, Approximate Geographic Center of Saskatchewan.

Tour 25. Prince Albert, Nipawin, Cumberland House, Squaw Rapids Hydroelectric Station.

Tour 26. Prince Albert, Candle Lake, Nipawin Provincial Park.

Tour 27. City Tour of Saskatoon.

Tour 28. City Tour of Regina.

NATIONAL PARKS. *Prince Albert National Park,* located less than 100 miles north of the city of Prince Albert, is the biggest national park in Saskatchewan. The park covers 1,496 square miles; has one townsite, Waskesiu; and is home to one of Canada's biggest white pelican colonies. Elk, moose, caribou, black bear, wolf, coyote, beaver, birds of prey, waterfowl, and buffalo inhabit the park. *Grasslands National Park,* near Val Marie, is being developed as a unique habitat for the original short-grass prairie on North America. It is in the southwest corner of the province.

PROVINCIAL PARKS. From the prairies, through the parklands, to the north, Saskatchewan has a provincial park to suit you—18 in all. There are also many regional parks and campgrounds. The park season is from Victoria Day to Labor Day. Some of the campgrounds stay open with limited services past this date. Up-to-the-minute information on camping may be obtained by calling *Tourism Saskatchewan* at 787-2300.

The parks have planned naturalist programs, but if you prefer not to plan your days, there are slide shows, campfire singsongs, team sports, tennis, golf, arts and crafts, swimming, fishing, boating, waterskiing, and hiking. Most parks offer complete amenities: laundry facilities, washrooms, showers, outdoor toilets, water standpipes, grocery stores, and cafeterias. There are cabins for rent at some of the provincial parks, and arrangements for accommodations can be made through the individual park superintendents.

Lac La Ronge: northeastern Saskatchewan, excellent for canoeing and fishing; 255 campsites, rental accommodations nearby, all amenities, swimming, fishing, and canoe outfitters.

Meadow Lake: 600 sq. miles of lake-studded forest; over 700 campsites, all amenities, swimming, natura trails, golf, rental accommodations, fishing and boat outfitters.

The Battlefords: west-central Saskatchewan; over 360 campsites, swimming, nature trails, 18-hole golf course, all amenities.

Greenwater Lake, Duck Mountain, Good Spirit: east-central; over 600 campsites; full facilities, swimming, boat rentals, nature trails, bicycle trails, tennis courts, golf course and cabin rentals.

Douglas, Daniel, and *Saskatchewan Landing:* created from building of Gardiner Dam, located around Lake Diefenbaker; over 260 campsites, amenities not complete, nature trails.

Pike Lake Provincial Park and *Blackstrap Recreational Area:* near Saskatoon; 60 campsites at Blackstrap but limited facilities, mainly a ski area; 250 campsites at Pike Lake, full amenities, swimming, nature trails, fishing, picnic areas, bicycle trails, tennis courts.

Buffalo Pound Park: 260 acres, 148 campsites, excellent services and facilities, ideal for water sports, swimming pool, nature trails, winter skiing at *White Track Ski Resort.*

Rowan's Ravine, Echo Valley, and *Katepwa:* in Qu'Appelle Valley; over 600 campsites, fishing, boating, waterskiing, swimming, playgrounds for kids, golf courses, picnic areas. Katepwa has no camping facilities.

Cypress Hills Provincial Park: southwestern Saskatchewan; geological freak of nature—see cactus, lodgepole pine, animal mutations such as white ants, and scorpions all alien to the prairie; excellent facilities. 466 campsites and rental lodging.

Moose Mountain: southeastern Saskatchewan; over 320 campsites, fully serviced; excellent recreational programs, fishing, hiking, riding, swimming, bicycle trails, lake cruises, golf.

FARM VACATIONS. The *Saskatchewan Farm Vacations Association,* Box 89, Blaine Lake, SK S0J 0J0 (306–497–2782), has more than 30 members willing to share their farms, and their chores, with you. Reservations are needed and can be obtained by contacting the individual farms or *Tourism Saskatchewan,* which also provides a list of the farms with a short description of each.

CHILDREN'S ACTIVITIES. Saskatchewan is a family province offering a variety of outdoor things to do for children as well as adults—provincial parks, zoos, fairgrounds, farm vacations, and fishing trips.

SPORTS. Summer: *Baseball* is a popular sport during the summer. Many towns have annual sports days with *hardball* and *softball* tournaments. Of course, the parks offer areas for *swimming, waterskiing, canoeing, fishing, hiking, golf,* and *tennis.* **Winter** activities include downhill and cross-country *skiing, snowshoeing, snowmobiling, hockey,* and *curling.* Almost every small town has at least one curling bonspiel a year.

CAMPING OUT. There are camping and tenting facilities located throughout the province. *Tourism Saskatchewan* can provide up-to-date information on the availability of sites in particular areas. Service is on a first-come, first-served basis in most areas.

The majority of campgrounds are open from Victoria Day to Labor Day only, but a few remain open offering limited service.

HISTORIC SITES. Most of Saskatchewan's historic sites have been preserved through historic parks. There are 9 of them open throughout the summer from Victoria Day to Labor Day. *Tourism Saskatchewan* has up-to-date information on all historic parks as well as the many museums and art galleries throughout the province.

St. Victor Petroglyphs Historic Park: St. Victor, 16 miles southwest of Assiniboia, is the site of this park, so named for the Indian rock carvings, or petroglyphs, on top of a sandstone outcropping. A picnic area and steps leading up to the carvings are provided.

Battleford National Historic Park: On Hwy. 29, near junction with Hwy. 16. Four of the buildings once used by the Northwest Mounted Police are located with Fort Battleford's reconstructed palisade; guard room, Sick Horse stable, officer's quarters and commanding officer's residence.

Cumberland House Historic Park: 100 miles northeast of Carrot River on Hwy. 123, it was the Hudson's Bay Company's first inland fur trading post. At the park, plaques describing the complete history of this area are erected.

Fort Carlton Historic Park: about four miles northwest of Carlton and 45 miles northwest of Saskatoon. Fort Carlton was headquarters for the Hudson's Bay Company during the mid-1800's and a favorite stopping place for famous travelers.

Fort Pitt Historic Park: 14 miles west of Frenchman Butte, it was established in 1829 as a Hudson's Bay Company post and played a critical role in the fur trade and settlement of the west.

Fort Wash National Park: 23 miles west of Cypress Hill Provincial Park, Northwest Mounted Police fortified post in 1800's. In 1942 RCMP chose the location for a remount ranch, largely because of historical associations.

Touchwood Hills Historic Park: Located 5 miles southeast of Punnichy on Hwy. No. 15, it was a Hudson's Bay Post which served as a provision center on the Fort Qu'Appelle-Touchwood Hills Trail as well as being a fur trading fort. A cairn is erected to describe the post's history.

Last Mountain House Historic Park: Located 5 miles north of Craven on Hwy. 20. Built by Issac Cowie in 1869, this fort stood on the northern edge of the great plains area. By 1872 the post was closed, as the buffalo herds had retreated southwest. Today, on site, is the reconstructed Master's house, men's house, and ice cellar.

Wood Mountain Historic Park: Located 3 miles south of Wood Mountain village, this fort played an important part in North American history. In 1874 a North West Mounted Police depot was set up at Wood Mountain. By 1877, almost the entire Sioux Nation under Chief Sitting Bull, fresh from a victory at the Battle of the Little Big Horn south of the border, was camped near Wood Mountain. The Sioux remained for four years; then finally hard times forced them to return to reservation life in the United States.

Cannington Manor Historic Park: Located 8 miles north and two miles east of Manor, this is a unique site. Cannington Manor was Captain Edward Pierce's dream come true of establishing a colony in the New World, based on agriculture, where he and others like him could pursue the life of English gentlemen. The original church, a museum in an old schoolhouse, an old log house, the blacksmith's shop, and carpenter's house can all be seen.

Steele Narrows Historic Park: Located 6 miles west of Loon Lake, this was the site of the last battle of the Riel Rebellion of 1885, the last armed conflict on Canadian soil. Big Bear and his band of Crees, holding 30 prisoners, met Major Sam Steele of the North West Mounted Police, with about 60 troopers, in battle here on June 3, 1885. Major Steele was victorious, and the prisoners were released a few days later. Today there are markers indicating the battlefield and a plaque describing the battle.

MUSEUMS AND GALLERIES. Most of the larger cities, and many of the small towns, which shared in Saskatchewan's history, have museums and art galleries. The cities' museums and art galleries have regular hours. Most galleries and museums have no admission charge. In smaller towns, the museums will be opened by request of the private owners.

Major attractions are the province's four *Western Development Museums,* each of which depicts a different Saskatchewan historical theme through extensive exhibits. The various museums and their themes are: Moose Jaw, the story of transportation; North Battleford, the story of agriculture; Saskatoon, the integrated story of western development; and Yorkton, the story of the people.

 SHOPPING. Saskatchewan has a number of small craft stores that offer original pottery, silkscreens, rock jewelry, potash clocks, embroidered leather, denim garments, purses, mitts, hats. There is a 5% sales tax on most items.

 **LIQUOR LAWS.** The drinking age is 19 years or older. Liquor is sold only in licensed liquor stores, licensed restaurants, cocktail lounges, dining rooms and beverage rooms, or by vendors. Retail liquor stores are operated throughout the province.

 RESTAURANTS. The people of Saskatchewan come from many different racial backgrounds—European, African, Asian, Australian. Each race brings its own culture, molding it into the Saskatchewan way of life. Every ethnic group is represented in the food and restaurants of Saskatchewan: Ukrainian, French, English, German, Romanian, Italian. There is a restaurant to meet each taste.

The major hotels in Saskatchewan have eating facilities ranging from coffeeshops to dining rooms. There are several top-flight entertainment centers which offer quality meals and top performers. There are also home-style restaurants, places that specialize in good eating only. For the tourist on the go there are also take-out and fast-food establishments. Costs are per person for the medium-priced meals on the menu: *Deluxe:* $30 and up, *Expensive,* $20–$30; *Moderate,* $15–20; *Inexpensive,* under $15. In most cases the prices include soup, entree, and dessert. Beverages are extra, and the 5% provincial tax and tips are not included.

Most places accept the following major credit cards: American Express, MasterCard and Visa; others may also be honored. Not all establishments accept credit cards, therefore we suggest you call for information.

ESTEVAN. *Inexpensive.* **The Old Homestead.** 400 King (634–6775). A pleasant relaxing atmosphere with background music. Varied menu and special children's menu. Located in the Estevan Shoppers Mall, lots of free parking.

LLOYDMINSTER. *Expensive:* **Wayside Inn.** Hwy. 16, just two blocks from Sask.-Alta. border (403–875–4404). Fine dining room, poolside restaurant.

MOOSE JAW. *Expensive:* **Hopkins Dining Parlour.** 65 Athabasca W. (692–5995). Located in a mansion from the early 20th century. Extended hours of operation.

Grant Hall Inn. 24 Fair Ford St. E. (692–2301). Good dining in recently renovated hotel. New cocktail lounge.

PRINCE ALBERT. *Inexpensive:* **Venice House Restaurant.** 1498 Central (764–6555). This is a family restaurant where courtesy and good, fast, friendly service are stressed. Has a varied menu. Free parking. Located in downtown Prince Albert.

SWIFT CURRENT. *Expensive:* **Wong's Kitchen.** South Service Rd. on Hwy. 1/TCH (773–6244). Serving Oriental and Canadian dishes, Wong's enjoys a reputation throughout Saskatchewan. Features live entertainment daily.

WEYBURN. *Moderate:* **El Rancho Pizza and Steak House.** 53 Government Rd. (842–1411). Feature steaks, seafood, and Italian dishes.

YORKTON. *Moderate:* **Gladstone Inn.** 185 Broadway W. (783–4827). Features German cuisine with a good wine list. Located at the corner of Broadway and Gladstone.

The Samovar and Coffee Shop. In the Holiday Inn, 110 Broadway E. (783–9781). Serves steak and Russian cuisine in dining room decorated in a colorful, Russian-style.

ALBERTA

Sunshine Country

by
SUSAN LEARNEY

Alberta is year-round sunshine and blue skies, friendly people, exciting cities, and spectacular scenery. More sunshine than any other part of the country along with a modern pioneer spirit of a vibrant and youthful population combine to set the mood for exploring the incredible natural beauty of one of Canada's youngest provinces.

Within a land area of 661,185 square kilometers (255,285 square miles), Alberta has four distinct scenic regions: magnificent mountains to the southwest, rolling prairie to the southeast, mixed forest and plains in the central area, and an exciting natural wilderness to the north.

The oldest part of the province is a small portion in the extreme northeast corner. It's part of the Canadian Shield, where the Pre-Cambrian rock at surface level is up to 3.5 billion years old. This rock core swoops underground, forming a basement beneath the province, that is 6,000 meters (19,700 feet) deep under its youngest portion, the Rocky Mountains. Massive rock movements lifted the mountains only in the last 60 million years or so. Between these two, the vast interior plain sweeps from the northwest, over the rest of the province. More than half of this plain is covered by northern forest and rolling parkland. The rest is semi-arid prairie.

Beneath this vast interior plain lies the Western Sedimentary Basin. Six hundred million years ago, Alberta alternated between dry land and inland seas. Marine and plant life evolved during this period. The decay of these life forms between 400 and 350 million years ago, formed the huge deposits of coal, oil, and natural gas lying beneath the surface of most of the province.

During the Mesozoic era, the time of the dinosaurs 225 to 70 million years ago, badlands were formed by the upraising of softer rock and inland flooding by oceans. Glacial action and erosion scoured the badlands, leaving them inarable, colored them with mineral deposits, and carved them into a myriad of distinctive shapes, such as coulees and hoodoos. Coulees are deep ravines cut through the ground by the force of flowing water. Hoodoos are above-ground formations of alternating layers of sandstone and rock. In exposed areas, winds erode the weaker sandstone layers, creating intriguing vertical columns held in place by the stronger rock cap. Some of the world's most significant dinosaur fossils exist in the Badlands region of central Alberta, near Drumheller and south along the Red Deer River. Others are found as far north as the Kleskun Hills near Grande Prairie.

The final retreat of the Ice Age, about 12,000 years ago, sculpted Alberta's great river systems, such as the Athabasca, Peace, and North Saskatchewan, and deposited the soil systems that exist today.

Alberta is a vertical province in a horizontal country. The rolling parkland, where grain and mixed farming predominate, stretches right up to the boundary with the Northwest Territories, permitting the most northerly agriculture in the country, and in the world.

Oil pumps dot the landscape throughout the province. Far to the north, the development of huge crude oil reserves in the tar sands was made feasible by the rising oil prices of the early 1970s. "Mega projects," with costs measured in billions of dollars to reap the oily black harvest of the tar sands, caused the meteoric rise to prominence of both Calgary and Edmonton.

Unlike other provinces, Alberta's two major cities also lie on a north–south axis. Early in the twentieth century, the two cities emerged along different paths to the future. Calgary evolved first as the transportation center for the ranching industry, then as the financial center for the oil industry. Edmonton grew as an administrative center, first for the province, as its capital, then for the petroleum industry, and it also served as the gateway to the north. During the 1960s and 1970s the two cities competed with each other for top position as Canada's fastest growing city. Today, they dominate the province. Together, their populations constitute more than half of the total number of people in the entire province. Their rivalry has been intense. But their emergence along different paths symbolizes the division between south and north in the historical evolution of the province as a whole.

Southern Alberta was dominated for thousands of years, by buffalo-hunting Plains Indians. Well into the 1880s the major population of the region was native. Up to the coming of white men, it was part of the huge territory, stretching south to Wyoming and north to the North Saskatchewan River, of the fierce Blackfoot nation, who violently repelled white intruders. The north was dominated by their traditional enemies, the Cree and the Athapaskan peoples, who cooperated with the fur traders.

North and central Alberta was first explored by voyageurs and British fur traders. In 1670, the Hudson's Bay Company had been given trading and administrative rights in all the territory whose waters drained into Hudson Bay. This area known as Rupert's Land extended all the way west to the Rockies. A hundred years later, the North West Company set itself up in direct competition. The two rival companies built fur posts throughout the northern portion of the province, vying with each other for dominance of the fur trade. The first known European in the province was a Hudson's Bay Company employee, who

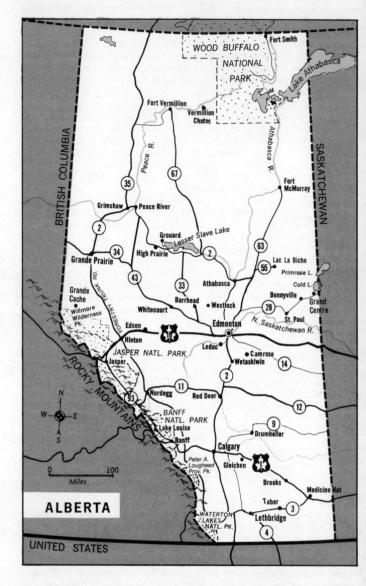

ALBERTA

wintered near Fort Edmonton in 1754. The first fur post was established by the North West Company in 1788, on the shore of Lake Athabasca. In 1821, the companies merged, and for another fifty years, the Hudson's Bay Company and the fur trade dominated this part of Rupert's Land.

In the wake of the fur traders came the missionaries. The first resident cleric, Methodist Reverend Robert Rundle, arrived in the province in 1840. He was followed by, among others, the father-and-son team of George and John McDougall, and the beloved Catholic priest,

Father Albert Lacombe. From bases near Fort Edmonton, the missionaries fanned out through the province to save Indian souls.

As a steady stream of fur trade traffic crossed the northern part of the province, an unsavory white influence began to pervade the south. In the late 1860s, American whiskey traders moved north from Fort Benton in Montana, building forts in southern Alberta from which they plied the Indians with cheap, vile alcoholic concoctions in return for buffalo robes. American wolf hunters also invaded the Blackfoot territory, and for a time, violence and lawlessness were rampant.

To the rescue came the newly formed North West Mounted Police (NWMP). A military-style force patterned after the Royal Irish Constabulary, the "redcoats" were instructed by the Canadian government to remove the American presence from Canadian soil and to restore law and order. After a grueling westward march under Assistant Commissioner J. F. Macleod, they arrived two months later, in 1874, in southern Alberta. From their base at the newly constructed Fort Macleod, they wiped out the whiskey trade within a few short years. Their red coats became the symbol of law and order throughout the land, to both white men and Indians alike.

In the 1870s the fur trade was declining, and the historic way of life of the Blackfoot was undergoing its most dramatic changes in 7,000 years. The buffalo, which had once blackened the prairie in herds numbering millions, had been overhunted by both Indians and whites and were nearing extinction. The Blackfoot were no longer able to stanch the flow of white men into the territory. Ranchers and settlers were moving into the lands sold by the Hudson's Bay Company to the government in 1869. Led by their great chief Crowfoot, and following the example of the Cree to the north a year earlier, the Blackfoot Indians surrendered their ancestral lands by signing Treaty No. 7, in 1877, at Blackfoot Crossing, near Cluny.

With Indian territory in the hands of the federal government and law and order assured by the "Mounties," the stage was set for the making of modern Alberta.

Much of the credit must surely go to William Van Horne, dynamic general manager of the Canadian Pacific Railway (CPR), a man of many talents, and "the ablest railroad general in the world." Charged with fulfilling the government's promise to British Columbia, in less than five short years he pushed the CPR across Alberta and through the Rockies. New towns sprang up along the line. Under the CPR tent town of Medicine Hat, natural gas was first discovered in Alberta. The NWMP's Fort Calgary became a major transportation center for the ranching industry. Within eighteen years, the fort had become a city.

A man of much vision, Van Horne also recognized the tourism potential of the Rockies. Apart from the sheer beauty of the area, warm sulphur springs were discovered in Banff, during railway construction. "Since we cannot bring the mountains to the people, we must bring the people to the mountains." So saying, Van Horne took pen in hand and helped design the now-classic, chateau-styled Banff Springs Hotel, completed in 1888.

As the CPR expanded it opened up the Rockies to underground coal mining. To the north, the Grand Trunk and Canadian Northern railways opened up huge areas of Alberta to settlement. During the last decade of the nineteenth century, and the first ten years of the twentieth, a flood of settlers poured into the territory via the new railways, spurred on by the enthusiastic immigration policies of the government and the promise of homestead land for $10 per quarter section (65 hectares, or 160 acres). In 1891 the population of the future province was 17,500. In 1911, six years after Alberta joined Confederation, the population had swelled to 373,000.

When the Dingman No. 1 well yielded oil at Turner Valley in 1914, it blew the lid off an economy sluggish after a slowdown in immigration and also feeling the effects of World War I. Over the next twenty years, Calgary was the chief beneficiary of the first and subsequent Turner Valley discoveries, and once again it looked as if southern and northern Alberta had different destinies.

In the north, Edmonton grew steadily, if unspectacularly, as capital of the province. But the 1930s became the era of the bush pilots. Aircraft, primitive and frail by today's standard, consolidated Edmonton's position as gateway to the far north. In the early 1940s, construction of the Alaska Highway both benefited the economy of Edmonton as the road's major supply center and reinforced the city's gateway position with road access to the far north.

Then, in 1947, just south of Edmonton, Leduce No. 1 oil well blew in, followed in quick succession by Redwater, Pembina, and Woodbend. By the 1960s and 1970s, all of Alberta was affected by the finds of huge oil deposits and tar sands. Economic power in Canada shifted westward. The population doubled in ten years, to 2.3 million. Until 1983, Alberta was the fastest growing province in the country, with a national prominence undreamed of at the beginning of the century.

Although declining oil prices and economic recession have since had their effect on its economy, Alberta's period of incredible wealth has left its mark. Albertans still pay the lowest income tax in the country, and there is no provincial sales tax. A legacy of public facilities, such as provincial and city parks, and centers for the arts, are there to be enjoyed by Albertans and visitors alike. The largest area of national parks in the country, with some of the world's greatest scenery, is in Alberta.

No matter what happens economically, Alberta will always have its friendly people, it scenery, and its sunshine.

CALGARY

Where the western prairie meets the foothills of the Rockies, nestled in a bend of the Bow River, is the city of Calgary. The glint of the western sun on the modern glass and steel of skyscrapers seems to belie Calgary's cherished frontier image.

Calgary literally sprang up in the last hundred years. But the area is scattered with the evidence of its early inhabitants. Campsites and buffalo kills, storage pits and tepee rings date back over 2,000 years. Just south of Calgary in Okotoks, a pictograph panel on Big Rock is thought to portray ancient religious customs.

Around the time of Christ, the Blackfoot moved in from the eastern woodlands and dominated the territory for centuries. The Sarcee came from the north around 1700, and the Stoney came later from Manitoba.

Wild, Wild Whiskey

White men first came to the area in the late 1700s. Cartographer David Thompson wintered near Calgary in 1787. The North West Company's Peter Fidler probably at least skirted the area in 1792. During the 1850s the Palliser Expedition, exploring all of the lands between Lake Superior and the Pacific, wandered through on their way to discovering the Kicking Horse Pass in the Rockies.

But it wasn't until the late 1860s that there was real activity in the area, and it was of a questionable nature! Briefly, unsettled southern

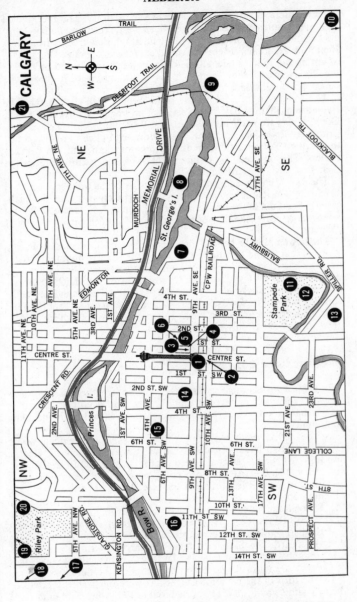

CALGARY

Calgary—Points of Interest

1) Calgary Tower
2) Olympic Interpretive Center
3) Convention Center
4) Glenbow Museum
5) Calgary Centre for the Performing Arts
6) Visitors Information
7) Fort Calgary
8) Calgary Zoo and Dinosaur Park
9) Sam Livingston Fish Hatchery
10) Inglewood Bird Sanctuary
11) Olympic Saddledome
12) Exhibition Grounds and Stampede Park
13) Reader Rock Garden
14) Devonian Gardens
15) Energeum
16) Planetarium
17) Calgary Olympic Park
18) McMahon Stadium
19) Jubilee Auditorium
20) Patrick Burns Memorial Garden
21) Calgary Airport

Alberta, more than any other part of the territory, saw the kind of action and violence of the wild American west. American buffalo hunters began to move north, followed by illicit whiskey traders from Fort Benton in Montana. These notorious characters operated on the idea of letting the Indians take all the risks, hunting buffalo and producing the highly prized robes and then paying them off with cheap, vile concoctions, for which the word "whiskey" is far too polite!

The Indians went wild on the stuff. Armed with six-shooters, the traders kept them at bay from a series of impregnable forts with names like Robber's Roost, Whiskey Gap, and Whoop-up. Violence was rampant. The newly formed North West Mounted Police were dispatched to southern Alberta to clean up the territory and rout the whiskey traders. They arrived in the summer of 1874, and set up operations at their first post, Fort Mcleod.

The NWMP's second post in southern Alberta was established in 1875. In 1876 its name was changed to Fort Calgary, after the birthplace in Scotland of the Assistant Commissioner, J. F. Macleod. Within a few short years, the first of several good fortunes came the way of Calgary.

The powers that be behind the construction of the Canadian Pacific Railway had to find a route west through the Rocky Mountains. After due consideration, they rejected a more northern route that would have used the easier Yellowhead Pass. Choosing instead the Kicking Horse, they aimed their steel rails right for Fort Calgary. The Canadian Pacific Railway laid out its townsite west of the Elbow River and south of the Bow. Calgary never looked back. Incorporated as a town in 1884, it grew to city status only nine years later.

A Sandstone Cowtown

In 1886, a devastating fire razed the wooden structures of downtown Calgary. City fathers decreed that the town be rebuilt of sandstone rather than wood. An aura of permanence developed in the fledgling community.

As the buffalo began to disappear from the prairie, Americans began driving in small herds of cattle from Montana. Missionaries George and John McDougall started a herd near their mission just to the west, at Morley. The NWMP provided both the security necessary for open grazing and a small local market for beef. The first of the large-scale ranching operations, the Cochrane Ranche Company, was started by M. H. Cochrane (later a Senator) just west of town, in 1881. As officers of the NWMP retired, they joined the ranching fraternity, as did several English gentlemen farmers, lured by the publicity given to North American cattle ranching in Britain. They arrived with sufficient capital to establish their own ranches. To this day, the cultural overtones of Calgary are more Anglo-Saxon than other Albertan cities.

By the turn of the century, Calgarians were unabashedly proud of their dynamic young city. They cried foul in 1905 when Edmonton was chosen the capital of the new province of Alberta. After all, it had taken Edmonton 110 years to become a city and Calgary only 18.

But, except for the crippling winter of 1906–07, the early fortunes of Calgary continued to rise with those of the ranching industry. To say that Calgary thrived as a cowtown is seriously understating the case. The city's first millionaire was Pat Burns, who built up the largest integrated meat packing business in Canada. The opening up of southern Alberta to cash crop farming in the early 1900s caused an explosive growth of the city. In ten short years, from 1901–11, the population rose to 43,000, an increase of about 1,000 percent!

Rail lines radiating in all directions assured Calgary's importance as a distribution center for the cattle industry, and as a transportation hub of western Canada.

The Last and the Best

Early in the century, a former American cowpuncher was promoting American wild west shows in Canada. Guy Weadick got the idea that people would pay to see demonstrations of the roundup skills of cowboys. By 1912, he had put together $100,000 in financing, with the help of such locals as Pat Burns. To launch his show, he combined forces with the Calgary Trade and Labour Council, who staged the annual Labour Day Parade. The combined procession included cowboys on horseback, the Duke and Duchess of Connaught, and 2,000 Indians in full ceremonial dress. The spectacle was viewed by 14,000. Over the six days of the hugely successful show, more than 40,000 spectators per day, watched legendary cowboys of the era, including some of Pancho Villa's bandits, competing for prize money of about $16,000 in the skills that earned them their daily bread. It was billed as "The Last and Best Great West Frontiers Days Celebration." As things turned out, it was definitely not the last, and perhaps not even the best. It merely foretold the birth of the single most important factor in Calgary's perpetual frontier image in the modern world, the annual Calgary Stampede.

Around this time, immigration to the west began to slow down, and World War I loomed on the horizon. In most of Alberta, the combined effect resulted in a general economic slowdown. But right in its midst, fortune smiled on Calgary again.

Bay Street West

The well known as Dingman No. 1 blew in 1914. The discovery of oil at Turner Valley, just southwest of Calgary, signaled the start of the industry that would focus world attention on Alberta during the 1970s and would be the making of modern Calgary. Alberta's first oil refinery opened in Calgary in 1923. Further important discoveries were made at Turner Valley in 1924 and 1936. Calgary's position in the oil industry was assured, especially after the recovery from World War II. With Edmonton, Calgary was one of the two or three fastest growing cities in Canada after World War II. Between the 1950s and 1960s, Calgary's population doubled, to a quarter of a million. By the 1970s, Calgary had become a world energy and financial center, and its population had doubled again. Today it has the third-highest number of corporate headquarters in the country, and it is called "the Bay Street of western Canada" (refering to Toronto's financial district, Canada's "Wall Street") because of the many banks represented there.

An Olympic-Size Ace in the Hole

Although hard hit during the early 1980s by the combined effects of economic recession and declining world oil prices, Calgary always seems to come up smiling. A submission that drew rave reviews from the International Olympics Committee won for the Calgary the 1988 Winter Olympics. Construction for this event has brought a chance to inject new life into the city, with facilities that will serve generations to come. Surrounded by ranchlands, grain fields, and petroleum reserves, all against the splendid backdrop of the Canadian Rockies, Calgary's future confidently awaits the guiding hand of a benevolent fate.

The Greatest Outdoor Show on Earth

But the image Calgary still likes best is that of a rough and ready cowtown. Calgarians don't just promote their city's frontier image, they revel in it. Look south of the briefcase of a business-suited professional and you're likely to see hand-tooled cowboy boots. White stetsons and bolo ties are Calgarian trademarks.

Guy Weadick's wild west show has become the "Greatest Outdoor Show on Earth"—the Calgary Stampede. Combined with the annual agricultural exhibition held since 1923, Stampede takes over the town. For the first half of every July, blue jeans become business dress. Revelry goes far into the night with fireworks, with dancing in the streets, in gambling casinos, and at grandstand shows. Then it starts all over again at dawn with outdoor flapjack breakfasts.

The ten days of competitions at Stampede Park that pit man against animal are launched with a massive, colorful Weadick-style parade. Cowboys compete for $500,000 in prize money in the skills that earned them livelihoods at round-up time—bareback and saddle bronco riding, bull riding, steer wrestling, and calf roping. Indian buffalo riding adds to the thrills. But the most spectacular sights and sounds are those of the Chuckwagon Races. Four wagons and thirty-two horses pound through a tight infield figure 8, then burst onto a racetrack for a mad dash to the finish. If you like rodeo, you'll love Stampede.

The Warmth of a Calgary Winter

Often, a solid ceiling of gray-blue cloud arches over the city. Beyond its clearly defined edge, near the horizon, sparkles the blue Albertan sky. When you see it, start unbuttoning your coat. A chinook is on the way.

Chinooks occur year-round, but are especially noticeable in winter, when the temperature can rise by as much as 25°C (45°F) in one hour. Prevailing westerly winds from the Pacific drop their moisture as they move east toward the Rockies. Forced to rise over the mountains, the winds are warmed and dried by the effect of increasing speed as they descend the eastern slopes and spread out over the prairie. Named after the Chinook tribe, which occupied the mouth of the Columbia River, from where the winds seemed to originate, chinooks can often cover most of southwestern Alberta. In the Calgary and Pincher Creek areas, the overall effect of frequent chinooks can reduce the devastating chill of a prairie winter to as little as thirty days.

EXPLORING CALGARY

Any tour of Calgary should start at the Calgary Tower, a 626-foot structure at the center of the city (9th Ave. S. and Center St.) This is one of Calgary's most distinctive landmarks. From the observation deck there is an unchallenged view of 96 kilometers (75 miles) in every direction. For a more relaxing view of the panoramic mountains and prairie, take advantage of the Tower's lounge and revolving dining rooms. There is a $2.25 elevator charge.

The tower is part of a complex housing the VIA Rail terminal, Palliser Hotel, the Olympic Interpretive Centre, and a number of retail stores and boutiques; it is connected by an enclosed elevated pedestrian walkway with the Glenbow Museum, the Convention Center and the Four Seasons Hotel.

The Glenbow Museum has an amazing collection of Indian and Inuit art and historical western Canadian artifacts from the days of the fur trade through the time of the oil boom. The wide variety of exhibits include a military section with armor and guns; a stamp and coin collection; sculpture, paintings and prints.

Just north is the Performing Arts Centre, which incorporates the historic Calgary Public Building. The Stephen Ave. Mall is a lively pedestrian area ideal for people-watching, sunning and shopping. The mall covers 4 blocks between 3rd St. W. and 1st St. E. Just east is the Burns Building, historic home of the cattle baron's meat market, and location of the Calgary Tourism and Convention Bureau. Continue north on 3rd St. W. to 7th Ave. and the Toronto Dominion Square. On the fourth level is the Devonian Gardens, a 2½-acre enclosed oasis with close to 1,600 subtropical plants, waterfalls, fountains and pools crisscrossed with bridges and paths. There are shops, snack bars, even a playground.

The Calgary Centennial Planetarium and Science Centre is 8 blocks west at 7th Ave. and 11th St. The observatory, model rockets, vintage aircraft and weather station display complement the 255-seat theater.

From here it is a brisk 12-block walk northeast to Princes Island Park on the south side of the Bow River. On the way, stop in at the Energeum, 5th Ave. S.W. and 6th St. The story of energy in Alberta is told in lively fashion with videos and models of oil fields. Princes Island is a good place, close to downtown, to let the kids run and work off steam. Several sculptures decorate the gardens. To get back to the center of town, walk south on 2nd or 4th St. W. to 9th Ave. S. and turn left to Center St.

If you are not in Calgary during the first two weeks of July, you can still see Stampede Park, a short ride south on the new light rail transit system (LRT),—where the famous Stampede takes place. There is a long season for both harness and thoroughbred racing at the park. Eat at one of the park's several restaurants or marvel at the new Olympic Saddledome, home of the hockey events, and built in the shape of—you guessed it—a colossal saddle! Nearby Reader Rock Gardens at 26th Ave. and 2nd St. S.E. also warrant a visit.

East of the Calgary Tower is Fort Calgary (950 9th Ave. S.E.). Multi-screen audiovisual presentations will take you back to frontier days. The outline of the original fort is traced by stumps in the ground.

Continue on 9th Ave. to 12th St., then turn left to St. George's Island for both the Calgary Zoo and Dinosaur Park. The zoo is Canada's second largest, with 1,400 representing 400 species. There is also a children's zoo. The 3-hectare (8.2-acre) Dinosaur Park boasts life-size replicas of dinosaurs that roamed Alberta in prehistoric times and an excellent collection of fossils housed in two buildings.

Retrace the route to 9th Ave., turn left and proceed to 20A St. S.E. and the Inglewood Bird Sanctuary, a unique river flats area that is a forested sanctuary for both migratory and resident birds. More than 217 species have been recorded. Admission is free.

Returning again to 9th Ave., travel west to the Blackfoot Trail, then south to Heritage Drive, and west to Heritage Park. The park is dedicated as "a living memorial to those who pioneered the early west." Two authentic town sites and 100 exhibits depict Alberta in the early part of this century and life as it was for early trappers, miners and settlers. It takes at least 3 hours to see the park fully. To get back downtown from here, retrace the route to Blackfoot Trail, then to 9th Ave. and head west to Center St. As you travel west out of Calgary, on Hwy. 1, a fifteen-minute drive from city center brings you, at the western city limit, to Canada Olympic Park, the venue for ski jumping, bobsled, and luge competitions of the 1988 Winter Olympics.

PRACTICAL INFORMATION FOR CALGARY

HOW TO GET THERE. By car: There is easy access by several interprovincial, state, and regional highways. **By train:** *Via Rail* serves Calgary. **By bus:** *Greyhound, Red Arrow, Brewster Grayline.* **By air:** Calgary is served by *Air Canada, Cascade Airways, C.P. Air, Continental, KLM, Pacific Western, Time Air, United, Wardair, Western,* and *Lufthansa.*

ACCOMMODATIONS. Calgary has a wide variety of hotels and motels ranging from luxurious to average. There is no provincial tax on accommodations, but some hotels and motels will charge for local phone calls. Price categories for double-occupancy are: *Deluxe,* $100 and up; *Expensive,* $70 to $100; *Moderate,* $50 to $70; *Inexpensive,* under $50.

During the first two weeks of July, the Calgary Stampede literally sells out the city. As a result, accommodation is at a premium and the cost of a room can jump 20 percent.

Most places accept the following major credit cards: American Express, MasterCard, and Visa; others may also be honored. Not all establishments accept credit cards, therefore we suggest you call for information.

Both the *YMCA* and *YWCA* have large facilities. Each offers complete Y-club amenities. YMCA, 332 6th Ave. S.E. YWCA, 320 5th Ave. S.W. Although the YWCA is for women only, they will accept children (boys under 7) on an overnight basis.

The Calgary Tourist and Convention Bureau offers a free year-round accommodation service. Contact 237–8th Ave. S.E., Calgary, Alta. T2G 0K8 (263–8510).

Deluxe

Delta Bow Valley Inn. 209 4th Ave. S.E., Calgary, Alta. T2G 0C6 (403–266–1980 or 800–661–1463). 400 rooms. A convenient location and all the services and amenities of a deluxe hotel.

Palliser Hotel. 133 9th Ave. S.W., Calgary Alta. T2P 2M3 (403–262–1234). An older CP hotel, but all 350 rooms have been recently updated, and the lobby is grand!

Skyline Hotel. 9th Ave. and Centre St. S., Calgary, Alta. T2G 5A6 (403–266 –7331). One of the top hotels in town. The rooms are all special and the tableware is silver. Hotel is adjacent to charming indoor garden.

Westin Hotel Calgary. 4th Ave. and 3rd St. S.W., Calgary, Alta. T2P 2S6 (403–266–1611 or 800–228–3000). This 554-room property is perhaps the finest in Calgary. Its Owls Nest dining room is rated one of Canada's top-10 eating establishments.

Expensive

Calgary Centre Inn. 202 4th Ave. S.W., Calgary, Alta. T2P 0H5 (403–262–7091 or 800–661–1463). There is a slight extra charge for water beds and 9-ft., heart-shaped playpens; air-conditioning, bar, licensed dining room, pool, and massive beer parlor.

Carriage House Motor Inn. 9030 Macleod Trail, Calgary, Alta. T2H 0M4 (403–253–1101). The works, from air conditioning to wheelchair services. Cable TV, direct-dial phones, in-room movies, cabarets, saunas, nightclub.

Chateau Airport. 2001 Airport Rd. N.E., Calgary, Alta. T2E 6Z8 (403–276–9681). 288 rooms and suites. Adjoining Calgary International Airport. Weekend rates and family plan available. Some rooms may be more expensive.

Crossroads Motor Hotel. 2120 16th Ave. N.E., Calgary, Alta. T2E 1L4 (403–291–4666). On Trans-Canada Hwy. at eastern entrance to city. 242 air-conditioned rooms. Western entertainment in its tavern. Suites available.

Holiday Inn. 4206 Macleod Trail S., Calgary, Alta. T2G 2R7 (403–287–2700). New and up to international standards. No charge for children under 18 in room with parents.

Moderate

Highlander Motor Hotel. 1818 16th Ave. N.W., Calgary, Alta. T2M 0L8 (403–289–1961). Older but well kept. Dining room is one of Calgary's best. Licensed coffee shop, bar, tavern, beer parlor, and cabaret.

Motel Village. Trans-Canada Hwy. and Crowchild Trail N.W. Not just one motel but an area of some two dozen, with a total of over 1,000 rooms. Most times, you have shopper's choice. During the popular season, you'll probably still find some accommodations here. Some rooms are more expensive.

Port-O-Call Inn. 1935 McKnight Blvd N.E., Calgary, Alta. T2E 6V4 (403–291–4600). 156 units. Executive suites, steamroom, racquetball courts, hot tubs and jacuzzi. Wheelchair facilities.

Westgate Motor Hotel. 3440 Bow Tr. S.W., Calgary, Alta. T3C 2E6 (403–249–3181). Good, clean operation and a good local watering hole. Big beer parlor, bar, and good dining room.

Westward Motor Inn. 119 12th Ave. S.W., Calgary, Alta. T2R 0G8 (403–266–4611). Comfortable, well-equipped rooms.

York Hotel. 7th Ave. and Centre St. S., Calgary, Alta. T2G 2C7 (403–262–5581). 135 rooms (some air-conditioned). Good family hotel. Color TV, dial telephones, sauna, beer parlor.

Inexpensive

Relax Inns. North, 2750 Sunridge, Calgary, Alta. T1Y 3R2 (403–291–1260). South, 9206 Mcleod Trail, Calgary, Alta. T2J 0P5 (403–253–7070). For both: 800–661–9563. Reasonably priced, clean—qualities that are attracting more and more believers. Convenient to highway.

HOSTELS. *Southern Alberta Hostelling.* 1414 Kensington Rd. N.W. Year-round accommodations near downtown area. Members, $9; nonmembers, $12 per night, single.

HOW TO GET AROUND. Getting around in Calgary is easy provided you remember to note the suffixes attached to street addresses. Streets run north–south, avenues run east–west. Calgary is divided into quadrants by Centre St. (N-S) and the Bow River and Memorial Drive (E-W). Suffixes (NW, NE, etc.) are attached to all street addresses. Forget the suffix and you may wind up on the opposite side of town.

By Public Transit and Taxi. Calgary has an excellent LRT system. Fare is $1, exact change. Taxi fares tend to be high by North American standards. The airport limo to downtown is a good deal compared to the bus, if three or more people share.

TOURIST INFORMATION. Comprehensive information about attractions, accommodations, prices, and maps is available by writing to *Travel Alberta,* Box 2500, Edmonton, Alta. T5J 0H4 or from *Calgary Tourist and Convention Bureau,* 237 8th Ave., S.E., Calgary, T2G 0K8 (263–8510).

SEASONAL EVENTS. March: *Rodeo Royal, Agricultural Round-up.* **May:** *Calgary International Horse Show.* **June:** *Spruce Meadows National* (equestrian). **July:** *Calgary Stampede* (rodeo). **September:** *Spruce Meadows Masters* (Equestrian). **December:** *Christmas Box Concert* and *Singing Christmas Tree.*

PARKS AND GARDENS. Calgary has over 11,000 acres of parkland within its boundaries. Some of the most important are Bowness, Confederation, Edworthy, Glenmore, Fish Creek, and Patric Burns Memorial. Be sure to visit *Reader Rock Gardens, Aviary at Zoo, Brewary Gardens, Devonian Gardens* (Downtown) and *Garden Terrace* (Convention Centre).

CHILDREN'S ACTIVITIES. *Bonzai Water Slide,* 8500 Macleod Trail S. is open June 15 to Labour Day. Full day, $8.00; half-day, $5.50. *St. George's Island Zoo* should be entertaining. *Calaway Park* is a 60-acre theme park with 15 rides, 3 miles west of Calgary on Hwy. 1. Admission: $10.95 per person; *Calgary Zoo* and *Dinosaur Park,* 9th Ave. and 12th St. S.E. Adults: $3.50; children under 12: $1.00.

SPORTS. Participant Sports. *Skiing* is also highly popular with *Canada Olympic Park* right in the city. The mountain runs of Fortress, Sunshine, Lake Louise, and Norquay offer skiing from November to May. Rentals of equipment are readily available in the city, and several bus packages provide economical and popular transportation packages. *Tennis, swimming, jogging,* and *hiking* facilities are numerous and free. There's lots of area for *cross-country skiing* in the winter. *Racquetball* and *health-exercise* facilities are numerous. And, of course, *horseback riding* is always available. Calgary has a city-wide *biking* trail that is widely used.

Spectator Sports. Aside from *rodeo,* Calgary is immensely proud of its Canadian *Football* League *Calgary Stampeders* and National *Hockey* League *Calgary Flames.* It has pro *baseball* and a host of semi-pro and amateur teams in a myriad of leagues.

CAMPING. For information, contact *K.O.A.* Box 10, Site 12, R.R. 1, Calgary, T2M 4N3 (288–0411). Open Apr. 15-Oct. 15. *Sunalta Trailer Parks, Ltd.,* Sub PO 55, Calgary, T3B 0H0 (288–7911). Open Apr. 1-Oct. 31.

MUSEUMS AND HISTORIC SITES. *The Glenbow/ Alberta Institute* is located on 9th Ave. at 1st St., S.E. Covers a broad spectrum of Alberta history. Its displays include one of greatest collections of guns and coins in existence, war trophies and equipment. Eskimo art and Indian artifacts, plus a fine carriage collection. Adults: $2; children under 12 free with adult.

Heritage Park is a living, working museum. An entire town lives within its 60 acres. Buildings are authentic and were brought here from their original settings in various parts of Alberta. Majority of people who run the community, i.e., paddlewheeler steamboat, mining train, blacksmith shop, general store, bakery, newspaper, are all retired career persons who now enjoy carrying on their life's work here. Adults: $4.00; children: $2.00.

Centennial Planetarium, 11th St. and 7th Ave. S.W., is a unique mixture of entertainment, education, thrills, and facts. It offers star shows, an observatory, and an aerospace museum. Star shows: afternoons, $3.00; evenings, $4.00.

Ft. Calgary, 750 9th Ave. S.E. On 30 acres of prairie, the ruins of the 1875 North West Mounted Police fort are marked for your wandering around enjoyment. Exhibits of artifacts and superb audio/visual/sensory presentation make a visit more than worthwhile. No admission charge.

Princess Patricia's Canadian Light Infantry Museum, at Currie Barracks, 4225 Crowchild Trail SW. Commemorates the regiment's years of service to Canada. The Original Color, on display, was handmade by HRH Princess Patricia. Admission free.

Sam Livingstone Fish Hatchery. 1440 17A St. S.E. Displays showing species and explaining habitats, breeding, and location of fish found in Alberta. Free admission.

PERFORMING ARTS. Music. *Calgary Philharmonic Orchestra* presents several series from classic to pop each season. *Mount Royal Woodwind Quintet,* performs regularly at the Leacock Theatre at Mount Royal College. *Music at Noon,* a noon time program offered September through April at the W.R. Castell Central Library. Further, Calgary is a recording center for all manner of contemporary groups and artists; consequently a full spectrum of entertainers may be heard at various locations throughout the year.

Choral. *Calgary Renaissance Singers and Players* is an unusual group performing at the University of Calgary Theatre. *Southern Alberta Opera Associa-*

tion presents three operas a year at the Jubilee Auditorium. *Devonian Gardens* features regular entertainment from concerts to impromptu sessions.

Theater. *Alberta Theatre Projects,* at the Calgary Centre for the Performing Arts (The Centre). Excellent group offering five plays per year. *Calgary Theatre Singers* present old-time favorites and musicals. *Loose Moose Theatre* offers innovative productions at the Pumphouse Theatre. *Lunchbox Theatre* performs irregularly in Bow Valley Square at noon hour. *Story Book Theatre* gives matinees every weekend at the Pumphouse Theatre. *Theatre Calgary* is a top professional organization with two series each season at The Centre.

Dance. *Alberta Ballet Company* is an excellent young company performing primarily at the Jubilee Auditorium.

SHOPPING. Try *The Calgary Cabin* and *Green's Lapidary* for special Albertan products.

RESTAURANTS. Alberta is cattle country and Calgary is the absolute heart of it all. It doesn't really matter what kind of beef you order, just as long as it's steak! The melt-in-your-mouth smoothness and special taste of Alberta sweet-grass-fed-and-grain-finished steak should not be missed. Calgary is also loaded with ethnic restaurants and gourmet menus. Naturally the fast-food takeouts and franchises are also in abundance.

Restaurants are listed by price category as follows: *Deluxe,* $50 and up; *Expensive,* $30–50; *Moderate,* $15–30; *Inexpensive,* under $15. Prices include an appetizer or soup, entrée, and dessert. Drinks and tips are not included.

Most places accept the following major credit cards: American Express, MasterCard, and Visa; others may also be honored. Not all establishments accept credit cards, therefore we suggest you call for information.

Deluxe

The Owls Nest. Westin Calgary. 320 4th Ave. S.W. One of the top ten restaurants in the country. Gourmet cooking with interesting selections. Worth the cost.

Caesars. 512 4th Ave. S.W. A simple but elegantly decorated restaurant. Possibly the finest food in Calgary. Steaks, ribs, seafood, and chicken.

The Calgary Tower. 9th Ave. at Centre St. International cuisine with a revolving dining room close to 600 feet above street level.

Don Quijote Restaurant. 1220 Kensington Rd. Seventy-six-item menu specializes in cuisine native to southern Spain. Specialties include roast suckling pig.

Franzl's Gasthaus. 2417–4 Street S.W. The feeling of a Rhine castle, the sounds of an "oompah band," and exquisite Bavarian food.

Hy's. 316 4th Ave. S.W. This is the original Hy's and still his best. The steaks are unbeatable in Calgary; the seafood nearly as good.

Inn on the Lake. Acadia Dr. and Lake Bonavista Dr. S.W. Fantastic view, plush decor, fine food.

Moose Factory. 1213 1st St. S.W. Two dining areas—two décors (Art Nouveau to intimate Modern). Dress regulations. Excellent menu. Piano/vocalists.

Omi of Japan. 615 2nd St. S.W. In the tradition of Japanese restaurants where you sit at the stove. Elaborate Samurai steak ceremony, excellent food.

The Red Carpet. Elbow Dr. and Glenmore Trail. Standard menu of steak, seafood, and prime rib, but sensational quality.

The Saddle Room. In the Saddledome at Stampede Park. Overlooks exhibit areas and has a great view of the Bow River Valley.

The Stagedoor. 830 9th Ave. S.W. Filled with mementos of the 20s, 30s, 40s, this charming restaurant features rack of lamb, curried shrimp, and prime rib of beef.

Three Greenhorns. 503 4th Ave. S.W. Good beef, carefully aged and prepared.

Tiki-Tiki. 718 8th Ave. S.W. Tropical, Polynesian, grass thatching—an enjoyable experience. Polynesian food and charcoal-broiled steaks.

Traders. In Skyline Hotel, 9th Ave. S.E. and Centre St. A fine dining room, elegant atmosphere, and excellent food.

Expensive

Black Angus. 1818 16th Ave. N.W. in the Highlander Motor Hotel. Fine food and service.

Casa D'Italia. 2820 Centre St. N. Excellent Italian food. Small, but with tasteful atmosphere.

Dilettante. 3rd floor, Scotia Centre, 225 7th Ave. S.W. Sophisticated. Outstanding wine list. Specialties include frogs' legs, truffles, steak Maubeuge, and lobster Newburg.

La Chaumiere. 121 17th Ave. S.E. Refreshingly French. Meticulous quality and service. Flaming duck, brandied tomatoes, steak Diane and crêpes.

Pardon My Garden. 4th Ave. and 4th St. S.W. Décor after fine, old garden of Calgary mansion. Crêpes, seafood, and steaks.

Taj Mahal. 4816 Macleod Trail S. Finest authentic Indian cuisine and atmosphere. Exotic delicacies. Curry.

Wellington's Fine Restaurant. 10325 Bonaventure Dr. S.E. A promise of gourmet delights fulfilled.

Moderate

Greek Korner Ristorante. 1604 14th St. S.W. Fried squid and pickled octopus are among the varied dishes.

Greek Village. 1212 17th Ave. S.W. Best Greek feeling in town. Superb food. Authentic décor.

Mother Tucker's. 345 10th Ave. S.W. Informal homespun with truly great food, fresh bread, homemade desserts.

Inexpensive

Francisco's. Hospitality Inn S., 135 Southland Dr. S.E. Mexican food in a California atmosphere.

Karouzo's. 2620 4th St. N.W. Listed primarily for the city's finest pizza experience.

Keg 'n Cleaver. 1101 5th St. S.W. Three of these in town, but the one addressed is tops. Steaks and prime rib are the specialties.

Old Spaghetti Factory. 628 9th Ave. S.W. Spaghetti and Italian foods served in a warehouse, redone in turn-of-the-century décor.

Phoenix Inn. 616 9th St. S.W. Best special is chop suey. Great Chinese smorgasbord.

 NIGHTCLUBS AND BARS. Calgary is an entertainment-loving city with hundreds of spots featuring professional talent. One notable completely in the Western character of Calgary is *Ranchman's* with two locations: 1117–1st St. S.W. and 9311 Macleod Tr. S. It features many popular artists along with drinking, dining, and dancing.

EDMONTON

The clean, modern skyline of Edmonton dominates the high banks of the river that gave it life. The North Saskatchewan River curves gracefully through the entire city, its breathtaking valley today providing mile after mile of parkland for Edmonton residents.

The river was an important part of the fur trade's vast network of waterways that traversed Canada from the Pacific all the way to the Gulf of St. Lawrence. Archeological evidence suggests that even 6,000 years ago, the bluffs of the North Saskatchewan were a gathering place for semi-nomadic hunters. History has assured Edmonton's position as a gateway, but it was the fur trade that first put Edmonton on the map.

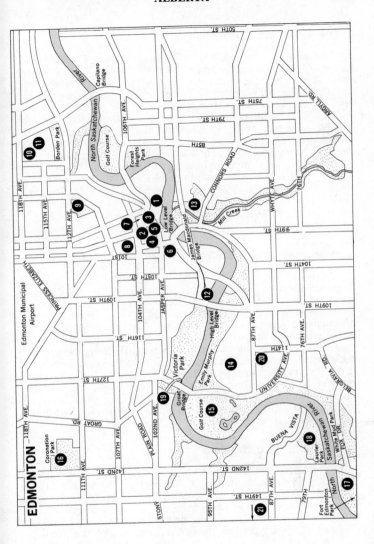

EDMONTON

Points of Interest

1) Convention Center & Aviation
   Hall of Fame
2) Art Gallery
3) Citadel Theater
4) City Hall
5) Civic Center
6) Vista 33 Observation AGT Bldg.
7) Post Office
8) CN Tower (Via Rail station)
9) Commonwealth Stadium
10) Northlands Park
11) Edmonton Northlands
12) Legislature Building
13) Muttart Conservatory
14) University of Alberta
15) Hawrelak Park
16) Space Sciences Center
17) Fort Edmonton Park
18) Valley Zoo
19) Provincial Museum
20) Jubilee Auditorium
21) Canada Fantasyland/West
    Edmonton Mall

The Athabasca Connection

A series of fur forts built in the vicinity between 1795 and 1830 dominated the western fur trade. All the forts were built along the north shore, in more hospitable territory, because all of the lands south, as far as Wyoming, were home to fierce warriors, the Blackfoot people, who didn't take kindly to strangers.

The first Fort Edmonton was built by the Hudson's Bay Company in 1795, near present-day Fort Saskatchewan. It was named for the birthplace (now a London suburb) of one of its clerks. The first fort of the rival North West Company was built nearby. Over their competitive years, the two companies built four sets of forts in the area. After their merger in 1821, two more forts were built, the last in 1830, on the present site of the Alberta Legislature Building. Fort Edmonton quickly became the western hub of the fur trade, providing access, via its connection with the Athabasca River, all the way from the Rockies to the fur-rich interior of the Lake Athabasca region.

Steamboats and Sawmills

But the fur trade encouraged lots of comings and goings, and not a great deal of permanent settlement. Real development outside the fort did not begin until the 1870s, after the decline of the fur trade and the government's acquisition of the Hudson's Bay Company's huge western land holdings. Steamboat and sternwheeler traffic took over the fur traders' water routes, and the beginnings of local industry dawned with the establishment of the Hudson's Bay Company's sawmill operation in 1875. As the Indians retreated from their ancestral lands, the settlement of Strathcona grew on the south shore of the river. With a population of about 1,000, compared to Strathcona's 500, Edmontonians in the early 1880s indulged in boundless optimism for their future, and eagerly awaited the coming of the national railroad.

The Yellowhead "By-Pass"

The route through the Rockies, via the Yellowhead, was endorsed by the Canadian Pacific Railway's chief engineer, Sir Sandford Fleming. It should have assured Edmonton's future. Edmontonians took it very personally when the final choice of the more southern Kicking Horse Pass took the railroad right through "upstart" Calgary in 1883. The historic rivalry between the two cities dates from this decision.

The Riel Rebellion

At the beginning of 1885, all of Canada seethed with rumors about the Métis and Indian unrest in Saskatchewan. Louis Riel, asked by the Métis to negotiate their grievances (mostly relating to land claims) with the federal government, had come to the conclusion that he had a divine mission to lead his people to victory over the federal government. At Duck Lake, on March 26, the Métis forces under Riel's lieutenant, Gabriel Dumont, launched a bloody battle with about 100 North West Military Police forces and volunteers under the command of Major L. N. Crozier. Within thirty minutes, Crozier lost one-quarter of his force, the Métis only five men. Edmontonians watched the developments closely, with mounting concern. One week later, the rebellion came much closer to home.

The Hudson Bay store at Frog Lake was a major point on the trail from Fort Carleton and Fort Pitt to Edmonton. On April 2, 1885, a band of Cree under Big Bear attacked the store, killing a priest and eight citizens. Big Bear and his Cree roamed eastward toward Fort Pitt, looting, killing, and taking prisoners. The Canadian militia, under Maj. Gen. T. B. Strange was dispatched from Calgary, arriving in Edmonton on April 20. From there they marched east, joining two forces sent north from Swift Current and Qu'Appelle. Métis resistance was finally broken at the three-day Battle of Batoche. By May 15, Riel had been arrested and Canada's largest armed revolt was over. Edmontonians heaved a sigh of relief and got on with their future.

The town continued to prosper. The first bank west of Winnipeg opened in Edmonton in 1889, and in 1891 Edmonton had its own power plant. That same year, the Canadian Northern Railway arrived in Strathcona. Travelers going on to Edmonton still had to descend the steep river banks by coach, then ferry across to the larger settlement, but at least the line brought more traffic to the vicinity. By 1892 Edmonton had achieved town status. The North Saskatchewan River was a hive of activity between the thriving communities of Edmonton and Strathcona.

Sternwheelers and Sluices

The first mention of gold in the river is found in reports of the Palliser Expedition of the 1850s. To the east of the fort, Thomas Clover was panning for gold, as early as 1862, on the sand bar that still bears his name. But by 1894, the river was frantic with prospecting activity. Early methods of panning for gold on the shores gave way to sluices. Dredging syndicates, using all sorts of machinery, mostly made from scrap parts, were mining the river bed. But the wealth of the traces found in the river was nothing compared to the great fortune awaiting Edmonton.

Back Door to the Klondike

There had been rumors of gold in the Canadian north for years. Edmontonians, busy mining their own river and developing their city, paid little attention. But when the news of George Carmack's big strike in the Klondike's Bonanza Creek hit town in 1897, the place went mad. Every community from Winnipeg to Victoria was affected by the Klondike gold rush, but none quite like Edmonton. Edmonton's historic fur trade connection with Lake Athabasca became the basis of the All-Canadian route to the goldfields. Miners and outfitters flocked into town. Within two years, the population, about 1,500, had doubled, and merchants were prospering. Few citizens of the town left for the goldfields themselves. Bigger money was to be made in town. Outfitters, not the least of which was the Hudson's Bay Company, made fortunes provisioning the expeditions heading north.

Most prospectors reached the Klondike by the coastal route, from Seattle to Skagway and overland to the Yukon gold fields. But the All-Canadian route, as it became officially known, had several advantages. It traveled between mountain valleys, eliminating the need to haul several hundred pounds of supplies over mountains. Edmontonians loudly promoted the fact that there was no duty chargeable on goods taken north from their city, since no part of the route went through Alaska. And it was a year-round route.

The All-Canadian route followed the fur trail north to Athabasca Landing. From there prospectors streamed north on the river, in canoes, on handbuilt scows and rafts, or by steamer, to Fort Chipewyan on Lake Athabasca. Via Slave River, they reached Fort Resolution on Great Slave Lake. From there, they went overland to the Mackenzie River, which connected in the delta with the Peel River. Another overland section, then down the Steward River, and they were finally in the gold fields. With good weather, and a minimum of accidents, a lucky prospector could cover the 1,900 miles to the gold fields in about sixty-five days.

A secondary route, the Assiniboine Trail, led northwest from Edmonton through the present St. Albert area to Fort Assiniboine in the Swan Hills, on to the Peace River Country, and into the gold fields via the Pelly River. But this route, through muskeg (spagnum bog) and wilderness was absolutely treacherous. Less used, it was more quickly littered with the graves of the unlucky. In short, it was a dismal failure.

Actually, both routes were tortuous, and few made it to the Klondike. Of about 2,000 fortune-seekers who left from Edmonton, only about one-quarter made it to the gold fields, and fewer still prospered when they got there.

Boom, Boom, and Boom

But Edmonton was never the same again. As the city entered the twentieth century, the optimism of its pioneers began to seem entirely justified. The town continued to prosper, especially as the wave of immigration sweeping over western Canada settled the vast agricultural region it serviced. In 1904, Edmonton became a city, and in 1905, to the shock and dismay of Calgarians, it was designated the capital of the new province of Alberta. Edmonton was finally linked with the national railway to the south by the Canadian Northern in 1905, and its neighbor, Strathcona, became the birthplace of the new University of Alberta. The first of several speculative land booms followed Edmonton's amalgamation with Strathcona in 1912. Another, in the 1920s, followed the resurgence after the economic slowdown during World War I.

During the 1930s, pioneering bush pilots, among them World War I flying aces Wop May and Punch Dickens, made aviation history, linking Edmonton by air with Canada's far north, assuring Edmonton's future as gateway to the Arctic.

Edmonton's fortunes, into the 1940s, were linked with its position as the provincial capital, and with those of the huge agricultural region it served. In 1941, Edmonton was still a relatively small city, population 92,000.

But then in 1942, the serious threat of a Japanese invasion proved the need to the United States military for an overland route to Alaska. Within eight months, the Alaska Highway was rammed through five mountain ranges and forested wilderness. American servicemen flooded into Edmonton as it became the center for construction of the road and for United States northern military operations.

Black Gold

But it was an event in 1947 that assured Edmonton's stunning rise in the last half of the twentieth century. In February, just south of town, Leduc No. 1 became the first major oil discovery north of Turner Valley; it was quickly followed by Pembina, Woodbend, and Redwater. Edmonton was suddenly surrounded with producing oil fields. Pumping "grasshoppers" began to dot farmer's fields all around the city. As Calgary became the financial center for the petroleum industry, Edmonton became its administrative service center, with thriving oil refining and petrochemical industries.

In the 1950s and 1960s, Edmonton, like Calgary, was one of the fastest-growing cities in Canada. Construction cranes were everywhere. In the 1970s, massive exploitation of Alberta's crude-oil reserves in the Fort McMurray area to the north were spurred on by the world energy crisis, and brought another construction boom to Edmonton. Canadians flocked to Edmonton from other provinces in unprecedented numbers. Suddenly it was a city of a half-million people.

As the petroleum industry grew in national importance, so did the provincial government of Alberta. More and more attention focused on Edmonton as the seat of that government. During the late 1970s the city achieved a national political prominence unimaginable to even its biggest early boosters.

Modern Edmonton is clean, vibrant, and young. The average age of its population of 700,000 is well below the national average. Although some historic buildings survive, especially in Old Strathcona, the most striking feature of the city's architecture is its newness. Modern office buildings and high rises dominate the landscape. The central area of Edmonton has been more or less continuously rebuilt since the 1950s and every part of the city shows the effects of construction booms of the 1960s and 1970s.

Like Calgary, Edmonton has been hard hit in the 1980s by the economic recession and declining world oil prices, but the hardiness of its pioneer spirit and optimism shows up in a burgeoning arts and cultural scene. For Edmontonians, surely the next economic boom is just over the horizon.

EXPLORING EDMONTON

Edmonton's most striking physical characteristic is the valley formed by the North Saskatchewan River, which flows right through the city. Seventeen miles of parks have been developed in the river valley, linked by hiking and bicycle trails. Pedestrian footbridges criss-cross the river.

The center of town is the intersection of Jasper Ave. (101st Ave.) and 100th St.—marked on its southeast side by the venerable Hotel Macdonald (closed for refurbishing between mid-1983 and 1987).

Two blocks east is Edmonton's stunning new Convention Center, an $84 million complex sunk into the river bank and home of Canada's Aviation Hall of Fame. Proceed north from 100th St. to 102nd Ave. to find Sir Winston Churchill Square and the Civic Center. Surrounding the square are a number of interesting buildings. At the southeast corner of 102nd Ave. and 100th St. is the Centennial Library, constructed in 1967 to celebrate Canada's 100th birthday. The Citadel Theater is nearby. A startling blend of brick and glass, it is western Canada's center for the performing arts. The Edmonton Art Gallery is to the north at the intersection of 99th St. and 102A Ave.; next door is a striking inverted pyramid, the Law Courts Building. At the north end of the square is City Hall, and to the west is Edmonton Center, a climate-controlled complex of shops, restaurants, office towers and hotel. Immediately north of the square, behind City Hall, are the CN Tower, which houses the Via Rail station, and the Central Post Office.

A walk back to Jasper Ave. from Sir Winston Churchill Square and then west takes you past several new office buildings—try the Bay (the descendant of the Hudson's Bay Company) for Canadian sculpture and art.

The Alberta Legislature is located south of Jasper Ave. on 108th St. Built on the site of an early Fort Edmonton trading post, it was completed in 1912. Tours of the building are available. The grounds, with manicured lawns, lovely gardens and a greenhouse, are open to the public and make for a delightful summer stop. If you walk down the hill through the grounds to 97th Ave. and cross the river on the James Macdonald Bridge, you'll come to the Muttart Conservatory, an imaginative botanical garden. Housed within five glass pyramids are tropical, desert, temperate and floral showcases. There is an excellent view of downtown from the reflecting pool at the base of the pyramids. (It is actually quite a long walk from the Legislature to the Muttart; a cab might be in order.)

Travel south of Jasper Ave. on 109th St. and cross the 160-ft. High Level Bridge (built in 1913). If you turn right onto 87th Ave., you'll reach the University of Alberta. Founded in 1908, this is Canada's second largest university, with more than 25,000 students. Buildings of interest are Rutherford House, 11153 Sask Dr., the former home of Alberta's first premier; the Hub Mall, a unique shopping center and residential complex, open to the public; the Geology Museum in the Earth Sciences; and the Walter C. MacKenzie Health Sciences Centre.

One of the visitor highlights of Edmonton is Fort Edmonton Park located on 158 acres of parkland on the south bank of the river, west of the University. A steam locomotive takes you from the parking lot to the reconstructed early trading post, from which the city grew. The park also has restorations of streets from 1885, 1905, and 1920. Also worth a visit and adjacent to the park is the John Janzen Nature Center.

As you leave Fort Edmonton, heading back toward the center of town, visit the Valley Zoo in Laurier Park—a must for children. The animal displays feature storybook characters and there are a miniature train, carousel and food concessions.

The drive from Laurier Park along 142nd St. to 102nd Ave. skirts three of Edmonton's most exclusive residential areas: Valleyview, Capital Heights and Old Glenora. Proceed right on 102nd Ave., east to the Provincial Museum at 128th St. Built in 1967, the museum displays artifacts of human and natural history in Alberta. One of the world's finest dinosaur exhibits, a superb collection of native crafts and remarkable geological section make this a rewarding stop. Also of interest is the beautiful old Lieutenant Governor's mansion, known as Government House. Admission is Free.

Proceed east on 102nd Ave and turn south at 124th St. to Jasper Ave. In the vicinity is the area known as Gallery Walk, with several small galleries and the Canadiana store. To get back downtown, proceed east on Jasper Ave. to 100th St.

A Fantasy Come True

Definitely worth at least one separate excursion is West Edmonton Mall, billed as the world's largest indoor playground and shopping center. Open seven days a week, year-round, the shopping mall has over 800 retail stores, including 5 large department stores. Fantasyland includes an Ice Palace, whose NHL-size surface is the practice home of the Oilers, and the tropical atmosphere of an indoor waterpark, with water slides, a wave lake, indoor beach, and underwater submarine rides. There are 28 midway rides. West Edmonton Mall is at Stony Plain Rd. (Hwy. 16) and 170th St. Shuttle bus service operates from 14 hotels in town.

PRACTICAL INFORMATION FOR EDMONTON

HOW TO GET THERE. By car: Major east-west access on the Yellowhead Highway (Highway 16), north-south on Highway 2. **By train:** *Via Rail* serves Edmonton. **By bus:** *Greyhound, Red Arrow.* **By air:** Edmonton is served by *Air Canada, America West, Continental, Time Air, Western, C.P. Air, Pacific Western, Wardair, United,* and *Northwest Orient.*

ACCOMMODATIONS. Edmonton has a variety of hotel and motel accommodations. There is no provincial tax on accommodations, but most hotels and motels will charge for local phone calls. Price categories for double-occupancy are: *Deluxe,* $90 and up; *Expensive,* $60–90; *Moderate,* $40–60; *Inexpensive,* under $40.

Reservations are recommended at all times. Many hotels have toll-free numbers; or rooms can be booked through travel agents.

Most places accept the following major credit cards: American Express, MasterCard, and Visa; others may also be honored. Not all establishments accept credit cards, therefore we suggest you call for information.

YMCA, 10030 102A Ave., Edmonton, Alta. T5J 0G5. *YWCA,* 10305 100th Ave., T5J 0G5. Accommodation from $12.00 up.

University of Alberta, 44 Lister Hall, U. of A., Edmonton, Alta T6G 2H6. Student residences are available from May through August only. (The residences involved are located at 87th Ave. and 116th St.)

Deluxe

Chateau Lacombe. 101st St. at Bellamy Hill, Edmonton, Alta. T5J 1N7 (403–428–6611 or 800–268–9411). One of Canada's fine hotels, with 320 rooms. A Canadian Pacific hotel.

Fantasyland Hotel. 17700–87 Ave., Edmonton, Alta. T5T 4V4 (403–444–3000 or 800–661–6454). At the West Edmonton Mall. 360 theme rooms and suites. Jacuzzis and lots of special effects in rooms, such as waterfalls.

Four Seasons Hotel. 10235 101 St., Edmonton, Alta. T5J 3E9 (403–428–7111). 314 rooms. Part of the Edmonton Centre shopping/business complex. Best dining room in town, excellent coffee shop, good pub, entertainment. Edmonton's best.

Ramada Renaissance Hotel. 10155 105th St., Edmonton, Alta. T5J 1E2 (403–423–4811). New in 1986. 300 rooms and suites. Downtown location, indoor pool, sauna, exercise facilities.

The Westin-Hotel Edmonton. 10135 100th St., Edmonton, Alta. T5J 0N7 (403–426–3636). 416 rooms and suites. Luxury accommodation with lobby, bar, pool, Carvery Dining Room.

Expensive

Alberta Place Apartment Hotel. 10049 103rd St., Edmonton, Alta. T5J 2W7 (403–423–1565). 85 suites; kitchens. Excellent downtown location. Good buy.

Convention Inn. 4404 Calgary Trail, Edmonton, Alta. T6H 5C2 (403–434–6415). Convenient southside location on Hwy. 2. 237 rooms, many in a new wing. Good dining room.

Edmonton Inn. Kingsway and 119th St., Edmonton, Alta. T5G 0X5 (403–454–9521). Interesting and well-managed hotel. 442 rooms. Edmonton's largest. Close to Municipal Airport.

Sheraton Edmonton. 10010 104th St., Edmonton, Alta. T5J 0Z1 (403–423–2450). 141 rooms, indoor pool, night club.

Terrace Inn. 4440 Calgary Trail, Edmonton, Alta. T6H 5C2 (403–437–6010). 228 rooms. Very attractive. Good selection of restaurants and lounges, entertainment, pool.

Moderate

Argyll Plaza Hotel. 9933 63rd Ave., Edmonton, Alta. T6E 6C9 (403–438–5876 or 800–661–6454). 48 rooms, indoor skating rink.

Capilano Motor Inn. 9125 50th St., Edmonton, Alta. T6B 2H3 (403–465–3355). Southeast location. 150 rooms. Air-conditioned, swimming pool, wheelchair facilities, licensed dining room, and lounge.

Mayfield Inn. Mayfield Rd. and 109th St., Edmonton, Alta. T5P 4K8 (403–484–0821). 250 rooms. Tennis courts, theater restaurant, licensed tavern, saunas. A fine complex, convenient to the west end.

Renford Inn on Whyte. 10620 Whyte Ave., Edmonton, Alta. T6E 2A7 (403–433–9411). 90 rooms and executive suites. Cable TV, sauna, health pool, dining, and lounge. Convenient to university.

Royal Park Apartment Hotel. 9835 106th St., Edmonton, Alta. T5K 1C3 (403–420–0809). 50 apartment suites, laundry, 24-hour TV, available by the day, week, or month.

Sandman Inn. 17635 Stony Plain Rd., Edmonton, Alta. T5S 1E3 (403–483–1385). 150 air-conditioned rooms. Swimming pool, all amenities.

Van Winkle Motor Inn. 5116 Calgary Trail, Edmonton, Alta. T6H 2H4 (403–434–7411). 196 units. TV, telephones, swimming pool, sauna, and exercise rooms.

Inexpensive

Relax Inns. South: 10320 45th Ave., Edmonton, Alta. T6H 5C4 (403–436–9770). West: 18320 Stony Plain Rd., Edmonton, Alta. T5S 1A7 (403–483–6031). For both: 800–661–9563. Each has 227 units. Clean, good highway locations—good value.

HOSTELS. Edmonton Hostel. 10422 91st St., Edmonton, Alta. T5H 1S6. Sleeping-bag accommodation at about $9 per night for CHA members or about $12 per night for nonmembers.

HOW TO GET AROUND. It's easy to get around in Edmonton. Streets run north–south, avenues run east–west. The center of town is Jasper Ave. and 100th St. **By Transit and Taxi.** Edmonton has an excellent LRT and bus system. Fare is $1 (exact change). Cabs may be hailed or ordered by telephone. Guided sightseeing tours are available from Royal Tours.

TOURIST INFORMATION. Comprehensive information about attractions, accommodations, prices and maps is available by writing to *Travel Alberta*, Box 2500, Edmonton, Alberta, Canada, T5J 2Z4, or from *Edmonton Convention & Tourism Authority*, No. 104, 9797 Jasper Ave., Edmonton, Alta. T5J 1N9.

SEASONAL EVENTS. March: *Western Superrodeo.* **June:** *Jazz City.* **July:** *Klondike Days.* City-wide extravaganza during last 2 weeks that includes "Sourdough Raft Race" on first Sunday (essentially a flotilla of junk on the river); the "Promenade" later that same day (200,000 participants in Klondike-period clothing parading through the streets); *Summerfest* (street entertainment). **August:** *Heritage Festival; Folk Music Festival; Fringe Theatre Event.* **November:** Largest *rodeo (Canadian Finals)* of fall season.

CHILDREN'S ACTIVITIES. *Muttart Conservatory,* 98th Ave. and 96A St. Unique glass pyramids offering plant species representative of specific world climatic zones. Adults $2.25; seniors and youth, $1.50; Children $1.

Canada Fantasyland, West Edmonton Mall. Indoor amusement park, water park, indoor ice palace, and petting zoo. Admission charge.

Edmonton Space Sciences Center, 142 St. and 111th Ave. in Coronation Park. Multi-media productions of astral activities. Free admission for exhibit galleries. Charges for star theater and IMAX film theater.

Valley Zoo, Buena Vista Rd. and 134th St. Story-book fairytales form the theme for the exhibition of 500 birds and animals. Adults, $2.25; children, $1; seniors and students, $1.75

SPORTS. Pride, joy and ecstasy could describe an Edmontonian's feeling for the three major professional teams, the *Eskimos* (CFL **football**), the *Oilers* (NHL **hockey**), and *Trappers* (PCL **baseball**). Yet, besides these clubs, there are hundreds of others, semi-pro and amateur, actively engaged in a myriad of competitive sports. Recreational participation in sports is a civic preoccupation. As a result, Edmonton is able to offer opportunities and facilities that are perhaps unequaled in Western Canada.

CAMPING. *Shakers Acres,* Box 59, Winterburn, T0E 2N0 (on Hwy. 16, west at Winterburn overpass). 178 sites with food service, indoor pool, laundry and showers, groceries, and gameroom.

Glowing Embers, Hwy. 16 west and Hwy. 60, 273 sites, hook-ups, laundromat, store.

Klondike Valley, Box 2, Site 3, R.R. 1, Edmonton, T6H 4N6. 150 sites, laundry, groceries, showers, firewood.

Rainbow Valley Campground, Whitemud Drive and 119 St. 80 sites, showers, laundry, store.

HISTORIC SITES. *Rutherford House,* 11153 Saskatchewan Dr. On the University Campus. The restored home of Alberta's first premier. Tours free.

John Walter Historic Site (southwest of Walterdale)– location of the 1st home built on south side of the North Saskatchewan River in 1874. Also, site of first telegraph office (1879).

MUSEUMS AND GALLERIES. Museums. *Canada's Aviation Hall of Fame* in the Convention Centre, 9797 Jasper Ave. Features memorabilia from famous aviators and bush pilots.

Fort Edmonton Park, Whitemud Dr. and Fox Dr. (exit on south end of Quesnell Bridge). 178-acre site consisting of the reconstruction of an 1846 fort, a farm, and a "living" town featuring specific dated streets that trace Edmonton's history. Adults $4.00, youth $2.50, Senior Citizens and children (6 to 12) $2.00, preschoolers free.

Edmonton Police Museum, 9620–103A Ave. at Police headquarters, depicts the history of law enforcement in Alberta. Free.

Provincial Museum of Alberta, 12845 102nd Ave. Wildlife, Native history and culture, geology, fossils, dinosaurs, and Alberta's pioneer past. Free.

Strathcona Science Park, south of Hwy. 16 east on 17th St. A collection of displays which describe and interpret how Alberta's natural resources are put to use; plus the evidence of man's existence in prehistoric times featuring an actual "dig" for artifacts to 3000 B.C. Admission is free.

Ukrainian Museum of Canada. 9543 110th Ave. Costumes, Easter eggs, dolls, and tapestries are displayed. Free.

Galleries. *Beaver House,* 10158 103rd St., Alberta art. Free admission. *Edmonton Art Gallery,* 2 Sir Winston Churchill Sq. Free. *Ring House Gallery* at the University of Alberta (south of the Faculty Club off Saskatchewan Dr.). Free.

PERFORMING ARTS. Music. The famous *Edmonton Symphony Orchestra* performs at the Jubilee Auditorium. *Edmonton Opera* features noted world stars within its numerous productions throughout the year. Music is very much a part of Edmonton's attitude and appetite, and the type of music played is as varied as the cultural background of the city.

Theater. *The Citadel Theatre,* with its most impressive facilities in uptown Edmonton, is close to being Canada's top-rated company. Its productions feature international name players. Additionally, Edmonton enjoys a healthy array of amateur companies that offer performances during various times of the year. One of the most successful dinner theaters in Canada is at the *Mayfield Inn.*

SHOPPING. Try *The Bay* for Inuit art and special Albertan products. West Edmonton Mall, 170 St. and Stony Plain Rd. 800 stores and services.

RESTAURANTS. Edmonton is a highly cosmopolitan city. As a result, it likes to boast that it has " . . . an enchanting potpourri of cultures and tastes . . . you can eat in over twenty-four different languages. . . . " Discovering just how diversified is the Edmonton palate can be an exciting and satisfying part of your visit. You don't have to be afraid to try ethnic eateries here. They have to be good, for those who patronize know the difference between genuine and a hopeful imitation.

Restaurants are listed by price category as follows: *Deluxe,* $50 and over; *Expensive,* $30–$50; *Moderate,* $15–$30; *Inexpensive,* under $15. Prices include an appetizer or soup, entrée, and dessert. Drinks and tips are not included.

Most places accept the following major credit cards: American Express, MasterCard, and Visa; others may also be honored. Not all establishments accept credit cards, therefore we suggest you call for information.

Deluxe

Beans and Barley. 10309 81st Ave. A beautiful room. Specials usually pleasant. "4-B" soup is a must, the spinach salad outstanding.

Four Seasons Room. Four Seasons Hotel, 102nd Ave. & 101st St. A fine dining room with broad, imaginative menu. Worth the money.

Oliver's. 11730 Jasper Ave. A formal setting for some of the best beef in town. An ambitious menu with something for everyone.

Victor's. 10405 Jasper Ave. A private elevator lifts you to a candlelit dining room. Prompt service and Continental cuisine. A well-run establishment.

Waldens. 10245 104th St. Lush greenery and skylights. Beef, veal and fresh fish daily. Excellent vegetables.

Expensive

Between Friends. 8615 51st Ave. An inventive kitchen crew prepares beef, veal, pork and lamb. Leave room for dessert.

Bruno's. 8223 109th St. Italian food with the accent on northern dishes. Homemade paté, hearty minestrone. Scallopine Grand Duke is memorable.

Cosmos Greek Village. 10312 111th St. Greek all the way in food, service, and atmosphere.

The Crêperie. 10220 103rd St. (The Boardwalk). 16 different selections of crêpes offered in this delightful eatery in a renovated warehouse.

The Japanese Village. 10126 100th St. Japanese style flavored with "Teppan" adds a plus to a great restaurant.

Ling Nan. 10582 104th St. One of Edmonton's venerable Chinese restaurants. Personal attention, very large selection.

Moderate

Bistro Praha. 10168 100A St. A bohemian gathering place. Large portions of hearty fare served in an air of informality.

Bones. 10220–103 St. (the Boardwalk). Hickory-smoked ribs and chicken. Good burgers. Enthusiastic service.

The Courtyard. Four Seasons Hotel. This is the less formal of the hotel's two restaurants. An excellent variety of food, carefully prepared.

Cucci's. Sun Life Bldg. 99th St. and Jasper Ave. Reasonably priced continental fare. Pleasant surroundings and attentive service.

Mongolian Food Experience. 100A St. and 101st Ave. and 102 Ave. and 125 St. The chef stir-fries vegetables and meat to your taste.

Red Diamond House. 7500 82 Ave. Not downtown but worth the trip. Reliable Cantonese cooking. Hot pots a specialty.

Steakboard. 10220 103rd St., located in the Boardwalk. Good steak and well-stocked salad bar. Steak sandwich is the best buy.

Trapper John's Trading Post. 10355–105 St. Western-town setting, with Campfire ribs, Goldmine Chicken and Fools' Gold. Good salad bar.

Inexpensive.

Swiss Chalet Chicken and Ribs. 3 locations. 17008 107 Ave., 5020 97 St., 4976 98 Ave. Reliable, solid fare.

Merryland. 7006 109th St. Basic Korean food and basic décor. Good food and value.

Strathcona Gasthaus. 8120 101st St. Hearty German fare and large portions. Excellent value in down-to-earth setting. Closes early. Unlicensed. No reservations, no credit cards.

 NIGHTCLUBS AND BARS. Edmonton takes a back seat to no city when it comes to night entertainment. Nightclubs, cabarets, taverns, lounges, and that infamous Alberta watering hole—the beer parlor—combine to provide a constant offering of local and international artists.

THE ROCKIES

Alberta's Rockies owe their rugged beauty to their extreme youth. Their bedrock is part of the Pre-Cambrian shield evident in the opposite, northeast corner of Alberta, and is about 3.5 billion years old. But the spectacular jagged peaks were created by colossal shifts and thrusting movements that literally shoved these massive mountains up out of the bowels of the earth during the Tertiary Age, less than fifty-eight million years ago. As rock mass ground against huge rock mass, the mountains were tilted and folded. Over the millions of years to the present, they have been carved by the combined effects of glacial action, wind, and erosion into some of the most beautiful and rugged scenery in the world.

There are three life zones in the mountains. The seemingly barren rock of the craggy peaks is above the treeline, an elevation of about 2,100 meters (almost 7,000 feet). This zone, high among gusting winds, resembles the Arctic tundra. Lichen and scrub grasses struggle for a toe-hold during a short growing season. In the sub-alpine zone, midway down the mountainsides, lesser winds and more moderate climate support thick stands of spruce and alpine fir. Beneath these two zones, on the slopes and valley bottoms, the montane forest supports a broad variety of life: trees—cottonwood, birch, poplar, spruce, pine, and fir—and animals—squirrels, chipmunks, beaver, muskrat, bear, elk, deer, moose, goat, and sheep.

EXPLORING THE ROCKIES

The Rockies were first sighted by a white man in 1754, from the area near Innisfail, on present Highway 2. During the early 1800s the mountains were explored by many white men, in search of routes to the west. David Thompson was one of the first to cross the Rockies—by the Athabasca and Yellowhead passes—on behalf of the fur trade. One notable group, under Captain John Palliser, explored the Rockies intensively from 1856 to 1860, as part of their mission to determine the suitability of western Canada for settlement. Several place names reveal the extent of their travels. Hector Lake is named for the group's famed naturalist and geologist, Sir Charles Hector, who, in turn, named Kicking Horse Pass after an incident with an unfriendly pack horse. The Palliser Expedition, while not optimistic about the future of western Canada, did feel that a railway through the Kicking Horse Pass would be feasible.

Twenty-three years later, as surveyors for the CPR roamed through the Rockies, three railway workers noticed the warm sulphurous waters bubbling out of the ground near Banff townsite. So many conflicting land claims were staked in the area that the government responded

ROCKY MOUNTAIN PARKS

Monkman Provincial Park

Continental Divide

Grande Cache

Cariboo Mountains

Willmore Wilderness Park

Scale
0 10 20 30 Miles
0 10 20 30 40 Kilometers

N

16

Yellowhead Hwy.

16 Edmonton

Jasper National Park

Mount Robson

40 Hinton

ALBERTA

Wells Gray Provincial Park

Jasper

2

Mount Robson Provincial Park

Mt. Edith Cavell

Icefield Parkway

Columbia Icefield

Forestry Trunk Road

Hamber Provincial Park

93

Peyto Lake
Bow Lake

Rocky Mountains Forest Reserve

11

Glacier National Park

Monashee Mountains

Yoho National Park

Banff National Park

Thompson River

Mt. Revelstoke National Park

Kicking Horse Pass

Lake Louise

Bow Valley Pkwy.

Kamloops

1

Revelstoke

Kootenay National Park

Banff

Canmore

1

Calgary

95

Radium Hot Springs

Mt. Assiniboine Provincial Park

Peter A. Lougheed Provincial Park

2

BRITISH COLUMBIA

97

Purcell Mountains

40

Vancouver

Columbia River

Kimberley

3

Crowsnest Hwy.

3

6

WASHINGTON

3

Waterton Lakes National Park

IDAHO MONTANA

395

95

93

Glacier National Park (US)

97

89

by setting aside a small surrounding parcel of land as Canada's first national park (1885). From that decision has grown the entire national parks system.

In the wake of the railroad came the coalminers and prospectors, swarming through the mountains in search of gold, copper, and silver. Briefly, towns like Silver City and Anthracite burst into existence and, when their mineral seams ran out, were surrendered to nature once more. Today, the best of the mountain scenery is preserved for those who pause to admire and who wish to take nothing away but photographs.

There are four distinct regions preserved in Alberta's Rockies, each worth the time it takes to explore them: two adjoining national parks, Banff and Jasper, Waterton Lakes National Park in the southwest corner of Alberta, and the Eastern Slopes, mostly wilderness and forest reserve. Between Banff and Jasper the incredible Icefield Parkway runs north–south for 230 kilometers (143 miles) through some of Canada's most spectacular scenery. As you explore the townsites of Banff and Jasper, let the existence of the parkway tantalize you into venturing farther through each park. Your senses will not be disappointed. And if you crave to commune with nature as much as with scenery, visit Waterton Lakes National Park. This little park will treat you to more wildlife than you can imagine in such a small area. The wilderness of the Eastern Slopes invites an active participation in the wonders of nature, from hiking, camping, and fishing to a full range of winter sports.

It's important to note here that the main roads will provide a lot, but not all, of the splendor of the Rockies. Do not hesitate to follow turnoffs and sideroads as you travel through the mountains. Every hiking trail and gentle footpath, every lake or river where boats and canoes can be rented, every primitive or modern campground offers vistas not available from main roads. Take the time to wander; your senses will be generously rewarded.

Banff National Park

Canada's first national park, Banff (6,594 square kilometers, 2,546 square miles) is located 130 kilometers west of Calgary on Highway 1. The park has recently been designated a UNESCO World Heritage Site. Just after you enter the park gates on Highway 1, the northeast face of Mount Rundle, viewed from the Valleyview picnic area, is a fine example of the violent upward thrusts that helped create the Rockies, pushing this portion of the mountain straight up out of the ground. At the next four-way junction, you can follow a 12-kilometer (7-mile) loop to Lake Minnewanka, the only lake in the park where power boats are permitted, and try some of the great fishing to be had at Two Jack Lake or Johnson Lake. Or you can turn left, following a secondary route into Banff townsite, up Tunnel Mountain, past a great view of Hoodoos and the large campground and winding back down the mountain into the town of Banff.

Banff Townsite

A circle of towering mountains—Rundle, Tunnel, Cascade, Norquay, and Sulphur—looms over Banff townsite, nestled in the Bow River Valley. Banff Avenue, the main street, follows a dog-leg curve through the main part of town, dead-ending across the Bow River at the Park Administration Office, with its lovely Cascade Gardens. To the extreme left, Spray Avenue leads up toward the Banff Springs (shown on our cover). Its baronial architecture dominates the town.

Sumptuous grounds, an imposing view, and a great golf course make it well worth a visit even if you're not a guest. A less sharp left turn on to Mountain Avenue leads you to the Upper Hot Springs. A sharp right takes you along Cave Avenue to the original springs at the Cave and Basin.

The town is always alive with people. In winter, skiers flock to enjoy some of the best snow conditions in the world at Norquay and Sunshine. The ski season can run from mid-November until the end of May. The rest of the year the town attracts hikers, climbers, and sightseers. In summer, its sidewalks teem with people. 1,100 kilometers (680 miles) of trails radiate from the townsite. There are canoe trips on the river, horseback riding, cycling, and climbing. Rental of all equipment is readily available.

Shops along Banff Avenue sell British woollens, Irish linen, and native and Canadian crafts. Gondola rides offer breathtaking views of the Rockies from Sunshine, Sulphur, and Mount Norquay, which also has a chairlift.

But *the* thing to do in Banff is to take a dip in the hot springs. Water in the Upper Hot Springs has a winter temperature of 29°C (48°F), 42°C (55°F) in summer. The discovery of the Cave and Basin Hot Springs in 1883 led to the formation of the park itself. Early bathers descended from a hole in the roof of the cave. Closed for many years, the pool has been renovated and is open from June to September. Historical and geological displays, open year-round, describe the effects of the warm sulphurous waters on the flora and fauna of the area.

There are many scenic drives from the townsite. You can meander partway up Tunnel Mountain to St. Julien Road, to the Banff Centre School of Fine Arts. From May to August, you can take in events at the Banff Centre Festival of the Arts. In the marshlands along Vermilion Lakes Road, you might well see beaver, moose, and a variety of birds. You can follow the spectacular switchback Mount Norquay Road that climbs 300 meters (980 feet) up the mountain to the base of the chairlift. Or, you can head towards Lake Louise on Highway 1, or the even more scenic route, the Bow Valley Parkway (Highway 1A).

Along the way you'll see Hole in the Wall Cavern, on the cliff of Mount Cory. The cavern was likely cut away by melting waters from the glacier that once filled the Bow Valley. You can follow the trail that begins at Johnson's Canyon Resort and proceeds 1 kilometer to the pleasant Lower Falls in Johnston Canyon. If you're feeling adventurous, continue the hike past the Upper Falls to the Ink Pots, in a meadow beyond the Upper Falls. Six cool springs bubble out of the ground year-round, their lovely aqua colors created by glacial sediments in the waters.

The Gem of the Rockies

Lake Louise may be the most famous lake in Canada. It is certainly one of the most photographed. Known as Lake of the Little Fishes to the Indians, it was named, perhaps most fittingly, Emerald Lake, by a member of a CPR survey crew in 1882. Within a short time it was renamed, though, to honor the daughter of Queen Victoria who was married to the Governor General of Canada.

From the village, the road climbs steadily for about 2 kilometers. Framing the lake, a perfect pictorial composition poses Beehive Mountain to the right, Fairview Mountain to the left, and the majestic Victoria glacier in the center. The calm, blue-green water reflects a perfect mirror image of the scene. Chateau Lake Louise sits like a castle on a hill, overlooking all this splendor.

The XV Olympic Winter Games

Calgary

February 13–28, 1988

In 1988, Calgary, at the eastern base of Canada's Rocky Mountains, will play host to the longest and largest Olympic Winter Games yet. Already a major tourist destination in summer, when the Stampede takes place, and a gateway to winter ski resorts, Calgary is going all out to prepare for over a million and a half visitors, well over a thousand athletes, and international media coverage of the event.

If you will be traveling to Calgary in late 1987 you can still see much that will enhance your appreciation of the games. You can ski at Nakiska and the Canmore Nordic Center and attend events at some of the venues. The Canada Olympic Center is open until August 1988, exciting visitors with special-effects films and hands-on computer simulations of Olympic events. Whether you will be at the games or in February or in Alberta any time in 1988, there's a lot of Olympic atmosphere to enjoy.

HISTORY

The ancient Olympic tradition was revived in 1896, but it was another thirty years before the Winter Olympics received separate recognition. Winter sports really came of age internationally during the 1920s, particularly after the pioneering of alpine ski racing by an Englishman, Sir Arnold Lunn. As a result of a decade of lobbying by several countries, a 1924 International Winter Sports Week in Chamonix, France, was dubbed, two years after the fact, the first Olympic Winter Games.

In spite of a relatively limited number of host countries able to offer the required environment and facilities, the Winter Olympics have continued to grow in prestige and popularity. The Chamonix Winter Olympics took place with 294 competitors from 11 coun-

1

tries. In 1988 Calgary will play host to about 1,500 athletes from 34 countries.

Calgary: A Modern Western City

Visitors to Calgary are always impressed with the friendly western spirit of its relatively youthful population of 625,000. The city itself is aglitter with the glass and steel of brand new buildings, especially in the downtown core, where virtually continuous rebuilding has gone on since the 1960s. Calgary's image is that of a place alive with energy, enthusiasm, and a justifiable optimism in its future.

There are many facets to this image. In its brief one hundred-year history, the city has mushroomed from a police post into the hub of Canada's western transportation network, the heart of the Canadian cattle-ranching industry, and the financial soul of the country's petroleum industry. It's also home to the legendary Calgary Stampede—the fantastic summer spectacle of rodeo skills that takes over the city every July, drawing one million visitors each year from around the world. And almost since its birth, Calgary has been a tourism gateway to the scenic splendors and the fabulous winter playground of the Canadian Rockies—Banff, Lake Louise, and more recently, Kananaskis Country.

In staging the Winter Games, the list of "firsts" that the host city has accumulated is impressive. For the first time there will be a full sixteen days of competitions. Calgary is both the first Canadian city to host the winter games, and the first major city anywhere in the world, served by its own international airport, to have the honor. Calgary is served by eight international airlines, making it one of the most easily accessible host cities ever. Where previous Winter Olympics have relied to a large extent on existing facilities, virtually all new venues have been constructed for these games—a real boon to a city that saw some tough economic times in the early 1980s. The venues, such as the world's first fully enclosed speed-skating oval, will wow athletes and spectators alike with their advanced construction techniques and state-of-the-art facilities. Even Hidy and Howdy, the Welcome Bears, score a first. They are the first male and female official Olympic mascots.

Calgary may be the first host city ever to deal with the prospect of several sudden springs, right in the middle of winter, a feat that has kept technical experts and planners busy for many months developing the sophisticated refrigeration and snowmaking techniques that will offset the untimely arrival of a chinook during the games. Chinooks, which are moist winds that blow in from the Pacific ocean and warm as they rise over the Rockies to head east, can suddenly dump warm air over southwestern Alberta causing a temperature change of over 25°C (45°F) in one hour. In some years, the overall effect of chinooks reduces Calgary's wintry chill to only about thirty days of cold weather. Olympic planners have installed refrigeration equipment that can cope with temperatures of up to

20°C (68°F) and 100 percent snowmaking capability on alpine ski runs.

The Rockies

Visitors to the 1988 Winter Olympics will be able to experience firsthand the splendor of some of the world's most spectacular scenery. Less than an hour from town, southwest of Calgary, Kananaskis Country is a huge recreational area under development by the provincial government. The scenery here rivals anything seen in the traditionally visited areas of Banff, Lake Louise, and Jasper. One of the beautiful mountains here is Mount Allan, where the alpine skiing events will be held.

A short drive further west of Calgary, right next door to magnificent Banff National Park is the town of Canmore. A former coal town, Canmore has been rejuvenated in recent years as a less expensive tourism alternative to Banff townsite, but it has had a virtual rebirth as an Olympic site. Olympic Village II is near the Recreational Center in town. It will house about 600 athletes competing at the Canmore Nordic Center. The Nordic Center is at the base of the imposing Mount Rundle, whose scenic beauty towers over nearby Banff townsite.

Building for the Olympics

The construction of permanent facilities—like the downtown Olympic Plaza, site of medals presentations; the new housing at the athletes' village that will become university student residences; and the Calgary Center for the Performing Arts, which will feature heavily in the Olympic Arts Festival—will result in a monumental legacy of training, recreation, and artistic facilities for Calgarians and their visitors from around the world. It has all been made possible by a tremendous level of financial and administrative cooperation among three levels of government—federal, provincial, and municipal—and a large measure of corporate sponsorship. The federal government is providing up to $45 million in operational funding, a $30-million Olympic Endowment Fund, and commemmorative coin and stamp programs. In addition, it is spending about $200 million to finance the construction, in whole or in part, of several venues. The provincial government has invested more than $55 million in Olympic construction. The city of Calgary is providing all necessary public services as well as cooperative funding of construction of several venues. Corporate sponsorship will further defray capital investment and operating costs.

Who Makes It All Work

The XV Winter Olympics' Organizing Committee (OCO '88) has been hard at work ever since Calgary got the nod from the International Olympic Committee (IOC) in September, 1981. It was Calgary's fourth bid for the Winter Games. After beating out

Vancouver in 1979 to receive the blessing of the Canadian Olympic Association, Calgary went on to compete internationally against Falun, and Cortina d'Ampezza, Italy, to become the IOC's choice for 1988.

The OCO staff has numbered about 300 in the last hectic year before the games began, overflowing an entire floor of office space in city hall. In spite of the almost inevitable cost overruns that plague such events preparations for the games are proceeding well. Ticket sales are booming, now that some early difficulties have been ironed out. OCO President Bill Pratt still radiates his usual confident smile.

There will also be as many as 10,000 volunteers, chosen by a computer that matches qualifications with needs. OCO '88 expects there may be four times as many volunteers as spaces available. The Olympic Volunteer Center is at McMahon Stadium on the University of Calgary campus.

PRACTICAL INFORMATION

If you want to attend the 1988 Winter Olympics, you'll have to hurry. Tickets have been on sale for over a year, and several events are sold out. As during Stampede accommodation prices are up and availability of prime space is already way down. And in the mountains, the ever-popular ski season will be well underway. If you can't attend the Olympics, but will be in town sometime before or after you can still taste Calgary's Olympic flavor by visiting the venues or the Olympic interpretive center (until August 1988). See the *Before and After* Section for details.

How to Get There

See the "How to Get There" section in the practical information for Calgary in the Alberta chapter of this book.

If you plan to drive to Calgary for the games, remember that, chinooks notwithstanding, you will be testing the heart of a Canadian winter. Snow tires are necessary for your car, and an engine-block heater might be a good idea. Bring warm winter clothing, especially windproof outerwear if you will be visiting the mountain venues. Keep the possibility of chinooks in the back of your mind, though, and bring at least one outfit suitable for those days when the temperature might soar from 10°C to 2°C (from 14°F to 68°F) by lunchtime.

Tourist Information

OCO '88 is your best bet for obtaining up-to-date information on the games. Their *Facts and Information* brochure gives complete descriptions of both events and venues. The *Come Together in*

Calgary brochure contains a complete schedule not only of medals competitions and demonstration events, and test competitions but also held during 1987 at the various venues, ticketing and accommodations information. OCO is producing regular updates of information right through to the beginning of the games, on ticket sales, accommodations, and Arts Festival events. Contact the *XV Winter Olympics Organizing Committee,* Box 1988, Station C, Calgary, Alberta, T2T 5R4 (403–262–1988).

Information can also be obtained from *The Olympic Mail Center,* Calgary Tourist and Convention Bureau, 237–8 Ave. S.E., Calgary, Alberta, T2G 0K8 (403–263–8510), and *Travel Alberta,* Box 2500, Edmonton, Alberta T5J 2Z4 (800–661–8888, from outside Alberta).

Ticket Sales

Of 1,669,000 tickets available, about 400,000 were reserved for media, and VIPs leaving about 1.2 million tickets for public sale. At press time, about 800,000 tickets were unsold.

For the past year, in North America, tickets have been sold on a mail-order basis. Mail-order forms are available through Royal Bank branches in Canada, major Canadian daily newspapers, and OCO '88. In other countries, about 50 appointed ticket agents around the world can also handle the travel and accommodation arrangements. OCO '88 can provide a list of ticket agents for all countries.

Tickets are being sold on a first-come-first-served basis. Payment by check, money order, or Visa credit card must accompany the application form. Tickets are being mailed out now.

At this point, though, probably the best way to order tickets is by phone. Contact OCO '88 (403–270–6088) for ticket orders and up-to-date information on sold-out events.

At press time, the following events were completely sold out: the opening and closing ceremonies; all figure skating; speed skating; and short track (demonstration event). See the *Olympics Events* Section for specifics on which events still had tickets available at press time.

Ticket prices range from $15 to $75 (Canadian), with almost two-thirds at $25 or less. The only free events are disabled skiing exhibitions to be held at Canada Olympic Park and Canmore Nordic Center.

Accommodations

Every year during the Calgary Stampede, accommodations are scarce and rates are higher than usual. Attendance at Olympic events is expected to parallel that of the Stampede, which averages 1,000,000 visitors per year, so the same situation exists. In Kananaskis, the newest Canadian Pacific hotel, the Lodge at Kananaskis, opened in June 1987, and two other hotels (still unnamed at press time) are expected to open in time for the games in the vicinity of Mount Allan. The town of Canmore, and nearby

Banff are stretching all their accommodation resources to house visitors. But it is well to remember that they are small towns and frequently booked to capacity during a *normal* ski season!

The *Olympic Housing Bureau* is providing the only comprehensive accommodations reservations and referral service. The Bureau can give information on availability, rates, location, and amenities for Calgary and the surrounding area, for hotels, motels, bed-and-breakfast and residential accommodations. Write to Olympic Housing Bureau, Box 4600, Station C, Calgary, AB T2T 5R4. If you plan to come to Calgary before or after the games, address your enquiry about accommodations to the Calgary Tourist and Convention Bureau, at the same address.

Ticket order forms also contain a section for accommodation requests. Check off this section when sending in your ticket order. Hurry: the allocation of space began last year!

Transportation

Within the city, there's no question that public transportation is your best bet. Except for some limited parking at demonstration events and designated areas for handicapped drivers, there is no public parking at venues within the city. The cost of public transportation is free for all ticketed events, including those at Canada Olympic Park. Just present your event ticket, and your ride is free. For unticketed events, such as medals presentations at Olympic Plaza, you must pay the regular transit fare.

Calgary has an excellent transit system. In addition to regular bus service, there is the new LRT system, known locally as C-trains, which has been extended in time for the games. There is also direct express bus service to several venues within the city, including Canada Olympic Park, from two large Park and Ride locations: in the northeast at 36 St. and McKnight Blvd. NE, and in the southwest at Glenmore Trail & Richard Rd. S.W. (near Mount Royal College).

Express public bus service is also provided from the Olympic terminal downtown on 3rd St. E. to Canada Olympic Park, Mount Allan, and Canmore. The service is free to Canada Olympic Park. Service to Mount Allan and Canmore costs $15.00 per person round-trip. Bus service operates for two hours before and after, and continuously during each event.

There is provision for free public parking near the venues at Canada Olympic Park, Mount Allan, and Canmore. At Canada Olympic Park, there is parking for 10,000 within walking distance of venue, but you must reserve your stall when buying your event tickets. At Mount Allan parking and free shuttle bus service for about 5,000 at two lots, one about 3km north of the main entrance, the other near the junction of hwys. I and 40, are available.

Canmore offers free parking for about 4,000 and free shuttle service to the Nordic Center. Shuttle service operates for two hours before and after, and continuously during the events. For detailed information on public transportation during the games, visit any of the Calgary Transit informations booths around the city.

BEFORE AND AFTER

If you're visiting Calgary prior to the games or later in 1988, you can still enjoy the Olympic atmosphere in several ways. The **Canada Olympic Center** is a *must-see* Olympic showcase. This $5-million state-of-the-art exhibition and information facility rivals the best pavilions of Expo '86. It was designed, constructed, and donated to the Calgary by the Canadian Pacific Group of Companies.

Have you ever stood at center ice while a hockey game surges all around you? Have you ever raced down a ski jump? You can experience this and more at the center. Your entry begins in the IMAX theater, with an 8-minute film with special effects. From there you are turned loose into a myriad of hands-on audio-visual and computer displays. The different games are described in detail. You can call up (on the computer) complete schedule and ticket-price information. A topographical model with narration familiarizes you with the venues; computer quizzes test your Olympic knowledge; and the TV control room simulates production of Olympic broadcasts.

The center will remain in operation until August 1988. Admission is free. It is located in downtown Calgary, on the second floor of Palliser Square, at the base of the Calgary Tower. Wheelchair access is by elevator from the main floor, near the information booth. Hours are Tues–Sat.: 10 A.M.–8 P.M., Sun.: noon–5 P.M., and closed Mondays.

Other Olympic locations such as Nakiska and the Canmore Nordic Center are open for public recreational skiing in winter. McMahon Stadium and the Saddledome offer regularly scheduled football and hockey games. Several of the locations for the Arts Festival events—the Jubilee Auditorium, the Glenbow Museum and the new Calgary Center for the Performing Arts—hold scheduled public performances and exhibitions. One of the feature exhibits of the Arts Festival is already on display at the Glenbow. (See Arts Festival Section.)

And the test competitions held during the year before the Winter Olympics offer a great chance for a preview of some Olympic venues. The remaining events to be held prior to the games are as follows:

Olympic Oval:
Speed-skating (World Cup) .... Nov. 1987

Saddledome:
Figure Skating (Skate Canada) .... Oct. 27–Nov. 1, 1987

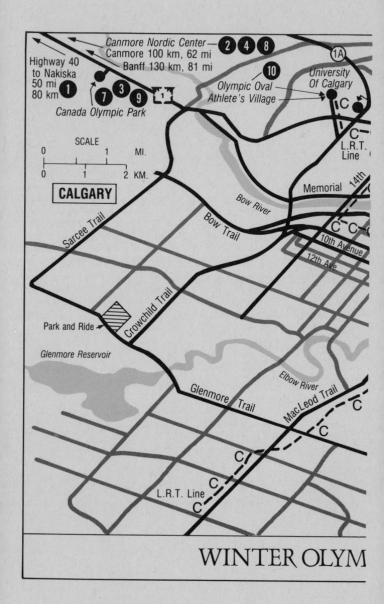

Canmore Nordic Center—
Canmore 100 km, 62 mi
Banff 130 km, 81 mi

Highway 40
to Nakiska
50 mi
80 km

Canada Olympic Park

Olympic Oval
Athlete's Village

University
Of Calgary

L.R.T.
Line

Memorial 14th

Bow River

Bow Trail

SCALE

0   1   MI.

0   1   2   KM.

CALGARY

Sarcee Trail

10th Avenue

12th. Ave.

Crowchild Trail

Park and Ride →

Glenmore Reservoir

Elbow River

Glenmore Trail

MacLeod Trail

L.R.T. Line

WINTER OLYM

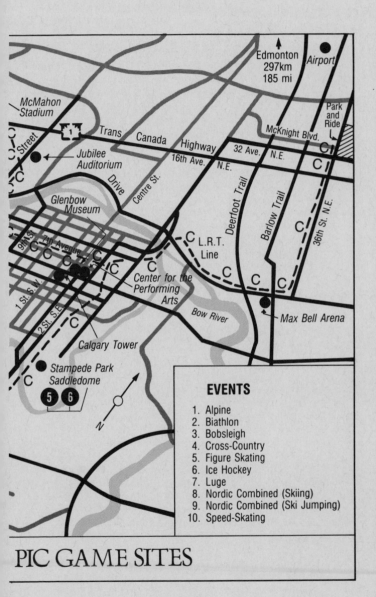

PIC GAME SITES

OLYMPIC EVENTS

Three months before the Winter Olympics begin, Olympic fever will hit Canada, and the Olympic torch will be flown from Olympia to Canada's most easterly major city, St. John's, Newfoundland. The torch relay will be the first visible, manifestly Canadian aspect of the games. Various amateur sports groups across the country will carry the torch, "by uniquely Canadian methods" (visions of snowshoes and dogsleds!) through all ten provinces and two territories—a distance of about 10,000 kilometers (6,000 miles)—to Calgary.

When the torch officially arrives in northwest Calgary, it will do so on the grounds of one of Calgary's proudest achievements, the University of Calgary, whose facilities will play a major role in the games. The main athletes' village is here, where $12 million in renovations to existing student housing, construction of two new residences and renovations to the dining center will cater exclusively to the needs of about 2,000 athletes, coaches, and other officials. Part of the village is the physical education building, where the expansion of facilities includes a new world-class sports-medicine clinic. It will later be open to students, faculty, and the general public. Also at the university, the Olympic Volunteer Center has been the hub of activity since 1986 for up to 10,000 volunteers required to help stage the games.

The university provides as well the location for the opening and closing ceremonies and speed-skating competitions.

Opening and Closing Ceremonies

The university-owned McMahon Stadium is considered "old" by Calgary standards. One of two or three facilities not built expressly for the games, the thirty-year old stadium has undergone an extensive $15.8-million facelift. New features include an entire floor of offices for the Olympic Volunteer Center, an outside elevator to the press booth, a special level of seating for handicapped spectators, new covered permanent seating on the east side of the stadium, and a complete new sound system. 50,000 spectators are expected to witness the opening and closing ceremonies in the "like new" stadium.

Many details of the ceremonies were still under wraps at press time. But OCO '88 has confidently placed the planning of the show in the capable hands of executive producer Paddy Samson, a well-known personality in the Canadian TV and film industries. The highlight of the opening ceremonies will be the arrival of the torch and the procession of the athletes. The show will feature ice (naturally) and will be a "uniquely Canadian event with a definite western flavor" according to one planner. Where other recent shows of this type have tended to focus on youth, these ceremonies will be designed to feature, and appeal to, all age ranges. Opening ceremonies begin at 1:15 P.M. (MST) on Saturday, February 13.

The closing ceremonies, staged in the early darkness of a wintry Calgary evening, will likely feature interesting lighting effects and fireworks. The dramatic moment when the torch is extinguished will be enhanced by the darkness. Closing ceremonies begin at 7:30 P.M. (MST) on Sunday, February 28.

Both events are completely sold out.

HOW TO GET THERE: There is special bus service from the two major Park and Ride locations (see *Transportation* Section). There are also 10 other Park and Ride locations along the LRT route. Take the LRT to University Station or use bus routes 20, 72, or 73.

Speed-skating

Also on the university campus is the totally new Olympic Oval, the world's first fully enclosed speed-skating oval. Completed at a cost of $39.9 million, paid for by the government of Canada, the 400-meter oval is roughly the length of two (Canadian) football fields, or large enough to house twenty-two tennis courts. Its unique design has the roof entirely supported from the outside, allowing maximum visibility for spectators. The structure is ringed with large windows, allowing natural light to flood the interior.

Speed-skating is an exciting individual competition for both men and women. Men's speed-skating is scheduled for Feb. 14, 17, 18, 20, and 21. Women's speed-skating will be held Feb. 22, 23, 26, 27, and 28. All dates are sold out.

HOW TO GET THERE: Take the LRT to the University Station, or use bus routes 20, 72, or 73. There is no express service. Limited parking is available. Take Memorial Drive west to Crowchild Trail then go north to University Drive.

Hockey and Figure Skating

Another major focus of Olympic activity is Stampede Park, where the world-famous rodeo takes place every July. Within the park are the main Press Center, the International Broadcast Center, and the Saddledome and the Stampede Coral—venues for two of the most popular Winter Olympic events.

Since its completion in 1983, the roofline of a huge saddle-shaped building has dominated Calgary's skyline. Structurally unique, the **Saddledome** has the largest concrete suspended roof in the world. There is no such thing as a bad seat. There are no posts or pillars to obstruct view, and no seat is more than 61 meters (200 feet) from center ice. The Saddledome is the playing home of the Calgary Flames of the National Hockey League, and has a seating capacity of 17,000. Early plans called for the closing ceremonies to be held here, but the Saddledome lost out to the larger seating capacity of McMahon Stadium.

Hockey is one of the most popular sports, with three matches scheduled for every day of the games except Tuesday, Feb. 23. Tickets are $20–$30 for preliminary games. Semi-finals tickets are $25–$45. Finals are sold out, as are evening games on Feb. 19, 21, 24, and 26 and afternoon games on Feb. 26 and 27.

The **Stampede Corral,** site of the compulsory figures portion of the skating competitions, was built in 1959, and has a seating capacity of over 6,400. **Figure skating** is one of the most visually elegant Olympic sports. Pairs competitions are scheduled for Feb. 14 and 16. Mens' figure skating will be held Feb. 17, 18, and 20. Dance competitions are scheduled for Feb. 21–23, and ladies' figure skating will be held Feb. 24, 25, and 27. All events are sold out.

HOW TO GET THERE: During the games there is no public parking within Stampede Park. Take the LRT to Erlton or Stampede stations, or use the express Park and Ride service (see *Transportation).*

Ski Jumping, Nordic Combined, Bobsleigh, and Luge

If you head west on the Trans-Canada Highway (Highway 1) toward the mountains, a fifteen minute drive from downtown brings you to **Canada Olympic Park.** Formerly known as Paskapoo, the site has been a recreational ski area for years, but its $60-million transformation by the government of Canada into an Olympic venue will provide a monumental legacy for Calgarians and training athletes for years to come.

Events at this venue are expected to draw well over 300,000 spectators. There are 70-meter and 90-meter jumps, and three training jumps. At the top of the 90-meter jump is a restaurant and media center. An amphitheater provides the outrun area (where jumpers land and stop) and the spectator gallery and is connected by a promenade to the bobsleigh and luge facility.

Ski jumping competitions will be held on Feb. 14 and 17; The 90-meter event (Feb. 20) is sold out. Ticket price is $20.

Nordic-combined competitions include ski jumping (held here) and cross-country skiing (held in Canmore Nordic Center—see below). The highest combined points totals determine medal standings. The jumping portion is scheduled for Feb. 23 and 27. Ticket price is $15, finals are $20.

The partly combined bobsleigh and luge run is said to be 25 years ahead of its time. A unique tuning fork design allows for individual start positions for both bobsleigh and luge. Sensors within the runs can tell athletes exactly where they gained or lost speed. The refrigeration plant includes 100 kilometers (60 miles) of pipe and can be used in temperatures up to 20°C. Because bobsleigh and luge are not widely practiced sports, training facilities for athletes are limited. This run is not only the first ever built in Canada but also only the second in North America (the other is in Lake Placid).

Its future importance as a training facility is without question to devotees of the sport.

Two-man **bobsleigh** events are scheduled for Feb. 20 and 21. Four-man events will be held Feb. 27and 28. Luge competitions are scheduled for Feb. 14–17 and 19. Ticket price for both bobsleigh and luge is $20.

HOW TO GET THERE: Drive west on Memorial Drive to Crowchild Trail, then north to the Trans-Canada Highway, then west. There is temporary parking for 10,000 cars within walking distance of the entrance. You must have reserved your stall when ordering tickets. Free express service leaves from the downtown Olympic terminal in Calgary and from the two Park and Ride locations in the city (see *Transportation*).

Alpine Skiing

As you travel southwest from Calgary, along the well-maintained Highway 40, the road curves at Porcupine Creek. Directly before you in the heart of Kananaskis Country, is majestic Mount Allan, the location of **Nakiska Ski Area**, which is the venue for alpine skiing. First in operation during the winter of 1986–87 (for public recreational skiing), this site is a source of pride and joy for Alberta. There are 30 ski runs, and one reserved for a training run, with a vertical rise of up to 854 meters (2,802 feet) to an elevation of 2,391 meters (7,844 feet) above sea level. A 70 percent pitch on the upper slopes will have athletes traveling at speeds of up to 130 kilometers (80 miles) per hour.

The government fought a difficult battle within the province before settling on Mount Allan. Conservationists were especially concerned about damage to the habitat of a herd of bighorn sheep who call the mountain home. To allay their fears, the logging, blasting, and heavy construction necessary to carve the ski runs out of the virgin mountainside were done only during summer months to minimize the disruption during the crucial winter and spring seasons. Lifts, snowmaking, communication, and utility lines are all constructed on a "corridor" concept for the same reason. A special "Olympic Platter Lift," necessary to obtain the required distance for men's downhill events, has been built as a temporary structure at the top of the mountain, to be removed immediately after the games.

Alpine skiing includes downhill, slalom, giant slalom, and super giant slalom events for both men and women. Men's downhill, Feb. 14, giant slalom, Feb. 25, and slalom, Feb. 27, are sold out. Tickets remain for the men's events, scheduled for Feb. 16, 21,. Ladies' events will be held Feb. 18–20, 22, 24, and 26. Ticket price is $25, finals are $30.

HOW TO GET THERE: From Calgary follow Highway 1 west to Highway 40, then south about 15km (9mi) to Nakiska. Parking and shuttle bus service is available from two lots, one about 3km north of the main entrance, the other near the junction of hwys. 1 and 40.

Direct round-trip bus service from the downtown Olympic terminal (3rd St. S) in Calgary is $15.00 per person.

Cross-Country Skiing, Nordic Combined, and Biathlon

Just outside the former coal-mining town of Canmore, near the gates of Banff National Park, is the **Canmore Nordic Center.** Since construction began in 1984, over 24,000 truckloads of dirt have been moved to "create" a natural setting at the base of Mount Rundle. The spectator area includes no seating, but has been designed to permit spectators to ski in and ski out after events. There are separate start and finish lines for cross-country and biathlon events, separate trails that intersect by a series of bridges, and separate day lodges. The cross-country day lodge has a magnificent fireplace and cafeteria, with a great view of the start and finish.

Cross-country skiing is an entirely different discipline than alpine skiing, calling for endurance over distances of up to 30 kilometers (18 miles). Ladies' events are scheduled for Feb. 14, 17, 21, and 25. Men's events will be held Feb. 15, 19, and 27. The men's 4 × 10km event (Feb. 22) is sold out. Ticket price is $15.

Nordic-combined includes ski jumping (see above) and cross-country skiing. The skiing portion is scheduled here for Feb. 24 and 28. Ticket price is $15, $20 for finals.

Biathlon events combine cross-country skiing with rifle marksmanship, in both standing and prone positions. It is a men-only event. Competitions are scheduled for Feb. 20, 23, and 26. Ticket price is $15.

HOW TO GET THERE: Take Highway 1 west from Calgary to Canmore (about a 55-minute drive). Free parking and shuttle service is on Three Sisters Drive, just west of town. Direct bus service leaves form the downtown Olympic terminal in Calgary (3rd St. S). The round trip is $15.00 per person.

DEMONSTRATION EVENTS

Three demonstration events are also scheduled. These are events not yet included in the Olympic roster, but likely to be so in future games. No medals are awarded.

Curling

In this game, 4-member teams compete against each other, alternately sliding heavy, polished granite rocks along an ice surface toward a circular target. The team whose rocks are closest to the target's center scores points. Points are totaled after ten "ends" are played, to determine the winner. The teams play against each other in small groups (round-robin) to determine semi-finalists. Round-robin events are scheduled for Feb. 15–18. Semi-finals, Feb. 20, and finals, Feb. 21 are both sold out. Ticket price is $20. Curling will be played at Max Bell Arena.

HOW TO GET THERE: Take Memorial Drive east, then south on Barlow Trail to the Max Bell Arena at 1001 Barlow Trail S.E. Although parking is limited, its availability makes driving possible. Take the NE leg of the LRT to Barlow/Max Bell Station, or use bus routes 26, 32, or 33.

Freestyle Skiing

Freestyle includes three types of alpine skiing. Aerials show a definite gymnastic style, ballet is more graceful and expressive and moguls are acrobatic performances on tough downhill terrain. Aerials and ballet demonstrations will take place at Canada Olympic Park on Feb. 21 and 25, respectively. Moguls demonstrations will be held at Nakiska on Feb. 22. Aerials and moguls events are sold out.

HOW TO GET THERE: See directions under ski jumping (Canada Olympic Park) and alpine skiing (Nakiska).

Short-Track Speed-Skating

This is virtually sprint speed-skating, around a laned oval in the fastest time possible. Demonstrations will take place at Father David Bauer Olympic Arena, on Feb. 22–25. All events are sold out.

HOW TO GET THERE: See directions for speed-skating. The arena is just southeast of the main entrance to the university campus.

Disabled Skiing Exhibitions

There will be competitions in alpine skiing for amputees at Canada Olympic Park on Feb. 16, and in cross-country skiing for the blind at the Canmore Nordic Center on Feb. 17. These events are for both men and women. There is no admission charge.

HOW TO GET THERE: See directions for ski jumping (Canada Olympic Park) and cross-country skiing (Canmore Nordic Center).

OLYMPIC ARTS FESTIVAL

Adding more excitement to the Olympic atmosphere is the Arts Festival (January 23–February 28). All over town, Calgary will sizzle with a stunning array of events, showcasing the talents of over 2,200 Canadian and international artists from 18 artistic disciplines. The theaters and concert hall of the Calgary Center for the Performing Arts, the Jubilee Auditorium, the Glenbow Museum—

indeed, virtually every concert hall, museum, and gallery in town—
will be used to stage the more than 600 performances, exhibitions,
and cultural events of the festival. There will be free on-site entertainment at the venues, the airport, and in the streets, provided by
more than 88 performing groups. It all begins at the Olympic
Saddledome with the opening gala—a stage and ice show reflecting the scope and variety of the Canadian and international talent
featured in the festival.

Some of the following highlights were among the details available at press time. The star-studded dance scene will feature performances by Canada's renowned National Ballet and Les Grands
Ballets Canadiens, as well as New York's Joffrey Ballet. The Alberta
Ballet Company will present its new production of *The Snow Maid-
en,* to the music of Tchaikovsky. In contemporary dance, at least six
new works will be presented by Canadian companies. Music will be
well represented by the National Arts Center Orchestra, the Calgary Philharmonic, the Olympic Jazz Youth Orchestra, and by
international orchestras and guest artists. The Calgary Opera Company will present the first ever Canadian production of *Porgy and
Bess.* Among the theater events will be Canada's famous Shaw
Festival.

Native art will be a strong component of the visual arts events.
A good example is the prestigious $2.6-million exhibition " The
Spirit Sings" at the Glenbow Museum.

For the first time in Olympic Arts Festivals, the literary arts will
be showcased as Canadian writers welcome the writers of the
world. Another first is the international Snow Sculpting contest in
Princes Island Park.

The excitement of the games is mirrored in the entertainment of
the Arts Festival. For the most up-to-date information on schedules
and ticket prices, see the official Olympic Ticket Brochure, or contact the Publicity Dept., Olympic Arts Fesitval, OCO '88, Box 1988,
Station C, Calgary, Alta. T2T 5R4 (403–262–1988).

For another perspective of the view, go out on the lake in a canoe rented from the concession near the Chateau. Try the leisurely 3 kilometer (2-mile) Saddle Back Trail, past Mirror Lake and Lake Agnes. For a closer look at the glacier, follow the 6.5-kilometer (4-mile) Plain of the Six Glaciers trail along the shore of Lake Louise.

The Great Divide

Two kilometers along the Lake Louise access road, Highway 1A branches west toward the Continental watershed. From here all waters flow either west to the Pacific, or east, ultimately to the Atlantic Ocean. At the picnic area, a creek demonstrates the principle by separating midstream, with one half flowing east, the other flowing west. The Kicking Horse Pass was the first pass crossed by a railroad in 1883.

Valley of the Ten Peaks

Thirteen kilometers (eight miles) to the east of the Lake Louise Road is the scene depicted on the back of the Canadian $20 bill. The emerald waters of Moraine Lake are surrounded by the ten glaciated summits of the Wenkchemna Peaks. Canoe and cabin rentals are available in the summer.

The Icefield Parkway

Less than one kilometer past Lake Louise village is the beginning of the Icefield Parkway, traveling 230 kilometers (143 miles) through Canada's most spectacular scenery to the townsite of Jasper. There are over 100 glaciers visible along the way. Wildlife abounds along its entire length, and the physical beauty of the mountain scenery defies description. The very names of some of its scenic viewpoints conjur up picture images: Panther Falls, Bridal Veil, Weeping Wall, Hanging Valley. Amid such continuous scenic splendor, it's possible only to describe some outstanding highlights along the way.

As the road climbs steadily toward Bow Summit, it approaches the upper limits of timberline. Bow Pass (2,068 meters/7,875 feet) is the highest point along the parkway. The glacial waters of beautifully tranquil Bow Lake reflect the surrounding snow-capped peaks. A few short generations ago, the Crowfoot Glacier used to resemble a three-towed crow's foot, but as the glacier has receded, only two toes remain today. Across the lake can be seen part of the Waputik Icefield, straddling the Great Divide. Bow Lake is the source of the Bow River, which flows east through Banff and Calgary, connecting down in the prairie with the South Saskatchewan River. Trails from here lead to Helen and Katherine Lakes and through the Dolomite Pass to Siffleur Wilderness on the eastern slopes.

A magnificent view of a classic Rocky Mountain lake can be had by following a short secondary road from here to the Peyto Lake Viewpoint. Along a short footpath from the viewpoint parking lot can be seen the dramatic Peyto Lake, 240 meters (914 feet) below in the Mistaya Valley. The color of the lake changes with the seasons, from a dark blue before meltoff in the spring to an emerald green in the summer, as melting glacial waters pick up silt on their way to the lake.

Farther along the Parkway at Saskatchewan River Crossing is the Park Warden station and interpretive center. Here too, is one of the few places along the Parkway where you can get gas, provisions, and light refreshments. Just south of the lodge, a viewpoint offers a great vista of the Mistaya, Howse, and Saskatchewan River Valleys. To the west can be seen the highest peak in the park, Mt. Forbes (3612 meters, 11,811 feet).

The Parker Ridge Trail ascends above the treeline through an Alpine meadow. From the crest of the ridge can be seen the Saskatchewan Glacier, the largest tongue of the Columbia Icefield.

Sunwapta Pass (2,035 meters, 6,654 feet) is the watershed divide of the North Saskatchewan River and the Athabasca River systems. The North Saskatchewan flows thousands of kilometers across the plains emptying, finally, into Hudson Bay. The Athabasca flows northward, to the Mackenzie River, ultimately draining into the Arctic Ocean. At Sunwapta also is the boundary between Banff and Jasper National Parks.

Just when you might be wearying of so much magnificence along the Icefield Parkway, the road bends slightly to the west, and before you looms the grandeur of the Columbia Icefield, 389 square kilometers (150 square miles) of ice and snow, and the largest body of ice in the Rockies. Glaciers are formed when a vast amount of snow is compacted into hard glacial ice. Visible from the highway are the north face of the glacier-draped Mount Athabasca and the Dome and Athabasca Glaciers.

The Athabasca Glacier is currently both advancing and retreating. The rate of melt at its toe is greater than its downward flow, thus it retreats at the rate of approximately 10 meters (38 feet) per year. As it retreats it leaves behind a glacial deposit, known as moraine, which is essentially rock debris. The interpretive center at the icefield houses a scale model of the entire Columbia Icefield area and offers an excellent audiovisual presentation.

Along the Parkway at Goat Lookout, pause to enjoy the panoramic view of the Athabasca River valley. Goats and other wildlife feed on the minerals in the white-clay soil found here. 6 kilometers (3.7 miles) farther along is the junction of Highway 93A.

For the rest of the trip to Jasper townsite, Highway 93A provides a 24-kilometer (15-mile) alternate and even more scenic route north, rejoining the Parkway 8 kilometers (5 miles) south of Jasper townsite. At the Athabasca Falls, the entire force of the mighty Athabasca River is funnelled through a narrow gorge, creating the awesome power of the falls. A new series of bridges, walkways, and viewpoints takes you very close to the action. Interpretive plaques describe the geology and the flora and fauna of the region. About 19 kilometers (12 miles) along Highway 93A, a narrow road winds for 14 kilometers (9 miles) to the base of Mount Edith Cavell, (3,363 meters, 10,997 feet), the highest peak in this area. It was named for a heroic British nurse who was executed by the Germans during World War I. A trail from the parking lot leads along the bottom of the valley, through boulders, rubble, and rock flour, formed by the grinding of rock around the tongue of the exquisite Angel glacier. Another trail leads up to Cavell Meadow.

Just before Highway 93A rejoins the Parkway, it passes Marmot Basin, a prime ski area in the winter.

Jasper National Park

Jasper National Park (10,880 square kilometers, 4,200 square miles), named for a trapper in the townsite in the early 1800s, was established in 1907, in anticipation of the construction of the Grand Trunk Railroad through the Yellowhead Pass. It is 362 kilometers (225 miles) west of Edmonton along the Yellowhead Highway.

Jasper Townsite

Located at the confluence of the Athabasca and Miette Rivers, Jasper Townsite is in a broad valley. Perhaps the sense of wider space has something to do with it, but Jasper definitely has a less frenetic atmosphere than Banff, even in peak summer season.

A nearby North West Company fur post acted as a supply depot for the mountain fur trade across the Athabasca Pass from about 1801, and continued after the merger with the Hudson's Bay Company until 1884. But the present townsite did not begin to develop until after the arrival of the Grand Trunk and Great Northern railways in 1911 and 1912. During the 1920s the CN absorbed both these lines, and Jasper town became a railway divisional point. Jasper Park Lodge was constructed during this period on the shores of Lac Beauvert. Construction of the all-weather road to Edmonton in 1927, combined with the railway access, spurred on the growth of the townsite as a tourist destination.

Jasper is a pretty place, with shops along its main street, Miette Avenue, selling a full range of souvenirs and Canadian and native crafts. But perhaps its chief attraction is the number of activities and beauty spots that are close at hand. A gondola ride up the Whistlers Mountain offers an opportunity for a fine view of the wide Athabasca valley, and to the west you can see the highest peak in the Canadian Rockies, Mount Robson (3954 meters, 12,929 feet) and Yellowhead Pass.

First known as Leather Pass because the Hudson's Bay Company obtained moose and caribou hides through this area in the 1820s, it was later named for the blond hunter and trapper, Pierre Hatsinaton, known as Tête Jaune. Yellowhead Pass offered a major route west to the Caribou goldfields in the 1850s but astoundingly, was rejected by the CPR thirty years later for their railroad route into British Columbia.

There are several interesting drives in the townsite area. The Pyramid Lake road leads 7 kilometers (4.3 miles) north to a pair of pretty lakes, Patricia and Pyramid, at the foot of Pyramid Mountain. This is a very popular picnic spot for residents and visitors.

One of Canada's top beauty spots is accessed by the Maligne Lake Road, about 3 kilometers (1.8 miles) east of town, off the Yellowhead Highway. Maligne Canyon is a spectacular limestone gorge, with turquoise pools, underground rivers, and cascading waterfalls. From the Visitor Center, many viewpoints and bridges allow you to see the best part of the gorge.

On Maligne Lake, 30 kilometers (18 miles) farther, boat rentals are available and a day lodge serves light refreshments. One of the most photographed scenes in the Canadian Rockies is Spirit Island in the center of the lake. The boat tour is the best way to enjoy this lovely vista. Closer to town, you can follow the road that travels through the grounds of Jasper Park Lodge to a branch that carries on to Annette and Edith Lakes in the Maligne Valley.

Forty-four kilometers (27 miles) east of the townsite, the Pocahantas turnoff leads 16 kilometers (10 miles) to the Miette Hot Springs. Crystal-clear mineral waters from three springs have to be cooled by the addition of cold water to create a bathing temperature of 39°C (102°F). New facilities for bathers and visitors opened in 1986.

Waterton Lakes National Park

In the southwest corner of Alberta, the western prairie abruptly meets the rock walls of the mountains in Waterton Lakes National Park. Established in 1895, it was united with Montana's impressive Glacier National Park in 1932 to form the world's first international peace park. Unique among the national parks, Waterton is small (525 square kilometers, 200 square miles) but encloses both prairie grasslands and rugged alpine environments within its boundaries.

It's a quiet place, unaccustomed to the crowds that frequent Banff and Jasper, and best enjoyed by those in tune with nature. Wild flowers bloom on the prairie and in alpine meadows. Trails throughout the park lead, by easy or arduous routes, past shimmering lakes and streams and tumbling waterfalls, climbing to alpine meadows and elevations of up to 2400 meters (7,850 feet). Evergreens, such as fir, pine, and spruce, cohabit with deciduous trees such as aspen, cottonwood, and maple. Antelope and coyote roam the prairie, and in the marshlands beaver and mink make their homes. Mountain goat, bighorn sheep, grizzly bear, and marmot frequent the alpine meadows and mountain ridgetops. There's even a small herd of Plains buffalo in a drive-through paddock.

The highest peak in the park is Mount Blakiston (2940 meters, 9,614 feet). The mountains include some of the oldest rock in the Rockies. The area has been sculpted by glacial action into a myriad of geological shapes, with rock colors ranging from purples and blue-grays to reds and ochres. Red Rock Canyon, 17 kilometers (9 miles) west of Waterton townsite, offers a chance to see a dramatic water-carved gorge from an easy hiking trail. The rocks here are colored by rusting deposits of iron.

Cameron Creek begins as a mountain stream, crashes into the town of Waterton at Cameron Falls, and continues on, more sedately, into Upper Waterton Lake. The majestic chateau-style Prince of Wales hotel guards a hilltop just north of the townsite. During its open season, May 1 to October 15 for most facilities, the townsite itself is a busy place, although less developed commercially than either Banff or Jasper. There are restaurants, motels, golf course, equipment and boat rentals, scenic boat tours, and a park information center.

The first discovery by white men of Alberta's oil was made in Waterton in 1886 by a local legend and colorful character, George "Kootenai" Brown. The first producing oil well in the province was Original Discovery Well No. 1, at Oil City. The ruins are now marked by a cairn on the Akamina Parkway leading through the townsite and on to Cameron Lake.

The Eastern Slopes

The eastern slopes of the Rockies provide superb opportunities for rugged outdoor adventure amid spectacular mountain and forest scenery. Liberally sprinkled with campgrounds and recreation areas, much of the eastern slopes is a provincial forest reserve.

This is a tremendous watershed area. The streams and rivers drain onto the prairies, supplying the largest portion of its water supply. The fishing is great and some of the world's most challenging whitewater is in this region. There are Rocky Mountain bighorn sheep, mountain goat, and grizzly bear, elk, deer, moose, and black bear. In some regions hunting is permitted in season. Trails for hiking, backpacking, snowshoeing and snowmobiling, and cross-country skiing interlace the eastern slopes.

In the central area are three designated wilderness areas, protected from development and habitation by man—Ghost River, Siffleur, and White Goat. These wilderness areas are available only to those hardy adventurers willing to do their exploring on foot. No vehicles of any kind are permitted, nor are horses or pack animals. No hunting, fishing, or trapping is allowed. North of Jasper National Park, Willmore Wilderness Park preserves the wild country, but here hunting and fishing are permitted in season, and horses and mountain bikes may be used.

The Forestry Trunk Road

North–south access to the spectacular scenery of the eastern slopes is by the 650-kilometer (400-mile) Forestry Trunk Road. The road runs south from Grande Prairie along the eastern slopes, intersecting the east–west highways, past cascading waterfalls, through the superb scenery of Highwood Pass (2,227 meters, 8,240 feet), Canada's highest drivable pass, terminating at the Crowsnest Highway (No. 3) at Coleman. Increasing stretches of this road, signed as Highway 40, are paved, such as the new section linking Grande Prairie and Grande Cache and the portion south of Highway 1 leading through Kananaskis Country; but much of the route is still gravel-surfaced backwoods road. This is not a route for towing large trailers. Services taken for granted on major routes are not readily available along portions of the Forestry Trunk Road. It would be wise to set out with a full tank, a good spare tire, and emergency equipment, including insect repellent. Major provisioning is available at the points where the east–west highways intersect the road—Grande Prairie, Hinton, Nordegg, Highwood, and Coleman.

Kananaskis Country

Kananaskis is a huge (4,000 square kilometers, 1,500 square miles), multi-purpose recreational area developed for year-round use by the provincial government. There are facilities for boating, fishing, camping, and picnicking, and trails for hiking, biking, and horseback and snowmobile riding.

Within the area, the terrain climbs through four zones, from sandstone foothills in the east, through the spruce and fir forests of the montane zone, past alpine meadows, and up to the highest altitudes where glaciers cover the barren mountain rock. Within Kananaskis, there are several regions. To the east are the Sibbald, Elbow, and Sheep Regions, reached respectively by highways 68 and 22 south from Highway 1, and Highway 546 from Turner Valley. South of Bragg Creek, off Highway 22, Elbow Falls tumbles over a limestone cliff, and at McLean Creek there are 190 kilometers (120 miles) of trails specifically designed for motorcycles, snowmobiles, and all-terrain and four-wheel drive vehicles.

Farther west, about a 50-minute drive from Calgary, Highway 40 runs south from Highway 1 through the Kananaskis Valley. Eight kilometers (5 miles) south is a former World War II prisoner of war camp, now a federal forestry research station. The Mount Lorette Fishing Ponds are specifically designed for wheelchair fishermen, but offer great fishing for all.

Five kilometers (3 miles) south is the Ribbon Creek area, and Nakiska at Mount Allan, the site of alpine skiing events of the 1988 Winter Olympics. Three chairlifts provide access to thirty ski runs, the highest of which is 2,400 meters (8,880 feet) long. The new 255-room CP resort village hotel is scheduled to open in June 1987. Two other hotels in the area are scheduled for completion in time for the Olympics.

Alberta's only 36-hole golf course is 4 kilometers (2.4 miles) farther south. Four 9-hole loops radiate from the clubhouse, allowing for varying combinations of play amid the spectacular mountain scenery.

Thirty kilometers (18 miles) farther south still is Peter A. Lougheed Provincial Park, a 508 square-kilometer (196 square-mile) wilderness park in a mountain setting. The park has camping facilities and trails for cycling, hiking, and cross-country skiing. There is also a grocery store, a cafeteria, and an especially well-staffed Visitor Center open year-round. Slide shows and interpretive displays describe the history and geography of the area. The park was formerly known as Kananaskis Provincial Park but was renamed in honor of Alberta's former premier.

PRACTICAL INFORMATION FOR THE ROCKIES

WHEN TO GO. Banff and Jasper National Parks are open year-round. In Waterton, although the park is open year-round, townsite facilities are open May 1–Oct.15. Kananaskis Country is open year-round. Winter in the Rockies is dominated by skiing, mostly downhill in the national parks. There are also lots of cross-country trails, especially on the Eastern Slopes. The townsites of Banff and Jasper are alive with après-skiers. Spring is a great time to see the Rockies without the crowds. The peaks are especially lovely, still capped with winter's snow. There are off-season rates widely available. In summer, the townsites and highways are jam-packed with crowds. Prices are higher, availability is lower. Campgrounds fill up early in the day. Days are warm and sunny, and the rivers swell with the snow melt from the mountains. Summer evenings can be cool after the sun sets behind the mountains. After Labour Day, the crowds diminish and prices drop.

HOW TO GET THERE. By Plane. The closest international airports are at Calgary for Banff, Waterton, and Kananaskis, and at Edmonton for Jasper. Banff has a grass strip for small planes, 8 kilometers (5 mi.) from town. The closest paved runway for charters and private aircraft is at Springbank, west of Calgary, off Hwy. 1. Jasper's grass strip is 10 km (6 mi.) east of town. *Hinton Airport's* paved runway accommodates private planes and small jets.

By Bus. To Banff and Lake Louise, *Brewster Grayline* offers year-round scheduled service from Calgary International Airport. *Greyhound* serves Jasper from Edmonton, and Waterton from Calgary.

By Train. VIA Rail provides transcontinental service to Banff and Jasper, and special package rates from several Canadian cities.

By Car. Access to the Rockies from Montana is via State Hwy. 89. From British Columbia and Alberta, east–west Highways. 3,1, and 16 access the mountains. To Waterton, Hwy. 5 west from Hwy. 2, and Hwy. 6 north from State Hwy. 89, or south from Hwy. 3. To Banff, east–west Hwy. 1. Hwy. 93 north from British Columbia enters Banff National Park between Banff and Lake Louise. Hwy. 11 from Red Deer gives easterly access just south of the park boundary between Banff and Jasper, at Saskatchewan River Crossing. To Jasper, east–west Hwy. 16. Between Lake Louise and Jasper, the Icefield Parkway runs north–south through both parks. Hwy. 40 (Forestry Trunk Road) runs north–south along the Eastern Slopes, providing the closest access to the wilderness areas. Kananaskis Country is accessed by Hwys. 66 and 40, south from Hwy. 1, west of Calgary, and by Hwys. 57 and 546 from Turner Valley. Peter A. Lougheed Provincial Park is accessed by Hwy. 40, south off Hwy. 1, west of Calgary, or by a secondary road leading south from Canmore.

ACCOMMODATIONS. Accommodations range from deluxe resorts and hotels to moderate motels. Several establishments offer off-season rates. During winter, there are often special rates and package prices for winter sports. Be sure to ask when booking. Price categories for double occupancy, in peak (summer) season are: *Super Deluxe*, $100 up; *Deluxe*, $90–$100; *Expensive*, $60–$90; *Moderate*, $40–$60. There is no provincial tax on accommodations, but some hotels and motels charge for local phone calls.

BANFF

Super Deluxe

Banff Park Lodge. Box 2200, Banff, Alta. TOL OCO. (403–762–4433 or 800–661–9266). 205 beautifully appointed rooms, in the heart of town. Lounge, pool, good restaurants.

Banff Springs Hotel. Box 960, Banff, Alta. T0L 0C0 (403–762–2211 or 800–268–9411). The famous chateau-style hotel that launched the CP chain. 560 rooms. Beautiful view of Bow Valley. 18-hole golf course.

Deluxe

Tunnel Mountain Chalets. Box 1137, Banff, Alta. TOL OCO. (403–762–4515). 75 rooms, each with full kitchen, queen-size bed, extra sleeping loft. Indoor pool, sauna and whirlpool. Barbecue area.

Expensive

Cascade Inn. Box 790, Banff, Alta. T0L 0C0 (403–762–3311). Clean rooms. Licensed lounge.

The Rimrock Inn. Box 1110, Banff, Alta. T0L 0C0. (403–762–3356 or 800–372–9270). On Sulphur Mountain. 100 rooms with view of Banff townsite. Close to Upper Hot Springs and Sulphur Mountain Gondola.

The Timberline Hotel. Box 69, Banff, Alta. T0L 0C0 (403–762–2281). An older hotel, and still gracious. Dining Room. Off Hwy. 1 east of town.

Moderate

Johnston's Canyon Resort. Box 875, Banff, Alta. T0L 0C0 (403–762–2971). 26 km (16 miles) west of Banff on Hwy. 1A. 41 rustic cabins. Adjacent to Johnston's Canyon and waterfalls. Seasonal.

Red Carpet Inn. Box 1800, Banff, Alta. T0L 0C0 (403–762–4184). 47 units, satellite TV, licensed dining.

ICEFIELD PARKWAY

Expensive

Num-Ti-Jah Lodge. Box 39, Lake Louise, Alta. T0L 1E0 (phone Mobile Operator Calgary; ask for Num-Ti-Jah Lodge at 135–9002). 28 units on Bow Lake. Seasonal.

The Crossing. Bag Service 333, Lake Louise, Alta. T0L 1E0 (403–721–3920). 66 units, satellite TV. Games room. Seasonal.

Moderate

Columbia Icefield Chalet. Box 1140, Banff, Alta. T0L 0C0 (403–762–2241). Seasonal. At Columbia Icefield. 22 rooms, gift shop.

JASPER TOWNSITE

Super Deluxe

Jasper Park Lodge. Jasper, Alta. T0E 1E0 (403–852–3301 or 800–268–8136). A superb establishment. 397 units with all amenities. Tennis courts, boating, fishing, golf, stables, luxurious dining and entertainment. Seasonal.

Deluxe

Becker's Roaring River Chalets. Box 579, Jasper, Alta. T0E 1E0 (403–852–3779). 49 bungalows, several with wood-burning fireplaces. 5 km (3 mi.) south of Townsite. Licensed dining. Seasonal.

Chateau Jasper. Box 1418, Jasper, Alta. T0E 1E0 (403–852–5644 or 800–661–9323). Downtown. 119 units, dining room and lounge.

Jasper Inn Motor Lodge. Box 879, Jasper, Alta. T0E 1E0 (403–852–4461 or 800–661–1933). 124 units with living rooms, fireplaces, balconies, queen-size beds, kitchens, indoor pools. A good bet for families.

Sawridge Hotel Jasper. Box 2080, Jasper, Alta. T0E 1E0 (403–852–5111 or 800–661–6427). 154 rooms, licensed dining and lounge. Wheelchair access.

Expensive

Marmot Lodge. Box 687, Jasper, Alta. T0E 1E0 (403–852–4471). 106 units, some with fireplace. Licensed dining and lounge. Pool. Wheelchair access.

Tonquin Motor Inn. Box 658, Jasper, Alta. T0E 1E0 (403–852–4987). 74 units. Laundry, Licensed dining.

Moderate

Pine Bungalows. Box 7, Jasper, Alta. T0E 1E0 (403–852–3491). 58 cabins, some with fireplace. Barbecue area. Seasonal.

Pyramid Lake Bungalows. Box 388, Jasper, Alta. T0E 1E0 (403–852–3536). 10 units on lakeside with boat rentals and fishing. Dining room. Seasonal.

Tekarra Lodge. Box 669, Jasper, Alta. T0E 1E0 (403–852–3058). 52 cabins and lodge rooms. Cabins more expensive, some with fireplaces. Dining room.

JASPER VICINITY

Moderate

Miette Hot Springs Resort. Box 907, Jasper, Alta. T0E 1E0 (403–866–3750). 38 units. Dining room, playground. Adjacent to Hot Springs. 17 km (10 mi.) east of Pocahontas. Seasonal.

Pocahontas Bungalows. Box 820, Jasper, Alta. T0E 1E0 (403–866–3732). 48 bungalows with kitchenettes. Games room. Near east park gate.

LAKE LOUISE

Super Deluxe

Chateau Lake Louise. Lake Louise, Alta. T0L 1E0 (403–522–3511 or 800–268–9411). Another famous CP hotel, on the shore of Lake Louise, 385 rooms. Magnificent dining room and lobby. Canoes, riding stables. Afternoon tea.

The Lake Louise Inn. Box 209, Lake Louise, Alta. T01 1E0 (403–522–3791). 186 varied units, some apartment, some hostelry. Licensed dining and swimming pool.

Expensive

Moraine Lake Lodge and Cabins. Box 70, Lake Louise, Alta. T01 1E0 (403–522–3733). Winter address: Box 1641, Westlock, Alta., T0G 2L0 (403–349–5093). 14 rustic log cabins, in the Valley of the Ten Peaks. Seasonal.

Moderate

Deer Lodge. Box 100, Lake Louise, Alta, T0L 1E0 (522–3747 or 800–661–1367). 74 rooms. Licensed dining and lounge. Afternoon tea. Magnificent property.

Post Hotel. Box 69, Lake Louise, Alta, T0L 1E0 (522–3989). 41 rooms, 7 with sink only, no bath. Licensed dining. Ski packages available.

PETER A. LOUGHEED PROVINCIAL PARK

Moderate

William Watson Lodge. Reservations by phone only (591–7222). Cabins, day lodge and campsites specifically designed for the disabled.

RIBBON CREEK (KANANASKIS)

Super Deluxe

The Lodge at Kananaskis. 133–9th Ave. S.W., Calgary T2P 2M3 (403–234–7877 or, from U.S., 800–828–7447; from most of Canada, 800–268–9411. 255 rooms in a resort village atmosphere. Tennis courts, swimming pool. Dining room, lounge. Time-share options available. Near Nakiska at Mount Allan, and Kananaskis Country Golf Course. A new star in the CP constellation. Newly opened in June 1987.

WATERTON LAKES NATIONAL PARK

Expensive

Aspen-Windflower Motel. Box 64, Waterton Park, Alta. T0K 2M0 (403–859–2255 or 800–552–8018). 53 motel and bungalow units. TV, sauna, complimentary coffee. Family units available. Seasonal.

Bayshore Inn. Box 38, Waterton Park, Alta. T0K 2M0 (403–852–2211 or 800–552–8008). 70 lakeshore units with private balconies. Licensed dining. Seasonal.

Emerald Bay Motel. Box 7, Waterton Park, Alta. T0K 2M0 (403–859–2620). 22 units overlooking marina. Complimentary coffee. Seasonal.

Prince of Wales Hotel. c/o Glacier Park Inc., East Glacier Park, MT 59434 (406–226–5551). 81 rooms. Licensed dining and lounge. Featured in most photos of Waterton Lake.

Moderate

Crandell Lodge Motel. Box 114, Waterton Park, Alta. T0K 2M0 (403–859–2288). 11 units, complimentary coffee, and kitchens.

El-Cortez Motel. Waterton Park, Alta. T0K 2M0 (859–2366; winter, 859–2373). 34 units. Two-and three-room units available.

HOSTELS. There are 15 hostels in the mountains. Overnight fees ranges from $3 to $9 for members, and from $7 to $12 for non-members. Full information is available from *Alberta Hostelling Association,* 1414 Kensington Rd. NW, Calgary, Alta. T2N 3P9 (283–5551) or 10926–88 Ave., Edmonton, Alta. T6E 0Z1 (439–3089).

TOURIST INFORMATION. Comprehensive information on all aspects of tourism in the Rockies can be obtained from *Travel Alberta,* Box 2500, Edmonton, Alta. T5J 2Z4 (800–661–8888 from most of U.S. and Canada). Travel Alberta also maintains information centers at Banff, Canmore, Crowsnest Pass, and in Kananaskis, at Gooseberry (weekends only), and Barrier Lake, and at entry points to the province, at Golden, British Columbia, and St. Mary, Montana.

Information on the national parks can be obtained from *Parks Canada,* Box 2989, Station M, Calgary, Alta. T2P 3H8 (292–4440) or by visiting the information centers located at Park Warden Offices in the townsites.

Information is also available from three Alberta tourism zones, at the following addresses. *Banff:* Tourist Committee, Banff–Lake Louise Chamber of Commerce, #1298, 94 Banff Ave., Banff, Alta. T0L 0C0 (762–3777). *Jasper:* Jasper Park Chamber of Commerce, Box 98, Jasper, Alta. T0E 1E0 (852–3858). *Waterton Lakes and Kananaskis:* Chinook Country Tourist Association, 2805 Scenic Dr., Lethbridge, Alta. T1K 5B7 (329–6777).

TELEPHONES. Local calls are 25 cents. Dial 411 for information. The Area Code for all of Alberta is 403. For long distance, dial 1 before the Area Code for direct-dial calls. Dial 0 before the Area Code for operator-assisted calls, such as collect or credit card calls.

EMERGENCY TELEPHONES. For all of Alberta, dial 911 for police, fire department, and ambulance and paramedics.

HOW TO GET AROUND. There is no scheduled transit service in any of the townsites, but there are tours of almost every description in all areas. **By Bus.** Bus service to ski locations is provided in the Banff area by *Pacific Western Transportation* (403–762–4558), in Jasper by *Brewster* (403–762

–2241 or 800–661–1152). **By Taxi.** Taxi service is provided by *Banff Taxi* and *Canmore Taxi* in Banff townsite, and by *Jasper Taxi* in Jasper townsite. There is no taxi service in Waterton townsite. **By Bicycle.** Cycle rentals are available through several outlets in Banff, Jasper, and Waterton townsites.

HINTS TO MOTORISTS. Fall comes early to the mountains and spring stays late. You can find yourself driving from a sunny day into a blinding snowstorm in a matter of miles. In winter, driving conditions can change suddenly. Portions of roads are often closed, due to snowfall or avalanche hazards. Check your spare tire, fill your tank, and make sure you have emergency equipment, such as flashlight, shovel, blanket, and candle for warmth, before setting out.

In summer, roads are often crowded, and vehicles frequently stop suddenly to view the wildlife.

Trailer Tips. Portions of Hwy. 40, along the Eastern Slopes, are not suitable for large trailers, nor are some of the winding mountain sideroads in the national parks. Travel Alberta's "Accommodation Guide" provides a list of trailer drop-off points and sewage dumping facilities.

HINTS TO HANDICAPPED TRAVELERS. Pedestrians with respiratory problems should exercise caution in the mountains, due to the high elevations. Many viewpoints have ramps or access trails, but some steps will be encountered. Travel Alberta's "Touring Guide" notes sightseeing locations that are wheelchair accessible. Especially designed for disabled users are Mount Lorette Fishing Ponds in Kananaskis and William Watson Lodge in Peter A. Lougheed Provincial Park.

Travel Alberta produces a brochure listing handicapped facilities, and its Accommodation Guide lists wheelchair-accessible hotels. The *Canadian Paraplegic Association* will supply information on accommodation for the disabled. Phone 403–438–5046 in Edmonton, 403–236–5060 in Calgary.

TOURS. By Bus. Tours of the Banff–Lake Louise area are offered by *Brewster* (403–762–2241 or 800–661–1152) and by *Pacific Western Transportation* (403–762–4558). Brewster also offers tours of the Jasper area (403–852–3332). In Waterton, *Glacier Park/Waterton Transport* offers tours in antique motor coaches. May 15–Sept. 15 (406–226–9311). Sept. 16–May 14 (602–248–2600).

By Boat. Banff area: Lake Minnewanka tours (the only lake in Banff Park where power boats are permitted) offered by *Minnewanka Tours* (762–3473). Jasper area: Two-hour boat tours to Spirit Island in Maligne Lake (852–3370). Waterton: *Shoreline Cruise* (859–2362) and the *International* (859–2455) offer cruises on Upper Waterton Lake, crossing the U.S. border. **By Raft.** River tours offered by *Rocky Mountain Raft Tours* (762–3632) and *Brewster* (762–2241) in Banff, and *Jasper Raft Tours* (852–3613) and *Jasper Mountain River Guides* (852–5879) in Jasper.

By Snowcoach. One of the most spectacular tours takes you right onto the Columbia Icefield. Phone *Brewster* (762–3441).

By Bicycle: Five-and fourteen-day cycle tours between Banff and Jasper offered by *Rocky Mountain Cycle Tours* (762–3477).

On Horseback. There are day- or week-long guided trips available originating out of Banff, Jasper, and Waterton. Travel Alberta's "Adventure Guide" lists full details.

On Foot. Guided hiking tours are available, with full information obtained from Travel Alberta.

On Skis. Helicopter skiing, with guide, takes you to the tops of slopes, lets you down, and picks you up at the bottom. Day packages available in Banff and Jasper.

NATIONAL AND PROVINCIAL PARKS. There is no charge for vehicles just passing through the national parks. A 24-hour vehicle pass costs $3, but a better bargain is a $10 season's pass, valid for all of Canada's national parks until Mar. 31 of the following year.

The townsites of the three mountain parks provide all visitor amenities—accommodation, restaurants, shopping, and sightseeing. Banff and Jasper townsites are year-round resorts. The season in Waterton townsite is May 1–Oct. 15.

Full information on parks regulations can be obtained from the parks information offices. For example, it is illegal and dangerous to feed the wildlife. Hunting in the parks is prohibited.

One of the best ways to become familiar with the mountains is to take advantage of the parks' interpretive programs, which cover a broad range of information from wildlife and nature lore to the history of the areas. Interpretive programs are offered in each of the townsites, and in many of the campgrounds.

There is no entry fee for provincial parks.

CAMPING. Camping may be the best way to enjoy the Rockies. Government campgrounds are well-maintained and offer a full range of services. Travel Alberta's "Accommodation Guide" carries a comprehensive section on federal, provincial, and private campgrounds. Federal campgrounds are open May–Oct., and fill up quickly during summer months. Campsite fees range from $3 to $9 depending on services. Provincial campsite fees are less expensive, and vary with the services offered. Two of the largest campgrounds are Tunnel Mountain in Banff, and Whistler, just south of Jasper, but there are many more in the national parks, and particularly along the Icefield Parkway. There are 140 campgrounds and recreation areas in the forest reserves of the Eastern Slopes, and 29 in Kananaskis Country.

FISHING. Six varieties of trout can be taken from mountain streams. During Aug. and Sept., the Rocky Mountain whitefish bites in almost all rivers. A fishing license ($10) is required for the national parks, and is valid for the season. In the provincial parks, angling is permitted year-round, subject to closed season for specific waters. A fishing license costs $5 for Albertans and Canadian visitors; $12 for non-Canadian visitors. A 3-day limited license is also available to non-Canadian visitors for $5

HUNTING. Hunting is not permitted in national or provincial parks. Firearms must be sealed at entry points to national parks. In provincial parks firearms must remain locked in your vehicle. Hunting in season is permitted in some areas of the Eastern Slopes. Full information on regulations can be obtained from *Fish and Wildlife Division,* Dept. of Energy & Natural Resources, Main Floor, North Tower, Petroleum Plaza, 9945–108 St., Edmonton, Alta. T5K 2C9.

SUMMER. Apart from sightseeing, there is a full range of summer activities in the mountains. Cycling, hiking, canoe and whitewater trips, instructed mountain climbing, horseback riding, and fishing are some of the more popular. Rentals of all necessary equipment can be arranged in the townsites. You must register with the Park Warden offices for any extensive trips and for mountain climbing.

The **Parks Interpretive Programs** are entertaining as well as informative.

The **Banff Centre Summer Festival** is a multimedia arts festival, running from May through Aug.

Great **golf** can be found in the mountains. All courses are 18-hole, except Kananaskis (36-hole). For reservations and tee-off times phone: *Banff Springs and Kananaskis Country Golf Course* (800–372–9201), *Canmore Golf Course* (678–4784) or *Jasper Park Lodge* (852–3301).

A dip in the **hot springs** can be refreshing and invigorating. In the Banff area, there are the Upper Hot Springs on Mountain Ave. and the Cave and Basin Springs on Cave Ave. In the Jasper area, Miette Hot Springs opened new facilities in 1986. Admission charge for each is under $2, and rental of suits, towels, and lockers is available.

For spectacular views, there are **gondola rides** to the tops of several mountains. In Banff, rides up Sulphur Mountain and Mount Norquay cost $6 or less for adults, less for children, small children free. The price for Sunshine's gondola ride varies with the season. Jasper Tramway takes you up Whistlers Mountain, just south of the townsite. Cost is under $7 for adults, less for children, and children under five are free.

WINTER ACTIVITIES. Winter in the mountains is for skiing, both downhill and cross-country, snowshoeing, and snowmobiling. **Downhill.** In the Banff area, there is fine skiing at Mount Norquay, Sunshine, and Lake Louise, and in Jasper at Marmot Basin. In Kananaskis Country there is Fortress Mountain and Nakiska at Mount Allan, with its new Olympic facilities. **Cross-country:** There are thousands of miles of trails throughout the mountains. Register with the Park Warden offices for any extended trips.

Snowmobiles are not allowed in the national parks, but they are permitted in Kananaskis and some areas of the forest reserves.

MUSEUMS. Museums in the Rockies tend to focus on the wildlife, geology, and history of the area. **Banff Townsite.** *Luxton Museum,* 1 Birch Ave. Features the early life of the Canadian Indian and wildlife of the area. Year-round. Admission: adults, $2; senior, $.50; students, $1; Children under 12, free with parents.

Natural History Museum. 112 Banff Ave. Features biological, geological evolution in the Rockies. Year-round. Admission: adults, $1.50; children 6–16, 75 cents; under 6 free. Family rate, $3.75.

Park Museum. 93 Banff Ave. Wide variety of birds and animals. Year-round. Free admission.

Whyte Museum of the Canadian Rockies. 111 Bear Ave. The archives of the Canadian Rockies. There are also exhibits of works by Canadian and international artists. Admission $1. Year-round.

Jasper Townsite. *The Den.* 105 Miette Ave. Over 100 species of native wildlife. Year-round. Small admission charge.

SHOPPING. Shops in the townsites sell souvenirs, British woollens, and Canadian and native crafts. Try *Quest* in Banff and *Quarks and Fribbles* in Jasper for Canadiana.

RESTAURANTS. You won't go hungry in the Rockies. Almost every hotel and motel in the townsites and on the main routes has a dining room, or at least a coffee shop on the premises. Reservations are rarely required for these, but during peak season it's good idea to inquire. The Super-Deluxe hotels usually have a range of rooms, from formal dining to coffee shops. For example, the Banff Springs Hotel has 13 restaurants. In these hotels, reservations are necessary for formal dining. In addition to restaurants in the townsites, there are, along trails, side roads, and major routes, numerous snack bars, teahouses, and concessions serving light refreshments. Price categories are: *Deluxe,* $30 and up; *Expensive,* $20–$30, *Moderate,* under $20. Price includes a complete meal for one, with hors d'oeuvres or soup, salad, main course, dessert, and coffee, but no other drinks or gratuities.

BANFF

Deluxe

Banff Springs Hotel. The Alhambra Room and the Alberta Restaurant have table d'hote menus. Worth a visit if only for the view (at 4,625 feet) and the sense of history. (See our cover.)

Le Beaujolais. Consistent quality in the French tradition. An attractive setting.

Expensive

Caboose. Steakhouse decorated in a railroad theme, adjacent to the train station.

Drifters. Good salad bar. Lots of beef and seafood on the menu.

Ticino. Swiss-Italian restaurant specializing in veal dishes, beef, cheese fondues, and steak.

Moderate

Banff Cafe. Informal, broad menu. A local favorite.

JASPER

Deluxe

Jasper Park Lodge. The main dining room, and the Henry House for steaks, both have a fine view. Reservations necessary.

Expensive

Chateau Jasper. Broad menu selection, in formal atmosphere.

Tekarra Lodge. Rustic and pleasant. Lamb a specialty.

Tonquin Prime Rib Village. As the name suggests, lots of beef on the menu. Clean and reliable.

Moderate

Diamond Motel. Good family meals amid mountain scenery.

L & W. Good burgers and pizza, in a casual atmosphere. Popular with locals.

LAKE LOUISE

Deluxe

Chateau Lake Louise. Fine, formal dining room. Afternoon tea served in the magnificent lobby, with a view of the lake.

Moderate

Chateau Lake Louise Coffee Shop. Large and friendly, and busy. Great view of the lake.

WATERTON LAKE

Expensive

Bayshore Inn. Broad menu with lots of beef. Right on the lake.

Prince of Wales Hotel. Fine dining room, great view, and friendly staff.

Tourist Cafe. Steak and home-cooked meals. Pies are a specialty.

Moderate

Pearl's Pantry. Great home cooking.

EXPLORING ALBERTA

The mountains and the major cities tell only a part of Alberta's story. There are still three distinctive regions to explore, each with a variety of scenery, history and special experiences for visitors.

Southern Alberta is mainly wide rolling prairie, cut by rivers and shaped by cliffs, rimrocks, and sandstone formations like the Hoodoos. Sagebrush wanders through desert-like areas in the extreme southeast, decorated with prickly pear cactus and oases studded with stands of cottonwood and willow trees.

In Central Alberta, the prairie gives way to the fertile black soil of the parkland, with broad valleys, stands of timber, and recreational lakes and rivers. The Red River tumbles down from the mountains, offering fine whitewater experiences, as it moves across the province, cutting a swath through the Badlands to the east.

The vastness of Northern Alberta is a land of many vistas—carefully tended farm fields dotted with oil pumps, mighty rivers and trophy fishing lakes, wide-open northern prairie, and lots of unspoiled forested wilderness.

Alberta has an excellent network of roads. We will use the east–west Trans-Canada Highway (No. 1) and the Yellowhead Highway (No. 16) as dividers between southern, central, and northern Alberta. The major north–south highway (No. 2) runs from the Montana border all the way to Athabasca, well north of Edmonton. Three cities on this highway, Calgary, Red Deer, and Edmonton will be our reference points for exploring the remaining three regions of Alberta—Calgary for southern, Red Deer for central, and Edmonton for northern, Alberta. In Central Alberta, some overlapping is inevitable, as this area is also easily accessible from Calgary and Edmonton.

EXPLORING FROM CALGARY

The Trans-Canada Highway (Hwy. 1)

The Trans-Canada Highway (No. 1) roughly divides southern and central Alberta. From Calgary west, the Trans-Canada Highway rises through the rolling ranchlands of the foothills into the Rockies, entering British Columbia via the Kicking Horse Pass, just west of Lake Louise.

An alternate route, Highway 1A, leads west from Calgary through the ranching town of Cochrane. One kilometer west is the provincial historic site of the Cochrane Ranche, the first large-scale ranching operation in Alberta, started in 1881. There are self-guided trails, a visitor center displaying artifacts found on archeological digs of the site of the original buildings, and picnic facilities among the wildflowers. Farther along Highway 1A is the Stoney Indian Reserve. Stoney Indian Park has camping and picnic facilities, with buffalo and horseback riding.

At Seebe, you can follow Highway 40 south to Kananaskis Country, or proceed west past Exshaw to rejoin the Trans-Canada Highway. Between Seebe and Canmore are several campgrounds. One of the prettiest is in Bow Valley Provincial Park, which offers splendid scenery from campsites along the Bow River.

Under the shadow of the Three Sisters peaks is the old coal town of Canmore, site of the cross-country skiing, nordic combined, and biathlon events of the 1988 Winter Olympics. The Canmore Nordic Centre includes 62 kilometers (38.5 miles) of skiing trails with links to the town itself and Banff National Park. From Canmore, a secondary road leads south to Peter A. Lougheed Provincial Park. The Trans-Canada Highway continues west through Banff National Park.

To the east, through progressively flattening prairie, the Trans-Canada Highway travels another 350 kilometers (217 miles) in a southeasterly direction, leaving Alberta just east of Medicine Hat. Forty kilometers (25 miles) east of Calgary, Highway 817 leads south to Wyndham–Carseland Provincial Park, also accessible by canoe from Calgary. The Blackfoot Museum at Gleichen contains historical artifacts from the time of the signing of Treaty No. 7 up to the present day. A fifteen-minute drive brings you to Cluny, 1 kilometer south of Highway 1. Just south of here is Blackfoot Crossing, the site of the signing of Treaty No. 7, and the grave of one its important signatories, Crowfoot, the last of the great Blackfoot chiefs.

In the region of Brooks are the Alberta Horticultural Research Centre, 4 kilometers (2.5 miles) to the east, and the Brooks Wildlife Centre, a farther 11 km east. Twelve kilometers (7 miles) south of Brooks on Highway 873 is Kinbrook Island Provincial Park, with camping, and sailing on Lake Newell. But a "must" detour from Brooks is 30 kilometers (19 miles) north. Follow signs from Highway 873 for Dinosaur Provincial Park. The park is a UNESCO World Heritage Site, designated in 1980. Against a landscape of hoodoos and gullies, each layer of sandstone and mudstone, deposited by rivers 75 million years ago, holds a wealth of fossils of various plant and animal species. No other area in the world, of comparable size, contains as broad a record of dinosaur life. Medicine Hat (population about 42,-000) is a park-studded picturesque city on the banks of the South Saskatchewan River, in the middle of the southern prairie. Over the years, there have been many explanations of its name, based on Indian legends. The most likely one tells the story of a Cree medicine man, who lost his headdress while fleeing a bloody battle with the Blackfoot. His disheartened people promptly surrendered and were massacred by the Blackfoot.

When the Canadian Pacific Railway passed through in 1883, a tent town sprang up around the station, and the town grew from there. In 1907, Rudyard Kipling described the place as a city "with all hell for a basement." The "basement" is a huge reserve of natural gas, first discovered by a Canadian Pacific Railway crew drilling for water, and available for the drilling all over town. Several small but vigorous industries owe their existence to this ready source of power. The city is dotted with petrochemical plants, and the Alta-glass glass blowing plant is definitely worth a visit. There is also local manufacturing of pottery, bricks, and tiles. A 38 kilometer (24 mile) trail system through parks along the South Saskatchewan River provides splendid views, picnic facilities, swimming, fishing, and boating.

East and south of Medicine Hat, on Highway 41, abruptly rising from the prairie, are the unique Cypress Hills. Now a provincial park that extends eastward into Saskatchewan, the Cypress Hills are one of the few areas in Canada that were not completely covered by glaciers. Rising 1,462 meters (5,567 feet) above the prairies, they are the highest point in mainland Canada between the Rockies and Labrador. With a more humid atmosphere than the prairie, this small region 7 kilometers (4 miles) wide supports a wealth of vegetation not found anywhere else in Canada, and over 200 species of birds. Evidence of human life in the area dates back over 7,000 years. About 3 kilometers (2 miles) into Saskatchewan, still within the park, is a reconstruction of historic Fort Walsh. During the late 1800s the area was a center for the illicit whiskey trade from Montana. In 1875, the North West Mounted Police constructed Fort Walsh near the site of a massacre of Assiniboine Indians by a party of American wolf hunters. Following Custer's Last Stand in 1876, the North West Mounted Police of Fort Walsh were called upon to negotiate with Sioux Indians who had followed Chief Sitting Bull across the United States border. Highway 41 continues as the Buffalo Trail along the route of the whiskey traders to the Montana border, connecting with Highway 232.

South on Highway 2

Due south of Calgary, Alberta is split by Highway 2 to the Montana border. In Okotoks, an 18,000-ton boulder sits in the middle of an open field, proof of the power of the glaciers. "Big Rock" has the same composition as Mount Edith Cavell, more than 300 kilometers (186 miles) to the northwest as the crow flies, and was carried here by glacial action. The rock's pictographs depict ancient native religious customs.

To the west, off Highway 2, Highway 7 leads to Turner Valley, site of the oil well that launched Alberta into the petroleum industry. Both that first well, Dingman No. 1, and the Royalite No. 4 are open to visitors. Turner Valley is also the gateway to the Bow-Crow forest reserve, and the Sheep River district of Kananaskis Country.

Just west of High River, further south on Highway 2, you can stop for afternoon tea—phone first for reservations (395–2418)—at the E. P. Ranch, owned for forty-two years by HRH Edward VIII.

Nanton is in the middle of some of Alberta's finest ranchlands. Spring water is piped from the Porcupine Hills, 10 kilometers (6 miles) west, to a large tap in the middle of town. Quench your parched throat here or buy bottled "Nanton Water" throughout Alberta. From Nanton, Highway 533 leads west to the Chain Lakes Provincial Park, with spectacular mountain views for campers.

Highway 2 passes through Claresholm south on its way to Fort Macleod. Just north of Fort Macleod and 20 kilometers (12 miles) west, beside Highway 516, is the Head-Smashed-In Buffalo Jump, a UNESCO World Heritage Site. The interpretive center describes how, for over 5,000 years, Plains Indians stampeded buffalo over this cliff before moving in for the kill.

The Fort Macleod area was the final stop of the North West Mounted Police's gruelling westward march in 1874. From the fort, established the same year, they wiped out the illicit whiskey trade in southern Alberta. In its heyday, the fort was the headquarters for the force, and, as a judicial seat, it was the site of many famous trials. The Fort Museum, a reconstruction of the famous fort, is open year-round, as are the heritage buildings on the main street. The entire Fort Macleod area is a Provincial Historic Site. Cardston, farther south, is named for Charles Ora Card, a son-in-law of Brigham Young, who in 1887, led forty Mormon families north to establish a settlement. The most striking feature in the town is Canada's only Mormon temple, a white granite structure that took ten years to complete. From Cardston, Highway 5 goes west 45 kilometers (28 miles) to the gate of Waterton National Park. Highway 2 continues south to the Montana border, connecting with Highway 89.

The Crowsnest Highway

This east–west highway (No.3) crosses Alberta through Fort Macleod. To the west, Highway 3 enters some of Alberta's prime coal mining territory, traveling through the Rockies to British Columbia via the Crowsnest Pass. At Pincher Creek, Highway 6 leads south to Waterton National Park, or farther south into Montana. 30 kilometers (19 miles) west of Pincher Creek, the ruins of the Leitch Collieries, a provincial historic site, have been stabilized for easy exploring. Hillcrest Mines was the scene of one of Canada's worst mining disasters in 1914, when an explosion killed 189 miners. In the Crowsnest Pass area is Turtle Mountain, where in 1903, 90 million tons of rocks crashed down on the town of Frank, killing seventy people. The Frank Slide interpretive center describes the coal mining and social history of the Pass area. On the south side of Highway 3 west of Coleman, a sign directs you to the only known evidence of volcanic action in Alberta. The rocks are about 100 million years old, twice as old as the Rockies.

To the east from Highway 2, about 43 kilometers (27 miles) along the Crowsnest Highway is Alberta's third largest city, Lethbridge (population about 60,000). Today Lethbridge is an irrigated oasis in the midst of the prairie, but its original name of Coalbanks gives a clue to early industry. Five hundred generations of Blackfoot inhabited this area before recorded history.

At the west end of town, on the Oldman River, is Indian Battle Park. The name of the park remembers the last great Indian battle in Canada, fought in 1870, along the coulee-scarred banks of the Oldman River, between the Blackfoot and the Cree. A reconstruction of the notorious whiskey-trading Fort Whoop-up is located in the park. Just north of the park, the Helen Schuler Coulee Center offers self-guided trails, nature walks, and interpretive programs.

In 1900, Alberta's first large-scale irrigation system was completed in Lethbridge. It was followed by several other irrigation projects in the area, notably the St. Marys River development after World War II. Today, pivot irrigation in the area even permits market gardening. The beautiful Nikka Yuko garden was created in 1967 as a gift to Canada by Lethbridge residents of Japanese descent. Japanese Canadians were relocated from Canada's west coast to Lethbridge at the onset of World War II.

South from Lethbridge, Highway 5 leads toward Highway 2, past the actual location of Fort Whoop-up (now a National Historic Site) and through the town of Magrath, home of the latest development in prairie skyscrapers. The "buffalo-slope" grain elevator is open to visitors.

Highway 4 goes south east through Raymond, site of the first ever Canadian rodeo in 1903, to the twenty-four-hour border crossing to Montana at Coutts.

About 20 kilometers (12 miles) north of Coutts, Highway 501 leads 48 kilometers (30 miles) east to the fascinating Writing-on-Stone Provincial Park, on the Milk River. Thousands of hoodoos have been weathered into haunting vertical shapes. The rocks are covered with ancient native pictographs which are explained by interpretive programs in the park. Highway 3 continues east through sagebrush country to Medicine Hat, via Taber, where the provincial park offers good fishing and a playground for the kids.

Hoodoos and Dinosaurs—Highway 9 Northeast

The badlands beckon you northeast from Calgary, through some of Alberta's finest wheat growing country, to the Drumheller region. Near Beiseker is a Hutterite colony, one of about ninety-nine in the province. For these followers of Jacob Hutter, agriculture has been a way of life sanctioned by religion since the 1500s. Each colony operates as an independent economic unit.

Shortly after ranchers first settled in the Drumheller region, Sam Drumheller bought what is now the whole townsite, and started coal mining all over town in 1911. Virtually a boom town for several years, Drumheller was affected by the decline of the coal industry after Alberta's major oil and gas discoveries in the 1940s. Today, the fossil-rich badlands along the Red Deer River focus world attention on the area.

It is important to note here that it is illegal in Alberta to remove dinosaur or other fossils. The Ministry of Culture appreciates reports of any significant new finds.

The Dinosaur Trail is a 48-kilometer (30-mile) loop that starts at the Dinosaur and Fossil Museum, on 1st St. E., in Drumheller's town center. The museum focuses on fossils, artifacts of prehistoric life, and the geological phenomena of the region. The trail makes a sharp left, past the Homestead Antique Museum, where an assortment of early automobiles, coal mining instruments, Indian relics, and pioneer furnishings rambles over a 4-hectare (10-acre) site.

Tyrrell Museum of Palaeontology

Ten minutes drive along the North Dinosaur Trail, among the hills of Midland Provincial Park, is the fabulous new Tyrrell Museum of Palaeontology. Dr. J. B. Tyrrell discovered the head of a petrified dinosaur in the area in the summer of 1884. Subsequent explorations have revealed some of the richest finds of dinosaur remains in the world. The museum dramatically presents the evolution of life on earth from its earliest beginnings. Displays take you through 3 billion years of history, right up to the present. Exhibits include over 800 fossil specimens, and forty dinosaur skeletons. Computer terminals, with science games, and film and video theaters bring history to life. Outdoor trails leading into the Badlands allow you to see the fossils in their natural locations. This $30 million facility includes a large cafeteria, bookstore, a "paleon-conservatory," an auditorium, and research facilities. It is open year-round, with no admission charge.

Farther along the trail, across the road from the Golf and Country Club, is the Little Church, which boasts a congregation of 10,000 per year—six at a time!

Horsethief Canyon Viewpoint, 4 kilometers (2 miles) along, provides a spectacular panorama of the prehistoric formation of the badlands. The walls of the canyon, descending 122 meters (400 feet), reveal a multitude of sedimentary strata deposited over 70 million years ago. The petrified oyster beds below are proof that this area was once part of a prehistoric inland sea.

The Dinosaur Trail continues on through oilfields and wheatfields, crossing the Red Deer River on the historic six-car Bleriot Cable Ferry. Near the ferry, wander among the Dinosaur Burial Grounds. The trail circles back to Drumheller.

For magnificent views of the hoodoos, drive east along the 60-kilometer (37-mile) East Coulee Drive, through the old mining towns of Wayne and Rosedale. The Rosedale Swinging Bridge leads to the Old Star Mine. Use caution when exploring the mine. Along this route too, is the Atlas Coal Mine, closed in 1979, which can be photographed from the road only.

The Wintering Hills, farther east, offer some interesting rambles through rolling ranchlands. From here, dotted by recreational lakes, the prairie stretches out as far as the eye can see. At Youngstown is the breeding ranch for the Calgary Stampede. Around Hanna, the pronghorn antelope roam freely. Some of the finest goose and duck hunting in North America is to be had in the Hanna–Oyen area.

Highway 2 North

Highway 2 runs north from Calgary through Airdrie, Didsbury, and Olds to the Innisfail area, where Anthony Henday became the first known white man to view the Rockies, in 1754. Five kilometers (3 miles) south of the town is the Royal Canadian Mounted Police Dog Training Centre, the only one of its kind in Canada. It is open daily, year-round.

Highway 54 leads 30 kilometers (19 miles) west to Markerville, home of Iceland's national poet, Stephan Stephansson. One of the western world's most prolific writers, Stephansson wrote most of his poetry in this house. The house, with displays of Icelandic crafts, is open May–September.

EXPLORING FROM RED DEER

Red Deer

The city of Red Deer (population about 46,000) was incorporated as Alberta's fifth city in 1913. The name is a translation of the Cree, Waskasoo Seepee, after the abundance of deer found in the area. Smack in the middle of thriving grain and cattle farming and an active oil industry, Red Deer boomed right along with Calgary and Edmonton. During the 1950s, it was probably Canada's fastest growing city. Today its equidistance from Calgary and Edmonton makes it a thriving center for conventions and meetings. The 11 kilometer (7-mile) Waskasoo Park provides first class recreational facilities interlaced with cycle, horseback, and pedestrian trails.

The David Thompson (Highway No.11)

To the west, the magnificent David Thompson Highway follows the route of the famous cartographer through farmlands, forests, foothills, and mountains, all the way to Saskatchewan River Crossing in Banff National Park.

Fifteen kilometers (9 miles) west of Red Deer, the resort town of Sylvan Lake comes alive in the summer. The lake's beautiful beach is right beside the highway, and there are fast-food outlets, souvenir shops, and a waterslide. Jarvis Bay Provincial Park nearby offers camping, fishing, boating, and swimming.

In the late 1700s, David Thompson wintered at Rocky Mountain House on his way to the mountains. Today, the National Historic Site commemorates a series of fur-trading forts built in the area by the Hudson's Bay Company and North West Company. Intended to promote trade with the Kootenay Indians of the Pacific slopes, the forts were unfortunately located in Blackfoot territory, and therefore relied on an uncertain clientele for trade. A self-guided trail interprets the history of the site. Fourteen kilometers (9 miles) west, off Highway 11, Crimson Lake Provincial Park has large campgrounds, good swimming, and several playgrounds. From here to the end of the highway, there are several small but attractive campgrounds, accessible from the main road.

The ghost town of Nordegg, once a thriving mining town, is now a major access point to the Forestry Trunk Road. Twenty-three kilometers (14 miles) west of Nordegg, on the Bighorn River, is Crescent Falls. Hike from the falls to the viewpoint at Bighorn Canyon.

Five kilometers (three miles) west is the access road to the Bighorn Dam, completed in 1972. Alberta's longest man-made lake was created in the process, named Abraham after a Stoney Indian. Across Abraham Lake is the peak of Mount Michener, which was officially named, in 1979, for and in the presence of one of Canada's most beloved Governors-General.

From here west, the highway parallels the magnificent North Saskatchewan River, and offers splendid mountain views. The grasslands of the Kootenay Plains Natural Area are a striking contrast to the rolling forest behind and craggy peaks ahead. In the area are Indian ceremonial grounds and camping and hiking trails to Siffleur Canyon and Falls.

Saskatchewan River Crossing is 37 kilometers (23 miles) inside Banff National Park.

Highway 12 to the east

Just north of Red Deer, at Lacombe, named for Alberta's beloved missionary, Highway 2 leads east through central Alberta. South from Highway 12, Highway 21 leads to Dry Island Buffalo Jump Provincial Park, 19 kilometers (12 miles) east of Huxley. Picnickers can view the flat-topped mesa or "dry island" in the midst of the badlands, then descend the cliff-like walls of the Red Deer River, over which Indians used to stampede buffalo.

The Stettler area, known in 1874 as Tail Creek Town, was the center of the western Métis buffalo hunt, with a rowdy floating population of up to 4,000. The eight buildings of the Stettler Town and Country Museum on Royal Canadian Mounted Police Road include an old train station and schoolhouse.

From Stettler, Highway 56 leads south, to the Badlands around Drumheller. Farther east along Highway 12, and north of Consort, the wooded oasis of Gooseberry Lake Provincial Park contrasts with its sun-baked beach. North of the park, on both sides of Highway 41, are the Neutral Hills, designated as a non-battle zone by warring Blackfoot and Cree.

North of Red Deer—East and West

It's about an hour's drive north on Highway 2 from Red Deer to Edmonton. Recreational areas on a plethora of lakes both to the east and west of the highway are equally accessible to, and serve the people of, both cities.

East of Highway 2, the Battle River, named for a series of Indian skirmishes, wanders through this entire region. Dozens of small communities dot the prime agricultural land of this area, providing services for small grain and mixed farming operations. There are 648 oil wells within a 32-kilometer (20-mile) radius of Camrose. The city also offers stock car races, industrial tours, and picnic facilities.

The Wainwright area was the locale of Buffalo National Park during the 1920s and 1930s. From the parking lot of Canadian Forces Base Wainwright, buffalo can be viewed today at the Bud Cotton Buffalo Paddock. Wainwright District Museum, open May–September, preserves the past of pioneers, the park, and the oil industry of the 1920s.

West of Highway 2 is one of Alberta's finest recreational lakes, Pigeon Lake. It's great for water sports and boating, and the provincial park has good camping facilities. To the northwest, in the heart of the great Pembina oilfields, is Alberta's first government-planned model town, Drayton Valley.

Southwest of Drayton Valley, 56 kilometers (35 miles) on Highway 620, the immense Brazeau Dam sits at the edge of a wilderness that stretches to the Rockies. The dam harnesses the power of the North Saskatchewan tributaries, the Elk and the Brazeau Rivers. Phone (894–3594) to arrange a tour.

North to Edmonton—Highway 2A

Highway 2A is an alternate route north from Morningside on Highway 2, connecting again with Highway 2 just south of Leduc. Ponoka is the site of a major Canadian rodeo each June. At the junction of Highway 13 is the city of Wetaskawin, whose name in Cree means Peace Hills.

EXPLORING FROM EDMONTON

Ringing Edmonton are several small communities, each with its own points of interest. Just south of the international airport, on Highway 2, the town of Leduc leapt into fame in 1947 when Leduc No. 1 oil well blew in.

Sherwood Park to the southeast is virtually a dormitory community for Edmonton. Fourteen kilometers (9 miles) south of the Sherwood Park Freeway, on Highway 14, is Polar Park, formerly known as the Alberta Game Farm. The park is now home to over 100 species of cold climate animals, which can be viewed in winter months, too, from 20 kilometers (12 miles) of cross-country trails. The warm water of Miquelon Lake, south from Highway 14 on Highway 833, is a major gathering place for migrating waterfowl. Within the provincial park there are a bird sanctuary, excellent beaches and camping facilities.

To the west of Edmonton, the Stony Plain Multicultural Heritage Centre offers demonstrations of pioneer crafts and samples of pioneer and ethnic foods. An art gallery and handicrafts shop feature works by Alberta artists.

St. Albert, immediately north of Edmonton, is where Father Albert Lacombe built his chapel, and named it for his patron saint. It is open May–September.

Northeast of Highway 2, outside St. Albert, is Alberta Wildlife Park, with 200 species of animals, petting zoo, and campground. Next door is Canada's largest barbecue restaurant and dance hall, the Red Barn.

Along the Yellowhead (Highway 16)

The Yellowhead Highway is a convenient divider between Central and Northern Alberta. To the east, 32 kilometers (20 miles) from Edmonton, is Canada's smallest National Park, Elk Island. Herds of elk, plains bison, and wood bison can be viewed in their natural habitat, from your car, or at closer range, in the paddock area. Eighteen kilometers (11 miles) east of Elk Island, in an area settled by Ukrainians, an early settlement is recreated at the Ukrainian Cultural Heritage Village. Farther east in Vegreville is the home of the world's largest *pysanka* (Easter Egg). Decorated in traditional Ukrainian design in bronze, gold, and silver, the 30-meter (98-foot) long egg weighs 2,270 kilograms (5,000 pounds) and was built to celebrate the Royal Canadian Mounted Police centennial in 1974. The federal agricultural research station at the east end of town conducts research on soil improvement and forage crops for northern Alberta. Open May–September by appointment. Phone (632–3985) for information.

Highway 16 continues east into Saskatchewan, right through Lloydminster (population about 9,000). Lloydminster's main street straddles the Alberta–Saskatchewan border. Merchants on the west side of the street used to do a roaring trade because Alberta has no sales tax, but now there is no sales tax anywhere in town. Lloydminster sits near a huge reserve of heavy oil.

To the West of Edmonton, the Yellowhead Highway travels through several resort towns, such as Alberta Beach, on its way to Jasper National Park. Sixty kilometers (37 miles) west of Edmonton, the sunny beach and campgrounds of Wabamun Lake Provincial Park are alive with Edmontonians in summer. There is excellent year-round fishing here (through holes in the ice in winter).

Near Evansburg, campsites are right beside the magnificent gorge in Pembina River Provincial Park.

Approximately halfway to Jasper, Edson is a major service center for the area. From Edson west to Hinton, the Coal Branch area, lying to the south of the Yellowhead, once throbbed with mining activity. Highway 40 south from Hinton passes right through the Luscar Cardinal River coal mine, with its huge open pit, on its way to Highway 3 in southern Alberta.

North from Hinton on Highway 40, five interconnecting lakes in William A. Switzer Provincial Park abound with fish. North of the park, Rock Lake Road leads 35 kilometers (22 miles) west into Willmore Wilderness Park. Highway 40 continues on through Grande Cache. Alberta's largest coal mining operation provides the industry for this completely modern town, carved out of the wilderness in 1968. It was named for the huge caches of fur stored there temporarily by early traders. Grande Cache provides northern access to Willmore and, via Highway 40, farther north to Grande Prairie.

Along the Yellowhead again, 27 kilometers (17 miles) west of Hinton are the gates of Jasper National Park.

NORTHERN ALBERTA—NEAR AND FAR

Northern Alberta is a special place. Nature still owns much of this region—only about ten percent of Alberta's population lives in this entire vast region north of Edmonton. Prairie grasslands contrast with forested wilderness. Although too cold for swimming, the fresh, clear water of its many lakes and magnificent rivers offer excellent boating and fishing for northern pike, walleye, whitefish, perch, and rainbow trout, to name just a few. The contrasts of this region continue in the facilities available to visitors. There are remote campsites and fishing locations, accessible only by plane or boat. There are completely modern campgrounds with showers and laundry facilities, and hotels and motels in many communities.

The "near" north is divided vertically by Highway 2, which continues north from Edmonton as far at Athabasca. Beyond Athabasca, the "far" north is roughly divided into vertical thirds, by the Mackenzie Highway (No.35) and Highway 63, to just north of Fort McMurray. Road systems provide access all the way through the scenic north of Alberta to its three boundaries with British Columbia, Northwest Territories, and Saskatchewan. There are many portions of gravel road, though, and much unspoiled wilderness. Headlight protectors and insect repellent are probably a good idea.

THE "NEAR NORTH"

Highway 2 North to Athabasca

Highway 2 north from Edmonton follows the Athabasca Trail, through St. Albert, and on past some of Alberta's richest farmland, settled by a variety of ethnic pioneers. This was the historic route of early fur traders and the gold seekers of '98. Today, the town of Athabasca is the home of Athabasca University, a correspondence university that uses distance as a teaching tool.

East on Highway 28

In the near north, Alberta is a rolling recreational paradise studded with trophy lakes and with heavy oil burbling just below ground. St. Paul originated as a Métis settlement, and today boasts Alberta's first bilingual cultural center, and the world's only UFO landing pad! Bonnyville started as a Northwest Canada fur post in 1789.

Grand Centre, in the middle of the Cold Lake tar sands, is the main service community for the agriculture, recreation, and oil industries of the region. Cold Lake Provincial Park offers a lovely white-sand beach along one of Alberta's most scenic lakes, with camping facilities and excellent fishing for lake trout.

South from Grand Centre, on Highway 897, is Frog Lake, the site of the massacre by Cree Indians during the Riel Rebllion of 1885. The monument, display, and the graves of eight of the nine victims are located three kilometers (two miles) east of Frog Lake Store, off Highway 897.

East on Highway 55

The area around Lac La Biche is dotted with at least fifty recreational lakes, within a 96-kilometer (60-mile) radius. The Lac La Biche Inn, built in 1916, served for a time as a hospital, and is now being restored to its former lavish grandeur as a resort hotel. Phone (623–4323) for tours. Sir Winston Churchill Provincial Park, on an island in the lake, is ringed with sandy beaches and surrounded by pine forest.

Northwest on the Grizzly Trail (Highway 33)

This alternate route northwest from Edmonton to Lesser Slave Lake roughly approximates the route of the Assiniboine Trail to the Klondike gold fields. Fort Assiniboine was historically a major stopping point on the long journey across western Canada, before the coming of the railroad. Accessed by Highway 18 west from Barrhead, Thunder Lake Provincial Park is a haven for boaters and water skiiers, and a nesting sight for the striking blue heron. The Swan Hills region is grizzly bear country!

Northwest to Alaska—Highway 43

West of Edmonton, just outside Stony Plain, Highway 43 runs northwest from the Yellowhead through fertile farmlands and untamed forested wilderness, meeting Mile "O" of the Alaska Highway at Dawson Creek, in British Columbia. At Whitecourt, "the gateway to Alaska," three waterways join the majestic Athabasca River. The Mcleod and Eagle Rivers, along with Beaver Creek, provide excellent fishing. The forested wilderness nearby abounds with big game—moose, elk, deer, and bear. Nineteen kilometers (12 miles) from Whitecourt are the two lakes of Carson–Pegasus Provincial Park. The Carson Lake campground is newly equipped with modern facilities, and the lake is stocked with rainbow trout. Pegasus Lake has a walk-in campground, right in the boreal forest, and fishing for northern pike, whitefish, and perch.

At the junction of Highways 34 and 43, surrounded by fields of wheat, oats, barley, and canola (rapeseed) is Valleyview. Two provincial parks, Williamson Lake, 15 kilometers (9 miles) west, and Youngs Point, 35 kilometers (22 miles) west, each have good fishing for northern pike, walleye, and perch. The largest community in the region is Grande Prairie (population about 24,000). Rolling plains, spruce and poplar forests, and oil fields make Grande Prairie a thriving service center for three major industries in the region. The city has its own symphony orchestra, art gallery, music conservatory, and a full season of live theater. Saskatoon Provincial Park, 25 kilometers (16 miles) west, named for the abundant wild berries in the area, is a nesting area for the rare trumpeter swan. Picnic and play amateur geologist, 19 kilometers (12 miles) to the northeast, at Kleskun Hill Park. The hills, formed by the erosion of glacial till, are part of an ancient sea bottom and hold fossils of dinosaurs and marine life.

Another scenic picnic location is O'Brien Provincial Park, on the Wapiti River, twenty minutes south of Grande Prairie, along the newly opened portion of Highway 40 which connects with Grande Cache.

THE "FAR NORTH"

Highway 63 Northeast

Known to fur traders and prospectors as Athabasca Landing, the town of Athabasca was connected by the water route of the great Athabasca River to the former fur post, Fort Chipewyan, at the west end of Lake Athabasca, high in the northeast corner of the province. Fort Chip is Alberta's oldest settlement, still accessible only by plane or boat in summer. From here, Alexander Mackenzie started his famous expeditions to two of Canada's oceans in the late 1700s. His route to the Arctic followed the Slave River, which now parallels the eastern boundary of Canada's largest national park.

Wood Buffalo National Park was established in 1922 to preserve Canada's last remaining large herd of wood bison, then numbering about 500. Today, 5,000 bison thrive in a wilderness of forests, meadows, and marshes, that also provides a habitat for caribou, black bear, the smaller creatures prized by the fur trade (such as beaver, muskrat, mink, and lynx), and migratory birds. The park is the only known nesting site for whooping cranes. Wood Buffalo is a true wilderness park, accessibly only by boat or plane, or by a dirt road that forms a loop through its northeast portion, from Fort Smith in the Northwest Territories.

Modern explorers can travel north from Athabasca by road, east on Highway 55, then north on Highway 63, as far as the great Athabasca tar sands, 34 kilometers (21 miles) north of Fort McMurray. Camp in the midnight twilight at Gregoire Provincial Park, or stay in Fort McMurray, 16 kilometers (10 miles) farther north.

Situated in the middle of 3.9 billion cubic meters of crude oil reserves, Fort McMurray saw a feverish building boom in the mid 1970s, to keep pace with a 100 percent population increase in just ten years. It all began with the great "mega projects," such as Great Canadian Oil Sands and Syncrude, in 1964. Crude oil is recovered from the tar sands by giving the oily slush a hot water bath. The sand falls to the bottom of the bath, allowing crude oil to be skimmed off the top. The interpretive center, at the corner of Highway 63 and Mackenzie Blvd., offers a multimedia presentation of the technology of oil-sand extraction. Tours to the Syncrude project (by appointment only) leave from the Tourist Information Center (791–4336) in town.

Highway 2—West and North

At Athabasca, Highway 2 breaks its long northerly run from the Montana border and veers westward along the south shore of Lesser Slave Lake, ultimately ending at Dawson Creek in British Columbia. Lesser Slave Lake is Alberta's longest lake accessible by car. At its east end is the town of Slave Lake. Lesser Slave Provincial Park, 35 kilometers (22 miles) north of town, on Highway 67, is famous for its wide, 8 kilometer (5 mile) long sandy beach. Campers can spot bald eagles, moose, deer, wolves, and bear in the neighborhood. At the west end of the lake, Grouard is named for the nineteenth-century missionary, Bishop Grouard, whose grave can be visited in the cemetery of St. Bernard Mission Church. Just north of High Prairie, in Winagami

Provincial Park, the kids might just find a beaver lodge, when they're not boating or waterskiing. West of High Prairie, Highway 2 takes a jog north and continues as an inverted U-shape to Grand Prairie. Fahler is known as the "Honey Capital of the World."

Bright yellow fields of canola (rapeseed) stretch for miles through Peace River Country. This area, which stretches all the way north to the Northwest Territories' border, is home to the most northerly commercial agriculture in the world. Introduced to the area during World War II, so as to provide lubricating oil for ships, canola has been a highly successful crop in the region and is now used for cooking, margarine, soap, and varnish.

The town of Peace River sits at the confluence of the mighty Peace, Smoky, and Heart rivers. The best sight of this breathtaking view is from the grave of Twelve-Foot Davis, on Judah Hill. Twelve-Foot Davis was a giant of generosity, not of stature. His nickname derives from his twelve-foot gold claim, staked between two much larger claims, in the early 1860s. His little plot yielded over $15,000, quite a tidy sum in those days. Natives and settlers alike benefited from his good fortune.

The Shaftsbury Trail travels through the wide, high valley of the Peace River, southwest of Grimshaw. The town of Dunvegan was a major fur fort in the early 1800s, and a mission site later in the century. St. Charles Mission Church is now an interpretive center, offering tours of the historic area May–September. The Dunvegan Bridge, spanning the 270-meter- (880-foot) high banks of the Peace River, is Alberta's only suspension bridge for vehicles.

Highway 67 North

The vast central area north of Lesser Slave Lake is served by secondary roads, plane, and boat. Highway 67 continues north as a secondary road for 432 kilometers (268 miles) along the Buffalo Head Hills, through yet another tar sands area, past large and fertile farms, to historic Fort Vermilion. Situated on the mighty Peace River, Fort Vermilion is over 200 years old, and was first established as an Northwest Canada fur-trading post.

The Mackenzie Highway (No. 35)

Nineteen kilometers (12 miles) west of Peace River, at Grimshaw, is Mile O of the Mackenzie Highway. The paved Mackenzie Highway travels 471 kilometers (293 miles) north to the border of the Northwest Territories, through the towns of Manning, named for a former Alberta premier, and High Level, the last major community before the northern border, crossing into the Northwest Territories to connect with Hay River.

PRACTICAL INFORMATION FOR ALBERTA

HOW TO GET THERE. By car: There is easy east/west access to Alberta via the Trans-Canada, Yellowhead, or the Crowsnest highways. From the south, State Hwy. 89, Interstate 15, and regional highway 232 connect with Alberta's north/south routes.

By train: *Via Rail* services Medicine Hat, Calgary, and Banff, also Edmonton and Jasper. Full transcontinental passenger service is through Calgary and Banff, Edmonton, and Jasper.

By bus: *Greyhound* is the major carrier to Alberta as well as through and around Alberta. Its head office in Canada is located in Calgary.

By Plane: Edmonton and Calgary are served by *Air Canada, Continental, Time Air, C.P. Air, Pacific Western, Western Airlines, Wardair* and *United.* Edmonton is also served by *America West* and *Northwest Orient;* Calgary by *Cascade Airways, KLM,* and *Lufthansa.*

 ACCOMMODATIONS in Alberta range from luxury hotels in the cities, to plain highway accommodation in small communities throughout the province. Price categories, for double occupancy, are: *Deluxe,* $90 and up; *Expensive,* $60 to $90; *Moderate,* $40 to $60; *Inexpensive,* under $40. There is no provincial tax on accommodations but some hotels and motels charge for local phone calls. Many hotels offer special rates and package prices for off-season and weekends, especially in the cities.

Most places accept the following major credit cards: American Express, MasterCard, and Visa; others may also be honored. Not all establishments accept credit cards, therefore we suggest you call for information.

ATHABASCA. *Moderate.* **Athabasca Inn.** Box 1526, Athabasca, Alta. T0G 0B0 (403–675–2294). 65 rooms, cable TV, licensed dining room and lounge.
Inexpensive. **Athabasca Lodge Motel.** On Hwy. 2. Box 1560, Athabasca, Alta. T0G 0B0 (403–675–2266). 27 units, satellite TV, outdoor pool.

BLAIRMORE. *Moderate.* **Blairmore Motel.** Box 1419, Blairmore, Alta. T0K 0E0 (403-562–2279). Two blocks south of Hwy. 3. 17 units, some family units, kitchenettes, TV.

BONNYVILLE. *Moderate.* **The Lakelander Motor Hotel.** Box 637, Bonnyville, Alta. T0A 0L0 (403–826–3309). Air-conditioned units, kitchenettes, licensed dining and cocktail lounges; sauna and other amenities. Good choice.
Midtown Motor Inn. Box 2490, Bonnyville, Alta. T0A 0L0 (403–826–2898). At 5215 50th Ave. 55 units, satellite TV, licensed dining and lounge.
Inexpensive. **Southview Motel.** Box 1077, Bonnyville, Alta. T0A 0L0 (403–826–3321). Kitchenettes, color TV, telephones.

BROOKS. *Moderate.* **Heritage Inn.** 2nd St. W., Box 907, Brooks, Alta. T0J 0J0 (403–362–6666). Room service, dining room, entertainment, and other amenities.
Inexpensive. **Plains Motel.** Box 1738, Brooks, Alta. T0J 0J0 (403–362–3367). At 1119 2nd St. W. A good, clean motel with 54 units, TV, telephones, sauna.
Tele-Star Motor Inn. Box 547, Brooks, Alta. T0J 0J0 (403–362–3466). 2 km south of Hwy. 1, on main access road. Cocktail lounge, air conditioning, kitchenettes, and licensed dining make this 51-unit motel a top choice in Brooks.

CAMROSE. *Inexpensive.* **Crystal Springs Motor Hotel.** 3911 48th Ave., Camrose, Alta. T4V 2Z1 (403–672–7741). 68 air-conditioned, clean, well-equipped units; in-house entertainment. Good choice for the Battle River zone.
Motel Johnson. 4772 46th St., Camrose, Alta. T4V 1G6 (403–672–4441). A good, clean operation; air conditioning, kitchenettes, complimentary coffee.
Norseman Inn. 6505 48th Ave., Camrose, Alta. T4V 3G8 (403–672–9171 or 800–661–1460). 80 rooms. Telephones, dining lounge, tavern. Close to shopping.

CANMORE. *Expensive.* **Rocky Mountain Chalet.** Box 725, Canmore, Alta. T0L 0M0 (403–678–5564). On Hwy. 1A at 17th St. 37 one- and two-bedroom units and lofts. Firelaces, kitchenettes.
Moderate. **AKAI Motel.** Box 687, Canmore, Alta. T0L 0M0 (403–678–4664). On Hwy. 1 service road. Air-conditioned comfort in neat, clean units. Complimentary coffee. Wheelchair-accessible units.
Rundle Mountain Motel. Box 147, Canmore, Alta. T0L 0M0 (403–678–5322). On service road, south side of Hwy. 1. 40 units. Playground.
Sundance Inn. Box 1400, Canmore, Alta. T0L 0M0 (403–678–5564). On Hwy. 1. 24 rooms, cable TV, dining room, and lounge.

CARDSTON. *Inexpensive.* **Evergreene Motel.** Box 838, Cardston, Alta. T0K 0K0 (403–653–4072). At junction of highwys 2 and 5. 20 units, complimentary coffee, color TV, free crib, parking for oversized vehicles.

Flamingo Motel. Box 92, Cardston, Alta. T0K 0K0 (403–653–3952). At south end of town. 20 units, including five 2-room suites; some wheelchair units and kitchenettes. Air-conditioned, complimentary coffee.

CLARESHOLM. *Inexpensive.* **Bluebird Motel.** Box 1888, Claresholm, Alta. T0L 0T0 (403–625–3395). On Hwy. 2 at north end of town. 23 units, some 2-room family units, cable TV, free coffee.

DRAYTON VALLEY. *Moderate.* **Black Gold Inn.** Box 2700, Drayton Valley, Alta. T0E 0M0 (403–542–3200). 100 units, cable TV, dining and tavern, laundry.

Inexpensive. **West-Wind Motor Inn.** Box 1287, Drayton Valley, Alta. T0E 0M0 (403–542–5375). At 4225 50th St. About 30 air-conditioned rooms, telephones, color TV, licensed dining room, tavern, and cocktail lounge.

DRUMHELLER. *Expensive.* **Drumheller Inn.** Box 3100, Drumheller, Alta. T0J 0Y0 (403–823–8400 or 800–661–1460). At 100 S. Railway Ave. 103 air-conditioned rooms. Breakfast free, children under 18 free with parents. Cable TV, entertainment.

Inexpensive. **Badlands Motel.** Box 2217, Drumheller, Alta. T0J 0Y0 (403–823–5155). On Dinosaur Trail. 21 units, including some family and apartment units. TV, play area.

Drumheller TraveLodge. Box 1810, Drumheller, Alta. T0J 0Y0 (403–823–3322 or 800–268–3330). Downtown. 55 units. Telephones, color TV.

Hoo-doo Motel. Box 310, Drumheller, Alta. T0J 0Y0 (403–823–5662). On Hwy. 9S. 32 units. TV, plug-ins. Senior discounts, children under 12 free with parents.

EDSON. *Moderate.* **Edson Motor Hotel.** Box 1418, Edson, Alta. T0E 0P0 (403–723–3381 or 800–661–1460). At Main St. and 1st Ave. 65 rooms, all amenities, some with kitchenettes.

FAIRVIEW. *Moderate.* **Dunvegan Motor Inn.** Box 1938, Fairview, Alta. T0H 1L0 (403–835–5100). 46 units, cable TV, dining room and lounge. Family rates.

FORT MACLEOD. *Moderate.* **Foothills Motel.** Box 516, 359 24th St., Fort Macleod, Alta. T0L 0Z0 (403–553–4434). 28 units, some 2-room. Satellite TV. Senior, family, and off-season rates.

Sunset Motel. Box 398, Fort Macleod, Alta. T0L 0Z0. Located at west entrance to town on Hwy. 3 (403–553–4448). 22 units, some 2-room units, all air-conditioned with kitchenettes; complimentary coffee.

FORT McMURRAY. *Expensive.* **Peter Pond Hotel.** 9713 Hardin St., Fort McMurray, Alta. T9H 3G4 (403–743–3301). 136 rooms and executive suites, TV, telephones. Licensed dining, cocktail lounge, tavern.

Inexpensive. **Twin Pine Motor Inn Motel.** 10024 Biggs Ave., Fort McMurray, Alta. T9H 1S3 (403–743–3391). Kitchenettes in 42 units, some executive suites, air-conditioning, TV, telephones.

GRANDE PRAIRE. *Moderate.* **Grande Prairie Inn.** 11633 100th St., Grande Praire, Alta. T8V 3Y4 (403–532–5221). 212 rooms, direct-dial phones, air-conditioning. Licensed dining and tavern. Swimming pool.

Inexpensive. **Golden Inn Hotel.** 11201 100th Ave., Grande Praire, Alta. T8V 5M6 (403–539–6000). 102 rooms, cable TV. Indoor pool and whirlpool. Dining room, tavern, entertainment.

Silver Crest Lodge. 11902 100th St., Grande Praire, Alta. T8V 4H5 (403–532–1040). 95 units, water beds, complimentary coffee.

HINTON. *Expensive.* **Crestwood Hotel.** Box 1700, Hinton, Alta. T0E 1B0 (403–865–4001). 96 rooms. Honeymoon/executive suites with whirlpool and in-room movies. Wheelchair facilities, swimming pool. Complimentary coffee.

Moderate. **Greentree Motor Lodge.** Box 938, Hinton, Alta. T0E 1B0 (403–865–3321, 800–661–1924). 100 units, sauna, all amenities. Swimming pool. Dining and cocktail lounge.

Tara Vista Motel. Box 187, Hinton, Alta. T0E 1B0 (403–865–3391). 28 units, TV, telephones, complimentary coffee.

Twin Pine Motor Inn. Box 1035, Hinton, Alta. T0E 1B0 (403–865–2281, 800–232–9412). 54 rooms, TV, telephones, dining room, complimentary coffee. Swimming pool. Wheelchair facilities.

LAC LA BICHE. *Moderate.* **Almac Motor Hotel.** Box 536, Lac la Biche, Alta. T0A 2C0 (403–623–4123). 80 units, kitchenettes, licensed dining, and tavern.

Inexpensive. **Parkland Hotel.** Box 659, Lac la Biche, Alta. T0A 2C0 (403–623–4424). 22 units, kitchen, radio and TV, telephones, complimentary coffee.

LACOMBE. *Inexpensive.* **Lacombe Motor Inn.** Box 1809, Lacombe, Alta. T0C 1S0 (403–782–6444). 44 rooms, cable TV, dining room.

LETHBRIDGE. *Expensive.* **Sandman Inn.** 421 Mayor Magrath Dr., Lethbridge, Alta. T1J 3L8 (403–328–1111). 139 rooms, sauna, convention facilities. Licensed dining. Swimming pool, wheelchair access.

Moderate. **Bridge Townhouse Motel.** 1026 Mayor Magrath Dr., Lethbridge, Alta. T1K 2P8 (403–327–4576). 37 air-conditioned rooms. Cable TV, direct-dial telephones, pool. Wheelchair facilities.

El Rancho Motor Hotel. 6 Mayor Magrath Dr., Lethbridge, Alta. T1J 3M2 (403–327–5701). 106 rooms, swimming pool, convention facilities, licensed dining.

Heidelberg Inn. 1303 Mayor Magrath Dr., Lethbridge, Alta. T1K 2R1 (403–329–0555 or 800–528–1234). 67 rooms, sauna, licensed dining, bar, and entertainment. Wheelchair facilities.

Lethbridge Lodge Hotel. 320 Scenic Dr., Lethbridge, Alta. T1J 4B4 (403–328–1123 or 800–661–1232). Family rates, indoor pool, complimentary coffee. A good choice.

Lodge Motel. Mayor Magrath Dr. and 7th Ave., Lethbridge, Alta. T1J 1M7 (403–329–0100). 94 units with kitchenettes. Swimming pool, sauna, Continental breakfast, and other amenities.

Inexpensive. **Park Plaza Hotel.** 1009 Mayor Magrath Dr., Lethbridge, Alta. T1K 2P7 (403–328–2366). 68 air-conditioned rooms, cable TV, telephone, licensed dining and lounge.

LLOYDMINSTER. *Expensive.* **Wayside Inn.** Box 1250, Lloydminster, Alta. T9V 1G1 (403–875–4404). At 5411 44th St. 99 rooms, with families in mind. Tennis, swimming, sauna, licensed dining.

Inexpensive. **Lodge Motel.** 6301 44th St., Lloydminster, Alta. T9V 2G6 (403–875–1919). 66 units, complimentary breakfast. Pets.

Thunderbird Motel. 5610 44th St., Lloydminster, Alta. T9V 0B6 (403–875–3371). 36 units, kitchens, TV, radio, telephones, complimentary coffee.

MEDICINE HAT. *Expensive.* **Best Western Flamingo Terrace.** 722 Redcliff Dr., Medicine Hat, Alta. T1A 5E3 (403–527–2268 or 800–528–1234). 94 units, some with 2 rooms for families. Laundromat. On Hwy. 1.

Moderate. **Continental Inn.** 954 7th St., Medicine Hat, Alta. T1A 7R7 (403–527–8844). 65 rooms. All amenities, sauna, licensed dining, cocktails, and tavern.

TraveLodge Motor Inn. 1100 Redcliff Dr. S.W., Medicine Hat, Alta. T1A 5E5 (403–527–2275). 92 units. All amenities, swimming pool, executive suites available.

Westlander Inn. Box 1032, Medicine Hat, Alta. T1A 7H1 (403–529–6721). On Hwy. 1 at east end of city (3216 13th Ave. S.E.). 40 rooms, all amenties. Licensed dining, cocktails, beer parlor, and entertainment. Best in 'Hat.

Inexpensive. **Assiniboia Inn.** Box 786, Medicine Hat, Alta. T1A 7G7 (403–526–2801). 63 clean hotel rooms, air conditioning, dining, color TV, telephones.

Bel Aire Motel. 633 14th St. S.W., Medicine hat, Alta. T1A 4V5 (403–526–2801). 12 units with kitchens, air conditioning, TV, radios, telephones. Off-season rates.

Park Lane Motor Hotel. 780 7th St. S.W., Medicine Hat, Alta. T1A 4L7 (403–527–2231). 79 units, air-conditioned, cable TV, telephones, swimming pool, licensed facilities. Family and off-season rates.

MILK RIVER. *Inexpensive.* **Southgate Inn.** Box 66, Milk River, Alta. T0K 1M0 (403–647–3733). 20 units. TV, weekly rates.

NANTON. *Inexpensive.* **Mid-way Motel.** Box 298, Nanton, Alta. T0L 1R0 (403–646–2170). 18 units, some with air-conditioning. Kitchenettes, satellite TV, one family unit.

OLDS. *Inexpensive.* **Sportman's Inn.** Box 1767, Olds, Alta. T0M 1P0 (403–556–3315). 44 units. Picnic, play area. Cable TV, telephones.

PEACE RIVER. *Moderate.* **Crescent Motel.** Box 670, Peace River, Alta. T0H 2X0 (403–624–2586). 95 units, some with queen-size beds, all with color TV, kitchens, and air-conditioning. Complimentary coffee.

PINCHER CREEK. *Inexpensive.* **Foothills Motel.** Box 2347, Pincher Creek, Alta. T0K 1W0 (403–627–3341). 30 units. Kitchens and most amenities, licensed dining.

Parkway Motel. Box 130, Pincher Creek, Alta. T0K 1W0 (403–627–3344). 41 units, some for families. Satellite TV, waterbeds. On Hwy. 6.

PONOKA. *Moderate.* **Ponoka Stampeder Inn.** Box 878, Ponoka, Alta. T0C 2H0 (403–783–5535). 58 units, TV, whirlpool, and exercise room.

Inexpensive. **Oasis Motel.** Box 1240, Ponoka, Alta. T0C 2H0 (403–783–3452 or 403–783–3804). 24 units, color TV, radio, telephones, air conditioning. Complimentary coffee.

Rancher Inn. Box 1898, Ponoka, Alta. T0C 2H0 (403–783–4441). 42 units. Telephones, color TV, coffee shop, tavern, dining room.

RED DEER. *Expensive.* **The Capri Centre.** 3310 Gaetz Ave., Red Deer, Alta. T4N 3X9 (403–346–2091). 262 rooms, all amenities. Swimming pool and licensed facilities and conference center.

Moderate. **Black Knight Inn.** 2929 Gaetz Ave., Red Deer, Alta. T4R 1H1 (403–343–6666). 100 rooms. Air-conditioning and amenities, swimming pool, licensed facilities, and entertainment. Pets accepted.

The Great West Inn. 6500 67th St., Red Deer, Alta. T4P 1A2 (403–342–6567). 99 rooms, health club, TV, licensed dining.

Red Deer Lodge. 4311 49th St., Red Deer, Alta. T4N 5Y7 (403–346–8841 or 800–662–7181). 240 rooms. Swimming pool and all amenities, including licensed dining and tavern.

Inexpensive. **Granada Motor Inn.** 4707 Ross St., Red Deer, Alta. T4N 1X3 (403–347–5551). 56 rooms, radios, color TV, telephones, air-conditioning. Wheelchair units. Licensed.

The Red Deer Inn. 4217 Gaetz Ave., Red Deer, Alta. T4N 3Z4 (403–346–6671). 64 rooms, all amenities, licensed dining and tavern.

ROCKY MOUNTAIN HOUSE. *Moderate.* **Tamarack Motor Inn.** Box 2860, Rocky Mountain House, Alta. T0M 1T0 (403–845–5252). 49 rooms, satellite TV, licensed dining room, tavern.

Walking Eagle Motor Inn. Box 1317, Rocky Mountain House, Alta. T0M 1T0 (403–845–2804). 82 rooms, air-conditioning, TV, licensed dining room.

ST. PAUL. *Inexpensive.* **Galaxy Motel.** Box 1265, St. Paul, Alta. T0A 3A0 (403–645–4441). 53 units with kitchens, TV, telephones, complimentary coffee.

Lakeland Motel. Box 2958, St. Paul, Alta. T0A 3A0 (403–645–3381). 22 units, some air-conditioned. Telephones, cable TV, kitchenettes.

SLAVE LAKE. *Expensive.* **Nash's Cabins.** Box 86, Slave Lake, Alta. T0G 2A0 (403–849–3977). Three log vabins, 5 km (3 mi.) north of Slave Lake on a private beach. Open May–Oct., reservations recommended.

Sawridge Motor Hotel. Box 879, Slave Lake, Alta. T0G 2A0 (403–849–4101). 120 rooms, some executive suites. Dining and tavern. Wheelchair facilities. Children under 12 free with parents.

STETTLER. *Inexpensive.* **Crusader Motor Inn.** Box 10, Stettler, Alta. T0C 2L0 (403–742–3371). At 6020 50th Ave. 33 units. Telephones, TV, licensed dining room, lounge.

Grandview Motel. Box 749, Stettler, Alta. T0C 2L0 (403–742–3391). On Hwy. 56 S. Telephones, TV, some refrigerators.

TURNER VALLEY. *Inexpensive.* **Turner Valley Inn.** 112 Flare Ave., Turner Valley, Alta. T0L 2A0 (403–933-7878). 27 rooms. Color TV. Children under 12 free with parents.

VALLEY VIEW. *Expensive.* **Raven Motor Inn.** Box 816, Valleyview, Alta. T0H 3N0 (403–524–3383). 35 air-conditioned units. Kitchenettes, TV, telephones, complimentary coffee, swimming pool.

Moderate. **Horizon Motels.** Box 1590, Valleyview, Alta. T0H 3N0 (403–524–3904). 63 units, most air-conditioned. Telephones, TV, licensed dining.

WAINWRIGHT. *Moderate.* **Buffalo Springs Flag Motor Inn.** Box 1646, Wainwright, Alta. T0B 4P0 (403–842–3371 or 800–661–1460). 30 units. Good dining facilities, telephones, color TV, and tavern. Weekend and family rates.

WETASKIWIN. *Moderate.* **Wayside Inn.** 4103 56th St., Wetaskiwin, Alta. T9A 1V2 (403–352–6681). 26 units. Most room amenities, kitchenettes, TV, fine dining, and cabaret facilities. Friendly.

WHITECOURT. *Inexpensive.* **Renford Motor Inn.** Box 1616, Whitecourt, Alta. T0E 2L0 (403–778–3133). 112 units, satellite TV, licensed dining, and lounge.

Rivers Motor Hotel. Box 1230, Whitecourt, Alta. T0E 2L0. 70 rooms. Telephones, TV, beer parlor.

TELEPHONES. The area code for all of Alberta is 403. For direct-dial, long distance calls, dial 1 before the area code. For operator-assistance, dial 0 before the area code. Local calls cost 25 cents. Dial 411 for local information.

HOW TO GET AROUND. By car. Alberta has over 150,000 km (90,000 mi.) of well-maintained highways and roads. Speed limits vary according to road conditions from 110 to 35 kph (70 to 22 mph). In general, the maximum highway speed limit in Alberta is 110 kph by day and 100 kph by night. Limits in school and playground zones are usually 30 kph in cities, 40 kph in rural areas. A note of caution: All mileages and speed limits are posted in kilometers.

By train. *VIA Rail* runs full trans-continental service through Calgary and Banff, Edmonton and Jasper. VIA Rail also maintains regular line service on a network throughout the province.

By bus. Full interprovincial bus coverage is provided by *Greyhound, Canadian Coachways, Brewster Transport, Lethbridge, Northern Bus Lines, Cardinal, Diversified (PWT), Grey Goose* and local companies.

By transit and taxi. The transit fare in both Edmonton and Calgary is $1; exact change required. Cabs are relatively expensive. The taxi trip from the airport is very expensive in Edmonton; in Calgary, for 3 or more people, it's more economical than the bus.

By plane. The prime provincial carriers are *Time Air, Pacific Western Air Lines* and, to a lesser degree, *Canadian Pacific.*

Information on the many **charter air services** can be obtained from the Alberta Aviation Council, 220 Terminal Building, Municipal Airport, Edmonton Alta. T5G 0W6 (451–5289).

FACTS AND FIGURES. Alberta, Canada's fourth largest province in land area, entered confederation on September 1, 1905. It was named by the Marquis of Lorne, then Governor General of Canada, in honor of his wife Princess Louise Caroline Alberta, fourth daughter of Queen Victoria. Its crest, issued by royal warrant in 1907, is a pictorial landscape of the province looking from east to west. It shows wheatfields, prairie, foothills, mountains, sky and a St. George's Cross. The flag of Alberta, adopted in 1968, bears the crest centered on a royal ultramarine blue background. Its floral emblem is the wild rose, and its tartan is primarily shades of green with interwoven stripes of blue, yellow and pink.

Bounded on the north by the Northwest Territories, on the west and southwest by British Columbia, on the south by Montana, and on the east by Saskatchewan, Alberta has a population of 2.3 million. Edmonton is its capital. Although the climate varies from area to area, Alberta has more sunshine than any other Canadian province, with year-round blue skies. Winters see heavy snowfall in the mountains and northern regions, cold conditions in the northern and eastern prairies, but moderate winters in the southwest. Summers are warm throughout. Trees leaf in the first and second weeks in May. The heaviest rainfall occurs in June.

TOURIST INFORMATION. Comprehensive literature on attractions and accommodations as well as maps can be obtained from *Travel Alberta,* Box 2500, Edmonton, Alta. T5J 2Z4 (800–661–8888 from the U.S. and most of Canada). Travel Alberta will also respond to questions about canoeing, hunting, fishing, skiing, and special events. The province is organized into 14 tourist zones. Travel Alberta will supply brochures on each, or requests for information can be made directly to individual zone at the addresses listed below.

Zone 1: *Chinook Country Tourist Association,* 2805 Scenic Dr., Lethbridge, Alta. T1K 5B7 (403–329–6777).

Zone 2 *(The Gateway): South-East Alberta Travel & Convention Bureau.* Box 605, Medicine Hat, Alta. T1A 7G5 (403–527–6422).

Zone 3: *The Big Country Tourist Association,* Box 2308, Drumheller, T0J 0Y0 (403–823–5885). There is a particularly interesting brochure with map on the Dinosaur Trail.

Zone 4: *David Thompson Country Tourist Council,* 4811 48th Ave., Red Deer, Alta. T4N 3T2 (403–342–2032).

Zone 5: *Battle River Tourist Association.* Box 1515, 6107 48th Ave., Camrose, Alta. T4V 1X4 (403–672–8555).

Zone 6: *The Lakeland Tourist Association,* Box 874, St. Paul, Alta. T0A 3A0 (403–645–2913).

Zone 7: *The Evergreen Tourist Association,* Box 2548, Edson, Alta. T0E 0P0 (403–723–4711).

Zone 8: *Land of the Mighty Peace Tourist Association,* Box 3210 Peace River, Alta. T0H 2X0 (403–624–4042).

Zone 9: *Jasper Park Chamber of Commerce,* Box 98, Jasper, Alta. T0E 1E0 (403–852–3858).

Zone 10: *Calgary Tourist and Convention Bureau,* 237 8th Ave. S.E., Calgary, Alta. T2G 0K8 (403–263–8510).

Zone 11: *Edmonton Convention and Tourism Authority,* #104, 9797 Jasper Ave., Edmonton, Alta. T5J 1N9 (403–422–5505).

Zone 12: *Tourist Committee Banff-Lake Louise Chamber of Commerce,* Box 1298, 94 Banff Ave., Banff, Alta. T0L 0C0 (403–762–3777).

Zone 13: *Game Country Travel Association,* Box 1254, Grande Prairie, Alta. T8V 4Z1 (403–539–6024).

Zone 14: *Midnight Twilight Tourist Association,* #1 Sturgeon Rd., St. Albert, Alta. T8N 0E8 (403–458–5600).

Travel Alberta maintains 20 information centers throughout the province and at entry points. 5 are year-round: in Calgary, Edmonton, Canmore, and in Kananaskis at Gooseberry Lake (weekends only) and Barrier Lake. Two are at U.S. border points: in St. Mary's, Montana (Rte. 89) and Milk River (Hwy. 4, north of I-15). One is in Golden, British Columbia.

TIME ZONE. Alberta is on Mountain Standard or Daylight Saving Time.

SEASONAL EVENTS. January: Height of ski season. The five big areas: *Sunshine Village, Lake Louise,* and *Mount Norquay,* all in Banff National Park, plus *Marmot Basin* in Jasper and *Fortress Mountain* and *Nakiska* in Kananaskis Country, are busy with slope activity and major competitions. Late January, *Banff Lake Louise Winter Festival.*

February: *Ski competitions* on all slopes. *Winter Carnivals* at Airdrie, Athabasca, Calgary, Edmonton, Grande Prairie, High River, Medicine Hat, and Red Deer. *Dog Sled Races* at Fox Creek. *North/Am International Snowmobile Races* at Wetaskiwin.

March: *Winter carnivals* at Strathmore, Swan Hills. *Figure Skating* at Leduc. The *rodeo* season begins (all indoor this time of year) with events at Calgary, Edmonton, Medicine Hat, and Lethbridge.

April: *Rodeos* at Camrose, Red Deer, Vermillion, Cardston, Lloydminster, Vulcan, and Drumheller. *Figure Skating* at Two Hills and Stony Plain. *Ski Competitions* on all slopes throughout the month.

May: *Calgary International Horse Show. Summer Showcase* at Banff opens, 1st-July 31. *Banff's Festival of the Arts* is on through summer. Many *rodeos,* including Leduc, Fox Creek, Taber, and Hobbema. At High River, the internationally acclaimed *Little Britches Rodeo* is an important event. In Edmonton is the *International Children's Festival.*

June: Two dozen *rodeos* throughout the province. One of the best is the *Ponoka Stampede. Horse shows* at Sundre, Claresholm, Edmonton and Red Deer. *Raft Race* at Big Valley. *Fish Derby* at Buck Lake. *International Folk Festival* at Red Deer. Edmonton's *Jazz City International Festival* begins in June, carries on into July.

July: July 1st is a national holiday and *Canada Day* celebrations are held in most communities in Alberta. 20 *rodeos* are scheduled this month; most important are; *Calgary Stampede, Medicine Hat Stampede, Whoop-Up Days* at Lethbridge, *Broncosaurus Days* at Drumheller, the *Professional* at Red Deer. *Fish Derby* at Buck Lake. In Edmonton *Klondike Days,* a glorification of the trek of '98. *Jet Boat Races* at Grande Cache, Edmonton, and Whitecourt. *Ukrainian Festival* at Vegreville, *Whitewater Canoe Races* at Sundre, Banff's *Indian Days,* hot-air balloons at Grande Prairie.

August: 1st is *Heritage Day* with major ethnic festivals in Edmonton and Calgary. Banff *Festival of the Arts, Fish Derby* at Bonnyville and Lac La Biche, and the *Red Deer International Air Show.* Ten *rodeos* occur and *horse shows* at Lloydminster, Didsbury, and Calgary. Also at Calgary is the *Annual Flower Show, Fringe Theater Event,* and *Folk Music Festival.*

September: Ft. McMurray, *Annual Blueberry Festival. Rodeos* and *golf tournaments* happening. At Peace River, a major festival occurs during the first two weeks of the month. *Spruce Meadows Masters* equestrian event in Calgary.

October: *Rodeos* at Bassano, Claresholm, Hanna, Vermilion, Caroline, Three Hills, and Hines Creek. An *Octoberfest* at Hinton, Medicine Hat, Red Deer.

November: The *Canadian Finals Rodeo* will be held in Edmonton, also annual *Farmfair.*

December: *Hockey* in every community. *Annual Christmas Carol Festival* at Foremost. In Calgary, the *Christmas Box Concert,* and the *Singing Christmas Tree,* also in Edmonton. *Curling Bonspiels* throughout the winter in many locations.

TOURS. By bus: Many bus tours through the Canadian west (including Alberta) are offered by tour companies whose main booking offices are in Toronto. These bus packages include variations of Alberta highlights; Calgary, Banff, Jasper, Edmonton. Two of the many are *UTL Holiday Tours,* 22 College Street; and *Horizon Holidays of Canada,* 44 Victoria Street, both from Toronto.

In Alberta, *Brewster Transport,* Box 1140, Banff or 130 Banff Ave. (762–3207), offers the most comprehensive Banff and Jasper bus plans. *Greyhound Bus Lines,* 222 1st Ave. S.W., Calgary, is able to get you around and about in Alberta. If you would like to see the cities, call *Grayline* in Calgary, *Royal Tours* in Edmonton. For tours through the Badlands by double-decker bus, call *Big Country Tours,* 15 Paul Place in Drumheller (823–8736).

By plane: *Time Air* lands at all major Alberta cities. *Air Charter Services* (located primarily at Calgary and Edmonton) are always available to take you into the most remote locations. Alberta Air Facilities maps and supplemental booklets are available from the *Alberta Aviation Council,* 220 Terminal Building, Municipal Airport, Edmonton, T5G 0W6 (451–5289).

By water: You can literally paddle your own canoe through Alberta. The province has charted every major waterway (and many minor ones, too). No other province has developed its waterways so extensively for visitor traffic. Six comprehensive guide books have been prepared, as well as a waterways map. All are available from *Travel Alberta* in Edmonton.

Commercial white water and quiet water raft tours are available in both Banff and Jasper.

On skis: All major ski resorts in Alberta offer guide service and instruction for cross country skiing, using hundreds of miles of summer hiking trails to see-the-sights.

NATIONAL PARKS. Alberta has five national parks: *Elk Island,* about 27 kms. (17 miles) west of Edmonton; *Waterton,* in the extreme southeast corner of the province; *Banff,* 130 km (80 mi.) west of Calgary; *Jasper,* 362 km (225 mi.) west of Edmonton; *Wood Buffalo* in the extreme northeast.

No pass through charge for any motor vehicle. To spend a day or less, a 24-hour stopping pass can be purchased for $3. Most convenient is to purchase a $10.00 annual national parks pass, good until March 31st of the year following at any national park in Canada. Annual angling licenses cost $10, valid for all national parks.

For safety reasons, visitors must register at a Parks Warden Office before embarking on or completing any climbing, extensive backpacking, hiking, or cross-country skiing expeditions. Use of open campfires is restricted to National Park Campsites specifically designed to accommodate them. Dogs and cats must be on leash. Use of firearms and bow string equipment is forbidden; all such equipment must be sealed at park entry points.

PROVINCIAL PARKS. There are 62 provincial parks in Alberta varying in size and facilities offered. For an overnight stay the charge is moderate and depends on services provided. Some parks will accept reservations. Contact Travel Alberta for details.

Most of Alberta's provincial parks provide picnicking and cooking facilities (including the wood). No firearms may be used, although they are allowed entry into the park providing they are kept locked securely within your vehicle.

The following provincial parks are among the most outstanding:

Cypress Hills Provincial Park: One of the largest, 64 km (40 mi.) southeast of Medicine Hat, the hills rise 2,000 feet above surrounding prairie: skiing, tobogganing, ice fishing, curling, skating, golf, swimming, and hiking. Reesor Lake and Elk Water Lake provide excellent water settings.

Chain Lakes Provincial Park: 39 km (23 mi.) west of Nanton. One of Alberta's most heavily stocked trout lakes, primarily set up to accommodate fishermen. Camping and boating.

Bragg Creek Provincial Park: 32 km (20 mi.) southwest of Calgary. Primarily a picnicking area; adjacent to the Rocky Mountains Forest Reserve; a scenic site of vast wilderness touring opportunities.

Bow Valley Provincial Park: 64 km (40 mi.) west of Calgary. Many types of glacial remnants; spectacular mountain terrain.

Crimson Lake Provincial Park: Located in the central foothills region, 14 km (9 mi.) northwest of Rocky Mountain House; suitable for swimming. Wildlife is abundant in the dense evergreen forest of this region;

Big Knife Provincial Park: 64 km (40 mi.) northeast of Stettler on site of an Indian battleground. The Battle River weaves through the park, providing a facility for boating.

Aspen Beach Provincial Park: 11 km (7 mi.) west of Lacombe; features the warm waters of Gull Lake for swimming and water skiing and a wide, sandy beach that is safe for children.

Big Hill Springs Provincial Park: 16 km (10 mi.) northeast of Cochrane, in the transition area between the Parkland and Foothills terrain. Spectacular bubbling springs provide water for 30 small waterfalls.

Jarvis Bay Provincial Park: On Sylvan Lake 19 km (12 mi.) west of Red Deer. Dense, unspoiled undergrowth; camping.

Miquelon Lake: 64 km (40 mi.) southeast of Edmonton; large warm-water lake and a wide, safe beach. Boating, swimming; picnicking and camping facilities are highly rated.

Pigeon Lake Provincial Park: 48 km (30 mi.) west of Wetaskiwin on the west shore of Pigeon Lake. One of Alberta's more popular lakes for watersports is developed for camping and picnicking. Its foliage of poplar, conifers, and under-brush provide a habitat for many types of birds. Waterfowl and birdwatching.

Saskatoon Island Park: 24 km (15 mi.) west of Grande Prairie; a bird watch-ing park.

Wabamum Lake Provincial Park: 64 km (40 mi.) west of Edmonton on highway 16. The natural beauty of the lake and its recreational qualities are the attractions. Angling is good for northern pike, yellow perch and lake whitefish.

Dinosaur Provincial Park: 22,000 acres located 42 km (26 mi.) northeast of Brooks. Noted for its magnificent badlands, dinosaur quarries and displays, a major portion of this park is restricted and accessible only by means of guided bus tour. Also self-guided nature trails and walks through areas of great histori-cal and geological interest.

Little Fish Provincial Park: 32 km (20 mi.) southeast of Drumheller is a popular Alberta sailboating lake.

Writing on Stone Provincial Park: 32 km (20 mi.) east of Milk River on highway number 4. One of the most interesting parks to visit. Contains vast badlands and hoodoos; the Milk River flows through its wooded and grassed picnic area. Indian stories (called pictographs) are inscribed on the rocks.

Lesser Slave Lake Provincial Park: 16 km (10 mi.) north of the town of Slave Lake. Massive lake and large sandy beaches.

Moonshine Provincial Park: 32 km (20 mi.) west of Spirit River. This park's current name reflects some of the goings-on in the surrounding forest at an earlier time. Known as Mirage Lake geographically, there is a rich variety of plant and animal life here.

Sir Winston Churchill Provincial Park: Located on an island in Lac La Biche with natural sandy beaches for sun bathing and swimming. The lake offers northern pike, yellow perch, and walleye.

Gregoire Lake Provincial Park: 40 km (25 mi.) southeast of Fort McMurray. Interesting hiking trails, a scenic shoreline and a good sandy beach with boat launching facilities are highlights. The park is within a boreal forest type of topography. Pike and perch fishing are excellent.

William A. Switzer Provincial Park. In the foothills 22km (14 mi) northwest of Hinton; surrounds a chain of 5 small lakes. Canoeing and hiking. Wildlife is abundant.

Williamson Provincial Park and *Youngspoint Provincial Park:* Both located on Sturgeon Lake 24 km (15 mi.) west of Valleyview off Highway 34. Two of northern Alberta's favorite campsites. Sturgeon Lake has all watersports and is noted for pike, walleye, and perch fishing.

Thunder Lake Provincial Park: 24 km (15 mi.) west of Barrhead on Highway 33. Boating is made interesting by islands in the lakes and many uninhabited coves. Thunder Lake is one of the few nesting sites of the majestic Blue Heron.

GARDENS. Three you might visit are: the *Nikka Yuko Centennial Garden* in **Lethbridge**, *Reader Rock Gardens* in **Calgary**, *Cascade Gardens* at the Administration Centre in **Banff** and the four indoor climatic pavilions of Edmonton's *Muttart Conservatory*. There are more . . . just ask.

FARM VACATIONS AND GUEST RANCHES. Rural families and visitors have discovered the two-way benefits of participating in Alberta's *Country Vacation* program. Facilities range from ranch to farm; from modern to rustic; from simple to most comfortable. All accommodations meet provincial health, fire, and municipal safety standards. Three basic types of accommodations are offered: room and board; housekeeping units; and camping areas. Facilities are available to families, children unaccompanied by adults, or adults (couples or singles). The plan is flexible. You can stay in your trailer, or tent, or live in the home with the family. You may arrange your own meals or share with the family. You can simply enjoy the farm atmosphere, or participate in farm chores.

The board and room rates vary slightly with the farm or ranch and the arrangement. In general, they are $18 a day or $125 a week for individuals, and $10 a day for children, 6 and under. Complete information and reservations can be obtained by contacting Travel Alberta, Box 2500, Edmonton, T5J 2Z4.

CHILDREN'S ACTIVITIES. Most provincial parks have hiking trails, hills to climb, fields to play in, water to splash in, and playgrounds to swing and slide around in. Children can also accompany you on trail riding, fishing trips, and ski trips. All ski instructors are using the short-ski method of teaching the sport. In **Calgary**, *St. George's Island Zoo* and *Calaway Park* are popular. In **Edmonton**, *Valley Zoo, Fantasyland,* and *Fort Edmonton* are your best bets.

SUMMER SPORTS. Participant sports. Nearly every town of any size has at least one *golf* course, *swimming* pool and *tennis* court. In major centers, you can participate in anything from *squash* to *chess*. Fly-in fishing and river rafting adventures are available. Details can be had by contacting Travel Alberta.

Spectator sports. The favorite spectator sports in the summer are *baseball, soccer, rodeos, lacrosse* . . . even *hockey* and *figure skating*.

WINTER SPORTS. In addition to some of the world's finest *skiing* in the Rockies, there are many other locations, at Edmonton, Camrose, Cypress Hills, Grande Prairie, Fort McMurray, Red Deer, Westlock—if not for downhill, certainly for cross-country skiing. There are also impressive facilities at the Olympic sites in Calgary. There are many areas for *snowmobiling*, but the machines are *not* allowed in national parks or many provincial parks. They are allowed in parts of the wilderness areas.

FISHING. Angling is permitted in Alberta 24 hours a day year-round, subject to closed season on specific waters. A fishing license for Albertans and visiting Canadians costs $5. For a visiting non-Canadian, it costs $12. A license is issued on an annual basis and is valid until the following March 31. A three-day-limit license is also available to visiting non-Canadians at $5. Angling permits are required by all fishermen except children under 16 years of age. A special trophy license ($5) is required for some lakes which offer specimens of unusual size. If sturgeon is what you are after, you should know that sturgeon is a protected species in many Alberta waters. A special sturgeon fishing license is required ($5). Spear fishermen must possess a $3 permit.

A fishing license is required for all national parks in Canada. It costs $10 and is good in every national park in Canada, again on an annual basis. Full information, sports fishing guide, and map may be obtained from Department of Energy

and Natural Resources, Main Fl., North Tower, Petroleum Plaza, 9945 108th
St., Edmonton, Alberta, T5K 2C9.

HUNTING. Hunting of any sort is not permitted in
Alberta's provincial or national parks. Further, revolv-
ers, pistols and fully automatic firearms are prohibited
in Canada. Persons entering Canada may possess and
bring in rifles, shotguns or fishing tackle but must provide Canadian Customs
with a description of such equipment and serial numbers of the guns so that the
articles may be readily cleared upon their return. Two hundred rounds of
ammunition per person are admitted duty free.

The province is noted for fine goose shooting. Waterfowl and upland game
birds such as ducks, pheasants, ptarmigan, grouse and partridge roam abundantly throughout the province. All hawks, owls, falcons and eagles are protected by law. Also, several species of game bird on the "Endangered Species List"
nest in Alberta (i.e., Whooping Crane). These birds are protected by law.
License fees for bird game are $5.00 for Canadians but nonresidents of Alberta,
and $50.00 for non-Canadians. An archery license is available for $3.00.

Big game hunting is still popular in Alberta. You can still hunt grizzly bear,
wolf, cougar, and a host of antlered animals. To be sure of the areas that can
be hunted and the license fees of specific game animals, prospective hunters must
acquire the summary and guide of big game regulations that is revised annually
by the Department of Energy, National Resources in Edmonton.

For some idea of costs: a non-Alberta resident (Canadian or otherwise) must
purchase a $4 Big Game or Bird Game Certificate. In addition, specific animal
licenses cost from $25 to $200, depending on the species. Further, nonresidents
must be accompanied by a guide. There are no trophy fees in Alberta and export
permits for game are issued free. Information on all hunting situations may be
obtained from either Travel Alberta or Department of Energy, National Resources, Main Fl., North Tower, Petroleum Plaza, 9945 108th St., Edmonton,
Alberta T5K 2C9.

CAMPING OUT. On every major roadway, at least
every 80 kms. (50 miles), a roadside campsite has been
established offering picnic shelters, fireplaces with wood
supplied, and drinking water.

The provincial park system also offers more camping opportunities at a very
moderate rate. These sites always incorporate recreational possibilities. There
are many well-maintained commercial (e.g., KOA), municipal, and club oriented camping and recreational vehicle parks. Most provide good camping amenities. Travel Alberta publishes an annual accommodations guide listing the
specifications and characteristics of every campground within the province. A
copy may be obtained by writing to *Travel Alberta,* Box 2500, Edmonton,
Alberta, Canada, T5J 2Z4.

TRAILER TIPS. Touring by trailer or motor home is
popular. All cities and many major towns provide facilities for service and maintenance of vehicles. While Alberta highways are more than suitable for safe driving,
advice should be sought before you attempt to travel the gravel roads of wilderness areas.

In most Alberta provincial parks, overnight camping is allowed. The cost is
included in the rate. Electrical hookup in provincial parks is additional per
night. Most private trailer parks are able to provide electrical, water, and sewage
hookups as well as showers and laundry services. *Travel Alberta's* accommodation guide lists well over 100 sewage dumping stations distributed conveniently
throughout the province. Calgary and Edmonton each have several such stations, while the major centers near Alberta points-of-entry are all able to accommodate these trailering needs.

HISTORIC SITES. Alberta abounds with historic sites. It all depends on where your interest lies: archeology, geology, anthropology, pioneer history, etc. Travel Alberta produces a brochure describing designated Provincial Historic Sites, which covers the full range of interests.

A few miles directly south of **Cluny** in the valley of the Bow River is the site of the signing of Treaty 7 in 1877. The Indians of the southern plains gathered here—representatives of Blackfoot, Blood, Peigans, Sarcee, and Stoneys—who surrendered their rights to their traditional way of life and to their territory to Queen Victoria.

Frank Slide in the **Crowsnest Pass,** between the towns of Blairmore and Bellevue on Highway 3, took the lives of more than 70 persons in 1903 when a gigantic wedge of limestone 2,100 feet high, 3,000 feet wide, and 500 feet thick crashed down from Turtle Mountain wiping out most of the town and taking the lives in approximately 100 seconds.

MUSEUMS. There are numerous museums in communities throughout the province. Some of the most important are: *The Luxton Museum* in **Banff,** which, although relatively small, contains one of Alberta's finest collections of Plains and Mountain native Indian paraphernalia.

The *Provincial Museum of Alberta* in **Edmonton** features excellent displays of natural and human history.

The *Glenbow Museum* in **Calgary** covers art and Indian and western Canadian history.

MUSIC. Both Calgary and Edmonton enjoy full philharmonic orchestras. Grande Prairie has its own symphony orchestra. Most cities possess performing groups.

SHOPPING. In Alberta, always popular are the Hudson's Bay blankets that have been in use since the days of Indian trade. Furs and fur products are choice items. Native people also produce clothing and tools of a bygone day and a high commercial standard. Artwork, produced by local artisans, includes pottery, ceramics, sculptures, and paintings. You will find at least one shop in the larger communities (*The Calgary Cabin* in Calgary, *Quest* in Banff, *The Bay* in Edmonton and *Quarks and Fribbles* in Jasper) that specializes in Albertan products.

LIQUOR LAWS. Legal age in Alberta is 18 years. Liquor and beer may be purchased only through Alberta Liquor stores. There are now wine boutiques, on a limited scale, in the province. In addition, beer supplies may be obtained from the majority of hotels. Liquor stores are closed Sunday, on major holidays, and days of election. There is no universal standard of opening hours. Some stores stay open until 11:30 P.M., others until 10:00 P.M., and many only until 6:00 P.M.

RESTAURANTS. This is cattle country, and Albertans are fiercely proud of the quality of beef that its grazing lands and grain yields. With good reason, too.

Restaurants are listed by price category as follows: *Deluxe,* $50 and over; *Expensive,* $30–50; *Moderate,* $15–30; *Inexpensive,* under $15. Prices include hors d' oeuvres or soup, salad, main course, dessert, and coffee, but not drinks or gratuities. Entertainment (particularly good music in an appealing atmosphere) is the general rule in *Deluxe* and *Expensive* categories.

Two pancake house chains—Smitty's Pancake House and Phil's Pancake House—both *inexpensive,* offer an extensive selection of appealing family foods.

Most places accept major credit cards.

CAMROSE. *Inexpensive.* **Bono's Family Restaurant.** A fine restaurant, specializing in seafood chowder, Alberta beef, and other excellent selections.

The Feedmill. Quiet. Relaxed in atmosphere and service. Good menu.

CLARESHOLM. *Inexpensive.* The Flying "N." One of Canada's top 10 restaurants, at a one-time Canadian Air Force Base. Extensive menu; the finest home-cooked food, served buffet-style.

DRUMHELLER. *Moderate.* The Corner Grill. Pizza tops the list on a wide menu.
Dick's Place. For western and Chinese.
Roman's Dining Lounge. Fresh food presented in a Neanderthal style.

EDSON. *Moderate.* Plainsman Motor Inn. A good, clean family restaurant.

FORT MACLEOD. *Moderate.* The Java Shop. Oven-baked chicken is superb.
Scarlet & Gold Inn. Mounted police atmosphere featuring steak and lobster.

GRANDE PRAIRIE. *Moderate.* Grande Prairie Motor Inn. Small, tastefully appointed dining room with a good menu. Excellent specialty is prime rib.

HINTON. *Inexpensive.* Husky House. Steak and eggs, plus a fair menu, good food, and a clean operation.

LETHBRIDGE. *Deluxe.* Anton's. In the Lethbridge Lodge Hotel. Formal dining and Sunday buffets.
El Rancho. Has long been one of the most popular eating establishments in Lethbridge.
Park Plaza Hotel. Southern Alberta elegance with flambés as delicious as they are spectacular. Lobster tails are superb. Menu imaginative.
Top of the Grandstand. Dine and dance country and western style. Try buffalo meat—as steaks, burgers, and roasts.
Moderate. Majorette Restaurant. Offers a choice of Western and Chinese cuisine. The menu is large enough to please an entire family.
Oz. Steak and seafood. Special food, and price specials.
The Panda Restaurant. Szechuan and Cantonese specialties.
Sven Eriksen's Family Restaurant. Definitely a better family-style restaurant, with good food.

MEDICINE HAT. *Deluxe.* Continental Inn. Gourmet menu. Excellent service in semi-formal atmosphere. Entertainment.
Old Mill Inn. An old flour mill has been converted into a spectacular dining experience. Menu features beef and seafoods.
The Westlander Inn. (Trans-Canada Hwy.) The ultimate in *Medicine Hat.* A first class operation in every aspect, rivaling those of many major cities. Gracious surroundings and service, exquisite food.
Moderate. Golden Dragon. Oriental menu is the specialty. Pleasant, quiet atmosphere.
Heidel Haus. Steaks. Old country decor. An upstairs loft offers dancing.
The Ming Tree. Lots of action; friendly faces, good food. Portions are large; specialty is chinese cuisine, but menu covers everything from steak to seafood to barbecued ribs.

PEACE RIVER. *Inexpensive.* Traveller's. Daytime smorgasbord. Interesting dining delights in evening with extensive menu.

PINCHER CREEK. *Deluxe.* Foothills Restaurant. Pleasing décor, home-cooked meals, and friendly service.
Expensive. Oasis Restaurant. Topping the ambitious menu are steak and lobster.

RED DEER. *Deluxe.* Capri Motor Hotel. The best in central Alberta. Gourmet cooking; good menu.

Killians. Flambes, steaks, and seafood.
Red Deer Lodge. Gracious gourmet dining on an international basis.
Moderate. **Crown and Anchor.** English-style pub and restaurant.
Ranch House. Excellent steaks at reasonable prices. Good salad bar. Best buy in Red Deer.

ST. ALBERT. *Moderate.* **New York Steak House.** Great steaks and onion soup.

SWAN HILLS. *Inexpensive.* **Millie's Place.** A family restaurant, great food.

WHITECOURT. *Moderate.* **Whitecourt Motor Inn.** A tastefully appointed dining room, with a well-thought-out menu.

BRITISH COLUMBIA

Gateway to the Pacific

by
GARRY MARCHANT

By the eighteenth century, most of the map of the New World was filled in except for the United States's Northwest and Canada's Pacific coast. Guarded by sea and mountains, British Columbia, the first gateway to North America for early man, had not yet been seen by Europeans. Early overland explorers called this land the "sea of mountains."

This rugged province encompasses the wettest climates in Canada as well as the driest, the warmest places as well as the coldest, the densest forest and the nearest thing the country has to a desert. British Columbia's diversity of climate results in more life zones with more kinds of plants and animals than there are in the rest of Canada combined.

The west coast province is 952,263 square kilometers (367,669 square miles) of mountains, lakes, rivers, ocean inlets, and even prairie. British Columbia, Canada's third largest province, is bigger than any United States state except Alaska and could encompass Washington, Oregon, and California combined. Its boundaries are the Pacific Ocean to the east, the Rockies and the province of Alberta to the west, the Yukon and Alaska to the north, and the American states of Washington, Idaho, and Montana to the south.

In British Columbia, as in most of English Canada, the first European settlers came from the British Isles, and to a lesser degree, the United States. Later arrivals, Chinese railway workers who stayed on, Japanese who came to farm and fish, and the great influxes from all over Europe at the turn of the century and after World War II, added the spice of variety to the racial makeup. Large-scale immigration from Asia in the past two decades has made British Columbia a cosmopolitan, multicultural province, especially in its cities.

The average British Columbian turns his wealth of nature into a playground. The province is the most outdoor-minded in Canada. Skiing, boating, hiking, jogging, and swimming are popular, as well as year-round tennis, and other games. And, while Canada has no single cultural center, British Columbia has more than its share of artists, musicians, and writers in residence, seduced by the mild climate as well as the intellectual stimulation. This is truly Canada's playground.

In the Beginning

Canada's Pacific Southwest Indians, the Haida, Kwakiutl, Cowichan, Sooke, and others, inhabited this land for at least 12,000 years and developed a highly advanced culture long before the arrival of the European. Evidence of their artwork can be seen in museums in Vancouver, Victoria, and northern Vancouver Island and in the totem poles all along the coast.

Much of British Columbian history—until quite recent times—is the story of competing fur traders and gold prospectors and, later, farmers, lumbermen, and fishermen. The pioneer feeling pervades the province, and even the larger cities seem only steps away from the wilderness.

Sir Francis Drake, in search of the Northwest Passage, may have sighted Vancouver Island in 1579. However, the next European, Juan Perez, a Spaniard from Mexico, sailed north as far as the Queen Charlotte Islands in 1774. The next year, Bodega y Quadra traveled north as far as Sitka, Alaska. Neither Spaniard landed in what is now British Columbia.

The real exploration of this coast began with the British Captain James Cook, who discovered Nootka Sound, Vancouver Island, in 1778. Cook, seeking the Northwest Passage, paused to refit his ships here. He was probably the first white man to land on this coast. Cook continued north to the Bering Sea and China, where the furs that his men bartered from the Indians were highly valued. Cook's account of his voyage and the fur trade, published in 1884, attracted widespread attention. In 1785 the first trading ships from England and the United States appeared on the coast and commerce began in British Columbia.

Ownership of these rich lands was disputed, however. Spain claimed the whole coast, and in 1789 the Spanish commander Martinez seized a number of British trading vessels in Nootka Sound. The dispute nearly broke out into war between Britain and Spain, until Spain reluctantly acknowledged that the area was open to all traders.

British Columbia Becomes British

In the 1790 Nootka Convention, Spain granted the northern Pacific Coast up to Russian Alaska to Britain. From 1792 to 1794, Captain George Vancouver explored and surveyed the coast for the British Admiralty. His charts were the first detailed representation of the wild, rugged coast. In 1795 the Spanish abandoned their last settlement in the area.

This was also the era of the great overland explorations. Long before the white man arrived, the Rocky mountains were a barrier between prairie buffalo and British Columbia's Kootenay Indians living west of the mountains. This seemingly impassable wall of rock confronted eastern Canadian fur traders who pushed west in the late eighteenth century. Tempted by the wealth of furs and access to sea routes, they probed for an opening through the barrier.

Montreal's North West Company (NWC) sent three young Scottish explorers to break this barrier and find a fur route through to the coast. In 1793 Alexander Mackenzie reached the Pacific Ocean near Bella Coola in the first overland crossing of the continent north of Mexico (and many years before Lewis and Clark). All three explorers reached the coast. Only David Thompson found a route the fur brigade could follow.

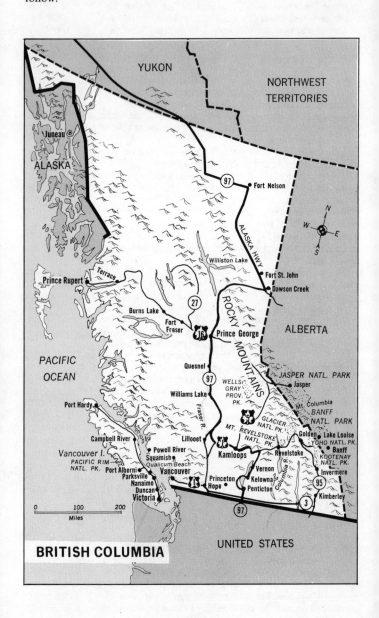

The Fur Trade

In 1805, the North West Company, the Hudson's Bay Company's (HBC) great fur trade rival, established trading posts west of the Rockies. Rival fur companies, staunch and long-time enemies, established forts and trading posts at strategic points along trading routes in a kind of continental chess game. Simon Fraser built a number of forts, including Fort Mcleod, the oldest continuously inhabited white settlement in British Columbia. These were years of tremendous energy and expansion, all fueled by the fur trade.

Despite all of the explorers, fur traders, adventurers, priests, and gold seekers crossing the massive barrier, their numbers were so few they still barely affected the vast wilderness.

In 1821 the giant Hudson's Bay Company, which had not been active west of the Rockies, swallowed up the North West Company. It became the only commercial—and political—force in the land for many decades. Their vast territory covered all of the land area from Spain's possessions in California up to Russian Alaska.

Hudson's Bay Company Governor George Simpson visited the Pacific coast in 1824–25, founding a new headquarters at Fort Vancouver on the Columbia River. The company added new posts in the coastal region, serviced by trading ships such as the famous *S.S. Beaver*. For a time, the company was all powerful in the whole British Columbia area.

Storm Clouds from the South

The private company could not hold on to such a vast, rich territory forever. A constant challenge came from the south, from Americans who resented the iron grip the company had on trade. The hold was gradually loosened by the waves of infiltration of American settlers. Following diplomatic wrangling between London and Washington, the 49th parallel was set as the border between British and American territories from the Rockies to the Pacific. The Hudson's Bay Company moved its headquarters to Victoria, as all of Vancouver Island remained British.

The British Parliament established the island as a crown colony in 1849 and appointed Richard Blanshard first governor. However, the company, solely interested in the fur trade, did nothing to encourage colonization of the island. The next governor, James Douglas, was also head of the Hudson's Bay Company's coast operation. Thus, the company had absolute control over the crown colony. In 1856 a seven-member Legislative Assembly was the first representative government in Western Canada.

Still, the colony grew slowly. In 1855 the total white population of Vancouver Island was only 774. The only white people on the mainland were attached to the company's fur-trading posts.

Gold!

As so often happens in history, the lure of gold dramatically altered events. When gold was discovered in the Fraser River in 1858, more than 25,000 men, mostly from the played-out claims of California, poured into the once-empty territory in a few months. Small fur-trading posts in the interior whose only visitors had been twice-yearly fur brigades now saw a daily stream of miners pass.

Most stayed only the summer, but later discoveries brought more men looking for their fortunes. In 1860–61, the great Cariboo riches were discovered, attracting even more gold seekers. The fur trader was no longer paramount in British Columbia.

The vast influx of unruly fortune seekers was a major headache for Governor Douglas. He controlled traffic up the Fraser, maintained law and order, and with a force of Royal Engineers built roads into the interior. Suddenly, the colony was growing.

A Province Is Born

The governor originally had no authority over the mainland. However, in 1858 the British Parliament created the colony of British Columbia on the mainland. Douglas became governor, provided he sever his connections with the Hudson's Bay Company. He was sworn in at Fort Langley, on the Fraser River, on November 19, 1858, the birth date of the Province of British Columbia.

Although the constitution provided for an optional legislative council, Douglas ruled the mainland by proclamations almost until his retirement in 1864.

New Westminster, a city on the Fraser, and a string of communities along travel routes to the interior, thrived along with the gold fields. Small-scale farming, lumbering, and fishing developed, but when the gold fields faltered, so did the communities. In 1866, the older Vancouver Island colony was annexed to British Columbia, with New Westminster as the capital. In 1869 Victoria became the capital, a position it still holds.

Union with Canada

At about this time, in 1867, the eastern colonies joined together to form a Confederation, the Dominion of Canada. The westcoast colony was still suffering from economic depression, and it appeared that only a union with the new country could save it. The new country wanted access to the Pacific, so negotiations for a union began.

British Columbia would only consent to union if a railway was built linking the country. Canada offered to begin work on the transcontinental railway within two years, and complete it within ten. On June 20, 1871, British Columbia became part of the Dominion of Canada. For the first time, the people had full, responsible government.

The railway across some of the world's most difficult terrain proved more difficult to build than to promise. A depression in the 1870s delayed construction, and in 1878 a secession resolution passed the British Columbia provincial assembly. However, after the first failure, the Canadian Pacific Railway (CPR), a private company, was founded in 1881 to attempt the task. Under the inspired leadership of American engineer William Van Horne, the line of steel was completed to the Pacific in five short years. It was one of the great engineering feats of the century, and assured Canada's existence coast to coast.

Into the Future

The combination of railway construction and major mineral discoveries brought money—and immigrants—to the province. For more than twenty years, Kootenay mines produced considerable wealth. Immigrants poured into the western province, in a period of rapid industrial development. Two new transcontinental railways—now part of the CNR—were built, and Vancouver became a major seaport. The completion of the Panama Canal in 1915, offering cheap water transportation to Europe, opened markets to British Columbia.

The development of the export trade through Vancouver and New Westminster was accompanied by development of forest industries, hydroelectric plants, and manufacturing. Forestry, mining, fishing, manufacturing—and tourism—all play an important part in British Columbia's economy today. In the twentieth century, with some setbacks and failures, British Columbia has developed steadily. In a short historical period, it has grown from a mere string of lonely fur trading posts to a dynamic, exciting, prosperous, and diverse province. British Columbia has always had the stunning mountains, lakes, and oceans; now it has sophisticated, ethnically-diverse, and culturally active cities to add to its appeal.

VANCOUVER

The rest of Canada looks with slight scorn—and a great deal of envy—at Vancouver, its third largest city. With an idyllic setting of forested mountains, rivers, and oceanfront, this city is a perfect outdoor playground—and its residents take full advantage of it. Only Hong Kong and Rio de Janeiro match Vancouver in natural beauty.

It is part of Canadian mythology that easterners are hardworking, serious people, but Vancouverites know how to enjoy life. Easterners call the coast city "Lotus Land." And while they are considered a bit hedonistic by other Canadians, Vancouver residents are comfortably secure in the knowledge that industrious Toronto, Montreal, and Ottawa career builders are only aspiring to be able one day to retire in British Columbia.

At about 1.3 million people, Vancouver, a small city by world standards, is remarkably cosmopolitan and sophisticated. Cultural events, international sports, fine restaurants, and elegant hotels are all here, if somewhat overshadowed by the awe-inspiring setting.

The city spreads out between Fraser River and the mountains to the north. Just a three-hour drive from Seattle, Washington, and 40 kilometers (25 miles) from the United States border, Metropolitan Vancouver covers 2,067 square kilometers (798 square miles), although Vancouver City comprises only 114 square kilometers (44 square miles).

Locals boast that they can ski and swim on the same day here, though no one knows why they would want to. Within the city limits, you can swim (nine miles of public beach); boat; waterski; golf (eighteen public, seven private courses); play tennis (152 courts), squash, or racketball; canoe; kayak (ocean or whitewater); or play baseball, football, or soccer at 344 playing fields. Hanggliding and alpine and cross-country ski slopes are twenty minutes from city center.

Even with all these natural blessings, Vancouver does not ignore culture. The city provides the highest per capita support for artists of any major Canadian city. It nurtures a dozen professional theater companies, two major universities, and the Vancouver Symphony Orchestra.

Although a tour bus or car is needed to reach some attractions, you can see many of the city's most interesting sights by public bus and on foot, armed only with maps and guides, provided free from the Vancouver Travel Infocenter.

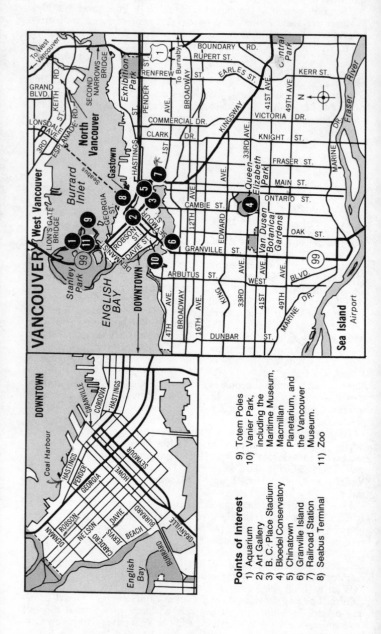

Points of Interest

1) Aquarium
2) Art Gallery
3) B. C. Place Stadium
4) Bloedel Conservatory
5) Chinatown
6) Granville Island
7) Railroad Station
8) Seabus Terminal
9) Totem Poles
10) Vanier Park, including the Maritime Museum, Macmillan Planetarium, and the Vancouver Museum.
11) Zoo

Harbor Center

To get your bearings—historical and geographical—take the glass-encased elevator forty floors up the side of the Harbor Center office block at 555 West Hastings St. On top, the enclosed Observation Deck gives a 360-degree, bird's-eye view of the city and surroundings. Plaques identify city landmarks, and through long-range telescopes you can, on a clear day, spot Mt. Baker in Washington State, British Columbia's capital, Victoria, and the Gulf Islands.

The award-winning Vancouver Discovery show, a 25-minute presentation of twenty-seven computer-linked projectors on a 37-foot screen, portrays Indian legends, the great Gastown fire, the dramatic growth of the city, and Vancouver today. Shows are on the hour.

The Ports of View restaurant on the Observation Deck provides light meals. The Harbor House restaurant, one floor above, offers more elegant fare, while revolving 360 degrees every sixty minutes. The restaurant refunds skylift admission.

Gastown Historical Area

From the Observation Deck, look east to the slash of red brick running along the harbor. This is Gastown, Vancouver's birthplace. In 1867, riverboat captain John "Gassy Jack" Deighton paddled a canoe around what is now Stanley Park with his wife, a dog, two chickens, six dollars, and a keg of whiskey. He landed near a lumber mill, and, within 24 hours, was serving drinks from a bar consisting of a plank across two barrels—and Vancouver was born.

The initial shantytown burned down in 1886, sparking a massive building boom—this time in concrete and brick. Eventually, the city shifted west, and old Gastown, then a slum, was almost demolished. But in the 1960s, a few square blocks of the old city were saved. The city laid brick sidewalks and cobbled streets to encourage pedestrian traffic, planted trees, and installed street furniture and fancy street lights patterned on the nineteenth-century originals. Thus was born one of Vancouver's favorite tourist spots (too touristy for some natives).

Gastown, mainly Water Street from Richards to Carrall, is a popular strolling area with expensive boutiques and cheap souvenir shops selling Canadian memorabilia like Hong Kong-made maple leaf tee-shirts, plastic totem poles, and moosehead ash trays. Huge import shops dispense geegaws and gimcrackery of the East, from smiling Buddha incense holders to rattan pistachio dispensers; urban cowboy stores sell stetsons and belt buckles; and antique stores sell—real antiques. Warm summer afternoons bring on an active street life from hot dog and crafts vendors to jugglers and would-be Willy Nelson drugstore cowboys.

Gastown's always-lively restaurant scene includes ethnic options from French to Indian, sidewalk cafes, seafood, and a railway diner still operating on a siding, Le Railcar.

Gastown's biggest draw for photographers is billed as the world's first steam-powered clock, a Rube Goldberg affair operated by chains, steel weights, and a one-cylinder steam engine, that plays the Westminster chimes from a steam whistle rescued from an old paddle-wheeler. At the other end of Gastown, a statue of Gassy Jack himself stands atop a whiskey barrel like a Hyde Park orator.

Chinatown

A few blocks southwest of Gastown, you can find Chinatown, on Pender Street from Shanghai Alley to Gore Street and especially the two blocks of Pender west of Main. This is a living, active community that is just incidentally fascinating for tourists. Vancouver's Chinese restaurants serve up some of the best Chinese food this side of the Pacific. Gaudy curio shops proffer inexpensive decorations, gifts, plastic temples and pagodas, household goods, and cheap clothes at bargain prices. Traditional merchants sell exotic potions of the East such as deer antlers, an aphrodisiac, ginseng, and dehydrated sea horses, while Oriental pop tunes blare out from electronics stores.

A curiosity is the building from 2 to 14 West Pender which, according to *Ripley's Believe It or Not,* is the narrowest building in the world; 96 feet long but only six feet wide. On the northwest corner of the intersection stands the building once inhabited by Dr. Sun Yat Sen while he plotted to overthrow the Manchu regime, and at Number 1 East Pender, *The Chinese Times,* Chinatown's oldest newspaper, is North America's largest Chinese-language periodical. Chinese craftsmen from Suchou have just completed North America's only authentic classical Chinese garden at Pender and Carrall Streets.

Granville Island

Granville Island, like Gastown, was salvaged from a previously desolated area, an industrial strip of factories with belching smokestacks, warehouses, and railway sidings. The reclaimed island under Granville Street Bridge now shelters a houseboat community, theaters, art galleries, the Emily Carr School of Art, crafts, shops, a book store, and boat supply stores for yuppie yachters.

The real action is in the public market, housed in a massive converted warehouse complete with skylights, exposed pipes, and tin sheeting. Nothing plastic here. No bargains either, but with-it "North Van" matrons and earnest earth people like to shop here for the ambience and variety. Under one large roof you will find fresh local produce stalls; cheese merchants; butcher shops; fishmongers selling fresh seafood such as pink salmon, oyster, and octopus; organic produce salesmen; bakeries; pasta producers; a French butcher specializing in pates; and the inevitable crafts. An amusing and talented one-man band often comes here to play requests on his ornate instrument of bells, whistles, and drums.

On a sunny day, the island is a pleasant retreat for lunch. Stands sell salads or muffins, pasta and pizzas, submarines, sausages, fish and chips, Greek specialties, or Italian food (but no alcohol). Tables and chairs are provided inside. Better yet, sit on the outdoor benches to watch yachts and tugs pass a few feet away and take in the majestic Coast Mountains that tower over the city across False Creek.

For more substantial food and drink, head for Mulvaney's, the Keg, or the popular Bridges, a collection of pubs and restaurants in a giant, canary-yellow warehouse with vast windows overlooking the city. The market is open from 9 A.M. to 6 P.M. every day except Monday. Public buses stop right outside the entrance and small motorboat ferries operate frequently from across False Creek. About the only time you can find a parking space is on Mondays, when the market is closed.

Robsonstrasse

Downtown Robson Street, especially between Burrard and Denman, has long been nicknamed Robsonstrasse for its high ethnic German content. There is not so much strasse left on Robson any longer. The egg man (who sold nothing but eggs) has gone, as well as some of the Schnitzel restaurants, both forced out by high rents. They have all been replaced by glittery, slick, and expensive bakeries, coffee shops, and boutiques.

Still, Robson is the most interesting street in the downtown area, with its delicatessens; cheese merchants; German, Lebanese, and Japanese restaurants; and fast-food shops.

A positive newcomer to the street is the new, spacious, two-story Public Market. Although too new to have the ambience, or the aromas, of the old European-run places, the market does have vegetable stalls and pasta makers, curry shops, bakers, butchers, and fishmongers. It is a perfect spot for an inexpensive, mix-and-match lunch from the second floor food stalls if you are in the neighborhood.

East of Burrard, near the Queen Elizabeth Theatre, the Robson Square complex is a lunchtime gathering place with a food fair and steps to sit on.

Trains and Totem Poles

For a break from the city, Stanley Park is 1,000 acres of natural rain forest and the largest urban park in the world. It is within walking distance of downtown, and free. Taking in the whole western tip of the downtown peninsula, the park has miles of hiking trails and recreational facilities, such as sandy bathing beaches, tennis courts, cricket pitches (an anachronism in North America), a giant checkerboard, pitch and putt courses, lawns for picnicking, a children's train, and summer theater under the stars. The Stanley Park Zoo started modestly in the 1870s with a black bear tied to a tree stump. Today, its menagerie includes monkeys, otters, Humboldt Penguins, and many more.

Lost Lagoon, at the entrance to the park, with its rushes and small islands is a nesting place for birds and marine life including Canada Geese and the rare Trumpeter Swan. Joggers head for Brockton Oval with its regulation-size cinder track, hot showers, and changing rooms.

The 10-kilometer (6 mile) Sea Wall path is popular with cyclists, earphoned roller skaters, wheezing joggers, and casual strollers. Bicycles, mopeds, and roller skates are available for rent outside the park, and cycling trail maps are available. The Sea Wall path is divided so vehicular traffic does not collide with strollers and bench-warmers.

Park sights include towering totem poles, the Japanese Monument, Lumberman's Arch, the statue of the Girl in a Wet Suit, Brockton Point Light House, the Nine O'Clock Gun that really fires at 9 P.M., Siwash Rock (a small, craggy island), and the Empress of Japan figurehead.

Dining facilities range from fish-and-chips and hotdog snack bars to the pleasant Teahouse Restaurant overlooking English Bay. For information, telephone Vancouver Parks & Recreation information (681–1141).

Fishy Fun

Near the Georgia Street entrance to the park is the largest aquarium in Canada with 6,000 species of aquatic creatures. Some 100 spectators can watch dolphins and killer whales perform at the Mammal complex. Visitors can touch sea stars and crabs hiding under rocks at the touch pools. World-famous sport fish such as Pacific salmon, Arctic grayling, and trout are exhibited in the Rufe Gallery in their natural habitats.

The new Tropical River Gallery displays animal life from the Amazon jungle, and the British Columbia Hall of Fishes exhibits local marine life from starfish to the world's largest octopus, the Giant Pacific. Native and exotic species displayed include wolf eels, sharks, piranha, poisonous stone-fish, lion fish, sea turtles, beluga whales, and thousands more.

They feed the sharks, sawfish, and giant sea bass on Wednesdays and Saturdays at 12 P.M.; turtles, sea otters, and harbor seals are fed daily. The Clamshell Gift Shop sells handicrafted gifts, books on the sea, and native art. The aquarium is open daily. Telephone (682–1118) for show times and rates.

Back to School

Across English Bay from Stanley Park, the University of British Columbia covers almost 1,000 acres on the tip of Point Grey, much of it still natural, rugged forest. Visitors are welcome and information booths at all entrances provide maps and literature. The campus is ideal for a quiet stroll. Attractions include the Nitobe Memorial Gardens, a traditional Japanese garden with a teahouse for ceremonial occasions; a rose garden with a collection of more than 1,500 rose bushes, including 168 varieties of all-America winners and miniatures; a fine arts gallery; botanical garden; and a geology museum.

On the cliffs of Point Grey on the University of British Columbia campus is the huge concrete and glass structure of the Museum of Anthropology, a stylized, twentieth-century version of an Indian post-and-beam longhouse.

The museum stores and displays more than 20,000 artifacts, more than half from the British Columbia West Coast, making it one of the most comprehensive collections of native West Coast art in the world. The Great Hall, with its 14-meter (45-foot) windows, displays some of the largest native pieces ever found; 12 to 14-meter-high (38 to 45-foot-high) totem poles recovered from Tsimshian and Kwakiutl villages, giant carved Kwakiutl housefront figures, and giant feast dishes—tub-sized bowls on wheels.

The towering windows, skylights, open spaces, and natural tones of the building protect the delicate wooden artifacts from the wet coastal climate while conveying the impression of the outdoors. "Visible storage" allows viewing of every artifact not on display. Visitors can participate in salmon barbecues, pole-raising ceremonies, and dancing and carving demonstrations, which often commemorate important museum events. From June to August, the museum is open Wednesdays to Sundays from 11 A.M. to 5 P.M. and on Tuesdays from 11 A.M. to 9 P.M. Admission is free on Tuesdays. Other days, adults, $2.50, children, students, and seniors, $1.00. Telephone (228–3825).

Wreck Beach below the University is Canada's most famous nude beach, crowded each summer with thousands of unclothed swimmers, sunners in search of the seamless tans, and nude hawkers selling everything from piña coladas to tanning lotion.

Seaview

Cities always look good from the water, and the easiest—and cheapest—way of getting a vantage point for Vancouver is on the blue-and-white, catamaran-hulled, 400-passenger ferries. The enclosed Seabus provides cheap transport between the North Shore and downtown. Seabuses for the 12-minute ride across Burrard Inlet leave every 15 minutes from the old C.P.R. station and the foot of Lonsdale Avenue in North Vancouver. Transfers are valid on all city buses (including Sea Bus and Skytrain) for 90 minutes from the issue time printed on the ticket; they are not valid for round-trip travel.

Skyview

In North Vancouver, just 20 minutes from downtown Vancouver, Canada's largest, most modern aerial tramway takes up to 100 passengers 3,700 feet up Grouse Mountain for a panoramic view of the city below. A popular ski resort in winter, Grouse has hiking trails, a lounge, cafeteria, restaurant (reservations requested for dinner), gift shops, Bavarian gardens, outdoor barbecues, hang-gliding demonstrations, chair lifts even higher up the mountain, helicopter tours, and an adventure playground. For most, getting up the skyride is adventure enough. Telephone (984–0661) for information.

A Swinging Time

The 137-meter (450-foot) suspension bridge, opened in 1899, swaying 230 feet over the Capilano River is an unnerving experience for the vertigo prone. But the view from the swinging footbridge (narrow enough to hang onto the railing on both sides) is a just reward for the moments of terror: the rushing river below, sometimes with canoes, kayaks, or even rafts braving the rapids; the narrow canyon; and the dense forest.

A 15-acre park of tall firs and cedars, complete with 200-foot waterfall and salmon and trout ponds, surrounds the swaying bridge. The Capilano Trading Post with its statues of Indians and totem poles; wishing well; and gift shops selling jade jewelry; peace pipes; tomahawks, and carvings, is a small Disneyland-like theme park. Open every day Sept.–June, 8 A.M. to 5 P.M., July & August, 8 A.M. to 10:30 P.M. Telephone (985–7474) for information.

The Skytrain

Vancouver's newest attraction is its Skytrain, a mass-transit system that is above ground most of the 22 kilometers (14 miles) between the central Waterfront station and New Westminster, the former provincial capital. The 27-minute run has been called the most scenic "subway" ride in the world. Your ticket is valid on the Seabus and local buses.

The "Royal City" (because its name was chosen by Queen Victoria) has a number of attractions including: the coach built for Lord and Lady Dufferin in 1876 in the museum; a vintage bicycle museum, including a bicycle-built-for-six; children's zoo; and Japanese Friendship Garden. Walking tours of historical sites and Victorian architecture can be arranged through Irving House Historic Avenue, 302 Royal Avenue.

More Scenic Spots

A little farther afield, but well worth the effort, is a jaunt out to Horseshoe Bay, ferry terminal for Nanaimo on Vancouver Island, the Sunshine Coast, and Bowen Island. If you have a car, you can do this in a circle tour, but it can be made inexpensively, if a little slowly, by public transit.

The blue West Vancouver–Horseshoe Bay bus follows the coast along Marine Drive through pleasant, wooded suburbs, offering magnificent vistas. Cedar-covered rock cliffs fall sharply to the sea; small, rocky islands rise from the sea; and a number of marinas house expensive yachts and small fishing boats. Horseshoe Bay is a pleasant seaside community some 14 kilometers (9 miles) from downtown.

The Troller neighbourhood pub brews its own beer, which it serves in a nautical setting. Local take-out fish-and-chips shops are popular with visitors and aggressive, noisy seagulls. From Horseshoe Bay, you can continue up the highway to Whistler or take the ferry to Vancouver Island, Bowen Island, or the Sunshine Coast. Coast Highway 101 leads to the Earls Cove-Saltery Bay ferry, ending in Lund (northern terminus of highway 101).

PRACTICAL INFORMATION FOR VANCOUVER

WHEN TO GO. Vancouver has a pleasant, though unpredictable, climate year round. Winters are mild, with at most a few weeks of snow, although some nearby peaks are snow-topped year-round. Despite its reputation for rain, Vancouver has more sunny days than most Canadian cities in June, July, and Aug. Still, it is wise to bring an umbrella or raincoat.

HOW TO GET THERE. By Plane. *Air Canada, Air New Zealand, British Airlines, Canadian Pacific Air Lines, Cathay Pacific, Continental, Japan Air Lines, KLM, Lufthansa, Pacific Western Air Lines, United, Western,* and *Qantas* fly into Vancouver International airport from Asia, Europe, and the United States. A number of commuter carriers connect Vancouver with the interior, with wheel, float, and ski-equipped aircraft. Private pilots should notify Canada Customs of date and estimated time of arrival in Canada.

By Car. From Seattle, take Interstate 5 north which becomes Hwy. 99 at the border. It is about a three-hour drive from Seattle to Vancouver, depending on border lineups. Trans-Canada Hwy. (Highway 1) approaches Vancouver from the east.

By Train. *VIA Rail* services on both *Canadian National* and *Canadian Pacific Railroad* lines terminate in Vancouver. For the adventurous, *British Columbia Rail* operates a service north to Prince George.

By Bus. *Greyhound* operates to eastern Canada and through Seattle directly on to San Francisco and Los Angeles. *Pacific Coachlines* serves Victoria from Vancouver. *Island Coach Lines* operates on Vancouver Island, and *Cascade* serves the Fraser Valley. *Maverick* services Nanaimo from Vancouver. Greyhound and a number of smaller lines operate throughout the province.

By Ferry. The *British Columbia Ferry* system, with the largest fleet in the world, operates services to Victoria and Nanaimo on Vancouver Island and to a number of Gulf Islands. In summer, the *Princess Marguerite* & the *Vancouver Island Princess* operate between Seattle and Victoria. Numerous cruise ships sail out of Vancouver for Alaska in the short summer season.

ACCOMMODATIONS. After a lull of many years, Vancouver has seen a boom in new hotel construction lately, particularly in the deluxe category. Accommodation should be no problem in the next few years. Rates for double occupancy are: *Deluxe,* more than $140; *Expensive,* $90–$140; *Moderate,* $70–$90; *Inexpensive,* less than $70. Most hotels accept American Express (AE), MasterCard (MC), and Visa (V) credit cards.

Deluxe

Coast Georgian Court. 773 Beatty St. (604–682–5555). An elegant European-flavored hotel near the stadium and the Queen Elizabeth theater.

Four Seasons. 791 W. Georgia St. (604–689–9333). A part of the Four Season's group, it manages to be quite large and refined at the same time. Fine cuisine, and views from higher rooms. One of the best in town.

Granville Island Hotel. 1235 Johnston St., Granville Island (604–683–7373). A small, unusual hotel romantically situated, with an excellent view. Rooms in this former warehouse are tastefully decorated in west coast cedar and original works by local artists.

Hotel Meridien. 845 Burrard St. (604–682–5511). Just opened in January, 1986, and despite the misplaced architecture, already considered one of the city's finest.

Hotel Vancouver. 900 W. Georgia St. (604–684–3131). One of Canada's great railway hotels in the traditional Chateaux-style architecture. This older hotel is a city landmark.

Hyatt Regency. 655 Burrard St. (604–687–6543). Excellent city-center location. 34 floors. Good bars and restaurants, popular for meetings and conventions.

Pagebrook Hotel. 1234 Hornby St. (604–688–1234). Centrally located full-service hotel with fitness center.

Pan Pacific. 300–999 Canada Place. (604–662–8111). New and flashy, its unexcelled waterfront location on top of the convention center and the cruise ship terminal give this large hotel a distinct advantage.

Vancouver Mandarin. 645 Howe St. (604–687–1122). The super-deluxe Mandarin group's first North American venture is considered the best hotel in Canada by some.

Wedgewood. 845 Hornby St. (604–689–7777). An older hotel remodelled, and renamed, by a local businesswoman. This has been a great success from its opening a few years ago.

Westin Bayshore. 1601 W. Georgia St. (604–682–3377). Grand location, slightly out from city center but next to Stanley Park and a yacht harbor. Overdressed doormen and a Trader Vic's are excusable lapses in taste.

Expensive

Century Plaza Travelodge. 1015 Burrard St. (604–687–0575). Next to St. Paul's Hospital. 30 stories. Has one of the fickle city's most popular night spots.

Delta Airport Inn. (604–278–9611). Close to the airport.

Delta River Inn. 3500 Cessna Dr. (604–278–1241). Close to the airport, on 10 acres of parkland overlooking the Fraser River.

Georgia Hotel. 801 W. Georgia St. (604–682–5566). One of the city's oldest, but recently renovated. Pleasant, central location and a good, lively pub in the basement.

Holiday Inn-Harborside. 1133 W. Hastings St. (604–689–9211). Good views, a 21st floor revolving restaurant and just slightly off city center.

International Plaza Hotel. 1999 Marine Dr. (604–984–0611). Across Lion's Gate Bridge, but the best on the North Shore.

Ming Court. 1160 Davie St. (604–685–1311). A major, and tasteful, refurbishing has turned this once very ordinary place into an attractive, first-class hotel, with bright lobby in marble and upgraded rooms and dining facilities. Back rooms overlook English Bay.

Pacific Palisades Hotel. 1277 Robson St. (604–688–0461). The suites in this hotel make it popular with the "Hollywood North" set taking up long-time residence.

Ramada Renaissance. 1733 Comox St. (604–688–7711). Grand views over English Bay and Stanley Park from this 36-story hotel just off busy Denman Street. The former apartment block has balconies and some rooms with kitchen facilities. Membership priveleges in the Denman Place Racquets Club, scenic rooftop bar, inefficient bellhop service. Former Denman Hotel.

Sheraton-Landmark Hotel. 1400 Robson St. (604–687–0511). At 42 stories, the tallest in town. A rooftop revolving restaurant and popular first floor club.

Moderate

Bosman's Motor Hotel. 1060 Howe St. (604–682–3171). Quiet, central. Heated outdoor pool.

Coast Vancouver Airport Hotel. 1041 SW Marine Dr. (604–263–1555). 15 minutes from city center. Fitness club.

Inn at False Creek. 1335 Howe St. (604–682–0229). Central hotel near English Bay.

Park Royal Hotel. 400 Clyde Ave. on the north shore (604–926–5511). Charming, secluded Tudor-style brick building with rooms and restaurant overlooking the Capilano River.

Sheraton Villa Inn. 4331 Dominion St. Burnaby (604–430–2828).

Inexpensive

Blue Boy Motor Hotel. 725 S.E. Marine (604–321–6611). A few miles south of city, close to the airport.

Nelson Place Hotel. 1006 Granville St. (604–681–6341). Near cinemas and shopping.

Relax Plaza Hotel. 3071 St. Edwards Dr. Richmond (604–278–5155). Near airport. Indoor pool and conference center.

Sunset Inn Apartment Hotel. 1111 Burnaby St. (604–684–8763). Walking distance to Stanley Park and downtown.

Sylvia. 1154 Gifford St. (604–681–9321). An ivy-covered, red-brick gem. Older, pleasant, place with an addition just tacked on. Drinks in the bar as the sun sets over the bay is one of Vancouver's great pleasures.

U.B.C. Conference Center. 5959 Student Union Mall (604–228–5441). Hotel with single units and suites. Fitness equipment.

TOURIST INFORMATION. The new *Vancouver Travel Infocenter*—which provides tourist information, reservations, and currency exchange—on 562 Burrard St., Vancouver, B.C. V6C 2J6, has information for the whole province. Telephone 683–2000; for reservations, 683–2772. For B.C. travel information, write or phone: Tourism British Columbia, Parliament Buildings, Victoria, B.C. V8V 1X4 (604–387–1642).

TELEPHONES. The area code for all of British Columbia is 604. Pay telephones are 25 cents for local calls. For local directory assistance, dial 411. For long distance, dial 1 before the area code and number. Dial 0 before the area code for operator assistance, collect calls, and third-party billing.

EMERGENCY TELEPHONE NUMBERS. In Vancouver, dial 911 for police, ambulance, and emergency inhalator.

HOW TO GET AROUND. From the airport. The *Hustle Bus* operates every 20 minutes from 6:20 A.M. to 12:20 A.M., stopping at major hotels and the bus depot. Adult fares, $10 round-trip, $6.00 one-way; children 4–12, $4.50. City buses also run regularly from airport level three.

By Public Transport. Fares range from $1.15 to $2.20. Tickets good for buses, the *Sea Bus* to North Vancouver, and the *Sky Train* to New Westminster (possibly the most scenic rapid transit ride in the world). Pay exact change to the driver, or buy a ticket from machines at the entrance to the Sea Bus or Sky Train stations.

By Car. It is easy to drive around Vancouver, although rush-hour traffic can be frustrating. Many of the city's attractions are a short drive from the city center.

By Taxi. Flag fall is $1.40, increasing by $2 a kilometer in small increments. Main companies are *Black Top, Yellow,* and *MacLures. Vancouver Taxi Ltd.* vehicles are designed to take wheelchairs.

HINTS TO MOTORISTS. Gas, sold by the liter, is more expensive here. Fill up before crossing the border into Canada. Road signs give metric distances. Seat belts are mandatory; helmets are currently not required for motorcyclists, but check for latest status on this. Drinking and driving is highly illegal, and no exceptions are made for tourists. Roadblocks appear during holiday season.

HINTS TO HANDICAPPED TRAVELERS. Listings in the official accommodations guide marked with a "W" indicate that the establishment is able to accommodate those confined to a wheelchair. More information is available from the *Canadian Parapalegic Association,* 780 S.W. Marine Drive, Vancouver, BC V6P 5Y7 (324–3611).

SEASONAL EVENTS. *Polar Bear Swim.* Every New Year's Day, whatever the weather, thousands of Vancouverites take part in the official, televised swim while the rest of Canada watches in wonder, from the comfort of their living rooms. *Chinese New Year.* The festival, in February or March, is celebrated with great noise and color by the Chinese community. *The Vancouver Sea Festival,* including the world championship bathtub races, is held in early July. *Pacific National Exhibition,* in late August, is a kind of county fair for city folk.

TOURS. *The Gray Line* offers a selection of city tours including a British double-decker bus excursion. *Town Tours* offers personalized tours by mini-bus. *City and Nature Tours* escorts quality tours with special attention to Vancouver's natural surroundings.

CITY PARKS AND GARDENS. Vancouver is a city of more than 157 parks. Five of the largest include *Stanley Park, Queen Elizabeth Park,* the *University of B.C. Endowment Lands, Van Dusen Botanical Gardens,* and *Jericho Park.*

CHILDREN'S ACTIVITIES. *Stanley Park* has an aquarium, an aquatic-life exhibit, whale shows, miniature train, and the children's zoo. Aquarium admission, adults, $5.00; children 5–12, $2.50; youths 13–18, $3.75; seniors, $2.50. Miniature train admission: $1.40, adults; $.75, children and seniors. Children's zoo same price as miniature train. Family zoo free. The *Arts, Science and Technology Centre* features hands-on exhibits and live science shows. Adults, $3.00; seniors and children, $1.50. *Granville Island* has a store exclusively for children and an innovative playground.

SPECTATOR SPORTS. All popular Canadian spectator sports are here. Canada's largest domed stadium, B.C. Place, is home of the British Columbia Lions professional **football** team. The Vancouver Canucks play **hockey** at the Pacific Coliseum, and the Vancouver Canadians play **baseball** at Nat Bailey Stadium. Exhibition Park features **thoroughbred** horse racing Apr.–Oct. Within a half-hour from downtown, Grouse, Seymour and Cypress Mountains offer day and night **skiing.** Year-round recreational alpine resort Whistler/Blackcomb is about two hours north of Vancouver. In the city, **golfers** enjoy some 20 public and private courses. **Boaters** can moor or rent at numerous marinas. City parks have many tennis courts, as do finer hotels.

HISTORIC SITES. *Old Hastings Mill Store Museum,* 1575 Alma St. (228–1213). The 1865 museum was Vancouver's first store and post office, surviving the great fire in 1886. Open 10 A.M.–4 P.M. daily June–Sept.; and 1 to 4 P.M. Sat. and Sun. in winter. Admission by donation. *Burnaby Village Museum,* Century Park, is a re-created, turn-of-the-century settlement. Adults, $3.00; children and seniors, $2.00. *Fort Langley National Historic Park,* is a restored Hudson's Bay Company Depot. The restored fort features demonstrations of early inhabitant activities from the 1850s period. Adults, $2.00, children 5–16, $1.00. seniors free.

MUSEUMS AND GALLERIES. *Vancouver Museum,* 1100 Chestnut St., Vanier Park, exhibits historic provincial artifacts. Adults, $2.50; children, students, seniors, $1.00. *The Maritime Museum,* 1905 Ogden St., Vanier Park, houses a fine collection of ship models, artifacts, and photographs. Next door the restored Royal Canadian Mounted Police vessel, the historic *St. Roch,* was the first to navigate the Northwest Passage both ways. Adults, $1.75; children and seniors, 75 cents. *Museum of Anthropology,* University of British Columbia, is an architectural masterpiece. The Great Hall houses exquisite Northwest Coast Indian totem poles and artwork. Adults, $2.50; students and seniors, $1.00; children, 6–12, $1.00.

Galleries. *Vancouver Art Gallery,* Robson at Hornby St., in the splendid old courthouse. Features works by Emily Carr. Adults, $2.50; students and seniors, $1.00; children under 12, free. Free admission Tues. *Burnaby Art Gallery,* 6344 Gilpin St. presents numerous shows and a Sun. tour at 2 P.M. Free.

 STAGE AND REVUES. Vancouver has some excellent theater, including the *Arts Club,* three locations; two are at Granville Island; the other is at 1181 Seymour St. *Firehall* and *Waterfront theaters* at Granville Island; and the *Queen Elizabeth Theatre,* Hamilton at Georgia. *City Stage,* 751 Thurlow St., features theatresports and the *Vancouver East Cultural Centre,* 1895 Venables, frequently presents experimental works. The gracious, restored *Orpheum Theatre,* Seymour at Smithe, hosts visiting artists as does the Queen Elizabeth Theatre, Check Vancouver newspapers or *Vancouver* magazine for current events.

 SHOPPING. Underground malls, Pacific Center and Royal Center, house department stores, shops, and restaurants. Robsonstrasse, Granville Island, and Gastown feature specialty shops and boutiques. Prices are somewhat higher than in other major Canadian cities. Good antique stores are found throughout Vancouver particularly on Main St. Fine European and English bone china is sold at Miller and Coe, 419 West Hastings and at the Canyon House at 3590 Capilano Rd. in North Vancouver. Gastown boutiques sell Indian and Inuit art.

 RESTAURANTS. Local food lovers say that, not too long ago, dining out in Vancouver was limited to steak and potatoes in a hotel restaurant, with wine brought in in a brown paper bag. While this is certainly an exaggeration, the city has come a long way in recent years, and some food critics hail Vancouver as Canada's best restaurant city.

Large scale immigration from Europe at the turn of the century, and especially after W W II, meant the introduction of German delicatessans, Italian trattorias, and Greek seafood places. Events in Asia, and Canada's lenient immigration policies, saw a further influx of immigrants in the 1970s. Already North America's most Asian city, Vancouver welcomed thousands more Vietnamese, Chinese, Malays, Filipinos, and Pakistanis. Again, the restaurant situation was enhanced. Today, there are few exotic cuisines not available here. A trend in recent years has been for good restaurants to locate away from city center. Some of the places listed below require a drive or a taxi ride to get to, but they are well worth the trip.

Restaurants are categorized according to the price of a three-course meal for one, not including beverages, tax, or tip. The categories are: *Deluxe,* more than $30 a person; *Expensive,* $20–$30; *Moderate,* $10–$20; and *Inexpensive,* less than $10. Most places accept major credit cards such as Visa (V), MasterCard (MC), American Express (AE), and Diners (D), but it pays to inquire.

CANADIAN

Moderate

La Quebecoise. 2537 Granville St. (733–5522). From La Belle Province comes Quebec specialties such as tourtiere, onion soup, and maple sugar pie.

Inexpensive

Fogg n' Suds on the Bay. 1215 Bidwell (669–9297). A former bordello, now offering Canada's largest selection of imported beers, more than 200.

Roosters's Quarters. 836 Denman (689–8023). Crispy Montreal-style barbecued chicken is the specialty here. The service is a little slow during busy lunch times, super-fast otherwise. The tasty gravy itself is worth the wait.

Tomahawk Barbecue. 1550 Philips Ave., North Vancouver (988–2612). Large helpings of standard, truck-stop dishes with cornball names (Chief Raven burgers). A good place to bulk up while looking at the Indian memorabilia. Hardy breakfasts.

CHINESE

Expensive

Grandview. 60 West Broadway (879–8885). The sizzly-hot Szechuan style food is much grander than the view here. A wide choice of vegetarian items, soups, and noodles.

The On On Tea Garden. 214 Keefer (685–7513). A former Prime Minister courted a former flower child in this popular Chinese cafe. A wide range of very good Cantonese-style dishes, even though the place has lost something of its earthy atmosphere now that they have a license and you don't have to brownbag the wine.

Tsui Hang Village. 615 Davie St. (683–6868). The best Chinese sea food in this seaside city, served in a restaurant with an aquarium decor. Chili and ginger crabs are especially good.

Inexpensive

The Green Door. In the lane behind 111 East Pender (685–4194). It takes an intrepid soul to walk down the dimly lit alley and into this stark, open restaurant behind a Chinese fishermen's gambling club. The decor is a stark green, but the food, cooked right before you, is cheap, plentiful, and tasty.

CONTINENTAL

Expensive

The Cristal. 645 Howe St. in the Mandarin Hotel (604–687–1122). Very formal (jacket and tie, even at lunch), excellent white-glove service, elegant decor inspired by Monet's works, and an imaginative and wide-ranging menu make this one of the top choices in town. You pay for what you get.

The William Tell. 765 Beatty St. (604–688–3504). One of Vancouver's best-known restaurateurs, Erwin Doebl, moved his establishment, name and all, to the Georgian Court Hotel, with mixed reviews. Fans say it is still the best in town, detractors that it lost something with the move into larger premises.

FRENCH

Expensive

Le Crocodile. 818 Thurlow St. (604–669–4298). Its fans consider this the best French restaurant in town. A simply decorated dining room and an imaginative menu. Reasonable fixed-price meals offered.

Moderate

La Brasserie de L'Horloge. 300 Water St. (604–685–4835). Across from the Gastown steam clock, as the name implies. The Gallic surliness does not detract from the food. The Devil's Chicken is especially good.

La Cote D'Azur. 1216 Robson St. (604–685–2629). The city's oldest French restaurant, in a pleasant old house, complete with fireplace, overlooking busy Robsonstrasse. Its reliable menu, with interesting specials, keeps the regulars coming back.

GREEK

Moderate

Orestes. 3116 West Broadway (604–732–1461). A lively college-aged atmosphere, and setting, and all those good Greek specialties.

Pasparos Taverna. 132 West 3rd St., North Vancouver (604–980–0331). Close to the other end of the Seabus run, its open verandah on a sunny day makes an ideal setting. Good for late evening wine, fish, and lamb.

Simpaticos. 2222 West Fourth Ave. (604–733–6824). Its whole-wheat pizza was voted the best in Canada by a national magazine several years ago. Also, standard Greek fare.

INDIAN

Moderate

India Gate. 616 Robson St. (684–4617). Reasonably priced, basic Punjabi Northern food.

Kilimanjaro Restaurant. 308 Water St. (604–681–9913). Authentic East African with Indian influence. Prawns Piri-Piri specialty consists of jumbo prawns marinated in garlic butter, paprika and congo peppers, basted with lime juice.

The Nirvana. 2313 Main St. (604–876–2911). You can't get it much more authentic, in food or atmosphere. A good, basic curry house.

ITALIAN

Expensive

Umberto's, La Cantina, and Il Giardino. 1376-82 Hornby St. (604–687–6316). Three side-by-side restaurants, each with its own specialty, are products of Italian whiz kid Umberto Menghi. He has expanded out to the Whistler ski resort, to San Francisco, and to Seattle, all on the strength of his consistently fine offerings. The restaurateur's latest venture is a string of small, inexpensive pasta places under the name Umbertinos.

Moderate

Francesco Alongi. 862 Richards St. (604–689–7018). An overwhelming decor and a would-be opera-star owner who bursts into song frequently make this a good bet for a lively evening.

Il Corsario Ristorante. 920 Commercial Dr. (604–255–1422). It is well worth the short drive or $5 taxi ride to Little Italy for this spacious restaurant. Friendly, lively, with loads of Latin charm (all ladies get a rose) and excellent Italian food. They make their own pasta, of course, an excellent linguine al pesto and a dynamite seafood platter.

JAPANESE

Moderate

Kamei Sushi. 811 Thurlow St. (604–684–4823). Ample servings, a sushi bar, and tatami rooms make this one of the most popular Japanese restaurants in town. Good lunch specials.

Koji. 347 E. Hastings St. (604–689–7351). One of the city's first Japanese restaurants remains one of its best.

Inexpensive

Shogun Sapporo Ramen House. 518 Hornby St. (604–689–2922). Big bowls of tasty noodles, rice dishes, or dumplings at bargain prices in an authentically Japanese cafe setting make this one of the best bets in the city center for lunch. Worth the inevitable line-ups.

NATIVE INDIAN

Expensive

Quilicum. 1724 Davie St. (604–681–7044). A rarity, a native Indian restaurant in a "longhouse" complete with totem poles, carved masks, drawings, and sculptures. The artwork is for sale. So is authentic Canadian Southwest Indian food—barbecued salmon, duck and rabbit, caribou stew, fiddleheads (a vegetable), and bannock bread. A unique experience along with a good meal.

SCANDINAVIAN

Moderate

Scanwich. 551 Howe St. (604–687–2415). Open-face sandwiches, roast beef, smoked salmon, etc. Famous for its coffees and excellent Danish pastry.

SEAFOOD

Moderate

A Kettle of Fish. 900 Pacific St. (604–682–6661). An almost overwhelming jungle of plants and vast skylights. Good choice of soups and chowders, fish, lobster, oysters, and clams barbecued or pan-fried.

Mulvaney's. #9 Greenhouse, Granville Island (604–685–6571). Borrowed New Orleans, with French-Quarter design, Louisiana jambalaya, and creole-style gumbo and seafood.

Inexpensive

The Only. 20 East Hastings (604–681–6546). Because they *only* have fish. No liquor license, no toilets, hardly any tables even. But only thick chowders cooked in cauldrons like Douglas fir trunks and fresh fish and seafood, steamed, broiled, or fried in butter.

SPANISH

Moderate

Las Tapas. 760 Cambie St. (604–669–1624). A big, open place with little corners, a bar, and a small outside verandah for those sunny days. A wide choice of "tapas" snacks, chicken and calamares, prawns, lamb, paella.

Inexpensive

The Bodega. 1277 Howe St. (604–684–8814). Punk rockers and stockbrokers, media types, and homesick Spaniards flock to this popular little bar for the atmosphere, reasonable drinks, and food, such as sizzling prawns in garlic oil, sausage, and grilled pork loin. **El Patio.** 891 Cambie St. With basically the same menu, and the same owner, should be almost as good with age.

STEAK

Expensive

Hy's Mansion. 1523 Davie St. (604–689–1111) and **Hy's Encore** 637 Hornby St. (604–683–7671). For meat lovers only, perhaps the best steak in town.

Moderate

Kegs. More than a dozen locations throughout Vancouver. If you can take the over-friendly, "Hi, my name is Randy and I'll be your server tonight" approach, a good deal for steaks, ribs, and drinks.

DINING WITH A VIEW

Moderate

Salmon House on the Hill. 2229 Folkstone Way, West Vancouver (604–926–3212). Fresh salmon barbecued over an open alder pit fire and a vista of the sea and city make this mountainside restaurant popular with out-of-town visitors. A short distance from downtown.

The Cannery. 2205 Commissioner St. (604–254–9606). An East End restaurant with a vista of the North Shore mountains, a genuine marine ambience, and good barbecued and poached fish.

The Teahouse. Ferguson Point, between Second and Third Beaches in Stanley Park (604–669–3281). Open, airy, set in Vancouver's favorite park. Views of English Bay, and a menu ranging from Crepes Florentine to grilled New York Steak.

 LIQUOR LAWS. Legal drinking age is 19. Liquor, wine, and beer are sold in provincial government liquor stores from Mon. to Sat. Beer to go is sold in hotel beer parlors. Sun., the small Granville Island brewery sells its own products, and a small selection of wine. Alcohol is served any 14 hours between 9 A.M. and 2 A.M., cabarets, 7 P.M. to 2 A.M. Since Expo 86, drinking establishments are open on Sundays. Also, a few stores selling only wine have recently opened.

 NIGHTLIFE. This port city has had a lively and varied nightlife since its founder first arrived, whiskey keg in tow. It is all here, the high life and the low, elegant, firelit diners and noisy, raunchy clubs. Local bars such as the Cecil, Flash One, The Drake, and Number Five Orange Street feature top-quality ecdysiasts (strippers)—one of whom won the grand prize in the first International Golden G-String Competition in Las Vegas recently. You will find live music, from punk to jazz, rock to country and canned disco all within easy reach.

Richards on Richards. Still the hottest club in town. Valet service, so it's important to have the right car.

Mardis Gras. Century Plaza Hotel, Burrard. Competing with Dick's on Dick's, very popular. Strict dress code, long lineups in the evening.

Club Soda. 1055 Homer St. The showcase club for rock acts, heading toward New Wave, so if you are old enough to drink legally, you probably won't like it.

The Railway Club. Technically a private club, but a small cover gets you in, and it is the best club in town for music lovers, from rock to jazz to pop. This is where most of them get their start.

Blarney Stone. 215 Carrall St. (687–4322). Lively Irish entertainment, good place to listen, sing, and drink, not to talk.

VICTORIA AND VANCOUVER ISLAND

Stretching 450 kilometers (280 miles) along the rugged coastline, Vancouver Island is North America's largest Pacific Island. Where Victoria has a tea-cosy-and-crumpets veneer, Vancouver Island is a rugged combination of snowy mountains, trout-filled lakes, fir and cedar forests, rich farmlands, and clean sandy beaches. The major industries are logging, fishing, mining and, increasingly, tourism.

The island, about 152 miles across at its widest point, juts below the 49th parallel. Most attractions (the tourist sights, beaches, restaurants, and resorts), follow the east coast Island Highway. Resorts, hotels, motels, and campgrounds offer overnight adequate accommodation. The wooded interior and the west coast are real wilderness, ideal for the experienced outdoorsman. Fishing, hunting, hiking, and camping on this lightly-populated island are all first rate.

Government ferries take about an hour and forty minutes to cover the 24 miles between the mainland and Vancouver Island, either at Nanaimo or Swartz Bay, near Victoria. Harbor-to-harbor float planes fly between Vancouver and Victoria in about twenty-five minutes. Most romantic is the four-hour trip from Seattle to downtown Victoria aboard the restored steamship *Princess Marguerite* (summer only).

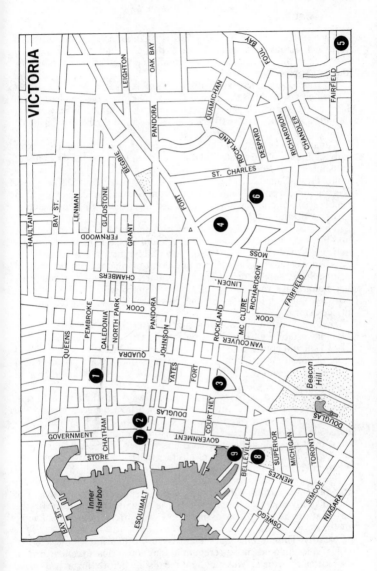

Victoria—Points of Interest

1) Arena
2) City Hall
3) Court House
4) Craigdarroch Castle
5) Gonzales Observatory
6) Government House
7) McPherson Playhouse (Centennial Square)
8) Parliament Buildings
9) Port Angeles Ferry

The Capital

Turn-of-the century Victoria, British Columbia's capital, inspired Rudyard Kipling to exclaim that the city had all the best of Bournemouth (the British seaside holiday spot) arranged "around the Bay of Naples."

To Canadians, Victoria, British Columbia, North America's most British city is "Behind the Tweed Curtain." Flower baskets hang from lamp posts, shops sell Harris tweed and Irish linen, locals play cricket and croquet, and visitors sightsee in red London double-decker buses or horsedrawn Tally-Ho carriages.

Canada's most westerly city has the country's gentlest climate, with only 27 inches of rain a year and a year-round average of six hours of sunshine a day. Mile "0"—the terminus of the 7,820-kilometer (4,860-mile) Trans-Canada Highway—is at Douglas Street and Dallas Road. Yet Victoria is on an island set apart from the mainland. The isolation sets it apart in character from bustling, aggressive, Vancouver across Georgia Strait.

This small city is easily seen on foot. Among the cobblestone streets and brick sidewalks, arcades, squares, and alleys, quaint shops sell furs and fine Royal Doulton or Wedgewood china; native art; English and Scottish woolens; and Hudson's Bay Point blankets, antiques, and old prints. Street names such as Bastion Square, Trounce Alley, and Market Square are reminiscent of a Victorian colony. In these hidden corners, you will find The English Sweet shop as well as the Gallery of the Arctic.

Historic Bastion Square, in the city center, is the site where James Douglas established Fort Victoria for the Hudson's Bay Company in 1843. The old courthouse is now the Maritime Museum with a collection of maritime artifacts including the *Tilikum* ,a 38-foot Indian dugout canoe and the 20-foot ketch *Trekka* which has sailed around the world.

Victoria's heart is the inner harbor, always bustling with ferries, seaplanes, and yachts from all over the world. Clustered around the harbor are the ivy-covered Empress Hotel, with its well-groomed gardens, and the stately, neo-Gothic British Columbia Parliament Buildings, built of local stone and wood and opened in 1898. At night it is brilliantly lit with thousands of electric lights, like a fairy-tale castle. Visitors can take guided tours of the building or stroll the grounds.

The Pacific Underseas Gardens, beside the Blackball Ferry terminal, is a natural aquarium with more than 5,000 species from the area. The world's only undersea theater where you actually descend beneath the sea features a live scuba diving show with Armstrong, the Pacific Octopus.

Nearby Thunderbird Park claims the world's finest collection of colorful totem poles and a ceremonial longhouse. The excellent British Columbia Provincial Museum here recalls life before the arrival of the white man.

For a somewhat contrived taste of Britain, the Royal London Wax Museum, on the inner harbor, offers a collection of 180 life-sized figures, including, of course, Queen Victoria herself. In the suburb of Esquimalt, a recreated Shakespearean-era English village includes Anne Hathaway's Cottage. The thatched cottage is authentically furnished with sixteenth-century antiques. On the same grounds, the Olde Englande Inn, almost completely furnished with antiques, offers afternoon teas daily.

Some fifteen establishments serving afternoon teas in Victoria, include: the Princess Mary, once a ship plying between Victoria and

Alaska, now a first-class seafood restaurant; the Old Country Gazebo Teahouse and Garden, with its circular white summer house on the outskirts of town; and the Crystal Gardens across from the Empress Hotel.

The Crystal Gardens were built in 1925 as a public salt-water swimming pool under a glass roof. They have been renovated into a tropical conservatory and aviary, an indoor garden with flamingos, parrots, fountains, and waterfalls. You can take tea from 2 until 5 P.M. under garden umbrellas on the Upper Terrace overlooking the lush, green, indoor jungle. Recitals and tea dances from an earlier era are held here on summer evenings.

High tea at the Empress Hotel, dowager of Victoria, is a local, albeit somewhat touristy, ritual. In this bit of genteel England preserved, recline in deep armchairs; nibble on scones or crumpets with honey butter, jam, and clotted cream or thin sandwiches; and sip blended tea, all from the finest china and silverware. The Empress's impressive guest list has included Winston Churchill, Bob Hope, and John Wayne. Richard Nixon honeymooned in this castle of pinnacles and turrets, verdigrised roofs, rich wood panels and beams, and intricate plaster decoration enriching lofty ceilings.

For more "British" Victoria, try the Oak Bay Beach Hotel's Snug, complete with fireplace and overlooking the Straits of Georgia. The dining room of this elegant, Tudor-style inn tastefully furnished with antiques serves good old English-style roast beef and Yorkshire pudding—and Canadian salmon.

Stately Victoria has a number of old residences worth exploring. Helmcken House, next to the museum, is British Columbia's oldest residence. Point Ellice House, another heritage building, is a treasure trove of Victoriana. Farther from the center of town, Craigdarroch Castle, a stone mansion worthy of the British Home Counties, was constructed in the 1880s by a coal millionaire for his wife. Craigflower Manor on Admiral's Road dates back to 1856.

To appreciate Victoria's wonderful natural setting, walk through centrally located 140-acre Beacon Hill Park overlooking the Pacific, and take the scenic Marine Drive. Along the way, stop at Oak Bay Marina, home of Canada's largest oceanarium, Sealand of the Pacific, where you can descend beneath the sea to look through windows at the marine life.

The drive takes you to Butchart Gardens 21 kilometers (13 miles) north of the city. These 35-acre gardens are the most popular and famous in this city of gardens, attracting half a million visitors a year. Proud locals claim these are among the most beautiful gardens in the world. On summer evenings the gardens, in a former quarry, are a colorful display of lights and fireworks. Live theater is performed on the grounds.

Riding the Rails

The Esquimalt & Nanaimo rail liner provides a scenic, relaxing day excursion into Canada's rugged, mountainous Pacific Southwest island. Known locally as the E & N, the dayliner is now operated by VIA Rail. You can ride the shiny coach to Courtenay and back, returning to Victoria in plenty of time for dinner, or stop at Duncan on the way to visit the forest museum.

VIA operates two 89-seat dayliners in the summer when traffic warrants it, one in the winter. The air-conditioned, self-contained, diesel-operated cars are capable of 90 miles per hour, but in this terrain, 45 miles per hour is more usual.

The dayliner leaves Victoria's Russell station every morning at 8:15 A.M. Pack a lunch—there is nothing to buy on the train, not even coffee. The fare from Victoria to Courtenay, the end of the line, is $20 one way; return fare varies depending on how long you spend in Courtenay.

Riding the dayliner past the Island's forests and lakes is the perfect way to relax; you simply enjoy the passing show, or at most, take photographs. The train passes the outskirts of old Victoria, an Indian reservation containing a longhouse painted with Indian symbols, mountains, lakes, canyons, and fjords. After passing the railway's only tunnel, it climbs to the Malahat Summit, at 1,000 feet, the highest point on the line.

From here, it passes stations and places with distinct Indian names—Cowichan, Shawnigan Lake, Koksilah River, Chemainus, Saanich, Qualicum Beach, and Nanaimo. And everywhere there is the West Coast forest, and signs of wildlife and birdlife—ducks, Canada geese, swans, eagles, and, of course, deer.

The train arrives in Nanaimo, the Island's Hub City, at 10:35 A.M. for a 25-minute stop. A coin machine dispenses food and beverages at the station, and a catering truck meets the train.

The E & N dayliner reaches Courtenay, the end of the line in the scenic Comox Valley, at 12:45 P.M. It departs again for the south half an hour later, arriving back in Victoria at 5:40 P.M. Passengers have a number of options: return directly by train; stay in the scenic Courtenay–Comox area for a few days and return by train; return by bus to Victoria ($19.60 one way); rent a car and explore farther along the Island to Campbell River, famous for its fishing, or even beyond; or return by ferry and bus or car to Powell River on the mainland and back to Vancouver.

The Island Highway

While Victoria may be British-tweedy, the rest of Vancouver Island is homespun plaid, logging boots, and jeans. Those with the time, and a car, should explore the island north of Victoria at a leisurely pace along the Island Highway or the uncrowded back roads.

On the outskirts of the city, you pass Goldstream Provincial park with a picnic spot under huge 600-year-old Douglas Fir. Beyond that, the road climbs to the Malahat Mountain Summit, high point on the highway, with scenic views of Saanich Inlet, the Gulf Island, the Lower Mainland, and Washington State.

Three miles south of the town of Duncan stands the Glass Castle, made from more than 180,000 bottles. Duncan itself is in the Cowichan Valley, home of the province's largest Indian band. The valley is known for the sweaters, hand-knit by local Cowichan Indians. In the British Columbia Forest Museum Park, 300-year-old Douglas Fir trees grow 56 meters (61 feet) tall and two meters across. The museum displays old and new logging machinery, and a steam locomotive takes visitors for rides around the park. The satellite earth station in Lake Cowichan runs 45-minute tours of facilities followed by a video presentation on satellite communications.

In Chemainus, larger than life-size murals on downtown buildings tell the Chemainus Valley history. Much older are the figures cut into a broad sandstone outcrop up to 10,000 years ago at Petroglyph Park just south of Nanaimo.

The symbol of Nanaimo, Vancouver Island's second largest city, is the Bastion, built as a Hudson's Bay Company fort in 1853 for protection from Indians. The builders boasted that a naked body could be drawn over the peeled logs without getting a splinter, though there is no evidence that it was ever tried. The Bastion now serves as a local museum.

Nanaimo founded the Bathtub Races, now an international sport practiced on several continents. Each July, as a highlight of Vancouver's Sea Festival, hundreds of outboard-motor-powered bathtubs race across Georgia Straight to Vancouver in a zany competition that is broadcast around the world.

North of Nanaimo, Highway 1 becomes Highway 19. You can leave the Island Highway at the Parksville turnoff to cross the island to the wild and rugged West Coast. Highway 4 passes through Cathedral Grove in Macmillan Provincial Park, with its towering, 800-year-old Douglas Fir trees before reaching Port Alberni.

Port Alberni's Sproat Lake is home base for the antique Martin Mars water bombers, the world's largest, with tail fins five stories high. The Forest Industries Flying Tankers still fight fires with these World War II veterans. Tours available on request outside of firefighting season.

From Port Alberni, gateway to the Pacific Rim National Park, the *MV Lady Rose,* built in Scotland in 1937, takes day-excursions along the narrow, fjord-like canal to the west coast of the island, visiting Bamfield and Ucluelet on alternate days.

Ucluelet is the start of Long Beach, an 11-kilometer (7-mile) stretch of fine, flat beach and rocky outcrops pounded by the Pacific. Bamfield, on the other side of the inlet, is the north end of the West Coast Trail, a former life-saving trail for ship-wrecked sailors. The 72-kilometer (45-mile) trail alongside the "Graveyard of the Pacific" takes five to eight days. For ambitious, experienced hikers only.

This is ideal whale-watching area. Some forty to fifty gray whales, weighing up to 30 tons, feed year-round off this coast, sea lions bask on offshore rocks, and harbor seals live among the sheltered coves. Thousands of migrating whales also pass on to California breeding grounds in the spring and back in the fall.

Back on the main Island Highway, the stretch between Parksville and Qualicum Beach, is a popular seaside recreation area of long beaches and warm tidal waters, perfect for beachcombing, fishing, swimming, and hiking. Nearby provincial parks, Englishman River Falls and Little Qualicum Falls, are convenient resting and picnicing spots. North of Qualicum Beach, the Comox Valley has two of the island's best ski areas: Forbidden Plateau, named for an eerie Indian legend, and Mt. Washington.

Just west of the highway, 500,000-acre Strathcona Provincial Park is the largest park on the island. From Great Central Lake Head, experienced hikers can reach Della Falls, at 1,443 feet North America's highest year-round falls. Camping is available in the park.

Campbell River, where the Campbell River pours into Discovery Passage, is a world-renowned fishing haven. Hollywood personalities and ordinary fishermen from as far away as Europe and Japan flock here to try their luck on the Tyee salmon, some weighing up to sixty pounds.

The museum in the Cape Mudge Indian Village on Quadra Island, near Campbell River, contains masks, carvings, and ceremonial objects confiscated by the Canadian government fifty years ago when potlatch dances and feasts were outlawed.

North of Campbell River, the paved road continues through increasingly wild country beyond normal tourist haunts. Alert Bay, reached by ferry seven times a day from Port McNeill, has the world's tallest totem pole, 54 meters (177 feet) high. Carved figures tell the story of the Kwakiutl Indians.

The paved highway terminates in Port Hardy, at the north end of the island. From here, you must turn back south or take the British

Columbia Ferries to Prince Rupert, Northern British Columbia, and more adventures.

PRACTICAL INFORMATION FOR VICTORIA
AND VANCOUVER ISLAND

WHEN TO GO. Southern Vancouver Island, particularly around Victoria, has the mildest climate in all of Canada, with short, mild winters. Farther north, and in the interior of the island, expect crisp, cold winters with lots of snow—ideal for skiing.

HOW TO GET THERE. By Plane. *Air Canada, Canadian Pacific Air Lines,* and *Pacific Western Air Lines* all connect Victoria with Vancouver and other mainland cities. Commuter airlines such as *Air BC* and *Burrard Air* operate small aircraft services.

By bus. *Pacific Coach Lines* operates services to Victoria. *Island Coach Lines* operates on the island. *Maverick Coach Lines* serves Nanaimo from Vancouver.

By ferry. British Columbia has the world's largest, most modern ferry fleet. *British Columbia Ferries* connect Vancouver Island and the mainland from Swartz Bay (Victoria) and Nanaimo. Smaller ferries connect with the Gulf Islands year round. For recorded schedule information, call (685–1021) in Vancouver, (656–0757) in Victoria or (753–6626) in Nanaimo. *Black Ball Transport* operates between Victoria and Port Angeles, Washington. *Washington State Ferries* operates daily year-round between Sidney, Victoria, and Anacortes, Washington, with San Juan Island ports of call. A refurbished steamship, *Princess Marguerite,* sails between Victoria and Seattle in summer.

ACCOMMODATIONS. Hotels and motels are arranged by price categories under the town or city where they are located. The cities are listed alphabetically. The price categories reflect the following cost for a double room: *Deluxe,* $100–$150; *Expensive,* $50–$80; *Moderate,* $30–$50; *Inexpensive,* under $30.

CAMPBELL RIVER. *Deluxe.* **April Point Lodge.** Box 1, Quathiaski Cove. On Quadra Island (604–285–3329). Seafront guest cottages on this secluded island. Excellent fishing. Charters available.

Expensive. **Coast Discovery Inn.** 975 Tyee Plaza (604–287–7155). Full-service hotel by the marina. Fishing packages available.

Moderate. **Austrian Chalet.** 462 South Island Hwy. (604–923–4231). Hotel with balconies overlooking Discovery Passage. Some with lofts. Indoor pool, whirlpool, sauna.

Vista Del Mar Motel. 920 South Island Hwy. (604–923–4271). A motel overlooking Georgia Straight. Boat launch nearby. Fishing guides arranged.

Inexpensive. **Rod and Reel Resort.** R.R. 2. (604–923–5250). Cottages with seafront view of mountains.

COURTENAY. *Expensive.* **The Westerly.** 1590 Cliffe Ave. (604–338–7741). River view. Indoor pool and racquet sport facilities.

Moderate. **The Kingfisher Inn.** 4330 S. Island Hwy. (604–338–1323). Waterfront hotel with tennis, outdoor heated pool and sauna. Fishing and skiing packages available.

DUNCAN. *Deluxe.* **Fairburn Farm.** 3310 Jackson Rd. (604–746–4637). Historic manor house on sprawling sheep farm. Hearty, home-cooked meals. Families welcome.

Expensive. **Cowichan Valley Inn.** 6457 Norcross Rd. 1 km north of town near B.C. (604–748–2722). Forest Museum. Waterbeds.

NANAIMO. *Deluxe.* **Coast Bastion Inn.** 11 Bastion St. (604–753–6601). All units with ocean view. Sauna, whirlpool, and exercise facilities.

Expensive. **Highlander Motor Inn.** 96 North Terminal Ave., near B.C. (604–754–6355). Ferries. Complimentary continental breakfast. Family rates available.

Tally-Ho Island Inns. 1 Terminal Ave. (604–753–2241). Centrally located with ocean view and heated outdoor pool.

PARKSVILLE. *Expensive.* **Tigh-Na-Mara.** R.R. 1, Site 114. (604–248–2072). Log lodge and cottages. Fireplaces, hot tub. Indoor pool. Fishing charters available.

Tuan Resort. Box 432 (604–248–6615). Oceanview cottages with fireplaces. Fishing. Adult oriented.

Moderate. **Vancouver Island Parksville Motel.** 414 W. Island Hwy. Parksville (604–248–3244). All ground-floor units, some kitchenettes. Complimentary coffee. Near beach.

PORT ALBERNI. *Expensive.* **Hospitality Motor Inn.** 3835 Redford St. (604–723–8111). Some waterbeds. Non-smoking rooms. Fishing charters available.

Timber Lodge Motor Inn. Port Alberni Highway. Near Mt. Arrowsmith (604–723–9415). Indoor pool and sauna. Enjoy free breakfast with room weekends.

Tyee Village Motel. 4151 Redford St. (604–723–8133). Non-smoking rooms available. Heated outdoor pool. Family and group rates.

QUALICUM BEACH. *Expensive.* **Best Western College Inn.** Box 99. (604–752–9262). Set in the former Qualicum Military College, overlooking the ocean. Large grounds. Lots of character.

VICTORIA. *Deluxe.* **Chateau Victoria.** 740 Burdett Ave. (604–382–4221). Downtown. Features roof-top dining. Kitchen units available.

Empress Hotel. 721 Government St. (604–384–8111). A fine, old-English style hotel overlooking the inner harbor. One of Canada's grand hotels. Famous for its afternoon teas.

Executive House Hotel. 777 Douglas St. (604–388–5111). Downtown. Kitchens available. Family rates.

Harbor Towers Hotel. 345 Quebec St. 604–385–2405. Near Parliament Buildings. Indoor pool and therapy pool. Bike rentals.

Laurel Point Inn. 680 Montreal St. (604–386–8721). Rooms have balconies and ocean view. Indoor and outdoor pools, tennis. Family rates.

Oak Bay Beach Hotel. 1175 Beach Dr. (604–598–4556). Traditional Victorian seaside hotel. High tea. Attractive gardens. Golf and marina nearby.

Victoria Regent. 1234 Wharf St. (604–386–2211). Balconies and terrace rooms overlooking the inner harbor. Some units have fireplaces.

Expensive. **Colony Motor Inn.** 2852 Douglas St. (604–385–2441). Indoor pool, sauna, whirlpool. Brass Rail pub can get noisy.

Inn on the Harbor. 427 Belleville St. (604–386–3451). Near ferries to Seattle and Port Angeles.

Captain's Palace. 309 Belleville St. (604–388–9191). Vintage accommodation with antiques and fresco ceilings. Complimentary breakfast with room.

Olde England Inn. (604–388–4353). Tudor Mansion in English Village. 6 km (4 miles) from town.

Moderate. **Craigmyle Guest House.** 1037 Craigdarroch Rd. (604–595–5411). Near Craigdarroch Castle. Share baths.

James Bay Inn. 270 Government St. (604–384–7151). Near lovely Beacon Hill Park and Parliament Buildings.

Inexpensive. **Slumber Lodge.** 3110 Douglas St. (604–388–4345). Indoor pool and sauna.

SALTSPRING ISLAND. *Deluxe.* **Hastings House.** Box 1110, 160 Upper Ganges, Ganges, (604–537–2362). Rated Canada's best resort, a refurbished manor house, barn, farmhouse, and post office. The top floor rooms of the manor house have fireplaces (wood always stacked outside your door), mullioned windows overlooking Ganges Bay, soft beds, and a breakfast hamper set outside the door each morning. Non-guests can stop by for the excellent Sun. brunch, which may include such imaginative dishes as snowcrab, spinach, and brie omelettes.

YELLOWPOINT. Inn of the Sea Resorts. Yellow Point Rd. (604–245–2211). Oceanview rooms with balconies. Heated outdoor pool and whirlpool. Fishing.

TOURIST INFORMATION. *Tourism British Columbia,* Parliament bldgs., Victoria, B.C. V8V 1X4 382–2127 or *Tourism Victoria,* 812 Wharf St., Victoria, BC V8W 1T3 (604–382–2127).

TELEPHONES. The area code for all of BC is 604. Pay telephones are 25 cents for local calls. For local directory assistance, dial 411. For long distance, dial 1 before the area code and number. Dial 0 before the area code for operator assistance, collect calls, and third-party billing.

HOW TO GET AROUND. From the airport to Victoria: There are buses to downtown, costing about $6. Call 388–9916 for information. **By bus:** *Island Coach Lines* makes numerous stops on the island.

TOURS. *Gray Line* offers tours of Victoria, starting with the Grand City Tour; $9, children $4.50. Butchart Gardens and the Saanich Peninsula tour is $17, children $8.50. All tours depart from the Empress Hotel. For more information call 388–5248. *Pacific Coach Lines* runs a number of tours out of Vancouver and Victoria. PCL has day trips out of Victoria to Nanaimo ($7.35 one way), and on to Campbell River and Port Hardy. A two-day Island Discovery trip ($82.50) starts with the ferry from Vancouver to Port Hardy and a bus ride down the east coast of the island, back on a ferry to Vancouver. For information in Vancouver call 872–8311; in Victoria call 388–5248.

SPECIAL INTEREST TOURS. If you're on Vancouver Island, take a trip on the M.V. *Lady Rose,* a mail, passenger, and cargo ship that leaves at 8 A.M. from Port Alberni and sails up the beautiful West Coast. Rugged country, plus you'll see the Pacific Rim Park. The trip takes all day. For information, call (604–723–8313).

Another great West Coast cruise is on the Gold River-based M.V. *Uchuck III,* which makes day trips to the logging communities of Tahsis and Zeballos and historic Nootka Island, where Captain Cook first landed in Canada. For information call (604–723–3132).

MUNICIPAL PARKS. In Victoria: *Beacon Hill Park,* between Douglas and Cook streets. Swans and one of the world's largest totem poles are in this beautiful city park. Free. *Thunderbird Park,* at Belleville and Douglas, has open-air displays of ethnic arts and crafts, totems and carvings.

MARINE LIFE. *Pacific Undersea Gardens,* 490 Belleville St., opposite Parliament Bldgs.; 382–5717. World's only undersea theater features a scuba show complete with octopus. Open May 20–September 15, 9 A.M.–9 P.M. daily; winter, 10 A.M.–5 P.M. Adults $4.50; children $2. *Sealand,* 1327 Beach Dr., has an aquarium and whale show. For more details call 598–3373.

GARDENS. *Butchart Gardens* (Box 4010, Station A, Victoria) is 14 miles north of Victoria on Hwy. 17. It is considered by some to be the floral showplace of North America. Admission $6.50; children, $1; teens, $3.50. Call 652–2066. Reduced winter rates.

PROVINCIAL PARKS. There are 330 provincial parks in British Columbia. Camping is available at 151 of them, including *Englishman River Falls, Little Qualicum Falls,* and *Strathcona,* for a small fee in summer. No reservations. For information you can call in Victoria 382–2127; in Vancouver 683–2000. Parks are open year-round.

NATIONAL PARKS. *Pacific Rim National Park* on Vancouver Island's west coast is a magnificent stretch of land that offers a range of outdoor activities. The 12-mile-long Long Beach attracts swimmers, beachcombers, and even surfers. Hiking trails abound—including the famous West Coast Trail, 45 miles of endurance-testing that once brought shipwreck survivors to safety. Sea lions frolic offshore. Open year-round. For more information write Box 280, Ucluelet, B.C. V0E 2S0; (604) 726–7721 or Parks Canada—Western Region, Box 2989, Station M, Calgary, AB T2P 3H8 (403-292-4440).

CAMPING. Camping in Canada's national and provincial parks is on a first-come, first-serve basis with nominal overnight fees. *Tourism Victoria* (812 Wharf St., 604–382–2127) can provide park information (especially about provincial parks), as can *National and Provincial Parks Association of Canada,* 47 Colborne St., Suite 308, Toronto, Ont. M5E 1E3. See sections on provincial and national parks, above.

SUMMER SPORTS. British Columbia offers every kind of sport. *Tourism Victoria* (See "Tourist Information") offers detailed information about all B.C. sports.
Boating: Sailing off Victoria and around the Gulf Islands is second to none. Charters are available from many companies including *Canoe Cove Charters,* P.O. Box 2099, Sidney V8L 4L4, phone 656–7131; *Sailwest Yacht Charters,* 1678 Cresswell Dr., Sidney V8L 4L4, phone 656–6348; and *Pacific Quest Charters,* Box 15, Schooner Cove Resort, Nanoose Bay V0R 2R0, phone 468–9721. **Canoes** can be rented at many resorts and at some inland hotels.

Fishing licenses can be obtained from sporting goods stores and marinas. See *Fishing,* Page 487, for fees. Separate fishing licenses are required in all national parks. The salmon fishing is great; there are also plentiful char, grayling, whitefish, bass, perch, trout. Port Alberni is a popular fresh- and saltwater fishing spot. Other popular fishing areas are Qualicum Beach, the Campbell River, and Sooke. Contact *Fish and Wildlife Branch,* Rm. 400, 1019 Wharf St., Victoria, B.C. V8W 2Z1; 387–6411 or *Fisheries and Oceans Dept.,* 666–3169, Vancouver.

Hiking is best in provincial and national parks where trails have been marked. The West Coast Trail in *Pacific Rim National Park* is well known as a fine, wild hiking trail—not recommended for beginners.

Hunting licenses cost $43 and up, depending on the game. Non-Canadian residents require a guide. Such licenses can also be obtained at sporting-goods stores.

Check the local telephone directories for **tennis** and **golf** facilities. You'll find over 110 golf courses in B.C. and countless tennis courts.

Mountain climbers will find parks the best place for climbing.

SKIING. It is hard to find better **skiing** elsewhere in North America. In fact, British Columbia has some of the most difficult and enjoyable runs anywhere in the world. Some areas are limited to the experts, but there are resorts that cater to every level of skier.

Forbidden Plateau is near Courtenay. Rentals available. Write 2050 Cliffe Ave., Courtenay, B.C. V9N 2L3; 334–4744. *Mount Washington Ski Resort* is 19 miles west of Courtenay. There's an on-mountain village. Rentals are available. Write 2040 Cliffe Ave., Courtenay, B.C. V9N 2L3; 338–1386.

CHILDREN'S ACTIVITIES. By and large, British Columbia is family territory; often the adults and the children end up enjoying the same things and seeing the same sights. In **Victoria**, at the Empress Hotel, is *Miniature World*, a unique and splendid show of miniature scenes. Near Victoria is *Fable Cottage Estate*, 5187 Cordova Bay Rd., 658–5741, with thatched cottages and animated characters. Open daily from last week of March-third week of October from 9:30 A.M. Admission charge. Farther north on the island is the *Forest Museum* around **Duncan;** for information call 382–2127. See also "Marine Life," above, for sea shows and aquariums, "Historic Sites and Houses," and "Museums," below.

HISTORIC SITES AND HOUSES. *Anne Hathaway's Cottage and Olde Englande Inn,* the world's only replica of the birthplace of Shakespeare's wife, is at 429 Lampson St., Victoria; 388–4353. Open June 1-September 30, 9 A.M.–9 P.M.; winter 10 A.M.–4 P.M. Admission $4, children $2.50. The inn is a historic house converted into a 50-bedroom hotel, some rooms with canopy beds. (See "Hotels and Motels," above.) *Bastion Square,* off Government Street, between Yates and Fort Streets at the foot of View Street. Established in 1843 as the original site of Fort Victoria. Several restored buildings are open for viewing. *Craigdarroch Castle,* an 1888 castle, 1050 Joan Crescent; 592–5323. Admission by donation; open 9 A.M.–9:00 P.M.; winter 10 A.M.–5:00 P.M. *Craigflower Manor,* an authentic 1853 home, 110 Island Hwy.; 387–3067. Admission free; open year-round, Wed.–Sat. 10 A.M.–3:45 P.M. *Helmcken House,* 638 Elliot St., 387–3440. A pioneer house with early medical instruments; admission free. *Parliament Buildings* (387–3046) offer six guided tours Mon.–Fri., 9:00 A.M.–5:00 P.M. during summer; no charge. *Victoria Heritage Village,* one block west of Parliament Bldgs.; 384–3232. Open daily 8:30 A.M.–10 P.M. summer. Check for off-season hours & rates; admission $5, children, $2.50. Attractions include changing of the guard, a haunted house, the "land of the little people," and Munchkin's garden café.

MUSEUMS. Campbell River has an *Indian Museum and Archives,* 287–3103. **Courtenay** has a *historical* museum; 334–3881. **Duncan:** *The B.C. Forest Museum,* 748 –9389, contains logging artifacts.
Victoria: *B.C. Provincial Museum,* 675 Belleville St.; 387–3701 for hours and programs. Superb heritage displays; admission free. *Classic Car Museum,* 813 Douglas St.; 382–7118. Open 9 A.M.–9 P.M.; year-round. Admission $4; children, 6–11 $1, students and seniors, $3. *Maritime Museum of B.C.,* 28 Bastion Sq.; 385–4222 for hours and admission charges. Outstanding exhibits, including a Captain Cook gallery. *Royal London Wax Museum,* 470 Belleville St.; 388–4461. Open May–Oct. 9 A.M.–9 P.M. ; winter 9:30 A.M.–6 P.M. Admission $4.50, children, $2.25, seniors, $3, students, $3.50.

GALLERIES. *Art Gallery of Greater Victoria,* 1040 Moss St.; 384–4101. Has European prints, English decorative art, Canadian historical and contemporary art, as well as a recognized collection of Japanese art. Admission $2; phone for other rates and hours. *Emily Carr Gallery,* 1107 Wharf St.; 387–3080. Rotating exhibits. No charge, phone for hours.

RESTAURANTS. Somewhat touristy Victoria offers first-class dining for a city this size. It can be a problem getting a table at many places during the height of the summer season, but is an especially good dining bet during the off season.
Restaurants are rated *Expensive,* more than $15; *Moderate,* $10–$15; *Inexpensive,* under $10.

Expensive

Bengal Room. Empress Hotel, 721 Government St. (384–8111). A buffet lunch Thurs. and Sun. in the elegant hotel offers curries with extensive condiment trays of coconuts, nuts, cucumbers in yogurt, hot and sweet chutney, all of which are attacked by cabinet ministers and bureaucrats from the nearby provincial legislative buildings.

Captain's Palace. 309 Belleville St. (388–9191). Quaint Victorian mansion facing the harbor, with just a few rooms upstairs and a popular restaurant.

The Chantecler. 4509 West Saanich Rd. (604–727–3344). Elegantly located in a Tudor mansion north of Victoria. Popular with proper locals. Menu may include venison, reindeer, and other game and seafood.

Chauney's. 614 Humboldt St. (604–385–4512). Good wine list, one of the city's best-known restaurants. Seafood.

Chez Daniel. 2522 Estevan St. (604–592–7424). Even though it is set out in Oak Bay, a few miles from downtown, you will likely need a reservation for this popular restaurant.

Chez Pierre. 512 Yates St. (388–7711). Victoria's oldest quality French restaurants, with all of the standard fare.

Deep Cove Chalet. 11190 Chalet Dr., Sidney (656–3541). Picturesque setting on a peninsula near the airport about 15 miles from downtown, windows overlooking the sea. French-style seafood.

Moderate

Periklis. 531 Yates St. (604–386–3313). Central location, bright decor, and the standard run of Greek food. Try the prawns in tomato sauce baked with cheese.

Pagliacci's. 1011 Broad St. (604–386–1662). For liveliness and live entertainment (usually jazz).

Inexpensive

Foo Hong. 564 Fisgard (386–9553). The place for Capital City aficionados of Middle Kingdom cooking. Warning: you might have to share a table with other diners, and it has no liquor license. Discreet brown-bagging overlooked upstairs.

Herald Street Caffe. 546 Herald St. (604–381–1441). Downtown, trendy. Homemade pastas in two sizes, interesting desserts.

R Normans. 1280 Fairfield Rd. (604–383–1615). The menu in this relatively new and very successful restaurant includes appetizers, like a lunchtime Spanish-type tapa bar. An eclectic collection of items.

Spinnakers. 308 Catherine St. (604–384–2112). For lovers of fine beer. They brew their own, and it is worth the slight extra cost.

OTHER RESTAURANTS ON VANCOUVER ISLAND

COURTENAY. The Old House. 100 17th St. (604 338–5406). Set in a restored house. Simple lunches, imaginative dinners.

QUALICUM BEACH. Old Dutch Inn. 110 Island Hwy. (604–752–6914). Another Island ethnic establishment.

SHAWNIGAN LAKE. Das Jager Haus. 2460 Renfrew Rd. (604–743–5322). As the name would imply, the full treatment—German decor and a schnitzel-inclined menu.

SOOKE. Sooke Harbor House. 1548 Whiffen Spit Rd. (604–642–3421). A small white farmhouse restaurant that rates high with gourmets.

EXPLORING INTERIOR BRITISH COLUMBIA

British Columbia is Canada's Cinderella province, the most beautiful and varied, with ten mountain ranges, lush forests, ranches and farmland, orchards, lakes, fast, clean rivers, and 8,948 kilometers (5,560 miles) of rugged coastline. As well, its two major cities, Vancouver and Victoria, have the finest climate in the country.

While the rest of Canada shivers under heavy blankets of snow, people on the coast are out picking the crocuses. And on New Year's Day, Canadians cluster around their TV sets to watch thousands of Vancouverites, many still in formal wear or costumes from the previous evening's celebrations, plunge into the Pacific in the annual Polar Bear Swim—rain or snow.

Sparkling-clear lakes and streams, snow-topped peaks etched against the deep blue sky, dense rain forests, and air scented with fresh-cut cedar so fresh and cool you can almost taste it, clean, safe cities with a hint of the foreign—all this spells British Columbia. Despite its vastness, it is easy to explore—if you take the time—with 12,800 kilometers (8,000 miles) of paved roads reaching from the scenic south right up to Yukon and Alaska.

The average British Columbian turns this wealth of nature into a playground. The province is the most outdoor-minded in Canada. Skiing, boating, hiking, jogging, and swimming are popular, as well as year-round tennis and other games. And, while Canada has no single cultural center, British Columbia has more than its share of artists, musicians, and writers in residence, seduced by the mild climate as well as the intellectual stimulation. This is truly Canada's playground.

The extensive province is divided into a number of distinct tourist regions.

SOUTHWESTERN BRITISH COLUMBIA

Steam Treat

The Royal Hudson 2860, a hissing, puffing anachronism, the largest steam locomotive in regular passenger service in North America, runs five times a week from late May until Labour Day (early September) from the North Vancouver railway station. During a six-hour, eighty-mile round-trip between Vancouver and Squamish, the old train roars past wild and rugged mountains, forests, waterfalls, and coastline. Across Burrard Inlet, it offers a sea-level view of Vancouver's ragged skyline and the sylvan silhouette of Stanley Park.

A two-hour stopover in the small town of Squamish allows time for a trek to Shannon Falls, cascading 213 meters (586 feet) down a cliff, a lunch in one of the small local cafes or fast-food stands, and a walk through town with its antique stores and, yes, souvenir shops. Precisely at 1:30 P.M., the locomotive puffs back into view from a spur line, and it is all aboard again for the ride back to Vancouver. The steam train arrives back in plenty of time for dinner.

Drive to the North Vancouver Station or take special buses marked Train Connection from Vancouver Bus depot. The excursion is popular, so book early through British Columbia Railway, 1311 West First St., North Vancouver, BC V7P 1A7 (604–987–5211) or Harbor Ferries, north foot of Denman St. (687–9558). Take the boat up, train back, or vice versa.

End of the Road

The famed Highway 101, which starts in Mexico City and runs the length of the United States Pacific coast, ends not at Seattle or Vancouver but at the tiny fishing village of Lund, more than 150 kilometers (93 miles) north of British Columbia's largest city.

A trip from Vancouver to the north end of the coastal highway (possible, but not really advisable, in one day) includes two ferry crossings past a beautiful, fjord-like countryside.

From downtown Vancouver, follow Highway 99 through Stanley Park (largest urban park in North America) and cross Lion's Gate Bridge to West Vancouver. Then, either turn right to the Upper Levels Highway (Highway 99–1) or continue along the lower road (the turning is well-marked). The Upper Levels provides a magnificent view of the city across the inlet. The lower road winds along the coast through pleasant forests and past marinas, parks, and fine homes. (Best go one way and return the other.)

The ferry terminal at Horseshoe Bay, 21 kilometers (13 miles) from downtown Vancouver, is well-marked from either road. Ferries leave about six times a day, crossing Howe Sound to Langdale. Contact British Columbia Ferry Corporation, 1045 Howe St., Vancouver, BC, V6Z 2A9 (604–685–1021) for rates and schedule.

The 115-meter (377-foot) ferry makes the 15.6-kilometer (9.7-mile) crossing in about 40 minutes. The ferry has a cafeteria with tolerable food.

From Langdale, Highway 101 continues its winding way northwest to Gibsons, where the popular *Beachcombers* T.V. series is filmed. Fishing is good, and clams and oysters are plentiful along the coast. Activities include swimming, beachcombing, camping, boating, golfing, hiking, and picnicking. This major center provides complete facilities for tourist and boater—motels, marinas, restaurants, and a forty-hectare (100-acre) campsite by the sea.

From Gibsons, the highway twists and turns 84 kilometers (52 miles) past forest and farms on the right and sheltered coves and rocky beaches on the left, to Earl's Cove and the next ferry terminal.

On the way, you pass Roberts Creek Provincial Park, Sechelt (with another Travel Infocenter), Madeira Park, and Pender Harbor. Possible side trips include Gray Creek Falls, Porpoise Bay, the Limestone Caves, Skookumchuk Rapids, and Irvines Landing, first populated by the Portuguese.

From Earl's Cove, the ferry winds through the small islands of Jervis Inlet for 50 minutes to Saltery Bay, the southern end of the final stretch of Highway 101. Saltery Bay is a scenic 35 kilometers (22 miles) from Powell River, the largest town on the Sunshine coast and jumping-off point to Vancouver Island.

There are twenty-four lakes within an hour's drive from the town, making it an ideal center for salt or fresh water fishing. From May to August, visitors can take guided tours of the world's three largest newsprint mills located in Powell River. A local curiosity is the log-pond breakwater made of ten floating concrete-hulled Liberty ships anchored in place and chained together. The ships, built in World War II as freighters or oil and gasoline barges, have provided an effective breakwater since they were installed in 1947.

Twenty-four kilometers (15 miles) north of Powell River, Highway 101 comes to an abrupt end. Lund, a quiet community, has a boat ramp, store, launderette, ice-shop, restaurant, tavern, and post office as well as boat rentals, fuel supplies, trailer parking, and safe anchorage. A quaint hotel, built at the turn of the century, was granted the first saloon license between Vancouver and the Yukon. This is as far as you can go along the North American west coast by road.

To the Rockies

You can fly, drive, or take a train from the Pacific coast to Banff/Lake Louise or Jasper, both in the heart of the Canadian Rockies. VIA rail departs Vancouver late every afternoon (call VIA for the latest schedule). Get a seat in the day coach (or take a sleeper) and meet other travelers in the restaurant, bar car, or dome car as you watch the sights of the city slip by. Get up early for a leisurely breakfast, then spend the day in the dome car watching some of the world's greatest scenery slip by. You might spot elk, bighorn sheep, moose, mountain goat, and both grizzly and black bear.

The Canyon

Highway 1, the world's longest national highway, follows the original transcontinental railway system, which united the country a century ago. During British Columbia's gold rush, prospectors and German hurdy-gurdy girls crossed the hair-raising Fraser Canyon road along the Cariboo Trail. The names of the claims reflect the nationality of most of the miners; Boston Bar, Texas Bar, and Yankee Doodle. Today, Hell's Gate Aerial Tramway crosses the river, offering a spectacular view of the boiling river below.

During the summer months, you may see whitewater rafters running the canyon. British Columbia's rivers rank with Idaho's Snake and Oregon's Rogue for whitewater enthusiasts, and some of the best are just two hours from downtown Vancouver. You can drive to the river put-in point; raft down the Fraser or Columbia, shooting Hell's Gate, Jaws, and Devil's Cauldron; and be back in your hotel in time for pre-dinner drinks. Local outfitters run two- and three-week rafting–camping trips in British Columbia, Yukon, and the Arctic as well.

OKANAGAN–SIMILKAMEEN

Scenic Okanagan Valley, in the middle of the province on the United States border, is a popular resort area for British Columbians on holiday. Local boosters call this "the land of beaches and peaches." Orchards covering low rolling hills, roadside fruit stands, small lakes and riverine beaches are a soft contrast to much of the province's more rugged beauty.

The rich orchards in the hilly country grow apricot, cherry, peaches, pears, plums, apples, and grapes. The Osoyoos Cherry Festival in late June and the Penticton Peach Festival in late July celebrate these industries. Winery tours are particularly popular throughout the region. The Okanagan Wine Festival features many wine-related events of all kinds, not least which is drinking it.

Cacti and unique flora and fauna thrive in Canada's hottest spot and only true desert, located on the east side of Osoyoos Lake. In Vaseaux Lake Provincial Park, you may see horned lizards, burrowing owls, bighorn sheep, and rare trumpeter swans. As a bonus, you can swim in Canada's warmest waters in Skaha Lake.

Lake Okanagan, the largest of many in the area, has room enough for seven provincial beach parks and Canada's longest floating bridge. It also houses a resident monster, the famous Ogopogo. Skeptics think Ogopogo is as mythical as the Loch Ness monster—and no one has collected the $1 million the local tourist board offers for positive proof the friendly monster really exists.

Such a popular holiday spot inevitably has its touristy aspects. Attractions for the youngsters include the Flintstone Bedrock City just out of Kelowna. Even if you don't see the real Ogopogo, and collect the million-dollar reward, there is a statue of what it is supposed to look like next to the *M.V. Fintry Queen*, a paddlewheeler in Kelowna.

The sprawling Okanagan Game Farm has more than 600 animals of 130 species, domestic and imported from far away.

An entire trading post has been assembled in the Kelowna Centennial Museum. McDougal's 1861 Trading Post illustrates the history of the local Indians, fur trading, and early agriculture. The museum includes a Chinese house and store from the long-gone China Town. Princeton's Pioneer Museum preserves the days of Granite Creek, and in Penticton, you can recall the past aboard the *SS Sicamous,* last paddlewheeler to cruise Okanagan Lake.

The area has twenty-two golf courses and the Similkameen Valley alone boasts forty-eight trout-filled lakes. You can cool off from Canada's hottest climate in "wild and wet" water slides along the lake with daredevil names such as Banzai Run and River Riot.

KOOTENAY COUNTRY

Historically, geography has influenced the Kootenays more than the rest of the province. A north–south line of steep-walled valleys provides a channel through which the Columbia and Kootenay Rivers flow to American states, forming natural transportation routes and economic links with the south.

Plants and animals on the Western flank of the interior wet belt are similar to those on the coast. To the east, the rugged landscape ranges from dry forest to alpine tundra. Silver, lead, zinc, and copper mines formed the backbone of the province's early mining industry.

"Silver, lead, and hell are raised in the Slocan, and unless you can take a hand in producing these articles, your services are not required." That was life in the boom towns according to a local newspaper in the 1890s. The town of Sandon, capital of the Silvery Slocan, had twenty-four hotels, twenty-three saloons, and an opera house for a population of about 2,000 residents.

That wild past lives on in a gallery of ghost towns such as Retallack, Sandon, and Zincton. A Heritage Walking Tour in Nelson, exploring some of the more than 350 heritage buildings, 50 of which have been restored to their original splendor, recalls the cities' 1890s bonanza days. In Rossland's Historical Museum, you can peek into the life of a hardrock miner on a tour of the LeRoi gold mine. If history is too much for you, you can windsurf at Lakeside Park, where paddlewheelers once churned upstream.

In Kaslo, the last of the Kootenay paddlewheelers, the *S.S. Moyie,* is now a museum after sixty years of carrying pioneers.

Kootenay Country offers ample natural splendors as well. From Stagleap on the Kootenay skyway, Canada's highest major road, look down on Creston surrounded by a fruitful valley and a wildlife preserve. Swans, geese, and hundreds of other species pass through the Creston Valley Wildlife Center, a 6,500-hectare (16,000-acre) sanctuary in the Kootenay Lake marshes. In the Valhallas, 60,000 hectares (148,000 acres) of pure mountain wilderness, you can hike over glaciers. Alpine lake water in Kokanee Glacier Park is so pure a beer is named after it. You can canoe the lake chain of Champion Lakes park near Trail, and broil yourself in the hot (up to 44°C) Nakusp Hot Springs.

In Boswell, on Kootenay Lake near the Idaho/Montana/Canada border, the town mortician has built his home entirely of embalming fluid bottles.

North on 3A is the world's longest free ferry ride across Kootenay Lake to Balfour. The road leads to Castlegar, then Grand Forks, home of the interesting Doukhobour sect of communal farmers who came to Canada to escape religious persecution in the late nineteenth century. Here you will see the distinctive Doukhobour architecture, and you can buy finely carved wooden soup ladles these Russian pacifist emigres make by hand. Grand Forks' Yale Hotel serves Doukhobour dishes such as *borscht, galooptsi, naleskini,* and *pyrohi.*

THE ROCKIES

Visible for hundreds of miles across the prairies, long before you reach
them, the Rocky Mountains rise abruptly from rolling foothills to form
an awesome rampart of jagged, icy peaks.

The earth's crust, buckling, threw up the Rockies long ago. They
owe their spectacular forms and color to sediments laid down over
millions of years. Yet in geological terms, the Rockies are mere infants,
so nature's forces have not yet eroded away their jagged beauty.

Life in these mountains has had to adapt to harsh, high-altitude
conditions. Trees that would grow tall lower down are stunted and
twisted by icy winds nearer the peaks. Flowers and shrubs, reproducing
quickly during the brief alpine spring, form carpets of brilliant colors
in the high meadows.

Animals summer in the rich alplands but retreat to sheltered lower
areas with the first snows of winter. Visitors, too, appear in the spring,
and, except for skiers, abandon the higher ground with the coming of
winter.

Two major routes cross the province from the Alberta border to
Vancouver, both competing for the title "The most beautiful drive in
North America." They traverse the most varied terrain in this immensely varied country, from ice fields to desert, sagebrush to rain
forest, and crossing ten mountain ranges and numerous large rivers.
Most traffic takes the better-known Trans-Canada Highway, through
Yoho National Park and the Monashee Mountains. This route passes
hot springs, ice fields, and glaciers of the Purcell, Selkirk and Rocky
Mountains. More than a hundred glaciers cover these mountain peaks,
and thirty of the Yoho's dramatic peaks are more than 3,000 meters
(9,800 feet) high.

The southern route follows Highway 93 from Banff, traversing narrow valleys of the Kootenay Mountains. You can stay the night in
Radium Hot Springs, where even grizzlies came to take the waters.
Steamy, odorless mineral water flows from the ground at up to 45°C
(57°F).

Kimberly, Canada's highest city, is ersatz Bavaria, complete with the
world's largest cuckoo clock and the Bavarian City Mining Company.
Fort Steele Provincial Historic Park is a restored "living" North West
Mounted Police fort and village. Visitors can pan for gold, ride a
stagecoach or steam train, and see some forty buildings including the
old police barracks.

High Country

Crossing the mountains from Edmonton or Calgary through tunnels,
switchbacks, and five national parks, brings you to the High Country,
central British Columbia's area of mountain vistas, cedar forests, and
cattle ranches. Highway 16 from Edmonton and Jasper passes through
Mount Robson Provincial Park. Mount Robson's 3,954-meter (12,972-
foot) peak is the highest in Canada.

"A Lake a Day as Long as You Stay" is the local motto—there are
200 to choose from around Kamloops alone. Graceful, old-fashioned
sternwheelers still cruise these waters in the leisurely fashion of a
bygone age. The *M.V. Phoebe Ann* takes day trips from Sicamous to
Seymour Arm; the *Sorrento Queen* takes 45-minute voyages along
Shuswap Lake from Sorrento, and the *Wanda Sue* cruises the Thompson River out of Kamloops. You can also rent your own houseboat on
Shuswap Lake.

The Kamloops Wildlife Park has buffalo, cougar, and other local animal species. South of Kamloops, Douglas Lake and the town of Quilchena is the heart of wild west, cattle country. Douglas Lake Ranch has one of the world's largest herds of Herefords roaming this "empire of grass."

The Quilchena Hotel was built in 1908 to serve cattle ranchers moving between Kamloops and Merritt. The bar sports bullet holes and a piano brought 'round Cape Horn. The new Coquihalla Toll Road, opened May 1985, connects Merritt to Hope.

CARIBOO CHILCOTIN

This expansive land cutting through the center of the province covers open rangelands, steep canyons, grass meadows, all the way to the coast rain forest. The interior plateau, stretching to the Coast Mountains, is one of British Columbia's prime cattle-ranching areas. The Fraser River bisects the central interior into the Cariboo to the east and the Chilcotin to the west. Tens of thousands of beef cattle still roam expanses of unfenced grassland on this 5,000-square mile plateau of rangeland. In Chilcotin, cattle have the right of way.

Some of the world's last real cowboys still ride herd here. You can see them at work in the Williams Lake Stampede on the July 1 weekend. American and Canadian cowboys compete in roping, riding, and steer wrestling. It is the biggest rodeo in Cariboo. During the great Cariboo gold rush, Barkerville boasted it was the largest town west of Chicago, north of San Francisco. The rowdiest and most flamboyant of the boom towns that grew up along the creeks, it had saloons, breweries, churches, and bakeries, a newspaper theater, and a cemetery. Barkerville Provincial Historic Park preserves more than 100 authentic buildings, displays, and businesses. You can pan for gold at the El Dorado or have a drink at the Root Beer Saloon.

A number of first-class resorts and guest ranches operate throughout the south Cariboo. Easiest access to this remote and rugged country is by British Columbia Rail excursion from North Vancouver to Lillooet and on to Quesnel and Prince George.

THE NORTHWEST

BC's vast, empty northwest, once New Caledonia, is ideal for adventurers and outdoorsmen. You don't even have to leave your car for game viewing up in the north. Moose, deer, and perhaps even bear and lynx often wander close to the roads. You can park almost anywhere and launch your boat or canoe; fishing and hunting are excellent. A number of hunting and fishing camps are based near Prince George, the center of the province, where the Yellowhead and Highway 97 meet. In Burns Lake and district, more than 500 lakes offer first-class sports fishing.

West on the Yellowhead, Vanderhoof, named for a Chicago publicity man hired to attract settlers to Western Canada, is the geographic center of the province. The Nechako Valley, with a bird sanctuary, is on a major Canada Goose flyway. Fort St. James was once a trading post and capital of New Caledonia. An old fort warehouse, clerk's house, and other fort buildings from the 1890s have been preserved on the site, now a national historic park.

Settlements grow smaller and distances increase along the lonely highway west. In the Kitwanga Valley, weathered totem poles recall earlier cultures. In the village of Kitwancool, the "Hole through the Ice," the world's oldest standing totem pole, is among more than twenty others more than a century old. A must for anyone interested in native Indian culture is the 'Ksan Village near Hazelton. Its six cedar longhouses decorated with carved poles and painted fronts, totem poles, smokehouses, and dugout canoes make it a showpiece of Gitskan Indian culture. You can watch carvers at work in one longhouse and buy Gitskan crafts in another.

Scenic wonders on these isolated roads include lava beds north of Terrace, and, in Stewart, off the main road, the luminous Bear Glacier. The Stuart–Cassiar highway branches north to the starkly beautiful Mt. Edziza Provincial Park and the Spastizi Plateau Provincial Wilderness Park. Past the Stikine River, you reach Dease Lake, and a special reward. Here in the "jade capital of the world" you may find a green mineral memento.

Back on the Yellowhead, some 800 km (500 miles) from Prince George, you reach Prince Rupert, "Halibut Capital of the World" and British Columbia's second port. Here, where the Skeena, the River of Mist, meets the sea, you can reach the top of Mt. Hays on the second steepest gondola ride in the world.

The Queen Charlottes, a ferry ride away, are lush, evergreen lands of mist and mystery. Ancient Haida totem poles and dugout canoes lie forgotten in silent forests and along the coast are a number of abandoned whaling stations. Naikoon Provincial Park preserves 707 square kilometers (273 square miles) of wilderness, with 97 kilometers of beaches. Bald eagles, peregrine falcons, killer and gray wales, porpoises, seal, and Sitka deer are commonly spotted in these isolated islands.

PEACE RIVER–ALASKA HIGHWAY

The extensive northeast corner of British Columbia includes wheat farms and silent, empty forests, trout lakes, and British Columbia's new coal-mining town, Tumbler Ridge. Settlers call the Peace River Country, a northern prairie of a million grain-growing acres, "the last, best west."

This is the land of the northern lights. Dawson Creek marks Mile 0 of the Alaska Highway. Built in only nine months by Canada and the United States Army, the 2,400-kilometer (1,500-mile) road winds through wild, dramatic country. A drive the length of the Alaskan Highway still rates one of the world's last remaining adventures. From Dawson Creek, the highway passes tranquil Charlie Lake to Summit Pass in Stone Mountain Provincial Park. Here you find pillars of sand, alpine meadow trails, and glacial lakes. In Muncho Lake Provincial Park, sheep and moose come down to the salt licks by the highway.

Liard River Hot Springs, at mile 493, is a tropical oasis that Indians called Paradise Valley. Water in the natural pool, bubbling up to 49°C (59°F), supports a variety of tropical vegetation. Monkey flower, ostrich fern, even orchids grow north of the 59th parallel. Not far from here, the road crosses the British Columbia–Yukon border.

PRACTICAL INFORMATION FOR
INTERIOR BRITISH COLUMBIA

WHEN TO GO. Summers are the most popular months for tourists to British Columbia. Although the coast and Vancouver Island have generally mild winters, the interior can be very cold in the winter months. However, downhill and cross-country skiers, snowshoers, ice skaters, and snowmobilers flock to the resorts for the cool, crisp sunny days that are perfect for winter sports.

HOW TO GET THERE. By Plane. All major Canadian airlines *Air Canada, Canadian Pacific Air Lines, Pacific Western Airlines*—a number of international air lines, and commuter lines such as *Air BC* serve the province. Vancouver is the main international gateway. There is an extensive air network within the province.

By Train. *VIA Rail* serves British Columbia from Eastern Canada. BC Rail operates from Vancouver to Prince George.

By Bus. *Trailways* and *Greyhound* operate throughout the province.

ACCOMMODATIONS. In the interior, these range from fine lodges with pleasant ambience and fine food to what the Spanish euphemistically call *muy rustica*. Most tend toward the latter, and visitors away from the cities should resign themselves to basic, motel-type rooms. It is the setting that counts. For a complete listing of hotels, motels, and trailer camps throughout the province, write *Tourism British Columbia,* Parliament Buildings, Victoria, BC V8V 1X4.

The price categories are: *Deluxe,* $80 and up; *Expensive,* $50–$80; *Moderate,* $40–$50; and *Inexpensive,* under $40.

ASHCROFT. *Deluxe.* **Sundance Guest Ranch.** (604–453–2554.) Open Mar.–Oct. Five km (3 mi.) south. Family oriented resort with trail rides, cookouts, tennis and swimming. One of Canada's largest dude riding herds.

CHILLIWACK. *Moderate.* **Friendship Inn Navaho.** 8583 Young Rd. (604–792–4671). Centrally located. Pool, jacuzzi, games room, some kitchens.

CLINTON—70-MILE HOUSE. *Deluxe.* **Flying U Guest Ranch.** Six miles east of 70-Mile House (604–456–7717). Picturesque working cattle ranch. Features horseback riding, canoeing, cross-country skiing in winter. Rates include meals.

CRANBROOK. **Mount Baker Hotel.** 1017 Baker St. (604–426–5277). Hot tubs. 24-hour satellite T.V.

Sandman Inn. 405 Cranbrook St. (604–426–4236). Indoor pool and sauna. Family rates.

Moderate. **Town and Country Motor Inn.** 600 Cranbrook St. (604–426–6683). Pleasant inner courtyard, pool, indoor sauna and whirlpool.

Inexpensive. **Nomad Motel.** 910 Cranbrook St. (604–426–6266). Some waterbeds. Heated pool in summer. Playground.

FAIRMONT HOT SPRINGS. *Deluxe.* **Fairmont Hot Springs Resort.** (604–345–6311.) Exclusive year-round resort. Facilities include hot outdoor mineral pools, riding, golf, tennis, and skiing.

FORT ST. JAMES. *Moderate.* **Stuart Lodge.** (604–996–7917.) Lakeside cottages 5 km (3 mi.) south of town.

GOLD BRIDGE. *Deluxe.* **Tyax Mountain Lake Resort.** Tyax Rd., V0K 1PO (604–238–2414). B.C.'s newest four-season wilderness retreat features heli-skiing and cross-country skiing in winter, heli-hiking, horseback-riding, tennis, and fishing in summer. Largest log lodge on the west coast.

HARRISON HOT SPRINGS. *Deluxe.* **The Harrison,** (604–796–2244). 129 km (80 mi.) from Vancouver, 240 km (155 mi.) from Seattle. Guests come here to take the waters of the hotel mineral pools and heated outdoor swimming pool. Rooms in the old wing are smaller, with more atmosphere, those in the new wing and tower larger, more comfortable.

Moderate. **Harrison Lakeshore Motel.** (604–796–2441.) Large units with lake view. Pool in summer.

HOPE. *Moderate.* **Imperial Motel.** 350 Hope–Princeton Hwy. (604–869–9951). Sauna, heated indoor pool.

KAMLOOPS. *Deluxe.* **Coast Canadian Inn.** 339 St. Paul St. (604–372–5201). Heated outdoor pool in summer.
Expensive. **David Thompson Motor Inn.** 650 Victoria St. (604–372–5282). Downtown. Outdoor pool.
Dome Motor Hotel. 555 West Columbia St. (604–374–0358). View. Roof-top piano bar.
Lac Le Jeune Resort. 15 miles south of Kamloops (604–372–2722). On the lake. Winter and summer recreational facilities.
The Place Inn. 1285 West Trans Canada Hwy. (604–374–5911). Full service hotel with summer and winter recreation packages.
Sandman Inn. 550 Columbia St. (604–374–1218).
Moderate. **Four Seasons Motel.** 1767 Trans Canada Hwy. 1 (604–372–2313). Barbecue and picnic area. Pool.
Inexpensive. **Village Hotel.** 377 Tranquille Rd. (604–376–8811).
Thrift Inn. 2459 Trans-Canada Hwy. 1 E., Kamloops (604–374–2488). Outdoor pool. (Seasonal.)

KELOWNA. *Expensive.* **Capri Hotel.** 1171 Harvey Ave. (604–860–6060). Pool and sauna.
Moderate–Deluxe. **Beacon Beach Resort.** Motel. 3766 Lakeshore Rd. (604–762–4225). Private beach. Lighted tennis courts. Welcomes families.
Moderate. **Stetson Village Inn.** 1455 Harvey Ave. (604–762–6000). Therapeutic pool. Efficiency units.
Willow Inn Hotel. 235 Queensway (604–762–2122). Water beds. Park and lake close by.
Kelowna TraveLodge. 1780 Gordon Dr. (604–762–3221). Indoor pool, whirlpool and sauna. Close to golf and shopping.
Inexpensive. **Western Budget Motel.** 2679 Hwy. 97N (604–860–4990).

NELSON. *Moderate.* **Slumber Lodge Motor Inn.** 153 Baker St. (604–352–3525). Sauna.

"108." *Expensive.* **108 Resort.** (604–791–5211.) Riding. Paved airstrip. 18-hole P.G.A. golf course, tennis, and riding. Cross-country skiing in winter.

PENTICTON. *Deluxe.* **Delta Lakeside.** 21 Lakeside Dr. (604–493–8221). On Lake Okanagan. Swimming, saunas, tennis, and exercise room.
Moderate. **Bowmont Motel.** 80 Riverside Dr. (604–492–0112). Welcomes families. Pool and play area.
Expensive. **Penticton TraveLodge.** 950 Westminster Ave. (604–492–0225). Outdoor pool. Indoor pool has waterslide.
Log Cabin Motel. 3287 Skaha Lake Rd. (604–492–3155). Outdoor pool and patio.
Stardust Motor Inn. 1048 Westminster Ave. (604–492–7015).

POWELL RIVER. *Expensive–Deluxe.* **Beach Gardens Resort Hotel.** 7074 Westminster St. (604–485–6267). Overlooking marina with boat rentals. Indoor pool. Tennis courts.

PRINCE GEORGE. *Deluxe.* **Coast Inn of the North.** 770 Brunswick St. (604–563–0121). Indoor pool. Japanese steakhouse.
Moderate. **Esther's Inn.** 1151 Commercial Dr. (604–562–4131). Indoor pool with waterslides, steam, sauna, whirlpool.
Connaught Motor Inn. 1550 Victoria St. (562–4441).
Sandman Inn. 1650 Central St. (604–563–8131). Near airport.

PRINCE RUPERT. *Expensive.* **Crest Motor Hotel.** 222 1st Ave W. (604–624 –6771). Harbor view. Fishing charters.

Highliner Inn. 815 1st Ave. W. (604–624–9060). Harbor view. Some housekeeping units. Beautician; goldsmith shop.

Prince Rupert Hotel. At 2nd Ave and 6th St. (624–6711).

PRINCETON. *Moderate.* **Evergreen Motel.** (604–295–7179.) 4 km (2 mi.) east of city center.

Ponderosa Motel. Box 238 (604–295–6244). Some housekeeping units. 24-hour movie channel, complimentary coffee.

RADIUM HOT SPRINGS. *Expensive.* **Radium Hot Springs Golf Resort.** 1 km south of Radium Hot Springs on Hwy. 95 (604–347–9311). Complete health spa, golf and tennis.

Moderate. **Big Horn Motel.** (604–347–9522.) Whirlpool, sauna and playground.

REVELSTOKE. *Expensive.* **McGregor Motor Inn.** Second St. and Connaught Ave. (604–837–2121). "Heli" skiing available.

Moderate. **Columbia Slumber Lodge.** 1601 Second St. W. (604–837–2191).

Revelstoke TraveLodge. 601 1st St. W. (604–837–2181). Families and small pets welcomed.

Inexpensive. **King Edward Motor Hotel.** (604–837–2104.) Central.

ROGERS PASS. *Expensive.* **Best Western Glacier Park Lodge.** (604–837– 2126.) 73 km (45 mi.) east of Revelstoke. Outdoor heated pool year-round.

SALMON ARM. *Expensive.* **Totem Pole Resort and Marina.** 27 km (17 mi.) off Hwy. 1 at Tappen (604–835–4567). Cedar homes and chalets on private lakeshore.

SMITHERS. *Moderate.* **Sandman Inn.** On Hwy. 16 (604–847–2637). Sauna. Family plan.

Inexpensive. **Florence Motel.** Highway 16 W. (604–847–2678). Barbecues. Complimentary coffee.

Tyee Motor Hotel. (604–847–2201.)

TRAIL. *Moderate.* **Ray-lyn Motel.** 118 Wellington St. Trail (604–368–5541). One mile west of city center. Courtesy coffee in rooms. Outdoor heated pool.

Inexpensive. **Glenwood Motel.** 2769 Glenwood Dr. (604–368–5522). Outdoor pool. Ski packages.

VALEMONT. *Moderate.* **Mountaineer Flag Inn.** (604–566–4477.) Country setting. Pool, sauna, squash courts. Cross-country ski packages.

VERNON. *Expensive.* **The Village Green Inn.** 4801 27th St. (604–542–3321). Pools, tennis. Winter ski packages.

WHISTLER. *Deluxe.* **Delta Mountain Inn.** In Whistler Village (604–932– 1982). Extensive exercise and recreation facilities. Cross-country ski and bike rentals.

Expensive. **Tantalus Lodge.** (604–932–4146.) In Whistler Village. Self-contained units with fireplaces and balconies. Pools. Golf adjacent.

TOURIST INFORMATION. *Tourism British Columbia,* Parliament Buildings, V8V 1X4. *Tourism Victoria* (604–382–2127). *Vancouver Travel Infocenter,* 683–6000.

SEASONAL EVENTS. January: Height of ski season. **February:** *Ski competitions* on all slopes. *Winter carnival,* Vernon, B.C.

April: *Rodeo* at Kamloops, B.C. *Ski Competitions* on all slopes throughout the month.

July: July 1st is a national holiday and *Dominion Day* celebrations are held in many communities. *Indian Days Festivals* in Kamloops, B.C. and Banff.

August: In Penticton, B.C.: *Peach Festival* and *Square Dance Jamboree;* in Kelowna, B.C. *International Regatta.*

December: *Hockey* in almost every community.

TOURS. Many bus tours through the Canadian west are offered by tour companies whose main booking offices are in Toronto; two such companies are: *UTL Holiday Tours,* 22 College St., (416) 967–3355, and *Horizon Holidays of Canada,* 44 Victoria St., (800) 268–7103. *Maverick Coach Lines,* 1375 Vernon Dr., Vancouver, (604) 255–1171, also has packages that take in the Canadian West.

In British Columbia, *Pacific Coach Lines* offers trips from Vancouver, such as a schedule up the Sunshine Coast for $38, an outing up the Fraser Valley to the delightful Harrison Hot Springs resort ($18), and a full day at Whistler ($20). For information in Vancouver call 662–3222. *Maverick* has a seven-day tour to Vancouver Island, the Inside Passage, Prince Rupert, and Prince George for $419. For information call (604) 255–1171.

Westours, 100 W. Harrison Plaza, Seattle, WA 98119, (208) 281–3535, provides several tours of B.C. of varying length.

SPECIAL-INTEREST TOURS. The adventurous might want to try a *raft* trip in the white waters of the Thompson and Fraser rivers. It helps to be a swimmer, but life jackets are provided. Most tours originate in Lytton and start at $50 for a one-day outing. Contact *West-Can Treks-Adventure Travel,* 3415 West Broadway, Vancouver. (604–734–1066).

HINTS TO MOTORISTS. Gas, sold by the liter, is more expensive here. Fill up before crossing the border into Canada. Road signs are in metric. Seat belts are mandatory, as are helmets for motorcyclists. Drinking and driving is highly illegal, and no exceptions are made for tourists. Roadblocks appear during holiday seasons.

HINTS TO HANDICAPPED TRAVELERS. Listings in the official accommodations guide marked with a "W" indicate that the establishment is able to accommodate those confined to a wheelchair. More information is available from the *Canadian Parapalegic Association,* 780 S. W. Marine Drive, Vancouver, BC V6P 5Y7, (604–324–3611).

PROVINCIAL PARKS. There are more than 330 provincial parks throughout British Columbia. Camping is available at most for a nominal fee in summer. No reservations. Popular parks are *Garibaldi, Manning,* and *Cathedral,* all of which are located in the southwest of the province. Open year-round. For information on the provincial parks in British Columbia's lower mainland, call 604–683–2000.

NATIONAL PARKS. For complete information on facilities write to *Parks Canada*—Western Region, Box 2989, Station M., Calgary, AB T2P 3H8 (403–292–4440). Or to *National and Provincial Parks Association of Canada,* 47 Colborne St., Suite 308, Toronto, ON M5E 1E3. Camping is on a first-come, first-serve basis. No pass-through charge for any motor vehicle. To spend a day or less, a 24-hour stopping pass can be purchased for $1. Most convenient is to purchase a $10 annual national parks pass, good until March 31st of the year following at any national park in Canada.

For safety reasons, visitors must register at a Parks Warden Office before embarking on or completing any climbing, extensive backpacking, hiking, or cross-country skiing expeditions. Use of open campfires is restricted to National Park Campsites specifically designed to accommodate them. Dogs and cats must be on leash. Use of firearms and bowstring equipment is forbidden; all such equipment must be sealed at park entry points. The parks are open year-round.

Glacier National Park (521 square miles) is in the Selkirk Mountains and contains over 100 glaciers as well as hemlock and cedar forests and excellent fishing streams. Write Box 350, Revelstoke, BC V0E 2S0; (604) 837–5515.

Kootenay National Park (543 square miles) is a narrow valley on the western slopes of the Rockies and includes colossal Sinclair Canyon and Radium Hot Springs. (P.O. Box 220, Radium Hot Springs, BC V0A 1M0; (604) 347–9615.)

Mount Revelstoke National Park (100 square miles), on the rugged western slopes of the Selkirks, is a mountaintop park with ski slopes and alpine meadows. Write P.O. Box 350, Revelstoke, BC V0E 2S0; (604) 837–5515.

Pacific Rim National Park (250 square miles) on the western slope of Vancouver Island is most famous for sandy Long Beach and the sea lions living on rocky offshore islets. Write P.O. Box 280, Ucluelet, BC V0R 3A0; 604–726–7721.

Yoho National Park (507 square miles)—"How Wonderful," in the local Indian language—has spectacular Yoho Glacier, Lake O'Hara, Takkakaw Falls, and a famous pass through the Rockies following Kicking Horse River. Write P.O. Box 99, Field, BC V0A 1G0; (604) 343–6324.

CAMPING. There are no reservations for camping in national and provincial parks, where in summer there are nominal overnight fees. (See the sections on these parks, below.)

FISHING. An annual saltwater fishing license for Canadians costs $5.00. For a nonresident or non-Canadian, it costs around $3.50 a day, $10 for 3 days, $20, annual. Available at sporting goods stores and marinas. A license is issued on an annual basis and is valid until the following March 31. Angling permits are required by all fishermen except children under 16 years of age. Freshwater licenses for 6 days cost $7, B.C. residents, $8, other Canadian residents, $12, non-Canadians. Annual licenses cost approximately double that amount.

A fishing license is required for all national parks in Canada. It costs $4.00 and is good in every national park in Canada, again on an annual basis. Full information, sports fishing guide, may be obtained from Ministry of Environment & Parks, Fish & Wildlife Branch, Parliament Buildings, Victoria, B.C. V8V 1X5 (604–387–4573).

HUNTING. The difficulty of reaching north central B.C. is rewarded by the abundance of game: mountain goat and sheep, black and grizzly bear, moose, caribou, deer, waterfowl. Nonresident hunters require a guide. Licenses start at $43, depending on the game. Canadian residents pay $17 to carry a firearm and hunt all game. You can contact the B.C. Fish and Game Association, 1607 Myrtle Ave., Victoria, for more information.

SUMMER SPORTS. You'll find over 110 **golf** courses in B.C. and countless **tennis** courts. **Watersports** are very popular and offered by most resorts. You can also swim at public or secluded beaches.

Mountain climbers will find parks the best place for climbing.

Yacht clubs in Victoria, on the Gulf Islands, and in Vancouver, and at many lakes can provide you with a boat for rent. **Canoeing** is also popular; canoes can be rented at resorts and at some inland hotels. Again, Tourism B.C. has up-to-date, detailed information on most sporting opportunities. It's best to check thoroughly on regulations, dates, and fees.

WINTER SPORTS. The **skiing** is nothing less than splendid. Here you can even find **helicopter glacier skiing.** Heli-skiing companies in the coastal mountains include *Whistler Heli-Ski,* Box 368, Whistler, B.C. V0N 1B0 (604–932–4105). Their newest terrain includes the sunny Chilcotins around Tyax Resort, near Gold Bridge. Also try *Mike Wiegele Helicopter Skiing,* Box 249, Banff, Alta. TOL OCO (403–762–5548). *Big White* in the Okanagan Valley is a popular resort (Box 2039, Station R, Kelowna, B.C. V1X 4K5; 765–4411), as are *Apex Alpine* (Box 489, Penticton, B.C. V2A 6K9; 292–8221) and *Silver Star* (#1,3001 43rd Ave., Vernon, B.C. V1T 3L4; 542–0166). One of the most popular ski resorts in British Columbia is *Whistler Mountain,* two hours north of Vancouver. The village of Whistler actually has two magnificent mountains (Whistler and Blackcomb), both offering a vertical drop of more than 4,000 feet. The village has full facilities including good hotels, restaurants, bars, discos and baby-sitting. For information and reservations contact the Whistler Resort Association, Box 1400, Whistler, BC V0N 1B0 (604–932–4222).

MUSEUMS AND GALLERIES. Barkerville: the whole town is restored and a museum in itself. **Courtenay:** *Courtenay & District Museum* features logging, mining, and pioneer history displays and a doll collection. **Dawson Creek:** *Station Museum* and *Park.* **Duncan:** *British Columbia Forest Museum* (logging artifacts). **Fort Langley:** renovated Hudson's Bay Company post. **Fort Steele:** North West Mounted Police post and re-created village. **Kamloops:** *Museum & Archives* display all aspects of local history. **Vernon:** *O'Keefe Ranch;* re-created old ranch.

RESTAURANTS. Most dining outside the big cities is just plain ordinary at best: Overcooked meat, pre-frozen French fries and a token slice of orange on the plate for garnish. The old trick of stopping where the truckers eat does not work either; you are likely to find yourself at a rural version of the worst all-night hotel coffee shop. There are some bright spots, however, like restaurants in interesting settings far from major population centers that offer superb dining prepared by people who genuinely care about food. For these we must be especially grateful.

The price categories, reflecting the cost of a three-course meal for one, without beverages, tax, or tip, are: *Expensive,* over $15; *Moderate,* $10–$15; and *Inexpensive,* under $10.

GOLDEN. *Expensive.* **Selkirk Inn.** (344–6315). Excellent cuisine, bar.

HARRISON HOT SPRINGS. The Black Forest Schnitzel House. Antlers on the wall, Rhineland murals, Teutonic knick-knackery, and a menu featuring Bavarian specials, salmon, and steaks.

HORSESHOE BAY. The Troller Pub. 6422 Bay St. (921–7616). Not so much for the food as for their own beer, brewed on the premises.

KAMLOOPS. *Expensive.* **David Thompson Dining Room.** 650 Victoria. Steak, lobster, prime ribs. Children's portions.
Minos. 262 Tranquille Rd. (376–2010). Another fine outpost of Greek food far, far from the sunny Mediterranean.
Chapters Viewpoint. 610 West Columbia. Overlooking the confluence of the Thompson and North Thompson Rivers. A wide-ranging menu.
Moderate: **China Village Restaurant.** 165 Victoria St. Chinese and North American food. Serves liquor.
Oriental Gardens. 545 Victoria St. Chinese (including authentic Szechuan) and Japanese.
Inexpensive: **Highlander Restaurant.** 444 Victoria St. Seafood, steaks, trout. Dancing. Serves liquor.

PENTICTON. *Moderate:* **Pilgrim House Motor Hotel Restaurant.** 1056 Eckhardt Ave. Specializing in prime beef.

PRINCE GEORGE. *Moderate:* **The Achillion.** 422 Dominion (564–1166). Surprisingly good Greek food in this northern town.
Outrigger Restaurant. 1208 6th Ave. (564–3888). South-Sea décor. Polynesian and Continental food.
Vienna Schnitzel Restaurant. 6th Ave. and Brunswick St. (563–7550). European cuisine in an Old World atmosphere. Entertainment.

PRINCE RUPERT. Smile's Seafood Cafe. 113 George Hills Way (624–3072). A good, basic seafood cafe worthy of the Halibut Capital of the World.
Moderate: **Crest Motor Hotel Restaurant,** 222 1st Ave. W. (624–6771). Continental cuisine in a dining room that overlooks the harbor.

POWELL RIVER. The Seahouse. 4448 Marine Ave. (485–9151). A pleasant surprise in this small seaside town.

VERNON. *Moderate:* **Vernon Lodge Hotel Restaurant.** 3914 32nd St. (545–3385). Good selection, especially seafood. Entertainment.

NORTHWEST TERRITORIES

Canada's Frontier

by
RAY PRICE and MAC MACKAY

Born in Surrey, England, Ray Price was a soldier, teacher, award-winning actor, and a professional cricket player. He wrote three books, Yellowknife, The Howling Arctic, *and* Trapper George. *Ray Price died in 1983.*

Mac Mackay, who travels extensively throughout Western Canada, has been a free-lance writer since 1976. He has been a columnist in both Canadian and U.S. publications.

The Northwest Territories is vast—over a million and a third square miles. On the east its shores are washed by the cold, gray waters of the Atlantic, and on the west only the Yukon Territory separates it from the borders of Alaska. Five provinces share its southern border, and its Arctic islands reach to within 200 miles of the North Pole.

The capital of the Northwest Territories is Yellowknife, a city of 10,000 which represents almost 25 percent of the total population of the entire Northwest Territories. A population that divides itself into roughly three equal parts: one-third Dene (Indian), one-third Inuit (Eskimo), and one third "Other."

Only in the last forty years has advancing civilization reached its tentacles into this exciting land of Inuit and Dene, of fur trader and explorer, and of missionary and trapper. Primitive people are being

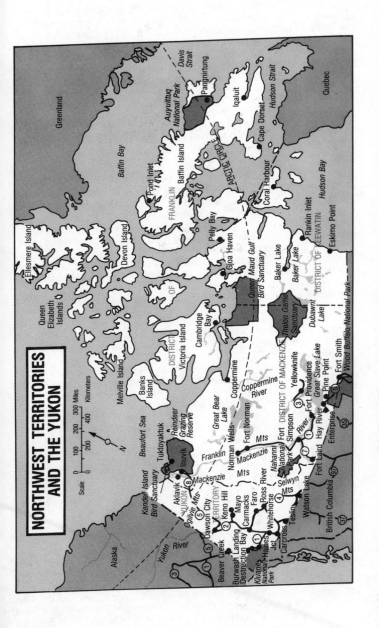

NORTHWEST TERRITORIES AND THE YUKON

wrenched into the world of aluminum and chrome, aircraft and schools, politics and plastics, precooked food, and deodorants.

These people have not taken kindly to some of the changes and are resisting the complete takeover of their land and lives by the forces of civilization that feed on oil, demand minerals, and threaten to lay waste the land of their fathers and home of their hopes.

The Northwest Territories is divided into regions, each one immense and each one offering to the visitor exciting and novel experiences—the Districts of Franklin, Keewatin, and Mackenzie.

THE DISTRICT OF FRANKLIN

In the east is the District of Franklin, a mass of water and land that embraces Baffin Island, all the High Arctic Islands, and is the biggest of the three. Iqaluit (formerly Frobisher Bay) is the largest community in this district. Situated on the shores of an inlet that plunges between the low rock hills of southern Baffin Island, it was originally named after the white discoverer of the land, Martin Frobisher, who landed there in 1576. He believed he had found fabulous deposits of gold, collected a considerable cargo, met and fought with the Natives, was ignominiously shot in the backside by a flint-tipped arrow, and then returned to England. Once back in the homeland he learned that the glorious gold was valueless iron pyrite.

Frobisher's voyages marked the beginning of great interest in the lands north and west of the British Isles. Slowly the whalers and the fur traders followed the paths of the explorers. The Davis Straits became known, and the cloud-haunted, ice-clad mountains of Baffin Island soon were familiar landmarks for those who sought wealth from the ocean.

Scattered across the white face of the District of Franklin are tiny Inuit communities. Few have populations numbering more than several hundred, and only where mining or the search for oil has become extensive is there any industrialization. Resolute Bay on the north shore of Lancaster Sound has become a center of activity and so has Nanisivik on the northwestern shore of Baffin Island.

Many oil companies are using Resolute Bay as a supply/distribution center. Here, there is an all-weather airstrip, and flights from Montreal and Vancouver terminate. Nordair has regular flights from the east, and Pacific Western Airlines, from the west. These flights usually call at the largest cities and towns en route.

At Nanisivik there is a mining development. In 1974, lead and zinc deposits were found, and it was deemed feasible to start mining operations. As a result, the tiny Inuit settlement that clings under towering cliffs to the shore of the Arctic Sea has become a center for wage earning activity. This is not welcomed by some of the free and easy Inuit whose prime love is the hunt and the never-ending battle for survival in a hostile environment.

Until the end of the Second World War there was minimal interest in what happened in the vast reaches of the District of Franklin. One of Canada's postwar prime ministers is quoted as saying, "We have governed Canada's North with a great absence of mind." Policed by a handful of Mounties, served by an occasional traveling doctor, ministered to by a few Anglican and Roman Catholic priests, and invaded by the Hudson's Bay Company for fur, both the land and the people remained beyond the ken of the average Canadian and far out of the reach of an embryonic tourist industry. During the last few years, however, more and more visitors have stepped tentatively into this vast land. Well to the fore have been archaeologists, geologists, and anthropologists, all of whom have made major contributions to our expanding knowledge of the Canadian Arctic. Numerous exciting discoveries have been made. Natural gas in abundance has been found and archaeological sites of considerable importance have been uncovered on Axel Heiberg, Bathurst, Coburg, Devon, Ellesmere, and Cornwallis islands. Aircraft, politics, radio, and economics have knifed aside the curtain of silence drawn across Canada's North, and she now lies open for us all to visit, to see, to enjoy, to begin to understand.

Exploring the District of Franklin

If you love the out-of-doors, enjoy hiking, mountaineering, fishing, and photography; and are prepared to rough it, then go to Baffin Island. Few of its settlements have hotels, and those, while adequate, are not luxurious. However, there are many opportunities for memorable holidays.

To be sure of a reasonable measure of comfort while visiting the most remote parts of North America, the wisest plan is to join one of the several Arctic tours that start in Montréal. These tours are varied in both route and price, and there are many different trips to choose from.

These tours give you a chance to see the very beautiful scenery of Baffin Island, visit several of its Inuit communities, and catch sight of some of the wildlife to be found on land and in the surrounding waters. Most travel is by air, although some side trips by boat are offered. Details of these tours may be obtained from Montréal-based travel agencies or from TravelArctic in Yellowknife.

For the most part, Baffin Island is not ready for an intensive and extensive tourist business. It is still a country for specialists: anthropologists, sociologists, photographers, geologists, writers, mountaineers, and the like. Visitors most likely to enjoy themselves are those who like roughing it, love fishing, are lured by the mountains, have the curiosity of a naturalist and the appreciation of a painter.

Pangnirtung

Pangnirtung, the gateway to the Auyuittuq National Park, is one of Baffin Island's most beautiful places, and has been called the "Switzerland of the Arctic." Ringed by mountains and washed by the waters of Cumberland Sound, it is a place that once visited is never forgotten. For many years whalers sailed into the Sound, and they were the first to bring some of the benefits of civilization to the Inuit People. Now it is fully civilized with an airstrip, Peyton Lodge, accommodating fifty persons, and a regular mail service. The latest television programs of the Canadian Broadcasting Corporation can also be viewed through facilities supplied by the communications satellite Anik.

Plunging north and east into the mountains is the Pangnirtung Fiord, one of the two main sledge routes through the Baffin mountains. The fiord also marks the entrance to the National Park.

The following services are available in Pangnirtung: nursing station; Royal Canadian Mounted Police; post office; Anglican Church; hotel with dining facilities; Hudson's Bay Store; Inuit Cooperative Weaving Shop; regular airline service via Nordair.

Auyuittuq National Park

This park has special treats for those seeking an exciting Arctic experience. Lying 1,500 miles northeast of Montréal, Canada's northernmost park covers 21,470 sq. kms. (8,290 square miles) of the island.

The Penny Highlands dominate the park, rising 7,000 feet above sea level, and carry on their peaks the Penny Ice Cap, 2,200 square miles of solid ice—a remnant of the last Ice Age. Glaciers, spawned by the ice cap, flow majestically into the surrounding valleys. The park can be reached by flying direct to Pangnirtung.

Here you will find wonderful camping spots and first-class opportunities to climb, fish, hike, read rocks, study nature, and take pictures. The Auyuittuq National Park can be explored year after year and still surprise, excite, and fill with wonder.

Holiday by Charter Aircraft

If funds are no problem, an exciting way to move comfortably around Baffin Island is by charter aircraft. Although some of the places can be reached on a scheduled run, a flight over Baffin Island's wild terrain and its formidable environs in a small aircraft can be an exciting, fascinating experience. Rarely visited places like Lake Harbour and Clyde River and Port Burwell on the south side of the Hudson Straits become reachable. It is usually possible to overnight in such places, although it is essential to make inquiries from the government offices in Yellowknife or the settlement manager. Letters can be addressed to the "Settlement Manager" in each of the above mentioned places. If writing to the settlements, please enclose a self-addressed return envelope to ensure a speedy, accurately directed answer.

The pilots of charter air companies know all the settlements and places of interest and will gladly share their expertise with you. Not only will charter air companies get you quickly and safely to less frequently visited places, they also can take you and your party to the finest spots for fishing, the greatest places for camping, and the best places to see the local fauna whether on land or sea.

A short flight (80 miles) from Frobisher Bay will take you to Lake Harbour, a small Inuit community that is still comparatively unaffected by the onrush of 20th-century technology. From there a longer hop will put you in Cape Dorset, the home of some of Canada's finest Inuit carvers, painters, and printmakers.

To complete a very exciting tour, fly on to Igloolik and see an island that has yielded some of the most interesting artifacts of early Inuit culture. The Hudson Bay has slowly receded during the centuries following the Ice Age, and as the shoreline has moved, the Inuit population has followed it. As archaeologists move toward the highest part of the island, tools and implements from more and more ancient peoples are uncovered.

The Inuit are proud of their heritage and will be glad to talk of their way of life and show you their carvings, paintings, prints, and beautiful fur garments. The latter are often for sale, although in recent years carvings, paintings, and garments have become expensive. Carvings frequently sell for well over $1,000.

Complete your trip by flying back via the far northern settlements of Arctic Bay and Pond Inlet, places ideal for the photographer and offering good chances to see whale, narwhal, and polar bear.

If you plan a trip like this, do not expect luxurious accommodations in the settlements. But in most places it is possible to obtain a good night's rest and reasonable food. The Inuit are cheerful, reasonable, and pleasant hosts.

Such a trip will give you ample opportunity for talking with Inuit— all of the younger generation read and speak English well—photographing their communities and their country and the Inuit themselves. Be courteous in your use of a camera; remember you are a guest in their homeland. They are hospitable, but do not like being treated as curiosities.

Should you travel in wintertime—during which there is often the best flying weather, although daylight hours are very short—side trips by dogteam or skidoo can be arranged. It is not easy to make such arrangements in advance. Inuit are not time or schedule conscious like the more regimented peoples in Western civilizations.

Keeping the above in mind, it is essential when planning such a once-in-a-lifetime trip to allow some room for possible, and indeed probable, delays. Weather in the eastern Arctic is frequently uncertain, and almost every year there are several days when radio communication becomes impossible. For example, this writer was stranded in Pangnirtung Fiord for nine days in 1972. The aircraft was damaged on landing and radio communication ruled out by sunspot activity. Eventually escape from the rapidly melting fiord had to be made by placing the aircraft's wheels onto toboggans and using them as skis when taking off.

It is unlikely that you will experience anything that unusual and frightening; however, anything can happen when touring Baffin Island and the surrounding land masses by small, chartered aircraft.

Charter Airline Services: Bradley Air Service Ltd., Box 477, Iqaluit, N.W.T. X0A 0H0, (819) 979–5810; Hall Beach, N.W.T. X0A 0K0, (819) 928–8927; Resolute, N.W.T. X0A 0V0, (819) 252–3981. Kenn Borek Air Ltd., Box 1159, Inuvik, N.W.T. X0E 0T0, (403) 979–3937; Box 210, Resolute, N.W.T. X0A 0V0, (819) 252–3849. Northwest Territorial Airways Ltd., Postal Service 9000, Yellowknife, N.W.T. X1A 2R3, (403) 920–2500.

Pond Inlet

Like Pangnirtung, it is set in spectacular scenery. Although it is on the far northern shore of Baffin Island, it is not a land of interminable snow and ice. Go there in the summer and see for yourself.

Take a boat trip to Bylot Island, 25 miles from the settlement. Here you will find a land of mountains and rivers, icebergs and sandstone, glaciers and snowfields, thousands of birds, and a sea alive with fish and mammals.

Pond Inlet can be reached from either the east of Canada or the west. Nordair flies from Montréal to Resolute, and Pacific Western Airlines flies from Edmonton or Calgary to Resolute, then from Resolute there is a feeder line operated by Kenn Borek Air to Pond Inlet.

A few years ago, Pond Inlet was especially honored by the Canadian government when a postage stamp was printed showing the spectacular view across the Inlet to the iceberg that for many years has been the source of the community's fresh water.

Write directly to Sauniq Hotel, Pond Inlet, N.W.T. X0A 0S0, (819) 899–8928, for up-to-date information concerning costs and the availability of accommodations. If Pond Inlet is your destination, then be sure to make your booking months in advance; accommodation is seriously limited.

Fishing

Arctic char, the salmon of the North, can be caught in the high tide waters of Cumberland Sound and the waters around Pond Inlet. This delicious fish, one of the most prized by sportsmen, frequently weighs in excess of 10 pounds. Boats are available from local people in Pangnirtung and Pond Inlet. Fish can also be caught in the unusually beautiful Summit Lake, high on the pass between the mountains.

Photography

There is magnificent unspoiled scenery to be photographed by the light of the midnight sun, under the fleeting, multicolored brilliance of the Aurora Borealis, or as the sun sweeps morning mists from river and sea.

For the wildlife photographer, there are subjects on both land and sea. Though sparse on land, some mammals can be seen by the alert photographer. Watch for the polar bear, lemming, fox, and very rarely, the barren ground caribou. Contrasted with all this rather sparse land-bound fauna, there is an abundance of life in the surrounding waters. Not infrequently, beluga, various species of seals, bowhead whales, and narwhals can all be spotted. The narwhal is of particular interest. It is a strange species of whale that grows one long tusk, a tooth that has been used for all sorts of things, including aphrodisiacs.

Hiking and Climbing

The majority of visitors to the Auyuittuq National Park come for the firsthand experience of the country that hiking affords. Difficult terrain and changeable weather demand considerable outdoor experience, careful selection of equipment, and adequate planning. The best time for hiking is from late June to early August, when the valleys are clear of snow.

Pangnirtung Pass has all the ingredients for a great hiking challenge: gravel flats, boulder-strewn moraines, glacial tongues, and icy streams to ford. A hiker will do well to travel at two miles per hour under these conditions. Overlord campground is located on the Weasal River Delta, some 20 miles from Pangnirtung very close to the boundary of the park. From here it is possible to walk to Summit Lake. Seven shelters are placed at strategic locations in Pangnirtung Pass. Each shelter holds a first-aid kit, and most of them have radiotelephones. Northwest Territorial publications emphasize the need for caution to all would-be travelers in the park. Winds can reach 100 miles per hour; freezing temperatures can occur during any month of the year; and avalanches and rockfalls are not uncommon.

Minimum equipment for a hiking trip into Auyuittuq National Park should include lightweight camping gear, warm windproof clothing, stout hiking boots, a camp stove, matches, maps, compass, and first-aid kit. A walking stick doubles as a probe to locate shallow points when fording streams. A lightweight rain suit should also be taken.

Climbers from Europe, Japan, and North America have been drawn to peaks such as Mount Asgard, Mount Odin, and Tete Blanche. These peaks range from 5,000 to 6,000 feet above sea level (1,500–2,000 m.). The best climbing months are June and July, although snow conditions in April and May are usually good. Travel to and from the best climbing areas is difficult. Location of supply bases and the drop-off of supplies require careful organization. Until the end of May or early

June, access is possible by ski-equipped aeroplane or snowmobile. During the best climbing period the only way to reach the mountains requires hard foot slogging over many miles or a helicopter.

Winter Sports

Snowmobiling, snowshoeing, and skiing: get away from mundane things in the spring of the year and enjoy fun in the snow at Pangnirtung and in the nearby National Park. Temperatures are moderate in April, May, and June, and the surrounding country can be explored by skidoo, ski, or snowshoe. Equipment can be rented from Inuit at Pangnirtung, and guides are also available.

Note: There is a special information bureau in Auyuittuq National Park. Information can be obtained at the park's office in Pangnirtung. Address your letters to: The Superintendent, Auyuittuq National Park, Pangnirtung, N.W.T. X0A 0R0. For their own safety, all park visitors are requested to register at the park's office in Pangnirtung or Broughton Island.

Practical Information for the District of Franklin

TRANSPORTATION SERVICES. Airlines. Scheduled Services: *Air Inuit Ltd.,* 9785 Ryan Ave., Dorval, Que. H9P 1A2, (514) 636–9445. Scheduled services to Cape Dorset from bases in northern Québec.

First Air Ltd., Box 477, Iqaluit, N.W.T. X0A 0H0, (819) 979–5810. *Boeing* 727 service is available from Ottawa to Iqaluit. Connections throughout Baffin Island and to Greenland.

Kenn Borek Air Ltd., Box 210, Resolute, N.W.T. X0A 0V0, (819) 252–3849. Scheduled flights between Resolute, Grise Fiord, Nanisivik, Arctic Bay, and Pond Inlet.

Nordair Ltd., Box 4000, Montreal International Airport, Dorval, Que. H4Y 1B8, (514) 636–7670. Daily service except Sunday from Toronto, Ottawa, Montreal, Iqaluit return. Twice weekly service to Hall Beach, Resolute and Nanisivik/Arctic Bay.

Northwest Territorial Airways Ltd., Postal Service 9000, Yellowknife, N.W.T. X1A 2R3, (403) 920–2500. Service to Iqaluit, Rankin Inlet, Cambridge Bay, Gjoa Haven, and Hall Beach. from Yellowknife.

Pacific Western Airlines, 2800–700–2nd St. S.W., Calgary, Alta. T2P 2W2, (403) 294–2000. Service from Cambridge Bay and Resolute to Yellowknife.

VEHICLE RENTALS. Cars and trucks are available in Iqaluit at *Arctic Resources Ltd.,* (819) 979–6465, and *Okata and Paton Ltd.,* (819) 979–6478; in Resolute at *Arctic Resources Ltd.,* (819) 252–3858.

ACCOMMODATIONS. Due to limited accommodation available in most Northwest Territories communities, please make reservations as early as possible. This is especially necessary for travel in the summer months. All hotels and motels listed in this section are open year-round unless noted otherwise. (At the time of publication, there are no bellhop services in most Northwest Territories hotels.)

Most places accept major credit cards; however, not all establishments accept credit cards, therefore we suggest you call for information.

CAMBRIDGE BAY. Ikaluktutiak Hotel. Box 38, Cambridge Bay, N.W.T. X0E 0C0, (403) 983–2215. 20-room motel accommodates 40 persons with shared accommodation and bath; TV. $80 and up, single. Major credit cards accepted.

CAPE DORSET. Kingnait Inn. Cape Dorset, N.W.T. X0A 0C0, (819) 897–8863. Accommodates 25 in 9 rooms with private baths; 3 rooms shared accommodation and bath. Located in the heart of the Inuit arts community. $130 single with meals.

IQALUIT. Frobisher Inn. Box 610, Iqaluit, N.W.T. X0A 0H0, (819) 979–5241. Located in the Astro Hill complex. Accommodation for 100 in 50 rooms with bath, TV, and telephones. Licensed dining lounge, cafe, laundry, fish freezing. $105 and up, single. Major credit cards.

PANGNIRTUNG. Peyton Lodge. Pangnirtung, N.W.T. X0A 0R0, (819) 473–8955. Open June-Sept. Accommodates 54 in 27 rooms. $125 single includes meals. Guided trips to spectacular Clearwater Fiord by boat for char fishing and sightseeing (seals, whales).

POND INLET. Sauniq Hotel. Pond Inlet, N.W.T. X0A 0S0, (819) 899–8928. Accommodates 38 in 19 rooms with shared accommodation, baths. TV, Dining lounge. $150 single includes meals.

FISHING OUTFITTERS AND LODGES. Alivuktuk Outfitting. Joavee Alivuktuk, Pangnirtung, NWT X0A 0R0, (819) 473–8721. Transportation to and from Auyuittuq National Park to points of interest around Cumberland Sound. Trips from ½ day to 1 week long from July 1 to September 1. Rates vary.

Banks Island Lodge. Sachs Harbour, N.W.T. X0E OZO, (403) 690–4191. Guided sightseeing trips by boat or on foot. Muskox, fox, seal, loons, king eider, falcons, snowy owl, Arctic wildflowers. $130 per day with meals.

Grise Fiord Lodge. Grise Fiord, N.W.T. X0A 0J0, (819) 980–9913. Tour Canada's northern-most community. Guided outings. Boat and snowmobile for wildlife sightings (bearded harp seal, ring seal, walrus, narwhal, beluga, muskox, polar bear, ivory gulls, fulmars, puffins). Tours can leave from Resolute.

High Arctic International Explorer Services Ltd. Bezal Jesudason, Box 200, Resolute, N.W.T. X0A 0V0, (819) 252–3875. Accommodates 15. World's northern-most fishing camp 410 miles north of Grise Fiord on Ellesmere Island. Excellent arctic char fishing.

High Arctic Lodge. Don and Marlene Hamilton, Box 1229, Revelstoke, B.C. V0E 2S0, (604) 837–2928. On Merkeley Lake, 85 miles northwest of Cambridge Bay on Victoria Island. Outpost camps in Hadley Bay area. Trophy arctic char and lake trout. Accommodates 12. July 13-Aug. 31. Meals, guides, flight from Cambridge Bay and side trips to outpost camp.

Koluctoo Bay Sports Fishing Camp. Toonoonik-Sahoonik Co-Op, Pond Inlet, N.W.T. X0A OSO. Arctic char fishing Aug.–Sept. 10.

Nuna-Kuuk Outfitting. Box 123, Iqaluit, N.W.T. X0A 0H0, (819) 979–6027. Whitewater rafting and kayaking at South Baffin, mid-July—mid-Sept.; equipment supplied. Dog-team trips by the hour or day, late Nov.-late June. Cross-country skiing with dog-team support, mid-Apr.-mid-June. Boat trips on Frobisher Bay, mid-July-mid-Oct. Eskimo dogs, kayaks, snow-surfing boards. York Sound camp, hiking, climbing, glacial skiing. Expeditions.

TOURIST INFORMATION. For *Baffin Island* and *High Arctic Islands,* write: Baffin Tourism Association, Box 820, Frobisher Bay, N.W.T. X0A 0H0, (819) 979–6551. For *central Arctic* including *Holman, Cambridge Bay,* and *Gjoa Haven,* write: Arctic Coast Tourist Association, Box 91, Cambridge Bay, N.W.T. X0E 0C0, (403) 983–2224. For *Banks Island,* write: Western Arctic Visitors Association, Box 1525, Inuvik, N.W.T. X0E 0T0, (403) 979–3756.

SEASONAL EVENTS. Iqaluit: *Toonik Tyme:* The arrival of spring in Iqaluit is marked by a carnival called Toonik Tyme. The week-long fiesta is filled with events: contests in seal skinning, igloo building, ice sculpturing, and the toughest power toboggan race of the world. The highlight is the choosing of a Mr. Toonik and a Queen held in late April. Write: Secretary Manager, Town Office, Iqaluit, N.W.T. XOA OHO.

PACKAGE TOURS. See under Practical Information for the District of Mackenzie.

THE DISTRICT OF KEEWATIN

Lying alongside the Province of Québec and nestling under the far reaching arm of the District of Franklin is the District of Keewatin. This mass of land and water embraces the whole of the Hudson and James bays and most of the barren lands of the Central Northern Plain. Its principal communities lie along the coast of the Hudson Bay and the Arctic Ocean.

The Hudson Bay was named after Henry Hudson, who sailed into it in 1611 and never returned. What happened to him is a matter for speculation and has become one of the mysteries that stays locked in the bosom of that fog-shrouded, ghost-inhabited inland sea. All that can be conjectured comes from stories handed down from generation to generation by the Inuit who have made their homes on the shores of the Bay.

After Henry Hudson, his son, and several faithful members of his crew were cast adrift by the mutinous crew, they disappeared from the page of factual, recorded history, but reappear in wraithlike fashion in the Inuit stories. The stories agree in a few particulars. A boatload of white men was discovered with all persons on board dead save the youngest—Henry Hudson's son. This boy was taken by the Inuit and tethered among the dogs. They were terrified by this strange apparition, a white-faced animal that looked like a human but could be a god. These new people they called *Kabloona,* which means "bushy eye-browed." One of Henry Hudson's most obvious characteristics was his heavy, bushy eyebrows.

The largest community in the Keewatin is Rankin Inlet, the administrative center.

Inuit are the only indigenous inhabitants of the Keewatin and until this century roamed over the vast inland plain in pursuit of the caribou or sallied onto the Bay's unfriendly waters for walrus, seal, and whale.

The Natives of the far Northern Region of Keewatin, who live on the shores of the Arctic Ocean, were those who saw the Franklin Party trek hopelessly to their death. These Inuit live in the most inaccessible part of Canada's inhabited North. Scarcely half a century has elapsed since missionaries first moved among them, and rare indeed were explorers who encountered them. In 1771 Samuel Hearne plunged north and west from Fort Churchill and reached the mouth of the Coppermine River; no one followed him until half a century or more later, and even then neither the trading companies nor the church reached those elusive, isolated, fascinating people. Today we can reach them by aircraft. The very adventurous tourist can visit their small communities and see an occasional relic of their culture.

Few now live in snowhouses at any time of the year. Occasionally they still build them when overnighting on the trail. Rather large, fully serviced houses have been supplied by the government, schools built, telephones installed, and television made available through Anik, the Canadian communications satellite. Girls wear pantyhose, boys play guitars, and liquor and cigarettes are readily available. In the space of very few years these people have traveled from the use of primitive tools of bone, sinew, and flint to the use of high-powered rifles, aircraft, and electric generators. No more are these people nomadic; no more are whole tribes on the move; no more are teepees being erected or snow-houses built. What they once were is only to be found in their carefully crafted carvings, prints, and garments; occasional relics; and the clear memories of their patriarchs.

Exploring the District of Keewatin

To see the great spreading tundra that sweeps across Canada's north-land, visit the Keewatin. Treeless, forbidding, almost uninhabited, it offers a new experience to those whose life is spent on concrete high-ways and admist the shining glass of thousand highrises.

Although many refer to the tundra as "the Barrens," it is anything but barren. It is a land of rock, low willows, a million streams, thou-sands of lakes thick with fish, vast herds of caribou, small groups of muskox, waterfowl by the millions, and crystal-clear skies flickering with Northern Lights or flashing with sunset colors that finger the entire horizon.

For an exciting and different trip that is of minimum cost, drive as far as Thompson in Northern Manitoba; the road is good all the way and well maintained. Then board a Canadian National train for Fort Churchill. Churchill is on the edge of the tundra and marks the border between the Northwest Territories and the province. Here you can see historic Fort Prince of Wales before moving deep into the territories.

From Churchill catch a plane to any of the small settlements along the coast of Hudson Bay—Calm Air has a scheduled service to most of them. These communities—Whale Cove, Eskimo Point, Rankin Inlet, Coral Harbour, Chesterfield Inlet, and Repulse Bay—are all Inuit villages. In each of them you will be able to visit the local Hud-son's Bay store or Inuit Cooperative, examine local works of art, talk with the native people, and travel into the surrounding area with rented equipment. The largest community, and the one with the best facilities for visitors, is Rankin Inlet. This settlement is a vibrant synthesis of the past and present.

What To Do at Rankin Inlet

Spend a few hours strolling through the town and browsing in the shops examining the Inuit craft and talking with the people. Wander to the lake or the shore of Hudson Bay. Photograph the disused head-frame of the old nickel mine—catch it silouetted against the low-slung midnight sun.

Thirty miles from Rankin Inlet, set in the mist-hung waters of the Hudson Bay, is Marble Island—an island of ghosts. Two centuries ago, 83-year-old James Knight, searching for the Northwest Passage, per-ished on this island together with all the crews of the ships with him. For more than a year those lonely, marooned British stayed alive, but slowly famine, scurvy, and accident destroyed each one until only the blacksmith remained. His body was discovered unburied, not far from the anvil on which he had worked. Legend has grown around the fate of these men, and for the Inuit it is a haunted, cursed land, not to be visited casually. Anyone visiting the island must crawl up the beach on hands and knees or else risk serious misfortune in the coming year. Boats and guides can be rented in Rankin Inlet.

Go in almost any direction and there will be rivers, lakes, or the sea to fish. Arctic char, a most delectable fish ranging in size from four to twenty pounds, and the fighting lake trout, as big as fifty pounds, can both be caught. Even if you are not a keen fisherman, you will enjoy being in this unspoiled country where there need be no noise other than the dip of a paddle and the swish of the canoe moving steadily forward.

Charter either a Peterhead boat or a small aircraft and head for Daly Bay. Quite likely you will see the Inuit out after seal, and perhaps you'll see a walrus.

Here taste life that is similar to the Inuit age-old ways—fishing for food, sleeping in tents, and watching keenly for the appearance of seal and walrus.

In the far north of the District of Keewatin there are three interesting communities, each of which has hotel accommodations: Pelly Bay, Spence Bay, and Gjoa Haven.

Whatever type of holiday you plan to spend in the Keewatin region of the Territories, it is essential that you have warm clothing, rubber boots, and sunglasses.

Practical Information for the District of Keewatin

HOW TO GET THERE. Scheduled air service is provided to each of these locations by *Northwest Territorial Airways Ltd.* Usually these schedules provide for two flights per week. To connect with these services, it is necessary to catch a *Pacific Western Airlines* flight out of one of the major western cities to Yellowknife. Northwest Territorial Airways will take you from there or you can fly all the way with Territorial Airways from Winnipeg.

ACCOMMODATIONS. Due to limited accommodation available in most Northwest Territories communities, please make reservations as early as possible. This is especially necessary for travel in the summer months. All hotels and motels listed in this section are open year-round unless noted otherwise. (At the time of publication, there are no bellhop services in most Northwest Territories hotels.)

Most places accept the following major credit cards: American Express, MasterCard and Visa; others may also be honored. Not all establishments accept credit cards, therefore we suggest you call for information.

BAKER LAKE. Iglu Hotel. Baker Lake, N.W.T. X0C 0A0, (819) 793–2801. Accommodates 55, shared accommodation, private baths. Lounge, dining room seats 50.

CORAL HARBOUR. Esunqarq Motel. Coral Harbour, N.W.T. X0C 0C0, (819) 925–9969. Accommodates 12 in 5 rooms with shared accommodation and baths.

ESKIMO POINT. Tugalik Inn. Eskimo Point, N.W.T. X0C 0E0, (819) 857–2919. Accommodates 22 in 10 rooms with shared accommodation, private baths; TV. Dining room.

GJOA HAVEN. Amundsen Hotel. Gjoa Haven, N.W.T. X0E 1J0, (403) 360–6176. Accommodates 12 in 6 rooms with shared accommodation and baths; TV, radio. Dining room has carving display. $95 and up, single.

PELLY BAY. Koomiut Hotel. Pelly Bay, N.W.T. X0E 1K0, (403) 769–7211. Accommodates 12 in 6 rooms, shared accommodation and baths; TV. Restaurant. Near craft shop.

RANKIN INLET. Rankin Inlet Lodge. Box 190, Rankin Inlet, N.W.T. X0C 0G0, (819) 645–2807. Accommodates 60 in 30 rooms; private baths, telephones. Licensed lounge, dining room. $95 and up, double. The lodge will outfit for fishing, natural history, and sightseeing. Major credit cards.

SANIKILUAQ. Amaulik Motel. Sanikiluaq, Belcher Islands, N.W.T. X0A 0W0, (819) 266–8860. Accommodates 24 in 8 rooms with shared accommodation and baths. $140 single includes meals.

FISHING OUTFITTERS AND LODGES. Canoe Arctic Inc. Box 130, Fort Smith, N.W.T. X0E 0P0, (403) 872–2308. Fly-in canoe trips in remote areas of taiga and tundra including Thelon and Coppermine Rivers. Photograph caribou, white wolves, musk-ox; rich in bird life and fine fishing.

Dubawnt Outpost Camp. Keewatin Arctic Camp Co., 801 P St., Lincoln, NE 68508, (402) 477–9249. Located at Outlet Bay, Dubawnt Lake. Accommodates 6 in 3 heated cabins. All-inclusive package with air charter from Stony Rapids, Sask. Daily maid service, comfortable beds, sleeping bags, meals, guides, boats, gas and motor. Separate dining tent with picture window. Radio at camp. Open July 10-August 30. Trophy lake trout. Observe caribou and musk-ox. Major credit cards.

Henik Lake Lodge. 801 P St., Lincoln, NE 68508, (402) 477–9249. On South Henik Lake, 250 miles northeast of Churchill, Manitoba and 850 miles north of Winnipeg. Open July-Sept. Accommodates 12 with meals, boats, guides, maid service, private baths, electricity, and fish freezer. Arctic char, lake trout, whitefish, and grayling. Observe caribou. Private airstrip.

Kasba Lake Lodge. D.E. Hill, Box 96, Parksville, B.C. V0R 2S0, (604) 248–3572. Located 265 miles (426 km.) northwest of Lynn Lake, Manitoba. Accommodates 38 in heated cabins. Meals served in main dining room. Lake trout, arctic grayling, pike, and whitefish. Fish filleting, freezing, and packaging availabl.e Rates U.S. $1,995 per week, all inclusive, from Saskatoon.

Lynx Tundra Camp. East Wind Arctic Tours & Outfitters Ltd., Box 2728A, Yellowknife, N.W.T. X1A 2R1, (403) 873–2170. Canoe outfitting and guiding services for barren-land trips, on Thelon, Eileen, and Snowdrift Rivers. One week to two months. All-inclusive packages from Yellowknife. Guided backpacking along esker systems in Thelon Valley. Trophy fishing for lake trout, grayling, pike, char.

Neultin Narrows Sub Arctic Camp. Bill and Beth Bennett, Box 1660, Campbellford, Ontario K0L 1L0, (705) 653–3280. In summer, Box 1229, Thompson, Man. R8N 1P1, (204) 284–3247. Just below the tree line, in Keewatin area north of Manitoba on Neultin Lake. Accommodates 10 in tents. Trophy lake trout, grayling, pike. Guests can view the old native camping structures on the nearby island.

Obre Lake Lodge. Lawrence Shewchuk, Box 1844, Red Lake, Ont. P0W 2M0, (807) 727–2450. In a sheltered bay on the shore of Obre Lake, north of the Saskatchewan-Manitoba border. Cabins set in a forested area, up from a sandy beach. Accommodates 14 people. Dining room. Airstrip.

Snowbird Lake Lodge. Snowbird Enterprises Ltd., Box 70184, St. Paul, Minnesota, U.S.A. 55107, (612) 228–9320. Located on Snowbird Lake 439 km. (273 miles) north of Lynn Lake, Manitoba. Accommodation for 20. Good cabins. Guides, boats, motors. Lake trout, arctic grayling, and northern pike.

Windy River Camp. Box 1660, Campbellford, Ontario K0L 1L0, (705) 653–3280. In summer, Box 1229, Thompson, Man. R8N 1P1. On north end of Nueltin Lake. Fastwater fishing for trout and grayling. Accommodates 10. Guests do own cooking. Open July 1 to September 15.

TRANSPORTATION SERVICES. Airlines. Scheduled service: *Air Inuit Ltd.* 9785 Ryan Ave., Dorval, Que. H9P 1A2, (514) 636–9445. Scheduled service to Sanikiluaq from bases in northern Québec.

Calm Air International Ltd. 60 Seal Rd., Thompson, Man. R8N 1S4, (204) 778–6471. HS 748, DC-4, Twin Otter, or Beech 200 service from Churchill, Manitoba to Eskimo Point, Whale Cove, Repulse Bay, Rankin Inlet, Baker Lake, Chesterfield Inlet and Coral Harbour.

First Air Ltd., Iqaluit, N.W.T. X0A 0H0, (819) 979–5810. Service from Coral Harbour to Iqaluit. From Hall Beach to Repulse Bay, Igloolik and Pelly Bay.

Nordair Inc., Box 4000, Montreal International Airport, Dorval, Que. H4Y 1B8, (514) 636–7670. Twice-weekly service from Hall Beach to Resolute, Nanisivik and Arctic Bay.

Northwest Territorial Airways Ltd., Postal Service 9000, Yellowknife, N.W.T. X1A 2R3, (403) 920–2500. Three flights weekly from Yellowknife to Rankin Inlet; two from Iqaluit. Weekly service to Spence Bay, Gjoa Haven, Pelly Bay from Yellowknife.

WHAT TO SEE. These far northern communities will be of special interest to those who enjoy the remote. They offer the chance to see people who, until the middle of this century, knew little about the rest of the world. At **Pelly Bay** there is an aboveground graveyard; a beautiful stone church built with loving care by Father Henry, who first went there in the early thirties; and rugged scenery that seems right for this windswept, icy corner of Canada. Each of these three northern settlements is the home of excellent carvers. Ivory carving is a specialty in Pelly Bay. These carvings can be examined and purchased and you can watch the carvers as they pursue their craft.

TOURIST INFORMATION. For Hudson Bay area write: Travel Keewatin, 272 Park Ave., Thunder Bay, Ont. P7B 1C5, (807) 345–3255. For north shore write: Arctic Coast Tourist Association, Box 91, Cambridge Bay, N.W.T. X0E 0C0, (403) 983–2224.

PACKAGE TOURS. See under Practical Information for the District of Mackenzie

THE DISTRICT OF MACKENZIE

West of the Keewatin is the District of Mackenzie, the best known area of Canada's Northwest Territories. In 1789, the year of the French Revolution, Alexander Mackenzie—one of Canada's great explorers, fur traders, and adventurers—traveled the length of the mighty river that now bears his name. In his wake came traders, Roman Catholic priests, Anglicans, and prospectors. One of the richest fur-bearing areas of Canada was now readied for exploitation.

After the fierce conflict of the Hudson's Bay Company and the Northwesters was resolved, Mackenzie Region became the sole province of the Hudson's Bay Company trader. Apart from a few explorers, individual adventurers, and (after 1850) hardworking missionaries, that vast repository of renewable resources was ignored. The Hudson's Bay Company enjoyed their unchallenged monopoly.

In 1870 the Hudson's Bay Company sold their right to the sole trading privileges in the Northwest Territories, and free traders began to move in. Then the discovery of gold in the Yukon shattered the silence forever. The introduction of steamboats made the Delta accessible, and more and more people invaded that vast land.

In 1919 oil was discovered at Norman Wells, and a decade later Gilbert Labine landed at Great Bear Lake and discovered radium. Things now moved fast. Aircraft were flying mail as far north as Aklavik; prospectors were looking for gold, base metals, and oil; white trappers were spreading into every nook and cranny of the magnificent mountains to the west and the vast expenses of tundra north of the tree line.

Gold was discovered in Yellowknife Bay in the early thirties, and another rush for riches was precipitated. From the prairie dust bowl, the hopefuls came. They came from newly established homesteads in the Peace River region and from every province of Canada and most of the states in America. Yellowknife was born and today is the capital of one and one third of a million square miles.

The Second World War slowed the pace of development in the Mackenzie District until the Japanese threatened the underbelly of Alaska and the need for a source of oil in the north became urgent. With frantic desperation a pipeline was built from Norman Wells to Whitehorse in the Yukon. The war ended as the line was completed, and oil was never pumped through it.

Near the end of the war, more gold was discovered in Yellowknife and a new rush followed the coming of peace. The population of Yellowknife swelled to several thousand, a new town was planned and built, and the foundations laid for the moment in 1967 when it was declared the capital.

As Yellowknife developed, so did other settlements in the Mackenzie River District: Fort Smith (once the capital), Hay River, Fort Simpson, Aklavik, Fort Macpherson, and then the brand-new town of Inuvik in 1960.

In the last few years the pressing need of the world for oil and gas has brought the Mackenzie region into sharp focus. The Dene are seeking a land claims settlement, oil companies are seeking more concessions, and the government is seeking solutions to the innumerable problems all these developments are causing.

Exploring the District of Mackenzie

The proposed Mackenzie Pipeline focused world attention on this area, and most of the settlements were mentioned by name on national and international radio and television. It is the most developed region of the Northwest Territories and the location of several of the Territories' largest communities, Yellowknife being both the biggest and the only city in a million-and-a-third square miles. It is the territorial capital.

How To Get There

Nearly all the communities can be reached by scheduled airline, and those that cannot are within easy reach of small chartered aircraft. The southern terminus for airline trips to the Mackenzie region is Edmonton. Pacific Western operates a fleet of jet aircraft that ensures fast, efficient service to Fort Smith, Hay River, Yellowknife, Norman Wells, and Inuvik. Feeder lines from these centers offer scheduled service to almost every other community in the Mackenzie, and where there is no such service, settlements can be reached by using small chartered aircraft.

Not only is the Mackenzie region easily accessible by air, but it is also feasible to drive to this part of the Northwest Territories. The road from Edmonton passes through such fascinating places as Whitecourt, Fox Creek, Peace River, High Level, and Indian Cabins on its way to the southern border of the Northwest Territories. Once in the territories, the Mackenzie Highway branches into an enticing system of roads, generally in such good condition as to surprise travelers. They reach the Slave River, the Northern Peace, cross the Hay and the Yellowknife, and provide free ferry service over the Liard and mammoth Mackenzie. The newly-built Liard Highway leaves the Alaska Highway just north of Fort Nelson, B.C., and follows the Liard River Valley north to meet the Mackenzie Highway 35 miles south of Fort Simpson.

Enjoy a Driving-Camping Tour

In this part of the Territories, you can take with you all those things that you might like to have along. Trailers, motor homes, boats, canoes —the many extras that make camping comfortable and more acceptable—need not be left behind. You do not have to be an expert outdoorsman to enjoy an exciting, fun-filled trip on the Mackenzie's roads, rivers, and lakes.

Before setting out on these northern gravel roads, be sure your vehicle is in good condition. It is the practice of seasoned travelers on these roads to carry extra gasoline and an extra spare tire, to cover the headlights with plastic, ensure the windshield (flying gravel from passing trucks not infrequently cracks them), protect the gas tank with a thick rubber sheath (ideal for this is a length of old conveyor belt), and take along a shovel, an axe, matches, a sleeping bag, and some food. These latter items are especially important if you are planning a winter trip when temperatures could drop very suddenly to minus forty degrees Fahrenheit *or* Celsius.

Note: If you have a trailer and a boat or put a canoe on top of your car, you will find endless opportunities to paddle or run your outboard in placid lakes and smooth, flowing rivers.

When driving north to Yellowknife, you drive through some of the world's finest fishing country. Should you never have fished in your life, now you have a chance—toss in a line and lure and watch northern pike, pickerel, and grayling fight for the hook.

The Mackenzie Highway

The Mackenzie Highway stretches one thousand miles from Edmonton to Yellowknife. Its hundreds of miles of wilderness, lakes, rivers, waterfalls, frontier settlements, and campgrounds provide challenge and interest all the way. (For those who do not like tents, trailers, or motor homes, there are motels and hotels reasonably spaced along the length of the highway.)

Once inside the Territories a variety of choice is open to you. You can drive the network of roads that links Fort Smith, Hay River, Pine Point, Enterprise, Fort Simpson, and Yellowknife, or you can hurry north to the mammoth Mackenzie and the Ingraham Trail that pushes out of Yellowknife to nowhere through what one writer called "a fish-laden Precambrian delight."

At Fort Smith you can visit the Wood Buffalo National Park, home for herds of northern bison and the almost extinct whooping crane; at Pine Point view the open pit mine of the biggest lead-zinc producer in North America; in Hay River watch the Northern Transportation riverboats preparing for their journey to the Arctic Ocean and all the while enjoy the forest. Watch for wildlife. Many animals can be seen by the alert observer—bear, wolf, lynx, and coyote to mention but a few. And be sure to train your glasses on the eagles that can be frequently seen soaring watchfully over the Great Slave Lake.

From Hay River drive to Fort Providence. Here you can buy beautifully worked pictures of dyed moose hair and garments of fur and skin, then move on to Rae, home of the Dogrib Indians (the largest Dene community in the north).

From there it is but seventy miles to Yellowknife, Canada's newest capital. Here is a modern city with high-rise buildings, hotels, restaurants, a museum, an old and new town, two gold mines, and a busy dock.

While in Yellowknife it would be a good idea to replenish your supplies. The city offers the best choice of stores in the north and, as a rule, the most competitive prices.

In Yellowknife

Guided bus tours of the city are available. These usually take about two hours and will give you a quick introduction to its exotic history. Tour information is available from the Yellowknife Chamber of Commerce, Box 906, Yellowknife, N.W.T. X1A 2N7, (403) 920–4944.

Boat trips on the Great Slave Lake. Four commercial companies offer a variety of cruises: Frontier Tours, Box 400, Yellowknife, N.W.T. X1A 2N3, (403) 873–4892; Raven Tours, Box 385, Yellowknife, N.W.T. X1A 2N3, (403) 873–4776; Snowcraft Cruises, Box 2006, Yellowknife, N.W.T. X1A 2P5, (403) 873–8858; and Yellowknife Traders, 2 Lessard Dr., Yellowknife, N.W.T. X1A 2G5, (403) 873–3020.

Charter air companies have immediately available aircraft to fly you to a lake or river of your choice, 10 miles away or 1,000 miles away. If you have time, a visit to one of the many beautiful, uninhabited lakes should be a priority.

When you leave Yellowknife and start the long drive south, plan to stay at all those places missed on the way north. With careful planning, and that's the secret of a successful trip into the Mackenzie region, you should not miss many of the interesting things there are to see and do when driving and camping along its highways.

Note: Camping permits are required for use of N.W.T. campgrounds and picnic areas at a cost ranging from $5 to $7 per day. Firewood, fireplaces, picnic tables, and washroom facilities are provided.

Adventure by Boat or Canoe

The Mackenzie River, one of the mightiest rivers in the world, can be traveled by canoe, kayak, speedboat, cabin cruiser, and even raft. More than a few northerners have used crude but serviceable craft to reach the far-off communities of Inuvik, Aklavik, and Fort Macpherson. Boats can be easily launched at Fort Providence or Fort Simpson and returned from the Arctic aboard one of the many Northern Transportation barges. Throughout the summer, tugs ply the river carrying a year's supplies to settlements and oil companies. Barges being brought up river are empty, so it is easy to have boats loaded and returned south. On the way down river, stops can be made at every settlement and supplies replenished. Food you have purchased can be supplemented with fish.

At the mouths of most of the creeks and rivers, grayling and pickerel can be caught, and should they not grab for your hook, you can be sure the ubiquitous northern pike will be there to swallow it.

Keep your eyes open wide for birds and beasts. Bear, moose, and larger game animals are only occasionally seen, but there are birds by the thousand: sandpipers, falcons, eagles, many kinds of geese, and more than twenty-five species of ducks. If you plan to travel the Mackenzie, you should allow two or three weeks for the trip.

Placid rivers, wide lakes, and torrential mountain streams all beckon to the boating and canoeing enthusiasts. In the Territories there is something for everyone who loves the water: tiny forest-ringed lakes within easy reach of every community; wide, windswept bodies of water closely akin to inland seas that demand seaworthy boats, navigational charts, and skillful seamanship; placid rivers that the most amateur of canoeists can enjoy safely; and rushing torrential mountain streams that challenge the experts, demanding the utmost in skill and determination. U-paddle canoes and kayaks are available in the Territories, as are small boats equipped with outboard motors. Canoes can be rented from the Hudson's Bay Company in much the same way as cars can in the south. A canoe may be picked up at one store and delivered to another. This makes a trip downriver possible without the arduous task of paddling back upstream. Arrangements for this type of rental should be made well in advance through Hudson's Bay Company, Northern Stores Department, 77 Main St., Winnipeg, Man. R3C 2R1, (204) 943–0880. Matters would be made especially simple if you have a credit card from "The Bay."

Should you want one of the greatest canoe experiences offered in Canada, then travel the South Nahanni River. This river has been made famous through books, legends, and films. It is an awesome river, tearing through rapids, plunging over the spectacular Virginia Falls (321 feet), twisting through canyons under 2,000-foot cliffs, wandering over spreading mud flats, and slipping by hot springs that may one day become a mecca for tourists. Excellent maps can be obtained from the government of Northwest Territories as well as interesting, essential descriptions of the river's hazards.

For less expert canoeists, why not follow the steps of Sir John Franklin and travel up the Yellowknife River, or paddle the shores of the innumerable lakes. The options are almost unlimited. In the old days, many trappers and hunters used to move from the Great Slave Lake to Great Bear Lake. This is a long trip, but one that can be made by determined persons who can read maps and like hard work. There are no serious hazards on the way. Distance makes careful preparation essential.

Should you prefer to be a passenger, a variety of choices is open to you. There are boat cruises on Great Slave Lake. These can be arranged for a few hours, a few days, or several weeks.

Hunting and Fishing

Presidents and royalty have come to the Northwest Territories to hunt and fish. Trout of such size that fishermen don't have to exaggerate are waiting to be lured from the depths of Great Slave Lake and the ice-cold waters of Great Bear Lake. Grayling, pickerel and northern pike will fight for your hook. If it is fish you are after, the Northwest Territories is the place to come. There are more than fifty fishing lodges and outfitters operating in the Territories, most of them in the Mackenzie region. Licenses are available in all communities. For the hunter, there is an impressive list of animals to be sought: black bear, grizzly, moose, Dall sheep, mountain goat, polar bear, musk-ox, and woodland caribou.

Because regulations for hunting are subject to change at short notice, it is advisable to contact the government office in Yellowknife for up-to-date information. Write to TravelArctic, Yellowknife, N.W.T. X1A 2L9. All nonresident hunters are required to use a licensed outfitter. Throughout the Mackenzie Region at all the strategic locations there are well-equipped outfitters who engage excellent guides. For hunting information and regulations write: Department of Renewable Resources, Government of the N.W.T., Box 1320, Yellowknife, N.W.T. X1A 2L9, (403) 920–8716.

Practical Information for the District of Mackenzie

TRANSPORTATION SERVICES. Bus Service: For those wishing to enjoy the Mackenzie Highway and who would prefer to leave the driving to someone else, there is a regularly scheduled, modern bus service operating over the highway except to Yellowknife and Rae during a 6-week period in the late fall and early spring, when freeze-up and breakup of the Mackenzie River occur.

Canadian Coachways System, 10324–103 Street, Edmonton, Alta., (403) 421 –4211. Daily services between Edmonton and Hay River via Peace River. Connections for Fort Providence, Rae, Edzo, and Yellowknife at Enterprise three times weekly, via N.W.T. Coachlines. Fares and schedules through any Greyhound Lines office or agency.

Frontier Coachlines, Box 400, Yellowknife, N.W.T. X1A 2N3, (403) 873–2911. Three-times-weekly service between Yellowknife and Hay River, with connections via Greyhound Lines to the south.

North of 60 Bus Lines, Hay River, N.W.T. X0E 0R0, (403) 874–6411. Service from Hay River to Pine Point and Fort Smith daily except Sundays and holidays.

Airlines. *Scheduled Services:*

Air Providence Ltd. Fort Providence, N.W.T. X0E 0L0, (403) 699–3551. Connecting Fort Providence to Yellowknife, Fort Simpson, and Hay River.

Kenn Borek Air Ltd. Box 1159, Inuvik, N.W.T. X0E 0T0, (403) 979–3937. Scheduled service from Inuvik to Aklavik, Fort McPherson, Tuktoyaktuk, Sachs Harbour, Paulatuk, Holman, and Coppermine.

Nahanni Air Services Ltd. Bag Service 2300, Norman Wells, N.W.T. X0E 0V0, (403) 587–2288. Norman Wells to Fort Good Hope, Fort Franklin, Fort Norman, Colville Lake, and Inuvik.

Northwest Territorial Airways Ltd. Postal Service 9000, Yellowknife, N.W.T. X1A 2R3, (403) 920–2500. Daily service from Yellowknife to Edmonton and Winnipeg. Regular service to Fort Simpson, Fort Nelson, B.C., Norman Wells, Rankin Inlet, Iqaluit, Coppermine, Cambridge Bay, Holman, Spence Bay, Gjoa Haven, Pelly Bay.

Pacific Western Airlines. 2800–700 2nd St. S.W., Calgary, Alta. T2P 2N2, (403) 294–2000. Scheduled jet passenger and cargo service from Edmonton and Calgary to Yellowknife and points north and east.

Ptarmigan Airways Ltd. Box 66, Yellowknife, N.W.T. X1A 2N1, (403) 873–4461. Scheduled service from Yellowknife to Lac La Martre, Rae Lakes, Snowdrift, Fort Resolution, Pine Point, and Hay River.

Ram Air Charter Ltd. Box 1530, Inuvik, N.W.T. X0E 0T0, (403) 979–3341. From Inuvik to Aklavik, Tuktoyaktuk, Fort McPherson, and Old Crow, Yukon.

Trans North Air. Box 4338, Whitehorse, Y.T. Y1A 3R1, (403) 668–2177. Inuvik from Mayo, Old Crow, and Whitehorse.

Other Scheduled Airlines: Air Canada serves the northern gateway airports of Edmonton, Winnipeg, and Montréal. *CP Air* serves Whitehorse as well as these 3 cities. A number of United States and other foreign airlines serve Canadian international airports, enabling travelers to easily reach their Northwest Territories destinations in comfort via modern airliners. Your travel agent can recommend the easiest route to the North.

CHARTER SERVICE. Charter aircraft, to take you into isolated settlements and historically famous Arctic adventure areas, are also conveniently available on reasonable advance notice. Charter aircraft rates are scaled according to the size of the aircraft used. Whether yours is a two-person or a busload, the most economically suitable aircraft can easily be chartered.

Adlair Aviation Ltd. Box 2946, Yellowknife, N.W.T. X1A 2R2, (403) 873–5161. Aircraft also based in Cambridge Bay.

Aero Arctic Helicopters Ltd., Box 1496, Yellowknife, N.W.T. X1A 2P1, (403) 873–5230. Aircraft and helicopters.

Air Providence Ltd. Fort Providence, N.W.T. X0E 0L0, (403) 699–3551.

Aklavik Flying Service Ltd. Box 1158, Inuvik, N.W.T. X0E 0T0, (403) 979–3190.

Buffalo Airways Ltd. Box 1479, Hay River, N.W.T. X0E 0R0, (403) 874–3333.

Carter Air Services Ltd. Box 510, Hay River, N.W.T. X0E 0R0, (403) 874–2281.

Edzo Air. Box 56, Rae, N.W.T. X0E 0Y0, (403) 371–3226. Wheels, skis, floats, aerial photography.

Fort Smith Air Services Ltd. Box 1017, Fort Smith, N.W.T. X0E 0P0, (403) 872–2312.

Inuvik Coastal Airways Ltd. Box 2629, Inuvik, N.W.T. X0E 0T0, (403) 979–3372.

Landa Aviation. Box 183, Hay River, N.W.T. X0E 0R0, (403) 874–3500. Wheels, skis, floats.

Latham Island Airways. Box 791, Yellowknife, N.W.T. X1A 2N6, (403) 920–2891.

La Ronge Aviation Services Ltd. Box 2489, Yellowknife, N.W.T. X1A 2P8, (403) 873–5330. Also based in La Ronge, Saskatchewan.

Liard Air Ltd. Box 3190, Fort Nelson, B.C. V0C 1R0, (604) 774–2909. Only air charter company based at Blackstone Landing, a convenient departure point for flights into Nahanni National Park.

Nahanni Air Services Ltd. Bag Service 2300, Norman Wells, N.W.T. X0E 0V0, (403) 587–2288. Arctic and mountain specialists.

Ptarmigan Airways Ltd. Box 66, Yellowknife, N.W.T. X1A 2N1, (403) 873–4461.

Ram Air Charter Ltd. Box 1530, Inuvik, N.W.T. X0E 0T0, (403) 979–3341.

Simpson Air Ltd. Box 260, Fort Simpson, N.W.T. X0E 0N0, (403) 695–2505. Wheels, skis, floats.

Wolverine Air Ltd. Box 316, Fort Simpson, N.W.T. X0E 0N0, (403) 695–2263. Charters to Nahanni National Park, Mackenzie Mountains.

 ACCOMMODATIONS. Due to limited accommodation available in most Northwest Territories communities, please make reservations as early as possible. This is especially necessary for travel in the summer months. All hotels and motels in this section are open year-round unless noted otherwise. (At the time of publication, there are no bellhop services in most Northwest Territories hotels.)

Most places accept the following major credit cards: American Express, MasterCard and Visa; others may also be honored. Not all establishments accept credit cards, therefore we suggest you call for information.

AKLAVIK. McLeod's Motel. Box 36, Aklavik, N.W.T. X0E 0A0, (403) 978–2218. Accommodates 10 in log building with shared accommodation and baths; kitchettes, TV.

COPPERMINE. Coppermine Inn. Coppermine, N.W.T. X0E 0E0, (403) 982–3333. Accommodation for 38 in 11 rooms, 5 A-frames, 2 motel units with shared accommodation and baths; TV. Dining room.

ENTERPRISE. Motel El Camino. Box 277, Hay River, N.W.T. X0E 0R0, (403) 984–3501. Accommodates 24 in 8 rooms, 6 with private bath. $30 and up, single. Service station, licensed lounge, general store, ice, and propane. Open all year. Near scenic spots: Louise Falls, Alexandra Falls, Escarpment Creek, the Hart Lake Fire Tower, and Lady Evelyn Falls on the Kakisa River.

FORT LIARD. HRY Holdings. Fort Liard, N.W.T. X0G 0A0, (403) 770–4441. Accommodates 12 in 8 air-conditioned rooms; private baths, 4 kitchenettes, TV. Craft shop, service station. Open all year. $59.50 and up, single.

FORT NORMAN. Bear Lodge. Fort Norman, N.W.T. X0E 0K0, (403) 588–4311. Accommodates 13 in 7 rooms with shared accommodation and baths. Arrange meals and rooms in advance. Overlooking Mackenzie River. Northwest Territories' oldest church nearby.

FORT PROVIDENCE. Big River Motel. Fort Providence, N.W.T. X0E 0L0, (403) 699–4301. On Highway 3 at junction to Fort Providence. Accommodates 22 in 6 units. Service station, meals, lounge, TV, laundry. $40 and up, single. Major credit cards.
Snowshoe Inn. Fort Providence, N.W.T. X0E 0L0, (403) 699–3511. Modern facilities overlooking the mighty Mackenzie River. Open all year. Accommodation for 63 in 35 units; private baths, telephones, TV, radio, kitchenettes. Cafe, licensed lounge, general store. The home of moosehair tufting and porcupine quill weaving. Fishing nearby. Major credit cards.

FORT SIMPSON. Fort Simpson Hotel. Box 248, Fort Simpson, N.W.T. X0E 0N0, (403) 695–2201. Located at the confluence of the Mackenzie and Liard rivers. Open all year. All-weather road to all points south. Accommodates 70 in 35 units; private baths, telephones, TV with cablevision. Restaurant, licensed air-conditioned dining room, cocktail lounge; ample parking and plug-ins.

FORT SMITH. Pelican Rapids Inn. Box 52, Fort Smith, N.W.T. X0E 0P0, (403) 872–2789. In downtown Fort Smith. Modern with all conveniences. 50 rooms with private baths, telephone, radio, TV, plug-ins, kitchenettes. Restaurant across the street. Major credit cards.
Pinecrest Hotel. Box 127, Fort Smith, N.W.T. X0E 0P0, (403) 872–2104. Accommodates 48 in 28 rooms, private and shared baths, TV, telephone. Cafe, licensed lounge. Open all year.

HAY RIVER. Caribou Motor Inn. Box 1114, Hay River, N.W.T. X0E 0R0, (403) 874–6706. In the new section of Hay River. Open all year. Accommodates 90 in 29 rooms; private baths, telephone, TV, plug-ins, kitchenettes. Licensed dining room, lounge. Major credit cards. $45 and up, single.
Migrator Motel. Box 1847, Hay River, N.W.T. X0E 0R0, (403) 874–6792. Accommodates 96 in 24 rooms; private baths, TV, telephone, plug-ins, kitchenettes. Movies available. $42 and up, single.
Ptarmigan Inn. Box 1000, Hay River, N.W.T. X0E 0R0, (403) 874–6781. Accommodates 164 in 41 air-conditioned rooms; private baths, satellite TV, radio, telephone. Lounge, cafe, licensed dining room. $62.50 and up, single. Major credit cards.

INUVIK. Eskimo Inn. Box 1740, Inuvik, N.W.T. X0E 0T0, (403) 979–2801. Open all year in downtown Inuvik. Accommodates 156 in 78 rooms, some with air-conditioning; private baths, refrigerators, telephone, satellite TV. Cocktail lounge, licensed dining room, cafe, smoke shop, craft store. $85 and up, single.
Finto Motor Inn. Box 1925, Inuvik, N.W.T. X0E 0T0, (403) 979–2647. Located at junction of Marine Bypass and Mackenzie Road. Accommodates 70; telephone, satellite TV, radio, refrigerators, laundry, truck rentals, plug-ins. $85 and up, single. Anton's licensed dining open for breakfast, lunch, dinner (French cuisine). Major credit cards.
Mackenzie Hotel. Box 1618, Inuvik, N.W.T. X0E 0T0, (403) 979–2861. Accommodates 60 in 32 rooms. 2 licensed lounges, coffee shop, licensed dining room, 150-seat night club. Open all year. $70 and up, single.

NORMAN WELLS. Mackenzie Valley Hotel. Box 125, Norman Wells, N.W.T. X0E 0V0, (403) 587–2511. Open all year. Accommodates 33 in 22 rooms; private baths, telephone, TV. French cuisine and pizza at licensed dining lounge and restaurant; gift shop. Vehicle rentals. The best in hospitality and meals are always available.
Rayuka Inn. Box 308, Norman Wells, N.W.T. X0E 0V0, (403) 587–2354. Accommodation for 20 in 10 rooms; private baths, telephone, TV, radio. Cafe, 2 licensed lounges.

PINE POINT. Pine Point Hotel. Box 148, Pine Point, N.W.T. X0E 0W0, (403) 393–2851. Accommodates 60 in 30 rooms, 6 suites; private baths, TV, radio, telephone. Licensed dining room, cocktail lounge, ice. $62 and up, single. Major credit cards. Nearby attractions include tours of the lead and zinc mine.

TUKTOYAKTUK. Hotel Tuk Inn. Box 193, Tuktoyaktuk, N.W.T. X0E 1C0, (403) 977–2381. Located on the main road between the airport and Tuktoyaktuk, just a stone's throw from the Arctic Ocean. Accommodates 35 in 15 rooms; private baths, TV, radio, telephone, kitchenettes. $95 and up, single. Airport limousine. Local tours, crafts available. Magnificent view of the pingos. Nigevik Restaurant features French, Italian, and local cuisine.

Pingo Park Lodge. Bag 6000, Tuktoyaktuk, N.W.T. X0E 1C0, (403) 977–2155. Near the ocean. 24 rooms, TV. Dining room. Harbor and pingo tours arranged.

YELLOWKNIFE. Explorer Hotel. Postal Service 7000, Yellowknife, N.W.T. X1A 2R3, (403) 873–3531. Accommodates 220 in 110 rooms in downtown area. Private baths, cable TV, telephone, air-conditioning. Executive suites with room service available. Airport courtesy van. Licensed dining room, lounges, cafe, gift shop. $99 and up, single. Major credit cards.

Gold Range Hotel. Box 698, Yellowknife, N.W.T. X1A 2N5, (403) 873–4441. Located in downtown Yellowknife. Open all year. Accommodates 72 in 42 rooms, 18 with private baths. All have telephones, TV.

Twin Pine Motor Inn. Box 596, Yellowknife, N.W.T. X1A 2N4, (403) 873–8511. This 44-room motel is located halfway between the old town of Yellowknife and the present city center. Accommodates 100 with breakfast service, kitchenettes, private baths, telephone, TV, radio. Major credit cards.

Yellowknife Inn. Box 490, Yellowknife, N.W.T. X1A 2N4, (403) 873–2601. Accommodates 300 in 150 rooms with telephones, TV, radio, ice. Open all year in the city center. Licensed dining room, lounge, cafe, tavern. Major credit cards. This is where the Northwest Territories Legislative Assembly meets.

YWCA. 5004 54th St. at Franklin, Yellowknife, N.W.T. X1A 2R6, (403) 920–2777. 33 furnished bachelor apartments; radio, TV. Also, hostel accommodation. Reservations accepted with daily, weekly, and monthly rates. Located within two blocks of restaurants, shopping, business, and theater. Complimentary morning coffee or tea; laundromat. In spite of its name, facilities are coed.

 FISHING OUTFITTERS AND LODGES. Arctic Circle Lodge. Box 503, Edmonton, Alta. T5J 2K1, (403) 458–3383. On Great Bear Lake, only 14 miles (22.4 kms.) from the Arctic Circle. Under all new management. Fishing for trophy lake trout, grayling, side trips for arctic char. All new boats and motors, excellent cuisine. Accommodates 34. All-inclusive from Edmonton.

Bathurst Inlet Lodge. Box 820, Yellowknife, N.W.T. X1A 2N6, (403) 873–2595. A small Inuit community north of the Arctic Circle. Hike to spectacular waterfalls and travel in comfort on the Arctic Ocean, retracing the paths of early explorers. Raft the Burnside River. Visit bird islands with nesting eider ducks, gulls, and loons. Fish for arctic char, lake trout, grayling. Bathurst caribou herd, musk-ox, grizzly, wolves, peregrine and gyrfalcon. For Arctic adventurers of all ages. All-inclusive weekly rate from Yellowknife. June 25-Aug. 15.

Blackford Lake Lodge. Taiga Sports Fishing Ltd., Box 1568, Yellowknife, N.W.T. X1A 2P2, (403) 873–3303. Located on Blackford Lake 96 kms. (60 miles) east of Yellowknife. Accommodates 10 in comfortable log cabins. Sauna and ice house. Excellent fishing: trout, walleye, northern pike, and whitefish. Food, fishing gear and sleeping bags must be brought by guests. Multiseason family and group rates available on request.

Brabant Lodge. Box 1095, Hay River, N.W.T. X0E 0R0; (403) 874–2600. On an island in the Mackenzie River 32 miles (51 kms.) by air from Hay River. Will accommodate up to 36 guests in comfortable cabins with modern plumbing or in lodge containing twin bedrooms. Boats, motors, fuel, cold storage, meals, and lodging provided. Cocktail lounge, telephone, guide service, and angling equipment available. Fishing excellent. Arctic grayling, pickerel, northern pike, whitefish. Side trips arranged. Hunting duck and goose in September. Open June 20-Sept. 15. Group rates available on request.

Branson's Lodge. Box 2600, Spruce Grove, Alta. T0E 2C0, (403) 962–6363. East side of Great Bear Lake, 5 miles (8 kms.) from Port Radium, scenic protected waters. Open July and August. Accommodation for 40. Carpet throughout; modern plumbing and heating. Licensed lounge. Side trips for arctic char, grayling, trout, Inuit villages. Visit abandoned mine, other local historic attractions. Licenses available. Convention facilities.

Colville Lake Lodge. B. W. Brown, Colville Lake, N.W.T. X0E 0H0. Located on south end of Colville Lake, 36 miles (58 kms.) above the Arctic Circle. Main lodge, situated in Hareskin Dene community, accommodates 12. Dining room. Four twin-engined boats. Outpost camp 25 miles (40 kms.) farther north has 2 cabins, boats, motors. Twenty-four hour fishing for trout and arctic grayling. Canoeing and camping equipment available. Log museum of native artifacts and gallery of Northern art.

Drum Lake Lodge. Paul Wright, Fort Norman, N.W.T. X0E 0K0, (403) 588–3161. Located on Wrigley Lake. Open June 15 to October 15. Accommodates 9. Lake trout, arctic grayling, and Dolly Varden. Fishing tackle available. Hunting trips arranged for N.W.T. residents. Private 1,000-foot (305 m.) airstrip.

Frontier Fishing Lodge. (Jerry Bricker's). Frontier Fishing Tours Ltd., Box 4550, Edmonton, Alta. T6E 5G4, (403) 433–4914. At Snowdrift on the east arm of Great Slave Lake, 115 miles (185 km.) from Yellowknife; 2,300-foot airstrip. Open mid-June to Mid-September. Accommodates 24 in lodge and cabins. Dining room, licensed facilities, sauna. Lake trout, arctic grayling, northern pike, and whitefish. Walk-in fish freezing facilities. Fish packed for return trip.

Great Bear Lake Lodge. (Plummer's). 1110 Sanford St., Winnipeg, Man. R3E 2Z9, (204) 774–5775. On Dease Arm. Open July and August. Accommodates 54 in 16 cabins with showers, flush toilets. Rates include charter flight and return from Winnipeg, boats, motors, fuel, guides, angling equipment, and cold storage. Dining room, telephone. Lake trout and arctic grayling. Plane at lodge for side trips to Tree River on Arctic Coast for char; 5,000-foot (1,524 m.) airstrip.

Great Bear Lodge. Box 2555, Yellowknife, N.W.T. X1A 2P9, (403) 920–2023. On Leith Peninsula on Great Bear Lake. Open July and August. Accommodates 54 at main lodge, outpost camp, and Neiland Bay Camp; Rates include boat, motors, guides, food, and lodging. Modern facilities, forced air heat, bar and rec room, native handicrafts, microwave telephone, 5,000-foot (1,800-m.) airstrip; lake trout, pike. Side-trips available for char and grayling.

Great Bear Trophy Lodge. Box 167, Norman Wells, N.W.T. X0E 0V0, (403) 587–2287. In Ford Bay on Smith Arm, west side of Great Bear Lake at Arctic Circle. Open July and August. Accommodates 44 in 22 rooms with bath, twin beds, electricity, wall-to-wall carpets. Rates are all-inclusive, Saskatoon return. Dining room, bar, lounge, commissary, telecommunications, boats, motors, and guides; 4,800-foot airstrip. Lake trout, arctic grayling, northern pike. Native villages and wild animals nearby. Charters arranged.

Great Slave Lake Lodge. Chummy Plummer, 1110 Sanford St., Winnipeg, Man. R3E 2Z9, (204) 772–8833. At Taltheilei Narrows, 90 miles (145 kms.) east of Yellowknife. Open June 15 to August 30. Accommodates 44. Charter propjet from and to Winnipeg. Private 5,200-foot (1,585-m.) airstrip. Meals, guides, boats, motors, gas, and care of fish. Modern plumbing, two-way radio, ice, bar, dining room. Lake trout, arctic grayling, northern pike, flyout for walleye.

Hanging Ice Fishing Lodge. Box 148, Pine Point, N.W.T. X0E 0W0, (403) 393–2851. New lodge northeast of Fort Smith, N.W.T. Lake trout, pickerel, northern pike. Opportunity to visit Fort Smith's *Northern Life Museum.* Lodge open May to October. Bring tackle. Boats, life jackets, linen supplied. Smokehouse, barbecue. Trophy fishing at Talston Lake outpost camp.

Indian Mountain Fishing Lodge. Box 687, Lumsden, Sask. S0G 3C0, (306) 731–3551. At McLeod Bay on Great Slave Lake. Open July and August. Accommodates 10 persons in 5 cabins. Float base. Guests arrange own float-plane transport. Superb trout and arctic grayling. Radiophone.

Namushka Lodge. Box 2304, Yellowknife, N.W.T. X1A 2P7, (403) 920–2495. On Harding Lake, 32 air miles (51 km.) east of Yellowknife. There are cooking facilities but guests prepare their own food. Lodge has showers, baths, boats and motors, fish freezer. Fish for lake trout, pike, walleye, and whitefish. Open June-Sept. Rockhounding, hiking, birdwatching (bald eagles).

Nonacho Lake Fishing Camp. Merlyn Carter, Carter Air Service Ltd., Box 510, Hay River, N.W.T. X0E 0R0, (403) 874–2281. On Nonacho Lake 200 miles (322 kms.) east of Hay River. Lake trout and northern pike. Cabin accommodation. Boats, motors, gas, sleeping bags, and housekeeping facilities (everything except food and fish tackle) supplied. Side trips can be arranged.

Pilot Lake Cabins. Kelly Clarke, Box 1283, Vermillion, Alta. T0B 4M0, (403) 853–2704. Fly-in cabins on Pilot Lake just 35 miles from Fort Smith. Boats, motors, and guide service available. Accommodates 15 in housekeeping cabins. The fishing is great, and it's an interesting place for rockhounds. Guests must supply their own fishing tackle and food. June 15-Sept. 15.

Prelude Lake Lodge. Box 2548, Yellowknife, N.W.T. X1A 2P8. On Prelude Lake, 20 road miles (32 kms.) east of Yellowknife. Open May 15 September 30. Accommodates 15 guests. Two- and 3-bed housekeeping cabins. Boats and rafts may be rented at hourly rate which includes gas and safety equipment. Restaurant, ice, tackle store, licensed dining lounge. Falls on Cameron River nearby.

Rutledge Lake Lodge. Box 342, Hay River, N.W.T. X0E 0R0, (403) 874–2571. Located 170 miles (274 kms.) east of Hay River. Fishing for lake trout and northern pike. Modern fully equipped housekeeping cabins. Rates include Zodiac boat, motors, gas, life jackets, sleeping bags. All you need is fishing tackle and food.

Sitidgi Lake Fishing Lodge. Andy McInnes, Box 1332, Inuvik, N.W.T. X0E 0T0, (403) 979–3349. 31 miles (51 kms.) from Inuvik. Accommodates 6 persons in 2 tents. Open June 15-Sept. 15; $150 per day, rates include meals and use of boats and motors. Main lodge building includes a dining room. Excellent fishing for lake trout, grayling, pike, whitefish very close by. Photograph moose, caribou, birdlife.

Thubun Lake Lodge. Jack and Bonnie Webb, Box 480, Hay River, N.W.T. X0E 0R0, (403) 874–2950. On Thubun Lake, 140 miles (227 km.) northeast of Hay River. Accommodates 22 in 3 housekeeping cabins. June 1-Sept. 30. Lake trout and northern pike. Boats, motors, gas, life jackets, nets, freezer, showers, telephone. Food, liquor, tackle. Full service guiding available. View bald eagles, peregrine falcons, wildlife.

Trophy Lodge. Reliance Sport Fishing Ltd., Box 670, Yellowknife, N.W.T. X1A 2N5, (403) 873–5420. At Fort Reliance on Great Slave Lake. 160 miles (257 kms.) east of Yellowknife. Open June 25-Sept. 1. Accommodation in housekeeping cabins with showers and fully equipped kitchens. Boats, motors, gas, fish freezing, tackle store. Can arrange charter flights to camp. Lake trout, arctic grayling; nearby attractions include Captain Back's chimneys and Parry Falls.

Trout Lake Dene Lodge. Trout Lake via Fort Simpson, N.W.T. X0E 0N0. Owned and operated by the Slavey Dene, this camp is a naturalist's paradise. It offers sandy beaches and pine forests, a variety of plants and wildlife, good northern fishing, a rare opportunity to observe the traditional ways of the Slavey people, and quiet seclusion at the only camp on the lake. Comfortable accommodation is provided in log housekeeping cabins. Boats, motors, guides, available. Family and group rates available.

Watta Lake Lodge. Arctic Fishing Lodges, Box 806, Yellowknife, N.W.T. X1A 2N6, (403) 873–4036. Located 68 kms. (42 miles) east of Yellowknife. Great fishing. Accommodates 12, plus 5 in tent camp. Open June 1-September 30. Rates $1,275 per week includes round-trip air charter from Yellowknife, boats, motors, meals, guides and some fishing equipment.

VEHICLE RENTALS. Many visitors prefer to fly to communities, then arrange ground transportation locally to see the area. The following is a list of car rental agencies in major centers.

Fort Simpson: *Tilden Rent-A-Car*, (403) 873–2911.

Fort Smith. *Avis Rent-A-Car*, J & M Enterprises, (403) 872–2211. *Tilden Rent-A-Car*, (403) 872–2777.

Hay River. *Hertz Rent-A-Car*, John's Cartage and Rental Services Ltd., (403) 874–6426. *Tilden Rent-A-Car*, (403) 874–6436. *Avis Rent-A-Car*, (403) 874–2571.

Inuvik: *Tilden Rent-A-Car*, (403) 979–3383.

Norman Wells: *Norman Wells Transportation Ltd.*, (403) 587–2416.

Yellowknife: *Avis Rent-A-Car*, Frame & Perkins Ltd., (403) 873–5648. *Tilden Rent-A-Car*, (403) 873–2911. *Hertz Rent-A-Car*, (403) 873–5043. *Budget Rent-A-Car*, (403) 873–3366.

WATER TRANSPORTATION. Cargo. Persons wishing to ship freight, cargo, or personal effects of any size will find that shipment by barge water transport in the Northwest Territories is economical and readily available in the summer.

Arctic Navigation & Transportation, 1900 425 1st St. S.W., Calgary, Alta. Telephone (403) 234–7524. Bases in Hay River, Inuvik, and Tuktoyaktuk.

Coastal Marine Ltd., Box 1778, Inuvik, N.W.T. X0E 0T0, (403) 979–3530. Barge service to the delta and coast.

Northern Transportation Co. Ltd., 9945 108 St., Edmonton, Alberta T5K 2G9. Mackenzie Valley and Hudson Bay Service, Hay River, Norman Wells, Inuvik, and Tuktoyaktuk.

Northwest Transport, Postal Service 7000, Yellowknife, N.W.T. X1A 2R3, (403) 873–3591. Hay River to all points on the Mackenzie River.

The Sportsman. Box 162, Yellowknife, N.W.T. X1A 2N3, (403) 873–2911.

Passengers. *Mackenzie River Cruises,* Box 65, Fort Simpson, N.W.T. X0E 0N0, (403) 695–2506. Explore miles and miles of virgin wilderness during an 8-day cruise on the Mackenzie. Choose upstream from Inuvik or downstream from Fort Simpson. Operates June through Sept. Travel by comfortable diesel-powered riverboat. Rates are $995 per person round-trip.

CANOES AND BOATS. Boats and motors can be rented on the spot in some communities; or large boats, complete with guides can be arranged to transport you on fishing or sightseeing jaunts. River trips in the Mackenzie district are an exciting reality this year with the offerings varying from wilderness boat camping to a luxury cruise.

Hudson's Bay Company. Northern Stores Department, 77 Main St., Winnipeg, Manitoba R3C 2R1, (204) 943–0880. Canoes may be rented from the Hudson's Bay Company with advance reservations made through their above address. Arrangements can be made to pick canoes up at one point and leave them at another where there is a Bay post.

TOURIST INFORMATION. For Great Slave and Great Bear Lakes area write: Northern Frontier Visitors Association, Box 1107, Yellowknife, N.W.T. X1A 2N8, (403) 873–3131. For northeast coast (Coppermine and Bathurst Inlet) write: Arctic Coast Tourist Association, Box 91, Cambridge Bay, N.W.T. X0E 0C0, (403) 983–2224. For upper Mackenzie River, Nahanni and Wood Buffalo National Parks write: Big River Travel Association, Box 185, Hay River, N.W.T. X0E 0R0, (403) 874–2422. For lower Mackenzie River and northwest shore write: Western Arctic Visitors Association, Box 1525, Inuvik, N.W.T. X0E 0T0, (403) 979–3756.

SPECIAL EVENTS. Hay River: *Ookpik Carnival:* Three-day carnival, mid-March, events include Ice Carnival, snowshoe and snowmobile races, log sawing, tea making, adult and teen dances, carnival queen contest, games of chance. For further information, write: Chairman, Recreation Board, Town Hall, Hay River, N.W.T. X0E 0R0.

Pine Point: *Karnival Kapers:* Enjoy a weekend after the long winter competing and being involved in the annual winter carnival. Highlight of the weekend is a two-day, 50-mile dogteam race with prizes totaling $2,000. Nail pounding, log sawing, snowmobile races, skating races, tea boiling, and many other novelty events. For further information, write: Karnival Kapers, Pine Point, N.W.T. X0E 0W0.

Tuktoyaktuk: *Beluga Jamboree:* Third week of April, with Inuit skill contests such as harpoon throwing, ice-hole digging, dogteam races, traditional games of physical skill. For further information, write: Hamlet Office, Tuktoyaktuk, N.W.T. X0E 1C0.

Yellowknife: *Caribou Carnival:* Winters are long and dark in Canada's north, but Yellowknife residents forget this aspect and accentuate the positive during the Caribou Carnival. It is a fun-filled three days, with the excitement and color of a local parade to start the action. Competitions are held in everything from ice sculpturing to tea making. Feature attraction is the *Dog Derby Race* open to all dog mushers in North America. To join the festivities, visit Yellowknife the last weekend in March and judge the celebration for yourself. For further information write Caribou Carnival Committee, Box 906, Yellowknife, N.W.T. X1A 2N7.

Annual Midnight Sun Golf Tournament: Gaining popularity as golfers from far and wide participate in this rollicking social event which tees off at midnight, June 21. Contact the President, Yellowknife Golf Club, Box 388, Yellowknife, N.W.T. X1A 2N3, for details and entry forms.

OTHER EVENTS. *Annual Northern Games:* Dates and locations to be announced early in year. A festival of traditional Inuit and Dene sports, dances, drumming, competitions, displays, crafts, and the "Good Woman" contest. Join the celebrations as northern people again gather from the N.W.T., Yukon, and Alaska. Write: Western Arctic Northern Games Association, Box 2656, Inuvik, N.W.T. X0E 0T0.

PACKAGE TOURS. There are many established package tours into the Northwest Territories. Each year new ones are being added.

Arctic Adventure Tour. Fully escorted 14-day holiday by ship, air, and private motorcoach. Visits Yellowknife, Inuvik, Tuktoyaktuk, Dawson City, Whitehorse, and Skagway, plus cruise of inside passage aboard. P & O's *Sun Princess.* Tours depart June, July, and August from Vancouver and Toronto. Write: Horizon Holidays Ltd., Horizon House, 160 John St., Toronto, Ont. M5V 2X8, (416) 585-9911.

Caribou Migration Naturalist Experience. A 5-day package from Yellowknife to a caribou camp on Courageous Lake. View caribou, barren-ground grizzly, possibly wolf, eagles, loons, and tundra flowers. Fishing also an option. Aug. Write: Qaivvik Ltd., Box 1538, Yellowknife, N.W.T. X1A 2P2, (403) 873-2074.

North Pole Expedition. Fly to the North Pole where you land, take photos, and drink a champagne toast. Includes a day in Resolute, two days in Grise Fiord, Eureka Weather Station on Ellesmere Island, and Tanquary Fiord. All-inclusive, 6-day tour from Montreal or Edmonton. For further information write: Canada North Outfitting Inc., Box 1230, Waterdown, Ont. L0R 2H0, (416) 689-7925.

North-West Expeditions Ltd. Raft trips on South Nahanni River. Spectacular scenery. Visits to hot springs. Operates from July to September. Write North-West Expeditions Ltd., 1616 Duranleau St., Vancouver, B.C. V6H 3S4, (604) 669-1100.

Special Odysseys (Special InteresTours). This company offers an interesting package of exciting, exotic tours to the High Arctic. Visit Ellesmere Island, stand at the North Pole, play midnight golf in Yellowknife and travel the sea-ice at Grise Fiord. Write: Special Odysseys, Box 37, Medina, WA 98039, (206) 455-1960.

Trekking in Auyuittuq National Park. Spring skiing trips through Pangnirtung Pass from Broughton Island to Pangnirtung. Apr. to mid-June, special equipment provided. Or backpack in picturesque Auyuittuq. Tours include qualified guide, accommodations, meals, and transportation from Ottawa/Montreal. Write: Tuullik Wilderness Adventures, Box 4201, Station E, Ottawa, Ont. K1S 5B2, (613) 230-8077.

THE YUKON

The Call of the Wild

by
RAY PRICE and MAC MACKAY

Yukon, the name of the river and the Territory, is an Indian word meaning "greatest." Indeed, superlatives are needed to describe the natural beauties of this land of jagged mountains, boundless waterways, infinite varieties of wildlife, and sharply contrasting seasons—a land that still maintains a frontier flavor despite a tumultuous era of exploitation that could have destroyed it forever.

Situated in the far northwest of Canada and extending northward beyond the Arctic Circle to the Beaufort Sea, the Yukon lies between Alaska on the west, the Northwest Territories on the east, and British Columbia on the south. More than twice the size of the British isles, the Yukon has vast mineral wealth within its 482,515 sq. kms. (186,290 square miles). Yet despite the fact that mining is, today, the Yukon's major industry, most of its resources remain unearthed because of its Arctic climate and rugged terrain. Perhaps these are also reasons why the Yukon was among the last areas of North America to attract the European explorer. Still sparsely settled, its population is around 23,-000, mostly concentrated in Whitehorse, its capital city. Fifteen percent are Native Indians; the rest are of European descent or mixed European and Indian stock.

One of the coldest regions in the world, it is a land of long, dark winters, harsh blizzards, and almost impenetrable mountains, rivaling in naked grandeur those in any part of the world. Yet summers are brilliant, shimmering with heat that drives the grizzly and the moose, the lynx and the coyote, the sheep, the mink, the wolf and the wolverine to cool themselves in the ubiquitous streams, pools, and rivers that define the territory.

A River of Gold

The land was shaped by the Yukon River which finds its source a scant 15 miles from the ocean into which it empties after wandering inland for more than 2,000 miles. Beginning high in the St. Elias Mountains, carving its way through the interior of the Territory, and slashing across the heart of Alaska, it finally cascades into Norton Sound through a sprawling delta of muskeg, sand, gravel, and mud. Into this river tumble the sparkling waters of its tributaries—the streams that carried the dust particles and nuggets of gold that were to make the Yukon world famous and thrust it, unprepared, into the industrial age. For gold was everywhere—on the sandbars and shoals scattered along the length of the Yukon; beneath the mud and silt of creeks and rivers whose waters found new channels; and caught in crevices and rocks that lay in the path of the tumbling mountain streams.

Furs before Gold

Before gold became the magnet in the late 19th century, the Yukon was already being exploited for its furs. Russian traders, coming west from their ports on the Alaskan Coast, moved steadily inland and the goods they traded moved faster and farther east. Evidence of Russian products could be found in the Mackenzie Delta and along the Peel and Porcupine Rivers long before the magic word "gold" had been uttered. As deliberately as the Russians moved eastward, so the British owned Hudson's Bay Company moved westward establishing Fort Yukon in 1847 in what is now Alaska. This far northwestern hold of the Hudson's Bay Company had to be relinquished when the Chilkat Indians attacked and destroyed the fort in 1852. As a result, like a snail encountering salt, the Hudson's Bay Company withdrew and entrenched itself more firmly to the east of the Mackenzie and Richardson Mountains.

During the first half of the 19th century as the fur trade flourished in the North, occasional rumors of gold were heard. The Hudson's Bay clerk at Fort Yukon spoke of it, and the Reverend Archdeacon Robert MacDonald, a "country-born" Anglican minister who later married an Indian, was reported to have dug it up by the spoonful; but for neither was gold important. The Company wanted furs and the Reverend was concerned with souls.

It was inevitable that rumors would spread south and that men would push north toward the rumors' source. Moving through the vastness of the Rockies, they trickled steadily into the Yukon.

Strike!

But it was not until 1896 that the first great strike was made by George Carmack, Skookum Jim, and Tagish Charlie who found gold by the fistful in Rabbit Creek, which flows into the Thronduike (hammer water) not far from where it joins the Yukon River. To the prospector, Thronduike became "Klondike" and Rabbit Creek "Bonanza Creek," names that are now synonymous with the world's last great gold rush.

No sooner was the news out than men flocked toward the North from almost every country in the world and by every known route and means of transport. There were three main routes to the Yukon. The most feasible was through Skagway and over the Chilkoot Pass; the second, possible though difficult, was an overland route that went up the crumpled hide of British Columbia; most improbable of all was an inland water route down the Peace, Slave and Mackenzie and up the Peel or Rat, Liard, and Gravel Rivers into the northeastern part of the Yukon.

Dawson City, Boom Town

Gold is an hypnotic word. It lured thousands into incredibly hazardous journeys, all too frequently resulting in accident, starvation, murder, financial ruin, the breakup of partnerships, and the end of dreams. Only a few—a very few—of those who prospected in the Klondike became rich and were able to live in comfort on the return from their frantic race to the lodestone of the Yukon.

Yet, for a short while, excitement ran high. Dawson City, the most famous gold rush city in the world, became a boom town that was as flamboyant as women, liquor, gambling, and the search for gold could make it. To the newly mobilized North West Mounted Police, the stampede provided one of the stiffest challenges it was ever to face. The possibility of fast wealth brought not only professional prospectors who preferred prospecting to discovery; greenhorns who willingly tossed aside their petty businesses; and monied investors looking for another world to conquer; but gangsters, card sharps, pimps, prostitutes, outlaws, fugitives from justice—an ugly spectrum of those whose aim was to mine the miners not the ground. Hotels burgeoned, gamblers thrived, whores grew rich, and swindlers grew fat. Dawson had come alive but the adrenalin of gold did not last. Colors faded in the pans and fewer and fewer prospectors hit paydirt. In only five years, the rush was almost over.

Thousands who had set out never reached the city of gold; and thousands who did returned empty handed. But the Yukon was never the same again. Many who came to make a quick stake and get out fast stayed on, captured by what the famed Yukon poet and balladeer Robert Service called the Spell of the Yukon: "Black mountains heaved to heaven,/Which the blinding sunsets blazon,/Black canyons where the rapids rip and roar."

Service was a prolific writer (he lived to be 84); his verse, his best selling novel *The Trail of Ninety-Eight,* and his ballads are a living chronicle of the period. Carl F. Klincke's biography of this colorful adventurer, published late in 1976, would be a fascinating resource for the Yukon traveler.

Whitehorse

Most who stayed behind gathered in Whitehorse, a community which came to prominence during the gold rush as a staging and distribution center; today it is the administrative center for the entire Yukon. A busy city, situated at the foot of Miles Canyon, with wide streets, good restaurants, several hotels and government offices, it was a natural place for boats to converge. At one time, there were more than 250 riverboats on the Yukon's rivers and, for a short while, Whitehorse became a river port—the rival of any on the Mississippi.

As Whitehorse grew, Dawson shrank, but it refused to die. Through the glittering days when its population was 40,000 to the dormant years, when scarcely 200 could be found, men and women have continued to make Dawson City their home.

The Beginnings of Change

Still virtually uninhabited except for its capital city, the Yukon has remained a territory since 1898, administered by a Commissioner appointed by the federal government and an elected Legislative Assembly, headed by a Government Leader. Yet there is no question but that this land of Carmack, Skookum Jim, and Robert Service, the Chilkat Indians, Russian traders, and the Hudson's Bay Company is beginning to experience change. A network of publicly operated radio stations reaches into every town and hamlet, and the television antenna and satellite dish are now part of the landscape.

The steady expansion of the highway network has also served to make much more of the Yukon accessible for the visitor and somewhat less formidable for its inhabitants. It is now possible to drive amid some of the Yukon's most spectacular scenery.

The Alaska Highway built during World War II by the American Army and Canadian engineers is the major land route into the Yukon from Southern Canada. It is a scenic adventure route that is maintained throughout the year. This highway started a new era in the Yukon, revitalizing historic communities and spawning new ones. At Watson Lake the highway meets the Robert Campbell Highway, which traverses the southeastern region of the Territory and joins the Klondike Highway at Carmacks.

The Klondike Highway follows the trail of '98 to Dawson City and the heart of the Yukon. In recent years the highway has been extended south via Carcross to Skagway, Alaska. At Carcross on the shores of Bennett Lake clusters of log cabins dating back to the gold rush can still be seen.

Another highway into Alaska is the Haines Road, which runs along the eastern edge of the St. Elias Mountains and connects Haines, Alaska, with Haines Junction, Yukon. Haines is a picture postcard fishing port nestling against the mountains. Ferry boats and cruise ships stop here and many travelers began their exploration of the Yukon by driving north through lush forests, then alongside the Chilkat River to northwestern B.C. and eventually Haines Junction, Yukon.

The newest and, in some ways, the most adventurous route that is now open for the motor tourist is the Dempster Highway. It links Dawson City to Inuvik in arctic Northwest Territories. This road is for the motorists who like rugged travel through uninhabited mountainous terrain. The highway snakes across the Richardson Mountains and slides into the sprawling delta of the Mackenzie River. Before setting out check road conditions; in wet weather it becomes very slippery and occasionally is closed. There are two ferry crossings on the way. Garage and restaurant services are very sparse; make sure you are well equipped. There are only two garages between Dawson City and the N.W.T. border.

From Dawson it is also possible to travel one of the Yukon's most spectacular routes, the Top of the World Highway. This route has to be one of the Yukon's most memorable—for lovers of tangled wilderness, tumbled mountains, and twisting rivers, this is a must.

There are yet other roads to travel—roads that now seem to lead to nowhere but give the camper, the canoeist, the fisherman, and the simple lover of the outdoors more opportunities to see the expansive wilderness of Canada's great northwest. There are roads whose names alone whet the appetite for adventure, Tagish Road, Canol Road, Nahanni Range Road, Atlin Road, Silver Trail to mention but a few.

Motorists, check your maps, check your vehicles, check the time you have available and then plunge into the Yukon, wandering where you will.

Exploring Whitehorse

Whitehorse, capital of the Yukon since 1953, covers an area of 420 sq. kms. (162 square miles), has a population of about 15,000, and offers all the facilities you'd expect in a modern city anywhere in North America. The city began as a stopping point on the route to the Klondike—the first place goldseekers could beach their boats after coming down the Miles Canyon and shooting the Whitehorse Rapids.

In 1900 the White Pass Railway was completed, thereby ensuring a future for the small community. It became an all important stop for travelers to and from the goldfields, linking the Yukon to Vancouver, Seattle and San Francisco. Riverboats sailed from its piers to Dawson City and the many other mining centers that flourished at the turn of the century.

Still in existence are old steam engines, Yukon-style coaches, the old telegraph office, and the McBride Museum, with its fine collection of Yukon relics. The Anglican Parish Church (1900), the first church built in the city, is now the old log museum. It was for a church concert here, in 1904, that one of its parishioners, the poet Robert Service, composed "The Ballad of Dangerous Dan McGrew."

Those who enjoy local customs might visit Whitehorse during its annual winter event, the Yukon Sourdough Rendezvous, a free-wheeling week of fun and relaxation, usually held during the last full week of February. Dog races, trials of strength, Native games, and evening entertainments in the bars and cabarets are all part of this winter festival.

Exploring Dawson City

Dawson City, incorporated in 1906, is located 240 kms. (150 miles) from the Arctic Circle where the Klondike flows into the Yukon River. In 1898, it was a thriving metropolis of 30,000–40,000 people; today 750 keep it alive. One-third of this population is Kutchin or part Kutchin Indian whose ancestors hunted here a thousand or more years before men came north for its gold. Today the city subsists on jobs provided by Territorial and Federal government agencies, tourism, and gold mining.

While in Dawson City, visit its museum; spot the Klondike and Yukon Rivers and surrounding goldfields from the Midnight Dome Viewpoint; see the old Bonanza Creek, and try your hand at goldpanning on Poverty Bar or at Claim #6 which is always open.

PRACTICAL INFORMATION FOR THE YUKON

HOW TO GET THERE. As thousands of Klondikers discovered in the 1890's, the Yukon was almost inaccessible. Now it can be reached in a variety of ways. **By air:** *CP Air* jet flights operate regularly between Vancouver, Edmonton, and Whitehorse for those who prefer comfort, speed, and convenience. Reservations can be made at any recognized travel agency.

By car: The Alaska Hwy., one of North America's greatest, was built during the Second World War to provide land access to Alaska. A fascinating trail that winds its way from Dawson Creek (not to be confused with Dawson City) in

Northern British Columbia to Fairbanks, Alaska, the highway is virtually all asphalt-surfaced but paving and highway upgrading continue. *Note:* Those who drive to the Yukon should take special precautions: Make sure your car is in good mechanical condition with good tires, including a good spare. Drive with lights on and protect headlights with plastic covers. Also protect radiator and paint with a wire-mesh screen placed across front of vehicle. Listen to radio reports of road condition given daily. When trucks pass, pull over to side of road but do not stop; avoid soft shoulders. Between the months of October and April when temperatures as low as -57° C. (-70°F.) have been recorded in the Yukon, emergency survival gear should be on board at all times—an axe, matches, sleeping bag, paper, kindling, sensible outdoor clothing, and food. The car should be properly winterized with light oil in the engine and transmission, a block heater, anti-freeze, and chains.

By bus: *Greyhound* travels the Alaska Hwy. Connections may be made at Dawson Creek, British Columbia, from Edmonton or Vancouver. The bus takes 31 hours from Edmonton to Whitehorse and 40 hours to Dawson City. Overnight stops on the road may be made at no extra cost; hotel reservations should be secured in advance.

By boat: The Inside Passage along the Pacific coastline is a spectacular way to travel to or depart from Yukon. Beginning in Seattle, Vancouver or Prince Rupert, the ships cruise along the Marine Highway which passes the scenic Queen Charlotte Islands. The *Alaska State Ferries* includes a fleet of registered ferryliners which transport passengers and vehicles within portions of southcentral and southwest Alaska. The ferry route also connects southeast Alaska with Prince Rupert in British Columbia. Drivers who plan to continue their travels through Yukon can disembark at Skagway, Alaska from where they can drive or take a motorcoach along the 110-mile Klondike Highway to Whitehorse and beyond. Another destination is Haines, Alaska where visitors can drive the Haines Road to the Alaska Highway.

 ACCOMMODATIONS. In view of the very heavy tourist flow through the Yukon Territory during the summer, you will be well advised to make hotel and motel reservations early in the year. Price ranges for double occupancy are: Expensive, $55 and up; Moderate, $40–$55; Inexpensive, under $40. Price will also be lower if room does not have private bath.

Most places accept the following major credit cards: American Express, MasterCard and Visa; others may also be honored. Not all establishments accept credit cards, therefore we suggest you call for information.

BEAVER CREEK. *Expensive:* **Alas/Kon Border Lodge.** Beaver Creek, Y.T. Y0B 1A0, (403) 862–7501. Dining room, lounge, liquor; open May 15-Sept. 27. From Oct.-Apr., contact Klondike Inn (Whitehorse) for Alas/Kon Border Lodge reservations.
Moderate: **Ida's Motel.** Beaver Creek, Y.T. Y0B 1A0, (403) 862–7223. Coffee shop, lounge, home cooking, liquor; open all year.

BURWASH LANDING. *Moderate:* **Burwash Landing Resort.** Mile 1093, Alaska Hwy., Y.T. Y1A 3V4, (403) 841–4441. Dining room, lounge, liquor, small store; open all year.

CARCROSS. *Moderate:* **Caribou Hotel.** Box 85, Carcross, Y.T. Y0B 1B0, (403) 821–4501. Cafe, lounge, liquor; open all year. One of the oldest hotels in Yukon.

CARMACKS. *Expensive:* **Carmacks Hotel.** Box 160, Carmacks, Y.T. Y0B 1C0, (403) 863–5221. Cafe, lounge, self-serve gas station, liquor, store; open all year.
Moderate. **Sunset Motel.** Carmacks, Y.T. Y0B 1C0, (403) 863–5266. Housekeeping units available, lounge, restaurant; open all year.
Braeburn Lodge. Mile 55, Klondike Hwy., Y.T. Y1A 4N1, radiotelephone 2M3987 (Fox Channel through Whitehorse). Located 47 mi. south of Carmacks midway to Whitehorse. Cafe; open all year.

DAWSON CITY. *Expensive:* **Eldorado Hotel.** 3rd and Princess, Box 338, Dawson City, Y.T. Y0B 1G0, (403) 993–5451. Restaurant, lounge, liquor, major credit cards; open all year.

Sheffield Dawson. 5th and Harper, Box 420, Dawson City, Y.T. Y0B 1G0, (403) 993–5542. Dining room, lounge, liquor, gift shop, open mid-May to mid-Sept. From Oct.-Apr., contact Sheffield Whitehorse for Sheffield Dawson reservations.

Gold Nugget Hotel. Box 86, Dawson City, Y.T. Y0B 1G0, (403) 993–5445. Open June 1-Aug. 31.

Eagle Plains Hotel. Bag 2735, Whitehorse, Y.T. Y1A 3V1, radiotelephone JL25889 (Rat Pass Channel through Fort Nelson, B.C.). 231 mi. north on Dempster Highway, midway between Dawson City and Inuvik, N.W.T. Licensed dining room, lounge, service station, liquor, laundromat, small store; open all year.

Klondike River Lodge. Dawson City, Y.T. Y0B 1G0, (403) 993–6892. 25 mi. south of Dawson City at the Dempster Highway cutoff. Restaurant, garage, liquor; open all year.

Moderate: **Downtown Hotel.** Box 780, Dawson City, Y.T. Y0B 1G0, (403) 993–5346. Dining room, lounge, liquor; open all year.

Midnight Sun Hotel. Queen and 3rd, Box 840, Dawson City, Y.T. Y0B 1G0, (403) 993–5495. Centrally located, dining room, lounge, coffee shop, saloon; open mid-May–mid-Sept. From Oct.–Apr. contact 5658 Halley Ave., Burnaby, B.C. V5H 2P8, (604) 437–8969.

Triple "J" Motel. Queen and 6th, Box 359, Dawson City, Y.T. Y0B 1G0, (403) 993–5323. Cafeteria, lounge, liquor, coin laundry; open May-Oct.

DESTRUCTION BAY. *Moderate:* **Talbot Arms Motel.** Destruction Bay, Y.T. Y0B 1H0, (403) 841–4461. Licensed dining room, lounge, liquor, service station; open all year.

FARO. *Expensive:* **Faro Hotel.** Box 238, Faro, Y.T. Y0B 1K0, (403) 994–2610. Coffee shop, lounge, liquor; open all year.

Little Salmon Lodge. Box 129, Faro, Y.T. Y0B 1K0, radiotelephone 2M4570 (Salmon Channel through Whitehorse). Located 34 mi. west of Faro on Campbell Highway. Dining room, licensed cafe, garage; open all year.

HAINES JUNCTION. *Expensive:* **Dezadeash Lodge.** Haines Junction, Y.T. Y0B 1L0, (403) 634–2315. Located 34 mi. south of Haines Junction on Haines Road. Restaurant, lounge, liquor, service station; open all year.

Gateway Motel. Haines Junction, Y.T. Y0B 1L0, (403) 634–2371. Lounge, liquor; open all year.

Moderate: **Kluane Park Inn.** Haines Junction, Y.T. Y0B 1L0, (403) 634–2261. Lounge, liquor; open all year.

Macintosh Lodge. Haines Junction, Y.T. Y0B 1L0, (403) 634–2301. Licensed dining room, liquor, laundromat; open all year.

MAYO-KENO. *Moderate:* **Chateau Mayo.** Box 66, Mayo, Y.T. Y0B 1M0, (403) 996–2366. Lounge, liquor; open all year.

North Star Motel. Box 34, Mayo, Y.T. Y0B 1M0, (403) 996–2231. Housekeeping facilities; open all year.

ROSS RIVER. *Moderate:* **Welcome Inn.** Ross River, Y.T. Y0B 1S0, (403) 969–2218. Housekeeping units, cafe, lounge, liquor; open all year.

TESLIN. *Moderate:* **North Lake Motel.** Teslin, Y.T. Y0A 1B0, (403) 390–2571. Cafe, tavern, liquor; open all year.

Yukon Motel. Teslin, Y.T. Y0A 1B0, (403) 390–2575. Restaurant, lounge, service station, liquor; open all year.

WATSON LAKE. *Moderate:* **Gateway Motor Inn.** Box 560, Watson Lake, Y.T. Y0A 1C0, (403) 536–7744. Licensed dining room, lounge, kitchenettes, liquor; open all year.

Watson Lake Hotel. Box 370, Watson Lake, Y.T. Y0A 1C0, (403) 536–7781. Licensed dining room, lounge, cafe, coin laundry, liquor; open all year.

WHITEHORSE. *Expensive:* **Airline Inn.** 16 Burns Rd., Whitehorse, Y.T. Y1A 4Y9, (403) 668–4400. Across highway from airport. Licensed dining room, lounge, indoor swimming pool, liquor.

Airport Chalet. 916 Alaska Hwy., Whitehorse, Y.T. Y1A 3E4, (403) 668–2166. Across highway from airport. Licensed dining room, lounge, cafe, liquor, self-serve gas and diesel.

Crystal Palace Hotel. Mile 866.5 Alaska Hwy., Y.T. Y1A 4S8, (403) 668–2727. Located 50 mi. east of Whitehorse on Alaska Highway. Licensed dining room, lounge, service station, liquor; open all year.

Gold Rush Inn. 411 Main St., Whitehorse, Y.T. Y1A 2B6, (403) 668–4500. Licensed dining room, lounge, housekeeping units with refrigerators.

Klondike Inn. 2288 Second Ave., Whitehorse, Y.T. Y1A 1C8, (403) 668–4747. Dining room, lounge, cabaret, coffee shop.

Sheffield Whitehorse. 2nd and Wood, Box 4250, Whitehorse, Y.T. Y1A 3T3, (403) 668–4700. Licensed dining room, lounge, travel agency, barber shop, art gallery, gift shop.

T & M Hotel. 401 Main St., Whitehorse, Y.T. Y1A 2B6, (403) 668–7644. Licensed dining room, lounge, liquor.

Taku Hotel. 4th and Main, Box 4308, Whitehorse, Y.T. Y1A 3T3, (403) 668–4545. Cafe, lounge. This is one of the oldest established hotels in the city and has a bar with atmosphere.

Moderate: **Capital Hotel.** 103 Main St., Whitehorse, Y.T. Y1A 2A7, (403) 667–2565. Lounge, 1898 decor.

Chilkoot Trail Inn. 4190 Fourth Ave., Whitehorse, Y.T. Y1A 1J8, (403) 668–4910. Close to shopping mall and theaters.

Edgewater Hotel. 101 Main St., Whitehorse, Y.T. Y1A 2A7, (403) 667–2572. Licensed dining room, coffee shop, lounge, liquor.

New North Motor Inn. 2141 Second Ave., Whitehorse, Y.T. Y1A 1C5, (403) 668–4646. Housekeeping units, licensed cafe, cabaret, quiet lounge, liquor.

Regina Hotel. 102 Wood St., Whitehorse, Y.T. Y1A 2E3, (403) 667–7801. Licensed dining room, lounge, liquor, heated parking.

Stratford Motel. Box 4629, Whitehorse, Y.T. Y1A 2R8, (403) 667–4243. Located downtown at 4th and Jarvis, kitchenettes, open May-Oct.

Whitehorse Centre Motor Inn. 206 Jarvis St., Whitehorse, Y.T. Y1A 2H1, (403) 668–4567. Centrally located, housekeeping units, lounge, free winter plug-ins, off-street parking.

Yukon Inn. 4220 Fourth Ave., Whitehorse, Y.T. Y1A 1K1, (403) 667–2527. Licensed dining room, cafe, tavern, cabaret, liquor.

TOURIST INFORMATION. For **Whitehorse,** write Whitehorse Chamber of Commerce, 302 Steele St., Whitehorse, Y.T. Y1A 2C5. For **Dawson City,** write Klondike Visitors Association, Box 389, Dawson City, Y.T. Y0B 1G0. Excellent information can also be obtained from: Tourism Yukon, Box 2703, Whitehorse, Y.T. Y1A 2C6.

PACKAGE TOURS. To see the Yukon in comfort and at reasonable cost, try one of the many well-paced organized tours. Some include Alaska and the western part of the Northwest Territories as well as the centrally located Yukon. The various tours offered by these operators are completely described in brochures which may be obtained by writing to each of the operators or by contacting your travel agent.

Anderson Tours, 153 Conneaut Lake Rd., Greenville, PA 16125. *Anik Tours,* 108–2223 Victoria Ave. E., Regina, Sask. S4N 6E4. *Atlas Travel Tours,* Box 4340, Whitehorse, Y.T. Y1A 3T5. *Gadabout Tours Inc.,* 700 E. Tahquitz Way, Palm Springs, CA 92262. *Goway Travel,* 40 Wellington St. E., Toronto, Ont. M5E 1C7. *Lone Star Travellers,* 5771 Enid, Houston, TX 77009. *Maupintours,* Box 807, Lawrence KS 66044. *Trek America,* Box 127, Staten Island, New York, NY 10309. *Princess Tours,* 1800–2121 Fourth Ave., Seattle, WA 98121. *Questors Tours,* 257 Park Ave. S., New York, NY 10010. *Rainbow Adventure Tours,* 3089 Third Ave., Whitehorse, Y.T. Y1A 5B3. *Senior Citizens Recreation Club,* Box 2233, 3210 Fiechtner Dr., Fargo, ND 58108. *Universal Fun Finders Tours,* 214–5809 MacLeod Tr. S., Calgary, Alta. T2H 0J9. *Weibe Tours,* 9647–45th Ave., Edmonton, Alta. T6E 5Z8. *Westours,* 300 Elliot Ave. W., Seattle WA 98119.

SPECIAL INTEREST TOURS. *Norline Coaches,* 3211A Third Ave., Whitehorse, Y.T. Y1A 1G6, has regular service between Whitehorse and Dawson City and offers daily transportation to points in Alaska.

Atlin Express operates between Whitehorse, Carcross, Tagish, and Atlin, B.C. Write *Atlin Express,* Box 175, Atlin, B.C. V0W 1A0.

Yukon River Cruises, Box 100034, Anchorage, AK 99510, (907) 276–8023 operates a cruise between Dawson City and Eagle, Alaska daily.

Between June and Sept., the *MV Anna Maria* travels the Yukon River between Dawson City and Whitehorse. Write: *Karpes and Pugh Yukon River Trading Co. Ltd.,* Box 5152, Whitehorse, Y.T. Y1A 4S3, (403) 668–4899.

The *Yukon Historical & Museums Association* offers free, guided walking tours of downtown Whitehorse.

WILDERNESS TOURS. *Ecosummer Yukon,* Box 5095, Whitehorse, Y.T. Y1A 4Z2. *Kluane Adventures,* Box 5466, Haines Junction, Y.T. Y0B 1L0, (403) 634–2282. *Old Squaw Lodge,* Bag Service 2711, Whitehorse, Y.T. Y1A 4K8, (403) 668–6732. *White Moose Tours & Outfitting Ltd.,* Box 236, Atlin, B.C. V0W 1A0, (403) 668–7336. *Wild and Woolly,* Box 53, Carcross, Y.T. Y0B 1B0. *Yukon Expeditions,* 127 Alsek Rd., Whitehorse, Y.T. Y1A 3K7, (403) 667–7960.

PHOTOGRAPHY. What an opportunity for the photographer-professional as well as amateur! At the height of summer, the midnight sun creates unique light conditions as do the flashing colors of the aurora borealis to be seen on many nights in the fall, winter, and spring. Be sure to use an ultra-filter (ultra-violet filter) as the air is very clean and clear and photographic contrast is high. The filter will cut down the amount of blue in your pictures and, at the same time, protect your lens. Also, as you are likely to encounter considerable dust, protect your camera and other gear with plastic bags.

Kluane Adventures, Box 5466, Haines Junction, Y.T. Y0B 1L0, (403) 634–2282. *Oldsquaw Lodge,* Bag Service 2711, Whitehorse, Y.T. Y1A 4K8, (403) 668–6732. *Pack Trails North Adventures,* Box 484, Watson Lake, Y.T. Y0A 1C0, (403) 536–2174. *Yukon Wilderness Unlimited,* Box 4126, Whitehorse, Y.T. Y1A 3S9, (403) 668–5244.

FISHING. The fish are there! Only a fishing license is necessary-the cost is $5 for Canadian residents for the season; $5 for nonresidents for 1 day, $10 for 5 days, and $20 for the season. Special National Park fishing license is $10 for season.

The most abundant species are lake trout, northern pike, and arctic grayling. Catch limits on these fish are generous and are outlined to the fisherman when the license is purchased. In recent years, the limit has been twenty pike per day, ten arctic grayling, and five lake trout. Less common are the Dolly Varden, rainbow trout, steelhead, and the king and coho salmon and the catch limit is less generous, too. Grayling and all trout less than eight inches long have to be returned to waters. Fishing lodges can be reached readily by road. For those in pursuit of a very special fishing experience, there are also fly-in camps. Many of the air charter companies in Yukon offer fly-in fishing packages to lakes either a short distance from a major center or to more distant lakes and rivers.

Trophy lake trout up to 40 pounds can be taken, spinning or trolling. Northern pike are there in the shallow, reedy bottoms; arctic grayling teem in the rivers, and whitefish, inconnu and rainbow trout are often just a cast away. Southwest Yukon also offers excellent salmon fishing in July. And in the far north, arctic char are popular with anglers anxious to add this unusual species to their list of accomplishments.

Fishing Camps and Lodges: *Brookland's Wilderness Camp,* Box 299, Atlin, B.C. V0W 1A0, radiotelephone 2M3940 (Fraser Channel through Whitehorse). *Johnnie John's Fishing Trips,* Carcross, Y.T. Y0B 1B0, (403) 821–3116. *Kluane Lake Tours,* Destruction Bay, Y.T. Y0B 1H0, (403) 841–4411. *Kluane Wilderness Lodge,* Box 5212, Whitehorse, Y.T. Y1A 4Z1, radiotelephone 2M3288 (Beaver Creek Channel through Whitehorse). *Peacock's Yukon Camps,* 77

Alsek Rd., Whitehorse, Y.T. Y1A 3K5, (403) 667–2846. *Tina Lake Wilderness Resort,* Box 5221, Whitehorse, Y.T. Y1A 4Z1, (403) 668–4059. *Wolf Lake Wilderness Camp,* Teslin, Y.T. Y0A 1B0, radiotelephone SQ707 (Teslin Channel through Whitehorse). *Yukon Fishing Safaris Ltd.,* Box 5209, Whitehorse, Y.T. Y1A 4Z1, (604) 785–0098.

HUNTING. The hunter is in his element in the Yukon. Among the mountains and river valleys are Dall sheep, the Stone and Fannin sheep, mountain goats, moose, barrenground and woodland caribou, black and brown bears, and the mighty grizzly. All **big game hunting** by nonresidents must be done in the company of a licensed guide. Hunting is only allowed during prescribed seasons. Any game or trophies to be taken home require export permits (free) from the Director of Game or any Government Agent. Open season on the black and grizzly bear is usually from mid-April to mid-June. Open season on moose (male only), caribou, and mountain goat (either sex) is from August 1 to November 30, mountain sheep (male only), August 1 to November 10. Dates are subject to change. Up-to-date regulations, fees, seasons, and limits may be obtained from Tourism Yukon, Box 2703, Whitehorse, Y.T. Y1A 2C6.

Bird hunting is permitted in the fall. Waterfowl as well as ruffed, willow, blue, and sharp-tailed grouse may be hunted from September 1 until November 30. Spruce (Franklin) grouse and ptarmigan seasons are September 1 to January 31 following. Licensed outfitters are controlled by the Yukon Territorial Government through the Game Branch. The Yukon is divided into Guiding Areas with one outfitter in each having exclusive rights.

Big Game Outfitters (usually prefer to conduct hunts for 14 days): *Stan Reynolds,* Box 108, Dawson City, Y.T. Y0B 1G0, radiotelephone SQ787 (Dawson Channel through Whitehorse). *Doug Low,* Tagish, Y.T. Y0B 1T0, (403) 399–3171. *Pete Jensen,* 58 Alsek Rd., Whitehorse, Y.T. Y1A 3K4, (403) 667–2030. *Rick Furniss,* Box 5364, Whitehorse, Y.T. Y1A 4Z2, (403) 667–2712. *Bonnet Plume Outfitters Ltd.,* Box 4840, Whitehorse, Y.T. Y1A 4N6, (403) 668–2888. *Dawn Marino,* Carmacks, Y.T. Y0B 1C0, (403) 863–5136. *Cam Drinan,* Ross River, Y.T. Y0B 1S0, (403) 969–2250. *Dave Coleman,* Box 5088, Whitehorse, Y.T. Y1A 4S3, (403) 668–5072. *Werner Koser,* Ross River, Y.T. Y0B 1S0, (403) 969–2210. *Dick Dickson,* 708 Minto Rd., Whitehorse, Y.T. Y1A 3X9, (403) 633–2228. *John Ostashek,* Box 4146, Whitehorse, Y.T. Y1A 3S6, (403) 668–7323. *John Drift,* Destruction Bay, Y.T. Y0B 1H0, radiotelephone YJ36478 (Destruction Bay Channel through Whitehorse). *Ron Hardie,* 25–5 Klondike Rd., Whitehorse, Y.T. Y1A 3L7, (403) 667–7182. *Lebarge Ranch & Outfitters,* Box 4458, Whitehorse, Y.T. Y1A 2R8, (403) 633–5273. *Clay Martin,* Box 4492, Whitehorse, Y.T. Y1A 2R8, (403) 633–6606. *David Young,* Site 12, Comp. 24, R.R. 1, Whitehorse, Y.T. Y1A 4Z6, (403) 668–4518. *Klaas Heynen,* 28 Alsek Rd., Whitehorse, Y.T. Y1A 3K2, (403) 667–2755. *Bob Hassard,* Teslin, Y.T. Y0A 1B0, (403) 390–2610. *Doug Smarch,* Teslin, Y.T. Y0A 1B0, (403) 390–2559. *Terry Wilkinson,* Box 484, Watson Lake, Y.T. Y0A 1C0, (403) 536–2174.

CANOEING. The Yukon's waterways are an open invitation to the canoeist. Each river has its own challengesome with rapids to be run and others to be circumnavigated. Before launching a canoe in the Yukon, obtain the best maps available and inform the Royal Canadian Mounted Police of your proposed route and estimated time of return. No law requires these precautions but police encourage all wilderness wanderers to adhere to them.

Experts favor the sturdy aluminum canoes although a few traditionalists still prefer thosemade of wood and canvas. Be sure to carry adequate emergency supplies and canoe repair outfits and know how to signal for help in the event of any emergency. Maps of the Yukon's rivers are available from many sources including *Igloo Sporting Goods,* 3097 Third Ave., Whitehorse, Y.T. Y1A 1E4.

Canoe Expeditions and Rentals: *Arctic Edge Canoe Expedition Outfitting,* Box 4896, Whitehorse, Y.T. Y1A 4N6, (403) 633–2443. *Karpes and Pugh Co.,* Box 5152, Whitehorse, Y.T. Y1A 4S3, (403) 668–4899. *Rainbow Adventure Tours Ltd.,* 3089 Third Ave., Whitehorse, Y.T. Y1A 5B3, (403) 668–5598. *Sunpath Expeditions,* Box 5272, Station F, Ottawa, Ont. K2C 3H5, (613) 731–8468. *Tatshenshini Expediting,* 1602 Alder St., Whitehorse, Y.T. Y1A 3W8,

(403) 633–2742. *Yukon Mountain and River Expeditions Ltd.,* Box 5405, White-horse, Y.T. Y1A 4Z2, (403) 668–2513. *Yukon Whitewater Recreation,* Box 4478, Whitehorse, Y.T. Y1A 2R8, (403) 667–6071.

TRAILER CAMPING. Trailer camps and tenting facilities are available on the growing network of roads at both Yukon government and commercial sites. Many commercial campsites have laundromats, electricity, food stores, telephones, and showers; most are located on the Klondike and Alaska Highways. Visitors are asked to camp in authorized areas only. For information, contact Tourism Yukon, Box 2703, Whitehorse, Y.T. Y1A 2C6.

HIKING AND CLIMBING. From the St. Elias Range, which has many peaks of more than 10,000 ft., and Mt. Logan, the highest point in Canada (19,850 ft.), to low rounded hills and flat river banks-there is something for everyone on foot. Maps should always be constant companions. For those who like to ramble through country that does not demand the skills of a mountaineer there are 155 miles of hiking trails in Kluane National Park. For more information write to Tourism Yukon, Box 2703, Whitehorse, Y.T. Y1A 2C6.

Outfitted Pack Trips: *Ecosummer Yukon,* Box 5095, Whitehorse, Y.T. Y1A 4Z2. *Jubilee Packtrain,* Box 5299, Whitehorse, Y.T. Y1A 4Z2, radiotelephone 2M5174 (White Mountain Channel through Whitehorse). *Pack Trails North Adventures,* Box 484, Watson Lake, Y.T. Y0A 1C0, (403) 536–2174. *Sky High Ranches,* Box 4482, Whitehorse, Y.T. Y1A 2R8, radiotelephone YS39074 (Whitehorse Channel). *Sundance Mountain Adventures,* Box 4801, Whitehorse, Y.T. Y1A 4N6.

MUSEUMS AND HISTORIC SITES. In **Keno,** a mining town of less than one hundred and one of the prettiest communities in the Yukon, there is the *Keno Mining Museum,* open 1 P.M.–5 P.M. June 1-Sept. 30.

Dawson City is home for a museum that boasts a collection of over 25,000 artifacts from the days of the gold rush. It also provides the visitor with a view of history right on its streets-the *Redfeather* and the *Monte Carlo,* two derelict saloons, still stand as mute reminders of the swinging nineties. Then, down by the river, sternwheel forever stilled, is the *Keno,* last of the riverboats to travel the Whitehorse-Dawson City route. See the largest wooden hull dredge (*Dredge #4*) in North America on Bonanza Creek. *Madame Tremblay's Store* features gowns and costumes of the gold rush era. Visit the displays in the *1901 Post Office.*

The well-known *MacBride Museum* is in **Whitehorse.** This museum contains an excellent display of Yukon animals. Historic places of interest worth visiting in the Yukon's largest community are the "Old Log Church," the S.S. *Klondike,* now a National Historic site, and the much-talked-about log "skyscrapers." The records of Yukon's history are preserved in the *Yukon Archives.* Open 9 A.M.–5 P.M., Tues.-Fri.

The *Kluane Museum of Natural History* in **Burwash Landing** is open daily during the summer, 9 A.M.–9 P.M. It features an interesting collection of natural history displays and historic artifacts including the tooth of a mammal 18,000 years old.

In **Teslin,** the *George Johnson Museum* is an impressive log structure which houses displays of traditional Indian arts and crafts as well as gold rush era relics.

ENTERTAINMENT. In **Dawson City** during the summer season (early June until roughly September 10), the *Gaslight Follies* in the Palace Grand Theatre is a vaudeville show, nightly except Tuesdays, at 8 P.M. *Diamond Tooth Gertie's Gambling Hall* is open nightly, except Sunday, 8 P.M.–2 A.M. offering legal gambling tables, bingo, bar, and three floor shows (9 and 11 P.M. and 1 A.M.) *Robert Service's Cabin* opens daily and free readings of his ballads can be heard at 10 A.M. and 3 P.M. Interpretations are presented at 1 P.M. daily in *Jack London's Cabin* (also free). The *Gold Room* located above the Canadian

Imperial Bank of Commerce offers tours of the assay equipment obtained from early mining operations. It's open daily, June-mid Sept., 10 A.M.–3 P.M.

In **Whitehorse,** the *Frantic Follies,* a popular gay nineties revue featuring high-kicking can-can girls, hilarious skits and rollicking good humor is held nightly in the Sheffield Whitehorse complex, June-mid-Sept. Tour a mine and pan for gold at *Black Mike's* just 22½ miles south of Whitehorse on the Alaska Highway. The *Yukon Conservation Society* provides nature hikes within the city area. Monthly exhibitions of local artists are held in the *Whitehorse Public Library Art Gallery* (free admission). A natural hot springs 17 miles north of the city just off the Klondike Highway has swimming, a picnic area, and a coffee shop. *Takhini Hot Springs* is open for bathing, 8 A.M.–10 P.M. The *Whitehorse Dam and Fish Ladder* is located at the end of Nisutlin Drive in the suburb of Riverdale. The fish ladder allows spawning salmon to bypass the hydro dam in late July and August. Pan for gold at *89 Below* on the banks of the Yukon River or savor a salmon barbecue at *Paradise Alley.* Ride through historic Miles Canyon on the *M.V. Schwatka,* a two-hour cruise departing daily. Miles Canyon presented the stampeders with formidable barriers in their attempts to reach the Klondike. Today a suspension bridge allows visitors to walk safely over the canyon to view the rapids. Tours of the Whitehorse area can be arranged by *Atlas Tours Ltd.,* Box 4340, Whitehorse, Y.T. Y1A 3T5 or through any local taxi company.

 RESTAURANTS. Your best bet for dining out in the Yukon Territory is to stick to the dining facilities in your hotel. There are about five restaurants in Dawson City that are open throughout the summer months. The following listing are suggestions for dining out in Whitehorse. Prices for a meal generally run under $10.

Most places accept the following major credit cards: American Express, MasterCard and Visa; others may also be honored. Not all establishments accept credit cards, therefore we suggest you call for information.

WHITEHORSE. Camelot Restaurant. 404 Wood St., (403) 668–5099. Open seven days a week from 11 A.M. Fully licensed. Family-priced meals. House specialties include reindeer and salmon.

The Cellar Dining Lounge. 101 Main St. in Edgewater Hotel, (403) 667–2573. Open seven days a week from 5:30 P.M. Fully licensed. Specializing in prime rib, king crab, lobster, barbecue ribs, and steaks.

Charlie's Dining Room. 2288 Second Ave. in Klondike Inn, (403) 668–4747. Open daily, 5–10 P.M. Named after the legendary Arizona Charlie Meadows. Set in an authentic 1898 atmosphere and features the finest cuisine. Fully licensed.

Christie's Downtown Place. 209 Main St., (403) 667–7671. Open Mon.–Sun., 11:00 A.M.–3:30 A.M. Licensed dining and take-out orders. Italian and Greek food, pizza, salad bar, steaks, chicken, ribs, and seafood.

Dairy Queen. Second Ave. and Elliott St., (403) 667–2272. Open Feb.-Nov., Mon.-Fri., 9:30 A.M.–11 P.M.; Sat., Sun., and holidays, 11 A.M.–11 P.M. Seats 116. Hamburgers, soft ice cream, take-out orders.

Golden Garter. 212 Main St., (403) 667–2626. Open mid-Feb.-Dec., Tues.-Sat., 6–10 P.M. Dining room seats 56. French cuisine, seafood. Licensed.

Greek Corner. 202 Strickland St., (403) 668–6266. Open for lunch, Thurs.–Fri., 11:30 A.M.–2:00 P.M. dinner, Mon.–Thurs., 5:00 P.M.–11:00 P.M., and Fri.–Sat., 5:00 P.M.–midnight. Greek cuisine and steaks. Fully licensed.

The Keg and Cleaver, Third Ave. and Jarvis St., (403) 668–4949. Open daily at 4:30 P.M. Licensed. Steak, seafood, never-ending salad bar.

Marina's. 95 Lewes Blvd., (403) 667–7878. Open Mon.–Thurs., 4:30 P.M.–1 A.M.; Fri. and Sat., 4:30 P.M.–2 A.M. Steaks, ribs, pizza. Fully licensed. Takeout available.

Mr. Mike's. 4114 Fourth Ave., (403) 667–2242. Open Mon.-Thurs., 11:30 A.M.–9 P.M.; Fri., 11:30 A.M.–10 P.M.; Sat., 11:30 A.M.–9 P.M.; Sun., noon–9 P.M. During the winter months: Sun., 4–9 P.M. Seats 99. Steaks, hamburgers, seafood, salad bar. Licensed. Family prices.

New Fireside Dining Lounge. 38 Lewes Blvd., (403) 668–4820. Chinese luncheon smorgasbord, Mon.-Fri., 11:30 A.M.–2 P.M. Dinner hours, 5–11 P.M. Family special: Chinese smorgasbord, Sun., 5–8 P.M. Open Sat., Sun., and holidays, 5–11 P.M. Seats 200. Western foods available. Fully licensed.

Oriental Restaurant. 210 Ogilvie St., (403) 668–6565. Open Sun.-Thurs., 4:30–11:30 P.M.; Fri. and Sat., 4:30 P.M.–1 A.M. Chinese smorgasbord, Mon.-Fri., 11:30 A.M.–2 P.M. Seats 100. Chinese cuisine, steak. Licensed.

FRENCH–ENGLISH TOURIST VOCABULARY

DAILY EXPRESSIONS

Can anyone here speak English?	Y a-t-il quelqu'un qui parle anglais?
Do you speak English?	Parlez-vous anglais?
Do you understand?	Comprenez-vous?
Don't mention it	Pas de quoi
I beg your pardon	Pardon! (pahrr'dong)
Good morning . . . day . . . afternoon	Bonjour
Good evening . . . night	Bonsoir
Goodbye	Au revoir
How are you?	Comment allez-vous?
How much . . . many?	Combien?
I don't know	Je ne sais pas
I don't understand	Je ne comprends pas
Yes	Oui
No	Non
Please speak more slowly	Parlez plus lentement, s'il vous plaît
Stop	Arrêtez
Go ahead	Continuez
Hurry	Dépêchez-vous
Wait here	Attendez ici
Come in!	Entrez! (ahn'tray)
Sit down	Asseyez-vous
Thank you very much	Merci bien
There is, there are	Il y a
Very good . . . well	Très bien
What is this?	Qu'est-ce que c'est? (kes-kuh-say)
What do you want?	Que voulez-vous?
Please	S'il vous plaît (seevooplay)
I'm sorry	Je regrette
You're welcome	Je vous en prie
What time is it?	Quelle heure est-il?
What is your name?	Comment vous appelez-vous?
With pleasure	Avec plaisir
You are very kind	Vous êtes bien aimable

DAYS OF THE WEEK

Sunday	Dimanche
Monday	Lundi
Tuesday	Mardi
Wednesday	Mercredi
Thursday	Jeudi
Friday	Vendredi
Saturday	Samedi

COMMON QUESTIONS

Is there . . .	Y a-t-il . . .
—a bus for . . . ?	—un autobus pour . . . ?
—a dining car?	—un wagon-restaurant . . . ?
—an English interpreter?	—un interprète anglais?
—a guide?	—un guide?
—a good hotel at . . . ?	—un bon hôtel à . . . ?
—a good restaurant here?	—un bon restaurant ici?
—a sleeper?	—une place dans le wagon-lit?
—time to get out?	—le temps de descendre?
—a train for . . . ?	—un train pour . . . ?
Where is . . .	Où est . . .
—the airport?	—l'aéroport?
—a bank?	—une banque?
—the bar?	—le bar?
—the barber's shop	—le coiffeur?

529

—the bathroom?   —la salle de bain?
—the ticket (booking) office?   —le guichet?
a chemist's shop (drugstore)?   —une pharmacie?
—the movies (cinema)?   —le cinéma?
—the cloakroom?   —le vestiaire?
—the British (American)   —le consulat d'Angleterre
    Consulate?   (d'Amérique)?
—the Customs office?   —la douane?
—a garage?   —un garage?
—a hairdresser? (barber)   —un coiffeur?
—the lavatory?   —le lavabo?
—the luggage?   —les bagages?
—the museum?   —le musée?
—the police station?   —le gendarmerie?
—the post office?   —le bureau de poste?
—the railway station?   —le gare?
—the theater?   —le théâtre?
—a tobacconist?   —un débit de tabac?
When . . .   Quand . . .
—is lunch?   —le déjeuner est-il servi?
—is dinner?   —le diner est-il servi?
—is the first (last) bus?   —le premier (dernier) autobus part-il?
—is the first (last) train?   —le premier (dernier) train part-il?
—does the theater open?   —ouvre-t-on le théâtre?
—will it be ready?   —sera-t-il (elle) prêt(e)?
—does the performance begin   —le séance commence-t-elle
    (end)?   (finit-elle)?
—will you be back?   —rentrerez-vous?
—can you return them?   —pouvez-vous me las rendre?
—can I have a bath?   —pourrais-je prendre un bain?
Which is . . .   Quel est . . .
—the way to . . . street?   —Par où va-t-on à la rue . . . ?
—the best hotel at . . . ?   —le meilleur hôtel de . . . ?
—the train (bus) for . . . ?   —le train (autobus) pour . . . ?
What is . . .   Quel est . . .
—the fare to . . . ?   —le prix du billet á . . . ?
the single fare?   le prix d'aller?
—the round trip (return) fare?   le prix d'aller et retour?
—the fare (taxi)?   —Je vous dois combien?
—the price?   —le prix?
—the price per day? per week?   —le prix par jour? par semaine?
—the price per kilo? (2.2 pounds)   Combien le kilo?
—the price per meter?   Combien le mètre?
    (39½ inches)
—the matter?   Ou'est-ce qu'il y a?
—the French for . . . ?   —Comment dit-on . . . en français?
Have you . . .   Avez-vous . . .
—any American (English)   —des cigarettes américaines
    cigarettes?   (anglaises)?
—a timetable?   —un indicateur?
—a room to let?   une chambre à louer?
—anything ready? (Food)   —quelque chose de prêt?
How often?   Combien de fois?
How long?   Combien de temps?

DAILY NEEDS

I want . . .   Je désire . . . Je voudrais . . .
—my bill   —l'addition (la note)
—to buy   —d'acheter
—cigars, cigarettes   —des cigares, cigarettes
—a dentist   —consulter un dentiste
—a dictionary   —un dictionnaire
—a doctor   —consulter un médicin
—something to drink   —prendre quelque chose à boire
—something to eat   —manger quelque chose
—some American (English)   —des journaux américains
    papers   (anglais)
—a haircut   —me faire couper les cheveux
—a shave   —me faire raser
—to go to   —aller à (au) . . .

—a porter	—un porteur
—to see . . .	—voir . . .
—to send a telegram	—envoyer un tétégramme
—some stamps	—des timbres
—a taxi	—un taxi
—to telephone	—téléphone
—the waiter	—parler avec le garçon
—some beer	—de la bière
—change for . . .	—la monnaie de . . .
—water	—de l'eau
—my key	—ma clé
—razor blades	—des lames de rasoir
—a road map	—une carte routière
—soap	—due savon

MENU TRANSLATOR

Meats (Viandes)

Agneau	Lamb	Jambon	Ham
Bifteck	Steak	Lapin	Rabbit
Boeuf	Beef	Lard	Bacon
Charcuterie	Pork cold cuts	Mouton	Mutton
Châteaubriand	Rump steak	Porc	Pork
Côte	Chop	Rosbif	Roast beef
Entrecôte	Rib steak	Saucisse	Sausage
Gigot d'agneau	Leg of Lamb	Veau	Veal
Gibier	Wild game		

Poultry (Volaille)

Canard	Duck	Oie	Goose
Caneton	Duckling	Pintade	Guinea hen
Coq	Young cock	Poulet	Chicken
Faisan	Pheasant		

Offal (Abats)

Cervelles	Brains	Langue	Tongue
Foie	Liver	Rognon	Kidney

Fish (Poisson)

Anguille	Eel	Perche	Bass
Maquereau	Mackerel	Saumon	Salmon
Morue	Cod	Truite	Trout

Shellfish (Coquillages, Crustaces)

Crevettes	Shrimp	Homard	Lobster
Ecrevisses	Crawfish	Huîtres	Oysters
Escargots	Snails	Langouste	Spiny rock lobster
Fruits de mer	Mixed shellfish	Moules	Mussels
Grenouilles	Frogs' legs	Palourdes	Clams

Vegetables (Légumes)

Aubergine	Eggplant	Epinards	Spinach
Chou	Cabbage	Haricots	Beans
Cresson	Watercress	Haricots verts	Green beans

Desserts (Desserts)

Beignets	Fritters	Glace	Ice cream
Gáteau	Cake	Tarte	Pie

Index

FODOR'S TRAVEL GUIDES

Here is a complete list of Fodor's Travel Guides, available in current editions; most are also available in a British edition published by Hodder & Stoughton.

U.S. GUIDES

Alaska
American Cities (Great Travel Values)
Arizona including the Grand Canyon
Atlantic City & the New Jersey Shore
Boston
California
Cape Cod & the Islands of Martha's Vineyard & Nantucket
Carolinas & the Georgia Coast
Chesapeake
Chicago
Colorado
Dallas/Fort Worth
Disney World & the Orlando Area (Fun in)
Far West
Florida
Forth Worth (see Dallas)
Galveston (see Houston)
Georgia (see Carolinas)
Grand Canyon (see Arizona)
Greater Miami & the Gold Coast
Hawaii
Hawaii (Great Travel Values)
Houston & Galveston
I-10: California to Florida
I-55: Chicago to New Orleans
I-75: Michigan to Florida
I-80: San Francisco to New York
I-95: Maine to Miami
Jamestown (see Williamsburg)
Las Vegas including Reno & Lake Tahoe (Fun in)
Los Angeles & Nearby Attractions
Martha's Vineyard (see Cape Cod)
Maui (Fun in)
Nantucket (see Cape Cod)
New England
New Jersey (see Atlantic City)
New Mexico
New Orleans
New Orleans (Fun in)
New York City
New York City (Fun in)
New York State
Orlando (see Disney World)
Pacific North Coast
Philadelphia
Reno (see Las Vegas)
Rockies
San Diego & Nearby Attractions
San Francisco (Fun in)
San Francisco plus Marin County & the Wine Country
The South
Texas
U.S.A.
Virgin Islands (U.S. & British)

Virginia
Waikiki (Fun in)
Washington, D.C.
Williamsburg, Jamestown & Yorktown

FOREIGN GUIDES

Acapulco (see Mexico City)
Acapulco (Fun in)
Amsterdam
Australia, New Zealand & the South Pacific
Austria
The Bahamas
The Bahamas (Fun in)
Barbados (Fun in)
Beijing, Guangzhou & Shanghai
Belgium & Luxembourg
Bermuda
Brazil
Britain (Great Travel Values)
Canada
Canada (Great Travel Values)
Canada's Maritime Provinces plus Newfoundland & Labrador
Cancún, Cozumel, Mérida & the Yucatán
Caribbean
Caribbean (Great Travel Values)
Central America
Copenhagen (see Stockholm)
Cozumel (see Cancún)
Eastern Europe
Egypt
Europe
Europe (Budget)
France
France (Great Travel Values)
Germany: East & West
Germany (Great Travel Values)
Great Britain
Greece
Guangzhou (see Beijing)
Helsinki (see Stockholm)
Holland
Hong Kong & Macau
Hungary
India, Nepal & Sri Lanka
Ireland
Israel
Italy
Italy (Great Travel Values)
Jamaica (Fun in)
Japan
Japan (Great Travel Values)
Jordan & the Holy Land
Kenya
Korea
Labrador (see Canada's Maritime Provinces)
Lisbon
Loire Valley
London

London (Fun in)
London (Great Travel Values)
Luxembourg (see Belgium)
Macau (see Hong Kong)
Madrid
Mazatlan (see Mexico's Baja)
Mexico
Mexico (Great Travel Values)
Mexico City & Acapulco
Mexico's Baja & Puerto Vallarta, Mazatlan, Manzanillo, Copper Canyon
Montreal (Fun in)
Munich
Nepal (see India)
New Zealand
Newfoundland (see Canada's Maritime Provinces)
1936 . . . on the Continent
North Africa
Oslo (see Stockholm)
Paris
Paris (Fun in)
People's Republic of China
Portugal
Province of Quebec
Puerto Vallarta (see Mexico's Baja)
Reykjavik (see Stockholm)
Rio (Fun in)
The Riviera (Fun on)
Rome
St. Martin/St. Maarten (Fun in)
Scandinavia
Scotland
Shanghai (see Beijing)
Singapore
South America
South Pacific
Southeast Asia
Soviet Union
Spain
Spain (Great Travel Values)
Sri Lanka (see India)
Stockholm, Copenhagen, Oslo, Helsinki & Reykjavik
Sweden
Switzerland
Sydney
Tokyo
Toronto
Turkey
Vienna
Yucatán (see Cancún)
Yugoslavia

SPECIAL-INTEREST GUIDES

Bed & Breakfast Guide: North America
Royalty Watching
Selected Hotels of Europe
Selected Resorts and Hotels of the U.S.
Ski Resorts of North America
Views to Dine by around the World

AVAILABLE AT YOUR LOCAL BOOKSTORE OR WRITE TO FODOR'S TRAVEL PUBLICATIONS, INC., 201 EAST 50th STREET, NEW YORK, NY 10022.